Note to Students

Accounting is a stimulating and rewarding field of study. To be successful, professionals in all areas of business, such as finance, production, marketing, personnel, and general management, must have an understanding of accounting. In addition, men and women whose careers are in nonbusiness areas often use their knowledge of accounting to perform their duties more effectively.

As you begin your study of accounting, you may find the following suggestions helpful:

- Read the learning objectives before you begin studying a chapter.
- Scan the chapter to get a feel for the material before you begin a detailed reading of the chapter.
- Briefly review the Glossary of Key Terms in the Chapter Review section to familiarize yourself with the terminology that will be emphasized in the chapter.
- As you read each chapter, you may wish to underline or highlight points that are important. Also, you should pay special attention to key terms that are identified in color when they are first defined in the chapter.
- After reading the chapter, carefully study the Chapter Review, giving special attention to the following items:

Key Points. The Key Points are summarized by learning objectives. You should be able to perform each of the learning objectives. If you cannot perform a learning objective, review the section of the chapter where it is discussed and illustrated.

Glossary of Key Terms. You should be able to define each key term. If you cannot, refer to the section of the chapter where the term is first presented and discussed.

Self-Examination Questions. Answer each of the self-examination questions. Check your answers by referring to the end of the chapter for the correct response and explanation.

Illustrative Problem. Study the illustrative problem and its suggested solution. Each illustrative problem applies the chapter's concepts and principles to a problem situation. If you have difficulty understanding the illustrative problem, refer to the section of the chapter where the applicable concepts and principles are discussed and illustrated.

- Work all assigned homework. In many cases, the homework is related to specific chapter illustrations, and you may find it helpful to review the relevant chapter sections before you begin a homework assignment.
- Take notes during class lectures and discussions. Pay special attention to the topics covered by your instructor in class.
- In reviewing for examinations, keep in mind those topics that your instructor has emphasized, and review your class notes and the text.
- If you feel you need additional aid, you will find the Study Guides that accompany this textbook helpful. The Study Guides can be ordered from South-Western Publishing Co. by your college or university bookstore.

Corporate
Financial
Accounting

FOURTH EDITION

CARL S. WARREN
Ph.D., C.P.A., C.M.A., C.I.A.
Professor of Accounting
University of Georgia, Athens

JAMES M. REEVE
Ph.D., C.P.A.
Professor of Accounting
University of Tennessee, Knoxville

PHILIP E. FESS
Ph.D., C.P.A.
Professor Emeritus of Accountancy
University of Illinois, Champaign-Urbana

COLLEGE DIVISION South-Western Publishing Co.

Cincinnati Ohio

Publisher: Mark Hubble
Sponsoring Editor: David L. Shaut
Senior Developmental Editor: Ken Martin
Production Editor: Shelley Brewer
Production House: York Production Services
Designer: Craig LaGesse Ramsdell
Cover and Internal Illustrator: David Lesh
Marketing Manager: Sharon Oblinger

AO66DA
Copyright © 1994
by South-Western Publishing Co.
Cincinnati, Ohio

ISBN: 0-538-83719-5

The complete version of this text is cataloged as follows:

Warren, Carl S.
    Financial and managerial accounting / Carl S. Warren, James M. Reeve, Philip E. Fess.
—4th ed.
        p.   cm.
    Rev. ed. of: Principles of financial & managerial accounting. 3rd ed. c1992.
    Includes index.
    ISBN 0-538-83336-X
    1. Accounting.   2. Managerial accounting.   I. Reeve, James M. II. Fess, Philip E.
    III. Warren, Carl S. Principles of financial & managerial accounting.   IV. Title.
HF5635.W27   1993
657—dc20   93-30522
                                                        CIP

International Thomson Publishing

South-Western Publishing Co. is an ITP Company. The ITP trademark is used under license.

1 2 3 4 5 6 7 8 9 KI 0 2 1 9 8 7 6 5 4 3
Printed in the United States of America

Preface

CORPORATE FINANCIAL ACCOUNTING opens the window to a full view of insightful accounting applications and innovative classroom supplements. Our text provides a fresh new perspective on a rapidly changing accounting environment. You'll find unique new features and interesting changes, based on recommendations by the Accounting Education Change Commission, extensive feedback from current users, and independent reviews by numerous scholars and educators. Take a look at the features that make financial accounting for corporations even more intriguing and more fun to teach and learn.

STUDENT CONNECTIONS TO THE BUSINESS WORLD

"You and Accounting." This new feature at the beginning of each chapter relates students' personal experience to the chapter's topic. Students are more motivated to study the chapter when they begin to appreciate the relevance of the accounting and business topics presented.

Using Accounting. Accounting does not operate in a vacuum, but instead is used within the rich context of today's business decisions. Also, accounting is not just for accountants. Accounting is important because almost all business managers use accounting information for planning and decision making. In each chapter, we provide examples of how accounting information is used by investors and managers to reach decisions. Many of the examples refer to actual business situations of real companies, so that students can become familiar with the kinds of decisions they will be asked to make in their future careers.

Enrichment Material. Excerpts from *The Journal of Accountancy, The Wall Street Journal, Business Week, Forbes,* or other well-known business periodicals appear in each chapter to enrich students' learning experience by providing real-world information relevant to the topics in the chapter.

Real-World Examples, Terms, and Survey Evidence. The text frequently uses actual organizational settings for many of the examples through the text. These settings introduce students to the actual terms used in service and merchandising companies. Thus, the text attempts to continue the student's introduction to the language of business by using the vocabulary of organizations. In addition, survey results are cited in order to show the use of certain alternative practices.

REAL WORLD FOCUS Each chapter includes at least one discussion question requiring students to interpret and

respond to real-world business situations. Some chapters also include a real-world exercise. These questions and exercises are based on actual business data from Maytag Corporation, Tandy Corporation, and other companies.

Ethics. Students are introduced to ethics in accounting in Chapter 1. An **Ethics Discussion Case** at the end of  the Discussion Questions in each chapter presents a scenario to stimulate student discussion of ethical dilemmas in today's business environment. **Videos** developed for the classroom dramatize selected ethics cases. Students can find the codes of professional conduct of the American Institute of Certified Public Accountants and the Institute of Management Accountants in an appendix at the end of the text for easy reference.

CONTEMPORARY COVERAGE

Perpetual Inventory Systems. Perpetual inventory systems are initially discussed in Chapter 5, with the introduction to merchandise transactions and financial statements for a merchandiser. The periodic system is discussed in an appendix. The discussion of cost flow assumptions (such as lifo and fifo) related to perpetual inventory systems is in Chapter 8. At this point, students are better able to handle the complexities of the physical flow of inventory and cost flows.

Internal Control. The discussion in Chapter 6 incorporates new examples of internal controls that students might encounter in their own experiences and in their future work environment. Similarly, internal controls are emphasized in Chapters 7–10. In each of these chapters, internal control exercises have been added.

International Accounting. The globalization of business and the impact on accounting are first recognized in the "Evolution of Financial Accounting." Also, numerous references to companies that engage in international business, such as Hershey Foods Corporation and Toys "R" Us, Inc., are cited throughout the text. In addition, Chapter 13 covers accounting for international transactions.

SKILLS-ORIENTED FEATURES FOR TOMORROW'S BUSINESS LEADERS

Financial Analysis and Interpretation. As a future business manager or accountant you will be expected to analyze and make decisions using accounting information. In this exercise, we provide an opportunity for students to develop these skills by analyzing Hershey Foods Corporation's financial data. Sometimes the data are reports or graphs. Other times, a dialogue with managers is the basis for the analysis.

WHAT DO YOU THINK This feature provides an opportunity for students to develop analytical reasoning skills by developing and supporting a position. Developing and supporting an opinion about how an issue should be decided is critical to success. Although there may not be a right answer, some positions are more easily defended than are others.

WhAT'S WRONG WiTH THiS? These end-of-chapter exercises challenge students to analyze and discover what is wrong with a financial statement, a report, or a management decision. They are ideal for a stimulating learning activity in the classroom.

SHARPEN YOUR COMMUNICATION SKILLS ► Several questions, exercises, problems, and the Mini-Case at the end of each chapter provide an opportunity for students to respond in an oral or written form. These assignments are designed to help students develop their ability to communicate effectively in an accounting and business environment. Additional writing assignments and some guidelines for using these assignments are provided in the *Instructor's Manual* that accompanies the text.

Mini-Cases. Each chapter contains a Mini-Case that simulates a real-world business situation. The Mini-Cases require students to use higher levels of cognitive learning and assist in summarizing chapter concepts. They can also be used as a group learning activity. Selected Mini-Cases are presented on **video** for an exciting classroom presentation.

Computer Applications. Students may use the **Solutions Software** to solve selected problems, including

SOLUTIONS SOFTWARE the comprehensive problems. The computer instructions for each of these problems, which involve a general ledger, are included in the text, following the manual instructions. The instructions are identified by the symbol at the left. Students may also use the software to solve several practice sets.

SPREADSHEET PROBLEM **Spreadsheet Template Diskettes** may also be used for solving selected exercises and problems. These diskettes include a spreadsheet tutorial and "what if" analysis for problems identified by the symbol at the left.

PRACTICAL PEDAGOGY

Reinforcing the Accounting Cycle. This text reinforces the accounting cycle by presenting it twice—once for a service enterprise (in Chapters 1–4) and once for a merchandising enterprise (in Chapter 5). This basic presentation gives students a clear understanding of the accounting process and helps them develop the analytical thinking skills that are essential for success in the accounting principles course.

Chapter 1 introduces and illustrates the **statement of cash flows** as one of the basic financial statements.

Chapter 3 presents the matching concept and all four basic types of adjusting entries. The discussion of recording prepaid expenses initially as expenses and unearned revenues initially as revenues is presented in **Appendix C**, which includes exercises. **Reversing entries** are covered in an appendix to Chapter 4.

Continuing Illustration of the Accounting Cycle. A continuing illustration in Chapters 1 through 5 covers the accounting cycle for a service enterprise and a merchandising enterprise. In Chapters 1–4, the enterprise offers computer consulting services. In Chapter 5, the enterprise becomes a merchandising enterprise that sells microcomputers and related software. This continuity facilitates student understanding and enables students to correlate the concepts and principles introduced in these chapters.

Technology for Classroom and Student Use. State-of-the-art technology supports a multimedia package for capturing the attention of visually oriented students. The text is available on CD-ROM. A **Videodisc** provides easy, instant access to videos, software, transparencies, and illustrations. A series of **videos** for classroom or student use reinforce accounting concepts and add the reality of the business world.

Use of Color. Extensive use of color throughout the text and captivating illustrations opening all the chapters draw students into the text. In addition, the chart below indicates how color is used to consistently highlight the material in the text.

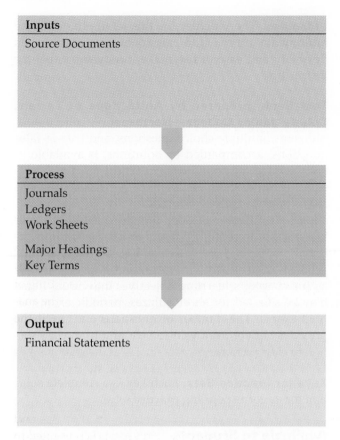

Inputs
Source Documents

Process
Journals
Ledgers
Work Sheets
Major Headings
Key Terms

Output
Financial Statements

Learning Objectives. Created to emphasize students' learning goals and actions, the learning objectives focus directly on the *action* objectives of studying each chapter.

- Each chapter begins with a listing of the learning objectives, providing a framework for the presentation of the chapter material.
- Each learning objective is repeated in the margin next to the start of the discussion to which the objective relates.
- The learning objectives are tied into the chapter review.
- All end-of-chapter exercises and problems are identified by learning objective.

Readability. To enhance clarity and understandability, the readability level was analyzed using a professional software program. An informal writing style and the active voice are used to enliven the text discussion of accounting issues.

Glossary. A glossary at the end of each chapter defines each key term. The learning objective number follows the definition to indicate where the term was discussed in the chapter. The key terms also appear in a complete glossary at the end of the text.

Classification of Accounts. A classification of the accounts on the financial statements, including the normal account balance, is presented on the inside back cover for students' use when reading the text and solving end-of-chapter materials.

Accounting for Merchandising Enterprises. The discussion of merchandising enterprises (Chapter 5) begins by presenting comparative income statements for service and merchandising enterprises. Differences between the two types of statements are then used as a basis for discussing merchandise transactions and financial statements for merchandising enterprises.

Accounting for Bonds Payable. The coverage of bonds payable is discussed in Chapter 11. The chapter presents the amortization of bond discounts and premiums using the straight-line method. This enables students to grasp the essential concepts involved in amortizing discounts and premiums. The more complex effective interest rate method is discussed in an appendix. This flexible presentation allows instructors who wish to omit the effective interest rate method to easily do so without interrupting the flow of the material.

ILLUSTRATIVE PROBLEM Each chapter review includes a problem and solution that are similar to a possible homework assignment. Students can build confidence in their abilities to apply a chapter's concepts and principles by reviewing this problem.

Self-Examination Questions. Each chapter review also includes a set of multiple-choice questions on the basic concepts of the chapter. Students can answer these questions and compare their answers with the correct ones provided at the end of the chapter. The explanations of both the correct and the incorrect answers are a subtle yet effective learning tool.

End-of-Chapter Materials. The end-of-chapter materials were carefully written by the authors to be both practical and comprehensive.

A **"B" Problem** is included for each **"A" Problem** in the text. These problems increase the variety and volume of assignment materials and give instructors a wide choice of subject matter and range of difficulty.

Five **Comprehensive Problems**—at the end of Chapters 4, 5, 10, 11, and 13—integrate and summarize the concepts and principles of several chapters. Instructors may assign these problems as mini practice sets for students to complete manually. As an alternative, these problems can be worked with the Solutions Software.

Check Figures. Check figures at the end of the text assist students in checking end-of-chapter problems. Agreement with the check figures indicates that a significant portion of the solution is basically correct.

SUPPLEMENTARY MATERIALS

CORPORATE FINANCIAL ACCOUNTING is part of a well-integrated educational package that includes materials designed for use by both the student and the instructor. These materials are carefully prepared and reviewed to maintain consistency and high quality throughout.

Available to Instructors

Annotated Edition. In addition to the text material for students, the unique instructor's edition contains points of emphasis, points of interest, teaching suggestions, discussion points, in-class exercises, real-world notes, and check figures.

Solutions Manual. This manual contains solutions to all end-of-chapter materials.

Instructor's Manual, prepared by Donna Chadwick of Sinclair Community College. This manual provides suggestions for cooperative learning activities and additional examples and illustrations for use in the classroom. Transparency masters for classroom use are also included.

Spreadsheet Applications. These template diskettes are used with Lotus® 1-2-3[1] or Microsoft® Excel[2]. They are complimentary to instructors at educational institutions that adopt this text.

Solutions Transparencies. Transparencies of solutions to the "A" problems and the comprehensive problems are available.

Teaching Transparencies. New teaching transparencies go beyond the text and add visual impact to the class lecture.

Videos. Six videotapes assist in classroom presentations. Part Opener videos show the real-world relevance of the material to be studied. Some of these Part Opener videos include interviews with executives, who highlight the importance of the accounting material to be covered. A set of Instructional Videos and Illustrative Problem videos may be used to review the key points of selected chapters. Selected Ethics Cases and Mini-Cases are dramatized on video. *Setting the Stage* includes 24 brief role-play segments that bring the world of financial accounting to life. *Luca Pacioli: Unsung Hero of the Renaissance* is a 25-minute documentary on the life of the father of accounting.

Videodisc. The videdisc for this text is the ultimate multimedia approach to classroom presentations. Its flexibility and ease of use make it a dynamic tool for instructors.

Test Bank, prepared by Anita Hope of Tarrant County Junior College—Northeast. A collection of problems, multiple-choice questions, and true-or-false questions, accompanied by solutions, is available in both printed and microcomputer (MicroEXAM) versions. The microcomputer versions are available in both IBM®[3] and Macintosh® formats.[4]

The Test Bank questions test three levels of learning—ability to recall key terms or key facts, computational ability, and analytical ability. Each question or problem is identified with its level of difficulty as well as the chapter's learning objective. Individual items may be selected for short quizzes, periodic exams, or final exams. The number of questions and problems provides variety from year to year and from class section to class section.

Keys for Practice Sets. Each key is a complete solution for its corresponding practice set.

Available to Students

Solutions Software, prepared by Dale H. Klooster and Warren W. Allen of Educational Technical Systems. This general ledger program is tailored specifically to CORPORATE FINANCIAL ACCOUNTING. It may be used with the IBM® PC, IBM® PS/2, the Tandy® 1000[5], and the Macintosh® microcomputers.

Working Papers. Appropriate printed forms for completing end-of-chapter problems and Mini-Cases are available.

Study Guide, prepared by Carl S. Warren and James M. Reeve. Designed to assist in comprehending the concepts and principles presented in the text, this publication includes an outline for each chapter as well as brief objective questions and problems. Solutions to the questions and problems are at the back of the Study Guide. The Study Guide also contains quiz and test hints to help students focus on their review of material. The Study Guide now features a **Continuing Problem, prepared by George Heyman of Oakton Community College.** This problem in Chapters 2–5 covers the accounting cycle for a single company.

---

[1] Lotus and 1-2-3 are registered trademarks of the Lotus Development Corporation. Any reference to Lotus or 1-2-3 refers to this footnote.
[2] Microsoft is a registered trademark of Microsoft Corporation.
[3] IBM is a registered trademark of International Business Machines Corporation. Any reference to the IBM Personal Computer or the IBM Personal System/2 refers to this footnote.
[4] Macintosh is a registered trademark of McIntosh Laboratory, Inc., and is used by Apple Computer, Inc., with its express permission.
[5] Tandy 1000 is a registered trademark of the Radio Shack Division of Tandy Corporation. Any reference to the Tandy 1000 microcomputer refers to this footnote.

Financial Accounting Tutor, prepared by Thomas P. Lawler of SUNY College at Geneseo. This interactive computerized tutorial provides step-by-step explanations and examples for students' review of accounting principles.

Practice Sets. Three practice sets offer a variety of options for synthesizing and reinforcing the text's coverage.

- **Mountain Bikes Inc., prepared by Jerry G. Kreuze of Western Michigan University,** is a corporation that uses a general journal.
- **First Designs Inc., prepared by Edward Krohn of Miami-Dade Community College—South,** is a departmentalized merchandising corporation.
- **SEMO Sporting Goods Supply Inc., prepared by Deborah F. Beard and Stephen C. DelVecchio of Southeast Missouri State University and John A. Elfrink of Ferris State University,** requires the preparation of correcting entries and financial statements for a wholesaling corporation.

Integrated Accounting: IBM, 4e, and Integrated Accounting: Macintosh, prepared by Dale H. Klooster and Warren W. Allen, are stand-alone, automated accounting packages intended for a first course in microcomputer accounting. Completion time for each is approximately 45–55 hours.

Electronic Spreadsheet Applications for Financial Accounting, prepared by Gaylord N. Smith of Albion College, is a supplemental text-workbook with template diskettes that include accounting applications and a Lotus 1-2-3 tutorial. The text-workbook requires approximately 20–25 hours for completion.

Writing for Accountants, by Aletha Hendrickson of the University of Maryland, is a handbook that emphasizes written and oral communication skills.

Ethical Issues in the Practice of Accounting, by W. Steve Albrecht of Brigham Young University, provides students with background material to stimulate discussions of ethics and increase students' awareness of ethical dilemmas faced by accountants.

Understanding Financial Statements, by Gus Gordon of the University of Southern Mississippi, develops an understanding of accounting statements, without the use of debits and credits.

ACKNOWLEDGMENTS

Throughout the textbook, relevant professional statements of the Financial Accounting Standards Board (including FASB Statement Nos. 105 and 107) and other authoritative publications are discussed, quoted, paraphrased, or footnoted. We are indebted to the American Accounting Association, the American Institute of Certified Public Accountants, and the Financial Accounting Standards Board for material from their publications.

In writing this text, we received extensive feedback from users of previous editions of our books as well as those who have not used our texts. We are most grateful for this input, and we continue to welcome your comments and suggestions.

The following faculty reviewed the manuscript and provided helpful comments:

Karen Adamson
Central Washington University

J. Bassieri
Cuesta College

Deborah Beard
Southeast Missouri State University

Linda Benz
Jefferson Community College

Steve Carter
North Harris County College

Donna Chadwick
Sinclair Community College

Wayne D. Claflin
St. Clair County Community College

Ken Coffey
Johnson County Community College

Paul Concilio
McLennon Community College

William D. Cooper
North Carolina A & T University

Sue Counte
Moraine Valley Community College

Robert H. Cox
Edison State Community College

Anna Cruz
Miami-Dade Community College—Wolfson

Larry Eaton
Gateway Technical College

Pat Evans
Auburn University

Estelle Faier
Metropolitan Community College

William E. Faulk
Northwestern Michigan College

Carl J. Fisher
Foothill College

Edward Fratentaro
Orange Coast College

Ann Gregory
South Plains College

Tim Helton
Joliet Junior College

George Heyman
Oakton Community College

Anita Hope
Tarrant County Junior College—Northeast

Morris Knapp
Miami-Dade Community College—Wolfson

James Lentz
Moraine Valley Community College

Larry F. Lofton
Hinds Community College

Gregory K. Lowry
Wilmington College

Daniel Luna
Raritan Valley Community College

Patrick McNabb
Ferris State University

Cynthia Middleton
University of Arkansas at Monticello

Donald H. Minyard
Auburn University

Anne Montminy
Brevard Community College

Greg Mostyn
Mission College

Susan Murphy
Monroe Community College

Terry J. Nunley
University of North Carolina at Charlotte

Alan Ransom
Cypress College

Robert Reas
Sinclair Community College

S. Gunter Samuelson
Suffolk County Community College

Jeanette Sanfillippo
Maryville University

James K. Smith
Baker College

John Uzzo
Northeastern (OK) State University

Joseph Williams
Itawamba Community College

The following faculty reviewed manuscript to verify the accuracy of solutions:

Pamela Anglin
Navarro College

Linda Benz
Jefferson Community College

Donald Brunner
Spokane Falls Community College

Brenda Hester
Volunteer State Community College

Donald MacGilvra
Shoreline Community College

William Phipps
Verson Regional Junior College

Jim Puthoff
Sinclair Community College

Donald Whisler
Spokane Falls Community College

Comments from the following faculty were useful in revising the Solutions Software:

Paul Concilio
McLennan Community College

Charles A. Konkol
University of Wisconsin–Milwaukee

John R. Stewart
University of Northern Colorado

We also deeply express our appreciation to the South-Western staff—editorial, production, art, advertising, marketing, and sales—for their input and assistance in helping us offer you this refreshing view of accounting.

Carl S. Warren
James M. Reeve
Philip E. Fess

CARL S. WARREN

Professor Carl S. Warren is the Arthur Andersen & Co. Alumni Professor of Accounting at the J.M. Tull School of Accounting at the University of Georgia, Athens. Professor Warren received his PhD from Michigan State University in 1973 and has taught accounting at the University of Iowa, Michigan State University, the University of Chicago, and the University of Georgia. He has received teaching awards from three different student organizations at the University of Georgia.

Professor Warren is a CPA and CMA. He received a Georgia Gold Key Award and a Certificate of Honorable Mention for his scores on the CPA examination. He received a Certificate of Distinguished Performance for his scores on the CMA examination. Professor Warren is also a Certified Internal Auditor (CIA) and Certified Fraud Examiner (CFE).

Professor Warren is a member of the American Institute of CPAs, the Georgia Society of CPAs, the Institute of Management Accountants, the Institute of Internal Auditors, the American Accounting Association, the Georgia Association of Accounting Educators, the National Association of Fraud Examiners, and the Financial Executives Institute. Professor Warren has served on numerous professional committees and editorial boards, including a term as a member of the Board of Examiners of the American Institute of CPAs. He has written seventeen textbooks and numerous articles in such journals as the *Journal of Accountancy*, the *Accounting Review*, the *Journal of Accounting Research*, the *CPA Journal, Cost and Management*, and *Managerial Planning*.

Professor Warren resides in Athens, Georgia, with his wife, Sharon, and two children. His daughter, Stephanie, attends Wake Forest University and his son, Jeffrey, is a senior in high school. Professor Warren's hobbies include golf, racquetball, and fishing.

JAMES M. REEVE

Professor James M. Reeve is Professor of Accounting at the University of Tennessee, Knoxville. Professor Reeve received his PhD from Oklahoma State University in 1980. He has received both the Ross and Keally Teaching Awards from the College of Business Administration at the University of Tennessee. In addition, he has twice received the MBA Faculty Recognition Award from the Tennessee Organization of MBAs. Professor Reeve is founder of the Cost Management Institute and a member of the Institutes for Productivity Through Quality faculty at the University of Tennessee.

Professor Reeve is a CPA and a member of the American Institute of CPAs, the American Accounting Association, the Institute of Management Accountants, and the Association for Manufacturing Excellence. He has served as a judge in the RIT/*USA Today* Quality Cup Competition. In addition, Professor Reeve has consulted on managerial accounting issues with numerous companies, including Procter & Gamble, AMOCO, Rockwell International, Harris Corporation, and Freddie Mac.

Professor Reeve has served on numerous professional committees and editorial boards. He has written over 40 articles, which have appeared in such journals as the *Accounting Review, Accounting Horizons, Journal of Management Accounting Research, Management Accounting, Journal of Cost Management*, and *Journal of Accounting Education*. Professor Reeve's research interests are in the role of managerial accounting information in organizational change and control.

Professor Reeve and his wife, Susan, have two sons, Joshua and Chase. His hobbies include golf, skiing, reading, and travel.

PHILIP E. FESS

Professor Philip E. Fess is the Arthur Andersen & Co. Alumni Professor of Accountancy Emeritus at the University of Illinois, Champaign-Urbana. Professor Fess received his PhD from the University of Illinois and has been involved in textbook writing for over twenty-five years. In addition to having more than 30 years of teaching experience, he has won numerous teaching awards, including the University of Illinois, College of Commerce Alumni Association Excellence in Teaching Award and the Illinois CPA Society Educator of the Year Award.

Professor Fess is a CPA and a member of the American Institute of CPAs, the Illinois Society of CPAs, and the American Accounting Association. He has served many professional associations in a variety of ways, including a term as a member of the Auditing Standards Board, editorial advisor to the *Journal of Accountancy*, and chairperson of the American Accounting Association Committee on CPA Examinations. Professor Fess has written more than 100 books and articles, which have appeared in such journals as the *Journal of Accountancy*, the *Accounting Review*, the *CPA Journal*, and *Management Accounting*. He has also served as an expert witness before the U.S. Tax Court and as a member of the Cost Advisory Panel for the Secretary of the Air Force.

Professor Fess and his wife, Suzanne, have three daughters: Linda, who is an Assistant Professor of Accountancy at Northern Illinois University; Ginny, who is a CPA and is employed by Solar Turbine Co.; and Martha, who is also a CPA and received a law degree from the University of San Diego. Professor Fess's hobby is tennis, and he has represented the United States in international tennis competition.

Brief Contents

Table of Contents

Part 1

Fundamentals of Financial Accounting Systems

Introduction: Evolution of Financial Accounting

Over the years, the evolution of financial accounting has been similar to other professions such as medicine and law. These professions continually change as society and the needs of society change. In recent years, for example, the practice of medicine has changed significantly with the invention and use of lasers. Likewise, the practice of law has changed to reflect new specializations, such as environmental law.

The objective of this introduction is to make you aware of how financial accounting has evolved. This awareness will help you understand the role and the importance of financial accounting in society and in your everyday life.

EARLY FINANCIAL ACCOUNTING

Just as you may keep a record of the money you spend, people throughout history have maintained records of their business activities. Some of these records were clay tablets that indicated the payment of wages in Babylon around 3600 B.C. Record keeping also existed in ancient Egypt and in the Greek city-states. Some of the earliest English records were compiled by William the Conqueror in the eleventh century. These early accounting records included only some of the financial activities of an entity. A systematic recording of all activities of an entity developed later in response to the needs of the commercial republics of Italy.

DOUBLE-ENTRY SYSTEM

How did the early recording of financial activities evolve into a system of financial accounting? The basic system of financial accounting, which is still used today, was invented by Luca Pacioli, a Franciscan monk. Pacioli was a mathematician who taught in various universities in Perugia, Naples, Pisa, and Florence. He was a close friend of Leonardo da Vinci, with whom he collaborated on a mathematics book. Pacioli did the text, and da Vinci drew the illustrations.

1

Pacioli invented what is known as the double-entry system of accounting. A description of the double-entry system was first published in Italy in 1494.[1] This system was strongly influenced by the financial needs of Venetian merchants. Goethe, the German poet, novelist, and scientist, described the double-entry system as "one of the most beautiful inventions of the human spirit, and every good businessman should use it in his economic undertakings."[2]

What is so special about the double-entry system? It is unique because it records financial activities in such a way that an equilibrium is created within the records. For example, assume that you borrow $1,000 from a bank. Within the double-entry system, the loan is recorded as $1,000 of cash received, and at the same time, an obligation is recorded for eventual repayment of the $1,000. Each of the $1,000 amounts is balanced by the other. In a complex business environment, in which an entity may be involved in thousands of transactions daily, this balancing is a valuable control that ensures the accuracy of the recording process.

Despite the enormous changes in business operations and their complexity since 1494, the basic elements of the double-entry system have remained virtually unchanged. This is a lasting tribute to the significance of Pacioli's invention and his contribution to society.

CORPORATE ORGANIZATION

In addition to the invention of the double-entry system, other major events significantly influenced the evolution of financial accounting. One such event was the Industrial Revolution. The Industrial Revolution occurred in England from the mid-eighteenth to the mid-nineteenth centuries. It changed the method of producing marketable goods from a handicraft method to a factory system.

As you might expect, the Industrial Revolution created a demand for large amounts of money or capital to build factories and purchase machinery. To meet this need for capital, the corporate form of organization was developed.

The corporate form of organization was first established in England in 1845. It soon spread rapidly to the United States, which became one of the world's leading industrial nations shortly after the Civil War. In the United States, large amounts of capital were essential for the development of new industries such as steel, transportation, mining, electric power, and communications. As in England, the corporation was the primary vehicle for raising the capital that was needed.

How does the corporate form of organization raise capital? If you answered "by issuing stock," you'd be correct. Corporate ownership is divided into shares of stock that can be readily transferred. The stockholders of a corporation normally do not exercise direct control over the operations of the corporation. The management of the corporation runs day-to-day operations, and the stockholders only indirectly control the corporation through electing a board of directors. The board of directors sets general policies and selects the officers who manage the corporation.

So, how did the corporate form of organization affect financial accounting? The corporate form affected the evolution of financial accounting because the stockholders needed information about how well management was running the corporation. Since stockholders are not directly involved in day-to-day operations, they must rely on financial accounting reports in evaluating management's performance.

As corporations grew larger, the number of individuals and institutions relying on financial accounting reports increased. Potential shareholders and creditors needed information. Government agencies required information for purposes of

---

[1] Several celebrations are planned in 1994 throughout the accounting profession to honor the 500th anniversary of Pacioli's invention.

[2] Goethe, Johann Wolfgang von, *Samtliche Werke,* edited by Edward von der Hellen (Stuttgart and Berlin: J. G. Cotta, 1902–1907), Vol XVII, p. 37.

taxation and regulation. Employees, union representatives, and customers requested information to judge the stability and profitability of corporations. Thus, largely because of the use of the corporate form of organization, financial accounting had to expand from serving the needs of a few owners to a public role of meeting the needs of a variety of interested parties.

PUBLIC ACCOUNTING

The corporate form of organization also created a need for an independent review or audit of reports prepared by the corporation's management. This audit was necessary to provide some assurance to users of the information that the reports were reliable. This audit function, called the attest function, was responsible for the development and growth of the public accounting profession. Unlike private accountants who work for a specific business entity, public accountants are independent of the enterprises whose reports they audit.

All states currently provide for the regulation and licensing of certified public accountants (CPAs). In 1944, fifty years after the enactment of the first CPA law, there were approximately 25,000 CPAs in the United States. During the next four decades, the number increased tenfold. Currently, the number exceeds 300,000 and is continuing to increase.

Although auditing is still a major service offered by CPAs, much of their time is also spent assisting in planning and controlling clients' operations. Such consulting services have increased dramatically in recent years. Today, consulting services are a major part of the practice of many public accounting firms.

INCOME TAX

We are all affected by income taxes. Since income taxes are based on records of financial activities, the development of the income tax significantly influenced the evolution of financial accounting, as you might expect.

The development of the federal income tax was made possible by the Sixteenth Amendment to the Constitution of the United States. The first federal income tax law was passed by the United States Congress in 1913. Currently, all business enterprises organized as corporations or partnerships, as well as many individuals and organizations, are required to file income tax returns. To meet this requirement, filers must maintain adequate financial records. Because of the complexity of the tax laws and regulations, more and more organizations and individuals depend on accountants. In addition to preparing tax returns, accountants advise clients on how to minimize their taxes.

GOVERNMENT INFLUENCE

Local, state, and federal governments also have had a significant influence on the evolution of financial accounting. Current accounting systems must record and report financial data for a variety of governmental laws and regulations.

What are some examples of such laws and regulations at the local, state, and federal levels? At the local level, commissions and boards levy property and sales taxes based on accounting data. At the state level, public service commissions often approve utility rates. Such rate-making processes use and analyze accounting data. At the federal level, in addition to the income tax, the Social Security and Medicare laws require accounting record keeping and reporting by almost all businesses and many individuals.

ACCOUNTING'S FUTURE

As the preceding paragraphs emphasize, financial accounting touches all of our lives in one way or another. Accounting data are essential to the functioning of modern society. As society changes, so too will accounting change. Although long-range predictions are risky, two areas of accounting are rapidly evolving and will likely be seeing significant change in the future: international accounting and social accounting.

International Accounting

Financial accounting changes to meet the needs of society. As a result, accounting rules and regulations differ significantly among countries, each of which has unique cultural and societal needs. These differences create major accounting problems when a firm has foreign operations in a country. In such cases, the firm must adapt its accounting system to the rules and regulations of each country. This increases the cost of recording accounting data and preparing financial accounting reports. It also has the potential of confusing the users of accounting reports.

There is a movement within the accounting profession to develop uniform international accounting standards. Working toward this goal are such international organizations as the International Accounting Standards Committee and the International Federation of Accountants.

Social Accounting

Accounting traditionally focuses on recording and reporting financial activities of business enterprises or other specific entities. Recently, there has been a suggestion that accounting should also record and report the impact of various organizations on society. This area of accounting is called social accounting.

As social accounting has evolved, three main areas have been identified for study. The first area is recording and reporting the impact of various organizations on matters that affect the overall quality of life in society. The second area is recording and reporting the impact of government programs on achieving specific social objectives. The third area is recording and reporting the impact of corporate social performance, which refers to the corporation's responsibilities in such areas as water and air pollution, conservation of natural resources, and equal employment practices.

The concept of social accounting is relatively simple as a theory. However, additional study and research are needed before socioeconomic costs and benefits of various activities can be recorded and reported. For example, the overall impact of a public utility's proposal to build a nuclear power plant is difficult to measure, record, and report.

DO YOU USE ACCOUNTING?

As this introduction suggests, we all use financial accounting to some degree. For some of us, our accounting involves recording checks in our checkbooks. For others, it may involve preparing our tax returns. As you begin your study of financial accounting, you should keep in mind the importance of accounting to your everyday life as well as its importance for your business career.

You and Accounting

How much are you worth? In financial terms, the first step in answering this question is to determine what you own. For example, if you own a car costing $12,000, your financial worth includes your $12,000 car. However, if you have a $10,000 loan outstanding on the car, your financial worth is only $2,000 ($12,000 - $10,000). Your financial worth may help you answer the question "Can I afford to buy a new stereo?"

Managers of business enterprises must daily answer questions similar to these. For example, a manager of a chain of pizza restaurants must decide whether to acquire delivery cars. The financial worth of the pizza restaurants may be a major factor in determining whether the cars can be acquired. That is, the financial worth of the restaurants may determine whether a loan can be obtained to finance the purchase of the cars.

In this chapter, we discuss the accounting framework by which business enterprises gather and report economic data. These data are then used in making decisions such as the one described here. You may also apply the concepts described in this chapter to your personal finances. For example, these concepts can be used to determine your financial worth.

Chapter 1
Accounting Concepts and Principles

LEARNING OBJECTIVES
After studying this chapter, you should be able to:

Objective 1
Define accounting as an information system.

Objective 2
Describe the profession of accounting, and list its specialized fields.

Objective 3
Summarize the development of generally accepted accounting principles and concepts, including the business entity concept and the cost principle.

Objective 4
List the characteristics of a business transaction.

Objective 5
State the accounting equation, and define each element of the equation.

Objective 6
Explain how business transactions can be stated in terms of the resulting changes in the three basic elements of the accounting equation.

Objective 7
Describe the financial statements of a corporation, and explain how they interrelate.

Accounting provides and interprets economic data for economic units within society. These economic units include profit enterprises and not-for-profit entities, such as churches, government agencies, and charities. In addition, accounting provides information for individual persons and family units. Regardless of the type of economic unit, accounting must provide economic data that are reliable and accurate.

The primary focus of this text is business enterprises organized for profit. Accountants for such enterprises must have a thorough understanding of accounting in order to process, interpret, and communicate economic data. Many others directly involved in the enterprise's activities also come in contact with accounting. For example, individuals engaged in such areas of business as finance, production, marketing, personnel, and general management must have an understanding of accounting. In addition, the importance of understanding accounting is not limited to those directly involved in managing a business. For example, an engineer in designing a product may consider the costs of alternative manufacturing processes. Likewise, lawyers use accounting data in tax cases and in settling lawsuits.

ACCOUNTING AS AN INFORMATION SYSTEM

Objective 1
Define accounting as an
information system.

Accounting plays an important role in our economic and social system. The decisions made by individuals, businesses, governments, and other entities determine the use of the nation's scarce resources. The goal of accounting is to record, report, and interpret economic data for use by decision makers.

Using Accounting

Do you use accounting information? The answer is yes. We all use accounting information in one form or another. For example, anyone who earns above a certain amount of income must file a tax return. If you are thinking about buying a new car, you use accounting information to determine whether you can afford the monthly payments. Similarly, your decision to attend college implies that you considered the benefits of attending (ability to obtain a higher-paying job) versus the related costs of attending (tuition, textbooks, and so on).

What is accounting? **Accounting**[1] is often called the language of business. Accounting can be viewed as an information system that provides essential information about the economic activities of an entity to various individuals or groups.

Accounting provides the conceptual framework for gathering economic data and the language for reporting these data. Who uses such information? Investors in a business enterprise need information about the enterprise's financial status and its future prospects. Bankers and creditors evaluate the financial condition of a business and assess the risks before making loans. Government agencies are concerned with the financial activities of business organizations for taxation and regulation. Employees and their unions are also interested in the condition and profit potential of the company that hires them. In directing the operations of a company, management depends on and uses accounting data.

The process of using accounting to provide information to users is illustrated in Exhibit 1. First, user groups are identified and their information needs determined. These needs determine which economic data are recorded by the accounting system. Finally, accounting reports are prepared summarizing the information

Exhibit 1
Accounting as a Provider of
Information to Users

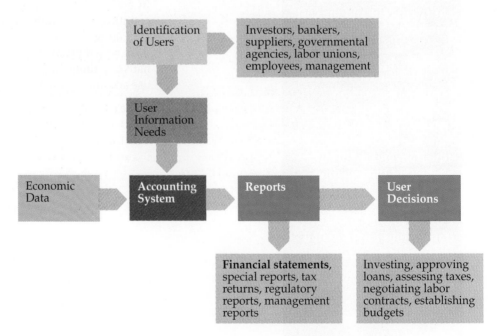

---

[1] A glossary of terms appears at the end of each chapter. The terms included in each glossary are printed in color the first time they are defined in the text.

for users. For example, to evaluate their investments, investors need information on the financial condition and results of operations of enterprises. Although the information for one group of users may differ from another, accounting can provide each group with useful information.

PROFESSION OF ACCOUNTING

Objective 2
Describe the profession of accounting, and list its specialized fields.

The profession of accounting has grown rapidly during the current century. The career opportunities in accounting and the number of accountants have both increased. The increase in number, size, and complexity of business enterprises has increased the demand for accounting services. In addition, new laws and regulations have also created a demand for accounting.

You may wonder whether there are job opportunities in accounting. The answer is yes. Employment opportunities in the profession of accountancy are expected to continue to grow and expand. In a report prepared by the U.S. Department of Labor, the accounting profession is projected to increase by 39.8% between the late 1980s and the year 2000.[2]

Accountants are engaged in either (1) private accounting or (2) public accounting. Accountants employed by a business firm or not-for-profit organization are said to be engaged in **private accounting**. Accountants and their staff who provide services on a fee basis are said to be engaged in **public accounting**.

Experience in private and public accounting has long been recognized as excellent training for top management positions. Many positions in industry and in state and federal agencies are held by individuals with education and experience in accounting. For example, in its 1990 Special Bonus Issue on "The Corporate Elite," *Business Week* reported that 31% of the chief executives of the 1,000 largest public corporations followed a finance-accounting career path. Merchandising-marketing was the career path for 27%, and engineering-technical was the career path for 22% of the chief executives.

Private Accounting

The scope of activities and duties of private accountants varies widely. Private accountants are frequently called management accountants. If they are employed by a manufacturing concern, they may be called industrial or cost accountants. The chief accountant in a business may be called the **controller**. Various state and federal agencies and other not-for-profit agencies also employ accountants.

The Institute of Certified Management Accountants, an affiliate of the Institute of Management Accountants (IMA), sponsors the **Certified Management Accountant (CMA)** program. The CMA certificate is evidence of competence in management accounting. To become a CMA, a college degree, two years of experience, and successful completion of a two-day examination are required. Continuing professional education is required for renewal of the CMA certificate.

The Institute of Internal Auditors sponsors a similar program for internal auditors. Internal auditors are accountants who review the accounting and operating procedures prescribed by their firms. Accountants who specialize in internal auditing may be granted the **Certified Internal Auditor (CIA)** certificate.

Public Accounting

In public accounting, an accountant may practice as an individual or as a member of a public accounting firm. Public accountants who have met a state's education, experience, and examination requirements may become **Certified Public Accountants (CPAs)**.

---

[2] U.S. Department of Labor, Bureau of Labor Statistics, *Occupational Projections and Training Data: 1991 Edition* (Washington: U.S. Government Printing Office), April 1991.

The requirements for obtaining the CPA certificate differ among the various states.[3] All states require a college education in accounting. In addition, a candidate must pass a two-day examination prepared by the American Institute of Certified Public Accountants (AICPA). How difficult is the CPA examination? Approximately 30% of the candidates pass each of the four parts of the CPA examination. Only about 10 to 20% pass the entire examination at one time.

Most states do not permit individuals to practice as CPAs until they have had from one to three years' experience in public accounting. Some states, however, accept similar employment in private accounting as equivalent experience.

All states require CPAs to obtain continuing professional education. CPAs who do not comply may lose their certificates and their right to practice. Although the details of this requirement may vary, most states require at least forty hours of continuing education per year.

Professional Ethics for Accountants

Ethics are moral principles that guide the conduct of individuals, whether they are acting alone or as members of a profession or business. Do all accountants agree on what is and is not ethical? No, individuals may differ on what is "right" or "wrong" in a given situation. However, proper ethical conduct implies a duty beyond that of law to act in the interests of society. At times, this may mean an individual must make personal sacrifices for the benefit of society. Often, such ethical conduct not only benefits society, but it promotes self-worth and is "good business." For example, a business that ignores the public welfare and pollutes the environment may find itself the focus of lawsuits and customer boycotts. Likewise, an automobile manufacturer that fails to correct a safety defect to save costs may later lose sales from the loss of consumer confidence.

Accountants in both private and public practice have developed standards to guide them in the conduct of their practices.[4] The Institute of Management Accountants (IMA) has prepared **standards of ethical conduct** to guide management accountants in serving their employers, their profession, and the public. As stated in these standards, management accountants have a responsibility to:[5]

1. Maintain an appropriate level of professional competence.
2. Refrain from disclosing confidential information.
3. Avoid conflicts of interest.
4. Communicate information fairly and objectively.

The American Institute of Certified Public Accountants (AICPA) has also developed standards to guide its members. The purpose of these standards, called **codes of professional conduct** or **codes of professional ethics**, is to instill public confidence in the public accounting profession. The standards require CPAs to:[6]

1. Exercise sensitive professional and moral judgments.
2. Act in a way that will serve the public interest, honor the public trust, and demonstrate commitment to professionalism.
3. Perform all professional responsibilities with integrity.
4. Maintain objectivity and be free of conflicts of interest.
5. Observe the profession's technical and ethical standards and continually improve competency.
6. Determine the scope and nature of professional services according to ethical standards.

The AICPA and state societies of CPAs can revoke a CPA's membership in their organizations for violations of the code of professional conduct. A state board of

[3] Information on a state's requirements is available from that state's board of accountancy.
[4] An ethics discussion case is provided at the end of each chapter to focus attention on meaningful ethical situations that accountants often face in practice.
[5] The text of the *Standards of Ethical Conduct For Management Accountants* (Institute of Management Accountants: Montvale, New Jersey, 1992) is reproduced in Appendix B.
[6] The text of the *Code of Professional Conduct* (American Institute of Certified Public Accountants: New York, 1992) is reproduced in Appendix B.

accountancy, the Securities and Exchange Commission (SEC), or other regulatory agencies may revoke or limit the CPA's ability to practice. This combination of review by the AICPA, state societies of CPAs, the SEC, and other regulatory agencies encourages ethical behavior by CPAs.

Codes of professional conduct change as society changes. However, ethical conduct is more than simply conforming to written standards of professional behavior. In a true sense, ethical conduct requires a personal commitment to honorable behavior.

Ethics in American Business

In October 1987, Touche Ross (now Deloitte & Touche) conducted a survey of 1,107 directors and top executives of corporations with $500 million or more in annual sales, deans of business schools, and members of Congress, seeking their opinions on ethics in American business. The survey's many interesting findings included the following:

- The United States has higher standards of business ethics than any other country in the world. Ethical standards are also considered high in the United Kingdom, Canada, Switzerland, and Germany, which respondents ranked in that order, followed by Japan.
- An enterprise actually strengthens its competitive position by maintaining high ethical standards.
- The four professions with the highest standards are clergy, accountants, teachers, and engineers, in that order. The ethical standards of businesspeople as a profes-

sional group are well regarded, particularly by bankers and accountants.
- A vast majority of the respondents believe that American business is ethical.
- Though respondents believe almost unanimously that the business community is troubled by ethical problems, they are very far from seeing a wholesale breakdown in American business ethics. Indeed, compared to a hundred years ago, during the age of the robber barons, business ethics are definitely better today.
- Legislation is the least effective way of encouraging ethical business behavior. Rather, the adoption of business codes of ethics is the most effective way. Indeed, the main reason for high ethical standards in a profession is that profession's own standards and accreditation.

Source: *Ethics in American Business*, Touche Ross, January 1988.

Specialized Accounting Fields

You may think that all accounting is the same. However, this is not true. Specialized fields in accounting have evolved as a result of technology advances and economic growth. The most important accounting fields are described in the following paragraphs.

Financial accounting is concerned with recording economic data for a business enterprise or other economic unit and periodically preparing reports from such records. The reports provide useful information for managers, owners, creditors, governmental agencies, and the public. Financial accountants use rules of accounting, termed **generally accepted accounting principles (GAAP)**. Business enterprises must follow these principles in preparing reports for use by their stockholders and the investing public. These rules ensure that accounting reports for different companies may be compared. The ability to compare company reports is essential if resources are to be divided efficiently among business organizations.

Auditing is a field of activity involving an independent review of the accounting records. In conducting an audit, CPAs examine the records supporting the financial reports of an enterprise. Based on this examination, CPAs provide an opinion on the fairness of the financial reports. An important element of evaluating "fairness" is agreement with generally accepted accounting principles. Many companies also employ a staff of internal auditors who determine if the operating units of a company are following management's policies and procedures.

Management accounting, often called **managerial accounting**, uses both historical and estimated data to aid management in running day-to-day operations and in planning future operations. The management accountant is often concerned with identifying alternative courses of action and preparing reports evaluating each alternative. For example, the accountant may aid the company treasurer in preparing alternative plans for future financing.

In recent years, CPAs have realized that their training and experience uniquely qualify them to advise management. This rapidly growing field of specialization by CPAs is called *management advisory services*.

Cost accounting focuses on estimating and controlling costs. It is concerned mainly with the costs of manufacturing activities and manufactured products. In addition, an important duty of the cost accountant is to record and explain cost data, both actual and prospective. Management uses these data in planning and controlling operations.

Tax accounting involves preparing tax returns and analyzing possible tax results of proposed decisions. Accountants in this field must be familiar with the tax statutes affecting their employer or clients. In addition, tax accountants must keep up to date on tax regulations and court decisions on tax cases.

Accounting systems is the special field concerned with the design and use of procedures for recording and reporting economic data. The systems accountant must design procedures to safeguard business properties and provide for an efficient information flow. Knowledge of data processing methods, including computer hardware and software, is required.

International accounting focuses on the special issues related to international trade. Because businesses of all sizes sell and buy goods in world markets, this field of accounting is increasing in importance. Accountants in this area must understand the influences of various countries' customs, laws, and taxation on business.

Not-for-profit accounting specializes in recording, reporting, and planning operations of federal, state, and other government agencies. In addition, other not-for-profit agencies, such as churches, charities, and educational institutions, employ accountants. Not-for-profit accounting focuses on adherence to restrictions and other standards required by law, organizations, or individual donors.

Social accounting is a new field of accounting. There are demands on the accounting profession to measure the social costs and benefits of various actions. For example, accountants in this field might measure and evaluate the environmental impact of acid rain. Other accountants might analyze and evaluate the use of welfare funds in a large city or the use of federal and state lands.

Accounting instruction provides a career for dedicated individuals to share their knowledge of and experience in accounting with their students. In addition to teaching and advising students, accounting instructors often perform research and write articles to expand accounting knowledge. They often actively participate in professional organizations. Many instructors maintain part-time accounting practices or consulting services.

There is some overlap among the various fields, and accountants are often experts in several fields. In addition, there may be further specialization within a field. For example, an auditor may become an expert in a single type of business such as retailing or banking. A tax accountant might become a specialist in oil- and gas-producing companies.

GENERALLY ACCEPTED ACCOUNTING PRINCIPLES AND CONCEPTS

Objective 3
Summarize the development of generally accepted accounting principles and concepts, including the business entity concept and the cost principle.

In accounting, as in the physical sciences, change is never-ending. Professional accountants, educators, and accounting organizations such as the AICPA constantly seek answers to accounting issues facing business. Generally accepted accounting principles and concepts develop from research, accepted accounting practices, and pronouncements of authoritative bodies.

Currently, the **Financial Accounting Standards Board (FASB)** is the primary authoritative body developing accounting principles. The FASB was organized in 1973 and is composed of seven members, four of whom must be CPAs drawn from practice. The FASB employs a full-time research and administrative staff and often uses task forces to study specific issues in financial accounting. As these issues arise, the FASB conducts extensive research to identify the primary concerns involved and possible solutions. Generally, after issuing discussion memoranda and preliminary proposals and evaluating comments from interested parties, the Board issues *Statements of Financial Accounting Standards*. These *Standards* become part of generally accepted accounting principles. To explain, clarify, or elaborate on existing standards, the Board also issues *Interpretations*, which have the same authority as the *Standards*. Since its inception, the FASB has issued over 100 *Statements* and *Interpretations*.[7]

In this chapter and throughout this text, we emphasize accounting principles and concepts. It is through this emphasis on the "why" of accounting as well as the "how" that you will gain an understanding of the full significance of accounting. In the following paragraphs, we discuss the business entity concept and the cost principle.

Business Entity Concept

The **business entity concept** is based on applying accounting to individual economic units in society, such as a business enterprise. The business entity concept requires that the first step in the practice of accounting is to identify the economic unit for which economic data are required. The data for the entity can then be recorded and analyzed and periodic reports prepared. A business entity could be identified as an individual, a not-for-profit organization such as a church, or an enterprise such as a real estate agency.

This textbook focuses on accounting concepts and principles for profit-making businesses. Such businesses are normally organized as sole proprietorships, partnerships, or corporations. A **sole proprietorship** is owned by one individual. A **partnership** is owned by two or more individuals. A **corporation** is organized under state or federal statutes as a separate legal entity. The ownership of a corporation is divided into shares of stock. The sole proprietorship is the most common business form. However, corporations receive over 90% of the total dollars of business receipts. These facts are shown in Exhibit 2.

In this text, we primarily illustrate the corporate form of organization.

Exhibit 2
Profit-Making Businesses

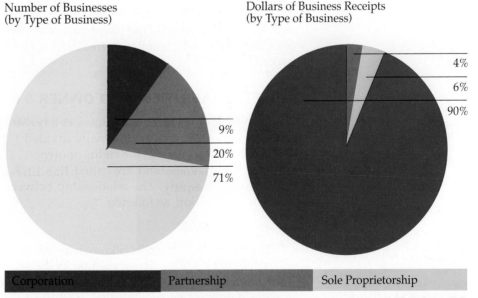

Number of Businesses
(by Type of Business)

Dollars of Business Receipts
(by Type of Business)

9%
20%
71%

4%
6%
90%

Corporation   Partnership   Sole Proprietorship

Source: U.S. Bureau of the Census, *Statistical Abstract of the United States:* 1991 (111th edition) Washington, DC.

[7] The FASB is also developing a broad conceptual framework for financial accounting. This framework is expected to take many years to complete. Six *Statements of Financial Accounting Concepts* have been published to date.

The Cost Principle

The properties and services bought by a business are recorded using the cost principle. By this principle, the actual cost of a property or service is entered into the accounting records. For example, if a building is bought for $150,000, that is the amount entered into the buyer's accounting records. The seller may have been asking $170,000 for the building up to the time of the sale. The buyer may have initially offered $130,000 for the building. The building may have been assessed at $125,000 for property tax purposes, and the buyer may have received an offer of $175,000 for the building the day after it was acquired. These latter amounts have no effect on the accounting records because they did not result in an exchange. *The exchange price, or cost, of $150,000 is the amount used in the accounting records for the building.*

Continuing the illustration, the $175,000 offer received by the buyer the day after the building was acquired indicates that it was a bargain purchase at $150,000. To use $175,000 in the accounting records, however, would record an illusory or unrealized profit. If, after buying the building, the buyer *should* accept the offer and sell the building for $175,000, a profit of $25,000 would then be realized and recorded. The new owner would record $175,000 as the cost of the building.

The use of cost in recording properties and services acquired is a basic concept of accounting. In exchanges between buyer and seller, both try to get the best price. Only the final amount agreed on is objective enough for accounting purposes. If the amounts for which properties were recorded were constantly revised upward and downward based on offers, appraisals, and opinions, accounting reports would soon become unstable and unreliable.

BUSINESS TRANSACTIONS

Objective 4
List the characteristics of a business transaction.

Are all economic events affecting a business entity recorded in an accounting system? No, only business transactions are recorded. A business transaction is an economic event or a condition that must be recorded by an entity. For example, the payment of a monthly telephone bill of $68 or the acquisition of land for $50,000 are business transactions.

A business transaction may lead to an event or a condition that results in another transaction. For example, the purchase of $1,750 of merchandise on credit will be followed later by the payment to the creditor. Each time a portion of the merchandise is sold, another transaction occurs. Each of these events must be recorded.

ASSETS, LIABILITIES, AND OWNER'S EQUITY

Objective 5
State the accounting equation, and define each element of the equation.

The properties owned by a business enterprise are called assets. The rights or claims to the properties are normally divided into two principal types: (1) the rights of creditors and (2) the rights of owners. The rights of creditors represent debts of the business and are called liabilities. The rights of the owners are called owner's equity. The relationship between the two may be stated in the form of an equation, as follows:

Assets = Liabilities + Owner's Equity

The preceding equation is known as the accounting equation. It is usual to place liabilities before owner's equity in the accounting equation because creditors have first rights to the assets. The claim of the owners is sometimes given greater emphasis by transposing liabilities to the other side of the equation, yielding:

Assets – Liabilities = Owner's Equity

To illustrate, if the assets owned by a business amount to $100,000 and the liabilities amount to $30,000, the owner's equity is equal to $70,000, as shown below:

Assets – Liabilities = Owner's Equity
$100,000 – $30,000 = $70,000

TRANSACTIONS AND THE ACCOUNTING EQUATION

Objective 6
Explain how business transactions can be stated in terms of the resulting changes in the three basic elements of the accounting equation.

All business transactions can be stated in terms of changes in the three elements of the accounting equation. You will see how business transactions affect the accounting equation by studying some typical transactions. For example, assume that on November 1, 1994, Computer King Corporation is organized by Pat King. Using Pat's knowledge of microcomputers, the business will offer computer consulting services for a fee. Each transaction or group of similar transactions during the first month of operations is described as follows. The effects of the transaction on the accounting equation are then shown.

Transaction a. Computer King Corporation issues shares of stock to Pat King in exchange for cash of $15,000. Stock issued to owners (stockholders), such as Pat King, is referred to as capital stock. The cash received for the stock is deposited in a bank account in the name of Computer King Corporation.

   This transaction increases the asset (cash), on the left side of the equation, by $15,000. To balance the equation, the owner's equity (capital stock) on the right side of the equation increases by the same amount. The effect of this transaction on Computer King Corporation's accounting equation is shown here.

Assets		Owner's Equity	
Cash	=	Capital Stock	
a. 15,000		15,000	Investment by stockholders

   You should note that the equation relates only to the business enterprise, Computer King Corporation. Pat King's personal assets, such as a home or personal bank account, and personal liabilities are excluded from the equation. This is an example of applying the business entity concept. The business is treated as a separate entity, with cash of $15,000 and owner's equity of $15,000.

Transaction b. Computer King Corporation buys land for $10,000 cash. The land is located near a shopping mall that contains three microcomputer stores. Pat King plans to rent office space and equipment for several months. If the business is a success, the company will build a building on the land.

   The purchase of the land changes the makeup of the assets but does not change the total assets. The items in the equation prior to this transaction and the effect of the transaction are shown next. The new amounts or *balances* of the items are also shown.

	Assets			Owner's Equity
	Cash	+	Land	= Capital Stock
	15,000			15,000
b.	–10,000		+10,000	
Bal.	5,000		10,000	15,000

Transaction c. During the month, Computer King Corporation buys supplies for $1,350, agreeing to pay the supplier in the near future. This type of transaction is called a purchase *on account*. The liability created is termed an account payable. Items such as supplies that will be used in the business in the future are called prepaid expenses, which are assets.

In practice, each purchase is normally recorded separately. However, to simplify this illustration, all the purchases of supplies are recorded together. The effect is to increase assets and liabilities by $1,350, as follows:

| | Assets | | | | Liabilities | + | Owner's Equity |
	Cash	+ Supplies	+ Land	=	Accounts Payable	+	Capital Stock
Bal.	5,000		10,000				15,000
c.		+1,350			+1,350		
Bal.	5,000	1,350	10,000		1,350		15,000

Transaction d. The amount charged to customers for goods or services sold to them is called **revenue**. Special terms may be used for certain kinds of revenue, such as *sales* for the sale of merchandise. Revenue from providing services is called *fees earned.* For example, a physician would record fees earned for services to patients. Other examples of revenue terms include *rent earned* for the use of real estate or other property, and *interest earned* for a bank.

The amount of revenue earned during a period is measured by the amount of assets received from customers for the goods sold or services rendered to them. Earning revenue through business operations increase owner's equity. Thus, revenue increases assets and increases owner's equity.

During its first month of operations, Computer King Corporation earns fees of $7,500, receiving the amount in cash. These transactions increase cash and the owner's equity by $7,500, as shown here.

| | Assets | | | | Liabilities | + | Owner's Equity | |
	Cash	+ Supplies	+ Land	=	Accounts Payable	+ Capital Stock	+ Retained Earnings	
Bal.	5,000	1,350	10,000		1,350	15,000		
d.	+7,500						+7,500	Fees earned
Bal.	12,500	1,350	10,000		1,350	15,000	7,500	

You should note that the increase in owner's equity from earning revenue is listed in the equation under "Retained Earnings." **Retained earnings** is the owner's equity created by the business operations (revenues less the expenses). Transactions affecting earnings are kept separate from transactions related to owners' investments (capital stock). This is useful in preparing reports to owners and creditors and in satisfying legal requirements that will be discussed later in the text.

Instead of requiring the payment of cash at the time services are provided or goods are sold, a business may accept payment at a later date. Such revenues are called **fees on account** or **sales on account.** In such cases, the firm has an **account receivable**, which is a claim against the customer. An account receivable is an asset, and the revenue is earned as if cash had been received. When customers pay their accounts, there is an exchange of one asset for another. Cash increases and accounts receivable decreases.

Transaction e. The amount of assets or services used in the process of earning revenue is called **expense**. Expenses include supplies used, wages of employees, and other assets and services used in operating the business. As you might have guessed, the effect of expenses on owner's equity is the opposite of the effect of revenues. Expenses decrease assets and decrease owner's equity.

For Computer King Corporation, the expenses paid during the month were as follows: wages, $2,125; rent, $800; utilities, $450; miscellaneous, $275. Miscellaneous expenses include small amounts paid for such items as postage due, coffee, and newspaper and magazine purchases. This group of transactions reduces cash and reduces owner's equity, as shown.

	Assets			=	Liabilities	+	Owner's Equity	
	Cash	+ Supplies	+ Land		Accounts Payable	+ Capital Stock	+ Retained Earnings	
Bal.	12,500	1,350	10,000	=	1,350	15,000	7,500	
e.	-3,650						-2,125	Wages expense
							- 800	Rent expense
							- 450	Utilities expense
							- 275	Misc. expense
Bal.	8,850	1,350	10,000		1,350	15,000	3,850	

Transaction f. During the month, Computer King Corporation pays $950 to creditors on account, thereby reducing both assets and liabilities. The effect on the equation is as follows:

	Assets			=	Liabilities		Owner's Equity	
	Cash	+ Supplies	+ Land		Accounts Payable	+ Capital Stock	+ Retained Earnings	
Bal.	8,850	1,350	10,000	=	1,350	15,000	3,850	
f.	- 950				- 950			
Bal.	7,900	1,350	10,000		400	15,000	3,850	

You should note that paying an amount on account is different from paying an amount for an expense. The payment of an expense reduces owner's equity, as illustrated in transaction (e). Paying an amount on account reduces the amount on a liability owed.

Transaction g. At the end of the month, the cost of the supplies on hand is $550. The remainder of the supplies ($1,350 - $550) were used in the operations of the business and are treated as an expense. This decrease of $800 in supplies and owner's equity is shown as follows:

	Assets			=	Liabilities		Owner's Equity	
	Cash +	Supplies +	Land		Accounts Payable	+ Capital Stock	+ Retained Earnings	
Bal.	7,900	1,350	10,000	=	400	15,000	3,850	
g.		- 800					- 800	Supplies expense
Bal.	7,900	550	10,000		400	15,000	3,050	

Transaction h. At the end of the month, Computer King Corporation pays $2,000 to stockholders (Pat King) as dividends. **Dividends** are distributions of earnings to stockholders. The payment of the dividends reduces both cash and owner's equity. The effect of this transaction is shown as follows:

	Assets			=	Liabilities		Owner's Equity	
	Cash +	Supplies +	Land		Accounts Payable	+ Capital Stock	+ Retained Earnings	
Bal.	7,900	550	10,000	=	400	15,000	3,050	
h.	-2,000						-2,000	Dividends
Bal.	5,900	550	10,000		400	15,000	1,050	

You should be careful not to confuse dividends with expenses. Dividends do not represent assets consumed or services used in the process of earning revenues. The decrease in owner's equity from the payment of dividends is listed in the equation under "Retained Earnings." This is because dividends are considered a distribution of earnings.

Summary. The transactions of Computer King Corporation are summarized as follows. The transactions are identified by letter, and the balance of each item is shown after each transaction.

	Cash +	Supplies +	Land	=	Accounts Payable +	Capital Stock +	Retained Earnings	
	Assets				**Liabilities**	**Owner's + Equity**		
a.	+15,000					+15,000		Investment by stockholders
b.	-10,000		+10,000					
Bal.	5,000		10,000			15,000		
c.		+1,350			+1,350			
Bal.	5,000	1,350	10,000		1,350	15,000		
d.	+ 7,500						+7,500	Fee earned
Bal.	12,500	1,350	10,000		1,350	15,000	7,500	
e.	- 3,650						-2,125	Wages expense
							- 800	Rent expense
							- 450	Utilities expense
							- 275	Misc. expenses
Bal.	8,850	1,350	10,000		1,350	15,000	3,850	
f.	- 950				- 950			
Bal.	7,900	1,350	10,000		400	15,000	3,850	
g.		- 800					-800	Supplies expense
Bal.	7,900	550	10,000		400	15,000	3,050	
h.	- 2,000						-2,000	Dividends
Bal.	5,900	550	10,000		400	15,000	1,050	

In reviewing the preceding illustration, you should note the following, which apply to all types of businesses:

1. The effect of every transaction can be stated in terms of increases or decreases in one or more of the accounting equation elements.
2. The two sides of the accounting equation are always equal.
3. The owner's equity is increased by amounts invested by stockholders (capital stock). In addition, owner's equity (retained earnings) is increased by revenues and decreased by expenses. Finally, owner's equity (retained earnings) is decreased by dividends distributed to stockholders. The effect of these four types of transactions on owner's equity is illustrated in Exhibit 3.

Exhibit 3
Effect of Transactions on Owner's Equity

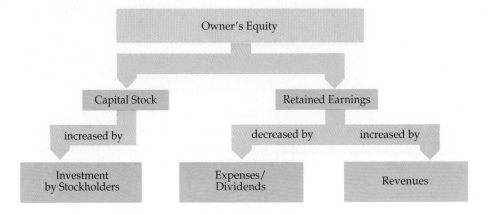

FINANCIAL STATEMENTS

Objective 7
Describe the financial statements of a corporation, and explain how they interrelate.

After transactions have been recorded and summarized, reports are prepared for users. The accounting reports that provide this information are called **financial statements**. The principal financial statements of a corporation are the income statement, the retained earnings statement, the balance sheet, and the statement of cash flows. The nature of the data presented in each statement is as follows:

Income statement. A summary of the revenue and the expenses of a business entity *for a specific period of time*, such as a month or a year.

Retained earnings statement. A summary of the changes in the earnings retained in the business entity *for a specific period of time*, such as a month or a year.

Balance sheet. A list of the assets, liabilities, and owner's equity of a business entity *as of a specific date*, usually at the close of the last day of a month or a year.

Statement of cash flows. A summary of the cash receipts and cash payments of a business entity *for a specific period of time*, such as a month or a year.

The basic features of the four statements and their interrelationships are illustrated in Exhibit 4. The data for the statements were taken from the summary of transactions of Computer King Corporation.

All financial statements should be identified by the name of the business, the title of the statement, and the *date* or *period of time*. The data presented in the income statement, the retained earnings statement, and the statement of cash flows are for a period of time. The data presented in the balance sheet are for a specific date.

You should note the indentions, captions, dollar signs, and rulings in the financial statements. They aid the reader by emphasizing the sections of the statements.

Using Accounting

Financial statements such as those illustrated in Exhibit 4 are useful in evaluating the financial position of a business entity and in predicting its future operating results and cash flows. For this reason, financial statements are used for a variety of business and investment decisions. For example, investors use financial statements as a basis for deciding whether to invest monies in a business and in evaluating the effectiveness of managers in running the entity.

Bank loan officers also use financial statements as a basis for granting loans. In many cases, loan agreements require that certain financial statement conditions be met by the borrower, such as maintaining a required level of assets in excess of liabilities. If you have applied for a loan, you were probably required to provide a financial statement similar to the balance sheet in Exhibit 4.

Income Statement

The excess of the revenue over the expenses incurred in earning the revenue is called **net income** or **net profit**. If the expenses of the enterprise exceed the revenue, the excess is a **net loss**. It is impractical to determine the exact amount of expense for each revenue transaction. Therefore, the net income or the net loss is reported for a period of time, such as a month or a year, rather than for each revenue transaction.

The net income (or net loss) is determined using a **matching** process involving two steps. First, revenue is recorded during the period. Second, expenses used in generating the revenue are **matched** against the revenue to determine the net income or the net loss. Generally, the revenue for providing a service is recorded after the service has been provided to the customer. The expenses incurred in generating revenue during a period are then recorded and are thus matched against the revenue.

The effects of revenue earned and expenses incurred during the month for Computer King Corporation were shown in the equation as increases and decreases in owner's equity (retained earnings). Net income for a period has the effect of increasing owner's equity (retained earnings) for the period, whereas a net loss has the effect of decreasing owner's equity (retained earnings) for the period.

The revenue, expenses, and net income of $3,050 for Computer King Corporation are reported in the income statement in Exhibit 4. The order in which the expenses are listed in the income statement varies among businesses. A common method used is to list them in the order of size, beginning with the larger items. Miscellaneous expense is usually shown as the last item, regardless of the amount.

Exhibit 4
Financial Statements

Computer King Corporation
Income Statement
For Month Ended November 30, 1994

Fees earned		$7 5 0 0 00
Operating expenses:		
Wages expense *payment for labor*	$2 1 2 5 00	
Rent expense	8 0 0 00	
Supplies expense	8 0 0 00	
Utilities expense	4 5 0 00	
Miscellaneous expense	2 7 5 00	
Total operating expenses		4 4 5 0 00
Net income		$3 0 5 0 00

Computer King Corporation
Retained Earnings Statement
For Month Ended November 30, 1994

Net income for November	$3 0 5 0 00	
Less dividends	2 0 0 0 00	
Retained earnings, November 30, 1994		$1 0 5 0 00

Computer King Corporation
Balance Sheet
November 30, 1994

Assets		Liabilities		
Cash	$5 9 0 0 00	Accounts payable		$ 4 0 0 00
Supplies	5 5 0 00	Stockholders' Equity		
Land	10 0 0 0 00	Capital Stock	$15 0 0 0 00	
Total assets	$16 4 5 0 00	Retained earnings	1 0 5 0 00	16 0 5 0 00
		Total liabilities and		
		stockholders' equity		$16 4 5 0 00

Computer King Corporation
Statement of Cash Flows
For Month Ended November 30, 1994

Cash flows from operating activities:		
Cash received from customers	$7 5 0 0 00	
Deduct cash payments for expenses and		
payments to creditors	4 6 0 0 00	
Net cash flow from operating activities		$2 9 0 0 00
Cash flows from investing activities:		
Cash payments for acquisition of land		(10 0 0 0 00)
Cash flows from financing activities:		
Cash received from sale of capital stock	$15 0 0 0 00	
Deduct cash dividends	2 0 0 0 00	
Net cash flow from financing activities		13 0 0 0 00
Net cash flow and Nov. 30, 1994 cash balance		$5 9 0 0 00

Retained Earnings Statement

The primary statement for analyzing changes in the owner's equity of a corporation is the retained earnings statement. The retained earnings statement is a connecting link between the income statement and the balance sheet.

Two types of transactions affect the retained earnings during the month: (1) the revenues and expenses that resulted in net income of $3,050 for the month and (2) dividends of $2,000 paid to stockholders. These transactions are summarized in the retained earnings statement for Computer King Corporation shown in Exhibit 4.

Since Computer King Corporation has been in operation for only one month, it has no retained earnings at the beginning of November. For December, however, there is a beginning balance—the balance at the end of November. This balance of $1,050 is reported on the retained earnings statement. To illustrate, assume that Computer King Corporation earned net income of $4,155 and paid dividends of $2,000 during December. The retained earnings statement for Computer King Corporation for December is shown here.

Computer King Corporation		
Retained Earnings Statement		
For Month Ended December 31, 1994		
Retained earnings, December 1, 1994		$1 0 5 0 00
Net income for the month	$4 1 5 5 00	
Less dividends	2 0 0 0 00	
Increase in retained earnings		2 1 5 5 00
Retained earnings, December 31, 1994		$3 2 0 5 00

Balance Sheet

The amounts of Computer King Corporation's assets, liabilities, and owner's equity at the end of November appear on the last line of the summary of transactions. With the addition of a heading, the balance sheet is prepared as shown in Exhibit 4. This form of balance sheet, called the **account form**, highlights the basic form of the accounting equation, with assets on the left side and the liabilities and owner's equity sections on the right side.[8] An alternative form of balance sheet, called the **report form**, presents the liability and owner's equity sections below the asset section. We illustrate this form of balance sheet in a later chapter.

The asset section of the balance sheet begins with cash. Cash is followed by receivables, supplies, prepaid insurance, and other assets. The assets are normally presented in the order that they will be converted into cash or used in operations. The assets of a more permanent nature, such as land, buildings, and equipment, are listed in that order.

In the liabilities and owner's equity sections of the balance sheet, the liabilities are presented first, followed by owner's equity. In the balance sheet in Exhibit 4, accounts payable is the only liability. When there are two or more categories of liabilities, each should be listed and the total amount of liabilities presented as shown.

	Liabilities	
Accounts payable	$12,900	
Wages payable	2,570	
Total liabilities		$15,470

[8] The nature and form of an account are discussed in the next chapter.

It is also normal on corporation balance sheets to refer to owner's equity as stockholders' equity. For Computer King Corporation, the November 30, 1994, stockholders' equity consists of $15,000 of capital stock and retained earnings of $1,050. The retained earnings amount of $1,050 is taken from the retained earnings statement.

Statement of Cash Flows

The statement of cash flows in Exhibit 4 consists of three sections: (1) operating activities, (2) investing activities, and (3) financing activities.

Cash flow from operating activities. This section reports a summary of cash receipts and cash payments from operations. The net cash flow from operating activities will normally differ from the amount of net income for the period. This difference occurs because revenues and expenses may not be recorded at the same time that cash is received from customers and cash is paid to creditors.[9]

Cash flow from investing activities. This section reports the cash transactions for the acquisition and sale of relatively long-term or permanent-type assets.

Cash flow from financing activities. This section reports the cash transactions related to cash investments by the stockholders, borrowings, and cash dividends.

Preparing the statement of cash flows requires concepts that we have not discussed in this chapter. For this reason, preparing the statement of cash flows is described and illustrated in a later chapter.

CHAPTER REVIEW

Key Points

Objective 1. Define accounting as an information system.
The goal of accounting is to record, report, and interpret economic data for use by decision makers. Accounting is often called the language of business. Accounting can be viewed as an information system that provides essential information about the economic activities of an entity to various individuals or groups.

Accounting provides the conceptual framework for gathering economic data and reporting these data to various users. Examples of users of accounting information include investors, bankers, creditors, government agencies, employees, and managers of the entity.

Objective 2. Describe the profession of accounting, and list its specialized fields.
Accountants are engaged in either (1) private accounting or (2) public accounting. Accountants in both private and public accounting must adhere to codes of professional ethics.

Specialized fields in accounting have evolved as a result

of technological advances and economic growth. The most important accounting fields are financial accounting, auditing, management accounting, cost accounting, tax accounting, accounting systems, international accounting, not-for-profit accounting, social accounting, and accounting instruction.

Objective 3. Summarize the development of generally accepted accounting principles, and concepts, including the business entity concept and the cost principle.
Generally accepted accounting principles have evolved to form a basis for accounting practice. The Financial Accounting Standards Board issues authoritative pronouncements on accounting principles.

The business entity concept is based on applying accounting to individual economic units in society. Profit-making businesses are normally organized as sole proprietorships, partnerships, or corporations.

The cost principle requires that properties and services bought by a business be recorded in terms of actual cost.

---

[9] Reconciling net income with cash flow from operating activities is discussed in a later chapter.

Objective 4. List the characteristics of a business transaction.

A business transaction is an economic event or a condition that must be recorded by an entity. Some business transactions cause future events or conditions that must also be recorded as transactions.

Objective 5. State the accounting equation, and define each element of the equation.

The properties owned by a business and the rights or claims to properties may be stated in the form of an equation, as follows: Assets = Liabilities + Owner's Equity.

Objective 6. Explain how business transactions can be stated in terms of the resulting changes in the three basic elements of the accounting equation.

All transactions can be stated in terms of the change in one or more of the three elements of the accounting equation. That is, the effect of every transaction can be stated in terms of increases or decreases in one or more of these elements, while maintaining the equality between the two sides of the equation.

Objective 7. Describe the financial statements of a corporation, and explain how they interrelate.

After transactions have been recorded and summarized, accounting reports (financial statements) are prepared for users. The principal financial statements of a corporation are the income statement, the retained earnings statement, the balance sheet, and the statement of cash flows.

Glossary of Key Terms

Accounting. The process of identifying, measuring, and communicating economic information to permit informed judgments and decisions by users of the information. **Objective 1**

Accounting equation. The expression of the relationship between assets, liabilities, and owner's equity; it is most commonly stated as Assets = Liabilities + Owner's Equity. **Objective 5**

Account form. The form of balance sheet with the asset section presented on the left-hand side and the liability and owner's equity sections presented on the right-hand side. **Objective 7**

Account payable. A liability created by a purchase made on credit. **Objective 6**

Account receivable. A claim against a customer for services rendered or goods sold on credit. **Objective 6**

Assets. Properties owned by a business enterprise. **Objective 5**

Balance sheet. A financial statement listing the assets, liabilities, and owner's equity of a business entity as of a specific date. **Objective 7**

Business entity concept. The concept that accounting applies to individual economic units and that each unit is separate from the persons who supply its assets. **Objective 3**

Business transaction. The occurrence of an economic event or a condition that must be recorded in the accounting records. **Objective 4**

Capital stock. Shares of ownership of a corporation. **Objective 6**

Corporation. A separate legal entity that is organized in accordance with state or federal statutes and in which ownership is divided into shares of stock. **Objective 3**

Cost principle. The principle that the monetary record for properties and services purchased by a business should be maintained in terms of actual cost. **Objective 3**

Dividends. A distribution of earnings of a corporation to its owners (stockholders). **Objective 6**

Expense. The amount of assets or services used in the process of earning revenue. **Objective 6**

Financial Accounting Standards Board (FASB). An authoritative body for the development of accounting principles. **Objective 3**

Generally accepted accounting principles (GAAP). Generally accepted guidelines for the preparation of financial statements. **Objective 2**

Income statement. A summary of the revenues and expenses of a business entity for a specific period of time. **Objective 7**

Liabilities. Debts of a business enterprise. **Objective 5**

Matching. The concept that expenses incurred in generating revenue should be matched against the revenue in determining the net income or net loss for the period. **Objective 7**

Net income. The final figure in the income statement when revenues exceed expenses. **Objective 7**

Net loss. The final figure in the income statement when expenses exceed revenues. **Objective 7**

Owner's equity. The rights of the owners in a business enterprise. **Objective 5**

Partnership. An unincorporated business owned by two or more individuals. **Objective 3**

Prepaid expenses. Purchased commodities or services that have not been used up at the end of an accounting period. **Objective 6**

Private accounting. The profession whose members are accountants employed by a business firm or not-for-profit organization. **Objective 2**

Public accounting. The profession whose members render accounting services on a fee basis. **Objective 2**

Report form. The form of balance sheet with the liability and owner's equity sections presented below the asset section. **Objective 7**

Retained earnings. Net income retained in a corporation. **Objective 6**

Retained earnings statement. A summary of the changes in the earnings retained in the business entity *for a specific period of time*, such as a month or a year. **Objective 7**

Revenue. The gross increase in owner's equity as a result of business and professional activities that earn income. **Objective 6**

Sole proprietorship. An unincorporated business owned by one individual. **Objective 3**

Statement of cash flows. A summary of the major cash receipts and cash payments for a period. **Objective 7**

Stockholders' equity. The equity of the stockholders of a corporation. **Objective 7**

Self-Examination Questions
Answers at end of chapter.

1. A profit-making business that is a separate legal entity and in which ownership is divided into shares of stock is known as a:
   A. sole proprietorship
   B. single proprietorship
   C. partnership
   D. corporation

2. The properties owned by a business enterprise are called:
   A. assets
   B. liabilities
   C. the accounting equation
   D. owner's equity

3. A list of assets, liabilities, and owner's equity of a business entity as of a specific date is:
   A. a balance sheet
   B. an income statement
   C. a retained earnings statement
   D. a statement of cash flows

4. If total assets increased $20,000 during a period of time and total liabilities increased $12,000 during the same period, the amount and direction (increase or decrease) of the period's change in owner's equity is:
   A. $32,000 increase
   B. $32,000 decrease
   C. $8,000 increase
   D. $8,000 decrease

5. If revenue was $45,000, expenses were $37,500, and dividends were $10,000, the amount of net income or net loss would be:
   A. $45,000 net income
   B. $7,500 net income
   C. $37,500 net loss
   D. $2,500 net loss

ILLUSTRATIVE PROBLEM

On October 1 of the current year, the assets, liabilities, and capital stock of E. F. Nelson, Attorney-at-Law, P.C., are as follows: Cash, $1,000; Accounts Receivable, $2,200; Supplies, $850; Land, $11,450; Accounts Payable, $2,030; Capital Stock, $10,000. E. F. Nelson, Attorney-at-Law, P.C., is organized as a professional corporation owned and operated by E. F. Nelson. The professional corporation status of the business is identified by the letters P.C. Currently, office space and office equipment are being rented, pending the construction of an office complex on land purchased last year. Business transactions during October are summarized as follows:

   a. Received cash from clients for services, $4,928.
   b. Paid creditors on account, $1,755.
   c. Received cash from E. F. Nelson as an additional investment and issued capital stock, $3,700.
   d. Paid office rent for the month, $1,200.
   e. Charged clients for legal services on account, $1,025.
   f. Purchased office supplies on account, $245.
   g. Received cash from clients on account, $2,000.
   h. Received invoice for paralegal services from Legal Aid Inc. for October (to be paid on November 10), $1,635.
   i. Paid the following: wages expense, $850; answering service expense, $250; utilities expense, $325; miscellaneous expense, $75.
   j. Determined that the cost of office supplies used during the month was $115.
   k. Paid dividends of $1,000.

Instructions
1. Determine the amount of retained earnings as of October 1 of the current year.
2. State the assets, liabilities, and owner's equity as of October 1 in equation form similar to that shown in this chapter. In tabular form below the equation, indicate the increases and decreases resulting from each transaction and the new balances after each transaction. Explain the nature of each increase and decrease in owner's equity by an appropriate notation at the right of the amount.
3. Prepare (a) an income statement for October, (b) a retained earnings statement for October, and (c) a balance sheet as of October 31.

Solution
1. Assets - Liabilities = Owner's Equity
   Assets - Liabilities = Capital Stock + Retained Earnings
   $15,500 - $2,030 = $10,000 + Retained Earnings
   $13,470 = $10,000 + Retained Earnings
   $3,470 = Retained Earnings

2.

		Assets			=	Liabilities	+	Owner's Equity	

			Accounts				Accounts	Capital	Retained	
	Cash	+ Receivable	+ Supplies	+ Land	=	Payable	+ Stock	+ Earnings	
Bal.	1,000	2,200	850	11,450		2,030	10,000	3,470	
a.	+4,928							+ 4,928	Fees earned
Bal.	5,928	2,200	850	11,450		2,030	10,000	8,398	
b.	-1,755					-1,755			
Bal.	4,173	2,200	850	11,450		275	10,000	8,398	
c.	+3,700						+ 3,700		Stockholders' investment
Bal.	7,873	2,200	850	11,450		275	13,700	8,398	
d.	-1,200							- 1,200	Rent expense
Bal.	6,673	2,200	850	11,450		275	13,700	7,198	
e.		+1,025						+ 1,025	Fees earned
Bal.	6,673	3,225	850	11,450		275	13,700	8,223	
f.			+ 245			+ 245			
Bal.	6,673	3,225	1,095	11,450		520	13,700	8,223	
g.	+2,000	-2,000							
Bal.	8,673	1,225	1,095	11,450		520	13,700	8,223	
h.						+1,635		- 1,635	Paralegal expense
Bal.	8,673	1,225	1,095	11,450		2,155	13,700	6,588	
i.	-1,500							- 850	Wages expense
								- 250	Answ. svc. exp.
								- 325	Utilities expense
								- 75	Misc. exp.
Bal.	7,173	1,225	1,095	11,450		2,155	13,700	5,088	
j.			- 115					- 115	Supplies expense
Bal.	7,173	1,225	980	11,450		2,155	13,700	4,973	
k.	-1,000							- 1,000	Dividends
Bal.	6,173	1,225	980	11,450		2,155	13,700	3,973	

3. a.

E. F. Nelson, Attorney-at-Law, P.C.

Income Statement

For Month Ended October 31, 19—

Fees earned		$5 9 5 3 00
Operating expenses:		
Paralegal expense	$1 6 3 5 00	
Rent expense	1 2 0 0 00	
Wages expense	8 5 0 00	
Utilities expense	3 2 5 00	
Answering service expense	2 5 0 00	
Supplies expense	1 1 5 00	
Miscellaneous expense	7 5 00	
Total operating expenses		4 4 5 0 00
Net income		$1 5 0 3 00

3. b.

E. F. Nelson, Attorney-at-Law, P.C.

Retained Earnings Statement

For Month Ended October 31, 19—

Retained earnings, October 1, 19—		$3 4 7 0 00
Net income for the month	$1 5 0 3 00	
Less dividends for the month	1 0 0 0 00	
Increase in retained earnings		5 0 3 00
Retained earnings, October 31, 19—		$3 9 7 3 00

ILLUSTRATIVE PROBLEM ILLUSTRATIVE PROBLEM ILLUSTRATIVE PROBLEM ILLUSTRATIVE PROBLEM

ILLUSTRATIVE PROBLEM

3. c.

E. F. Nelson, Attorney-at-Law, P.C.
Balance Sheet
October 31, 19—

Assets		Liabilities		
Cash	$6 1 7 3 00	Accounts payable		$2 1 5 5 00
Accounts receivable	1 2 2 5 00	Stockholders' Equity		
Supplies	9 8 0 00	Capital stock	$13 7 0 0 00	
Land	11 4 5 0 00	Retained earnings	3 9 7 3 00	17 6 7 3 00
Total assets	$19 8 2 8 00	Total liabilities and		
		stockholders' equity		$19 8 2 8 00

DISCUSSION QUESTIONS

1. Name some of the categories of individuals and institutions who use accounting information.
2. Distinguish between private accounting and public accounting.
3. Describe in general terms the requirements that an individual must meet for (a) the CMA certificate and (b) the CPA certificate.
4. What are ethics?
5. Name some of the specialized fields in accounting.
6. How are generally accepted accounting principles (GAAP) established?
7. Identify each of the following abbreviations:
   a. AICPA   d. CPA
   b. CIA   e. FASB
   c. CMA   f. GAAP
8. a. Name the three principal forms of profit-making business organizations.
   b. Which of these forms is identified with the greatest number of businesses?
   c. Which of these forms is the dominant form in terms of dollars of business activity?
9. What is meant by the cost principle?
10. On February 8, Allen Delivery Service Inc. extended an offer of $90,000 for land that had been priced for sale at $100,000. On February 20, Allen Delivery Service Inc. accepted the seller's counteroffer of $95,000. At what amount should the land be recorded by Allen Delivery Service Inc.?
11. a. Land with an assessed value of $60,000 for property tax purposes is acquired by a business enterprise for $75,000. At what amount should the land be recorded by the purchaser?
    b. Ten years later, the plot of land in (a) has an assessed value of $110,000, and the business enterprise receives an offer of $150,000 for it. Should the monetary amount assigned to the land in the business records now be increased and, if so, by what amount?
    c. Assuming that the land acquired in (a) was sold for $175,000, (1) by how much would the owner's equity increase, and (2) at what amount would the purchaser record the land?
12. Name the three elements of the accounting equation.
13. If the assets owned by a business enterprise total $250,000, what is the amount of the liabilities and owner's equity of the enterprise?
14. a. An enterprise has assets of $210,000 and liabilities of $145,000. What is the amount of its owner's equity?
    b. An enterprise has assets of $450,000 and owner's equity of $200,000. What is the total amount of its liabilities?
    c. An enterprise has liabilities of $400,000 and owner's equity of $150,000. What is the total amount of its assets?
    d. A corporation has assets of $750,000, liabilities of $400,000, and capital stock of $200,000. What is the amount of its retained earnings?
15. Describe how the following business transactions affect the three elements of the accounting equation.

   a. Issued capital stock for cash.

   b. Received cash for services performed.

   c. Purchased supplies for cash.

   d. Paid for utilities used in the business.

   e. Purchased supplies on account.

16. a. A vacant lot acquired for $50,000, on which there is a balance owed of $35,000, is sold for $65,000 in cash. What is the effect of the sale on the total amount of the seller's (1) assets, (2) liabilities, and (3) owner's equity?

   b. After receiving the $65,000 cash in (a), the seller pays the $35,000 owed. What is the effect of the payment on the total amount of the seller's (1) assets, (2) liabilities, and (3) owner's equity?

17. Operations of a service enterprise for a particular month are summarized as follows:
   Services sold: on account, $15,000; for cash, $80,000.
   Expenses incurred: on account, $46,000; for cash, $35,000.
   What was the amount of the enterprise's (a) revenue, (b) expenses, and (c) net income?

18. Describe the difference between an account receivable and an account payable.

19. A business enterprise had revenues of $112,000 and operating expenses of $120,000. Did the enterprise (a) incur a net loss or (b) realize a net income?

20. A business enterprise had revenues of $202,500 and operating expenses of $170,000. Did the enterprise (a) incur a net loss or (b) realize a net income?

21. Name the two types of transactions that increase the owner's equity of a corporation.

22. Indicate whether each of the following types of transactions will (a) increase owner's equity or (b) decrease owner's equity:

   1. issuance of capital stock   3. expenses

   2. revenues   4. dividends

23. Give the title of a corporation's four major financial statements illustrated in this chapter, and briefly describe the nature of the information provided by each.

24. Indicate whether the data in each of the following financial statements (a) cover a period of time or (b) are for a specific date:

   1. balance sheet

   2. income statement

   3. retained earnings statement

   4. statement of cash flows

25. What particular item of financial or operating data appears on (a) both the income statement and the retained earnings statement, and (b) both the balance sheet and the retained earnings statement?

26. House of Vision Inc. had owner's equity of $260,000 at the beginning of the period. At the end of the period, the company had total assets of $345,000 and total liabilities of $95,000. (a) What was the net income or net loss for the period, assuming no additional sale of capital stock and no dividends? (b) What was the net income or net loss for the period, assuming that dividends of $30,000 had been paid during the period?

27. Name the three types of activities reported in the statement of cash flows.

28. Indicate whether each of the following activities would be reported on the statement of cash flows as (a) an operating activity, (b) an investing activity, or (c) a financing activity:

   1. cash received by issuing capital stock

   2. cash paid for land

   3. cash received from fees earned

   4. cash paid for expenses

 **REAL WORLD FOCUS** 29. The 1993 annual report of LA-Z-BOY Chair Company reported total assets of $401,064,000 and total liabilities of $137,678,000 on April 24, 1993. What was the owner's equity at April 24, 1993.

ETHICS DISCUSSION CASE

Joan Kelley, president of Kelley Enterprises, applied for a $100,000 loan from Pioneer National Bank. The bank requested financial statements from Kelley Enterprises as a basis for granting the loan. Joan Kelley has told her accountant to provide the bank with a balance sheet. Joan Kelley has decided to omit the other financial statements because there was a net loss during the past year.

 **SHARPEN YOUR COMMUNICATION SKILLS**   Discuss whether Joan Kelley is behaving in an ethical manner by omitting some of the financial statements.

WHAT DO YOU
THINK
?

Many companies, especially those in high-technology markets, such as electronics, often spend large amounts of money in researching and developing new products. For example, a pharmaceutical company may spend millions of dollars developing a new drug long before the drug is actually approved for sale by the Federal Drug Administration (FDA). Do you think the amounts spent on researching and developing new products by a company should be initially recorded as assets or as expenses?

FINANCIAL ANALYSIS AND INTERPRETATION

The relationship between liabilities and stockholders' equity is often used in analyzing a corporation's ability to withstand adverse business conditions. It is also used to indicate the margin of safety for creditors. The ratio is computed as follows:

$$\text{Ratio of Liabilities to Stockholders' Equity} = \frac{\text{Total Liabilities}}{\text{Total Stockholders' Equity}}$$

better → less

The lower the ratio, the better the corporation can withstand poor business conditions and still meet its commitments to creditors. Moreover, the lower the ratio, the greater is the protection to the creditors. For example, a ratio of 1:1 indicates that the liabilities and stockholders' equity are equal and the protection to the creditors is 100%. If the ratio decreases to .5:1, the protection to the creditors is 200%; that is, the corporation may suffer a loss equal to 20% of liabilities before the amount of the assets drops below the amount of the liabilities.

a. Determine the ratio of liabilities to stockholders' equity for Hershey Foods Corporation at the end of 1992 and 1991. (The financial statements for Hershey Foods Corporation appear in the annual report of the corporation, presented at the end of Chapter 13.)

SHARPEN YOUR ▶
COMMUNICATION SKILLS
b. What conclusions regarding the margin of protection to the creditors can be drawn from your analysis?

EXERCISES

EXERCISE 1-1
PROFESSIONAL ETHICS
Objective 2

A fertilizer manufacturing company wants to relocate in Collier County. A 13-year-old report from a fired researcher at the company says the company's product is releasing toxic byproducts. The company has suppressed that report. A second report commissioned by the company shows there is no problem with the fertilizer.

REAL WORLD FOCUS   Source: "Business Leaders Ponder Ethical Questions," *Naples Daily News*, May 12, 1991, p. 1E.

SHARPEN YOUR ▶
COMMUNICATION SKILLS
Should the company's chief executive officer reveal the context of the unfavorable report in discussions with Collier County representatives? Discuss.

EXERCISE 1-2
BUSINESS ENTITY CONCEPT
Objective 3

La Croix Inc., owned by Jere Jansen and Lolly Cross, specializes in media advertising for small business enterprises. Jere Jansen serves as president, and Lolly Cross serves as the sales representative and aids in advertising design and artwork. One of La Croix Inc.'s primary customers is Dr. Jose Gomez, a local physician who places several promotional ads each week in the *Hickory Banner Herald*, a daily newspaper.

The following transactions were completed during a period:

a. Lolly Cross purchased $10,000 additional capital stock from La Croix Inc.
b. Jere Jansen purchased art supplies for use in developing the week's advertisements, $180.
c. Dr. Gomez treated Jere Jansen's son for a sore throat. Jere Jansen paid Dr. Gomez $80 for the office visit and medication.
d. Jere Jansen purchased a tuxedo to wear to a hospital awards banquet honoring Dr. Gomez, $550.
e. *Hickory Banner Herald* purchased $2,500 of ink and paper supplies for the month's printing needs.
f. Dr. Gomez placed a help-wanted advertisement for a receptionist in the *Hickory Banner Herald*.

g. The *Hickory Banner Herald* billed La Croix Inc. $850 for last month's advertisements placed by La Croix Inc.

h. Lolly Cross paid $150 to Baby Wanted Inc. for childcare services for her daughters.

i. La Croix paid $400 to Dr. Gomez for life insurance physical examinations on Jere Jansen and Lolly Cross. The insurance policies name La Croix Inc. as beneficiary.

j. La Croix Inc. billed Dr. Gomez for services rendered in the preceding month, $1,100.

k. La Croix Inc. received a bill from Northeast Telephone Inc. mobile phone use for Lolly Cross' cellular telephone, $69. Lolly uses the cellular telephone extensively in the field to contact potential customers, arrange meetings, and the like.

l. Lolly Cross sent flowers on behalf of La Croix Inc. to Dr. Gomez's wife, congratulating her husband on his election as president of the local chapter of the medical association, $60.

m. Jere Jansen and Lolly Cross received dividends from La Croix, based on the amount of shares they owned, $1,500.

n. Lolly Cross purchased groceries for her family, $180.

o. Lolly Cross purchased tickets to a local charity baseball game, $30. La Croix Inc. will be listed as a sponsor of the game in the program.

Indicate which of the preceding transactions should be recorded by La Croix Inc. in its accounting records.

EXERCISE 1-3
ACCOUNTING EQUATION
Objective 5

Determine the missing amount for each of the following:

	Assets	Liabilities	Owner's Equity
a.	X	$15,500	$21,500
b.	$62,750	X	30,000
c.	57,000	19,000	X

EXERCISE 1-4
ASSET, LIABILITY, OWNER'S
EQUITY ITEMS
Objective 6

Indicate whether each of the following represents (1) an asset, (2) a liability, or (3) owner's equity:

a. accounts payable
b. cash
c. fees earned
d. land
e. supplies
f. wages expense
g. dividends

EXERCISE 1-5
TRANSACTIONS
Objective 6

The following selected transactions were completed by Cavin Delivery Service Inc. during August:

1. Received cash from issuing capital stock, $15,000.
2. Paid rent for August, $2,500.
3. Billed customers for delivery services on account, $2,900.
4. Received cash from cash customers, $3,250.
5. Paid advertising expense, $625.
6. Purchased supplies for cash, $750.
7. Received cash from customers on account, $700.
8. Paid creditors on account, $550.
9. Determined that $575 of supplies had been used during the month.
10. Paid cash dividends, $2,000.

Indicate the effect of each transaction on the accounting equation by listing the numbers identifying the transactions, (1) through (10), in a vertical column, and inserting at the right of each number the appropriate letter from the following list:

a. Increase in one asset, decrease in another asset.
b. Increase in an asset, increase in a liability.
c. Increase in an asset, increase in owner's equity.
d. Decrease in an asset, decrease in a liability.
e. Decrease in an asset, decrease in owner's equity.

EXERCISE 1-6
NATURE OF
TRANSACTIONS
Objective 6

Carmine Darby Inc. is a service business. Summary financial data for July are presented in equation form as follows. Each line designated by a number indicates the effect of a transaction on the equation. Each increase and decrease in owner's equity, except transaction (5), affects net income.

	Cash	+ Supplies	+ Land	= Liabilities	+ Capital Stock	+ Retained Earnings
Bal.	4,500	750	15,000	3,750	10,000	6,500
1.	+9,000					+9,000
2.	-3,250					-3,250
3.	-2,300			-2,300		
4.		+600		+ 600		
5.	-1,950					-1,950
6.	-4,000		+ 4,000			
7.		-680				- 680
Bal.	2,000	670	19,000	2,050	10,000	9,620

a. Describe each transaction.
b. What is the amount of net decrease in cash during the month?
c. What is the amount of net increase in retained earnings during the month?
d. What is the amount of the net income for the month?
e. How much of the net income for the month was retained in the business?

EXERCISE 1-7
NATURE OF NET INCOME
AND DIVIDENDS
Objective 7

The income statement of a corporation for the month of October indicates a net income of $35,000. During the same period, cash dividends of $36,000 were paid. Would it be correct to say that the corporation incurred a net loss of $1,000 during the month? Discuss.

EXERCISE 1-8
NET INCOME AND
OWNER'S EQUITY FOR
FOUR ENTERPRISES
Objective 7

Four different corporations, A, B, C, and D, show the same balance sheet data at the beginning and end of a year. These data, exclusive of the amount of owner's equity, are summarized as follows:

	Total Assets	Total Liabilities
Beginning of the year	$525,000	$190,000
End of the year	620,000	265,000

On the basis of these data and the following additional information for the year, determine the net income (or loss) of each company for the year. (*Suggestion:* First determine the amount of increase or decrease in owner's equity during the year.)

Company A: No additional capital stock was issued, and no dividends were paid.
Company B: No additional capital stock was issued, and dividends of $40,000 were paid.
Company C: Capital stock of $50,000 was issued, and no dividends were paid.
Company D: Capital stock of $50,000 was issued, and dividends of $40,000 were paid.

EXERCISE 1-9
BALANCE SHEET ITEMS
Objective 7

From the following list of selected items taken from the records of A-1 Appliance Service Inc. as of a specific date, identify those that would appear on the balance sheet:

1. Accounts Payable
2. Cash
3. Fees Earned
4. Land
5. Retained Earnings
6. Supplies
7. Supplies Expense
8. Utilities Expense
9. Wages Expense
10. Wages Payable

EXERCISE 1-10
INCOME STATEMENT ITEMS
Objective 7

Based on the data presented in Exercise 1-9, identify those items that would appear on the income statement.

EXERCISE 1-11
RETAINED EARNINGS
STATEMENT
Objective 7

Financial information related to JB Inc. for the month ended September 30, 1994, is as follows:

Net income for September	$ 4,750
Dividends paid during September	3,000
Retained earnings, September 1, 1994	39,950

Prepare a retained earnings statement for the month ended September 30, 1994.

EXERCISE 1-12
INCOME STATEMENT
Objective 7

Chavez Inc. was organized on June 1. A summary of the revenue and expense transactions for June are as follows:

Fees earned	$5,400
Wages expense	1,700
Miscellaneous expense	50
Rent expense	900
Supplies expense	250

Prepare an income statement for the month ended June 30.

EXERCISE 1-13
MISSING AMOUNTS FROM
BALANCE SHEET AND
INCOME STATEMENT DATA
Objective 7

One item is omitted in each of the following summaries of balance sheet and income statement data for four different corporations, I, II, III, and IV.

	I	II	III	IV
Beginning of the year:				
Assets	$270,000	$70,000	$90,000	(d)
Liabilities	160,000	35,000	76,000	$22,750
End of the year:				
Assets	315,000	95,000	94,000	79,000
Liabilities	185,000	25,000	87,000	52,000
During the year:				
Additional issuance of				
capital stock	(a)	12,000	5,000	20,000
Dividends	20,000	18,000	(c)	23,000
Revenue	87,750	(b)	88,100	99,000
Expenses	72,750	32,000	89,600	78,000

Determine the amounts of the missing items, identifying them by letter. (*Suggestion:* First determine the amount of increase or decrease in owner's equity during the year.)

EXERCISE 1-14
BALANCE SHEETS; NET
INCOME
Objective 7

Financial information related to L. Keaton Interiors Inc. for May and June of the current year is as follows:

	May 31, 19—	June 30, 19—
Accounts Payable	$ 7,720	$ 9,900
Accounts Receivable	10,300	13,400
Capital Stock	7,500	7,500
Retained Earnings	?	?
Cash	10,150	12,050
Supplies	975	750

1. Prepare balance sheets for L. Keaton Interiors Inc. as of May 31 and as of June 30 of the current year.
2. Determine the amount of net income for June, assuming no additional issuances of capital stock or dividends during the month.
3. Determine the amount of net income for June, assuming no additional issuances of capital stock and dividends of $4,000 during the month.

WhAT'S WRONG
WITH THIS?

How many errors can you find in the following financial statements for Cox Realty Corporation, prepared after the first month of operations?

COX REALTY CORPORATION
Income Statement
For Month Ended June 30, 19—

Sales commissions		$7 1 0 0 00
Operating expenses:		
Office salaries expense	$2 1 5 0 00	
Rent expense	1 8 0 0 00	
Automobile expense	4 0 0 00	
Supplies expense	1 2 5 00	
Miscellaneous expense	2 5 0 00	
Total operating expenses		4 7 2 5 00
Net income		$2 3 7 5 00

Retained Earnings Statement
June 30, 19—

Issuance of capital stock during the month		$7 5 0 0 00
Net income for the month	$1 8 7 5 00	
Plus dividends	1 5 0 0 00	
Increase in retained earnings		3 3 7 5 00
Retained earnings, June 30, 19—		$10 8 7 5 00

Balance Sheet
June 30, 19—

Assets			Liabilities	
Cash		$ 8 2 5 0 00	Supplies	$ 3 2 5 00
Accounts payable		2 0 0 00	Stockholders' Equity	
Total assets		$ 8 4 5 0 00	Retained earnings	10 8 7 5 00
			Total liabilities and	
			stockholders' equity	$11 2 0 0 00

PROBLEMS

Series A

PROBLEM 1-1A
TRANSACTIONS
Objective 6

Ruth Ruhl organized Ruhl Corporation on April 1 of the current year. Ruhl Corporation completed the following transactions during April:

a. Received cash from issuing capital stock, $8,000.
b. Received cash from fees earned, $2,500.
c. Purchased supplies (stationery, stamps, pencils, and so on) on account, $1,950.
d. Paid creditors on account, $975.
e. Billed customers for fees earned, $9,250.
f. Paid automobile expenses (including rental charges) for month, $980, and miscellaneous expenses, $775.
g. Paid rent on office and equipment for the month, $4,000.
h. Paid office salaries, $1,500.
i. Determined that the cost of supplies on hand was $925; therefore, the cost of supplies used was $1,025.
j. Paid dividends, $1,200.

Instructions

1. Indicate the effect of each transaction and the balances after each transaction using the following tabular headings:

Assets			=	Liabilities	Owner's + Equity	
Cash + Accounts Receivable + Supplies			=	Accounts Payable	Capital + Stock	Retained + Earnings

By appropriate notations at the right of each change, indicate the nature of each increase and decrease in owner's equity.

2. Briefly explain why issuing capital stock and revenues increased owner's equity, whereas distributing dividends and expenses decreased owner's equity.

SHARPEN YOUR COMMUNICATION SKILLS

PROBLEM 1-2A
FINANCIAL STATEMENTS
Objective 7

Following are the amounts of the assets and liabilities of Pelican Travel Inc. at October 31, 1995, the end of the current year, and its revenue and expenses for the year ended on that date. The items are listed in alphabetical order. The capital stock was $10,000 throughout the year; retained earnings was $4,500 at November 1, 1994, the beginning of the year; and dividends of $5,000 were paid during the current year.

Accounts payable	$ 210
Accounts receivable	20,000
Cash	16,500
Miscellaneous expense	1,750
Rent expense	24,000
Fees earned	84,530
Supplies	865
Supplies expense	1,125
Utilities expense	4,500
Wages expense	25,500

Instructions

1. Prepare an income statement for the current year ended October 31, 1995.
2. Prepare a retained earnings statement for the current year ended October 31, 1995.
3. Prepare a balance sheet as of October 31, 1995.

PROBLEM 1-3A
FINANCIAL STATEMENTS
Objective 7

Mary Hall established Mary's Services Corporation on April 1 of the current year. The effect of each transaction and the balances after each transaction for April are as follows:

	Assets				Liabilities + Owner's Equity			
		Accounts			Accounts	Capital	Retained	
	Cash +	Receivable +	Supplies	=	Payable +	Stock +	Earnings	
a.	+ 5,000					+5,000		Issuance of capital stock
b.	+ 6,200						+6,200	Fees earned
Bal.	11,200					5,000	6,200	
c.			+725		+725			
Bal.	11,200		725		725	5,000	6,200	
d.	- 225				-225			
Bal.	10,975		725		500	5,000	6,200	
e.	- 1,800						- 1,800	Rent expense
Bal.	9,175		725		500	5,000	4,400	
f.	- 1,600						- 1,250	Auto expense
							- 350	Misc. expense
Bal.	7,575		725		500	5,000	2,800	
g.	- 1,900						-1,900	Salaries expense
Bal.	5,675		725		500	5,000	900	
h.			-450				- 450	Supplies expense
Bal.	5,675		275		500	5,000	450	
i.		+1,900					+1,900	Fees earned
Bal.	5,675	1,900	275		500	5,000	2,350	
j.	- 2,000						-2,000	Dividends
Bal.	3,675	1,900	275		500	5,000	350	

Instructions

1. Prepare an income statement for the month ended April 30.
2. Prepare a retained earnings statement for the month ended April 30.
3. Prepare a balance sheet as of April 30.

PROBLEM 1-4A
TRANSACTIONS;
FINANCIAL STATEMENTS
Objectives 6, 7

On August 1 of the current year, Doris Lusk organized Lusk Realty Inc. During the month of August, Lusk Realty Inc. completed the following transactions:

a. Received cash from issuance of capital stock, $7,500.
b. Earned sales commissions, receiving cash, $14,100.
c. Purchased supplies (stationery, stamps, pencils, and so on) on account, $750.
d. Paid creditor on account, $500.
e. Paid rent on office and equipment for the month, $4,100.
f. Paid dividends, $2,000.
g. Paid automobile expenses (including rental charge) for month, $1,900, and miscellaneous expenses, $350.
h. Paid office salaries, $4,150.
i. Determined that the cost of supplies used was $550.

Instructions

1. Indicate the effect of each transaction and the balances after each transaction using the following tabular headings:

Assets		Liabilities	+	Owner's Equity	
				Capital	Retained
Cash + Supplies	=	Accounts Payable	+	Stock +	Earnings

By appropriate notations at the right of each change, indicate the nature of each increase and decrease in owner's equity.

2. Prepare an income statement for August, a retained earnings statement for August, and a balance sheet as of August 31.

PROBLEM 1-5A
TRANSACTIONS;
FINANCIAL STATEMENTS
Objectives 6, 7

Dry Cleaners Corporation is owned and operated by Karen Guy. Currently, a building and equipment are being rented, pending expansion to new facilities. The actual work of dry cleaning is done by another company at wholesale rates. The assets and the liabilities of the business on May 1 of the current year are as follows: Cash, $6,250; Accounts Receivable, $12,100; Supplies, $900; Land, $25,000; Accounts Payable, $7,800; Capital Stock, $15,000. Business transactions during May are summarized as follows:

a. Received cash from cash customers for dry cleaning sales, $10,750.
b. Paid rent for the month, $2,000.
c. Purchased supplies on account, $820.
d. Paid creditors on account, $7,800.
e. Charged customers for dry cleaning sales on account, $6,920.
f. Received monthly invoice for dry cleaning expense for May (to be paid on June 10), $7,700.
g. Paid the following: wages expense, $2,400; truck expense, $1,580; utilities expense, $960; miscellaneous expense, $630.
h. Received cash from customers on account, $8,100.
i. Determined the cost of supplies used during the month, $970.

Instructions

1. Determine the amount of retained earnings as of May 1 of the current year.
2. State the assets, liabilities, and owner's equity as of May 1 in equation form similar to that shown in this chapter. In tabular form below the equation, indicate increases and decreases resulting from each transaction and the new balances after each transaction. Explain the nature of each increase and decrease in owner's equity by an appropriate notation at the right of the amount.
3. Prepare (a) an income statement for May, (b) a retained earnings statement for May, and (c) a balance sheet as of May 31.

PROBLEM 1-6A
FINANCIAL STATEMENTS
Objective 7

Following are the amounts of the assets and liabilities of Graf Services Inc. at December 31, the end of the current year, and its revenue and expenses for the year ended on that date. The items are listed in alphabetical order. The retained earnings was $10,450 at January 1, the beginning of the current year; and dividends of $10,000 were paid during the current year.

Accounts payable	$ 3,100
Accounts receivable	31,000
Advertising expense	3,000
Capital stock	10,000
Cash	17,200
Fees earned	99,250
Miscellaneous expense	1,250
Rent expense	12,000
Supplies	2,750
Supplies expense	4,800
Taxes expense	4,500
Utilities expense	8,100
Wages expense	29,700
Wages payable	1,500

Instructions

1. Prepare an income statement for the current year ended December 31.
2. Prepare a retained earnings statement for the current year ended December 31.
3. Prepare a balance sheet as of December 31 of the current year.

Series B

PROBLEM 1-1B
TRANSACTIONS
Objective 6

David Key organized DK Inc. on October 1 of the current year. DK Inc. completed the following transactions during October:

a. Received cash from issuing capital stock, $5,000.
b. Received cash from fees earned, $6,250.
c. Paid rent on office and equipment for the month, $2,500.
d. Purchased supplies on account, $850.
e. Paid creditors on account, $625.
f. Paid automobile expenses for month, $780, and miscellaneous expenses, $250.
g. Paid office salaries, $1,500.
h. Determined that the cost of supplies on hand was $275; therefore, the cost of supplies used was $575.
i. Billed customers for fees earned, $2,350.
j. Paid dividends, $1,000.

Instructions

1. Indicate the effect of each transaction and the balances after each transaction using the following tabular headings:

Assets	=	Liabilities	Owner's + Equity

Cash + Accounts Receivable + Supplies	=	Accounts Payable +	Capital Stock +	Retained Earnings

By appropriate notations at the right of each change, indicate the nature of each increase and decrease in owner's equity.

SHARPEN YOUR ▶
COMMUNICATION SKILLS

2. Briefly explain why issuing capital stock and revenues increased owner's equity, whereas distributing dividends and expenses decreased owner's equity.

PROBLEM 1-2B
FINANCIAL STATEMENTS
Objective 7

Following are the amounts of the assets and liabilities of Cole Travel Service Inc. at June 30, 1995, the end of the current year, and its revenue and expenses for the year ended on that date. The items are listed in alphabetical order. The capital stock was $7,500 throughout the year; retained earnings was $5,400 at July 1, 1994, the beginning of the current year; and dividends of $8,000 were paid during the current year.

Accounts payable	$ 1,100	Supplies	$ 675
Accounts receivable	17,500	Supplies expense	4,550
Cash	6,125	Taxes expense	1,800
Fees earned	68,775	Utilities expense	8,500
Miscellaneous expense	825	Wages expense	24,900
Rent expense	9,900		

Instructions

1. Prepare an income statement for the current year ended June 30.
2. Prepare a retained earnings statement for the current year ended June 30.
3. Prepare a balance sheet as of June 30 of the current year.

PROBLEM 1-3B
FINANCIAL STATEMENTS
Objective 7

Jack Hyde established Jack's Services Corporation on July 1 of the current year. The effect of each transaction and the balances after each transaction for July are as follows:

		Assets			=	Liabilities + Owner's Equity			
			Accounts			Accounts	Capital	Retained	
		Cash +	Receivable +	Supplies	=	Payable +	Stock +	Earnings	
a.		+2,500					+2,500		Issuance of capital stock
b.		+5,000						+5,000	Fees earned
Bal.		7,500					2,500	5,000	
c.				+550		+550			
Bal.		7,500		550		550	2,500	5,000	
d.		-2,000						-2,000	Rent expense
Bal.		5,500		550		550	2,500	3,000	
e.		- 250				-250			
Bal.		5,250		550		300	2,500	3,000	
f.			+1,750					+1,750	Fees earned
Bal.		5,250	1,750	550		300	2,500	4,750	
g.		-1,155						- 780	Auto expense
								- 375	Misc. expense
Bal.		4,095	1,750	550		300	2,500	3,595	
h.		-1,000						-1,000	Salaries expense
Bal.		3,095	1,750	550		300	2,500	2,595	
i.				-125				- 125	Supplies expense
Bal.		3,095	1,750	425		300	2,500	2,470	
j.		-1,200						-1,200	Dividends
Bal.		1,895	1,750	425		300	2,500	1,270	

Instructions

1. Prepare an income statement for the month ended July 31.
2. Prepare a retained earnings statement for the month ended July 31.
3. Prepare a balance sheet as of July 31.

PROBLEM 1-4B
TRANSACTIONS;
FINANCIAL STATEMENTS
Objectives 6, 7

On July 1 of the current year, Leo Egan organized Egan Realty Inc. During the month of July, Egan Realty Inc. completed the following transactions:

a. Received cash from issuing capital stock, $5,000.
b. Earned sales commissions, receiving cash, $11,100.
c. Purchased supplies (stationery, stamps, pencils, and so on) on account, $825.
d. Paid creditor on account, $500.
e. Paid rent on office and equipment for the month, $3,600.
f. Paid dividends, $1,000.
g. Paid automobile expenses (including rental charge) for month, $900, and miscellaneous expenses, $550.
h. Paid office salaries, $2,950.
i. Determined that the cost of supplies used was $425.

Instructions

1. Indicate the effect of each transaction and the balances after each transaction using the following tabular headings:

Assets		Liabilities	+	Owner's Equity	
Cash + Supplies	=	Accounts Payable + Capital Stock + Retained Earnings			

By appropriate notations at the right of each change, indicate the nature of each increase and decrease in owner's equity.

2. Prepare an income statement for July, a retained earnings statement for July, and a balance sheet as of July 31.

PROBLEM 1-5B
TRANSACTIONS;
FINANCIAL STATEMENTS
Objectives 6, 7

Spotless Cleaners Inc. is owned and operated by Tom Courier. Currently, a building and equipment are being rented, pending expansion to new facilities. The actual work of dry cleaning is done by another company at wholesale rates. The assets and the liabilities of the business on June 1 of the current year are as follows: Cash, $5,400; Accounts Receivable, $6,750; Supplies, $560; Land, $10,000; Accounts Payable, $3,880; Capital Stock, $10,000. Business transactions during June are summarized as follows:

a. Paid rent for the month, $1,450.
b. Charged customers for dry cleaning sales on account, $7,150.
c. Paid creditors on account, $1,680.
d. Purchased supplies on account, $310.
e. Received cash from cash customers for dry cleaning sales, $3,600.
f. Received cash from customers on account, $3,750.
g. Received monthly invoice for dry cleaning expense for June (to be paid on July 10), $3,400.
h. Paid the following: wages expense, $1,800; truck expense, $725; utilities expense, $510; miscellaneous expense, $190.
i. Determined the cost of supplies used during the month, $570.

Instructions
1. Determine the amount of retained earnings as of June 1 of the current year.
2. State the assets, liabilities, and owner's equity as of June 1 in equation form similar to that shown in this chapter. In tabular form below the equation, indicate increases and decreases resulting from each transaction and the new balances after each transaction. Explain the nature of each increase and decrease in owner's equity by an appropriate notation at the right of the amount.
3. Prepare (a) an income statement for June, (b) a retained earnings statement for June, and (c) a balance sheet as of June 30.

PROBLEM 1-6B
FINANCIAL STATEMENTS
Objective 7

Following are the amounts of the assets and liabilities of Bennett Consultants Corp. at July 31, 1995, the end of the current year, and its revenue and expenses for the year ended on that date. The items are listed in alphabetical order. The retained earnings was $107,890 on August 1, 1994, the beginning of the current year. During the current year, dividends of $50,000 were paid.

Accounts payable	$ 78,000
Accounts receivable	69,750
Advertising expense	30,000
Capital stock	50,000
Cash	64,515
Land	150,000
Miscellaneous expense	8,125
Rent expense	165,000
Fees earned	827,500
Supplies	6,250
Supplies expense	19,750
Taxes expense	33,500
Utilities expense	65,750
Wages expense	412,000
Wages payable	11,250

Instructions
1. Prepare an income statement for the current year ended July 31, 1995.
2. Prepare a retained earnings statement for the current year ended July 31, 1995.
3. Prepare a balance sheet as of July 31, 1995.

MINI-CASE VINES TENNIS SERVICES

Ana Gage, a junior in college, has been seeking ways to earn extra spending money. As an active sports enthusiast, Ana plays tennis regularly at the Vines Tennis Club, where her family has a membership. The president of the club recently approached Ana with the proposal that she manage the club's tennis courts on weekends. Ana's primary duty would be to supervise the operation of the club's four indoor and six outdoor courts, including court reservations. In return for her services, the club would pay Ana $60 per weekend, and Ana could keep whatever she earned from lessons and the fees from the use of the ball machine. The club and Ana agreed to a one-month trial, after which both would consider an arrangement for the remaining two years of Ana's college career. On this basis, Ana organized Vines Tennis Services. During September, Ana managed the tennis courts and entered into the following transactions:

a. Opened a business account by depositing $300.
b. Paid $150 for tennis supplies (practice tennis balls, and the like).
c. Paid $75 for the rental of videotape equipment to be used in offering lessons during September.
d. Arranged for the rental of two ball machines during September for $100. Paid $50 in advance, with the remaining $50 due October 1.
e. Received $950 for lessons given during September.
f. Received $150 in fees from the use of the ball machines during September.
g. Paid $300 for salaries of part-time employees who answered the telephone and took reservations while Ana was giving lessons.
h. Paid $75 for miscellaneous expenses.
i. Received $240 from the club for managing the tennis courts during September.

j. Determined that supplies on hand at the end of the month totaled $80.
k. Withdrew $600 for personal use on September 30.

As a friend and accounting student, you have been asked by Ana to aid her in assessing the venture.

Instructions

1. Small businesses such as Vines Tennis Services are often organized as sole proprietorships. The accounting for sole proprietorships is similar to that for a corporation, except for owner's equity. Instead of Capital Stock and Retained Earnings, an item entitled Ana Gage, Capital can be used to indicate owner's equity in the accounting equation. Indicate the effect of each transaction and the balances after each transaction using the following tabular headings:

Assets		Liabilities	+ Owner's Equity
Cash + Supplies	=	Accounts Payable	+ A. Gage, Capital

Explain the nature of each increase and decrease in owner's equity by an appropriate notation at the right of the amount.

2. Prepare an income statement for September.
3. a. Assume that Ana Gage could earn $8 per hour working 20 hours per weekend as a waitress. Evaluate which of the two alternatives, working as a waitress or operating Vines Tennis Services, would provide Ana with the most income per month.
   b. ▮▮▮▮▶ Discuss any other factors that you believe Ana should consider before discussing a long-term arrangement with Vines Tennis Club.

ANSWERS TO SELF-EXAMINATION QUESTIONS

1. **D** A corporation, organized in accordance with state or federal statutes, is a separate legal entity in which ownership is divided into shares of stock (answer D). A sole proprietorship, sometimes called a single proprietorship (answers A and B), is an unincorporated business enterprise owned by one individual. A partnership (answer C) is an unincorporated business enterprise owned by two or more individuals.

2. **A** The properties owned by a business enterprise are called assets (answer A). The debts of the business are called liabilities (answer B), and the equity of the owners is called owner's equity (answer D). The relationship between assets, liabilities, and owner's equity is expressed as the accounting equation (answer C).

3. **A** The balance sheet is a listing of the assets, liabilities, and owner's equity of a business entity at a specific date (answer A). The income statement (answer B) is a summary of the revenue and expenses of a business entity for a specific period of time. The retained earnings statement (answer C) summarizes the changes in the earnings retained in a corporation during a specific period of time.

The statement of cash flows (answer D) summarizes the cash receipts and cash payments for a specific period of time.

4. **C** The accounting equation is:

Assets = Liabilities + Owner's Equity

Therefore, if assets increased by $20,000 and liabilities increased by $12,000, owner's equity must have increased by $8,000 (answer C), as indicated in the following computation:

$$
\begin{aligned}
\text{Assets} &= \text{Liabilities} + \text{Owner's Equity} \\
\$20{,}000 &= \$12{,}000 + \text{Owner's Equity} \\
\$20{,}000 - \$12{,}000 &= \text{Owner's Equity} \\
\$8{,}000 &= \text{Owner's Equity}
\end{aligned}
$$

5. **B** Net income is the excess of revenue over expenses, or $7,500 (answer B). If expenses exceed revenue, the difference is a net loss. Dividends are the opposite of the owner's investing in the business and do not affect the amount of net income or net loss.

You and Accounting

Rico's Pizzeria is hiring students part-time to deliver pizzas. If you are hired, you will be using your own car. You will be paid $.20 per mile for each mile driven plus $5.00 an hour and tips. If your car has a standard odometer, how would you determine the number of miles driven each day delivering pizzas?

One method would be to record the reading of the odometer before work and then at quitting time. The difference would be the miles driven. For example, if the odometer read 56,743 at the start of work and 56,889 at the end of work, the miles driven would be 146 miles. However, this method is subject to error if you copy down the wrong odometer reading or make a math error. Is there a better method that would be more efficient and less subject to error?

If your car has a trip odometer, you could set the trip odometer to zero when you begin work and simply read it at the end of work for the miles driven. You could also check the accuracy of the trip odometer by recording the standard odometer readings as described in the preceding paragraph. If the estimates of the miles driven agreed, you could be confident that you are being paid for the actual miles driven.

In running a business, managers need to have similar information readily available. Such information is useful for analyzing the effects of transactions on the business and for making decisions. For example, a manager needs to know how much cash is available, how much has been spent, and what services have been provided customers. In this chapter, you will read about methods used to analyze transactions. In addition, you will read about how managers rely on the accounting system to check the accuracy of information.

Chapter 2
Analyzing Transactions

Basic concepts, principles, and methods of recording transactions were presented in Chapter 1. The preparation of financial statements summarizing the effects of transactions on an enterprise was also illustrated.

In this chapter, we will describe additional concepts, principles, and methods used to analyze transactions. We will also discuss how errors may occur and how they are detected by the accounting process. Finally, we will discuss methods of correcting errors.

USEFULNESS OF AN ACCOUNT

Objective 1
Explain how an account can be
used for analyzing the effects of
transactions on financial
statements.

Transactions can be analyzed and summarized by using the accounting equation,
Assets = Liabilities + Owner's Equity. Although transactions can be summarized
in this way, such a format is not practical for actual accounting systems.

Accounting systems provide information on business transactions for use by
management in directing operations and in preparing financial statements. How
do accounting systems provide this information? The effects of transactions on
each item that appears on the financial statements are kept in a separate record. For
example, since cash appears on the balance sheet, the increases and decreases in
cash are kept in a separate record. Likewise, increases and decreases in supplies,
land, accounts payable, and the other balance sheet items are kept in separate
records. Similar records would be kept for income statement items, such as fees
earned, wages expense, and rent expense.

The record used to summarize increases and decreases in individual financial
statement items is called an **account**. A group of accounts for a business entity is a
ledger. The ledger is used in preparing the financial statements of a business.

CHART OF ACCOUNTS

Objective 2
Prepare a chart of accounts for a
service enterprise.

To determine the most useful type and number of accounts, a company must analyze its expected operations and volume of business. In addition, the extent to
which reports are needed for taxes, managerial decisions, and credit purposes must
be considered. For example, the type and number of accounts needed by a small
retailer would be different from those needed by an attorney or a real estate agency.

The system of accounts for an enterprise is called its **chart of accounts**. In a chart
of accounts, the accounts are normally listed in the order in which they appear in
the financial statements. The balance sheet accounts are usually listed first, in the
order of assets, liabilities, and owner's equity. The income statement accounts are
then listed in the order of revenues and expenses. Each of these major account classifications is briefly described below.

Assets are physical items (tangible) or rights (intangible) that have value and
that are owned by the business entity. Examples of tangible assets include cash, accounts receivable, supplies, prepaid expenses (such as insurance), buildings,
equipment, and land. An example of an intangible asset is patent rights.

Liabilities are debts owed to outsiders (creditors). Liabilities are often identified on the balance sheet by titles that include the word *payable*. Examples of liabilities include accounts payable, notes payable, and wages payable. Revenue received in advance, such as magazine subscriptions received by a publisher or
tuition received by a college, is also classified as a liability. Revenue received in advance is often called *unearned* revenue.

Owner's equity is the claim against the assets of the business after the total liabilities are deducted. For a corporation, the owner's equity on the balance sheet is
called stockholders' equity and is represented by the balance of the **capital stock**
and **retained earnings** accounts. A **dividends** account represents distributions of
earnings to stockholders.

Revenues are increases in owner's equity as a result of rendering services or
selling products to customers. Examples of revenues include fees earned, fares
earned, commissions revenue, rent income, and interest income.

Assets used up or services consumed in the process of generating revenues are
expenses. Examples of typical expenses include wages expense, rent expense, utilities expense, supplies expense, interest expense, and miscellaneous expense.

The accounts in an enterprise's chart of accounts are numbered to permit indexing and for use as references. Although accounts in the ledger may be numbered in order as in the pages of this book, a flexible system of indexing is desired.
Such a system has the advantage of allowing the later addition of new accounts in
their proper order without affecting other account numbers. For example, the chart
of accounts in Exhibit 1 does not include all of Computer King Corporation's accounts. Additional accounts will be introduced in later chapters.

In the chart of accounts in Exhibit 1, each account number has two digits. The first digit indicates the major classification of the ledger in which the account is located. Accounts beginning with 1 represent assets; 2, liabilities; 3, owner's equity; 4, revenue; and 5, expenses. The second digit indicates the location of the account within its class. For a large enterprise with many departments or operations, it is common for each account number to have four or more digits. For example, Procter and Gamble's account numbers have over 30 digits to reflect different operations, and regions.

Exhibit 1
Chart of Accounts for Computer King Corporation

Balance Sheet Accounts	Income Statement Accounts
1. Assets	4. Revenue
11 Cash	41 Fees Earned
12 Accounts Receivable	5. Expenses
14 Supplies	51 Wages Expense
15 Prepaid Insurance	52 Rent Expense
17 Land	54 Utilities Expense
18 Office Equipment	55 Supplies Expense
2. Liabilities	59 Miscellaneous Expense
21 Accounts Payable	
23 Unearned Rent	
3. Owner's Equity	
31 Capital Stock	
32 Retained Earnings	
33 Dividends	

CHARACTERISTICS OF AN ACCOUNT

Objective 3
Explain the characteristics of an account.

The simplest form of an account has three parts. First, each account has a title, which is the name of the item recorded in the account. Second, each account has a space for recording increases in the amount of the item. Third, each account has a space for recording decreases in the amount of the item. The account form presented below is called a **T account** because it is similar to the letter T.

Title	
Left side	Right side
debit	*credit*

The left side of the account is called the **debit** side and the right side is called the **credit** side.[1] Amounts entered on the left side of an account, regardless of the account title, are called **debits** to the account. When debits are entered in an account, the account is said to be **debited** (or charged). Amounts entered on the right side of an account are called **credits**, and the account is said to be **credited**. Debits and credits are sometimes abbreviated as *Dr.* and *Cr.*

---

[1] The terms *debit* and *credit* are derived from the Latin *debere* and *credere*.

In the cash account shown below, transactions involving receipts of cash are listed vertically on the debit side of the account. The transactions involving cash payments have been listed in similar fashion on the credit side of the account. If at any time the total of the cash receipts is needed, the entries on the debit side of the account may be added and the total ($10,950) inserted below the last debit.[2] The total of the cash payments, $6,850 in the example, may be inserted on the credit side in a similar manner. Subtracting the smaller sum from the larger, $10,950 – $6,850, identifies the amount of cash on hand. This amount is called the **balance of the account**. The cash account in the example has a balance of $4,100. This amount may be inserted in the account, next to the total of the debit column. In this way, the balance is identified as a **debit balance**. If a balance sheet were to be prepared at this time, cash of $4,100 would be reported.

		Cash	
	3,750		850
	4,300		1,400
	2,900		700
4,100	10,950		2,900
			1,000
			6,850

ANALYZING AND SUMMARIZING TRANSACTIONS IN ACCOUNTS

Objective 4
List the rules of debit and credit and the normal balances of accounts.

In this section, we will discuss how transactions are analyzed and summarized in accounts. In addition, we will discuss how accounts are useful in summarizing the effects of transactions on the financial statements.

The Computer King Corporation transactions from Chapter 1, with dates added, are used as the basis for our illustrations. First, we illustrate how transactions (a), (b), (c), and (f) are analyzed and summarized in balance sheet accounts. Next, we illustrate how transactions (d), (e), and (g) are analyzed and summarized in income statement accounts. Finally, we illustrate how the payment of dividends, transaction (h), is analyzed and summarized in the accounts.

Balance Sheet Accounts

Balance sheet accounts consist of the assets, liabilities, and owner's equity accounts. Pat King's first transaction (a) was to deposit $15,000 in a bank account in the name of Computer King Corporation. After the deposit on November 1, the balance sheet for the business is as follows:

Computer King Corporation
Balance Sheet
November 1, 1994

Assets		Owner's Equity	
Cash	$15,000	Capital Stock	$15,000

Every business transaction affects an enterprise's financial statements and at least two accounts. The effect of the above transaction on the balance sheet is to increase cash and owner's equity. This effect is shown in the accounts as a $15,000 debit to Cash and a $15,000 credit to Capital Stock.

The effects of a transaction on a business and its accounts is initially entered in a record called a **journal**. In the journal, the transaction's effects are stated in a formal manner. The title of the account to be debited is listed first, followed by the amount to be debited. The title of the account to be credited is listed below and to the right of the debit, followed by the amount to be credited. This process of record-

---

[2] The figures should be small or identified in some other way to avoid mistaking the amount for an additional debit.

ing a transaction in the journal is called **journalizing**. The form of presentation is called a **journal entry**, as shown below.

Entry a.   Nov. 1   Cash   15,000
                         Capital Stock   15,000

The effects of this transaction are shown in the accounts by transferring the amount and the date of the journal entry to Cash and Capital Stock, as follows:

Cash		Capital Stock	
Nov. 1 15,000		Nov. 1	15,000

The amount of the asset, which is reported on the left side of the balance sheet, is transferred to the left (debit) side of Cash. The owner's equity in the business, which is reported on the right side of the balance sheet, is transferred to the right (credit) side of Capital Stock. When other assets are acquired, the increases will also be recorded as debits to asset accounts. Likewise, other increases in owner's equity will be recorded as credits to owner's equity accounts.

On November 5 (transaction b), Computer King Corporation bought land for $10,000, paying cash. This transaction increases one asset account and decreases another. It can be expressed as a $10,000 increase (debit) to Land and a $10,000 decrease (credit) to Cash. The journal entry for this transaction is shown below.

Entry b.   Nov. 5   Land   10,000
                         Cash   10,000

The effect of this entry is shown in the accounts of Computer King Corporation as follows:

Cash	Land	Capital Stock
Nov. 1 15,000 Nov. 5 10,000	Nov. 5 10,000	Nov. 1 15,000

On November 10 (transaction c), Computer King Corporation purchased supplies on account for $1,350. This transaction increases an asset account and increases a liability account. It can be expressed as a $1,350 increase (debit) to Supplies and a $1,350 increase (credit) to Accounts Payable. The journal entry for this transaction is shown below. To simplify the illustration, the effect of entry (c) and the remaining journal entries for Computer King Corporation will be shown in the accounts later.

Entry c.   Nov. 10   Supplies   1,350
                          Accounts Payable   1,350

On November 30 (transaction f), Computer King Corporation paid creditors on account, $950. This transaction decreases a liability account and decreases an asset account. It can be expressed as a $950 decrease (debit) to Accounts Payable and a $950 decrease (credit) to Cash. The journal entry for this transaction is shown below.

Entry f.   Nov. 30   Accounts Payable   950
                          Cash   950

In the preceding examples, you should observe that the left side of asset accounts is used for recording increases and the right side is used for recording decreases. Also the right side of liability and owner's equity accounts is used to record increases. It naturally follows that the left side of such accounts is used to record decreases. The left side of all accounts, whether asset, liability, or owner's equity, is the debit side and the right side is the credit side. Thus, a debit may be either an increase or a decrease, depending on the account affected. A credit may likewise be either an increase or a decrease, depending on the account. The general rules of debit and credit for balance sheet accounts may therefore be stated as follows:

	Debit	Credit
Asset accounts	Increase (+)	Decrease (–)
Liability accounts	Decrease (–)	Increase (+)
Owner's equity (stockholders' equity) accounts	Decrease (–)	Increase (+)

The rules of debit and credit may also be stated in relationship to the accounting equation, as shown below.

Balance Sheet Accounts

ASSETS		LIABILITIES	
Asset Accounts		Liability Accounts	
Debit for increases	Credit for decreases	Debit for decreases	Credit for increases

OWNER'S EQUITY	
Owner's Equity Accounts	
Debit for decreases	Credit for increases

Income Statement Accounts

The analysis of business transactions affecting the income statement focuses on how each transaction affects owner's equity. Transactions that increase revenue will increase owner's equity. Just as increases in owner's equity are recorded as credits, increases in revenue accounts are recorded as credits. Transactions that increase expense will decrease owner's equity. Just as decreases in owner's equity are recorded as debits, increases in expense accounts are recorded as debits.

Computer King Corporation's transactions (d), (e), and (g) illustrate the analysis of transactions and the rules of debit and credit for revenue and expense accounts. On November 18 (transaction d), Computer King Corporation received fees of $7,500 from customers for services. This transaction increases an asset account and increases a revenue account. It can be expressed as a $7,500 increase (debit) to Cash and a $7,500 increase (credit) to Fees Earned. The journal entry for this transaction is shown below.

Entry d.   Nov. 18   Cash   7,500
                               Fees Earned   7,500

Throughout the month, Computer King Corporation incurred the following expenses: wages, $2,125; rent, $800; utilities, $450; miscellaneous, $275. To simplify the illustration, the entry to journalize the payment of these expenses is recorded on November 30 (transaction e), as shown below. This transaction increases various expense accounts and decreases an asset account.

Entry e.   Nov. 30   Wages Expense   2,125
                               Rent Expense   800
                               Utilities Expense   450
                               Miscellaneous Expense   275
                               Cash   3,650

Regardless of the number of accounts, the sum of the debits is always equal to the sum of the credits in a journal entry. This equality of debit and credit for each transaction is inherent in the accounting equation: Assets = Liabilities + Owner's Equity. It is also because of this double equality that the system is known as **double-entry accounting**

On November 30, Computer King Corporation recorded the amount of supplies used in the operations during the month (transaction g). This transaction increases an expense account and decreases an asset account. The journal entry for transaction (g) is shown below.

Entry g.   Nov. 30   Supplies Expense   800
                           Supplies   800

The general rules of debit and credit for analyzing transactions affecting income statement accounts are stated below.

	Debit	Credit
Revenue accounts	Decrease (–)	Increase (+)
Expense accounts	Increase (+)	Decrease (–)

The rules of debit and credit for income statement accounts may also be summarized in relationship to the owner's equity in the accounting equation, as shown below.

Income Statement Accounts

Debit for decreases in owner's equity		Credit for increases in owner's equity	
Expense Accounts		Revenue Accounts	
Debit for increases	Credit for decreases	Debit for decreases	Credit for increases

Dividends

A corporation may from time to time distribute earnings from operations by paying dividends to its stockholders. The payment of dividends has the effect of decreasing owner's equity. Just as decreases in owner's equity are recorded as debits, dividends are recorded as debits. Debits to the dividends account are normally thought of as increasing dividends rather than as decreasing owner's equity.

On November 30 (transaction h), Computer King Corporation paid dividends of $2,000 to its stockholders. This transaction increases the dividends account and decreases the cash account. The journal entry for transaction (h) is shown below.

Entry h.   Nov. 30   Dividends   2,000
                           Cash   2,000

Taking the Human Spirit into Account

Double-entry bookkeeping is one of the most beautiful discoveries of the human spirit. . . . It came from the same spirit which produced the systems of Galileo and Newton and the subject matter of modern physics and chemistry. By the same means, it organizes perceptions into a system, and one can character- *ize it as the first Cosmos constructed purely on the basis of mechanistic thought. . . . Without too much difficulty, we can recognize in double-entry bookkeeping the ideas of gravitation, of the circulation of the blood and of the conservation of matter.*

Source: From the novel, *Wilhelm Meister's Lehrjahre (Apprenticeship)*, written in 1795–6 by the German poet Johann Wolfgang von Goethe, translated by the German political economist Werner Sombart (1863–1941).

Normal Balances of Accounts

The sum of the increases recorded in an account is usually equal to or greater than the sum of the decreases recorded in the account. For this reason, the normal balances of all accounts are positive rather than negative. For example, the total debits (increases) in an asset account will ordinarily be greater than the total credits (decreases). Thus, asset accounts normally have debit balances.

The rules of debit and credit and the normal balances of the various types of accounts are summarized as follows:

	Increase (Normal Balance)	Decrease
Balance sheet accounts:		
Asset	**Debit**	Credit
Liability	**Credit**	Debit
Owner's Equity or Stockholders' Equity:		
Capital Stock	**Credit**	Debit
Retained Earnings	**Credit**	Debit
Dividends	**Debit**	Credit
Income statement accounts:		
Revenue	**Credit**	Debit
Expense	**Debit**	Credit

When an account that normally has a debit balance actually has a credit balance, or vice versa, an error may have occurred or an unusual situation may exist. For example, a credit balance in the office equipment account could result only from an error. On the other hand, a debit balance in an accounts payable account could result from an overpayment.

ILLUSTRATION OF ANALYZING AND SUMMARIZING TRANSACTIONS

Objective 5

Analyze and summarize the financial statement effects of transactions.

How does a transaction occur in a business enterprise? A transaction is initiated by the action of a manager or other authorized employee, who normally generates a business document. For example, an invoice is a business document used for purchasing supplies.[3] A billing statement is a business document used for providing services. On the basis of business documents, the effects of transactions on the financial statements are analyzed and recorded. As we discussed in the preceding section, a transaction is first recorded in a journal. Periodically the journal entries are transferred to the accounts in the ledger. This process of transferring the debits and credits from the journal entries to the accounts is called **posting**. The flow of a transaction from its authorization to its posting in the accounts is shown in the diagram below.

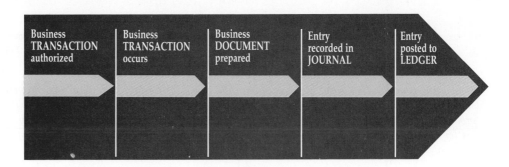

The ability to analyze the effects of transactions on financial statements is an essential skill for a successful career in business. As we illustrated earlier in the chapter, the double-entry accounting system is a very powerful tool in this analysis. Using this system to analyze transactions can be summarized as follows:

---

[3] In computerized accounting systems, some transactions are automatically authorized when certain events occur. For example, the salaries of managers may be paid automatically at the end of each pay period.

1. Determine whether an asset, a liability, owner's equity, revenue, or expense is affected.
2. Determine whether the affected asset, liability, owner's equity, revenue, or expense increases or decreases.
3. Determine whether the effect of the transaction should be recorded as a debit or as a credit in an asset, liability, owner's equity, revenue, or expense account.

In practice, businesses use a variety of formats for recording journal entries. A business may use one all-purpose journal, or it may use several journals. In the latter case, each journal is used to record different types of transactions, such as cash receipts or cash payments.[4] The journals may be part of either a manual accounting system or a computerized accounting system.

To illustrate a manual accounting system for recording and posting transactions, the December transactions of Computer King Corporation will be used. The first transaction in December occurred on December 1.

Dec. 1. Computer King Corporation paid a premium of $2,400 for a comprehensive insurance policy covering liability, theft, and fire. The policy covers a two-year period.

Analysis: Advance payments of expenses such as insurance are prepaid expenses, which are assets. For Computer King Corporation, the asset acquired for the cash payment is insurance protection for 24 months. The asset Prepaid Insurance increases and is debited for $2,400. The asset Cash decreases and is credited for $2,400.

The recording of this transaction in an all-purpose journal and its posting to accounts in the ledger is shown in Exhibit 2.

Exhibit 2
Diagram of the Recording and Posting of a Debit and a Credit

JOURNAL — Page 2 ③

	DATE	DESCRIPTION		POST. REF.	DEBIT	CREDIT
①	1994 Dec. 1	Prepaid Insurance	④	15	2 400 00	
		Cash	④	11		2 400 00
		Premium on 2-year policy				

④ ② ②

ACCOUNT *Prepaid Insurance* — ACCOUNT NO. *15* ④

	DATE	ITEM	POST. REF.	DEBIT	CREDIT	BALANCE DEBIT	BALANCE CREDIT
①	1994 Dec. 1		2	2 400 00		2 400 00	

③

ACCOUNT *Cash* — ACCOUNT NO. *11* ④

	DATE	ITEM	POST. REF.	DEBIT	CREDIT	BALANCE DEBIT	BALANCE CREDIT
①	Nov. 30		1		2 000 00	5 900 00	
	Dec. 1		2		2 400 00	3 500 00	

③

[4] Examples of special journals are presented in Appendix D. The use of computerized accounting systems is discussed in later chapters after the basics of accounting systems have been presented.

In the journal, you should note where the date of the transaction is recorded. Also note that the entry is explained as the payment of an insurance premium. Such explanations may be omitted when the nature of the transaction is obvious. Also, for complex transactions, such as a long-term rental arrangement, it may be more efficient to reference the rental agreement or other business document.

You will note that the T account form is not used in this illustration. Although the T account clearly separates debit entries and credit entries, it is inefficient for summarizing a large quantity of transactions. In practice, the T account is usually replaced with the standard form shown in Exhibit 2.

The debits and credits for each journal entry are posted to the accounts in the order that they occur in the journal. In posting to the standard account, ① the date is entered and ② the amount of the entry is entered. For future reference, ③ the journal page number is inserted in the Posting Reference column of the account, and ④ the account number is inserted in the Posting Reference column of the journal.

The remaining December transactions for Computer King Corporation are analyzed in the following paragraphs. These transactions are posted to the ledger in Exhibit 3. To simplify and reduce repetition, some of the December transactions are stated in summary form. For example, cash received for services is normally recorded on a daily basis. In this example, however, only summary totals are recorded at the middle and end of the month. Likewise, all fees earned on account during December are recorded at the middle and end of the month. In practice, each fee earned is recorded separately.

Dec. 1. Computer King Corporation paid rent for December, $800. The company from which Computer King Corporation is renting its store space now requires the payment of rent on the 1st of each month, rather than at the end of the month.

Analysis: Similar to the advance payment of the insurance premium in the preceding transaction, the advance payment of rent is an asset. However, the asset prepaid insurance will not completely expire for 24 months, while the asset prepaid rent will expire in one month. When an asset that is purchased will be used up in a short period of time, such as a month, it is normal to debit an expense account initially. This avoids having to transfer the balance from an asset account (Prepaid Rent) to an expense account (Rent Expense) at the end of the month. Thus, when the rent for December is prepaid at the beginning of the month, Rent Expense is debited for $800 and Cash is credited for $800.

			JOURNAL			Page 2	
	DATE		DESCRIPTION	POST. REF.	DEBIT	CREDIT	
1	1994 Dec.	1	Rent Expense	52	8 0 0 00		1
2			Cash	11		8 0 0 00	2
3							3

Dec. 1. Computer King Corporation received an offer from a local retailer to rent the land purchased on November 5th. The retailer plans to use the land as a parking lot for its employees and customers. Computer King Corporation agreed to rent the land for three months, payable in advance. Computer King Corporation received $360 for three months' rent beginning December 1st.

Analysis: By agreeing to rent the land and accepting the $360, Computer King Corporation has incurred an obligation (liability) to the retailer. This obligation is to make the land available for use for three months and not to interfere with its use.

The liability created by receiving the revenue in advance is called **unearned revenue**. Thus, the $360 received is an increase in an asset and is debited to Cash. The liability account Unearned Rent increases and is credited for $360. As time passes, the unearned rent liability will decrease and will become revenue.

4					4
5	1	Cash	11	3 6 0 00	5
6		Unearned Rent	23		3 6 0 00	6

Dec. 4. Purchased office equipment on account from Executive Supply Co. for $1,800.

Analysis: The asset account Office Equipment increases and is therefore debited for $1,800. The liability account Accounts Payable increases and is credited for $1,800.

7					7
8	4	Office Equipment	18	1 8 0 0 00	8
9		Accounts Payable	21		1 8 0 0 00	9

Dec. 6. Paid $180 for a newspaper advertisement.

Analysis: An expense increases and is debited for $180. The asset Cash decreases and is credited for $180. Expense items that are expected to be minor in amount are normally included as part of the miscellaneous expense. Thus, Miscellaneous Expense is debited for $180.

10					10
11	6	Miscellaneous Expense	59	1 8 0 00	11
12		Cash	11		1 8 0 00	12

Dec. 11. Paid creditors $400.

Analysis: This payment decreases the liability account Accounts Payable, which is debited for $400. Cash also decreases and is credited for $400.

13					13
14	11	Accounts Payable	21	4 0 0 00	14
15		Cash	11		4 0 0 00	15

Dec. 13. Paid receptionist and part-time assistant $950 for two weeks' wages.

Analysis: This transaction is similar to the December 6th transaction, where an expense account is increased and Cash is decreased. Thus, Wages Expense is debited for $950 and Cash is credited for $950.

16					16
17	13	Wages Expense	51	9 5 0 00	17
18		Cash	11		9 5 0 00	18

Dec. 16. Received $3,100 from fees earned for the first half of December.

Analysis: Cash increases and is debited for $3,100. The revenue account Fees Earned increases and is credited for $3,100.

19						19
20	16	Cash	11	3 1 0 0 00		20
21		Fees Earned	41		3 1 0 0 00	21

Dec. 16. Fees earned on account totaled $1,750 for the first half of December.

Analysis: When an enterprise agrees that payment for services provided or goods sold can be accepted at another date, the firm has an **account receivable**, which is a claim against the customer. The account receivable is an asset, and the revenue is earned even though no cash has been received. Thus, Accounts Receivable increases and is debited for $1,750. The revenue account Fees Earned increases and is credited for $1,750.

22						22
23	16	Accounts Receivable	12	1 7 5 0 00		23
24		Fees Earned	41		1 7 5 0 00	24

Dec. 20. Paid $900 to Executive Supply Co. on the $1,800 debt owed from the December 4 transaction.

Analysis: Similar to transaction of December 11.

25						25
26	20	Accounts Payable	21	9 0 0 00		26
27		Cash	11		9 0 0 00	27

Dec. 21. Received $650 from customers in payment of their accounts.

Analysis: When customers pay amounts owed for services they have previously received, one asset increases and another asset decreases. Thus, Cash is debited for $650, and Accounts Receivable is credited for $650.

28						28
29	21	Cash	11	6 5 0 00		29
30		Accounts Receivable	12		6 5 0 00	30

Dec. 23. Paid $1,450 for supplies.

Analysis: The asset account Supplies increases and is debited for $1,450. The asset account Cash decreases and is credited for $1,450.

31						31
32	23	Supplies	14	1 4 5 0 00		32
33		Cash	11		1 4 5 0 00	33

Dec. 27. Paid receptionist and part-time assistant $1,200 for two weeks' wages.

Analysis: Similar to transaction of December 13.

34							34
35		27	Wages Expense	51	1 2 0 0 00		35
36			Cash	11		1 2 0 0 00	36

Dec. 31. Paid $310 telephone bill for the month.

Analysis: Similar to transaction of December 6. The expense account Utilities Expense is debited for $310 and Cash is credited for $310.

37							37
38	Dec.	31	Utilities Expense	54	3 1 0 00		38
39			Cash	11		3 1 0 00	39

Dec. 31. Paid $225 electric bill for the month.

Analysis: Similar to the preceding transaction.

40							40
41		31	Utilities Expense	54	2 2 5 00		41
42			Cash	11		2 2 5 00	42

Dec. 31. Received $2,870 from fees earned for the second half of December.

Analysis: Similar to transaction of December 16.

43							43
44		31	Cash	11	2 8 7 0 00		44
45			Fees Earned	41		2 8 7 0 00	45

Dec. 31 Fees earned on account totaled $1,120 for the second half of December.

Analysis: Similar to transaction of December 16.

46							46
47		31	Accounts Receivable	12	1 1 2 0 00		47
48			Fees Earned	41		1 1 2 0 00	48

Dec. 31. Computer King Corporation paid dividends of $2,000 to stockholders.

Analysis: The transaction resulted in an increase in the amount of dividends and is recorded by a $2,000 debit to Dividends. The decrease in cash is recorded by a $2,000 credit to Cash.

49							49
50		31	Dividends	33	2 0 0 0 00		50
51			Cash	11		2 0 0 0 00	51

The journal for Computer King Corporation since it was organized on November 1 is shown in Exhibit 3. Exhibit 3 also shows the ledger after the transactions for both November and December have been posted.

Exhibit 3
Journal and Ledger—Computer King Corporation

	DATE		DESCRIPTION	POST. REF.	DEBIT	CREDIT	
1	1994 Nov.	1	Cash	11	15 0 0 0 00		1
2			Capital Stock	31		15 0 0 0 00	2
3							3
4		5	Land	17	10 0 0 0 00		4
5			Cash	11		10 0 0 0 00	5
6							6
7		10	Supplies	14	1 3 5 0 00		7
8			Accounts Payable	21		1 3 5 0 00	8
9							9
10		18	Cash	11	7 5 0 0 00		10
11			Fees Earned	41		7 5 0 0 00	11
12							12
13		30	Wages Expense	51	2 1 2 5 00		13
14			Rent Expense	52	8 0 0 00		14
15			Utilities Expense	54	4 5 0 00		15
16			Miscellaneous Expense	59	2 7 5 00		16
17			Cash	11		3 6 5 0 00	17
18							18
19		30	Accounts Payable	21	9 5 0 00		19
20			Cash	11		9 5 0 00	20
21							21
22		30	Supplies Expense	55	8 0 0 00		22
23			Supplies	14		8 0 0 00	23
24							24
25		30	Dividends	33	2 0 0 0 00		25
26			Cash	11		2 0 0 0 00	26
27							27
28	Dec.	1	Prepaid Insurance	15	2 4 0 0 00		28
29			Cash	11		2 4 0 0 00	29
30							30
31		1	Rent Expense	52	8 0 0 00		31
32			Cash	11		8 0 0 00	32

JOURNAL — Page 1

JOURNAL — Page 2

	DATE		DESCRIPTION	POST. REF.	DEBIT	CREDIT	
1	1994 Dec.	1	Cash	11	3 6 0 00		1
2			Unearned Rent	23		3 6 0 00	2
3							3
4		4	Office Equipment	18	1 8 0 0 00		4
5			Accounts Payable	21		1 8 0 0 00	5
6							6
7		6	Miscellaneous Expense	59	1 8 0 00		7
8			Cash	11		1 8 0 00	8
9							9
10		11	Accounts Payable	21	4 0 0 00		10
11			Cash	11		4 0 0 00	11
12							12
13		13	Wages Expense	51	9 5 0 00		13
14			Cash	11		9 5 0 00	14
15							15
16		16	Cash	11	3 1 0 0 00		16
17			Fees Earned	41		3 1 0 0 00	17
18							18
19		16	Accounts Receivable	12	1 7 5 0 00		19
20			Fees Earned	41		1 7 5 0 00	20

			POST. REF.	DEBIT	CREDIT	
22	20	Accounts Payable	21	9 0 0 00		22
23		Cash	11		9 0 0 00	23
24						24
25	21	Cash	11	6 5 0 00		25
26		Accounts Receivable	12		6 5 0 00	26
27						27
28	23	Supplies	14	1 4 5 0 00		28
29		Cash	11		1450 00	29
30						30
31	27	Wages Expense	51	1 2 0 0 00		31
32		Cash	11		1 2 0 0 00	32

JOURNAL

Page 3

	DATE	DESCRIPTION	POST. REF.	DEBIT	CREDIT	
1	1994 Dec. 31	Utilities Expense	54	3 1 0 00		1
2		Cash	11		3 1 0 00	2
3						3
4	31	Utilities Expense	54	2 2 5 00		4
5		Cash	11		2 2 5 00	5
6						6
7	31	Cash	11	2 8 7 0 00		7
8		Fees Earned	41		2 8 7 0 00	8
9						9
10	31	Accounts Receivable	12	1 1 2 0 00		10
11		Fees Earned	41		1 1 2 0 00	11
12						12
13	31	Dividends	33	2 0 0 0 00		13
14		Cash	11		2 0 0 0 00	14

ACCOUNT Cash

ACCOUNT NO. 11

DATE	ITEM	POST. REF.	DEBIT	CREDIT	BALANCE DEBIT	BALANCE CREDIT
1994 Nov. 1		1	15 0 0 0 00		15 0 0 0 00	
5		1		10 0 0 0 00	5 0 0 0 00	
18		1	7 5 0 0 00		12 5 0 0 00	
30		1		3 6 5 0 00	8 8 5 0 00	
30		1		9 5 0 00	7 9 0 0 00	
30		1		2 0 0 0 00	5 9 0 0 00	
Dec. 1		2		2 4 0 0 00	3 5 0 0 00	
1		2		8 0 0 00	2 7 0 0 00	
1		2	3 6 0 00		3 0 6 0 00	
6		2		1 8 0 00	2 8 8 0 00	
11		2		4 0 0 00	2 4 8 0 00	
13		2		9 5 0 00	1 5 3 0 00	
16		2	3 1 0 0 00		4 6 3 0 00	
20		2		9 0 0 00	3 7 3 0 00	
21		2	6 5 0 00		4 3 8 0 00	
23		2		1 4 5 0 00	2 9 3 0 00	
27		2		1 2 0 0 00	1 7 3 0 00	
31		3		3 1 0 00	1 4 2 0 00	
31		3		2 2 5 00	1 1 9 5 00	
31		3	2 8 7 0 00		4 0 6 5 00	
31		3		2 0 0 0 00	2 0 6 5 00	

ACCOUNT   *Accounts Receivable*   ACCOUNT NO. *12*

DATE		ITEM	POST. REF.	DEBIT	CREDIT	BALANCE DEBIT	BALANCE CREDIT
1994 Dec.	16		2	1 7 5 0 00		1 7 5 0 00	
	21		2		6 5 0 00	1 1 0 0 00	
	31		3	1 1 2 0 00		2 2 2 0 00	

ACCOUNT   *Supplies*   ACCOUNT NO. *14*

DATE		ITEM	POST. REF.	DEBIT	CREDIT	BALANCE DEBIT	BALANCE CREDIT
1994 Nov.	10		1	1 3 5 0 00		1 3 5 0 00	
	30		1		8 0 0 00	5 5 0 00	
Dec.	23		2	1 4 5 0 00		2 0 0 0 00	

ACCOUNT   *Prepaid Insurance*   ACCOUNT NO. *15*

DATE		ITEM	POST. REF.	DEBIT	CREDIT	BALANCE DEBIT	BALANCE CREDIT
1994 Dec.	4		2	2 4 0 0 00		2 4 0 0 00	

ACCOUNT   *Land*   ACCOUNT NO. *17*

DATE		ITEM	POST. REF.	DEBIT	CREDIT	BALANCE DEBIT	BALANCE CREDIT
1994 Nov.	5		1	10 0 0 0 00		10 0 0 0 00	

ACCOUNT   *Office Equipment*   ACCOUNT NO. *18*

DATE		ITEM	POST. REF.	DEBIT	CREDIT	BALANCE DEBIT	BALANCE CREDIT
1994 Dec.	4		2	1 8 0 0 00		1 8 0 0 00	

ACCOUNT   *Accounts Payable*   ACCOUNT NO. *21*

DATE		ITEM	POST. REF.	DEBIT	CREDIT	BALANCE DEBIT	BALANCE CREDIT
1994 Nov.	10		1		1 3 5 0 00		1 3 5 0 00
	30		1	9 5 0 00			4 0 0 00
Dec.	4		2		1 8 0 0 00		2 2 0 0 00
	11		2	4 0 0 00			1 8 0 0 00
	20		2	9 0 0 00			9 0 0 00

ACCOUNT   *Unearned Rent*   ACCOUNT NO. *23*

DATE		ITEM	POST. REF.	DEBIT	CREDIT	BALANCE DEBIT	BALANCE CREDIT
1994 Dec.	1		2		3 6 0 00		3 6 0 00

ACCOUNT   *Capital Stock*   ACCOUNT NO. *31*

DATE		ITEM	POST. REF.	DEBIT	CREDIT	BALANCE DEBIT	BALANCE CREDIT
1994 Nov.	1		1		15 0 0 0 00		15 0 0 0 00

ACCOUNT   *Dividends*   ACCOUNT NO. *33*

DATE		ITEM	POST. REF.	DEBIT	CREDIT	BALANCE DEBIT	BALANCE CREDIT
1994 Nov.	30		1	2 0 0 0 00		2 0 0 0 00	
Dec.	31		3	2 0 0 0 00		4 0 0 0 00	

ACCOUNT   *Fees Earned*   ACCOUNT NO. *41*

DATE		ITEM	POST. REF.	DEBIT	CREDIT	BALANCE DEBIT	BALANCE CREDIT
1994 Nov.	18		1		7 5 0 0 00		7 5 0 0 00
Dec.	16		2		3 1 0 0 00		10 6 0 0 00
	16		2		1 7 5 0 00		12 3 5 0 00
	31		3		2 8 7 0 00		15 2 2 0 00
	31		3		1 1 2 0 00		16 3 4 0 00

ACCOUNT   *Wages Expense*   ACCOUNT NO. *51*

DATE		ITEM	POST. REF.	DEBIT	CREDIT	BALANCE DEBIT	BALANCE CREDIT
1994 Nov.	30		1	2 1 2 5 00		2 1 2 5 00	
Dec.	13		2	9 5 0 00		3 0 7 5 00	
	27		2	1 2 0 0 00		4 2 7 5 00	

ACCOUNT   *Rent Expense*   ACCOUNT NO. *52*

DATE		ITEM	POST. REF.	DEBIT	CREDIT	BALANCE DEBIT	BALANCE CREDIT
1994 Nov.	30		1	8 0 0 00		8 0 0 00	
Dec.	1		2	8 0 0 00		1 6 0 0 00	

ACCOUNT   *Utilities Expense*   ACCOUNT NO. *54*

DATE		ITEM	POST. REF.	DEBIT	CREDIT	BALANCE DEBIT	BALANCE CREDIT
1994 Nov.	30		1	4 5 0 00		4 5 0 00	
Dec.	31		3	3 1 0 00		7 6 0 00	
	31		3	2 2 5 00		9 8 5 00	

ACCOUNT   *Supplies Expense*   ACCOUNT NO. *55*

DATE		ITEM	POST. REF.	DEBIT	CREDIT	BALANCE DEBIT	BALANCE CREDIT
1994 Nov.	30		1	8 0 0 00		8 0 0 00	

ACCOUNT	*Miscellaneous Expense*				ACCOUNT NO. *59*	
		POST.			BALANCE	
DATE	ITEM	REF.	DEBIT	CREDIT	DEBIT	CREDIT
1994 Nov. 30		1	2 7 5 00		2 7 5 00	
Dec. 6		2	1 8 0 00		4 5 5 00	

TRIAL BALANCE

Objective 6
Prepare a trial balance and explain how it can be used to discover errors.

How can you be sure that you have not made an error in posting the debits and credits to the ledger? One way is to determine the equality of the debits and credits in the ledger. This equality should be proved at the end of each accounting period, if not more often. Such a proof, called a **trial balance**, may be in the form of a computer printout or in the form shown in Exhibit 4.[5]

Exhibit 4
Trial Balance

Computer King Corporation
Trial Balance
December 31, 1994

Cash	2 0 6 5 00	
Accounts Receivable	2 2 2 0 00	
Supplies	2 0 0 0 00	
Prepaid Insurance	2 4 0 0 00	
Land	10 0 0 0 00	
Office Equipment	1 8 0 0 00	
Accounts Payable		9 0 0 00
Unearned Rent		3 6 0 00
Capital Stock		15 0 0 0 00
Dividends	4 0 0 0 00	
Fees Earned		16 3 4 0 00
Wages Expense	4 2 7 5 00	
Rent Expense	1 6 0 0 00	
Utilities Expense	9 8 5 00	
Supplies Expense	8 0 0 00	
Miscellaneous Expense	4 5 5 00	
	32 6 0 0 00	32 6 0 0 00

The first step in preparing the trial balance is to determine the balance of each account in the ledger. When the standard account form is used, the balance of each account appears in the balance column on the same line as the last posting to the account.

The trial balance does not provide complete proof of the accuracy of the ledger. It indicates only that the debits and the credits are equal. This proof is of value, however, because errors often affect the equality of debits and credits. If the two totals of a trial balance are not equal, an error has occurred. In the remainder of this chapter, we will discuss procedures for discovering and correcting errors.

---

[5] A trial balance is not a formal statement, but is used by the accountant to verify the accuracy of the accounting records. Thus, financial statement captions, subtotals, and dollar signs are normally omitted from a trial balance.

DISCOVERY AND CORRECTION OF ERRORS

Objective 7
Discover errors in recording transactions and correct them.

Errors will sometimes occur in journalizing and posting transactions. The following paragraphs describe and illustrate how you can discover and correct errors.

Discovery of Errors

As mentioned previously, the trial balance is one of the primary ways for discovering errors in the ledger. However, it indicates only that the debits and credits are equal. If the two totals of the trial balance are not equal, it is probably due to one or more of the following types of errors:

1. Error in preparing the trial balance, such as:
    a. One of the columns of the trial balance was incorrectly added.
    b. The amount of an account balance was incorrectly recorded on the trial balance.
    c. A debit balance was recorded on the trial balance as a credit, or vice versa, or a balance was omitted entirely.
2. Error in determining the account balances, such as:
    a. A balance was incorrectly computed.
    b. A balance was entered in the wrong balance column.
3. Error in recording a transaction in the ledger, such as:
    a. An erroneous amount was posted to the account.
    b. A debit entry was posted as a credit, or vice versa.
    c. A debit or a credit posting was omitted.

Among the types of errors that will not cause an inequality in the trial balance totals are the following:

1. Failure to record a transaction or to post a transaction.
2. Recording the same erroneous amount for both the debit and the credit parts of a transaction.
3. Recording the same transaction more than once.
4. Posting a part of a transaction correctly as a debit or credit but to the wrong account.

It is obvious that care should be used in recording transactions in the journal and in posting to the accounts. The need for accuracy in determining account balances and reporting them on the trial balance is equally obvious.

Errors in the accounts may be discovered in various ways: (1) by audit procedures, (2) by chance, or (3) by looking at the trial balance. If the two trial balance totals are not equal, the amount of the difference between the totals should be determined before searching for the error.

The amount of the difference between the two totals of a trial balance sometimes gives a clue as to the nature of the error or where it occurred. For example, a difference of 10, 100, or 1,000 between two totals is often the result of an error in addition. A difference between totals can also be due to the omission of a debit or a credit posting. If the difference is divisible evenly by 2, the error may be due to the posting of a debit as a credit, or vice versa. For example, if the debit total is $20,640 and the credit total is $20,236, the difference of $404 may indicate that a credit posting of $404 was omitted or that a credit of $202 was incorrectly posted as a debit.

Two other common types of errors are known as transpositions and slides. A **transposition** is the erroneous rearrangement of digits, such as writing $542 as $452 or $524. In a **slide**, the entire number is erroneously moved one or more spaces to the right or the left, such as writing $542.00 as $54.20 or $5,420.00. If an error of either type has occurred and there are no other errors, the difference between the two trial balance totals can be evenly divided by 9.

When you search for a trial balance difference along the lines suggested by the preceding paragraphs, you will often find the error. If you do not find the error, the steps in the accounting process must be retraced, beginning with the last step and working back to the entries in the journal. Usually, errors causing the trial balance totals to be unequal will be discovered before all of the steps are retraced. While there are no standard rules for searching for errors, the steps presented below are usually followed:

1. Prove the accuracy of the trial balance totals by re-adding the columns.
2. Compare the listings in the trial balance with the balances shown in the ledger. Make certain that no accounts have been omitted.
3. Recompute the balance of each account in the ledger.
4. Trace the postings in the ledger back to the journal. Place a small check mark beside each item in the ledger and also in the journal. If the error is not found, examine each account to see if there is an entry without a check mark. Do the same with the entries in the journal.
5. Prove the equality of the debits and the credits in the journal.

Correction of Errors

When errors in journalizing and posting transactions are discovered, the procedures used to correct them vary according to the nature of the error and when the error is discovered. We will discuss these procedures in the following paragraphs.

An error in an account title or amount in the journal may be discovered before the entry is posted. In this case, the correction may be made by drawing a line through the error and inserting the correct title or amount directly above. If there is any chance of questions arising later, the person responsible may initial the correction.

An entry in the journal may be prepared correctly, but may be incorrectly posted to the account. In this case, the incorrect posting may be corrected by drawing a line through the error and posting the item correctly. As indicated above, if there is any chance of questions arising later, the person responsible may initial the correction.

An incorrect account title may appear in a journal entry and the error may not be discovered until after posting is completed. In this case, it is best to journalize and post a correcting entry. To illustrate, assume that on May 5 a purchase of office equipment was incorrectly journalized and posted as a $12,500 debit to Supplies. The credit was correctly journalized and posted as a $12,500 credit to Accounts Payable. Before a correcting entry is made, it is best to determine (1) the debit(s) and credit(s) of the entry in which the error occurred and (2) the debit(s) and credit(s) that should have been recorded. T accounts may be helpful in making this analysis, as in the following example:

Entry in which error occurred:

Supplies		Accounts Payable	
12,500			12,500

Entry that should have been recorded:

Office Equipment		Accounts Payable	
12,500			12,500

Comparison of the two sets of T accounts shows that the incorrect debit of $12,500 to Supplies may be corrected by debiting Office Equipment for $12,500 and crediting Supplies for $12,500. The following correcting entry is then journalized and posted:

JOURNAL							Page 30	
	DATE	DESCRIPTION	POST. REF.	DEBIT		CREDIT		
1	1994 May 31	Office Equipment	18	12 5 0 0 00				1
2		Supplies	14			12 5 0 0 00		2
3		To correct erroneous						3
4		debit to Supplies on May 5.						4
5		See invoice from Bell						5
6		Office Equipment Co. *C.W.*						6

The procedures for correcting errors are summarized in Exhibit 5.

Exhibit 5
Procedures for Correcting Errors

Error	Correction Procedure
Journal entry incorrect, but not posted.	Draw line through the error and insert correct title or amount.
Journal entry correct, but posted incorrectly.	Draw line through the error and post correctly.
Journal entry incorrect and posted.	Journalize and post a correcting entry.

MATERIALITY CONCEPT

Objective 8
Describe and apply the materiality concept.

Generally accepted accounting principles should be applied to all significant items in preparing the financial statements. Insignificant items may be treated in the easiest manner. Determining what is and what is not significant or material requires judgment. Precise criteria cannot be developed.

The Financial Accounting Standards Board's *Statement of Financial Accounting Concepts, No. 2* defines **materiality** as follows:

The omission or misstatement of an item in a financial report is material if, in light of the surrounding circumstances, the magnitude of the item is such that it is probable that the judgment of a reasonable person relying upon the report would have been changed or influenced by the inclusion or correction of the item.[6]

In assessing the materiality of an item, the size of the item, its nature, and relationship to other items in the financial statements should be considered. For example, an error in classifying a $10,000 asset on a balance sheet with total assets of $10,000,000 would probably be immaterial. If the assets totaled only $100,000, however, the error would be material. If the $10,000 were a note receivable from an officer of the enterprise, it might well be material even in the first case. Assume further that the loan increased to $100,000 between the end of the fiscal period and the issuance of the financial statements. In this case, the nature of the item, its amount at the balance sheet date, and its subsequent increase in amount should be disclosed in the statements.

The materiality concept may also be applied to recording transactions. For example, many companies record small expenditures for assets as an expense of the period rather than as an asset. In setting the dollar cutoff for such expenditures, factors such as the following should be considered: (1) the amount of assets, (2) the number of such expenditures, (3) the nature and expected life of the assets, and (4) the effect on reported net income.

A common use of the materiality concept is the practice of omitting cents in preparing financial statements. Many large companies round financial

---

[6] *Statement of Financial Accounting Concepts, No. 2,* "Qualitative Characteristics of Accounting Information" (Stamford: Financial Accounting Standards Board, 1980), par. 132.

statement items to thousands or even millions of dollars for reporting purposes. For example, the 1992 edition of *Accounting Trends & Techniques* indicated that 51 of 600 (8%) companies reported amounts to the nearest dollar, 388 (65%) to the nearest thousand dollars, and 161 (27%) to the nearest million dollars.

Some companies use "whole-dollar" accounting in which the cents amounts are eliminated from accounting records at the earliest possible point in the accounting process. Any differences introduced into the accounts by rounding tend to balance out, and any final difference is usually not material. There may be some accounts, however, such as those with customers and creditors, for which it may not be feasible to use "whole-dollar" accounting.

Concerning the Gnat and the Camel

This is the story as it comes to us: An accountant . . . was [asked] to check the cash of a concern, which may be called the XYZ Corporation. This concern among its activities included a selling department where goods of small value were sold in fairly large quantities. When the cash of the selling department was counted it was found that the amount on hand was, let us say, $2.04—a fictitious amount greater than the actual sum—more than it should have been. Now this incident happened in the city of New York where, as all citizens know to their sorrow, there is a two percent tax on sales. Evidently, therefore, this excessive sum of $2.04 represented the sale of some article for $2, plus a tax of four cents. . . . Apparently a careless member of the staff had sold such an article, placed the proceeds in the till and forgotten to make the proper record of the whole stupendous transaction. The carelessness was unpardonable, of course. No member of any staff anywhere should forget anything. However, the error occurred and the perspicacious young [accountant] discovered it, as he could not very well avoid doing. He found the unaccountable excess and, like a well-trained man, conscious of his complete efficiency, he set to work to trace the mistake and to expose the guilty person. Here was a chance for him to demonstrate his incalculable value to his firm. . . . Such wrongdoing must not escape unchallenged. Relying upon his supposed authority he began a search, a veritable inquisition, and after two or three days of earnest ef-

fort, during which he had interrupted the work of the entire . . . office and had. . . considerable . . . time expended, he was compelled to admit that he could not find a shortage in the inventory to account for the surplus cash, nor could he rightfully determine who had committed the crime. At last he regretfully reported the matter to his superior and confessed himself defeated. What the superior had to say about the matter is not recorded; but one can imagine the attitude of the [superior] and can form a reasonably accurate notion of the comments which were made. . . .

This little story bears a moral which every accountant may well take to heart. It might be unwise to say that errors should be overlooked or that carelessness should be condoned. But surely there is no sense whatever in a ridiculous adherence to meticulous detail when the sole purpose is to trace something which is not worth tracing. . . . What the [accountant] should have done in the present case is clear. He should have made a note of the excess, and, after spending a few minutes in trying to trace it to its source, he should have gone on to weightier things. It is a great pity that this sort of incident ever occurs; but we are told that the case before us is not unique. There are many little fellows who revel in the most microscopic minutiae. They can't help it. They probably were born that way, but they should never, never, be employed in the work of accountancy, which, after all, is a matter of principles, not of pin points.

Source: A. P. Richardson, *The Journal of Accountancy* (October, 1936), pp. 233-235.

CHAPTER REVIEW

Key Points

Objective 1. Explain how an account can be used for analyzing the effects of transactions on financial statements.

The record used for the purpose of recording individual transactions is an account. A group of accounts is called a ledger.

Objective 2. Prepare a chart of accounts for a service enterprise.

The system of accounts that make up a ledger is called a chart of accounts. The accounts are numbered and listed in the order in which they appear in the balance sheet and the income statement.

Objective 3. Explain the characteristics of an account.

The simplest form of an account, a T account, has three parts. First, each account has a title, which is the name of the item recorded in the account. Second, each account has a left side, called the debit side. Third, each account has a right side, called the credit side. Amounts entered on the left side of an account, regardless of the account title, are called debits to the account. Amounts entered on the right side of an account are called credits. Periodically, the debits and the credits in an account are summed and the balance of the account is determined.

Objective 4. List the rules of debit and credit and the normal balances of accounts.

General rules of debit and credit have been established for recording increases or decreases to asset, liability, owner's equity, revenue, expense, and dividend accounts. Each transaction is recorded so that the sum of the debits is always equal to the sum of the credits.

Transactions are initially entered in a record called a journal. The data in the journal entry are transferred to the proper accounts by a process known as posting.

The sum of the increases recorded in an account is usually equal to or greater than the sum of the decreases recorded in the account. For this reason, the normal balance of an account is indicated by the side of the account (debit or credit) that receives the increases.

The rules of debit and credit and normal account balances are summarized in the following table:

	Increase (Normal Balance)	Decrease
Balance sheet accounts:		
Asset	**Debit**	Credit
Liability	**Credit**	Debit
Owner's Equity or Stockholders' Equity:		
Capital Stock	**Credit**	Debit
Retained Earnings	**Credit**	Debit
Dividends	**Debit**	Credit
Income statement accounts:		
Revenue	**Credit**	Debit
Expense	**Debit**	Credit

Objective 5. Analyze and summarize the financial statement effects of transactions.

A two-column journal with a debit column and a credit column is used for recording initial transactions in an accounting system. In practice, the T account is usually replaced with the standard four-column account. Journal entries are periodically posted to the accounts.

Objective 6. Prepare a trial balance and explain how it can be used to discover errors.

A trial balance is prepared by listing the accounts from the ledger and their balances. If the two totals of the trial balance are not equal, an error has occurred.

Objective 7. Discover errors in recording transactions and correct them.

Errors may be discovered (1) by audit procedures, (2) by chance, or (3) by looking at the trial balance. The procedures for correcting errors are summarized in Exhibit 5.

Objective 8. Describe and apply the materiality concept.

The materiality concept requires accountants to consider the relative importance of any event, accounting procedure, or change in procedure that affects the financial statements. Generally accepted accounting principles should be applied to all material items in preparing the financial statements. Immaterial items may be treated in the easiest manner.

Glossary of Key Terms

Account. The form used to record additions and deductions for each individual asset, liability, owner's equity, revenue, and expense. **Objective 1**

Assets. Physical items (tangible) or rights (intangible) that have value and that are owned by the business entity. **Objective 2**

Balance of the account. The amount of difference between the debits and the credits that have been entered into an account. **Objective 3**

Chart of accounts. The system of accounts that make up the ledger for a business enterprise. **Objective 2**

Credit. (1) The right side of an account; (2) the amount entered on the right side of an account; (3) to enter an amount on the right side of an account. **Objective 3**

Debit. (1) The left side of an account; (2) the amount entered

on the left side of an account; (3) to enter an amount on the left side of an account. **Objective 3**

Dividends. The distribution of earnings of a corporation to its stockholders. **Objective 2**

Double-entry accounting. A system for recording transactions, based on recording increases and decreases in accounts so that debits always equal credits. **Objective 4**

Expenses. Assets used up or services consumed in the process of generating revenues. **Objective 2**

Journal. The initial record in which the effects of a transaction on accounts are recorded. **Objective 4**

Journalizing. The process of recording a transaction in a journal. **Objective 4**

Ledger. The group of accounts used by an enterprise. **Objective 1**

Liabilities. Debts owed to outsiders (creditors). **Objective 2**

Materiality. The concept that recognizes the practicality of ignoring small or insignificant deviations from generally accepted accounting principles. **Objective 8**

Owner's equity. The claim of owners against the assets of the business after the total liabilities are deducted. **Objective 2**

Posting. The process of transferring debits and credits from a journal to the accounts. **Objective 4**

Revenues. Increases in owner's equity as a result of providing services or selling products to customers. **Objective 2**

Slide. The erroneous movement of all digits in a number, one or more spaces to the right or the left, such as writing $542 as $5,420. **Objective 7**

T account. A form of account resembling the letter T. **Objective 3**

Transposition. The erroneous arrangement of digits in a number, such as writing $542 as $524. **Objective 7**

Trial balance. A summary listing of the titles and balances of the accounts in the ledger. **Objective 6**

Self-Examination Questions
Answers at end of chapter.

1. A debit may signify:
   - A. an increase in an asset account
   - B. a decrease in an asset account
   - C. an increase in a liability account
   - D. an increase in the capital stock account

2. The type of account with a normal credit balance is:
   - A. an asset
   - B. a dividend
   - C. a revenue
   - D. an expense

3. A debit balance in which of the following accounts would indicate a likely error?
   - A. Accounts Receivable
   - B. Cash
   - C. Accounts Payable
   - D. Miscellaneous Expense

4. The receipt of cash from customers in payment of their accounts would be recorded by a:
   - A. debit to Cash; credit to Accounts Receivable
   - B. debit to Accounts Receivable; credit to Cash
   - C. debit to Cash; credit to Accounts Payable
   - D. debit to Accounts Payable; credit to Cash

5. The form listing the titles and balances of the accounts in the ledger on a given date is the:
   - A. income statement
   - B. balance sheet
   - C. retained earnings statement
   - D. trial balance

ILLUSTRATIVE PROBLEM

Judy K. Schmidt, M.D., has been practicing as a pediatrician for three years as the owner and sole stockholder of Child Care Inc., a professional services corporation. During June, Child Care Inc. completed the following transactions:

June 1. Paid office rent for June, $600.
2. Purchased equipment on account, $2,100.
5. Received cash on account from patients, $4,150.
8. Purchased X-ray film and other supplies on account, $145.
9. One of the items of equipment purchased on June 2 was defective. It was returned with the permission of the supplier, who agreed to reduce the account for the amount charged for the item, $125.
12. Paid cash to creditors on account, $1,250.
16. Sold X-ray film to another doctor at cost, receiving cash, $63. (Record the credit in the supplies account.)
17. Paid cash for renewal of a two-year property insurance policy, $370.
20. Discovered that the balance of the cash account and of the accounts payable account as of June 1 were overstated by $50. A payment of that amount to a creditor in May had not been recorded. Journalize the $50 payment as of June 20.
23. Paid cash for laboratory analyses, $245.
27. Paid dividends, $1,250.
30. Recorded the cash received in payment of services (on a cash basis) to patients during June, $1,720.
30. Paid salaries of receptionist and nurses, $1,725.
30. Paid gas and electricity expense, $157.
30. Paid water expense, $29.
30. Recorded fees charged to patients on account for services performed in June, $4,145.
30. Paid telephone expense, $74.
30. Paid miscellaneous expenses, $132.

Schmidt's account titles, numbers, and balances as of June 1 (all normal balances) are listed as follows: Cash, 11, $3,123; Accounts Receivable, 12, $6,725; Supplies, 13, $290; Prepaid Insurance, 14, $365; Equipment, 18, $19,745; Accounts Payable, 22, $765; Capital Stock, 31, $10,000; Retained Earnings, 32, $19,483; Dividends, 33; Professional Fees, 41; Salary Expense, 51; Rent Expense, 53; Laboratory Expense, 55; Utilities Expense, 56; Miscellaneous Expense, 59.

Instructions

1. Open a ledger of standard four-column accounts for Child Care Inc. as of June 1 of the current year. Enter the balances in the appropriate balance columns and place a check mark (✔) in the posting reference column. (It is advisable to verify the equality of the debit and credit balances in the ledger before proceeding with the next instruction.)
2. Journalize each transaction in a two-column journal.
3. Post the journal to the ledger, extending the month-end balances to the appropriate balance columns after each posting.
4. Prepare a trial balance as of June 30.

Solution   2. and 3.

JOURNAL

Page 27

	DATE		DESCRIPTION	POST. REF.	DEBIT	CREDIT	
1	19-- June	1	Rent Expense	53	6 0 0 00		1
2			Cash	11		6 0 0 00	2
3							3
4		2	Equipment	18	2 1 0 0 00		4
5			Accounts Payable	22		2 1 0 0 00	5
6							6
7		5	Cash	11	4 1 5 0 00		7
8			Accounts Receivable	12		4 1 5 0 00	8
9							9
10		8	Supplies	13	1 4 5 00		10
11			Accounts Payable	22		1 4 5 00	11
12							12
13		9	Accounts Payable	22	1 2 5 00		13
14			Equipment	18		1 2 5 00	14
15							15
16		12	Accounts Payable	22	1 2 5 0 00		16
17			Cash	11		1 2 5 0 00	17
18							18
19		16	Cash	11	6 3 00		19
20			Supplies	13		6 3 00	20
21							21
22		17	Prepaid Insurance	14	3 7 0 00		22
23			Cash	11		3 7 0 00	23
24							24
25		20	Accounts Payable	22	5 0 00		25
26			Cash	11		5 0 00	26
27							27
28		23	Laboratory Expense	55	2 4 5 00		28
29			Cash	11		2 4 5 00	29
30							30
31		27	Dividends	33	1 2 5 0 00		31
32			Cash	11		1 2 5 0 00	32
33							33
34		30	Cash	11	1 7 2 0 00		34
35			Professional Fees	41		1 7 2 0 00	35

JOURNAL
Page 28

	DATE	DESCRIPTION	POST. REF.	DEBIT	CREDIT	
1	30	Salary Expense	51	1 7 2 5 00		1
2		Cash	11		1 7 2 5 00	2
3						3
4	30	Utilities Expense	56	1 5 7 00		4
5		Cash	11		1 5 7 00	5
6						6
7	30	Utilities Expense	56	2 9 00		7
8		Cash	11		2 9 00	8
9						9
10	30	Accounts Receivable	12	4 1 4 5 00		10
11		Professional Fees	41		4 1 4 5 00	11
12						12
13	30	Utilities Expense	56	7 4 00		13
14		Cash	11		7 4 00	14
15						15
16	30	Miscellaneous Expense	59	1 3 2 00		16
17		Cash	11		1 3 2 00	17

1. and 3.

ACCOUNT Cash
ACCOUNT NO. 11

DATE		ITEM	POST. REF.	DEBIT	CREDIT	BALANCE DEBIT	BALANCE CREDIT
19-- June	1	Balance	✓			3 1 2 3 00	
	1		27		6 0 0 00	2 5 2 3 00	
	5		27	4 1 5 0 00		6 6 7 3 00	
	12		27		1 2 5 0 00	5 4 2 3 00	
	16		27	6 3 00		5 4 8 6 00	
	17		27		3 7 0 00	5 1 1 6 00	
	20		27		5 0 00	5 0 6 6 00	
	23		27		2 4 5 00	4 8 2 1 00	
	27		27		1 2 5 0 00	3 5 7 1 00	
	30		27	1 7 2 0 00		5 2 9 1 00	
	30		28		1 7 2 5 00	3 5 6 6 00	
	30		28		1 5 7 00	3 4 0 9 00	
	30		28		2 9 00	3 3 8 0 00	
	30		28		7 4 00	3 3 0 6 00	
	30		28		1 3 2 00	3 1 7 4 00	

ACCOUNT Accounts Receivable
ACCOUNT NO. 12

DATE		ITEM	POST. REF.	DEBIT	CREDIT	BALANCE DEBIT	BALANCE CREDIT
19-- June	1	Balance	✓			6 7 2 5 00	
	5		27		4 1 5 0 00	2 5 7 5 00	
	30		28	4 1 4 5 00		6 7 2 0 00	

ILLUSTRATIVE PROBLEM ILLUSTRATIVE PROBLEM ILLUSTRATIVE PROBLEM ILLUSTRATIVE PROBLEM

ACCOUNT *Supplies*   **ACCOUNT NO.** *13*

DATE		ITEM	POST. REF.	DEBIT	CREDIT	BALANCE DEBIT	BALANCE CREDIT
19-- June	1	Balance	√			2 9 0 00	
	8		27	1 4 5 00		4 3 5 00	
	16		27		6 3 00	3 7 2 00	

ACCOUNT *Prepaid Insurance*   **ACCOUNT NO.** *14*

DATE		ITEM	POST. REF.	DEBIT	CREDIT	BALANCE DEBIT	BALANCE CREDIT
19-- June	1	Balance	√			3 6 5 00	
	17		27	3 7 0 00		7 3 5 00	

ACCOUNT *Equipment*   **ACCOUNT NO.** *18*

DATE		ITEM	POST. REF.	DEBIT	CREDIT	BALANCE DEBIT	BALANCE CREDIT
19-- June	1	Balance	√			19 7 4 5 00	
	2		27	2 1 0 0 00		21 8 4 5 00	
	9		27		1 2 5 00	21 7 2 0 00	

ACCOUNT *Accounts Payable*   **ACCOUNT NO.** *22*

DATE		ITEM	POST. REF.	DEBIT	CREDIT	BALANCE DEBIT	BALANCE CREDIT
19-- June	1	Balance	√				7 6 5 00
	2		27		2 1 0 0 00		2 8 6 5 00
	8		27		1 4 5 00		3 0 1 0 00
	9		27	1 2 5 00			2 8 8 5 00
	12		27	1 2 5 0 00			1 6 3 5 00
	20		27	5 0 00			1 5 8 5 00

ACCOUNT *Capital Stock*   **ACCOUNT NO.** *31*

DATE		ITEM	POST. REF.	DEBIT	CREDIT	BALANCE DEBIT	BALANCE CREDIT
19-- June	1	Balance	√				10 0 0 0 00

ACCOUNT *Retained Earnings*   **ACCOUNT NO.** *32*

DATE		ITEM	POST. REF.	DEBIT	CREDIT	BALANCE DEBIT	BALANCE CREDIT
19-- June	1	Balance	√				19 4 8 3 00

ACCOUNT *Dividends*   **ACCOUNT NO.** *33*

DATE		ITEM	POST. REF.	DEBIT	CREDIT	BALANCE DEBIT	BALANCE CREDIT
19-- June	27		27	1 2 5 0 00		1 2 5 0 00	

ACCOUNT   *Professional Fees*   ACCOUNT NO. *41*

DATE	ITEM	POST. REF.	DEBIT	CREDIT	BALANCE DEBIT	BALANCE CREDIT
19-- June 30		27		1 7 2 0 00		1 7 2 0 00
30		28		4 1 4 5 00		5 8 6 5 00

ACCOUNT   *Salary Expense*   ACCOUNT NO. *51*

DATE	ITEM	POST. REF.	DEBIT	CREDIT	BALANCE DEBIT	BALANCE CREDIT
19-- June 30		28	1 7 2 5 00		1 7 2 5 00	

ACCOUNT   *Rent Expense*   ACCOUNT NO. *53*

DATE	ITEM	POST. REF.	DEBIT	CREDIT	BALANCE DEBIT	BALANCE CREDIT
19-- June 1		27	6 0 0 00		6 0 0 00	

ACCOUNT   *Laboratory Expense*   ACCOUNT NO. *55*

DATE	ITEM	POST. REF.	DEBIT	CREDIT	BALANCE DEBIT	BALANCE CREDIT
19-- June 23		27	2 4 5 00		2 4 5 00	

ACCOUNT   *Utilities Expense*   ACCOUNT NO. *56*

DATE	ITEM	POST. REF.	DEBIT	CREDIT	BALANCE DEBIT	BALANCE CREDIT
19-- June 30		28	1 5 7 00		1 5 7 00	
30		28	2 9 00		1 8 6 00	
30		28	7 4 00		2 6 0 00	

ACCOUNT   *Miscellaneous Expense*   ACCOUNT NO. *59*

DATE	ITEM	POST. REF.	DEBIT	CREDIT	BALANCE DEBIT	BALANCE CREDIT
19-- June 30		28	1 3 2 00		1 3 2 00	

ILLUSTRATIVE PROBLEM ILLUSTRATIVE

4.

Child Care Inc.				
Trial Balance				
June 30, 19--				
Cash	3 1 7 4 00			
Accounts Receivable	6 7 2 0 00			
Supplies	3 7 2 00			
Prepaid Insurance	7 3 5 00			
Equipment	21 7 2 0 00			
Accounts Payable			1 5 8 5 00	
Capital Stock			10 0 0 0 00	
Retained Earnings			19 4 8 3 00	
Dividends	1 2 5 0 00			
Professional Fees			5 8 6 5 00	
Salary Expense	1 7 2 5 00			
Rent Expense	6 0 0 00			
Laboratory Expense	2 4 5 00			
Utilities Expense	2 6 0 00			
Miscellaneous Expense	1 3 2 00			
	36 9 3 3 00		36 9 3 3 00	

DISCUSSION QUESTIONS

1. What is an account?
2. Differentiate between an account and a ledger.
3. What is the name of the listing of accounts in the ledger?
4. Describe in general terms the sequence of accounts in the ledger.
5. Do the terms *debit* and *credit* signify increase or decrease, or may they signify either? Explain.
6. What is the name of the record in which a transaction is initially entered?
7. Define posting.
8. Indicate whether each of the following is recorded by a debit or by a credit: (a) increase in an asset account, (b) decrease in a liability account, (c) increase in a revenue account.
9. Explain why the rules of debit and credit are the same for liability accounts and owner's equity accounts.
10. What is the effect (increase or decrease) of debits to expense accounts (a) in terms of owner's equity and (b) in terms of expense?
11. What is the effect (increase or decrease) of credits to revenue accounts (a) in terms of owner's equity and (b) in terms of revenue?
12. Identify each of the following accounts as asset, liability, owner's equity, revenue, or expense, and state in each case whether the normal balance is a debit or a credit.
    a. Accounts Payable   f. Accounts Receivable
    b. Equipment   g. Fees Earned
    c. Salary Expense   h. Capital Stock
    d. Dividends   i. Supplies
    e. Cash   j. Rent Expense
13. On June 1 the accounts payable account had a normal balance of $11,725. During June the account was debited for a total of $13,500 and credited for a total of $14,000. (a) What was the balance of the account on June 30? (b) Was the balance in (a) a debit or a credit?
14. Liebrandt Corporation adheres to a policy of depositing all cash receipts in a bank account and making all payments by check. The cash account as of June 30 has a credit balance of $575 and there is no undeposited cash on hand. (a) Assuming that there were no errors in journalizing or posting, what is the explanation of this unusual balance? (b) Is the $575 credit balance in the cash account an asset, a liability, owner's equity, a revenue, or an expense?

15. During the month, a business enterprise has a substantial number of transactions affecting each of the following accounts. State for each account whether it is likely to have (a) debit entries only, (b) credit entries only, or (c) both debit and credit entries.

    1. Fees Earned
    2. Cash
    3. Miscellaneous Expense
    4. Accounts Payable
    5. Dividends
    6. Accounts Receivable
    7. Supplies Expense

16. Rearrange the following in proper sequence: (a) entry posted to ledger, (b) business transaction occurs, (c) entry recorded in journal, (d) business document prepared, (e) business transaction authorized.

17. Describe the three procedures required to post the credit portion of the following journal entry (Fees Earned is account no. 41):

	JOURNAL				Page 32	
DATE	DESCRIPTION	POST. REF.	DEBIT	CREDIT	
19-- June 11	Accounts Receivable	12	8 7 5 00		1
	Fees Earned			8 7 5 00	2

18. In examining an entry that has been recorded in the journal, what indicates that the entry has been posted to the accounts?

19. Justice Inc. performed services in June for a specific customer and the fee was $6,200. Payment was received in the following July. (a) Was the revenue earned in June or July? (b) What accounts should be debited and credited in (1) June and (2) July?

20. a. Describe the form known as a trial balance.
    b. What proof is provided by a trial balance?

21. If the two totals of a trial balance are equal, does it mean that there are no errors in the accounting records? Explain.

22. When a trial balance is prepared, an account balance of $36,750 is listed as $3,675 and an account balance of $4,500 is listed as $5,400. Identify the transposition and the slide.

23. When a purchase of supplies of $690 for cash was recorded, both the debit and the credit were journalized and posted as $960. (a) Would this error cause the trial balance to be out of balance? (b) Would the answer be the same if the $690 entry had been journalized correctly, but the debit to Cash had been posted as $960?

24. Indicate which of the following errors, each considered individually, would cause the trial balance totals to be unequal:
    a. A payment of $950 to a creditor was posted as a debit of $950 to Accounts Payable and a debit of $950 to Cash.
    b. Payment of cash dividends of $2,000 was journalized and posted as a debit of $200 to Salary Expense and a credit of $200 to Cash.
    c. A payment of $5,000 for equipment purchased was posted as a debit of $5,000 to Equipment and a credit of $50,000 to Cash.
    d. A receipt of $500 from an account receivable was journalized and posted as a debit of $500 to Cash and a credit of $500 to Sales.
    e. A fee of $2,500 earned and due from a client was not debited to Accounts Receivable or credited to a revenue account, because the cash had not been received.

25. How is a correction made when an error in an account title or amount in the journal is discovered before the entry is posted?

26. In journalizing and posting the entry to record the purchase of supplies on account, the accounts receivable account was credited in error. What is the preferred procedure to correct the error?

27. The acquisition of a $2,500 piece of equipment was recorded as an expense. Would this error be material (a) if total assets were $50,000 and annual net income was $5,000? (b) if total assets were $5,000,000 and annual net income was $500,000?

28. A business reported $75,094,500 and $8,271,100 of net revenues and net income respectively for the past year. Early in the current year, suspicions that the business had recorded revenues too early led to an investigation. The investigation disclosed that $418,000 of revenues applicable to the current year had been recorded in the past year. Determine (a) the corrected net income for the past year and (b) the percent error in the reported net income for the past year. (Adapted from 1987 annual report of Matrix Science Corporation.)

ETHICS DISCUSSION CASE

At the end of the current month, Ted Beam prepared a trial balance for Ace Services Corporation. The credit side of the trial balance exceeds the debit side by a significant amount. Ted has decided to add the difference to the balance of the miscellaneous expense account in order to complete the preparation of the current month's financial statements by a 5 o'clock deadline. Ted will look for the difference next week when there is more time. Discuss whether Ted Beam is behaving in an ethical manner.

SHARPEN YOUR COMMUNICATION SKILLS

WHAT DO YOU THINK

?

The college or university that you attend probably requires you to pay tuition before you are allowed to enroll and attend classes. What journal entry do you think would be used by the college or university to record the receipt of your tuition payments? Identify the nature of each account in your entry.

FINANCIAL ANALYSIS AND INTERPRETATION

A single item appearing in a financial statement is often useful in interpreting the financial results of an enterprise. However, comparing this item in a current statement with the same item in the prior statement often enhances the usefulness of the financial information. Such comparisons often take two forms: (1) the amount of the increase or decrease and (2) the percent of the increase or decrease for the current item when compared to the same item in the prior period. For example, the amount of the prior period's revenue and the amount of the change and the percent of change determined is indicated in the illustration below:

	1993	1992	Increase Amount	(Decrease) Percent
Revenues	$120,000	$100,000	$20,000	20%

a. For Hershey Foods Corporation, comparing 1992 with 1991, determine the amount of change and the percent of change for
  1. net sales (revenues) and
  2. selling, marketing, and administrative expenses.

SHARPEN YOUR COMMUNICATION SKILLS

b. What conclusions can be drawn from these analyses of the net sales and the selling, marketing, and administrative expenses?

EXERCISES

EXERCISE 2-1
CHART OF ACCOUNTS
Objective 2

RB Corp. is a newly organized enterprise. The list of accounts to be opened in the general ledger is as follows:

Accounts Payable	Miscellaneous Expense
Accounts Receivable	Prepaid Insurance
Capital Stock	Rent Expense
Cash	Retained Earnings
Dividends	Supplies Expense
Equipment	Unearned Rent
Fees Earned	Wages Expense

List the accounts in the order in which they should appear in the ledger of RB Corp. and assign account numbers. Each account number is to have two digits: the first digit is to indicate the major classification ("1" for assets, etc.), and the second digit is to identify the specific account within each major classification ("11" for Cash, etc.).

EXERCISE 2-2
IDENTIFY TRANSACTIONS
Objectives 3, 4

The nine transactions recorded by Gross Corp. during June, its first month of operations, are indicated in the following T accounts:

Cash		Accounts Receivable		Supplies	
(1) 15,000	(2) 1,500	(5) 12,500	(7) 8,500	(2) 1,500	(9) 450
(7) 8,500	(3) 3,950				
	(4) 3,725				
	(6) 5,000				
	(8) 2,500				

Equipment		Accounts Payable		Capital Stock	
(3) 13,950		(6) 5,000	(3) 10,000		(1) 15,000

Dividends		Service Revenue		Operating Expenses	
(8) 2,500			(5) 12,500	(4) 3,725	
				(9) 450	

Indicate for each debit and each credit: (a) whether an asset, liability, owner's equity, dividends, revenue, or expense account was affected and (b) whether the account was increased (+) or decreased (-). Answers should be presented in the following form (transaction (1) is given as an example):

	Account Debited		Account Credited	
Transaction	Type	Effect	Type	Effect
(1)	asset	+	owner's equity	+

EXERCISE 2-3
TRIAL BALANCE
Objective 6

Based upon the data presented in Exercise 2-2, prepare a trial balance, listing the accounts in their proper order.

EXERCISE 2-4
RETAINED EARNINGS
ACCOUNT BALANCE
Objective 3

SHARPEN YOUR ▶
COMMUNICATION SKILLS

As of January 1, Retained Earnings had a credit balance of $20,000. During the year, dividends totaled $18,000 and the business incurred a net loss of $6,000.

a. Calculate the balance of Retained Earnings as of the end of the year.
b. Assuming that there have been no recording errors, will the balance sheet prepared at December 31 balance? Explain.

EXERCISE 2-5
CASH ACCOUNT BALANCE
Objective 3

SHARPEN YOUR ▶
COMMUNICATION SKILLS

During the month, a business received $897,500 in cash and paid out $890,000 in cash.

a. Do the data indicate that the business earned $7,500 during the month? Explain.
b. If the balance of the cash account was $32,500 at the beginning of the month, what was the cash balance at the end of the month?

EXERCISE 2-6
ACCOUNT BALANCES
Objective 3

a. On July 1 the cash account balance was $12,750. During July, cash receipts totaled $26,000 and the July 31 balance was $14,000. Determine the cash payments made during July.
b. On July 1 the accounts receivable account balance was $19,900. During July, $21,000 was received from customers on account. If the July 31 balance was $22,500, determine the fees billed to customers on account during July.
c. During July, $30,500 was paid to creditors on account and purchases on account were $27,700. If the July 31 balance of Accounts Payable was $25,000, determine the account balance on July 1.

EXERCISE 2-7
TRANSACTIONS
Objectives 4, 5

Rago Corporation has the following accounts in its ledger: Cash; Accounts Receivable; Supplies; Office Equipment; Accounts Payable; Capital Stock; Retained Earnings; Dividends; Fees Earned; Rent Expense; Advertising Expense; Utilities Expense; Miscellaneous Expense.

Journalize the following selected transactions, completed during May of the current year, in a two-column journal:

May   1. Paid rent for the month, $1,500.
        3. Paid cash for supplies, $270.
        5. Paid advertising expense, $350.
        5. Purchased office equipment on account, $4,200.
        8. Received cash from customers on account, $5,600.
      12. Paid creditor on account, $2,150.
      15. Paid cash dividend, $1,800.
      25. Paid cash for repairs to office equipment, $90.
      27. Paid telephone bill for the month, $195.
      29. Fees earned and billed to customers for the month, $9,150.
      31. Paid electricity bill for the month, $430.

EXERCISE 2-8
TRANSACTIONS AND
T ACCOUNTS
Objectives 3, 4, 5

SPREADSHEET
PROBLEM

The following selected transactions were completed during November of the current year:

1. Purchased supplies on account, $720.
2. Billed customers for fees earned, $2,210.
3. Received cash from customers on account, $1,100.
4. Paid creditors on account, $500.

a. Journalize the foregoing transactions in a two-column journal, using the appropriate number to identify the transactions.
b. Post the entries prepared in (a) to the following T accounts: Cash, Supplies, Accounts Receivable, Accounts Payable, Fees Earned. To the left of each amount posted in the accounts, place the appropriate number to identify the transactions.

EXERCISE 2-9
TRIAL BALANCE
Objective 6

The accounts in the ledger of Pogue Corporation as of August 31 of the current year are listed in alphabetical order as follows. All accounts have normal balances. The balance of the cash account has been intentionally omitted.

Accounts Payable	$ 19,710	Miscellaneous Expense	$ 9,900
Accounts Receivable	20,500	Notes Payable	25,000
Cash	?	Prepaid Insurance	3,150
Capital Stock	20,000	Rent Expense	48,000
Retained Earnings	100,290	Wages Expense	190,000
Dividends	28,000	Supplies	4,100
Fees Earned	325,000	Supplies Expense	5,900
Insurance Expense	5,000	Unearned Rent	10,000
Land	125,000	Utilities Expense	41,500

Prepare a trial balance, listing the accounts in their proper order and inserting the missing figure for cash.

EXERCISE 2-10
ERRORS IN TRIAL BALANCE
Objective 6

The following preliminary trial balance of Brett Carpet Services Inc. does not balance:

Brett Carpet Services Inc.
Trial Balance
December 31, 19--

Cash	53,000	
Accounts Receivable	16,200	
Prepaid Insurance		3,300
Equipment	4,500	
Accounts Payable		10,050
Unearned Rent		480
Capital Stock	25,000	
Retained Earnings	36,250	
Dividends		14,000
Service Revenue		64,940
Wages Expense		33,400
Advertising Expense	5,200	
Miscellaneous Expense		1,380
	140,150	127,550

When the ledger and other records are reviewed, you discover the following: (1) the debits and credits in the cash account total $53,000 and $37,300, respectively; (2) a billing of $800 to a customer on account was not posted to the accounts receivable account; (3) a payment of $2,100 made to a creditor on account was not posted to the accounts payable account; (4) the balance of the unearned rent account is $840; (5) the correct balance of the equipment account is $45,000; and (6) each account has a normal balance. Prepare a corrected trial balance.

EXERCISE 2-11
EFFECT OF ERRORS ON
TRIAL BALANCE
Objective 6

The following errors occurred in posting from a two-column journal:

1. A credit of $150 to Cash was posted as $510.
2. A debit of $1,000 to Cash was posted to Wages Expense.
3. A debit of $750 to Supplies was posted twice.
4. A credit of $500 to Accounts Payable was posted as a debit.
5. An entry debiting Accounts Receivable and crediting Fees Earned for $4,000 was not posted.
6. A debit of $750 to Wages Expense was posted as $570.
7. A credit of $1,730 to Accounts Receivable was not posted.

Considering each case individually (i.e., assuming that no other errors had occurred), indicate: (a) by "yes" or "no" whether the trial balance would be out of balance; (b) if answer to (a) is "yes," the amount by which the trial balance totals would differ; and (c) whether the debit or credit column of the trial balance would have the larger total. Answers should be presented in the following form (error (1) is given as an example):

Error	(a) Out of Balance	(b) Difference	(c) Larger Total
(1)	yes	$360	credit

EXERCISE 2-12
ENTRIES TO CORRECT
ERRORS
Objective 7

A number of errors in journalizing and posting transactions are described as follows:

a. A $500 purchase of supplies on account was recorded as a debit to Cash and a credit to Accounts Payable.
b. A dividend of $2,500 was recorded as a debit to Miscellaneous Expense and a credit to Cash.
c. Rent of $800 paid for the current month was recorded as a debit to Supplies Expense and a credit to Cash.

Journalize the entries to correct the errors.

**WhAT'S WRONG
WITH THiS?**
■
■
▲
■

How many errors can you find in the following trial balance? All accounts have normal balances.

Mason Corporation
Trial Balance
For Month Ended October 31, 19--

Cash	4,010	
Accounts Receivable		14,400
Prepaid Insurance	2,400	
Equipment	41,200	
Accounts Payable	5,850	
Salaries Payable		750
Capital Stock		15,000
Retained Earnings		34,600
Dividends		9,000
Service Revenue	37,900	
Salary Expense	18,400	
Advertising Expense	4,200	
Miscellaneous Expense	490	
	94,100	94,100

PROBLEMS

Series A

PROBLEM 2-1A
ENTRIES INTO T ACCOUNTS
AND TRIAL BALANCE
Objectives 3, 4, 6

Lisa Kent, architect, organized a professional services corporation known as Lisa Kent, Architect, P.C., on February 1 of the current year. During February she opened the office and completed the following transactions connected with her practice:

a. Received cash from issuance of capital stock, $10,000. The cash was deposited in a bank account under the corporation's name.
b. Paid February rent for office and workroom, $1,500.
c. Purchased used automobile for $9,500, paying $2,500 cash and giving a non-interest-bearing note for the remainder.
d. Purchased office and drafting room equipment on account, $6,000. *A.P—e, Eq D*
e. Paid cash for supplies, $900. *Cash-CR ; S-DR*
f. Paid cash for insurance policies, $850.
g. Received cash from client for plans delivered, $2,100. *Cash-DR*
h. Paid cash for miscellaneous services, $75.
i. Paid cash to creditors on account, $3,000. *Ac.P -D   Cash-CR*
j. Paid installment due on note payable, $400.
k. Received invoice for blueprint service, due in March, $110. *get bill*
l. Recorded fee earned on plans delivered, payment to be made in March, $3,150. *Fee*
m. Paid salary of assistant, $1,250.
n. Paid gas, oil, and repairs on automobile for February, $115.

Instructions

1. Record the foregoing transactions directly in the following T accounts, without journalizing: Cash; Accounts Receivable; Supplies; Prepaid Insurance; Automobiles; Equipment; Notes Payable; Accounts Payable; Capital Stock; Professional Fees; Rent Expense; Salary Expense; Automobile Expense; Blueprint Expense; Miscellaneous Expense. To the left of the amount entered in the accounts, place the appropriate letter to identify the transaction.
2. Determine the balances of the T accounts having two or more debits or credits. A memorandum balance should also be inserted in accounts having both debits and credits, in the manner illustrated in the chapter. For accounts with entries on one side only (such as Professional Fees), there is no need to insert the memorandum balance in the item column. For accounts containing only a single debit and a single credit (such as Notes Payable), the memorandum balance should be inserted in the appropriate item column. Accounts containing a single entry only (such as Prepaid Insurance) do not need a memorandum balance.
3. Prepare a trial balance for Lisa Kent, Architect, P.C., as of February 28 of the current year.

PROBLEM 2-2A
JOURNAL ENTRIES AND
TRIAL BALANCE
Objectives 3, 4, 6

On July 1 of the current year, Janet Lopez established Lopez Realty Inc., which completed the following transactions during July:

a. Issued capital stock for cash, $5,000.
b. Paid rent on office and equipment for the month, $3,000.
c. Purchased supplies (stationery, stamps, pencils, ink, etc.) on account, $4,500.
d. Paid creditor on account, $2,900.
e. Earned sales commissions, receiving cash, $29,750.
f. Paid automobile expenses (including rental charge) for month, $2,900, and miscellaneous expenses, $1,950.
g. Paid office salaries, $8,000.
h. Determined that the cost of supplies used was $1,325.
i. Paid cash dividends, $1,000.

Instructions

1. Journalize entries for transactions (a) through (i), using the following account titles: Cash; Supplies; Accounts Payable; Capital Stock; Dividends; Sales Commissions; Office Salaries Expense; Rent Expense; Automobile Expense; Supplies Expense; Miscellaneous Expense.
2. Prepare T accounts, using the account titles in (1). Post the journal entries to these accounts, placing the appropriate letter to the left of each amount to identify the trans-

actions. Determine the account balances, after all posting is complete, for all accounts having two or more debits or credits. A memorandum balance should also be inserted in accounts having both debits and credits, in the manner illustrated in the chapter. For accounts with entries on one side only, there is no need to insert a memorandum balance in the item column. For accounts containing only a single debit and a single credit, the memorandum balance should be inserted in the appropriate item column.

3. Prepare a trial balance as of July 31, 19--.
4. Determine the following:
   a. Amount of total revenue recorded in the ledger.
   b. Amount of total expenses recorded in the ledger.
   c. Amount of net income for July.

S O L U T I O N S
S O F T W A R E

Instructions for Solving Problem 2-2A Using Solutions Software

1. Load opening balances.
2. Enter your name in the Student Name field in the General Information data entry window. Set the run date to July 31 of the current year.
3. Use the Save As command to save the opening balances file to your drive and directory. Name the file XXX2-2A (where XXX is your initials).
4. Select the General Journal Entries option and key the journal entries. Use July 31 as the date of each transaction. Leave the reference field blank. (Note: To review the chart of accounts, select F-1.)
5. Display a journal entries report.
6. Display a detailed general ledger.
7. Display a trial balance.
8. Display an income statement.
9. Display a retained earnings statement.
10. Display a balance sheet.
11. Save your data file to disk.
12. End the session.

PROBLEM 2-3A
JOURNAL ENTRIES AND
TRIAL BALANCE
Objectives 4, 5, 6

On June 5 of the current year, Tom Morgan established a corporation to be known as Morgan Decorators Inc. During the remainder of the month, Morgan Decorators Inc. completed the following business transactions:

June 5. Issued capital stock for cash, $15,000.
       5. Paid rent for period of June 5 to end of month, $950.
       7. Purchased office equipment on account, $6,250.
       8. Purchased a used truck for $15,000, paying $7,500 cash and giving a note payable for the remainder.
      10. Purchased supplies for cash, $525.
      12. Received cash for job completed, $600.
      15. Paid wages of employees, $800.
      20. Paid premiums on property and casualty insurance, $725.
      22. Recorded jobs completed on account and sent invoices to customers, $1,950.
      24. Received an invoice for truck expenses, to be paid in July, $310.
      26. Received cash for job completed, $650. This job had not been recorded previously.
      28. Purchased supplies on account, $190.
      29. Paid utilities expense, $390.
      29. Paid miscellaneous expenses, $95.
      30. Received cash from customers on account, $1,300.
      30. Paid wages of employees, $1,200.
      30. Paid creditor a portion of the amount owed for equipment purchased on June 7, $2,500.
      30. Paid cash dividends, $2,000.

Instructions

1. Journalize each transaction in a two-column journal, referring to the following chart of accounts in selecting the accounts to be debited and credited. (Do not insert the account numbers in the journal at this time.)

11 Cash

12 Accounts Receivable

13 Supplies

14 Prepaid Insurance

16 Equipment

18 Truck

21 Notes Payable

22 Accounts Payable

31 Capital Stock

33 Dividends

41 Fees Earned

51 Wages Expense

53 Rent Expense

54 Utilities Expense

55 Truck Expense

59 Miscellaneous Expense

2. Post the journal to a ledger of four-column accounts, inserting appropriate posting references as each item is posted. Extend the balances to the appropriate balance columns after each transaction is posted.

3. Prepare a trial balance for Morgan Decorators Inc. as of June 30.

SOLUTIONS SOFTWARE

Instructions for Solving Problem 2-3A Using Solutions Software

1. Load opening balances.

2. Enter your name in the Student Name field in the General Information data entry window. Set the run date to June 30 of the current year.

3. Use the Save As command to save the opening balances file to your drive and directory. Name the file XXX2-3A (where XXX is your initials).

4. Select the General Journal Entries option and key the journal entries. Leave the reference field blank. (Note: To review the chart of accounts, select F-1.)

5. Display a journal entries report.

6. Display a detailed general ledger.

7. Display a trial balance.

8. Display an income statement.

9. Display a retained earnings statement.

10. Display a balance sheet.

11. Save your data file to disk.

12. End the session.

PROBLEM 2-4A
JOURNAL ENTRIES AND
TRIAL BALANCE
Objectives 4, 5, 6

During June of the current year, Frank Saul, M.D., completed the following transactions in his practice organized as a professional services corporation:

June 1. Paid office rent for June, $2,000.

  2. Purchased equipment on account, $10,500.

  3. Purchased X-ray film and other supplies on account, $725.

  6. Received cash on account from patients, $10,025.

  6. Paid cash to creditors on account, $5,240.

  8. Sold X-ray film to another doctor at cost, receiving cash, $75. (Record the credit in the supplies account.)

  10. Paid cash for renewal of property insurance policy, $495.

  15. Paid cash for laboratory analyses, $395.

  20. Discovered that the balance of the cash account was understated and the accounts receivable account was overstated as of June 1 by $100. A cash receipt of that amount on account from a patient in May had not been recorded. Journalized the $100 receipt as of June 20.

  24. One of the items of equipment purchased on June 2 was defective. It was returned with the permission of the supplier, who agreed to reduce the account for the amount charged for the item, $550.

  26. Paid cash dividends, $2,750.

  30. Recorded fees charged to patients on account for services performed in June, $7,770.

  30. Recorded the cash received in payment of services (on a cash basis) to patients during June, $9,610.

  30. Paid salaries of receptionist and nurses, $4,050.

  30. Paid miscellaneous expenses, $420.

  30. Paid gas and electricity expense, $610.

  30. Paid water expense, $130.

  30. Paid telephone expense, $280.

The chart of accounts of Frank Saul, M.D., P.C. and the balances of accounts as of June 1 (all normal balances) are as follows:

11	Cash	$ 5,075
12	Accounts Receivable	15,110
13	Supplies	1,140
14	Prepaid Insurance	3,70
18	Equipment	52,200
22	Accounts Payable	9,850
31	Capital Stock	25,000
32	Retained Earnings	42,375
33	Dividends	-0-
41	Professional Fees	-0-
51	Salary Expense	-0-
53	Rent Expense	-0-
55	Utilities Expense	-0-
56	Laboratory Expense	-0-
59	Miscellaneous Expense	-0-

Instructions

1. Enter the June 1 account balances in the appropriate balance column of a four-column account. Place a check mark (✔) in the posting reference column. (It is advisable to verify the equality of the debit and credit balances in the ledger before proceeding with the next instruction.)
2. Journalize each transaction in a two-column journal.
3. Post the journal to the ledger, extending the account balance to the appropriate balance column after each posting.
4. Prepare a trial balance as of June 30.
5. Assuming that the expenses that have not been recorded (such as supplies expense and insurance expense) total $2,950 for the month, determine the following amounts:
   a. Net income for the month of June.
   b. Increase or decrease in stockholders' equity during June.
   c. Stockholders' equity as of June 30.

PROBLEM 2-5A
JOURNAL ENTRIES AND
TRIAL BALANCE
Objectives 4, 5, 6

Lakeside Realty Inc. acts as an agent in buying, selling, renting, and managing real estate. The account balances at the end of March of the current year are as follows:

11	Cash	36,150	
12	Accounts Receivable	28,750	
13	Prepaid Insurance	1,100	
14	Office Supplies	715	
16	Land	-0-	
21	Accounts Payable		6,175
22	Notes Payable		-0-
31	Capital Stock		10,000
32	Retained Earnings		30,840
33	Dividends	2,000	
41	Fees Earned		125,500
51	Salary and Commission Expense	92,100	
52	Rent Expense	4,500	
53	Advertising Expense	3,900	
54	Automobile Expense	2,750	
59	Miscellaneous Expense	550	
		172,515	172,515

The following business transactions were completed by Lakeside Realty Inc. during April of the current year:

April 1. Paid rent on office for month, $1,500.
        3. Purchased office supplies on account, $375.
        5. Paid insurance premiums, $1,650.
        7. Received cash from clients on account, $18,200.
       15. Paid salaries and commissions for the first half of the month, $16,650.
       15. Purchased land for a future building site for $55,000, paying $11,000 in cash and giving a note payable for the remainder.

15. Recorded revenue earned and billed to clients during first half of month, $19,100.
18. Paid creditors on account, $4,150.
20. Returned a portion of the office supplies purchased on April 3, receiving full credit for their cost, $75.
23. Received cash from clients on account, $16,700.
24. Paid advertising expense, $1,550.
27. Discovered an error in computing a commission; received cash from the salesperson for the overpayment, $350.
28. Paid automobile expense (including rental charges for an automobile), $715.
29. Paid miscellaneous expenses, $215.
30. Recorded revenue earned and billed to clients during second half of the month, $16,300.
30. Paid salaries and commissions for the second half of the month, $19,850.
30. Paid cash dividends, $2,000.

Instructions

1. Record the April 1 balance of each account in the appropriate balance column of a four-column account, write *Balance* in the item section, and place a check mark (✔) in the posting reference column.
2. Journalize the transactions for April in a two-column journal.
3. Post to the ledger, extending the account balance to the appropriate balance column after each posting.
4. Prepare a trial balance of the ledger as of April 30.

PROBLEM 2-6A
ERRORS IN TRIAL BALANCE
Objectives 6, 7

If the working papers correlating with the textbook are not used, omit Problem 2-6A.

The following records of Donahue TV Repair Inc. are presented in the working papers:

Journal containing entries for the period March 1–31.
Ledger to which the March entries have been posted.
Preliminary trial balance as of March 31, which does not balance.

Locate the errors, supply the information requested, and prepare a corrected trial balance, proceeding in accordance with the following detailed instructions. The balances recorded in the accounts as of March 1 and the entries in the journal are correctly stated. If it is necessary to correct any posted amounts in the ledger, a line should be drawn through the erroneous figure and the correct amount inserted above. Corrections or notations may be inserted on the preliminary trial balance in any manner desired. It is not necessary to complete all of the instructions if equal trial balance totals can be obtained earlier. However, the requirements of instructions (6) and (7) should be completed in any event.

Instructions

1. Verify the totals of the preliminary trial balance, inserting the correct amounts in the schedule provided in the working papers.
2. Compute the difference between the trial balance totals.
3. Compare the listings in the trial balance with the balances appearing in the ledger and list the errors found in the space provided in the working papers.
4. Verify the accuracy of the balance of each account in the ledger and list the errors found in the space provided in the working papers.
5. Trace the postings in the ledger back to the journal, using small check marks to identify items traced. Correct any amounts in the ledger that may be necessitated by errors in posting and list the errors in the space provided in the working papers.
6. Journalize as of March 31 the payment of $125 for advertising expense. The bill had been paid on March 31 but was inadvertently omitted from the journal. Post to the ledger. (Revise any amounts necessitated by posting this entry.)
7. Prepare a new trial balance.

PROBLEM 2-7A
CORRECTED TRIAL
BALANCE
Objectives 6, 7

Carpet Installation Corp. has the following trial balance as of August 31 of the current year:

Cash	4,400	
Accounts Receivable	6,400	
Supplies	1,010	
Prepaid Insurance	150	
Equipment	35,500	
Notes Payable		15,000
Accounts Payable		4,620
Capital Stock		6,000
Retained Earnings		29,300
Dividends	7,000	
Fees Earned		49,980
Wages Expense	28,500	
Rent Expense	6,400	
Advertising Expense	320	
Gas, Electricity, and Water Expense	3,150	
	92,830	104,900

The debit and credit totals are not equal as a result of the following errors:

a. The balance of cash was overstated by $500.
b. A cash receipt of $240 was posted as a debit to Cash of $420.
c. A debit of $1,000 for dividends was posted as a credit to Capital Stock.
d. The balance of $3,200 in Advertising Expense was entered as $320 in the trial balance.
e. A debit of $725 to Accounts Receivable was not posted.
f. A return of $125 of defective supplies was erroneously posted as a $215 credit to Supplies.
g. The balance of Notes Payable was overstated by $5,000.
h. An insurance policy acquired at a cost of $200 was posted as a credit to Prepaid Insurance.
i. Miscellaneous Expense, with a balance of $945, was omitted from the trial balance.
j. A debit of $710 in Accounts Payable was overlooked when determining the balance of the account.

SPREADSHEET
PROBLEM

SHARPEN YOUR ▶
COMMUNICATION SKILLS

Instructions

1. Prepare a corrected trial balance as of August 31 of the current year.
2. Does the fact that the trial balance in (1) is balanced mean that there are no errors in the accounts? Explain.

Series B

PROBLEM 2-1B
ENTRIES INTO T ACCOUNTS
AND TRIAL BALANCE
Objectives 3, 4, 6

Hector Cruz, architect, organized a professional services corporation known as Hector Cruz, Architect, P.C., on November 1 of the current year. During the month, he completed the following transactions connected with his professional practice:

a. Received cash from issuance of capital stock, $10,000. The cash was deposited in a bank account under the corporation's name.
b. Purchased used automobile for $14,300, paying $3,300 cash and giving a non-interest-bearing note for the remainder.
c. Paid November rent for office and workroom, $1,200.
d. Paid cash for supplies, $225.
e. Purchased office and drafting room equipment on account, $4,200.
f. Paid cash for insurance policies on automobile and equipment, $510.
g. Received cash from a client for plans delivered, $1,725.
h. Paid cash to creditors on account, $2,100.
i. Paid cash for miscellaneous expenses, $65.
j. Received invoice for blueprint service, due in following month, $75.
k. Recorded fee earned on plans delivered, payment to be made in December, $2,500.

l. Paid salary of assistant, $1,000.

m. Paid cash for miscellaneous expenses, $68.

n. Paid installment due on note payable, $300.

o. Paid gas, oil, and repairs on automobile for November, $70.

Instructions

1. Record the foregoing transactions directly in the following T accounts, without journalizing: Cash; Accounts Receivable; Supplies; Prepaid Insurance; Automobiles; Equipment; Notes Payable; Accounts Payable; Capital Stock; Professional Fees; Rent Expense; Salary Expense; Automobile Expense; Blueprint Expense; Miscellaneous Expense. To the left of each amount entered in the accounts, place the appropriate letter to identify the transaction.

2. Determine the balances of the T accounts having two or more debits or credits. A memorandum balance should also be inserted in accounts having both debits and credits, in the manner illustrated in the chapter. For accounts with entries on one side only (such as Professional Fees), there is no need to insert the memorandum balance in the item column. For accounts containing only a single debit and a single credit (such as Notes Payable), the memorandum balance should be inserted in the appropriate item column. Accounts containing a single entry only (such as Prepaid Insurance) do not need a memorandum balance.

3. Prepare a trial balance for Hector Cruz, Architect, P.C., as of November 30 of the current year.

PROBLEM 2-2B
JOURNAL ENTRIES AND
TRIAL BALANCE
Objectives 3, 4, 6

On July 1 of the current year, Rob Petrie established Midstate Realty Inc., which completed the following transactions during the month:

a. Issued capital stock for cash, $15,000.

b. Paid rent on office and equipment for the month, $12,000.

c. Purchased supplies (stationery, stamps, pencils, ink, etc.) on account, $5,900.

d. Paid creditor on account, $4,000.

e. Earned sales commissions, receiving cash, $41,500.

f. Paid cash dividends, $1,000.

g. Paid automobile expenses (including rental charge) for month, $3,900, and miscellaneous expenses, $1,950.

h. Paid office salaries, $10,000.

i. Determined that the cost of supplies used was $2,250.

Instructions

1. Journalize entries for transactions (a) through (i), using the following account titles: Cash; Supplies; Accounts Payable; Capital Stock; Dividends; Sales Commissions; Rent Expense; Office Salaries Expense; Automobile Expense; Supplies Expense; Miscellaneous Expense.

2. Prepare T accounts, using the account titles in (1). Post the journal entries to these accounts, placing the appropriate letter to the left of each amount to identify the transactions. Determine the account balances, after all posting is complete, for all accounts having two or more debits or credits. A memorandum balance should also be inserted in accounts having both debits and credits, in the manner illustrated in the chapter. For accounts with entries on one side only, there is no need to insert a memorandum balance in the item column. For accounts containing only a single debit and a single credit, the memorandum balance should be inserted in the appropriate item column.

3. Prepare a trial balance as of July 31, 19--.

4. Determine the following:

   a. Amount of total revenue recorded in the ledger.

   b. Amount of total expenses recorded in the ledger.

   c. Amount of net income for July.

Instructions for Solving Problem 2-2B Using Solutions Software
1. Load opening balances.
2. Enter your name in the Student Name field in the General Information data entry window. Set the run date to July 31 of the current year.
3. Use the Save As command to save the opening balances file to your drive and directory. Name the file XXX2-2B (where XXX is your initials).
4. Select the General Journal Entries option and key the journal entries. Use July 31 as the date of each transaction. Leave the reference field blank. (Note: To review the chart of accounts, select F-1.)
5. Display a journal entries report.
6. Display a detailed general ledger.
7. Display a trial balance.
8. Display an income statement.
9. Display a retained earnings statement.
10. Display a balance sheet.
11. Save your data file to disk.
12. End the session.

PROBLEM 2-3B
JOURNAL ENTRIES AND
TRIAL BALANCE
Objectives 4, 5, 6

On July 10 of the current year, Jane Morse established a corporation known as Morse Decorators Corp. During the remainder of the month, Morse Decorators Corp. completed the following business transactions:

July 10. Issued capital stock for cash, $10,000.
　　　10. Paid rent for period of July 10 to end of month, $600.
　　　11. Purchased a truck for $9,000, paying $3,000 cash and giving a note payable for the remainder.
　　　12. Purchased equipment on account, $1,700.
　　　14. Purchased supplies for cash, $885.
　　　14. Paid premiums on property and casualty insurance, $420.
　　　15. Received cash for job completed, $510.
　　　16. Purchased supplies on account, $240.
　　　17. Paid wages of employees, $600.
　　　21. Paid creditor for equipment purchased on July 12, $1,700.
　　　24. Recorded jobs completed on account and sent invoices to customers, $2,100.
　　　26. Received an invoice for truck expenses, to be paid in August, $225.
　　　26. Received cash for job completed, $1,050. This job had not been recorded previously.
　　　27. Paid utilities expense, $205.
　　　27. Paid miscellaneous expenses, $73.
　　　28. Received cash from customers on account, $1,420.
　　　31. Paid wages of employees, $1,350.
　　　31. Paid cash dividends, $1,500.

Instructions

1. Journalize each transaction in a two-column journal, referring to the following chart of accounts in selecting the accounts to be debited and credited. (Do not insert the account numbers in the journal at this time.)

11 Cash	41 Fees Earned
12 Accounts Receivable	51 Wages Expense
13 Supplies	53 Rent Expense
14 Prepaid Insurance	54 Utilities Expense
16 Equipment	55 Truck Expense
18 Truck	59 Miscellaneous Expense
21 Notes Payable	
22 Accounts Payable	
31 Capital Stock	
33 Dividends	

2. Post the journal to a ledger of four-column accounts, inserting appropriate posting references as each item is posted. Extend the balances to the appropriate balance columns after each transaction is posted.
3. Prepare a trial balance for Morse Decorators Corp. as of July 31.

**SOLUTIONS
SOFTWARE**

Instructions for Solving Problem 2-3B Using Solutions Software

1. Load opening balances.
2. Enter your name in the Student Name field in the General Information data entry window. Set the run date to July 31 of the current year.
3. Use the Save As command to save the opening balances file to your drive and directory. Name the file XXX2-3B (where XXX is your initials).
4. Select the General Journal Entries option and key the journal entries. Leave the reference field blank. (Note: To review the chart of accounts, select F-1.)
5. Display a journal entries report.
6. Display a detailed general ledger.
7. Display a trial balance.
8. Display an income statement.
9. Display a retained earnings statement.
10. Display a balance sheet.
11. Save your data file to disk.
12. End the session.

PROBLEM 2-4B
JOURNAL ENTRIES AND
TRIAL BALANCE
Objectives 4, 5, 6

During June of the current year, Chris Dunn, M.D., completed the following transactions in her practice organized as a professional services corporation:

May 1. Paid office rent for May, $2,100.
    2. Purchased equipment on account, $8,500.
    5. Purchased X-ray film and other supplies on account, $850.
    6. Received cash on account from patients, $8,925.
    7. Paid cash to creditors on account, $5,620.
    10. Sold X-ray film to another doctor at cost, receiving cash, $75. (Record the credit in the supplies account.)
    10. Paid cash for renewal of property insurance policy, $545.
    15. Paid cash for laboratory analyses, $345.
    20. Discovered that the balance of the cash account was understated and the accounts receivable account was overstated as of May 1 by $100. A cash receipt of that amount on account from a patient in April had not been recorded. Journalized the $100 receipt as of May 20.
    24. One of the items of equipment purchased on May 2 was defective. It was returned with the permission of the supplier, who agreed to reduce the account for the amount charged for the item, $250.
    26. Paid cash dividends, $2,200.
    28. Paid miscellaneous expenses, $420.
    30. Paid gas and electricity expense, $510.
    30. Paid water expense, $130.
    30. Paid telephone expense, $225.
    31. Recorded fees charged to patients on account for services performed in May, $8,200.
    31. Recorded the cash received in payment of services (on a cash basis) to patients during May, $9,910.
    31. Paid salaries of receptionist and nurses, $4,650.

The chart of accounts and the balances of accounts for Chris Dunn, M.D., P.C., as of May 1 (all normal balances) are as follows:

11	Cash	$ 5,925	41	Professional Fees	-0-
12	Accounts Receivable	15,160	51	Salary Expense	-0-
13	Supplies	1,240	53	Rent Expense	-0-
14	Prepaid Insurance	3,500	55	Utilities Expense	-0-
18	Equipment	55,600	56	Laboratory Expense	-0-
22	Accounts Payable	9,850	59	Miscellaneous Expense	-0-
31	Capital Stock	15,000			
32	Retained Earnings	56,575			
33	Dividends	-0-			

Instructions

1. Enter the May 1 account balances in the appropriate balance column of a four-column account. Place a check mark (✔) in the posting reference column. (It is advisable to verify the equality of the debit and credit balances in the ledger before proceeding with the next instruction.)

2. Journalize each transaction in a two-column journal.
3. Post the journal to the ledger, extending the balances to the appropriate balance column after each posting.
4. Prepare a trial balance as of May 31.
5. Assuming that the expenses that have not been recorded (such as supplies expense and insurance expense) total $1,850 for the month, determine the following amounts:
   a. Net income for the month of May.
   b. Increase or decrease in retained earnings during May.
   c. Stockholders' equity as of May 31.

PROBLEM 2-5B
JOURNAL ENTRIES AND
TRIAL BALANCE
Objectives 4, 5, 6

Combs Realty Inc. acts as an agent in buying, selling, renting, and managing real estate. The account balances at the end of April of the current year are as follows:

11 Cash	39,500	
12 Accounts Receivable	28,600	
13 Prepaid Insurance	750	
14 Office Supplies	625	
16 Land	-0-	
21 Accounts Payable		9,250
22 Notes Payable		-0-
31 Capital Stock		10,000
32 Retained Earnings		53,025
33 Dividends	20,000	
41 Fees Earned		157,750
51 Salary and Commission Expense	122,100	
52 Rent Expense	9,000	
53 Advertising Expense	4,900	
54 Automobile Expense	3,950	
59 Miscellaneous Expense	600	
	230,025	230,025

The following business transactions were completed by Combs Realty Inc. during May of the current year:

May 1. Paid rent on office for month, $2,500.
    2. Purchased office supplies on account, $425.
    3. Paid insurance premiums, $1,925.
    9. Received cash from clients on account, $21,000.
    15. Paid salaries and commissions for the first half of the month, $19,650.
    15. Purchased land for a future building site for $50,000, paying $10,000 in cash and giving a note payable for the remainder.
    15. Recorded revenue earned and billed to clients during first half of month, $20,900.
    18. Paid creditors on account, $5,650.
    20. Returned a portion of the office supplies purchased on May 2, receiving full credit for their cost, $50.
    29. Received cash from clients on account, $19,200.
    29. Paid advertising expense, $2,150.
    29. Discovered an error in computing a commission; received cash from the salesperson for the overpayment, $500.
    30. Paid automobile expense (including rental charges for an automobile), $850.
    30. Paid miscellaneous expenses, $215.
    31. Recorded revenue earned and billed to clients during the second half of the month, $19,300.
    31. Paid salaries and commissions for the second half of the month, $19,850.
    31. Paid cash dividends, $10,000.

Instructions
1. Record the May 1 balance of each account in the appropriate balance column of a four-column account, write *Balance* in the item section, and place a check mark (✔) in the posting reference column.
2. Journalize the transactions for May in a two-column journal.
3. Post to the ledger, extending the account balance to the appropriate balance column after each posting.
4. Prepare a trial balance of the ledger as of May 31.

If the working papers correlating with the textbook are not used, omit Problem 2-6B.

PROBLEM 2-6B
ERRORS IN TRIAL BALANCE
Objectives 6, 7

The following records of Donahue TV Repair Inc. are presented in the working papers:

Journal containing entries for the period March 1-31.
Ledger to which the March entries have been posted.
Preliminary trial balance as of March 31, which does not balance.

Locate the errors, supply the information requested, and prepare a corrected trial balance, proceeding in accordance with the following detailed instructions. The balances recorded in the accounts as of March 1 and the entries in the journal are correctly stated. If it is necessary to correct any posted amounts in the ledger, a line should be drawn through the erroneous figure and the correct amount inserted above. Corrections or notations may be inserted on the preliminary trial balance in any manner desired. It is not necessary to complete all of the instructions if equal trial balance totals can be obtained earlier. However, the requirements of instructions (6) and (7) should be completed in any event.

Instructions
1. Verify the totals of the preliminary trial balance, inserting the correct amounts in the schedule provided in the working papers.
2. Compute the difference between the trial balance totals.
3. Compare the listings in the trial balance with the balances appearing in the ledger and list the errors found in the space provided in the working papers.
4. Verify the accuracy of the balance of each account in the ledger and list the errors found in the space provided in the working papers.
5. Trace the postings in the ledger back to the journal, using small check marks to identify items traced. Correct any amounts in the ledger that may be necessitated by errors in posting, and list the errors in the space provided in the working papers.
6. Journalize as of March 31 the payment of $160 for gas and electricity. The bill had been paid on March 31 but was inadvertently omitted from the journal. Post to the ledger. (Revise any amounts necessitated by posting this entry.)
7. Prepare a new trial balance.

PROBLEM 2-7B
CORRECTED TRIAL
BALANCE
Objectives 6, 7

Wells Photography Inc. has the following trial balance as of October 31 of the current year:

Cash	4,735	
Accounts Receivable	9,925	
Supplies	1,277	
Prepaid Insurance	330	
Equipment	32,500	
Notes Payable		5,000
Accounts Payable		3,025
Capital Stock		5,000
Retained Earnings		27,490
Dividends	6,750	
Fees Earned		80,750
Wages Expense	48,150	
Rent Expense	750	
Advertising Expense	5,250	
Gas, Electricity, and Water Expense	3,150	
	112,817	121,265

The debit and credit totals are not equal as a result of the following errors:

a. The balance of cash was understated by $1,000.
b. A cash receipt of $540 was posted as a debit to Cash of $450.
c. A debit of $175 to Accounts Receivable was not posted.
d. A return of $252 of defective supplies was erroneously posted as a $225 credit to Supplies.
e. An insurance policy acquired at a cost of $310 was posted as a credit to Prepaid Insurance.

f. The balance of Notes Payable was understated by $2,500.
g. A credit of $75 in Accounts Payable was overlooked when the balance of the account was determined.
h. A debit of $750 for a cash dividend was posted as a credit to Retained Earnings.
i. The balance of $7,500 in Rent Expense was entered as $750 in the trial balance.
j. Miscellaneous Expense, with a balance of $915, was omitted from the trial balance.

SPREADSHEET PROBLEM

SHARPEN YOUR COMMUNICATION SKILLS

Instructions

1. Prepare a corrected trial balance as of October 31 of the current year.
2. Does the fact that the trial balance in (1) is balanced mean that there are no errors in the accounts? Explain.

MINI-CASE PECK CADDY SERVICES

During June through August, Fran Peck is planning to manage and operate Peck Caddy Service at Flamingo Golf and Country Club. Fran will rent a small maintenance building from the country club for $100 per month and will offer caddy services, including cart rentals, to golfers. Fran has had no formal training in record keeping. During June, she kept notes of all receipts and expenses in a shoe box.

An examination of Fran's shoe box records for June revealed the following:

June 1. Withdrew $1,000 from personal bank account to be used to operate the caddy service.
1. Paid rent to Flamingo Golf and Country Club, $100.
2. Paid for golf supplies (practice balls, etc.), $190.
2. Paid miscellaneous expenses, $50.
3. Arranged for the rental of forty regular (pulling) golf carts and ten gasoline-driven carts for $1,000 per month. Paid $500 in advance, with the remaining $500 due June 20.
7. Purchased supplies, including gasoline, for the golf carts on account, $325. Flamingo Golf and Country Club has agreed to allow Fran to store the gasoline in one of its fuel tanks at no cost.
15. Cash receipts for June 1-15, $990.
15. For June 1-15, accepted IOUs from customers on account, $210.
15. Paid salary of part-time employees, $110.
17. Paid cash to creditors on account, $180.
20. Paid remaining rental on golf carts, $500.
22. Purchased supplies, including gasoline, on account, $280.
25. Received cash in payment of IOUs on account, $150.
28. Paid miscellaneous expenses, $60.
30. Cash receipts for June 16-30, $1,475.

30. For June 16-30, accepted IOUs from customers on account, $150.
30. Paid electricity (utilities) expense, $55.
30. Paid telephone (utilities) expense, $30.
30. Paid salary of part-time employees, $110.
30. Supplies on hand at the end of June, $170.

Fran has asked you several questions concerning her financial affairs to date, and she has asked you to assist with her record keeping and reporting of financial data.

Instructions:

1. To assist Fran with her record keeping, prepare a chart of accounts that would be appropriate for Peck Caddy Services.
Note: Small business enterprises such as Peck Caddy Services are often organized as sole proprietorships. The accounting for sole proprietorships is similar to that for a corporation, except that the owner's equity accounts differ. Specifically, instead of the account for Capital Stock, a capital account entitled Fran Peck, Capital is used to record investments in the business. In addition, instead of a dividends account, withdrawals from the business enterprise are debited to Fran Peck, Drawing. A sole proprietorship has no retained earnings account.

2. Prepare an income statement for June in order to help Fran assess the profitability of Peck Caddy Services. For this purpose, the use of T accounts may be helpful in analyzing the effects of each of the June transactions.

3. Based on Fran's records of receipts and payments, calculate the amount of cash on hand on June 30. For this purpose, a T account for cash may be useful.

4. A count of the cash on hand on June 30 totaled $420. Briefly discuss the possible causes of the difference between the amount of cash computed in (3) and the actual amount of cash on hand.

ANSWERS TO SELF-EXAMINATION QUESTIONS

1. **A** A debit may signify an increase in asset accounts (answer A) or a decrease in liability and capital stock accounts. A credit may signify a decrease in asset accounts (answer B) or an increase in liability and capital stock accounts (answers C and D).

2. **C** Liability, capital stock, and revenue (answer C) accounts have normal credit balances. Asset (answer A), dividend (answer B), and expense (answer D) accounts have normal debit balances.

3. **C** Accounts Receivable (answer A), Cash (answer B), and Miscellaneous Expense (answer D) would all normally have debit balances. Accounts Payable should normally have a credit balance. Hence, a debit balance in Accounts Payable (answer C) would indicate a likely error in the recording process.

4. **A** The receipt of cash from customers on account increases the asset Cash and decreases the asset Accounts Receivable, as indicated by answer A. Answer B has the debit and credit reversed, and answers C and D involve transactions with creditors (accounts payable) and not customers (accounts receivable).

5. **D** The trial balance (answer D) is a listing of the titles and balances of the accounts in the ledger on a given date, so that the equality of the debits and credits in the ledger can be verified. The income statement (answer A) is a summary of revenue and expenses for a period of time, the balance sheet (answer B) is a presentation of the assets, liabilities, and owner's equity on a given date, and the retained earnings statement (answer C) is a summary of the changes in retained earnings for a period of time.

You and Accounting

Assume that you rented an apartment last month and signed a nine-month lease. When you signed the lease agreement, you were required to pay the final month's rent of $500. This amount is not returnable to you.

You are now applying for a student loan at a local bank. The loan application requires a listing of all your assets. Should you list the $500 deposit as an asset?

The answer to this question is "yes." The deposit is an asset to you until you receive the use of the apartment in the ninth month.

A business enterprise faces similar accounting problems at the end of a period. A business must determine what assets, liabilities, and owner's equity should be reported on its balance sheet. It must also determine what revenues and expenses should be reported on its income statement. In this chapter, you will read about one of the accounting concepts that is the basis for preparing financial statements.

Chapter 3
The Matching Concept and the Adjusting Process

LEARNING OBJECTIVES
After studying this chapter, you should be able to:

Objective 1
Explain how the matching concept relates to the accrual basis of accounting.

Objective 2
Explain why adjustments are necessary and list the characteristics of adjusting entries.

Objective 3
Journalize entries for accounts requiring adjustment.

Objective 4
Enter adjustments on a work sheet and prepare an adjusted trial balance.

Transactions are recorded as they occur, as illustrated in Chapter 2. At the end of an accounting period, the ledger accounts must be analyzed and, if necessary, updated to ensure that revenues and expenses are properly matched. This matching concept ensures that the income statement fairly presents the results of operations for a period and the balance sheet fairly presents the financial condition at the end of the period.

In this chapter, you will study the matching concept and how accounts are updated at the end of the accounting period. Accounts that normally require updating are described, and the journal entries necessary to update the accounts are illustrated. The chapter concludes with a discussion of the use of the work sheet in the adjustment process.

THE MATCHING CONCEPT

Objective 1
Explain how the matching concept relates to the accrual basis of accounting.

Revenues and expenses may be reported on the income statement, using either (1) the **cash basis** of accounting or (2) the **accrual basis** of accounting. When the cash basis is used, revenues are reported in the period in which cash is received and expenses are reported in the period in which cash is paid. For example, fees are recorded when cash is received from clients and wages expense is recorded when cash is paid to employees. The net income (or net loss) is the difference between the cash receipts (revenues) and the cash payments (expenses).

Small service enterprises that have few receivables and payables often use the cash basis of accounting. For example, accountants, attorneys, physicians, and real estate agents often use the cash basis. Also, most individuals use the cash basis of accounting in their personal financial records. For most businesses, however, the cash basis will not provide accurate financial statements for user needs. For this reason, the accrual basis will be emphasized in the remainder of this text.

Using Accounting

Although you probably use the cash basis of accounting, you may at times be asked to provide financial information in addition to the amount of cash you have on hand or in the bank. For example, when you apply for a loan, the financial institution will usually ask you to list the fair market value of your assets and liabilities on the loan application. In addition, sources of income and major monthly expenditures, such as mortgage or other loan payments, must also be listed. In this way, the loan officer of the financial institution can assess your ability to repay the loan.

When the accrual basis of accounting is used, revenues are reported in the period in which they are earned. Expenses are reported in the period in which they are incurred in producing revenues. For example, revenue is recorded as services are provided to customers. Cash may be received from customers at this time or at a later date if the services are provided on account. Likewise, wages expense is recorded in the period when the employees work and not when the cash is paid.

Generally accepted accounting principles require the use of the accrual basis. The accrual basis ensures that the expenses incurred are properly **matched** with the revenues they generate. In this way, the income statement will properly report the revenues earned, the expenses incurred, and the resulting income or loss for the period. The accounting principle that requires the matching of revenues and expenses is called the **matching concept** or **matching principle**.

The matching concept requires an analysis and updating of some accounts at the end of an accounting period. This process of analyzing and updating accounts in the ledger is called the **adjusting process**. In the following paragraphs, we will further describe this process.

NATURE OF THE ADJUSTING PROCESS

Objective 2
Explain why adjustments are necessary and list the characteristics of adjusting entries.

At the end of an accounting period, many of the balances of accounts in the ledger can be reported, without change, in the financial statements. For example, the balance of the cash account is normally the amount reported on the balance sheet as the cash on hand at the end of the accounting period.

Some accounts in the ledger, however, require updating. For example, the balances listed for prepaid expenses are normally overstated because the use of these assets is not recorded on a day-to-day basis. The balance of the supplies account usually represents the cost of supplies at the beginning of the period plus the cost of supplies acquired during the period. The day-to-day use of supplies is not recorded, since to do so would require many entries with small amounts. In addition, the total amount of supplies is small relative to other assets, and managers usually do not require day-to-day information on the amount of supplies on hand.

Another example of a prepaid expense account that requires updating is Prepaid Insurance. The balance in Prepaid Insurance represents the beginning balance plus the cost of insurance policies acquired during the period. Journal entries are not made daily for the premiums as they expire. To make such entries would be costly and unnecessary.

The journal entries at the end of an accounting period to bring the accounts up to date and to properly match revenues and expenses are called **adjusting entries**. By their nature, *all adjusting entries affect at least one income statement account and one balance sheet account*. Thus, an adjusting entry will always involve a revenue or an expense account and an asset or a liability account.

Is there an easy way to know when an adjusting entry is needed? Yes, two basic classifications of items require adjusting entries. The first class of items, **deferrals**, is created by recording a transaction in a way that delays or defers the recognition of an expense or a revenue. Deferrals may be either deferred expenses or deferred revenues, as described below.

Deferred expenses are items that have been initially recorded as assets but are expected to become expenses over time or through the normal operations of the enterprise. The supplies and prepaid insurance discussed in the preceding paragraphs are examples of deferred expenses. The supplies become an expense as they are used, and the prepaid insurance becomes an expense as time passes and the insurance expires. Deferred expenses are often called **prepaid expenses**.

Deferred revenues are items that have been initially recorded as liabilities but are expected to become revenues over time or through the normal operations of the enterprise. Examples of deferred revenues include tuition received by a college at the beginning of the term and magazine subscriptions received in advance by a publisher. The tuition is earned throughout the term as students attend class. The subscriptions are earned as the magazines are published and distributed. Deferred revenues are often called **unearned revenues**.

The second class of items that give rise to adjusting entries is accruals. **Accruals** are created by the failure to record an expense that has been incurred or a revenue that has been earned. Accruals may be either accrued expenses or accrued revenues, as described below.

Accrued expenses are expenses that have been incurred *but have not been recorded* in the accounts. Examples of accrued expenses include unrecorded wages owed to employees at the end of a period and unrecorded interest owed on loans. Accrued expenses are often called **accrued liabilities**.

Accrued revenues are revenues that have been earned *but have not been recorded* in the accounts. Examples of accrued revenues include unrecorded fees earned by an attorney or unrecorded commissions earned by a real estate agent. Accrued revenues are often called **accrued assets.**

How do you tell the difference between deferrals and accruals? Deferrals normally arise when cash is received or paid in the current period, but the related revenue or expense is to be recorded in a later period. Accruals normally arise when a revenue or expense is recorded in the current period, but the related cash is received or paid in a later period. These differences are illustrated in Exhibit 1.

Exhibit 1
Deferrals and Accruals

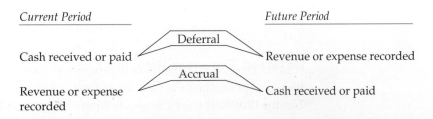

RECORDING ADJUSTING ENTRIES

Objective 3
Journalize entries for accounts requiring adjustment.

The examples of adjusting entries that follow are based on the ledger of Computer King Corporation, as reported in the December 31 trial balance in Exhibit 2.

Exhibit 2
Unadjusted Trial Balance for Computer King

Computer King Corporation Trial Balance December 31, 1994		
Cash	2 0 6 5 00	
Accounts Receivable	2 2 2 0 00	
Supplies	2 0 0 0 00	
Prepaid Insurance	2 4 0 0 00	
Land	10 0 0 0 00	
Office Equipment	1 8 0 0 00	
Accounts Payable		9 0 0 00
Unearned Rent		3 6 0 00
Capital Stock		15 0 0 0 00
Dividends	4 0 0 0 00	
Fees Earned		16 3 4 0 00
Wages Expense	4 2 7 5 00	
Rent Expense	1 6 0 0 00	
Utilities Expense	9 8 5 00	
Supplies Expense	8 0 0 00	
Miscellaneous Expense	4 5 5 00	
	32 6 0 0 00	32 6 0 0 00

An expanded chart of accounts for Computer King Corporation is shown in Exhibit 3. The additional accounts that will be used in this chapter are shown in color.

Exhibit 3
Expanded Chart of Accounts for Computer King Corporation

Balance Sheet Accounts	Income Statement Accounts
1. Assets	4. Revenue
11 Cash	41 Fees Earned
12 Accounts Receivable	42 Rent Income
14 Supplies	5. Expenses
15 Prepaid Insurance	51 Wages Expense
17 Land	52 Rent Expense
18 Office Equipment	53 Depreciation Expense
19 Accumulated Depreciation	54 Utilities Expense
2. Liabilities	55 Supplies Expense
21 Accounts Payable	56 Insurance Expense
22 Wages Payable	59 Miscellaneous Expense
23 Unearned Rent	
3. Owner's Equity	
31 Capital Stock	
32 Retained Earnings	
33 Dividends	

To simplify the examples, T accounts are used. The adjusting entries are shown in color in the accounts to separate them from other transactions.

Deferred Expenses (Prepaid Expenses)

The concept of adjusting the accounting records was introduced in Chapters 1 and 2 in the illustration for Computer King Corporation. In that illustration, supplies were purchased on November 10 (transaction c). The supplies used during November were recorded on November 30 (transaction g). In practice, this matching of revenues and expenses is part of the normal adjusting process that takes place only at the end of the accounting period, which is typically monthly and at least quarterly.

The balance in Computer King Corporation's supplies account on December 31 is $2,000. Some of these supplies (computer diskettes, paper, envelopes, etc.) were used during December and some are still on hand. If either amount is known, the other can be readily determined. It is normally easier to determine the cost of the supplies on hand at the end of the month than it is to keep a record of those used daily. Assuming that the inventory of supplies on December 31 is $760, the amount to be transferred from the asset account to the expense account is $1,240, computed as follows:

Supplies available (balance of account)	$2,000
Supplies on hand (inventory)	760
Supplies used (amount of adjustment)	$1,240

As discussed in Chapter 2, increases in expense accounts are recorded as debits and decreases in asset accounts are recorded as credits. Hence, at the end of December, the supplies expense account should be debited for $1,240 and the supplies account should be credited for $1,240 to record the supplies used during December. The adjusting journal entry and T accounts for Supplies and Supplies Expense are as follows:

Supplies Expense	1,240	
Supplies		1,240

Supplies				Supplies Expense	
Bal.	2,000	Dec. 31	1,240	Bal.	800
760				Dec. 31	1,240
					2,040

After the adjustment has been recorded and posted, the supplies account has a debit balance of $760. This balance represents an asset that will become an expense in a future period.

The debit balance of $2,400 in Computer King Corporation's prepaid insurance account represents a December 1 prepayment of insurance for 24 months. At the end of December, the insurance expense account should be increased (debited) and the prepaid insurance account should be decreased (credited) by $100, the insurance for one month. The adjusting journal entry and the T accounts for Prepaid Insurance and Insurance Expense are as follows:

Insurance Expense	100	
Prepaid Insurance		100

Prepaid Insurance				Insurance Expense	
Bal.	2,400	Dec. 31	100	Dec. 31	100
	2,300				

After the adjustment has been recorded and posted, the prepaid insurance account has a debit balance of $2,300. This balance represents an asset that will become an expense in future periods. The insurance expense account has a debit balance of $100, which is an expense of the current period.

What is the effect of omitting adjusting entries? If the preceding adjustments for supplies ($1,240) and insurance ($100) are not recorded, the financial statements prepared as of December 31 will be misstated. On the income statement, Supplies Expense and Insurance Expense will be understated by a total of $1,340 and net income will be overstated by $1,340. On the balance sheet, Supplies and Prepaid Insurance will be overstated by a total of $1,340. Since net income increases retained earnings, retained earnings will also be overstated by $1,340 on the balance sheet and the retained earnings statement. The effects of omitting these adjusting entries on the income statement and balance sheet are shown below.

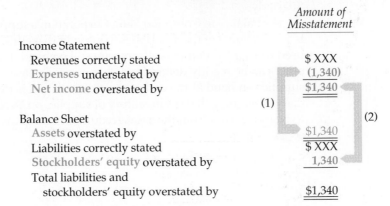

	Amount of Misstatement
Income Statement	
Revenues correctly stated	$ XXX
Expenses understated by	(1,340)
Net income overstated by	$1,340
Balance Sheet	
Assets overstated by	$1,340
Liabilities correctly stated	$ XXX
Stockholders' equity overstated by	1,340
Total liabilities and stockholders' equity overstated by	$1,340

Arrows (1) and (2) indicate how omitting adjusting entries affects both the income statement and the balance sheet. Arrow (1) indicates the effects on the expenses and assets. Arrow (2) indicates the effect of the overstated net income on stockholders' equity. On the balance sheet, the assets and the total liabilities and stockholders' equity are misstated by the same amount.

Supplies and prepaid insurance are two examples of prepaid expenses that may require adjustment at the end of an accounting period. Other examples of prepaid expenses that may require adjustment are prepaid advertising and prepaid interest.

Prepayments of expenses are sometimes made at the beginning of the period in which they will be *entirely consumed*. On December 1, for example, Computer King Corporation paid rent of $800 for the month of December. On December 1, the rent payment represents the asset prepaid rent. The prepaid rent expires daily, and at the end of December the entire amount has become an expense (rent expense). In cases such as this, the initial payment is recorded as an expense rather than as an asset. Thus, if the payment is recorded as a debit to Rent Expense, no adjusting entry is needed at the end of the period.[1]

Deferred Revenue (Unearned Revenue)

According to Computer King Corporation's trial balance on December 31, the balance in the unearned rent account is $360. This balance represents the receipt of three months' rent on December 1 for December, January, and February. At the end of December, the unearned rent account should be decreased by $120 (debited) and the rent income account should be increased by $120 (credited). The $120 represents the rental income for one month ($360 ÷ 3). The adjusting journal entry and T accounts are shown below.

Unearned Rent	120	
Rent Income		120

Unearned Rent				Rent Income	
Dec. 31	120	Bal.	360	Dec. 31	120
			240		

After the adjustment has been recorded and posted, the unearned rent account, which is a liability, has a credit balance of $240. This balance represents a deferral

---

[1] This alternative treatment of recording the cost of supplies, rent, and other prepayments of expenses is discussed in Appendix C.

that will become revenue in a future period. The rent income account has a balance of $120, which is revenue of the current period.

If the preceding adjustment of unearned rent and rent income is not recorded, the financial statements prepared on December 31 will be misstated. On the income statement, Rent Income and the net income will be understated by $120. On the balance sheet, Unearned Rent will be overstated by $120, and Retained Earnings will be understated by $120. The effects of omitting this adjusting entry are shown below.

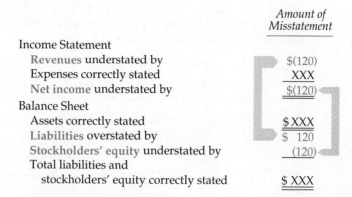

	Amount of Misstatement
Income Statement	
Revenues understated by	$(120)
Expenses correctly stated	XXX
Net income understated by	$(120)
Balance Sheet	
Assets correctly stated	$ XXX
Liabilities overstated by	$ 120
Stockholders' equity understated by	(120)
Total liabilities and stockholders' equity correctly stated	$ XXX

The only unearned revenue for Computer King Corporation was unearned rent. Other examples of unearned revenue that may require adjustment include tuition received in advance by a school, an annual retainer fee received by an attorney, premiums received in advance by an insurance company, and amounts received in advance by an advertising firm for advertising services to be rendered in the future.[2]

Accrued Expenses (Accrued Liabilities)

Some types of services, such as insurance, are normally paid for before they are used. These prepayments are deferrals. Other types of services are paid for *after* the service has been performed. For example, wages expense accumulates or *accrues* hour by hour and day by day, but payment may be made only weekly, biweekly, or monthly. The amount of such an accrued but unpaid item at the end of the accounting period is both an expense and a liability. For this reason, such accruals are called **accrued expenses** or **accrued liabilities**. In the case of wages expense, if the last day of a pay period is not the last day of the accounting period, the accrued expense and the related liability must be recorded in the accounts by an adjusting entry. This adjusting entry is necessary so that expenses are properly matched to the period in which they were incurred.

At the end of December, accrued wages for Computer King Corporation were $250. This amount is an additional expense of December and is debited to the wages expense account. It is also a liability as of December 31 and is credited to Wages Payable. The adjusting journal entry and T accounts are shown below.

Wages Expense	250	
Wages Payable		250

Wages Expense			Wages Payable	
Bal.	4,275		Dec. 31	250
Dec. 31	250			
	4,525			

---

[2] An alternative treatment of recording revenues received in advance of their being earned is discussed in Appendix C.

After the adjustment has been recorded and posted, the debit balance of the wages expense account is $4,525, which is the wages expense for the two months, November and December. The credit balance of $250 in Wages Payable is the amount of the liability for wages owed as of December 31.

The accrual of the wages expense for Computer King Corporation is summarized in Exhibit 4. You should note that Computer King paid wages of $950 on December 13 and $1,200 on December 27. These payments represent biweekly payroll payments made on alternate Fridays for the pay periods ending on those days. The wages of $250 earned for Monday and Tuesday, December 30 and 31, are accrued at December 31. The wages paid on January 10 totaled $1,275, which included the $250 accrued wages of December 31.

Exhibit 4
Accrued Wages

1. Wages are paid on the second and fourth Fridays for the two-week periods ending on those Fridays. The payments were $950 on December 13 and $1,200 on December 27.

2. The wages accrued for Monday and Tuesday, December 30 and 31, are $250.

3. Wages paid on Friday, January 10, total $1,275.

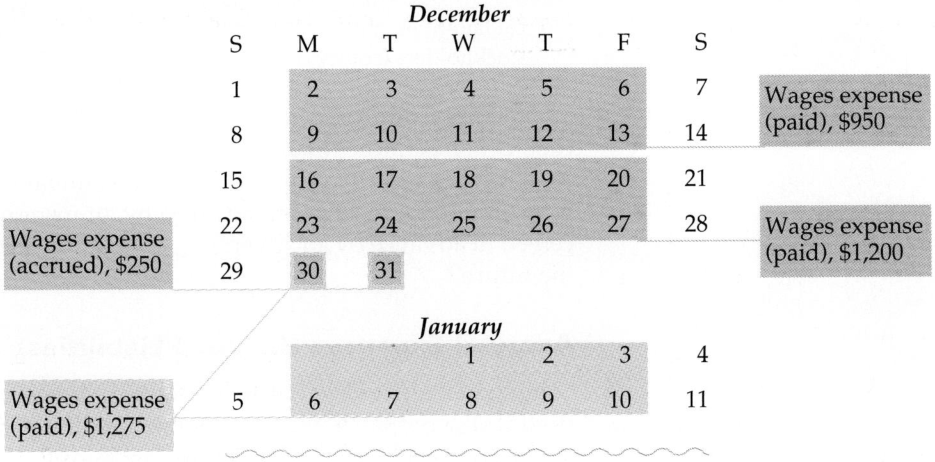

What would be the effect on the financial statements if the adjustment for wages ($250) is not recorded? The income statement for the period and the balance sheet as of December 31 will be misstated. On the income statement, Wages Expense will be understated by $250, and the net income will be overstated by $250. On the balance sheet, Wages Payable will be understated by $250, and Retained Earnings will be overstated by $250. These effects of omitting the adjusting entry are shown below.

	Amount of Misstatement
Income Statement	
Revenues correctly stated	$ XXX
Expenses understated by	(250)
Net income overstated by	$ 250
Balance Sheet	
Assets correctly stated	$ XXX
Liabilities understated by	$(250)
Stockholders' equity overstated by	250
Total liabilities and stockholders' equity correctly stated	$ XXX

Accrued wages is an example of an accrued expense that must be recorded by an adjusting entry. Other accrued expenses include accrued interest on notes payable and accrued taxes.

Accrued Revenues (Accrued Assets)

All assets belonging to a business at the end of an accounting period and all revenue earned during a period should be recorded in the ledger. During an accounting period, some revenues are recorded only when cash is received. Thus, at the end of an accounting period there may be items of revenue that have been earned *but have not been recorded.* In such cases, the amount of the revenue should be recorded by debiting an asset account and crediting a revenue account. Because of the dual nature of such accruals, they are called **accrued revenues** or **accrued assets.**

To illustrate, assume that Computer King Corporation signed an agreement with Dankner Co. on December 15. The agreement provides that Computer King Corporation will be on call to answer questions and render assistance to Dankner Co.'s employees concerning computer problems. The services provided will be billed to Dankner Co. on the fifteenth of each month at a rate of $20 per hour. As of December 31, Computer King Corporation had provided 25 hours of assistance to Dankner Co. Although the revenue of $500 (25 hours × $20) will be billed and collected in January, Computer King Corporation earned the revenue in December. The adjusting journal entry and T accounts to record the claim against the customer (an account receivable) and the revenue earned in December are shown below.

Accounts Receivable	500	
Fees Earned		500

Accounts Receivable		Fees Earned	
Bal.	2,220	Bal.	16,340
Dec. 31	500	Dec. 31	500
	2,720		16,840

If the adjustment for the accrued asset ($500) is not recorded, the income statement for the period and the balance sheet as of December 31 will be misstated. On the income statement, Fees Earned and the net income will be understated by $500. On the balance sheet, Accounts Receivable and Retained Earnings will be understated by $500. These effects of omitting the adjusting entry are shown below.

	Amount of Misstatement
Income Statement	
Revenues understated by	$(500)
Expenses correctly stated	XXX
Net income understated by	$(500)
Balance Sheet	
Assets understated by	$ (500)
Liabilities correctly stated	$XXX
Stockholders' equity understated by	(500)
Total liabilities and	
stockholders' equity understated by	$ (500)

Accrued fees is an example of an accrued revenue that must be recorded by an adjusting entry to properly match revenues and expenses. Other accruals that would require similar treatment include accrued interest on notes receivable and accrued rent on property rented to others.

Plant Assets

Tangible assets that are owned by a business enterprise, are permanent or have a long life, and are used in the business are called **plant assets** or **fixed assets**. In a sense, plant assets are a type of long-term deferred expense. However, because of their nature and long life, they are discussed separately from other deferred expenses, such as supplies and prepaid insurance.

Computer King Corporation's plant assets include office equipment that is used much like the supplies are used to generate revenue. Unlike supplies, however, there is no visible reduction in the quantity of the equipment. Instead, as time passes, the equipment loses its ability to provide useful services. This decrease in usefulness is called *depreciation*.

All plant assets, except land, lose their usefulness. Any decrease in an asset used to generate revenue is an expense. However, it is difficult to objectively measure the decrease in usefulness of a plant asset. For this reason, **depreciation** in accounting is the systematic allocation of a plant asset's cost to expense. This allocation occurs over the asset's estimated life during which it is expected to generate revenue. Methods of computing depreciation are discussed and illustrated in a later chapter.

The adjusting entry to record depreciation is similar to the adjusting entry for supplies used, in which an expense account is debited and an asset account is credited. The account debited is a depreciation expense account. However, the asset account Office Equipment is not credited because both the original cost of a plant asset and the amount of depreciation recorded since its purchase are normally reported on the balance sheet. The account credited is an **accumulated depreciation account**, which is reported on the balance sheet as a deduction from the asset account. Accumulated depreciation accounts are called **contra accounts** or **contra asset accounts** because they are reported as deductions from the related asset accounts.

Normal titles for plant asset accounts and their related contra asset accounts are as follows:

Plant Asset	Contra Asset
Land	None—Land is not depreciated
Buildings	Accumulated Depreciation—Buildings
Equipment	Accumulated Depreciation—Equipment

The ledger could have a separate account for each of a number of buildings. Equipment may also be subdivided according to function, such as Delivery Equipment, Store Equipment, and Office Equipment, with a related accumulated depreciation account for each plant asset account.

The adjusting entry to record depreciation for December for Computer King Corporation is illustrated in the following journal entry and T accounts. The estimated amount of depreciation for the month is assumed to be $50.

Depreciation Expense	50	
Accumulated Depreciation—Office Equipment		50

Office Equipment			Accumulated Depreciation	
Bal.	1,800		Dec. 31	50

Depreciation Expense	
Dec. 31	50

The $50 increase in the accumulated depreciation account represents a subtraction from the $1,800 cost recorded in the related plant asset account. The difference between the two balances is the unexpired, undepreciated, or unallocated cost. This amount ($1,750) is called the **book value of the asset**. The book value may be presented on the balance sheet in the following manner:

Office equipment	$1,800	
Less accumulated depreciation	50	$1,750

You should note that the market value of a plant asset normally differs from its book value. This is because depreciation is an allocation method, not a valuation method. That is, depreciation allocates the cost of a plant asset to expense over its estimated life. Depreciation does not attempt to measure changes in market values, which may vary significantly from year to year.

If the previous adjustment for depreciation ($50) is not recorded, the financial statements as of December 31 will be misstated. On the income statement, Depreciation Expense will be understated by $50, and the net income will be overstated by $50. On the balance sheet, Office Equipment and Retained Earnings will be overstated by $50. The effects of omitting the adjustment for depreciation are shown below.

	Amount of Misstatement
Income Statement	
Revenues correctly stated	$ XX
Expenses understated by	(50)
Net income overstated by	$ 50
Balance Sheet	
Assets overstated by	$ 50
Liabilities correctly stated	$ XX
Stockholders' equity overstated by	50
Total liabilities and stockholders' equity overstated by	$ 50

WORK SHEET

Objective 4
Enter adjustments on a work sheet and prepare an adjusted trial balance.

Before adjusting entries such as those described above can be prepared, the relevant data must be assembled. For example, the cost of supplies on hand and the wages accrued at the end of the period must be determined. Such data and analyses are summarized by accountants in **working papers**.

A working paper often used by accountants to summarize adjusting entries and assist in the preparation of the financial statements is the **work sheet**. The name of the business, the type of working paper (work sheet), and the period of time should be listed at the top of the work sheet, as shown in Exhibit 5. Such work sheets can be prepared quickly with the use of computer spreadsheet programs.

Trial Balance Columns

The trial balance discussed in Chapter 2 may be prepared directly on the work sheet. The work sheet in Exhibit 5 shows the trial balance for Computer King Corporation at December 31, 1994.

Adjustments Columns

The adjustment data are entered on the work sheet in the Adjustments columns. Both the debit and the credit amounts are inserted for the proper accounts for each adjustment. Cross-referencing the debit and credit of each adjustment by letters is useful in reviewing the work sheet. It is also helpful when the adjusting entries are recorded in the journal.

The order in which the adjustments are entered on the work sheet is not important. Most accountants enter the adjustments in the order in which the data are assembled. If the titles of some of the accounts to be adjusted do not appear in the trial balance, they should be inserted in the Account Title column, below the trial balance totals, as needed. The adjustments for Computer King Corporation which were explained and illustrated earlier in the chapter have been entered on the work sheet in Exhibit 6 on page 101.

Exhibit 5
Work Sheet with Trial Balance Entered

Computer King Corporation
Work Sheet
For Two Months Ended December 31, 1994

	Trial Balance		Adjustments		Adjusted Trial Balance		Income Statement		Balance Sheet	
	Dr.	Cr.	Dr.	Cr.	Dr.	Cr.	Dr.	Cr.	Dr.	Cr.
Cash	2,065									
Accounts Receivable	2,220									
Supplies	2,000									
Prepaid Insurance	2,400									
Land	10,000									
Office Equipment	1,800									
Accounts Payable		900								
Unearned Rent		360								
Capital Stock		15,000								
Dividends	4,000									
Fees Earned		16,340								
Wages Expense	4,275									
Rent Expense	1,600									
Utilities Expense	985									
Supplies Expense	800									
Miscellaneous Expense	455									
	32,600	32,600								

> The work sheet is used for assembling data and summarizing the effects of adjusting entries. It also aids in the preparation of financial statements.

Explanations for the entries in the Adjustments columns of the work sheet follow:

(a) **Supplies**. The supplies account has a debit balance of $2,000. The cost of the supplies on hand at the end of the period is $760. Therefore, the supplies expense for December is the difference between the two amounts, or $1,240. The adjustment is entered by writing (1) **$1,240** in the Adjustments Debit column on the same line as Supplies Expense and (2) **$1,240** in the Adjustments Credit column on the same line as Supplies.

(b) **Prepaid Insurance**. The prepaid insurance account has a debit balance of $2,400, which represents the prepayment of insurance for 24 months beginning December 1. Thus, the insurance expense for December is $100 ($2,400 ÷ 24). The adjustment is entered by writing (1) **$100** in the Adjustments Debit column on the same line as Insurance Expense and (2) **$100** in the Adjustments Credit column on the same line as Prepaid Insurance.

(c) **Unearned Rent**. The unearned rent account has a credit balance of $360, which represents the receipt of three months' rent, beginning with December. Thus, the rent income for December is $120. The adjustment is entered by writing (1) **$120** in the Adjustments Debit column on the same line as Unearned Rent, (2) Rent Income in the Account Title column, and (3) **$120** in the Adjustments Credit column on the same line as Rent Income.

(d) **Wages**. Wages accrued but not paid at the end of December total $250. This amount is an increase in expenses and an increase in liabilities. The adjust-

Exhibit 6
Work Sheet with Trial Balance and Adjustments Entered

Computer King Corporation
Work Sheet
For Two Months Ended December 31, 1994

Account Title	Trial Balance		Adjustments		Adjusted Trial Balance		Income Statement		Balance Sheet	
	Dr.	Cr.	Dr.	Cr.	Dr.	Cr.	Dr.	Cr.	Dr.	Cr.
Cash	2,065									
Accounts Receivable	2,220		(e) 500							
Supplies	2,000			(a)1,240						
Prepaid Insurance	2,400			(b) 100						
Land	10,000									
Office Equipment	1,800									
Accounts Payable		900								
Unearned Rent		360	(c) 120							
Capital Stock		15,000								
Dividends	4,000									
Fees Earned		16,340		(e) 500						
Wages Expense	4,275		(d) 250							
Rent Expense	1,600									
Utilities Expense	985									
Supplies Expense	800		(a)1,240							
Miscellaneous Expense	455									
	32,600	32,600								
Insurance Expense			(b) 100							
Rent Income				(c) 120						
Wages Payable				(d) 250						
Depreciation Expense			(f) 50							
Accumulated Depreciation				(f) 50						
			2,260	2,260						

Accounts are added, as needed, to complete the adjustments.	(a) Supplies used, $1,240 ($2,000 – $760).
	(b) Insurance expired, $100.
	(c) Rent earned from amount received in advance, $120.

(d) Wages accrued but not paid, $250.
(e) Fees earned but not received, $500.
(f) Depreciation of office equipment, $50.

ment is entered by writing (1) **$250** in the Adjustments Debit column on the same line as Wages Expense, (2) Wages Payable in the Account Title column, and (3) **$250** in the Adjustments Credit column on the same line as Wages Payable.

(e) **Accrued Fees**. Fees accrued at the end of December but not recorded total $500. This amount is an increase in an asset and an increase in revenue. The adjustment is entered by writing (1) **$500** in the Adjustments Debit column on the same line as Accounts Receivable and (2) **$500** in the Adjustments Credit column on the same line as Fees Earned.

(f) **Depreciation**. Depreciation of the office equipment is $50 for December. The adjustment is entered by writing (1) Depreciation Expense in the Account Title column, (2) **$50** in the Adjustments Debit column on the same line as Depreciation Expense, (3) Accumulated Depreciation in the Account Title column, and (4) **$50** in the Adjustments Credit column on the same line as Accumulated Depreciation.

The Adjustments columns are totaled to verify the mathematical accuracy of the adjustment data. The total of the Debit column must equal the total of the Credit column.

Adjusted Trial Balance Columns

The data in the Trial Balance columns are added to or subtracted from the adjustments data and extended to the Adjusted Trial Balance columns, as shown on the work sheet in Exhibit 7. For example, the cash account is extended at its original amount of $2,065, since no adjustments affected Cash. Accounts Receivable has an initial balance of $2,220 and a debit adjustment (increase) of $500. The amount to be extended is the debit balance of $2,720. The same procedure is continued until all account balances have been extended to the Adjusted Trial Balance columns. The Debit and Credit columns are then totaled to verify the equality of the Debit and Credit columns.

Exhibit 7
Work Sheet with Trial Balance,
Adjustments, and Adjusted Trial
Balance Entered

Computer King Corporation
Work Sheet
For Two Months Ended December 31, 1994

Account Title	Trial Balance Dr.	Trial Balance Cr.	Adjustments Dr.	Adjustments Cr.	Adjusted Trial Balance Dr.	Adjusted Trial Balance Cr.	Income Statement Dr.	Income Statement Cr.	Balance Sheet Dr.	Balance Sheet Cr.
Cash	2,065				2,065					
Accounts Receivable	2,220		(e) 500		2,720					
Supplies	2,000			(a)1,240	760					
Prepaid Insurance	2,400			(b) 100	2,300					
Land	10,000				10,000					
Office Equipment	1,800				1,800					
Accounts Payable		900				900				
Unearned Rent		360	(c) 120			240				
Capital Stock		15,000				15,000				
Dividends	4,000				4,000					
Fees Earned		16,340		(e) 500		16,840				
Wages Expense	4,275		(d) 250		4,525					
Rent Expense	1,600				1,600					
Utilities Expense	985				985					
Supplies Expense	800		(a)1,240		2,040					
Miscellaneous Expense	455				455					
	32,600	32,600								
Insurance Expense			(b) 100		100					
Rent Income				(c) 120		120				
Wages Payable				(d) 250		250				
Depreciation Expense			(f) 50		50					
Accumulated Depreciation				(f) 50		50				
			2,260	2,260	33,400	33,400				

> The adjusted trial balance amounts are determined by extending the trial balance amounts plus or minus the adjustments. For example, the Wages Expense debit of $4,525 is the trial balance amount of $4,275 plus the $250 adustment debit.

Completing the Work Sheet

We will complete the work sheet, including the use of the Income Statement and Balance Sheet columns, in Chapter 4. Also, we will discuss the use of the work sheet in preparing financial statements and the journalizing and posting of the adjusting entries. Finally, we will illustrate how to prepare the accounting records for the next accounting period.

CHAPTER REVIEW

Key Points

Objective 1. Explain how the matching concept relates to the accrual basis of accounting.

The accrual basis of accounting requires the use of an adjusting process at the end of the accounting period to match revenues and expenses properly. Revenues are reported in the period in which they are earned, and expenses are matched with the revenues they generate.

Objective 2. Explain why adjustments are necessary and list the characteristics of adjusting entries.

At the end of an accounting period, some of the amounts listed on the trial balance are not necessarily current balances. For example, amounts listed for prepaid expenses are normally overstated because the use of these assets has not been recorded on a daily basis. A delay of the recognition of an expense already paid or a revenue already received is called a deferral.

Some revenues and expenses related to a period may not be recorded at the end of the period, since these items are normally recorded only when cash has been received or paid. A revenue or expense that has not been paid or recorded is called an accrual.

The entries required at the end of an accounting period to bring accounts up to date and to ensure the proper matching of revenues and expenses are called adjusting entries. Adjusting entries require a debit or a credit to a revenue or an expense account and an offsetting debit or credit to an asset or a liability account.

Adjusting entries affect amounts reported in the income statement and the balance sheet. Thus, if an adjusting entry is not recorded, these financial statements will be incorrect (misstated).

Objective 3. Journalize entries for accounts requiring adjustment.

Adjusting entries illustrated in this chapter include deferred (prepaid) expenses, deferred (unearned) revenues, accrued expenses (accrued liabilities), and accrued revenues (accrued assets). In addition, the adjusting entry necessary to record depreciation on plant assets was illustrated.

Objective 4. Enter adjustments on a work sheet and prepare an adjusted trial balance.

The work sheet illustrated in this chapter has trial balance, adjustments, adjusted trial balance, income statement, and balance sheet columns. Adjustments are entered on the work sheet in the Adjustments columns. The adjustments are added to or subtracted from the trial balance amounts, and the resulting amounts are extended to the Adjusted Trial Balance columns. The Debit and Credit columns are then totaled to verify the equality of the Debit and Credit columns.

Glossary of Key Terms

Accruals. Expenses that have been incurred or revenues that have been earned, but have not been recorded. **Objective 2**

Accrual basis. Revenues are recognized in the period earned and expenses are recognized in the period incurred in the process of generating revenues. **Objective 1**

Accrued expenses. Expenses that have been incurred but not recorded in the accounts. Sometimes called accrued liabilities. **Objective 2**

Accrued revenues. Revenues that have been earned but not recorded in the accounts. Sometimes called accrued assets. **Objective 2**

Accumulated depreciation account. The contra asset account used to accumulate the depreciation recognized to date on plant assets. **Objective 3**

Adjusting entries. Entries required at the end of an accounting period to bring the ledger up to date. **Objective 2**

Adjusting process. The process of updating the accounts at the end of a period. **Objective 1**

Book value of the asset. The difference between the balance of a plant asset account and its related accumulated depreciation account. **Objective 3**

Cash basis. Revenue is recognized in the period cash is received, and expenses are recognized in the period cash is paid. **Objective 1**

Contra accounts. Accounts that are offset against other accounts. **Objective 3**

Deferrals. Delays in the recognition of expenses that have been incurred or revenues that have been received. **Objective 2**

Deferred expenses. Items that are initially recorded as assets but are expected to become expenses over time or through the normal operations of the enterprise. Sometimes called prepaid expenses. **Objective 2**

Deferred revenues. Items that are initially recorded as liabilities but are expected to become revenues over time or through the normal operations of the enterprise. Sometimes called unearned revenues. **Objective 2**

Depreciation. In a general sense, the decrease in usefulness of plant assets other than land. In accounting, refers to the systematic allocation of a plant asset's cost to expense. **Objective 3**

Matching concept. The concept that all expenses incurred should be matched with the revenue they generate during a period of time. **Objective 1**

Plant assets. Tangible assets that are owned by a business enterprise, are permanent or have a long life, and are used in the business. **Objective 3**

Work sheet. A working paper used to summarize adjusting entries and assist in the preparation of financial statements. **Objective 4**

Self-Examination Questions
Answers at end of chapter.

1. Which of the following items represents a deferral?
   A. Prepaid insurance   C. Fees earned
   B. Wages payable   D. Accumulated depreciation

2. If the supplies account, before adjustment on May 31, indicated a balance of $2,250, and supplies on hand at May 31 totaled $950, the adjusting entry would be:
   A. debit Supplies, $950; credit Supplies Expense, $950
   B. debit Supplies, $1,300; credit Supplies Expense, $1,300
   C. debit Supplies Expense, $950; credit Supplies, $950
   D. debit Supplies Expense, $1,300; credit Supplies, $1,300

3. The balance in the unearned rent account for Jones Corp. as of December 31 is $1,200. If Jones Corp. failed to record the adjusting entry for $600 of rent earned during December, the effect on the balance sheet and income statement for December is:
   A. assets understated $600; net income overstated $600
   B. liabilities understated $600; net income understated $600
   C. liabilities overstated $600; net income understated $600
   D. liabilities overstated $600; net income overstated $600

4. If the estimated amount of depreciation on equipment for a period is $2,000, the adjusting entry to record depreciation would be:
   A. debit Depreciation Expense, $2,000; credit Equipment, $2,000
   B. debit Equipment, $2,000; credit Depreciation Expense, $2,000
   C. debit Depreciation Expense, $2,000; credit Accumulated Depreciation, $2,000
   D. debit Accumulated Depreciation, $2,000; credit Depreciation Expense, $2,000

5. If the equipment account has a balance of $22,500 and its accumulated depreciation account has a balance of $14,000, the book value of the equipment is:
   A. $36,500   C. $14,000
   B. $22,500   D. $8,500

ILLUSTRATIVE PROBLEM

Two years ago, K. L. Waters organized Star Realty Inc. At March 31, 1995, the end of the current year, the trial balance of Star Realty Inc. is as follows:

Cash	2,425	
Accounts Receivable	5,000	
Supplies	1,870	
Prepaid Insurance	620	
Office Equipment	41,650	
Accumulated Depreciation		9,700
Accounts Payable		925
Unearned Fees		1,250
Capital Stock		5,000
Retained Earnings		15,930
Dividends	1,200	
Fees Earned		39,125
Wages Expense	12,415	
Rent Expense	3,600	
Utilities Expense	2,715	
Miscellaneous Expense	435	
	71,930	71,930

The data needed to determine year-end adjustments are as follows:

a. Supplies *on hand* at March 31, 1995	$ 480
b. Insurance premiums *expired* during the year	315
c. *Depreciation* on equipment during the year	1,950
d. Wages *accrued but not paid* at March 31, 1995	140
e. Accrued fees *earned but not recorded* at March 31, 1995	1,000
f. *Unearned fees* on March 31, 1995	750

Instructions
1. Enter the March 31, 1995, trial balance on a work sheet.
2. Using the adjustment data, enter the necessary adjustments on the work sheet.
3. Extend the adjustment data on the work sheet to the Adjusted Trial Balance columns.

Solution

1, 2, 3

Star Realty Inc.
Work Sheet
For Year Ended March 31, 1995

	ACCOUNT TITLE	TRIAL BALANCE DEBIT	TRIAL BALANCE CREDIT	ADJUSTMENTS DEBIT	ADJUSTMENTS CREDIT	ADJUSTED TRIAL BALANCE DEBIT	ADJUSTED TRIAL BALANCE CREDIT
1	Cash	2 4 2 5 00				2 4 2 5 00	
2	Accounts Receivable	5 0 0 0 00		(e)1 0 0 0 00		6 0 0 0 00	
3	Supplies	1 8 7 0 00			(a)1 3 9 0 00	4 8 0 00	
4	Prepaid Insurance	6 2 0 00			(b) 3 1 5 00	3 0 5 00	
5	Office Equipment	41 6 5 0 00				41 6 5 0 00	
6	Accumulated Depreciation		9 7 0 0 00		(c)1 9 5 0 00		11 6 5 0 00
7	Accounts Payable		9 2 5 00				9 2 5 00
8	Unearned Fees		1 2 5 0 00	(f) 5 0 0 00			7 5 0 00
9	Capital Stock		5 0 0 0 00				5 0 0 0 00
10	Retained Earnings		15 9 3 0 00				15 9 3 0 00
11	Dividends	1 2 0 0 00				1 2 0 0 00	
12	Fees Earned		39 1 2 5 00		(e)1 0 0 0 00		40 6 2 5 00
13					(f) 5 0 0 00		
14	Wages Expense	12 4 1 5 00		(d) 1 4 0 00		12 5 5 5 00	
15	Rent Expense	3 6 0 0 00				3 6 0 0 00	
16	Utilities Expense	2 7 1 5 00				2 7 1 5 00	
17	Miscellaneous Expense	4 3 5 00				4 3 5 00	
18		71 9 3 0 00	71 9 3 0 00				
19	Supplies Expense			(a)1 3 9 0 00		1 3 9 0 00	
20	Insurance Expense			(b) 3 1 5 00		3 1 5 00	
21	Depreciation Expense			(c)1 9 5 0 00		1 9 5 0 00	
22	Wages Payable				(d) 1 4 0 00		1 4 0 00
				5 2 9 5 00	5 2 9 5 00	75 0 2 0 00	75 0 2 0 00

DISCUSSION QUESTIONS

1. How are revenues and expenses reported on the income statement under (a) the cash basis of accounting and (b) the accrual basis of accounting?

2. Fees for services provided are billed to a customer during 1994. The customer remits the amount owed in 1995. During which year would the revenues be reported on the income statement under (a) the cash basis? (b) the accrual basis?

3. Employees performed services in 1994 but the wages were not paid until 1995. During which year would the wages expense be reported on the income statement under (a) the cash basis? (b) the accrual basis?

4. Is the matching concept related to (a) the cash basis of accounting or (b) the accrual basis of accounting?

ILLUSTRATIVE PROBLEM ILLUSTRATIVE PROBLEM ILLUSTRATIVE PROBLEM ILLUSTRATIVE PROBLEM

5. Is the balance listed for cash on the trial balance, before the accounts have been adjusted, the amount that should normally be reported on the balance sheet? Explain.

6. Is the balance listed for supplies on the trial balance, before the accounts have been adjusted, the amount that should normally be reported on the balance sheet? Explain.

7. Why are adjusting entries needed at the end of an accounting period?

8. What is the difference between *adjusting entries* and *correcting entries*?

9. Identify the five different categories of adjusting entries frequently required at the end of an accounting period.

10. If the effect of the credit portion of an adjusting entry is to increase the balance of a liability account, which of the following statements describes the effect of the debit portion of the entry?
    a. Increases the balance of a revenue account.
    b. Increases the balance of an expense account.
    c. Increases the balance of an asset account.

11. Does every adjusting entry have an effect on the determination of the amount of net income for a period? Explain.

12. What is the nature of the balance in the prepaid insurance account at the end of the accounting period (a) before adjustment? (b) after adjustment?

13. On May 1 of the current year, an enterprise paid the May rent on the building that it occupies. (a) Do the rights acquired at May 1 represent an asset or an expense? (b) What is the justification for debiting Rent Expense at the time of payment?

14. At December 31, the end of the first *month* of the year, the usual adjusting entry transferring supplies used to an expense account is inadvertently omitted. Which items will be incorrectly stated, because of the error, on (a) the income statement for the year and (b) the balance sheet as of December 31? Also indicate whether the items in error will be overstated or understated.

15. At the end of January, the first *month* of the year, the usual adjusting entry transferring rent earned to a revenue account from the unearned rent account was omitted. Which items will be incorrectly stated, because of the error, on (a) the income statement for January, (b) the retained earnings statement for January and (c) the balance sheet as of January 31? Also indicate whether the items in error will be overstated or understated.

16. Accrued salaries of $3,000 owed to employees for December 30 and 31 are not taken into consideration in preparing the financial statements for the year ended December 31. Which items will be erroneously stated, because of the error, on (a) the income statement for the year and (b) the balance sheet as of December 31? Also indicate whether the items in error will be overstated or understated.

17. Assume that the error in Question 16 was not corrected and that the $3,000 of accrued salaries was included in the first salary payment in January. Which items will be erroneously stated, because of failure to correct the initial error, on (a) the income statement for the month of January and (b) the balance sheet as of January 31?

18. The adjusting entry for accrued fees was omitted at December 31, the end of the current year. Which items will be in error, because of the omission, on (a) the income statement for the current year and (b) the balance sheet as of December 31? Also indicate whether the items in error will be overstated or understated.

19. What are plant assets?

20. What is depreciation?

21. In accounting for depreciation on equipment, what is the name of the account that would be referred to as a contra asset account?

22. (a) Explain the purpose of the two accounts: Depreciation Expense and Accumulated Depreciation. (b) What is the normal balance of each account? (c) Is it customary for the balances of the two accounts to be equal in amount? (d) In what financial statements, if any, will each account appear?

23. What term is applied to the difference between the balance in a plant asset account and its related accumulated depreciation account?

24. The adjusting entry for depreciation of equipment was omitted at December 31, the end of the current year. Which items will be in error, because of the omission, on (a) the income statement for the current year and (b) the balance sheet as of December 31? Also indicate whether the items in error will be overstated or understated.

25. Classify the following items as (a) deferred expense (prepaid expense), (b) deferred revenue (unearned revenue), (c) accrued expense (accrued liability), or (d) accrued revenue (accrued asset).

1. Utilities owed but not yet paid.
2. Fees received but not yet earned.
3. Salary owed but not yet paid.
4. A two-year premium paid on a fire insurance policy.
5. Fees earned but not yet received.
6. Taxes owed but payable in the following period.
7. Supplies on hand.
8. Tuition collected in advance by a university.

26. Identify each of the following accounts as (a) revenue, (b) expense, (c) asset, or (d) liability:

   1. Rent Income   5. Supplies
   2. Wages Payable   6. Unearned Rent
   3. Supplies Expense   7. Fees Earned
   4. Accounts Receivable   8. Wages Expense

27. What is a work sheet?

28. Dow Chemical Company reported *Plant Properties* of $21,444 million and *Accumulated Depreciation* of $12,643 million at December 31, 1992. What was the book value of the plant assets at December 31, 1992?

29. The balance sheet for Tandy Corporation as of June 30, 1992, includes the following accrued expenses as liabilities:

Accrued payroll and bonuses	$51,986,000
Accrued sales and payroll taxes	16,509,000
Accrued insurance	42,556,000
Accrued interest	11,386,000

The net income for Tandy Corporation for the year ended June 30, 1992, was $183,847,000. (a) If the accrued expenses had not been recorded at June 30, 1992, how much would net income have been misstated for the fiscal year ended June 30, 1992? (b) What is the percentage of the misstatement in (a) to the reported net income of $183,847,000?

ETHICS DISCUSSION CASE

Paul Martinez opened Martinez Real Estate Inc., a small corporation, on January 11 of the current year. A CPA friend explained the accrual basis of reporting revenue and expenses, explained that it was the most widely used method, and suggested its use for Martinez Real Estate Inc. Martinez decided that the accrual basis was too complicated and unnecessary for his business. He decided to use the cash basis for preparing financial statements, even though a large amount of receivables and payables existed at the end of the year.

SHARPEN YOUR COMMUNICATION SKILLS ▶

Discuss whether Paul Martinez behaved in an ethical manner by using the cash basis for preparing the financial statements for Martinez Real Estate Inc.

WHAT DO YOU THINK

?

On December 30, 1993, you buy a Ford Explorer. The Explorer comes with a three-year, 50,000-mile warranty. On January 21, 1994, you return the Explorer to the dealership for some basic repairs covered under the warranty. The cost of the repairs to the dealership is $150. In what year, 1993 or 1994, should Ford Motor Co. recognize the cost of the warranty repairs as an expense?

FINANCIAL ANALYSIS AND INTERPRETATION

Analytical procedures can take many forms. One form would be comparing an item on the current statement with the same item on a prior statement. For example, the net income for the current year may be compared to the net income of the prior year. Also, an item in the current statement may be compared to other items in the same statement. For example, the amount of the net income for the current year can be compared with the amount of the revenues for the same year.

a. Determine for Hershey Foods Corporation:

1. the amount of the change and percent of change in net income for the year ended December 31, 1992.
2. the percentage relationship between net income and net sales (net income divided by net sales) for the years ended December 31, 1992 and 1991.

SHARPEN YOUR COMMUNICATION SKILLS ► b. What conclusions can be drawn from the analyses performed in (a)?

EXERCISES

EXERCISE 3-1
DETERMINATION OF
PLANT ASSET'S BOOK
VALUE
Objective 3

The balance in the equipment account is $75,000 and the balance in the accumulated depreciation—equipment account is $25,000.

a. What is the book value of the equipment?   75,000 − 25,000 = 50,000

SHARPEN YOUR COMMUNICATION SKILLS ► b. Does the balance in the accumulated depreciation account mean that the equipment's loss of value is $25,000? Explain.

EXERCISE 3-2
ADJUSTING ENTRY FOR
SUPPLIES
Objective 3

The balance in the supplies account, before adjustment at the end of the year, is $3,725. Journalize the adjusting entry required if the amount of supplies on hand at the end of the year is $1,575.

$$\begin{array}{r} 3725 \\ \underline{1575} \\ 2150 \end{array}$$

Supplies Expense (O/E−) 2150
    Supplies (A−)   2150

EXERCISE 3-3
ADJUSTING ENTRIES FOR
PREPAID INSURANCE
Objective 3

The balance in the prepaid insurance account, before adjustment at the end of the year, is $8,650. Journalize the adjusting entry required under each of the following *alternatives* for determining the amount of the adjustment: (a) the amount of insurance expired during the year is $4,900; (b) the amount of unexpired insurance applicable to future periods is $3,750.

(O/E−) Insurance Expense   4,900
    (A−) Prepaid Insur.   4,900

EXERCISE 3-4
ADJUSTING ENTRIES FOR
PREPAID INSURANCE
Objective 3

The prepaid insurance account had a balance of $4,750 at the beginning of the year. The account was debited for $5,150 for premiums on policies purchased during the year. Journalize the adjusting entry required at the end of the year for each of the following situations: (a) the amount of unexpired insurance applicable to future periods is $4,300; (b) the amount of insurance expired during the year is $5,100.

Bal. 4,750 (b) Ins. Exp 5,100   (a) Pr. Ins 4,300
Pur. 5,150 (b) Pr. Ins. (A−) 5,100
left 4,300

EXERCISE 3-5
ADJUSTING ENTRIES FOR
UNEARNED FEES
Objective 3

The balance in the unearned fees account, before adjustment at the end of the year, is $6,000. Journalize the adjusting entry required if the amount of unearned fees at the end of the year is $3,500.

EXERCISE 3-6
ADJUSTING ENTRIES
FOR ACCRUED SALARIES
Objective 3

A business enterprise pays weekly salaries of $15,000 on Friday for a five-day week ending on that day. Journalize the necessary adjusting entry at the end of the accounting period, assuming that the period ends (a) on Tuesday, (b) on Wednesday.

EXERCISE 3-7
ADJUSTING ENTRIES FOR
PREPAID AND ACCRUED
TAXES
Objective 3

A business enterprise was organized on March 1 of the current year. On March 2, the enterprise prepaid $9,600 to the city for taxes (license fees) for the *next* 12 months, and debited the prepaid taxes account. The same enterprise is also required to pay in January an annual tax (on property) for the *previous* calendar year. The estimated amount of the property tax for the current year is $12,600. (a) Journalize the two adjusting entries required to bring the accounts affected by the two taxes up to date as of December 31, the end of the current year. (b) What is the amount of tax expense for the current year?

EXERCISE 3-8
DETERMINE SUPPLIES
PURCHASED AND WAGES
PAID
Objective 3

Selected account balances at December 31, the end of the first year of operations after the adjusting entries have been posted, are shown in the following T accounts:

Supplies		Supplies Expense	
Bal.	750	Bal.	1,050

Wages Payable		Wages Expense	
	Bal.	300	Bal.	11,900

Determine (a) the amount of supplies purchased during the year and (b) the amount of wages paid during the year.

EXERCISE 3-9
ADJUSTING ENTRY FOR
ACCRUED FEES
Objective 3

**SHARPEN YOUR ►
COMMUNICATION SKILLS**

At the end of the current year, $4,950 of fees have been earned but have not been billed to clients.

a. Journalize the adjusting entry to record the accrued fees.

b. If the cash basis rather than the accrual basis had been used, would an adjusting entry have been necessary? Explain.

EXERCISE 3-10
ADJUSTING ENTRIES
FOR UNEARNED AND
ACCRUED FEES
Objective 3

The balance in the unearned fees account, before adjustment at the end of the year, is $9,000. Of these fees, $6,500 have been earned. In addition, $3,750 of fees have been earned but have not been billed. Journalize the adjusting entries (a) to adjust the unearned fees account and (b) to record the accrued fees.

EXERCISE 3-11
ADJUSTING ENTRY
FOR DEPRECIATION
Objective 3

The estimated amount of depreciation on equipment for the current year is $420. Journalize the adjusting entry to record the depreciation.

EXERCISE 3-12
ADJUSTING ENTRIES
FOR DEPRECIATION;
EFFECT OF ERROR
Objective 3

On December 31, a business enterprise estimates depreciation on equipment used during the first year of operations to be $2,500. (a) Journalize the adjusting entry required as of December 31. (b) If the adjusting entry in (a) were omitted, which items would be erroneously stated on (1) the income statement for the year and (2) the balance sheet as of December 31?

EXERCISE 3-13
ADJUSTING ENTRIES FOR
SUPPLIES AND
DEPRECIATION
Objective 3

The balance in the supplies account, before adjustment at the end of the year, is $1,950. The amount of supplies on hand at the end of the year was determined to be $600. The estimated depreciation on equipment used during the year is $690. Journalize the adjusting entries required at the end of the year to recognize (a) supplies used during the year and (b) depreciation expense for the year.

WhAT'S WRONG
WITH THiS?

The accountant for Lakeside Laundromat Inc. prepared the following portion of a work sheet. How many errors can you find in the accountant's work?

LAKESIDE LAUNDROMAT INC.
Work Sheet
For Year Ended July 31, 1995

Account Title	Trial Balance Dr.	Trial Balance Cr.	Adjustments Dr.	Adjustments Cr.	Adjusted Trial Balance Dr.	Adjusted Trial Balance Cr.
Cash	17,790				17,790	
Laundry Supplies	4,750		(a) 2,910		7,660	
Prepaid Insurance	2,825			(b) 1,500	1,325	
Laundry Equipment		85,600				85,600
Accumulated Depreciation	55,700			(c) 5,720	61,420	
Accounts Payable		4,950				4,950
Capital Stock		7,500				7,500
Retained Earnings		23,400				23,400
Dividends	8,000				8,000	
Laundry Revenue		76,900				76,900
Wages Expense	24,500		(d) 850		25,350	
Rent Expense	15,575				15,575	
Utilities Expense	8,500				8,500	
Miscellaneous Expense	910				910	
	138,550	198,350				
Laundry Supplies Expense			(a) 2,910		2,910	
Insurance Expense			(b) 1,500		1,500	
Depreciation Expense				(c) 5,720	5,720	
Wages Payable			(d) 850			850
			14,740	7,220	156,660	199,200

PROBLEMS

Series A

PROBLEM 3-1A
ADJUSTING ENTRIES
Objective 3

On December 31, the end of the current year, the following data were accumulated to assist the accountant in preparing the adjusting entries:

a. The supplies account balance on December 31 is $1,450. The supplies on hand on December 31 are $695.

b. The unearned rent account balance on December 31 is $2,700, representing the receipt of an advance payment on December 1 of three months' rent from tenants.

c. Wages accrued but not paid at December 31 are $3,100.

d. Fees accrued but unbilled at December 31 are $7,500.

e. Depreciation on office equipment for the year is $550.

Instructions

1. Journalize the adjusting entries required at December 31.

SHARPEN YOUR
COMMUNICATION SKILLS ▶

2. Briefly explain the difference between adjusting entries and entries that would be made to correct errors.

PROBLEM 3-2A
ADJUSTING ENTRIES
Objective 3

Selected account balances before adjustment for Midstate Realty Inc. at December 31, the end of the current year, are shown below.

	Debits	Credits
Accounts Receivable	$11,250	
Supplies	3,600	
Prepaid Rent	26,000	
Equipment	42,500	
Accumulated Depreciation		$10,900
Wages Payable		—
Unearned Fees		6,000
Fees Earned		87,950
Wages Expense	29,400	
Rent Expense	—	
Depreciation Expense	—	
Supplies Expense	—	

Data needed for year-end adjustments are as follows:

a. Unbilled fees at December 31	$ 8,650
b. Supplies on hand at December 31	1,275
c. Rent expired during year	24,000
d. Depreciation on equipment during year	4,750
e. Unearned fees at December 31	2,350
f. Wages accrued but not paid at December 31	750

Instructions

Journalize the six adjusting entries required at December 31, based upon the data presented.

PROBLEM 3-3A
ADJUSTING ENTRIES
Objectives 3, 4

If the working papers correlating with the textbook are not used, omit Problem 3-3A.
A portion of the work sheet for JL Rhodes Services Corp. for the current year ending December 31 is presented in the working papers.

Instructions

1. Enter the data for the six adjustments in the two Adjustments columns of the work sheet. (Although the sequence in which the accounts are analyzed is not important, we suggest that you begin your analysis with Cash and proceed downward in the order that the accounts are listed on the work sheet.) Cross-reference the debit and credit for each adjustment by letters. Total the Adjustments columns after all adjustment data have been entered.
2. Assume that the adjusting entries were omitted for (a) supplies used and (b) accrued wages. Indicate the effect of each error, considered individually, on net income for the current year and assets, liabilities, and owner's (stockholders') equity at December 31. Record your answers by inserting the dollar amount in the appropriate spaces of the following table. Insert -0- if the error does not affect the item.

	Error (a)		Error (b)	
	Over-stated	Under-stated	Over-stated	Under-stated
1. Net income for the year would be	$	$	$	$
2. Assets at December 31 would be	$	$	$	$
3. Liabilities at December 31 would be	$	$	$	$
4. Owner's (stockholders') equity at December 31 would be	$	$	$	$

PROBLEM 3-4A
ADJUSTING ENTRIES
Objective 3

As of June 30, 1995, the end of the current year, the accountant for Hoover Corporation prepared a trial balance and an adjusted trial balance. The two trial balances are as follows:

Hoover Corporation
Trial Balance
June 30, 1995

	Unadjusted		Adjusted	
Cash	12,825		12,825	
Accounts Receivable	19,500		19,500	
Supplies	8,950		3,635	
Prepaid Insurance	3,750		1,250	
Equipment	92,150		92,150	
Accumulated Depreciation—Equipment		53,480		66,270
Automobiles	56,500		56,500	
Accumulated Depreciation—Automobiles		28,250		36,900
Accounts Payable		8,310		8,730
Salaries Payable		—		3,400
Unearned Service Fees		5,000		1,225
Capital Stock		10,000		10,000
Retained Earnings		45,470		45,470
Dividends	18,600		18,600	
Service Fees Earned		261,200		264,975
Salary Expense	172,300		175,700	
Rent Expense	18,000		18,000	
Supplies Expense	—		5,315	
Depreciation Expense—Equipment	—		12,790	
Depreciation Expense—Automobiles	—		8,650	
Utilities Expense	4,700		5,120	
Taxes Expense	2,725		2,725	
Insurance Expense	—		2,500	
Miscellaneous Expense	1,710		1,710	
	411,710	411,710	436,970	436,970

SPREADSHEET
PROBLEM

Instructions
Journalize the seven entries that adjusted the accounts at June 30. None of the accounts were affected by more than one adjusting entry.

PROBLEM 3-5A
ADJUSTING ENTRIES
Objective 3

Carey Corporation prepared the following trial balance at the end of its first year of operations:

Carey Corporation
Trial Balance
June 30, 19—

Cash	5,150	
Accounts Receivable	2,500	
Supplies	800	
Equipment	17,900	
Accounts Payable		750
Unearned Fees		2,000
Capital Stock		5,000
Retained Earnings		5,000
Dividends	2,000	
Fees Earned		35,750
Wages Expense	8,500	
Rent Expense	8,000	
Utilities Expense	2,750	
Miscellaneous Expense	900	
	48,500	48,500

In preparation for making the adjusting entries, the following data were assembled:

a. Fees earned but unbilled on June 30 were $2,550.
b. Supplies on hand on June 30 were $310.
c. Depreciation on equipment was estimated to be $1,100 for the year.
d. The balance in unearned fees represented the March 1 receipt in advance for services to be provided. Only $900 of the services were provided between March 1 and June 30.
e. Unpaid wages accrued on June 30 were $175.

Instructions

Journalize the adjusting entries necessary on June 30.

Instructions for Solving Problem 3-5A Using Solutions Software

1. Load opening balances.
2. Enter your name in the Student Name field in the General Information data entry window. Set the run date to June 30 of the current year.
3. Save the opening balances file to your drive and directory.
4. Key the adjusting entries. Key ADJ.ENT. in the reference field.
5. Display the adjusting entries.
6. Display the financial statements.
7. Save your data file to disk.
8. End the session.

PROBLEM 3-6A
WORK SHEET AND
ADJUSTING ENTRIES
Objectives 3, 4

The accountant for Elster Bowl Inc. prepared the following trial balance at December 31, the end of the current year:

Elster Bowl Inc.
Trial Balance
December 31, 19—

Cash	9,700	
Prepaid Insurance	3,400	
Supplies *prev. recorded*	1,950	
Land	50,000	
Building	141,500	
Accumulated Depreciation—Building		91,700
Equipment	90,100	
Accumulated Depreciation—Equipment		65,300
Accounts Payable		7,500
Unearned Rent — *Liability*		6,000
Capital Stock		15,000
Retained Earnings		55,700
Dividends	20,000	
Bowling Revenue		218,400
Salaries and Wages Expense	80,200	
Utilities Expense	28,200	
Advertising Expense	19,000	
Repairs Expense	11,500	
Miscellaneous Expense	4,050	
	459,600	459,600

The data needed to determine year-end adjustments are as follows:

a. Unexpired insurance at December 31	$ 700
b. Supplies on hand at December 31	450
c. Depreciation of building for the year	1,620
d. Depreciation of equipment for the year	5,500
e. Rent unearned at December 31	2,000
f. Accrued salaries and wages at December 31	2,000

SPREADSHEET
PROBLEM

SOLUTIONS
SOFTWARE

Instructions

1. Enter the trial balance on a ten-column work sheet.
2. Enter the data for the six adjustments in the Adjustments columns of the work sheet. Add additional accounts as needed.
3. Complete the Adjusted Trial Balance columns in the work sheet.
4. On the basis of the adjustment data in the work sheet, journalize the adjusting entries.

Instructions for Solving Problem 3-6A Using Solutions Software

1. Load opening balances.
2. Enter your name in the Student Name field in the General Information data entry window. Set the run date to December 31 of the current year.
3. Save the opening balances file to your drive and directory.
4. Key the adjusting entries. Key ADJ.ENT. in the reference field.
5. Display the adjusting entries.
6. Display the financial statements.
7. Save your data file to disk.
8. End the session.

PROBLEM 3-7A
ADJUSTING ENTRIES AND
ERRORS
Objective 3

At the end of June, the first month of operations, the following selected data were taken from the financial statements:

Net income for June	$39,750
Total assets at June 30	89,700
Total liabilities at June 30	30,200
Total stockholders' equity at June 30	59,500

In preparing the financial statements, adjustments for the following data were overlooked:

a. Supplies used during June, $1,750.
b. Unbilled fees earned at June 30, $3,900.
c. Depreciation on equipment for June, $300.
d. Accrued wages at June 30, $2,500.

Instructions

1. Journalize the entries to record the omitted adjustments.
2. Determine the correct amount of net income for June and the total assets, liabilities, and stockholders' equity at June 30. In addition to indicating the corrected amounts, indicate the effect of each omitted adjustment by completing the following columnar table. Adjustment (a) is presented as an example.

	Net Income	Total Assets	Total Liabilities	Total Stockholders' Equity
Reported amounts	$39,750	$89,700	$30,200	$59,500
Corrections:				
Adjustment (a)	– 1,750	– 1,750	0	– 1,750
Adjustment (b)	_____	_____	_____	_____
Adjustment (c)	_____	_____	_____	_____
Adjustment (d)	_____	_____	_____	_____
Corrected amounts	_____	_____	_____	_____

Series B

PROBLEM 3-1B
ADJUSTING ENTRIES
Objective 3

On December 31, the end of the current year, the following data were accumulated to assist the accountant in preparing the adjusting entries:

a. Fees accrued but unbilled at December 31 are $8,250.
b. The supplies account balance on December 31 is $2,100. The supplies on hand on December 31 are $535.
c. Wages accrued but not paid at December 31 are $4,350.
d. The unearned rent account balance on December 31 is $3,000, representing the receipt of an advance payment on December 1 of three months' rent from tenants.
e. Depreciation on office equipment for the year is $600.

**SHARPEN YOUR
COMMUNICATION SKILLS** ►

Instructions
1. Journalize the adjusting entries required at December 31.
2. Briefly explain the difference between adjusting entries and entries that would be made to correct errors.

PROBLEM 3-2B
ADJUSTING ENTRIES
Objective 3

Selected account balances before adjustment for Centrex Realty Inc. at December 31, the end of the current year, are shown below.

	Debits	Credits
Accounts Receivable	$ 9,250	
Supplies	2,700	
Prepaid Rent	14,500	
Equipment	50,500	
Accumulated Depreciation		$16,900
Wages Payable	—	
Unearned Fees		6,600
Fees Earned		89,850
Wages Expense	30,750	
Rent Expense	—	
Depreciation Expense	—	
Supplies Expense	—	

Data needed for year-end adjustments are as follows:

a.	Supplies on hand at December 31	$ 750
b.	Depreciation on equipment during year	4,950
c.	Rent expired during year	18,000
d.	Wages accrued but not paid at December 31	525
e.	Unearned fees at December 31	2,250
f.	Unbilled fees at December 31	4,750

Instructions
Journalize the six adjusting entries required at December 31, based upon the data presented.

If the working papers correlating with the textbook are not used, omit Problem 3-3B.

PROBLEM 3-3B
ADJUSTING ENTRIES
Objectives 3, 4

A portion of the work sheet for JL Rhodes Services Corp. for the current year ending December 31 is presented in the working papers.

Instructions
1. Enter the data for the six adjustments in the two Adjustments columns of the work sheet. (Although the sequence in which the accounts are analyzed is not important, we suggest that you begin your analysis with Cash and proceed downward in the order that the accounts are listed on the work sheet.) Cross-reference the debit and credit for each adjustment by letters. Total the Adjustments columns after all adjustment data have been entered.
2. Assume that the adjusting entries were omitted for (a) insurance expired and (b) accrued service revenue. Indicate the effect of each error, considered individually, on net income for the current year and assets, liabilities, and owner's equity (stockholders' equity) at December 31. Record your answers by inserting the dollar amount in the appropriate spaces of the following table. Insert -0- if the error does not affect the item.

	Error (a)		Error (b)	
	Over-stated	Under-stated	Over-stated	Under-stated
1. Net income for the year would be	$	$	$	$
2. Assets at December 31 would be	$	$	$	$
3. Liabilities at December 31 would be	$	$	$	$
4. Owner's (stockholders') equity at December 31 would be	$	$	$	$

PROBLEM 3-4B
ADJUSTING ENTRIES
Objective 3

As of December 31, the end of the current year, the accountant for Linke Corporation prepared a trial balance and an adjusted trial balance. The two trial balances are as follows:

Linke Corporation
Trial Balance
December 31, 19—

	Unadjusted		Adjusted	
Cash	19,750		19,750	
Accounts Receivable	10,400		10,400	
Supplies	9,880		3,460	
Prepaid Insurance	2,700		700	
Land	47,500		47,500	
Buildings	107,480		107,480	
Accumulated Depreciation—Buildings		79,600		84,400
Trucks	72,000		72,000	
Accumulated Depreciation—Trucks		32,800		50,900
Accounts Payable		8,920		9,520
Salaries Payable		—		1,450
Unearned Service Fees		7,500		920
Capital Stock		10,000		10,000
Retained Earnings		83,890		83,890
Dividends	24,000		24,000	
Service Fees Earned		170,680		177,260
Salary Expense	81,200		82,650	
Depreciation Expense—Trucks	—		18,100	
Rent Expense	9,600		9,600	
Supplies Expense	—		6,420	
Utilities Expense	6,200		6,800	
Depreciation Expense—Buildings	—		4,800	
Taxes Expense	1,720		1,720	
Insurance Expense	—		2,000	
Miscellaneous Expense	960		960	
	393,390	393,390	418,340	418,340

SPREADSHEET
PROBLEM

Instructions
Journalize the seven entries that adjusted the accounts at December 31. None of the accounts were affected by more than one adjusting entry.

PROBLEM 3-5B
ADJUSTING ENTRIES
Objective 3

Fuller Corporation prepared the following trial balance at the end of its first year of operations:

Fuller Corporation
Trial Balance
April 30, 19—

Cash	5,650	
Accounts Receivable	1,500	
Supplies	1,300	
Equipment	19,900	
Accounts Payable		750
Unearned Fees		2,000
Capital Stock		5,000
Retained Earnings		9,500
Dividends	2,500	
Fees Earned		36,750
Wages Expense	9,500	
Rent Expense	9,000	
Utilities Expense	3,750	
Miscellaneous Expense	900	
	54,000	54,000

unearned Fees
deposit slip + job descr.

need gds

Prepaid Ins

ins policies

did money but not worked

In preparation for making the adjusting entries, the following data were assembled: *1,300 − 310 = 990 − used up.*

a. Supplies on hand on April 30 were $310.
b. Fees earned but unbilled on April 30 were $3,025.
c. Depreciation on equipment was estimated to be $950 for the year.
d. Unpaid wages accrued on April 30 were $210.
e. The balance in unearned fees represented the March 1 receipt in advance for services to be provided. Only $800 of the services were provided between March 1 and April 30.

Instructions
Journalize the adjusting entries necessary on April 30.

Instructions for Solving Problem 3-5B Using Solutions Software
1. Load opening balances.
2. Enter your name in the Student Name field in the General Information data entry window. Set the run date to April 30 of the current year.
3. Save the opening balances file to your drive and directory.
4. Key the adjusting entries. Key ADJ.ENT. in the reference field.
5. Display the adjusting entries.
6. Display the financial statements.
7. Save your data file to disk.
8. End the session.

PROBLEM 3-6B
WORK SHEET AND
ADJUSTING ENTRIES
Objectives 3, 4

The accountant for Midtown Bowl Corp. prepared the following trial balance at December 31, the end of the current year:

Midtown Bowl Corp.
Trial Balance
December 31, 19—

Cash	10,200	
Prepaid Insurance	3,900	
Supplies	2,450	
Land	50,000	
Building	141,500	
Accumulated Depreciation—Building		95,700
Equipment	90,100	
Accumulated Depreciation—Equipment		65,300
Accounts Payable		7,500
Unearned Rent		4,000
Capital Stock		8,000
Retained Earnings		62,700
Dividends	20,000	
Bowling Revenue		218,400
Salaries and Wages Expense	78,700	
Utilities Expense	28,200	
Advertising Expense	19,000	
Repairs Expense	13,500	
Miscellaneous Expense	4,050	
	461,600	461,600

The data needed to determine year-end adjustments are as follows:

a.	Unexpired insurance at December 31	$ 825
b.	Supplies on hand at December 31	450
c.	Depreciation of building for the year	1,500
d.	Depreciation of equipment for the year	5,500
e.	Rent unearned at December 31	2,000
f.	Accrued salaries and wages at December 31	1,900

SPREADSHEET
PROBLEM

SOLUTIONS
SOFTWARE

Instructions

1. Enter the trial balance on a ten-column work sheet.
2. Enter the data for the six adjustments in the Adjustments columns of the work sheet. Add additional accounts as needed.
3. Complete the Adjusted Trial Balance columns in the work sheet.
4. On the basis of the adjustment data in the work sheet, journalize the adjusting entries.

Instructions for Solving Problem 3-6B Using Solutions Software

1. Load opening balances.
2. Enter your name in the Student Name field in the General Information data entry window. Set the run date to December 31 of the current year.
3. Save the opening balances file to your drive and directory.
4. Key the adjusting entries. Key ADJ.ENT. in the reference field.
5. Display the adjusting entries.
6. Display the financial statements.
7. Save your data file to disk.
8. End the session.

PROBLEM 3-7B
ADJUSTING ENTRIES AND
ERRORS
Objective 3

At the end of July, the first month of operations, the following selected data were taken from the financial statements:

Net income for July	$ 60,500
Total assets at July 31	127,250
Total liabilities at July 31	46,500
Total stockholders' equity at July 31	80,750

In preparing the financial statements, adjustments for the following data were overlooked:

a. Unbilled fees earned at July 31, $5,900.
b. Supplies used during July, $3,100.
c. Depreciation on equipment for July, $1,300.
d. Accrued wages at July 31, $3,250.

Instructions

1. Journalize the entries to record the omitted adjustments.
2. Determine the correct amount of net income for July and the total assets, liabilities, and stockholders' equity at July 31. In addition to indicating the corrected amounts, indicate the effect of each omitted adjustment by completing the following columnar table. Adjustment (a) is presented as an example.

	Net Income	Total Assets	Total Liabilities	Total Stockholders' Equity
Reported amounts	$60,500	$127,250	$46,500	$80,750
Corrections:				
Adjustment (a)	+ 5,900	+ 5,900	0	+ 5,900
Adjustment (b)	_____	_____	_____	_____
Adjustment (c)	_____	_____	_____	_____
Adjustment (d)	_____	_____	_____	_____
Corrected amounts	══════	══════	══════	══════

MINI-CASE A-1 TELEVISION REPAIR INC.

Several years ago your father opened A-1 Television Repair. He made a small initial investment and added money from his personal bank account as needed. He withdrew money for living expenses at irregular intervals. As the business grew, he incorporated the business and hired an assistant. He is now considering adding more employees, purchasing additional service trucks, and purchasing the building which he now rents. To secure funds for the expansion, your father submitted a loan application to the bank and included the most recent financial statements (shown at right) prepared from accounts maintained by a part-time bookkeeper.

After reviewing the financial statements, the loan officer at the bank asked your father if he used the accrual basis of accounting for revenues and expenses. Your father responded that he did and that is why he included an account for "Amounts Due from Customers." The loan officer then asked whether or not the accounts were adjusted prior to the preparation of the statements. Your father answered that they had not been adjusted.

Instructions:

1. ▓▓▓▓▬ Why do you think that the loan officer suspected that the accounts had not been adjusted prior to the preparation of the statements?
2. Indicate possible accounts that might need to be adjusted before an accurate set of financial statements could be prepared.

A-1 Television Repair Inc.
Income Statement
For the Year Ended December 31, 19—

Service revenue		$76,900
Less: Rent paid	$18,000	
Wages paid	16,500	
Supplies paid	7,000	
Utilities paid	3,100	
Insurance paid	3,000	
Miscellaneous payments	2,150	49,750
Net income		$27,150

A-1 Television Repair Inc.
Balance Sheet
December 31, 19—

Assets	
Cash	$ 3,750
Amounts due from customers	2,100
Truck	15,000
Total assets	$20,850
Equities	
Capital stock	$ 5,000
Retained earnings	15,850
Total stockholders' equity	$20,850

ANSWERS TO SELF-EXAMINATION QUESTIONS

1. **A** A deferral is the delay in recording an expense already paid, such as prepaid insurance (answer A). Wages payable (answer B) is considered an accrued expense or accrued liability. Fees earned (answer C) is a revenue item. Accumulated depreciation (answer D) is a contra account to a plant asset.

2. **D** The balance in the supplies account, before adjustment, represents the amount of supplies available. From this amount ($2,250) is subtracted the amount of supplies on hand ($950) to determine the supplies used ($1,300). Since increases in expense accounts are recorded by debits and decreases in asset accounts are recorded by credits, answer D is the correct entry.

3. **C** The failure to record the adjusting entry debiting Unearned Rent, $600, and crediting Rent Income, $600, would have the effect of overstating liabilities by $600 and understating net income by $600 (answer C).

4. **C** Since increases in expense accounts (such as depreciation expense) are recorded by debits and it is customary to record the decreases in usefulness of plant assets as credits to accumulated depreciation accounts, answer C is the correct entry.

5. **D** The book value of a plant asset is the difference between the balance in the asset account and the balance in the related accumulated depreciation account, or $22,500 − $14,000, as indicated by answer D ($8,500).

You and Accounting

Have you ever ridden in a taxi? When you get in, you tell the driver where you want to go, and the driver lowers the meter lever (flag) to start the meter running. At the end of the trip, the driver stops the meter. You then pay the driver for the amount indicated on the meter. As the next passenger is picked up, the driver lowers the lever, and the cycle starts all over again.

Businesses also go through a cycle of activities. At the beginning of the cycle, management plans where it wants the business to go and begins the necessary actions to achieve its operating goals. Throughout the cycle, which is normally one year, the accountant records the operating activities (transactions) of the enterprise. At the end of the cycle, the accountant prepares financial statements, which summarize the operating activities for the year. The accountant then prepares the accounts for the recording of the operating activities in the next cycle. In this chapter, you will read about the completion of the accounting cycle for a business.

Chapter 4
Completing the Accounting Cycle

LEARNING OBJECTIVES
After studying this chapter, you should be able to:

Objective 1
Prepare a work sheet.

Objective 2
Prepare financial statements from a work sheet.

Objective 3
Journalize and post the adjusting entries.

Objective 4
Journalize and post the closing entries, and prepare a post-closing trial balance.

Objective 5
Explain what is meant by the fiscal year and the natural business year.

Objective 6
List the seven basic steps of the accounting cycle.

We described and illustrated the matching concept and the adjusting process in Chapter 3. We also introduced the work sheet, which assists in the year-end procedures. In this chapter, we complete the discussion of the work sheet, including its use in preparing financial statements. In addition, we discuss journalizing and posting the adjusting entries. Finally, we conclude the chapter by discussing how to prepare the accounting records for the next accounting period.

WORK SHEET

Objective 1
Prepare a work sheet.

In Chapter 3, we illustrated the use of a work sheet for assembling data and summarizing the effects of adjusting entries on the accounts. The December 31, 1994, trial balance for Computer King Corporation was prepared directly on the work sheet. The adjustments were then entered in the Adjustments Debit and Credit columns, and the Trial Balance amounts were extended through these columns to the Adjusted Trial Balance columns, as shown again in Exhibit 1. In the following paragraphs, we describe how extending the Adjusted Trial Balance amounts to Income Statement and Balance Sheet columns can aid in preparing the financial statements.

Exhibit 1
Work Sheet with Trial Balance,
Adjustments, and Adjusted Trial
Balance Entered

Computer King Corporation
Work Sheet
For Two Months Ended December 31, 1994

Account Title	Trial Balance Dr.	Trial Balance Cr.	Adjustments Dr.	Adjustments Cr.	Adjusted Trial Balance Dr.	Adjusted Trial Balance Cr.	Income Statement Dr.	Income Statement Cr.	Balance Sheet Dr.	Balance Sheet Cr.
Cash	2,065				2,065					
Accounts Receivable	2,220		(e) 500		2,720					
Supplies	2,000			(a)1,240	760					
Prepaid Insurance	2,400			(b) 100	2,300					
Land	10,000				10,000					
Office Equipment	1,800				1,800					
Accounts Payable		900				900				
Unearned Rent		360	(c) 120			240				
Capital Stock		15,000				15,000				
Dividends	4,000				4,000					
Fees Earned		16,340		(e) 500		16,840				
Wages Expense	4,275		(d) 250		4,525					
Rent Expense	1,600				1,600					
Utilities Expense	985				985					
Supplies Expense	800		(a)1,240		2,040					
Miscellaneous Expense	455				455					
	32,600	32,600								
Insurance Expense			(b) 100		100					
Rent Income				(c) 120		120				
Wages Payable				(d) 250		250				
Depreciation Expense			(f) 50		50					
Accumulated Depreciation				(f) 50		50				
			2,260	2,260	33,400	33,400				

Accounts are added, as needed, to complete the adjustments.

The adjustments on the work sheet are used in preparing the adjusting journal entries.

The adjusted trial balance amounts are determined by extending the trial balance amounts plus or minus the adjustments. For example, the Wages Expense debit of $4,525 is the trial balance amount of $4,275 plus the $250 adjustment debit.

Income Statement and Balance Sheet Columns

The Income Statement Debit and Credit columns are directly to the right of the Adjusted Trial Balance columns in the work sheet. The Balance Sheet Debit and Credit columns are directly to the right of the Income Statement columns.

The work sheet may be expanded to include Retained Earnings Statement columns. However, because of the few items affecting retained earnings (net income or net loss and dividends), separate columns for the retained earnings statement are normally not included in the work sheet.

Completing the Work Sheet

The work sheet is completed by extending the Adjusted Trial Balance amounts to the Income Statement and Balance Sheet columns. The amounts for assets, liabilities, capital stock, retained earnings, and dividends are extended to the Balance Sheet columns. The amounts for revenues and expenses are extended to the Income Statement columns.

In the Computer King Corporation work sheet, the first account listed is Cash, and the balance appearing in the Adjusted Trial Balance Debit column is $2,065. This amount should be extended to the proper column. Cash is an asset, it is listed on the balance sheet, and it has a debit balance. Thus, the $2,065 is extended to the Debit column of the Balance Sheet section. The $2,720 balance of Accounts Receivable is extended in similar fashion. The same procedure is continued until all account balances have been extended to the proper columns, as shown in Exhibit 2.

After all the balances have been extended, each of the four statement columns is added, as shown in Exhibit 3 on page 126. The difference between the two Income Statement columns is the amount of the net income or the net loss for the period. Likewise, the difference between the two Balance Sheet columns is also the amount of the net income or net loss for the period.

If the Income Statement Credit column total (representing total revenue) is greater than the Income Statement Debit column total (representing total expenses), the difference is the net income. If the Income Statement Debit column total is greater than the Income Statement Credit column total, the difference is a net loss. For Computer King Corporation, the computation of net income is as follows:

Total of Credit column (revenues)	$16,960
Total of Debit column (expenses)	9,755
Net income (excess of revenues over expenses)	$ 7,205

As shown in Exhibit 3, the amount of the net income, $7,205, is inserted in the Income Statement Debit column and the Balance Sheet Credit column. The term *Net income* is inserted in the Account Title column. If there had been a net loss instead of net income, the amount would have been entered in the Income Statement Credit column and the Balance Sheet Debit column. The term *Net loss* would then be inserted in the Account Title column. Inserting the net income or net loss into the statement columns on the work sheet shows the effect of transferring the net balance of the revenue and expense accounts to the owner's equity. We discuss the journalizing of this transfer later in this chapter.

After the net income or net loss has been entered on the work sheet, each of the four statement columns is totaled. The totals of the two Income Statement columns must be equal. The totals of the two Balance Sheet columns must also be equal.

FINANCIAL STATEMENTS

Objective 2
Prepare financial statements from a work sheet.

The work sheet is an aid in preparing the income statement, the retained earnings statement, and the balance sheet, which are presented in Exhibit 4 on page 126. In the following paragraphs, we discuss these financial statements for Computer King

Exhibit 2
Work Sheet with Amounts
Extended to Income Statement
and Balance Sheet Columns

Computer King Corporation
Work Sheet
For Two Months Ended December 31, 1994

Account Title	Trial Balance Dr.	Trial Balance Cr.	Adjustments Dr.	Adjustments Cr.	Adjusted Trial Balance Dr.	Adjusted Trial Balance Cr.	Income Statement Dr.	Income Statement Cr.	Balance Sheet Dr.	Balance Sheet Cr.
Cash	2,065				2,065				2,065	
Accounts Receivable	2,220		(e) 500		2,720				2,720	
Supplies	2,000			(a)1,240	760				760	
Prepaid Insurance	2,400			(b) 100	2,300				2,300	
Land	10,000				10,000				10,000	
Office Equipment	1,800				1,800				1,800	
Accounts Payable		900				900				900
Unearned Rent		360	(c) 120			240				240
Capital Stock		15,000				15,000				15,000
Dividends	4,000				4,000				4,000	
Fees Earned		16,340		(e) 500		16,840		16,840		
Wages Expense	4,275		(d) 250		4,525		4,525			
Rent Expense	1,600				1,600		1,600			
Utilities Expense	985				985		985			
Supplies Expense	800		(a)1,240		2,040		2,040			
Miscellaneous Expense	455				455		455			
	32,600	32,600								
Insurance Expense			(b) 100		100		100			
Rent Income				(c) 120				120		
Wages Payable				(d) 250		250				250
Depreciation Expense			(f) 50		50		50			
Accumulated Depreciation				(f) 50		50				50
			2,260	2,260	33,400	33,400				

The revenue and expense amounts are extended to the Income Statement columns.

The asset, liability, capital stock, and dividends amounts are extended to the Balance Sheet columns.

Corporation, which were prepared from the completed work sheet in Exhibit 3. The basic form of the statements is similar to those presented in Chapter 1.

Income Statement

The income statement is normally prepared directly from the accounts listed in the work sheet. The order of the expenses may be changed, however. On the income statement, the expenses are normally presented in order of size, from largest to smallest.

Retained Earnings Statement

The first item normally presented on the retained earnings statement is the balance of the retained earnings account at the beginning of the period. Since Computer King Corporation began operations on November 1, the retained earnings statement in Exhibit 4 begins with the net income for the two months ended December 31, 1994. The amount of dividends are then deducted to arrive at the retained earnings as of December 31, 1994.

For the following period, there would be a beginning balance of retained earnings for Computer King Corporation. As we noted, this beginning balance would be reported as the first amount on the retained earnings statement. For example, assume that during 1995, Computer King Corporation earned net income of $159,595 and paid dividends of $24,000. The retained earnings statement for the year ending December 31, 1995, for Computer King Corporation is as follows:

Computer King Corporation		
Retained Earnings Statement		
For Year Ended December 31, 1995		
Retained earnings, January 1, 1995		$ 3 2 0 5 00
Net income for the year	$159 5 9 5 00	
Less dividends	24 0 0 0 00	
Increase in retained earnings		135 5 9 5 00
Retained earnings, December 31, 1995		$138 8 0 0 00

For Computer King Corporation, the amount of dividends was less than the net income. If the dividends had exceeded the net income, the order of the net income and the dividends could have been reversed. The difference between the two items would then be deducted from the beginning Retained Earnings balance. Other factors, such as a net loss, may also require some change in the form of the retained earnings statement, as shown in the following example:

Retained earnings, January 1, 19—		$45,000
Net loss for the year	$ 5,600	
Dividends	9,500	
Decrease in retained earnings		15,100
Retained earnings, December 31, 19—		$29,900

Some accountants prefer to debit dividends directly to Retained Earnings. When you are preparing a retained earnings statement and there is no dividends account in the ledger, you will need to refer to the retained earnings account to determine the beginning balance of Retained Earnings and the amount of the dividends paid during the period.

Balance Sheet

The balance sheet in Exhibit 4 has been expanded by adding subsections for current assets, plant assets, and current liabilities. Many companies prepare such a balance sheet, which is described as a classified balance sheet. We describe some of the sections and subsections that may be used in a classified balance sheet in the following paragraphs. We introduce additional sections in later chapters.

ASSETS. Assets are commonly divided into classes for presentation on the balance sheet. Two of these classes are (1) current assets and (2) plant assets.

Exhibit 3
Completed Work Sheet With Net
Income Shown

Computer King Corporation
Work Sheet
For Two Months Ended December 31, 1994

Account Title	Trial Balance Dr.	Trial Balance Cr.	Adjustments Dr.	Adjustments Cr.	Adjusted Trial Balance Dr.	Adjusted Trial Balance Cr.	Income Statement Dr.	Income Statement Cr.	Balance Sheet Dr.	Balance Sheet Cr.
Cash	2,065				2,065				2,065	
Accounts Receivable	2,220		(e) 500		2,720				2,720	
Supplies	2,000			(a)1,240	760				760	
Prepaid Insurance	2,400			(b) 100	2,300				2,300	
Land	10,000				10,000				10,000	
Office Equipment	1,800				1,800				1,800	
Accounts Payable		900				900				900
Unearned Rent		360	(c) 120			240				240
Capital Stock		15,000				15,000				15,000
Dividends	4,000				4,000				4,000	
Fees Earned		16,340		(e) 500		16,840		16,840		
Wages Expense	4,275		(d) 250		4,525		4,525			
Rent Expense	1,600				1,600		1,600			
Utilities Expense	985				985		985			
Supplies Expense	800		(a)1,240		2,040		2,040			
Miscellaneous Expense	455				455		455			
	32,600	32,600								
Insurance Expense			(b) 100		100		100			
Rent Income				(c) 120				120		
Wages Payable				(d) 250		250				250
Depreciation Expense			(f) 50		50		50			
Accumulated Depreciation				(f) 50		50				50
			2,260	2,260	33,400	33,400	9,755	16,960	23,645	16,440
Net income							7,205			7,205
							16,960	16,960	23,645	23,645

The difference between the Income Statement column totals is the net income (or net loss) for the period. The difference between the Balance Sheet column totals is also the net income (or net loss) for the period.

Exhibit 4
Financial Statements
Prepared from Work Sheet

Computer King Corporation
Income Statement
For Two Months Ended December 31, 1994

Fees earned	$16 8 4 0 00		
Rent income	1 2 0 00		
Total revenues		$16 9 6 0 00	
Expenses:			
Wages expense	$ 4 5 2 5 00		
Supplies expense	2 0 4 0 00		
Rent expense	1 6 0 0 00		
Utilities expense	9 8 5 00		
Insurance expense	1 0 0 00		
Depreciation expense	5 0 00		
Miscellaneous expense	4 5 5 00		
Total expenses		9 7 5 5 00	
Net income		$ 7 2 0 5 00	

Computer King Corporation
Retained Earnings Statement
For Two Months Ended December 31, 1994

Net income for November and December	$ 7 2 0 5 00	
Less dividends	4 0 0 0 00	
Increase in retained earnings		$ 3 2 0 5 00
Retained earnings, December 31, 1994		$ 3 2 0 5 00

Computer King Corporation
Balance Sheet
December 31, 1994

Assets				Liabilities		
Current assets:				Current liabilities:		
Cash	$ 2 0 6 5 00			Accounts payable	$ 9 0 0 00	
Accounts receivable	2 7 2 0 00			Wages payable	2 5 0 00	
Supplies	7 6 0 00			Unearned rent	2 4 0 00	
Prepaid insurance	2 3 0 0 00			Total liabilities	$ 1 3 9 0 00	
Total current assets		$ 7 8 4 5 00				
Plant assets:				Stockholders' Equity		
Land	$10 0 0 0 00			Capital stock	$15 0 0 0 00	
Office equipment	$1 8 0 0 00			Retained earnings	3 2 0 5 00	
Less accumulated depreciation	5 0 00	1 7 5 0 00		Total stockholders' equity	18 2 0 5 00	
Total plant assets			11 7 5 0 00	Total liabilities and		
Total assets			$19 5 9 5 00	stockholders' equity	$19 5 9 5 00	

Current Assets. Cash and other assets that are expected to be converted to cash or sold or used up usually within one year or less, through the normal operations of the business, are called **current assets.** In addition to cash, the current assets usually owned by a service business are notes receivable and accounts receivable, and supplies and other prepaid expenses. Notes receivable and accounts receivable are current assets because they will usually be converted to cash within one year or less.

Notes receivable are written claims against debtors who promise to pay the amount of the note and possibly interest at an agreed rate to a specified person or bearer. Accounts receivable are also claims against debtors but are less formal than notes and do not provide for interest. Accounts receivable normally arise from providing services or selling merchandise on account.

Plant Assets. The plant assets or fixed assets section may also be described as **property, plant, and equipment.** Plant assets include equipment, machinery, buildings, and land. With the exception of land, such assets depreciate over a period of time, as we discussed in Chapter 3. The cost, accumulated depreciation, and book value of each major type of plant asset is normally reported on the balance sheet.

LIABILITIES. Liabilities are debts of the business entity owed to outsiders (creditors). The two most common classes of liabilities are (1) current liabilities and (2) long-term liabilities.

Current Liabilities. Liabilities that will be due within a short time (usually one year or less) and that are to be paid out of current assets are called **current liabilities.** The most common liabilities in this group are notes payable and accounts payable. These liabilities are like their receivable counterparts, except that the debtor–creditor relationship is reversed. Other current liability accounts commonly found in the ledger are Wages Payable, Interest Payable, Taxes Payable, and Unearned Fees.

Long-Term Liabilities. Liabilities that will not be due for a long time (usually more than one year) are called **long-term liabilities.** If Computer King Corporation had long-term liabilities, they would be reported below the current liabilities. As long-term liabilities come due and are to be paid within one year, they are classified as current liabilities. If they are to be renewed rather than paid, they would continue to be classified as long term. When an asset is pledged as security for a liability, the obligation may be called a mortgage note payable or a mortgage payable.

STOCKHOLDERS' EQUITY. The stockholders' claim against the assets of the business entity is presented on the balance sheet below the liabilities section. The stockholders' equity is added to the total liabilities, and this total must be equal to the total assets.

Using Accounting

The classified balance sheet is used extensively by loan officers of financial institutions in assessing the debt-paying ability of borrowers. The excess of current assets over current liabilities, called working capital, indicates the ability of the business enterprise to pay currently maturing debt. The relationship of long-term liabilities to total stockholders' equity indicates the margin of safety for long-term creditors.

It also indicates the ability of the enterprise to withstand a poor business climate. Many times, a loan agreement will include conditions that the borrower must meet, such as a certain level of working capital, for the loan to remain outstanding. Such conditions are often referred to as loan covenants. Managers pay close attention to such covenants in planning and controlling operations.

JOURNALIZING AND POSTING ADJUSTING ENTRIES

Objective 3
Journalize and post the adjusting entries.

At the end of the accounting period, the adjustment data appearing in the work sheet are normally used to record the adjusting entries in the journal. After all the adjusting entries have been posted, the ledger is in agreement with the data reported on the financial statements. The adjusting entries are dated as of the last day of the period even though they are usually recorded at a later date. Each entry may be supported by an explanation, but a caption above the first adjusting entry is acceptable.

The adjusting entries for Computer King Corporation are as follows. The accounts to which they have been posted appear in the ledger in Exhibit 6.

	DATE		DESCRIPTION	POST. REF.	DEBIT	CREDIT	
			Adjusting Entries				
1	1994 Dec.	31	Supplies Expense	55	1 2 4 0 00		1
2			Supplies	14		1 2 4 0 00	2
3							3
4		31	Insurance Expense	56	1 0 0 00		4
5			Prepaid Insurance	15		1 0 0 00	5
6							6
7		31	Unearned Rent	23	1 2 0 00		7
8			Rent Income	42		1 2 0 00	8
9							9
10		31	Wages Expense	51	2 5 0 00		10
11			Wages Payable	22		2 5 0 00	11
12							12
13		31	Accounts Receivable	12	5 0 0 00		13
14			Fees Earned	41		5 0 0 00	14
15							15
16		31	Depreciation Expense	53	5 0 00		16
17			Accumulated Depreciation—				17
18			Office Equipment	19		5 0 00	18

JOURNAL — Page 4

NATURE OF THE CLOSING PROCESS

Objective 4
Journalize and post the closing entries, and prepare a post-closing trial balance.

At the end of an accounting period, the revenue and expense account balances are reported in the income statement. The balance of the dividends account is reported on the retained earnings statement. Since revenues, expenses, and dividends are reported for each period, the balances of these accounts should be zero at the beginning of the next period. The zero balances allow entries in these accounts in the next period to be separate from the preceding period's entries.

How are the end-of-the-period balances of revenues, expenses, and dividends converted to zero? The balance of the dividends account is zeroed out by transferring it directly to Retained Earnings. To zero out the revenue and expense accounts, their balances are transferred to an account called **Income Summary**. The balance of Income Summary is then transferred to the retained earnings account.

Because Income Summary has the effect of clearing the revenue and expense accounts of their balances, it may be described as a **clearing account**. Other titles used for this account include Revenue and Expense Summary, Profit and Loss Summary, and Income and Expense Summary.

The process of transferring the balances of revenue, expense, and dividends accounts is called the **closing process**. These accounts are then said to be *closed*. The entries that achieve this transfer are called **closing entries**.[1]

[1] It is possible to close the revenue and expense accounts without using a clearing account. Instead, the balances of these accounts are debited directly to Retained Earnings.

Because revenue, expense, and dividends accounts are periodically closed, they are sometimes called temporary accounts or nominal accounts. You should note that the balances of the accounts reported in the balance sheet are carried forward from year to year. Because of their permanent nature, balance sheet accounts are sometimes called real accounts.

Journalizing and Posting Closing Entries

You should be careful to note that Income Summary is used *only* at the end of the period. At the beginning of the closing process, Income Summary has no balance. During the closing process, Income Summary will be debited and credited for various amounts. The balance closed out of Income Summary is the net income or net loss for the period. At the end of the closing process, Income Summary will again have no balance.

Four journal entries close the temporary accounts of a corporation at the end of the period. These entries are as follows:

1. Debit each revenue account for the amount of its balance, and credit Income Summary for the total revenue.
2. Debit Income Summary for the total expense, and credit each expense account for the amount of its balance.
3. Debit Income Summary for the amount of its balance (net income), and credit Retained Earnings for the same amount. (The accounts debited and credited are reversed if there is a net loss.)
4. Debit Retained Earnings for the amount of the dividends account balance, and credit Dividends for the same amount.

The account titles and balances needed in preparing the closing entries may be obtained from either the (1) work sheet, (2) income statement and retained earnings statement, or (3) ledger. If a work sheet is used, the data for the first two entries appear in the Income Statement columns. The amount for the third entry is the net income or net loss appearing at the bottom of the work sheet. The dividends account balance appears in the Balance Sheet Debit column of the work sheet.

The closing entries for Computer King Corporation are as follows:

	DATE		DESCRIPTION	POST. REF.	DEBIT	CREDIT	
1			Closing Entries				1
2	1994 Dec.	31	Fees Earned	41	16 8 4 0 00		2
3			Rent Income	42	1 2 0 00		3
4			Income Summary	34		16 9 6 0 00	4
5							5
6		31	Income Summary	34	9 7 5 5 00		6
7			Wages Expense	51		4 5 2 5 00	7
8			Rent Expense	52		1 6 0 0 00	8
9			Depreciation Expense	53		5 0 00	9
10			Utilities Expense	54		9 8 5 00	10
11			Supplies Expense	55		2 0 4 0 00	11
12			Insurance Expense	56		1 0 0 00	12
13			Miscellaneous Expense	59		4 5 5 00	13
14							14
15		31	Income Summary	34	7 2 0 5 00		15
16			Retained Earnings	32		7 2 0 5 00	16
17							17
18		31	Retained Earnings	32	4 0 0 0 00		18
19			Dividends	33		4 0 0 0 00	19

JOURNAL — Page 5

A flowchart of the closing process for Computer King Corporation is shown in Exhibit 5. The balances in the accounts are those shown in the Trial Balance columns of the work sheet in Exhibit 1.

Exhibit 5
Flowchart of Closing Process for Computer King Corporation

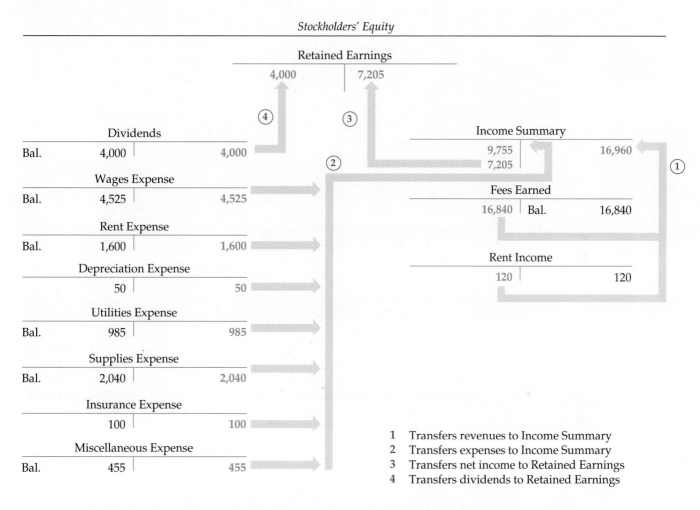

1   Transfers revenues to Income Summary
2   Transfers expenses to Income Summary
3   Transfers net income to Retained Earnings
4   Transfers dividends to Retained Earnings

After the closing entries have been posted to the ledger, the balance in Retained Earnings should agree with the amount reported on the retained earnings statement and the balance sheet. In addition, the revenue, expense, and dividends accounts should have zero balances.

The ledger of Computer King Corporation after the adjusting and closing entries have been posted appears in Exhibit 6. Each posting of an adjusting entry and a closing entry is identified in the item section of the account as an aid. It is not necessary that this be done in actual practice.

After the entry to close an account has been posted, a line is normally inserted in both Balance columns opposite the final entry. The next period's transactions for the revenue, expense, and dividends accounts will be posted directly below the closing entry.

Post-Closing Trial Balance

The last accounting procedure for a period is to prepare a trial balance after the closing entries have been posted. The purpose of the **post-closing** (after closing) **trial balance** is to make sure that the ledger is in balance at the beginning of the

Exhibit 6
Ledger for Computer King Corporation

ACCOUNT Cash   ACCOUNT NO. 11

DATE		ITEM	POST. REF.	DEBIT	CREDIT	BALANCE DEBIT	BALANCE CREDIT
1994 Nov.	1		1	15 0 0 0 00		15 0 0 0 00	
	5		1		10 0 0 0 00	5 0 0 0 00	
	18		1	7 5 0 0 00		12 5 0 0 00	
	30		1		3 6 5 0 00	8 8 5 0 00	
	30		1		9 5 0 00	7 9 0 0 00	
	30		1		2 0 0 0 00	5 9 0 0 00	
Dec.	1		2		2 4 0 0 00	3 5 0 0 00	
	1		2		8 0 0 00	2 7 0 0 00	
	1		2	3 6 0 00		3 0 6 0 00	
	6		2		1 8 0 00	2 8 8 0 00	
	11		2		4 0 0 00	2 4 8 0 00	
	13		2		9 5 0 00	1 5 3 0 00	
	16		2	3 1 0 0 00		4 6 3 0 00	
	20		2		9 0 0 00	3 7 3 0 00	
	21		2	6 5 0 00		4 3 8 0 00	
	23		2		1 4 5 0 00	2 9 3 0 00	
	27		2		1 2 0 0 00	1 7 3 0 00	
	31		3		3 1 0 00	1 4 2 0 00	
	31		3		2 2 5 00	1 1 9 5 00	
	31		3	2 8 7 0 00		4 0 6 5 00	
	31		3		2 0 0 0 00	2 0 6 5 00	

ACCOUNT Accounts Receivable   ACCOUNT NO. 12

DATE		ITEM	POST. REF.	DEBIT	CREDIT	BALANCE DEBIT	BALANCE CREDIT
1994 Dec.	16		2	1 7 5 0 00		1 7 5 0 00	
	21		2		6 5 0 00	1 1 0 0 00	
	31		3	1 1 2 0 00		2 2 2 0 00	
	31	Adjusting	4	5 0 0 00		2 7 2 0 00	

ACCOUNT Supplies   ACCOUNT NO. 14

DATE		ITEM	POST. REF.	DEBIT	CREDIT	BALANCE DEBIT	BALANCE CREDIT
1994 Nov.	10		1	1 3 5 0 00		1 3 5 0 00	
	30		1		8 0 0 00	5 5 0 00	
Dec.	23		2	1 4 5 0 00		2 0 0 0 00	
	31	Adjusting	4		1 2 4 0 00	7 6 0 00	

ACCOUNT Prepaid Insurance   ACCOUNT NO. 15

DATE		ITEM	POST. REF.	DEBIT	CREDIT	BALANCE DEBIT	BALANCE CREDIT
1994 Dec.	1		2	2 4 0 0 00		2 4 0 0 00	
	31	Adjusting	4		1 0 0 00	2 3 0 0 00	

Exhibit 6 (continued)
Ledger for Computer King Corporation

ACCOUNT   *Land*   ACCOUNT NO. *17*

DATE	ITEM	POST. REF.	DEBIT	CREDIT	BALANCE DEBIT	BALANCE CREDIT
1994 Nov. 5		1	10 000 00		10 000 00	

ACCOUNT   *Office Equipment*   ACCOUNT NO. *18*

DATE	ITEM	POST. REF.	DEBIT	CREDIT	BALANCE DEBIT	BALANCE CREDIT
1994 Dec. 4		2	1 800 00		1 800 00	

ACCOUNT   *Accumulated Depreciation*   ACCOUNT NO. *19*

DATE	ITEM	POST. REF.	DEBIT	CREDIT	BALANCE DEBIT	BALANCE CREDIT
1994 Dec. 31	Adjusting	4		50 00		50 00

ACCOUNT   *Accounts Payable*   ACCOUNT NO. *21*

DATE	ITEM	POST. REF.	DEBIT	CREDIT	BALANCE DEBIT	BALANCE CREDIT
1994 Nov. 10		1		1 350 00		1 350 00
30		1	950 00			400 00
Dec. 4		2		1 800 00		2 200 00
11		2	400 00			1 800 00
20		2	900 00			900 00

ACCOUNT   *Wages Payable*   ACCOUNT NO. *22*

DATE	ITEM	POST. REF.	DEBIT	CREDIT	BALANCE DEBIT	BALANCE CREDIT
1994 Dec. 31	Adjusting	4		250 00		250 00

ACCOUNT   *Unearned Rent*   ACCOUNT NO. *23*

DATE	ITEM	POST. REF.	DEBIT	CREDIT	BALANCE DEBIT	BALANCE CREDIT
1994 Dec. 1		2		360 00		360 00
31	Adjusting	4	120 00			240 00

ACCOUNT   *Capital Stock*   ACCOUNT NO. *31*

DATE	ITEM	POST. REF.	DEBIT	CREDIT	BALANCE DEBIT	BALANCE CREDIT
1994 Nov. 1		1		15 000 00		15 000 00

ACCOUNT   *Retained Earnings*   ACCOUNT NO. *32*

DATE	ITEM	POST. REF.	DEBIT	CREDIT	BALANCE DEBIT	BALANCE CREDIT
1994 Dec. 31	Closing	5		7 205 00		7 205 00
31	Closing	5	4 000 00			3 205 00

Exhibit 6 (continued)
Ledger for Computer King Corporation

ACCOUNT Dividends ACCOUNT NO. 33

DATE		ITEM	POST. REF.	DEBIT	CREDIT	BALANCE DEBIT	BALANCE CREDIT
1994 Nov.	30		1	2 0 0 0 00		2 0 0 0 00	
Dec.	31		3	2 0 0 0 00		4 0 0 0 00	
	31	Closing	5		4 0 0 0 00	—	—

ACCOUNT Income Summary ACCOUNT NO. 34

DATE		ITEM	POST. REF.	DEBIT	CREDIT	BALANCE DEBIT	BALANCE CREDIT
1994 Dec.	31	Closing	5		16 9 6 0 00		16 9 6 0 00
	31	Closing	5	9 7 5 5 00			7 2 0 5 00
	31	Closing	5	7 2 0 5 00		—	—

ACCOUNT Fees Earned ACCOUNT NO. 41

DATE		ITEM	POST. REF.	DEBIT	CREDIT	BALANCE DEBIT	BALANCE CREDIT
1994 Nov.	18		1		7 5 0 0 00		7 5 0 0 00
Dec.	16		2		3 1 0 0 00		10 6 0 0 00
	16		2		1 7 5 0 00		12 3 5 0 00
	31		3		2 8 7 0 00		15 2 2 0 00
	31		3		1 1 2 0 00		16 3 4 0 00
	31	Adjusting	4		5 0 0 00		16 8 4 0 00
	31	Closing	5	16 8 4 0 00		—	—

ACCOUNT Rent Income ACCOUNT NO. 42

DATE		ITEM	POST. REF.	DEBIT	CREDIT	BALANCE DEBIT	BALANCE CREDIT
1994 Dec.	31	Adjusting	4		1 2 0 00		1 2 0 00
	31	Closing	5	1 2 0 00		—	—

ACCOUNT Wages Expense ACCOUNT NO. 51

DATE		ITEM	POST. REF.	DEBIT	CREDIT	BALANCE DEBIT	BALANCE CREDIT
1994 Nov.	30		1	2 1 2 5 00		2 1 2 5 00	
Dec.	13		2	9 5 0 00		3 0 7 5 00	
	27		2	1 2 0 0 00		4 2 7 5 00	
	31	Adjusting	4	2 5 0 00		4 5 2 5 00	
	31	Closing	5		4 5 2 5 00	—	—

ACCOUNT Rent Expense ACCOUNT NO. 52

DATE		ITEM	POST. REF.	DEBIT	CREDIT	BALANCE DEBIT	BALANCE CREDIT
1994 Nov.	30		1	8 0 0 00		8 0 0 00	
Dec.	1		2	8 0 0 00		1 6 0 0 00	
	31	Closing	5		1 6 0 0 00	—	—

Exhibit 6 (continued)
Ledger for Computer King Corporation

ACCOUNT *Depriciation Expense* ACCOUNT NO. 53

DATE		ITEM	POST. REF.	DEBIT	CREDIT	BALANCE DEBIT	BALANCE CREDIT
1994 Dec.	31	Adjusting	4	5 0 00		5 0 00	
	31	Closing	5		5 0 00	—	—

ACCOUNT *Utilities Expense* ACCOUNT NO. 54

DATE		ITEM	POST. REF.	DEBIT	CREDIT	BALANCE DEBIT	BALANCE CREDIT
1994 Nov.	30		1	4 5 0 00		4 5 0 00	
Dec.	31		3	3 1 0 00		7 6 0 00	
	31		3	2 2 5 00		9 8 5 00	
	31	Closing	5		9 8 5 00	—	—

ACCOUNT *Supplies Expense* ACCOUNT NO. 55

DATE		ITEM	POST. REF.	DEBIT	CREDIT	BALANCE DEBIT	BALANCE CREDIT
1994 Nov.	30		1	8 0 0 00		8 0 0 00	
Dec.	31	Adjusting	4	1 2 4 0 00		2 0 4 0 00	
	31	Closing	5		2 0 4 0 00	—	—

ACCOUNT *Insurance Expense* ACCOUNT NO. 56

DATE		ITEM	POST. REF.	DEBIT	CREDIT	BALANCE DEBIT	BALANCE CREDIT
1994 Dec.	31	Adjusitng	4	1 0 0 00		1 0 0 00	
	31	Closing	5		1 0 0 00	—	—

ACCOUNT *Miscellaneous Expense* ACCOUNT NO. 59

DATE		ITEM	POST. REF.	DEBIT	CREDIT	BALANCE DEBIT	BALANCE CREDIT
1994 Nov.	30		1	2 7 5 00		2 7 5 00	
Dec.	6		2	1 8 0 00		4 5 5 00	
	31	Closing	5		4 5 5 00	—	—

next period. You should note that the accounts and amounts in the post-closing trial balance should agree exactly with the accounts and amounts listed on the balance sheet at the end of the period. The post-closing trial balance for Computer King Corporation is shown in Exhibit 7.

Exhibit 7
Post-Closing Trial Balance

Computer King Corporation Post-Closing Trial Balance December 31, 1994		
Cash	2 0 6 5 00	
Accounts Receivable	2 7 2 0 00	
Supplies	7 6 0 00	
Prepaid Insurance	2 3 0 0 00	
Land	10 0 0 0 00	
Office Equipment	1 8 0 0 00	
Accumulated Depreciation		5 0 00
Accounts Payable		9 0 0 00
Wages Payable		2 5 0 00
Unearned Rent		2 4 0 00
Capital Stock		15 0 0 0 00
Retained Earnings		3 2 0 5 00
	19 6 4 5 00	19 6 4 5 00

Instead of preparing a formal post-closing trial balance, the accounts may be listed directly from the ledger, using a printing calculator or a computer. The calculator tape or computer printout, in effect, becomes the post-closing trial balance. Without such a listing, the cause of an inequality of trial balance totals may be difficult to determine.

FISCAL YEAR

Objective 5
Explain what is meant by the
fiscal year and the natural
business year.

The maximum length of an accounting period is usually one year, which includes a complete cycle of business activities. Income, property taxes, and other financial reporting requirements are often based on yearly periods.

In the Computer King illustration, the length of the accounting period was two months, November and December. Computer King Corporation began operations November 1, with Pat King as its sole stockholder. Since Pat King decided to adopt a calendar-year accounting period, Computer King Corporation's accounts were closed on December 31, 1994. In future years, the financial statements for Computer King Corporation will be prepared for twelve months ending on December 31 each year.

The annual accounting period adopted by an enterprise is known as its **fiscal year** (not "physical" year). Fiscal years begin with the first day of the month selected and end on the last day of the following twelfth month. The period most commonly used is the calendar year. Other periods are not unusual, however. For example, an enterprise may adopt a fiscal year that ends when business activities have reached the lowest point in the enterprise's annual operating cycle. Such a fiscal year is called the **natural business year**.

The 1992 edition of *Accounting Trends & Techniques*, published by the American Institute of Certified Public Accountants, reported the following results of a survey of 600 industrial and merchandising companies concerning the month of their fiscal year end:

Percentage of companies with fiscal
years ending in the month of:

January	4%	July	3%
February	2	August	3
March	2	September	5
April	1	October	4
May	3	November	3
June	10	December	60

Closing the Books

Habit is a wonderful saver of mental effort. But too close adherence to habit in business limits efficiency by shutting off initiative.

This is particularly true in the adherence of general business to the habit of following a fixed date for closing the so-called fiscal year.

The best date for closing the books and preparing financial statements for the "fiscal" year is when business is in its most liquid condition—when bank loans and other liabilities are lowest, accounts receivable reduced, and especially, when the inventory is at a minimum.

The most logical date for closing your "fiscal" year is that time when *your* business is logically over for the twelve months—when stocks are lowest, when prices are normal, when selling is not being forced, when you are not buying heavily, when profits can be most accurately determined, when your accounting department is not working nights, or when your bank is not burdened with December 31 reports. In other words, close your books when *your* business is most naturally through with the rush of *your* year, when proper time and attention can be given, and when your public accountants can serve you best.

Source: *Management and Administration* (May 1924), p. 503.

The financial history of a business enterprise may be shown by a series of balance sheets and income statements. If the life of a business enterprise is expressed by a line moving from left to right, the series of balance sheets and income statements may be graphed as follows:

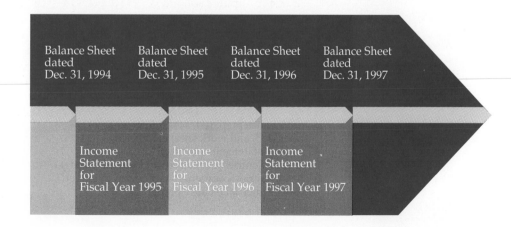

ACCOUNTING CYCLE

Objective 6
List the seven basic steps of the accounting cycle.

We have presented, in this chapter and Chapters 2 and 3, the primary accounting procedures of a fiscal period. This sequence of procedures is called the **accounting cycle**. It begins with the analysis and the journalizing of transactions and ends with the post-closing trial balance. The most important output of the accounting cycle is the financial statements.

You should thoroughly understand the basic steps of the accounting cycle. These steps are listed here and are shown, by number, in the flowchart in Exhibit 8.

1. Transactions analyzed and recorded in journal.
2. Transactions posted to ledger.
3. Trial balance prepared, adjustment data assembled, and work sheet completed.
4. Financial statements prepared.
5. Adjusting entries journalized and posted to ledger.
6. Closing entries journalized and posted to ledger.
7. Post-closing trial balance prepared.

Exhibit 8
Accounting Cycle

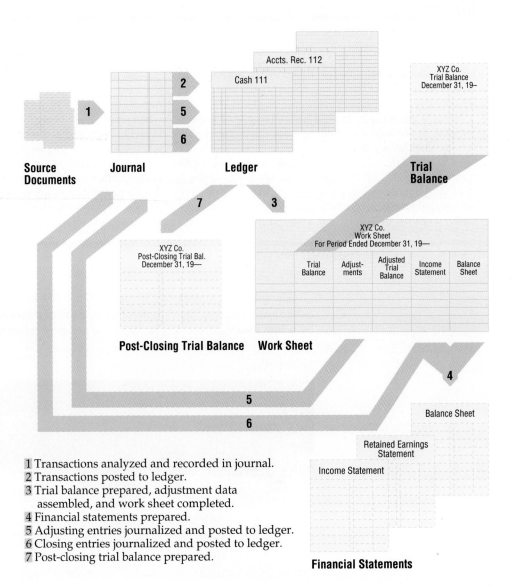

1 Transactions analyzed and recorded in journal.
2 Transactions posted to ledger.
3 Trial balance prepared, adjustment data assembled, and work sheet completed.
4 Financial statements prepared.
5 Adjusting entries journalized and posted to ledger.
6 Closing entries journalized and posted to ledger.
7 Post-closing trial balance prepared.

APPENDIX

REVERSING ENTRIES

Some of the adjusting entries recorded at the end of an accounting period have an important effect on otherwise routine transactions that occur in the following period. A typical example is accrued wages owed to employees at the end of a period. If there has been an adjusting entry for accrued wages expense, the first payment of wages in the following period will include the accrual. In the absence of some special provision, Wages Payable must be debited for the amount owed for the earlier period, and Wages Expense must be debited for the portion of the payroll that represents expense for the later period. However, an optional entry—the reversing entry—may be used to simplify the analysis and recording of this first payroll entry in a period. As the term implies, a **reversing entry** is the exact reverse of the adjusting entry to which it relates. The amounts and accounts are the same as the adjusting entry; the debits and credits are reversed.

We illustrate reversing entries by using the data for Computer King Corporation's accrued wages, which we present in Chapter 3. These data are summarized in Exhibit 9.

Exhibit 9
Accrued Wages

1. Wages are paid on the second and fourth Fridays for the two-week periods ending on those Fridays. The payments were $950 on December 13 and $1,200 on December 27.
2. The wages accrued for Monday and Tuesday, December 30 and 31, are $250.
3. Wages paid on Friday, January 10, total $1,275.

The adjusting entry to record the accrued wages of December 30 and 31 is as follows:

	DATE	DESCRIPTION	POST. REF.	DEBIT	CREDIT	
		JOURNAL			Page 4	
1	1994 Dec. 31	Wages Expense	51	2 5 0 00		1
2		Wages Payable	22		2 5 0 00	2
3						3

After the adjusting entry has been posted, Wages Expense will have a debit balance of $4,525, and Wages Payable will have a credit balance of $250, as shown in the accounts at the bottom of the page. After the closing process is completed, Wages Expense will have a zero balance and will be ready for entries in the next period. Wages Payable, on the other hand, has a balance of $250. Without the use of a reversing entry, it is necessary to record the $1,275 payroll on January 10 as a debit of $250 to Wages Payable, a debit of $1,025 to Wages Expense, and a credit of $1,275 to Cash. The employee who records this entry must refer to the prior period's adjusting entries to determine the amount of the debits to Wages Payable and Wages Expense.

Because the January 10 payroll is not recorded in the usual manner, there is a greater chance that an error may occur. This chance of error is reduced by recording a reversing entry as of the first day of the fiscal period. For example, the reversing entry for the accrued wages expense is as follows:

	DATE	DESCRIPTION	POST. REF.	DEBIT	CREDIT	
		JOURNAL			Page 6	
1	1995 Jan. 1	Wages Payable	22	2 5 0 00		1
2		Wages Expense	51		2 5 0 00	2
3						3

The reversing entry transfers the $250 liability from Wages Payable to the credit side of Wages Expense. The nature of the $250 is unchanged—it is still a liability. When the payroll is paid on January 10, Wages Expense is debited, and Cash is credited for the entire amount of the payment, $1,275. After this entry is posted, Wages Expense has a debit balance of $1,025. This amount is the wages expense for the period January 1–10. The sequence of entries, including adjusting, closing, and reversing entries, is illustrated in the following accounts:

ACCOUNT *Wages Payable*   ACCOUNT NO. *22*

						BALANCE	
DATE	ITEM	POST. REF.	DEBIT	CREDIT	DEBIT	CREDIT	
1994 Dec. 31	Adjusting	4		2 5 0 00		2 5 0 00	
1995 Jan. 1	Reversing	6	2 5 0 00		—		

ACCOUNT *Wages Expense*   ACCOUNT NO. *51*

					BALANCE		
DATE	ITEM	POST. REF.	DEBIT	CREDIT	DEBIT	CREDIT
1994 Nov. 30		1	2 1 2 5 00		2 1 2 5 00	
Dec. 13		2	9 5 0 00		3 0 7 5 00	
27		2	1 2 0 0 00		4 2 7 5 00	
31	Adjusting	4	2 5 0 00		4 5 2 5 00	
31	Closing	5		4 5 2 5 00	—	—
1995 Jan. 1	Reversing	6		2 5 0 00		2 5 0 00
10		6	1 2 7 5 00		1 0 2 5 00	

In addition to accrued expenses (accrued liabilities), reversing entries may be journalized for accrued revenues (accrued assets). For example, the following reversing entry could be recorded for Computer King Corporation's accrued fees earned:

	JOURNAL			Page 6	
DATE	DESCRIPTION	POST. REF.	DEBIT	CREDIT	
1995 Jan. 1	Fees Earned	41	5 0 0 00		
	Accounts Receivable	12		5 0 0 00	

Reversing entries may also be journalized for prepaid expenses that are initially recorded as expenses and unearned revenues that are initially recorded as revenues. These situations are described and illustrated in Appendix C.

As we mentioned, the use of reversing entries is optional. However, with the increased use of computerized accounting systems, data entry personnel may be inputting routine accounting entries. In such an environment, reversing entries may be useful, since these individuals may not recognize the impact of adjusting entries on the related transactions in the following period.

CHAPTER REVIEW

Key Points

Objective 1. Prepare a work sheet.

The work sheet is prepared by first entering a trial balance in the Trial Balance columns. The adjustments are then entered in the Adjustments Debit and Credit columns. The Trial Balance accounts plus or minus adjustments are extended to the Adjusted Trial Balance columns. The work sheet is completed by extending the Adjusted Trial Balance amounts of assets, liabilities, capital stock, retained earnings, and dividends to the Balance Sheet columns. The Adjusted Trial Balance amounts of revenues and expenses are extended to the Income Statement columns. The net income (or net loss) for the period is entered on the work sheet in the Income Statement Debit (or Credit) column and the Balance Sheet Credit (or Debit) column. Each of the four statement columns is then totaled.

Objective 2. Prepare financial statements from a work sheet.

The income statement is normally prepared directly from the accounts listed in the work sheet. On the income statement, the expenses are normally presented in the order of size, from largest to smallest.

The basic form of the retained earnings statement is prepared by listing the beginning balance of retained earnings, adding net income, and deducting dividends.

Various sections and subsections are often used in preparing a balance sheet. Two common classes of assets are current assets and plant assets. Cash and other assets that are normally expected to be converted to cash or sold or used up within one year or less are called current assets. Plant assets may also be called property, plant, and equipment. The cost, accumulated depreciation, and book value of each major type of plant asset is normally reported on the balance sheet.

Two common classes of liabilities are current liabilities and long-term liabilities. Liabilities that will be due within a short time (usually one year or less) and that are to be paid out of current assets are called current liabilities. Liabilities that will not be due for a long time (usually more than one year) are called long-term liabilities.

The stockholders' claim against the assets is presented below the liabilities section and added to the total liabilities. The total liabilities and total stockholders' equity must equal the total assets.

Objective 3. Journalize and post the adjusting entries.

At the end of the accounting period, the adjusting entries appearing in the work sheet are recorded in the journal and posted to the ledger. This brings the ledger into agreement with the data reported on the financial statements.

Objective 4. Journalize and post the closing entries, and prepare a post-closing trial balance.

The four entries required in closing the temporary accounts of a corporation are:

1. Debit each revenue account for the amount of its balance, and credit Income Summary for the total revenue.
2. Debit Income Summary for the total expense, and credit each expense account for the amount of its balance.
3. Debit Income Summary for the amount of its balance (net income), and credit Retained Earnings for the same amount. (Debit and credit are reversed if there is a net loss.)
4. Debit Retained Earnings for the amount of the dividends account balance, and credit Dividends for the same amount.

After the closing entries have been posted to the ledger, the balance in the retained earnings account will agree with the amount reported on the retained earnings statement and balance sheet. In addition, the revenue, expense, and dividends accounts will have zero balances.

The last step of the accounting cycle is to prepare a post-closing trial balance. The purpose of the post-closing trial balance is to make sure that the ledger is in balance at the beginning of the next period.

Objective 5. Explain what is meant by the fiscal year and the natural business year.

The annual accounting period adopted by an enterprise is known as its fiscal year. An enterprise may adopt a fiscal year that ends when business activities have reached the lowest point in the enterprise's annual operating cycle. Such a fiscal year is called the natural business year.

Objective 6. List the seven basic steps of the accounting cycle.

The basic steps of the accounting cycle are:

1. Transactions analyzed and recorded in a journal.
2. Transactions posted to the ledger.
3. Trial balance prepared, adjustment data assembled, and work sheet completed.
4. Financial statements prepared.
5. Adjusting entries journalized and posted to ledger.
6. Closing entries journalized and posted to ledger.
7. Post-closing trial balance prepared.

Glossary of Key Terms

Accounting cycle. The sequence of basic accounting procedures during a fiscal period. **Objective 6**

Closing entries. Entries necessary to eliminate the balances of temporary accounts in preparation for the following accounting period. **Objective 4**

Current assets. Cash or other assets that are expected to be converted to cash or sold or used up, usually within a year or less, through the normal operations of a business. **Objective 2**

Current liabilities. Liabilities that will be due within a short time (usually one year or less) and that are to be paid out of current assets. **Objective 2**

Fiscal year. The annual accounting period adopted by an enterprise. **Objective 5**

Income Summary. The account used in the closing process for transferring the revenue and expense account balances to Retained Earnings at the end of the period. **Objective 4**

Long-term liabilities. Liabilities that are not due for a long time (usually more than one year). **Objective 2**

Natural business year. A year that ends when a business's activities have reached the lowest point in its annual operating cycle. **Objective 5**

Nominal accounts. Revenue or expense accounts that are periodically closed to the income summary account; temporary owner's equity accounts. **Objective 4**

Post-closing trial balance. A trial balance prepared after all the temporary accounts have been closed. **Objective 4**

Real accounts. Balance sheet accounts. **Objective 4**

Temporary accounts. Revenue or expense accounts that are periodically closed to the income summary account; nominal accounts. **Objective 4**

Self-Examination Questions
Answers at end of chapter.

1. Which of the following accounts would be extended from the Adjusted Trial Balance columns of the work sheet to the Balance Sheet columns?
   A. Utilities Expense
   B. Rent Income
   C. Dividends
   D. Miscellaneous Expense

2. Which of the following accounts would be classified as a current asset on the balance sheet?
   A. Office Equipment
   B. Land
   C. Accumulated Depreciation
   D. Accounts Receivable

3. Which of the following entries closes the dividends account at the end of the period?
   A. Debit the dividends account, credit the income summary account.
   B. Debit the retained earnings account, credit the dividends account.
   C. Debit the income summary account, credit the dividends account.
   D. Debit the dividends account, credit the retained earnings account.

4. Which of the following accounts would not be closed to the income summary account at the end of a period?
   A. Fees Earned   C. Rent Expense
   B. Wages Expense   D. Accumulated Depreciation

5. Which of the following accounts would not be included in a post-closing trial balance?
   A. Cash   C. Accumulated Depreciation
   B. Fees Earned   D. Retained Earnings

ILLUSTRATIVE PROBLEM

Two years ago, K. L. Waters organized Star Realty Inc. At March 31, 1995, the end of the current fiscal year, the trial balance of Star Realty Inc. is as follows:

Star Realty Inc.
Trial Balance
March 31, 1995

Account	Debit	Credit
Cash	2 4 2 5 00	
Accounts Receivable	5 0 0 0 00	
Supplies	1 8 7 0 00	
Prepaid Insurance	6 2 0 00	
Office Equipment	32 6 5 0 00	
Accumulated Depreciation		9 7 0 0 00
Accounts Payable		9 2 5 00
Unearned Fees		1 2 5 0 00
Capital Stock		5 0 0 0 00
Retained Earnings		15 9 3 0 00
Dividends	10 2 0 0 00	
Fees Earned		39 1 2 5 00
Wages Expense	12 4 1 5 00	
Rent Expense	3 6 0 0 00	
Utilities Expense	2 7 1 5 00	
Miscellaneous Expense	4 3 5 00	
	71 9 3 0 00	71 9 3 0 00

The following adjustment data have been entered on the ten-column work sheet.

a. Supplies on hand at March 31, 1995, are $480.
b. Insurance premiums expired during the year are $315.
c. Depreciation of equipment during the year is $1,950.
d. Wages accrued but not paid at March 31, 1995, are $140.
e. Accrued fees earned but not recorded at March 31, 1995, are $1,000.
f. Unearned fees on March 31, 1995, are $750.

Instructions

1. Complete the ten-column work sheet.
2. Prepare an income statement, a retained earnings statement, and a balance sheet.
3. On the basis of the adjustment data in the work sheet, journalize the adjusting entries.
4. On the basis of the data in the work sheet, journalize the closing entries.

Solution

1.

Star Realty Inc.
Work Sheet
For Year Ended March 31, 1995

Account Title	Trial Balance Dr.	Trial Balance Cr.	Adjustments Dr.	Adjustments Cr.	Adjusted Trial Balance Dr.	Adjusted Trial Balance Cr.	Income Statement Dr.	Income Statement Cr.	Balance Sheet Dr.	Balance Sheet Cr.
Cash	2,425				2,425				2,425	
Accounts Receivable	5,000		(e)1,000		6,000				6,000	
Supplies	1,870			(a)1,390	480				480	
Prepaid Insurance	620			(b) 315	305				305	
Office Equipment	32,650				32,650				32,650	
Accumulated Depreciation		9,700		(c)1,950		11,650				11,650
Accounts Payable		925				925				925
Unearned Fees		1,250	(f) 500			750				750
Capital Stock		5,000				5,000				5,000
Retained Earnings		15,930				15,930				15,930
Dividends	10,200				10,200				10,200	
Fees Earned		39,125		(e)1,000		40,625		40,625		
				(f) 500						
Wages Expense	12,415		(d) 140		12,555		12,555			
Rent Expense	3,600				3,600		3,600			
Utilities Expense	2,715				2,715		2,715			
Miscellaneous Expense	435				435		435			
	71,930	71,930								
Supplies Expense			(a)1,390		1,390		1,390			
Insurance Expense			(b) 315		315		315			
Depreciation Expense			(c)1,950		1,950		1,950			
Wages Payable				(d) 140		140				140
			5,295	5,295	75,020	75,020	22,960	40,625	52,060	34,395
Net Income							17,665			17,665
							40,625	40,625	52,060	52,060

2.

Star Realty Inc.
Income Statement
For Year Ended March 31, 1995

Fees earned		$40 6 2 5 00
Operating expenses:		
Wages expense	$12 5 5 5 00	
Rent expense	3 6 0 0 00	
Utilities expense	2 7 1 5 00	
Depreciation expense	1 9 5 0 00	
Supplies expense	1 3 9 0 00	
Insurance expense	3 1 5 00	
Miscellaneous expense	4 3 5 00	
Total operating expenses		22 9 6 0 00
Net income		$17 6 6 5 00

Star Realty Inc.
Retained Earnings Statement
For Year Ended March 31, 1995

Retained earnings, April 1, 1994		$15 9 3 0 00
Net income for the year	$17 6 6 5 00	
Less dividends	10 2 0 0 00	
Increase in retained earnings		7 4 6 5 00
Retained earnings, March 31, 1995		$23 3 9 5 00

Star Realty Inc.
Balance Sheet
March 31, 1995

Assets			Liabilities		
Current assets:			Current liabilities:		
Cash	$ 2 4 2 5 00		Accounts payable	$ 9 2 5 00	
Accounts receivable	6 0 0 0 00		Unearned fees	7 5 0 00	
Supplies	4 8 0 00		Wages payable	1 4 0 00	
Prepaid insurance	3 0 5 00		Total liabilities		$ 1 8 1 5 00
Total current assets		$ 9 2 1 0 00	Stockholders' Equity		
Plant assets:			Capital stock	$ 5 0 0 0 00	
Office equipment	$32 6 5 0 00		Retained earnings	23 3 9 5 00	
Less accumulated			Total stockholders' equity		28 3 9 5 00
depreciation	11 6 5 0 00	21 0 0 0 00	Total liabilities and		
Total assets		$30 2 1 0 00	stockholders' equity		$30 2 1 0 00

3.

			JOURNAL							Page 42	
	DATE		DESCRIPTION	POST. REF.	DEBIT		CREDIT				
1			Adjusting Entries								1
2	1995 Mar.	31	Supplies Expense		1 3 9 0 00						2
3			Supplies				1 3 9 0 00				3
4											4
5		31	Insurance Expense		3 1 5 00						5
6			Prepaid Insurance				3 1 5 00				6
7											7
8		31	Depreciation Expense		1 9 5 0 00						8
9			Accumulated Depreciation				1 9 5 0 00				9
10											10
11		31	Wages Expense		1 4 0 00						11
12			Wages Payable				1 4 0 00				12
13											13
14		31	Accounts Receivable		1 0 0 0 00						14
15			Fees Earned				1 0 0 0 00				15
16											16
17		31	Unearned Fees		5 0 0 00						17
18			Fees Earned				5 0 0 00				18

ILLUSTRATIVE PROBLEM

4.

	JOURNAL			Page 43		
DATE	DESCRIPTION	POST. REF.	DEBIT		CREDIT	
	Closing Entries					1
1995 Mar. 31	Fees Earned		40 6 2 5 00			2
	Income Summary				40 6 2 5 00	3
						4
31	Income Summary		22 9 6 0 00			5
	Wages Expense				12 5 5 5 00	6
	Rent Expense				3 6 0 0 00	7
	Utilities Expense				2 7 1 5 00	8
	Miscellaneous Expense				4 3 5 00	9
	Supplies Expense				1 3 9 0 00	10
	Insurance Expense				3 1 5 00	11
	Depreciation Expense				1 9 5 0 00	12
						13
31	Income Summary		17 6 6 5 00			14
	Retained Earnings				17 6 6 5 00	15
						16
31	Retained Earnings		10 2 0 0 00			17
	Dividends				10 2 0 0 00	18

DISCUSSION QUESTIONS

1. Is the work sheet a substitute for the financial statements? Discuss.
2. The balances for the accounts listed here appeared in the Adjusted Trial Balance columns of the work sheet. Indicate whether each balance should be extended to (a) the Income Statement columns or (b) the Balance Sheet columns.
   - (1) Retained Earnings
   - (2) Fees Earned
   - (3) Accounts Payable
   - (4) Wages Expense
   - (5) Supplies
   - (6) Unearned Fees
   - (7) Utilities Expense
   - (8) Dividends
   - (9) Accounts Receivable
   - (10) Wages Payable
3. Balances for each of the following accounts appear in the Adjusted Trial Balance columns of the work sheet. Identify each as (a) asset, (b) liability, (c) revenue, or (d) expense.
   - (1) Unearned Rent
   - (2) Supplies
   - (3) Salary Expense
   - (4) Rent Income
   - (5) Prepaid Advertising
   - (6) Insurance Expense
   - (7) Accounts Receivable
   - (8) Land
   - (9) Fees Earned
   - (10) Supplies Expense
   - (11) Salary Payable
   - (12) Prepaid Insurance
4. In the Income Statement columns of the work sheet, the Debit column total is greater than the Credit column total before the amount for the net income or net loss has been included. Would the income statement report a net income or a net loss? Explain.
5. In the Balance Sheet columns of the work sheet for McReynolds Inc. for the current year, the Debit column total is $91,500 greater than the Credit column total before the amount for net income or net loss has been included. Would the income statement report a net income or a net loss? Explain.
6. Describe the nature of the assets that compose the following sections of a balance sheet: (a) current assets, (b) plant assets.
7. Identify each of the following as (a) a current asset or (b) a plant asset:
   - (1) supplies
   - (2) cash
   - (3) building
   - (4) accounts receivable
   - (5) equipment
   - (6) land
8. What is the difference between a current liability and a long-term liability?
9. What type of accounts are referred to as temporary accounts?
10. Are adjusting and closing entries in the journal dated as of the last day of the fiscal period or as of the day the entries are actually made? Explain.

11. Why are closing entries required at the end of an accounting period?

12. What is the difference between adjusting entries and closing entries?

13. Describe the four entries that close the temporary accounts.

14. What type of accounts are closed by transferring their balances to Income Summary (a) as a debit, (b) as a credit?

15. To what account is the income summary account closed?

16. To what account is the dividends account closed?

17. From the following list, identify the accounts that should be closed to Income Summary at the end of the fiscal year:

a. Accounts Payable	g. Equipment
b. Salaries Payable	h. Supplies Expense
c. Fees Earned	i. Retained Earnings
d. Salaries Expense	j. Dividends
e. Depreciation Expense—Buildings	k. Land
f. Supplies	l. Accumulated Depreciation—Buildings

18. Which of the following accounts will usually appear in the post-closing trial balance?

a. Accounts Receivable	g. Equipment
b. Accumulated Depreciation	h. Wages Expense
c. Cash	i. Capital Stock
d. Supplies	j. Fees Earned
e. Depreciation Expense	k. Dividends
f. Wages Payable	

19. What is the purpose of the post-closing trial balance?

20. What term is applied to the annual accounting period adopted by a business enterprise?

21. What is the natural business year?

22. Why might a department store select a fiscal year ending January 31, rather than a fiscal year ending December 31?

23. Rearrange the following steps in the accounting cycle in proper sequence:

a. Adjusting entries journalized and posted to ledger.

b. Post-closing trial balance prepared.

c. Closing entries journalized and posted to ledger.

d. Transactions analyzed and recorded in journal.

e. Financial statements prepared.

f. Trial balance prepared, adjustment data assembled, and work sheet completed.

g. Transactions posted to ledger.

REAL WORLD FOCUS   24. The fiscal years for several well-known companies were as follows:

Company	Fiscal Year Ending
K Mart	January 30
J.C. Penney	January 26
Zayre Corp.	January 26
Toys "R" Us, Inc.	February 3
Federated Department Stores	February 2
The Limited, Inc.	February 2

What general characteristic shared by these companies explains why they do not have fiscal years ending December 31?

ETHICS DISCUSSION CASE

McRee Inc.'s fiscal year ends October 31. During the first week of November, McRee Inc.'s accountant prepared the work sheet for the year ended October 31, 1995. After the financial statements were prepared, the accountant journalized and posted the adjusting and closing entries. The accountant dated the adjusting and closing entries October 31, 1995, even though the entries were actually prepared and entered on November 6, 1995.

SHARPEN YOUR COMMUNICATION SKILLS   Evaluate whether the accountant behaved in an ethical manner in dating the adjusting and closing entries October 31, 1995.

WHAT DO YOU THINK

Do you think the United States federal government should be required to publish financial statements similar to those illustrated in this chapter?

FINANCIAL ANALYSIS AND INTERPRETATION

The ability of a business to meet its financial obligations (debts) as they come due is called solvency. There are many ways in which financial statement data can be analyzed to provide insight into the solvency of a business. One financial measure that relates to a business's ability to pay its debts is working capital. Working capital is the excess of the current assets of an enterprise over its current liabilities, as indicated below:

Working Capital = Current Assets – Current Liabilities

Working capital is especially useful in making monthly or other period-to-period comparisons for a company.

a. Determine the working capital for Hershey Foods Corporation as of December 31, 1992 and 1991.

SHARPEN YOUR COMMUNICATION SKILLS

b. What conclusions concerning the company's ability to meets its financial obligations can you draw from these data?

EXERCISES

EXERCISE 4-1
INCOME STATEMENT
Objective 2

The following account balances were taken from the Adjusted Trial Balance columns of the work sheet for Finney Corporation for the current fiscal year ended June 30:

Fees Earned	$92,500
Salaries Expense	37,100
Rent Expense	18,000
Utilities Expense	8,500
Supplies Expense	2,050
Miscellaneous Expense	1,750
Insurance Expense	1,500
Depreciation Expense	2,100

Prepare an income statement.

EXERCISE 4-2
INCOME STATEMENT; NET LOSS
Objective 2

The following revenue and expense account balances were taken from the ledger of Henderson Inc. after the accounts had been adjusted on October 31, the end of the current fiscal year:

Depreciation Expense	$ 4,000
Insurance Expense	3,900
Miscellaneous Expense	2,250
Rent Expense	24,000
Service Revenue	71,200
Supplies Expense	3,100
Utilities Expense	8,500
Wages Expense	26,750

Prepare an income statement.

EXERCISE 4-3
RETAINED EARNINGS
STATEMENT
Objective 2

Selected accounts from the ledger of Sampras Services Inc., for the current fiscal year ended December 31, are as follows:

Retained Earnings					Dividends			
Dec. 31	30,000	Jan. 1	62,500	Mar. 31	7,500	Dec. 31	30,000
		Dec. 31	40,250	June 30	7,500		
				Sep. 30	7,500		
				Dec. 31	7,500		

Income Summary			
Dec. 31	548,150	Dec. 31	588,400
31	40,250		

SPREADSHEET
PROBLEM

Prepare a retained earnings statement for the year.

EXERCISE 4-4
RETAINED EARNINGS
STATEMENT; NET LOSS
Objective 2

Selected accounts from the ledger of Chang Corporation, for the current fiscal year ended March 31, are as follows:

Retained Earnings					Dividends			
Mar. 31	24,000	Apr. 1	60,500	June 30	6,000	Mar. 31	24,000
31	10,500			Sep. 30	6,000		
				Dec. 31	6,000		
				Mar. 31	6,000		

Income Summary			
Mar. 31	623,400	Mar. 31	612,900
		31	10,500

Prepare a retained earnings statement for the year.

EXERCISE 4-5
BALANCE SHEET
CLASSIFICATION
Objective 2

SHARPEN YOUR
COMMUNICATION SKILLS

At the balance sheet date, a business enterprise owes a mortgage note payable of $250,000, the terms of which provide for monthly payments of $5,000.

Explain how the liability should be classified on the balance sheet.

EXERCISE 4-6
BALANCE SHEET
Objective 2

After all the accounts have been closed on June 30, the end of the current fiscal year, the balances of selected accounts from the ledger of Leeds Inc. are as follows:

Accounts Payable	$12,750
Accounts Receivable	9,920
Accumulated Depreciation—Equipment	21,100
Capital Stock	15,000
Cash	6,150
Equipment	60,600
Prepaid Insurance	3,100
Prepaid Rent	2,400
Retained Earnings	33,320
Salaries Payable	3,750
Supplies	4,750
Unearned Fees	1,000

Prepare a classified balance sheet.

EXERCISE 4-7
CLOSING ENTRIES
Objective 4

Prior to the completion of the closing process, Income Summary had total debits of $357,500 and total credits of $378,000.

▶ SHARPEN YOUR
COMMUNICATION SKILLS

Briefly explain the purpose served by the income summary account and the nature of the entries that resulted in the $357,500 and the $378,000.

EXERCISE 4-8
CLOSING ENTRIES
Objective 4

After all revenue and expense accounts have been closed at the end of the fiscal year, Income Summary has a debit of $795,500 and a credit of $867,500. At the same date, Retained Earnings has a credit balance of $99,500, and Dividends has a balance of $36,000. (a) Journalize the entries required to complete the closing of the accounts. (b) State the amount of Retained Earnings at the end of the period.

EXERCISE 4-9
CLOSING ENTRIES
Objective 4

After the accounts have been adjusted at February 28, the end of the fiscal year, the following balances were taken from the ledger of Dunn Services Corporation:

Retained Earnings	$27,250
Dividends	6,000
Fees Earned	55,000
Wages Expense	21,500
Rent Expense	9,000
Supplies Expense	5,500
Miscellaneous Expense	2,000

Journalize the four entries required to close the accounts.

EXERCISE 4-10
POST-CLOSING TRIAL
BALANCE
Objective 4

The accountant prepared the following post-closing trial balance:

Parrish Repairs Inc.
Post-Closing Trial Balance
July 31, 19—

Cash	8,500	
Accounts Receivable	11,250	
Supplies	900	900
Equipment	31,500	31,500
Accumulated Depreciation—Equipment	15,130	15,130
Accounts Payable	6,250	6250
Salaries Payable		3,500
Unearned Rent	4,000	4,000
Capital Stock	5,000	5,000
Retained Earnings	18,270	18,270
	68,400	35,900
	52,150	52,150

Prepare a corrected post-closing trial balance. Assume that all accounts have normal balances and that the amounts shown are correct.

APPENDIX EXERCISE 4-11
ADJUSTING AND
REVERSING ENTRIES

On the basis of the following data, journalize (a) the adjusting entries at December 31, 1995, the end of the current fiscal year, and (b) the reversing entries on January 1, 1996, the first day of the following year.

1. Sales salaries are uniformly $9,000 for a five-day workweek, ending on Friday. The last payday of the year was Friday, December 27.
2. Accrued fees earned but not recorded at December 31, $2,750.

**APPENDIX
EXERCISE 4-12**
ENTRIES POSTED
TO THE WAGES
EXPENSE ACCOUNT

Portions of the wages expense account of an enterprise are as follows:

ACCOUNT   Wages Expense   ACCOUNT NO.   53

Date	Item	Post. Ref.	Dr.	Cr.	Balance Dr.	Balance Cr.
19—						
Dec. 27	(1)	51	7,500		245,500	
31	(2)	52	3,000		248,500	
31	(3)	53		248,500	—	—
19—						
Jan. 2	(4)	54		3,000		3,000
7	(5)	55	7,500		4,500	

a. Indicate the nature of the entry (payment, adjusting, closing, reversing) from which each numbered posting was made.
b. Journalize the complete entry from which each numbered posting was made.

WhAT'S WRONG WITH THiꙅ?

How many errors can you find in the following balance sheet?

Eastland Services Corp.
Balance Sheet
For Year Ended July 31, 1995

Assets			Liabilities		
Current assets:			Current liabilities:		
Cash		$ 6,170	Accounts receivable	$ 5,390	
Accounts payable		5,390	Net loss	15,500	
Supplies		590	Total liabilities		$ 20,890
Prepaid insurance		840			
Land		20,000			
Total current assets		$ 32,995			
Plant assets:			Stockholders' Equity		
Building	$55,500		Wages payable	$ 975	
Plus accumulated depreciation	23,525	$79,025	Capital stock	25,000	
Equipment	$28,250		Retained earnings	44,515	
Plus accumulated depreciation	17,340	45,590	Total stockholders' equity		70,490
Total plant assets		224,615	Total liabilities and		
Total assets		$257,610	stockholders' equity		$ 91,380

PROBLEMS

Series A

The trial balance of Suds Inc. at July 31, 1995, the end of the current fiscal year, and the data needed to determine year-end adjustments are as follows:

PROBLEM 4-1A
WORK SHEET AND
RELATED ITEMS
Objectives 1, 2, 3, 4

Suds Inc.
Trial Balance
July 31, 1995

Cash	6,290	
Laundry Supplies	3,850	
Prepaid Insurance	2,400	
Laundry Equipment	81,600	
Accumulated Depreciation		52,700
Accounts Payable		3,950
Capital Stock		10,000
Retained Earnings		23,900
Dividends	16,600	
Laundry Revenue		66,900
Wages Expense	22,900	
Rent Expense	14,400	
Utilities Expense	8,500	
Miscellaneous Expense	910	
	157,450	157,450

a. Laundry supplies on hand at July 31 are $940.
b. Insurance premiums expired during the year are $1,500.
c. Depreciation of equipment during the year is $5,220.
d. Wages accrued but not paid at July 31 are $850.

SPREADSHEET
PROBLEM

Instructions

1. Record the trial balance on a ten-column work sheet, and complete the work sheet.
2. Prepare an income statement, a retained earnings statement, and a balance sheet.
3. On the basis of the adjustment data in the work sheet, journalize the adjusting entries.
4. On the basis of the data in the work sheet, journalize the closing entries.

SOLUTIONS
SOFTWARE

Instructions for Solving Problem 4-1A Using Solutions Software

1. Load opening balances.
2. Enter your name in the Student Name field in the General Information data entry window. Set the run date to July 31, 1995.
3. Save the opening balances file to your drive and directory.
4. Key the adjusting entries. Key ADJ.ENT. in the reference field.
5. Display the adjusting entries.
6. Display the financial statements.
7. Save a backup copy of your data file.
8. Perform period-end closing.
9. Display a post-closing trial balance.
10. Save your data file to disk.
11. End the session.

PROBLEM 4-2A
ADJUSTING AND CLOSING
ENTRIES; RETAINED
EARNINGS STATEMENT
Objectives 2, 3

On April 30, 1995, the end of the current fiscal year, the accountant for Riley Corporation prepared a trial balance, journalized and posted the adjusting entries, prepared an adjusted trial balance, prepared the financial statements, and completed the other procedures required at the end of the accounting cycle. The two trial balances as of April 30, one before adjustments and the other after adjustments, are as follows:

Riley Corporation
Trial Balance
April 30, 1995

	Unadjusted		Adjusted	
Cash	7,325		7,325	
Accounts Receivable	16,900		20,900	
Supplies	6,920		1,610	
Prepaid Insurance	1,275		350	
Equipment	69,750		69,750	
Accumulated Depreciation—Equipment		33,480		36,270
Accounts Payable		4,310		4,530
Salaries Payable		—		3,480
Taxes Payable		—		1,200
Unearned Rent		750		500
Capital Stock		5,000		5,000
Retained Earnings		28,975		28,975
Dividends	18,300		18,300	
Service Fees Earned		181,200		185,200
Rent Income		—		250
Salary Expense	112,300		115,780	
Rent Expense	15,600		15,600	
Supplies Expense	—		5,310	
Depreciation Expense—Equipment	—		2,790	
Utilities Expense	2,720		2,940	
Taxes Expense	915		2,115	
Insurance Expense	—		925	
Miscellaneous Expense	1,710		1,710	
	253,715	253,715	265,405	265,405

SPREADSHEET
PROBLEM

SHARPEN YOUR
COMMUNICATION SKILLS

Instructions
1. Journalize the eight entries that were required to adjust the accounts at April 30. None of the accounts were affected by more than one adjusting entry.
2. Journalize the entries that were required to close the accounts at April 30.
3. Prepare a retained earnings statement for the fiscal year ended April 30, 1995. There were no additional investments during the year.
4. If the balance of Dividends had been $75,000 instead of $18,300, what would the balance of Retained Earnings have been on April 30, 1995? Explain how this balance would be reported on the balance sheet.

PROBLEM 4-3A
LEDGER ACCOUNTS AND
WORK SHEET AND
RELATED ITEMS
Objectives 1, 2, 3, 4

If the working papers correlating with this textbook are not used, omit Problem 4-3A.
The ledger and trial balance of Salazar Corp. as of January 31, 1995, the end of the first month of its current fiscal year, are presented in the working papers.

Instructions
1. Complete the ten-column work sheet. Data needed to determine the necessary adjusting entries are as follows:
   a. Service revenue accrued at January 31 is $700.
   b. Supplies on hand at January 31 are $450.
   c. Insurance premiums expired during January are $80.
   d. Depreciation of the building during January is $110.
   e. Depreciation of equipment during January is $115.
   f. Unearned rent at January 31 is $100.
   g. Wages accrued at January 31 are $975.
2. Prepare an income statement, a retained earnings statement, and a balance sheet.
3. Journalize and post the adjusting entries, inserting balances in the accounts affected.
4. Journalize and post the closing entries. Indicate closed accounts by inserting a line in both Balance columns opposite the closing entry. Insert the new balance of the retained earnings account.
5. Prepare a post-closing trial balance.

PROBLEM 4-4A
WORK SHEET AND
FINANCIAL STATEMENTS
Objectives 1, 2

Beacon Inc. prepared the following trial balance at June 30, 1995, the end of the current fiscal year:

Beacon Inc.
Trial Balance
June 30, 1995

Cash	11,500	
Accounts Receivable	12,500	
Prepaid Insurance	2,400	
Supplies	1,950	
Land	40,000	
Building	100,500	
Accumulated Depreciation—Building		81,700
Equipment	72,400	
Accumulated Depreciation—Equipment		63,800
Accounts Payable		6,100
Unearned Rent		1,500
Capital Stock		7,500
Retained Earnings		53,000
Dividends	24,000	
Fees Revenue		161,200
Salaries and Wages Expense	60,200	
Advertising Expense	19,000	
Utilities Expense	18,200	
Repairs Expense	8,100	
Miscellaneous Expense	4,050	
	374,800	374,800

The data needed to determine year-end adjustments are as follows:

   a. Accrued fees revenue at June 30 is $1,500.
   b. Insurance expired during the year is $1,050.
   c. Supplies on hand at June 30 are $450.
   d. Depreciation of building for the year is $1,620.
   e. Depreciation of equipment for the year is $5,160.
   f. Accrued salaries and wages at June 30 are $1,950.
   g. Unearned rent at June 30 is $500.

Instructions

1. Record the trial balance on a ten-column work sheet, and complete the work sheet.
2. Prepare an income statement for the year ended June 30.
3. Prepare a retained earnings statement for the year ended June 30.
4. Prepare a balance sheet as of June 30.
5. Compute the percent of net income to total revenue for the year.

SOLUTIONS
SOFTWARE

Instructions for Solving Problem 4-4A Using Solutions Software

 1. Load opening balances.
 2. Enter your name in the Student Name field in the General Information data entry window. Set the run date to June 30, 1995.
 3. Save the opening balances file to your drive and directory.
 4. Key the adjusting entries. Key ADJ.ENT. in the reference field.
 5. Display the adjusting entries.
 6. Display the financial statements.
 7. Save a backup copy of your data file.
 8. Perform period-end closing.
 9. Display a post-closing trial balance.
10. Save your data file to disk.
11. End the session.

PROBLEM 4-5A
LEDGER ACCOUNTS, WORK
SHEET, AND RELATED
ITEMS
Objectives 1, 2, 3, 4

The trial balance of Jordan Repair Inc. at July 31, 1995, the end of the current year, and the data needed to determine year-end adjustments are as follows:

Jordan Repair Inc.
Trial Balance
July 31, 1995

11 Cash	6,491	
13 Supplies	4,295	
14 Prepaid Insurance	1,735	
16 Equipment	30,650	
17 Accumulated Depreciation—Equipment		9,750
18 Trucks	23,300	
19 Accumulated Depreciation—Trucks		6,400
21 Accounts Payable		2,015
31 Capital Stock		5,000
32 Retained Earnings		25,426
33 Dividends	18,000	
41 Service Revenue		89,950
51 Wages Expense	33,925	
53 Rent Expense	9,600	
55 Truck Expense	8,350	
59 Miscellaneous Expense	2,195	
	138,541	138,541

a. Supplies on hand at July 31 are $302.
b. Insurance premiums expired during year are $990.
c. Depreciation of equipment during year is $3,380.
d. Depreciation of trucks during year is $4,400.
e. Wages accrued but not paid at July 31 are $693.

Instructions

1. For each account listed in the trial balance, enter the balance in the appropriate Balance column of a four-column account, and place a check mark (✔) in the Posting Reference column.
2. Record the trial balance on a ten-column work sheet, and complete the work sheet.
3. Prepare an income statement, a retained earnings statement, and a balance sheet.
4. Journalize and post the adjusting entries, inserting balances in the accounts affected. The following additional accounts from Jordan Repair Inc.'s chart of accounts should be used: Wages Payable, 22; Supplies Expense, 52; Depreciation Expense—Equipment, 54; Depreciation Expense—Trucks, 56; Insurance Expense, 57.
5. Journalize and post the closing entries. (Income Summary is account 34 in the chart of accounts.) Indicate closed accounts by inserting a line in both Balance columns opposite the closing entry. Insert the new balance of the retained earnings account.
6. Prepare a post-closing trial balance.

SOLUTIONS
SOFTWARE

Instructions for Solving Problem 4-5A Using Solutions Software

1. Load opening balances.
2. Enter your name in the Student Name field in the General Information data entry window. Set the run date to July 31, 1995.
3. Save the opening balances file to your drive and directory.
4. Key the adjusting entries. Key ADJ.ENT. in the reference field.
5. Display the adjusting entries.
6. Display the financial statements.
7. Save a backup copy of your data file.
8. Perform period-end closing.
9. Display a post-closing trial balance.
10. Save your data file to disk.
11. End the session.

Series B

PROBLEM 4-1B
WORK SHEET AND
RELATED ITEMS
Objectives 1, 2, 3, 4

The trial balance of E-Z Laundry Inc. at October 31, 1995, the end of the current fiscal year, and the data needed to determine year-end adjustments are as follows:

E-Z Laundry Inc.
Trial Balance
October 31, 1995

Cash	13,100	
Laundry Supplies	6,560	
Prepaid Insurance	2,750	
Laundry Equipment	84,100	
Accumulated Depreciation		45,200
Accounts Payable		6,100
Capital Stock		9,000
Retained Earnings		27,060
Dividends	18,000	
Laundry Revenue		140,900
Wages Expense	51,400	
Rent Expense	36,000	
Utilities Expense	13,650	
Miscellaneous Expense	2,700	
	228,260	228,260

a. Laundry supplies on hand at October 31 are $3,050.
b. Insurance premiums expired during the year are $1,800.
c. Depreciation of equipment during the year is $4,600.
d. Wages accrued but not paid at October 31 are $1,750.

Instructions

1. Record the trial balance on a ten-column work sheet, and complete the work sheet.
2. Prepare an income statement, a retained earnings statement, and a balance sheet.
3. On the basis of the adjustment data in the work sheet, journalize the adjusting entries.
4. On the basis of the data in the work sheet, journalize the closing entries.

Instructions for Solving Problem 4-1B Using Solutions Software

1. Load opening balances.
2. Enter your name in the Student Name field in the General Information data entry window. Set the run date to October 31, 1995.
3. Save the opening balances file to your drive and directory.
4. Key the adjusting entries. Key ADJ.ENT. in the reference field.
5. Display the adjusting entries.
6. Display the financial statements.
7. Save a backup copy of your data file.
8. Perform period-end closing.
9. Display a post-closing trial balance.
10. Save your data file to disk.
11. End the session.

PROBLEM 4-2B
ADJUSTING AND CLOSING
ENTRIES; RETAINED
EARNINGS STATEMENT
Objectives 2, 3

As of December 31, the end of the current fiscal year, the accountant for Furstner Corporation prepared a trial balance, journalized and posted the adjusting entries, prepared an adjusted trial balance, prepared the financial statements, and completed the other procedures required at the end of the accounting cycle. The two trial balances as of December 31, one before adjustments and the other after adjustments, are as follows:

Furstner Corporation
Trial Balance
December 31, 19—

	Unadjusted		Adjusted	
Cash	13,650		13,650	
Accounts Receivable	10,380		13,960	
Supplies	9,750		3,330	
Prepaid Insurance	2,400		800	
Land	42,500		42,500	
Buildings	116,000		116,000	
Accumulated Depreciation—Buildings		77,600		82,400
Equipment	82,000		82,000	
Accumulated Depreciation—Equipment		32,800		50,900
Accounts Payable		7,120		7,520
Salaries Payable		—		1,450
Taxes Payable		—		920
Unearned Rent		900		600
Capital Stock		25,000		25,000
Retained Earnings		99,890		99,890
Dividends	21,000		21,000	
Service Fees Earned		140,680		144,260
Rent Income		—		300
Salary Expense	71,200		72,650	
Depreciation Expense—Equipment	—		18,100	
Rent Expense	9,000		9,000	
Supplies Expense	—		6,420	
Utilities Expense	4,550		4,950	
Depreciation Expense—Buildings	—		4,800	
Taxes Expense	600		1,520	
Insurance Expense	—		1,600	
Miscellaneous Expense	960		960	
	383,990	383,990	413,240	413,240

SPREADSHEET
PROBLEM

SHARPEN YOUR
COMMUNICATION SKILLS

Instructions

1. Journalize the nine entries that were required to adjust the accounts at December 31. None of the accounts were affected by more than one adjusting entry.
2. Journalize the entries that were required to close the accounts at December 31.
3. Prepare a retained earnings statement for the fiscal year ended December 31.
4. If the balance of Dividends had been $130,000 instead of $21,000, what would the balance of Retained Earnings have been on December 31? Explain how this balance would be reported on the balance sheet.

PROBLEM 4-3B
LEDGER ACCOUNTS AND
WORK SHEET AND
RELATED ITEMS
Objectives 1, 2, 3, 4

If the working papers correlating with this textbook are not used, omit Problem 4-3B.
The ledger and trial balance of Salazar Corp. as of January 31, 1995, the end of the first month of its current fiscal year, are presented in the working papers.

Instructions

1. Complete the ten-column work sheet. Data needed to determine the necessary adjusting entries are as follows:
   a. Service revenue accrued at January 31 is $750.
   b. Supplies on hand at January 31 are $550.60.
   c. Insurance premiums expired during January are $72.50.
   d. Depreciation of the building during January is $125.
   e. Depreciation of equipment during January is $95.
   f. Unearned rent at January 31 is $100.
   g. Wages accrued but not paid at January 31 are $1,006.50.

2. Prepare an income statement, a retained earnings statement, and a balance sheet.
3. Journalize and post the adjusting entries, inserting balances in the accounts affected.
4. Journalize and post the closing entries. Indicate closed accounts by inserting a line in both Balance columns opposite the closing entry. Insert the new balance of the retained earnings account.
5. Prepare a post-closing trial balance.

PROBLEM 4-4B
WORK SHEET AND
FINANCIAL STATEMENTS
Objectives 1, 2

Willis Corporation prepared the following trial balance at June 30, 1995, the end of the current fiscal year:

Willis Corporation
Trial Balance
June 30, 1995

Cash	7,200	
Accounts Receivable	6,500	
Prepaid Insurance	3,400	
Supplies	1,950	
Land	50,000	
Building	137,500	
Accumulated Depreciation—Building		51,700
Equipment	90,100	
Accumulated Depreciation—Equipment		35,300
Accounts Payable		7,500
Unearned Rent		3,000
Capital Stock		40,000
Retained Earnings		123,700
Dividends	20,000	
Fees Revenue		198,400
Salaries and Wages Expense	80,200	
Advertising Expense	28,200	
Utilities Expense	19,000	
Repairs Expense	11,500	
Miscellaneous Expense	4,050	
	459,600	459,600

The data needed to determine year-end adjustments are as follows:
   a. Accrued fees revenue at June 30 are $1,200.
   b. Insurance expired during the year is $2,700.
   c. Supplies on hand at June 30 are $450.
   d. Depreciation of building for the year is $1,620.
   e. Depreciation of equipment for the year is $5,500.
   f. Accrued salaries and wages at June 30 are $2,000.
   g. Unearned rent at June 30 is $1,500.

Instructions
1. Record the trial balance on a ten-column work sheet, and complete the work sheet.
2. Prepare an income statement for the year ended June 30.
3. Prepare a retained earnings statement for the year ended June 30.
4. Prepare a balance sheet as of June 30.
5. Compute the percent of net income to total revenue for the year.

SOLUTIONS
SOFTWARE

Instructions for Solving Problem 4-4B Using Solutions Software
   1. Load opening balances.
   2. Enter your name in the Student Name field in the General Information data entry window. Set the run date to June 30, 1995.
   3. Save the opening balances file to your drive and directory.
   4. Key the adjusting entries. Key ADJ.ENT. in the reference field.
   5. Display the adjusting entries.
   6. Display the financial statements.
   7. Save a backup copy of your data file.
   8. Perform period-end closing.
   9. Display a post-closing trial balance.
   10. Save your data file to disk.
   11. End the session.

PROBLEM 4-5B
LEDGER ACCOUNTS, WORK
SHEET, AND RELATED
ITEMS
Objectives 1, 2, 3, 4

The trial balance of Lee Repair Inc. at December 31, 1995, the end of the current year, and the data needed to determine year-end adjustments are as follows:

Lee Repair Inc.
Trial Balance
December 31, 1995

11	Cash	6,825	
13	Supplies	4,820	
14	Prepaid Insurance	2,000	
16	Equipment	32,200	
17	Accumulated Depreciation—Equipment		9,050
18	Trucks	42,000	
19	Accumulated Depreciation—Trucks		27,100
21	Accounts Payable		4,015
31	Capital Stock		5,000
32	Retained Earnings		20,800
33	Dividends	18,000	
41	Service Revenue		99,950
51	Wages Expense	37,925	
53	Rent Expense	9,600	
55	Truck Expense	9,350	
59	Miscellaneous Expense	3,195	
		165,915	165,915

a. Supplies on hand at December 31 are $860.
b. Insurance premiums expired during year are $1,050.
c. Depreciation of equipment during year is $6,080.
d. Depreciation of trucks during year is $5,500.
e. Wages accrued but not paid at December 31 are $700.

Instructions
1. For each account listed in the trial balance, enter the balance in the appropriate Balance column of a four-column account, and place a check mark (✔) in the Posting Reference column.
2. Record the trial balance on a ten-column work sheet, and complete the work sheet.
3. Prepare an income statement, a retained earnings statement, and a balance sheet.
4. Journalize and post the adjusting entries, inserting balances in the accounts affected. The following additional accounts from Lee Repair Inc.'s chart of accounts should be used: Wages Payable, 22; Supplies Expense, 52; Depreciation Expense—Equipment, 54; Depreciation Expense—Trucks, 56; Insurance Expense, 57.
5. Journalize and post the closing entries. (Income Summary is account 34 in the chart of accounts.) Indicate closed accounts by inserting a line in both Balance columns opposite the closing entry. Insert the new balance of the retained earnings account.
6. Prepare a post-closing trial balance.

SOLUTIONS
SOFTWARE

Instructions for Solving Problem 4-5B Using Solutions Software
1. Load opening balances.
2. Enter your name in the Student Name field in the General Information data entry window. Set the run date to December 31, 1995.
3. Save the opening balances file to your drive and directory.
4. Key the adjusting entries. Key ADJ.ENT. in the reference field.
5. Display the adjusting entries.
6. Display the financial statements.
7. Save a backup copy of your data file.
8. Perform period-end closing.
9. Display a post-closing trial balance.
10. Save your data file to disk.
11. End the session.

MINI-CASE NO-PEST INC.

Assume that you recently accepted a position with the Second National Bank as an assistant loan officer. As one of your first duties, you have been assigned the responsibility of evaluating a loan request for $75,000 from No-Pest Inc., a small corporation. In support of the loan application, Jean Wicks, the sole stockholder, submitted the following "Statement of Accounts" (trial balance) for the first year of operations ended December 31, 1995:

No-Pest Inc.
Statement of Accounts
December 31, 1995

Cash	4,120	
Billings Due from Others	7,740	
Supplies (chemicals, etc.)	14,950	
Trucks	32,750	
Equipment	16,150	
Amounts Owed to Others		4,700
Investment in Business		47,500
Service Revenue		97,650
Wages Expense	60,100	
Utilities Expense	6,900	
Rent Expense	4,800	
Insurance Expense	1,400	
Other Expenses	940	
	149,850	149,850

Instructions:

1. ▆▆▆ ▸Explain to Jean Wicks why a set of financial statements (income statement, retained earnings statement, and balance sheet) would be useful to you in evaluating the loan request.
2. In discussing the Statement of Accounts with Jean Wicks, you discovered that the accounts had not been adjusted at December 31. Through analysis of the Statement of Accounts, indicate possible adjusting entries that might be necessary before an accurate set of financial statements could be prepared.
3. Assuming that an accurate set of financial statements will be submitted by Jean Wicks in a few days, what other considerations or information would you require before making a decision on the loan request?

COMPREHENSIVE PROBLEM 1

For the past several years, Lance Fox has operated a consulting business from his home on a part-time basis. As of September 1, Fox decided to move to rented quarters, devote full time to the business, and incorporate the business as Fox Consulting Corp. Fox Consulting Corp. entered into the following transactions during September:

Sep. 1. Issued capital stock for the following assets received from Lance Fox: cash, $6,000; accounts receivable, $1,000; supplies, $1,250; and office equipment, $6,200. There were no liabilities received.
2. Paid three months' rent on a lease rental contract, $2,400.
2. Paid the premiums on property and casualty insurance policies, $1,800.
4. Received cash from clients as an advance payment for services to be performed and recorded them as unearned fees, $2,500.
4. Purchased additional office equipment on account from Payne Company, $2,000.
6. Received cash from clients on account, $600.
9. Paid cash for a newspaper advertisement, $80.
11. Paid Payne Company for part of the debt incurred on September 4, $1,100.
12. Recorded services performed on account for the period September 1–12, $1,200.
13. Paid part-time receptionist for two weeks' salary, $400.
17. Recorded cash from cash clients for fees earned during the first half of September, $2,100.
17. Paid cash for supplies, $950.
20. Recorded services performed on account for the period September 13–20, $1,100.
24. Recorded cash from cash clients for fees earned for the period September 17–24, $1,850.
27. Received cash from clients on account, $1,200.
27. Paid part-time receptionist for two weeks' salary, $400.

Sep. 30. Paid telephone bill for September, $65.
    30. Paid electricity bill for September, $140.
    30. Recorded cash from cash clients for fees earned for the period September 25–30, $850.
    30. Recorded services performed on account for the remainder of September, $500.
    30. Paid cash dividends, $1,200.

Instructions

1. Journalize each transaction in a two-column journal, referring to the following chart of accounts in selecting the accounts to be debited and credited. (Do not insert the account numbers in the journal at this time.)

11 Cash	41 Fees Earned
12 Accounts Receivable	51 Salary Expense
14 Supplies	52 Rent Expense
15 Prepaid Rent	53 Supplies Expense
16 Prepaid Insurance	54 Depreciation Expense
18 Office Equipment	55 Insurance Expense
19 Accumulated Depreciation	59 Miscellaneous Expense
21 Accounts Payable	
22 Salaries Payable	
23 Unearned Fees	
31 Capital Stock	
32 Retained Earnings	
33 Dividends	

2. Post the journal to a ledger of four-column accounts.
3. Prepare a trial balance as of September 30, on a ten-column work sheet, listing all the accounts in the order given in the ledger. Complete the work sheet, using the following adjustment data:
   a. Insurance expired during September is $250.
   b. Supplies on hand on September 30 are $1,420.
   c. Depreciation of office equipment for September is $750.
   d. Accrued receptionist salary on September 30 is $100.
   e. Rent expired during September is $800.
   f. Unearned fees on September 30 are $1,100.
4. Prepare an income statement, a retained earnings statement, and a balance sheet.
5. Journalize and post the adjusting entries.
6. Journalize and post the closing entries. (Income Summary is account 34 in the chart of accounts.) Indicate closed accounts by inserting a line in both Balance columns opposite the closing entry. Insert the new balance in the retained earnings account.
7. Prepare a post-closing trial balance.

SOLUTIONS
SOFTWARE

Instructions for Solving Comprehensive Problem 1 Using Solutions Software

1. Load opening balances.
2. Enter your name in the Student Name field in the General Information data entry window. Set the run date to September 30 of the current year.
3. Save the opening balances file to your drive and directory.
4. Select the General Journal Entries option, and key the journal entries. Leave the reference field blank. (Note: To review the chart of accounts, select F-1.)
5. Display a journal entries report.
6. Display a trial balance.
7. Key the adjusting entries. Key ADJ.ENT. in the reference field.
8. Display the adjusting entries.
9. Display the financial statements.
10. Save a backup copy of your data file.
11. Perform period-end closing.
12. Display a post-closing trial balance.
13. Save your data file to disk.
14. End the session.

ANSWERS TO SELF-EXAMINATION QUESTIONS

1. **C** The dividends account (answer C) would be extended to the Balance Sheet columns of the work sheet. Utilities Expense (answer A), Rent Income (answer B), and Miscellaneous Expense (answer D) would all be extended to the Income Statement columns of the work sheet.

2. **D** Cash or other assets that are expected to be converted to cash or sold or used up within one year or less, through the normal operations of the business, are classified as current assets on the balance sheet. Accounts Receivable (answer D) is a current asset since it will normally be converted to cash within one year. Office Equipment (answer A), Land (answer B), and Accumulated Depreciation (answer C) are all reported in the plant asset section of the balance sheet.

3. **B** The entry to close the dividends account is to debit the retained earnings account and credit the dividends account (answer B).

4. **D** Since all revenue and expense accounts are closed at the end of the period, Fees Earned (answer A), Wages Expense (answer B), and Rent Expense (answer C) would all be closed to Income Summary. Accumulated Depreciation (answer D) is a contra asset account that is not closed.

5. **B** Since the post-closing trial balance includes only balance sheet accounts (all the revenue, expense, and dividends accounts are closed), Cash (answer A), Accumulated Depreciation (answer C), and Retained Earnings (answer D) would appear on the post-closing trial balance. Fees Earned (answer B) is a temporary account that is closed prior to the preparation of the post-closing trial balance.

You and Accounting

When you purchase merchandise at a store and pay cash, the clerk normally uses a cash register to record the sale. The cash register is designed to record the sale electronically or on a tape within the machine.

After the sale has been "rung up," the clerk provides you with a receipt similar to the one shown here.

```
        INGLES #426
        ATHENS GA

                         10/02/92

GROCERY                      2.99L
GROCERY                      1.00L
FZ FOOD                      1.29L
SUBTOTAL                     5.28
TAX                           .32
TOTAL                        5.60

CASH                        10.00

CHANGE                       4.40

# ITEMS      3


   THANK YOU C123 R03 T12:38
```

The receipt indicates the items purchased, the subtotal of the purchases, the sales tax, the total due, the amount of cash received, and the amount of change. In this example, three items were purchased totaling $5.28, sales tax of $.32 (6%) was charged, the total due was $5.60, the clerk was given $10.00, and change of $4.40 was received. The receipt also indicates that the sale was made by Store #426 of the Ingles chain located in Athens, Georgia. The date and time of the sale and other data used internally by the store are also indicated.

Chapter 5
Accounting for Merchandising Enterprises

LEARNING OBJECTIVES
After studying this chapter, you should be able to:

Objective 1
Compare a service enterprise's income statement to a merchandising enterprise's income statement.

Objective 2
Journalize the entries for merchandise transactions, including:
a. Merchandise purchases
b. Merchandise sales
c. Merchandise transportation costs

Objective 3
Journalize the entries for merchandise transactions from both the buyer's and the seller's point of view.

Objective 4
Prepare a chart of accounts for a merchandising enterprise.

Objective 5
Prepare a work sheet for a merchandising enterprise.

Objective 6
Prepare an income statement, a retained earnings statement, and a balance sheet for a merchandising enterprise.

Objective 7
Journalize the adjusting entries for a merchandising enterprise.

Objective 8
Journalize the closing entries for a merchandising enterprise.

We described and illustrated the accounting for service enterprises in preceding chapters. In this chapter, we focus on the accounting principles and concepts for merchandising enterprises, which purchase merchandise for sale to customers. It is this buying and selling of merchandise that makes the activities of merchandising enterprises different from the activities of service enterprises.

INCOME STATEMENTS FOR MERCHANDISING ENTERPRISES

Objective 1
Compare a service enterprise's income statement to a merchandising enterprise's income statement.

How do the revenue activities of a college, university, or hospital, which are service enterprises, differ from those of Wal-Mart or K Mart, which are merchandising enterprises? These differences are highlighted in the following condensed income statements for each type of enterprise:

Service Enterprise		*Merchandising Enterprise*	
Fees earned	$XXX	Sales	$XXX
Operating expenses	XXX	Cost of merchandise sold	XXX
Net income	$XXX	Gross profit	$XXX
		Operating expenses	XXX
		Net income	$XXX

The revenue-generating activities of a service enterprise involve providing services to customers. On the income statement for a service enterprise, the revenues from services are reported as fees earned. The operating expenses incurred in providing the services are subtracted from the fees earned to arrive at net income.

In contrast, the revenue-generating activities of a merchandise enterprise involve the buying and selling of merchandise. A merchandising enterprise must first purchase merchandise to sell to its customers. When this merchandise is sold, the revenue is reported as sales, and its cost is recognized as an expense called the cost of merchandise sold. The cost of merchandise sold is subtracted from sales to arrive at gross profit. This amount is called gross profit because from it the operating expenses are deducted to arrive at net income. We discuss in the remainder of this chapter the transactions that affect these identifying features of the merchandising enterprise income statement—sales, cost of merchandise sold, and gross profit.

Merchandise that is not sold at the end of an accounting period is called **merchandise inventory**. Merchandise inventory is reported as a current asset on the balance sheet of a merchandising enterprise.

ACCOUNTING FOR PURCHASES

Objective 2a
Journalize the entries for merchandise purchases.

There are two systems for accounting for merchandise purchased for sale: perpetual and periodic. In the **perpetual inventory system**, each purchase and sale of merchandise is recorded in an inventory account. In this way, the inventory records always (perpetually) disclose the amount of merchandise on hand and the amount sold. In the **periodic inventory system**, no attempt is made to keep detailed inventory records of the amounts on hand throughout the period. Instead, a detailed listing of the merchandise on hand (called a **physical inventory**) at the end of the accounting period is prepared. This physical inventory listing is used to determine the cost of the inventory on hand at the end of the period and the cost of the merchandise sold during the period.

The use of computers and standard bar codes makes perpetual inventory systems practical for even small merchandise enterprises. For this reason, we use the perpetual inventory system in the following illustrations. We describe and illustrate the periodic inventory system in the appendix at the end of this text.

Under the perpetual inventory system, purchases of merchandise for sale are recorded in the merchandise inventory account in the ledger. When purchases are made for cash, the transaction is recorded as follows:

| Jan. 3 | Merchandise Inventory
    Cash
      Purchases from supplier,
      Bowen Co. | 2,510 | 2,510 |

Purchases of merchandise on account are recorded as follows:

| Jan. 4 | Merchandise Inventory
    Accounts Payable
      Purchases from supplier,
      Thomas Corporation. | 9,250 | 9,250 |

Purchases Discounts

The terms of a purchase are normally indicated on the **invoice** or bill that the seller sends to the buyer. An example of such an invoice is shown in Exhibit 1.

Exhibit 1
Invoice

Wallace 3800 Mission Street
Electronics San Francisco,CA 94110-1732
Supply

Made in USA.

SOLD TO

Computer King Corporation
1000 Peachtree Street
Atlanta, GA 30309-1000

CUSTOMER'S ORDER NO. & DATE
412 Jan. 10,1996
REFER TO INVOICE NO.
106-8

DATE SHIPPED	HOW SHIPPED AND ROUTE	TERMS	INVOICE DATE
Jan.12 1996	Western Trucking Co.	2/10, n/30	Jan. 12,1996
FROM	**F.O.B.**	**PREPAID OR COLLECT?**	
San Francisco	Atlanta	Prepaid	
QUANTITY	**DESCRIPTION**	**UNIT PRICE**	**AMOUNT**
20	392E Monitors	75.00	1,500.00

The terms agreed on by the buyer and the seller as to when payments for merchandise are to be made are called the **credit terms**. If payment is required on delivery, the terms are said to be *cash* or *net cash*. Otherwise, the buyer is allowed an amount of time, known as the **credit period**, in which to pay.

The credit period usually begins with the date of the sale as shown on the invoice. If payment is due within a stated number of days after the date of the invoice, such as 30 days, the terms are said to be *net 30 days*. These terms may be written as n/30.[1] If payment is due by the end of the month in which the sale was made, it may be written as *n/eom*.

As a means of encouraging payment before the end of the credit period, the seller may offer a discount to the buyer for the early payment of cash. For example, a seller may offer a buyer a 2% discount if payment is received within 10 days of the

---

[1] The word *net* as used here does not have the usual meaning of a number after deductions have been subtracted, as in *net income*.

invoice date. If the buyer does not take the discount, the total amount is due within 30 days. These terms are expressed as *2/10, n/30* and are read as *2% discount if paid within 10 days, net amount due within 30 days*. The credit terms of 2/10, n/30 are summarized in Exhibit 2.

Exhibit 2
Credit Terms

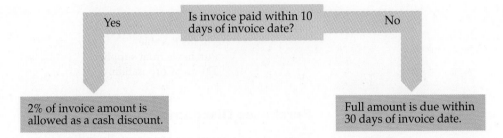

Discounts taken by the buyer for early payment of an invoice are called **purchases discounts**. These discounts are viewed as a reduction in the cost of the merchandise purchased. Most businesses design their accounting systems so that all available discounts are taken. Thus, throughout this chapter, we assume that all discounts are taken.[2]

Using Accounting

Do you pay your bills, such as utility bills and credit card bills, as soon as they are received? The terms of payment on each bill (the credit terms) may allow you to delay payment a week or more.

Most bills that you receive do not offer discounts for early payment. Rather, the bills normally indicate only a due date and a penalty for late payment. Many times, you receive these bills days or even weeks before they are due. In such cases, it is to your advantage to file the bill by its due date in a folder or other organizer, such as a desk calendar, and mail the payment a few days before it is due. In this way, you have the opportunity to earn additional interest on the balance in your checking account or savings account.

Since most buyers will take advantage of purchases discounts, buyers using perpetual inventory systems normally record merchandise purchases at their net cost. *Net cost* is the invoice price less any discounts. For example, for the invoice in Exhibit 1, the net cost is $1,470 [$1,500 – .02 ($1,500)]. The entries recorded by Computer King Corporation for this invoice in Exhibit 1 and its payment at the end of the discount period are as follows:

Jan. 11	Merchandise Inventory	1,470	
	Accounts Payable		1,470
	Invoice 106-8 from Wallace		
	Electronics Supply.		

Jan. 21	Accounts Payable	1,470	
	Cash		1,470
	Payment of Invoice 106-8 from Wallace		
	Electronics Supply.		

[2] In the next chapter, we will discuss the accounting for discounts not taken.

Purchases Returns and Allowances

When merchandise is returned (**purchases return**) or a price adjustment (**purchases allowance**) is requested, the buyer usually notifies the seller in writing. The details may be stated in a letter, or the buyer (debtor) may use a **debit memorandum** form. This form, shown in Exhibit 3, informs the seller (creditor) of the amount the buyer proposes to debit to the account payable due the seller. It also states the reasons for the return or the request for a price reduction.

Exhibit 3
Debit Memorandum

Computer King Corporation
1000 Peachtree Street, Atlanta, GA 30309-1000   No.18

DEBIT MEMORANDUM

TO   **DATE**

Power Electronics   July 7,1996
1614 LaSalle Street
Chicago, IL 60602-2391

WE DEBIT YOUR ACCOUNT AS FOLLOWS

5 No. 8241 Printer Covers, your   @ 18.00   90.00
Invoice No. 7291, are being
returned via parcel post. Our
order specified No. 825x.

The buyer may use a copy of the debit memorandum as the basis for an entry or may wait for confirmation from the seller. The seller confirms the return or allowance by issuing a **credit memorandum**. In either event, Accounts Payable must be debited, and Merchandise Inventory must be credited. To illustrate, the entry by Computer King Corporation to record the return of the merchandise indicated in the debit memo in Exhibit 3 is as follows:

July 7	Accounts Payable	90	
	Merchandise Inventory		90
	Debit Memo No. 18.		

When merchandise subject to a purchase discount is returned, the amount of the entry is for the net cost of the merchandise returned. For example, assume that on May 2, Computer King Corporation purchases $5,000 of merchandise subject to terms 2/10, n/30. On May 4, Computer King returns $3,000 of the merchandise, and on May 12, Computer King pays the original invoice, less the return. The entries to record the preceding transactions are as follows:

May 2	Merchandise Inventory	4,900	
	Accounts Payable		4,900
	($5,000 less 2% × $5,000)		
May 4	Accounts Payable	2,940	
	Merchandise Inventory		2,940
	($3,000 less 2% × $3,000)		
May 12	Accounts Payable	1,960	
	Cash		1,960
	($2,000 less 2% × $2,000)		

ACCOUNTING FOR SALES

Objective 2b
Journalize the entries for merchandise sales.

Merchandise sales are usually identified in the ledger as *Sales*. Sometimes an enterprise will use a more exact title, such as *Sales of Merchandise*.

A business may sell merchandise for cash. Cash sales are normally rung up (entered) on a cash register. At the end of the day, the sales are recorded as follows:

Jan. 3	Cash		1,800	
	Sales			1,800
	Cash sales for the day.			

Under the perpetual inventory system, the cost of merchandise sold and the reduction in merchandise inventory are also recorded on the date of sale. In this way, the merchandise inventory account will indicate the amount of merchandise that should be on hand. At the end of the period, the balance of the cost of merchandise sold account is reported on the income statement, along with the related sales for the period. To illustrate, assume that the cost of merchandise sold on January 3 was $1,200. The entry to record the cost of merchandise sold and the reduction in the merchandise inventory is as follows:

Jan. 3	Cost of Merchandise Sold		1,200	
	Merchandise Inventory			1,200
	Cost of merchandise			
	sold for the day.			

How do retailers record sales made with the use of Mastercard or VISA? Sales to customers who use bank credit cards are usually treated as cash sales. The credit card receipts (slips) for these sales are deposited by the seller directly into the bank. The credit card slips, cash, and checks received for the sales make up the total deposit.

Normally, banks charge service fees for handling credit card sales. These service fees should be debited to an expense account. An entry at the end of a month to record the payment of service charges on bank credit card sales is shown here.

Jan. 31	Bank Credit Card Expense		48	
	Cash			48
	Service charges on bank			
	credit card sales for			
	the month.			

Sales may also be made by accepting a customer's nonbank credit card (such as American Express). These sales must be reported directly to the card company before cash is received. Therefore, such sales create a receivable with the card company. Before the card company pays cash, it normally deducts a service fee. For example, assume that nonbank credit card sales of $1,000 are made and reported to the card company on January 20. The cost of the merchandise sold was $550. On January 27, the card company deducts a service fee of $50 and sends $950 to the seller. These transactions are recorded by the seller as follows:

Jan. 20	Accounts Receivable	1,000	
	Sales		1,000
	American Express		
	credit card sales.		
20	Cost of Merchandise Sold	550	
	Merchandise Inventory		550
27	Cash	950	
	Nonbank Credit Card Expense	50	
	Accounts Receivable		1,000
	Receipt of cash from		
	American Express for		
	sales reported on		
	January 20.		

A business may sell merchandise on account. Such sales result in a debit to Accounts Receivable and a credit to Sales. An example of an entry for a sale on account of $510 follows. The cost of merchandise sold was $280.

Jan. 12	Accounts Receivable	510	
	Sales		510
	Invoice No. 7172 to		
	Sims Co.		
12	Cost of Merchandise Sold	280	
	Merchandise Inventory		280

The Battle of Credit Cards

The decade of the 1990s is shaping up as the decade in which critical battles will be fought among the major credit card companies—Discover, VISA, Mastercard, and American Express. One particular area in which battle lines are being drawn is service fees. The following excerpts from an article in *Business Week* illustrate how pressures from VISA, Mastercard, and Discover have caused American Express (AmEx) to, in some cases, lower its service fees charged to retailers.

In mid-April . . . a group of Boston restaurants . . . staged a modern-day version of the Boston Tea Party. The eateries threatened to boycott American Express Co. cards and complained that the merchant fees it collects every time a diner charges a meal were too high. AmEx responded by shaving off half a percentage point from its 3.25% fee to larger restaurants that file their charge records electronically.

Three weeks later . . . U-Haul's chief financial officer . . . fired off a letter to [American Express] . . . demanding a similar reduction. Why should U-Haul, which rang up $88 million a year in AmEx charges, pay a higher fee than restaurants with only $10 million a year in AmEx charges? If U-Haul got the same break, it would save about half a million a year in fees. . . .

. . . Like most merchants, U-Haul pays about one percentage point more if a customer uses an AmEx card rather than a VISA, Discover, or MasterCard. U-Haul is . . . talking to other card issuers about whether more patronage from their cardholders would make up for the loss of AmEx's. Says [a] U-Haul treasury analyst, "Will we lose business if we don't take the card? It's a guessing game."

. . . Whatever the impact on American Express of the merchant uprising, there is no question that AmEx is suffering from white-hot competition in the credit-card business. . . . AmEx's overall strategy is to stress to merchants its upscale cardholders, who charge an average of $3,409 a year vs. VISA's $1,122 per card. . . .

Source: Lea Nathans Sprio, Geoffrey Smith, and Maria Shao, "AmEx Fights to Discourage Defectors," *Business Week* (July 1, 1991), pp. 56–58.

Sales Discounts

As we mentioned in our discussion of purchase transactions, a seller may offer the buyer credit terms that include a discount for early payment, such as 2/10, n/30. Such discounts are referred to by the seller as sales discounts. When a buyer takes advantage of such a discount by paying within the discount period, the seller debits the sales discounts account. For example, if cash is received within the discount period (10 days) from the credit sale of $1,500, shown on the invoice in Exhibit 1, the transaction would be recorded by Wallace Electronics Supply, as follows:

Jan. 22	Cash	1,470	
	Sales Discounts	30	
	Accounts Receivable		1,500
	Collection on Invoice		
	No. 106-8 to Computer King		
	Corporation, less discount.		

Sales discounts are considered to be a reduction in the amount initially recorded in Sales. In this sense, the balance of the sales discounts account is viewed as a contra (or offsetting) account to Sales.

Sales Returns and Allowances

Merchandise sold may be returned by the buyer (**sales return**). In addition, the buyer may be allowed a reduction from the initial price at which the goods were sold because of defects or for other reasons (**sales allowance**). If the return or allowance is for a sale on account, the seller usually issues the buyer a **credit memorandum**. This memorandum shows the amount and the reason for which the buyer's account receivable is to be credited. A credit memorandum is illustrated in Exhibit 4.

Exhibit 4
Credit Memorandum

Computer King Corporation   No.32
1000 Peachtree Street, Atlanta, GA 30309-1000

CREDIT MEMORANDUM

TO   **DATE**

Berry Company   January 13,1996
7608 Melton Avenue
Los Angeles, CA 90025-3942

WE CREDIT YOUR ACCOUNT AS FOLLOWS

1 Model 393F Printer   225.00

The effect of a sales return or allowance is to reduce sales revenue and cash or accounts receivable. To reduce sales, the sales account could be debited. However, the balance of the sales account would then represent net sales for the period. Because of the loss in revenue and the related expense that may result from returns and allowances, management closely monitors the amount of returns and allowances. If it becomes too large, management may take appropriate action to reduce returns and allowances. For this reason, sales returns and allowances are recorded in a separate account entitled *Sales Returns and Al-*

lowances. Because sales returns and allowances reduce the amount initially recorded in Sales, the sales returns and allowances account is a contra (or offsetting) account to Sales.

Sales Returns and Allowances is debited for the amount of the return or allowance. If the original sale is on account, Accounts Receivable is credited. Since the merchandise inventory is kept up to date in a perpetual system, the cost of the merchandise returned is added to the merchandise inventory account. The cost of merchandise returned must also be credited to the cost of merchandise sold account since this account was debited when the original sale was recorded.

To illustrate, assume that the cost of the merchandise returned in Exhibit 4 was $140. The credit memo in Exhibit 4 would be recorded by Computer King Corporation, as follows:

Jan. 13	Sales Returns and Allowances	225	
	Accounts Receivable		225
	Credit Memo No. 32.		
13	Merchandise Inventory	140	
	Cost of Merchandise Sold		140
	Cost of merchandise returned, Credit Memo No. 32.		

What if the buyer pays for the merchandise and the merchandise is later returned? In this case, a credit may be issued and applied against other accounts receivable owed by the buyer, or a cash refund may be issued. If the credit is to be applied against the buyer's other receivables, entries similar to the preceding are recorded. If a cash refund is made for merchandise returned or for an allowance, Sales Returns and Allowances is debited, and Cash is credited.

Sales Taxes

Almost all states and many other taxing units levy a tax on sales of merchandise.[3] The liability for the sales tax is incurred at the time the sale is made.

At the time of a cash sale, the seller collects the sales tax. When a sale is made on account, the tax is charged to the buyer by debiting Accounts Receivable. The seller credits the sales account for only the amount of the sale and credits the tax to Sales Tax Payable. For example, a sale of $100 on account, subject to a tax of 6%, is recorded by the following entry:

Aug. 12	Accounts Receivable	106	
	Sales		100
	Sales Tax Payable		6
	Invoice No. 339.		

The amount of the sales tax that has been collected is normally paid to the taxing unit on a regular basis. An entry to record such a payment is as follows:

| Sep. 15 | Sales Tax Payable | 2,900 | |
| | Cash | | 2,900 |

---

[3] Enterprises that purchase merchandise for resale to others are normally exempt from paying sales taxes on their purchases. Only *final* buyers of merchandise normally pay sales taxes.

Trade Discounts

Many wholesalers of merchandise publish periodic catalogs that are used by buyers in ordering merchandise. Rather than updating their catalogs frequently, wholesalers publish price updates, which may involve large discounts from the list prices in their catalogs. In addition, sellers frequently offer certain classes of buyers, such as government agencies or buyers who order large quantities, special discounts called **trade discounts**.

Sellers and buyers do not normally record the list prices of merchandise and the related trade discounts in their accounts. For example, assume that a seller offers for sale an item with a list price of $1,000 and a 40% trade discount. The seller records the sale of the item at $600 [$1,000 less the trade discount of $400 ($1,000 x 40%)]. Likewise, the buyer records the purchase at $600. For accounting purposes, only the final price—$600 in this example—is important.

TRANSPORTATION COSTS

Objective 2c
Journalize the entries for merchandise transportation costs.

The terms of a sales agreement between a buyer and a seller should indicate when the ownership (title) of the merchandise passes to the buyer. The point at which the title of the merchandise passes to the buyer determines which party, the buyer or the seller, must pay the transportation costs.[4]

The ownership of the merchandise may pass to the buyer when the seller delivers the merchandise to the transportation company or freight carrier. In this case, the terms are said to be **FOB shipping point**. This shipping term means that the seller delivers the merchandise *free on board* to the shipping point. The buyer pays the transportation costs to the final destination.

The ownership of the merchandise may pass to the buyer when the merchandise is received by the buyer. In this case, the terms are said to be **FOB destination**. This shipping term means that the seller delivers the merchandise *free on board* to the buyer's final destination. The seller pays the transportation costs to the final destination.

Sometimes FOB shipping point and FOB destination are expressed in terms of the location at which the title to the merchandise passes to the buyer. For example, assume that a seller located in Philadelphia ships merchandise to a buyer located in Chicago. In this case, the terms FOB shipping point could be expressed as *FOB Philadelphia*. Likewise, the terms FOB destination could be expressed as *FOB Chicago*.

Shipping terms, the passage of title, and whether the buyer or seller is to pay the transportation costs are summarized as follows:

	FOB Shipping Point	FOB Destination
Ownership (title) passes to buyer when merchandise is	delivered to freight carrier	delivered to buyer
Transportation costs are paid by	buyer	seller

When merchandise is purchased on terms of FOB shipping point, the transportation costs are paid by the buyer. Such costs are part of the total cost of acquiring inventory and should be added to the cost of the inventory by debiting the merchandise inventory account.

When the terms of shipment are FOB destination, the amounts paid by the seller for delivery are debited to Transportation Out, Delivery Expense, or a similarly titled account. The total of such costs incurred during a period is reported on the seller's income statement as an expense.

---

[4] The passage of title also determines whether the buyer or seller must pay other costs, such as the cost of insurance while the merchandise is in transit.

As a convenience or courtesy to the buyer, the seller may prepay the transportation costs even though the terms are FOB shipping point. The seller will then add the transportation costs to the invoice. The buyer will debit Merchandise Inventory for the total amount of the invoice, including transportation costs.

To illustrate, assume that on June 10, Computer King Corporation sells merchandise to Reeve Company on account, $900, terms FOB shipping point, n/30. Computer King Corporation pays the transportation costs of $50 and adds them to the invoice. The cost of the merchandise sold is $480. The entries by Computer King Corporation (the seller) are shown here.

June 10	Accounts Receivable	900	
	Sales		900
10	Accounts Receivable	50	
	Cash		50
10	Cost of Merchandise Sold	480	
	Merchandise Inventory		480

The entry by Reeve Company (the buyer) on receipt of the invoice is as follows:

| June 10 | Merchandise Inventory | 950 | |
| | Accounts Payable | | 950 |

Transportation costs are not subject to sales or purchase discounts. Thus, if the terms had been 2/10, n/30 in the preceding illustration, the cost of the merchandise to Reeve Company would have been $932, computed as follows:

Invoice from Computer King Corporation, including prepaid transportation of $50		$950
Amount subject to discount	$900	
Rate of discount	2%	
Amount of purchases discount		18
Amount of payment		$932

ILLUSTRATION OF ACCOUNTING FOR MERCHANDISE TRANSACTIONS

Objective 3
Journalize the entries for merchandise transactions from both the buyer's and the seller's point of view.

Each merchandising transaction, as described in the preceding paragraphs, affects a buyer and a seller. The following illustration summarizes the principles and concepts of accounting for merchandising transactions by presenting the entries that the seller and the buyer would record. In this example, the seller is Scully Company, and the buyer is Burton Co.

	Scully Company (Seller)			*Burton Co. (Buyer)*		
July 1. Scully Company sold merchandise on account to Burton Co., $5,000, terms FOB destination, n/30. The cost of the merchandise sold was $3,500.	Accounts Receivable	5,000		Merchandise Inventory	5,000	
	Sales		5,000	Accounts Payable		5,000
	Cost of Merchandise Sold	3,500				
	Merchandise Inventory		3,500			

	Scully Company (Seller)		Burton Co. (Buyer)	
July 3. Scully Company paid transportation costs of $250 for delivery of merchandise sold to Burton Co. on July 1.	Transportation Out *(Exp %)* 250 Cash	250	No entry. *not his exp.*	

July 9. Scully Company issued Burton Co. a credit memorandum for merchandise returned, $1,000. The merchandise had been purchased by Burton Co. on account on July 1. The cost of the merchandise returned was $700.	Sales Returns & Allowances 1,000 *— to debit sales — offset of sales*
	   Accounts Receivable
	
	Merchandise Inventory *put back* 700
	   Cost of Merchandise Sold *take out*
		1,000
		
		700
			Accounts Payable *(L−)* 1,000
			   Merchandise Inventory *(A−)*
				1,000

July 11. Scully Company received payment from Burton Co. for purchase of July 1.	Cash *(A+)* 4,000
	   Accounts Receivable *(A−)*
		4,000	Accounts Payable 4,000
			   Cash
				4,000

July 13. Scully Company sold merchandise on account to Burton Co., $12,000, terms FOB shipping point, 2/10, n/eom. Scully Company prepaid transportation costs of $500, which were added to the invoice. The cost of the merchandise sold was $7,200.	Accounts Receivable 12,000
	   Sales
	
	Accounts Receivable 500
	   Cash
	
	Cost of Merchandise Sold 7,200
	   Merchandise Inventory
		12,000
		
		500
		
		7,200
			Merchandise Inventory 12,260
			   Accounts Payable
			   [$12,000 − (2% × $12,000) + $500]
				12,260

July 28. Scully Company received payment from Burton Co. for purchase of July 13, less discount.	Cash 12,260
	Sales Discounts 240
	   Accounts Receivable
		12,500	Accounts Payable 12,260
			   Cash
				12,260

July 30. Scully Company sold merchandise on account to Burton Co., $7,500, terms FOB shipping point, n/45. The cost of the merchandise sold was $4,500.	Accounts Receivable 7,500
	   Sales
	
	Cost of Merchandise Sold 4,500
	   Merchandise Inventory
		7,500
		
		4,500
			Merchandise Inventory 7,500
			   Accounts Payable
				7,500

July 31. Burton Co. paid transportation charges of $150 on July 30 purchase from Scully Company.	No entry.		*Transp. Expense* Merchandise Inventory 150 Cash	150

CHART OF ACCOUNTS FOR A MERCHANDISING ENTERPRISE

Objective 4
Prepare a chart of accounts for a merchandising enterprise.

When Computer King Corporation opened a merchandising outlet selling microcomputers and software on January 1, 1995, it stopped providing consulting services. As a result of this change in the type of its transactions, Computer King Corporation's chart of accounts changed. A new chart of accounts for Computer King Corporation is shown in Exhibit 5. The accounts related to merchandising transactions are shown in color.

Exhibit 5
Chart of Accounts for Computer King Corporation, Merchandising Enterprise

Balance Sheet Accounts	Income Statement Accounts
100 Assets	400 Revenues
110 Cash	410 Sales
111 Notes Receivable	411 Sales Returns and Allowances
112 Accounts Receivable	412 Sales Discounts
113 Interest Receivable	500 Costs and Expenses
115 Merchandise Inventory	510 Cost of Merchandise Sold
116 Office Supplies	520 Sales Salaries Expense
117 Prepaid Insurance	521 Advertising Expense
120 Land	522 Depreciation Expense—Store Equipment
123 Store Equipment	529 Miscellaneous Selling Expense
124 Accumulated Depreciation—Store Equipment	530 Office Salaries Expense
125 Office Equipment	531 Rent Expense
126 Accumulated Depreciation—Office Equipment	532 Depreciation Expense—Office Equipment
200 Liabilities	533 Insurance Expense
210 Accounts Payable	534 Office Supplies Expense
211 Salaries Payable	539 Misc. Administrative Expense
212 Unearned Rent	600 Other Income
215 Notes Payable	610 Rent Income
300 Stockholders' Equity	611 Interest Income
310 Capital Stock	700 Other Expense
311 Retained Earnings	710 Interest Expense
312 Dividends	
313 Income Summary	

Computer King Corporation is now using three-digit account numbers, which are assigned in a manner that permits the addition of new accounts as they are needed. The first digit indicates the major financial statement classification (1 for assets, 2 for liabilities, and so on). The second digit indicates the subclassification (11 for current assets, 21 for current liabilities, and so on). The third digit identifies the specific account (110 for Cash, 210 for Accounts Payable, and so on).

Computer King Corporation is using a more complex numbering system because it has a greater variety of transactions. As enterprises grow, the types of transactions and the complexities of transactions usually increase. For example, a rapidly growing enterprise may borrow funds to expand its operations by issuing notes payable. The enterprise may also accept notes receivable from major customers for sales of merchandise. Interest expense may be incurred on the notes payable, and interest income may be earned on the notes receivable. Thus, such transactions would require the inclusion of Notes Receivable, Notes Payable, Interest Income, and Interest Expense in the chart of accounts.

The growth of an enterprise also creates a need for more detailed information for use in managing the enterprise. For example, a wages expense account may be adequate for managing a small service enterprise with one or two employees. However, a merchandising enterprise normally uses two or more payroll accounts, such as Sales Salaries Expense and Office Salaries Expense. Moreover, the chart of accounts for a merchandising enterprise normally classifies expenses as selling or administrative expenses.

WORK SHEET FOR MERCHANDISING ENTERPRISES

Objective 5
Prepare a work sheet for a merchandising enterprise.

At the end of the accounting period, a work sheet may be used to assist in the preparation of adjusting entries, closing entries, and financial statements. Exhibit 6 illustrates a work sheet for a merchandising enterprise. In this work sheet, the trial balance differs slightly from trial balances presented earlier. All the accounts, including accounts that have no balances, are listed in the order that they appear in the ledger.

The work sheet in Exhibit 6 for Computer King Corporation is for the year ended December 31, 1996. As we mentioned, Computer King Corporation opened a retail store in January 1995. The account balances in Exhibit 6 reflect Computer King Corporation's second year of operations as a merchandising enterprise.

Exhibit 6
Work Sheet for Merchandising Enterprise

Computer King Corporation
Work Sheet
For Year Ended December 31, 1996

Account Title	Trial Balance Dr.	Cr.	Adjustments Dr.	Cr.	Adjusted Trial Balance Dr.	Cr.	Income Statement Dr.	Cr.	Balance Sheet Dr.	Cr.
Cash	52,950				52,950				52,950	
Notes Receivable	40,000				40,000				40,000	
Accounts Receivable	60,880				60,880				60,880	
Interest Receivable			(a) 200		200				200	
Merchandise Inventory	63,950			(b) 1,800	62,150				62,150	
Office Supplies	1,090			(c) 610	480				480	
Prepaid Insurance	4,560			(d) 1,910	2,650				2,650	
Land	10,000				10,000				10,000	
Store Equipment	27,100				27,100				27,100	
Accum. Depr.—Store Equip.		2,600		(e) 3,100		5,700				5,700
Office Equipment	15,570				15,570				15,570	
Accum. Depr.—Office Equip.		2,230		(f) 2,490		4,720				4,720
Accounts Payable		22,420				22,420				22,420
Salaries Payable				(g) 1,140		1,140				1,140
Unearned Rent		2,400	(h) 600			1,800				1,800
Notes Payable (final payment, 2000)		25,000				25,000				25,000
Capital Stock		15,000				15,000				15,000
Retained Earnings		138,800				138,800				138,800
Dividends	18,000				18,000				18,000	
Sales		720,185				720,185		720,185		
Sales Returns and Allowances	6,140				6,140		6,140			
Sales Discounts	5,790				5,790		5,790			
Cost of Merchandise Sold	523,505		(b) 1,800		525,305		525,305			
Sales Salaries Expense	59,250		(g) 780		60,030		60,030			
Advertising Expense	10,860				10,860		10,860			
Depr. Exp.—Store Equip.			(e) 3,100		3,100		3,100			
Miscellaneous Selling Expense	630				630		630			
Office Salaries Expense	20,660		(g) 360		21,020		21,020			
Rent Expense	8,100				8,100		8,100			
Depr. Exp.—Office Equip.			(f) 2,490		2,490		2,490			
Insurance Expense			(d) 1,910		1,910		1,910			
Office Supplies Expense			(c) 610		610		610			
Misc. Administrative Expense	760				760		760			
Rent Income				(h) 600		600		600		
Interest Income		3,600		(a) 200		3,800		3,800		
Interest Expense	2,440				2,440		2,440			
	932,235	932,235	11,850	11,850	939,165	939,165	649,185	724,585	289,980	214,580
Net Income							75,400			75,400
							724,585	724,585	289,980	289,980

(a) Interest earned but not received on notes receivable, $200.
(b) Merchandise inventory shrinkage for period, $1,800.
(c) Office supplies used, $610 ($1,090 − $480).
(d) Insurance expired, $1,910.
(e) Depreciation of store equipment, $3,100.
(f) Depreciation of office equipment, $2,490.
(g) Salaries accrued but not paid
    (sales salaries, $780; office salaries, $360), $1,140.
(h) Rent earned from amount received in advance, $600.

The data needed for adjusting the accounts of Computer King Corporation are as follows:

Interest accrued on notes receivable on December 31, 1996		$ 200
Physical merchandise inventory on December 31, 1996		62,150
Office supplies on hand on December 31, 1996		480
Insurance expired during 1996		1,910
Depreciation during 1996 on: Store equipment		3,100
Office equipment		2,490
Salaries accrued on December 31, 1996: Sales salaries	$780	
Office salaries	360	1,140
Rent income earned during 1996		600

There is no specific order in which to analyze the accounts in the work sheet, assemble the adjustment data, and make the adjusting entries. However, you can normally save time by selecting the accounts in the order in which they appear on the trial balance. Using this approach, the adjustment for accrued interest is listed first (entry (a) on the work sheet), followed by the adjustment for merchandise inventory shrinkage (entry (b) on the work sheet), and so on. Except for the merchandise inventory shrinkage, we have previously discussed all the adjustments on the work sheet. In the following paragraphs, we discuss the nature of the merchandise inventory shrinkage adjustment and the completion of the work sheet.

Merchandise Inventory Shrinkage

What is merchandise inventory shrinkage? Under the perpetual inventory system, a separate merchandise inventory account is maintained in the ledger. Throughout the accounting period, this account shows the amount of merchandise that should be on hand at any time. However, merchandise enterprises may experience some loss of inventory due to shoplifting, employee theft, or errors in recording or counting inventory. As a result, the physical inventory taken at the end of the accounting period may differ from the amount of inventory shown in the inventory records. Normally, the amount of merchandise that should be on hand as indicated by the balance of the merchandise inventory account is larger than the total amount of merchandise counted during the physical inventory. For this reason, the difference is often called **inventory shrinkage** or **inventory shortage**.

To illustrate, Computer King Corporation's inventory records indicate that $63,950 of merchandise should be on hand on December 31, 1996. The physical inventory taken on December 31, 1996, however, indicates that only $62,150 of merchandise is actually on hand. Thus, the inventory shrinkage for the year ending December 31, 1996, is $1,800 ($63,950–$62,150). This amount is recorded by the following adjusting entry:

Dec. 31	Cost of Merchandise Sold	1,800	
	Merchandise Inventory		1,800

After this entry has been recorded and posted, the accounting records agree with the actual physical inventory at the end of the period. Since no system of procedures and safeguards can totally eliminate it, inventory shrinkage is often considered a normal cost of operations. If the amount of the shrinkage is abnormally large, it may be disclosed separately on the income statement. In such cases, the shrinkage may be recorded in a separate account, such as Loss From Merchandise Inventory Shrinkage.

Completing the Work Sheet

After all the necessary adjustments have been entered on the work sheet, the Adjustments columns are totaled to prove the equality of debits and credits. As we illustrated in previous chapters, the balances of the accounts in the Trial Balance columns and the amount of any adjustments are extended to the Adjusted Trial Balance columns.[5] The Adjusted Trial Balance columns are then totaled to prove the equality of debits and credits.

The process of extending the balances, as adjusted, to the statement columns usually begins with Cash and moves down the work sheet, item by item. After all the items have been extended to the statement columns, the four columns are totaled, and the net income or net loss is determined. For Computer King Corporation, the difference between the credit and the debit columns of the Income Statement section is $75,400, the amount of the net income. The difference between the debit and the credit columns of the Balance Sheet section is also $75,400, which is the increase in stockholders' equity (retained earnings) as a result of the net income. Agreement between the two balancing amounts is evidence of debit–credit equality and mathematical accuracy.

FINANCIAL STATEMENTS FOR MERCHANDISING ENTERPRISES

Objective 6
Prepare an income statement, a retained earnings statement, and a balance sheet for a merchandising enterprise.

The basic financial statements for a merchandising enterprise are similar to those for a service enterprise. As we discussed earlier, the income statements differ in the reporting of revenue (sales), cost of merchandise sold, and gross profit. The balance sheets are similar, except that merchandise inventory is included as a current asset on the balance sheet of a merchandising enterprise. The retained earnings statement and the statement of cash flows do not differ significantly for service and merchandising enterprises.

In the following paragraphs, we describe and illustrate the income statement, balance sheet, and retained earnings statement for Computer King Corporation merchandising enterprise. These statements are prepared from the work sheet in Exhibit 6.

Income Statement

There are two widely used forms for the income statement: multiple step and single step. The 1992 edition of *Accounting Trends & Techniques* reported that 64% of the 600 industrial and merchandising companies surveyed use the multiple-step form, whereas 36% use the single-step form.

MULTIPLE-STEP FORM. The **multiple-step income statement** contains several sections, subsections, and subtotals. The amount of detail presented in these sections varies from company to company. For example, instead of reporting gross sales, sales returns and allowances, and sales discounts, some companies just report net sales.

The multiple-step income statement for Computer King Corporation is presented in Exhibit 7. We discuss the various sections of this income statement in the following paragraphs.

Revenue from Sales. The total amount charged customers for merchandise sold, for cash and on account, is reported in this section. Sales returns and allowances and sales discounts are deducted from this total to yield net sales.

Cost of Merchandise Sold. The cost of merchandise sold during the period may also be called the **cost of goods sold** or the **cost of sales**.

Gross Profit. The excess of net sales over cost of merchandise sold is called **gross profit**. It is sometimes called **gross profit on sales** or **gross margin**.

Operating Expenses. Most merchandising enterprises classify operating expenses as either selling expenses or administrative expenses. However, depending on the decision-making needs of managers and other users of the financial statements, other classifications could be used.

---

[5] Some accountants prefer to eliminate the Adjusted Trial Balance columns and to extend the adjusted balances directly to the statement columns. Such a work sheet is often used if there are only a few adjustment items.

Exhibit 7
Multiple-Step Income Statement

Computer King Corporation
Income Statement
For Year Ended December 31, 1996

Revenue from sales:

Sales *(Revenue)*   *Gross sales* $720,185

Less: Sales returns and allowances *Debit*		$ 6,140	
Sales discounts *o/e −*		5,790	11,930
Net Sales			$708,255
Cost of merchandise sold			525,305
Gross profit			$182,950

Operating expenses:

Selling expenses:

Sales salaries expense	$ 60,030		
Advertising expense	10,860		
Depreciation expense—store equipment	3,100		
Miscellaneous selling expense	630		
Total selling expenses		$ 74,620	

Administrative expenses:

Office salaries expense	$ 21,020		
Rent expense	8,100		
Depreciation expense—office equipment	2,490		
Insurance expense	1,910		
Office supplies expense	610		
Miscellaneous administrative expense	760		
Total administrative expenses		34,890	
Total operating expenses			109,510
Income from operations			$ 73,440

Other income:

Interest income	$ 3,800		
Rent income	600		
Total other income		$ 4,400	
Other expense:			
Interest expense		2,440	1,960
Net income			$ 75,400

Expenses that are incurred directly in the selling of merchandise are **selling expenses**. They include such expenses as salespersons' salaries, store supplies used, depreciation of store equipment, and advertising.

Expenses incurred in the administration or general operations of the business are **administrative expenses** or **general expenses**. Examples of these expenses are office salaries, depreciation of office equipment, and office supplies used.

Expenses that are related to both administrative and selling functions may be divided between the two classifications. In small businesses, however, such expenses as rent, insurance, and taxes are commonly reported as administrative expenses. Transactions for small, infrequent expenses are often reported as Miscellaneous Selling Expense or Miscellaneous Administrative Expense.

Income from Operations. The excess of gross profit over total operating expenses is called **income from operations** or **operating income**. The relationships of income from operations to total assets and to net sales are important factors in judging the efficiency and profitability of operations. If operating expenses are greater than the gross profit, the excess is called a **loss from operations**.

Other Income and Other Expense. Revenue from sources other than the primary operating activity of a business is classified as **other income** or **nonoperating income**. In a merchandising enterprise, these items include income from interest, rent, dividends, and gains resulting from the sale of plant assets.

Expenses that cannot be traced directly to operations are identified as **other expense** or **nonoperating expense**. Interest expense that results from financing activities and losses incurred in the disposal of plant assets are examples of these items.

Other income and other expense are offset against each other on the income statement. If the total of other income exceeds the total of other expense, the difference is added to income from operations. If the reverse is true, the difference is subtracted from income from operations.

Net Income. The final figure on the income statement is called **net income** (or **net loss**). It is the net increase (or net decrease) in the owner's equity as a result of the period's profit-making activities.

SINGLE-STEP FORM. In the single-step income statement, the total of all expenses is deducted *in one step* from the total of all revenues. Such a statement is shown in Exhibit 8 for Computer King Corporation. The statement has been condensed to focus attention on its primary features. Such condensing is not essential for the single-step form.

Exhibit 8
Single-Step Income Statement

Computer King Corporation Income Statement For Year Ended December 31, 1996		
Revenues:		
Net sales		$708,255
Interest income		3,800
Rent income		600
Total revenues		$712,655
Expenses:		
Cost of merchandise sold	$525,305	
Selling expenses	74,620	
Administrative expenses	34,890	
Interest expense	2,440	
Total expenses		637,255
Net income		$ 75,400

The single-step form has the advantage of emphasizing total revenues and total expenses as the factors that determine net income. A criticism of the single-step form is that such amounts as gross profit and income from operations are not readily available for analysis.

Retained Earnings Statement

The retained earnings statement shows the changes in retained earnings during the period resulting from net income (or net loss) and dividends. The retained earnings statement for Computer King Corporation is shown in Exhibit 9.

Exhibit 9
Retained Earnings Statement

Computer King Corporation Retained Earnings Statement For Year Ended December 31, 1996		
Retained earnings, January 1, 1996		$138,800
Net income for year	$75,400	
Less dividends	18,000	
Increase in retained earnings		57,400
Retained earnings, December 31, 1996		$196,200

Balance Sheet

As we discussed and illustrated in previous chapters, the balance sheet may be presented with Assets on the left-hand side and the Liabilities and Stockholders' Equity on the right-hand side. This form of the balance sheet is called the **account form**. The balance sheet may also be presented in a downward sequence in three sections. The total of the Assets section equals the combined total of the Liabilities and Stockholders' Equity sections. This form of balance sheet is called the **report form**. The report form of balance sheet for Computer King Corporation is shown in Exhibit 10. In this balance sheet, note that merchandise inventory at the end of the period is reported as a current asset, and the current portion of the note payable is $5,000.

Exhibit 10
Report Form of Balance Sheet

[Handwritten margin notes: Unearned rent — current; wages — current; security deposit on building — Returned; "could be turned in cash or used in 1 year"]

Computer King Corporation			
Balance Sheet			
December 31, 1996			
Assets			
Current assets:			
Cash		$ 52,950	
Notes receivable		40,000	
Accounts receivable		60,880	
Interest receivable		200	
Merchandise inventory		62,150	
Office supplies		480	
Prepaid insurance		2,650	
Total current assets			$219,310
Plant assets:			
Land		$ 10,000	
Store equipment	$27,100		
Less accumulated depreciation	5,700	21,400	
Office equipment	$15,570		
Less accumulated depreciation	4,720	10,850	
Total plant assets			42,250
Total assets			$261,560
Liabilities			
Current liabilities:			
Accounts payable		$ 22,420	
Note payable (current portion)		5,000	
Salaries payable		1,140	
Unearned rent		1,800	
Total current liabilities			$ 30,360
Long-term liabilities:			
Note payable (final payment, 2000)			20,000
Total liabilities			$ 50,360
Stockholders' Equity			
Capital stock		$ 15,000	
Retained earnings		196,200	
Total stockholders' equity			211,200
Total liabilities and stockholders' equity			$261,560

We've Only Just Begun

It is important for the management of a retailer to look beyond the financial statements to the intangibles of sound operating philosophies. One company that has been highly successful in doing this is Wal-Mart. The following excerpts from an article in *Retail Control* describe some of the reasons for Wal-Mart's success.

. . . *Relentless innovation and remorseless boosterism delivered $21 billion of new market value to Wal-Mart's shareholders over the past five years.* . . .

. . . *[There] hasn't been much growth in discount retailing during the [recent] past . . . [but] Wal-Mart's earnings have grown at an average rate of 31 percent annually for the past five years.* . . .

. . . *[Wal-Mart] is fueled by values like self-respect, initiative, and belonging. Wal-Mart employees, called associates, "are constantly being challenged by one another and forced to laugh at themselves"* . . . *"They take pride in the fact that they are working to create perhaps the finest company in the world and their individual contributions are recognized."*

. . . *To fuel competition among department managers, Wal-Mart tracks each department's sales as a percentage of total sales for each store. . . . At this year's annual meeting, department managers who ranked No. 1 by this measure were honored.* . . .

. . . *"Wal-Mart is making a contribution . . . of a magnitude previously not dreamt of in business." And, says the company motto, "We've only just begun."*

Source: Gregory J. Millman, "These Companies Add Value for Shareholders," *Retail Control* (November 1991), pp. 16–18.

ADJUSTING ENTRIES

Objective 7
Journalize the adjusting entries for a merchandising enterprise.

During the process of preparing the work sheet, we completed the analyses required to make the adjustments. Thus we do not need to refer to the basic data when we journalize the adjusting entries. After we have posted these entries, the balances of all asset, liability, revenue, and expense accounts equal the amounts reported in the financial statements. The adjusting entries for Computer King Corporation are as follows:

	DATE		DESCRIPTION	POST. REF.	DEBIT	CREDIT	
1			Adjusting Entries				1
2	1996 Dec.	31	Interest Receivable	113	2 0 0 00		2
3			Interest Income	611		2 0 0 00	3
4							4
5		31	Cost of Merch. Sold	510	1 8 0 0 00		5
6			Merchandise Inv.	115		1 8 0 0 00	6
7							7
8		31	Office Supplies Expense	534	6 1 0 00		8
9			Office Supplies	116		6 1 0 00	9
10							10
11		31	Insurance Expense	533	1 9 1 0 00		11
12			Prepaid Insurance	117		1 9 1 0 00	12
13							13
14		31	Depreciation Expense—				14
15			Store Equip.	522	3 1 0 0 00		15
16			Accumulated Depr.—				16
17			Store Equip.	124		3 1 0 0 00	17
18							18
19		31	Depreciation Expense—				19
20			Office Equip.	532	2 4 9 0 00		20
21			Accumulated Depr.—				21
22			Office Equip.	126		2 4 9 0 00	22
23							23
24		31	Sales Salaries Expense	520	7 8 0 00		24
25			Office Salaries Expense	530	3 6 0 00		25
26			Salaries Payable	211		1 1 4 0 00	26
27							27
28		31	Unearned Rent	212	6 0 0 00		28
29			Rent Income	610		6 0 0 00	29

JOURNAL   Page 28

CLOSING ENTRIES

Objective 8
Journalize the closing entries for a merchandising enterprise.

The closing entries are recorded in the journal immediately following the adjusting entries.[6] The closing entries for Computer King Corporation are as follows:

[6] Computerized accounting systems may be designed so that, when properly authorized, closing entries are automatically prepared and posted.

			JOURNAL			Page 29

	DATE		DESCRIPTION	POST. REF.	DEBIT	CREDIT	
1			Closing Entries				1
2	1996 Dec.	31	Sales	410	720 185 00		2
3			Rent Income	610	6 00 00		3
4			Interest Income	611	3 800 00		4
5			Income Summary	313		724 585 00	5
6							6
7		31	Income Summary	313	649 185 00		7
8			Sales Returns and Allowances	411		6 140 00	8
9			Sales Discounts	412		5 790 00	9
10			Cost of Merchandise Sold	510		525 305 00	10
11			Sales Salaries Expense	520		60 030 00	11
12			Advertising Expense	521		10 860 00	12
13			Depr. Expense—Store Equip.	522		3 100 00	13
14			Miscellaneous Selling Expense	529		6 30 00	14
15			Office Salaries Expense	530		21 020 00	15
16			Rent Expense	531		8 100 00	16
17			Depr. Expense—Office Equip.	532		2 490 00	17
18			Insurance Expense	533		1 910 00	18
19			Office Supplies Expense	534		6 10 00	19
20			Misc. Administrative Exp.	539		7 60 00	20
21			Interest Expense	710		2 440 00	21
22							22
23		31	Income Summary	313	75 400 00		23
24			Retained Earnings	311		75 400 00	24
25							25
26		31	Retained Earnings	311	18 000 00		26
27			Dividends	312		18 000 00	27

As we discussed in previous chapters, the effect of the closing entries is to clear all the temporary owner's equity accounts of their balances, reducing them to zero. The first entry closes all income statement accounts with *credit* balances by transferring the total to the credit side of Income Summary. The second entry closes all income statement accounts with *debit* balances by transferring the total to the debit side of Income Summary. For a merchandising enterprise, the income statement accounts with credit balances include the sales account and the other revenue accounts. The income statement accounts with debit balances include the cost of merchandise sold account and the contra sales accounts.

The balance of Income Summary, after the first two closing entries have been posted, is the net income or net loss for the period. The third closing entry transfers this balance to Retained Earnings. The income summary account after the closing entries have been posted is as follows:

ACCOUNT *Income Summary*							ACCOUNT NO. *313*		
	DATE		ITEM	POST. REF.	DEBIT	CREDIT	BALANCE		
							DEBIT	CREDIT	
	1996 Dec.	31	Revenue, etc.	29		724 585 00		724 585 00	
		31	Expense, etc	29	649 185 00			75 400 00	
		31	Net income	29	75 400 00				

The fourth closing entry transfers the balance of Dividends to Retained Earnings. Thus, the effect of closing the temporary owner's equity accounts is a net increase or a net decrease in the retained earnings account. The stockholders' equity accounts and the asset, contra asset, and liability accounts are the only accounts with balances after the closing entries have been posted. To verify the debit–credit equality of the balances of these accounts, a post-closing trial balance is normally prepared. The account balances should be the same as the amounts appearing on the balance sheet in Exhibit 10.

CHAPTER REVIEW

Key Points

Objective 1. Compare a service enterprise's income statement to a merchandising enterprise's income statement.

The primary differences between a service enterprise and a merchandising enterprise relate to the revenue activities of the enterprises. Merchandising enterprises purchase merchandise for selling to customers.

On a merchandise enterprise's income statement, revenue from selling merchandise is reported as sales. The cost of the merchandise sold is subtracted from sales to arrive at gross profit. The operating expenses are subtracted from gross profit to arrive at net income.

Merchandise inventory, which is merchandise not sold, is reported as a current asset on a merchandise enterprise's balance sheet.

Objective 2a. Journalize the entries for merchandise purchases.

Purchases of merchandise for cash or on account are recorded by debiting Merchandise Inventory. For purchases of merchandise on account, the credit terms may allow cash discounts for early payment. Such purchases discounts are viewed as a reduction in the cost of the merchandise purchased. Since most buyers will take advantage of purchases discounts, merchandise purchases are normally recorded at their net cost. Net cost is the invoice price less any discounts.

When merchandise is returned or a price adjustment is granted, the buyer records the adjustment as a credit to Merchandise Inventory.

Objective 2b. Journalize the entries for merchandise sales.

Sales of merchandise for cash or on account are recorded in the ledger as a credit to Sales. The cost of merchandise sold and the reduction in merchandise inventory are also recorded on the date of the sale.

For sales of merchandise on account, the credit terms may allow sales discounts for early payment. Such discounts are recorded by the seller as a debit to Sales Discounts. Sales discounts are reported as a deduction from the amount initially recorded in Sales. Likewise, when merchandise is returned or a price adjustment is granted, the seller records the adjustment as a debit to Sales Returns and Allowances.

The liability for sales tax is incurred at the time the sale is made and is recorded by the seller as a credit to the sales tax payable account. When the amount of the sales tax is paid to the taxing unit, Sales Tax Payable is debited, and Cash is credited.

Many wholesalers offer trade discounts, which are discounts off the list prices of merchandise. Neither the seller nor the buyer normally records the list price and the trade discount.

Objective 2c. Journalize the entries for merchandise transportation costs.

When merchandise is shipped FOB shipping point, the buyer pays the transportation costs and debits Merchandise Inventory. When merchandise is shipped FOB destination, the seller pays the transportation costs and debits Transportation Out, Delivery Expense, or a similarly titled account. If the seller pays transportation costs as a convenience to the buyer, the seller debits Accounts Receivable for the costs.

Objective 3. Journalize the entries for merchandise transactions from both the buyer's and the seller's point of view.

The illustration in this chapter summarizes the principles and concepts of accounting for merchandising transactions by presenting the entries that the seller and the buyer would record.

Objective 4. Prepare a chart of accounts for a merchandising enterprise.

The chart of accounts for a merchandising enterprise is more complex than that for a service enterprise and normally includes accounts such as Sales, Sales Discounts, Sales Returns and Allowances, and Cost of Merchandise Sold.

Objective 5. Prepare a work sheet for a merchandising enterprise.

The preparation of a work sheet for a merchandising enterprise is similar to that for a service enterprise, except for the merchandise inventory shrinkage. The normal adjusting entry is to debit Cost of Merchandise Sold and credit Merchandise Inventory for the amount of the shrinkage.

Objective 6. Prepare an income statement, a retained earnings statement, and a balance sheet for a merchandising enterprise.

The income statement for a merchandising enterprise reports sales, cost of merchandise sold, and gross profit. The balance sheet reports merchandise inventory as a current asset.

There are two widely used forms for the income statement: multiple step and single step. The multiple-step income statement contains several sections, subsections, and subtotals. In the single-step income statement, the total of all expenses is deducted from the total of all revenues.

The balance sheet may be prepared using the account form or the report form. The account form lists assets on the left-hand side and liabilities and owner's equity on the right-hand side of the statement. The report form lists assets, liabilities, and owner's equity in a downward sequence.

Objective 7. Journalize the adjusting entries for a merchandising enterprise.

The adjusting entries for a merchandising enterprise are prepared from the work sheet Adjustments columns. After the adjusting entries have been posted, the balances of all asset, liability, revenue, and expense accounts equal the amounts reported in the financial statements.

Objective 8. Journalize the closing entries for a merchandising enterprise.

The first closing entry for a merchandise enterprise closes all income statement accounts with credit balances, which includes the sales account. The second entry closes all income statement accounts with debit balances, which include the expense accounts and the contra sales accounts. The closing entries reduce the balances of all the temporary accounts to zero.

Glossary of Key Terms

Account form of balance sheet. A form of balance sheet with assets on the left-hand side and liabilities and stockholders' equity on the right-hand side. **Objective 6**

Administrative expenses. Expenses incurred in the administration or general operations of a business. **Objective 6**

Credit memorandum. The form issued by a seller to inform a buyer that a credit has been posted to the buyer's account receivable. **Objective 2b**

Debit memorandum. The form issued by a buyer to inform a seller that a debit has been posted to the seller's account payable. **Objective 2a**

FOB destination. Terms of agreement between buyer and seller whereby ownership passes when merchandise is received by the buyer, and the seller pays the transportation costs. **Objective 2c**

FOB shipping point. Terms of agreement between buyer and seller whereby ownership passes when merchandise is delivered to the freight carrier, and the buyer pays the transportation costs. **Objective 2c**

Gross profit. The excess of net sales over the cost of merchandise sold. **Objective 6**

Income from operations. The excess of gross profit over total operating expenses. **Objective 6**

Invoice. The bill provided by the seller (who refers to it as a *sales invoice*) to a buyer (who refers to it as a *purchase invoice*) for items purchased. **Objective 2a**

Merchandise inventory. Merchandise on hand and available for sale to customers. **Objective 1**

Multiple-step income statement. An income statement with several sections, subsections, and subtotals. **Objective 6**

Other expense. An expense that cannot be traced directly to operations. **Objective 6**

Other income. Revenue from sources other than the primary operating activity of a business. **Objective 6**

Periodic inventory system. A system of inventory accounting in which only the revenue from sales is recorded each time a sale is made. The cost of merchandise on hand at the end of a period is determined by a detailed listing (physical inventory) of the merchandise on hand. **Objective 2a**

Perpetual inventory system. A system of inventory accounting in which both the revenue from sales and the cost of merchandise sold are recorded each time a sale is made so that the records continually disclose the amount of the inventory on hand. **Objective 2a**

Physical inventory. The detailed listing of merchandise on hand. **Objective 2a**

Purchases discounts. An available discount taken by a buyer for early payment of an invoice. **Objective 2a**

Purchases returns and allowances. Reductions in purchases, resulting from merchandise being returned to the seller or from the seller's reduction in the original purchase price. **Objective 2a**

Report form of balance sheet. A form of balance sheet with the liabilities and owner's equity sections below the asset section. **Objective 6**

Sales discounts. An available discount granted by a seller for early payment of an invoice; a contra account to Sales. **Objective 2b**

Sales returns and allowances. Reductions in sales, resulting from merchandise being returned by customers or from the seller's reduction in the original sales price; a contra account to Sales. **Objective 2b**

Selling expenses. Expenses incurred directly in the sale of merchandise. **Objective 6**

Single-step income statement. An income statement in which the total of all expenses is deducted in one step from the total of all revenues. **Objective 6**

Trade discounts. Special discounts from published list prices offered by sellers to certain classes of buyers. **Objective 2b**

Self-Examination Questions
Answers at end of chapter.

1. If merchandise purchased on account is returned, the buyer may inform the seller of the details by issuing:
   A. a debit memorandum
   B. a credit memorandum
   C. an invoice
   D. a bill

2. If merchandise is sold on account to a customer for $1,000, terms FOB shipping point, 1/10, n/30, and the seller prepays $50 in transportation costs, the amount of the discount for early payment would be:
   A. $0
   B. $5.00
   C. $10.00
   D. $10.50

3. The income statement in which the total of all expenses is deducted from the total of all revenues is termed:
   A. multiple-step form
   B. single-step form
   C. account form
   D. report form

4. On a multiple-step income statement, the excess of net sales over the cost of merchandise sold is called:
   A. operating income
   B. income from operations
   C. gross profit
   D. net income

5. Which of the following expenses would normally be classified as Other expense on a multiple-step income statement?
   A. Depreciation expense— office equipment
   B. Sales salaries expense
   C. Insurance expense
   D. Interest expense

ILLUSTRATIVE PROBLEM

A work sheet for Hadley Corp., shown on the next page, has been completed through the Adjustments columns.

Instructions
1. Complete the work sheet for Hadley Corp.
2. Prepare a multiple-step income statement.
3. Prepare a retained earnings statement.
4. Prepare an account form of balance sheet assuming that the current portion of the note payable is $7,500.
5. Journalize the adjusting entries.
6. Journalize the closing entries.

Solution

1.

Hadley Corp.
Work Sheet
For Year Ended October 31, 1995

Account Title	Trial Balance Dr.	Trial Balance Cr.	Adjustments Dr.	Adjustments Cr.	Adjusted Trial Balance Dr.	Adjusted Trial Balance Cr.	Income Statement Dr.	Income Statement Cr.	Balance Sheet Dr.	Balance Sheet Cr.
Cash	26,400				26,400				26,400	
Accounts Receivable	62,200				62,200				62,200	
Merchandise Inventory	159,000			(a) 3,000	156,000				156,000	
Prepaid Insurance	6,800			(b) 4,300	2,500				2,500	
Store Supplies	1,250			(c) 660	590				590	
Office Supplies	800			(d) 480	320				320	
Store Equipment	65,000				65,000				65,000	
Accum. Depr.—Store Equip.		20,100		(e) 5,850		25,950				25,950
Office Equipment	19,600				19,600				19,600	
Accum. Depr.—Office Equip.		8,100		(f) 2,160		10,260				10,260
Accounts Payable		36,400				36,400				36,400
Salaries Payable				(g) 2,700		2,700				2,700
Unearned Rent		1,000	(h) 500			500				500
Note Payable (final payment, 2004)		75,000				75,000				75,000
Capital Stock		12,000				12,000				12,000
Retained Earnings		100,420				100,420				100,420
Dividends	8,000				8,000				8,000	
Sales		540,000				540,000		540,000		
Sales Returns and Allowances	4,300				4,300		4,300			
Sales Discounts	2,500				2,500		2,500			
Cost of Merchandise Sold	330,420		(a) 3,000		333,420		333,420			
Sales Salaries Expense	43,200		(g) 1,800		45,000		45,000			
Advertising Expense	15,000				15,000		15,000			
Depr. Exp.—Store Equip.			(e) 5,850		5,850		5,850			
Store Supplies Expense			(c) 660		660		660			
Miscellaneous Selling Expense	970				970		970			
Office Salaries Expense	30,000		(g) 900		30,900		30,900			
Rent Expense	8,500				8,500		8,500			
Insurance Expense			(b) 4,300		4,300		4,300			
Depr. Exp.—Office Equip.			(f) 2,160		2,160		2,160			
Office Supplies Expense			(d) 480		480		480			
Misc. Administrative Expense	830				830		830			
Rent Income				(h) 500		500		500		
Interest Expense	8,250				8,250		8,250			
	793,020	793,020	19,650	19,650	803,730	803,730	463,120	540,500	340,610	263,230
Net Income							77,380			77,380
							540,500	540,500	340,610	340,610

2.

Hadley Corp. Income Statement For Year Ended October 31, 1995			

Revenue from sales:			
Sales		$540,000	
Less: Sales returns and allowances	$ 4,300		
Sales discounts	2,500	6,800	
Net sales			$533,200
Cost of merchandise sold			333,420
Gross profit			$199,780
Operating expenses:			
Selling expenses:			
Sales salaries expense	$ 45,000		
Advertising expense	15,000		
Depreciation expense—store equipment	5,850		
Store supplies expense	660		
Miscellaneous selling expense	970		
Total selling expenses		$ 67,480	
Administrative expenses:			
Office salaries expense	$ 30,900		
Rent expense	8,500		
Insurance expense	4,300		
Depreciation expense—office equipment	2,160		
Office supplies expense	480		
Miscellaneous administrative expense	830		
Total administrative expenses		47,170	
Total operating expenses			114,650
Income from operations			$ 85,130
Other income:			
Rent income		$ 500	
Other expense:			
Interest expense		8,250	7,750
Net income			$ 77,380

3.

Hadley Corp. Retained Earnings Statement For Year Ended October 31, 1995		

Retained earnings, November 1, 1994		$100,420
Net income for the year	$77,380	
Less dividends	8,000	
Increase in retained earnings		69,380
Retained earnings, October 31, 1995		$169,800

4.

Hadley Corp.			
Balance Sheet			
October 31, 1995			

Assets

Current assets:
Cash		$ 26,400	
Accounts receivable		62,200	
Merchandise inventory		156,000	
Prepaid insurance		2,500	
Store supplies		590	
Office supplies		320	
Total current assets			$248,010

Plant assets:
Store equipment	$65,000		
Less accumulated depreciation	25,950	$ 39,050	
Office equipment	$19,600		
Less accumulated depreciation	10,260	9,340	
Total plant assets			48,390
Total assets			$296,400

Liabilities

Current liabilities:
Accounts payable	$ 36,400	
Note payable (current portion)	7,500	
Salaries payable	2,700	
Unearned rent	500	
Total current liabilities		$ 47,100

Long-term liabilities:
Note payable (final payment, 2004)		67,500
Total liabilities		$114,600

Stockholders' Equity

Capital stock	$ 12,000	
Retained earnings	169,800	181,800
Total liabilities and stockholders' equity		$296,400

5.

	DATE		DESCRIPTION	POST. REF.	DEBIT	CREDIT	
1			**Adjusting Entries**				1
2	1995 Oct.	31	Cost of Merchandise Sold		3 0 0 0 00		2
3			Merchandise Inventory			3 0 0 0 00	3
4							4
5		31	Insurance Expense		4 3 0 0 00		5
6			Prepaid Insurance			4 3 0 0 00	6
7							7
8		31	Store Supplies Expense		6 6 0 00		8
9			Store Supplies			6 6 0 00	9
10							10
11		31	Office Supplies Expense		4 8 0 00		11
12			Office Supplies			4 8 0 00	12
13							13

ILLUSTRATIVE PROBLEM ILLUSTRATIVE PROBLEM ILLUSTRATIVE PROBLEM ILLUSTRATIVE PROBLEM ILLUSTRATIVE PROBLEM

5. (cont.)

	DATE		DESCRIPTION	POST. REF.	DEBIT	CREDIT	
14							14
15		31	Depr. Expense—Store Equip.		5 8 5 0 00		15
16			Accumulated Depr.—Store Equip.			5 8 5 0 00	16
17							17
18		31	Depr. Expense—Office Equipment		2 1 6 0 00		18
19			Accumulated Depr.—Office Equip.			2 1 6 0 00	19
20							20
21		31	Sales Salaries Expense		1 8 0 0 00		21
22			Office Salaries Expense		9 0 0 00		22
23			Salaries Payable			2 7 0 0 00	23
24							24
25		31	Unearned Rent		5 0 0 00		25
26			Rent Income			5 0 0 00	26

6.

	DATE		DESCRIPTION	POST. REF.	DEBIT	CREDIT	
1			**Closing Entries**				1
2	1995 Oct.	31	Sales		540 0 0 0 00		2
3			Rent Income		5 0 0 00		3
4			Income Summary			540 5 0 0 00	4
5							5
6		31	Income Summary		463 1 2 0 00		6
7			Sales Returns and Allowances			4 3 0 0 00	7
8			Sales Discounts			2 5 0 0 00	8
9			Cost of Merchandise Sold			333 4 2 0 00	9
10			Sales Salaries Expense			45 0 0 0 00	10
11			Advertising Expense			15 0 0 0 00	11
12			Depr. Expense—Store Equipment			5 8 5 0 00	12
13			Store Supplies Expense			6 6 0 00	13
14			Miscellaneous Selling Expense			9 7 0 00	14
15			Office Salaries Expense			30 9 0 0 00	15
16			Rent Expense			8 5 0 0 00	16
17			Insurance Expense			4 3 0 0 00	17
18			Depr. Expense—Office Equipment			2 1 6 0 00	18
19			Office Supplies Expense			4 8 0 00	19
20			Miscellaneous Administrative Exp.			8 3 0 00	20
21			**Interest Expense**			8 2 5 0 00	22
22							23
23		31	Income Summary		77 3 8 0 00		24
24			Retained Earnings			77 3 8 0 00	25
25							26
26		31	Retained Earnings		8 0 0 0 00		27
27			Dividends			8 0 0 0 00	28

DISCUSSION QUESTIONS

1. What distinguishes a merchandising enterprise from a service enterprise?
2. If sales were $250,000 and the cost of merchandise sold was $175,000, what was the amount of the gross profit?   *$75,000*
3. If sales were $410,000 and the gross profit was $150,000, what was the amount of the cost of merchandise sold? *$ 260,000*
4. Can a business enterprise earn a gross profit but incur a net loss? Explain.
5. In which type of system for accounting for merchandise held for sale is there no attempt to record the cost of merchandise sold until the end of the period, when a physical inventory is taken?
6. What is the name of the account in which purchases of merchandise are recorded in a perpetual inventory system?
7. Ames Company purchased merchandise on account from a supplier for $2,000, terms 1/10, n/30. Ames Company returned $500 of the merchandise and received full credit. (a) If Ames Company pays the invoice within the discount period, what is the amount of cash required for the payment? (b) Under a perpetual inventory system, what account is credited by Ames Company to record the return?
8. The debits and credits from four related transactions are presented in the following T accounts. (a) Describe each transaction. (b) What is the rate of the discount, and on what amount was it computed?

Cash			Accounts Payable			
	(2)	100	(3)	980	(1)	4,900
	(4)	3,920	(4)	3,920		

Merchandise Inventory			
(1)	4,900	(3)	980
(2)	100		

9. What is the name of the account in which sales of merchandise are recorded?
10. How does the accounting for sales to customers using bank credit cards, such as Mastercard and VISA, differ from accounting for sales to customers using nonbank credit cards, such as American Express?
11. The credit period during which the buyer of merchandise is allowed to pay usually begins with what date?
12. Boggs Company ordered $1,000 of merchandise from Sherrill Company on June 1, terms 1/10, n/30. Although Sherrill Company shipped the merchandise on June 6, the merchandise was not received by Boggs Company until June 7. The invoice received with the merchandise was dated June 6. What is the last date Boggs Company could pay the invoice and still receive the discount?
13. What is the meaning of (a) 1/10, n/60; (b) n/30; (c) n/eom?
14. What is the term applied to discounts for early payment of an invoice (a) by the seller, (b) by the buyer?
15. What is the nature of (a) a credit memorandum issued by the seller of merchandise, (b) a debit memorandum issued by the buyer of merchandise?
16. After the amount due on a sale of $5,000, terms 1/10, n/eom, is received from a customer within the discount period, the seller consents to the return of the entire shipment. (a) What is the amount of the refund owed to the customer? (b) What accounts should be debited and credited by the seller to record the return and the refund?
17. The debits and credits for three related transactions are presented in the following T accounts. Describe each transaction.

Cash			Sales		
(5)	9,310			(1)	10,000

Accounts Receivable				Sales Discounts	
(1)	10,000	(3)	500	(5)	190
		(5)	9,500		

Merchandise Inventory				Sales Returns and Allowances	
(4)	300	(2)	6,000	(3)	500

Cost of Merchandise Sold			
(2)	6,000	(4)	300

18. Who bears the transportation costs when the terms of sale are (a) FOB shipping point, (b) FOB destination?

19. Merchandise is sold on account to a customer for $10,000, terms FOB shipping point, 1/10, n/30. The seller paid the transportation costs of $250. Determine the following: (a) amount of the sale, (b) amount debited to Accounts Receivable, (c) amount of the discount for early payment, (d) amount due within the discount period.

20. A retailer is considering the purchase of ten units of a specific item from either of two suppliers. Their offers are as follows:
    A: $500 a unit, total of $5,000, 2/10, n/30, plus transportation costs of $275.
    B: $520 a unit, total of $5,200, 1/10, n/30, no charge for transportation.
    Which of the two offers, A or B, yields the lower price?

21. A sale of merchandise on account for $200 is subject to a 6% sales tax. (a) Should the sales tax be recorded at the time of sale or when payment is received? (b) What is the amount of the sale? (c) What is the amount debited to Accounts Receivable? (d) What is the title of the account to which the $12 is credited?

22. What is the normal balance of the following accounts: (a) sales returns and allowances, (b) merchandise inventory, (c) sales discounts, (d) transportation out, (e) sales, (f) cost of merchandise sold?

23. Name three accounts that would normally appear in the chart of accounts of a merchandise enterprise but would not appear in the chart of accounts of a service enterprise.

24. Differentiate between the multiple-step and the single-step forms of the income statement.

25. What major advantages and disadvantages does the single-step form of income statement have in comparison to the multiple-step statement?

26. For the fiscal year, sales were $1,250,000, sales discounts were $10,100, sales returns and allowances were $40,000, and the cost of merchandise sold was $720,000. What was the amount of net sales and gross profit?

27. The following expenses were incurred by a merchandising enterprise during the year. In which expense section of the income statement should each be reported: (a) selling, (b) administrative, or (c) other?
    (1) Interest expense on notes payable.
    (2) Salaries of office personnel.
    (3) Advertising expense.
    (4) Insurance expense on store equipment.
    (5) Rent expense on office building.
    (6) Depreciation expense on office equipment.
    (7) Office supplies used.
    (8) Salary of sales manager.

28. What type of revenue is reported in the Other Income section of the multiple-step income statement?

29. Differentiate between the account form and the report form of balance sheet.

30. From the following list, identify the accounts that should be closed to Income Summary at the end of the fiscal year: (a) Accounts Receivable, (b) Cost of Merchandise Sold, (c) Merchandise Inventory, (d) Sales, (e) Sales Discounts, (f) Sales Returns and Allowances, (g) Supplies, (h) Supplies Expense, (i) Salaries Expense, (j) Salaries Payable.

REAL WORLD FOCUS

31. It is not unusual for a customer to drive into some Texaco, Mobil, or BP gasoline stations and discover that the cash price per gallon is 3 or 4 cents less than the credit price per gallon. As a result, many customers pay cash rather than use their credit cards. Why would a gasoline station owner establish such a policy?

ETHICS DISCUSSION CASE

On March 1, 1995, Katz Company purchased $5,000 of merchandise, terms 1/10, n/30, from C. L. Allan Co. Even though the discount period had expired on March 15, 1995, Kay Williams subtracted the discount of $50 when she processed the documents for payment by the treasurer.

SHARPEN YOUR COMMUNICATION SKILLS ▶ Discuss whether Kay Williams behaved in an ethical manner by subtracting the discount, even though the discount period had expired.

WHAT DO YOU
THINK

Purchases of merchandise are often subject to discounts, such as 2/10, n/30. Assume that on December 31, 1995, an enterprise has $500,000 of accounts payable outstanding, which are subject to a 2/10, n/30 purchases discount. Thus, only $490,000 of cash will need to be paid to pay the accounts payable within the discount period. On its balance sheet as of December 31, 1995, should the enterprise report accounts payable of $500,000 or $490,000?

FINANCIAL ANALYSIS AND INTERPRETATION

Profitability refers to an enterprise's ability to earn profits or net income. This ability depends on the efficiency of operations as well as the assets available to the enterprise. Thus, profitability analysis focuses primarily on the relationship between the operating results (the income statement) and the assets used (the balance sheet).

One ratio that may be used to assess profitability is the ratio of net sales to assets. It indicates how effectively a firm uses its assets and is computed as follows:

$$\text{Ratio of Net Sales to Assets} = \frac{\text{Net Sales}}{\text{Total Assets}}$$

a. Using total assets at the end of each year, determine the ratio of net sales to total assets for Hershey Foods Corporation for the years ended December 31, 1992 and 1991.

SHARPEN YOUR ► b. What conclusions can be drawn from these ratios concerning the trend in profitability?
COMMUNICATION SKILLS

EXERCISES

EXERCISE 5-1
DETERMINATION
OF GROSS PROFIT
Objective 1

During the current year, merchandise is sold for $200,000 cash and for $375,000 on account. The cost of the merchandise sold is $490,000.

a. What is the amount of the gross profit?

SHARPEN YOUR ► b. Will the income statement necessarily report a net income? Explain.
COMMUNICATION SKILLS

EXERCISE 5-2
DETERMINATION OF
AMOUNTS TO BE PAID ON
INVOICES
Objective 2

Determine the amount to be paid in full settlement of each of the following invoices, assuming that credit for returns and allowances was received prior to payment and that all invoices were paid within the discount period.

	Merchandise	Transportation	Terms	Returns and Allowances
a.	$10,000	—	FOB destination, n/30	$ 500
b.	8,000	—	FOB destination, 2/10, n/30	—
c.	6,000	—	FOB shipping point, 1/10, n/30	1,000
d.	4,000	$90	FOB shipping point, 1/10, n/30	100
e.	2,000	50	FOB shipping point, 2/10, n/30	750

EXERCISE 5-3
PURCHASE-RELATED
TRANSACTIONS
Objective 2

Leonard Co. purchases $6,000 of merchandise from a supplier on account, terms FOB destination, 1/10, n/30. Leonard Co. returns $500 of the merchandise, receiving a credit memorandum, and then pays the amount due within the discount period. Journalize Leonard Co.'s entries to record (a) the purchase, (b) the merchandise return, and (c) the payment.

EXERCISE 5-4
PURCHASE-RELATED
TRANSACTIONS
Objective 2

Journalize entries for the following related transactions of Drysdale Company:

a. Purchased $10,000 of merchandise from Craig Co. on account, terms 1/10, n/30.
b. Paid the amount owed on the invoice within the discount period.
c. Discovered that $2,500 of the merchandise was defective and returned items, receiving credit.
d. Purchased $1,200 of merchandise from Craig Co. on account, terms 1/10, n/30.
e. Received a check for the balance owed from the return in (c), after deducting for the purchase in (d).

EXERCISE 5-5
SALES-RELATED
TRANSACTIONS,
INCLUDING THE USE
OF CREDIT CARDS
Objective 2

Journalize the entries for the following transactions:

a. Sold merchandise for cash, $12,500. The cost of the merchandise sold was $7,500.
b. Sold merchandise on account, $10,000. The cost of the merchandise sold was $6,000.
c. Sold merchandise to customers who used Mastercard and VISA, $4,750. The cost of the merchandise sold was $2,850.
d. Sold merchandise to customers who used American Express, $3,100. The cost of the merchandise sold was $1,860.
e. Paid an invoice from First National Bank for $250, representing a service fee for processing Mastercard and VISA sales.
f. Received $2,910 from American Express Company after a $190 collection fee had been deducted.

EXERCISE 5-6
SALES RETURNS AND
ALLOWANCES
Objective 2

During the year, sales returns and allowances totaled $89,950. The accountant recorded all the returns and allowances by debiting the sales account and crediting Cost of Merchandise Sold.

**SHARPEN YOUR ▶
COMMUNICATION SKILLS**

Was the accountant's method of recording returns acceptable? Explain. In your explanation, include the advantages of using a sales returns and allowances account.

EXERCISE 5-7
SALES TAX TRANSACTIONS
Objective 2

Journalize the entries to record the following selected transactions:

a. Sold $5,000 of merchandise on account, subject to a sales tax of 6%. The cost of the merchandise sold was $3,000.
b. Paid $1,650 to the state sales tax department for taxes collected.

EXERCISE 5-8
SALES-RELATED
TRANSACTIONS
Objectives 2, 3

Coyles Co. sells merchandise to Westbury Co. on account, $6,900, terms 2/15, n/30. The cost of the merchandise sold is $3,900. Coyles Co. issues a credit memorandum for $750 for merchandise returned and subsequently receives the amount due within the discount period. The cost of the merchandise returned is $450. Journalize Coyles Co.'s entries for (a) the sale, including the cost of the merchandise sold, (b) the credit memorandum, including the cost of the returned merchandise, and (c) the receipt of the check for the amount due from Westbury Co.

EXERCISE 5-9
PURCHASE-RELATED
TRANSACTIONS
Objectives 2, 3

Based on the data presented in Exercise 5-8, journalize Westbury Co.'s entries for (a) the purchase, (b) the return of the merchandise for credit, and (c) the payment of the invoice within the discount period.

EXERCISE 5-10
CHART OF ACCOUNTS
Objective 4

Kline Corporation is a newly organized enterprise with the following list of accounts, arranged in alphabetical order:

Accounts Payable	Miscellaneous Selling Expense
Accounts Receivable	Notes Payable (short-term)
Accumulated Depreciation—Office Equipment	Notes Receivable (short-term)
Accumulated Depreciation—Store Equipment	Office Equipment
Advertising Expense	Office Salaries Expense
Capital Stock	Office Supplies
Cash	Office Supplies Expense
Cost of Merchandise Sold	Prepaid Insurance
Depreciation Expense—Office Equipment	Rent Expense
Depreciation Expense—Store Equipment	Retained Earnings
Dividends	Salaries Payable
Income Summary	Sales
Insurance Expense	Sales Returns and Allowances
Interest Expense	Sales Discounts
Interest Income	Sales Salaries Expense
Interest Receivable	Store Equipment
Land	Store Supplies
Merchandise Inventory	Store Supplies Expense
Miscellaneous Administrative Expense	

Construct a chart of accounts, assigning account numbers and arranging the accounts in balance sheet and income statement order, as illustrated in Exhibit 5. Each account number is to comprise three digits: The first digit is to indicate the major classification ("1" for assets, and so on), the second digit is to indicate the subclassification ("11" for current assets, and so on), and the third digit is to identify the specific account ("110" for Cash, and so on).

EXERCISE 5-11
DETERMINATION OF
AMOUNTS FOR ITEMS
OMITTED FROM INCOME
STATEMENT
Objective 6

Three items are omitted in each of the following four lists of income statement data. Determine the amounts of the missing items, identifying them by letter.

Sales	$ (a)	$610,000	$990,000	$757,500
Sales returns and allowances	9,000	17,000	(e)	30,500
Sales discounts	3,000	8,000	10,000	(g)
Net sales	150,000	(c)	965,000	(h)
Cost of merchandise sold	90,000	375,000	(f)	540,000
Gross profit	(b)	(d)	390,000	180,000

EXERCISE 5-12
SINGLE-STEP INCOME
STATEMENT
Objective 6

Summary operating data for Solar Products Company during the current year ended June 30, 1995, are as follows: cost of merchandise sold, $925,000; administrative expenses, $145,000; interest expense, $27,500; rent income, $30,000; net sales, $1,500,000; and selling expenses, $210,000. Prepare a single-step income statement.

EXERCISE 5-13
MULTIPLE-STEP INCOME
STATEMENT
Objective 6

Selected account titles and related amounts appearing in the Income Statement and Balance Sheet columns of the work sheet of Vincent Company for the year ended December 31 are listed in alphabetical order as follows:

Administrative Expenses	$ 79,500
Building	312,500
Capital Stock	100,000
Cash	58,500
Cost of Merchandise Sold	836,300
Dividends	60,000
Interest Expense	2,500
Merchandise Inventory	230,000
Notes Payable	25,000
Office Supplies	10,600
Retained Earnings	200,000
Salaries Payable	4,220
Sales	1,275,000
Sales Discounts	10,200
Sales Returns and Allowances	34,300
Selling Expenses	132,700
Store Supplies	7,700

All selling expenses have been recorded in the account entitled *Selling Expenses*, and all administrative expenses have been recorded in the account entitled *Administrative Expenses*.

a. Prepare a multiple-step income statement for the year.

▶ b. Compare the major advantages and disadvantages of the multiple-step and single-step forms of income statements.

EXERCISE 5-14
CLOSING ENTRIES
Objective 8

Based on the data presented in Exercise 5-13, journalize the closing entries.

EXERCISE 5-15
ADJUSTING ENTRY FOR
MERCHANDISE INVENTORY
SHRINKAGE
Objective 7

Wilkes Inc. perpetual inventory records indicate that $129,500 of merchandise should be on hand on December 31, 1995. The physical inventory indicates that $127,300 of merchandise is actually on hand. Journalize the adjusting entry for the inventory shrinkage for Wilkes Inc. for the year ended December 31, 1995.

WhAT'S WRONG
WITH THIS?

How many errors can you find in the following income statement?

Baxter Company
Income Statement
For Year Ended December 31, 19—

Revenue from sales:			
Sales			$1,200,000
Add: Sales returns and allowances	$28,000		
Sales discounts	9,500	37,500	
Gross Sales			$1,237,500
Cost of merchandise sold			795,000
Income from operations			$ 442,500
Operating expenses:			
Selling expenses		$ 125,000	
Transportation in on merchandise sold		6,300	
Administrative expenses		87,200	
Total operating expenses			218,500
Gross profit			$ 224,000
Other expense:			
Interest expense			7,500
Net loss			$ 216,500

PROBLEMS

Series A

PROBLEM 5-1A
PURCHASE-RELATED
TRANSACTIONS
Objective 2

The following selected transactions were completed by Willis Company during July of the current year:

July 1. Purchased merchandise from Larkin Co., $4,800, terms FOB destination, n/30.
      3. Purchased merchandise from Toomes Co., $10,000, terms FOB shipping point, 1/10, n/eom. Prepaid transportation costs of $200 were added to the invoice.

July   5. Purchased merchandise from Warwich Co., $5,000, terms FOB destination, 2/10, n/30.

       8. Issued debit memorandum to Warwich Co. for $1,000 of merchandise returned from purchase on July 5.

      13. Paid Toomes Co. for invoice of July 3, less discount.

      15. Paid Warwich Co. for invoice of July 5, less debit memorandum of July 8 and discount.

      18. Purchased merchandise from Astro Company, $8,250, terms FOB shipping point, n/eom.

      18. Paid transportation charges of $220 on July 18 purchase from Astro Company.

      19. Purchased merchandise from Hatcher Co., $4,500, terms FOB destination, 2/10, n/30.

      29. Paid Hatcher Co. for invoice of July 19, less discount.

      31. Paid Larkin Co. for invoice of July 1.

      31. Paid Astro Company for invoice of July 18.

Instructions

Journalize entries to record the transactions of Willis Company for July.

PROBLEM 5-2A
SALES-RELATED
TRANSACTIONS
Objective 2

The following selected transactions were completed by Lawrence Supply Co., which sells primarily to wholesalers but occasionally sells to retail customers:

July   1. Sold merchandise on account to Griffin Company, $4,000, terms FOB destination, 2/10, n/30. The cost of the merchandise sold was $2,400.

       1. Paid transportation costs of $95 on merchandise sold on July 1.

       2. Sold merchandise for $600 plus 5% sales tax to cash customers. The cost of merchandise sold was $350.

       3. Sold merchandise on account to Vance Co., $2,500, terms FOB shipping point, n/eom. The cost of merchandise sold was $1,800.

       5. Sold merchandise for $1,200 plus 5% sales tax to customers who used Mastercards. Deposited credit card receipts into the bank. The cost of merchandise sold was $750.

       8. Sold merchandise on account to Vance Co., $1,500, terms FOB shipping point, n/eom. The cost of merchandise sold was $900.

      11. Received check for amount due from Griffin Company for sale on July 1.

      12. Sold merchandise to customers who used American Express cards, $3,500. The cost of merchandise sold was $2,100.

      13. Sold merchandise on account to Monroe Co., $6,500, terms FOB shipping point, 1/10, n/30. The cost of merchandise sold was $3,900.

      15. Issued credit memorandum for $500 to Monroe Co. for merchandise returned from sale on July 13. The cost of the merchandise returned was $300.

      16. Sold merchandise on account to Davis Co., $10,000, terms FOB destination, 2/15, n/30. The cost of merchandise sold was $6,000.

      18. Sold merchandise on account to Braggs Company, $7,500, terms FOB shipping point, 1/10, n/30. Added $85 to the invoice for transportation costs prepaid. The cost of merchandise sold was $4,500.

      23. Received check for amount due from Monroe Co. for sale on July 13 less credit memorandum of July 15 and discount.

      24. Issued credit memorandum for $250 to Davis Co. for allowance for damaged merchandise sold on July 16.

      26. Received $9,410 from American Express for $10,000 of sales reported during the week of July 11–17.

      28. Received check for amount due from Braggs Company for sale of July 18.

      30. Received check for amount due from Vance Co. for sales of July 3 and July 8.

      31. Paid Ace Delivery Service $770 for merchandise delivered during July to local customers under shipping terms of FOB destination.

Aug. 4. Paid First National Bank $480 for service fees for handling Mastercard sales during July.

      10. Paid $875 to state sales tax division for taxes owed on July sales.

      15. Received check for amount due from Davis Co. for sale of July 16, less credit memorandum of July 24.

Instructions

Journalize entries to record the transactions of Lawrence Supply Co.

PROBLEM 5-3A
SALES-RELATED AND
PURCHASE-RELATED
TRANSACTIONS
Objective 2

The following were selected from among the transactions completed by Freeman Company during November of the current year:

Nov. 3. Purchased office supplies for cash, $120.
5. Purchased merchandise on account from Butler Co., list price $20,000, trade discount 37.5%, terms FOB destination, 1/10, n/30.
6. Sold merchandise for cash, $2,950. The cost of the merchandise sold was $1,450.
7. Purchased merchandise on account from Mattox Co., $6,400, terms FOB shipping point, 2/10, n/30, with prepaid transportation costs of $190 added to the invoice.
7. Returned $2,500 of merchandise purchased on November 5 from Butler Co.
11. Sold merchandise on account to Bowles Co., list price $2,250, trade discount 20%, terms 1/10, n/30. The cost of the merchandise sold was $880.
15. Paid Butler Co. on account for purchase of November 5, less return of November 7 and discount.
16. Sold merchandise on nonbank credit cards and reported accounts to the card company, $3,850. The cost of the merchandise sold was $1,900.
17. Paid Mattox Co. on account for purchase of November 7, less discount.
19. Purchased merchandise for cash, $3,500.
21. Received cash on account from sale of November 11 to Bowles Co., less discount.
24. Sold merchandise on account to Clemons Co., $4,200, terms 1/10, n/30. The cost of the merchandise sold was $2,025.
28. Received cash from card company for nonbank credit card sales of November 16, less $190 service fee.
30. Received merchandise returned by Clemons Co. from sale on November 24, $2,700. The cost of the returned merchandise was $1,310.

Instructions
Journalize the transactions.

SOLUTIONS
SOFTWARE

Instructions for Solving Problem 5-3A Using Solutions Software

1. Load opening balances.
2. Enter your name in the Student Name field in the General Information data entry window. Set the run date to November 30 of the current year.
3. Save the opening balances file to your drive and directory.
4. Select the General Journal Entries option, and key the journal entries. Leave the reference field blank. Note: To review the chart of accounts, select F-1.
5. Display a journal entries report.
6. Display a trial balance.
7. Key the adjusting entries, based on the following data:

    Insurance expired on November 30 $400
    Office supplies on hand on November 30   300
   Key ADJ.ENT. in the reference field.

8. Display the adjusting entries. Key ADJ.ENT. in the Reference Restriction area of the Selection Options screen.
9. Display the financial statements.
10. Save a backup copy of your data file.
11. Perform period-end closing.
12. Display a post-closing trial balance.
13. Save your data file to disk.
14. End the session.

PROBLEM 5-4A
SALES-RELATED AND
PURCHASE-RELATED
TRANSACTIONS FOR
SELLER AND BUYER
Objectives 2, 3

The following selected transactions were completed during October between Sims Company and J. C. Power Co.:

Oct. 4. Sims Company sold merchandise on account to J. C. Power Co., $10,000, terms FOB destination, 1/15, n/eom. The cost of the merchandise sold was $6,000.
4. Sims Company paid transportation costs of $600 for delivery of merchandise sold to J. C. Power Co. on October 4.
10. Sims Company sold merchandise on account to J. C. Power Co., $15,000, terms FOB shipping point, n/eom. The cost of the merchandise sold was $9,000.

Oct. 12. J. C. Power Co. returned $2,000 of merchandise purchased on account on October 4 from Sims Company. The cost of the merchandise returned was $1,200.

   14. J. C. Power Co. paid transportation charges of $200 on October 10 purchase from Sims Company.

   18. Sims Company sold merchandise on account to J. C. Power Co., $18,000, terms FOB shipping point, 2/10, n/30. Sims Company paid transportation costs of $1,500, which were added to the invoice. The cost of the merchandise sold was $10,800.

   19. J. C. Power Co. paid Sims Company for purchase of October 4, less discount and less return of October 11.

   28. J. C. Power Co. paid Sims Company on account for purchase of October 18, less discount.

   31. J. C. Power Co. paid Sims Company on account for purchase of October 10.

Instructions

Journalize the October transactions for (1) Sims Company and (2) J. C. Power Co.

PROBLEM 5-5A
WORK SHEET FOR
MERCHANDISING
ENTERPRISE
Objective 5

The accounts in the ledger of Iyer Inc., with the unadjusted balances on July 31, the end of the current fiscal year, are as follows:

Cash	$ 18,500
Notes Receivable	50,000
Accounts Receivable	53,340
Merchandise Inventory	88,500
Prepaid Insurance	4,200
Store Supplies	2,100
Store Equipment	154,200
Accumulated Depreciation—Store Equipment	84,600
Accounts Payable	32,000
Salaries Payable	—
Unearned Rent	7,600
Capital Stock	50,000
Retained Earnings	191,640
Dividends	26,000
Sales	790,500
Cost of Merchandise Sold	465,800
Sales Salaries Expense	79,800
Advertising Expense	34,850
Depreciation Expense—Store Equipment	—
Store Supplies Expense	—
Miscellaneous Selling Expense	1,600
Office Salaries Expense	83,700
Rent Expense	45,000
Heating and Lighting Expense	37,400
Taxes Expense	7,850
Insurance Expense	—
Miscellaneous Administrative Expense	3,500
Rent Income	—

The data needed for year-end adjustments on July 31 are as follows:

Physical merchandise inventory on July 31		$80,000
Insurance expired during the year		1,060
Store supplies on hand on July 31		820
Depreciation for the current year		9,300
Accrued salaries on July 31:		
Sales salaries	$1,500	
Office salaries	1,200	2,700
Rent income earned during the year		3,800

Instructions

Prepare a work sheet for the fiscal year ended July 31. List all accounts in the order given.

Instructions for Solving Problem 5-5A Using Solutions Software
1. Load opening balances.
2. Enter your name in the Student Name field in the General Information data entry window. Set the run date to July 31 of the current year.
3. Save the opening balances file to your drive and directory.
4. Key the adjusting entries. Key ADJ.ENT. in the reference field.
5. Display the adjusting entries. Key ADJ.ENT. in the Reference Restriction area of the Selection Options screen.
6. Display the financial statements.
7. Save a backup copy of your data file.
8. Perform period-end closing.
9. Display a post-closing trial balance.
10. Save your data file to disk.
11. End the session.

PROBLEM 5-6A
WORK SHEET, INCOME
STATEMENT, AND CLOSING
ENTRIES
Objectives 5, 6, 8,

A partially completed work sheet for Sycamore Corp. for the current year ended April 30 is as follows:

Sycamore Corp.
Work Sheet
For Year Ended April 30, 19—

Account Title	Trial Balance Dr.	Trial Balance Cr.	Adjustments Dr.	Adjustments Cr.
Cash	28,500			
Accounts Receivable	88,300			
Merchandise Inventory	114,700			(a) 9,500
Prepaid Insurance	11,500			(b) 6,900
Store Supplies	2,300			(c) 1,400
Office Supplies	1,500			(d) 900
Store Equipment	166,600			
Accum. Depr.—Store Equip.		68,000		(e) 8,100
Office Equipment	49,300			
Accum. Depr.—Office Equip.		12,000		(f) 3,000
Accounts Payable		29,500		
Salaries Payable				(g) 4,700
Unearned Rent		2,400	(h) 1,600	
Note Payable (due 1999)		100,000		
Capital Stock		50,000		
Retained Earnings		86,100		
Dividends	30,000			
Sales		760,000		
Sales Returns and Allowances	12,000			
Sales Discounts	7,500			
Cost of Merchandise Sold	446,800		(a) 9,500	
Sales Salaries Expense	64,000		(g) 3,500	
Advertising Expense	13,000			
Depr. Expense—Store Equip.			(e) 8,100	
Store Supplies Expense			(c) 1,400	
Misc. Selling Expense	4,400			
Office Salaries Expense	31,000		(g) 1,200	
Rent Expense	24,000			
Depr. Expense—Office Equip.			(f) 3,000	
Insurance Expense			(b) 6,900	
Office Supplies Expense			(d) 900	
Misc. Administrative Expense	1,100			
Rent Income				(h) 1,600
Interest Expense	11,500			
	1,108,000	1,108,000	36,100	36,100

SPREADSHEET
PROBLEM

SOLUTIONS
SOFTWARE

Instructions

1. Complete the work sheet for Sycamore Corp.

2. Prepare a single-step income statement for the year ended April 30.

3. Journalize the closing entries for Sycamore Corp.

Instructions for Solving Problem 5-6A Using Solutions Software

1. Load opening balances.
2. Enter your name in the Student Name field in the General Information data entry window. Set the run date to April 30 of the current year.
3. Save the opening balances file to your drive and directory.
4. Key the adjusting entries. Key ADJ.ENT. in the reference field.
5. Display the adjusting entries. Key ADJ.ENT. in the Reference Restriction area of the Selection Options screen.
6. Display the financial statements.
7. Save a backup copy of your data file.
8. Perform period-end closing.
9. Display a post-closing trial balance.
10. Save your data file to disk.
11. End the session.

PROBLEM 5-7A
MULTIPLE-STEP INCOME
STATEMENT AND REPORT
FORM OF BALANCE SHEET
Objective 6

The following selected accounts and their normal balances appear in the Income Statement and Balance Sheet columns of the work sheet of Merz Corp. for the fiscal year ended January 31, 1995:

Cash	$ 39,000
Notes Receivable	120,000
Accounts Receivable	212,000
Merchandise Inventory	100,000
Office Supplies	5,600
Prepaid Insurance	3,400
Office Equipment	35,000
Accumulated Depreciation—Office Equipment	12,800
Store Equipment	72,000
Accumulated Depreciation—Store Equipment	24,200
Accounts Payable	45,600
Salaries Payable	2,400
Note Payable (final payment, 2004)	56,000
Capital Stock	100,000
Retained Earnings	291,000
Dividends	15,000
Sales	1,400,000
Sales Returns and Allowances	12,100
Sales Discounts	11,900
Cost of Merchandise Sold	1,100,000
Sales Salaries Expense	123,200
Advertising Expense	22,800
Depreciation Expense—Store Equipment	6,400
Miscellaneous Selling Expense	1,600
Office Salaries Expense	31,150
Rent Expense	16,350
Depreciation Expense—Office Equipment	12,700
Insurance Expense	3,900
Office Supplies Expense	1,300
Miscellaneous Administrative Expense	1,600
Interest Income	21,000
Interest Expense	6,000

Instructions

1. Prepare a multiple-step income statement.
2. Prepare a retained earnings statement.

(continued)

3. Prepare a report form of balance sheet, assuming that the current portion of the note payable is $6,000.

► 4. Briefly explain (a) how multiple-step and single-step income statements differ and (b) how report form and account form balance sheets differ.

PROBLEM 5-8A
SINGLE-STEP INCOME
STATEMENT AND
ACCOUNT FORM OF
BALANCE SHEET
Objective 6

Selected accounts and related amounts for Merz Corp. for the fiscal year ended January 31, 1995, are presented in Problem 5-7A.

Instructions
1. Prepare a single-step income statement.
2. Prepare a retained earnings statement.
3. Prepare an account form of balance sheet, assuming that the current portion of the note payable is $6,000.

PROBLEM 5-9A
PREPARATION OF WORK
SHEET, FINANCIAL
STATEMENTS, AND
ADJUSTING AND CLOSING
ENTRIES
Objectives 5, 6, 7, 8

The accounts and their balances in the ledger of Gant Inc. on December 31 of the current year are as follows:

Cash	$ 68,175
Accounts Receivable	112,500
Merchandise Inventory	230,000
Prepaid Insurance	9,700
Store Supplies	4,250
Office Supplies	2,100
Store Equipment	112,000
Accumulated Depreciation—Store Equipment	40,300
Office Equipment	50,000
Accumulated Depreciation—Office Equipment	17,200
Accounts Payable	66,700
Salaries Payable	—
Unearned Rent	1,200
Note Payable (final payment, 2000)	105,000
Capital Stock	100,000
Retained Earnings	120,510
Dividends	40,000
Income Summary	—
Sales	995,000
Sales Returns and Allowances	11,900
Sales Discounts	7,100
Cost of Merchandise Sold	576,200
Sales Salaries Expense	86,400
Advertising Expense	30,000
Depreciation Expense—Store Equipment	—
Store Supplies Expense	—
Miscellaneous Selling Expense	1,335
Office Salaries Expense	54,000
Rent Expense	36,000
Insurance Expense	—
Depreciation Expense—Office Equipment	—
Office Supplies Expense	—
Miscellaneous Administrative Expense	1,650
Rent Income	—
Interest Expense	12,600

The data needed for year-end adjustments on December 31 are as follows:

Physical merchandise inventory on December 3		$220,000
Insurance expired during the year		7,260
Supplies on hand on December 31:		
Store supplies		1,700
Office supplies		400
Depreciation for the year:		
Store equipment		9,500
Office equipment		4,800
Salaries payable on December 31:		
Sales salaries	$2,750	
Office salaries	1,150	3,900
Unearned rent on December 31		400

Instructions

1. Prepare a work sheet for the fiscal year ended December 31, listing all accounts in the order given.
2. Prepare a multiple-step income statement.
3. Prepare a retained earnings statement.
4. Prepare a report form of balance sheet, assuming that the current portion of the note payable is $15,000.
5. Journalize the adjusting entries.
6. Journalize the closing entries.

Series B

PROBLEM 5-1B
PURCHASE-RELATED
TRANSACTIONS
Objective 2

The following selected transactions were completed by Wilton Company during May of the current year:

May 1. Purchased merchandise from Duncan Co., $5,750, terms FOB destination, n/30.
       3. Purchased merchandise from Darwin Co., $10,000, terms FOB shipping point, 2/10, n/eom. Prepaid transportation costs of $250 were added to the invoice.
       5. Purchased merchandise from Thompson Co., $5,000, terms FOB destination, 1/10, n/30.
       8. Issued debit memorandum to Thompson Co. for $1,000 of merchandise returned from purchase on May 5.
    13. Paid Darwin Co. for invoice of May 3, less discount.
    15. Paid Thompson Co. for invoice of May 5, less debit memorandum of May 8 and discount.
    18. Purchased merchandise from Moat Company, $8,250, terms FOB shipping point, n/eom.
    18. Paid transportation charges of $220 on May 18 purchase from Moat Company.
    19. Purchased merchandise from Hatcher Co., $7,500, terms FOB destination, 2/10, n/30.
    29. Paid Hatcher Co. for invoice of May 19, less discount.
    31. Paid Duncan Co. for invoice of May 1.
    31. Paid Moat Company for invoice of May 18.

Instructions
Journalize entries to record the transactions of Wilton Company for May.

PROBLEM 5-2B
SALES-RELATED
TRANSACTIONS
Objective 2

The following selected transactions were completed by Buller Co., which sells primarily to wholesalers but occasionally sells to retail customers:

May 1. Sold merchandise on account to McGee Company, $12,000, terms FOB destination, 1/10, n/30. The cost of merchandise sold was $7,200.
       1. Paid transportation costs of $255 on merchandise sold on May 1.
       2. Sold merchandise for $700 plus 6% sales tax to cash customers. The cost of merchandise sold was $400.
       3. Sold merchandise on account to Boskie Co., $2,500, terms FOB shipping point, n/eom. The cost of merchandise sold was $1,300.
       5. Sold merchandise for $1,200 plus 6% sales tax to customers who used VISA Cards. Deposited credit card receipts into the bank. The cost of merchandise sold was $800.

May 8. Sold merchandise on account to Boskie Co., $4,500, terms FOB shipping point, n/eom. The cost of merchandise sold was $2,700.

11. Received check for amount due from McGee Company for sale on May 1.

12. Sold merchandise to customers who used American Express cards, $2,500. The cost of merchandise sold was $1,600.

13. Sold merchandise on account to Monroe Co., $6,500, terms FOB shipping point, 1/10, n/30. The cost of merchandise sold was $4,000.

15. Issued credit memorandum for $500 to Monroe Co. for merchandise returned from sale on May 13. The cost of the merchandise returned was $360.

16. Sold merchandise on account to Felder Co., $5,000, terms FOB destination, 2/15, n/30. The cost of merchandise sold was $3,000.

18. Sold merchandise on account to Stockton Company, $7,500, terms FOB shipping point, 1/10, n/30. Paid $110 for transportation costs and added them to the invoice. The cost of merchandise sold was $5,000.

23. Received check for amount due from Monroe Co. for sale on May 13 less credit memorandum of May 15 and discount.

24. Issued credit memorandum for $250 to Felder Co. for allowance for damaged merchandise sold on May 16.

26. Received $7,410 from American Express for $8,000 of sales reported during the week of May 12–18.

28. Received check for amount due from Stockton Company for sale of May 18.

30. Received check for amount due from Boskie Co. for sales of May 3 and May 8.

31. Paid Ace Delivery Service $670 for merchandise delivered during May to local customers under shipping terms of FOB destination.

June 4. Paid American National Bank $380 for service fees for handling Mastercard sales during May.

10. Paid $375 to state sales tax division for taxes owed on May sales.

15. Received check for amount due from Felder Co. for sale of May 16, less credit memorandum of May 24.

Instructions

Journalize entries to record the transactions of Buller Co.

PROBLEM 5-3B
SALES-RELATED AND
PURCHASE-RELATED
TRANSACTIONS
Objective 2

The following were selected from among the transactions completed by Montrose Company during May of the current year:

May 3. Purchased merchandise on account from Floyd Co., list price $5,000, trade discount 20%, terms FOB shipping point, 2/10, n/30, with prepaid transportation costs of $120 added to the invoice.

5. Purchased merchandise on account from Kramer Co., $8,500, terms FOB destination, 1/10, n/30.

6. Sold merchandise on account to C. F. Howell Co., list price $4,000, trade discount 30%, terms 2/10, n/30. The cost of the merchandise sold was $1,125.

8. Purchased office supplies for cash, $150.

10. Returned $1,300 of merchandise purchased on May 5 from Kramer Co.

13. Paid Floyd Co. on account for purchase of May 3, less discount.

14. Purchased merchandise for cash, $10,500.

15. Paid Kramer Co. on account for purchase of May 5, less return of May 10 and discount.

16. Received cash on account from sale of May 6 to C. F. Howell Co., less discount.

19. Sold merchandise on nonbank credit cards and reported accounts to the card company, $2,450. The cost of the merchandise sold was $980.

22. Sold merchandise on account to Comer Co., $3,480, terms 2/10, n/30. The cost of the merchandise sold was $1,400.

24. Sold merchandise for cash, $4,350. The cost of the merchandise sold was $1,750.

25. Received merchandise returned by Comer Co. from sale on May 22, $1,480. The cost of the returned merchandise was $600.

31. Received cash from card company for nonbank credit card sales of May 19, less $140 service fee.

Instructions
Journalize the transactions.

Instructions for Solving Problem 5-3B Using Solutions Software

1. Load opening balances.
2. Enter your name in the Student Name field in the General Information data entry window. Set the run date to May 31 of the current year.
3. Save the opening balances file to your drive and directory.
4. Select the General Journal Entries option, and key the journal entries. Leave the reference field blank. Note: To review the chart of accounts, select F-1.
5. Display a journal entries report.
6. Display a trial balance.
7. Key the adjusting entries, based on the following data:

Insurance expired on May 31	$400
Office supplies on hand on May 31	300

   Key ADJ.ENT. in the reference field.
8. Display the adjusting entries. Key ADJ.ENT. in the Reference Restriction area of the Selection Options screen.
9. Display the financial statements.
10. Save a backup copy of your data file.
11. Perform period-end closing.
12. Display a post-closing trial balance.
13. Save your data file to disk.
14. End the session.

PROBLEM 5-4B
SALES-RELATED AND
PURCHASE-RELATED
TRANSACTIONS FOR
SELLER AND BUYER
Objectives 2, 3

The following selected transactions were completed during April between Swalm Company and Parker Company:

Apr. 3. Swalm Company sold merchandise on account to Parker Company, $12,500, terms FOB shipping point, 2/10, n/30. Swalm Company paid transportation costs of $600, which were added to the invoice. The cost of the merchandise sold was $7,500.

8. Swalm Company sold merchandise on account to Parker Company, $16,000, terms FOB destination, 1/15, n/eom. The cost of the merchandise sold was $10,500.

8. Swalm Company paid transportation costs of $800 for delivery of merchandise sold to Parker Company on April 8.

11. Parker Company returned $4,000 of merchandise purchased on account on April 8 from Swalm Company. The cost of the merchandise returned was $2,500.

13. Parker Company paid Swalm Company for purchase of April 3, less discount.

23. Parker Company paid Swalm Company for purchase of April 8, less discount and less return of April 11.

24. Swalm Company sold merchandise on account to Parker Company, $8,000, terms FOB shipping point, n/eom. The cost of the merchandise sold was $5,000.

27. Parker Company paid transportation charges of $300 on April 24 purchase from Swalm Company.

30. Parker Company paid Swalm Company on account for purchase of April 24.

Instructions
Journalize the April transactions for (1) Swalm Company and (2) Parker Company.

PROBLEM 5-5B
WORK SHEET FOR
MERCHANDISING
ENTERPRISE
Objective 5

The accounts in the ledger of Marden Corporation, with the unadjusted balances on June 30, the end of the current fiscal year, are as follows:

Cash	$ 15,100
Notes Receivable	50,000
Accounts Receivable	67,600
Merchandise Inventory	100,000
Prepaid Insurance	5,800
Store Supplies	4,950
Store Equipment	50,500
Accumulated Depreciation—Store Equipment	30,130
Accounts Payable	26,800
Salaries Payable	—
Unearned Rent	4,600
Capital Stock	60,000
Retained Earnings	109,870
Dividends	15,000
Sales	600,500
Cost of Merchandise Sold	352,000
Sales Salaries Expense	61,500
Advertising Expense	25,800
Depreciation Expense—Store Equipment	—
Store Supplies Expense	—
Miscellaneous Selling Expense	3,750
Office Salaries Expense	39,000
Rent Expense	24,000
Heating and Lighting Expense	9,660
Taxes Expense	5,100
Insurance Expense	—
Miscellaneous Administrative Expense	2,140
Rent Income	—

The data needed for year-end adjustments on June 30 are as follows:

Physical merchandise inventory on June 30		$91,700
Insurance expired during the year		3,800
Store supplies on hand on June 30		870
Depreciation for the current year		10,500
Accrued salaries on June 30:		
Sales salaries	$2,600	
Office salaries	1,650	4,250
Rent income earned during the year		3,800

Instructions

Prepare a work sheet for the fiscal year ended June 30. List all accounts in the order given.

**SOLUTIONS
SOFTWARE**

Instructions for Solving Problem 5-5B Using Solutions Software

1. Load opening balances.
2. Enter your name in the Student Name field in the General Information data entry window. Set the run date to June 30 of the current year.
3. Save the opening balances file to your drive and directory.
4. Key the adjusting entries. Key ADJ.ENT. in the reference field.
5. Display the adjusting entries. Key ADJ.ENT. in the Reference Restriction area of the Selection Options screen.
6. Display the financial statements.
7. Save a backup copy of your data file.
8. Perform period-end closing.
9. Display a post-closing trial balance.
10. Save your data file to disk.
11. End the session.

PROBLEM 5-6B
WORK SHEET, INCOME
STATEMENT, AND CLOSING
ENTRIES
Objectives 5, 6, 8

A partially completed work sheet for McNair Inc. for the current year ended October 31 is
as follows:

McNair Inc.
Work Sheet
For Year Ended October 31, 19—

Account Title	Trial Balance Dr.	Trial Balance Cr.	Adjustments Dr.		Adjustments Cr.	
Cash	14,400					
Accounts Receivable	86,300					
Merchandise Inventory	120,500				(a)	12,100
Prepaid Insurance	10,500				(b)	7,600
Store Supplies	3,800				(c)	2,200
Office Supplies	1,200				(d)	750
Store Equipment	159,600					
Accum. Depr.—Store Equip.		53,000			(e)	10,500
Office Equipment	47,300					
Accum. Depr.—Office Equip.		12,000			(f)	3,800
Accounts Payable		30,500				
Salaries Payable					(g)	4,100
Unearned Rent		2,400	(h)	1,600		
Note Payable (due 1999)		80,000				
Capital Stock		40,000				
Retained Earnings		109,200				
Dividends	29,000					
Sales		820,000				
Sales Returns and Allowances	7,000					
Sales Discounts	8,500					
Cost of Merchandise Sold	502,900		(a)	12,100		
Sales Salaries Expense	70,000		(g)	3,200		
Advertising Expense	28,000					
Depr. Expense—Store Equip.			(e)	10,500		
Store Supplies Expense			(c)	2,200		
Misc. Selling Expense	2,400					
Office Salaries Expense	35,000		(g)	900		
Rent Expense	10,000					
Depr. Expense—Office Equip.			(f)	3,800		
Insurance Expense			(b)	7,600		
Office Supplies Expense			(d)	750		
Misc. Administrative Expense	1,100					
Rent Income					(h)	1,600
Interest Expense	9,600					
	1,147,100	1,147,100	42,650		42,650	

Instructions

1. Complete the work sheet for McNair Inc.
2. Prepare a single-step income statement for the year ended October 31.
3. Journalize the closing entries for McNair Inc.

Instructions for Solving Problem 5-6B Using Solutions Software

1. Load opening balances.
2. Enter your name in the Student Name field in the General Information data entry window. Set the run date to October 31 of the current year.
3. Save the opening balances file to your drive and directory.
4. Key the adjusting entries. Key ADJ.ENT. in the reference field.

(continued)

5. Display the adjusting entries. Key ADJ.ENT. in the Reference Restriction area of the Selection Options screen.
6. Display the financial statements.
7. Save a backup copy of your data file.
8. Perform period-end closing.
9. Display a post-closing trial balance.
10. Save your data file to disk.
11. End the session.

PROBLEM 5-7B
MULTIPLE-STEP INCOME
STATEMENT AND REPORT
FORM OF BALANCE SHEET
Objective 6

The following selected accounts and their normal balances appear in the Income Statement and Balance Sheet columns of the work sheet of Kilgore Inc. for the fiscal year ended November 30, 1995:

Cash	$ 105,000
Notes Receivable	50,000
Accounts Receivable	92,000
Merchandise Inventory	100,000
Office Supplies	1,600
Prepaid Insurance	6,800
Office Equipment	24,000
Accumulated Depreciation—Office Equipment	10,800
Store Equipment	40,500
Accumulated Depreciation—Store Equipment	18,900
Accounts Payable	32,000
Salaries Payable	1,700
Note Payable (final payment, 2004)	35,000
Capital Stock	50,000
Retained Earnings	244,010
Dividends	25,000
Sales	1,000,000
Sales Returns and Allowances	9,000
Sales Discounts	8,500
Cost of Merchandise Sold	770,300
Sales Salaries Expense	88,000
Advertising Expense	16,300
Depreciation Expense—Store Equipment	4,600
Miscellaneous Selling Expense	1,000
Office Salaries Expense	30,900
Rent Expense	12,150
Depreciation Expense—Office Equipment	3,700
Insurance Expense	2,750
Office Supplies Expense	900
Miscellaneous Administrative Expense	1,150
Interest Income	5,400
Interest Expense	3,660

Instructions
1. Prepare a multiple-step income statement.
2. Prepare a retained earnings statement.
3. Prepare a report form of balance sheet, assuming that the current portion of the note payable is $3,500.

**SHARPEN YOUR ►
COMMUNICATION SKILLS**

4. Briefly explain (a) how multiple-step and single-step income statements differ and (b) how report form and account form balance sheets differ.

PROBLEM 5-8B
SINGLE-STEP INCOME
STATEMENT AND
ACCOUNT FORM OF
BALANCE SHEET
Objective 6

Selected accounts and related amounts for Kilgore Inc. for the fiscal year ended November 30, 1995, are presented in Problem 5-7B.

Instructions
1. Prepare a single-step income statement.
2. Prepare a retained earnings statement.
3. Prepare an account form of balance sheet, assuming that the current portion of the note payable is $3,500.

PROBLEM 5-9B
PREPARATION OF WORK
SHEET, FINANCIAL
STATEMENTS, AND
ADJUSTING AND CLOSING
ENTRIES
Objectives 5, 6, 7, 8

The accounts and their balances in the ledger of Dietz Inc. on December 31 of the current year are as follows:

Cash	$ 59,575
Accounts Receivable	116,100
Merchandise Inventory	235,000
Prepaid Insurance	10,600
Store Supplies	3,750
Office Supplies	1,700
Store Equipment	115,000
Accumulated Depreciation—Store Equipment	40,300
Office Equipment	52,000
Accumulated Depreciation—Office Equipment	17,200
Accounts Payable	66,700
Salaries Payable	—
Unearned Rent	1,200
Note Payable (final payment, 2000)	105,000
Capital Stock	50,000
Retained Earnings	170,510
Dividends	40,000
Income Summary	—
Sales	997,500
Sales Returns and Allowances	15,500
Sales Discounts	6,000
Cost of Merchandise Sold	571,200
Sales Salaries Expense	86,400
Advertising Expense	29,450
Depreciation Expense—Store Equipment	—
Store Supplies Expense	—
Miscellaneous Selling Expense	1,885
Office Salaries Expense	60,000
Rent Expense	30,000
Insurance Expense	—
Depreciation Expense—Office Equipment	—
Office Supplies Expense	—
Miscellaneous Administrative Expense	1,650
Rent Income	—
Interest Expense	12,600

The data needed for year-end adjustments on December 31 are as follows:

Physical merchandise inventory on December 31		$220,000
Insurance expired during the year		6,760
Supplies on hand on December 31:		
Store supplies		1,800
Office supplies		500
Depreciation for the year:		
Store equipment		9,500
Office equipment		4,800
Salaries payable on December 31:		
Sales salaries	$3,050	
Office salaries	1,550	4,600
Unearned rent on December 31		400

Instructions

1. Prepare a work sheet for the fiscal year ended December 31, listing all accounts in the order given.
2. Prepare a multiple-step income statement.
3. Prepare a retained earnings statement.
4. Prepare a report form of balance sheet, assuming that the current portion of the note payable is $15,000.
5. Journalize the adjusting entries.
6. Journalize the closing entries.

MINI-CASE BROOKS VIDEO COMPANY

Your sister operates Brooks Video Company, a videotape distributorship that is in its third year of operation. The following income statement was recently prepared for the year ended May 31, 1995:

BROOKS VIDEO COMPANY
Income Statement
For Year Ended May 31, 1995

Revenues:		
Net sales		$307,000
Interest income		500
Total revenues		$307,500
Expenses:		
Cost of merchandise sold	$214,900	
Selling expenses............................	46,080	
Administrative expenses.............	24,780	
Interest expense	6,000	
Total expenses..........................		291,760
Net income		$ 15,740

Your sister is considering a proposal to increase net income by offering sales discounts of 2/15, n/30, and by shipping all merchandise FOB shipping point. Currently, no sales discounts are allowed and merchandise is shipped FOB destination. It is estimated that these credit terms will increase net sales by 10%. The ratio of the cost of merchandise sold to net sales is 70% and is not expected to change

under the proposed plan. All selling and administrative expenses are expected to remain unchanged, except for store supplies, miscellaneous selling, office supplies, and miscellaneous administrative expenses, which are expected to increase proportionately with increased net sales. The amounts of these preceding items for the year ended May 31, 1995, were as follows:

Store supplies expense.........................	$1,600
Miscellaneous selling expense...........	1,020
Office supplies expense......................	840
Miscellaneous administrative exp	600

The other income and other expense items will remain unchanged. The shipment of all merchandise FOB shipping point will eliminate all transportation out expenses, which for the year ended May 31, 1995, were $14,160.

Instructions

1. Prepare a projected single-step income statement for the year ending May 31, 1996, based on the proposal.
2. a. ▪▪ ▸ Based on the projected income statement in (1), would you recommend the implementation of the proposed changes?
   b. ▪▪ ▸ Describe any possible concerns you may have related to the proposed changes described in (1).

COMPREHENSIVE PROBLEM 2

Oliver Inc. is a merchandising enterprise. The account balances for Oliver Inc. as of May 1, 1995 (unless otherwise indicated) are as follows:

110	Cash	$ 39,160
111	Notes Receivable	—
112	Accounts Receivable	60,220
113	Interest Receivable	—
115	Merchandise Inventory	123,900
116	Prepaid Insurance	3,750
117	Store Supplies	2,550
123	Store Equipment	44,300
124	Accumulated Depreciation	12,600
210	Accounts Payable	38,500
211	Salaries Payable	—
310	Capital Stock	50,000
311	Retained Earnings, June 1, 1994	123,270
312	Dividends	4,500
313	Income Summary	—
410	Sales	741,600
411	Sales Returns and Allowances	13,600
412	Sales Discounts	5,200
510	Cost of Merchandise Sold	518,040
520	Sales Salaries Expense	74,400
521	Advertising Expense	18,000
522	Depreciation Expense	—
523	Store Supplies Expense	—
529	Miscellaneous Selling Expense	2,800
530	Office Salaries Expense	29,400
531	Rent Expense	24,500
532	Insurance Expense	—
539	Miscellaneous Administrative Expense	1,650
611	Interest Income	—

During May, the last month of the fiscal year, the following transactions were completed:

May 1. Paid rent for May, $2,500.
      1. Received a $10,000 note receivable from a customer on account.
      2. Purchased merchandise on account, terms 2/10, n/30, FOB shipping point, $22,000.
      3. Paid transportation charges on purchase of May 2, $860.
      4. Purchased merchandise on account, terms n/30, FOB destination, $16,200.
      5. Sold merchandise on account, terms 2/10, n/30, FOB shipping point, $8,500. The cost of the merchandise sold was $5,000.
      8. Received $14,900 cash from customers on account, no discount.
     10. Sold merchandise for cash, $18,300. The cost of the merchandise sold was $11,000.
     11. Paid $12,800 to creditors on account.
     12. Paid for merchandise purchased on May 2, less discount.
     13. Received merchandise returned on sale of May 5, $1,000. The cost of the merchandise returned was $600.
     14. Paid advertising expense for last half of May, $2,000.
     15. Received cash from sale of May 5, less return and discount.
     18. Paid sales salaries of $1,500 and office salaries of $500.
     18. Received $28,500 cash from customers on account, after discounts of $400 had been deducted.
     19. Purchased merchandise for cash, $6,400.
     19. Paid $13,150 to creditors on account.
     20. Sold merchandise on account, terms 1/10, n/30, FOB shipping point, $16,000. The cost of the merchandise sold was $9,600.
     21. For the convenience of the customer, paid shipping charges on sale of May 20, $600.
     21. Purchased merchandise on account, terms 1/10, n/30, FOB destination, $15,000.
     22. Paid for merchandise purchased on May 4.
     24. Returned $3,000 of damaged merchandise purchased on May 21, receiving credit from the seller.
     25. Refunded cash on sales made for cash, $400. The cost of the merchandise returned was $240.
     27. Paid sales salaries of $1,200 and office salaries of $400.
     28. Sold merchandise on account, terms 2/10, n/30, FOB shipping point, $24,700. The cost of the merchandise sold was $15,000.
     29. Purchased store supplies for cash, $350.
     30. Received cash from sale of May 20, less discount, plus transportation paid on May 21.
     31. Paid for purchase of May 21, less return and discount.
     31. Sold merchandise on account, terms 2/10, n/30, FOB shipping point, $17,400. The cost of the merchandise sold was $10,000.
     31. Purchased merchandise on account, terms 1/10, n/30, FOB destination, $19,700.

Instructions

1. Enter the balances of each of the accounts in the appropriate balance column of a four-column account. Write *Balance* in the item section, and place a check mark (✔) in the Posting Reference column.
2. Journalize the transactions for May.
3. Post the journal to the ledger, extending the month-end balances to the appropriate balance columns after all posting is completed.
4. Prepare a trial balance as of May 31 on a ten-column work sheet, listing all the accounts in the order given in the ledger. Complete the work sheet for the fiscal year ended May 31, using the following adjustment data:

a. Interest accrued on notes receivable on May 31, 1995		$ 100
b. Physical merchandise inventory on May 31, 1995		140,643
c. Insurance expired during the year		2,250
d. Store supplies on hand on May 31, 1995		750
e. Depreciation for the current year		8,860
f. Accrued salaries on May 31, 1995:		
Sales salaries	$400	
Office salaries	140	540

(continued)

5. Prepare a multiple-step income statement, a retained earnings statement, and a report form of balance sheet.
6. Journalize and post the adjusting entries.
7. Journalize and post the closing entries.
8. Prepare a post-closing trial balance.

SOLUTIONS SOFTWARE

Instructions for Solving Comprehensive Problem 2 Using Solutions Software
1. Load opening balances.
2. Enter your name in the Student Name field in the General Information data entry window. Set the run date to May 31 of the current year.
3. Save the opening balances file to your drive and directory.
4. Select the General Journal Entries option, and key the journal entries. Leave the reference field blank. Note: To review the chart of accounts, select F-1.
5. Display a journal entries report.
6. Display a trial balance.
7. Key the adjusting entries. Key ADJ.ENT. in the reference field.
8. Display the adjusting entries. Key ADJ.ENT. in the Reference Restriction area of the Selection Options screen.
9. Display the financial statements.
10. Save a backup copy of your data file.
11. Perform period-end closing.
12. Display a post-closing trial balance.
13. Save your data file to disk.
14. End the session.

ANSWERS TO SELF-EXAMINATION QUESTIONS

1. **A** A debit memorandum (answer A), issued by the buyer, indicates the amount the buyer proposes to debit to the accounts payable account. A credit memorandum (answer B), issued by the seller, indicates the amount the seller proposes to credit to the accounts receivable account. An invoice (answer C) or a bill (answer D), issued by the seller, indicates the amount and terms of the sale.

2. **C** The amount of discount for early payment is $10 (answer C), or 1% of $1,000. Although the $50 of transportation costs paid by the seller are debited to the customer's account, the customer is not entitled to a discount on that amount.

3. **B** The single-step form of income statement (answer B) is so named because the total of all expenses is deducted in one step from the total of all revenues. The multiple-step form (answer A) includes numerous sections and subsections with several subtotals. The account form (answer C) and the report form (answer D) are two common forms of the balance sheet.

4. **C** Gross profit (answer C) is the excess of net sales over the cost of merchandise sold. Operating income (answer A) or income from operations (answer B) is the excess of gross profit over operating expenses. Net income (answer D) is the final figure on the income statement after all revenues and expenses have been reported.

5. **D** Expenses such as interest expense (answer D) that cannot be associated directly with operations are identified as *Other expense* or *Nonoperating expense*. Depreciation expense—office equipment (answer A) is an administrative expense. Sales salaries expense (answer B) is a selling expense. Insurance expense (answer C) is a mixed expense with elements of both selling expense and administrative expense. For small businesses, insurance expense is usually reported as an administrative expense.

Part 2

Financial Accounting Systems - Assets

You and Accounting

When you receive the monthly statement for your checking account, you may simply accept the bank statement as correct. However, banks can make mistakes. For example, at the bottom right-hand corner of each check returned from the bank is a magnetic coding that has been entered by a bank clerk. This coding indicates the amount of the check. If the clerk enters the coding incorrectly, then the check will be processed for a wrong amount. To illustrate, the following check written for $25 was incorrectly processed as $250:

Ed Smith
1026 3rd Ave., So.
Lansing, Wisconsin 58241

7406

7/23 19 95   64-7088/2611

PAY TO THE
ORDER OF   *Jones Co.* $ 25 00/100

Twenty Five Dollars and no/100 _____ DOLLARS

**FIRST FEDERAL
SAVINGS BANK
OF WISCONSIN**
LANSING, WISCONSIN

FOR   *Ed Smith*

⑆2611708891⑆ 04 33 503662⑆ 7406 ⑆0000025000⑆

Not only can banks make errors, but so can you. To find both types of errors, the balance of your checking account should be brought into agreement, or reconciled, monthly with your bank statement balance. In this chapter, you will see how businesses reconcile their monthly bank statements as one feature of a system for accounting for and controlling cash. The basic techniques of reconciling a business bank account also apply to your individual checking account.

Chapter 6
Accounting Systems and Cash

Managers need information for use in planning and controlling the operations of a business enterprise. The accounting system of an enterprise provides this information, in addition to reports for external users, such as investors and creditors. In this chapter, we will discuss the basic principles of accounting systems, including internal controls. In addition, we will discuss the basic principles of accounting systems design and implementation, including data processing methods. We will apply these principles to the design of systems for controlling cash and the accounting for cash transactions.

PRINCIPLES OF ACCOUNTING SYSTEMS

Objective 1
Describe the basic principles of accounting systems.

The methods and procedures used by an enterprise to record and report financial data make up the **accounting system**. Accounting systems vary from business to business. For example, the accounting system for a not-for-profit hospital will differ significantly from the accounting system for a retailer. This variation is due to differences in management's information needs, the type and number of transactions to be recorded, and the information needs of external users of financial statements. However, there are a number of broad principles that apply to all systems.

Cost-Benefit Balance

An accounting system must be designed to meet the specific information needs of a business. However, providing information is costly. Thus, a major consideration in designing an accounting system is balancing the benefits against the cost of the information. In general, the benefits should be at least equal to the cost of producing the information. Because of improving technology and declining costs, many enterprises have switched from manual accounting systems to computerized accounting systems. The basic principles of accounting systems that we discussed in the following paragraphs are applicable to both types of systems.

Effective Reports

To be effective, the reports generated by an accounting system must be prepared in a timely, clear, and concise manner. When these reports are prepared, the needs and knowledge of the user should be considered. For example, managers may need a variety of detailed reports for planning and controlling operations on a daily or weekly basis. In contrast, regulatory agencies often require uniform reports at established intervals, such as quarterly or yearly.

Ability to Adapt to Future Needs

Businesses operate in a changing environment. This environment may include changes beyond the control of a business, such as new government regulations, changes in accounting principles, or changes in computer technology. An accounting system must be able to adapt to the changing needs for information in such an environment. For example, regulatory agencies such as the Securities and Exchange Commission and the Internal Revenue Service often change the information and reports they require of businesses.

Accounting systems reflect the organizational structure and the information needs of individuals within the business. As individuals or lines of authority and responsibility within a business change, the accounting system must also adapt and change. To be effective, the accounting system must support all levels of management.

Adequate Internal Controls

An accounting system provides information that management reports to owners, creditors, and other interested parties. In addition, the system should aid management in planning and controlling operations. The detailed policies and procedures used to direct operations, protect assets, and provide reasonable assurance that the business's objectives are achieved are called **internal controls**. The general principles for an adequate internal control structure are discussed later in this chapter.

ACCOUNTING SYSTEMS INSTALLATION AND REVISION

Objective 2
List the three phases of accounting systems installation and revision.

Designing and installing an accounting system for an enterprise requires a thorough knowledge of the enterprise's operations. In addition, accounting systems must be continually reviewed for possible revisions in order to keep pace with the changing information needs of enterprises. For example, some areas of the system, such as the types and design of forms and the number and titles of accounts, continually change as the enterprise grows and adapts to its environment. This process of installing or changing an accounting system is made up of three phases: (1) analysis, (2) design, and (3) implementation.

Systems Analysis

Systems analysis usually begins with a review of the organizational structure and the job descriptions of personnel. This review is followed by a study of the forms, records, procedures, processing methods, and reports used by the enterprise. The source of such information is usually found in the firm's *Systems Manual*.

The data needed by an enterprise to satisfy its information needs is called its **database**. The goal of systems analysis is to determine these needs, the sources of information, and weaknesses in the procedures and the data processing methods being used.

In addition to analyzing and reviewing the current system, the systems analyst should also assess management's plans for changes in operations (volume, products, territories, etc.). Such changes usually require changes in the current system.

Systems Design

Accounting systems are changed as a result of the kind of systems analysis described above. Such changes may involve only minor changes from the existing system, such as revision of a particular form and the related procedures and processing methods. In contrast, a complete revision of the entire system may be required.

System designers must have a general knowledge of different accounting systems and methods of processing transactions, both manual and computerized. A successful systems design depends upon the creativity, imagination, and ability of the systems designer to evaluate alternatives. The basic principles of accounting systems are also necessary for a successful design.

In the preceding chapters, we described and illustrated manual accounting systems. Such systems are usually easy to understand and use. In addition, understanding a manual accounting system helps you understand how computerized accounting systems function. Computerized accounting systems use electronic technology and media to perform more rapidly the same processing functions as manual accounting systems.

In many cases, a manual accounting system adequately meets a firm's information needs. In other cases, the simple manual systems described in preceding chapters can be modified in order to meet the needs of an enterprise more efficiently. For example, as the number of customers increases, the ledger becomes unwieldy when a separate account for each customer is included. Thus, the individual customers' accounts are normally placed in a separate ledger called a **subsidiary ledger**. This subsidiary ledger is represented in the principal ledger (now called the **general ledger**) by a summarizing account, called a **controlling account**. The balance in the accounts receivable controlling account in the general ledger must equal the sum of the balances of the accounts in the subsidiary ledger.[1]

The concept of the subsidiary ledger can be extended to any group of individual accounts with a common characteristic. For example, a subsidiary ledger for creditors' accounts payable may be used, with Accounts Payable serving as the controlling account in the general ledger. When a perpetual inventory system is used, a subsidiary ledger for merchandise inventory may be used, with Merchandise Inventory serving as the controlling account in the general ledger.

---

[1] Another means by which manual systems can be modified to reduce costs and more efficiently process accounting data is to use special journals. In each special journal, selected kinds of transactions are recorded. The basic features of special journals and a more detailed discussion of subsidiary ledgers are presented in Appendix F.

Systems Implementation

The final phase of systems installation or revision is to carry out, or implement, the systems design. New or revised forms, records, procedures, and equipment must be installed, and any that are no longer useful must be withdrawn. All personnel responsible for operating the system must be carefully trained and supervised until the system is fully operational.

Major revisions of a system, such as changing from a centralized computer system to a decentralized, micro-computer-based data processing system, must be carefully planned. Managers must have reasonable assurance that the new system will provide complete and accurate information. Therefore, many companies implement new or revised systems in stages over a period of time. Weaknesses and conflicting or unnecessary elements in the design are easier to detect when the implementation is gradual rather than all at once. In addition, this approach reduces the chances that essential operating information will be unavailable during the systems implementation.

Another approach to new system implementation is to conduct a parallel test. In a parallel test, the old and new systems are run at the same time. The outputs of both systems are then compared. Parallel tests are costly, since two systems are being run. However, many managers believe this additional cost is worth the assurance that the new system is complete and accurate. In addition, this approach guarantees that essential operating information will be available from the old system if the new system does not function properly.

Accounting Systems, Profit Measurement, and Management

A Greek restaurant owner in Canada had his own system of accounting. He kept his accounts payable in a cigar box on the left-hand side of his cash register, his daily cash returns in the cash register, and his receipts for paid bills in another cigar box on the right.

When his youngest son graduated as an accountant, he was appalled by his father's primitive methods. "I don't know how you can run a business that way," he said. "How do you know what your profits are?"

"Well, son," the father replied, "when I got off the boat from Greece, I had nothing but the pants I was wearing. Today, your brother is a doctor. You are an accountant. Your sister is a speech therapist. Your mother and I have a nice car, a city house, and a country home. We have a good business, and everything is paid for. . . ."

"So, you add all that together, subtract the pants, and there's your profit!"

INTERNAL CONTROL STRUCTURE

Objective 3
List, define, and give examples of the three elements of the internal control structure.

The objective of an internal control structure is to provide assurance that an enterprise's goals and objectives are achieved. The internal control structure also exists to protect assets from theft or misuse. In a small business where it is possible for the owner-manager to supervise employees directly, the control structure may be very simple. As the number of employees and the complexities of an enterprise increase, it becomes more difficult for the owner-manager to supervise and control all phases of operations. As a result, more authority is delegated to employees. Managers, in turn, rely more on the internal control structure to motivate employees to act in a way that is consistent with the enterprise's goals and objectives. In such cases, the internal control structure can become very complex.

An **internal control structure** consists of an enterprise's (1) accounting system, (2) control environment, and (3) control procedures.[2] In the following paragraphs, we will briefly discuss the basic principles underlying each of these three elements of internal control structure.

---

[2] *Statements on Auditing Standards, No. 55*, "Consideration of the Internal Control Structure in a Financial Statement Audit" (New York: American Institute of Certified Public Accountants, 1988).

The Accounting System

The accounting system is an integral part of the internal control structure of an enterprise. It provides management with data necessary to plan and direct operations. We discussed the principles of an effective accounting system earlier in this chapter.

The Control Environment

What is an enterprise's control environment? An enterprise's control environment is the overall attitude of management and employees about the importance of controls. One of the factors that influences the control environment of an enterprise is management's philosophy and operating style. A management that overemphasizes operating goals may indirectly encourage employees to overstate or misreport operating data. For example, one of the largest company frauds in history involved the Equity Funding Corporation of America. In the 1970s, this company recorded over $2 billion of fictitious insurance policies. One of the factors that contributed to this fraud was top management's overemphasis on improving operating results.

A management that often deviates from established control policies and procedures may also be indicating to employees that controls are not important. On the other hand, a management that emphasizes the importance of controls and encourages adherence to control policies will create an effective control environment.

Another factor that influences the control environment is the enterprise's organizational structure, which is the framework for planning and controlling operations. For example, a merchandising enterprise might organize each of its stores as relatively separate business units. Each store manager may be given full authority over pricing and other operating activities. In such a structure, each store manager would have the responsibility for establishing an effective control environment.

Personnel policies and procedures also affect the control environment. Personnel policies involve the hiring, training, evaluating, compensating, and promoting of employees. The human resource area also includes the development of job descriptions, employee codes of ethics, and conflict-of-interest policies. Such policies and procedures can enhance the internal control environment if they provide reasonable assurance that only competent, honest employees are hired and retained.

Control Procedures

Control procedures are those policies and procedures that management has established to provide reasonable assurance that enterprise goals will be achieved. In the following paragraphs, we will briefly discuss control procedures that can be integrated throughout the accounting system.

COMPETENT PERSONNEL, ROTATION OF DUTIES, AND MANDATORY VACATIONS. The successful operation of an accounting system requires procedures to ensure that people are able to perform the duties to which they are assigned. Hence, it is necessary that all accounting employees be adequately trained and supervised to perform their jobs. It may also be advisable to rotate clerical personnel periodically from job to job. In addition to increasing their understanding of the system, the knowledge that an employee's work may be performed by others encourages adherence to prescribed procedures. For nonclerical personnel such as managers, mandatory vacations normally are used rather than job rotations. During vacation periods, the relevant job responsibilities are performed by other managers.

Rotation of duties and mandatory vacations may prevent errors and fraud and may also lead to the detection of errors or fraud. For example, an accounts receivable clerk should be periodically rotated to another job or required to take a vacation. If the clerk steals customers' cash payments, the thefts will likely be discovered when a new clerk bills customers for amounts they have already paid.

ASSIGNMENT OF RESPONSIBILITY. If employees are to work efficiently, their responsibilities must be clearly defined. Control procedures should provide assurance that no overlapping or undefined areas of responsibility exist and that employees are held accountable for their responsibilities. For example, if a certain cash register is to be used by two or more salesclerks, the clerks should be assigned separate cash drawers and register keys. In this way, the clerks are held responsible for their individual cash drawers, and a daily proof of cash can be obtained for each clerk.

SEPARATION OF RESPONSIBILITIES FOR RELATED OPERATIONS. To decrease the possibility of inefficiency, errors, and fraud, responsibility for a sequence of related operations should be divided among two or more persons. For example, the responsibilities for purchasing, receiving, and paying for merchandise should be divided among three persons or departments. If one individual orders merchandise, verifies the receipt of the merchandise, and pays the supplier, the following abuses are possible:

1. Orders may be placed on the basis of friendship with a supplier, rather than on price, quality, and other objective factors.
2. The quantity and the quality of merchandise received may not be verified.
3. Merchandise may be stolen by the employee.
4. The validity and accuracy of invoices may be verified carelessly, thus causing the payment of false or inaccurate invoices.

The "checks and balances" provided by dividing responsibilities among various departments requires no duplication of effort. The business documents prepared as a result of the work of each department are designed to coordinate and support those prepared by the other departments.

SEPARATION OF ACCOUNTING, CUSTODY OF ASSETS, AND OPERATIONS. Control policies and procedures should establish the responsibilities for various business activities. To reduce the possibility of errors and fraud, the following functions should be separated:

1. Accounting for the enterprise's transactions.
2. Custody of the firm's assets.
3. Engaging in the enterprise's operating activities.

When these functions are separated, the accounting records serve as an independent check on the individuals who have custody of the assets and who engage in the business operations. For example, the employees entrusted with handling cash receipts from credit customers should not record cash receipts in the accounting records. To do so would allow employees to borrow or steal cash and hide the theft in the records. Likewise, if those engaged in operating activities also record the results of operations, they could distort the accounting reports to show favorable results. For example, a store manager whose year-end bonus is based upon operating profits might be tempted to record fictitious sales in order to receive a larger bonus.

PROOFS AND SECURITY MEASURES. Proofs and security measures should be used to safeguard business assets and ensure reliable accounting data. This control procedure applies to many different techniques, such as authorization, approval, and reconciliation procedures. For example, a control procedure might require reports to verify the receipt of all sales returns before credit is approved and granted to a customer. Other examples of control procedures include the use of bank accounts and other measures to ensure the safety of cash and other valuable documents. Using a cash register that displays the amount recorded for each sale and provides for the customer a printed receipt can be an effective part of the internal control structure.

Companies may obtain insurance to protect against losses from employee fraud. Such insurance, called a fidelity bond, normally requires background checks on all employees covered. If a claim is paid, insurance companies normally take legal action against the employees responsible. Such legal action tends to deter employee fraud and enhances the internal control structure.

INDEPENDENT REVIEW. To determine whether internal control procedures are being effectively applied, the control structure should be periodically reviewed and evaluated. In large businesses, internal auditors who are independent of operations normally have this responsibility. An example of the use of internal auditors for review of internal control procedures is described in the annual report of Rose's Stores Inc. as follows:

To meet its responsibilities with respect to financial information, management maintains and enforces internal accounting policies, procedures, and controls which are designed to provide reasonable assurance that assets are safeguarded and that transactions are properly recorded and executed in accordance with management's authorization. The concept of reasonable assurance is based on the recognition that the cost of controls should not exceed the expected benefits. Management maintains an internal audit function and an internal control function which are responsible for evaluating the adequacy and application of financial and operating controls and for testing compliance with Company policies and procedures.

Internal auditors should report any weaknesses and recommend changes to correct them. For example, a review of cash payments may disclose that invoices were not paid within the discount period, even though enough cash was available.

BANK RECONCILIATIONS AS A CONTROL OVER CASH

As you might expect, because of the ease with which money can be transferred, cash is the asset most likely to be diverted and used improperly by employees. In addition, many transactions either directly or indirectly affect the receipt or the payment of cash. A business must therefore use special controls for safeguarding cash.

The Bank Account as a Tool for Controlling Cash

Objective 4
Prepare a bank reconciliation and journalize any necessary entries.

One of the main tools for controlling cash is the bank account. To maximize control over cash, all cash received should be deposited in a bank account. Likewise, all cash payments should be disbursed from a bank account. When such a system is strictly followed, there is a double record of cash—one by the business and the other by the bank. Thus, when the amount of cash recorded by the business is compared and reconciled with the amount of cash recorded by the bank, any errors and misuse or thefts may be detected.

The forms used by a business with a bank account are a signature card, deposit ticket, check, and record of checks drawn. These forms are described below.

SIGNATURE CARD.
When you open a checking account, you sign a **signature card**. This card is used by the bank to verify the signature on checks that you have written. Also, when you open an account, the bank assigns an identifying number to the account.

DEPOSIT TICKET. The details of a deposit are listed by the depositor on a printed form supplied by the bank. These **deposit tickets** may be prepared in duplicate. The bank teller stamps or initials a copy of the deposit ticket and gives it to the depositor as a receipt. Other types of receipts may also be used to give the depositor written proof of the date and the total amount of the deposit.

CHECK. A **check** is a written instrument signed by the depositor, ordering the bank to pay a sum of money to an individual or entity. There are three parties to a check—the drawer, the drawee, and the payee. The **drawer** is the one who signs the check, ordering payment by the bank. The **drawee** is the bank on which the check is drawn. The **payee** is the party to whom payment is to be made.

When checks are issued to pay bills, they are recorded as credits to Cash on the day issued. The credit to Cash is recorded even though the checks will not be presented by the payee to the drawer's bank until a later date. Likewise, when checks are received from customers, they are recorded as debits to Cash.

Check forms may be obtained in many styles. The name and the address of the depositor are often printed on each check. In addition, checks are normally prenumbered, so that they can easily be kept track of as an aid to internal control. Most banks use automatic sorting and posting equipment. This equipment requires that the bank's identification number and the depositor's account number be printed on each check. These numbers are usually printed along the lower margin in machine-readable magnetic ink. When the check is presented for payment, the amount for which it is drawn is inserted next to the account number, also in magnetic ink. At the beginning of this chapter, we illustrated a check that had been processed by a bank.

RECORD OF CHECKS DRAWN. A record of the basic details of a check should be prepared at the time the check is written. A copy of each check written or a stub from which the check is detached may be used as the basis for recording cash payments. A small booklet called a **transactions register** may also be used.

The invoice number or other data may be inserted in spaces provided on the check or on an attachment to the check. Normally, checks issued to a creditor on account are sent with a form that identifies the specific invoice that is being paid. The purpose of this form, sometimes called a **remittance advice**, is to make sure that proper credit is recorded in the accounts of the creditor. In this way, mistakes are less likely to occur. A check and remittance advice is shown in Exhibit 1.

Exhibit 1
Check and Remittance Advice

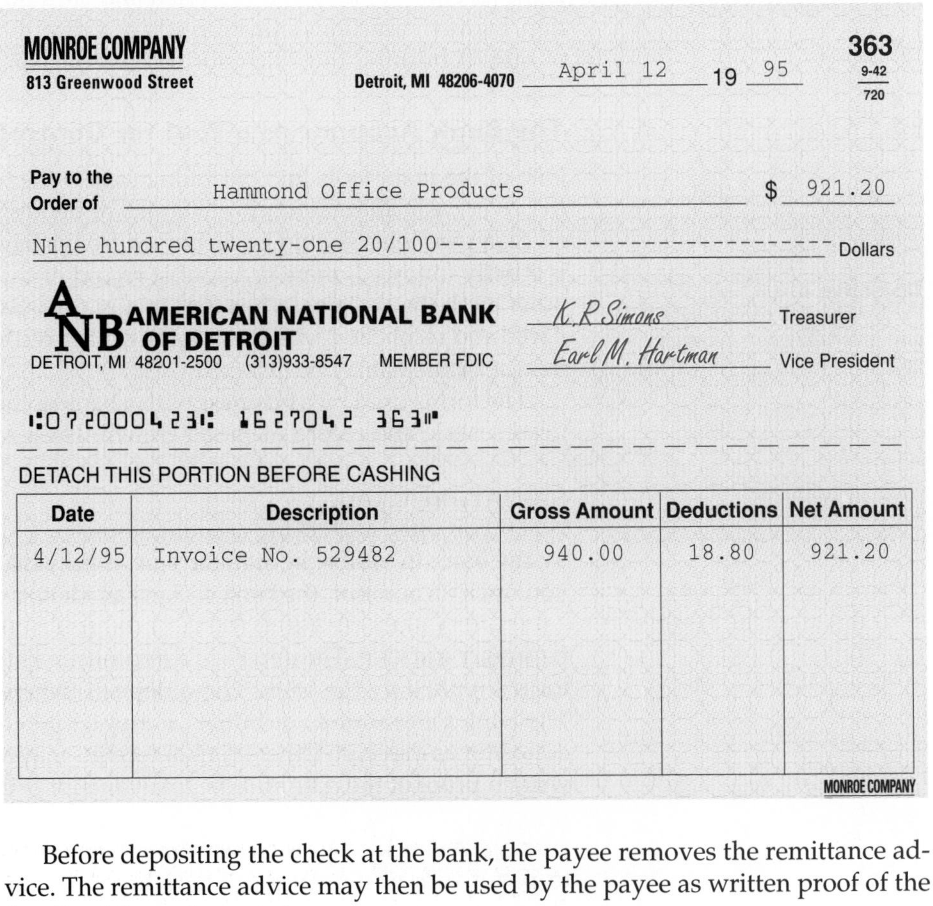

Date	Description	Gross Amount	Deductions	Net Amount
4/12/95	Invoice No. 529482	940.00	18.80	921.20

Before depositing the check at the bank, the payee removes the remittance advice. The remittance advice may then be used by the payee as written proof of the details of the cash receipt.

Bank Statement

Banks usually maintain a record of all checking account transactions. A summary of all transactions, called a **statement of account**, is mailed to the depositor, usually once each month. Like any account with a customer or a creditor, the bank statement shows the beginning balance, additions, deductions, and the balance at the end of the period.

The depositor's checks received by the bank during the period may accompany the bank statement, arranged in the order of payment. The paid or canceled checks are perforated or stamped "Paid," together with the date of payment. Debit or credit memorandums describing other entries in the depositor's account may also be enclosed with the statement. For example, the bank may have debited the depositor's account for service charges or for deposited checks returned because of insufficient funds. It may have credited the account for receipts from notes receivable left for collection, for loans to the depositor, or for interest.[3] A typical bank statement is shown in Exhibit 2.

Exhibit 2
Bank Statement

```
                                                        PAGE  1
 A                          ACCOUNT NUMBER  1627042
 NB                MEMBER FDIC    FROM   6/30/95      TO   7/31/95
AMERICAN NATIONAL BANK           BALANCE                  4,233.60
OR DETROIT                       22  DEPOSITS          13,749.75
DETROIT, MI 48201-2500  (313)933-8547   52  WITHDRAWS  15,013.57

                                  2  OTHER DEBITS
                                     AND CREDITS           390.00 CR
   MONROE COMPANY
   813 GREENWOOD STREET           NEW BALANCE            3,359.78
   DETROIT, MI 48206-4070


     *--CHECKS AND OTHER DEBITS---*---DEPOSITS--*---DATES--*--BALANCE--*
    819.40     122.54                  585.75     07/01    3,862.41
    369.50     732.26      20.15       421.53     07/02    3,162.03
    600.00     190.70      52.50       781.30     07/03    3,100.13
     25.93     160.00                  662.50     07/05    3,576.31
     36.80     181.02                  503.18     07/07    3,862.06
 ================================================================
     32.26     535.09                  932.00     07/29    3,404.40
     21.10     126.20                  705.21     07/30    3,962.31
              SC 18.00     MS          408.00     07/30    4,352.31
     26.12   1,615.13                  648.72     07/31    3,359.78

     EC--ERROR CORRECTION            OD--OVERDRAFT
     MS--MISCELLANEOUS               PS--PAYMENT STOPPED
     NSF--NOT SUFFICIENT FUNDS       SC--SERVICE CHARGE

     ***                    ***                    ***

        THE RECONCILEMENT OF THIS STATEMENT WITH YOUR RECORDS IS ESSENTIAL.
          ANY ERROR OR EXCEPTION SHOULD BE RETORTED IMMEDIATELY.
```

Bank Reconciliation

When all cash receipts are deposited in the bank and all payments are made by check, the cash account is often called *Cash in Bank*. This account in the business enterprise's (the depositor's) ledger is an asset account with a debit balance. The bank records amounts deposited by customers as a liability.[4] The liability account used is supported by a subsidiary ledger that contains individual accounts for each customer. Thus, the depositor's cash in bank account has a reciprocal account in the bank's customers subsidiary ledger.

---

[3] Although interest-bearing checking accounts are common for individuals, Federal Reserve Regulation Q prohibits the paying of interest on corporate checking accounts.
[4] Banks often use the account title *Demand Deposits* to record deposits payable upon demand (checking account deposits).

You might think that the balance of the cash in bank account in the depositor's records should always equal the balance of the customer's account in the bank's subsidiary ledger. However, the balances are not likely to be equal on any specific date because of either or both of the following: (1) delay by either party in recording transactions and (2) errors by either party in recording transactions.

Usually, there is a time lag of one day or more between the date a check is written and the date that it is presented to the bank for payment. If the depositor mails deposits to the bank or uses the night depository, a time lag between the date of the deposit and the date that it is recorded by the bank is also probable. Conversely, the bank may debit or credit the depositor's account for transactions about which the depositor will not be informed until later. Examples are service or collection fees charged by the bank and the proceeds of notes receivable sent to the bank for collection.

The depositor or the bank may record transactions incorrectly. For example, a depositor may incorrectly post to Cash in Bank a check written for $4,500 as $450. Likewise, a bank may incorrectly enter the amount of a check, as we illustrated at the beginning of this chapter.

To determine the reasons for any differences in the balance of Cash in Bank and the ending cash balance shown on the bank statement, a bank reconciliation should be prepared. A **bank reconciliation** is divided into two sections. The first section begins with the cash balance according to the bank statement and ends with the adjusted balance. The second section begins with the cash balance according to the depositor's records and ends with the adjusted balance. The two amounts designated as the adjusted balance must be equal. The form and the content of the bank reconciliation are outlined as follows:

Cash balance according to **bank statement**		$XXX
Add: Additions by depositor not on bank statement	$XX	
Bank errors	XX	XX
		$XXX
Deduct: Deductions by depositor not on bank statement	$XX	
Bank errors	XX	XX
Adjusted balance		$XXX
Cash balance according to **depositor's records**		$XXX
Add: Additions by bank not recorded by depositor	$XX	
Depositor errors	XX	XX
		$XXX
Deduct: Deductions by bank not recorded by depositor	$XX	
Depositor errors	XX	XX
Adjusted balance		$XXX

The following steps are useful in finding the reconciling items and determining the adjusted balance of Cash in Bank:

1. Individual deposits listed on the bank statement are compared with unrecorded deposits appearing in the preceding period's reconciliation and with deposit receipts or other records of deposits. *Deposits not recorded by the bank are added to the balance according to the bank statement.*
2. Paid checks are compared with outstanding checks appearing on the preceding period's reconciliation and with checks recorded. *Checks issued that have not been paid by the bank are outstanding and are deducted from the balance according to the bank statement.*
3. Bank credit memorandums are compared to entries in the journal. For example, a bank would issue a credit memorandum for a note receivable and interest that it collected for a customer. *Credit memorandums that have not been recorded are added to the balance according to the depositor's records.*
4. Bank debit memorandums are compared to entries recording cash payments. For example, a bank normally issues debit memorandums for service charges and check printing charges. A bank also issues debit memorandums for not-

sufficient-funds checks. A **not-sufficient-funds (NSF) check** is a customer's check that was recorded and deposited but was not paid when it was presented to the customer's bank for payment. NSF checks are normally charged back to the customer's account receivable. *Debit memorandums that have not been recorded are deducted from the balance according to the depositor's records.*

5. Errors discovered during the preceding steps are listed separately on the reconciliation. For example, if an amount has been recorded incorrectly by the depositor, the amount of the error should be added to or deducted from the Cash in Bank balance. Similarly, errors by the bank should be added to or deducted from the cash balance according to the bank statement.

ILLUSTRATION OF BANK RECONCILIATION. The bank statement for Monroe Company in Exhibit 2 shows a balance of $3,359.78 as of July 31. The balance in Cash in Bank in Monroe Company's ledger as of the same date is $2,249.99. The following reconciling items are revealed by using the steps outlined above:

Deposit of July 31 not recorded on bank statement	$ 816.20
Checks outstanding: No. 812, $1,061.00; No. 878, $435.39; No. 883, $48.60	1,544.99
Note plus interest of $8 collected by bank (credit memorandum), not recorded in the journal	408.00
Bank service charges (debit memorandum) not recorded in the journal	18.00
Check No. 879 for $732.26 to Taylor Co. on account, recorded in the journal as $723.26	9.00

The bank reconciliation based on the bank statement and the reconciling items is as follows:

Monroe Company
Bank Reconciliation
July 31, 1995

Cash balance according to bank statement		$3,359.78
Add deposit of July 31, not recorded by bank		816.20
		$4,175.98
Deduct outstanding checks:		
No. 812	$1,061.00	
No. 878	435.39	
No. 883	48.60	1,544.99
Adjusted balance		$2,630.99
Cash balance according to depositor's records		$2,249.99
Add note and interest collected by bank		408.00
		$2,657.99
Deduct: Bank service charges	$ 18.00	
Error in recording Check No. 879	9.00	27.00
Adjusted balance		$2,630.99

ENTRIES BASED ON BANK RECONCILIATION. No entries are necessary on the depositor's records as a result of the information included in the first section of the bank reconciliation. This section begins with the cash balance according to the bank statement. However, the bank should be notified of any errors that need to be corrected on its records.

Any addition or deduction items in the second section of the bank reconciliation must be recorded in the depositor's accounts. This section begins with the cash balance according to the depositor's records. Entries should be made for bank memorandums not recorded by the depositor and any depositor's errors.

The entries for Monroe Company, based on the bank reconciliation above, are as follows:

July 31	Cash in Bank	408	
	Notes Receivable		400
	Interest Income		8
	Note collected by bank.		
31	Miscellaneous Administrative Expense	18	
	Accounts payable—Taylor Co.	9	
	Cash in Bank		27
	Bank service charges and error		
	in recording Check No. 879.		

After the above entries have been posted, Cash in Bank will have a debit balance of $2,630.99. This balance agrees with the adjusted cash balance shown on the bank reconciliation. It is the amount of cash available as of July 31 and the amount that would be reported on the balance sheet on that date.

IMPORTANCE OF BANK RECONCILIATION. The bank reconciliation is an important part of the system of internal control. It is a means of comparing recorded cash, as shown by the accounting records, with the amount of cash reported by the bank. It thus provides for finding and correcting errors and irregularities. To enhance internal control, the bank reconciliation should be prepared by an employee who does not take part in and record cash transactions with the bank. Without a proper separation of these duties, cash is more likely to be embezzled. For example, an employee who takes part in all of these duties could prepare an unauthorized check, omit it from the accounts, and cash it. To hide the theft, the employee could understate the amount of the outstanding checks on future bank reconciliations by the amount of the unauthorized check.

Using Accounting

How you reconcile your bank account may be slightly modified from the steps shown above for a business enterprise. You should first scan your bank statement for any bank debit or credit entries that you have not yet recorded. Examples of such entries include service charges (debit entry) and interest earned (credit entry). You should then enter these amounts in your check book (register) and determine the balance of cash in the bank. At this point, the balance of cash in the bank according to your check book should be the correct amount of cash on hand. Any differences between your balance and the bank's balance are normally caused by (1) deposits in transit that have not yet been recorded by the bank and (2) outstanding checks that have not yet been recorded by the bank. Thus, your bank reconciliation can take the following form:

Cash balance according to bank statement	$XXX
Add: Deposits not on bank statement	XX
Deduct: Outstanding checks	XX
Adjusted cash balance	$XXX

Any errors made by either the bank or by you would require further investigation before the bank balance and your balance would agree.

INTERNAL CONTROL OF CASH RECEIPTS

Objective 5
Summarize basic procedures for achieving internal control over cash receipts, including the use of cash change funds and the cash short and over account.

Retailers normally use special control procedures for safeguarding and handling the large volume of cash receipts. To protect cash from theft and misuse, a business enterprise must control cash from the time it is received until it can be deposited in a bank. Such procedures are called **protective controls**.

Procedures that are designed to detect theft or misuse of cash are called **detective controls**. In a sense, detective controls are also preventive in nature, since employees are less likely to steal or misuse cash if they know there is a good chance they will be detected.

Department stores and other retail businesses normally receive cash from two main sources: (1) over the counter from cash customers and (2) by mail from credit customers making payments on account. Cash is received over the counter when a customer pays cash for the purchase of merchandise. One of the most important controls to protect cash received in over-the-counter sales is a cash register. When the clerk (cashier) enters the amount of the sale, the cash register normally displays the amount to the customer. The customer can then verify the accuracy of the purchase, which serves as an additional control.

The recording of the sale in the cash register establishes the initial accountability for the cash received. Most cash registers are designed to record this initial data on paper tapes. In addition, most businesses prohibit cashiers from changing or otherwise altering the cash register tapes without the approval of a supervisor.

At the end of the day or work shift, the cashiers count the cash in their cash drawers and record the amounts on cash or sales memorandum forms. The cashiers' supervisor removes the cash register tapes on which total receipts were recorded. The supervisor counts the cash and compares the total with the memoranda and the tapes, noting any differences. Normally, the cash is then placed in a store safe until it can be deposited in the bank. The tapes and memorandums are forwarded to the Accounting Department, where they become the basis for journal entries.

Cash is received in the mail when customers pay their bills. This cash is usually in the form of checks and money orders. Most companies' invoices are designed so that customers return a remittance advice with these payments. The employee who opens the incoming mail should initially compare the amount of cash received with the amount shown on the remittance advice. The employee should note any differences. If a customer does not return a remittance advice, an employee prepares one on a form designed for such use. Like the cash register, this record of cash received establishes the initial accountability for the cash. It also helps ensure that the posting to the customer's account is accurate.

All cash received in the mail is sent to the Cashier's Department. An employee there combines it with the receipts from cash sales and prepares a bank deposit ticket. The remittance advices and their summary totals are delivered to the Accounting Department. An accounting clerk then prepares the journal entries and posts to the customer accounts in the subsidiary ledger.

After the cash is deposited in the bank, the duplicate deposit tickets or other bank receipt forms are returned to the Accounting Department. An accounting clerk then compares the total amount deposited with the amount recorded as the cash receipt. This control helps ensure that all the cash is deposited and that no cash is lost or stolen on the way to the bank. Any shortages are thus promptly detected.

The separation of the duties of the Cashier's Department, which handles cash, and the Accounting Department, which records cash, is a preventive control. If Accounting Department employees both handled and recorded cash, an employee could steal cash and change the accounting records to hide the theft.

An important detective control for the handling of cash receipts is the use of a bank account and the bank reconciliation. Bank reconciliations are useful in detecting errors by both the bank and the business in recording cash receipts. Bank reconciliations may also be useful in detecting thefts of cash. For example, assume that an assistant store manager decides to borrow (take) cash from the daily deposits on the way to the bank. The assistant store manager then alters the daily deposit slip from the bank to show the amount of cash that should have been deposited. When the store manager prepares the bank reconciliation at the end of the month, the amount stolen will be evident because the daily deposits on the bank statement will not agree with the store's records. By preparing a bank reconciliation on a timely basis, the loss is detected before large amounts are stolen.

Cash Change Funds

Retail stores and other businesses that receive cash directly from customers must keep some currency and coins on hand in order to make change. This cash is recorded in a cash change fund account.

The cash change fund may be established by drawing a check for the required amount, debiting Cash on Hand, and crediting Cash in Bank. No additional charges or credits to the cash on hand account are necessary unless the amount of the fund is increased or decreased.

The cash on hand may be divided up among the various cash registers and drawers. The amount in each cash register or drawer is recorded for later use in reconciling cash sales for the day. The total amount of cash received during the day is deposited, and the original amount of the change fund is retained. The desired makeup of the fund is maintained by exchanging bills or coins at the bank.

Cash Short and Over

The amount of cash on hand at the end of each day should be the beginning amount of cash in each cash register plus the cash sales for the day. However, the amount of actual cash on hand at the end of the day often differs from this amount. This occurs because of errors in recording cash sales or errors in making change.

Differences in the amount of cash counted and the amount of cash in the records are normally recorded in an account entitled Cash Short and Over. For example, the following entry records one day's cash sales, when the actual cash received is less than the amount indicated by the cash register tally:

Cash in Bank	4,577.60	
Cash Short and Over	3.16	
Sales		4,580.76

If there is a debit balance in the cash short and over account at the end of a period, it is an expense that may be included as a miscellaneous administrative expense in the income statement. If there is a credit balance, it is revenue that may be listed in the Other income section. If the balance becomes larger than may be accounted for by minor errors in making change, management should take any necessary corrective measures.

INTERNAL CONTROL OF CASH PAYMENTS

Objective 6
Summarize basic procedures for achieving control over cash payments, including the use of a voucher system, a discounts lost account, and a petty cash account.

It is common practice for business enterprises to require that all payments of cash be made by check signed by an authorized individual. As an additional control, some firms require two signatures on all checks or on checks which are larger than a certain amount. It is also common to use a check protector, which imprints amounts on the check that are not easily removed or changed.

In a small business, an owner-manager may sign all checks based upon personal knowledge of all goods and services purchased. In large business enterprises, however, disbursing officials are seldom able to have such a complete knowledge of business transactions. In such enterprises, the issuance of purchase orders, inspection of goods received, and verification of invoices is divided among the employees of several departments. These activities must be coordinated with the final issuance of checks to creditors. One system used for this purpose is the voucher system.

Basic Features of the Voucher System

A **voucher system** is a set of methods and procedures for authorizing and recording liabilities and cash payments. A voucher system normally uses (1) vouchers, (2) a file for unpaid vouchers, and (3) a file for paid vouchers. As in all accounting systems, many differences in detail are possible. The following discussion refers to a medium-size merchandising enterprise with separate departments for purchasing, receiving, accounting, and disbursing.

VOUCHERS. The term voucher is widely used in accounting. In a general sense, a voucher is any document that serves as proof of authority to pay cash, such as an invoice approved for payment. A voucher may also be a document that serves as evidence that cash has been paid, such as a canceled check.

In a voucher system, a **voucher** is a special form on which is recorded relevant data about a liability and the details of its payment. A voucher form is shown in Exhibit 3.

Exhibit 3
Voucher

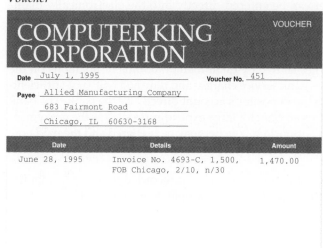

Vouchers are normally prenumbered for control purposes. Each voucher provides space for the name and address of the creditor, the date, and a summary of the basic details of the supporting document. Such basic details in the voucher shown include the invoice number and the amount and terms of the invoice. One half of the back of the voucher is devoted to the account distribution and the other half to summaries of the voucher and the details of payment. Spaces are also provided for the signature or initials of certain employees.

A voucher must be prepared for every expenditure. A check may not be issued except in payment of a properly authorized voucher. Vouchers may be paid immediately after they are prepared or at a later date, depending upon the credit terms.

A voucher is normally prepared by the Accounting Department on the basis of an invoice or a memorandum that serves as support for the expenditure. A voucher is usually prepared only after the following steps have been completed and noted on the invoice:

1. The invoice is compared with a copy of the purchase order to verify quantities, prices, and terms.
2. The invoice is compared with the receiving report to verify receipt of the items billed.
3. The arithmetical accuracy of the invoice is proved.

After all data except details of payment have been inserted, the invoice or other supporting evidence is attached to the voucher. The voucher is then given to the proper official for approval.

UNPAID VOUCHER FILE. After a voucher has been approved, it is recorded as a credit to Accounts Payable and a debit to the appropriate account or accounts. For example, the entry to record the voucher prepared by Computer King Corporation, illustrated in Exhibit 3, is as follows:

Merchandise Inventory	1,470	
Accounts Payable		1,470

After a voucher has been recorded, it is filed in an unpaid voucher file. The amount due on each voucher represents the credit balance of an account payable.

When a voucher is to be paid, it is removed from the unpaid voucher file. The date, the number, and the amount of the check written in payment are listed on the back of the voucher. Paid vouchers and supporting documents should be stamped PAID or otherwise canceled to prevent accidental or intentional reuse.

In a computerized accounting system, the due date, amount of payment, and other details of the voucher can be entered directly into the electronically maintained unpaid voucher file. As the payment for a voucher becomes due, the computer automatically prints the necessary check for mailing to the vendor.

An exception to the general rule that vouchers be prepared for all expenditures may be made for bank charges shown by debit memorandums or notations on the bank statement. Such items as bank service charges and returned NSF (not-sufficient-funds) checks are charged to the depositor's account directly by the bank. The bank may also charge the depositor's account for large expenditures such as the repayment of a loan. In this latter case, a supporting voucher may be prepared and the paid note attached as evidence of the obligation and its payment.

PAID VOUCHER FILE. The payment of a voucher is recorded in the same manner as the payment of an account payable. For example, Computer King's entry to record the check issued in payment of the voucher in Exhibit 3 is as follows:

Accounts Payable	1,470	
Cash in Bank		1,470

After payment, vouchers are usually filed in numerical order in a paid voucher file. They are then readily available for examination by employees needing information about a certain expenditure. Eventually the paid vouchers are destroyed according to the firm's policies concerning the retention of records.

THE VOUCHER SYSTEM AND MANAGEMENT. The voucher system not only provides effective accounting controls but also aids management in fulfilling its responsibilities. For example, the voucher system ensures that all payments are for valid liabilities. In addition, up-to-date information is always available for use in predicting future cash requirements. This in turn enables management to make the best use of cash resources. Invoices on which cash discounts are allowed are highlighted for payment within the discount period. Other invoices are highlighted for payment on the final day of the credit period. This aids management in maintaining a favorable credit standing. Borrowing can also be planned more accurately, with a savings in interest costs.

Purchases Discounts Lost

In previous examples, we assumed that all invoices subject to a purchases discount were paid within the discount period. Even if the buyer has to borrow to make the payment within the discount period, it is normally to the buyer's advantage to do so. To illustrate, assume that Computer King Corporation borrows money to pay the invoice shown in Exhibit 3. The last day of the discount period in which the $30 discount can be taken is July 8, 1995. The money is borrowed for the remaining 20 days of the credit period. If an annual interest rate of 12% and a 360-day year are assumed, the interest on the loan of $1,470 ($1,500 – $30) is $9.80 ($1,470 × 12% × 20/360). The net savings to Computer King Corporation is $20.20, computed as follows:

Discount of 2% on $1,500	$30.00
Interest for 20 days at rate of 12% on $1,470	9.80
Savings from borrowing	$20.20

The approximate interest rate earned on taking a discount on a purchase with credit terms of 2/10, n/30 is 36%. As shown in the following calculation, this rate is estimated by annualizing 2% for 20 days.

$$2\% \times \frac{360 \text{ days}}{20 \text{ days}} = 2\% \times 18 = 36\%$$

In this example, as long as Computer King Corporation can borrow the necessary amount at a rate of less than 36%, it should take advantage of the discount and pay within the discount period.

In practice, purchases discounts may be missed due to oversight, errors in recording due dates, or other reasons. When discounts are missed, any discounts not taken are recorded in an expense account called *Discounts Lost*.[5] The balance of this account represents the cost of failing to take cash discounts. If the balance becomes large, management can take action to avoid losing discounts in the future.

To illustrate, assume that the discount on the invoice in Exhibit 3 is not taken. When the invoice is paid on July 28, the payment is recorded as follows:

Accounts Payable	1,470	
Discounts Lost	30	
Cash in Bank		1,500

Overpayments of Accounts Payable—Can It Happen?

The business of Howard Schultz & Associates (HS&A) is reviewing payments of accounts payable. HS&A scours its clients' books, looking for duplicate payments, failures to get promised discounts, and inaccurate calculations. Some of the findings that HS&A has discovered for its clients are listed below. The magnitude of these findings indicates the importance of strong controls over cash payments of accounts payable.

. . . The typical amount recovered for a company amounts to about one-tenth of 1 percent of the total payments made to sup- *pliers. That doesn't sound like much, but for a company with $250 million in payments, it would mean a recovery of about $250,000. . . .*

The average [amount recovered is] more than $300,000 for [a] client. . . .

For . . . a "fast-growing major discount chain" . . . HS&A recovered . . . $4.5 million. . . .

HS&A once discovered a quarter-million-dollar overpayment on a single order . . . [HS&A] even unearthed a double payment made to itself. The money was refunded immediately. . . .

Source: Thomas Buell, Jr., "Demand Grows for Auditor," *The Naples Daily News* (January 12, 1992), p. 14F.

Petty Cash

As in your own day-to-day life, most businesses frequently need cash to pay small amounts, such as postage due or for small purchases of urgently needed supplies. Payment by check in such cases could result in unnecessary delay and expense. Yet,

[5] If the amount of the discounts lost is not significant, the merchandise inventory or cost of merchandise sold accounts may be debited instead of Discounts Lost. However, the disadvantage of debiting these accounts is that management cannot easily identify the amount of discounts lost during the period. Therefore, corrective action may not be taken.

these small payments may occur frequently enough to amount to a significant total amount. Thus, it is desirable to retain control over such payments. For this purpose, a special cash fund called a **petty cash fund** is used.

A petty cash fund is established by first estimating the amount of cash needed for disbursements from the fund during a period, such as a week or a month. If a voucher system is used, a voucher is prepared for this amount. The voucher is recorded as a debit to Petty Cash and a credit to Accounts Payable. The check drawn to pay the voucher is recorded as a debit to Accounts Payable and a credit to Cash in Bank.

The money obtained from cashing the check is placed in the custody of a specific employee who is authorized to disburse monies from the fund. Restrictions may also be placed on the maximum amount and the nature of fund disbursements. Each time monies are disbursed from the fund, the fund custodian records the essential details on a petty cash receipt form. In addition, the signature of the payee and the initials of the custodian of the fund are written on the form as proof of the payment. A typical petty cash receipt is illustrated in Exhibit 4.

Exhibit 4
Petty Cash Receipt

PETTY CASH RECEIPT

No. 121   Date   August 1, 1995

Paid to   Metropolitan Times   Amount

For   Daily newspaper   3 | 70

Charge to   Miscellaneous Administrative Expense

Payment received:

S.O. Hall   Approved by   _N.E.R_

A petty cash fund is normally replenished at periodic intervals or when it is depleted or reaches a minimum amount. When a petty cash fund is replenished, the accounts debited are determined by summarizing the petty cash receipts. If a voucher system is used, the voucher is recorded as a debit to the various expense and asset accounts and a credit to Accounts Payable. The check in payment of the voucher is recorded in the usual manner.

To illustrate the entries that would be made in accounting for petty cash, assume that a voucher system is used and that a petty cash fund of $100 is established on August 1. At the end of August, the petty cash receipts indicate expenditures for the following items: office supplies, $28; postage (office supplies), $22; store supplies, $35; and daily newspapers (miscellaneous administrative expense), $3.70. The entries to establish and replenish the petty cash fund are as follows:

Aug. 1	Petty Cash	100.00	
	Accounts Payable		100.00
1	Accounts Payable	100.00	
	Cash in Bank		100.00
31	Office Supplies	50.00	
	Store Supplies	35.00	
	Miscellaneous Administrative Expense	3.70	
	Accounts Payable		88.70
31	Accounts Payable	88.70	
	Cash in Bank		88.70

Replenishing the petty cash fund restores it to its original amount of $100. You should note that there is no entry in Petty Cash when the fund is replenished. Petty Cash is debited only when the fund is initially set up or when the permanent amount of the fund is increased or decreased at some later time.

Other Cash Funds

Cash funds may also be established to meet other special needs of a business. For example, money may be advanced for travel expenses as needed. Periodically, after expense reports have been received, the expenses are recorded and the fund is replenished. A similar procedure may be used to provide a cash operating fund for a sales office located in another city. The amount of the fund may be deposited in a local bank and the sales representative may be authorized to draw checks for payment of rent, salaries, and other operating expenses. Each month, the representative sends the invoices, bank statement, paid checks, bank reconciliation, and other business documents to the home office. The data are audited, the expenditures are recorded, and a replenishing check is returned for deposit in the local bank.

Like petty cash funds, disbursements from other cash funds are not recorded in the accounts until the funds are replenished. To bring the accounts up to date, such funds should always be replenished at the end of an accounting period. The amount of monies in these funds will then agree with the balances in the fund accounts. At the same time, the expenses and the assets for which payments have been made will be recorded in the proper period.

PRESENTATION OF CASH ON THE BALANCE SHEET

Objective 7
Summarize how cash is presented in the balance sheet.

Cash is the most liquid asset, and therefore it is listed as the first asset in the Current Assets section of the balance sheet. Most companies combine all their cash accounts and present only a single cash amount on the balance sheet.

A company may have cash in excess of its operating needs. In such cases, it may invest in highly liquid investments in order to earn interest. These investments are called **cash equivalents**.[6] Examples of cash equivalents include United States Treasury Bills, notes issued by major corporations (referred to as commercial paper), and money market funds. Companies that have invested excess cash in cash equivalents usually report *Cash and cash equivalents* as one amount on the balance sheet.

Cash and cash equivalents normally do not require special disclosures in the notes to the financial statements. However, if the ability to withdraw cash is restricted, the restrictions should be disclosed. For example, companies with foreign operations often have cash deposits in foreign banks. These deposits may be subject to foreign laws that limit withdrawals to certain amounts. Such limitations should be disclosed in the notes to the financial statements.

A bank often requires a business to maintain in a bank account a minimum cash balance. Such a balance is called a **compensating balance**. This requirement is generally imposed by the bank as a part of a loan agreement or line of credit. A line of credit is a pre-approved amount the bank is willing to lend to a customer upon request. Compensating balance requirements should be disclosed in notes to the financial statements. An example of such a note is shown below for K Mart Corporation:

. . . In support of lines of credit, it is expected that compensating balances will be maintained on deposit with the banks, which will average 10% of the line to the extent that it is not in use and an additional 10% on the portion in use, whereas other lines require fees in lieu of compensating balances. . . .

---

[6] To be classified as a cash equivalent, it is expected that the investment will be converted to cash within 90 days.

CASH TRANSACTIONS AND ELECTRONIC FUNDS TRANSFER

Objective 8
Define electronic funds transfer and give an example of how it is used to process cash transactions.

Most cash transactions are in the form of currency or check. The broad principles discussed in earlier sections provide the basis for developing an effective system to control such cash transactions. However, the use of electronic funds transfer is changing the form in which many cash transactions are executed. This, in turn, affects the processing and controlling of cash transactions.

Electronic funds transfer (EFT) can be defined as a payment system that uses computerized electronic instructions rather than paper (money, checks, etc.) to effect a cash transaction. For example, a business may pay its employees by means of EFT. Under such a system, employees may authorize the deposit of their payroll checks directly in a checking account. For each pay period, the business's computer produces a payroll file with computer-sensitive notations for relevant payroll data. This file is transmitted over telephone lines to the banks indicated by the employees. The banks then credit each employee's account. Similar cash payments might be made for other authorized payments. The federal government currently processes several million social security checks through EFT.

EFT may also be used for retail sales. Through a point-of-sale (POS) system, a customer pays for goods at the time of purchase by presenting a plastic card. The card is used to transfer monies from the customer's checking account to the retailer's account at the bank.

Some companies are using EFT systems to process both cash payments and cash receipts. For example, General Electric Co. estimates that 40%-50% of its payments to creditors and its collections from customers are processed by EFT systems.

Studies have indicated that EFT systems generally reduce the cost of processing certain cash transactions and contribute to better control over cash receipts and cash payments. Offsetting these advantages are problems of protecting the privacy of information stored in computers and difficulties in documenting purchase and sale transactions.

Controlling EFT Systems

Many companies use EFT to transfer cash among various bank accounts, to make investments, and to pay vendors. Control weaknesses and some relatively simple steps to safeguard electronically transferred funds were described in a *Journal of Accountancy* article, as follows:

The key element in most EFT systems is the telephone. Once a . . . cash manager has established an EFT facility with a bank, he or she usually only needs to call the bank (or make contact through a computer hookup), identify himself and specify the dollar amount to be transferred from a particular account at the disbursing bank, as well as the account and bank to which funds are to be transferred. . . . As a result of these calls, hundreds of billions of dollars are transferred through the banking system every business day. . . .

When cash disbursements are made by written check, most companies' control procedures . . . [provide] reasonable assurance that cash disbursements . . . are being made [properly]. When an EFT system is used] . . . several relatively inexpensive and easily implemented control procedures can be added to traditional controls to reduce the risk of losing funds during electronic transfers. . . .

- *Passwords. Companies should instruct banks not to accept transfer instructions from any caller who is unable to provide*

an established password. . . .
- *Additional authorization. The vast majority of fund transfers by most companies are routine, such as transfers between their own bank accounts and transfers to investment accounts in the company's name. These reasonably could be considered relatively low risk, since funds never leave the company's accounts. Transfers to outside accounts, on the other hand, generally are much less frequent and obviously involve much higher risk.*

To minimize the risk of lost funds . . . additional authorizations [should be required] before unusual transfers are completed. . . .

- *After the transfer. The traditional bank account reconciliation process is an effective control except for the time lag involved. . . . To overcome this weakness, an ongoing reconciliation system can be used with EFTs. Banks should be instructed to provide the transaction advice for each fund transfer on a timely basis. . . .*

Transaction advices should be sent directly to a person not involved in the EFT process. This person should be instructed to match the advices on the day they are received with the internal cash receipt or disbursement records, as well as with required internal documentation. . . .

Source: Michael J. Fischer, "Electronic Funds Transfers: Controlling the Risk," *The Journal of Accountancy* (June 1988), pp. 130-134.

CHAPTER REVIEW

Key Points

Objective 1. Describe the basic principles of accounting systems.

Although accounting systems vary from business to business, the following principles apply to all systems:

1. The cost of the information must be balanced against its benefits.
2. Reports must be prepared with the needs and the knowledge of the user considered.
3. The system must be able to adapt to changing needs.
4. Internal controls must be adequate.

Objective 2. List the three phases of accounting systems installation and revision.

The three phases of accounting system installation and revision are (1) analysis of information needs, (2) design of the system, and (3) implementation of the systems design.

Objective 3. List, define, and give examples of the three elements of the internal control structure.

The three elements of the internal control structure of an entity are (1) the accounting system, (2) the control environment, and (3) the control procedures. The accounting system provides the information needed by management to plan and direct operations in achieving enterprise goals. Procedures for recording transactions are part of the accounting system. The control environment is the overall attitude of management and employees about the importance of controls. The existence of employee codes of ethics and conflict-of-interest policies contributes to the effectiveness of a control environment. Control procedures are those policies and procedures that management has established to provide reasonable assurance that enterprise goals will be achieved. Control procedures include the rotation of duties and mandatory vacations.

Objective 4. Prepare a bank reconciliation and journalize any necessary entries.

The first section of the bank reconciliation begins with the cash balance according to the bank statement. This balance is adjusted for the depositor's changes in cash that do not appear on the bank statement and for any bank errors. The second section begins with the cash balance according to the depositor's records. This balance is adjusted for the bank's changes in cash that do not appear on the depositor's records and for any depositor errors. The adjusted balances for the two sections must be equal.

No entries are necessary on the depositor's records as a result of the information included in the first section of the bank reconciliation. However, the items in the second section must be journalized on the depositor's records.

Objective 5. Summarize basic procedures for achieving internal control over cash receipts, including the use of cash change funds and the cash short and over account.

To protect cash from theft and misuse, business enterprises use protective and detective controls. One of the most important controls to protect cash received in over-the-counter sales is a cash register. A remittance advice is a protective control for cash received through the mail. The separation of the duties of handling cash and recording cash is also a protective control.

Retail stores and other businesses that receive cash directly from customers must keep some currency and coins in a cash change fund in order to make change. Differences in the amount of cash counted and the amount of cash in the records are normally recorded in Cash Short and Over.

Objective 6. Summarize basic procedures for achieving control over cash payments, including the use of a voucher system, a discounts lost account, and a petty cash account.

A voucher system can assist in achieving control over cash payments. A voucher system is a set of methods and procedures for authorizing and recording liabilities and cash payments. A voucher system uses vouchers, a file for unpaid vouchers, and a file for paid vouchers.

Because of the importance of taking advantage of all purchases discounts, a business may use a separate account, called Discounts Lost, to account for any discounts not taken during the discount period. When this procedure is used with a voucher system, all vouchers are prepared and recorded at the net amount, assuming that the discount will be taken.

A petty cash fund may be used by a business to make small payments that occur frequently, for which payment by check would cause unnecessary delay and expense. The money in a petty cash fund is placed in the custody of a specific employee, who authorizes payments from the fund according to restrictions as to maximum amount and purpose. Periodically or when the amount of money in the fund is depleted or reduced to a minimum amount, the fund is replenished.

Objective 7. Summarize how cash is presented in the balance sheet.

Cash is listed as the first asset in the Current Assets section of the balance sheet. Companies that have invested excess cash in highly liquid investments usually report *Cash and cash equivalents* on the balance sheet.

Objective 8. Define electronic funds transfer and give an example of how it is used to process cash transactions.

Electronic funds transfer (EFT) is a payment system that uses computerized electronic impulses rather than paper (money, checks, etc.) to effect cash transactions. EFT may be used in processing cash payments and cash receipts and in processing retail sales.

Glossary of Key Terms

Accounting system. The methods and procedures used by an enterprise to record and report financial data for use by management and external users. **Objective 1**

Bank reconciliation. The method of analysis that details the items that are responsible for the difference between the cash balance reported in the bank statement and the balance of the cash account in the ledger. **Objective 4**

Cash equivalents. Highly liquid investments that are usually reported on the balance sheet with cash. **Objective 7**

Controlling account. The account in the general ledger that summarizes the balances of the accounts in a subsidiary ledger. **Objective 2**

Electronic funds transfer (EFT). A payment system that uses computerized electronic impulses rather than paper (money, checks, etc.) to effect a cash transaction. **Objective 8**

General ledger. The primary ledger, when used in conjunction with subsidiary ledgers, that contains all of the balance sheet and income statement accounts. **Objective 2**

Internal controls. The detailed policies and procedures used by an enterprise to direct operations and provide reasonable assurance that the enterprise objectives are achieved. **Objective 1**

Internal control structure. Consists of the following three elements: (1) the accounting system, (2) the control environment, and (3) the control procedures. **Objective 3**

Petty cash fund. A special cash fund used to pay relatively small amounts. **Objective 6**

Subsidiary ledger. A ledger containing individual accounts with a common characteristic. **Objective 2**

Voucher. A document that serves as evidence of authority to pay cash. **Objective 6**

Voucher system. Records, methods, and procedures employed in verifying and recording liabilities and paying and recording cash payments. **Objective 6**

Self-Examination Questions

Answers at end of chapter.

1. The detailed procedures used by management to direct operations so that enterprise goals can be achieved are called:
   A. internal controls
   B. systems analysis
   C. systems design
   D. systems implementation

2. In preparing a bank reconciliation, the amount of checks outstanding would be:
   A. added to the cash balance according to the bank statement
   B. deducted from the cash balance according to the bank statement
   C. added to the cash balance according to the depositor's records
   D. deducted from the cash balance according to the depositor's records

3. Journal entries based on the bank reconciliation are required for:
   A. additions to the cash balance according to the depositor's records
   B. deductions from the cash balance according to the depositor's records

   C. both A and B
   D. neither A nor B

4. A voucher system is used and all vouchers for purchases are recorded at the net amount. When a purchase is made for $500 under terms 1/10, n/30:
   A. Merchandise Inventory would be debited for $495
   B. Discounts Lost would be debited for $5 if the voucher is not paid within the discount period
   C. the discount lost would be reported as an expense on the income statement if the voucher is not paid until after the discount period has expired
   D. all of the above

5. A petty cash fund is:
   A. used to pay relatively small amounts
   B. established by estimating the amount of cash needed for disbursements of relatively small amounts during a specified period
   C. reimbursed when the amount of money in the fund is reduced to a predetermined minimum amount
   D. all of the above

ILLUSTRATIVE PROBLEM

The bank statement for Dunlap Company for April 30 indicates a balance of $10,443.11. Dunlap Company uses a voucher system in controlling cash payments. All cash receipts are deposited each evening in a night depository, after banking hours. The accounting records indicate the following summary data for cash receipts and payments for April:

Cash balance as of April 1	$ 5,143.50
Total cash receipts for April	28,971.60
Total amount of checks issued in April	26,060.85

Comparison of the bank statement and the accompanying canceled checks and memorandums with the records reveals the following reconciling items:

a. The bank had collected for Dunlap Company $912 on a note left for collection. The face of the note was $900.

b. A deposit of $1,852.21, representing receipts of April 30, had been made too late to appear on the bank statement.

c. Checks outstanding totaled $3,265.27.

d. A check drawn for $79 had been erroneously charged by the bank as $97.

e. A check for $10 returned with the statement had been recorded in the check register as $100. The check was for the payment of an obligation to Davis Equipment Company for the purchase of office supplies on account.

f. Bank service charges for April amounted to $8.20.

Instructions

1. Prepare a bank reconciliation for April.
2. Journalize the entries that should be made by Dunlap Company.

Solution

1.

Dunlap Company
Bank Reconciliation
April 30, 19--

Cash balance according to bank statement		$10,443.11 *31,016.30*
Add: Deposit of April 30 not recorded by bank	$1,852.21 *6917.75*	
Bank error in charging check for $97 instead of $79	18,00	1,870.21
		$12,313.32
Deduct: Outstanding checks		3,265.27 *15,391.50*
Adjusted balance		$ 9,048.05
Cash balance according to depositor's records		$ 8,054.25* *20,100.30*
Add: Proceeds of note collected by bank, including		
$12 interest	$ 912.00 *3045*	
Error in recording check	90.00	1,002.00
		$ 9,056.25
Deduct: Bank service charges		8.20
Adjusted balance		$ 9,048.05

*$5,143.50 + $28,971.60 − $26,060.85

Handwritten: *100 − 10* / *19 − 91* *R*

2.

Cash in Bank	1,002.00	
Notes Receivable		900.00
Interest Income		12.00
Accounts Payable		90.00
Miscellaneous Administrative Expense	8.20	
Cash in Bank		8.20

DISCUSSION QUESTIONS

1. Why is the accounting system of an enterprise an information system?
2. What are internal controls?
3. What is the objective of systems analysis?
4. Name and describe the three elements of the internal control structure.
5. How does a policy of rotating clerical employees from job to job aid in strengthening the control procedures within the control environment?
6. Why should the responsibility for a sequence of related operations be divided among different persons?
7. Why should the employee who handles cash receipts not have the responsibility for maintaining the accounts receivable records?
8. Why should the employee who handles cash receipts not be responsible for approving sales returns and allowances?
9. In an attempt to improve operating efficiency, one employee was made responsible for all purchasing, receiving, and storing of merchandise. Is this organizational change wise from an internal control standpoint? Explain.

ILLUSTRATIVE PROBLEM ILLUSTRATIVE PROBLEM ILLUSTRATIVE

10. In an attempt to improve operating efficiency, one employee was made responsible for maintaining all personnel records, for timekeeping, for preparing payroll records, and for distributing payroll checks. Is this organizational change wise from an internal control standpoint? Explain.

11. The ticket seller at a movie theater doubles as a ticket taker for a few minutes each day while the ticket taker is on a break. Which control procedure of an enterprise's system of internal control is violated in this situation?

12. Why should the responsibility for maintaining the accounting records be separated from the responsibility for operations?

13. How does a periodic review by internal auditors strengthen the internal control structure?

14. What is the term applied (a) to the ledger containing the individual customer accounts, and (b) to the single account summarizing accounts receivable?

15. Why is cash the asset that often warrants the most attention in the design of an effective internal control structure?

16. Distinguish between the drawer and the payee of a check.

17. The balance of Cash in Bank is likely to differ from the cash balance reported by the bank statement. What two factors are likely to be responsible for the difference?

18. What is the purpose of preparing a bank reconciliation?

19. Do items reported on the bank statement as credits represent (a) additions made by the bank to the depositor's balance, or (b) deductions made by the bank from the depositor's balance?

20. What entry should be made if a check received from a customer and deposited is returned by the bank for lack of sufficient funds (an NSF check)?

21. Identify each of the following reconciling items as: (a) an addition to the cash balance according to the bank statement, (b) a deduction from the cash balance according to the bank statement, (c) an addition to the cash balance according to the depositor's records, or (d) a deduction from the cash balance according to the depositor's records. (None of the transactions reported by bank debit and credit memorandums have been recorded by the depositor.)

    1. Check for $27 charged by bank as $72.
    2. Check drawn by depositor for $90 but recorded as $900.
    3. Outstanding checks, $8,515.50.
    4. Deposit in transit, $3,279.12.
    5. Note collected by bank, $5,200.00.
    6. Check of a customer returned by bank to depositor because of insufficient funds, $212.50.
    7. Bank service charges, $40.10.

22. Which of the reconciling items listed in Question 21 necessitate an entry in the depositor's accounts?

23. The procedures used for over-the-counter receipts are as follows: At the close of each day's business, the sales clerks count the cash in their respective cash drawers, after which they determine the amount recorded by the cash register tapes and prepare the memorandum cash form, noting any discrepancies. An employee from the cashier's office counts the cash, compares the total with the memorandum, and takes the cash to the cashier's office. (a) Indicate the weak link in internal control. (b) How can the weakness be corrected?

24. The mailroom employees send all remittances and remittance advices to the cashier. The cashier deposits the cash in the bank and forwards the remittance advices and duplicate deposit slips to the Accounting Department. (a) Indicate the weak link in internal control in the handling of cash receipts. (b) How can the weakness be corrected?

25. The combined cash count of all cash registers at the close of business is $4 less than the cash sales indicated by the cash register tapes. (a) In what account is the cash shortage recorded? (b) Are cash shortages debited or credited to this account?

26. In which section of the income statement would a credit balance in Cash Short and Over be reported?

27. The controller approves all vouchers before they are submitted to the treasurer for payment. What procedure should the treasurer perform to ensure that the documents accompanying the vouchers and supporting the payments are not "reused" to support future vouchers improperly?

28. The accounting clerk pays all obligations by prenumbered checks. What are the strengths and weaknesses in the internal control over cash payments in this situation?

29. What are the advantages of recording purchases at the net amount?

30. As a general rule, all cash payments should be made by check. Explain why some cash payments are made in coins and currency from a petty cash fund.

31. What account or accounts are debited when recording the voucher (a) establishing a petty cash fund and (b) replenishing a petty cash fund?

32. The petty cash account has a debit balance of $500. At the end of the accounting period, there is $93 in the petty cash fund, along with petty cash receipts totaling $407. Should the fund be replenished as of the last day of the period? Discuss.

33. a. What is meant by the term *cash equivalents*?
    b. How are cash equivalents reported in the financial statements?

34. a. What is meant by the term *compensating balance* as applied to the checking account of a firm?
    b. How is the compensating balance reported in the financial statements?

35. What is meant by *electronic funds transfer*?

36. In the Equity Funding fraud, approximately $2 billion of insurance policies that were claimed to have been sold by the company were bogus. The bogus policies, which were supported by falsified policy applications, were listed along with real policies on Equity Funding's computer tapes (records). These computer tapes were kept in a separate room where they were easily accessible by Equity Funding personnel, including the computer programmers. In addition, computer programmers and other company personnel had access to the computer. What general weaknesses in Equity Funding's internal controls contributed to the occurrence and the size of the fraud?

REAL WORLD FOCUS

37. Between September 3 and September 22, seventeen prenumbered checks totaling $1,129,232.39 were forged and cashed on the accounts of Perini Corporation, a construction company based in the Boston suburb of Framingham. Perini Corporation kept its supply of blank prenumbered checks in an unlocked storeroom with items such as styrofoam coffee cups. Every clerk and secretary had access to this storeroom. It was later discovered that someone had apparently stolen two boxes of prenumbered checks. The numbers of the missing checks matched the numbers of the out-of-sequence checks cashed by the banks. What fundamental principle of control over cash was violated in this case?

ETHICS DISCUSSION CASE

During the preparation of the bank reconciliation for Klaus Co., Jane Ellet, the assistant controller, discovered that Banco National Bank erroneously recorded a $700 check written by Klaus as $70. Jane has decided not to notify the bank, but to wait for the bank to detect the error. Jane plans to record the $630 error as Other Income if the bank fails to detect the error within the next three months.

SHARPEN YOUR COMMUNICATION SKILLS

Discuss whether Jane Ellet is behaving in an ethical manner.

WhAT'S WRONG WITH THIS?

One of the purposes of an internal control structure is to prevent and detect embezzlement and fraud by employees. Do you think a company should "spend whatever it takes" to eliminate the possibility of employee embezzlement and fraud?

FINANCIAL ANALYSIS AND INTERPRETATION

Corporations generally issue annual reports to their stockholders and other interested parties. These annual reports include a Management Responsibility (or Management Report) section as well as financial statements. The Management Responsibility section discusses responsibility for the financial statements and normally includes an assessment of the company's internal control system. The financial statements include a report of the enterprise's cash and cash equivalents.

a. What does the annual report for Hershey Foods Corporation indicate about the internal control system?

b. What is Hershey's amount of cash and cash equivalents at December 31, 1992?

continued

c. What is the makeup of Hershey's cash equivalents at December 31, 1992?
d. In which financial statement for Hershey Foods Corporation are the major inflows and outflows of cash and cash equivalents for 1992 reported?

EXERCISES

EXERCISE 6-1
INTERNAL CONTROLS
Objective 3

Susan Voltz has recently been hired as the manager of Lizzy's Deli Inc. Lizzy's is a national chain of franchised delicatessens. During her first month as store manager, Susan encountered the following internal control situations:

a. Lizzy's has one cash register. Prior to Susan's joining the deli, each employee working on a shift would take a customer order, accept payment, and then prepare the order. Susan made one employee on each shift responsible for taking orders and accepting the customer's payment. Other employees prepare the orders.
b. Since only one employee uses the cash register, that employee is responsible for counting the cash at the end of the shift and verifying that the cash in the drawer matches the amount of cash sales recorded by the cash register. Susan expects each cashier to balance the drawer to the penny every time—no exceptions.
c. Susan caught an employee putting a box of 100 single-serving bags of potato chips in his car. Not wanting to create a scene, Susan smiled and said, "I don't think you're putting those chips on the right shelf. Don't they belong inside the deli?" The employee returned the chips to the stockroom.

SHARPEN YOUR COMMUNICATION SKILLS ▶ State whether you agree or disagree with Susan's handling of each situation and explain your answer.

EXERCISE 6-2
INTERNAL CONTROLS
Objective 3

Fashions Now Inc. is a retail store specializing in women's clothing. The store has established a liberal return policy for the holiday season in order to encourage gift purchases. Any item purchased during November and December may be returned through January 31, with a receipt, for cash or exchange. If the customer does not have a receipt, cash will still be refunded for any item under $25. If the item is more than $25, a check is mailed to the customer.

Whenever an item is returned, a store clerk completes a return slip, which the customer signs. The return slip is placed in a special box. The store manager visits the return counter approximately once every two hours to authorize the return slips. Clerks are instructed to place the returned merchandise on the proper rack on the selling floor as soon as possible.

This year, returns at Fashions Now Inc. have reached an all-time high. There are a large number of returns under $25 without receipts.

SHARPEN YOUR COMMUNICATION SKILLS ▶ a. How can sales clerks employed at Fashions Now Inc. use the store's return policy to steal money from the cash register?

SHARPEN YOUR COMMUNICATION SKILLS ▶ b. 1. What internal control weaknesses do you see in the return policy that make cash thefts easier?
2. Would issuing a store credit in place of a cash refund for all merchandise returned without a receipt reduce the possibility of theft? List some advantages and disadvantages of issuing a store credit in place of a cash refund.
3. Assume that Fashions Now Inc. is committed to the current policy of issuing cash refunds without a receipt. What changes could be made in the store's procedures regarding customer refunds in order to improve internal control?

EXERCISE 6-3
BANK RECONCILIATION
Objective 4

The following data are accumulated for use in reconciling the bank account of C. C. Davidson Inc. for February:

a. Cash balance according to the depositor's records at February 28, $5,530.20.
b. Cash balance according to the bank statement at February 28, $9,100.50.
c. Checks outstanding, $4,111.20.
d. Deposit in transit, not recorded by bank, $780.40.
e. A check for $140 in payment of a voucher was erroneously recorded in the check register as $410.
f. Bank debit memorandum for service charges, $30.50.

SPREADSHEET
PROBLEM

Prepare a bank reconciliation.

EXERCISE 6-4
ENTRIES FOR BANK
RECONCILIATION
Objective 4

Using the data presented in Exercise 6-3, journalize the entry or entries that should be made by the depositor.

EXERCISE 6-5
ENTRY FOR NOTE
COLLECTED BY BANK
Objective 4

Accompanying a bank statement for Cross Corp. is a credit memorandum for $5,075, representing the principal ($5,000) and interest ($75) on a note that had been collected by the bank. The depositor had been notified by the bank at the time of the collection but had made no entries. Journalize the entry that should be made by the depositor to bring the accounting records up to date.

EXERCISE 6-6
ENTRY FOR CASH SALES
Objective 5

The actual cash received from cash sales was $7,160.70, and the amount indicated by the cash register total was $7,155.20. Journalize the entry to record the cash receipts and cash sales.

EXERCISE 6-7
EVALUATION OF INTERNAL
CONTROLS OF CASH
Objectives 4, 5, 6

The following procedures were recently installed by Nero Corporation:

a. The bank reconciliation is prepared by the accountant.
b. Each cashier is assigned a separate cash register drawer, to which no other cashier has access.
c. All sales are rung up on the cash register and a receipt is given to the customer. All sales are recorded on a tape locked inside the cash register.
d. Checks received through the mail are given daily to the accounts receivable clerk for recording collections on account and for depositing in the bank.
e. At the end of a shift, each cashier counts the cash in his or her drawer, unlocks the tape, and compares the amount of cash with the amount on the tape to determine cash shortages and overages.
f. Vouchers and all supporting documents are perforated with a PAID designation after being paid by the treasurer.
g. Disbursements are made from the petty cash fund only after a petty cash receipt has been completed and signed by the payee.

Indicate whether each of the procedures of internal control over cash represents (1) a strength or (2) a weakness.

EXERCISE 6-8
INTERNAL CONTROL OVER
CASH RECEIPTS
Objective 5

SHARPEN YOUR ►
COMMUNICATION SKILLS

Jeanette Jones works at the drive-through window of Bob's Burgers. Occasionally, when a drive-through customer orders, Jeanette fills the order and pockets the customer's money. She does not ring up the order on the cash register.

Identify the internal control weaknesses that exist at Bob's Burgers, and discuss what can be done to prevent this theft.

EXERCISE 6-9
PROCEDURES FOR
INTERNAL CONTROL OF
CASH PAYMENTS
Objective 6

SHARPEN YOUR ►
COMMUNICATION SKILLS

H. L. Stricker Inc. is a medium-size merchandising enterprise. When its current income statement was reviewed, it was noted that, in spite of a sufficient bank balance, a significant amount of available cash discounts had been lost because of failure to make timely payments. In addition, it was discovered that several purchases invoices had been paid twice.

Outline procedures for the payment of vendors' invoices, so that the possibilities of losing available cash discounts and of paying an invoice a second time will be minimized.

EXERCISE 6-10
INTERNAL CONTROL OVER
CASH PAYMENTS
Objective 6

NDT Corporation, a communications equipment manufacturer, recently fell victim to an embezzlement scheme masterminded by one of its employees. To understand the scheme, it is necessary to review NDT's procedures for the purchase of services.

The purchasing agent is responsible for ordering services (such as repairs to a photocopy machine or office cleaning) after receiving a service requisition from an authorized manager. However, since no tangible goods are delivered, a receiving report is not prepared. When the Accounting Department receives an invoice billing NDT for a service call, the accounts payable clerk calls the manager who requested the service in order to verify that it was performed.

The embezzlement scheme involves Rob Ryan, the manager of plant and facilities. Rob arranged for his uncle's company, Ralph's Industrial Supply and Service, to be placed on NDT's approved vendor list. Rob did not disclose the family relationship.

On several occasions, Rob would submit a requisition for services to be provided by Ralph's Industrial Supply and Service. However, the service requested was really not needed and it was never performed. Ralph would bill NDT for the service and then split the cash payment with Rob.

SHARPEN YOUR ►
COMMUNICATION SKILLS

Explain what changes should be made to NDT's procedures for ordering and paying for services in order to prevent such occurrences in the future.

EXERCISE 6-11
PURCHASES DISCOUNTS
LOST
Objective 6

Journalize the entries to record the following transactions by Dill Inc.:

a. Purchased merchandise on October 1, terms 3/10, n/30, $10,000.
b. Paid the invoice on October 31.

EXERCISE 6-12
BORROWING TO TAKE A
PURCHASES DISCOUNT
Objective 6

In Exercise 6-11, compute the following:

a. The net savings to Dill Inc. from borrowing at 12% to take the discount.
b. The approximate interest rate earned on taking a discount on a purchase with credit terms of 3/10, n/30.

EXERCISE 6-13
PETTY CASH FUND ENTRIES
Objective 6

Journalize the entries to record the following:

a. Voucher No. 5 is prepared to establish a petty cash fund of $150.
b. Check No. 4 is issued in payment of Voucher No. 5.
c. The amount of cash in the petty cash fund is now $17.30. Voucher No. 59 is prepared to replenish the fund, based on the following summary of petty cash receipts: office supplies, $52.15; miscellaneous selling expense, $50.60; miscellaneous administrative expense, $28.70. (Since the amount of the check to replenish the fund plus the balance in the fund do not equal $150, record the discrepancy in the cash short and over account.)
d. Check No. 55 is issued by the disbursing officer in payment of Voucher No. 59. The check is cashed and the money is placed in the fund.

EXERCISE 6-14
CASH CHANGE FUND
ENTRIES
Objective 6

Journalize the entries for the following transactions:

a. Voucher No. 31 is prepared to establish a change fund of $500.
b. Check No. 25 is issued in payment of Voucher No. 31.
c. Cash sales for the day, according to the cash register tapes, were $4,655.30, and cash on hand is $5,156.50. A bank deposit ticket was prepared for $4,656.50.

WhAT'S WROnG WITH THi2?

How many errors can you find in the following bank reconciliation prepared as of the end of the current month?

Wright Company
Bank Reconciliation
For Month Ended April 30, 19--

Cash balance according to bank statement		$10,767.76
Add deposit of April 29, not recorded by bank		510.06
		$11,277.82
Deduct outstanding checks:		
No. 721	$ 345.95	
739	172.75	
743	359.60	
744	601.50	1,479.80
Adjusted balance		$ 9,801.02
Cash balance according to depositor's records		$ 7,491.32
Add: Proceeds of note collected by bank:		
Principal	$2,500.00	
Interest	75.00 $2,575.00	
Service charges	19.50	2,594.50
		$10,085.82
Deduct: Check returned because of insufficient funds	$ 266.80	
Error in recording April 15 deposit of $497 as $479	18.00	284.80
Adjusted balance		$9,801.02

PROBLEMS

Series A

PROBLEM 6-1A
BANK RECONCILIATION
AND ENTRIES
Objective 4

SPREADSHEET
P R O B L E M

The cash in bank account for A. C. Forrest Co. at June 30 of the current year indicates a balance of $20,100.30. The bank statement indicates a balance of $31,016.30 on June 30. Comparison of the bank statement and the accompanying canceled checks and memorandums with the records reveals the following reconciling items:

a. Checks outstanding totaled $15,391.50.
b. A deposit of $6,917.75, representing receipts of June 30, had been made too late to appear on the bank statement.
c. The bank had collected $3,045 on a note left for collection. The face of the note was $2,900.
d. A check for $91 returned with the statement had been recorded incorrectly as $19. The check was for the payment of an obligation to Leeco for the purchase of office equipment on account.
e. A check drawn for $55 had been incorrectly charged by the bank as $550.
f. Bank service charges for June amounted to $35.75.

Instructions
1. Prepare a bank reconciliation.
2. Journalize the necessary entries. The accounts have not been closed, and the voucher system is used.

PROBLEM 6-2A
BANK RECONCILIATION
AND ENTRIES
Objective 4

The cash in bank account for Conner Co. at August 1 of the current year indicated a balance of $18,443.90. During August, the total cash deposited was $30,650.75, and checks written totaled $31,770.25. The bank statement indicated a balance of $26,465.50 on August 31. Comparison of the bank statement, the canceled checks, and the accompanying memorandums with the records revealed the following reconciling items:

a. Checks outstanding totaled $8,003.84.
b. A deposit of $2,148.21, representing receipts of August 31, had been made too late to appear on the bank statement.
c. The bank had collected for Conner Co. $3,650 on a note left for collection. The face of the note was $3,500.
d. A check for $470 returned with the statement had been incorrectly charged by the bank as $740.
e. A check for $84.20 returned with the statement had been recorded by Conner Co. as $8.42. The check was for the payment of an obligation to Bartles Co. on account.
f. Bank service charges for August amounted to $18.75.

Instructions
1. Prepare a bank reconciliation as of August 31.
2. Journalize the necessary entries. The accounts have not been closed.

PROBLEM 6-3A
BANK RECONCILIATION
AND RELATED ENTRIES
Objective 4

Sorter Corporation uses the voucher system in controlling cash payments. All cash receipts are deposited each Wednesday and Friday in a night depository, after banking hours. The data required to reconcile the bank statement as of April 30 have been taken from various documents and records and are reproduced as follows:

CASH IN BANK ACCOUNT:
  Balance as of April 1 $8,317.40

CASH RECEIPTS FOR MONTH OF APRIL   7,679.58

DUPLICATE DEPOSIT TICKETS:
  Date and amount of each deposit in April:

Date	Amount	Date	Amount	Date	Amount
April 1	$908.50	April 10	$896.61	April 22	$897.34
3	854.17	15	882.95	24	942.71
8	840.50	17	946.74	29	510.06

CHECKS WRITTEN:
   Number and amount of each check issued in April:

Check No.	Amount	Check No.	Amount	Check No.	Amount
740	$237.50	747	Void	754	$249.75
741	495.15	748	$450.90	755	172.75
742	501.90	749	640.13	756	113.95
743	671.30	750	376.77	757	907.95
744	506.88	751	299.37	758	359.60
745	117.25	752	537.01	759	601.50
746	298.66	753	380.95	760	486.39

Total amount of checks issued in April $8,405.66

APRIL BANK STATEMENT:
   Balance as of April 1 $ 8,447.20
   Deposits and other credits   10,502.77
   Checks and other debits   (8,082.21)
   Balance as of April 30 $10,867.76

Date and amount of each deposit in April:

Date	Amount	Date	Amount	Date	Amount
April 1	$690.25	April 9	$840.50	April 18	$964.74
2	908.50	11	896.61	23	897.34
4	854.17	16	882.95	25	942.71

CHECKS ACCOMPANYING APRIL BANK STATEMENT:
   Number and amount of each check, rearranged in numerical sequence:

Check No.	Amount	Check No.	Amount	Check No.	Amount
731	$162.15	744	$506.88	751	$299.37
738	251.40	745	117.25	752	537.01
739	60.55	746	298.66	753	380.95
740	237.50	748	450.90	754	249.75
741	495.15	749	640.13	756	113.95
742	501.90	750	376.77	757	907.95
743	671.30			760	486.39

BANK MEMORANDUMS ACCOMPANYING APRIL BANK STATEMENT:

Date	Description	Amount
April 9	Bank credit memo for note collected:	
	Principal	$2,500.00
	Interest	125.00
28	Bank debit memo for check returned because of	
	insufficient funds	291.90
30	Bank debit memo for service charges	44.40

BANK RECONCILIATION FOR PRECEDING MONTH:

Sorter Corporation
Bank Reconciliation
March 31, 19—

Cash balance according to bank statemen		$8,447.20
Add deposit for March 31, not recorded by bank		690.25
		$9,137.45
Deduct outstanding checks:		
No. 731	$162.15	
736	345.95	
738	251.40	
739	60.55	820.05
Adjusted balance		$8,317.40
Cash balance according to depositor's records		$8,352.50
Deduct service charges		35.10
Adjusted balance		$8,317.40

[Handwritten note in left margin:] Beg. Balance out + Cash Receipts – Cash Disbursement End Balance

Instructions

1. Prepare a bank reconciliation as of April 30. If errors in recording deposits or checks are discovered, assume that the errors were made by the company. Assume that all deposits are from cash sales. All checks are in payment of vouchers.
2. Journalize the necessary entries. The accounts have not been closed.
3. What is the amount of Cash in Bank that should appear on the balance sheet as of April 30?
4. Assume that in preparing the bank reconciliation, you note that a canceled check for $450 has been incorrectly recorded by the bank as $540. Briefly explain how the error would be included in the bank reconciliation and how it should be corrected.

SHARPEN YOUR COMMUNICATION SKILLS ►

PROBLEM 6-4A
TRANSACTIONS FOR PETTY CASH, ADVANCES TO SALESPERSONS FUND; CASH SHORT AND OVER
Objectives 5, 6

Crump Company has just adopted the policy of depositing all cash receipts in the bank and of making all payments by check in conjunction with the voucher system. The following transactions were selected from those completed in May of the current year:

May 2. Recorded Voucher No. 1 to establish a petty cash fund of $200 and a change fund of $500.
  2. Issued Check No. 419 in payment of Voucher No. 1.
  4. Recorded Voucher No. 5 to establish an advances to salespersons fund of $1,000.
  4. Issued Check No. 422 in payment of Voucher No. 5.
  17. The cash sales for the day, according to the cash register tapes, totaled $3,970.60. The combined count of all cash on hand (including the change fund) totaled $4,473.20.
  29. Recorded Voucher No. 44 to reimburse the petty cash fund for the following disbursements, each evidenced by a petty cash receipt:

  May 3. Store supplies, $21.50.
    5. Express charges on merchandise purchased, $16.00.
    8. Office supplies, $12.75.
    11. Office supplies, $9.20.
    17. Postage stamps, $52 (Office Supplies).
    19. Repair to office calculator, $37.50 (Miscellaneous Administrative Expense).
    22. Postage due on special delivery letter, $1.05 (Miscellaneous Administrative Expense).
    23. Express charges on merchandise purchased, $20.
    27. Office supplies, $11.10.
  29. Issued Check No. 452 in payment of Voucher No. 44.
  30. The cash sales for the day, according to the cash register tapes, totaled $4,055.50. The count of all cash on hand (including the change fund) totaled $4,551.60.
  31. Recorded Voucher No. 49 to replenish the advances to salespersons fund for the following expenditures for travel: Frank Abott, $212.50; Jeff Marlow, $356.50; Nancy Powell, $272.10.
  31. Issued Check No. 460 in payment of Voucher No. 49.

Instructions
Journalize the transactions.

PROBLEM 6-5A
ENTRIES FOR VOUCHER
SYSTEM
Objective 6

The following selected transactions were completed by a company that uses a voucher system and a perpetual inventory system, and records all invoices at their net price.

Sep. 3. Recorded Voucher No. 540 for $800, payable to Jones Supply Co., for office supplies purchased, terms n/eom.
    8. Recorded Voucher No. 542 for $9,000, payable to Cox Co., for merchandise purchased, terms 1/10, n/30.
    9. Recorded Voucher No. 548 for $1,400, payable to Collins Inc., for merchandise purchased, terms 2/10, n/30.
    19. Issued Check No. 264 in payment of Voucher No. 548.
    29. Recorded Voucher No. 560 for $225.14 to replenish the petty cash fund for the following disbursements: store supplies, $92.88; office supplies, $84.95; miscellaneous administrative expense, $42.45; miscellaneous selling expense, $34.86.
    30. Issued Check No. 270 in payment of Voucher No. 560.
    30. Issued Check No. 277 in payment of Voucher No. 542.
    30. Issued Check No. 289 in payment of Voucher No. 540.

Instructions
Journalize the transactions.

SOLUTIONS
SOFTWARE

Instructions for Solving Problem 6-5A Using Solutions Software
1. Load opening balances.
2. Enter your name in the Student Name field in the General Information data entry window. Set the run date to September 30 of the current year.
3. Save the opening balances file to your drive and directory.
4. Select the General Journal Entries option and key the journal entries. Leave the reference field blank. (Note: To review the chart of accounts, select F-1.)
5. Display a journal entries report.
6. Display a trial balance.
7. Save your data file to disk.
8. End the session.

Series B

PROBLEM 6-1B
BANK RECONCILIATION
AND ENTRIES
Objective 4

The cash in bank account for R. O. Dibble Co. at May 31 of the current year indicated a balance of $14,460. The bank statement indicated a balance of $19,391.40 on May 31. Comparison of the bank statement and the accompanying canceled checks and memorandums with the records reveals the following reconciling items:

a. Checks outstanding totaled $5,950.
b. A deposit of $4,215.50, representing receipts of May 31, had been made too late to appear on the bank statement.
c. The bank had collected $3,120 on a note left for collection. The face of the note was $3,000.
d. A check for $120 returned with the statement had been recorded incorrectly as $210. The check was for the payment of an obligation to Buck & Co. for the purchase of office supplies on account.
e. A check drawn for $63 had been incorrectly charged by the bank as $36.
f. Bank service charges for May amounted to $40.10.

SPREADSHEET
PROBLEM
$

Instructions
1. Prepare a bank reconciliation.
2. Journalize the necessary entries. The accounts have not been closed. The voucher system is used.

PROBLEM 6-2B
BANK RECONCILIATION
AND ENTRIES
Objective 4

The cash in bank account for Powlen Co. at June 1 of the current year indicated a balance of $12,881.40. During June, the total cash deposited was $40,500.40, and checks written totaled $38,850.47. The bank statement indicated a balance of $18,880.45 on June 30. Comparison of the bank statement, the canceled checks, and the accompanying memorandums with the records revealed the following reconciling items:

a. Checks outstanding totaled $4,180.27.
b. A deposit of $2,481.70, representing receipts of June 30, had been made too late to appear on the bank statement.
c. A check for $190 had been incorrectly charged by the bank as $100.
d. A check for $570.45 returned with the statement had been recorded by Powlen Co. as $750.45. The check was for the payment of an obligation to Scott and Son on account.
e. The bank had collected for Powlen Co. $2,400 on a note left for collection. The face of the note was $2,000.
f. Bank service charges for June amounted to $19.45.

Instructions
1. Prepare a bank reconciliation as of June 30.
2. Journalize the necessary entries. The accounts have not been closed.

PROBLEM 6-3B
BANK RECONCILIATION
AND RELATED ENTRIES
Objective 4

Rundle Company uses the voucher system in controlling cash payments. All cash receipts are deposited each Wednesday and Friday in a night depository, after banking hours. The data required to reconcile the bank statement as of July 31 have been taken from various documents and records and are reproduced as follows.

CASH IN BANK ACCOUNT:
  Balance as of July 1 .... $9,578.00

CASH RECEIPTS IN JULY 6,232.60

DUPLICATE DEPOSIT TICKETS:
  Date and amount of each deposit in July:

Date	Amount	Date	Amount	Date	Amount
July 2	$619.50	July 12	$780.70	July 23	$731.45
5	701.80	16	600.10	26	601.50
9	819.24	19	701.26	30	677.05

CHECKS WRITTEN IN JULY:
  Number and amount of each check issued in July:

Check No.	Amount	Check No.	Amount	Check No.	Amount
614	$243.50	621	$409.50	628	$737.70
615	650.10	622	Void	629	329.90
616	279.90	623	Void	630	882.80
617	395.50	624	707.01	631	981.56
618	535.40	625	658.63	632	62.40
619	220.10	626	550.03	633	310.08
620	238.87	627	318.73	634	103.30

Total amount of checks issued in July $8,615.01

JULY BANK STATEMENT:
  Balance as of July 1 $ 9,422.80
  Deposits and other credits   11,436.35
  Checks and other debits   (8,583.61)
  Balance as of July 31 $12,275.54

Date and amount of each deposit in July:

Date	Amount	Date	Amount	Date	Amount
July 1	$780.80	July 11	$819.24	July 21	$701.26
3	619.50	13	780.70	24	731.45
6	701.80	17	600.10	28	601.50

CHECKS ACCOMPANYING JULY BANK STATEMENT:
Number and amount of each check, rearranged in numerical sequence:

Check No.	Amount	Check No.	Amount	Check No.	Amount
580	$310.10	618	$535.40	626	$550.03
612	92.50	619	230.10	627	318.73
613	137.50	620	238.87	629	329.90
614	243.50	621	409.50	630	882.80
615	650.10	624	707.01	631	981.56
616	279.90	625	658.63	632	62.40
617	395.50			633	310.08

BANK MEMORANDUMS ACCOMPANYING JULY BANK STATEMENT:

Date	Description	Amount
July 14	Bank credit memo for note collected:	
	Principal	$5,000.00
	Interest	100.00
20	Bank debit memo for check returned because of	
	insufficient funds	225.40
31	Bank debit memo for service charges	34.10

BANK RECONCILIATION FOR PRECEDING MONTH:

Rundle Company
Bank Reconciliation
June 30, 19—

Cash balance according to bank statement		$ 9,422.80
Add deposit for June 30, not recorded by bank		780.80
		$10,203.60
Deduct outstanding checks:		
No. 580	$310.10	
602	85.50	
612	92.50	
613	137.50	625.60
Adjusted balance		$ 9,578.00
Cash balance according to depositor's records		$ 9,605.70
Deduct service charges		27.70
Adjusted balance		$ 9,578.00

Instructions

1. Prepare a bank reconciliation as of July 31. If errors in recording deposits or checks are discovered, assume that the errors were made by the company. Assume that all deposits are from cash sales. All checks are in payment of vouchers.
2. Journalize the necessary entries. The accounts have not been closed.
3. What is the amount of Cash in Bank that should appear on the balance sheet as of July 31?

SHARPEN YOUR COMMUNICATION SKILLS ►

4. Assume that in preparing the bank reconciliation, you note that a canceled check for $800 has been incorrectly recorded by the bank as $900. Briefly explain how the error would be included in the bank reconciliation and how it should be corrected.

PROBLEM 6-4B
TRANSACTIONS FOR PETTY CASH, ADVANCES TO SALESPERSONS FUND; CASH SHORT AND OVER
Objectives 5, 6

Jordan Company has just adopted the policy of depositing all cash receipts in the bank and of making all payments by check in conjunction with the voucher system. The following transactions were selected from those completed in June of the current year:

June 1. Recorded Voucher No. 1 to establish a petty cash fund of $250 and a change fund of $500.
      1. Issued Check No. 699 in payment of Voucher No. 1.
      3. Recorded Voucher No. 5 to establish an advances to salespersons fund of $1,000.

June 4. Issued Check No. 702 in payment of Voucher No. 5.

   15. The cash sales for the day, according to the cash register tapes, totaled $2,995.60. The combined count of all cash on hand (including the change fund) totaled $3,498.20.

   26. Recorded Voucher No. 38 to reimburse the petty cash fund for the following disbursements, each evidenced by a petty cash receipt:

   June 4. Store supplies, $26.50.
         6. Express charges on merchandise purchased, $15.50.
         8. Office supplies, $14.75.
         9. Office supplies, $9.20.
        12. Postage stamps, $52 (Office Supplies).
        16. Repair to adding machine, $29.50 (Miscellaneous Administrative Expense).
        20. Repair to typewriter, $31.50 (Miscellaneous Administrative Expense).
        22. Postage due on special delivery letter, $1.05 (Miscellaneous Administrative Expense).
        24. Express charges on merchandise purchased, $19.50.

   26. Issued Check No. 737 in payment of Voucher No. 38.

   30. The cash sales for the day, according to the cash register tapes, totaled $3,009.50. The count of all cash on hand (including the change fund) totaled $3,505.60.

   30. Recorded Voucher No. 43 to replenish the advances to salespersons fund for the following expenditures for travel: Susan Reeser, $219.50; Frank Sampson, $333.40; Alice Yates, $275.10.

   30. Issued Check No. 740 in payment of Voucher No. 43.

Instructions

Journalize the transactions.

PROBLEM 6-5B
ENTRIES FOR VOUCHER
SYSTEM
Objective 6

The following selected transactions were completed by a company that uses a voucher system and a perpetual inventory system, and records all invoices at their net price.

Jan. 3. Recorded Voucher No. 1015 for $2,500, payable to Edwards Supply Co., for office supplies purchased, terms n/30.

    5. Recorded Voucher No. 1020 for $8,000, payable to Fair Co., for merchandise purchased, terms 2/10, n/eom.

   10. Recorded Voucher No. 1028 for $2,500, payable to Clinton Inc., for merchandise purchased, terms 1/10, n/30.

   20. Issued Check No. 795 in payment of Voucher No. 1028.

   30. Recorded Voucher No. 1040 for $239.84 to replenish the petty cash fund for the following disbursements: store supplies, $92.88; office supplies, $69.95; miscellaneous administrative expense, $42.45; miscellaneous selling expense, $34.56.

   31. Issued Check No. 806 in payment of Voucher No. 1040.

   31. Issued Check No. 821 in payment of Voucher No. 1020.

   31. Issued Check No. 835 in payment of Voucher No. 1015.

Instructions

Journalize the transactions.

SOLUTIONS
SOFTWARE

Instructions for Solving Problem 6-5B Using Solutions Software

1. Load opening balances.
2. Enter your name in the Student Name field in the General Information data entry window. Set the run date to January 31 of the current year.
3. Save the opening balances file to your drive and directory.
4. Select the General Journal Entries option and key the journal entries. Leave the reference field blank. (Note: To review the chart of accounts, select F-1.)
5. Display a journal entries report.
6. Display a trial balance.
7. Save your data file to disk.
8. End the session.

MINI-CASE   CRIER & COMPANY

The records of Crier & Company indicate a July 31 cash in bank balance of $21,931.05, which includes undeposited receipts for July 30 and 31. The cash balance on the bank statement as of July 31 is $18,704.95. This balance includes a note of $5,000 plus $150 interest collected by the bank but not recorded in the cash receipts journal. Checks outstanding on July 31 were as follows: No. 470, $950.20; No. 479, $510; No. 490, $616.50; No. 996, $227.40; No. 997, $720; and No. 999, $351.50.

On July 3, the cashier resigned, effective at the end of the month. Before leaving on July 31, the cashier prepared the following bank reconciliation:

Cash balance per books, July 31		$21,931.05
Add outstanding checks:		
No. 996	$227.40	
997	720.00	
999	351.50	1,198.90
		$23,129.95
Less undeposited receipts		4,425.00
Cash balance per bank, July 31		$18,704.95
Deduct unrecorded note with interest		5,150.00
True cash, July 31		$13,554.95

Calculator Tape of Outstanding Checks

```
     0.00  *
   227.40  +
   720.00  +
   351.50  +
 1,198.90  *
```

Subsequently, the owner of Crier & Company discovered that the cashier had stolen all undeposited receipts in excess of the $4,425 on hand on July 31. The owner, a close family friend, has asked your help in determining the amount that the former cashier has stolen.

Instructions

1. Determine the amount the cashier stole from Crier & Company. Show your computations in good form.
2. How did the cashier attempt to conceal the theft?
3. a. ▪▪▪ ► Identify two major weaknesses in internal controls, which allowed the cashier to steal the undeposited cash receipts.
   b. ▪▪▪ ► Recommend improvements in internal controls, so that similar types of thefts of undeposited cash receipts can be prevented.

ANSWERS TO SELF-EXAMINATION QUESTIONS

1. **A** The policies and procedures established by an enterprise to provide reasonable assurance that the enterprise's goals will be achieved are called internal controls (answer A). The three phases of installing or changing an accounting system are (1) analysis (answer B), (2) design (answer C), and (3) implementation (answer D). Systems analysis is the determination of the informational needs, sources of such information, and deficiencies in the procedures and data processing methods presently used. Systems design refers to the design of a new system or change in the present system based on the systems analysis. The carrying out of proposals for the design of a system is called systems implementation.

2. **B** On any specific date, the cash in bank account in a depositor's ledger may not agree with the reciprocal account in the bank's ledger because of delays and/or errors by either party in recording transactions. The purpose of a bank reconciliation, therefore, is to determine the reasons for any differences between the two account balances. All errors should then be corrected by the depositor or the bank, as appropriate. In arriving at the adjusted (correct) cash balance according to the bank statement, outstanding checks must be deducted (answer B) to adjust for checks that have been written by the depositor but that have not yet been presented to the bank for payment.

3. **C** All reconciling items that are added to and deducted from the cash balance according to the depositor's records on the bank reconciliation (answer C) require that journal entries be made by the depositor to correct errors made in recording transactions or to bring the cash account up to date for delays in recording transactions.

4. **D** A major advantage of recording purchases at the net amount (answer A) is that the cost of failing to take discounts is recorded in the accounts (answer B) and then reported as an expense on the income statement (answer C).

5. **D** To avoid the delay, annoyance, and expense that is associated with paying all obligations by check, relatively small amounts (answer A) are paid from a petty cash fund. The fund is established by estimating the amount of cash needed to pay these small amounts during a specified period (answer B), and it is then reimbursed when the amount of money in the fund is reduced to a predetermined minimum amount (answer C).

You and Accounting

At one time or another, most people borrow money in order to buy such items as a stereo system, a car, or a home. When you borrow money, the lender generally charges interest on the outstanding balance. For example, when you borrow money to buy a car, you must pay the lender interest on the money borrowed. In this chapter, you will learn how to estimate the amount of interest you can expect to pay when you borrow money. In turn, you will be able to determine whether the lender is computing your interest accurately and truthfully according to the lending agreement.

Chapter 7
Receivables and Temporary Investments

LEARNING OBJECTIVES
After studying this chapter, you should be able to:

Objective 1
List the common classifications of receivables.

Objective 2
Summarize and provide examples of internal control procedures that apply to receivables.

Objective 3
State the accounting implications of promissory notes.

Objective 4
Journalize the entries for notes receivable transactions, including discounted notes receivable and dishonored notes receivable.

Objective 5
Name and describe two methods of accounting for uncollectible receivables.

Objective 6
Journalize the entries for the allowance method of accounting for uncollectibles, and estimate uncollectible receivables based on sales and on an analysis of receivables.

Objective 7
Journalize the entries for the direct write-off of uncollectible receivables.

Objective 8
Describe the accounting for receivables from installment sales.

Objective 9
Define temporary investments, give an example of two kinds of temporary investments, and explain how temporary investments are valued on the balance sheet.

Objective 10
Prepare the Current Assets section of a balance sheet that includes temporary investments and receivables.

For many businesses, the revenue from sales on account is one of the largest factors influencing the amount of net income. As credit is granted, the resulting receivables may represent a significant portion of the total current assets. In this chapter, we will discuss the accounting for such receivables as well as the accounting for notes receivable. As the receivables are collected, the cash is recorded and accounted for in the manner discussed in prior chapters. If the amount of cash on hand exceeds the business's immediate cash needs, the excess cash may be invested in securities until it is needed. We conclude this chapter with a discussion of the accounting for such temporary investments.

CLASSIFICATIONS OF RECEIVABLES

Objective 1
List the common classifications of receivables.

What do we mean by the term *receivables?* **Receivables** includes all money claims against other entities, including people, business firms, and other organizations. Receivables are acquired by business enterprises in various kinds of transactions, the most common of which is the sale of merchandise or services on credit.

Credit may be granted on open account or on the basis of a formal instrument of credit, such as a promissory note. A **promissory note**, often simply called a **note**, is a written promise to pay a sum of money on demand or at a definite time. Notes are often used for credit periods of more than sixty days, such as an installment plan for equipment sales. Notes may also be used in settlement of an open account and in borrowing or lending money.

To the creditor, a claim supported by a note has some advantages over a claim in the form of an account receivable. By signing a note, the debtor recognizes the debt and agrees to pay it according to the terms listed. A note is therefore a stronger legal claim if there is court action. It is also more liquid than an open account because the holder can usually sell it more readily to a bank or other financial agency in exchange for cash.

The enterprise owning a note refers to it as a **note receivable.** If notes and accounts receivable originate from sales transactions, they are sometimes called **trade receivables.** Unless otherwise described, accounts and notes receivable may be assumed to have originated from credit sales in the usual course of business.

Other receivables include interest receivable, loans to officers or employees, and loans to affiliated companies. As an aid in classifying receivables properly on the balance sheet, a general ledger account should be maintained for each type of receivable. Subsidiary ledgers may also be maintained, as necessary.

All receivables that are expected to be realized in cash within a year are presented in the Current Assets section of the balance sheet. Those that are not currently collectible, such as long-term loans, should be listed under the caption *Investments* below the Current Assets section.

INTERNAL CONTROL OF RECEIVABLES

Objective 2
Summarize and provide examples of internal control procedures that apply to receivables.

The principles of internal control discussed in prior chapters can be used to establish procedures to safeguard receivables. These controls include separating the business operations from the accounting for receivables. In this way, the accounting records can serve as an independent check on operations. Thus, the employee who handles the accounting for notes and accounts receivables should not be involved with the operating aspects of approving credit or collecting receivables. Separating these functions reduces the possibility of errors and misusing funds.

To further illustrate the internal control principle of separating related operating functions, assume that salespersons have been given authority to approve credit. If the salespersons are paid salaries plus commissions, say 10% of sales, they can increase their commissions by approving poor credit risks. Thus, the credit approval function is normally assigned to an individual outside the sales area.

Within the accounting function, related functions should also be separated. In this way, the work of one employee serves as a check on the work of another employee. For example, the responsibilities for maintaining the accounts receivable customers' (subsidiary) ledger and for the general ledger should be separated. The work of the accounts receivable clerk can be checked by comparing the total of the individual account balances in the customers' (subsidiary) ledger with the balance of the accounts receivable controlling account that is maintained by the general ledger clerk. If one individual performed both functions, this control would be lacking.

For most businesses, the primary receivables are notes receivable and accounts receivable. Generally, notes receivable are recorded in a single general ledger account. If there are many notes, the general ledger account can be supported by a notes receivable register or a subsidiary ledger. The register would contain details of each note, such as the name of the maker, place of payment, amount, term, interest rate, and due date. Reference to the due date section directs attention to those notes that are due for payment. In this way, the maker of the note can be notified when the note is due, and the risk that the maker will overlook the due date is minimized.

Control over accounts receivable begins with the proper credit approval of the sale by an authorized company official. Procedures for granting credit should be developed by the credit department of the company. Likewise, procedures for authorizing adjustments of accounts receivable, such as for sales returns and allowances and sales discounts, should be developed. Collection procedures should also be established to ensure timely collection of accounts receivable and to minimize losses from uncollectible accounts.

CHARACTERISTICS OF NOTES RECEIVABLE

Objective 3
State the accounting implications of promissory notes.

As we indicated earlier in the chapter, a note is a written promise to pay a sum of money on demand or at a definite time. As in the case of a check, it must be payable to the order of a certain person or firm or to the bearer. It must also be signed by the person or firm that makes the promise. The **payee** is the person to whom the note is payable, and the one making the promise is called the **maker.** The face amount of the note is called the **principal.** In the example in Exhibit 1 , Pearland Company is the payee, Selig Company is the maker, and the principal is $2,500.

Exhibit 1
Promissory Note

$ __2,500.00__   Fresno, California __March 16__ 19 __95__

__Ninety days__   AFTER DATE __We__ PROMISE TO PAY TO

THE ORDER OF __Pearland Company__

__Two thousand five hundred 00/100 – – – – – – – – – – – –__ DOLLARS

PAYABLE AT __First National Bank__

VALUE RECEIVED WITH INTEREST AT __10%__
NO. __14__ DUE __June 14, 1995__   *H.B. Lane*
                                        TREASURER, *SELIG COMPANY*

Notes have several characteristics that have accounting implications. We describe these characteristics in the following paragraphs.

Due Date

The date a note is to be paid is called the **due date** or **maturity date.** The period of time between the issuance date and the due date of a short-term note may be stated in either days or months. When the term of a note is stated in days, the due date is the specified number of days after its issuance. To illustrate, the due date of the 90-day note in Exhibit 1 is determined as follows:

Term of the note		90
March (days)	31	
Date of note	16	15
Number of days remaining		75
April (days)		30
		45
May (days)		31
Due date, June		14

When the term of a note is stated as a certain number of months after the is-suance date, the due date is determined by counting the number of months from the issuance date. Thus a three-month note dated June 5 would be due on September 5. In those cases in which there is no date in the month of maturity that corresponds to the issuance date, the due date becomes the last day of the month. For example, a two-month note dated July 31 would be due on Sep-tember 30.

Interest-Bearing Notes and Non-Interest-Bearing Notes

A note that specifies an interest rate for the period between the issuance date and the due date is called an **interest-bearing note.** A **non-interest-bearing note** does not specify an interest rate. The note in Exhibit 1 is an interest-bearing note.

Interest

As you are probably aware, interest rates must be stated in terms of a time period. Rates for interest-bearing notes are usually stated in terms of one year, regardless of the actual period of time involved. Thus, the interest on $2,000 for one year at 12% is $240 (12% of $2,000); the interest on $2,000 for one-fourth of one year at 12% is $60 (1/4 of $240).

Notes covering a period of time longer than one year normally provide that the interest be paid semiannually, quarterly, or at some other stated interval. The time involved in business credit transactions is usually less than one year, and the in-terest provided for by a note is payable at the time the note is paid. In computing interest for a period of less than one year, agencies of the federal government use the actual number of days in the year. For example, 90 days is 90/365 of one year. To simplify the computations, we will use 360 days. Thus, 90 days is considered to be 90/360 of one year.

The basic formula for computing interest is as follows:

Principal $\times$ Rate $\times$ Time = Interest

To illustrate the use of the formula, the $62.50 interest for the $2,500, 90-day, 10% note in Exhibit 1 is computed as follows:

$$\$2,500 \times \frac{10}{100} \times \frac{90}{360} = \$62.50 \text{ interest}$$

One of the commonly used shortcut methods of computing interest is called the 60-day, 6% method. The 6% annual rate is converted to the effective rate of 1% for a 60-day period (60/360 of 6%). Accordingly, the interest on any amount for 60 days at 6% is determined by moving the decimal point in the principal two places to the left. For example, the interest on $1,500 at 6% for 60 days is $15. The amount obtained by moving the decimal point must be adjusted (1) for interest rates greater or less than 6% and (2) for periods of time greater or less than 60 days. For exam-ple, the interest on $1,500 at 6% for 90 days is $22.50 (90/60 of $15). The interest on $1,500 at 12% for 60 days is $30 (12/6 of $15).

When the term of a note is stated in months instead of in days, each month may be considered as being 1/12 of a year. Alternatively, the actual number of days in the term may be counted. For example, the interest on a three-month note dated June 1 could be computed on the basis of 3/12 of a year or on the basis of 92/365 of a year. Banks usually charge interest for the exact number of days. To simplify, we will consider a month as 1/12 of a year.

Using Accounting

The concept of interest is useful in your everyday life. For example, credit card balances that remain unpaid at the end of the month incur an interest charge expressed in terms of a percent per month. Interest charges of 1½% per month are common. Such charges approximate an annual interest rate of 18% per year (1½% × 12). Thus, if you can borrow money at less than 18%, you are better off borrowing the money and paying off the credit card balance than incurring the monthly interest charges on the unpaid credit card balance. Likewise, many companies charge penalties for late payment of bills. For example, a utility bill might be due on the 15th of the month, with a late charge of 5% if paid after the 15th. If the bill remains unpaid after 30 days, the utility stops services. If you pay late and incur the 5% late charge, you are, in effect, borrowing the amount of the bill for an extra 15 days. But the extra 15 days costs you 5%, which approximates an annual rate of 120% [(360 days ÷ 15 days) × 5%]. Again, you would be better off borrowing to avoid the late charge.

Maturity Value

The amount that is due at the maturity or due date is called the **maturity value.** The maturity value of a non-interest-bearing note is the face amount. The maturity value of an interest-bearing note is the sum of the face amount and the interest. In the note in Exhibit 1, the maturity value is $2,562.50 ($2,500 face amount plus $62.50 interest).

ACCOUNTING FOR NOTES RECEIVABLE

Objective 4
Journalize the entries for notes receivable transactions, including discounted notes receivable and dishonored notes receivable.

The typical retail enterprise makes most of its sales for cash or on account. If the account of a customer becomes past due, the creditor may insist that the account be converted into a note. In this way, the debtor is given more time to make payment. Also, if the creditor needs more funds, the note may be endorsed and sold to a bank or other financial agency. Notes may also be received by retail firms that sell merchandise on long-term credit. For example, a dealer in household appliances may require a down payment at the time of sale and accept a note or a series of notes for the remainder. Such arrangements usually provide for monthly payments.

When a note is received from a customer to apply on account, the facts are recorded by debiting the notes receivable account and crediting Accounts Receivable and the account of the customer from whom the note is received. To illustrate, assume that the account of Glenn Enterprises, which has a balance of $9,200, is past due. A 90-day, non-interest-bearing note for that amount, dated May 16, 1995, is accepted in settlement of the account. The note receivable is recorded at its face value, and the entry to record the transaction is as follows:

May 16	Notes Receivable	9,200	
	Accounts Receivable—Glenn Enterprises		9,200
	Received 90-day, non-interest-bearing		
	note dated May 16, 1995.		

When the $9,200 due on the note is collected, the following entry is recorded:

| Aug. 14 | Cash | 9,200 | |
| | Notes Receivable | | 9,200 |

Interest-Bearing Notes Receivable

If the note received from a customer on account is interest-bearing, interest must be recorded. For example, assume that a 30-day, 12% note dated November 21,

1995, is accepted in settlement of the account of W.A Bunn Co., which has a balance of $6,000. The entry to record the transaction is as follows:

Nov. 21	Notes Receivable	6,000	
	Accounts Receivable—W. A. Bunn Co.		6,000
	Received 30-day, 12% note dated		
	November 21, 1995.		

At the time the note matures, the entry to record the receipt of $6,060 ($6,000 principal plus $60 interest) is as follows:

Dec. 21	Cash	6,060	
	Notes Receivable		6,000
	Interest Income		60

If an interest-bearing note matures in a later fiscal period, the interest accrued in the period in which the note is received must be recorded. For example, assume that a 90-day, 12% note dated December 1 is received from Crawford Company in settlement of its account, which has a balance of $4,000. The entry to record the receipt of the note is similar to the November 21 entry above. On December 31, the following adjusting entry is necessary to record the $40 interest earned for 30 days in December ($4,000 × 30/360 × 12/100):

| Dec. 31 | Interest Receivable | 40 | |
| | Interest Income | | 40 |

The interest income account is closed at December 31. The amount of interest income is reported in the Other Income section of the income statement for the year ended December 31, 1995.

Discounting Notes Receivable

Although it is not a common transaction, a company in need of cash may transfer its notes receivable to a bank by endorsement. The **discount** (interest) charged by the bank is computed on the maturity value of the note for the period that the bank must hold the note. This period, called the **discount period,** is the time that will pass between the date of the transfer and the due date of the note. The amount of the **proceeds** paid to the endorser is the excess of the maturity value over the discount.

For example, assume that a 90-day, 12% note receivable for $1,800, dated April 8, is discounted at the payee's bank on May 3 at the rate of 14%. The data used in determining the effect of the transaction are as follows:

Face value of note dated April 8	$1,800.00
Interest on note (90 days at 12%)	54.00
Maturity value of note due July 7	$1,854.00
Discount on maturity value (65 days from May 3 to July 7, at 14%)	46.87
Proceeds	$1,807.13

The same information is presented graphically in Exhibit 2. In reading the data, follow the direction of the arrows.

Exhibit 2
Diagram of Discounting a Note
Receivable

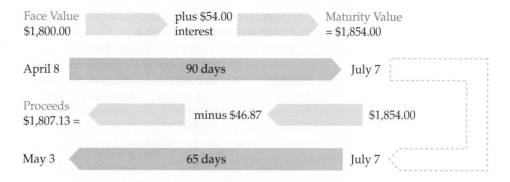

The excess of the proceeds from discounting the note, $1,807.13, over its face value, $1,800, is recorded as interest income. The entry for the transaction is as follows:

May 3	Cash	1,807.13	
	Notes Receivable		1,800.00
	Interest Income		7.13

What if the proceeds from discounting a note receivable are less than the face value? When this situation occurs, the excess of the face value over the proceeds is recorded as interest expense. The length of the discount period and the difference between the interest rate and the discount rate determines whether interest expense or interest income will result from discounting.

Without a statement limiting responsibility, the endorser of a note is committed to paying the note if the maker defaults. Such potential obligations will become actual liabilities only if certain events occur in the future. These potential obligations are called **contingent liabilities**. Thus, the endorser of a note that has been discounted has a contingent liability until the due date. If the maker pays the promised amount at maturity, the contingent liability is removed without any action on the part of the endorser. If, on the other hand, the maker defaults and the endorser is notified according to legal requirements, the liability becomes an actual one.

Significant contingent liabilities should be disclosed on the balance sheet or in an accompanying note. In a later chapter, we will discuss disclosure requirements for contingent liabilities.

Dishonored Notes Receivable

If the maker of a note fails to pay the debt on the due date, the note is said to be *dishonored*. A **dishonored note receivable** is no longer negotiable. For this reason the holder usually transfers the claim, including any interest due, to the accounts receivable account. For example, assume that a $6,000, 30-day, 12% note received and recorded on November 21 has been dishonored at maturity. The entry to charge the note, including the interest, back to the customer's account is as follows:

Dec. 21	Accounts Receivable—W. A. Bunn Co.	6,060	
	Notes Receivable		6,000
	Interest Income		60
	Dishonored note and interest.		

If there had been some assurance that the maker would pay the note within a short time, action could be delayed until the matter is resolved. However, for future reference in extending credit, it may be desirable that the customer's account disclose the dishonor of the note.

When a discounted note receivable is dishonored, the holder usually notifies the endorser of that fact and asks for payment. If the request for payment and notification of dishonor are timely, the endorser is legally obligated to pay the amount due on the note. The entire amount paid to the holder by the endorser, including the interest, should be debited to the account receivable of the maker. For example, assume that the $1,800, 90-day, 12% note discounted on May 3 (Exhibit 2) is dishonored at maturity by the maker, Pryor & Co. The entry to record the payment by the endorser is as follows:

| July 7 | Accounts Receivable—Pryor & Co. | 1,854 | |
| | Cash | | 1,854 |

In some cases, the holder of a dishonored note gives the endorser a notarized statement of the facts of the dishonor. The fee for this statement, known as a **protest fee,** is charged to the endorser, who in turn charges it to the maker of the note. For example, if the bank charges a protest fee of $12 in connection with the dishonored Pryor & Co. note, the entry to record the payment by the endorser is as follows:

| July 7 | Accounts Receivable—Pryor & Co. | 1,866 | |
| | Cash | | 1,866 |

UNCOLLECTIBLE RECEIVABLES

Objective 5
Name and describe two methods of accounting for uncollectible receivables.

Regardless of the care used in granting credit and the collection procedures used, a part of the claims from sales to customers on credit will normally not be collectible. The operating expense incurred because of the failure to collect receivables is called an expense or a loss from **uncollectible accounts, doubtful accounts,** or **bad debts**.[1]

When does an account become uncollectible? There is no general rule for determining when an account or a note becomes uncollectible. The fact that a debtor fails to pay an account according to a sales contract or dishonors a note on the due date does not necessarily mean that the account will be uncollectible. Bankruptcy of the debtor is one of the most significant indications of partial or complete uncollectibility of a receivable. Other indications that an account may be uncollectible include the closing of the customer's business and the failure of repeated attempts to collect.

There are two methods of accounting for receivables that are believed to be uncollectible. The **allowance method** provides in advance for uncollectible receivables.[2] The other procedure, called the **direct write-off method** or **direct charge-off method,** recognizes the expense only when certain accounts are judged to be worthless.

ALLOWANCE METHOD OF ACCOUNTING FOR UNCOLLECTIBLES

Objective 6
Journalize the entries for the allowance method of accounting for uncollectibles, and estimate uncollectible receivables based on sales and on an analysis of receivables.

Most large business enterprises estimate currently the uncollectible portion of their trade receivables. The provision for future uncollectibility is made by an adjusting entry at the end of a fiscal period. As with all periodic adjustments, this entry serves two purposes. First, it provides for the reduction of the value of the receivables to the amount of cash expected to be realized in the future, called the **net realizable value.** Second, it matches the uncollectible expense of the current period with the related revenues of the period.

---

[1] If both notes and accounts are involved, both may be included in the expense account title, as in *Uncollectible Notes and Accounts Expense,* or *Uncollectible Receivables Expense.* Because of its wide usage and simplicity, *Uncollectible Accounts Expense* will be used in this text.
[2] The allowance method is not acceptable for determining the federal income tax of most taxpayers.

To illustrate the allowance method, assumed data for a new business firm, Richards Company, is used. The enterprise began business in August and chose to use the calendar year as its fiscal year. The accounts receivable account, shown below, has a balance of $105,000 at the end of the period.

ACCOUNT ACCOUNTS RECEIVABLE   ACCOUNT NO. 114

Date		Item	Post. Ref.	Debit	Credit	Balance Debit	Balance Credit
19–							
Aug.	31			20,000		20,000	
Sep.	30			25,000		45,000	
	30				15,000	30,000	
Oct.	31			40,000		70,000	
	31				25,000	45,000	
Nov.	30			38,000		83,000	
	30				23,000	60,000	
Dec.	31			75,000		135,000	
	31				30,000	105,000	

Among the customer accounts making up the $105,000 balance in Accounts Receivable are a number of balances that are past due. No specific accounts are believed to be totally uncollectible at this time. However, it seems likely that some will be collected only in part and that others will become worthless. Based on a careful study, it is estimated that a total of $3,000 will eventually prove to be uncollectible. The net realizable value of the accounts receivable is therefore $102,000 ($105,000 − $3,000). The $3,000 reduction in value is the uncollectible accounts expense for the period.

Because the $3,000 reduction in accounts receivable is an estimate, it cannot be credited to specific customer accounts or to the accounts receivable controlling account. Instead, a contra asset account entitled Allowance for Doubtful Accounts is credited. The adjusting entry to record the expense and the reduction in the asset is as follows:

Page 4

Dec. 31	*Adjusting Entry* Uncollectible Accounts Expense	717	3,000	
	Allowance for Doubtful Accounts	115		3,000

The two accounts to which the entry is posted are illustrated as follows:

ACCOUNT UNCOLLECTIBLE ACCOUNTS EXPENSE   ACCOUNT NO. 717

Date		Item	Post. Ref.	Debit	Credit	Balance Debit	Balance Credit
19–							
Dec.	31	Adjusting		3,000		3,000	

ACCOUNT ALLOWANCE FOR DOUBTFUL ACCOUNTS   ACCOUNT NO. 115

Date		Item	Post. Ref.	Debit	Credit	Balance Debit	Balance Credit
19–							
Dec.	31	Adjusting			3,000		3,000

The debit balance of $105,000 in Accounts Receivable is the amount of the total claims against customers on open account. The credit balance of $3,000 in Allowance for Doubtful Accounts is the amount to be deducted from Accounts Receivable to determine the net realizable value.

Uncollectible accounts expense is normally reported on the income statement as an administrative expense. This classification is used because the credit-granting and collection duties are the responsibilities of departments within the administrative area. At the end of the period, the $3,000 balance in Uncollectible Accounts Expense is closed to Income Summary.

The accounts receivable may be listed on the balance sheet at the net amount of $102,000, with a notation in parentheses showing the amount of the allowance. Alternately, the details may be presented as shown below in the Current Assets section of the balance sheet. When the allowance account includes provision for doubtful notes as well as accounts, it should be deducted from the total of Notes Receivable and Accounts Receivable.

Current assets:		
Cash		$ 21,600
Accounts receivable	$105,000	
Less allowance for doubtful accounts	3,000	102,000

match expense with the year sale

Write-Offs to the Allowance Account

When an account is believed to be uncollectible, it is written off against the allowance account as follows:

Jan. 21	Allowance for Doubtful Accounts	610	
	Accounts Receivable—John Parker		610
	To write off the uncollectible account.		

During the year, as accounts or portions of accounts are determined to be uncollectible, they are written off against Allowance for Doubtful Accounts. Authorization for write-offs should originate with the credit manager or other designated officer. The authorizations, which should be written, serve as support for the accounting entry.

The total amount written off against the allowance account during a period will rarely be equal to the amount in the account at the beginning of the period. The allowance account will have a credit balance at the end of the period if the write-offs during the period are less than the beginning balance. It will have a debit balance if the write-offs exceed the beginning balance. After the year-end adjusting entry is recorded, the allowance account will have a credit balance.

An account receivable that has been written off against the allowance account may later be collected. In such cases, the account should be reinstated by an entry that is the exact reverse of the write-off entry. For example, assume that the account of $610 written off in the preceding journal entry is later collected. The entry to reinstate the account would be as follows:

June 10	Accounts Receivable—John Parker	610	
	Allowance for Doubtful Accounts		610
	To reinstate account written off earlier in the year.		

The cash received in payment would be recorded as a receipt on account as follows:

June 10	Cash	610	
	Accounts Receivable—John Parker		610

The two preceding entries can be combined. However, recording two separate entries in the customer's account, with proper notation, provides useful credit information.

Estimating Uncollectibles

How is the amount of uncollectible accounts estimated? The estimate of uncollectibles at the end of a fiscal period is based on past experience and forecasts of future business activity. When the general economic environment is favorable, the amount of the expense should normally be less than when the trend is in the opposite direction. The estimate of uncollectibles is usually based on either (1) the amount of sales for the period or (2) the amount and the age of the receivable accounts at the end of the period.

ESTIMATE BASED ON SALES. Accounts receivable are acquired as a result of sales on account. The amount of such sales during the year may therefore be used to estimate the amount of uncollectible accounts. The amount of this estimate is added to whatever balance exists in Allowance for Doubtful Accounts. For example, assume that the allowance account has a credit balance of $700 before adjustment. It is estimated from past experience that 1% of credit sales will be uncollectible. If credit sales for the period are $300,000, the adjusting entry for uncollectible accounts at the end of the period is as follows:

| Dec. 31 | Uncollectible Accounts Expense | 3,000 | |
| | Allowance for Doubtful Accounts | | 3,000 |

After the adjusting entry has been posted, the balance in the allowance account is $3,700. If there had been a debit balance of $200 in the allowance account before the year-end adjustment, the amount of the adjustment would still have been $3,000. The balance in the allowance account, after the adjusting entry has been posted, would be $2,800 ($3,000 − $200).

Instead of credit sales, total sales (including those made for cash) may be used in estimating the percentage of uncollectible accounts. Using total sales is less costly, since total sales is available in the sales account in the ledger. In contrast, a separate analysis may be required to determine credit sales. If the ratio of credit sales to cash sales does not change very much from year to year, estimates using total sales will be acceptable. In the above example, if 3/4 of 1% is used to estimate uncollectibles, based upon total sales of $400,000, the same estimate of $3,000 would result.

If the amount of write-offs is always greater or less than the amount provided by the adjusting entry, the percentage applied to the sales data should be revised. A new business enterprise, having no prior credit experience, may estimate uncollectible percentages using data from trade association journals and other industry publications.

The estimate-based-on-sales method of estimating the uncollectible accounts expense is widely used. Its advantages are that it is simple and it emphasizes the matching of uncollectible accounts expense with the related sales of the period.

ESTIMATE BASED ON ANALYSIS OF RECEIVABLES. The process of analyzing each account receivable in terms of the length of time it is past due is called aging the receivables. The base point for determining age is the due date of the account. The number and length of the time intervals used varies according to the credit terms granted to customers. Exhibit 3 shows an example of a typical aging of accounts receivable.

Exhibit 3
Aging of Accounts Receivable

Customer	Balance	Not Due	Days Past Due						
			1-30	31-60	61-90	91-180	181-365	over 365
Ashby & Co.	$ 150			$ 150				
B. T. Barr	610					$ 350	$260	
Brock Co.	470	$ 470						
J. Zimmer Co.	160							160
Total	$86,300	$75,000	$4,000	$3,100	$1,900	$1,200	$800	$300

The aging schedule is completed by adding the columns to determine the total amount of receivables in each age group. A sliding scale of percentages, based on experience, is used to estimate the amount of uncollectibles in each group. The manner in which the data may be presented is shown in Exhibit 4.

Exhibit 4
Estimate of Uncollectible Accounts

		Estimated Uncollectible Accounts	
Age Interval	Balance	Percent	Amount
Not due	$75,000	2%	$1,500
1–30 days past due	4,000	5	200
31–60 days past due	3,100	10	310
61–90 days past due	1,900	20	380
91–180 days past due	1,200	30	360
181–365 days past due	800	50	400
Over 365 days past due	300	80	240
Total	$86,300		$3,390

% not to collect · *16,000*

The estimate of uncollectible accounts is $3,390 in Exhibit 4. This amount is deducted from accounts receivable to yield the accounts receivable net realizable value. It is also the amount of the desired balance of the allowance account at the end of the period. The excess of this amount over the balance of the allowance account before adjustment is the amount of the uncollectible accounts expense for the period.

To continue the example, assume that the allowance account has a credit balance of $510 before adjustment. The amount to be added to this balance is therefore $2,880 ($3,390 − $510). The adjusting entry is as follows:

Dec. 31	Uncollectible Accounts Expense	2,880	
	Allowance for Doubtful Accounts		2,880

After the adjusting entry has been posted, the credit balance in the allowance account is $3,390, the desired amount. If there had been a debit balance of $300 in the allowance account before the year-end adjustment, the amount of the adjustment would have been $3,690 ($3,390 desired balance + $300 debit balance).

Estimates of uncollectible accounts expense based on analyzing receivables are less common than estimates based on sales volume. The primary advantage of analyzing receivables is that it emphasizes the current net realizable value of the receivables.

The Older It Gets

A properly designed accounting system should provide for the careful screening of credit, prompt reporting of delinquent accounts, and effective collection procedures for delinquent accounts. As illustrated in the following article from a public accounting firm's newsletter, collection success depends on quick collection efforts.

There is a direct relationship between the age of outstanding receivables and the chance of successfully collecting [them]. . . . [The] Commercial Law League of America published the following data showing the precise correlation between the age of the receivable and the chance of collection:

Period of Delinquency	Collection Likelihood
1 month	94%
2 months	85%
3 months	74%
6 months	48%
9 months	43%
1 year	27%
2 years	14%

Source: "The Older It Gets," *The Advisor* (Spring 1988), p. 2

DIRECT WRITE-OFF METHOD OF ACCOUNTING FOR UNCOLLECTIBLES

Objective 7
Journalize the entries for the direct write-off of uncollectible receivables.

The allowance method illustrated in the preceding paragraphs emphasizes reporting uncollectible accounts expense in the period in which the sales occur. This emphasis on matching expenses with related revenue is the preferred method of accounting for uncollectible receivables. However, there are situations in which it is impossible to estimate, with reasonable accuracy, the uncollectibles at the end of the period. Also, if an enterprise sells most of its goods or services on a cash basis, the amount of its expense from uncollectible accounts is usually small in relation to its revenue. The amount of its receivables at any time is also likely to represent a relatively small part of its total current assets. In such cases, it is acceptable to delay recognition of uncollectible expense until the accounts are determined to be worthless. Thus, under the direct write-off method, an allowance account and an adjusting entry are not needed at the end of the period. The entry to write off an account when it is determined to be uncollectible is as follows:

May 10	Uncollectible Accounts Expense	420	
	Accounts Receivable—D. L. Ross		420
	To write off uncollectible account.		

What if a customer later pays on an account that has been written off? If an account that has been written off is collected later, the account should be reinstated. If the recovery is in the same period as the write-off, the earlier entry should be reversed to reinstate the account. For example, assume that the account written off in the May 10 entry is collected in November of the same fiscal year. The entry to reinstate the account is as follows:

Nov. 21	Accounts Receivable—D. L. Ross	420	
	Uncollectible Accounts Expense		420
	To reinstate account written		
	off earlier in the year.		

The receipt of cash in payment of the reinstated amount is recorded in the usual manner. That is, Cash is debited and Accounts Receivable is credited.

When an account that has been written off is collected in a later fiscal year, it may be reinstated by debiting Accounts Receivable and crediting Uncollectible Accounts Expense. An alternative is to credit some other appropriately titled account, such as Recovery of Uncollectible Accounts Written Off. The credit balance in such an account at the end of the period may then be reported on the income statement as a deduction from Uncollectible Accounts Expense. In either case, only the net uncollectible expense is reported.

RECEIVABLES FROM INSTALLMENT SALES

Objective 8
Describe the accounting for receivables from installment sales.

In some businesses, especially in the retail field, it is common to make sales on the installment plan. In a typical installment sale, the buyer makes a down payment and agrees to pay the remainder in periodic payments over a period of time. The seller may retain title to the goods or may use other contractual means to make repossession of the goods easier if the buyer defaults on the payments. Despite such provisions, installment sales should normally be recorded in the same manner as any other sale on account. That is, the revenue is considered to be realized at the point of sale. Under the **point-of-sale method**, revenue is considered to be realized at the time title to the merchandise passes to the buyer.

In rare cases, collecting receivables from installment sales may not be reasonably assured. In these cases, the **installment method** of realizing revenue may be used.[3] Under this method, revenue is realized upon the receipt of cash. Each cash receipt is considered to be (1) part cost of merchandise sold and (2) part gross profit on the sale.

To illustrate, assume that in the first year of operations, a dealer in household appliances had total installment sales of $300,000, with a related cost of $180,000 of merchandise sold. Assume also that collections of the installment accounts receivable are spread over three years as follows: first year, $140,000; second year, $100,000; third year, $60,000. Under the point-of-sale method, all of the revenue would be recognized in the first year, and the gross profit realized in that year would be as follows:

Point-of-sale method:	
Installment sales	$300,000
Cost of merchandise sold	180,000
Gross profit	$120,000

Under the installment method, gross profit is allocated according to the amount of receivables collected in each year. This allocation is based on the percent of gross profit to sales. The rate of gross profit to sales is determined as follows:

$$\frac{\text{Gross Profit}}{\text{Installment Sales}} = \frac{\$120,000}{\$300,000} = 40\%$$

The amounts reported as gross profit for each of the three years in the illustration, based on collections of installment accounts receivable, are as follows:

Installment method:		
1st year collections:	$140,000 × 40%	$ 56,000
2d year collections:	100,000 × 40%	40,000
3d year collections:	60,000 × 40%	24,000
Total	$300,000	$120,000

TEMPORARY INVESTMENTS

Objective 9
Define temporary investments, give an example of two kinds of temporary investments, and explain how temporary investments are valued on the balance sheet.

A business may have excess cash that is not needed immediately for operations. Rather than allow this excess cash to be idle until it is needed, a business may invest all or a part of it in income-yielding securities. Since these investments can be quickly sold and converted to cash as needed, they are called **temporary investments** or **marketable securities**. Although such investments may be retained for number of years, they continue to be classified as temporary, provided that two conditions are met. First, the securities are readily marketable and thus can be sold for cash at any time. Second, it is the intent of management to sell the securities at such time as the enterprise needs more cash for operations.

Temporary investments include investments in stocks and bonds. **Stocks** are

---

[3] *Opinions of the Accounting Principles Board, No. 10,* "Omnibus Opinion—1966" (New York: American Institute of Certified Public Accountants, 1966), par. 12

equity securities issued by corporations. **Bonds** are debt securities issued by corporations and various government agencies. Stocks and bonds held as temporary investments are classified on the balance sheet as current assets. They may be listed after *Cash*, or they may be combined with cash and cash equivalents and described as *Cash, cash equivalents, and marketable securities*.

A temporary investment in a portfolio of debt securities is normally carried at cost. However, the **carrying amount** (also called **basis**) of a temporary investment in equity securities is the lower of its total cost or market value. The market value is determined at the date of the balance sheet.[4] The carrying amount is based on comparing the *total* cost and the *total* market value of the investment, not the cost and market price of *each item*. To illustrate, the following portfolio of temporary investments in equity securities is valued at the lower of the total cost ($690,000) or total market ($660,000):

Temporary Investment Portfolio	Cost	Market	Unrealized Gain (Loss)
Equity security A	$150,000	$100,000	$(50,000)
Equity security B	200,000	200,000	—
Equity security C	180,000	210,000	30,000
Equity security D	160,000	150,000	(10,000)
Total	$690,000	$660,000	$(30,000)

The above marketable equity securities are reported at a cost of $690,000 in the Current Assets section of the balance sheet in Exhibit 5. An allowance for decline to market value of $30,000 is subtracted to yield the carrying amount of $660,000. The unrealized loss of $30,000 is included in determining net income and reported as a separate item on the income statement.

If the total market value of the investment portfolio later rises, the unrealized loss is reversed and included in net income. It is reported separately in the Other Income section of the income statement, and the amount reported on the balance sheet is adjusted. However, the carrying value cannot exceed the original cost.[5]

TEMPORARY INVESTMENTS AND RECEIVABLES IN THE BALANCE SHEET

Objective 10
Prepare the Current Assets section of a balance sheet that includes temporary investments and receivables.

Temporary investments and all receivables that are expected to be realized in cash within a year are presented in the Current Assets section of the balance sheet. It is normal to list the assets in the order of their liquidity. This is the order in which they are expected to be converted to cash during normal operations. Exhibit 5 shows the presentation of temporary investments and receivables in a partial balance sheet for Pilar Enterprises.

Exhibit 5
Temporary Investments and Receivables in Balance Sheet

Pilar Enterprises
Balance Sheet
December 31, 19—

Assets

Current assets:		
Cash		$119,500
Marketable equity securities	$690,000	
Less allowance for decline to market	30,000	660,000
Notes receivable		250,000
Accounts receivable	$445,000	
Less allowance for doubtful accounts	15,000	430,000
Interest receivable		14,500

[4] *Statement of Financial Accounting Standards, No. 12,* "Accounting for Certain Marketable Securities" (Stamford: Financial Accounting Standards Board, 1975), par. 8.
[5] The discussion of temporary investments in this chapter focuses on the concepts applicable to their presentations on the financial statements. Other aspects of accounting for investments, such as dividend income and interest income, are discussed in a later chapter.

Disclosures related to temporary investments and receivables are presented either on the face of the financial statements or in the accompanying notes. Such disclosures include the market (fair) value of the temporary investments and receivables.[6] Generally, the market value of receivables approximates their carrying value. In addition, if unusual credit risks exist within the receivables, the nature of the risks should be disclosed. For example, if the majority of the receivables are due from one customer or are due from customers located in one area of the country or one industry, these facts should be disclosed.[7] An illustration of a credit risk disclosure taken from the 1991 financial statements of Deere & Company is shown below.

> *Credit receivables have significant concentrations of credit risk in the agricultural, industrial, lawn and grounds care, and recreational (non-Deere equipment) business sectors. At October 31, 1991 and 1990, the portions of credit receivables related to the agricultural equipment business were 60 percent and 56 percent, those related to the industrial equipment business were 12 percent and 14 percent, those related to the lawn and grounds care equipment business were seven percent and eight percent, and those related to the recreational equipment business were 21 percent and 22 percent, respectively. On a geographic basis, there is not a disproportionate concentration of credit risk in any area. . . .*

[6] *Statement of Financial Accounting Standards, No. 107*, "Disclosures about Fair Value of Financial Instruments," (Norwalk: Financial Accounting Standards Board, 1991), par. 10.
[7] *Statement of Financial Accounting Standards, No. 105*, "Disclosure of Information about Financial Instruments with Off-Balance Sheet Risk and Financial Instruments with Concentrations of Credit Risk," (Norwalk: Financial Accounting Standards Board, 1990), par. 20, and *Statement of Financial Accounting Standards, No. 107, op. cit.*, par. 13.

CHAPTER REVIEW

Key Points

Objective 1. List the common classifications of receivables.
The common classes of receivables include accounts receivable and notes receivable. Accounts and notes receivable originating from sales transactions are called trade receivables.

Objective 2. Summarize and provide examples of internal control procedures that apply to receivables.
The internal controls that apply to receivables include the separation of responsibilities for related functions. In this way, the work of one employee can serve as a check on the work of another employee. Other controls are the use of subsidiary ledgers and authorization procedures for credit approval and adjustments of accounts.

Objective 3. State the accounting implications of promissory notes.
The accounting implications of a promissory note include the recognition of interest and the determination of the due date and the maturity value of the note. The basic formula for computing interest on a note is: Principal × Rate × Time = Interest. The due date is the date a note is to be paid, and the period of time between the issuance date and the due date is normally stated in either days or months. The maturity value of an interest-bearing note is the sum of the face amount and the interest. The maturity value of a non-interest-bearing note is the face value of the note.

Objective 4. Journalize the entries for notes receivable transactions, including discounted notes receivable and dishonored notes receivable.
A note received in settlement of an account receivable is recorded as a debit to Notes Receivable and a credit to Accounts Receivable. When a note matures, Cash is debited, Notes Receivable is credited, and Interest Income is credited for any interest. A note receivable may be discounted at a bank. In this case, Cash is debited for the proceeds, Notes Receivable is credited, and any interest income or interest expense is recorded.

If the maker of a note that has been discounted fails to pay the debt on the due date, the note is said to be dishonored. When the holder of a dishonored note has been paid by the endorser, the amount of the endorser's claim against the maker of the note is debited to an accounts receivable account.

Objective 5. Name and describe two methods of accounting for uncollectible receivables.

The two methods of accounting for uncollectible receivables are the allowance method and the direct write-off method. The allowance method provides in advance for uncollectible receivables. The direct write-off method recognizes the expense only when the account is judged to be uncollectible.

Objective 6. Journalize the entries for the allowance method of accounting for uncollectibles, and estimate uncollectible receivables based on sales and on an analysis of receivables.

An adjusting entry made at the end of the fiscal period provides for (1) the reduction of the value of the receivables to the amount of cash expected to be realized from them in the future and (2) the allocation to the current period of the expected expense resulting from such reduction. The adjusting entry debits Uncollectible Accounts Expense and credits Allowance for Doubtful Accounts. When an account is believed to be uncollectible, it is written off against the allowance account.

When the estimate of uncollectibles is based upon the amount of sales for the fiscal period, the adjusting entry at the end of the period is made without regard to the balance of the allowance account. When the estimate of uncollectibles is based upon the amount and the age of the receivable accounts at the end of the period, the adjusting entry is recorded so that the balance of the allowance account will equal the estimated uncollectibles at the end of the period.

The allowance account, which will have a credit balance after the adjusting entry has been posted, is a contra asset account. The uncollectible accounts expense is generally reported on the income statement as an administrative expense.

Objective 7. Journalize the entries for the direct write-off of uncollectible receivables.

Under the direct write-off method, the entry to write off an account debits Uncollectible Accounts Expense and credits Accounts Receivable. Neither an allowance account nor an adjusting entry is needed at the end of the period.

Objective 8. Describe the accounting for receivables from installment sales.

Revenue from sales made on the installment plan should normally be accounted for by the point-of-sale method, under which revenue is realized at the time title passes to the buyer. When the collection of the receivables is not reasonably assured, the installment method may be used. Under this method, the gross profit from installment sales is recognized according to the amount of receivables collected each year, based upon the percent of gross profit to sales.

Objective 9. Define temporary investments, give an example of two kinds of temporary investments, and explain how temporary investments are valued on the balance sheet.

Temporary investments are income-yielding securities that can be quickly sold and converted to cash. Such investments include stocks and bonds. Stocks are equity securities, and bonds are debt securities issued by corporations and various government agencies. A temporary investment in debt securities is normally carried at cost on the balance sheet. However, a temporary investment in equity securities must be carried at the lower of its total cost or total market value at the balance sheet date.

Objective 10. Prepare the Current Assets section of a balance sheet that includes temporary investments and receivables.

Temporary investments and all receivables that are expected to be realized in cash within a year are presented in the Current Assets section of the balance sheet. It is normal to list the assets in the order of their liquidity, which is the order in which they can be converted to cash in normal operations.

Glossary of Key Terms

Aging the receivables. The process of analyzing the accounts receivable and classifying them according to various age groupings, with the due date being the base point for determining age. **Objective 6**

Allowance method. A method of accounting for uncollectible receivables, whereby advance provision for the uncollectibles is made. **Objective 5**

Carrying amount. The amount at which a temporary investment is reported on the balance sheet; also called basis or book value. **Objective 9**

Contingent liabilities. Potential obligations that will materialize only if certain events occur in the future. **Objective 4**

Direct write-off method. A method of accounting for uncollectible receivables, whereby an expense is recognized only when specific accounts are judged to be uncollectible. **Objective 5**

Discount. The interest deducted from the maturity value of a note receivable. **Objective 4**

Dishonored note receivable. A note that the maker fails to pay on its due date. **Objective 4**

Installment method. The method of recognizing revenue, whereby each receipt of cash from installment sales is considered to be part cost of merchandise sold and part gross profit. **Objective 8**

Marketable securities. Investments in securities that can be readily sold when cash is needed. **Objective 9**

Maturity value. The amount due at the maturity or due date of a note. **Objective 3**

Note receivable. A written promise to pay, representing an amount to be received by a business. **Objective 1**

Point-of-sale method. The method of recognizing revenue, whereby the revenue is determined to be realized at the time that title passes to the buyer. **Objective 8**

Proceeds. The net amount available from discounting a note. **Objective 4**

Promissory note. A written promise to pay a sum in money on demand or at a definite time. **Objective 1**

Temporary investments. Investments in securities that can be readily sold when cash is needed. **Objective 9**

Self-Examination Questions

Answers at end of chapter.

1. What is the maturity value of a 90-day, 12% note for $10,000?
   A. $8,800
   B. $10,000
   C. $10,300
   D. $11,200

2. On June 16, an enterprise discounts a 60-day, 10% note receivable for $15,000, dated June 1, at the rate of 12%. The proceeds are:
   A. $15,000.00
   B. $15,021.25
   C. $15,250.00
   D. $15,478.75

3. At the end of the fiscal year, before the accounts are adjusted, Accounts Receivable has a balance of $200,000 and Allowance for Doubtful Accounts has a credit balance of $2,500. If the estimate of uncollectible accounts determined by aging the receivables is $8,500, the current provision to be made for uncollectible accounts expense is:
   A. $2,500
   B. $6,000
   C. $8,500
   D. $11,000

4. At the end of the fiscal year, Accounts Receivable has a balance of $100,000 and Allowance for Doubtful Accounts has a balance of $7,000. The expected net realizable value of the accounts receivable is:
   A. $7,000
   B. $93,000
   C. $100,000
   D. $107,000

5. Under what caption would a temporary investment in stock be reported in the balance sheet?
   A. Current assets
   B. Plant assets
   C. Investments
   D. Current liabilities

ILLUSTRATIVE PROBLEM

Rodriguez Company uses the allowance method of accounting for uncollectible accounts receivable. Selected transactions completed by Rodriguez Company are as follows:

Jan. 28. Sold merchandise on account to Lakeland Co., $10,000.

Mar. 1. Accepted a 60-day, 12% note for $10,000 from Lakeland Co. on account.

Apr. 11. Wrote off a $4,500 account from Exdel Co. as uncollectible.

16. Loaned $7,500 cash to Thomas Glazer, receiving a 90-day, 14% note.

30. Received the interest due from Lakeland Co. and a new 90-day, 14% note as a renewal of the loan. (Record both the debit and the credit to the notes receivable account.)

May 1. Discounted the note from Thomas Glazer at the First National Bank at 10%.

June 13. Reinstated the account of Exdel Co., written off on April 11, and received $4,500 in full payment.

July 15. Received notice from First National Bank that Thomas Glazer dishonored his note. Paid the bank the maturity value of the note plus a $20 protest fee.

29. Received from Lakeland Co. the amount due on its note of April 30.

Aug. 14. Received from Thomas Glazer the amount owed on the dishonored note, plus interest for 30 days at 15%, computed on the maturity value of the note and the protest fee.

Dec. 16. Accepted a 60-day, 12% note for $6,000 from Harden Company on account.

31. It is estimated that 2% of the credit sales of $958,600 for the year ended December 31 will be uncollectible.

Instructions

1. Journalize the transactions.
2. Journalize the adjusting entry to record the accrued interest on December 31.

Solution

1.

Jan.	28	Accounts Receivable—Lakeland Co.	10,000.00	
		Sales		10,000.00
Mar.	1	Notes Receivable—Lakeland Co.	10,000.00	
		Accounts Receivable—Lakeland Co.		10,000.00
Apr.	11	Allowance for Doubtful Accounts	4,500.00	
		Accounts Receivable—Exdel Co.		4,500.00
	16	Notes Receivable—Thomas Glazer	7,500.00	
		Cash		7,500.00
	30	Notes Receivable—Lakeland Co.	10,000.00	
		Cash	200.00	
		Notes Receivable—Lakeland Co.		10,000.00
		Interest Income		200.00
May	1	Cash	7,600.78	
		Notes Receivable—Thomas Glazer		7,500.00
		Interest Income		100.78

Face value	$7,500.00
Interest on note (90 days at 14%)	262.50
Maturity value	$7,762.50
Discount on maturity value (75 days at 10%)	161.72
Proceeds	$7,600.78

June	13	Account Receivable—Exdel Co.	4,500.00	
		Allowance for Doubtful Accounts		4,500.00
	13	Cash	4,500.00	
		Accounts Receivable—Exdel Co.		4,500.00
July	15	Accounts Receivable—Thomas Glazer	7,782.50	
		Cash		7,782.50
	29	Cash	10,350.00	
		Notes Receivable—Lakeland Co.		10,000.00
		Interest Income		350.00
Aug.	14	Cash	7,879.78	
		Accounts Receivable—Thomas Glazer		7,782.50
		Interest Income		97.28
		($7,782.50 × 15% × 30/360)		
Dec.	16	Notes Receivable—Harden Company	6,000.00	
		Accounts Receivable—Harden Company		6,000.00
	31	Uncollectible Accounts Expense	19,172.00	
		Allowance for Doubtful Accounts		19,172.00

2.

Dec.	31	Interest Receivable	30.00	
		Interest Income		30.00
		($6,000 × 12% × 15/360)		

DISCUSSION QUESTIONS

1. For a business, what are the advantages of a note receivable in comparison to an account receivable?
2. What are trade receivables?
3. In what section of the balance sheet should a note receivable be listed if its term is (a) 90 days, (b) 5 years?
4. The accounts receivable clerk is also responsible for handling cash receipts. Which principle of internal control is violated in this situation?
5. Carey Company issued a promissory note to Stevens Company. (a) Who is the payee? (b) What is the title of the account used by Stevens Company in recording the note?

6. If a note provides for payment of principal of $10,000 and interest at the rate of 10%, will the interest amount to $1,000? Explain.

7. The following questions refer to a 90-day, 9% note for $5,000, dated May 1: (a) What is the face value of the note? (b) What is the amount of interest payable at maturity? (c) What is the maturity value of the note? (d) What is the due date of the note?

8. At the end of the fiscal year, an enterprise holds a $3,600, 10%, 90-day note receivable accepted from a customer thirty days earlier. What is the amount of interest accrued at the end of the fiscal year?

9. The payee of a 60-day, 9% note for $5,000, dated April 20, endorses it to a bank on May 10. The bank discounts the note at 10%, paying the endorser $5,018.61. Identify or determine the following as they relate to the note: (a) face value, (b) maturity value, (c) due date, (d) number of days in the discount period, (e) proceeds, (f) interest income or expense recorded by endorser, (g) amount payable to the bank if the maker defaults.

10. Arnould Co. received a 60-day note dated July 7 from a customer on account. Arnould Co. discounted the note at the bank on July 22. (a) Did Arnould Co. have a contingent liability on July 22 after the note was discounted? (b) If the answer in (a) is "yes," when does the contingent liability expire?

11. During the year, notes receivable of $150,000 were discounted at a bank by an enterprise. By the end of the year, $112,500 of these notes have matured. What is the amount of the endorser's contingent liability for notes receivable discounted at the end of the year?

12. The maker of a $6,000, 8%, 90-day note receivable failed to pay the note on the due date. What entry should be made in the accounts of the payee to record the dishonored note receivable?

13. A discounted note receivable is dishonored by the maker and the endorser pays the bank the face of the note, $8,000, the interest, $120, and a protest fee of $15. What entry should be made in the accounts of the endorser to record the payment?

14. The series of six transactions recorded in the following T accounts were related to a sale to a customer on account and receipt of the amount owed. Briefly describe each transaction.

Cash				Sales		
(4)	19,305	(5)	19,540	(2)	500	(1)	20,000
(6)	19,600						

Notes Receivable				Interest Income		
(3)	19,500	(4)	19,500			(6)	60

Accounts Receivable				Interest Expense		
(1)	20,000	(2)	500	(4)	195		
(5)	19,540	(3)	19,500				
		(6)	19,540				

15. Which of the two methods of accounting for uncollectible accounts provides for the recognition of the expense at the earlier date?

16. What kind of an account (asset, liability, etc.) is Allowance for Doubtful Accounts, and is its normal balance a debit or a credit?

17. Give the adjusting entry to increase Allowance for Doubtful Accounts by $5,900.

18. After the accounts are adjusted and closed at the end of the fiscal year, Accounts Receivable has a balance of $201,250 and Allowance for Doubtful Accounts has a balance of $12,250. (a) What is the expected net realizable value of the accounts receivable? (b) If an account receivable of $1,000 is written off against the allowance account, what will be the expected net realizable value of the accounts receivable after the write-off, assuming that no other changes in either account have occurred in the meantime?

19. A firm has consistently adjusted its allowance account at the end of the fiscal year by adding a fixed percent of the period's net sales on account. After five years, the balance in Allowance for Doubtful Accounts has become disproportionately large in relationship to the balance in Accounts Receivable. Give two possible explanations.

20. Evans Company has decided to write off the $750 balance of an account owed by a customer. Give the entry to record the write-off in the general ledger (a) assuming

that the allowance method is used and (b) assuming that the direct write-off method is used.

21. Which of the two methods of estimating uncollectibles, when advance provision for uncollectible receivables is made, provides for the most accurate estimate of the current net realizable value of the receivables?

22. Is revenue from sales of merchandise on account more commonly recognized at the time of sale or at the time of cash receipt?

23. During the current year, merchandise costing $480,000 was sold on the installment plan for $800,000. The down payments and the installment payments received during the current year totaled $300,000. What is the amount of gross profit realized in the current year, applying (a) the point-of-sale method and (b) the installment method of revenue recognition?

24. Under what caption should securities held as a temporary investment be reported on the balance sheet?

25. A company has two equity securities that it holds as temporary investments. If they have a total cost of $210,000 and a fair market value of $202,750, at what amount should these securities be reported in the Current Assets section of the company's balance sheet?

REAL WORLD FOCUS

26. Hilton Hotels Corporation owns and operates casinos at several of its hotels, located primarily in Nevada. At the end of a recent fiscal year, the following accounts and notes receivable were reported (in thousands):

Hotel accounts and notes receivable	$75,796
Less Allowance for doubtful accounts	3,256
	$72,540
Casino accounts receivable	$26,334
Less Allowance for doubtful accounts	6,654
	$19,680

(a) Compute the percentage of allowance for doubtful accounts to the gross hotel accounts and notes receivable for the end of the fiscal year. (b) Compute the percentage of the allowance for doubtful accounts to the gross casino accounts receivable for the end of the fiscal year. (c) Discuss possible reasons for the difference in the two ratios computed in (a) and (b).

ETHICS DISCUSSION CASE

Andrew Wilson, vice-president of operations for Palmer National Bank, has instructed the bank's computer programmer to program the bank's computers to calculate interest on depository accounts (payables) using the 365-day year and to calculate interest on loans (receivables) using the 360-day year.

SHARPEN YOUR COMMUNICATION SKILLS ▶   Discuss whether Andrew Wilson is behaving in an ethical manner.

WHAT DO YOU THINK

?

Temporary investments in equity securities are carried at the lower of total cost or market value. Do you think it would be better if generally accepted accounting principles required that such investments be carried at market value, regardless of the original cost?

FINANCIAL ANALYSIS AND INTERPRETATION

Businesses that grant long credit terms usually have larger accounts receivable balances than those granting short credit terms. In either case, it is desirable to collect receivables as promptly as possible. The cash collected from receivables improves solvency, and prompt collection also lessens the risk of loss from uncollectible accounts.

There are two financial measures that are especially useful in evaluating the efficiency in collecting accounts receivable: (1) accounts receivable turnover and (2) number of days' sales in receivables. The accounts receivable turnover is computed as follows:

$$\text{Accounts receivable turnover} = \frac{\text{Net sales on account}}{\text{Average accounts receivable}}$$

The average accounts receivable can be determined by adding the beginning and ending accounts receivable balances and dividing by two.

The number of days' sales in receivables is an estimate of the length of time the accounts receivable have been outstanding and is computed as follows:

$$\text{Number of days' sales in receivables} = \frac{\text{Accounts receivable, end of year}}{\text{Average daily sales on account}}$$

Average daily sales on account is determined by dividing net sales on account by 365 days.

An improvement in the efficiency in collecting accounts receivable is indicated by an increase in the accounts receivable turnover and a decrease in the number of days' sales in receivables.

a. For Hershey Foods Corporation, assume that all sales are credit sales and that the accounts receivable were $142,971,000 at December 31, 1990.
  1. Compute the accounts receivable turnover for 1992 and 1991
  2. Compute the number of days' sales in receivables at December 31, 1992 and 1991.

SHARPEN YOUR COMMUNICATION SKILLS b. What conclusions can be drawn from these analyses regarding Hershey's efficiency in collecting receivables?

EXERCISES

EXERCISE 7-1
INTERNAL CONTROL PROCEDURES
Objective 2

Simpson Carpet Company sells carpeting. Over 80% of all carpet sales are on credit. The following procedures are used by Simpson to process this large number of credit sales and the subsequent collections.

a. All credit sales to a first-time customer must be approved by the Credit Department. Salespersons will assist the customer in filling out a credit application, but an employee in the Credit Department is responsible for verifying employment and checking the customer's credit history before granting credit.

b. Simpson's standard credit period is 60 days. The Credit Department may approve an extension of this repayment period of up to one year. Whenever an extension is granted, the customer signs a promissory note. Up to 35% of the credit sales in any one year are for repayment periods exceeding 60 days.

c. A formal ledger is not maintained for customers who sign promissory notes. Simpson simply keeps a copy of each signed note in a file cabinet. These unpaid notes are filed by due date.

d. Simpson employs an accounts receivable clerk. The clerk is responsible for recording customer credit sales (based on sales tickets), receiving cash from customers, giving customers credit for their payments, and handling all customer billing complaints.

e. The general ledger control account for Accounts Receivable is maintained by the General Accounting Department at Simpson. This department records total credit sales, based on credit sale information from the store's electronic cash register, and total customer receipts, based on the bank deposit slip.

SHARPEN YOUR COMMUNICATION SKILLS State whether each of these procedures is appropriate or inappropriate, considering the principles of internal control. If the procedure is inappropriate, state which internal control principle is violated.

EXERCISE 7-2
DETERMINATION OF DUE DATE AND INTEREST ON NOTES
Objective 3

Determine the due date and the amount of interest due at maturity on the following notes:

Date of Note	Face Amount	Term of Note	Interest Rate
a. March 11	$ 5,000	30 days	9%
b. May 20	6,000	60 days	10%
c. May 30	10,000	75 days	12%
d. June 9	15,000	90 days	10%
e. July 11	17,500	120 days	12%

EXERCISE 7-3
ENTRIES FOR NOTES
RECEIVABLE
Objectives 3, 4

SPREADSHEET
PROBLEM

Wallace Company issued a 90-day, 9% note for $10,000, dated May 10, to Preston Company on account.

a. Determine the due date of the note.

b. Determine the maturity value of the note.

c. Journalize the entries to record the following: (1) receipt of the note by the payee, and (2) receipt by the payee of payment of the note at maturity.

EXERCISE 7-4
ENTRIES FOR NOTE
RECEIVABLE, INCLUDING
YEAR-END ENTRIES
Objective 4

The following selected transactions were completed by Thompson Co. during the current year:

Dec. 1. Received from Barr Co., on account, a $10,000, 90-day, 12% note dated December 1.
     31. Recorded an adjusting entry for accrued interest on the note of December 1.
     31. Closed the interest income account. The only entry in this account originated from the December 31 adjustment.

Journalize the transactions.

EXERCISE 7-5
DISCOUNTING NOTE
RECEIVABLE
Objective 4

Geraldi Co. holds a 120-day, 9% note for $20,000, dated March 20, that was received from a customer on account. On April 19, the note is discounted at the bank at the rate of 10%.

a. Determine the maturity value of the note.
b. Determine the number of days in the discount period.
c. Determine the amount of the discount.
d. Determine the amount of the proceeds.
e. Journalize the entry to record the discounting of the note on April 19.

EXERCISE 7-6
ENTRIES FOR RECEIPT AND
DISCOUNTING OF NOTE
RECEIVABLE AND
DISHONORED NOTE
Objective 4

Journalize the following transactions in the accounts of L.L. McLean Company:

Mar. 1. Received a $40,000, 60-day, 12% note dated March 1 from Sutcliffe Company on account.
     16. Discounted the note at First National Bank at 14%.
Apr. 30. The note is dishonored by Sutcliffe; paid the bank the amount due on the note, plus a protest fee of $50.
June 29. Received the amount due on the dishonored note plus interest for 60 days at 12% on the total amount charged to Sutcliffe Company on April 30.

EXERCISE 7-7
ENTRIES FOR RECEIPT AND
DISHONOR OF NOTES
RECEIVABLE
Objectives 4, 6

Journalize the following transactions in the accounts of Sandburg Co.:

July 1. Received a $20,000, 30-day, 12% note dated July 1 from Grace Co. on account.
     10. Received a $12,000, 60-day, 12% note dated July 10 from O'Neil Co. on account
     31. The note dated July 1 from Grace Co. is dishonored and the customer's account is charged for the note, including interest.
Sep. 9. The note dated July 10 from O'Neil Co. is dishonored and the customer's account is charged for the note, including interest.
Oct. 14. Cash is received for the amount due on the dishonored note dated July 1 plus interest for 75 days at 12% on the total amount debited to Grace Co. on July 31.
     30. Wrote off against the allowance account the amount charged to O'Neil Co. on September 9 for the dishonored note dated July 10.

EXERCISE 7-8
PROVISION FOR DOUBTFUL
ACCOUNTS
Objective 6

At the end of the current year, the accounts receivable account has a debit balance of $290,000, and net sales for the year total $3,100,000. Determine the amount of the adjusting entry to record the provision for doubtful accounts under each of the following assumptions:

a. The allowance account before adjustment has a credit balance of $1,750. (1) Uncollectible accounts expense is estimated at ½ of 1% of net sales. (2) Analysis of the accounts in the customer's ledger indicates doubtful accounts of $16,000.

b. The allowance account before adjustment has a debit balance of $1,500. (1) Uncollectible accounts expense is estimated at ¾ of 1% of net sales. (2) Analysis of the accounts in the customer's ledger indicates doubtful accounts of $20,000.

EXERCISE 7-9
ENTRIES FOR
UNCOLLECTIBLE
RECEIVABLES USING
ALLOWANCE METHOD
Objective 6

Journalize the following transactions in the accounts of Loveday Company, which uses the allowance method of accounting for uncollectible receivables:

Feb.   9. Sold merchandise on account to B. C. Burr, $5,500
Aug. 19. Received $2,500 from B. C. Burr and wrote off the remainder owed on the sale of February 9 as uncollectible.
Dec. 30. Reinstated the account of B. C. Burr that had been written off on August 19 and received $3,000 cash in full payment.

EXERCISE 7-10
ENTRIES FOR
UNCOLLECTIBLE
ACCOUNTS USING DIRECT
WRITE-OFF METHOD
Objective 7

Journalize the following transactions in the accounts of Henderson and Co., which uses the direct write-off method of accounting for uncollectible receivables:

Jan. 11. Sold merchandise on account to John Lang, $3,000.
June 1. Received $2,000 from John Lang and wrote off the remainder owed on the sale of January 11 as uncollectible.
Dec. 10. Reinstated the account of John Lang that had been written off on June 1 and received $1,000 cash in full payment.

EXERCISE 7-11
GROSS PROFIT BY POINT-
OF-SALE AND
INSTALLMENT METHODS
Objective 8

SPREADSHEET
PROBLEM

Diana Company makes all sales on the installment plan. Data related to merchandise sold during the current fiscal year are as follows:

Sales	$950,000
Cash received on the $950,000 of installments contracts	350,000
Cost of merchandise sold	665,000

Determine the amount of gross profit that would be recognized for the current fiscal year according to (a) the point-of-sale method and (b) the installment method.

EXERCISE 7-12
TEMPORARY EQUITY
SECURITIES IN FINANCIAL
STATEMENTS
Objective 9

As of December 31 of the first year of operations, Knight Company has the following portfolio of temporary equity securities:

	Cost	Market
Security A	$65,500	$67,000
Security B	21,000	19,100
Security C	39,250	35,000
Security D	40,250	41,500

**SHARPEN YOUR
COMMUNICATION SKILLS**

Describe how the portfolio of temporary equity securities would affect the year-end balance sheet and income statement of Knight Company.

**WHAT'S WRONG
WITH THIS?**

Can you find any errors in the following partial balance sheet?

Lane Company
Balance Sheet
December 31, 19--

Assets		
Current assets:		
Cash		$ 95,000
Marketable equity securities (cost)	$460,000	
Plus allowance for increase to market	30,000	490,000
Notes receivable		250,000
Accounts receivable	$445,000	
Plus allowance for doubtful accounts	15,000	460,000
Interest receivable		9,000

PROBLEMS

Series A

PROBLEM 7-1A
SALES, NOTES RECEIVABLE,
DISCOUNTING NOTES
RECEIVABLE
TRANSACTIONS
Objective 4

The following were selected from among the transactions completed by Gonzales Co. during the current year:

Jan. 15. Loaned $10,000 cash to Jose Montes, receiving a 90-day, 10% note.
Feb. 1. Sold merchandise on account to Bryant and Son, $6,000.
      20. Sold merchandise on account to C. D. Connors Co., $7,500.
Mar. 2. Received from C. D. Connors Co. the amount of the invoice of February 20, less 1% discount.
      3. Accepted a 60-day, 12% note for $6,000 from Bryant and Son on account.
Apr. 15. Received the interest due from Jose Montes and a new 90-day, 12% note as a renewal of the loan of January 15. (Record both the debit and the credit to the notes receivable account.)
May   2. Received from Bryant and Son the amount due on the note of March 3.
July 10. Sold merchandise on account to Song Yu and Co., $30,000.
      14. Received from Jose Montes the amount due on his note of April 15.
Aug. 9. Accepted a 60-day, 12% note for $30,000 from Song Yu and Co. on account.
Sep. 8. Discounted the note from Song Yu and Co. at the American National Bank at 14%.
Oct. 8. Received notice from the American National Bank that Song Yu and Co. had dishonored its note. Paid the bank the maturity value of the note.
      28. Received from Song Yu and Co. the amount owed on the dishonored note, plus interest for 20 days at 12% computed on the maturity value of the note.

Instructions
Journalize the transactions.

Instructions for Solving Problem 7-1A Using Solutions Software
1. Load the opening balances.
2. Enter your name in the Student Name field in the General Information data entry window. Set the run date to December 31 of the current year.
3. Save the opening balances file to your drive and directory.
4. Key the journal entries.
5. Display the journal entries.
6. Display a trial balance.
7. Save your data file to disk.
8. End the session.

PROBLEM 7-2A
DETAILS OF NOTES
RECEIVABLE, INCLUDING
DISCOUNTING
Objective 4

During the current fiscal year, Stone Co. received the following notes. Notes (1), (2), (3), and (4) were discounted on the dates and at the rates indicated.

	Date	Face Amount	Term	Interest Rate	Date Discounted	Discount Rate
1.	Oct. 1	$ 6,000	60 days	10%	Oct. 16	12%
2.	Oct. 11	10,000	30 days	12%	Oct. 21	14%
3.	Oct. 28	6,200	90 days	14%	Dec. 27	12%
4.	Nov. 8	8,000	60 days	12%	Nov. 23	16%
5.	Dec. 11	14,400	60 days	11%	—	—
6.	Dec. 26	18,000	30 days	12%	—	—

Instructions
1. Determine for each note (a) the due date and (b) the amount of interest due at maturity, identifying each note by number.
2. Determine for each of the first four notes (a) the maturity value, (b) the discount period, (c) the discount, (d) the proceeds, and (e) the interest income or interest expense, identifying each note by number.

(continued)

3. Journalize the entries to record the discounting of notes (2) and (4) at a bank.
4. Journalize the adjusting entry to record the accrued interest on Notes (5) and (6) on December 31.

PROBLEM 7-3A
NOTES RECEIVABLE
ENTRIES
Objective 4

The following data relate to notes receivable and interest for Goldberg Co. (All notes are dated as of the day they are received.)

Apr. 1. Received a $7,500, 14%, 60-day note on account.
     11. Received a $30,000, 12%, 120-day note on account.
May 16. Received a $24,000, 13%, 60-day note on account.
     21. Received a $12,000, 12%, 30-day note on account.
     31. Received $7,675 on note of April 1.
June 20. Received $12,120 on note of May 21.
     26. Received a $9,000, 12%, 30-day note on account.
July 15. Received $24,520 on note of May 16.
     26. Received $9,090 on note of June 26.
Aug. 9. Received $31,200 on note of April 11.

Instructions
Journalize entries to record the transactions.

PROBLEM 7-4A
ENTRIES RELATED TO
UNCOLLECTIBLE
ACCOUNTS
Objective 6

The following transactions, adjusting entries, and closing entries were completed during the current fiscal year ended December 31:

Feb. 1. Received 75% of the $8,000 balance owed by Nixon Co., a bankrupt business, and wrote off the remainder as uncollectible.
May 17. Reinstated the account of Barbara Lyman, which had been written off in the preceding year as uncollectible. Journalized the receipt of $675 cash in full payment of Lyman's account.
June 9. Wrote off the $7,250 balance owed by Larkin Co., which has no assets.
Oct. 30. Reinstated the account of Viscano Co., which had been written off in the preceding year as uncollectible. Journalized the receipt of $2,500 cash in full payment of the account.
Dec. 31. Wrote off the following accounts as uncollectible (compound entry): Davis Co., $3,950; Nance Co., $4,600; Powell Distributors, $6,500; J. J. Stevens, $4,200.
     31. Based on an analysis of the $695,000 of accounts receivable, it was estimated that $32,700 will be uncollectible. Journalized the adjusting entry.
     31. Journalized the entry to close the appropriate account to Income Summary.

Instructions
1. Record the following January 1 credit balance in the account indicated:

    115   Allowance for Doubtful Accounts $29,050
    313   Income Summary   —
    718   Uncollectible Accounts Expense   —

2. Journalize the transactions and the adjusting and closing entries described. After it has been journalized, post each entry to the three selected accounts affected and extend the new balances.
3. Determine the expected net realizable value of the accounts receivable as of December 31.
4. Assuming that, instead of basing the provision for uncollectible accounts on an analysis of receivables, the adjusting entry on December 31 had been based on an estimated loss of 3/4 of 1% of the net sales of $4,000,000 for the year, determine the following:
   a. Uncollectible accounts expense for the year.
   b. Balance in the allowance account after the adjustment of December 31.
   c. Expected net realizable value of the accounts receivable as of December 31.

PROBLEM 7-5A
COMPARISON OF TWO
METHODS OF
ACCOUNTING FOR
UNCOLLECTIBLE
RECEIVABLES
Objectives 6, 7

Lebaron Company has just completed its fourth year of operations. The direct write-off method of recording uncollectible accounts expense has been used during the entire period. Because of substantial increases in sales volume and amount of uncollectible accounts, the firm is considering the possibility of changing to the allowance method. Information is requested as to the effect that an annual provision of 1% of sales would have had on the amount of uncollectible accounts expense reported for each of the past four years. It is also considered desirable to know what the balance of Allowance for Doubtful Accounts would have been at the end of each year. The following data have been obtained from the accounts:

Year	Sales	Uncollectible Accounts Written Off	Year of Origin of Accounts Receivable Written Off as Uncollectible			
			1st	2d	3d	4th
1st	$400,000	$2,000	$2,000			
2d	600,000	2,950	1,500	$1,450		
3d	850,000	4,700	700	2,400	$1,600	
4th	900,000	6,000		1,900	2,500	$1,600

SPREADSHEET
PROBLEM

Instructions

1. Assemble the desired data, using the following columnar captions:

	Uncollectible Accounts Expense			Balance of
Year	Expense Actually Reported	Expense Based on Estimate	Increase in Amount of Expense	Allowance Account, End of Year

SHARPEN YOUR
COMMUNICATION SKILLS

2. Experience during the first four years of operations indicated that the receivables were either collected within two years or had to be written off as uncollectible. Does the estimate of 1% of sales appear to be reasonably close to the actual experience with uncollectible accounts originating during the first two years? Explain.

PROBLEM 7-6A
INSTALLMENT SALES
Objective 8

Puckett Co. makes all sales on the installment basis and recognizes revenue at the point of sale. Condensed income statements and the amounts collected from customers for each of the first three years of operations are as follows:

	First Year	Second Year	Third Year
Sales	$398,750	$340,000	$382,000
Cost of merchandise sold	271,150	227,800	248,300
Gross profit	$127,600	$112,200	$133,700
Operating expenses	60,000	51,500	62,250
Net income	$ 67,600	$ 60,700	$ 71,450
Collected from sales of first year	$121,250	$157,500	$120,000
Collected from sales of second year		95,000	145,000
Collected from sales of third year			99,000

Instructions

1. Determine the gross profit percentage for each year.
2. Determine the amount of net income or loss that would have been reported in each year if the installment method of recognizing revenue had been used, ignoring the possible effects of uncollectible accounts on the computation.

PROBLEM 7-7A
INSTALLMENT SALE AND
REPOSSESSION
Objective 8

Martino Video uses the installment method of recognizing gross profit for sales made on the installment plan. Details of a particular installment sale, amounts collected from the buyer, and the repossession of the item sold are as follows:

First year:
    Sold for $800 a television set having a cost of $640; received a down payment of $150.

Second year:
    Received 12 monthly payments of $25 each.

Third year:
    The buyer defaulted on the monthly payments, the set was repossessed, and the remaining 14 installments were canceled. The set was sold for $250.

Instructions

1. Determine the gross profit to be recognized in the first year.
2. Determine the gross profit to be recognized in the second year.
3. Determine the gain or loss to be recognized from the repossession and sale of the set in the third year. (*Suggestion:* First determine the amount of the unrecovered cost in the canceled installments. The gain or loss will then be the difference between this unrecovered cost and the sales price of the repossessed set.)

PROBLEM 7-8A
FINANCIAL STATEMENTS
Objective 10

The following data for Chen Inc. were selected from the ledger, after adjustment at December 31, the end of the current fiscal year:

Accounts payable	$ 26,100
Accounts receivable	57,500
Accumulated depreciation, building	175,000
Accumulated depreciation, office equipment	49,750
Administrative expenses	73,500
Allowance for decline to market of marketable equity securities	1,100
Allowance for doubtful accounts	1,500
Building	335,000
Capital stock	150,000
Cash	29,500
Cost of merchandise sold	520,000
Dividends	60,000
Interest income	6,100
Land	65,000
Marketable equity securities	60,000
Merchandise inventory	74,200
Notes receivable	40,000
Office equipment	79,750
Office supplies	5,600
Prepaid insurance	5,200
Retained earnings	305,900
Salaries payable	2,900
Sales	805,000
Sales discounts	6,500
Selling expenses	110,500
Unrealized loss from decline to market of marketable equity securities	1,100

Instructions

1. Prepare an income statement in multiple-step form.
2. Prepare a statement of owner's equity.
3. Prepare a balance sheet in report form.

SOLUTIONS SOFTWARE

Instructions for Solving Problem 7-8A Using Solutions Software

1. Load the opening balances.
2. Enter your name in the Student Name field in the General Information data entry window. Set the run date to December 31 of the current year.
3. Save the opening balances file to your drive and directory.
4. Display a trial balance. (Use these account balances as the basis for the adjusting entries.)
5. Key the adjusting entries. Key ADJ.ENT. in the reference field. The data needed for year-end adjustments are as follows:
   a. Office supplies on hand, $5,600.
   b. Insurance expired, $1,500.
   c. Depreciation expense on building, $25,000.
   d. Depreciation expense on office equipment, $9,750.
   e. Uncollectible accounts expense, $1,000.
   f. Decline in market value of temporary investments, $1,100.
6. Display the adjusting entries. Key ADJ.ENT. in the Reference Restriction area of the Selection Options screen.

7. Display the financial statements.
8. Save a backup copy of your data file.
9. Perform period-end closing.
10. Display a post-closing trial balance.
11. Save your data file to disk.
12. End the session.

Series B

PROBLEM 7-1B
SALES, NOTES RECEIVABLE,
DISCOUNTING NOTES
RECEIVABLE
TRANSACTIONS
Objective 4

The following were selected from among the transactions completed by J.J. Borge Co. during the current year:

Jan. 31. Sold merchandise on account to Perras Co., $10,000.
Mar. 2. Accepted a 60-day, 12% note for $10,000 from Perras Co. on account.
May 1. Received from Perras Co. the amount due on the note of March 2.
June 1. Sold merchandise on account to Kohl's for $5,000.
       5. Loaned $9,000 cash to Frank Gary, receiving a 30-day, 14% note.
      11. Received from Kohl's the amount due on the invoice of June 1, less 2% discount.
July 5. Received the interest due from Frank Gary and a new 60-day, 14% note as a renewal of the loan of June 5. (Record both the debit and the credit to the notes receivable account.)
Sep. 3. Received from Frank Gary the amount due on his note of July 5.
       4. Sold merchandise on account to Alice Gow, $4,000.
Oct. 4. Accepted a 60-day, 12% note for $4,000 from Alice Gow on account.
Nov. 3. Discounted the note from Alice Gow at the Pelican National Bank at 10%.
Dec. 3. Received notice from Pelican National Bank that Alice Gow had dishonored her note. Paid the bank the maturity value of the note.
      18. Received from Alice Gow the amount owed on the dishonored note, plus interest for 15 days at 10% computed on the maturity value of the note.

Instructions
Journalize the transactions.

SOLUTIONS
SOFTWARE

Instructions for Solving Problem 7-1B Using Solutions Software
1. Load the opening balances.
2. Enter your name in the Student Name field in the General Information data entry window. Set the run date to December 31 of the current year.
3. Save the opening balances file to your drive and directory.
4. Key the journal entries.
5. Display the journal entries.
6. Display a trial balance.
7. Save your data file to disk.
8. End the session.

PROBLEM 7-2B
DETAILS OF NOTES
RECEIVABLE, INCLUDING
DISCOUNTING
Objective 4

During the last six months of the current fiscal year, Brackett Co. received the following notes. Notes (1), (2), (3), and (4) were discounted on the dates and at the rates indicated.

	Date	Face Amount	Term	Interest Rate	Date Discounted	Discount Rate
1.	Mar. 1	$15,000	60 days	12%	Mar. 21	10%
2.	May 10	12,000	60 days	12%	May 20	15%
3.	July 11	30,000	90 days	10%	Aug. 10	12%
4.	Sep. 1	20,000	90 days	11%	Oct. 1	12%
5.	Dec. 11	18,000	60 days	12%	—	—
6.	Dec. 16	36,000	30 days	13%	—	—

SPREADSHEET
PROBLEM

Instructions
1. Determine for each note (a) the due date and (b) the amount of interest due at maturity, identifying each note by number.
2. Determine for each of the first four notes (a) the maturity value, (b) the discount period, (c) the discount, (d) the proceeds, and (e) the interest income or interest expense, identifying each note by number.

(continued)

3. Journalize entries to record the discounting of notes (2) and (3) at a bank.

4. Journalize the adjusting entry to record the accrued interest on Notes (5) and (6) on December 31.

PROBLEM 7-3B
NOTES RECEIVABLE
ENTRIES
Objective 4

The following data relate to notes receivable and interest for French Co. (All notes are dated as of the day they are received.)

Apr. 1. Received a $30,000, 12%, 60-day note on account.
     21. Received an $18,000, 14%, 90-day note on account.
May 16. Received a $12,000, 15%, 90-day note on account.
     21. Received a $10,800, 13%, 30-day note on account.
     31. Received $30,600 on note of April 1
June 20. Received $10,917 on note of May 21.
     21. Received a $7,000, 12%, 30-day note on account.
July 20. Received $18,630 on note of April 21.
     21. Received $7,070 on note of June 21.
Aug.14. Received $12,450 on note of May 16.

Instructions
Journalize entries to record the transactions.

PROBLEM 7-4B
ENTRIES RELATED TO
UNCOLLECTIBLE
ACCOUNTS
Objective 6

The following transactions, adjusting entries, and closing entries were completed by Bradford Company during the current fiscal year ended December 31:

Feb. 1. Reinstated the account of Nancy Boyle, which had been written off in the preceding year as uncollectible. Journalized the receipt of $1,025 cash in full payment of Boyle's account.
     28. Wrote off the $8,500 balance owed by D'Arrigo Co., which is bankrupt.
May 7. Received 60% of the $5,000 balance owed by C.D. Clark Co., a bankrupt business, and wrote off the remainder as uncollectible.
July 29. Reinstated the account of Louis Jaeger, which had been written off two years earlier as uncollectible. Recorded the receipt of $625 cash in full payment.
Dec. 30. Wrote off the following accounts as uncollectible (compound entry): Boyd Co., $1,050; Engel Co., $1,760; Loach Furniture, $2,775; Briana Parker, $620.
Dec. 31. Based on an analysis of the $335,500 of accounts receivable, it was estimated that $15,200 will be uncollectible. Journalized the adjusting entry.
     31. Journalized the entry to close the appropriate account to Income Summary.

Instructions
1. Record the following January 1 credit balance in the account indicated:

115	Allowance for Doubtful Accounts	$17,955
313	Income Summary	—
718	Uncollectible Accounts Expense	—

2. Journalize the transactions and the adjusting and closing entries described. After it has been journalized, post each entry to the three selected accounts affected and extend the new balances.

3. Determine the expected net realizable value of the accounts receivable as of December 31.

4. Assuming that, instead of basing the provision for uncollectible accounts on an analysis of receivables, the adjusting entry on December 31 had been based on an estimated loss of ½ of 1% of the net sales of $2,500,000 for the year, determine the following:
   a. Uncollectible accounts expense for the year.
   b. Balance in the allowance account after the adjustment of December 31.
   c. Expected net realizable value of the accounts receivable as of December 31.

PROBLEM 7-5B
COMPARISON OF TWO
METHODS OF
ACCOUNTING FOR
UNCOLLECTIBLE
RECEIVABLES
Objectives 6, 7

Lantz Company has just completed its fourth year of operations. The direct write-off method of recording uncollectible accounts expense has been used during the entire period. Because of substantial increases in sales volume and amount of uncollectible accounts, the firm is considering the possibility of changing to the allowance method. Information is requested as to the effect that an annual provision of 1% of sales would have had on the amount of uncollectible accounts expense reported for each of the past four years. It is also considered desirable to know what the balance of Allowance for Doubtful Accounts would have been at the end of each year. The following data have been obtained from the accounts:

Year	Sales	Uncollectible Accounts Written Off	Year of Origin of Accounts Receivable Written Off as Uncollectible			
			1st	2d	3d	4th
1st	$600,000	$2,600	$2,600			
2d	700,000	3,500	1,950	$1,550		
3d	850,000	7,600	1,200	3,400	$3,000	
4th	950,000	8,550		2,300	2,950	$3,300

SPREADSHEET
PROBLEM

Instructions

1. Assemble the desired data, using the following columnar captions:

Year	Uncollectible Accounts Expense			Balance of Allowance Account, End of Year
	Expense Actually Reported	Expense Based on Estimate	Increase in Amount of Expense	

SHARPEN YOUR
COMMUNICATION SKILLS

2. Experience during the first four years of operations indicated that the receivables were either collected within two years or had to be written off as uncollectible. Does the estimate of 1% of sales appear to be reasonably close to the actual experience with uncollectible accounts originating during the first two years? Explain.

PROBLEM 7-6B
INSTALLMENT SALES
Objective 8

D. J. Aguilera Co. makes all sales on the installment basis and recognizes revenue at the point of sale. Condensed income statements and the amounts collected from customers for each of the first three years of operations are as follows:

	First Year	Second Year	Third Year
Sales	$300,000	$340,000	$440,000
Cost of merchandise sold	195,000	224,400	281,600
Gross profit	$105,000	$115,600	$158,400
Operating expenses	62,500	68,500	98,400
Net income	$ 42,500	$ 47,100	$ 60,000
Collected from sales of first year	$ 75,000	$125,000	$100,000
Collected from sales of second year		110,000	180,000
Collected from sales of third year			115,000

Instructions

1. Determine the gross profit percentage for each year.
2. Determine the amount of net income or loss that would have been reported in each year if the installment method of recognizing revenue had been used, ignoring the possible effects of uncollectible accounts on the computation.

PROBLEM 7-7B
INSTALLMENT SALE AND
REPOSSESSION
Objective 8

Higuera Video uses the installment method of recognizing gross profit for sales made on the installment plan. Details of a particular installment sale, amounts collected from the buyer, and the repossession of the item sold are as follows:

First year:
    Sold for $900 a television set having a cost of $720; received a down payment of $150.
Second year:
    Received 12 monthly payments of $30 each.
Third year:
    The buyer defaulted on the monthly payments, the set was repossessed, and the remaining 13 installments were canceled. The set was sold for $350.

Instructions

1. Determine the gross profit to be recognized in the first year.
2. Determine the gross profit to be recognized in the second year.
3. Determine the gain or loss to be recognized from the repossession and sale of the set in the third year. (*Suggestion:* First determine the amount of the unrecovered cost in the canceled installments. The gain or loss will then be the difference between this unrecovered cost and the sales price of the repossessed set.)

PROBLEM 7-8B
FINANCIAL STATEMENTS
Objective 10

The following data for Landsburg Inc. were selected from the ledger, after adjustment at December 31, the end of the current fiscal year:

Accounts payable	$ 29,250
Accounts receivable	88,000
Accumulated depreciation, building	162,500
Accumulated depreciation, office equipment	47,250
Administrative expenses	82,250
Allowance for decline to market	
of marketable equity securities	2,400
Allowance for doubtful accounts	8,400
Building	363,000
Capital stock	150,000
Cash	40,500
Cost of merchandise sold	610,000
Dividends	75,000
Interest income	5,100
Land	80,000
Marketable equity securities	75,000
Merchandise inventory	95,100
Notes receivable	50,000
Office equipment	79,750
Office supplies	5,500
Prepaid insurance	7,000
Retained earnings	453,400
Salaries payable	5,950
Sales	935,000
Sales discounts	8,500
Selling expenses	137,250
Unrealized loss from decline to	
market of marketable equity securities	2,400

Instructions

1. Prepare an income statement in multiple-step form.
2. Prepare a statement of owner's equity.
3. Prepare a balance sheet in report form.

Instructions for Solving Problem 7-8B Using Solutions Software

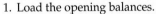

1. Load the opening balances.
2. Enter your name in the Student Name field in the General Information data entry window. Set the run date to December 31 of the current year.
3. Save the opening balances file to your drive and directory.
4. Display a trial balance. (Use these account balances as the basis for the adjusting entries.)
5. Key the adjusting entries. Key ADJ.ENT. in the reference field. The data needed for year-end adjustments are as follows:
   a. Office supplies on hand, $5,500.
   b. Insurance expired, $1,500.
   c. Depreciation expense on building, $25,000.
   d. Depreciation expense on office equipment, $9,750.
   e. Uncollectible accounts expense, $5,000.
   f. Decline in market value of temporary investments, $2,400.
6. Display the adjusting entries. Key ADJ.ENT. in the Reference Restriction area of the Selection Options screen.
7. Display the financial statements.
8. Save a backup copy of your data file.
9. Perform period-end closing.
10. Display a post-closing trial balance.
11. Save your data file to disk.
12. End the session.

MINI-CASE HARDING'S

For several years, sales have been on a "cash only" basis. On January 1, 1990, however, Harding's began offering credit on terms of n/30. The amount of the adjusting entry to record the estimated uncollectible receivables at the end of each year has been ½ of 1% of credit sales, which is the rate reported as the average for the industry. Credit sales and the year-end credit balances in Allowance for Doubtful Accounts for the past four years are as follows:

Year	Credit Sales	Allowance for Doubtful Accounts
1990	$6,000,000	$ 6,000
1991	6,700,000	10,000
1992	6,200,000	14,500
1993	5,500,000	19,500

Janet Harding, president of Harding's, is concerned that the method used to account for and write off uncollectible receivables is unsatisfactory. She has asked for your advice in the analysis of past operations in this area and for recommendations for change.

Instructions

1. Determine the amount of (a) the addition to Allowance for Doubtful Accounts and (b) the accounts written off for each of the four years.

2. a. ▨▨▨ ► Advise Janet Harding as to whether the estimate of ½ of 1% of credit sales appears reasonable.

   b. ▨▨ ► Assume that after discussing (a) with Janet Harding, she asked you what action might be taken to determine what the balance of Allowance for Doubtful Accounts should be at December 31, 1993, and possible changes, if any, you might recommend in accounting for uncollectible receivables. How would you respond?

ANSWERS TO SELF-EXAMINATION QUESTIONS

1. **C** Maturity value is the amount that is due at the maturity or due date. The maturity value of $10,300 (answer C) is determined as follows:

Face amount of note	$10,000
Plus interest ($10,000 × 90/360 × 12/100)	300
Maturity value of note	$10,300

2. **B** The proceeds of $15,021.25 (answer B) are determined as follows:

Face value of note dated June 1	$15,000.00
Interest on note (60 days at 10%)	250.00
Maturity value of note due July 31	$15,250.00
Discount on maturity value (45 days, from June 16 to July 31, at 12%)	228.75
Proceeds	$15,021.25

3. **B** The estimate of uncollectible accounts, $8,500 (answer C), is the amount of the desired balance of Allowance for Doubtful Accounts after adjustment. The amount of the current provision to be made for uncollectible accounts expense is thus $6,000 (answer B), which is the amount that must be added to the Allowance for Doubtful Accounts credit balance of $2,500 (answer A), so that the account will have the desired balance of $8,500.

4. **B** The amount expected to be realized from accounts receivable is the balance of Accounts Receivable, $100,000, less the balance of Allowance for Doubtful Accounts, $7,000, or $93,000 (answer B).

5. **A** Securities held as temporary investments are classified on the balance sheet as current assets (answer A).

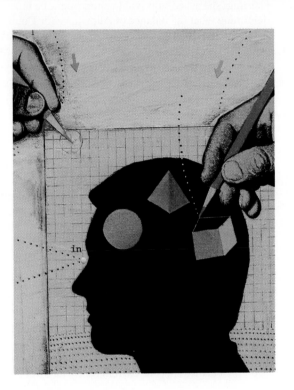

You and Accounting

Assume that you purchased a Sony Compact Disc (CD)/Receiver in June of last year. You planned on attaching three pairs of speakers to the system. Initially, however, you could afford only one pair of speakers, which cost $160. In August and October, you purchased the second and third pairs of speakers at higher prices. The pair of speakers bought in August cost $170, and the pair of speakers bought in October cost $180.

Over the holidays, you take the CD/Receiver and one pair of speakers home. Unfortunately, someone breaks into your dorm room and steals your other two pairs of speakers. Luckily, your parents' homeowners insurance policy will cover the theft, but the insurance company needs to know the cost of the speakers that were stolen.

All the speakers are identical. To respond to the insurance company, however, you will need to identify which pairs of speakers were stolen. Were they the first and second pairs, which cost a total of $330? Or were they the second and third pairs, which cost a total of $350? Whichever assumption you make may determine the amount that you receive from the insurance company.

Merchandise enterprises make similar assumptions when identical merchandise is purchased at different costs. At the end of a period, some of the merchandise will be on hand, and some will have been sold. But which costs relate to the sold merchandise, and which costs relate to the merchandise on hand? If you sell one pair of your speakers, what is the cost of those speakers? In this chapter, you will read about this cost issue as well as other similar issues.

Chapter 8
Inventories

LEARNING OBJECTIVES
After studying this chapter, you should be able to:

Objective 1
Summarize and provide examples of internal control procedures that apply to inventories.

Objective 2
List the procedures for determining the actual quantities in inventory.

Objective 3
Compute the cost of inventory under the perpetual inventory system, using the following costing methods:
   First-in, first-out
   Last-in, first-out
   Average cost

Objective 4
Compute the cost of inventory under the periodic inventory system, using the following costing methods:
   First-in, first-out
   Last-in, first-out
   Average cost

Objective 5
Compare the use of the three inventory costing methods.

Objective 6
Compute the proper valuation of inventory at other than cost, using the lower-of-cost-or-market and net realizable value concepts.

Objective 7
Prepare a balance sheet presentation of merchandise inventory.

Objective 8
Estimate the cost of inventory, using the retail method and the gross profit method.

Objective 9
Describe the inventories of manufacturing enterprises.

Objective 10
Describe the accounting for long-term construction contracts.

The buying and selling of merchandise is the primary activity in operating a wholesale or retail business. The sale of merchandise provides the major source of revenue for such enterprises. The cost of merchandise sold is often the largest deduction from sales in determining net income. Moreover, merchandise inventory is usually the largest current asset of such a firm. In this chapter, we describe and illustrate several topics related to merchandise inventory. These include the use of cost flow assumptions in determining the cost of inventory.

INTERNAL CONTROL OF INVENTORIES

Objective 1
Summarize and provide examples of internal control procedures that apply to inventories.

What is included in inventory? The term **inventory** is used to indicate (1) merchandise held for sale in the normal course of business and (2) materials in the process of production or held for production. In this chapter, we focus primarily on inventory of merchandise purchased for resale. We also briefly discuss inventories of raw materials and partially processed materials of a manufacturing enterprise.

The cost of inventories is a significant item on the financial statements of many businesses. Because of the importance of inventory, an enterprise should have effective internal controls over its inventory. The objective of these controls is to ensure that the inventory is safeguarded and properly reported in the financial statements. As we discussed in earlier chapters, internal controls can be either preventive or detective. In the following paragraphs, we discuss types of preventive and detective controls over inventory.

Internal controls for safeguarding inventory begin with developing and using security measures to protect the inventory from damage or employee theft. For example, inventory should be stored in a warehouse or other area to which access is restricted to authorized employees. The storage area should also be climate controlled to prevent damage to the inventory from heat or cold. Further, when the enterprise is not operating or the business is not open, the storage area should be locked.

When you have been shopping, you may have noticed how retail stores protect inventory from customer theft. Retail stores often use such devices as two-way mirrors, cameras, and security guards. High-priced items are often displayed in locked cabinets, or they may be tagged so that an alarm is set off if the tagged merchandise is taken out of the store.

Another control over inventory includes using a voucher system similar to the one described in an earlier chapter. In such a system, using prenumbered receiving reports establishes the initial accountability for inventory. These receiving reports are reconciled to the initial purchase order and the vendor's invoice before the purchase is recorded. Moreover, requisition forms authorizing withdrawals of merchandise from storage can be used to control inventory.

Using a perpetual inventory system for merchandise often provides an effective means of control over inventory. The amount of each type of merchandise on hand is always readily available in a subsidiary **inventory ledger**. In addition, the subsidiary ledger can be an aid in maintaining inventory quantities at optimum levels. Frequent comparisons of balances with predetermined maximum and minimum levels allow for the timely reordering of merchandise and prevent the ordering of excess inventory.

To ensure the accuracy of the amount of inventory reported in the financial statements, a merchandising enterprise should take a **physical inventory**. The knowledge that a physical inventory will be taken also serves to deter (prevent) possible employee thefts or misuses of inventory.

Any errors in reporting inventory affect both the balance sheet and income statement. For example, an error in taking the physical inventory has the effect of misstating ending inventory, current assets, and total assets on the balance sheet. In a perpetual inventory system, the physical inventory is compared to the recorded inventory in order to determine the amount of inventory shrinkage or shortage. As we discussed in a previous chapter, an adjusting entry records this amount by debiting Cost of Merchandise Sold and crediting Merchandise Inventory. Thus, misstating the physical inventory will misstate the amount of inventory shrinkage, which in turn, misstates the cost of merchandise sold. As a result, gross profit, net income, retained earnings, and total stockholders' equity will also be misstated.

Falsified Inventory and Income Inflate Company's Value

The importance of inventory to financial statements is recognized even by those who attempt to manipulate a company's statements in a fraudulent manner. One example of such inventory fraud is described in the following excerpt from an article in *The Wall Street Journal*:

Until last year, Crazy Eddie Inc. steadily recorded superb gains in sales and earnings, apparently because of rapid expansion of its electronics stores, adept sales-floor techniques and catchy commercials.

But the now-troubled company's latest court and regulatory filings suggest another element: a possible scheme by founder Eddie Antar and others to falsify inventory and profit reports. . . .

. . . Crazy Eddie says its former management—led by Mr. Antar—created "phantom" inventory and profits, then destroyed records in a cover-up. The purpose, the company says . . . was to "artificially inflate the net worth of the company" and the value of stock owned by Mr. Antar and others.

For instance, Crazy Eddie says the former management inflated the March 1987 inventory count at one warehouse by $10 million, by drafting phony count sheets and, among other things, improperly including $4 million in merchandise that was [recorded as] being returned to suppliers. Stores were also packed with unrecorded [purchases] prior to physical [inventory] counts. . . .

Source: Jeffrey A. Tannenbaum, "Filings by Crazy Eddie Suggest Founder Led Scheme to Inflate Company's Value," *The Wall Street Journal* (May 31, 1988), p. 28.

DETERMINING ACTUAL QUANTITIES IN THE INVENTORY

Objective 2
List the procedures for determining the actual quantities in inventory.

How do you "take" an inventory? The first step in this process is to determine the quantity of each kind of merchandise owned by the enterprise. The specific procedures for determining inventory quantities and assembling the data differ among companies. A common practice is to use teams made up of two persons. One person counts, weighs, or otherwise determines quantity, and the other lists the description and the quantity on inventory count sheets. The quantities indicated for high-cost items may be checked by a second count team during the inventory-taking process. It is also recommended that the second count team check quantities of other items selected at random from the inventory count sheets.

All the merchandise owned by the business on the inventory date, and only such merchandise, should be included in the inventory. For merchandise in transit, the party (the seller or the buyer) who has title to the merchandise on the inventory date must be determined. To determine who has title, it may be necessary to examine purchases and sales invoices of the last few days of the current period and the first few days of the following period.

As we discussed in a previous chapter, shipping terms are often helpful in determining when title passes. When goods are purchased or sold **FOB shipping point**, title usually passes to the buyer when the goods are shipped. When the terms are **FOB destination**, title usually does not pass to the buyer until the goods are delivered.

To illustrate, assume that merchandise purchased FOB shipping point is shipped by the seller on the last day of the buyer's fiscal period. The merchandise does not arrive until the following period and thus is not available for counting by the inventory crew. However, such merchandise should be included in the buyer's inventory because title has passed. A debit to Merchandise Inventory and a credit to Accounts Payable should be recorded by the buyer as of the end of the current period.

Another example, though less common, further illustrates the importance of carefully examining transactions involving shipments of merchandise. Manufacturers sometimes ship merchandise to retailers who act as the manufacturer's agent when selling the merchandise. The manufacturer retains title until the goods are sold. Such merchandise is said to be shipped *on consignment* to the retailers. The unsold merchandise is a part of the manufacturer's (consignor's) inventory even though the merchandise is in the hands of the retailers. Likewise, the consigned merchandise should not be included in the retailer's (consignee's) inventory.

INVENTORY COSTING METHODS UNDER A PERPETUAL INVENTORY SYSTEM

Objective 3

Compute the cost of inventory under the perpetual inventory system, using the following costing methods:

First-in, first-out

Last-in, first-out

Average cost

As we described in an earlier chapter, all merchandise increases and decreases in a perpetual system are recorded in a manner similar to the recording of increases and decreases in cash. The merchandise inventory account at the beginning of an accounting period indicates the merchandise on hand on that date. Purchases are recorded by debiting Merchandise Inventory and crediting Cash or Accounts Payable. On the date of each sale, the cost of the merchandise sold is recorded by debiting Cost of Merchandise Sold and crediting Merchandise Inventory. Thus, the merchandise inventory account constantly (perpetually) discloses the balance of merchandise on hand. At the end of the period, the balance in the merchandise inventory account, adjusted for any inventory shrinkage, is reported on the balance sheet. The balance in the cost of merchandise sold account is reported on the income statement.

What costs should be included in inventory? The purchase price of merchandise, less any purchases discounts, is part of the cost of inventory. In addition, costs incurred in acquiring the merchandise, such as transportation, customs duties, and insurance against losses in transit, are normally included in the cost of inventory. However, some costs of acquiring merchandise, such as the salaries of Purchasing Department employees and other administrative costs, are not easily allocated to the inventory. Therefore, these costs are treated as operating expenses of the period.

A major accounting issue arises in using the perpetual system when identical units of a commodity are acquired at different unit costs during a period. In such cases, when an item is sold, it is necessary to determine its unit cost so that the proper accounting entry can be recorded. To illustrate, assume that three identical units of Commodity X are available for sale during the first ten days in January. One of these units was in the inventory at the beginning of the year, and the other two were purchased on January 4 and January 9. The costs per unit are as follows:

Commodity X		Units	Cost
Jan. 1	Inventory	1	$ 9
4	Purchase	1	13
9	Purchase	1	14
Total		3	$36
Average cost per unit			$12

Assume that one unit is sold on January 10. If this unit can be identified with a specific purchase, the **specific identification method** can be used to determine the cost of the unit sold. For example, if the unit sold was purchased on January 4, the cost assigned to the unit is $13.

The specific identification method is not practical unless each unit can be identified accurately. An automobile dealer, for example, may be able to use this method. For businesses that buy and sell units that are identical, however, a flow of costs must be assumed. That is, an assumption must be made as to which unit was sold and which units are still on hand. The three most common cost flow assumptions are as follows:

1. Cost flow is in the order in which the costs were incurred—first-in, first-out.
2. Cost flow is in the reverse order in which the costs were incurred—last-in, first-out.
3. Cost flow is an average of the costs.

The cost of the unit of Commodity X sold and the cost of the two remaining units are shown here for each of the cost flow assumptions.

| | Commodity X Costs | | |
	Units Available	Unit Sold	Units Remaining
1. In order in which costs were incurred (first-in, first-out)	$36	– $9	= $27
2. In reverse order in which costs were incurred (last-in, first-out)	36	– 14	= 22
3. In accordance with average costs	36	– 12	= 24

The three most widely used inventory costing methods (which correspond to the three assumptions of cost flows) are:

1. First-in, first-out (fifo)
2. Last-in, first-out (lifo)
3. Average cost

The chart in Exhibit 1 shows the extent these three methods are used.

Exhibit 1
Inventory Costing Methods

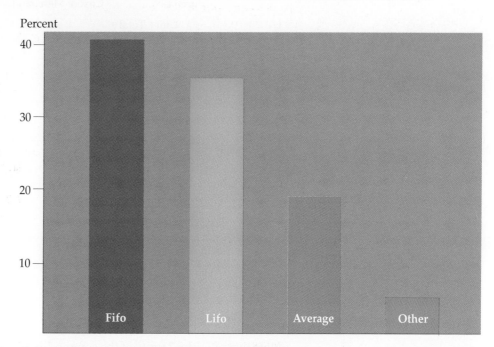

Percent

Source: *Accounting Trends & Techniques*, 46th ed. (New York: American Institute of Certified Public Accountants, 1992).

Using Accounting

Individuals may purchase marketable securities of a company over time at different costs per share. Alternatively, an investor may purchase shares in a mutual fund at various costs. When such investments are sold, the investor must either specifically identify which shares are sold or make a cost flow assumption similar to that for inventories, such as the first-in, first-out assumption. This must be done so that the individual investor can report the proper amounts for income tax purposes.

First-In, First-Out Method

When the first-in, first-out (fifo) method of costing inventory is used, costs are assumed to be charged against revenue in the order in which they were incurred. Hence the inventory remaining is assumed to be made up of the most recent costs. We illustrate this method using the following data for merchandise identified as Commodity 127B:

Commodity 127B	Units	Cost
Jan. 1 Inventory	10	$20
4 Sale	7	
10 Purchase	8	21
22 Sale	4	
28 Sale	2	
30 Purchase	10	22

To illustrate the first-in, first-out method of cost flow in a perpetual inventory system, Exhibit 2 shows the inventory ledger account for Commodity 127. The number of units on hand after each transaction, together with total costs and unit costs, appear in the inventory section of the account.

Exhibit 2
Perpetual Inventory Account (Fifo)

Commodity 127B

Date	Purchases Quantity	Purchases Unit Cost	Purchases Total Cost	Cost of Merchandise Sold Quantity	Cost of Merchandise Sold Unit Cost	Cost of Merchandise Sold Total Cost	Inventory Quantity	Inventory Unit Cost	Inventory Total Cost
Jan. 1							10	20	200
4				7	20	140	3	20	60
10	8	21	168				3 / 8	20 / 21	60 / 168
22				3 / 1	20 / 21	60 / 21	7	21	147
28				2	21	42	5	21	105
30	10	22	220				5 / 10	21 / 22	105 / 220

Note that after the 7 units of the commodity were sold on January 4, there was an inventory of 3 units at $20 each. The 8 units purchased on January 10 were acquired at a unit cost of $21, instead of $20. Therefore, the inventory after the January 10 purchase is reported on two lines—3 units at $20 each and 8 units at $21 each. Next, note that the $81 cost of the 4 units sold on January 22 is comprised of the remaining 3 units at $20 each and 1 unit at $21. At this point, 7 units are in inventory at a cost of $21 per unit. The remainder of the illustration can be explained in a similar manner.

Most businesses dispose of goods in the order in which the goods are purchased. This would be especially true of perishables and goods whose styles or models often change. Thus, the fifo method is often consistent with the physical movement of merchandise in an enterprise. To the extent that this is the case, the fifo method provides results that are about the same as those obtained by identifying the specific costs of each item sold and in inventory.

Last-In, First-Out Method

When the last-in, first-out method is used in a perpetual inventory system, the cost of the units sold is the cost of the most recent purchases. To illustrate, Exhibit 3 shows the ledger account for Commodity 127B, prepared on a lifo basis.

Exhibit 3
Perpetual Inventory Account
(Lifo)

Commodity 127B

	Purchases			Cost of Merchandise Sold			Inventory		
Date	Quantity	Unit Cost	Total Cost	Quantity	Unit Cost	Total Cost	Quantity	Unit Cost	Total Cost
Jan. 1							10	20	200
4				7	20	140	3	20	60
10	8	21	168				3	20	60
							8	21	168
22				4	21	84	3	20	60
							4	21	84
28				2	21	42	3	20	60
							2	21	42
30	10	22	220				3	20	60
							2	21	42
							10	22	220

Comparing the ledger accounts for the fifo perpetual system and the lifo perpetual system indicates that the accounts are the same through the January 10 purchase. Using the lifo perpetual system, however, the cost of the 4 units sold on January 22 is the cost of the units from the January 10 purchase ($21 per unit). The cost of the 7 units in inventory after the sale on January 22 is the cost of the 3 units remaining from the beginning inventory and the cost of the 4 units remaining from the January 10 purchase. The remainder of the lifo illustration can be explained in a similar manner.

When the lifo method is used, the inventory ledgers are sometimes maintained in units only. The units are converted to dollars when the financial statements are prepared at the end of the period.

The use of the lifo method was originally limited to rare situations in which the units sold were taken from the most recently acquired goods. For tax reasons, its use has greatly increased during the past few decades. Lifo is now often used even when it does not represent the physical flow of goods.

Average Cost Method

When the **average cost method** is used in a perpetual inventory system, an average unit cost for each type of commodity is computed each time a purchase is made rather than at the end of the period. This unit cost is then used to determine the cost of each sale until another purchase is made and a new average is computed. This averaging technique is called a **moving average**. Since the average cost method is not often used for merchandise enterprises using perpetual inventory systems, we do not illustrate it in this chapter.

Computerized Perpetual Inventory Systems

A perpetual inventory system may be maintained using manually kept records. However, such a system is often too costly and too time consuming for enterprises with a large number of inventory items or many purchase and sales transactions. In such cases, the record keeping is often computerized.

An example of using computers in maintaining perpetual inventory records for retail stores is described as follows:

1. The relevant details for each inventory item, such as a description, quantity, and unit size, are stored in an inventory record. The individual inventory records make up the computerized inventory ledger.

2. Each time an item is purchased or returned by a customer, the inventory data are entered into the computer and stored. Hourly, daily, or at some other interval, the computerized inventory ledger (detailed inventory records) is updated.

3. Each time an item is sold, a sales clerk passes an electronic wand (optical scanner) over the price tag attached to the merchandise. The electronic wand *reads* the magnetic code on the price tag. The inventory data provided in the magnetic code are immediately entered into the computer and stored. Periodically, these data are used to update the computerized inventory ledger (detailed inventory records).

4. After a physical inventory is taken, the inventory count data are entered into the computer. These data are compared with the current balances, and a listing of the overages and shortages is printed. The inventory balances are then adjusted to the quantities determined by the physical count.

By entering additional data, this system can be extended to aid in maintaining inventory quantities at optimal levels. For example, data on the most economical quantity to be purchased in a single order, and the minimum quantity to be maintained for each item can be entered into the computer records. The computer software is then programmed to compare these data with data on the book inventories. As necessary, the computer program begins the purchasing activity by preparing purchase orders.

The system can also be extended to aid in processing the related accounting transactions. For example, as cash sales are entered on an electronic cash register, the sales data are accumulated and used for the daily accounting entries. These entries debit Cash and credit Sales as well as debit Cost of Merchandise Sold and credit Merchandise Inventory.

INVENTORY COSTING METHODS UNDER A PERIODIC INVENTORY SYSTEM

Objective 4

Compute the cost of inventory under the periodic inventory system, using the following costing methods:

First-in, first-out

Last-in, first-out

Average cost

When the periodic inventory system is used, only revenue is recorded each time a sale is made. No entry is made at the time of the sale to record the cost of the merchandise sold. At the end of the accounting period, a physical inventory is taken to determine the cost of the inventory on hand and the cost of the merchandise sold.

Like the perpetual inventory system, a cost flow assumption must be made when identical units of a commodity are acquired at different unit costs during a period. In such cases, the first-in, first-out (fifo); last-in, first-out (lifo); or average cost method is normally used.

First-In, First-Out Method

To illustrate the use of the first-in, first-out method in a periodic inventory system, we assume the following data for a commodity:

Jan. 1	Inventory:	200 units at $ 9	$ 1,800
Mar. 10	Purchase:	300 units at 10	3,000
Sep. 21	Purchase:	400 units at 11	4,400
Nov. 18	Purchase:	100 units at 12	1,200
	Available for sale during year	1,000	$10,400

The physical count on December 31 shows that 300 units of the commodity are on hand. Using the fifo method, the cost of these units is determined as follows:

Most recent costs, Nov. 18:	100 units at $12	$1,200
Next most recent costs, Sep. 21:	200 units at 11	2,200
Inventory, Dec. 31:	300	$3,400

Deducting the inventory of $3,400 from the $10,400 of merchandise available for sale yields $7,000 as the cost of merchandise sold. The $7,000 cost of merchandise sold is made up of the earliest costs incurred for this commodity. Exhibit 4 shows the relationship of the inventory at December 31 and the cost of merchandise sold during the year.

Exhibit 4
First-In, First-Out Flow of Costs

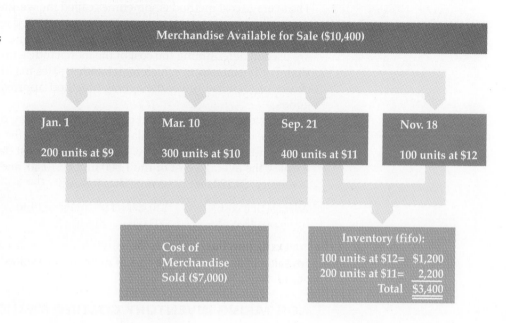

Last-In, First-Out Method

When the last-in, first-out (lifo) method of inventory costing is used, the inventory remaining is assumed to comprise the earliest costs. Based on the data in the fifo example, the cost of the 300 units of inventory is determined as follows:

Earliest costs, Jan. 1:	200 units at $ 9	$1,800
Next earliest costs, Mar. 10:	100 units at 10	1,000
Inventory, Dec. 31:	300	$2,800

Deducting the inventory of $2,800 from the $10,400 of merchandise available for sale yields $7,600 as the cost of merchandise sold. The $7,600 cost of merchandise sold is made up of the most recent costs incurred for this commodity. Exhibit 5

Exhibit 5
Last-In, First-Out Flow of Costs

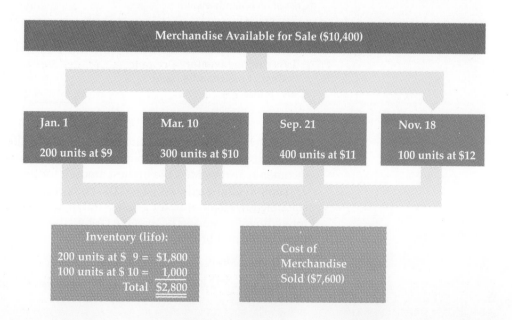

shows the relationship of the inventory at December 31 and the cost of merchandise sold during the year.

Average Cost Method

The average cost method is sometimes called the **weighted average method**. When this method is used, costs are assumed to be matched against revenue according to an average of the unit costs of the goods sold. The same weighted average unit costs are used in determining the cost of the merchandise inventory at the end of the period. For businesses in which merchandise sales may be made up of various purchases of identical units, the average method approximates the physical flow of goods.

The weighted average unit cost is determined by dividing the total cost of the units of each commodity available for sale during the period by the related number of units of that commodity. Using the same cost data as in the fifo and lifo examples, the average cost of the 1,000 units, $10.40, and the cost of the 300 units in inventory, $3,120, are determined as follows:

Average unit cost: $10,400 ÷ 1,000 units = $10.40
Inventory, Dec. 31:   300 units at $10.40 = **$3,120**

Deducting the inventory of **$3,120** from the **$10,400** of merchandise available for sale yields **$7,280** as the cost of merchandise sold.

COMPARING INVENTORY COSTING METHODS

Objective 5
Compare the use of the three inventory costing methods.

A different cost flow is assumed for each of the three alternative methods of costing inventories. You should note that if the cost of units had remained stable, all three methods would have yielded the same results. Since prices do change, however, the three methods will normally yield different amounts for (1) the ending inventory, (2) the cost of the merchandise sold for the period, and (3) the gross profit (and net income) for the period. Using the preceding examples for the periodic inventory system and assuming that net sales were $15,000, the following partial income statements indicate the effects of each method when prices are rising:[1]

	First-In, First-Out		Average Cost		Last-In, First-Out	
Net sales		$15,000		$15,000		$15,000
Cost of merchandise sold:						
Beginning inventory	$1,800		$1,800		$1,800	
Purchases	8,600		8,600		8,600	
Merchandise available for sale	$10,400		$10,400		$10,400	
Less ending inventory	3,400		3,120		2,800	
Cost of merchandise sold		7,000		7,280		7,600
Gross profit		$8,000		$7,720		$7,400

As shown in the income statements, the fifo method yielded the lowest amount for the cost of merchandise sold and the highest amount for gross profit (and net income). It also yielded the highest amount for the ending inventory. On the other hand, the lifo method yielded the highest amount for the cost of merchandise sold, the lowest amount for gross profit (and net income), and the lowest amount for ending inventory. The average cost method yielded results that were between those of fifo and lifo.

---

[1] Similar results would also occur when comparing inventory costing methods under a perpetual inventory system.

Use of the First-In, First-Out Method

When the fifo method is used, as we discussed earlier, the costs of the units sold are assumed to be in the order in which they were incurred. During a period of inflation or rising prices, the earlier unit costs are lower than the more recent unit costs, as shown in the preceding fifo example. Much of the benefit of the larger amount of gross profit is lost, however, because the inventory must be replaced at ever higher prices. When the rate of inflation reaches double digits, as it did during the 1970s, the larger gross profits that result from the fifo method are often called *inventory profits* or *illusory profits*.

You should note that in a period of deflation or declining prices, this effect is just the opposite. The fifo method, compared to the other methods, yields the lowest amount of gross profit. A major criticism of the fifo method is its tendency to pass through the effects of inflationary and deflationary trends to gross profit. An advantage of the fifo method, however, is that the balance sheet will report the ending merchandise inventory at an amount that is about the same as its current replacement cost.

Use of the Last-In, First-Out Method

When the lifo method is used during a period of inflation or rising prices, the results are opposite those of the other two methods. As shown in the preceding example, the lifo method will yield a lower amount of inventory at the end of the period, a higher amount of cost of merchandise sold, and a lower amount of gross profit than the other two methods. The reason for these effects is that the cost of the most recently acquired units most nearly approximates the cost of their replacement. In a period of inflation, the more recent unit costs are higher than the earlier unit costs. Thus, it can be argued that the lifo method more nearly matches current costs with current revenues. This latter point was one reason that **Chrysler Corporation** changed from the fifo method to the lifo method in the 1980s, as stated in the following footnote that accompanied **Chrysler's** financial statements:

Chrysler changed its method of accounting from first-in, first-out (fifo) to last-in, first-out (lifo) for substantially all of its domestic productive inventories. The change to lifo was made to more accurately match current costs with current revenues.

During periods of rising prices, using lifo offers an income tax savings. The income tax savings results because lifo reports the lowest amount of net income of the three methods. During the double-digit inflationary period of the 1970s, many businesses changed from fifo to lifo to take advantage of tax savings.

Again, you should note that in a period of deflation or falling price levels, this effect is just the opposite. The lifo method yields the highest amount of gross profit. The major argument for using lifo is its tendency to minimize the effect of price trends on gross profit. A criticism of using lifo, however, is that the ending merchandise inventory on the balance sheet may be quite different from its current replacement cost. In such cases, however, the financial statements normally include a note that states the estimated difference between the lifo inventory and the inventory if fifo had been used. An example of such a note accompanied the 1992 statements of **The Walgreen Co.**, as shown.

Inventories are valued on a . . . last-in, first-out (LIFO) cost . . . basis. At August 31, 1992 and 1991, inventories would have been greater by $360,344,000 and $325,431,000 respectively, if they had been valued on a lower of first-in, first-out (FIFO) cost or market basis.

Inflation and Adoption of LIFO

The effects of using lifo and some of the reasons that the method is adopted (or not adopted) by businesses were discussed in an article in *Management Accounting*. Some excerpts from that article follow.

The primary advantage of lifo is that in today's inflationary environment lifo defers (not avoids) income taxes by reducing income. The improved cash flow, then, can be profitably invested or used to reduce borrowings. . . .

In addition to deferring income taxes, though, lifo has a great deal of theoretical justification. By matching current costs against current sales, lifo produces a truer picture of income; that is, the quality of income produced by the use of lifo is higher because it more nearly approximates disposable income. . . .

Even though the primary advantage of lifo—reduced tax payments—is a function of lower income, the negative earnings im-

pact ironically continues to cloud corporate managers' decisions about the adoption of lifo. Managers fear that lower reported earnings will [have unfavorable effects on the stock price, executive compensation contracts, and credit ratings. . . .]

Another concern about lifo commonly expressed by corporate managers is misstatement of the inventories on the lifo balance sheet. Particularly over a period of rapidly rising inventory quantities and prices, the use of lifo can lead to a valuation of inventories that is significantly less than current replacement cost. However, this misstatement can be mitigated by presenting inventories valued on a non-lifo basis and deducting the lifo valuation [allowance to reduce the balance sheet inventory to the lifo amount, as follows:]

Inventory	XXX
Less reduction to lifo cost	XXX
Total	XXX

Source: Clayton T. Rumble, "So You Still Have Not Adopted Lifo," *Management Accounting* (October 1983), pp. 59–67.

Use of the Average Cost Method

As you might have guessed, the average cost method of inventory costing is, in a sense, a compromise between fifo and lifo. The effect of price trends is averaged in determining the cost of merchandise sold and the ending inventory. For a series of purchases, the average cost will be the same, regardless of the direction of price trends. For example, a complete reversal of the sequence of unit costs presented in the preceding illustration would not affect the reported cost of merchandise sold, gross profit, or ending inventory.

Selection of an Inventory Costing Method

The preceding comparisons show the importance attached to the selection of the inventory costing method. Often enterprises apply one method to one class of inventory and a different method to another class. For example, a computer retailer might use the fifo method for its microcomputer inventory and the lifo method for software and other inventory. The method(s) used may also be changed for a valid reason. The effect of any change in method and the reason for the change should be disclosed in the financial statements for the period in which the change occurred.

VALUATION OF INVENTORY AT OTHER THAN COST

Objective 6
Compute the proper valuation of inventory at other than cost using the lower-of-cost-or-market and net realizable value concepts.

As we discussed earlier in the chapter, cost is the primary basis for evaluating inventories. In some cases, however, inventory is valued at other than cost. Two such cases arise when (1) the cost of replacing items in inventory is below the recorded cost and (2) the inventory is not salable at normal sales prices. This latter case may be due to imperfections, shop wear, style changes, or other causes.

Valuation at Lower of Cost or Market

If the cost of replacing an item in inventory is lower than the original purchase cost, the **lower-of-cost-or-market method** is used to value the inventory. *Market*, as used in the phrase *lower of cost or market*, is the cost to replace the merchandise on the inventory date. This market value is based on quantities normally purchased from the usual source of supply.

The lower-of-cost-or-market method provides two advantages. First, the gross profit (and net income) is reduced in the period in which the decline occurred. Second, an approximately normal gross profit will be realized during the period in which the item is later sold.

To illustrate, assume that merchandise with a unit cost of $70 has sold at $100 during the period, yielding a gross profit of $30 a unit, or 30% of sales. Assume also that at the end of the year, there is a single unit in the inventory and that its replacement cost has declined to $63. In such a case, it would be expected that the selling price would also decline, if it has not already done so. Assuming a reduction in the selling price to $90, the gross profit based on the replacement cost of $63 would be $27, which is also 30% of the selling price.

The valuation of the unit in the inventory at $63 reduces gross profit of the prior period by $7 and permits a normal gross profit of $27 to be realized on its sale in the following period. If the unit had been valued at its original cost of $70, the gross profit determined for the past year would have been $7 greater. Likewise, the gross profit for the sale of the item in the following period would have been $7 less.

To apply the lower-of-cost-or-market method, the cost and the replacement cost can be determined for (1) each item in the inventory, (2) major classes or categories, or (3) the inventory as a whole. In practice, the cost and replacement cost of each item are usually determined. To illustrate, assume that there are 400 identical units of Commodity A in the inventory, each acquired at a unit cost of $10.25. If at the inventory date the item would cost $10.50 to replace, the cost price of $10.25 would be multiplied by 400 to determine the inventory value. On the other hand, if the item could be replaced at $9.50 a unit, the replacement cost of $9.50 would be used for valuation purposes. The table in Exhibit 6 illustrates one way of organizing inventory data in applying the lower-of-cost-or-market method to each inventory item.

Exhibit 6
Determining Inventory at Lower of Cost or Market

Commodity	Inventory Quantity	Unit Cost Price	Unit Market Price	Total Cost	Total Lower of C or M
A	400	$10.25	$ 9.50	$ 4,100	$ 3,800
B	120	22.50	24.10	2,700	2,700
C	600	8.00	7.75	4,800	4,650
D	280	14.00	14.75	3,920	3,920
Total				$15,520	$15,070

Although accumulating the data for total cost is not necessary, as shown in Exhibit 6, it provides management with the amount of the reduction in inventory value caused by the decline in market prices. The amount of the market decline, $450 ($15,520 - $15,070), may be reported as a separate item on the income statement. Otherwise, the market decline will be included in the cost of merchandise sold. Regardless, net income will be reduced by the amount of the market decline.

Valuation at Net Realizable Value

As you would probably expect, obsolete, spoiled, or damaged merchandise and other merchandise that can be sold only at prices below cost should be written down. Such merchandise should be valued at net realizable value. **Net realizable value** is the estimated selling price less any direct cost of disposal, such as sales commissions. For example, assume that damaged merchandise costing $1,000 can be sold for only $800, and direct selling expenses are estimated to be $150. This inventory should be valued at $650 ($800 – $150), which is its net realizable value.

PRESENTATION OF MERCHANDISE INVENTORY ON THE BALANCE SHEET

Objective 7
Prepare a balance sheet presentation of merchandise inventory.

As we discussed in an earlier chapter, merchandise inventory is usually presented in the Current Assets section of the balance sheet, following receivables. Both the method of determining the cost of the inventory (fifo, lifo, or average) and the method of valuing the inventory (cost, or lower of cost or market) should be shown. These details may be disclosed in parentheses on the balance sheet or in a footnote to the financial statements. Exhibit 7 shows how parentheses may be used.

Exhibit 7
Merchandise Inventory on the Balance Sheet

Afro-Arts Company Balance Sheet December 31, 1995		
Assets		
Current assets:		
Cash		$19,400
Accounts receivable	$80,000	
Less allowance for doubtful accounts	3,000	77,000
Merchandise inventory—at lower of cost (first-in, first-out method) or market		216,300

It is not unusual for large enterprises with varied activities to use different costing methods for different segments of their inventories. The following note taken from the financial statements of Chrysler Corp. illustrates this:

Automotive inventories are valued at the lower of cost or market. The cost of substantially all domestic automotive inventories is recorded on a Last-In, First-Out (LIFO) basis.

Aerospace inventories are stated at the lower of cost or market, with cost recognized on a First-In, First-Out (FIFO) basis.

ESTIMATING INVENTORY COST

Objective 8
Estimate the cost of inventory, using the retail method and the gross profit method.

In practice, it may be necessary to know the amount of inventory when it is impractical to take a physical inventory or to maintain perpetual inventory records. For example, an enterprise that uses a periodic inventory system may need monthly income statements, but taking a physical inventory each month may be too costly. Moreover, when a disaster such as a fire has destroyed the inventory, an enterprise will need to determine the amount of the loss. In this case, taking a physical inventory is impossible, and even if perpetual inventory records have been kept, the accounting records may also have been destroyed. In such cases, the inventory cost can be estimated by using (1) the retail method or (2) the gross profit method.

Retail Method of Inventory Costing

The retail inventory method of estimating inventory cost is based on the relationship of the cost of merchandise available for sale to the retail price of the same merchandise. To use this method, the retail prices of all merchandise acquired are accumulated. Next, the inventory at retail is determined by deducting sales for the period from the retail price of the goods that were available for sale during the period. The estimated inventory cost is then calculated by multiplying the inventory at retail by the ratio of cost to selling (retail) price for the merchandise available for sale, as we illustrate in Exhibit 8.

Exhibit 8
Determining Inventory by
the Retail Method

	Cost	Retail
Merchandise inventory, January 1	$19,400	$ 36,000
Purchases in January (net)	42,600	64,000
Merchandise available for sale	$62,000	$100,000

Ratio of cost to retail price: $\dfrac{\$62,000}{\$100,000} = 62\%$

	Retail
Sales for January (net)	70,000
Merchandise inventory, January 31, at retail	$ 30,000
Merchandise inventory, January 31, at estimated cost	
($30,000 x 62%)	$ 18,600

When the inventory is estimated as the percent of cost to selling price, we assume that the *mix* of the items in the ending inventory is the same as the entire stock of merchandise available for sale. In Exhibit 8, for example, it is unlikely that the retail price of every item comprised exactly 62% cost and 38% gross profit. It is assumed, however, that the weighted average of the cost percentages of the merchandise in the inventory ($30,000) is the same as in the merchandise available for sale ($100,000). When the inventory is made up of different classes of merchandise with very different gross profit rates, the cost percentages and the inventory should be developed for each class of inventory.

One of the major advantages of the retail method is that it provides inventory figures for use in preparing monthly or quarterly statements. Department stores and similar merchandisers usually determine gross profit and operating income each month but take a physical inventory only once a year. In addition, comparing the estimated ending inventory with the physical ending inventory, both at retail prices, will help identify inventory shortages resulting from shoplifting and other causes. Management can then take appropriate actions.

The retail method may also be used to facilitate taking a physical inventory at the end of the year. In this case, the items counted are recorded on the inventory sheets at their retail (selling) prices instead of their cost prices. The physical inventory at selling price is then converted to cost by applying the ratio of cost to selling (retail) price for the merchandise available for sale.

To illustrate, assume that the data in Exhibit 8 are for an entire fiscal year rather than for only January. If the physical inventory taken at the end of the year totaled $29,000, priced at retail, this amount would be converted to cost rather than the $30,000. Thus, the inventory at cost would be $17,980 ($29,000 x 62%) instead of $18,600 ($30,000 x 62%). The $17,980 would be used for the year-end financial statements and for income tax purposes.

Gross Profit Method of Estimating Inventories

The **gross profit method** uses the gross profit estimated for the period to estimate the inventory at the end of the period. The gross profit is usually estimated from the actual rate for the preceding year, adjusted for any changes made in the cost and sales prices during the current period. By using the gross profit rate, the dollar amount of sales for a period can be divided into its two components: (1) gross profit and (2) cost of merchandise sold. The latter amount may then be deducted from the cost of merchandise available for sale to yield the estimated cost of merchandise on hand.

Exhibit 9 illustrates the gross profit method for estimating a company's inventory on January 31. In this example, the inventory on January 1 is assumed to be $57,000, the net purchases during the month are $180,000, and the net sales during the month are $250,000. In addition, the historical gross profit was 30% of net sales.

Exhibit 9
Estimating Inventory by Gross Profit Method

Merchandise inventory, January 1		$ 57,000
Purchases in January (net)		180,000
Merchandise available for sale		$237,000
Sales in January (net)	$250,000	
Less estimated gross profit ($250,000 x 30%)	75,000	
Estimated cost of merchandise sold		175,000
Estimated merchandise inventory, January 31		$ 62,000

The gross profit method is useful for estimating inventories for monthly or quarterly financial statements. It is also useful in estimating the cost of merchandise destroyed by fire or other disaster.

INVENTORIES OF MANUFACTURING ENTERPRISES

Objective 9
Describe the inventories of manufacturing enterprises.

In the preceding discussion, we presented the principles and procedures for inventory in the context of a merchandising enterprise. These same principles and procedures, with some modification, also apply to inventories of a manufacturing enterprise.

Manufacturing businesses maintain three inventory accounts instead of a single merchandise inventory account. Separate accounts are maintained for (1) goods in the state in which they are to be sold **(finished goods)**, (2) goods in the process of manufacture **(work in process)**, and (3) goods in the state in which they were acquired **(materials)**. The balances in these inventory accounts may be presented in the balance sheet in the following manner:

Inventories:		
Finished goods	$300,000	
Work in process	55,000	
Materials	123,000	$478,000

The finished goods inventory and work in process inventory consist of three separate categories of manufacturing costs: direct materials, direct labor, and factory overhead. **Direct materials** represent the cost of materials that are an integral part of the manufactured product. **Direct labor** represents the cost of wages of employees who are directly involved in converting materials into the manufactured product. **Factory overhead** includes all the remaining costs of manufacturing the product, such as wages for factory supervision, supplies used in the manufacturing process, property taxes, and depreciation on factory equipment.

LONG-TERM CONSTRUCTION CONTRACTS

Objective 10
Describe the accounting for long-term construction contracts.

Enterprises engaged in large construction projects may take years to complete a contract. For example, assume that a contractor begins a project that will require three years to complete at a total contract price of $50,000,000. Also assume that the total estimated cost to be incurred over the three-year period is $44,000,000. Using the point-of-sale method, no revenue or expense would be recognized until the project is completed. Thus, the entire net income from the contract would be reported in the third year. This method of realizing revenue from long-term contracts is called the **completed-contract method**.

Whenever the total cost of a long-term contract and the project's progress can be reasonably estimated, revenue is often realized over the entire life of the contract by the **percentage-of-completion method**.[2] The amount of revenue realized in a period is determined on the basis of the estimated percentage of the contract that has been completed during the period. The percentage of completion can be estimated by comparing the amount of incurred costs with the estimated total costs. Other methods of estimating the percentage of completion include using estimates developed by engineers, architects, or other qualified personnel.

[2] *Accounting Research and Terminology Bulletins—Final Edition*, "No. 45, Long-term Construction-type Contracts" (New York: American Institute of Certified Public Accountants, 1961), par. 15.

Continuing with the preceding example, assume that by the end of the first fiscal year the contract is estimated to be one-fourth completed. The costs incurred during the first year were $11,200,000. Using the percentage-of-completion method, the revenue realized and the income for the year are as follows:

Revenue realized ($50,000,000 × 25%)	$12,500,000
Costs incurred	11,200,000
Income (Year 1)	$ 1,300,000

The 1992 edition of *Accounting Trends & Techniques* indicated that 67% of the surveyed companies with long-term contracts used the percentage-of-completion method. This method involves estimates and hence possible inaccuracies in determining and reporting revenue. However, the financial statements are often considered more informative and more useful than if the completed-contract method is used.

Whichever method is used to recognize revenue on a long-term contract, it should be disclosed in the financial statements. The following excerpt taken from a note to the financial statements of Martin Marietta Corporation is an example of such a disclosure:

Revenue Recognition

Sales under long-term contracts generally are recognized under the percentage-of-completion method, and include a proportion of the earnings expected to be realized on the contract. . . . Other sales are recorded upon shipment of products or performance of services.

CHAPTER REVIEW

Key Points

Objective 1. Summarize and provide examples of internal control procedures that apply to inventories.
Internal control procedures for inventories include those developed to protect the inventories from damage, employee theft, and customer theft. In addition, a physical inventory count should be taken periodically to detect shortages as well as to deter employee thefts.

Objective 2. List the procedures for determining the actual quantities in inventory.
The first step in "taking" an inventory is to count the merchandise on hand. Count teams are often made up of two persons—one who counts and the other who records the quantities and descriptions on inventory count sheets. A second count team may be used to check quantities of high-cost items and other items selected at random. Care must be used to include all merchandise in transit that is owned. Consigned merchandise should not be included in the consignee's inventory.

Objective 3. Compute the cost of inventory under the perpetual inventory system, using the following costing methods:

First-in, first-out
Last-in, first-out
Average cost
In a perpetual inventory system, the number of units and the cost of each type of merchandise are recorded in a subsidiary inventory ledger, with a separate account for each type of merchandise. Inventory costs and the amounts charged against revenue are illustrated using the fifo and lifo methods.

Objective 4. Compute the cost of iinventory under the periodic inventory system, using the following costing methods:
First-in, first out
Last-in, first-out
Average cost
In a periodic inventory system, a physical inventory is taken to determine the cost of the inventory and the cost of merchandise sold. Inventory costs snd the amounts charged against revenue are illustrated using fifo, lifo, and average cost methods.

Objective 5. Compare the use of the three inventory costing methods.

The three inventory costing methods will normally yield different amounts for (1) the ending inventory, (2) the cost of the merchandise sold for the period, and (3) the gross profit (and net income) for the period. During periods of inflation, the fifo method yields the lowest amount for the cost of merchandise sold, the highest amount for gross profit (and net income), and the highest amount for the ending inventory. The lifo method yields the opposite results. During periods of deflation, the preceding effects are reversed. The average cost method yields results that are between those of fifo and lifo.

Objective 6. Compute the proper valuation of inventory at other than cost, using the lower-of-cost-or-market and net realizable value concepts.

If the market price of an item of inventory is lower than its cost, the lower market price is used to compute the value of the item. Market price is the cost to replace the merchandise on the inventory date. It is possible to apply the lower of cost or market to each item in the inventory, to major classes or categories, or to the inventory as a whole.

Merchandise that can be sold only at prices below cost should be valued at net realizable value, which is the estimated selling price less any direct cost of disposal.

Objective 7. Prepare a balance sheet presentation of merchandise inventory.

Merchandise inventory is usually presented in the Current Assets section of the balance sheet, following receivables. Both the method of determining the cost of the inventory (fifo, lifo, or average) and the method of valuing the inventory (cost, or lower of cost or market) should be shown.

Objective 8. Estimate the cost of inventory, using the retail method and the gross profit method.

In using the retail method to estimate inventory, the retail prices of all merchandise acquired are accumulated. The inventory at retail is determined by deducting sales for the period from the retail price of the goods that were available for sale during the period. The inventory at retail is then converted to cost on the basis of the ratio of cost to selling (retail) price for the merchandise available for sale.

In using the gross profit method to estimate inventory, the estimated gross profit is deducted from the sales to determine the estimated cost of merchandise sold. This amount is then deducted from the cost of merchandise available for sale to determine the estimated ending inventory.

Objective 9. Describe the inventories of manufacturing enterprises.

Manufacturing enterprises maintain three separate inventory accounts for (1) goods in the state in which they are to be sold (finished goods), (2) goods in the process of manufacture (work in process), and (3) goods in the state in which they were acquired (materials). The finished goods inventory and work in process inventory consist of three separate manufacturing costs: direct materials, direct labor, and factory overhead.

Objective 10. Describe the accounting for long-term construction contracts.

Enterprises engaged in large, long-term construction projects may determine revenue and income by the completed-contract method or percentage-of-completion method. Under the latter method, the revenue to be recognized each year of the life of the contract is based on the estimated percentage of the contract that has been completed during each year.

Glossary of Key Terms

Average cost method. The method of inventory costing that is based on the assumption that costs should be charged against revenue in accordance with the weighted average unit costs of the items sold. **Objective 3**

Completed-contract method. The method that recognizes revenue from long-term construction contracts when the project is completed. **Objective 10**

Direct labor. The cost of wages of employees who are directly involved in converting materials into the manufactured project. **Objective 9**

Direct materials. The cost of materials that are an integral part of the manufactured product. **Objective 9**

Factory overhead. All the remaining costs of manufacturing the product that are not included in direct materials or direct labor. **Objective 9**

Finished goods. Manufactured goods in the state in which they are to be sold. **Objective 9**

First-in, first-out (fifo) method. A method of inventory costing based on the assumption that the costs of merchandise sold should be charged against revenue in the order in which the costs were incurred. **Objective 3**

Gross profit method. A means of estimating inventory on hand based on the relationship of gross profit to sales. **Objective 8**

Last-in, first-out (lifo) method. A method of inventory costing based on the assumption that the most recent merchandise costs incurred should be charged against revenue. **Objective 3**

Lower-of-cost-or-market method. A method of valuing inventory that reports the inventory at the lower of its cost or current market value (replacement cost). **Objective 6**

Materials. Goods in the state in which they were acquired for use in a manufacturing process. **Objective 9**

Net realizable value. The amount at which merchandise that can be sold only at prices below cost should be valued; it is determined as the estimated selling price less any direct costs of disposal. **Objective 6**

Percentage-of-completion method. A method of recognizing revenue from long-term contracts over the entire life of the contract. **Objective 10**

Physical inventory. The detailed listing of merchandise on hand. **Objective 1**

Retail inventory method. A means of estimating inventory based on the relationship of the cost and the retail price of merchandise. **Objective 8**

Work in process. Goods in the process of manufacture. **Objective 9**

Self-Examination Questions
Answers at end of chapter.

1. If the inventory shrinkage at the end of the year is overstated by $7,500, the error will cause an:
   A. understatement of cost of merchandise sold for the year by $7,500
   B. overstatement of gross profit for the year by $7,500
   C. overstatement of merchandise inventory for the year by $7,500
   D. understatement of net income for the year by $7,500

2. The inventory costing method that is based on the assumption that costs should be charged against revenue in the order in which they were incurred is:
   A. fifo   C. average cost
   B. lifo   D. perpetual inventory

3. The following units of a particular item were purchased and sold during the period:
   Beginning inventory   40 units at $20
   First purchase   50 units at $21
   Second purchase   50 units at $22
   First sale   110 units
   Third purchase   50 units at $23
   Second sale   45 units

What is the unit cost of the 35 units on hand at the end of the period as determined under the perpetual inventory system by the lifo costing method?
   A. $20 and $23   C. $20
   B. $20 and $21   D. $23

4. The following units of a particular item were available for sale during the period:
   Beginning inventory   40 units at $20
   First purchase   50 units at $21
   Second purchase   50 units at $22
   Third purchase   50 units at $23

What is the unit cost of the 35 units on hand at the end of the period, as determined under the periodic inventory system by the fifo costing method?
   A. $20   C. $22
   B. $21   D. $23

5. If merchandise inventory is being valued at cost and the price level is steadily rising, the method of costing that will yield the highest net income is:
   A. lifo   C. average
   B. fifo   D. periodic

ILLUSTRATIVE PROBLEM

Stewart Co.'s beginning inventory and purchases during the fiscal year ended March 31, 1995, were as follows:

		Units	Unit Cost	Total Cost
April 1, 1994	Inventory	1,000	$50.00	$ 50,000
April 10, 1994	Purchase	1,200	52.50	63,000
April 25, 1994	Sold 800 units			
May 30, 1994	Purchase	800	55.00	44,000
June 5, 1994	Sold 1,500 units			
August 26, 1994	Purchase	2,000	56.00	112,000
September 9, 1994	Sold 1,000 units			
October 15, 1994	Purchase	1,500	57.00	85,500
December 31, 1994	Purchase	700	58.00	40,600
January 11, 1995	Sold 1,400 units			
January 18, 1995	Purchase	1,350	60.00	81,000
February 3, 1995	Sold 1,100 units			
March 21, 1995	Purchase	450	62.00	27,900
Total		9,000		$504,000

Instructions

1. Determine the cost of inventory on March 31, 1995, using the perpetual inventory system and each of the following inventory costing methods:
   a. first-in, first-out
   b. last-in, first-out
2. Determine the cost of inventory on March 31, 1995, using the periodic inventory system and each of the following inventory costing methods:
   a. first-in, first-out
   b. last-in, first-out
   c. average cost
3. Assume that during the fiscal year ended March 31, 1995, sales were $536,000 and the estimated gross profit rate was 40%. Estimate the ending inventory at March 31, 1995, using the gross profit method.

Solution

1. a. First-in, first-out method:

Date	Purchases			Cost of Merchandise Sold			Inventory		
	Quantity	Unit Cost	Total Cost	Quantity	Unit Cost	Total Cost	Quantity	Unit Cost	Total Cost
Apr. 1							1,000	50	50,000
10	1,200	52.50	63,000				1,000	50	50,000
							1,200	52.50	63,000
25				800	50	40,000	200	50	10,000
							1,200	52,50	63,00
May 30	800	55	44,000				200	50	10,000
							1,200	52.50	63,000
							800	55	44,000
June 5				200	50	10,000	700	55	38,500
				1,200	52.50	63,000			
				100	55	5,500			
Aug. 26	2,000	56	112,000				700	55	38,500
							2,000	56	112,000
Sept. 9				700	55	38,500	1,700	56	95,200
				300	56	16,800			
Oct. 15	1,500	57	85,500				1,700	56	95,200
							1,500	57	85,500
Dec. 31	700	58	40,600				1,700	56	95,200
							1,500	57	85,500
							700	58	40,600
Jan. 11	1,400			1,400	56	78,400	300	56	16,800
							1,500	57	85,500
							700	58	40,600
18	1,350	60	81,000				300	56	16,800
							1,500	57	85,500
							700	58	40,600
							1,350	60	81,000
Feb. 3				300	56	16,800	700	57	39,900
				800	57	45,600	700	58	40,600
							1,350	60	81,000
Mar. 21	450	62	27,900				700	57	39,900
							700	58	40,600
							1,350	60	81,000
							450	62	27,900

b. Last-in, first-out method:

Date	Purchases			Cost of Merchandise Sold			Inventory		
	Quantity	Unit Cost	Total Cost	Quantity	Unit Cost	Total Cost	Quantity	Unit Cost	Total Cost
Apr. 1							1,000	50	50,000
10	1,200	52.50	63,000				1,000	50	50,000
							1,200	52.50	63,000
25				800	52.50	42,000	1,000	50	50,000
							400	52.50	21,000
May 30	800	55	44,000				1,000	50	50,000
							400	52.50	21,000
							800	55	44,000
June 5				800	55	44,000	700	50	35,000
				400	52.50	21,000			
				300	50	15,000			
Aug. 26	2,000	56	112,000				700	50	35,000
							2,000	56	112,000
Sept. 9				1,000	56	56,000	700	50	35,000
							1,000	56	56,000
Oct. 15	1,500	57	85,500				700	50	35,000
							1,000	56	56,000
							1,500	57	85,500

1. b. continued

Date	Purchases			Cost of Merchandise Sold			Inventory		
	Quantity	Unit Cost	Total Cost	Quantity	Unit Cost	Total Cost	Quantity	Unit Cost	Total Cost
Dec. 31	700	58	40,600				700	50	35,000
							1,000	56	56,000
							1,500	57	85,500
							700	58	40,600
Jan. 11				700	58	40,600	700	50	35,000
				700	57	39,900	1,000	56	56,000
							800	57	45,600
18	1,350	60	81,000				700	50	35,000
							1,000	56	56,000
							800	57	45,600
							1,350	60	81,000
Feb. 3				1,100	60	66,000	700	50	35,000
							1,000	56	56,000
							800	57	45,600
							250	60	15,000
Mar. 21	450	62	27,900				700	50	35,000
							1,000	56	56,000
							800	57	45,600
							250	60	15,000
							450	62	27,900

2. a. First-in, first-out method:

450 units at $62	$ 27,900
1,350 units at $60	81,000
700 units at $58	40,600
700 units at $57	39,900
3,200 units	$189,400

b. Last-in, first-out method:

1,000 units at $50.00	$ 50,000
1,200 units at $52.50	63,000
800 units at $55.00	44,000
200 units at $56.00	11,200
3,200 units	$168,200

c. Average cost method:

Average cost per unit: $504,000 ÷ 9,000 units = $56
Inventory, March 31, 1995:   3,200 units at $56 = $179,200

3.
Merchandise inventory, April 1, 1994		$ 50,000
Purchases (net), April 1, 1994–March 31, 1995		454,000
Merchandise available for sale		$504,000
Sales (net), April 1, 1994–March 31, 1995	$536,000	
Less estimated gross profit ($536,000 x 40%)	214,400	
Estimated cost of merchandise sold		321,600
Estimated merchandise inventory, March 31, 1995		$182,400

DISCUSSION QUESTIONS

1. What security measures may be used by retailers to protect merchandise inventory from customer theft?
2. Which inventory system provides the more effective means of controlling inventories (perpetual or periodic)? Why?
3. Before inventory purchases are recorded, the receiving report should be reconciled to what documents?
4. What document should be presented by an employee requesting inventory items to be released from the company's warehouse?

5. Why is it important to periodically take a physical inventory if the perpetual system is used?

6. The inventory shrinkage at the end of the year was understated by $10,000. (a) Did the error cause an overstatement or an understatement of the gross profit for the year? (b) Which items on the balance sheet at the end of the year were overstated or understated as a result of the error?

7. When does title to merchandise pass from the seller to the buyer if the terms of shipment are (a) FOB shipping point, (b) FOB destination?

8. Bradley Co. sold merchandise to Midland Company on December 31, FOB shipping point. If the merchandise is in transit on December 31, the end of the fiscal year, which company would report it in its financial statements? Explain.

9. A manufacturer shipped merchandise to a retailer on a consignment basis. If the merchandise is unsold at the end of the period, in whose inventory should the merchandise be included?

10. What are the two most widely used inventory costing methods?

11. Which of the three methods of inventory costing—fifo, lifo, or average cost—is based on the assumption that costs should be charged against revenue in the reverse order in which they were incurred?

12. Do the terms *fifo* and *lifo* refer to techniques used in determining quantities of the various classes of merchandise on hand? Explain.

13. Does the term *last-in* in the lifo method mean that the items in the inventory are assumed to be the most recent (last) acquisitions? Explain.

14. Under which method of cost flow are (a) the earliest costs assigned to inventory, (b) the most recent costs assigned to inventory, (c) average costs assigned to inventory?

15. The following units of a particular item were available for sale during the year:

Beginning inventory	20 units at $50
Sale	15 units at $90
First purchase	30 units at $54
Sale	25 units at $93
Second purchase	40 units at $65
Sale	35 units at $98

The firm uses the perpetual system, and there are 15 units of the item on hand at the end of the year. What is the total cost of the ending inventory according to (a) fifo, (b) lifo?

16. If merchandise inventory is being valued at cost and the price level is steadily rising, which of the three methods of costing—fifo, lifo, or average cost—will yield (a) the highest inventory cost, (b) the lowest inventory cost, (c) the highest gross profit, (d) the lowest gross profit?

17. Which of the three methods of inventory costing—fifo, lifo, or average cost—will in general yield an inventory cost most nearly approximating current replacement cost?

18. If inventory is being valued at cost and the price level is steadily rising, which of the three methods of costing—fifo, lifo, or average cost—will yield the lowest annual income tax expense? Explain.

19. Can a company change its method of costing inventory? Explain.

20. In the phrase *lower of cost or market*, what is meant by *market*?

21. The cost of a particular inventory item is $410, the current replacement cost is $400, and the selling price is $525. At what amount should the item be included in the inventory according to the lower-of-cost-or-market basis?

22. Because of imperfections, an item of merchandise cannot be sold at its normal selling price. How should this item be valued for financial statement purposes?

23. How is the method of determining the cost of the inventory and the method of valuing it disclosed in the financial statements?

24. An enterprise using the retail method of inventory costing determines that merchandise inventory at retail is $500,000. If the ratio of cost to retail price is 65%, what is the amount of inventory to be reported on the financial statements?

25. What uses can be made of the estimate of the cost of inventory determined by the gross profit method?

26. Name the three inventory accounts for a manufacturing business, and describe what each balance represents at the end of an accounting period.

27. Name and describe the three categories of manufacturing costs included in the cost of finished goods and the cost of work in process.

28. What are the advantages and disadvantages of using the percentage-of-completion method for reporting income on long-term construction projects?

29. The following footnote was taken from the 1992 financial statements of The Walgreen Co.:

Inventories are valued on a . . . last-in, first-out (LIFO) cost . . . basis. At August 31, 1992 and 1991, inventories would have been greater by $360,344,000 and $325,431,000 respectively, if they had been valued on a lower of first-in, first-out (FIFO) cost or market basis.

Additional data are as follows:

Earnings before income taxes, 1992 $353,005,000
Total lifo inventories, August 31, 1992   994,168,000

REAL W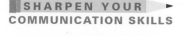**RLD FOCUS**

Based on the preceding data, determine (a) what the total inventories at August 31, 1992, would have been, using the fifo method, and (b) what the earnings before income taxes for the year ended August 31, 1992, would have been if fifo had been used instead of lifo.

ETHICS DISCUSSION CASE

Lemke Co. is experiencing a decrease in sales and operating income for the fiscal year ending December 31, 1995. Betty Arnett, controller of Lemke Co., has suggested that all orders received before the end of the fiscal year be shipped by midnight, December 31, 1995, even if the shipping department must work overtime. Since Lemke Co. ships all merchandise FOB shipping point, it would record all such shipments as sales for the year ending December 31, 1995, thereby offsetting some of the decreases in sales and operating income.

Discuss whether Betty Arnett is behaving in an ethical manner.

SHARPEN YOUR ►
COMMUNICATION SKILLS

WHAT DO YOU
THINK

?

Should the Financial Accounting Standards Board (FASB) mandate only one cost flow assumption for inventories rather than allowing companies to choose among first-in, first-out; last-in, first-out; or average cost flow assumptions?

FINANCIAL ANALYSIS AND INTERPRETATION

A merchandising enterprise should keep enough inventory on hand to meet the needs of its customers. At the same time, however, too much inventory reduces solvency by tying up funds, and it increases expenses such as storage expense. Moreover, excess inventory increases the risk of losses due to prices declining or the inventory becoming obsolete.

As with many types of financial analyses, it is possible to determine more than one measure to express the relationship between the cost of merchandise sold (cost of sales) and inventory. Two such measures are the inventory turnover and the number of days' sales in inventory. The inventory turnover is computed as follows:

$$\text{Inventory Turnover} = \frac{\text{Cost of Merchandise Sold}}{\text{Average Inventory}}$$

The average inventory can be determined by dividing the sum of the inventories at the beginning and end of the year by 2.

Generally, an increase in the turnover indicates an improvement in managing inventory. However, differences in companies and industries are too great to allow a more specific statement as to what is a good inventory turnover. For example, a firm selling food should have a higher turnover than a firm selling furniture. However, for each business, there is a reasonable turnover rate. A turnover lower than this rate could mean that inventory is not being managed properly. In such cases, management should investigate to determine the causes of the lower inventory rate.

The number of days' sales in inventory is computed as follows:

$$\begin{array}{c}\text{Number of Days' Sales} \\ \text{in Inventory}\end{array} = \frac{\text{Inventory, End of Year}}{\text{Average Daily Cost of Merchandise Sold}}$$

The average daily cost of merchandise sold is determined by dividing the cost of merchandise sold by 365.

The number of days' sales in inventory is a rough measure of the length of time it takes to acquire, sell, and replace the inventory. Generally, a decrease in the number of days' sales in inventory indicates an improvement in managing the inventory.

a. Hershey Foods Corporation has inventories of $379,108,000 at December 31, 1990. For the years ended December 31, 1992 and 1991, determine:

(1) the inventory turnover

(2) the number of days' sales in inventory

SHARPEN YOUR ▶
COMMUNICATION SKILLS
b. What conclusions can be drawn from these analyses concerning Hershey's efficiency in managing inventory?

EXERCISES

EXERCISE 8-1
INTERNAL CONTROL OF
INVENTORIES
Objective 1

Amis Hardware Store currently uses a periodic inventory system. Jim Amis, the owner, is considering the purchase of a computer system that would make it feasible to switch to a perpetual inventory system.

Jim is unhappy with the periodic inventory system because it does not provide timely information on inventory levels. Jim has noticed several occasions when the store runs out of good-selling items while too many poor-selling items are on hand.

Jim is also concerned about lost sales while a physical inventory is being taken. Amis Hardware currently takes a physical inventory twice a year. To minimize distractions, the store is closed on the day inventory is taken. Jim believes closing the store is the only way to get an accurate inventory count.

SHARPEN YOUR ▶
COMMUNICATION SKILLS
Will switching to a perpetual inventory system strengthen Amis Hardware's control over inventory items? Will switching to a perpetual inventory system eliminate the need for a physical inventory count? Explain.

EXERCISE 8-2
INTERNAL CONTROL OF
INVENTORIES
Objective 1

Govan Luggage Shop is a small retail establishment located in a large shopping mall. This shop has implemented the following procedures regarding inventory items:

a. Since the shop carries mostly high-quality, designer luggage, all inventory items are tagged with a control device that activates an alarm if a tagged item is removed from the store.

b. Since the display area of the store is limited, only a sample of each piece of luggage is kept on the selling floor. Whenever a customer selects a piece of luggage, the salesclerk gets the appropriate piece from the store's stockroom. Since all salesclerks need access to the stockroom it is not locked. The stockroom is adjacent to the break room used by all mall employees.

c. Whenever Govan receives a shipment of new inventory, the items are taken directly to the stockroom. Govan's accountant uses the vendor's invoice to record the amount of inventory received.

SHARPEN YOUR ▶
COMMUNICATION SKILLS
State whether each of these procedures is appropriate or inappropriate considering the principles of internal control. If the procedure is inappropriate, state which internal control principle is violated.

EXERCISE 8-3
PERPETUAL INVENTORY
USING FIFO
Objective 3

Beginning inventory, purchases, and sales data for Commodity E29 are as follows:

Jan.	1	Inventory	15	units at $45
	6	Sale	5	units
	9	Purchase	15	units at $47
	15	Sale	18	units
	22	Sale	3	units
	30	Purchase	10	units at $48

The enterprise maintains a perpetual inventory system, costing by the first-in, first-out method. Determine the cost of the merchandise sold for each sale and the inventory balance after each sale, presenting the data in the form illustrated in Exhibit 2.

EXERCISE 8-4
PERPETUAL INVENTORY
USING LIFO
Objective 3

Beginning inventory, purchases, and sales data for Commodity A40 for May are as follows:

Inventory: Purchases:
  May 1   30 units at $30   May 4   20 units at $31
Sales: 20   15 units at $32
  May 11   15 units
      17   10 units
      27   10 units

Assuming that the perpetual inventory system is used, costing by the lifo method, determine the cost of the inventory balance at May 31, presenting data in the form illustrated in Exhibit 3.

EXERCISE 8-5
PERIODIC INVENTORY BY
THREE METHODS
Objective 4

The units of an item available for sale during the year were as follows:

Jan.	1	Inventory	40 units at $39
Apr.	4	Purchase	30 units at $40
July	20	Purchase	40 units at $42
Sep.	30	Purchase	30 units at $41

SPREADSHEET
PROBLEM

There are 45 units of the item in the physical inventory at December 31. The periodic inventory system is used. Determine the inventory cost by the (a) first-in, first-out method; (b) last-in, first-out method; (c) average cost method.

EXERCISE 8-6
PERIODIC INVENTORY BY
THREE METHODS; COST OF
MERCHANDISE SOLD
Objective 4

The units of an item available for sale during the year were as follows:

Jan.	1	Inventory	15 units at $60
Mar.	4	Purchase	10 units at $62
June	7	Purchase	20 units at $65
Nov.	15	Purchase	15 units at $70

There are 20 units of the item in the physical inventory at December 31. The periodic inventory system is used. Determine the inventory cost and the cost of merchandise sold by three methods, presenting your answers in the following form:

SPREADSHEET
PROBLEM

	Cost	
Inventory Method	Merchandise Inventory	Merchandise Sold
a. First-in, first-out	$	$
b. Last-in, first-out		
c. Average cost		

EXERCISE 8-7
LOWER-OF-COST-OR-
MARKET INVENTORY
Objective 6

On the basis of the following data, determine the value of the inventory at the lower of cost or market. Assemble the data in the form illustrated in Exhibit 6.

Commodity	Inventory Quantity	Unit Cost Price	Unit Market Price
43B	8	$340	$350
19H	17	110	105
33P	12	275	260
90R	35	60	65
45T	20	95	100

EXERCISE 8-8
MERCHANDISE INVENTORY
ON THE BALANCE SHEET
Objective 7

Based on the data in Exercise 8-7 and assuming that cost was determined by the fifo method, show how the merchandise inventory would appear on the balance sheet.

EXERCISE 8-9
RETAIL INVENTORY
METHOD
Objective 8

On the basis of the following data, estimate the cost of the merchandise inventory at June 30 by the retail method:

		Cost	Retail
June 1	Merchandise inventory	$244,500	$370,500
June 1–30	Purchases (net)	164,700	249,500
June 1–30	Sales (net)		259,000

EXERCISE 8-10
GROSS PROFIT INVENTORY
METHOD
Objective 8

The merchandise inventory was destroyed by fire on March 20. The following data were obtained from the accounting records:

Jan. 1	Merchandise inventory	$172,250
Jan. 1–March 20	Purchases (net)	212,250
	Sales (net)	380,000
	Estimated gross profit rate	40%

a. Estimate the cost of the merchandise destroyed.
b. Briefly describe the situations in which the gross profit method is useful.

**SHARPEN YOUR
COMMUNICATION SKILLS**

EXERCISE 8-11
PERCENTAGE-OF-
COMPLETION METHOD
Objective 10

During the current year, Cross Construction Company obtained a contract to build an apartment building. The total contract price was $9,000,000, and the estimated construction costs were $7,950,000. During the current year, the project was estimated to be 40% completed, and the costs incurred totaled $3,110,000. Under the percentage-of-completion method of revenue recognition, what amount of (a) revenue, (b) cost, and (c) income should be recognized from the contract for the current year?

**WhAT'S WRONG
WITH THIS?**

During 1995, it was discovered that the inventory shrinkage at the end of 1994 had been overstated by $50,000. Instead of correcting the error, the accountant decided to understate the inventory shrinkage of 1995 by $50,000. The accountant reasoned that the two errors would balance each other, and the error in 1994 would be balanced out by the error in 1995. Are there any flaws in the accountant's reasoning?

PROBLEMS

Series A

PROBLEM 8-1A
FIFO PERPETUAL
INVENTORY
Objective 3

The beginning inventory of Commodity 37D and data on purchases and sales for a three-month period are as follows:

Date		Transaction	Number of Units	Per Unit	Total
April	1	Inventory	9	$220	$1,980
	5	Purchase	25	225	5,625
	12	Sale	10	300	3,000
	22	Sale	6	300	1,800
May	4	Purchase	10	230	2,300
	6	Sale	8	310	2,480
	21	Sale	5	310	1,550
	28	Purchase	15	235	3,525
June	5	Sale	9	315	2,835
	13	Sale	10	315	3,150
	19	Purchase	10	240	2,400
	26	Sale	8	320	2,560

Instructions
1. Record the inventory, purchases, and cost of merchandise sold data in a perpetual inventory record similar to the one illustrated in Exhibit 2 using the first-in, first-out method.
2. Determine the total sales and the total cost of Commodity 37D sold for the period. Journalize the entries in the sales and cost of merchandise sold accounts. Assume that all sales were on account.
3. Determine the gross profit from sales of Commodity 37D for the period.

PROBLEM 8-2A
LIFO PERPETUAL
INVENTORY
Objective 3

The beginning inventory of Commodity 37D and data on purchases and sales for a three-month period are shown in Problem 8-1A.

Instructions
1. Record the inventory, purchases, and cost of merchandise sold data in a perpetual inventory record similar to the one illustrated in Exhibit 3 using the last-in, first-out method.
2. Determine the total sales, the total cost of Commodity 37D sold, and the gross profit from sales for the period.

PROBLEM 8-3A
PERIODIC INVENTORY BY
THREE METHODS
Objective 4

House of Television uses the periodic inventory system. Details regarding the inventory of television sets at January 1, purchases invoices during the year, and the inventory count at December 31 are summarized as follows:

Model	Inventory, January 1	Purchases Invoices 1st	Purchases Invoices 2d	Purchases Invoices 3d	Inventory Count, December 31
B91	4 at $150	6 at $150	8 at $155	7 at $155	5
F10	3 at 210	3 at 215	5 at 213	4 at 225	3
H21	2 at 520	2 at 530	2 at 530	2 at 536	3
J39	6 at 520	8 at 531	4 at 549	6 at 542	8
P80	9 at 213	7 at 215	6 at 222	6 at 225	8
T15	6 at 305	3 at 310	3 at 316	4 at 321	5
V11	—	4 at 220	4 at 230	—	2

Instructions

1. Determine the cost of the inventory on December 31 by the first-in, first-out method. Present data in columnar form using the following headings:

Model	Quantity	Unit Cost	Total Cost

If the inventory of a particular model comprises one entire purchase plus a portion of another purchase acquired at a different unit cost, use a separate line for each purchase.

2. Determine the cost of the inventory on December 31 by the last-in, first-out method, following the procedures indicated in (1).
3. Determine the cost of the inventory on December 31 by the average cost method using the columnar headings indicated in (1).

SHARPEN YOUR
COMMUNICATION SKILLS ▶

4. Discuss which method (fifo or lifo) would be preferred for income tax purposes in periods of (a) rising prices and (b) declining prices.

PROBLEM 8-4A
LOWER-OF-COST-OR-
MARKET INVENTORY
Objective 6

If the working papers correlating with the textbook are not used, omit Problem 8-4A.
Data on the physical inventory of Lyons Co. as of December 31, the end of the current fiscal year, are presented in the working papers. The quantity of each commodity on hand has been determined and recorded on the inventory sheet. Unit market prices have also been determined as of December 31 and recorded on the sheet. The inventory is to be determined at cost and also at the lower of cost or market using the first-in, first-out method. Quantity and cost data from the last purchases invoice of the year and the next-to-the-last purchases invoice are summarized as follows:

Description	Last Purchases Invoice Quantity Purchased	Last Purchases Invoice Unit Cost	Next-to-the-Last Purchases Invoice Quantity Purchased	Next-to-the-Last Purchases Invoice Unit Cost
A71	20	$ 60	40	$ 59
C22	25	190	15	190
D82	15	145	15	142
E34	150	25	100	27
F17	6	550	15	540
J19	75	16	100	17
K41	8	400	5	410
P21	500	6	500	7
R72	70	17	50	16
T15	5	250	4	260
V55	1,000	10	500	10
AC2	100	45	100	46
BB7	5	410	5	400
BD1	100	20	100	19
CC1	50	15	40	16
EB2	40	29	50	28
FF7	55	28	50	28
GE4	6	690	5	700

Instructions

Record the appropriate unit costs on the inventory sheet, and complete the pricing of the inventory. When there are two different unit costs applicable to an item, proceed as follows:

1. Draw a line through the quantity, and insert the quantity and unit cost of the last purchase.
2. On the following line, insert the quantity and unit cost of the next-to-the-last purchase. The first item on the inventory sheet has been completed as an example.

PROBLEM 8-5A
ADJUSTING ENTRIES;
FINANCIAL STATEMENTS
Objectives 6, 7

Worden Sales is a distributor of imported motorcycles. Its unadjusted trial balance as of the end of the current fiscal year is as follows:

Cash	27,900	
Accounts Receivable	49,500	
Allowance for Doubtful Accounts		275
Merchandise Inventory	90,200	
Equipment	30,000	
Accumulated Depreciation—Equipment		12,250
Accounts Payable		24,500
Notes Payable		10,000
Capital Stock		10,000
Retained Earnings		61,750
Dividends	6,000	
Sales		535,700
Cost of Merchandise Sold	395,800	
Operating Expenses (controlling account)	55,175	
Rent Income		1,200
Interest Expense	1,100	
	655,675	655,675

Data needed for adjustments at December 31:

a. Merchandise inventory at December 31 is valued at lower of fifo cost or market. Worden Sales uses a perpetual inventory system. The physical inventory on December 31 indicated an inventory shrinkage of $5,600.
b. Uncollectible accounts expense for current year, estimated at $1,725.
c. Depreciation of equipment for current year, $5,500.

Instructions

1. Journalize the necessary adjusting entries. All selling and administrative expenses are included in the operating expenses controlling account.
2. Prepare the following without the use of a conventional work sheet: (a) an income statement, (b) a retained earnings statement, and (c) a balance sheet in report form.

Instructions for Solving Problem 8-5A Using Solutions Software

1. Load the opening balances.
2. Enter your name in the Student Name field in the General Information data entry window. Set the run date to December 31 of the current year.
3. Save the opening balances file to your drive and directory.
4. Key the adjusting entries. Key ADJ.ENT. in the reference field.
5. Display the adjusting entries. Key ADJ.ENT. in the Reference Restriction area of the Selection Options screen.
6. Display the financial statements.
7. Save a backup copy of your data file.
8. Perform period-end closing.
9. Display a post-closing trial balance.
10. Save your data file to disk.
11. End the session.

PROBLEM 8-6A
RETAIL METHOD; GROSS
PROFIT METHOD
Objective 8

Selected data on merchandise inventory, purchases, and sales for Wright Co. and C. F. Jones Co. are as follows:

	Cost	Retail
Wright Co.		
Merchandise inventory, January 1	$377,100	$579,100
Transactions during January:		
Purchases	186,600 ⎱	298,400
Purchases discounts	2,100 ⎰	
Sales		340,500
Sales returns and allowances		5,500
C. F. Jones Co.		
Merchandise inventory, July 1	$517,900	
Transactions during July and August:		
Purchases	425,500	
Purchases discounts	3,600	
Sales	570,250	
Sales returns and allowances	5,250	
Estimated gross profit rate	35%	

SPREADSHEET
PROBLEM

Instructions

1. Determine the estimated cost of the merchandise inventory of Wright Co. on January 31 by the retail method, presenting details of the computations.
2. a. Estimate the cost of the merchandise inventory of C. F. Jones Co. on August 31 by the gross profit method, presenting details of the computations.
   b. Assume that C. F. Jones Co. took a physical inventory on August 31 and discovered that $565,000 of merchandise was on hand. What was the estimated loss of inventory due to theft or damage during July and August?

PROBLEM 8-7A
PERCENTAGE-OF-
COMPLETION METHOD
Objective 10

Munoz Company began construction on three contracts during 1993. The contract prices and construction activities for 1993, 1994, and 1995 were as follows:

Contract	Contract Price	1993 Costs Incurred	1993 Percent Completed	1994 Costs Incurred	1994 Percent Completed	1995 Costs Incurred	1995 Percent Completed
1	$ 5,000,000	$1,810,000	40%	$1,575,000	35%	$1,090,000	25%
2	10,000,000	2,550,000	30	2,625,000	30	2,695,000	30
3	8,000,000	3,710,000	50	3,815,000	50	—	—

SPREADSHEET
PROBLEM

Instructions

Determine the amount of revenue and the income to be recognized for each of the years, 1993, 1994, and 1995. Revenue is to be recognized by the percentage-of-completion method.

Series B

PROBLEM 8-1B
FIFO PERPETUAL
INVENTORY
Objective 3

The beginning inventory of soybeans at SW Co-Op and data on purchases and sales for a three-month period are as follows:

Date	Transaction	Number of Bushels	Per Unit	Total
July 1	Inventory	25,000	$6.10	$152,500
10	Purchase	75,000	6.15	461,250
15	Sale	35,000	7.00	245,000
25	Sale	30,000	7.00	210,000
Aug. 8	Sale	10,000	7.10	71,000
12	Purchase	50,000	6.20	310,000
17	Sale	35,000	7.20	252,000
28	Sale	20,000	7.15	143,000
Sep. 5	Purchase	60,000	6.10	366,000
17	Sale	40,000	7.00	280,000
20	Purchase	30,000	6.00	180,000
30	Sale	45,000	7.00	315,000

Instructions

1. Record the inventory, purchases, and cost of merchandise sold data in a perpetual inventory record similar to the one illustrated in Exhibit 2 using the first-in, first-out method.
2. Determine the total sales and the total cost of soybeans sold for the period. Journalize the entries in the sales and cost of merchandise sold accounts. Assume that all sales were on account.
3. Determine the gross profit from sales of soybeans for the period.

PROBLEM 8-2B
LIFO PERPETUAL
INVENTORY
Objective 3

The beginning inventory of soybeans at SW Co-Op and data on purchases and sales for a three-month period are shown in Problem 8-1B.

Instructions

1. Record the inventory, purchases, and cost of merchandise sold data in a perpetual inventory record similar to the one illustrated in Exhibit 3 using the last-in, first-out method.
2. Determine the total sales, the total cost of soybeans sold, and the gross profit from sales for the period.

PROBLEM 8-3B
PERIODIC INVENTORY BY
THREE METHODS
Objective 4

A-1 Television uses the periodic inventory system. Details regarding the inventory of television sets at July 1, 1994, purchases invoices during the year, and the inventory count at June 30, 1995, are summarized as follows:

Model	Inventory, July 1	Purchases Invoices 1st	2d	3d	Inventory Count, June 30
A37	6 at $238	4 at $250	8 at $260	10 at $266	12
E15	6 at 77	5 at 82	8 at 89	8 at 99	10
L10	2 at 108	2 at 110	3 at 128	3 at 130	3
O18	8 at 88	4 at 79	3 at 85	6 at 92	8
K72	2 at 250	2 at 260	4 at 271	4 at 275	4
S91	5 at 160	4 at 170	4 at 175	7 at 180	8
V17	—	4 at 150	4 at 200	2 at 205	5

SPREADSHEET
PROBLEM
$

Instructions

1. Determine the cost of the inventory on June 30, 1995, by the first-in, first-out method. Present data in columnar form using the following headings:

Model	Quantity	Unit Cost	Total Cost

If the inventory of a particular model comprises one entire purchase plus a portion of another purchase acquired at a different unit cost, use a separate line for each purchase.

2. Determine the cost of the inventory on June 30, 1995, by the last-in, first-out method, following the procedures indicated in (1).
3. Determine the cost of the inventory on June 30, 1995, by the average cost method using the columnar headings indicated in (1).
4. Discuss which method (fifo or lifo) would be preferred for income tax purposes in periods of (a) rising prices and (b) declining prices.

PROBLEM 8-4B
LOWER-OF-COST-OR-
MARKET INVENTORY
Objective 6

If the working papers correlating with the textbook are not used, omit Problem 8-4B.

Data on the physical inventory of Klein Company as of December 31, the end of the current fiscal year, are presented in the working papers. The quantity of each commodity on hand has been determined and recorded on the inventory sheet. Unit market prices have also been determined as of December 31 and recorded on the sheet. The inventory is to be determined at cost and also at the lower of cost or market using the first-in, first-out method. Quantity and cost data from the last purchases invoice of the year and the next-to-the-last purchases invoice are summarized as follows:

Description	Last Purchases Invoice		Next-to-the-Last Purchases Invoice	
	Quantity Purchased	Unit Cost	Quantity Purchased	Unit Cost
A71	20	$ 60	30	$ 59
C22	25	210	20	205
D82	10	145	25	142
E34	150	25	100	24
F17	10	560	10	570
J19	100	15	100	14
K41	10	380	5	385
P21	500	6	500	6
R72	80	17	50	18
T15	5	250	4	260
V55	700	9	500	9
AC2	100	45	50	46
BB7	5	420	5	425
BD1	100	20	75	19
CC1	60	16	40	17
EB2	50	29	25	28
FF7	75	26	60	25
GE4	5	710	5	715

SPREADSHEET
PROBLEM

Instructions

Record the appropriate unit costs on the inventory sheet, and complete the pricing of the inventory. When there are two different unit costs applicable to an item, proceed as follows:
1. Draw a line through the quantity, and insert the quantity and unit cost of the last purchase.
2. On the following line, insert the quantity and unit cost of the next-to-the-last purchase. The first item on the inventory sheet has been completed as an example.

PROBLEM 8-5B
ADJUSTING ENTRIES;
FINANCIAL STATEMENTS
Objectives 6, 7

Boyd Imports is a distributor of imported motorcycles. Its unadjusted trial balance as of the end of the current fiscal year is as follows:

Cash	27,550	
Accounts Receivable	67,500	
Allowance for Doubtful Accounts		275
Merchandise Inventory	95,200	
Equipment	37,500	
Accumulated Depreciation—Equipment		20,000
Accounts Payable		24,500
Notes Payable		10,000
Capital Stock		25,000
Retained Earnings		61,675
Dividends	5,000	
Sales		850,200
Cost of Merchandise Sold	695,800	
Operating Expenses (controlling account)	63,200	
Rent Income		1,200
Interest Expense	1,100	
	992,850	992,850

Data needed for adjustments at December 31:
a. Merchandise inventory at December 31 is valued at lower of fifo cost or market. Boyd Imports uses a perpetual inventory system. The physical inventory on December 31 indicated an inventory shrinkage of $5,600.
b. Uncollectible accounts expense for current year, estimated at $1,900.
c. Depreciation of equipment for current year, $6,800.

Instructions
1. Journalize the necessary adjusting entries. All selling and administrative expenses are included in the operating expenses controlling account.
2. Prepare the following without the use of a conventional work sheet: (a) an income statement, (b) a retained earnings statement, and (c) a balance sheet in report form.

(Continued)

SOLUTIONS SOFTWARE

Instructions for Solving Problem 8-5B Using Solutions Software
1. Load the opening balances.
2. Enter your name in the Student Name field in the General Information data entry window. Set the run date to December 31 of the current year.
3. Save the opening balances file to your drive and directory.
4. Key the adjusting entries. Key ADJ.ENT. in the reference field.
5. Display the adjusting entries. Key ADJ.ENT. in the Reference Restriction area of the Selection Options screen.
6. Display the financial statements.
7. Save a backup copy of your data file.
8. Perform period-end closing.
9. Display a post-closing trial balance.
10. Save your data file to disk.
11. End the session.

PROBLEM 8-6B
RETAIL METHOD; GROSS
PROFIT METHOD
Objective 8

Selected data on merchandise inventory, purchases, and sales for Heims Co. and G. N. Palmer Co. are as follows:

	Cost	Retail
Heims Co.		
Merchandise inventory, July 1	$259,800	$370,000
Transactions during July:		
Purchases	366,840 ⎤	521,000
Purchases discounts	2,940 ⎦	
Sales		600,000
Sales returns and allowances		5,000
G. N. Palmer Co.		
Merchandise inventory, April 1	$317,500	
Transactions during April and May:		
Purchases	410,250	
Purchases discounts	5,250	
Sales	625,000	
Sales returns and allowances	5,000	
Estimated gross profit rate	40%	

SPREADSHEET PROBLEM

Instructions
1. Determine the estimated cost of the merchandise inventory of Heims Co. on July 31 by the retail method, presenting details of the computations.
2. a. Estimate the cost of the merchandise inventory of G. N. Palmer Co. on May 31 by the gross profit method, presenting details of the computations.
   b. Assume that G. N. Palmer Co. took a physical inventory on May 31 and discovered that $338,750 of merchandise was on hand. What was the estimated loss of inventory due to theft or damage during April and May?

PROBLEM 8-7B
PERCENTAGE-OF-
COMPLETION
METHOD
Objective 10

T. Rodriguez Company began construction on three contracts during 1993. The contract prices and construction activities for 1993, 1994, and 1995 were as follows:

Contract	Contract Price	1993 Costs Incurred	1993 Percent Completed	1994 Costs Incurred	1994 Percent Completed	1995 Costs Incurred	1995 Percent Completed
1	$ 6,000,000	$2,175,000	40%	$3,250,000	60%	—	—
2	4,000,000	600,000	20	1,375,000	40	$1,500,000	40%
3	3,500,000	455,000	15	985,000	30	1,575,000	50

Instructions
Determine the amount of revenue and the income to be recognized for each of the years, 1993, 1994, and 1995. Revenue is to be recognized by the percentage-of-completion method.

MINI-CASE GARVEY COMPANY

Garvey Company began operations in 1994 by selling a single product. Data on purchases and sales for the year were as follows:

Purchases

Date	Units Purchased	Unit Cost	Total Cost
April 5	5,000	$13.20	$ 66,000
May 2	5,000	14.00	70,000
June 4	5,000	14.20	71,000
July 10	5,000	15.00	75,000
August 7	3,000	15.25	45,750
October 5	2,000	15.50	31,000
November 1	1,000	15.75	15,750
December 10	1,000	17.00	17,000
	27,000		$391,500

Sales

April	2,000 units	September	3,500 units
May	2,000	October	2,250
June	3,500	November	2,250
July	4,000	December	1,000
August	3,500		

Total sales $454,000

On January 3, 1995, the president of the company, Laura Garvey, asked for your advice on costing the 3,000-unit physical inventory that was taken on December 31, 1994. Moreover, since the firm plans to expand its product line, she asked for your advice on the use of a perpetual inventory system in the future.

Instructions

1. Determine the cost of the December 31, 1994 inventory under the periodic system using the (a) first-in, first-out method, (b) last-in, first-out method, and (c) average cost method.
2. Determine the gross profit for the year under each of the three methods in (1).
3. a. ▇▇▇ ► In your opinion, which of the three inventory costing methods best reflects the results of operations for 1994? Why?
   b. ▇▇▇ ► In your opinion, which of the three inventory costing methods best reflects the replacement cost of the inventory on the balance sheet as of December 31, 1994? Why?
   c. ▇▇▇ ► Which inventory costing method would you choose to use for income tax purposes? Why?
   d. ▇▇▇ ► Discuss the advantages and disadvantages of using a perpetual inventory system. From the data presented in this case, is there any indication of the adequacy of inventory levels during the year?

ANSWERS TO SELF-EXAMINATION QUESTIONS

1. **D** The overstatement of inventory shrinkage by $7,500 at the end of the year will cause the cost of merchandise sold for the year to be overstated by $7,500, the gross profit for the year to be understated by $7,500, the merchandise inventory to be understated by $7,500, and the net income for the year to be understated by $7,500 (answer D).

2. **A** The fifo method (answer A) is based on the assumption that costs are charged against revenue in the order in which they were incurred. The lifo method (answer B) charges the most recent costs incurred against revenue, and the average cost method (answer C) charges a weighted average of unit costs of items sold against revenue. The perpetual inventory system (answer D) is a system that continuously discloses the amount of inventory.

3. **A** The lifo method of costing is based on the assumption that costs should be charged against revenue in the reverse order in which costs were incurred. Thus the old-est costs are assigned to inventory. Thirty of the 35 units would be assigned a unit cost of $20 (since 10 of the beginning inventory units were sold on the first sale), and the remaining 5 units would be assigned a cost of $23 (answer A).

4. **D** The fifo method of costing is based on the assumption that costs should be charged against revenue in the order in which they were incurred (first-in, first-out). Thus the most recent costs are assigned to inventory. The 35 units would be assigned a unit cost of $23 (answer D).

5. **B** When the price level is steadily rising, the earlier unit costs are lower than recent unit costs. Under the fifo method (answer B), these earlier costs are matched against revenue to yield the highest possible net income. The periodic inventory system (answer D) is a system and not a method of costing.

You and Accounting

Assume that your parents have offered to buy you a car for your 20th birthday, provided that you agree to pay all operating costs. You have found a 1980 Porsche 911 at a local car dealership. The sales manager has offered to sell you the car "as is" for $12,000. One of your friends who is a mechanic has inspected the car and has indicated that it needs a tune-up and new tires, shocks, and brakes. Should you ask your parents to pay for this mechanical work?

Normally, the cost of the car and the cost of getting it ready for use are costs of purchasing the car. Thus, you may be able to convince your parents to pay for the additional mechanical work. Once that work is completed, however, other mechanical work such as periodic tune-ups would normally be considered an operating cost.

In this chapter, you will read about issues similar to the preceding example. For example, business enterprises must determine and record the total cost of assets acquired. You will also read about other issues related to plant assets, such as accounting for costs that may significantly enhance or improve an asset after it is purchased.

Chapter 9
Plant Assets and Intangible Assets

In the prior chapters, we have discussed assets that are classified as current assets. Such assets include cash or assets that are expected to be realized in cash or sold or used up normally within one year. In this chapter, we describe and illustrate accounting principles and concepts for long-term assets of a relatively permanent nature. Such assets include land, buildings, equipment, patents, and copyrights. We also discuss the costs of acquiring such assets, accounting for their depreciation, depletion, or amortization, and accounting for their disposal.

LEARNING OBJECTIVES
After studying this chapter, you should be able to:

Objective 1
Define and give examples of plant assets and intangible assets.

Objective 2
Identify and list the costs of acquiring a plant asset.

Objective 3
Describe the nature of depreciation of plant assets.

Objective 4
Compute depreciation, using the following methods: straight-line, units-of-production, declining-balance, and sum-of-the-years-digits.

Objective 5
Compute depreciation, using the composite-rate method.

Objective 6
Classify plant asset costs as either capital expenditures or revenue expenditures.

Objective 7
Journalize entries for the disposal of plant assets.

Objective 8
Define a lease and summarize the accounting rules related to the leasing of plant assets.

Objective 9
Describe internal controls over plant assets and provide examples of such controls.

Objective 10
Compute depletion and journalize the entry for depletion.

Objective 11
Journalize the entries for acquiring and amortizing intangible assets, such as patents, copyrights, and goodwill.

Objective 12
Describe how depreciation expense is reported in an income statement and prepare a balance sheet that includes plant assets and intangible assets.

Objective 13
Describe the arguments for and against reporting replacement cost for plant assets.

NATURE OF PLANT ASSETS AND INTANGIBLE ASSETS

Objective 1
Define and give examples of plant assets and intangible assets.

Plant assets are long-term or relatively permanent tangible assets that are used in the normal business operations. They are owned by the enterprise and are not held for sale in the ordinary course of business. Other descriptive titles for such assets are **fixed assets** or **property, plant, and equipment**. These assets may also be described in more specific terms, such as equipment, furniture, tools, machinery, buildings, and land.

Long-term assets that are without physical attributes and not held for sale but are useful in the operations of an enterprise are classified as **intangible assets**. Intangible assets include such items as patents, copyrights, and goodwill.

There is no standard rule as to the minimum length of life necessary for an asset to be classified as a plant asset or an intangible asset. Such assets must be capable of repeated use or benefit and are normally expected to last more than a year. However, an asset need not actually be used on an ongoing basis or even often. For example, items of standby equipment held for use in the event of a breakdown of regular equipment or for use only during peak periods of activity are included in plant assets.

Assets acquired for resale in the normal course of business are not classified as plant assets, regardless of their permanent nature or the length of time they are held. For example, undeveloped land or other real estate acquired as an investment for resale should be listed on the balance sheet in the asset section entitled *Investments*.

COSTS OF ACQUIRING PLANT ASSETS

Objective 2
Identify and list the costs of acquiring a plant asset.

What is included in the cost of a plant asset? The cost of acquiring a plant asset includes all expenditures necessary to get it in place and ready for use. For example sales tax, transportation charges, insurance while in transit, special foundations, and installation costs should be added to the asset's purchase price in determining the cost of a plant asset. Similarly, when a secondhand asset is purchased, the initial costs of getting it ready for use, such as expenditures for new parts, repairs, and painting, should be included as part of the asset cost. These expenditures should be debited to the asset account. On the other hand, costs related to acquiring a plant asset should be excluded from the asset account if they are not necessary for getting the asset ready for use and thus do not increase the asset's usefulness. For example, costs resulting from errors in installing an asset, from vandalism, or from other unusual occurrences do not increase the usefulness of the asset and should be treated as an expense.

The cost of constructing a building includes the fees paid to architects and engineers for plans and supervision. In addition, insurance incurred during construction and all other necessary expenditures related to the project are included in the cost of the building. Generally, interest incurred during the construction period on money borrowed to finance construction should also be treated as part of the cost of the building.[1]

The cost of land includes not only the negotiated price but also broker's commissions, title fees, surveying fees, and other expenditures of obtaining title. If delinquent real estate taxes are paid by the buyer, they also are charged to the land account. If unwanted buildings are located on land acquired for a plant site, the cost of their razing or removal, less any salvage recovered, is a cost of the land. The cost of leveling or otherwise changing the contour of the land is also a cost of the land.

Other expenditures related to land may be charged to Land, Buildings, or Land Improvements, depending upon the nature of the expenditure. If a prop-

---

[1] *Statement of Financial Accounting Standards, No. 34*, "Capitalization of Interest Cost" (Stamford: Financial Accounting Standards Board, 1979), par. 6.

erty owner pays for the initial cost of paving a public street bordering the land, either by direct payment or by special tax assessment, the paving may be considered part of the cost of the land. On the other hand, the cost of constructing walkways to and around a building may be added to the cost of the building if the walkways are expected to last only as long as the building. Expenditures for improvements that are neither as permanent as the land nor directly related to a building may be set apart in a land improvements account. Some of the more usual items of this nature are trees and shrubs, fences, outdoor lighting, and paved parking areas.

NATURE OF DEPRECIATION

Objective 3
Describe the nature of depreciation of plant assets.

As time passes, all plant assets except land lose their ability to provide services.[2] As a result, the cost of a plant asset should be transferred to an expense account, in a systematic manner, during the asset's expected useful life. This periodic cost expiration is called **depreciation**.

Factors that cause a decline in the ability of a plant asset to provide services may be divided into two categories. First, physical depreciation caused by wear and tear from use and from the action of the elements decreases usefulness. Second, functional depreciation caused by inadequacy and obsolescence decreases usefulness. A plant asset becomes inadequate if its capacity is not able to meet the demands of increased production. A plant asset is obsolete if the item that it produces is no longer in demand or if a newer machine can produce an item of better quality at the same or a lower cost. Advances in technology during this century have made obsolescence an increasingly important cause of depreciation.

The meaning of the term *depreciation* as used in accounting is often misunderstood because the same term is also used in business to mean a decline in the market value of an asset. However, the amount of a plant asset's unexpired cost reported in the balance sheet usually does not agree with the amount that could be realized from its sale. Plant assets are held for use in an enterprise rather than for sale. It is assumed that the enterprise will continue as a **going concern**. Thus, a decision to dispose of a plant asset is based mainly on the usefulness of the asset to the enterprise and not on its market value.

Another common misunderstanding is that depreciation accounting provides cash needed to replace plant assets as they wear out. The cash account is neither increased nor decreased by the periodic entries that transfer the cost of plant assets to depreciation expense accounts. The misunderstanding probably occurs because depreciation, unlike most expenses, does not require an outlay of cash in the period in which it is recorded.

Using Accounting

Although depreciation is a major expense for many business enterprises, it does not require an immediate outlay of cash. However, depreciable plant assets must eventually be replaced in order for the enterprise to remain in operation. In evaluating the liquidity of a business enterprise, bankers and other creditors rely upon the statement of cash flows. The most common method of preparing this statement adds back depreciation to net income in determining cash flows from operations. This latter figure provides users with an indication of the ability of the enterprise to meet its liabilities, some of which may be incurred in acquiring plant assets.

[2] As discussed in this section, land is assumed to be used only as a location or site. Land acquired for its mineral deposits or other natural resources will be considered later in the chapter.

ACCOUNTING FOR DEPRECIATION

Objective 4
Compute depreciation, using the following methods:

Straight-line method
Units-of-production method
Declining-balance method
Sum-of-the-years-digits method

Three factors are considered in determining the amount of depreciation expense to be recognized each period. These three factors are the (a) plant asset's initial cost, (b) its expected useful life, and (c) its estimated value at the end of its useful life. This third factor is called the **residual value, scrap value, salvage value,** or **trade-in value.** Exhibit 1 shows the relationship among the three factors and the periodic depreciation expense.

Exhibit 1
Factors that Determine
Depreciation Expense

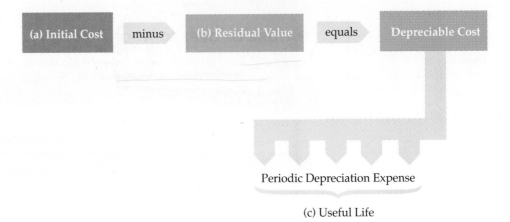

If a plant asset is expected to have no residual value at the time that it is taken out of service, then its initial cost should be spread over its expected useful life as depreciation expense. Also, if a plant asset's estimated residual value at the time it is taken out of service is expected to be very small compared to the cost of the asset, this value may be ignored and the entire cost spread over the asset's expected useful life. If a plant asset is expected to have a significant residual value, the difference between its initial cost and this value is the cost (called **depreciable cost**) that should be spread over the asset's useful life as depreciation expense.

Neither *the period of usefulness* of a plant asset nor its *residual value* at the end of that period can be accurately determined until the asset is taken out of service. However, in determining the amount of the periodic depreciation, these two related factors must be estimated at the time the asset is placed in service. There are no set rules for estimating either factor, and both factors may be affected by management policies. For example, a company that provides its salespersons with a new automobile every year will have different estimates than a company that keeps its cars for five years. Such variables as climate, use, and maintenance will also affect the estimates.

Where can we find estimates of the useful life of plant assets? Estimates are available from various trade association and other publications. For federal income tax purposes, the Internal Revenue Service has also established guidelines for useful lives. These guidelines may also be helpful in determining depreciation for financial reporting purposes.

In addition to the many factors that may affect the useful life of an asset, various degrees of accuracy may be used in the computations. A month is normally the smallest unit of time used. When this period of time is used, all assets placed in or taken out of service during the first half of a month are treated as if the event occurred on the first day of that month. Likewise, all plant asset additions and deductions during the second half of a month are treated as if the event occurred on the first day of the next month. In the absence of any statement to the contrary, this practice is assumed throughout this chapter.

It is not necessary that an enterprise use a single method of computing depreciation for all its depreciable assets. The methods used in the accounts and financial statements may also differ from the methods used in determining income taxes and property taxes. The four methods used most often are: (1) straight-line, (2) units-of-production, (3) declining-balance, and (4) sum-of-the-years-digits. Exhibit 2 shows the extent of the use of these methods in financial statements.

Exhibit 2
Use of Depreciation Methods

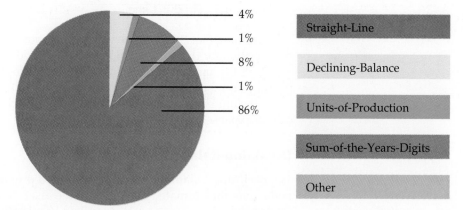

Source: *Accounting Trends & Techniques*, 46th ed. (New York: American Institute of Certified Public Accountants, 1992).

Straight-Line Method

The **straight-line depreciation method** provides for equal amounts of periodic expense over the estimated useful life of the asset. For example, assume that the cost of a depreciable asset is $16,000, its estimated residual value is $1,000, and its estimated life is 5 years. The annual depreciation is computed as follows:

$$\frac{\$16,000 \text{ cost} - \$1,000 \text{ estimated residual value}}{5 \text{ years estimated life}} = \$3,000 \text{ annual depreciation}$$

When an asset is used for only part of a year, the annual depreciation is prorated. For example, assume that the fiscal year ends on December 31 and that the asset in the above example is first used on October 15. The depreciation for the first fiscal year of use would be $750 ($3,000 × 3/12), computed on the basis of 3 months. If usage had begun on October 16, the depreciation for the year would have been $500 ($3,000 × 2/12).

For ease in applying the straight-line method, the annual depreciation may be converted to a percentage of depreciable cost. This percentage is determined by dividing 100 by the number of years of useful life. For example, a useful life of 20 years converts to a 5% (100 ÷ 20) rate, 8 years converts to a 12.5% (100 ÷ 8) rate, and so on.[3] To further illustrate, the straight-line rate in the above example is 20% (100 ÷ 5). The annual depreciation of $3,000 can be computed by multiplying the depreciable cost of $15,000 by this rate.

The straight-line method is simple and is widely used. It provides a reasonable allocation of costs to periodic expense when the usage of the asset and the related revenues from its use are about the same from period to period.

Units-of-Production Method

The **units-of-production depreciation method** yields depreciation expense that varies with the amount of the asset's usage. In applying this method, the useful life of the asset is expressed in terms of units of productive capacity, such as hours or miles. Depreciation is first computed for each unit of production. The total depreciation expense for each accounting period is then determined by multiplying

[3] The depreciation rate may also be expressed as a fraction. For example, the annual straight-line rate for an asset with a 3-year useful life is ⅓.

the unit depreciation by the number of productive units used during the period. For example, assume that a machine with a cost of $16,000 and an estimated residual value of $1,000 is expected to have an estimated life of 10,000 operating hours. The depreciation for a unit of one hour is computed as follows:

$$\frac{\$16,000 \text{ cost} - \$1,000 \text{ estimated residual value}}{10,000 \text{ estimated hours}} = \$1.50 \text{ hourly depreciation}$$

Assuming that the machine was in operation for 2,200 hours during a year, the depreciation for that year would be $3,300 ($1.50 × 2,200 hours).

When the amount of use of a plant asset varies from year to year, the units-of-production method is more appropriate than the straight-line method. In such cases, the units-of-production method better matches the allocation of cost (depreciation expense) with the related revenue.

Declining-Balance Method

The **declining-balance depreciation method** provides for a declining periodic expense over the estimated useful life of the asset. To apply this method, the annual straight-line depreciation rate described previously is doubled. For example, the declining-balance rate for an asset with an estimated life of 5 years is 40%—double the straight-line rate of 20% (100 ÷ 5).

This rate is then multiplied by the cost of the asset for the first year of use. After the first year, the rate is multiplied by the declining **book value** (cost minus accumulated depreciation) of the asset. To illustrate, the annual declining-balance depreciation for an asset with an estimated 5-year life and a cost of $16,000 is shown below.

Year	Cost	Accum. Depr. at Beginning of Year	Book Value at Beginning of Year	Rate	Depreciation for Year	Book Value at End of Year
1	$16,000	—	$16,000.00	40%	$6,400.00	$9,600.00
2	16,000	$ 6,400.00	9,600.00	40%	3,840.00	5,760.00
3	16,000	10,240.00	5,760.00	40%	2,304.00	3,456.00
4	16,000	12,544.00	3,456.00	40%	1,382.40	2,073.60
5	16,000	13,926.40	2,073.60	40%	829.44	1,244.16

You should note that when the declining-balance method is used, the estimated residual value is not considered in determining the depreciation rate. It is also ignored in computing the periodic depreciation, except that the asset should not be depreciated below its estimated residual value. In the above example, it was assumed that the estimated residual value at the end of the fifth year approximates the book value of $1,244.16. If the estimated residual value were $1,500, the depreciation for the fifth year would have been $573.60 ($2,073.60 – $1,500.00) instead of $829.44.

In the example above, the first use of the asset is assumed to have occurred at the beginning of the fiscal year. This is normally not the case in practice, however, and depreciation for the first partial year of use must be computed. For example, assume that the asset above had been placed in service at the end of the third month of the fiscal year. In this case, only a portion (9/12) of the first full year's depreciation of $6,400 is allocated to the first fiscal year. Thus, depreciation of $4,800 (9/12 × $6,400) is allocated to the first partial year of use. The method of computing the depreciation for the following years would not be affected. Thus, the depreciation for the second fiscal year would be $4,480 [40% × ($16,000 – $4,800)].

Sum-of-the-Years-Digits Method

Under the **sum-of-the-years-digits depreciation method**, depreciation expense is determined by multiplying the original cost of the asset less its estimated residual value by a smaller fraction each year. Thus, the sum-of-the-years-digits method is similar to the declining-balance method, in that the depreciation expense declines each year.

The denominator of the fraction used in determining the depreciation expense is the sum of the digits of the years of the asset's useful life. For example, an asset with a useful life of 5 years would have a denominator of 15 (5 + 4 + 3 + 2 + 1).[4] The numerator of the fraction is the number of years of useful life remaining at the beginning of each year for which depreciation is being computed. Thus, the numerator decreases each year by 1. For a useful life of 5 years, the numerator is 5 the first year, 4 the second year, 3 the third year, and so on.

The following depreciation schedule illustrates the sum-of-the-years-digits method for an asset with a cost of $16,000, an estimated residual value of $1,000, and an estimated useful life of 5 years:

Year	Cost Less Residual Value	Rate	Depreciation for Year	Accum. Depr. at End of Year	Book Value at End of Year
1	$15,000	5/15	$5,000	$ 5,000	$11,000
2	15,000	4/15	4,000	9,000	7,000
3	15,000	3/15	3,000	12,000	4,000
4	15,000	2/15	2,000	14,000	2,000
5	15,000	1/15	1,000	15,000	1,000

What if the plant asset is not placed in service at the beginning of the year? When the date an asset is first put into service is not the beginning of a fiscal year, each full year's depreciation must be allocated between the two fiscal years benefited. To illustrate, assume that the asset in the above example was put into service at the beginning of the fourth month of the first fiscal year. The depreciation for that year would be $3,750 ($9/12 \times 5/15 \times $15,000$). The depreciation for the second year would be $4,250, computed as follows:

$3/12 \times 5/15 \times $15,000$	$1,250
$9/12 \times 4/15 \times $15,000$	3,000
Total depreciation for second fiscal year	$4,250

Comparing Depreciation Methods

The straight-line method provides for uniform periodic charges to depreciation expense over the life of the asset. The units-of-production method provides for periodic charges to depreciation expense that vary, depending upon the amount of usage of the asset.

Both the declining-balance and the sum-of-the-years-digits methods provide for a higher depreciation charge in the first year the asset is used, followed by a gradually declining periodic charge. For this reason, these methods are frequently called accelerated depreciation methods. They are most appropriate for situations in which the decline in an asset's productivity or earning power is greater in the early years of its use than in later years. Further, using these methods is often justified because repairs tend to increase with the age of an asset. The reduced amounts of depreciation in later years are thus offset to some extent by increased repairs expenses.

Exhibit 3 compares the periodic depreciation charges for the straight-line method and the accelerated methods. This comparison is based on an asset cost of $16,000, an estimated life of 5 years, and an estimated residual value of $1,000.

---

[4] The denominator can also be determined from the following formula: $S = N[(N + 1)/2]$, where S = sum of the digits and N = number of years of estimated life.

Exhibit 3
Comparison of Depreciation
Methods

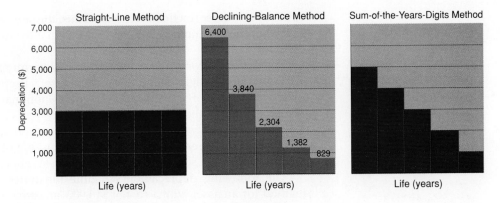

Depreciation for Federal Income Tax

Can a business enterprise choose any depreciation method it wishes for tax purposes? No, each of the four depreciation methods we described in the preceding paragraphs could be used to determine depreciation expense for federal income tax purposes for plant assets acquired prior to 1981. The two accelerated depreciation methods (declining-balance and sum-of-the-years-digits) are widely used for tax purposes. Acceleration of the *write-off* of the asset reduces the income tax liability in the earlier years. Thus, the amount of cash available to pay for the asset or for other purposes is increased in those years.

For plant assets acquired after 1980 and before 1987, either the straight-line method or the Accelerated Cost Recovery System (ACRS) could be used for federal income tax purposes. ACRS provided for depreciation deductions that were similar to those that would be computed using the 150-percent declining-balance method.[5] For most business property, ACRS provided for three classes of useful life. Each class of useful life was often much shorter than the actual useful life of the asset in that class.

Under the Tax Reform Act of 1986, Modified ACRS (MACRS) provides for eight classes of useful life for plant assets acquired after 1986. The two most common classes, other than real estate, are the 5-year class and the 7-year class.[6] The 5-year class includes automobiles and light-duty trucks, and the 7-year class includes most machinery and equipment. The depreciation deduction for these two classes approximates the use of the declining-balance method using twice the straight-line rate.

The Internal Revenue Service has prescribed methods that use annual percentages (rates) in determining depreciation for each class of asset. In using these rates, residual value is ignored, and all plant assets are assumed to be put in service in the middle of the year and taken out of service in the middle of the year. Thus, for the 5-year-class assets, for example, depreciation is spread over six years, as shown in the following MACRS schedule of depreciation rates:

Year	5-Year-Class Depreciation Rates
1	20.0%
2	32.0
3	19.2
4	11.5
5	11.5
6	5.8
	100.0%

[5] The 150-percent declining-balance method uses 150% of the straight-line rate, in contrast to double the straight-line rate (or 200%) as illustrated earlier in this chapter for the declining-balance method.
[6] Real estate is classified into 27½-year classes and 31½-year classes and is depreciated by the straight-line method.

Two (Legal) Sets of Books

Many companies use one method of depreciation for financial reporting purposes (frequently the straight-line method) and a different method of depreciation for income tax purposes (often an accelerated method). The advantages of maintaining two sets of accounts is addressed in the following excerpt from an article in *The Wall Street Journal*:

When you're dealing with the tax folks, quick depreciation . . . of equipment outlays makes a lot of sense. It cuts . . . profits and [therefore cuts] taxes . . . . [Such a policy also] leaves more cash for other uses. But good tax strategy can be bad business strategy.

David A. Tonneson, a Wakefield, Mass., accountant who specializes in advising small businesses, says the biggest mistake his clients make is to immediately deduct too much from profits [for depreciation of] equipment and installation costs. This results in undervalued [bases for] assets and makes borrowing more funds or selling the company more difficult. Small start-up

companies would be wiser to [spread depreciation over future years more evenly]. Though this boosts reported income [in the early years], it boosts their asset base, permitting them to borrow more and sell their concern for more.

Mr. Tonneson says one of his clients lost a chance for a $1 million contract because it had used accelerated depreciation for its equipment. Using straight-line depreciation, the equipment would have been valued on the books at $525,000, or enough to collateralize a $420,000 loan from a bank. But after accelerated depreciation, the books only showed the equipment at $300,000, so the bank would supply only a $240,000 loan. The company needed $400,000 to gear up for the new order. It lost the sale.

Many new small-business owners aren't aware that they can use accelerated depreciation [MACRS] to report income to the tax authorities but can keep their asset [book] values up by using straight-line depreciation to report to shareholders. . . . While this does entail keeping two sets of books, "it's well worth it."

Source: Lee Berton, "Dos and Don'ts," *The Wall Street Journal* (June 10, 1988), p. 34R.

Revision of Periodic Depreciation

Earlier in this chapter, we indicated that two of the factors that must be considered in computing the periodic depreciation of a plant asset are (1) its estimated residual value and (2) its estimated useful life. These factors must be estimated at the time the asset is placed in service. Revisions of these estimates are normal and tend to be recurring. When such revisions occur, the revised estimates are used to determine the depreciation expense to be charged to future periods.

To illustrate, assume that a plant asset was purchased for $130,000, was originally estimated to have a useful life of 30 years, and was estimated to have a residual value of $10,000. The asset has been depreciated for 10 years by the straight-line method. At the end of ten years, the asset's book value (undepreciated cost) is $90,000, determined as follows:

Asset cost	$130,000
Less accumulated depreciation ($4,000 per year × 10 years)	40,000
Book value (undepreciated cost), end of tenth year	$ 90,000

During the eleventh year, it is estimated that the remaining useful life is 25 years (instead of 20) and that the residual value is $5,000 (instead of $10,000). The depreciation expense for each of the remaining 25 years is $3,400, computed as follows:

Book value (undepreciated cost), end of tenth year	$90,000
Less revised estimated residual value	5,000
Revised remaining depreciable cost	$85,000
Revised annual depreciation expense ($85,000 ÷ 25)	$ 3,400

You should note that the revisions of the estimates used in determining depreciation does not affect the amounts of depreciation expense recorded in earlier years. The use of estimates and the resulting revisions of such estimates are inherent in the accounting process. Therefore, when such revisions are made, the amounts recorded for depreciation expense in the past are not corrected. Only future depreciation expense amounts are affected.[7]

Recording Depreciation

Depreciation may be recorded by an entry at the end of each month or an adjustment at the end of the year. As we discussed in an earlier chapter, the entry to record depreciation is a debit to Depreciation Expense and a credit to a contra asset account entitled Accumulated Depreciation or Allowance for Depreciation. The use of a contra asset account allows the original cost to remain unchanged in the plant asset account. This amount is useful for computing periodic depreciation, preparing the balance sheet presentation of both cost and accumulated depreciation, and reporting for property tax and income tax purposes.

An exception to recording depreciation only monthly or annually is made when a plant asset is sold, traded in, or scrapped. As we will illustrate, a disposal is recorded by removing from the accounts both the cost of the asset and its related accumulated depreciation as of the date of the disposal. Depreciation for the current period should be recorded before the disposal of the asset is recorded.

Subsidiary Ledgers for Plant Assets

When depreciation is computed on a large number of individual assets, a subsidiary ledger is usually maintained. For example, assume that an enterprise owns 200 items of office equipment with a total cost of $100,000. Unless the business is new, the equipment would have been acquired over a number of years. The individual cost, estimated residual value, and estimated useful life would be different in each case. In addition, the makeup of the assets will continually change because of acquisitions and disposals.

The subsidiary records for depreciable assets may be maintained by a manual system or a computerized system. In either case, a separate ledger account may be maintained for each asset. The subsidiary ledger account shown in Exhibit 4 provides spaces for recording the acquisition and the disposal of the asset, the depreciation charged each period, the accumulated depreciation to date, and the book value. Other relevant data useful to management may also be included.

Exhibit 4
An Account in the Office Equipment Ledger

PLANT ASSET RECORD

Account No.: 123-215   General Ledger Account: Office Equipment
Item: SF 490 Copier
Serial No.: AT 47-3926
From Whom Purchased: Hamilton Office Machines Co.
Estimated Useful Life: 10 Years   Estimated Residual Value: $500   Depr. per Year: $240

Date	Asset Debit	Asset Credit	Asset Balance	Accum. Depr. Debit	Accum. Depr. Credit	Accum. Depr. Balance	Book Value
04/08/93	2,900		2,900				2,900
12/31/93					180	180	2,720
12/31/94					240	420	2,480

The number assigned to the account in Exhibit 4 is made up of the number of the controlling account in the general ledger, Office Equipment (123), followed by the number assigned to the specific item of office equipment purchased (215). A tag or plaque with the account number is attached to the asset for control purposes. Depreciation for the year in which the asset was acquired, computed for

[7] The correction of material or large errors made in computing depreciation in prior periods is discussed in a later chapter.

nine months on a straight-line basis, is $180. Depreciation for the following year is $240. The subsidiary ledger can therefore provide the data for the adjusting entries for depreciation at the end of each year.

When an asset is disposed of, the asset section of the subsidiary account is credited and the accumulated depreciation section is debited. Thus the balances of both sections are reduced to zero. The account is then removed from the ledger and filed for future reference.

Subsidiary ledgers for plant assets are useful to accountants in (1) determining periodic depreciation expense, (2) recording the disposal of individual items, (3) preparing tax returns, and (4) preparing insurance claims in the event of insured losses. The subsidiary account forms may also be expanded for accumulating data on the operating efficiency of the asset. Such information as number of breakdowns, length of time out of service, and cost of repairs may be useful to management. For example, when new equipment is to be purchased, these data may be useful in deciding upon size, model, and the best vendor.

Depreciation of Plant Assets of Low Unit Cost

Subsidiary ledgers are not usually maintained for classes of plant assets that are made up of individual items of low unit cost. Examples of such items are hand tools and other small portable equipment, dies, molds, patterns, and spare parts. Because of hard usage, breakage, and pilferage, such assets may be relatively short-lived and may require frequent replacement.

For plant assets with a low unit cost, the usual depreciation methods are generally not practical. One method of accounting for such assets is to treat them as expenses when they are acquired. Another method of accounting for assets with a low unit cost is to treat them as assets when they are acquired. Then, at the end of the year, an inventory of the items on hand is taken and their current value is estimated. The difference between this value and the assets' original cost or last year's value is debited to an expense account and credited to the plant asset account.

COMPOSITE-RATE DEPRECIATION METHOD

Objective 5
Compute depreciation, using the composite-rate method.

In the preceding examples, we computed depreciation for each individual plant asset. This procedure is normally used in the exercises and problems at the end of this chapter. Another method, called the composite-rate depreciation method, determines depreciation for groups of assets, using a single rate. The basis for grouping may be estimates of useful lives or other common traits. The groupings may be expanded to include all assets within a class, such as office equipment or factory equipment.

When depreciation is computed on the basis of a group of assets with differing useful lives, a rate based on an average must be developed. This rate is computed by (1) determining the annual depreciation for each asset, (2) determining the total annual depreciation, and (3) dividing the total annual depreciation by the total cost of the assets. An example of the composite-rate method is shown below.

Asset No.	Cost	Estimated Residual Value	Estimated Life	Annual Depreciation
101	$ 20,000	$4,000	10 years	$ 1,600
102	15,600	1,500	15 years	940
147	41,000	1,000	8 years	5,000
Total	$473,400			$49,707

$$\frac{\$49,707 \text{ annual depreciation}}{\$473,400 \text{ cost}} = 10.5\% \text{ composite rate}$$

Although new assets of differing useful lives and residual values will be added to the group and old assets will be taken out of service, the *mix* is assumed to remain relatively unchanged. Thus, the depreciation rate based on averages (10.5% in the example) also remains unchanged for an indefinite time in the future.

A composite rate can be applied to the total asset cost on a monthly basis, or some reasonable assumption regarding the timing of increases and decreases in the group may be made. A common practice is to assume that all additions and disposals occur uniformly throughout the year. The average of the beginning and the ending balances of the asset account is then multiplied by the composite rate. Another approach is to assume that all additions and disposals during the first half of the year occur as of the first day of the year. All additions and disposals during the second half of the year are then assumed to have occurred on the first day of the following year.

When assets within the composite group are taken out of service, no gain or loss is recognized. Instead, the asset account is credited for the cost of the asset, and the accumulated depreciation account is debited for the excess of the cost over the amount realized from the disposal. Any deficiency in the amount of depreciation recorded on the shorter-lived assets is presumed to be balanced by excessive depreciation on the longer-lived assets.

CAPITAL AND REVENUE EXPENDITURES

Objective 6
Classify plant asset costs as either capital expenditures or revenue expenditures.

The costs of acquiring plant assets, adding to plant assets, and adding utility to plant assets for more than one accounting period are called **capital expenditures**. Such expenditures are either debited to the asset account or debited to the related accumulated depreciation account. Costs that benefit only the current period or costs incurred in order to maintain normal operating efficiency are called **revenue expenditures**. Such expenditures are debited to expense accounts.

It is important for a business to distinguish between capital and revenue expenditures so that its revenues and expenses are properly matched. Capital expenditures will affect the depreciation expense of more than one period, while revenue expenditures will affect the expenses of only the current period.

Capital Expenditures

We discussed accounting for the initial costs of acquiring plant assets earlier in the chapter. In the following paragraphs, we discuss accounting for capital expenditures after a plant asset has been acquired—(a) additions, (b) betterments, and (c) extraordinary repairs.

ADDITIONS TO PLANT ASSETS. An expenditure for an addition to a plant asset should be debited to the related plant asset account. The cost of an addition should be depreciated over the estimated useful life of the addition. For example, the cost of adding an air conditioning system to a building or of adding a wing to a building should be accounted for as a capital expenditure.

BETTERMENTS. An expenditure that increases the operating efficiency or capacity for the remaining useful life of a plant asset is called a **betterment**. Such an expenditure should be debited to the related plant asset account. For example, if the power unit attached to a machine is replaced by one of greater capacity, the cost should be debited to the machine account. Also, the cost and the accumulated depreciation related to the old power unit should be removed from the accounts. The cost of the new power unit is depreciated over its estimated useful life or the remaining useful life of the machine, whichever is shorter.

EXTRAORDINARY REPAIRS. An expenditure that increases the useful life of an asset beyond its original estimate is called an **extraordinary repair**. Such an expenditure should be debited to the related accumulated depreciation account. In such cases, the repairs are said to restore or *make good* a portion of the depreciation accumulated in prior years. The depreciation for future periods should be computed on the basis of the revised book value of the asset and the revised estimate of the remaining useful life.

To illustrate, assume that a machine costing $50,000 has no estimated residual value and an estimated useful life of 10 years. Assume also that the machine has been depreciated for 6 years by the straight-line method ($5,000 annual depreciation). At the beginning of the seventh year, an $11,500 extraordinary repair increases the remaining useful life of the machine to 7 years (instead of 4). The repair of $11,500 should be debited to Accumulated Depreciation. The annual depreciation for the remaining 7 years of use would be $4,500, computed as follows:

Cost of machine		$50,000
Less Accumulated Depreciation balance:		
Depreciation for first 6 years ($5,000 × 6)	$30,000	
Deduct debit for extraordinary repairs	11,500	
Balance of Accumulated Depreciation		18,500
Revised book value of machine after extraordinary repair		$31,500
Annual depreciation ($31,500 ÷ by 7 years remaining useful life)		$ 4,500

Revenue Expenditures

Expenditures for normal maintenance and repairs are classified as revenue expenditures. For example, the cost of replacing spark plugs in an automobile or the cost of repainting a building should be debited to expense accounts.

Small expenditures that are insignificant in amount are also normally debited to repair expense accounts, even though they may have the qualities of capital expenditures. The saving in time and record-keeping effort justifies the small loss of accuracy. Some businesses establish a minimum dollar amount required to classify an item as a capital expenditure.

Summary of Capital and Revenue Expenditures

Exhibit 5 summarizes the accounting for capital and revenue expenditures related to plant assets.

Exhibit 5
Capital and Revenue
Expenditures

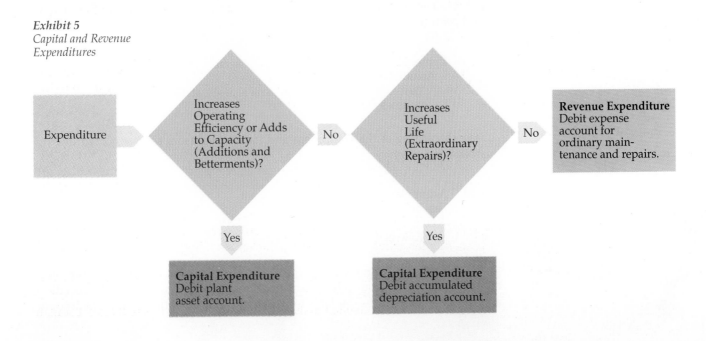

DISPOSAL OF PLANT ASSETS

Plant assets that are no longer useful may be discarded, sold, or traded for other plant assets. The details of the entry to record a disposal will vary. In all cases, however, the book value of the asset must be removed from the accounts. The entry for this purpose is a debit to the asset's accumulated depreciation account for its balance on the date of disposal and a credit to the asset account for the cost of the asset.

It is important to note that a plant asset should not be removed from the accounts only because it has been fully depreciated. If the asset is still used by the enterprise, the cost and accumulated depreciation should remain in the ledger. This maintains accountability for the asset in the ledger. If the book value of the asset were removed from the ledger, the accounts would contain no evidence of the continued existence of the asset. In addition, the cost and the accumulated depreciation data on such assets are often needed for property tax and income tax reports.

Discarding Plant Assets

When plant assets are no longer useful to the business and have no residual or market value, they are discarded. If the asset has been fully depreciated, no loss is realized. For example, assume that an item of equipment acquired at a cost of $25,000 is fully depreciated at December 31, the end of the preceding fiscal year. On February 14, the equipment is discarded as worthless. The entry to record the discarding of the asset is as follows:

Feb. 14	Accumulated Depreciation—Equipment	25,000	
	Equipment		25,000
	To write off equipment discarded.		

You should be careful to note that the depreciation for a plant asset must be brought up to date prior to removing it from service. In the preceding example, the equipment was fully depreciated at the end of the preceding fiscal year. If, however, the asset had not been fully depreciated, depreciation should be recorded prior to removing the asset from service and from the accounting records.

To illustrate, assume that equipment costing $6,000 is depreciated at an annual straight-line rate of 10%. In addition, assume that on December 31 of the preceding fiscal year, the accumulated depreciation balance, after adjusting entries, is $4,750. Finally, assume that the asset is removed from service on the following March 24. The entry to record the depreciation for the three months of the current period prior to the asset's removal from service is as follows:

Mar. 24	Depreciation Expense—Equipment	150	
	Accumulated Depreciation—Equipment		150
	To record current depreciation on equipment discarded ($600 × 3/12).		

The discarding of the equipment and its removal from service is recorded by the following entry:

Mar. 24	Accumulated Depreciation—Equipment	4,900	
	Loss on Disposal of Plant Assets	1,100	
	Equipment		6,000
	To write off equipment discarded.		

In the preceding example, a loss of $1,100 is recorded. A loss on the discarding of a plant asset will occur whenever the balance of the accumulated depreciation account ($4,900 in this example) is less than the balance in the equipment account

($6,000 in this example). Losses on the discarding of plant assets are nonoperating items and are normally reported in the Other expense section of the income statement.

Sale of Plant Assets

The entry to record the sale of a plant asset is similar to the entries illustrated above, except that the cash or other asset received must also be recorded. If the selling price is more than the book value of the asset, the transaction results in a gain. If the selling price is less than the book value, there is a loss.

To illustrate, assume that equipment is acquired at a cost of $10,000 and is depreciated at an annual straight-line rate of 10%. The equipment is sold for cash on October 12 of the eighth year of its use. The balance of the accumulated depreciation account as of the preceding December 31 is $7,000. The entry to update the depreciation for the nine months of the current year is as follows:

Oct. 12	Depreciation Expense—Equipment	750	
	Accumulated Depreciation—Equipment		750
	To record current depreciation on equipment sold ($10,000 × 3/4 × 10%).		

After the current depreciation is recorded, the book value of the asset is $2,250 ($10,000 − $7,750). The entries to record the sale, assuming three different selling prices, are as follows:

Sold at book value, for $2,250. No gain or loss.	Oct. 12	Cash	2,250	
		Accumulated Depreciation—Equipment	7,750	
		Equipment		10,000

Sold below book value, for $1,000. Loss of $1,250.	Oct. 12	Cash	1,000	
		Accumulated Depreciation—Equipment	7,750	
		Loss on Disposal of Plant Assets	1,250	
		Equipment		10,000

Sold above book value, for $3,000. Gain of $750.	Oct. 12	Cash	3,000	
		Accumulated Depreciation—Equipment	7,750	
		Equipment		10,000
		Gain on Disposal of Plant Assets		750

Exchanges of Similar Plant Assets

Old equipment is often traded in for new equipment having a similar use. The trade-in allowance is deducted from the price of the new equipment, and the balance owed is paid according to the credit terms. This balance is often called **boot**. The trade-in allowance granted by the seller may be greater or less than the book value of the old equipment traded in.

GAINS ON EXCHANGES. At one time, it was acceptable to recognize gains on exchanges of similar plant assets. For example, a trade-in allowance of $1,500 on equipment with a book value of $1,000 would have resulted in a gain of $500. However, such gains are no longer recognized for financial reporting purposes. This is based on the theory that revenue occurs from the production and sale of goods produced by plant assets and not from the exchange of similar plant assets.

When the trade-in allowance exceeds the book value of an asset traded in and no gain is recognized, the cost of the new asset is the amount of boot given plus the book value of the old asset. For example, assume the following exchange:

Similar equipment acquired (new):

Price of new equipment	$5,000
Trade-in allowance on old equipment	1,100
Boot given (cash)	$3,900

Equipment traded in (old):

Cost of old equipment	$4,000	
Accumulated depreciation at date of exchange	3,200	
Book value at June 19, date of exchange		**800**
Cost of new equipment		$4,700

The entry to record this exchange and the assumed payment of cash is as follows:

June 19	Accumulated Depreciation—Equipment	3,200	
	Equipment	4,700	
	Equipment		4,000
	Cash		3,900

Not recognizing the $300 gain ($1,100 trade-in allowance minus $800 book value) at the time of the exchange reduces future depreciation expense. That is, the depreciation expense for the new asset is based on a cost of $4,700 rather than on the quoted price of $5,000. In effect, the unrecognized gain of $300 reduces the total amount of depreciation taken during the life of the equipment by $300.

In exchanges as described above, gains are also not recognized for federal income tax purposes. Specifically, the Internal Revenue Code (IRC) does not recognize gains when (1) the asset acquired by the taxpayer is similar in use to the asset given in exchange and (2) any boot involved is given (rather than received) by the taxpayer. Thus, in the above example, the cost of the new equipment for federal income tax purposes is $4,700.

LOSSES ON EXCHANGES. If the trade-in allowance is less than the book value of the old equipment, losses are recognized. To illustrate, assume the following exchange:

Similar equipment acquired (new):

Price of new equipment	$10,000
Trade-in allowance on old equipment	2,000
Boot given (cash)	$ 8,000

Equipment traded in (old):

Cost of old equipment	$ 7,000
Accumulated depreciation at date of exchange	4,600
Book value at September 7, date of exchange	$ 2,400

The amount of the loss recognized on the exchange is the excess of the book value of the equipment traded in ($2,400) over the trade-in allowance ($2,000), or $400. The entry to record the exchange is as follows:

Sep. 7	Accumulated Depreciation—Equipment	4,600	
	Equipment	10,000	
	Loss on Disposal of Plant Assets	400	
	Equipment		7,000
	Cash		8,000

For federal income tax purposes, losses are not recognized when (1) the asset acquired by the taxpayer is similar in use to the asset given in exchange and (2) any boot involved is given (rather than received) by the taxpayer. The cost of the new equipment is determined by adding the boot given to the book value of the equipment traded in. In the above example, the cost of the new equipment for federal income tax purposes is determined as follows:

Book value of equipment traded in	$ 2,400	
Boot given (cash)	8,000	
Cost of new equipment	$10,400	

The unrecognized loss of $400 at the time of the exchange increases the cost of the new equipment. Thus, the total amount of depreciation expense increases by $400 during the useful life of the equipment.

SUMMARY OF ACCOUNTING FOR EXCHANGES. Exhibit 6 summarizes the accounting for exchanges of similar plant assets for financial and income tax reporting, based on the following data:

Exhibit 6
Summary Illustration—
Accounting for Exchanges of
Similar Plant Assets

Quoted price of new equipment acquired	$15,000
Cost of old equipment traded in	$12,500
Accumulated depreciation at date of exchange	10,100
Book value at date of exchange	$ 2,400

CASE ONE (GAIN): Trade-in allowance is more than book value of asset traded in.
Trade-in allowance, $3,000; boot given, $12,000 ($15,000 – $3,000)

	Financial Reporting	Income Tax Reporting
Cost of new asset	Boot plus book value of asset traded in, $14,400 ($12,000 + $2,400)	Boot plus book value of asset traded in, $14,400 ($12,000 + $2,400)
Gain recognized	None	None

Entry	Equipment 14,400
	Accumulated Depreciation 10,100
	  Equipment 12,500
	  Cash 12,000
		Equipment 14,400
		Accumulated Depreciation 10,100
		  Equipment 12,500
		  Cash 12,000

CASE TWO (LOSS): Trade-in allowance is less than book value of asset traded in.
Trade-in allowance, $2,000; boot given, $13,000 ($15,000 – $2,000)

	Financial Reporting	Income Tax Reporting
Cost of new asset	Quoted price of new asset acquired, $15,000	Boot plus book value of asset traded in, $15,400 ($13,000 + $2,400)
Loss recognized	$400	None

Entry	Equipment 15,000
	Accumulated Depreciation 10,100
	Loss on disposal 400
	  Equipment 12,500
	  Cash 13,000
		Equipment 15,400
		Accumulated Depreciation 10,100
		  Equipment 12,500
		  Cash 13,000

LEASING PLANT ASSETS

Objective 8
Define a lease and summarize the accounting rules related to the leasing of plant assets.

You are probably familiar with leases. Instead of owning a plant asset, a business may acquire the use of a plant asset through a lease. For example, automobiles, computers, and airplanes are often leased. A **lease** is a contract for the use of an asset for a stated period of time. The two parties to a lease contract are the lessor and the lessee. The **lessor** is the party who owns the asset. The **lessee** is the party to whom the rights to use the asset are granted by the lessor. The lessee is obligated to make periodic rent payments for the lease term.

All leases are classified by the lessee as either capital leases or operating leases. **Capital leases** include one or more of the following elements:

1. The lease transfers ownership of the asset to the lessee at the end of the lease term.
2. The lease contains an option for a bargain purchase of the asset by the lessee.
3. The lease term extends over most of the economic life of the asset.
4. The lease requires rental payments that approximate the fair market value of the asset.[8]

A capital lease is accounted for as if the lessee has, in fact, purchased the asset. Thus, under a capital lease, the lessee debits an asset account for the fair market value of the asset. The offsetting credit is to a long-term lease liability account. The accounting for capital leases is discussed in detail in more advanced accounting texts.

Leases that do not meet the preceding criteria for a capital lease are classified as **operating leases**. The lease payments under an operating lease are accounted for as rent expense by the lessee. The rentals of assets described in the earlier chapters of this text were accounted for as operating leases. Neither future lease obligations nor the future rights to use the asset are recognized in the accounts. However, the lessee must disclose future lease commitments in footnotes to the financial statements.[9]

INTERNAL CONTROL OF PLANT ASSETS

Objective 9
Describe internal controls over plant assets and provide examples of such controls.

Because of the dollar value and the long-term nature of plant assets, it is important to design and implement effective internal controls over plant assets. Such controls should begin with authorization and approval procedures for the purchase of plant assets. Procedures should also exist to ensure that plant assets are acquired at the lowest possible costs. One procedure to achieve this objective is to require competitive bids from preapproved vendors.

Like the assets we discussed in earlier chapters, plant assets should be safeguarded from possible theft, misuse, or other damage. For example, plant assets that are highly marketable and susceptible to theft, such as computers, should be locked or otherwise safeguarded when not in use. Likewise, procedures should exist for training employees to properly operate plant assets such as equipment and machinery. Plant assets should also be insured against theft, fire, flooding, or other disasters.

As soon as a plant asset is received, it should be inspected and tagged for control purposes and an entry made in the plant asset subsidiary ledger. A company that maintains a computerized subsidiary ledger may use bar-coded tags, similar to the one on the back of this textbook, so that plant asset data can be directly scanned into computer records.

A physical inventory of plant assets should be taken periodically in order to verify the accuracy of the accounting records. Such an inventory would detect missing, obsolete, or idle plant assets. In addition, plant assets should be inspected periodically in order to determine their state of repair.

Careful control should also be exercised over the disposal of plant assets. All disposals should be properly authorized and approved. Fully depreciated assets should be retained in the accounting records until disposal has been authorized and they are removed from service. In this way, accountability for the asset is maintained throughout the period of ownership.

---

[8] *Statement of Financial Accounting Standards, No. 13*, "Accounting for Leases" (Stamford: Financial Accounting Standards Board, 1976), par. 7.
[9] *Ibid.*, par. 16.

DEPLETION

Objective 10
Compute depletion and
journalize the entry for
depletion.

The periodic allocation of the cost of metal ores and other minerals removed from the earth is called **depletion.** This allocation to expense is based upon a depletion rate that is computed by dividing the cost of the mineral deposit by its estimated size. The amount of periodic depletion is determined by multiplying the quantity extracted during the period by the depletion rate.

To illustrate, assume that an enterprise paid $400,000 for the mining rights to a mineral deposit estimated at 1,000,000 tons of ore. The depletion rate is $.40 per ton ($400,000 ÷ 1,000,000 tons). If 90,000 tons are mined during the year, the periodic depletion is $36,000 (90,000 tons × $.40). The entry to record the depletion is shown below.

	Adjusting Entry		
Dec. 31	Depletion Expense	36,000	
	Accumulated Depletion		36,000

Like the accumulated depreciation account, the accumulated depletion account is a contra asset account. It is reported on the balance sheet as a deduction from the cost of the mineral deposit.

In determining income subject to the federal income tax, complex Internal Revenue Code (IRC) rules regarding depletion deductions must be applied. In some cases, it is possible for the total depletion deductions to be more than the cost of the property. You can find a detailed discussion of the tax law and the regulations regarding depletion in tax textbooks.

INTANGIBLE ASSETS

Objective 11
Journalize the entries for
acquiring and amortizing
intangible assets, such as patents,
copyrights, and goodwill.

The basic principles of accounting for intangible assets are like those described earlier for plant assets. The major concerns are (1) determining the initial cost and (2) recognizing the periodic cost expiration, called **amortization.** Amortization results from the passage of time or a decline in the usefulness of the intangible asset. In the following paragraphs, we discuss these concerns as they affect patents, copyrights, and goodwill.

Patents

Manufacturers may acquire exclusive rights to produce and sell goods with one or more unique features. Such rights are granted by **patents,** which the federal government issues to inventors. These rights continue in effect for 17 years. An enterprise may purchase patent rights from others, or it may obtain patents developed by its own research and development efforts.

The initial cost of a purchased patent should be debited to an asset account. This cost should be written off, or amortized, over the years of the patent's expected usefulness. This period of time may be less than the remaining legal life of the patent. The estimated useful life of the patent may also change as technology or consumer tastes change. The straight-line method of amortization is used unless it can be shown that another method is better.[10]

A separate contra asset account is normally not credited for the write-off or amortization of patents. The credit is normally recorded directly in the patents account. This practice is common for all intangible assets.

To illustrate, assume that at the beginning of its fiscal year an enterprise acquires patent rights for $100,000. The patent had been granted 6 years earlier by the Federal Patent Office. Although the patent will not expire for 11 years, its re-

[10] *Opinions of the Accounting Principles Board, No. 17,* "Intangible Assets" (New York: American Institute of Certified Public Accountants, 1970), par. 30.

maining useful life is estimated as 5 years. The entry to amortize the patent at the end of the fiscal year is as follows:

Adjusting Entry		
Dec. 31	Amortization Expense—Patents	20,000	
	Patents		20,000

Assume that after two years of use it appears that this patent will have only two years of remaining usefulness. The cost to be amortized in the third year is $30,000, which is the balance of the asset account, $60,000 ($100,000 – $40,000), divided by two years.

Rather than purchase patent rights, an enterprise may incur significant costs in developing patents through its own research and development efforts. Such costs, called **research and development costs**, are accounted for as current operating expenses in the period in which they are incurred.[11]

The expensing of research and development costs in the period they are incurred is justified for two reasons. First, there is a high degree of uncertainty about the future benefits from research and development efforts. In fact, most research and development efforts do not result in patents. Second, even if a patent is granted, it may be difficult to objectively estimate its cost. If many research projects are in process at the same time, for example, it is difficult to separate the costs of one project from another.

Whether patent rights are purchased or developed internally, an enterprise often incurs significant legal fees related to patents. For example, legal fees may be incurred in filing for patents or in defending the legal rights to patents. Such fees should be debited to an asset account and then amortized over the years of usefulness of the patents.

Copyrights

The exclusive right to publish and sell a literary, artistic, or musical composition is granted by a **copyright**. Copyrights are issued by the federal government and extend for 50 years beyond the author's death. The costs of a copyright include all costs of creating the work plus any administrative or legal costs of obtaining the copyright. A copyright that is purchased from another should be recorded at the price paid for it. Because of the uncertainty regarding the useful life of a copyright, it is normally amortized over a short period of time.

Goodwill

In business, goodwill refers to an intangible asset of an enterprise that is created from such favorable factors as location, product quality, reputation, and managerial skill. Goodwill allows an enterprise to earn a rate of return on its investment that is often in excess of the normal rate for other firms in the same business.

Generally accepted accounting principles permit the recording of goodwill in the accounts only if it is objectively determined by a transaction. An example of such a transaction is the purchase or sale of a business. In addition, goodwill should be amortized over its estimated useful life. The estimated useful life of goodwill, however, cannot exceed 40 years.[12]

FINANCIAL REPORTING FOR PLANT ASSETS AND INTANGIBLE ASSETS

Objective 12
Describe how depreciation expense is reported in an income statement and prepare a balance sheet that includes plant assets and intangible assets.

How should plant assets and intangible assets be reported in the financial statements? The amount of depreciation and amortization expense of a period should be reported separately in the income statement or disclosed in a footnote. A gen-

---

[11] *Statement of Financial Accounting Standards, No. 2,* "Accounting for Research and Development Costs" (Stamford: Financial Accounting Standards Board, 1974), par. 12.
[12] *Opinions of the Accounting Principles Board, No. 17,* "Intangible Assets," *op. cit.,* par. 29.

eral description of the method or methods used in computing depreciation should also be reported.[13]

The balance of each major class of plant assets should be disclosed in the balance sheet or in footnotes. The related accumulated depreciation should also be disclosed, either by major class or in total.[14] If there are too many classes of plant assets, a single amount may be presented in the balance sheet, supported by a separate detailed listing.

Intangible assets are usually reported in the balance sheet in a separate section immediately following plant assets. The balance of each major class of intangible assets should be disclosed at an amount net of amortization taken to date.

Exhibit 7 is a partial balance sheet that shows the reporting of plant assets and intangible assets.

Exhibit 7
Plant Assets and Intangible Assets in the Balance Sheet

Clinton Door Co.
Balance Sheet
December 31, 19—
Assets

	Cost	Accumulated Depreciation	Book Value	
Total current assets				$462,500
Plant assets:				
Land	$ 30,000	—	$ 30,000	
Buildings	110,000	$ 26,000	84,000	
Factory equipment	650,000	192,000	458,000	
Office equipment	120,000	13,000	107,000	
Total plant assets	$910,000	$231,000		679,000
Intangible assets:				
Patents			$ 75,000	
Goodwill			$ 50,000	
Total intangible assets				125,000

REPLACEMENT COST OF PLANT ASSETS

Objective 13
Describe the arguments for and against reporting replacement cost for plant assets.

In preceding illustrations, we recorded plant assets at the cost actually incurred in acquiring them (historical cost), and we based depreciation on this cost. This principle is generally accepted for financial reporting purposes. The basic financial statements, therefore, do not indicate the effect of changes in price levels on plant assets and depreciation. In periods of inflation, which have been common in the past, many accountants have questioned the usefulness of financial statements that ignore the effects of inflation on operations.

To indicate the nature of the problem, assume that plant assets acquired by an enterprise ten years ago for $1,000,000 are now to be replaced with similar assets which, at present price levels, will cost $2,000,000. Assume further that during the ten-year period the plant assets had been fully depreciated and that the net income of the enterprise had amounted to $5,000,000. Although the initial outlay of $1,000,000 for the plant assets was recovered through depreciation charges, the amount represents only one half of the cost of replacing the assets. Instead of considering the current value of the new assets to have doubled compared to a decade earlier, the dollars recovered have declined to one half of their earlier value. From either point of view, the firm has suffered a loss in purchas-

[13] *Opinions of the Accounting Principles Board, No. 22,* "Disclosure of Accounting Policies" (New York: American Institute of Certified Public Accountants, 1972), par. 13.
[14] *Opinions of the Accounting Principles Board, No. 12,* "Omnibus Opinion—1967" (New York: American Institute of Certified Public Accountants, 1967), par. 5.

ing power, which is the same as a loss of capital. In addition, $1,000,000 of the net income reported during the period is illusory, since it must be used to replace the assets.

Using historical cost in accounting for plant assets ensures objectivity. Therefore, in spite of inflationary trends, historical-cost financial statements are considered to be better than statements based on movements in the price level. Many accountants, however, recommend that businesses provide supplemental information that indicates the replacement cost, or current cost, of plant assets and the depreciation based on such cost. This supplemental information would match current costs for depreciation against current revenues. It would therefore give a net income figure that would be useful in evaluating operating results. For example, a net income figure determined after considering plant asset depreciation based on replacement cost would be especially useful in evaluating the amount of net income available for dividends.

There are many obstacles to using replacement costs in accounting for plant assets. For many businesses, such as a steel company with its many buildings and special machinery and equipment, it would be difficult to determine replacement costs with reasonable accuracy. In addition, if replacement costs were used, the process of estimating costs would have to be repeated each year, which would further increase the subjectivity of the accounting method. For reasons such as these, the use of replacement costs in accounting for plant assets has been generally restricted to experimental situations involving supplementary data.

Replacement Costs for Assets

Over the years, there has been much discussion and controversy over the relevance of using original cost for reporting plant assets on the balance sheet and for determining depreciation expense for the income statement. The Securities and Exchange Commission views on this topic are addressed in the following excerpts from an article in *The Wall Street Journal:*

Under federal law, the SEC has the mandate to determine accounting principles for publicly traded companies. But it has generally ceded that authority to private-sector accounting bodies such as the Financial Accounting Standards Board. However, the SEC may now be shaking up the world of accounting.

Although no one is suggesting that the SEC will revamp financial statements altogether, it wants to force companies to go a long way toward putting up-to-date values on assets currently on their books at historical cost—the original purchase price. It has launched an aggressive campaign in Congress and with the accounting profession to get fast action. . . .

At the root of SEC's new zeal are lessons drawn from the thrift [savings and loan] crisis. [SEC Chairman Richard C.] Breeden cites 1978 numbers that show the thrift industry with a positive net worth. But a harder look—using current instead of historical accounting—shows that the industry was already ailing, with a negative net worth of as much as $118 billion. . . .

A major advantage of historical-cost accounting, . . . argues [John Robbins, a managing partner at the accounting firm of Kenneth Leventhal & Co.], is that value is determined by competing interests—a buyer and a seller agreeing on a price. Rely-

ing on a company's current valuation requires appraisals. "There's only one danger with doing an appraisal: Believing it," he says. The wild real-estate appraisals emerging from the devastated thrift industry have increased that anxiety.

But that hasn't stopped some companies from relying more heavily on internal systems of current accounting. "We may not be accurate in our current cost estimates," says David G. Harmer, FMC Corp.'s comptroller, "but we're a hell of a lot closer than erroneous historical-cost basis. We know [those] are understated." . . .

Mr. Harmer cites a metal-fabrication press, which bends and shapes metal. To determine the replacement cost of a press bought in 1982 for $522,000, the company would add 19%—the change in the wholesale price index over the seven years—to arrive at a replacement cost of $621,000.

Since the company assumes that the press has a 12-year life, it then would deduct depreciation from both numbers, putting the replacement value at $257,000. That's still 19% higher than what accounting rules force the company to show on its books. . . .

. . . FMC's numbers . . . also show why many companies oppose the plan: FMC estimates that 1989 operating profit (before interest expense and taxes), reported at $347 million, would have been 10% to 15% lower using current-cost accounting. . . .

. . . SEC [Commissioner Philip] Lochner sees [some other] stumbling block[s]. "What is the current value of Coca-Cola's trademarks? Your guess is as good as theirs," he says. "But we all know it's worth more than the $1 or so it's carried for on Coke's books." (Actually, it's on the books at zero.) . . .

Source: Kevin G. Salwen and Robin Goldwyn Blumenthal, "What's It Worth? Tackling Accounting, SEC Pushes Changes with Broad Impact," *The Wall Street Journal* (September 27, 1990), p. 1.

CHAPTER REVIEW

Key Points

Objective 1. Define and give examples of plant assets and intangible assets.

Plant assets are long-term tangible assets that are owned by the enterprise and are used in the normal operations of the business. Examples of plant assets are equipment, buildings, and land. Long-term assets that are without physical attributes but are used in the business are classified as intangible assets. Examples of intangible assets are patents, copyrights, and goodwill.

Objective 2. Identify and list the costs of acquiring a plant asset.

The initial cost of a plant asset includes all expenditures necessary to get it in place and ready for use. For example, sales tax, transportation charges, insurance in transit, special foundations, and installation costs are all included in the cost of a plant asset.

Objective 3. Describe the nature of depreciation of plant assets.

Depreciation recognizes that, as time passes, all plant assets except land lose their ability to provide services. As a result, the cost of a plant asset should be transferred to an expense account, in a systematic manner, during the asset's expected useful life. This periodic cost expiration is called depreciation.

Objective 4. Compute depreciation, using the following methods: straight-line method, units-of-production method, declining-balance method, and sum-of-the-years-digits method.

In computing depreciation, three factors need to be considered: (1) the plant asset's initial cost, (2) the useful life of the asset, and (3) the residual value of the asset.

The straight-line method spreads the initial cost less the residual value equally over the useful life. The units-of-production method spreads the initial cost less the residual value equally over the units expected to be produced by the asset during its useful life.

The declining-balance method is applied by multiplying the declining book value of the asset by twice the straight-line rate. The sum-of-the-years-digits method is applied by multiplying the cost less the residual value by a smaller fraction each year.

Objective 5. Compute depreciation, using the composite-rate method.

Depreciation is computed under the composite-rate method by using a single rate for a group of assets.

Objective 6. Classify plant asset costs as either capital expenditures or revenue expenditures.

Costs for additions to plant assets and other costs related to improving efficiency or capacity are classified as capital expenditures. Costs for additions to an asset and costs that add to the utility of the asset for more than one period (called betterments) are also classified as capital expenditures. Also, costs that increase the useful life of an asset beyond the original estimate are a type of capital expenditure and are called extraordinary repairs. Expenditures that benefit only the current period or that maintain normal operating efficiency are debited to expense accounts and are classified as revenue expenditures.

Objective 7. Journalize entries for the disposal of plant assets.

The journal entries to record disposals of plant assets will vary. In all cases, however, any depreciation for the current period should be recorded, and the book value of the asset is then removed from the accounts. The entry to remove the book value from the accounts is a debit to the asset's accumulated depreciation account and a credit to the asset account for the cost of the asset. For assets retired from service, a loss may be recorded for any remaining book value of the asset.

When a plant asset is sold, the book value is removed and the cash or other asset received is also recorded. If the selling price is more than the book value of the asset, the transaction results in a gain. If the selling price is less than the book value, there is a loss.

When a plant asset is exchanged for another of similar nature, no gain is recognized on the exchange. The acquired asset's cost is adjusted for any gains. A loss on an exchange of similar assets is recorded.

Objective 8. Define a lease and summarize the accounting rules related to the leasing of plant assets.

A lease is a contract for the use of an asset for a period of time. A capital lease is accounted for as if the lessee has purchased the asset. The lease payments under an operating lease are accounted for as rent expense for the lessee.

Objective 9. Describe internal controls over plant assets and provide examples of such controls.

Internal controls over plant assets should include procedures for authorizing the purchase of assets. Once acquired, plant assets should be safeguarded from theft, misuse, or damage. A physical inventory of plant assets should be taken periodically.

Objective 10. Compute depletion and journalize the entry for depletion.

The amount of periodic depletion is computed by multiplying the quantity of minerals extracted during the period by a depletion rate. The depletion rate is computed by dividing the cost of the mineral deposit by its estimated size. The entry to record depletion debits a depletion expense account and credits an accumulated depletion account.

Objective 11. Journalize the entries for acquiring and amortizing intangible assets, such as patents, copyrights, and goodwill.

The initial cost of an intangible asset should be debited to an asset account. This cost should be written off, or amortized, over the years of the asset's expected usefulness by debiting an expense account and crediting the intangible asset account.

Objective 12. Describe how depreciation expense is reported in an income statement and prepare a balance sheet that includes plant assets and intangible assets.

The amount of depreciation expense and the method or methods used in computing depreciation should be disclosed in the financial statements. In addition, each major class of plant assets should be disclosed, along with the related accumulated depreciation. Intangible assets are usually presented in the balance sheet in a separate section immediately following plant assets. Each major class of intangible assets should be disclosed at an amount net of the amortization recorded to date.

Objective 13. Describe the arguments for and against reporting replacement cost for plant assets.

Plant assets are recorded at cost, and depreciation is based on this cost for financial reporting purposes. However, many accountants recommend that businesses provide supplemental information that indicates the replacement cost, or current cost, of plant assets and the depreciation based on such costs. Such supplemental information would be especially useful in evaluating operating results in periods of inflation.

Glossary of Key Terms

Accelerated depreciation methods. Depreciation methods that provide for a high depreciation expense in the first year of use of an asset and a gradually declining expense thereafter. **Objective 4**

Amortization. The periodic expense attributed to the decline in usefulness of an intangible asset. **Objective 11**

Betterment. An expenditure that increases operating efficiency or capacity for the remaining useful life of a plant asset. **Objective 6**

Boot. The balance owed the supplier when an old asset is traded for a new asset. **Objective 7**

Capital expenditures. Costs that add to the utility of assets for more than one accounting period. **Objective 6**

Capital leases. Leases that include one or more of four provisions that result in treating the leased assets as purchased assets in the accounts. **Objective 8**

Composite-rate depreciation method. A method of depreciation based on the use of a single rate that applies to entire groups of assets. **Objective 5**

Declining-balance depreciation method. A method of depreciation that provides declining periodic depreciation expense over the estimated life of an asset. **Objective 4**

Depletion. The cost of metal ores and other minerals removed from the earth. **Objective 10**

Depreciation. The periodic cost expiration for the use of all plant assets except land. **Objective 3**

Extraordinary repair. An expenditure that increases the useful life of an asset beyond the original estimate. **Objective 6**

Goodwill. An intangible asset that attaches to a business as a result of such favorable factors as location, product superiority, reputation, and managerial skill. **Objective 11**

Intangible assets. Long-lived assets that are useful in the operations of an enterprise, are not held for sale, and are without physical qualities. **Objective 1**

Operating leases. Leases that do not meet the criteria for capital leases and thus are accounted for as operating expenses. **Objective 8**

Plant assets. Relatively permanent tangible assets used in the operations of a business enterprise. **Objective 1**

Residual value. The estimated recoverable cost of a depreciable asset as of the time of its removal from service. **Objective 4**

Revenue expenditures. Expenditures that benefit only the current period. **Objective 6**

Straight-line depreciation method. A method of depreciation that provides for equal periodic depreciation expense over the estimated life of an asset. **Objective 4**

Sum-of-the-years-digits depreciation method. A method of depreciation that provides for declining periodic depreciation expense over the estimated life of an asset. **Objective 4**

Units-of-production depreciation method. A method of depreciation that provides for depreciation expense based on the expected productive capacity of an asset. **Objective 4**

Self-Examination Questions
Answers at end of chapter.

1. Which of the following expenditures incurred in connection with the acquisition of machinery is a proper charge to the asset account?
   A. Transportation charges   C. Both A and B
   B. Installation costs   D. Neither A nor B

2. What is the amount of depreciation, using the sum-of-the-years-digits method, for the first year of use for equipment costing $9,500, with an estimated residual value of $500 and an estimated life of 3 years?
   A. $4,500   B. $3,166.67   C. $3,000   D. $2,500

3. An example of an accelerated depreciation method is:
   A. straight-line   C. units-of-production
   B. sum-of-the-years-digits   D. composite-rate

4. A plant asset priced at $100,000 is acquired by trading in a similar asset that has a book value of $25,000. Assuming that the trade-in allowance is $30,000 and that $70,000 cash is paid for the new asset, what is the cost of the new asset for financial reporting purposes?
   A. $100,000   C. $70,000
   B. $95,000   D. $30,000

5. Which of the following is an example of an intangible asset?
   A. Patents   C. Copyrights
   B. Goodwill   D. All of the above

ILLUSTRATIVE PROBLEM

Florence Company acquired new equipment at a cost of $75,000 at the beginning of the fiscal year. The equipment has an estimated life of 5 years and an estimated residual value of $6,000. Patrick Florence, the president, has requested information regarding alternative depreciation methods.

Instructions

1. Determine the annual depreciation for each of the five years of estimated useful life of the equipment, the accumulated depreciation at the end of each year, and the book value of the equipment at the end of each year by (a) the straight-line method, (b) the declining-balance method (at twice the straight-line rate), and (c) the sum-of-the-years-digits method.
2. Assume that the equipment was depreciated under the declining-balance method. In the first week of the fifth year, the equipment was traded in for similar equipment priced at $90,000. The trade-in allowance on the old equipment was $8,000, and cash was paid for the balance.
   a. Journalize the entry to record the exchange.
   b. What is the cost basis of the new equipment for computing the amount of depreciation allowable for income tax purposes?

Solution

1.

	Year	Depreciation Expense	Accumulated Depreciation, End of Year	Book Value, End of Year
a.	1	$13,800	$13,800	$61,200
	2	13,800	27,600	47,400
	3	13,800	41,400	33,600
	4	13,800	55,200	19,800
	5	13,800	69,000	6,000
b.	1	$30,000	$30,000	$45,000
	2	18,000	48,000	27,000
	3	10,800	58,800	16,200
	4	6,480	65,280	9,720
	5	3,720*	69,000	6,000
c.	1	$23,000	$23,000	$52,000
	2	18,400	41,400	33,600
	3	13,800	55,200	19,800
	4	9,200	64,400	10,600
	5	4,600	69,000	6,000

*The asset is not depreciated below the estimated residual value of $6,000.

2.

a.
Accumulated Depreciation—Equipment	65,280	
Equipment	90,000	
Loss on Disposal of Plant Assets	1,720	
Equipment		75,000
Cash		82,000

b.
Book value of old equipment	$ 9,720
Boot given (cash)	82,000
Cost basis of new equipment for income tax purposes	$91,720

DISCUSSION QUESTIONS

1. Which of the following qualities are characteristic of plant assets? (a) tangible, (b) intangible, (c) capable of repeated use in the operations of the business, (d) held for sale in the normal course of business, (e) used continuously in the operations of the business, (f) long-lived.
2. Tols Office Equipment Co. has a fleet of automobiles and trucks for use by salespersons and for delivery of office supplies and equipment. Holmes Auto Sales Co. has automobiles and trucks for sale. Under what caption would the automobiles and trucks be reported on the balance sheet of (a) Tols Office Equipment Co., (b) Holmes Auto Sales Co.?
3. W. C. Simons Co. acquired an adjacent vacant lot with the hope of selling it in the future at a gain. The lot is not intended to be used in Simons' business operations. Where should such real estate be listed in the balance sheet?
4. Tomlin Company solicited bids from several contractors to construct an addition to its office building. The lowest bid received was for $120,000. Tomlin Company decided to construct the addition itself at a cost of $105,000. What amount should be recorded in the building account?
5. Which of the following expenditures incurred in acquiring factory equipment should be debited to the asset account? (a) sales tax on purchase price, (b) transportation charges, (c) insurance while in transit, (d) cost of special foundation, (e) new parts to replace those damaged in unloading, (f) fee paid to factory representative for installation.
6. Which of the following expenditures incurred in purchasing a secondhand printing press should be debited to the asset account? (a) transportation charges, (b) installation costs, (c) repair of vandalism damage that occurred during installation, (d) replacement of worn-out parts.
7. To increase its parking area, Pineridge Shopping Center acquired adjoining land for $95,000 and a building located on the land for $50,000. The net cost of razing the building and leveling the land was $10,000, after amounts received from the sale of salvaged building materials were deducted. What accounts should be debited for (a) the cost of the land ($95,000), (b) the cost of the building ($50,000), (c) the net cost of preparing the land ($10,000)?
8. Are the amounts at which plant assets are reported in the balance sheet their approximate market values as of the balance sheet date? Discuss.
9. a. Does the recognition of depreciation in the accounts provide a special cash fund for the replacement of plant assets? Explain.
   b. Describe the nature of depreciation as the term is used in accounting.
10. Name the three factors that need to be considered in determining the amount of periodic depreciation.
11. West Company purchased a machine that has a manufacturer's suggested life of 12 years. The company plans to use the machine on a special project that will last 4 years. At the completion of the project, the machine will be sold. Over how many years should the machine be depreciated?
12. Is it necessary for an enterprise to use the same method of computing depreciation (a) for all classes of its depreciable assets, (b) in the financial statements and in the determination of income taxes?
13. Of the four common depreciation methods, which is most widely used?
14. A plant asset with a cost of $87,500 has an estimated residual value of $7,500 and an estimated useful life of 4 years. What is the amount of the annual depreciation computed by the straight-line method?
15. A plant asset with a cost of $95,000 has an estimated residual value of $5,000 and an estimated productive capacity of 600,000 units. What is the amount of depreciation computed by the units-of-production method for a year in which production is (a) 60,000 units, (b) 40,000 units?
16. Convert each of the following estimates of useful life to a straight-line depreciation rate, stated as a percentage, assuming that the residual value of the plant asset is to be ignored: (a) 4 years, (b) 5 years, (c) 10 years, (d) 20 years, (e) 25 years, (f) 40 years, (g) 50 years.
17. The declining-balance method, at double the straight-line rate, is to be used for an asset with a cost of $100,000, estimated residual value of $10,000, and estimated useful life of 10 years. What is the depreciation for the first fiscal year, assuming that the asset was placed in service at the beginning of the year?

18. An asset with a cost of $26,000, an estimated residual value of $1,000, and an estimated useful life of 4 years is to be depreciated by the sum-of-the-years-digits method. (a) What is the denominator of the depreciation fraction? (b) What is the amount of depreciation for the first full year of use? (c) What is the amount of depreciation for the second full year of use?

19. a. Under what conditions is the use of an accelerated depreciation method most appropriate?

    b. Why are the accelerated depreciation methods used frequently for income tax purposes?

    c. What is the Modified Accelerated Cost Recovery System (MACRS), and under what conditions is it used?

20. A plant asset with a cost of $205,000 has an estimated residual value of $5,000, an estimated useful life of 40 years, and is depreciated by the straight-line method. (a) What is the amount of the annual depreciation? (b) What is the book value at the end of the twentieth year of use? (c) If at the start of the twenty-first year it is estimated that the remaining life is 25 years and that the residual value is $5,000, what is the depreciation expense for each of the remaining 25 years?

21. The cost of the equipment in a composite group is $600,000 and the annual depreciation, computed on the individual items, totals $60,000. (a) What is the composite straight-line depreciation rate? (b) What would the rate be if the total depreciation amounted to $66,000 instead of $60,000?

22. a. Differentiate between capital expenditures and revenue expenditures.

    b. Why are some items that have the characteristics of capital expenditures treated as revenue expenditures?

23. Immediately after a used truck is acquired, a new motor is installed and the tires are replaced at a total cost of $3,950. Is this a capital expenditure or a revenue expenditure?

24. For some of the plant assets of an enterprise, the balance in Accumulated Depreciation is exactly equal to the cost of the asset. (a) Is it permissible to record additional depreciation on the assets if they are still useful to the enterprise? Explain. (b) When should an entry be made to remove the cost and the accumulated depreciation from the accounts?

25. In what sections of the income statement are gains and losses from the disposal of plant assets presented?

26. A plant asset priced at $120,000 is acquired by trading in a similar asset and paying cash for the difference between trade-in allowance and the price of the new asset. (a) Assuming that the trade-in allowance is $50,000, what is the amount of boot given? (b) Assuming that the book value of the asset traded in is $40,000, what is the cost of the new asset for financial reporting purposes? (c) What is the cost of the new asset for the computation of depreciation for federal income tax purposes?

27. Assume the same facts as in Question 26, except that the book value of the asset traded in is $60,000. (a) What is the cost of the new asset for financial reporting purposes? (b) What is the cost of the new asset for the computation of depreciation for federal income tax purposes?

28. Differentiate between a capital lease and an operating lease.

29. Describe the internal controls for acquiring plant assets.

30. Why is an inventory of plant assets necessary?

31. What is the term applied to the periodic charge for (a) ore removed from a mine, (b) the write-off of the cost of an intangible asset?

32. a. Over what period of time should the cost of a patent acquired by purchase be amortized?

    b. In general, what is the required treatment for research and development costs?

33. How should (a) plant assets and (b) intangible assets be reported in the balance sheet?

34. Is the use of replacement cost generally accepted for accounting for plant assets and depreciation?

35. What is an argument for and against the use of replacement costs for plant assets?

REAL W⬤RLD FOCUS 36. A company has developed a tract of land into a ski resort. The company has cut the trees, cleared and graded the land and hills, and constructed ski lifts. (a) Should the tree cutting, land clearing, and grading costs of constructing the ski slopes be debited to the land account? (b) If such costs are debited to Land, should they be depreciated?

Source: "Technical Issues Feature," *Journal of Accountancy* (December 1987), p. 82.

REAL WORLD FOCUS   37. A revision of depreciable plant asset lives resulted in an increase in the remaining lives of certain plant assets. The company would like to include, as income of the current period, the cumulative effect of the changes, which reduce the depreciation expense of past periods. Is this in accordance with generally accepted accounting principles? Discuss.

Source: "Q's and A's Technical Hotline," *Journal of Accountancy* (December 1991), p. 89.

REAL WORLD FOCUS   38. The financial statements of La-Z-Boy Chair Company contain the following footnote:

The Company has several long-term leases covering manufacturing facilities. The lease agreements require the Company to insure and maintain the facilities and provide for annual payments, which include interest. These leases give the Company the option to purchase the facilities for nominal amounts, or in some instances to renew the leases for extended periods at nominal annual rentals.

Would these leases be classified as operating or capital leases? Discuss.

ETHICS DISCUSSION CASE

Alice Parker, CPA, is an assistant to the controller of Wilson Co. In her spare time, Alice also prepares tax returns and performs general accounting services for clients. Frequently, Alice performs these services after her normal working hours, using Wilson Co.'s microcomputers and laser printers. Occasionally, Alice's clients will call her at the office during regular working hours.

SHARPEN YOUR ►   Discuss whether Alice Parker is performing in an ethical manner.
COMMUNICATION SKILLS

WHAT DO YOU THINK

Should the Financial Accounting Standards Board (FASB) require that plant assets be reported at current replacement cost?

FINANCIAL ANALYSIS AND INTERPRETATION

Long-term liabilities (debt) are often secured by mortgages on plant assets. The ratio of total plant assets to long-term liabilities (debt) is a solvency measure that indicates the margin of safety to the debtors. It also indicates the ability of the enterprise to borrow additional funds on a long-term basis. The ratio of plant assets to long-term liabilities (debt) is computed as follows:

$$\text{Ratio of Plant Assets to Long-Term Liabilities (debt)} = \frac{\text{Plant Assets (Net)}}{\text{Long-Term Liabilities (debt)}}$$

a. For Hershey Foods Corporation, compute the ratio of plant assets (property, plant, and equipment) to long-term liabilities (debt) as of December 31, 1992 and 1991.

SHARPEN YOUR ► b. What conclusions can be drawn from these ratios concerning Hershey's ability to borrow additional funds on a long-term basis?
COMMUNICATION SKILLS

EXERCISES

EXERCISE 9-1
DETERMINING COST OF LAND
Objective 2

Lancaster Company acquired an adjacent lot to construct a new warehouse, paying $10,000 and giving a non-interest-bearing short-term note for $50,000. Legal fees paid were $2,500, delinquent taxes assumed were $4,000, and fees paid to remove an old building from the land were $5,500. Materials salvaged from the demolition of the building were sold for $1,000. A contractor was paid $112,500 to construct a new warehouse. Determine the cost of the land to be reported on the balance sheet.

EXERCISE 9-2
NATURE OF DEPRECIATION
Objective 3

Flowers Co. reported $725,000 for equipment and $510,000 for accumulated depreciation—equipment on its balance sheet.

▓SHARPEN YOUR ►
COMMUNICATION SKILLS

Does this mean (a) that the replacement cost of the equipment is $725,000 and (b) that $510,000 is set aside in a special fund for the replacement of the equipment? Explain.

EXERCISE 9-3
DEPRECIATION BY UNITS-OF-PRODUCTION METHOD
Objective 4

A diesel-powered generator with a cost of $170,000 and estimated salvage value of $20,000 is expected to have a useful operating life of 50,000 hours. During November, the generator was operated 360 hours.

Determine the depreciation for the month.

EXERCISE 9-4
DEPRECIATION BY UNITS-OF-PRODUCTION METHOD
Objective 4

Prior to adjustment at the end of the year, the balance in Trucks is $109,600, and the balance in Accumulated Depreciation—Trucks is $53,500. Details of the subsidiary ledger are as follows:

Truck No.	Cost	Estimated Residual Value	Estimated Useful Life	Accumulated Depreciation at Beginning of Year	Miles Operated During Year
1	$45,000	$5,000	200,000 miles	$22,500	25,000 miles
2	17,600	2,600	100,000	7,700	20,000
3	28,000	4,000	150,000	23,300	4,500
4	19,000	1,000	200,000	—	12,000

a. Determine the depreciation rates per mile and the amount to be credited to the accumulated depreciation section of each of the subsidiary accounts for the miles operated during the current year.

b. Journalize the entry to record depreciation for the year.

EXERCISE 9-5
DEPRECIATION BY THREE METHODS
Objective 4

A plant asset acquired on January 2 at a cost of $220,000 has an estimated useful life of 10 years. Assuming that it will have no residual value, determine the depreciation for each of the first two years (a) by the straight-line method, (b) by the declining-balance method, using twice the straight-line rate, and (c) by the sum-of-the-years-digits method.

EXERCISE 9-6
DEPRECIATION BY THREE METHODS
Objective 4

A piece of machinery acquired at the beginning of the fiscal year at a cost of $45,200 has an estimated residual value of $2,000 and an estimated useful life of 8 years. Determine the following: (a) the amount of annual depreciation by the straight-line method, (b) the amount of depreciation for the **second year** computed by the declining-balance method (at twice the straight-line rate), (c) the amount of depreciation for the **second year** computed by the sum-of-the-years-digits method.

EXERCISE 9-7
DEPRECIATION BY ACCELERATED DEPRECIATION METHODS
Objective 4

An item of equipment acquired at a cost of $33,000 has an estimated residual value of $3,000 and an estimated useful life of 5 years. It was placed in service on April 1 of the current fiscal year, which ends on December 31. Determine the depreciation for the current fiscal year and for the following fiscal year by (a) the declining-balance method, at twice the straight-line rate, and (b) the sum-of-the-years-digits method.

EXERCISE 9-8
REVISION OF DEPRECIATION
Objective 4

An item of equipment acquired on January 5, 1990, at a cost of $32,500, has an estimated residual value of $2,500 and an estimated useful life of 10 years. Depreciation has been recorded for the first four years ended December 31, 1993, by the straight-line method. Determine the amount of depreciation for the current year ended December 31, 1994, if the revised estimated residual value is $2,100 and the revised estimated remaining useful life (including the current year) is 8 years.

EXERCISE 9-9
COMPOSITE DEPRECIATION RATE
Objective 5

A composite depreciation rate of 15% is applied annually to a plant asset account. Details of the account for the fiscal year ended December 31 are as follows:

Machinery

Jan. 1 Balance	297,750	May 1	16,500
Mar. 2	27,250	Sep. 7	11,750
Apr. 29	14,000	Dec. 15	15,500
Aug. 22	20,500		
Nov. 14	17,500		

Determine the depreciation for the year according to each of the following assumptions: (a) that all additions and retirements have occurred uniformly throughout the year, (b) that additions and retirements during the first half of the year occurred on the first day of that year and those during the second half occurred on the first day of the succeeding year.

EXERCISE 9-10
MAJOR REPAIR TO PLANT ASSET
Objective 6

A number of major structural repairs on a building were completed at the beginning of the current fiscal year at a cost of $90,000. The repairs are expected to extend the life of the building 10 years beyond the original estimate. The original cost of the building was $800,000, and it has been depreciated by the straight-line method for 25 years. The residual value is expected to be negligible and has been ignored. The balance of the related accumulated depreciation account after the depreciation adjustment at the end of the preceding year is $400,000.

a. What has the amount of annual depreciation been in past years?
b. To what account should the cost of repairs ($90,000) be debited?
c. What is the book value of the building after the repairs have been recorded?
d. What is the amount of depreciation for the current year using the straight-line method (assuming that the repairs were completed at the very beginning of the year)?

EXERCISE 9-11
ENTRIES FOR SALE OF PLANT ASSET
Objective 7

A piece of equipment acquired on January 3, 1991, at a cost of $57,500, has an estimated useful life of 5 years, an estimated residual value of $7,500, and is depreciated by the straight-line method.

a. What was the book value of the equipment at December 31, 1994, the end of the fiscal year?
b. Assuming that the equipment was sold on July 1, 1995, for $9,000, journalize the entries to record (1) depreciation for the six months of the current year ending December 31, 1995, and (2) the sale of the equipment.

EXERCISE 9-12
DISPOSAL OF PLANT ASSET
Objective 7

A piece of equipment acquired on January 3, 1991, at a cost of $25,000, has an estimated useful life of 4 years and an estimated residual value of $5,000.

a. What was the annual amount of depreciation for the years 1991, 1992, and 1993, using the straight-line method of depreciation?
b. What was the book value of the equipment on January 1, 1994?
c. Assuming that the equipment was sold on January 2, 1994, for $8,500, journalize the entry to record the sale.
d. Assuming that the equipment had been sold for $11,500 on January 2, 1994, instead of $8,500, journalize the entry to record the sale.

EXERCISE 9-13
ENTRIES FOR LOSS ON TRADE OF PLANT ASSET
Objective 7

On July 1, Lewis Co. acquired a new computer with a list price of $125,000. Lewis received a trade-in allowance of $15,000 on an old computer of a similar type, paid cash of $30,000, and gave a series of five notes payable for the remainder. The following information about the old computer is obtained from the account in the office equipment ledger: cost, $82,500; accumulated depreciation on December 31, the end of the preceding fiscal year, $50,000; annual depreciation, $15,000. Journalize the entries to record: (a) the current depreciation of the old computer to the date of trade-in, (b) the transaction on July 1 for financial reporting purposes.

EXERCISE 9-14
ENTRIES FOR GAIN ON TRADE OF PLANT ASSET
Objective 7

On July 1, Klaus Co. acquired a new computer with a list price of $130,000. Klaus received a trade-in allowance of $20,000 on an old computer of a similar type, paid cash of $20,000, and gave a series of five notes payable for the remainder. The following information about the old computer is obtained from the account in the office equipment ledger: cost, $82,500; accumulated depreciation on December 31, the end of the preceding fiscal year, $62,500; annual depreciation, $15,000. Journalize the entries to record: (a) the current depreciation of the old computer to the date of trade-in, (b) the transaction on July 1 for financial reporting purposes.

EXERCISE 9-15
DEPRECIABLE COST OF
ASSET ACQUIRED BY
EXCHANGE
Objective 7

On the first day of the fiscal year, a delivery truck with a list price of $30,000 was acquired in exchange for an old delivery truck and $26,000 cash. The old truck had a book value of $2,500 at the date of the exchange.

a. Determine the following:
   1. Depreciable cost for financial reporting purposes.
   2. Depreciable cost for income tax purposes.
b. Assuming that the book value of the old delivery truck was $5,000, determine the following:
   1. Depreciable cost for financial reporting purposes.
   2. Depreciable cost for income tax purposes.

EXERCISE 9-16
INTERNAL CONTROL OF
PLANT ASSETS
Objective 9

Programs Co. is a computer software company marketing software products in the United States and Canada. While Programs Co. has over 30 sales offices, all accounting is handled at the company's headquarters in Dayton, Ohio.

Programs Co. keeps all its plant asset records on a computerized system. The computer maintains a subsidiary ledger of all plant assets owned by the company and calculates depreciation automatically. Whenever a manager at one of the thirty sales offices wants to purchase a plant asset, a purchase request is submitted to headquarters for approval. Upon approval, the plant asset is purchased and the invoice is sent back to headquarters so that the asset can be entered into the plant asset system.

A manager who wants to dispose of a plant asset simply sells or disposes of the asset and notifies headquarters to remove the asset from the system. Company cars and personal computers are frequently purchased by employees when they are disposed of. Most pieces of office equipment are traded in when new assets are acquired.

SHARPEN YOUR COMMUNICATION SKILLS ►

What internal control weakness exists in the procedures used to acquire and dispose of plant assets at Programs Co.?

EXERCISE 9-17
DEPLETION ENTRIES
Objective 10

Grace Co. acquired mineral rights for $3,000,000. The mineral deposit is estimated at 15,000,000 tons. During the current year, 600,000 tons were mined and sold for $750,000.

a. Determine the amount of depletion expense for the current year.
b. Journalize the adjusting entry to recognize the expense.

EXERCISE 9-18
AMORTIZATION ENTRIES
Objective 11

Mercedes Company acquired patent rights on January 3, 1991, for $59,500. The patent has a useful life equal to its legal life of 17 years. On January 5, 1994, Mercedes successfully defended the patent in a lawsuit at a cost of $19,600.

a. Determine the patent amortization expense for the current year ended Dec. 31, 1994.
b. Journalize the adjusting entry to recognize the amortization.

WhAT'S WRONG WITH THIS?
■
■
▲
■

How many errors can you find in the following partial balance sheet?

Prague Company
Balance Sheet
December 31, 19—

Assets

	Replacement Cost	Accumulated Depreciation	Book Value	
Total current assets:				$397,500
Plant assets:				
Land	$ 50,000	$ 20,000	$ 30,000	
Buildings	160,000	76,000	84,000	
Factory equipment	450,000	192,000	258,000	
Office equipment	120,000	73,000	47,000	
Patents	60,000	—	60,000	
Goodwill	45,000	—	45,000	
Total plant assets	$885,000	$361,000		524,000

PROBLEMS

Series A

PROBLEM 9-1A
ALLOCATION OF
PAYMENTS AND RECEIPTS
TO PLANT ASSET
ACCOUNTS
Objective 2

The following payments and receipts are related to land, land improvements, and buildings acquired for use in a business enterprise. The receipts are identified by an asterisk.

a.	Cost of real estate acquired as a plant site: Land	$ 175,000
	Building	50,000
b.	Finder's fee paid to real estate agency	15,000
c.	Fee paid to attorney for title search	900
d.	Delinquent real estate taxes on property, assumed by purchaser	18,500
e.	Cost of razing and removing building	11,250
f.	Proceeds from sale of salvage materials from old building	1,500*
g.	Cost of filling and grading land	13,500
h.	Architect's and engineer's fees for plans and supervision	105,000
i.	Premium on 1-year insurance policy during construction	9,000
j.	Cost of paving parking lot to be used by customers	17,500
k.	Cost of trees and shrubbery planted	10,000
l.	Special assessment paid to city for extension of water main to the property	4,500
m.	Cost of repairing windstorm damage during construction	3,500
n.	Cost of repairing vandalism damage during construction	800
o.	Proceeds from insurance company for windstorm and vandalism damage	3,300*
p.	Interest incurred on building loan during construction	85,000
q.	Money borrowed to pay building contractor	1,000,000*
r.	Payment to building contractor for new building	1,250,000
s.	Refund of premium on insurance policy (i) canceled after 10 months	750*

Instructions

SPREADSHEET
PROBLEM

1. Assign each payment and receipt to Land (permanently capitalized), Land Improvements (limited life), Building, or Other Accounts. Indicate receipts by an asterisk. Identify each item by letter and list the amounts in columnar form, as follows:

Item	Land	Land Improvements	Building	Other Accounts
	$	$	$	$

SHARPEN YOUR COMMUNICATION SKILLS

2. The costs assigned to the land, which is used as a plant site, will not be depreciated, while the costs assigned to land improvements will be depreciated. Explain this seemingly contradictory application of the concept of depreciation.

PROBLEM 9-2A
COMPARISON OF FOUR
DEPRECIATION METHODS
Objective 4

King Company purchased equipment on January 2, 1993, for $90,000. The equipment was expected to have a useful life of 3 years, or 7,000 operating hours, and a residual value of $6,000. The equipment was used for 2,000 hours during 1993, 2,800 hours in 1994, and 2,200 hours in 1995.

Instructions

Determine the amount of depreciation expense for the years ended December 31, 1993, 1994, and 1995 by (a) the straight-line method, (b) the units-of-production method, (c) the declining-balance method, using twice the straight-line rate, and (d) the sum-of-the-years-digits method. Also determine the total depreciation expense for the three years by each method. The following columnar headings are suggested for recording the depreciation expense amounts:

	Depreciation Expense			
Year	Straight-line method	Units-of-production method	Declining-balance method	Sum-of-the-years-digits method
1993				
1994				
1995				
Total				

PROBLEM 9-3A
DEPRECIATION BY FOUR
METHODS; PARTIAL YEARS
Objective 4

Robb Company purchased equipment on July 1, 1993, for $72,000. The equipment was expected to have a useful life of 3 years, or 6,900 operating hours, and a residual value of $3,000. The equipment was used for 700 hours during 1993, 2,800 hours in 1994, 2,400 hours in 1995, and 1,000 hours in 1996. The equipment was sold for $3,000 on July 1, 1996.

Instructions

Determine the amount of depreciation expense for the years ended December 31, 1993, 1994, 1995, and 1996 by (a) the straight-line method, (b) the units-of-production method, (c) the declining-balance method, using twice the straight-line rate, and (d) the sum-of-the-years-digits method.

PROBLEM 9-4A
DEPRECIATION BY THREE
METHODS; TRADE OF
PLANT ASSET
Objectives 4, 7

An item of new equipment, acquired at a cost of $80,000 at the beginning of a fiscal year, has an estimated useful life of 4 years and an estimated residual value of $5,000. The manager requested information regarding the effect of alternative methods on the amount of depreciation expense each year. Upon the basis of the data presented to the manager, the declining-balance method was selected.

In the first week of the fourth year, the equipment was traded in for similar equipment priced at $200,000. The trade-in allowance on the old equipment was $15,000, cash of $15,000 was paid, and a note payable was issued for the balance.

SPREADSHEET
PROBLEM

Instructions

1. Determine the annual depreciation expense for each of the estimated 4 years of use, the accumulated depreciation at the end of each year, and the book value of the equipment at the end of each year by (a) the straight-line method, (b) the declining-balance method (at twice the straight-line rate), and (c) the sum-of-the-years-digits method. The following columnar headings are suggested for each schedule:

Year	Depreciation Expense	Accumulated Depreciation, End of Year	Book Value, End of Year

2. For financial reporting purposes, determine the cost of the new equipment acquired in the exchange.
3. Journalize the entry to record the exchange.
4. What is the cost of the new equipment for purposes of computing the amount of depreciation allowable for income tax purposes?
5. Journalize the entry to record the exchange, assuming that the trade-in allowance was $5,000 instead of $15,000.
6. What is the cost of the new equipment for purposes of computing the amount of depreciation allowable for income tax purposes, assuming the data presented in Instruction (5)?

PROBLEM 9-5A
CORRECTING ENTRIES
Objectives 2, 6, 7

The following recording errors occurred and were discovered during the current year:

a. The $750 cost of repairing factory equipment damaged in the process of installation was charged to Factory Equipment.
b. The sale of a computer for $475 was recorded by a $475 credit to Office Equipment. The original cost of the computer was $1,450, and the related balance in Accumulated Depreciation at the beginning of the current year was $925. Depreciation of $100 accrued during the current year, prior to the sale, had not been recorded.
c. Property taxes of $5,000 were paid on real estate acquired during the year and were debited to Property Tax Expense. Of this amount, $4,000 was for taxes that were delinquent at the time the property was acquired.
d. Office equipment with a book value of $11,200 was traded in for similar equipment with a list price of $60,000. The trade-in allowance on the old equipment was $15,000, and a note payable was given for the balance. A gain on the disposal of plant assets of $3,800 was recorded.
e. The $1,100 cost of a major motor overhaul expected to prolong the life of a truck two years beyond the original estimate was debited to Delivery Expense. The truck was acquired new four years earlier.
f. A $450 charge for incoming transportation on an item of factory equipment was debited to Transportation In.
g. The cost of a razed building, $30,000, was debited to Loss on Disposal of Plant Assets and credited to Building. The building and the land on which it was located had been

acquired at a total cost of $110,000 ($80,000 debited to Land, $30,000 debited to Building) as a parking area for the adjacent plant.

h. The fee of $7,500 paid to the wrecking contractor to raze the building in (g) was debited to Miscellaneous Expense.

i. The $7,750 cost of repainting several interior rooms of a building was debited to Building. The building had been owned and occupied for 20 years.

Instructions

Journalize the entries to correct the errors during the current year. Identify each entry by letter.

PROBLEM 9-6A
TRANSACTIONS FOR PLANT ASSETS, INCLUDING TRADE
Objectives 2, 6, 7

The following transactions, adjusting entries, and closing entries were completed by Stucky Furniture Co. during 3 fiscal years ending on June 30. All are related to the use of delivery equipment. The declining-balance method (at twice the straight-line rate) of depreciation is used.

1993–1994 Fiscal Year

July 3. Purchased a used delivery truck for $15,000, paying cash.
      6. Paid $1,000 to replace the automatic transmission and install new brakes on the truck. (Debit Delivery Equipment.)
Dec. 7. Paid garage $215 for changing the oil, replacing the oil filter, and tuning the engine on the delivery truck.
June 30. Recorded depreciation on the truck for the fiscal year. The estimated useful life of the truck is 8 years, with a residual value of $3,000.
    30. Closed the appropriate accounts to the income summary account.

1994–1995 Fiscal Year

Aug. 29. Paid garage $240 to tune the engine and make other minor repairs on the truck.
Oct. 31. Traded in the used truck for a new truck priced at $28,000, receiving a trade-in allowance of $12,000 and paying the balance in cash. (Record depreciation to date in 1994.)
June 30. Recorded depreciation on the truck. It has an estimated trade-in value of $2,750 and an estimated life of 10 years.
    30. Closed the appropriate accounts to the income summary account.

1995–1996 Fiscal Year

Apr. 1. Purchased a new truck for $30,000, paying cash.
     2. Sold the truck purchased October 31, 1994, for $20,500. (Record depreciation for the year.)
June 30. Recorded depreciation on the remaining truck. It has an estimated residual value of $4,500 and an estimated useful life of 8 years.
    30. Closed the appropriate accounts to the income summary account.

Instructions

Journalize the transactions and the adjusting and closing entries. Post to the following accounts in the ledger and extend the balances after each posting:

    122   Delivery Equipment
    123   Accumulated Depreciation—Delivery Equipment
    616   Depreciation Expense—Delivery Equipment
    617   Truck Repair Expense
    812   Gain on Disposal of Plant Assets

If the working papers correlating with the textbook are not used, omit Problem 9-7A.

PROBLEM 9-7A
PLANT ASSET
TRANSACTIONS AND
SUBSIDIARY PLANT LEDGER
Objectives 4, 7

Langford Press Co. maintains a subsidiary equipment ledger for the printing equipment and accumulated depreciation accounts in the general ledger. A small portion of the subsidiary ledger, the two controlling accounts, and a journal are presented in the working papers. The company computes depreciation on each individual item of equipment. Transactions and adjusting entries affecting the printing equipment are described as follows:

1993

June 30. Purchased a binder (Model G, Serial No. C3721) from Kunz Manufacturing Co. on account for $108,000. The estimated useful life of the asset is 12 years, it is expected to have no residual value, and the straight-line method of depreciation is to be used. (This is the only transaction of the year that directly affected the printing equipment account.)

Dec. 31. Recorded depreciation for the year in subsidiary accounts 125-30 to 125-32 and inserted the new balances. (An assistant recorded the depreciation and the new balances in accounts 125-1 to 125-29.)

    31. Journalized and posted the annual adjusting entry for depreciation on printing equipment. The depreciation for the year, recorded in subsidiary accounts 125-1 to 125-29, totaled $61,200, to which was added the depreciation entered in accounts 125-30 to 125-32.

1994

Sep. 30. Purchased a Model 722 rotary press from Gross Press Co., priced at $60,000, giving the Model G3 flatbed press (Account No. 125-31) in exchange, plus $20,000 cash and a series of ten $2,500 notes payable, maturing at 6-month intervals. The estimated useful life of the new press is 10 years, and it is expected to have a residual value of $6,250. (Recorded depreciation to date in 1994 on item traded in.)

Instructions

1. Journalize the transaction of June 30. Post to Printing Equipment in the general ledger and to Account No. 125-32 in the subsidiary ledger.
2. Journalize the adjusting entry on December 31 and post to Accumulated Depreciation—Printing Equipment in the general ledger.
3. Journalize the entries required by the purchase of printing equipment on September 30. Post to Printing Equipment and to Accumulated Depreciation—Printing Equipment in the general ledger and to Account Nos. 125-31 and 125-33 in the subsidiary ledger.
4. If the rotary press purchased on September 30 had been depreciated by the declining-balance method at twice the straight-line rate, determine the depreciation on this press for the fiscal years ending (a) December 31, 1994, and (b) December 31, 1995.

PROBLEM 9-8A
INCOME STATEMENT AND
BALANCE SHEET
Objectives 5, 11, 12

The trial balance of Martin Corp. at the end of the current calendar year, before adjustments, is as follows:

Cash	30,100	
Accounts Receivable	60,200	
Allowance for Doubtful Accounts		500
Merchandise Inventory	178,700	
Prepaid Expense	11,250	
Land	50,000	
Buildings	225,000	
Accumulated Depreciation—Buildings		86,000
Office Equipment	31,100	
Accumulated Depreciation—Office Equipment		11,600
Store Equipment	51,500	
Accumulated Depreciation—Store Equipment		21,400
Delivery Equipment	57,850	
Accumulated Depreciation—Delivery Equipment		21,750
Patents	18,000	
Accounts Payable		40,200
Notes Payable (short-term)		20,000
Capital Stock		100,000
Retained Earnings		329,750
Dividends	70,000	
Sales (net)		996,950
Cost of Merchandise Sold	702,350	
Operating Expenses (controlling account)	140,500	
Interest Expense	1,600	
	1,628,150	1,628,150

Data needed for year-end adjustments:

a. Estimated uncollectible accounts at December 31, $6,100.
b. Insurance and other prepaid operating expenses expired during the year, $7,250.
c. The physical count of merchandise inventory at December 31, $171,000. Martin Corp. uses the perpetual inventory system.
d. Depreciation is computed at composite rates on the average of the beginning and the ending balances of the plant asset accounts. The beginning balances and rates are as follows:

Office Equipment, $27,900; 10%   Delivery Equipment, $57,150; 20%
Store Equipment, $48,500; 8%   Buildings, $225,000; 2%

e. Amortization of patents, computed for the year, $3,000.
f. Accrued liabilities at the end of the year, $3,000, of which $300 is for interest on the notes and $2,700 is for wages and other operating expenses.

Instructions

1. Prepare a multiple-step income statement for the current year.
2. Prepare a balance sheet in report form, presenting the plant assets in the manner illustrated in this chapter.

SOLUTIONS SOFTWARE

Instructions for Solving Problem 9-8A Using Solutions Software

1. Load opening balances.
2. Enter your name in the Student Name field in the General Information data entry window. Set the run date to December 31 of the current year.
3. Save the opening balances file to your drive and directory.
4. Key the adjusting entries. Key ADJ.ENT. in the reference field.
5. Display the adjusting entries.
6. Display the financial statements.
7. Save a back-up copy of your data file.
8. Perform period-end closing.
9. Display a post-closing trial balance.
10. Save your data file to disk.
11. End the session.

PROBLEM 9-9A
AMORTIZATION AND
DEPLETION ENTRIES
Objectives 10, 11

Data related to the acquisition of timber rights and intangible assets during the current year ended December 31 are as follows:

a. Timber rights on a tract of land were purchased for $50,000 on February 5. The stand of timber is estimated at 500,000 board feet. During the current year, 75,000 board feet of timber were cut.
b. Goodwill in the amount of $160,000 was purchased on January 4. It is decided to amortize over the maximum period allowable.
c. Governmental and legal costs of $24,800 were incurred on July 10 in obtaining a patent with an estimated economic life of 8 years. Amortization is to be for one-half year.

Instructions

1. Determine the amount of the amortization or depletion expense for the current year for each of the foregoing items.
2. Journalize the adjusting entries to record the amortization or depletion expense for each item.

Series B

PROBLEM 9-1B
ALLOCATION OF
PAYMENTS AND RECEIPTS
TO PLANT ASSET
ACCOUNTS
Objective 2

The following payments and receipts are related to land, land improvements, and buildings acquired for use in a business enterprise. The receipts are identified by an asterisk.

a.	Cost of real estate acquired as a plant site: Land	$ 150,000
	Building	40,000
b.	Delinquent real estate taxes on property, assumed by purchaser	8,750
c.	Cost of razing and removing building	5,800
d.	Fee paid to attorney for title search	900
e.	Cost of filling and grading land	9,700
f.	Architect's and engineer's fees for plans and supervision	60,000
g.	Premium on 1-year insurance policy during construction	5,500
h.	Payment to building contractor for new building	750,000
i.	Cost of repairing windstorm damage during construction	1,500
j.	Cost of paving parking lot to be used by customers	12,500
k.	Cost of trees and shrubbery planted	15,000
l.	Special assessment paid to city for extension of water main to the property	2,500
m.	Cost of repairing vandalism damage during construction	500
n.	Interest incurred on building loan during construction	39,000
o.	Cost of floodlights installed on parking lot	13,500
p.	Proceeds from sale of salvage materials from old building	1,100*
q.	Money borrowed to pay building contractor	600,000*
r.	Proceeds from insurance company for windstorm damage	1,000*
s.	Refund of premium on insurance policy (g) canceled after 11 months	350*

Instructions

1. Assign each payment and receipt to Land (permanently capitalized), Land Improvements (limited life), Building, or Other Accounts. Indicate receipts by an asterisk. Identify each item by letter and list the amounts in columnar form, as follows:

Item	Land	Land Improvements	Building	Other Accounts
	$	$	$	$

SPREADSHEET
PROBLEM

SHARPEN YOUR
COMMUNICATION SKILLS ▶

2. The costs assigned to the land, which is used as a plant site, will not be depreciated, while the costs assigned to land improvements will be depreciated. Explain this seemingly contradictory application of the concept of depreciation.

PROBLEM 9-2B
COMPARISON OF FOUR
DEPRECIATION METHODS
Objective 4

Taylor Company purchased equipment on January 3, 1993, for $99,000. The equipment was expected to have a useful life of 3 years, or 9,000 operating hours, and a residual value of $9,000. The equipment was used for 3,000 hours during 1993, 3,800 hours in 1994, and 2,200 hours in 1995.

Instructions

Determine the amount of depreciation expense for the years ended December 31, 1993, 1994, and 1995 by (a) the straight-line method, (b) the units-of-production method, (c) the declining-balance method, using twice the straight-line rate, and (d) the sum-of-the-years-digits method. Also determine the total depreciation expense for the three years by each method. The following columnar headings are suggested for recording the depreciation expense amounts:

	Depreciation Expense			
Year	Straight-line method	Units-of-production method	Declining-balance method	Sum-of-the-years-digits method
1993				
1994				
1995				
Total				

PROBLEM 9-3B
DEPRECIATION BY FOUR
METHODS; PARTIAL YEARS
Objective 4

XL Company purchased machinery on July 1, 1993, for $90,000. The equipment was expected to have a useful life of 3 years, or 14,000 operating hours, and a residual value of $6,000. The equipment was used for 1,400 hours during 1993, 5,600 hours in 1994, 4,800 hours in 1995, and 2,200 hours in 1996.

Instructions

Determine the amount of depreciation expense for the years ended December 31, 1993, 1994, 1995, and 1996 by (a) the straight-line method, (b) the units-of-production method, (c) the declining-balance method, using twice the straight-line rate, and (d) the sum-of-the-years-digits method.

PROBLEM 9-4B
DEPRECIATION BY THREE
METHODS; TRADE OF
PLANT ASSET
Objectives 4, 7

An item of new equipment, acquired at a cost of $125,000 at the beginning of a fiscal year, has an estimated useful life of 5 years and an estimated residual value of $5,000. The manager requested information regarding the effect of alternative methods on the amount of depreciation expense each year. Upon the basis of the data presented to the manager, the declining-balance method was selected.

In the first week of the fifth year, the equipment was traded in for similar equipment priced at $170,000. The trade-in allowance on the old equipment was $20,000, cash of $25,000 was paid, and a note payable was issued for the balance.

SPREADSHEET
PROBLEM

Instructions

1. Determine the annual depreciation expense for each of the estimated 5 years of use, the accumulated depreciation at the end of each year, and the book value of the equipment at the end of each year by (a) the straight-line method, (b) the declining-balance method (at twice the straight-line rate), and (c) the sum-of-the-years-digits method. The following columnar headings are suggested for each schedule:

Year	Depreciation Expense	Accumulated Depreciation, End of Year	Book Value, End of Year

2. For financial reporting purposes, determine the cost of the new equipment acquired in the exchange.
3. Journalize the entry to record the exchange.
4. What is the cost of the new equipment for purposes of computing the amount of depreciation allowable for income tax purposes?
5. Journalize the entry to record the exchange, assuming that the trade-in allowance was $10,000 instead of $20,000.
6. What is the cost of the new equipment for purposes of computing the amount of depreciation allowable for income tax purposes, assuming the data presented in Instruction (5)?

PROBLEM 9-5B
CORRECTING ENTRIES
Objectives 2, 6, 7

The following recording errors occurred and were discovered during the current year:

a. The $900 cost of repairing equipment damaged in the process of installation was charged to Equipment.
b. Store equipment with a book value of $6,700 was traded in for similar equipment with a list price of $50,000. The trade-in allowance on the old equipment was $10,500, and a note payable was given for the balance. A gain on the disposal of plant assets of $3,800 was recorded.
c. Property taxes of $5,000 were paid on real estate acquired during the year and were debited to Property Tax Expense. Of this amount, $3,000 was for taxes that were delinquent at the time the property was acquired.
d. The sale of a computer for $1,750 was recorded by a $1,750 credit to Office Equipment. The original cost of the computer was $7,800, and the related balance in Accumulated Depreciation at the beginning of the current year was $6,000. Depreciation of $800 accrued during the current year, prior to the sale, had not been recorded.
e. The $2,250 cost of a major motor overhaul expected to prolong the life of a truck two years beyond the original estimate was debited to Delivery Expense. The truck was acquired new four years earlier.
f. The $12,500 cost of repainting several interior rooms of a building was debited to Building. The building had been owned and occupied for 20 years.

g. The cost of a razed building, $25,000, was debited to Loss on Disposal of Plant Assets and credited to Building. The building and the land on which it was located had been acquired at a total cost of $100,000 ($75,000 debited to Land, $25,000 debited to Building) as a parking area for the adjacent plant.

h. The fee of $4,000 paid to the wrecking contractor to raze the building in (g) was debited to Miscellaneous Expense.

i. A $250 charge for incoming transportation on an item of store equipment was debited to Transportation In.

Instructions

Journalize the entries to correct the errors during the current year. Identify each entry by letter.

PROBLEM 9-6B
TRANSACTIONS FOR PLANT
ASSETS, INCLUDING TRADE
Objectives 2, 6, 7

The following transactions, adjusting entries, and closing entries were completed by Keck Furniture Co. during a 3-year period. All are related to the use of delivery equipment. The declining-balance method (at twice the straight-line rate) of depreciation is used.

1993

Jan. 2. Purchased a used delivery truck for $10,800, paying cash.
      5. Paid $1,200 for major repairs to the truck.
Sep. 17. Paid garage $225 for miscellaneous repairs to the truck.
Dec. 31. Recorded depreciation on the truck for the fiscal year. The estimated useful life of the truck is 4 years, with a residual value of $1,800.
      31. Closed the appropriate accounts to the income summary account.

1994

June 30. Traded in the used truck for a new truck priced at $25,000, receiving a trade-in allowance of $5,000 and paying the balance in cash. (Record depreciation to date in 1994.)
Nov. 4. Paid garage $195 for miscellaneous repairs to the truck.
Dec. 31. Recorded depreciation on the truck. It has an estimated trade-in value of $4,500 and an estimated life of 5 years.
      31. Closed the appropriate accounts to the income summary account.

1995

Oct. 1. Purchased a new truck for $24,400, paying cash.
      2. Sold the truck purchased June 30, 1994, for $15,000. (Record depreciation for the year.)
Dec. 31. Recorded depreciation on the remaining truck. It has an estimated residual value of $1,500 and an estimated useful life of 8 years.
      31. Closed the appropriate accounts to the income summary account.

Instructions

Journalize the transactions and the adjusting and closing entries. Post to the following accounts in the ledger and extend the balances after each posting:

    122   Delivery Equipment
    123   Accumulated Depreciation—Delivery Equipment
    616   Depreciation Expense—Delivery Equipment
    617   Truck Repair Expense
    812   Gain on Disposal of Plant Assets

If the working papers correlating with the textbook are not used, omit Problem 9-7B.

PROBLEM 9-7B
PLANT ASSET
TRANSACTIONS AND
SUBSIDIARY PLANT LEDGER
Objectives 4, 7

Dunn Press Co. maintains a subsidiary equipment ledger for the printing equipment and accumulated depreciation accounts in the general ledger. A small portion of the subsidiary ledger, the two controlling accounts, and a journal are presented in the working papers. The company computes depreciation on each individual item of equipment. Transactions and adjusting entries affecting the printing equipment are described as follows:

1993

Sep. 1. Purchased a power binder (Model 14B, Serial No. 6725) from King Manufacturing Co. on account for $60,000. The estimated useful life of the asset is 10 years, it is expected to have no residual value, and the straight-line method of depreciation is to be used. (This is the only transaction of the year that directly affected the printing equipment account.)

Dec. 31. Recorded depreciation for the year in subsidiary accounts 125-30 to 125-32 and inserted the new balances. (An assistant recorded the depreciation and the new balances in accounts 125-1 to 125-29.)

31. Journalized and posted the annual adjusting entry for depreciation on printing equipment. The depreciation for the year, recorded in subsidiary accounts 125-1 to 125-29, totaled $68,200, to which was added the depreciation entered in accounts 125-30 to 125-32.

1994
Mar. 31. Purchased a Model 4B rotary press from Carson Press, priced at $50,000, giving the Model G3 flatbed press (Account No. 125-31) in exchange, plus $7,500 cash and a series of four $5,000 notes payable, maturing at 6-month intervals. The estimated useful life of the new press is 10 years, and it is expected to have a residual value of $2,000. (Recorded depreciation to date in 1994 on item traded in.)

Instructions
1. Journalize the transaction of September 1. Post to Printing Equipment in the general ledger and to Account No. 125-32 in the subsidiary ledger.
2. Journalize the adjusting entry on December 31 and post to Accumulated Depreciation—Printing Equipment in the general ledger.
3. Journalize the entries required by the purchase of printing equipment on March 31. Post to Printing Equipment and to Accumulated Depreciation—Printing Equipment in the general ledger and to Account Nos. 125-31 and 125-33 in the subsidiary ledger.
4. If the rotary press purchased on March 31 had been depreciated by the declining-balance method at twice the straight-line rate, determine the depreciation on this press for the fiscal years ending (a) December 31, 1994, and (b) December 31, 1995.

PROBLEM 9-8B
INCOME STATEMENT AND
BALANCE SHEET
Objectives 5, 11, 12

The trial balance of Treadway Inc. at the end of the current calendar year, before adjustments, is as follows:

Cash	30,700	
Accounts Receivable	62,600	
Allowance for Doubtful Accounts		500
Merchandise Inventory	179,200	
Prepaid Expense	10,750	
Land	55,000	
Buildings	225,000	
Accumulated Depreciation—Buildings		90,000
Office Equipment	41,100	
Accumulated Depreciation—Office Equipment		17,600
Store Equipment	52,200	
Accumulated Depreciation—Store Equipment		22,100
Delivery Equipment	57,850	
Accumulated Depreciation—Delivery Equipment		21,750
Patents	18,000	
Accounts Payable		43,200
Notes Payable (short-term)		30,000
Capital Stock		100,000
Retained Earnings		330,250
Dividends	70,000	
Sales (net)		999,750
Cost of Merchandise Sold	706,550	
Operating Expenses (controlling account)	144,600	
Interest Expense	1,600	
	1,655,150	1,655,150

Data needed for year-end adjustments:
a. Estimated uncollectible accounts at December 31, $7,200.
b. The physical count of merchandise inventory at December 31, $171,000. Treadway Inc. uses the perpetual inventory system.

    c. Insurance and other prepaid operating expenses expired during the year, $6,750.
    d. Depreciation is computed at composite rates on the average of the beginning and the ending balances of the plant asset accounts. The beginning balances and rates are as follows:

Office Equipment, $37,900; 10%   Delivery Equipment, $57,150; 20%
Store Equipment, $49,200; 8%   Buildings, $225,000; 2%

    e. Amortization of patents computed for the year, $3,000.
    f. Accrued liabilities at the end of the year, $2,000, of which $250 is for interest on the notes and $1,750 is for wages and other operating expenses.

Instructions

1. Prepare a multiple-step income statement for the current year.
2. Prepare a balance sheet in report form, presenting the plant assets in the manner illustrated in this chapter.

SOLUTIONS SOFTWARE

Instructions for Solving Problem 9-8B Using Solutions Software

1. Load opening balances.
2. Enter your name in the Student Name field in the General Information data entry window. Set the run date to December 31 of the current year.
3. Save the opening balances file to your drive and directory.
4. Key the adjusting entries. Key ADJ.ENT. in the reference field.
5. Display the adjusting entries.
6. Display the financial statements.
7. Save a back-up copy of your data file.
8. Perform period-end closing.
9. Display a post-closing trial balance.
10. Save your data file to disk.
11. End the session.

PROBLEM 9-9B
AMORTIZATION AND
DEPLETION ENTRIES
Objectives 10, 11

Data related to the acquisition of timber rights and intangible assets during the current year ended December 31 are as follows:

    a. Timber rights on a tract of land were purchased for $60,000 on March 5. The stand of timber is estimated at 500,000 board feet. During the current year, 50,000 board feet of timber were cut.
    b. Goodwill in the amount of $150,000 was purchased on January 3. It is decided to amortize over the maximum period allowable.
    c. Governmental and legal costs of $20,000 were incurred on July 1 in obtaining a patent with an estimated economic life of 8 years. Amortization is to be for one-half year.

Instructions

1. Determine the amount of the amortization or depletion expense for the current year for each of the foregoing items.
2. Journalize the adjusting entries required to record the amortization or depletion for each item.

MINI-CASE WILDE AND COMPANY

Ann Wilde, president of Wilde and Company, is considering the purchase of plant assets on July 1, 1994, for $120,000. The plant assets have a useful life of 5 years and no residual value. In the past, all plant assets have been leased. For tax purposes, Wilde is considering depreciating the plant assets by the straight-line method. She discussed the matter with her CPA and learned that, although the straight-line method could be elected, it was to her advantage to use the modified accelerated cost recovery system (MACRS) for tax purposes. She asked for your advice as to which method to use for tax purposes.

Instructions

1. Compute depreciation for each of the years (1994, 1995, 1996, 1997, 1998, and 1999) of useful life by (a) the straight-line method and (b) MACRS. In using the straight-line method, one-half year's depreciation should be computed for 1994 and 1999. Use the MACRS rates presented in the chapter.
2. Assuming that income before depreciation and income tax is estimated to be $200,000 uniformly per year and that the income tax rate is 30%, compute the net income for each of the years 1994, 1995, 1996, 1997, 1998, and 1999 if (a) the straight-line method is used and (b) MACRS is used.
3. What factors would you present for Wilde's consideration in the selection of a depreciation method?

ANSWERS TO SELF-EXAMINATION QUESTIONS

1. **C** All expenditures necessary to get a plant asset (such as machinery) in place and ready for use are proper charges to the asset account. In the case of machinery acquired, the transportation charges (answer A) and the installation costs (answer B) are both (answer C) proper charges to the machinery account.
2. **A** The periodic charge for depreciation under the sum-of-the-years-digits method is determined by multiplying a fraction by the original cost of the asset after the estimated residual value has been subtracted. The denominator of the fraction, which remains constant, is the sum of the digits representing the years of life, or 6 (3+2+1) in this question. The numerator of the fraction, which changes each year, is the number of years of life remaining at the beginning of the year for which depreciation is being computed, or 3 for the first year, 2 for the second year, and 1 for the third year in this question. The $4,500 (answer A) of depreciation for the first year is determined as follows:
3. **B** Depreciation methods that provide for a higher depreciation charge in the first year of the use of an asset and a gradually declining periodic charge thereafter are called accelerated depreciation methods. Examples of such methods are the sum-of-the-years-digits (answer B) and the declining-balance methods.
4. **B** The acceptable method of accounting for an exchange of similar assets in which the trade-in allowance ($30,000) exceeds the book value of the old asset ($25,000) requires that the cost of the new asset be determined by adding the amount of boot given ($70,000) to the book value of the old asset ($25,000), which totals $95,000.
5. **D** Long-lived assets that are useful in operations, not held for sale, and without physical qualities are called intangible assets. Patents, goodwill, and copyrights are examples of intangible assets (answer D).

$$\frac{\text{Years of Life Remaining at Beginning of Year}}{\text{Sum of Digits for Years of Life}} \times \left[\text{Cost} - \begin{array}{c}\text{Estimated}\\ \text{Residual Value}\end{array}\right]$$

$$\frac{3}{3+2+1} \times (\$9{,}500 - \$500) = \frac{1}{2} \times \$9{,}000 = \$4{,}500$$

Part 3

Financial Accounting Systems - Liabilities and Equity

You and Accounting

Have you ever checked the accuracy of your payroll check? For each pay period, your paycheck is less than the total amount you earned during the period. Various deductions from your total earnings are made for such items as federal income tax and FICA tax. For example, if you worked 20 hours last week at $10 per hour, you are paid weekly, you are single with no dependents, and your employer withholds federal income tax and FICA tax, your payroll check could appear as follows:

JACOBS TRUCKING CO.
306 Greene St.
Waynesburg, PA 15370

Tina Nelson
22 Valley Farm Dr.
Waynesburg, PA 15370

Check Number: 186252
Pay Period Ending: 12/27/94

HOURS & EARNINGS / TAXES & DEDUCTIONS

DESCRIPTION	AMOUNT	DESCRIPTION	CURRENT AMOUNT	Y-T-D AMOUNT
Rate of Pay Reg.	10	FICA Tax	15.00	780.00
Rate of Pay O.T.	15	Fed. Income Tax	27.00	1,560.00
Hours Worked Reg.	20			
Hours Worked O.T.	0			
Net Pay	158.00			
Total Gross Pay	200.00	Total	42.00	2,340.00
Total Gross Y-T-D	10,400.00			

STATEMENT OF EARNINGS. DETACH AND KEEP FOR YOUR RECORDS

JACOBS TRUCKING CO.
306 Greene St.
Waynesburg, PA 15370
Pay Period Ending: 12/27/94

Sargent Savings & Loan
32 Bonita Avenue, Suite 20
Washington, PA 15301

186252

24-2/531

PAY ONE HUNDRED FIFTY EIGHT AND 00/100 . . . . **DOLLARS**

$***158.00

To the Order of

TINA NELSON
22 VALLEY FARM DR.
WAYNESBURG, PA 15370

Ben W. Jacobs

⑆291337⑆ ⑆153111123⑆ ⑆938540 2⑆

In this chapter you will learn how to verify whether you are being paid the correct amount each pay period.

Chapter 10
Payroll, Notes Payable, and Other Current Liabilities

LEARNING OBJECTIVES
After studying this chapter, you should be able to:

Objective 1
Determine employer's liabilities for payroll, including liabilities arising from employee earnings and deductions from earnings.

Objective 2
Record payroll and payroll taxes, using a payroll register, employees' earnings records, and a general journal.

Objective 3
Journalize entries for employee fringe benefits, including vacation pay and pensions.

Objective 4
Journalize entries for short-term notes payable.

Objective 5
Journalize entries for product warranties.

Objective 6
Describe the accounting for contingent liabilities.

Payables are the opposite of receivables. They are debts owed by an enterprise to its creditors. Money claims against a firm may be created in many ways. For example, payables are created by purchases of merchandise or services on account, loans from banks, and purchases of equipment and marketable securities on a credit basis. At a point in time, a business may also owe its employees for wages or salaries accrued, banks or other creditors for interest accrued on notes, and governmental agencies for taxes.

We have discussed some types of current liabilities, such as accounts payable, in earlier chapters. In this chapter, we will discuss additional types of current liabilities, including liabilities arising from payrolls, vacation pay, pensions, notes payable, and product warranties.

PAYROLL AND PAYROLL TAXES

We are all familiar with the term *payroll*. In accounting the term **payroll** refers to the amount paid to employees for services provided during a period. An enterprise's payroll is usually significant for several reasons. First, employees are sensitive to payroll errors and irregularities. Maintaining good employee morale requires that the payroll be paid on a timely, accurate basis. Second, payroll expenditures are subject to various federal and state regulations. Finally, payroll expenditures and related payroll taxes have a significant effect on the net income of most business enterprises. Although the amount of such expenses varies widely, it is not unusual for a business to expend nearly a third of its revenue for payroll and payroll-related expenses.

Liability for Employee Earnings

The term **salary** usually refers to payment for managerial, administrative, or similar services. The rate of salary is normally expressed in terms of a month or a year. The term **wages** usually refers to payment for manual labor, both skilled and unskilled. The rate of wages is normally stated on an hourly or weekly basis. In practice, the terms salary and wages are often used interchangeably.

The basic salary or wage of an employee may be increased by commissions, bonuses, profit sharing, or cost-of-living adjustments. Although payment is usually made in cash, it may take such forms as securities, notes, lodging, or other property or services. Generally, the form of payment has no effect on how salaries and wages are treated by either the employer or the employee.

Salary and wage rates are determined by agreement between the employer and the employees. Enterprises engaged in interstate commerce must follow the requirements of the Fair Labor Standards Act. Employers covered by this legislation, which is commonly called the Federal Wage and Hour Law, are required to pay a minimum rate of $1\frac{1}{2}$ times the regular rate for all hours worked in excess of 40 hours per week. Exemptions are provided for executive, administrative, and certain supervisory positions. Premium rates for overtime or for working at night, holidays, or other less desirable times are fairly common, even when not required by law. In some cases, the premium rates may be as much as twice the base rate.

To illustrate the computation of the earnings of an employee, assume that John T. McGrath is employed at the rate of $20 per hour. Any hours in excess of 40 hours per week are paid at a rate of $1\frac{1}{2}$ times the normal rate, or $30 ($20 + $10) per hour. For the week ended December 27, McGrath's time card indicates that he worked 50 hours. His earnings for that week are computed as follows:

Earnings at base rate (40 × $20)	$ 800
Earnings at overtime rate (10 × $30)	300
Total earnings	$1,100

Deductions from Employee Earnings

The total earnings of an employee for a payroll period, including bonuses and overtime pay, are called **gross pay**. From this amount is subtracted one or more **deductions** to arrive at the net pay. **Net pay** is the amount the employer must pay the employee. The deductions for federal taxes are usually the largest deduction. Deductions may also be required for state or local income taxes. Other deductions may be made for medical insurance, contributions to pensions, and for items authorized by individual employees.

FICA TAX. Most of us have FICA tax withheld from our payroll checks. Employers are required by the Federal Insurance Contributions Act (FICA) to withhold a portion of the earnings of each of their employees. The amount of **FICA tax** withheld is the employees' contribution to two federal programs. The first program, referred to as social security, is for old age, survivors, and disability insurance. The second program, referred to as Medicare, is for health insurance.

The amount of tax employers are required to withhold from each employee is normally based on the amount of earnings paid in the calendar year. Although both the schedule of future tax rates and the maximum amount subject to tax are revised often by Congress, such changes have little effect on the basic payroll system.[1] In this text, we will use a combined rate of 7.5% on the first $60,000 of annual earnings and a rate of 1.5% on annual earnings in excess of $60,000.

To illustrate, assume that John T. McGrath's annual earnings prior to the current payroll period total $59,200. Assume also that the current period earnings are $1,100. The FICA tax of $64.50 is determined as follows:[2]

Earnings subject to 7.5% FICA tax		
($60,000 − $59,200)	$800.00	
FICA tax rate	7.5%	
FICA tax		$60.00
Earnings subject to 1.5% FICA tax		
($59,200 + $1,100 − $60,000)	$300.00	
FICA tax rate	1.5%	
FICA tax		4.50
Total FICA tax		$64.50

Your Social Security Taxes

In its 1936 publication, *Security in Your Old Age*, the Social Security Board set forth the following explanation of how the social security tax would affect a worker's paycheck:

The taxes called for in this law will be paid both by your employer and by you. For the next 3 years you will pay maybe 15 cents a week, maybe 25 cents a week, maybe 30 cents or more, according to what you earn. That is to say, during the next 3 years, beginning January 1, 1937, you will pay 1 cent for every dollar you earn, and at the same time your employer will pay 1 cent for every dollar you earn, up to $3,000 a year. Twenty-six million other workers and their employers will be paying at the same time.

After the first 3 years—that is to say, beginning in 1940— you will pay, and your employer will pay, 1½ cents for each dollar you earn, up to $3,000 a year. This will be the tax for 3 years, and then beginning in 1943, you will pay 2 cents, and so will your employer, for every dollar you earn for the next three years. After that, you and your employer will each pay half a cent more for 3 years, and finally, beginning in 1949, twelve years from now, you and your employer will each pay 3 cents on each dollar you earn, up to $3,000 a year. That is the most you will ever pay.

The rate on January 1, 1993, is 7.65 cents per dollar earned (7.65%). The social security portion is 6.2% on the first $57,600 of earnings. The Medicare portion is 1.45% on all earnings.

Source: Arthur Lodge, "That Is the Most You Will Ever Pay," *Journal of Accountancy* (October 1985), p. 44.

FEDERAL INCOME TAX. Except for certain types of employment, all employers must withhold a portion of employee earnings for payment of the employees' federal income tax. As a basis for determining the amount to be withheld, each employee completes and submits to the employer an "Employee's Withholding Allowance Certificate," often called a W-4. Exhibit 1 is an example of a completed W-4 form.

You may recall filling out a W-4 form. On the W-4, an employee indicates marital status, the number of withholding allowances, and whether any additional withholdings are authorized. A single employee may claim one withholding allowance. A married employee may claim an additional allowance for a spouse. An

---

[1] The FICA rates for 1993 are 6.2% for the first $57,600 of earnings and 1.45% for earnings in excess of $57,600.

[2] Tables are available from the Internal Revenue Service for determining FICA withholding.

Exhibit 1
Form W-4

---------------- **Cut here and give the certificate to your employer. Keep the top portion for your records.** ----------------

Form **W-4**	**Employee's Withholding Allowance Certificate**	OMB No. 1545-0010
Department of the Treasury Internal Revenue Service	▶ **For Privacy Act and Paperwork Reduction Act Notice, see reverse.**	19**93**

1 Type or print your first name and middle initial	Last name		2 Your social security number
John T.	McGrath		381–48–9120

Home address (number and street or rural route)	3 ☒ Single ☐ Married ☐ Married, but withhold at higher Single rate.
1830 4th Street	**Note:** *If married, but legally separated, or spouse is a nonresident alien, check the Single box.*

City or town, state, and ZIP code	4 If your last name differs from that on your social security card, check
Clinton, Iowa 52732–6142	here and call 1-800-772-1213 for more information · · · ▶ ☐

5 Total number of allowances you are claiming (from line G above or from the worksheets on page 2 if they apply) .	**5**	1
6 Additional amount, if any, you want withheld from each paycheck	**6**	$

7 I claim exemption from withholding for 1993 and I certify that I meet **ALL** of the following conditions for exemption:
 ● Last year I had a right to a refund of **ALL** Federal income tax withheld because I had **NO** tax liability; **AND**
 ● This year I expect a refund of **ALL** Federal income tax withheld because I expect to have **NO** tax liability; **AND**
 ● This year if my income exceeds $600 and includes nonwage income, another person cannot claim me as a dependent.
 If you meet all of the above conditions, enter "EXEMPT" here . . . . ▶ | **7**

Under penalties of perjury, I certify that I am entitled to the number of withholding allowances claimed on this certificate or entitled to claim exempt status.

Employee's signature ▶	Date ▶ June 2	19 93
8 Employer's name and address (Employer: Complete 8 and 10 only if sending to the IRS)	9 Office code (optional)	10 Employer identification number

Cat. No. 10220Q

employee may also claim an allowance for each dependent other than a spouse. Each allowance claimed reduces the amount of federal income tax withheld from the employee's check.

The amount that must be withheld for income tax differs, depending upon each employee's gross pay and completed W-4. Most employers use wage bracket withholding tables furnished by the Internal Revenue Service to determine the amount to be withheld.[3]

Exhibit 2 is an example of a wage bracket withholding table. This table is for a single employee who is paid weekly. Other tables are used for employees who are married or who are paid biweekly, semimonthly, monthly, or at other time periods. Unlike FICA tax, there is no ceiling on the amount of employee earnings subject to federal income tax withholding.

In using the withholding table, you would first locate the employee's wage bracket in the left-hand column. Then locate the number of withholding allowances across the horizontal columns. The intersection of the employee's wage bracket with the appropriate withholding allowance column indicates the federal withholding. For example, assume that John T. McGrath, who is single and has declared one withholding allowance, made $1,100 for the week ended December 27. Using the withholding table in Exhibit 2, the amount of federal income tax withheld is $238.

OTHER DEDUCTIONS. Deductions from gross earnings for payment of taxes are required. Neither the employer nor the employee has any choice in the matter. In addition, however, there may be other deductions authorized by individual employees. For example, you as an employee may authorize deductions for the purchase of U.S. Savings Bonds, for contributions to charitable organizations, for premiums on employee insurance, or for retirement annuities. A union contract may also require the deduction of union dues.

Computing Employee Net Pay

Gross earnings less payroll deductions equals the amount to be paid to an employee for the payroll period. This amount is the **net pay**, which is often called the **take-home pay**. The amount to be paid John T. McGrath for the week ended December 27 is $772.50, as shown below.

---

[3] Current federal income tax withholding tables are available from the Internal Revenue Service as part of *Circular E,* "Employer's Tax Guide."

Gross earnings for the week		$1,100.00
Deductions:		
FICA tax	$ 64.50	
Federal income tax	238.00	
U.S. savings bonds	20.00	
United Fund	5.00	
Total deductions		327.50
Net pay		**$ 772.50**

We illustrated the determination of the gross earnings and the FICA tax and federal income tax withheld for McGrath earlier in the chapter. We assumed that the deductions for the purchase of bonds and for the United Fund contribution were authorized by McGrath.

Exhibit 2
Wage Bracket
Withholding Table

WEEKLY PAYROLL PERIOD—continued SINGLE PERSONS

Wages: $550–$1,200 and over

And the wages are—		And the number of withholding allowances claimed is—										
At least	But less than	0	1	2	3	4	5	6	7	8	9	10
		The amount of income tax to be withheld shall be—										
$550	$560	$95	$82	$70	$60	$53	$46	$40	$33	$26	$20	$13
560	570	98	85	73	61	54	48	41	35	28	21	15
570	580	100	88	76	63	56	49	43	36	29	23	16
580	590	103	91	78	66	57	51	44	38	31	24	18
590	600	106	94	81	69	59	52	46	39	32	26	19
600	610	109	96	84	72	60	54	47	41	34	27	21
610	620	112	99	87	74	62	55	49	42	35	29	22
620	630	114	102	90	77	65	57	50	44	37	30	24
630	640	117	105	92	80	68	58	52	45	38	32	25
640	650	120	108	95	83	70	60	53	47	40	33	27
650	660	123	110	98	86	73	61	55	48	41	35	28
660	670	126	113	101	88	76	64	56	50	43	36	30
670	680	128	116	104	91	79	66	58	51	44	38	31
680	690	131	119	106	94	82	69	59	53	46	39	33
690	700	134	122	109	97	84	72	61	54	47	41	34
700	710	137	124	112	100	87	75	62	56	49	42	36
710	720	140	127	115	102	90	78	65	57	50	44	37
720	730	142	130	118	105	93	80	68	59	52	45	39
730	740	145	133	120	108	96	83	71	60	53	47	40
740	750	148	136	123	111	98	86	74	62	55	48	42
750	760	151	138	126	114	101	89	76	64	56	50	43
760	770	154	141	129	116	104	92	79	67	58	51	45
770	780	156	144	132	119	107	94	82	70	59	53	46
780	790	159	147	134	122	110	97	85	72	61	54	48
790	800	162	150	137	125	112	100	88	75	63	56	49
800	810	165	152	140	128	115	103	90	78	66	57	51
810	820	168	155	143	130	118	106	93	81	68	59	52
820	830	170	158	146	133	121	108	96	84	71	60	54
830	840	173	161	148	136	124	111	99	86	74	62	55
840	850	176	164	151	139	126	114	102	89	77	65	57
850	860	179	166	154	142	129	117	104	92	80	67	58
860	870	182	169	157	144	132	120	107	95	82	70	60
870	880	184	172	160	147	135	122	110	98	85	73	61
880	890	187	175	162	150	138	125	113	100	88	76	63
890	900	190	178	165	153	140	128	116	103	91	79	66
900	910	193	180	168	156	143	131	118	106	94	81	69
910	920	196	183	171	158	146	134	121	109	96	84	72
920	930	198	186	174	161	149	136	124	112	99	87	75
930	940	201	189	176	164	152	139	127	114	102	90	77
940	950	204	192	179	167	154	142	130	117	105	93	80
950	960	207	194	182	170	157	145	132	120	108	95	83
960	970	210	197	185	172	160	148	135	123	110	98	86
970	980	212	200	188	175	163	150	138	126	113	101	89
980	990	215	203	190	178	166	153	141	128	116	104	91
990	1,000	218	206	193	181	168	156	144	131	119	107	94
1,000	1,010	221	208	196	184	171	159	146	134	122	109	97
1,010	1,020	224	211	199	186	174	162	149	137	124	112	100
1,020	1,030	226	214	202	189	177	164	152	140	127	115	103
1,030	1,040	230	217	204	192	180	167	155	142	130	118	105
1,040	1,050	233	220	207	195	182	170	158	145	133	121	108
1,050	1,060	236	222	210	198	185	173	160	148	136	123	111
1,060	1,070	239	225	213	200	188	176	163	151	138	126	114
1,070	1,080	242	228	216	203	191	178	166	154	141	129	117
1,080	1,090	245	231	218	206	194	181	169	156	144	132	119
1,090	1,100	248	234	221	209	196	184	172	159	147	135	122
1,100	1,110	251	238	224	212	199	187	174	162	150	137	125
1,110	1,120	254	241	227	214	202	190	177	165	152	140	128
1,120	1,130	257	244	230	217	205	192	180	168	155	143	131
1,130	1,140	261	247	233	220	208	195	183	170	158	146	133
1,140	1,150	264	250	236	223	210	198	186	173	161	149	136
1,150	1,160	267	253	239	226	213	201	188	176	164	151	139
1,160	1,170	270	256	242	229	216	204	191	179	166	154	142
1,170	1,180	273	259	246	232	219	206	194	182	169	157	145
1,180	1,190	276	262	249	235	222	209	197	184	172	160	147
1,190	1,200	279	265	252	238	224	212	200	187	175	163	150

$1,200 and over   Use Table 1(a) for a **SINGLE person** on page 29.

Liability for Employer's Payroll Taxes

So far, we have discussed payroll taxes from the employees' point of view. These taxes are assessed against employees and are withheld by employers. Most employers are also subject to federal and state payroll taxes based on the amount paid their employees. Such taxes are an operating expense of the business.

FICA TAX. Employers are required to contribute to the Federal Insurance Contributions Act (FICA) program for each employee. The tax rates are the same as those we discussed earlier for employees.

FEDERAL UNEMPLOYMENT COMPENSATION TAX. Unemployment insurance provides temporary payments to those who become unemployed as a result of layoffs due to economic causes beyond their control. Types of employment subject to the unemployment insurance program are similar to those covered by the FICA tax. The tax of .8% is levied on employers only, rather than on both employers and employees.[4] It is applied to only the first $7,000 of the earnings of each covered employee during a calendar year. The rate and the maximum earnings subject to federal unemployment compensation tax are often revised by Congress. The funds collected by the federal government are not paid directly to the unemployed, but are allocated among the states for use in state programs.

STATE UNEMPLOYMENT COMPENSATION TAX. The amounts paid as benefits to unemployed persons are obtained, for the most part, by taxes levied upon employers only. A very few states also require employee contributions. The rates of tax and the tax bases vary. In most states, employers who provide stable employment for their employees are granted reduced rates. The employment experience and the status of each employer's tax account are reviewed annually, and the tax rates are adjusted accordingly.[5]

ACCOUNTING SYSTEMS FOR PAYROLL AND PAYROLL TAXES

Objective 2
Record payroll and payroll taxes, using a payroll register, employees' earnings records, and a general journal.

You as an employee of an enterprise would expect to and are entitled to be paid at regular intervals at the end of each payroll period. Regardless of the number of employees, the payroll system must be designed to process payroll data quickly and accurately.

In designing payroll systems, the requirements of various federal, state, and local agencies for payroll data are considered. Payroll data must not only be maintained for each payroll period, but also for each employee. Periodic reports using payroll data must be submitted to governmental agencies. The payroll data itself must be retained for possible inspection by the various agencies.

Payroll systems should also be designed to provide useful data for management decision-making needs. Such needs might include settling employee grievances and negotiating retirement or other benefits with employees.

Although payroll systems differ among enterprises, the major components common to most payroll systems are the payroll register, employee's earnings record, and payroll checks. We discuss and illustrate each of these major components below. We have kept the illustrations relatively simple, and they may be modified in practice to meet the needs of each individual enterprise.

Payroll Register

The payroll register is a multicolumn form used in assembling and summarizing the data needed each payroll period. Its design varies according to the number and classes of employees and the extent to which computers are used. Exhibit 3 shows a form suitable for a small number of employees.

---

[4] The rate on January 1, 1993, was 6.2%, which may be reduced to 0.8% for credits for state unemployment compensation tax.
[5] As of January 1, 1993, the maximum state rate recognized by the federal unemployment system was 5.4% of the first $7,000 of each employee's earnings during a calendar year.

The nature of the data appearing in the payroll register is evident from the columnar headings. The number of hours worked and the earnings and deduction data are inserted in their proper columns. The sum of the deductions for each employee is then deducted from the total earnings to yield the amount to be paid. The check numbers are recorded in the payroll register as evidence of payment.

The last two columns of the payroll register are used to accumulate the total wages or salaries to be charged to the various expense accounts. This process is usually called **payroll distribution**. If a large number of accounts are to be debited, the data may be accumulated on a separate payroll distribution sheet.

The format of the payroll register in Exhibit 3 aids in determining the mathematical accuracy of the payroll before checks are issued to employees. All columnar totals should be cross-verified, as shown below.

Earnings:
Regular	$13,328.00	
Overtime	574.00	
Total		$13,902.00

Deductions:
FICA tax	$ 851.60	
Federal income tax	3,332.00	
U.S. savings bonds	680.00	
United Fund	470.00	
Accounts receivable	50.00	
Total		5,383.60
Paid—net amount		$ 8,518.40

Accounts debited:
Sales Salaries Expense		$11,122.00
Office Salaries Expense		2,780.00
Total (as above)		$13,902.00

RECORDING EMPLOYEES' EARNINGS. Amounts in the payroll register may be posted directly to the accounts. An alternative is to use the payroll register as a supporting record for a compound journal entry. The entry based on the payroll register in Exhibit 3 follows.

Dec. 27	Sales Salaries Expense	11,122.00	750
	Office Salaries Expense	2,780.00	
	FICA Tax Payable		851.60
	Employees Federal Income Tax Payable		3,332.00
	Bond Deductions Payable		680.00
	United Fund Deductions Payable		470.00
	Accounts Receivable—Fred G. Elrod		50.00
	Salaries Payable		8,518.40
	Payroll for week ended December 27.		

The total expense incurred for the services of employees is recorded by the debits to the salary expense accounts. Amounts withheld from employees' earnings have no effect on the debits to these accounts. Five of the credits in the preceding entry increase liability accounts and one credit decreases the accounts receivable account.

RECORDING AND PAYING PAYROLL TAXES. It is important for you to note that all employer's payroll taxes become liabilities when the related payroll is *paid* to employees. In addition, employers are required to compute and report payroll

Exhibit 3
Payroll Register

			PAYROLL FOR WEEK ENDING	
		EARNINGS		
Employee Name	Total Hours	Regular	Overtime	Total
Abrams, Julie S.	40	500.00		500.00
Elrod, Fred G.	44	392.00	58.80	450.80
Gomez, Jose C.		840.00		840.00
McGrath, John T.	50	800.00	300.00	1,100.00
Wilkes, Glenn K.	40	480.00		480.00
Zumpano, Michael W.		600.00		600.00
Total		13,328.00	574.00	13,902.00

taxes on a *calendar-year* basis. The calendar year must be used for payroll taxes, even if a different fiscal year is used for financial reporting and income tax purposes.

To illustrate the accounting implications of the preceding requirement, assume that Everson Company's fiscal year ends on April 30. Also, assume that Everson Company owes its employees $26,000 of wages on December 31. The following portions of the $26,000 of wages are subject to payroll taxes on December 31:

	Earnings Subject to Payroll Taxes
FICA—Social Security and Medicare (7.5%)	$18,000
FICA—Medicare only (1.5%)	8,000
State and Federal Unemployment Compensation	1,000

If the payroll is paid on December 31, the payroll taxes will be based on the preceding amounts. If the payroll is paid on January 2, however, the *entire* $26,000 will be subject to payroll taxes.

Each time the payroll is prepared, the amounts of employer payroll taxes should be determined. The payroll tax expense accounts are then debited and related liability accounts credited.

To illustrate, the payroll register in Exhibit 3 indicates that the amount of FICA tax withheld is $851.60. Since the employer must match the employees' FICA contributions, the employer's FICA payroll tax will also be $851.60. Further, assume that the earnings subject to state and federal unemployment compensation taxes are $2,710. Multiplying this amount by the state (5.4%) and federal (.8%) unemployment tax rates yields the unemployment compensation taxes shown below.

FICA tax	$ 851.60
State unemployment compensation tax (5.4% × $2,710)	146.34
Federal unemployment compensation tax (.8% × $2,710)	21.68
Total payroll tax expense	$1,019.62

The entry to journalize the payroll tax expense for the week and the liability for the taxes accrued is shown below. Payment of the liabilities for payroll taxes is recorded in the same manner as the payment of other liabilities.

Dec. 27	Payroll Tax Expense	1,019.62	
	FICA Tax Payable		851.60
	State Unemployment Tax Payable		146.34
	Federal Unemployment Tax Payable		21.68
	Payroll taxes for week ended December 27.		

DECEMBER 27, 19--

	DEDUCTIONS					PAID		ACCOUNTS DEBITED	
FICA Tax	Federal Income Tax	U.S. Savings Bonds	Miscel-laneous		Total	Net Amount	Check No.	Sales Salaries Expense	Office Salaries Expense
37.50	74.00	20.00	UF	10.00	141.50	358.50	6857	500.00	
33.81	62.00		UF	50.00	145.81	304.99	6858		450.80
12.60	173.00	25.00	UF	10.00	220.60	619.40	6859	840.00	
64.50	238.00	20.00	UF	5.00	327.50	772.50	6860	1,100.00	
36.00	69.00	10.00			115.00	365.00	6880	480.00	
45.00	71.00	5.00	UF	2.00	123.00	477.00	6881		600.00
851.60	3,332.00	680.00	UF	470.00	5,383.60	8,518.40		11,122.00	2,780.00
			AR	50.00					

Miscellanous Deductions UF–United Fund; AR–Accounts Receivable

FICA contributions (both the employees' and employer's amounts) and federal income taxes must be deposited periodically in a federal depository bank. An "Employer's Quarterly Federal Tax Return" (Form 941) must be filed by the end of the first month following each calendar quarter. Exhibit 4 shows a portion of a completed Form 941.

Exhibit 4
Form 941

Form 941
(Rev. January 1992)
Department of the Treasury
Internal Revenue Service

4141

Employer's Quarterly Federal Tax Return

▶ See Circular E for more information concerning employment tax returns.

Please type or print.

2	Total wages and tips subject to withholding, plus other compensation ▶	2	40,180	50	
3	Total income tax withheld from wages, tips, pensions, annuities, sick pay, gambling, etc. ▶	3	6,520	00	
4	Adjustment of withheld income tax for preceding quarters of calendar year (see instructions) . ▶	4			
5	Adjusted total of income tax withheld (line 3 as adjusted by line 4—see instructions) . . .	5	6,520	00	
6a	Taxable social security wages (Complete line 7) $ 40,180 50 × 12.4% (.124) =	6a	4,982	38	
b	Taxable social security tips $ × 12.4% (.124) =	6b			
7	Taxable Medicare wages and tips . . . . $ × 2.9% (.029) =	7			
8	Total social security and Medicare taxes (add lines 6a, 6b, and 7)	8	4,982	38	
9	Adjustment of social security and Medicare taxes (see instructions for required explanation) .	9			
10	Adjusted total of social security and Medicare taxes (line 8 as adjusted by line 9—see instructions) . ▶	10	4,982	38	
11	Backup withholding (see instructions)	11			
12	Adjustment of backup withholding tax for preceding quarters of calendar year	12			
13	Adjusted total of backup withholding (line 11 as adjusted by line 12)	13			
14	**Total taxes** (add lines 5, 10, and 13)	14	11,502	38	
15	Advance earned income credit (EIC) payments made to employees, if any . . . . ▶	15			
16	Net taxes (subtract line 15 from line 14). **This should equal line IV below** (plus line IV of Schedule A (Form 941) if you have treated backup withholding as a separate liability) . . .	16	11,502	38	
17	**Total deposits for quarter**, including overpayment applied from a prior quarter, from your records . ▶	17	11,502	38	
18	**Balance due** (subtract line 17 from line 16). This should be less than $500. Pay to Internal Revenue Service . ▶	18	0		

Unemployment compensation tax returns and payments are required by the federal government on an annual basis. Earlier payments are required when the tax exceeds a certain minimum. Unemployment compensation tax returns and payments are required by most states on a basis similar to that required by the federal government.

Employee's Earnings Record

The amount of each employee's earnings to date must be readily available at the end of each payroll period. This cumulative amount is required in order to compute each employee's earnings subject to FICA tax and federal and state unemployment taxes. Without this cumulative amount, there would be no means of determining the employee's FICA tax withholding and employer's payroll taxes. It is essential, therefore, that a detailed payroll record be maintained for each employee. This record is called an **employee's earnings record**.

Exhibit 5
Employee's Earnings Record

John T. McGrath
1830 4th Street
Clinton, IA 52732-6142   **PHONE: 555-3148**

MARRIED   NUMBER OF
           WITHHOLDING   PAY
           ALLOWANCES: 1   RATE: $800.00 Per Week
OCCUPATION: Salesperson   EQUIVALENT HOURLY RATE: $20

| | | | | EARNINGS | |
Period Ended	Total Hours	Regular Earnings	Overtime	Total Earnings	Cumulative Total
SEP. 27	51	800.00	330.00	1,130.00	45,700.00
THIRD QUARTER		10,400.00	4,770.00	15,170.00	
OCT. 4	50	800.00	300.00	1,100.00	46,800.00
NOV. 15	48	800.00	240.00	1,040.00	54,000.00
NOV. 22	50	800.00	300.00	1,100.00	55,100.00
NOV. 29	46	800.00	180.00	980.00	56,080.00
DEC. 6	50	800.00	300.00	1,100.00	57,180.00
DEC. 13	46	800.00	180.00	980.00	58,160.00
DEC. 20	48	800.00	240.00	1,040.00	59,200.00
DEC. 27	50	800.00	300.00	1,100.00	60,300.00
FOURTH QUARTER		10,400.00	4,200.00	14,600.00	
YEARLY TOTAL		41,600.00	18,700.00	60,300.00	

Exhibit 5 shows a portion of the employee's earnings record for John T. Mc-Grath. The relationship between this record and the payroll register can be seen by tracing the amounts entered on McGrath's earnings record for December 27 back to its source—the fourth line of the payroll register in Exhibit 3.

In addition to spaces for recording data for each payroll period and the cumulative total of earnings, the employee's earnings record has spaces for quarterly totals and the yearly total. These totals are used in various reports for tax, insurance, and other purposes. One such report is the Wage and Tax Statement, commonly called a Form W-2. You may recall receiving a W-2 form for use in preparing your individual tax return. This form must be provided annually to each employee as well as to the Social Security Administration. The amounts reported in the example of a Form W-2 shown below were taken from John T. McGrath's employee's earnings record.

a Control number	22222	Void ☐	For Official Use Only ▶		
b Employer's identification number 61-8436524				**1** Wages, tips, other compensation 60,300.00	**2** Federal income tax withheld 14,181.00
c Employer's name, address, and ZIP code McDermott Supply Co. 415 5th Ave. So. Dubuque, Iowa 52736-0142				**3** Social security wages 60,000.00	**4** Social security tax withheld 4,504.50
				5 Medicare wages and tips	**6** Medicare tax withheld
				7 Social security tips	**8** Allocated tips
d Employee's social security number 381-48-9120				**9** Advance EIC payment	**10** Dependent care benefits
e Employee's name (first, middle initial, last) John T. McGrath 1830 4th St. Clinton, Iowa 52732-6142				**11** Nonqualified plans	**12** Benefits included in Box 1
				13 See Instrs. for Box 13	**14** Other
				15 Statutory employee ☐ Deceased ☐ Pension plan ☐ Legal rep. ☐ 942 emp. ☐ Subtotal ☐ Deferred compensation ☐	
f Employee's address and ZIP code					
16 State Employer's state I.D. No.	**17** State wages, tips, etc.	**18** State income tax	**19** Locality name	**20** Local wages, tips, etc.	**21** Local income tax

Cat. No. 10134D   Department of the Treasury—Internal Revenue Service

Form **W-2** Wage and Tax Statement **1993**

Copy A For Social Security Administration

For Paperwork Reduction Act Notice,
see separate instructions.

OMB No. 1545-0008

SOC. SEC. NO.: 381-48-9120   EMPLOYEE NO.: 814

DATE OF BIRTH: February 15, 1974

DATE EMPLOYMENT TERMINATED:

| | DEDUCTIONS | | | | | PAID | |
FICA Tax	Federal Income Tax	U.S. Bonds	Other		Total	Net Amount	Check No.
84.75	247.00	20.00			351.75	778.25	6175
1,137.75	3,185.00	260.00	UF	40.00	4,622.75	10,547.25	
82.50	238.00	20.00	UF	5.00	345.50	754.50	6225
78.00	220.00	20.00			318.00	722.00	6530
82.50	238.00	20.00			340.50	759.50	6582
73.50	203.00	20.00			296.50	683.50	6640
82.50	238.00	20.00	UF	5.00	345.50	754.50	6688
73.50	203.00	20.00			296.50	683.50	6743
78.00	220.00	20.00			318.00	722.00	6801
64.50	238.00	20.00	UF	5.00	327.50	772.50	6860
1,072.50	3,090.00	260.00	UF	15.00	4,437.50	10,162.50	
4,504.50	14,181.00	1,040.00	UF	100.00	19,825.50	40,474.50	

Payroll Checks

At the end of each pay period, one of the major outputs of the payroll system is a series of **payroll checks**. These checks are prepared from the payroll register, in which each line applies to an employee. Normally, the payroll check includes a detachable statement showing the details of how the net pay was computed. Exhibit 6 is a payroll check for John T. McGrath.

When the voucher system is used, it is necessary to prepare a voucher for the net amount to be paid the employees. The voucher is then recorded as a debit to Salaries Payable and a credit to Accounts Payable. The payment of the voucher is recorded in the usual manner. If the voucher system is not used, the payment is recorded by a debit to Salaries Payable and a credit to Cash.

The compound journal entry to record the employee payroll should precede the employer payroll tax entries just described. The information for the employee payroll entry is taken from the payroll register. Also, the entire amount paid is normally recorded as a single amount, regardless of the number of employees. There is no need to record each payroll check separately in the journal, since all of the details are available in the payroll register.

Exhibit 6
Payroll Check

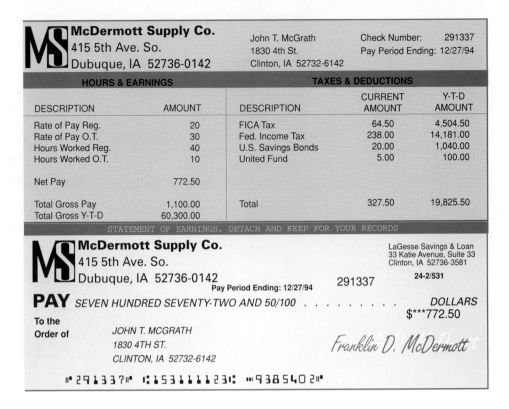

MS McDermott Supply Co. 415 5th Ave. So. Dubuque, IA 52736-0142		John T. McGrath 1830 4th St. Clinton, IA 52732-6142	Check Number: 291337 Pay Period Ending: 12/27/94	
HOURS & EARNINGS		**TAXES & DEDUCTIONS**		
DESCRIPTION	AMOUNT	DESCRIPTION	CURRENT AMOUNT	Y-T-D AMOUNT
Rate of Pay Reg.	20	FICA Tax	64.50	4,504.50
Rate of Pay O.T.	30	Fed. Income Tax	238.00	14,181.00
Hours Worked Reg.	40	U.S. Savings Bonds	20.00	1,040.00
Hours Worked O.T.	10	United Fund	5.00	100.00
Net Pay	772.50			
Total Gross Pay	1,100.00	Total	327.50	19,825.50
Total Gross Y-T-D	60,300.00			

STATEMENT OF EARNINGS. DETACH AND KEEP FOR YOUR RECORDS

MS McDermott Supply Co.
415 5th Ave. So.
Dubuque, IA 52736-0142
Pay Period Ending: 12/27/94

LaGesse Savings & Loan
33 Katie Avenue, Suite 33
Clinton, IA 52736-3581

291337   24-2/531

PAY *SEVEN HUNDRED SEVENTY-TWO AND 50/100* . . . . **DOLLARS**
$***772.50

To the
Order of   JOHN T. MCGRATH
1830 4TH ST.
CLINTON, IA 52732-6142

Franklin D. McDermott

⑈291337⑈ ⑆153111123⑆ ⑈938540 2⑈

For paying their payroll, most employers use payroll checks drawn on a special bank account. After the data for the payroll period have been recorded and summarized in the payroll register, a single check for the total amount to be paid is written on the firm's regular bank account. This check is then deposited in the special payroll bank account. Individual payroll checks are written from the payroll account, and the numbers of the payroll checks are inserted in the payroll register.

The use of payroll checks relieves the treasurer or other executives of the task of signing a large number of regular checks each payday. The task of signing payroll checks may be given to a paymaster, or a check-signing machine may be used to imprint the checks with the treasurer's signature.

Another advantage of using a separate payroll bank account is that the task of reconciling the bank statements is simplified. The paid payroll checks are returned by the bank with a bank statement for the payroll account. If all the payroll checks have been cashed by employees, the balance of the payroll account should be zero or the amount initially required by the bank to open the account. This is because the amount of each deposit is equal to the total amount of payroll checks written. Any payroll checks not cashed by employees will appear as outstanding checks on the bank reconciliation. After a period of time, funds for payroll checks that have not been cashed are transferred to the regular bank account. This establishes control over these items and prevents the theft or misuse of uncashed payroll checks.

Currency may be used to pay payroll. For example, currency is often used for payment of part-time workers or for employees who are paid at remote locations where cashing checks is difficult. In such cases, a single check, payable to Payroll, is written for the entire amount to be paid. The check is then cashed at the bank and the money is inserted in individual pay envelopes. The employees should be asked for identification and should be required to sign a receipt when picking up their pay envelopes. Journalizing the payroll is the same as if payroll checks were used.

Payroll System Diagram

You may find Exhibit 7 useful in following the flow of data within the payroll segment of an accounting system. The diagram indicates the relationships among the primary components of the payroll system we described in this chapter. The need to update the employee's earnings record is indicated by the dotted line.

Exhibit 7
Flow of Data in a Payroll System

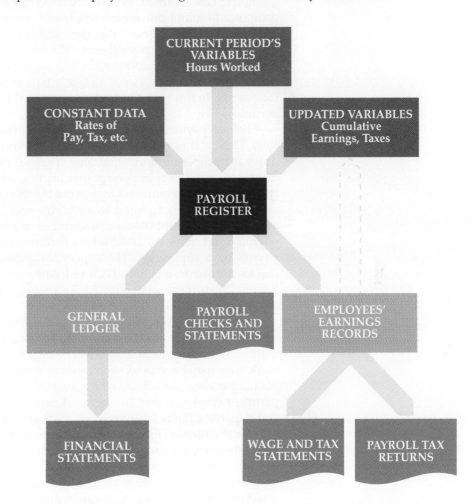

Our focus in the preceding discussion has been on the outputs of a payroll system: the payroll register, payroll checks, the employee's earnings record, and tax and other reports. As shown in the diagram in Exhibit 7, the inputs into a payroll system may be classified as either constants or variables. Constants are data that remain unchanged from payroll to payroll and thus do not need to be inputted into the system each pay period. Variables are data that change from payroll to payroll and thus must be inputted into the system each pay period.

Examples of constants include such data as each employee's name and social security number, marital status, number of income tax withholding allowances, rate of pay, payroll category (office, sales, etc.), and department where employed. The FICA tax rates and various tax tables are also constants that apply to all employees. Examples of variables include such data as the number of hours or days worked for each employee during the payroll period, days of sick leave with pay, vacation credits, and cumulative earnings and taxes withheld. If salespersons are paid commissions, the amount of their sales would also vary from period to period.

Internal Controls for Payroll Systems

The processing of payroll, as we discussed above, requires the input of a large amount of data, along with numerous, sometimes complex, computations. These factors, combined with the large dollar amounts involved, require controls to ensure that payroll payments are timely and accurate. In addition, the system must also provide adequate safeguards against theft or other misuse of funds.

One scheme to misuse payroll funds, which you may recall, was portrayed in the movie *Superman III*. In this movie, actor Richard Pryor played a computer programmer, Gus Gorman, who embezzled payroll funds. Gus programmed the computer to round down each employee's payroll amount to the nearest penny. The amount "rounded out" was then added to Gus's payroll check. For example, if an employee's total payroll was $458.533, the payroll program would pay the employee $458.53 and add the $.003 to a special account. The total in this special account would be transferred to Gus's paycheck at the end of the processing of the payroll. In this way, Gus's check increased from $143.80 to $85,000 in one pay period.

The cash payment controls we discussed in the cash chapter also apply to payrolls. Thus, it is normally desirable to use a voucher system that includes procedures for proper authorization and approval of payroll. When a check-signing machine is used, it is important that blank payroll checks and access to the machine be carefully controlled to prevent the theft or misuse of payroll funds.

It is especially important to authorize and approve in writing the additions and deletions of employees and changes in pay rates. For example, numerous payroll frauds have occurred where fictitious employees have been added to the payroll by a supervisor. The supervisor then cashes the fictitious employees' checks. Similar frauds have occurred where employees have been fired, but the Payroll Department is not notified. As a result, payroll checks to the fired employees are prepared and cashed by a supervisor.

To prevent or detect frauds such as those we described above, employees' attendance records should be controlled. For example, many companies use "In and Out" cards on which employees record their time of arrival to and departure from work. You may have used such cards in a part-time or summer job. These cards are inserted in a time clock, which automatically records the time. A Payroll Department employee may be stationed near the time clock during normal arrival and departure times in order to verify that employees only "clock in" once and only for themselves. Employee identification cards or badges may also be used to verify that only authorized employees are clocking in and are permitted entrance to work areas. When payroll checks are distributed, employee identification cards may be used to deter one employee from picking up another's check.

Other controls include verification and approval of all payroll rate changes. In addition, in a computerized system, all program changes should be properly approved and tested by employees who are independent of the payroll system. This would prevent or detect any changes such as those portrayed in the movie mentioned above. The use of a special payroll bank account, as we discussed earlier in the chapter, also enhances control over payroll.

EMPLOYEES' FRINGE BENEFITS

Objective 3
Journalize entries for employee fringe benefits, including vacation pay and pensions.

Many companies provide their employees a variety of benefits in addition to salary and wages earned. These benefits are often called **fringe benefits**. Such benefits may take many forms, including vacations, pension plans, and health, life, and disability insurance. When the employer pays part or all of the cost of the fringe benefits, these costs must be recognized as expenses. To properly match revenues and expenses, the estimated cost of these benefits should be recorded as an expense during the period in which the employee earns the benefit. In the following paragraphs, we discuss applying this matching concept to vacation pay and pension costs.

Vacation Pay

Most employers grant vacation rights, sometimes called compensated absences, to their employees. To properly match revenues and expense, employees' vacation pay should be accrued as a liability as the vacation rights are earned.[6] The entry to accrue vacation pay may be recorded in total at the end of each fiscal year, or it may be recorded at the end of each pay period. To illustrate this latter case, assume that employees earn one day of vacation for each month worked during the year. Assume also that the estimated vacation pay for the payroll period ending May 5 is $2,000. The entry to record the accrued vacation pay for this pay period is shown below.

May 5	Vacation Pay Expense	2,000	
	Vacation Pay Payable		2,000
	Vacation pay for week ended May 5.		

If employees are required to take all their vacation time within one year, the vacation payable is reported on the balance sheet as a current liability. If employees are allowed to accumulate their vacation time from year to year, the estimated portion of vacation payable that is applicable to time that will not be taken within one year is reported as a long-term liability on the balance sheet.

When payroll is prepared for the period in which the employees have taken vacations, the vacation payable is reduced. The entry debits Vacation Pay Payable and credits Salaries Payable and the other related accounts for recording taxes and withholdings.

Pensions

In the past twenty years, retirement pension plans have increased rapidly in number, variety, and complexity. Although such plans vary from employer to employer, pension benefits are normally based on employee age, years of service, and salary level. In 1974, Congress enacted the Employee Retirement Income Security Act (ERISA), which set forth guidelines for safeguarding employee benefits.

Pension plans may be classified as contributory or noncontributory, funded or unfunded, and qualified or unqualified. A **contributory plan** requires the employer to withhold a portion of each employee's earnings as a contribution to the plan. The employer then makes a contribution according to the provisions of the plan. A **noncontributory plan** requires the employer to bear the entire cost.

A **funded plan** requires the employer to set aside funds to meet future pension benefits by making payments to an independent funding agency. The funding agency is responsible for managing the assets of the pension fund and for disbursing the pension benefits to employees. For many pension plans, insurance companies serve as the funding agency. An **unfunded plan** is managed entirely by the employer instead of by an independent agency.

A **qualified plan** is designed to comply with federal income tax requirements. Plans meeting these requirements allow the employer to deduct pension contributions for tax purposes and exempt the pension fund income from tax. Most pension plans are qualified.

The accounting for pension plans is usually very complex due to the uncertainties of projecting future pension obligations. Such obligations depend upon such factors as employee life expectancies, expected employee compensation levels, and investment income on pension contributions. Pension funding obligations are estimated by using sophisticated mathematical and statistical models.

The employer's cost of an employee's pension plan in a given period is called the **net periodic pension cost**. This cost is debited to an operating expense ac-

---

[6] *Statement of Financial Accounting Standards, No. 43,* "Accounting for Compensated Absences" (Stamford: Financial Accounting Standards Board, 1980), par. 6.

count, Pension Expense.[7] Cash is credited if the pension cost is fully funded. If the pension cost is partially funded, any unfunded amount is credited to Unfunded Pension Liability. For example, assume that the pension plan of Flossmoor Industries requires an annual pension cost of $25,000, and Flossmoor Industries pays $15,000 to the fund trustee, Equity Insurance Company. The entry to record the transaction is as follows:

Pension Expense	25,000	
Cash		15,000
Unfunded Pension Liability		10,000

If the unfunded pension liability is to be paid within one year, it will be classified on the balance sheet as a current liability. That portion of the liability to be paid beyond one year is classified as a long-term liability.

An entity's financial statements should fully disclose the nature of its pension plans and pension obligations. These disclosures are usually included as footnotes to the financial statements. They should include the net periodic pension cost and a description of the plan, which includes such items as the employees covered and the accounting and funding policies used. In addition, any changes that affect the ability to compare pension costs and obligations among years should be disclosed.

When a pension plan is first adopted or later changed, the employer must decide whether to grant employees credit for prior years' service. If a company does grant credit to employees for prior service, a prior service cost obligation is recognized. A prior service cost is normally funded over a number of years, thus creating a long-term prior service pension liability. The complex nature of accounting for prior service costs is left for more advanced accounting study.

Postretirement Benefits Other Than Pensions

In addition to pension benefits described above, employees may earn during their term of employment rights to benefits from their employer for themselves and their dependents after they retire. Such benefits, called **postretirement benefits**, may include dental care, eye care, medical care, life insurance, tuition assistance for dependents, tax services, and legal services. Like pensions, postretirement plans may be either funded or unfunded, contributory or noncontributory, and may involve obligations for prior service of the employee.

Generally accepted accounting principles require the recognition of postretirement benefit expense in the financial statements as the employees earn the rights to the benefits.[8] The entry to recognize benefits earned in the current year is to debit Postretirement Benefits Expense. Cash is credited if the benefits are fully funded. If the benefits are not fully funded, a credit is made to a postretirement benefits plan liability account. You may read about additional complexities of accounting for postretirement benefits in more advanced textbooks.

---

[7] *Statement of Financial Accounting Standards, No. 87*, "Employers' Accounting for Pensions" (Stamford: Financial Accounting Standards Board, 1985), par. 6.

[8] *Statement of Financial Accounting Standards, No. 106*, "Employers' Accounting for Postretirement Benefits Other Than Pensions" (Norwalk: Financial Accounting Standards Board, 1990).

Using Accounting

Because accounting standards require recognizing postretirement benefits as they are earned by employees, some companies have begun to reduce or even eliminate such benefits for future retirees. In the past, companies recorded the cost of such benefits as they were paid to retirees. Thus, managers were often willing to grant postretirement benefits, knowing that the expense would be deferred to the future. Quite often the managers granting the rights would themselves be retired at that time. Thus, granting such rights in the past would not affect the current financial statements significantly and the investors' and other users' evaluations of management's performance. Under the current accounting standards, managers are more concerned about granting such rights to future retirees.

Employee Stock Options

Stock options are rights given by a corporation to its employees to purchase shares of the corporation's stock at a stated price. Employee stock options generally involve an element of salary expense when the employees have the right to purchase the corporation's stock at a price below market value. In such a case, the expense is the difference between the market price of the stock and the amount the employees are required to pay for it. The amount of the expense is debited to an appropriate expense account and credited to an owner's equity account. The details of accounting for employee stock options are discussed in more advanced accounting texts.

Income-Sharing Bonuses

Many enterprises pay managers an annual bonus in addition to a regular salary. The amount of the bonus is often based on some measure of productivity, such as income or profit of the enterprise. Such income-sharing bonuses are treated in the same manner as salaries.

The method used in determining the amount of an income-sharing bonus should be stated in the contract between the employer and the managers. When the bonus is expressed as a percentage of income, the percentage may be applied to one of the following four income measures:

1. Income before deducting the bonus and income taxes.
2. Income after deducting the bonus but before deducting income taxes.
3. Income before deducting the bonus but after deducting income taxes.
4. Net income after deducting both the bonus and income taxes.

Determining a 10% bonus using each of the four income measures is shown below. In these illustrations, the employer's income before deducting the bonus and income taxes is $150,000, and the income tax rate is 40%. Bonus and income taxes are abbreviated as B (bonus) and T (taxes).

1. Bonus based on income before deducting bonus and taxes.

$$B = .10 \ (\$150,000)$$
$$\textbf{Bonus} = \textbf{\$15,000}$$

2. Bonus based on income after deducting bonus but before deducting taxes.

$$B = .10(\$150,000 - B)$$

Simplifying: $$B = \$15,000 - .10B$$
Transposing: $$1.10B = \$15,000$$
$$\textbf{Bonus} = \textbf{\$13,636.36}$$

3. Bonus based on income before deducting bonus but after deducting taxes.

B equation: $$B = .10(\$150,000 - T)$$
T equation: $$T = .40(\$150,000 - B)$$

Substituting for T in the B equation and solving for B:

$$B = .10[\$150,000 - .40(\$150,000 - B)]$$

Simplifying:	$B = .10(\$150,000 - \$60,000 + .40B)$
Simplifying:	$B = \$15,000 - \$6,000 + .04B$
Transposing:	$.96B = \$9,000$

$$\text{Bonus} = \$9,375$$

4. Bonus based on net income after deducting bonus and taxes.

B equation:	$B = .10(\$150,000 - B - T)$
T equation:	$T = .40(\$150,000 - B)$

Substituting for T in the B equation and solving for B:

$$B = .10[\$150,000 - B - .40(\$150,000 - B)]$$

Simplifying:	$B = .10(\$150,000 - B - \$60,000 + .40B)$
Simplifying:	$B = \$15,000 - .10B - \$6,000 + .04B$
Transposing:	$1.06B = \$9,000$

$$\text{Bonus} = \$8,490.57$$

You probably have noticed that in the preceding examples, the amount of the bonus ranges from a high of $15,000 to a low of $8,490.57. It is obvious that strictly following the bonus agreement is important. If the bonus is to be shared by all of the managers, the agreement must also indicate how the bonus is divided among the managers. A common method is to express the bonus as a percentage of total earnings for the year. For example, if the bonus was $15,000 and total manager earnings before the bonus were $100,000, the bonus for each of the managers could be stated as 15% of their earnings.

Using Accounting

Since management's bonuses are normally based upon financial statement amounts, managers have a personal interest in the selection of accounting principles and the determination of accounting estimates. For example, a chief executive officer (CEO) who plans to retire in the near future might select accounting principles that tend to increase reported income, such as straight-line depreciation and the first-in, first-out inventory costing method, so as to increase their bonus. Likewise, such managers might tend to bias accounting estimates, such as uncollectible accounts expense, in favor of reporting more income.

SHORT-TERM NOTES PAYABLE

Objective 4
Journalize entries for short-term notes payable.

Notes may be issued to creditors to temporarily satisfy an account payable created earlier. They may also be issued at the time merchandise or other assets are purchased. For example, assume that an enterprise issues a 90-day, 12% note for $1,000, dated August 1, 1994, to Murray Co. for a $1,000 overdue account. The entry to record the issuance of the note is as follows:

Aug. 1	Accounts Payable—Murray Co.	1,000	
	Notes Payable		1,000
	Issued a 90-day, 12% note on account.		

At the time the note matures, the entry to record the payment of $1,030 ($1,000 principal plus $30 interest) is as follows:

Oct. 30	Notes Payable	1,000	
	Interest Expense	30	
	Cash		1,030

The interest expense account is closed at December 31, and the amount is reported in the Other Expense section of the income statement for the year ended December 31, 1994.

The preceding entries for notes payable are similar to those we discussed in an earlier chapter for notes receivable. Notes payable entries are presented from the viewpoint of the borrower, while notes receivable entries are presented from the viewpoint of the creditor or lender. To illustrate, the following entries are journalized for a borrower (Bowden Co.), who issues a note payable to a creditor (Coker Co.):

	Bowden Co. (Borrower)		Coker Co. (Creditor)	

May 1. Bowden Co. purchased merchandise on account from Coker Co., $10,000, 2/10, n/30.	Purchases 10,000
	    Accounts Payable 10,000
			Accounts Receivable 10,000
			    Sales 10,000	

May 31. Bowden Co. issued a 60-day, 12% note for $10,000 to Coker Co. on account.	Accounts Payable 10,000
	    Notes Payable 10,000
			Notes Receivable 10,000
			    Accounts Receivable 10,000	

July 30. Bowden Co. paid Coker Co. the amount due on the note of May 31. Interest: $10,000 × 12% × 60/360	Notes Payable 10,000
	Interest Expense 200
	    Cash 10,200
			Cash 10,200
			    Interest Income 200
			    Notes Receivable 10,000	

Notes may also be issued when money is borrowed from banks. Although the terms may vary, many banks would accept from the borrower an interest-bearing note for the amount of the loan. For example, assume that on September 19 a firm borrows $4,000 from the First National Bank by giving the bank a 90-day, 15% note. The entry to record the receipt of cash and the issuance of the note is as follows:

| Sep. 19 | Cash | 4,000 | |
| | Notes Payable | | 4,000 |

On the due date of the note (December 18), the borrower owes $4,000, the principal of the note, plus interest of $150. The entry to record the payment of the note is as follows:

Dec. 18	Notes Payable	4,000	
	Interest Expense	150	
	Cash		4,150

Sometimes a borrower will issue a non-interest-bearing note to the bank rather than an interest-bearing note. The face amount of the note is the amount that is to be paid at maturity. Although such a note does not specify an interest rate, the bank sets a rate of interest and deducts the interest from the maturity value of the note. The borrower is given the remainder. This deduction of interest from the maturity value is called **discounting**. The rate used in computing the amount deducted is called the **discount rate,** and the deduction is called the **discount**. The net amount received by the borrower is called the **proceeds**.

To illustrate, assume that on August 10 an enterprise issues to a bank a $4,000, 90-day, non-interest-bearing note, which the bank discounts at a rate of 15%. The amount of the discount is $150, and the proceeds are $3,850. The entry to record the issuance of the note is as follows:

Aug. 10	Cash	3,850	
	Interest Expense	150	
	Notes Payable		4,000

Cash is debited for the proceeds received from the bank from issuance of the note. Since most discounted notes mature within a short period of time, the amount of the discount is normally debited to Interest Expense at the time of issuance. If the accounting period ends before the maturity date of the note, an adjusting entry should be prepared, allocating the interest expense between accounting periods. Notes Payable is credited for the face amount of the note, which is also its maturity value.

When the note in the preceding illustration is paid, the following entry is recorded:

| Nov. 8 | Notes Payable | 4,000 | |
| | Cash | | 4,000 |

Short-term notes payable are presented in the Current Liabilities section of the balance sheet. If the market (fair) value of short-term notes payable differs from the carrying (book) value, the market value of the notes should be disclosed in notes to the financial statements.[9] In most cases, however, the carrying value of short-term notes payable approximates the market value, and such disclosures are unnecessary.

PRODUCT WARRANTY LIABILITY

Objective 5
Journalize entries for product warranties.

At the time of sale, a company may grant a warranty on a product. You may be familiar with warranties on electronic equipment and automobiles. To match revenues and expenses properly, warranty costs should be recognized as expenses in the same period in which the revenues to which they relate are recorded. In other words, estimated warranty costs should be recognized as expenses in the period in which the sale is recorded.[10] Later, when the product is repaired or replaced, the liability will be reduced.

To illustrate, assume that during June a company sells $60,000 of a product, on which there is a 36-month warranty for repairing defects in the product. Past experience indicates that the average cost to repair defects is 5% of the sales price. The entry to record the estimated warranty expense for June is as follows:

June 30	Product Warranty Expense	3,000	
	Product Warranty Payable		3,000
	Product warranty for June, 5% × $60,000.		

When the defective product is repaired, the repair costs are recorded by debiting Product Warranty Payable and crediting Cash, Supplies, or other appropriate accounts.

CONTINGENT LIABILITIES

Objective 6
Describe the accounting for contingent liabilities.

As we discussed earlier, contingent liabilities are potential obligations that will become liabilities only if certain events occur in the future. If the liability is probable and the amount of the liability can be reasonably estimated, it should be recorded in the accounts. Examples of such liabilities include vacation pay payable and product warranty payable. Although the vacation pay liability depends upon employees taking vacations, the liability is probable and is reasonably estimated. Likewise, although the product warranty liability depends upon customers presenting products for repair, the liability is probable and is reasonably estimated.

---

[9] *Statement of Financial Accounting Standards, No. 107*, "Disclosures about Fair Value of Financial Instruments" (Norwalk: Financial Accounting Standards Board, 1991), pars. 10 and 13.
[10] *Statement of Financial Accounting Standards, No. 5*, "Accounting for Contingencies" (Stamford: Financial Accounting Standards Board, 1975), pars. 8 and 24.

If the amount of the potential obligation cannot be reasonably estimated, the facts of the contingency should be disclosed.[11] For example, the following footnote taken from the annual report of Harley-Davidson, Inc., describes a potential liability for environmental contamination:

6. Commitments and Contingencies

The Company is involved in various environmental matters, including soil contamination at its York, Pennsylvania facility (the Facility), with various governmental and environmental agencies. During the third quarter of 1991, the Company discovered additional soil contamination at the Facility in an area formerly owned and used by the U.S. Navy and AMF, (the predecessor corporation of Minstar) from whom the Company was purchased in 1981. Based on the preliminary information available to the Company, the Company is unable to determine what remediation will be necessary, what the costs of such remediation will be and what the Company's share of such costs might be, relative to either the Navy's share or other former owner's share. The Company is therefore unable to determine at this time whether the potential liability relating to this matter will have a material effect on the Company's financial condition. Based on preliminary information available to the Company and admission by the Navy in the pending . . . action, the Company believes that the Navy should be liable for a substantial portion of the on-going investigation and future cleanup of the Facility.

Common examples of contingent liabilities disclosed in notes to the financial statements are litigation, guarantees, and discounting receivables. The 1992 edition of *Accounting Trends & Techniques* indicated that 60% of the surveyed companies disclosed contingencies for litigations, 39% for guarantees, and 12% for discounting receivables. We briefly discuss these contingent liabilities below.

Litigation

Most companies have lawsuits filed against them at one time or another. In many cases, litigation takes many months or years to complete. Although it is often difficult to estimate the amount of the liability, if any, the litigation should be disclosed. An example of a note in the financial statements of Pier 1 Imports, Inc., disclosing a contingent liability arising from litigation, is shown below.

Note 9—Litigation

In August 1988, a suit was filed in the 113th District Court of Harris County, Texas against Wolfe Nursery, Inc. (a wholly owned subsidiary of the Company), an apartment complex owner, a chemical distributor, a chemical manufacturer, and others, alleging that the improper use of chemicals and a failure to warn resulted in personal injury, and in certain cases, wrongful death. The plaintiffs seek $90 million. One defendant, a chemical manufacturer, has settled with the plaintiffs and has been dismissed from the lawsuit. The Company continues to deny liability in this action and intends to vigorously pursue all available defenses. The Company believes that its ultimate liability, if any, will not have a material adverse effect on the Company.

Guarantees

Companies sometimes guarantee a loan for another company, often an affiliate, supplier, or major customer. In such cases, the company is obligated to pay the loan if the borrower fails to make payment. Such a contingency may be disclosed in a note to the financial statements, such as that shown below for PepsiCo, Inc.:

At year-end 1991 and 1990, PepsiCo was contingently liable under direct and indirect guarantees aggregating $86 million and $97 million, respectively. The guarantees are primarily issued to support financial arrangements of certain restaurant and bottling franchises and PepsiCo joint ventures. PepsiCo manages the risk associated with these guar-

---

[11] *Statement of Financial Accounting Standards, No. 5, "Accounting for Contingencies"* (Stamford: Financial Accounting Standards Board, 1975), pars. 8, 10, 12.

antees by performing appropriate credit reviews in addition to retaining certain rights as a franchisor or joint venture partner.

Discounted Receivables

The contingent liability arising from discounting a note receivable was discussed in a previous chapter. A similar obligation may also arise from the sale of receivables. The contingent liability exists until the due date for discounted receivables. An example of a note disclosing such an obligation is shown below for The Wurlitzer Company.

7 (in part): Commitments and Contingent Liabilities

During the year ended March 31, . . . the Company negotiated an agreement to sell at face value approximately $6,100,000 of accounts receivable to an outside finance company. Cash proceeds of the sale were approximately $6,000,000: the remaining $100,000 is held by the outside finance company as security for the uncollected recourse receivables. At March 31, . . . the Company remained contingently liable on approximately $1,900,000 of the sold receivables; however, management believes that the allowance for doubtful accounts will be adequate for any such uncollectible receivables.

CHAPTER REVIEW

Key Points

Objective 1. Determine employer's liabilities for payroll, including liabilities arising from employee earnings and deductions from earnings.

An employer's liability for payroll is calculated by determining employees' total earnings for a payroll period, including bonuses and overtime pay. From this amount is subtracted employee deductions to arrive at the net pay to be paid each employee. Employer's liabilities for employee deductions are recognized at the time the payroll is recorded. Most employers also incur liabilities for payroll taxes, such as FICA tax, federal unemployment compensation tax, and state unemployment compensation tax.

Objective 2. Record payroll and payroll taxes, using a payroll register, employees' earnings records, and a general journal.

The payroll register is a multicolumn form used in assembling and summarizing the data needed each payroll period. The data recorded in the payroll register include the number of hours worked and the earnings and deduction data for each employee. The sum of the deductions for each employee is subtracted from the total earnings to yield the amount to be paid. Check numbers are recorded in the payroll register as evidence of payment to each employee. The payroll register also includes columns for accumulating total wages or salaries to be debited to the various expense accounts.

Amounts in the payroll register may be posted directly to the accounts. Alternatively, the payroll register may be used as a supporting record for recording the payroll for the period in the general journal. The payroll register is supported by a detailed payroll record for each employee, called an employee's earnings record.

Objective 3. Journalize entries for employee fringe benefits, including vacation pay and pensions.

Fringe benefits should be recognized as expenses of the period in which the employees earn the benefits. Fringe benefits are recorded by debiting an expense account and crediting a liability account. For example, the entry to record accrued vacation pay debits Vacation Pay Expense and credits Vacation Pay Payable.

Objective 4. Journalize entries for short-term notes payable.

A note issued to a creditor to temporarily satisfy an account payable is recorded as a debit to Accounts Payable and a credit to Notes Payable. At the time the note is paid, Notes Payable and Interest Expense are debited and Cash is credited. Notes may also be issued to purchase merchandise or other assets or to borrow money from a bank. When a non-interest-bearing note is issued to a bank, Interest (discount) Expense is debited for the interest deduction at the time of issuance, Cash is debited for the proceeds, and Notes Payable is credited for the face value of the note.

Objective 5. Journalize entries for product warranties.

If a company grants a warranty on a product, an estimated warranty expense and liability should be recorded in the period of the sale. The expense and the liability are recorded by debiting Product Warranty Expense and crediting Product Warranty Payable.

Objective 6. Describe the accounting for contingent liabilities.

Contingent liabilities are potential obligations that will become liabilities only if certain events occur in the future. If the liability is probable and the amount of the liability can be reasonably estimated, it should be recorded in the accounts. If the amount cannot be reasonably estimated, the details of the contingency should be disclosed in the financial statements.

Glossary of Key Terms

Contingent liabilities. Potential obligations that will become liabilities only if certain events occur in the future. **Objective 6**

Discount. The interest deducted from the maturity value of a note. **Objective 4**

Discount rate. The rate used in computing the interest to be deducted from the maturity value of a note. **Objective 4**

Employee's earnings record. A detailed record of each employee's earnings. **Objective 2**

FICA tax. Federal Insurance Contributions Act tax used to finance federal programs for old-age and disability benefits (social security) and health insurance for the aged (Medicare). **Objective 1**

Gross pay. The total earnings of an employee for a payroll period. **Objective 1**

Net pay. Gross pay less payroll deductions; the amount the employer is obligated to pay the employee. **Objective 1**

Payroll. The total amount paid to employees for a certain period. **Objective 1**

Payroll register. A multicolumn form used to assemble and summarize payroll data at the end of each payroll period. **Objective 2**

Postretirement benefits. Rights to benefits that employees earn during their term of employment for themselves and their dependents after they retire. **Objective 3**

Proceeds. The net amount available from discounting a note. **Objective 4**

Stock options. Rights given by a corporation to its employees to purchase shares of the corporation's stock at a stated price. **Objective 3**

Self-Examination Questions
Answers at end of chapter.

1. An employee's rate of pay is $20 per hour, with time and a half for all hours worked in excess of 40 during a week. The FICA rate is 7.5% on the first $60,000 of annual earnings and 1.5% on earnings in excess of $60,000. The following additional data are available:

Hours worked during current week   45
Year's cumulative earnings prior to current week $59,400
Federal income tax withheld   212

Based on these data, the amount of the employee's net pay for the current week is:

A. $620.50   C. $666.75
B. $641.50   D. $687.75

2. Which of the following taxes are employers usually not required to withhold from employees?
A. Federal income tax   C. FICA tax
B. Federal unemployment   D. State and local income
   compensation tax   taxes

3. With limitations on the maximum earnings subject to the tax, employers do not incur operating costs for which of the following payroll taxes?
A. FICA tax   C. State unemployment
B. Federal unemployment   compensation tax
   compensation tax   D. Employees' federal
                              income tax

4. An enterprise issued a $5,000, 60-day, 12% note to the bank. The amount due at maturity is:
A. $4,900   C. $5,100
B. $5,000   D. $5,600

5. An enterprise issued a $5,000, 60-day, non-interest-bearing note to the bank, and the bank discounts the note at 12%. The proceeds are:
A. $4,400   C. $5,000
B. $4,900   D. $5,100

ILLUSTRATIVE PROBLEM

Selected transactions of Grainger Company, completed during the fiscal year ended December 31, are as follows:

Mar. 1. Purchased merchandise on account from Perry Co., $15,000.
Apr. 10. Issued a 60-day, 12% note for $15,000 to Perry Co. on account.
June 9. Paid Perry Co. the amount owed on the note of April 10.
Aug. 1. Issued a 90-day, non-interest-bearing note for $30,000 to Atlantic Coast National Bank. The bank discounted the note at 15%.
Oct. 30. Paid Atlantic Coast National Bank the amount due on the note of August 1.
Dec. 27. Journalized the entry to record the biweekly payroll. A summary of the payroll record follows:

	Salary distribution:		
	Sales	$50,800	
	Officers	25,800	
	Office	6,400	$83,000
	Deductions:		
	FICA tax	$ 4,820	
	Federal income tax withheld	13,280	
	State income tax withheld	3,840	
	Savings bond deductions	630	
	Medical insurance deductions	960	23,530
	Net amount		$59,470

30. Issued a check in payment of employees' federal income tax of $13,280 and FICA tax of $9,640 due.
31. Issued a check for $8,600 to the pension fund trustee to fully fund the pension cost for December.
31. Journalized an entry to record the employees' accrued vacation pay, $32,200.
31. Journalized an entry to record the estimated accrued product warranty liability, $41,360.

Instructions

Journalize the preceding transactions.

Solution

Mar. 1	Purchases	15,000	
	Accounts Payable—Perry Co.		15,000
Apr. 10	Accounts Payable—Perry Co.	15,000	
	Notes Payable		15,000
June 9	Notes Payable	15,000	
	Interest Expense	300	
	Cash		15,300
Aug. 1	Cash	28,875	
	Interest Expense	1,125	
	Notes Payable		30,000
Oct. 30	Notes Payable	30,000	
	Cash		30,000
Dec. 27	Sales Salaries Expense	50,800	
	Officers Salaries Expense	25,800	
	Office Salaries Expense	6,400	
	FICA Tax Payable		4,820
	Employees Federal Income Tax Payable		13,280
	Employees State Income Tax Payable		3,840
	Bond Deductions Payable		630
	Medical Insurance Payable		960
	Salaries Payable		59,470
30	Employees Federal Income Tax Payable	13,280	
	FICA Tax Payable	9,640	
	Cash		22,920
31	Pension Expense	8,600	
	Cash		8,600
31	Vacation Pay Expense	32,200	
	Vacation Pay Payable		32,200
31	Product Warranty Expense	41,360	
	Product Warranty Payable		41,360

DISCUSSION QUESTIONS

1. What term is frequently used to refer to the total amount paid to employees for a certain period?
2. What is (a) gross pay? (b) net, or take-home, pay?
3. What programs are funded by the FICA (Federal Insurance Contributions Act) tax?
4. a. Identify the federal taxes that most employers are required to withhold from employees.
   b. Give the titles of the accounts to which the amounts withheld are credited.
5. For each of the following payroll-related taxes, indicate whether there is a ceiling on the annual earnings subject to the tax: (a) FICA tax, (b) federal income tax, (c) federal unemployment compensation tax.
6. An employee earns $18 per hour and 1½ times that rate for all hours in excess of 40 per week. If the employee worked 50 hours during the current week, what was the gross pay for the week?
7. Based on the data presented in Question 6, calculate the net pay for the current week assuming that gross pay prior to the current week totaled $49,760, the FICA tax rate was 7.5% (with earnings up to $60,000 subject to the 7.5% rate), and federal income tax to be withheld was $195.
8. Identify the payroll taxes levied against employers.
9. Why are deductions from employees' earnings classified as liabilities for the employer?
10. Do payroll taxes levied against employers become liabilities at the time the liabilities for wages are incurred or at the time the wages are paid?
11. Taylor Company, with 20 employees, is expanding operations. It is trying to decide whether to hire one employee full-time for $25,000 or two employees part-time for a total of $25,000. Would any of the employer's payroll taxes discussed in this chapter have a bearing on this decision? Explain.
12. For each of the following payroll-related taxes, indicate whether they generally apply to (a) employees only, (b) employers only, (c) both employees and employers:
    1. FICA tax
    2. Federal income tax
    3. Federal unemployment compensation tax
    4. State unemployment compensation tax
13. What type of information is recorded in the employee's earnings record and for what purpose is this information used?
14. An employer pays the employees in currency, and the pay envelopes are prepared by an employee rather than by the bank. (a) Why would it be advisable to obtain from the bank the exact amount of money needed for a payroll? (b) How could the exact number of each bill and coin denomination needed be determined efficiently in advance?
15. What are the principal reasons for using a special payroll checking account?
16. A company uses a weekly payroll period and a special bank account for payroll. (a) When should deposits be made in the account? (b) How is the amount of the deposit calculated? (c) Is it necessary to have in the general ledger an account entitled "Cash—Special Payroll Account"? Explain. (d) The bank statement for the payroll bank account for the month ended June 30 indicates a bank balance of $7,127.50. Assuming that the bank has made no errors, what does this amount represent?
17. In a payroll system, what type of input data are referred to as (a) constants, (b) variables?
18. To strengthen internal controls, what department should provide written authorizations for the addition of names to the payroll?
19. Explain how a payroll system that is properly designed and operated tends to ensure (a) that wages paid are based upon hours actually worked, and (b) that payroll checks are not issued to fictitious employees.
20. What are employee fringe benefits? Give three examples of such fringe benefits.
21. To match revenues and expenses properly, should the expense for employee vacation pay be recorded in the period during which the vacation privilege is earned or during the period in which the vacation is taken? Discuss.
22. Differentiate between a contributory and a noncontributory pension plan.
23. Identify several factors that influence the future pension obligation of an enterprise.
24. How does prior service cost arise in a new or revised pension plan?
25. Where should the unfunded pension liability be reported on the balance sheet?
26. What are some examples of postretirement benefits other than pensions that employees may earn for themselves and their dependents after they retire?

27. What are employee stock options?

28. If an employee is granted an income-sharing bonus, is the amount of the bonus (a) part of the employee's earnings and (b) deductible as an expense of the enterprise in determining the federal income tax?

29. The general manager of a business enterprise is entitled to an annual income-sharing bonus of 6%. For the current year, income before bonus and income taxes is $250,000, and income taxes are estimated at 35% of income before income taxes. Calculate the amount of the bonus, assuming that the bonus is based on net income after deducting both bonus and income taxes.

30. A bank has two alternatives in making a $30,000 loan: (1) accepting a $30,000, 60-day, 10% note or (2) discounting a $30,000 non-interest-bearing note at 10%. Which alternative is more favorable to the bank? Explain.

31. A business enterprise issued a 90-day, 10% note for $15,000 to a creditor on account. Give the entries to record (a) the issuance of the note and (b) the payment of the note at maturity, including interest of $375.

32. In borrowing money from a bank, an enterprise issued a $50,000, 60-day, non-interest- bearing note, which the bank discounted at 12%. Are the proceeds $50,000? Explain.

33. When should the liability associated with a product warranty be recorded? Discuss.

34. A business firm is contesting a suit for damages of a substantial amount, brought by a customer for an alleged faulty product. Is this a contingent liability for the defendant? If so, should it be disclosed in financial statements issued during the period of litigation? Discuss.

35. The 1992 annual report for Compaq Computer Corporation reported $73 million of product warranties in the current liability section of its December 31, 1992 balance sheet:

   a. What entry would have been made to record the accrued product warranty costs at December 31, 1992, assuming that no entry had been made in prior years?

   b. How would costs of repairing a defective product be recorded?

36. The "Questions and Answers Technical Hotline'' in the *Journal of Accountancy* included the following question:

   Several years ago, Company B instituted legal action against Company A. Under a memorandum of settlement and agreement, Company A agreed to pay Company B a total of $17,500 in three installments—$5,000 on March 1, $7,500 on July 1 and the remaining $5,000 on December 31. Company A paid the first two installments during its fiscal year ended September 30. Should the unpaid amount of $5,000 be presented as a current liability at September 30?

   How would you answer this question?

ETHICS DISCUSSION CASE

Ellen Burks, a CPA and staff assistant for a local CPA firm, noticed on her payroll stub covering the two-week period of April 5–18 that her overtime pay had been computed on the basis of 2 times her regular pay rate, rather than 1½ times her regular rate. Ellen has decided to cash the payroll check. If her employer later catches the error, Ellen plans to deny having originally noticed the mistake.

   Discuss whether Ellen Burks is behaving in an ethical manner.

SHARPEN YOUR COMMUNICATION SKILLS ▶

WHAT DO YOU THINK

Should managers' bonuses be based upon accounting income as reported in the income statement?

FINANCIAL ANALYSIS AND INTERPRETATION

Several measures can be used to assess the ability of an enterprise to pay its current liabilities. Two such analyses that are of special interest to short-term creditors are the current ratio and the acid-test ratio.

The current ratio is computed by dividing current assets by current liabilities, as indicated below:

$$\text{Current ratio} = \frac{\text{Current assets}}{\text{Current liabilities}}$$

The acid-test ratio or quick ratio is the ratio of the total quick assets to the total current liabilities. Quick assets are cash and other current assets that can be quickly converted to cash. Quick assets normally include cash, marketable securities, and receivables. The ratio is computed as follows:

$$\text{Acid-test ratio} = \frac{\text{Quick assets}}{\text{Current liabilities}}$$

The current ratio does not consider the makeup of the current assets. The acid-test ratio measures the "instant" debt-paying ability of the company and focuses on the assets that can generally be converted to cash rather quickly to meet current liabilities.

    a. For Hershey Foods Corporation, compute as of December 31, 1992 and 1991:
        1. the current ratio, and
        2. the acid-test ratio. (In computing the acid-test ratio consider the "investment interest" to be a short-term receivable.)
    b. What conclusions can be drawn from these data as to Hershey's ability to meet its current liabilities?

EXERCISES

EXERCISE 10-1
SUMMARY PAYROLL DATA
Objectives 1, 2

In the following summary of data for a payroll period, some amounts have been intentionally omitted:

Earnings:			Deductions:	
1. At regular rate	?		4. FICA tax	$ 6,500
2. At overtime rate	$6,100		5. Income tax withheld	10,750
3. Total earnings	?		6. Medical insurance	1,050
			7. Union dues	?
			8. Total deductions	19,450
			9. Net amount paid	75,550

Accounts debited:	
10. Factory Wages	$71,500
11. Sales Salaries	?
12. Office Salaries	7,500

    a. Calculate the amounts omitted in lines (1), (3), (7), and (11).
    b. Journalize the entry to record the payroll.
    c. Journalize the entry to record the voucher for the payroll.
    d. Journalize the entry to record the payment of the voucher.

**SHARPEN YOUR ▶
COMMUNICATION SKILLS**

    e. From the data given in this exercise and your answer to (a), would you conclude that this payroll was paid sometime during the first few weeks of the calendar year? Explain.

EXERCISE 10-2
INTERNAL CONTROL
PROCEDURES
Objective 2

Gem City Sounds is a retail store specializing in the sale of jazz compact disks and cassettes. The store employs 3 full-time and 10 part-time workers. The store's weekly payroll averages $1,800 for all 13 workers.

Gem City Sounds uses a personal computer to assist with the preparation of paychecks.

Each week, the store's accountant collects employee time cards and enters the hours worked into the payroll program. The payroll program calculates each employee's pay and prints a paycheck. The accountant uses a check-signing machine to sign the paychecks. Next, a voucher is prepared to transfer funds from the store's regular bank account to the payroll account. This voucher is authorized by the store's owner.

For the week of May 10, the accountant accidentally recorded 400 hours worked instead of 40 hours for one of the full-time employees. Does Gem City have internal controls in place to catch this error? If so, how will this error be detected?

EXERCISE 10-3
INTERNAL CONTROL
PROCEDURES
Objective 2

Smart Shop Inc. is a small manufacturer of home workshop power tools. The company employs 30 production workers and 10 administrative persons. The following procedures are used to process the company's weekly payroll:

a. Smart Shop maintains a separate checking account for payroll checks. Each week, the total net pay for all employees is transferred from the company's regular bank account to the payroll account.
b. Paychecks are signed by using a check-signing machine. This machine is located in the main office, so that it can be easily accessed by anyone needing a check signed.
c. All employees are required to record their hours worked by clocking in and out on a time clock. Employees must clock out for lunch break. Due to congestion around the time clock area at lunch time, management has not objected to having one employee clock in and out for an entire department.
d. Whenever an employee receives a pay raise, the supervisor must fill out a wage adjustment form, which is signed by the company president. This form is used to change the employee's wage rate in the payroll system.
e. Whenever a salaried employee is terminated, Personnel authorizes Payroll to remove the employee from the payroll system. However, this procedure is not required when an hourly worker is terminated. Hourly employees only receive a paycheck if their time card shows hours worked. The computer automatically drops an employee from the payroll system when that employee has six consecutive weeks with no hours worked.

▌SHARPEN YOUR   ►
COMMUNICATION SKILLS

State whether each of the procedures is appropriate or inappropriate after considering the principles of internal control. If a procedure is inappropriate, state what action must be taken to correct it.

EXERCISE 10-4
PAYROLL TAX ENTRIES
Objective 2

According to a summary of the payroll of O'Hare Publishing Co., the amount of earnings for the payroll paid on November 30 of the current year was $540,000. Of this amount, $510,000 was subject to the 7.5% FICA tax rate and $30,000 was subject to the 1.5% FICA tax rate. Also, $15,000 was subject to state and federal unemployment taxes.

a. Calculate the employer's payroll taxes expense on the payroll, using the following rates: state unemployment, 4.3%; federal unemployment, 0.8%.
b. Journalize the entry to record the accrual of payroll taxes.

EXERCISE 10-5
ACCRUED VACATION PAY
Objective 3

A business enterprise provides its employees with varying amounts of vacation per year, depending on the length of employment. The estimated amount of the current year's vacation pay is $186,000. Journalize the adjusting entry required on January 31, the end of the first month of the current year, to record the accrued vacation pay.

EXERCISE 10-6
PENSION PLAN ENTRIES
Objective 3

Tice Company maintains a funded pension plan for its employees. The plan requires quarterly installments to be paid to the funding agent, Interstate Insurance Company, by the fifteenth of the month following the end of each quarter. If the pension cost is $75,000 for the quarter ended December 31, journalize entries to record (a) the accrued pension liability on December 31 and (b) the payment to the funding agent on January 15.

EXERCISE 10-7
INCOME-SHARING BONUS
Objective 3

The general manager of a business enterprise is entitled to an annual income-sharing bonus of 5%. For the current year, income before bonus and income taxes is $400,000, and income taxes are estimated at 35% of income before income taxes.

Calculate the amount of the bonus, assuming that (a) the bonus is based on income before deductions for bonus and income taxes, and (b) the bonus is based on income after deductions for bonus and income taxes.

EXERCISE 10-8
ENTRIES FOR DISCOUNTING
NOTES
Objective 4

Clark Co. issues a 60-day, non-interest-bearing note for $100,000 to First National Bank and Trust Co., and the bank discounts the note at 12%.

a. Journalize the maker's entries to record:
   1. the issuance of the note.
   2. the payment of the note at maturity.
b. Journalize the payee's entries to record:
   1. the receipt of the note.
   2. the receipt of payment of the note at maturity.

EXERCISE 10-9
CALCULATION OF
INTEREST ON NOTES ISSUED
Objective 4

In negotiating a 90-day loan, an enterprise has the option of either (1) issuing a $250,000, non-interest-bearing note that will be discounted at the rate of 10%, or (2) issuing a $250,000 note that bears interest at the rate of 10% and that will be accepted at face value.

a. Calculate the amount of the interest expense for each option.
b. Calculate the amount of the proceeds for each option.

SHARPEN YOUR ►
COMMUNICATION SKILLS

c. Which option is more favorable to the borrower? Explain.

EXERCISE 10-10
PLANT ASSET PURCHASES
WITH NOTE
Objective 4

On June 30, Candice Company purchased land for $200,000 and a building for $670,000, paying $150,000 cash and issuing a 10% note for the balance, secured by a mortgage on the property. The terms of the note provide for 18 semiannual payments of $40,000 on the principal plus the interest accrued from the date of the preceding payment. Journalize the entry to record (a) the transaction on June 30, (b) the payment of the first installment on December 31, and (c) the payment of the second installment the following June 30.

EXERCISE 10-11
ACCRUED PRODUCT
WARRANTY
Objective 5

Blair Company warrants its products for one year. The estimated product warranty is 2% of sales. If sales were $750,000 for January, journalize the adjusting entry required at January 31, the end of the first month of the current year, to record the accrued product warranty.

WhAT'S WRONG
WITH THi?

The fiscal year for K. L. Clark Co. ends on June 30. However, the company computes and reports payroll taxes on the calendar-year basis. What is wrong with these procedures for accounting for payroll taxes?

PROBLEMS

Series A

PROBLEM 10-1A
ENTRIES FOR PAYROLL
AND PAYROLL TAXES
Objectives 1, 2

The following information relative to the payroll for the week ended December 30 was obtained from the records of D. N. Bonnar Co.:

Salaries:		Deductions:	
Sales salaries	$ 86,500	Income tax withheld	$18,050
Warehouse salaries	18,980	FICA tax withheld	8,175
Office salaries	9,520	Group insurance	1,350
	$115,000	U.S. savings bonds	1,200

Tax rates assumed:
   FICA, 7.5% on first $60,000 and 1.5% on excess of $60,000 of employee annual earnings
   State unemployment (employer only), 4.2%   4,830
   Federal unemployment, 0.8%   920

Instructions

1. Assuming that the payroll for the last week of the year is to be paid on December 31, journalize the following entries:

    a. December 30, to record the payroll.

    b. December 30, to record the employer's payroll taxes on the payroll to be paid on December 31. Of the total payroll for the last week of the year, $9,000 is subject to unemployment compensation taxes.

2. Assuming that the payroll for the last week of the year is to be paid on January 5 of the following year, journalize the following entries:

    a. December 31, to record the payroll.

    b. January 5, to record the employer's payroll taxes on the payroll to be paid on January 5.

If the working papers correlating with the textbook are not used, omit Problem 10-2A.

PROBLEM 10-2A
PAYROLL REGISTER
Objectives 1, 2

The payroll register for C. L. Pugh Co. for the week ended December 12 of the current fiscal year is presented in the working papers.

Instructions

1. Journalize the entry to record the payroll for the week.
2. Assuming the use of a voucher system and payment by regular check, journalize the entries to record the payroll voucher and the issuance of the checks to employees.
3. Journalize the entry to record the employer's payroll taxes for the week. Assume the following tax rates: state unemployment, 3.1%; federal unemployment, 0.8%. Of the earnings, $1,020 is subject to unemployment taxes.
4. Journalize the entries to record the following selected transactions:

    Dec. 16. Prepared a voucher, payable to Burbank National Bank, for employees' income taxes, $937.00, and FICA taxes, $766.06.

        16. Issued a check to Burbank National Bank in payment of the voucher.

PROBLEM 10-3A
WAGE AND TAX
STATEMENT DATA AND
EMPLOYER FICA TAX
Objectives 1, 2

Graham Company began business on January 2 of last year. Salaries were paid to employees on the last day of each month, and both FICA tax and federal income tax were withheld in the required amounts. An employee who is hired in the middle of the month receives half the monthly salary for that month. All required payroll tax reports were filed and the correct amount of payroll taxes was remitted by the company for the calendar year. Before the Wage and Tax Statements (Form W-2) could be prepared for distributing to employees and filing with the Social Security Administration, the employees' earnings records were inadvertently destroyed.

None of the employees resigned or were discharged during the year, and there were no changes in salary rates. The FICA tax was withheld at the rate of 7.5% on the first $60,000 of salary and at the rate of 1.5% on salary in excess of $60,000. Data on dates of employment, salary rates, and employees' income taxes withheld, which are summarized as follows, were obtained from personnel records and payroll records.

Employee	Date First Employed	Monthly Salary	Monthly Income Tax Withheld
Alvarez	Jan. 16	$2,800	$ 471
Cruz	Nov. 1	2,500	394
Funk	Jan. 2	4,200	895
Little	July 16	3,400	636
Powell	Jan. 2	5,400	1,374
Soong	May 1	3,600	652
Wilson	Feb. 16	4,000	864

SPREADSHEET
PROBLEM

Instructions

1. Calculate the amounts to be reported on each employee's Wage and Tax Statement (Form W-2) for the year, arranging the data in the following form:

Employee	Gross Earnings	Federal Income Tax Withheld	FICA Tax Withheld

2. Calculate the following employer payroll taxes for the year: (a) FICA; (b) state unemployment compensation at 4.2% on the first $7,000 of each employee's earnings; (c) federal unemployment compensation at 0.8% on the first $7,000 of each employee's earnings; (d) total.

PROBLEM 10-4A
PAYROLL REGISTER
Objectives 1, 2

The following data for Butler Co. relate to the payroll for the week ended December 7, 1994:

Employee	Hours Worked	Hourly Rate	Weekly Salary	Federal Income Tax	U.S. Savings Bonds	Accumulated Earnings, Nov. 30
A	40	$20.00		$166	$25.00	$38,880
B	42	20.00		265	37.50	40,500
C			$1,200	300	50.00	60,000
D	40	11.00		68		22,000
E	40	15.00		115	25.00	30,000
F	48	12.75		125		15,300
G	40	14.00		93	25.00	28,000
H			350	35		2,100
I	20	11.00		15		2,700
J	40	15.00		81		30,000

Employees C and H are office staff, and all of the other employees are sales personnel. All sales personnel are paid 1½ times the regular rate for all hours in excess of 40 hours per week. The FICA tax rate is 7.5% on the first $60,000 of annual earnings and 1.5% of annual earnings in excess of $60,000 for each employee. The next payroll check to be used is No. 818.

SPREADSHEET
PROBLEM

Instructions
1. Prepare a payroll register for Butler Co., similar to the one in Exhibit 3, for the week ended December 7, 1994.
2. Journalize the entry to record the payroll for the week.

PROBLEM 10-5A
PAYROLL ACCOUNTS AND
YEAR-END ENTRIES
Objectives 1, 2

The following accounts, with the balances indicated, appear in the ledger of Becker Company on December 1 of the current year:

212	Salaries Payable	—
213	FICA Tax Payable	$ 6,000
214	Employees Federal Income Tax Payable	7,500
215	Employees State Income Tax Payable	13,260
216	State Unemployment Tax Payable	1,710
217	Federal Unemployment Tax Payable	360
218	Bond Deductions Payable	715
219	Medical Insurance Payable	3,875
611	Sales Salaries Expense	631,300
711	Officers Salaries Expense	311,800
712	Office Salaries Expense	85,500
719	Payroll Taxes Expense	92,430

The following transactions relating to payroll, payroll deductions, and payroll taxes occurred during December:

Dec. 2. Prepared Voucher No. 637 for $715, payable to Marine National Bank, to purchase U.S. savings bonds for employees.
2. Issued Check No. 620 in payment of Voucher No. 637.
3. Prepared Voucher No. 638 for $13,500, payable to Marine National Bank for $6,000 of FICA tax and $7,500 of employees' federal income tax due.
3. Issued Check No. 621 in payment of Voucher No. 638.
14. Journalized the entry to record the biweekly payroll. A summary of the payroll record follows:

Salary distribution:		
Sales	$30,600	
Officers	15,200	
Office	3,800	$49,600
Deductions:		
FICA tax	$ 3,250	
Federal income tax withheld	7,790	
State income tax withheld	1,920	
Savings bond deductions	315	
Medical insurance deductions	480	13,755
Net amount		$35,845

14. Prepared Voucher No. 646, payable to Payroll Bank Account, for the net amount of the biweekly payroll.

14. Issued Check No. 627 in payment of Voucher No. 646.

14. Journalized the entry to record payroll taxes on employees' earnings of December 14: FICA, $3,250; state unemployment tax, $163; federal unemployment tax, $35.

17. Prepared Voucher No. 647 for $14,290, payable to Marine National Bank for $6,500 of FICA tax and $7,790 of employees' federal income tax due.

17. Issued Check No. 633 in payment of Voucher No. 647.

18. Prepared Voucher No. 650 for $3,875, payable to Wilson Insurance Company, for the semiannual premium on the group medical insurance policy.

19. Issued Check No. 639 in payment of Voucher No. 650.

28. Journalized the entry to record the biweekly payroll. A summary of the payroll record follows:

Salary distribution:		
Sales	$28,500	
Officers	15,200	
Office	3,800	$47,500
Deductions:		
FICA tax	$ 3,010	
Federal income tax withheld	7,565	
State income tax withheld	1,845	
Savings bond deductions	315	12,735
Net amount		$34,765

28. Prepared Voucher No. 684, payable to Payroll Bank Account, for the net amount of the biweekly payroll.

28. Issued check No. 671 in payment of Voucher No. 684.

28. Journalized the entry to record payroll taxes on employees' earnings of December 28: FICA, $3,010; state unemployment tax, $160; federal unemployment tax, $33.

30. Prepared Voucher No. 690 for $630, payable to Marine National Bank, to purchase U.S. savings bonds for employees.

30. Issued Check No. 680 in payment of Voucher No. 690.

30. Prepared Voucher No. 691 for $13,260, payable to Marine National Bank, for employees' state income tax due on December 31.

30. Issued Check No. 681 in payment of Voucher No. 691.

Instructions

1. Journalize the transactions.
2. Journalize the adjusting entry on December 31 to record salaries for the incomplete payroll period. Salaries accrued are as follows: sales salaries, $2,950; officers salaries, $1,640; office salaries, $410. The payroll taxes are immaterial and are not accrued. Post to the accounts.

SOLUTIONS SOFTWARE

Instructions for Solving Problem 10-5A Using Solutions Software

1. Load opening balances.
2. Enter your name in the Student Name field in the General Information data entry window. Set the run date to December 31 of the current year.
3. Save the opening balances file to your drive and directory.
4. Select the General Journal entries option and key the journal entries. Leave the reference field blank.
5. Display a journal entries report.
6. Display a trial balance.
7. Key the adjusting entries for payroll only. All other adjustments have been made. Key ADJ.ENT. in the reference field.
8. Display the financial statements.
9. Save a backup copy of your data file.
10. Perform period-end closing.
11. Display a post-closing trial balance.
12. Save your data file to disk.
13. End the session.

PROBLEM 10-6A
INCOME-SHARING
BONUSES
Objective 3

The Chief Operating Officer (COO) of TX Co. is entitled to an annual income-sharing bonus of 5%. For the current year, income before bonus and income taxes is $309,000, and income taxes are estimated at 40% of income before income taxes.

Instructions
1. Calculate the amount of the bonus, assuming that:
    a. The bonus is based on income before deductions for bonus and income taxes.
    b. The bonus is based on income after deduction for bonus but before deduction for income taxes.
    c. The bonus is based on income after deduction for income taxes but before deduction for bonus.
    d. The bonus is based on income after deductions for bonus and income taxes.

**SHARPEN YOUR
COMMUNICATION SKILLS** ►

2. a. Which bonus plan would the COO prefer? Discuss.
    b. Would this plan always be the COO's choice, regardless of TX Co.'s income level? Discuss.

PROBLEM 10-7A
PURCHASES AND NOTES
PAYABLE TRANSACTIONS
Objectives 3, 4, 5

The following items were selected from among the transactions completed by Landon Co. during the current year:

Jan. 15. Purchased merchandise on account from Wyatt Co., $7,800.

Mar. 1. Purchased merchandise on account from Evans Co., $9,600.

6. Issued a 30-day, 12% note for $7,800 to Wyatt Co., on account.

10. Paid Evans Co. for the invoice of March 1, less 1% discount.

Apr. 5. Paid Wyatt Co. the amount owed on the note on March 6.

July 15. Borrowed $8,000 from Royal National Bank, issuing a 90-day, 13% note.

25. Issued a 120-day, non-interest-bearing note for $20,000 to Barnett State Bank. The bank discounted the note at the rate of 15%.

Oct. 13. Paid Royal National Bank the interest due on the note of July 15 and renewed the loan by issuing a new 30-day, 15% note for $8,000. (Journalize both the debit and credit to the notes payable account.)

Nov. 12. Paid Royal National Bank the amount due on the note of October 13.

22. Paid Barnett State Bank the amount due on the note of July 25.

Dec. 1. Purchased office equipment from Bunn Equipment Co. for $57,500, paying $7,500 and issuing a series of ten 12% notes for $5,000 each, coming due at 30-day intervals.

31. Paid the amount due Bunn Equipment Co. on the first note in the series issued on December 1.

31. Paid $27,500 of the annual pension cost of $40,000. (Record both the payment and unfunded pension liability.)

Instructions
1. Journalize the transactions.
2. Journalize the adjusting entries for each of the following accrued expenses for the current year:
    a. Vacation pay $15,000
    b. Product warranty cost   12,750
3. Journalize the adjusting entry for the accrued interest at December 31 on the nine notes owed to Bunn Equipment Co.
4. Assume that a single note for $50,000 had been issued on December 1 instead of the series of ten notes and that its terms required principal payments of $5,000 each 30 days, with interest at 12% on the principal balance before applying the $5,000 payment. Calculate the amount that would have been due and payable on December 31.

**SOLUTIONS
SOFTWARE**

Instructions for Solving Problem 10-7A Using Solutions Software
1. Load opening balances.
2. Enter your name in the Student Name field in the General Information data entry window. Set the run date to December 31 of the current year.
3. Save the opening balances file to your drive and directory.
4. Select the General Journal Entries option and key the journal entries. Leave the reference field blank. Note: To review the chart of accounts, select F-1.
5. Display a journal entries report.
6. Display a trial balance.
7. Key the adjusting entries. Key ADJ.ENT. in the reference field.

(continued)

8. Display the financial statements.
9. Save a backup copy of your data file.
10. Perform period-end closing.
11. Display a post-closing trial balance.
12. Save your data file to disk.
13. End the session.

Series B

PROBLEM 10-1B
ENTRIES FOR PAYROLL
AND PAYROLL TAXES
Objectives 1,2

The following information relative to the payroll for the week ended December 30 was obtained from the records of E. Thurmond Co.:

Salaries:		Deductions:	
Sales salaries	$148,700	Income tax withheld	$33,850
Warehouse salaries	21,280	FICA tax withheld	8,460
Office salaries	12,020	U.S. savings bonds	4,400
	$182,000	Group insurance	2,800

Tax rates assumed:
   FICA, 7.5% on first $60,000 and 1.5% on excess of $60,000 of employee annual earnings
   State unemployment (employer only), 3.8%
   Federal unemployment, 0.8%

Instructions

1. Assuming that the payroll for the last week of the year is to be paid on December 31, journalize the following entries:
   a. December 30, to record the payroll.
   b. December 30, to record the employer's payroll taxes on the payroll to be paid on December 31. Of the total payroll for the last week of the year, $15,000 is subject to unemployment compensation taxes.
2. Assuming that the payroll for the last week of the year is to be paid on January 4 of the following fiscal year, journalize the following entries:
   a. December 30, to record the payroll.
   b. January 4, to record the employer's payroll taxes on the payroll to be paid on January 4.

PROBLEM 10-2B
PAYROLL REGISTER
Objectives 1, 2

If the working papers correlating with the textbook are not used, omit Problem 10-2B.
The payroll register for L. C. Herbert Co. for the week ended December 12 of the current fiscal year is presented in the working papers.

Instructions

1. Journalize the entry to record the payroll for the week.
2. Assuming the use of a voucher system and payment by regular check, journalize the entries to record the payroll voucher and the issuance of the checks to employees.
3. Journalize the entry to record the employer's payroll taxes for the week. Assume the following tax rates: state unemployment, 3.8%; federal unemployment, 0.8%. Of the earnings, $1,020 is subject to unemployment taxes.
4. Journalize the entries to record the following selected transactions:

   Dec. 15. Prepared a voucher, payable to Second National Bank, for employees' income taxes, $937.00, and FICA taxes, $766.06.
       15. Issued a check to Second National Bank in payment of the voucher.

PROBLEM 10-3B
WAGE AND TAX
STATEMENT DATA AND
EMPLOYER FICA TAX
Objectives 1, 2

Griffin Company began business on January 2 of last year. Salaries were paid to employees on the last day of each month, and both FICA tax and federal income tax were withheld in the required amounts. An employee who is hired in the middle of the month receives half the monthly salary for that month. All required payroll tax reports were filed and the correct amount of payroll taxes was remitted by the company for the calendar year. Before the Wage and Tax Statements (Form W-2) could be prepared for distributing to employees and filing with the Social Security Administration, the employees' earnings records were inadvertently destroyed.

None of the employees resigned or were discharged during the year, and there were no changes in salary rates. The FICA tax was withheld at the rate of 7.5% on the first $60,000 of salary and at the rate of 1.5% on salary in excess of $60,000. Data on dates of employment, salary rates, and employees' income taxes withheld, which are summarized as follows, were obtained from personnel records and payroll records.

Employee	Date First Employed	Monthly Salary	Monthly Income Tax Withheld
Allen	June 2	$2,500	$ 417
Cox	Jan. 2	4,200	854
Gower	Mar. 1	3,800	748
Nunn	Jan. 2	4,000	810
Quinn	Nov. 15	3,600	652
Ruiz	Apr. 15	2,800	461
Wu	Jan. 16	5,300	1,261

Instructions

1. Calculate the amounts to be reported on each employee's Wage and Tax Statement (Form W-2) for the year, arranging the data in the following form:

Employee	Gross Earnings	Federal Income Tax Withheld	FICA Tax Withheld

2. Calculate the following employer payroll taxes for the year: (a) FICA; (b) state unemployment compensation at 3.8% on the first $7,000 of each employee's earnings; (c) federal unemployment compensation at 0.8% on the first $7,000 of each employee's earnings; (d) total.

PROBLEM 10-4B
PAYROLL REGISTER
Objectives 1, 2

The following data for Butler Co. relate to the payroll for the week ended December 7, 1994:

Employee	Hours Worked	Hourly Rate	Weekly Salary	Federal Income Tax	U.S. Savings Bonds	Accumulated Earnings, Nov. 30
A	44	$20.00		$280	$37.50	$44,700
B	40	20.00		166	25.00	38,880
C			$1,120	270	50.00	60,000
D	40	15.00		81		30,000
E	40	15.00		115	25.00	30,000
F	48	12.75		125		15,300
G	40	14.00		93	25.00	28,000
H			400	40		3,200
I	20	11.00		15		2,700
J	40	11.00		68		22,000

Employees C and H are office staff, and all of the other employees are sales personnel. All sales personnel are paid 1½ times the regular rate for all hours in excess of 40 hours per week. The FICA tax rate is 7.5% on the first $60,000 of annual earnings and 1.5% of annual earnings in excess of $60,000 for each employee. The next payroll check to be used is No. 981.

Instructions
1. Prepare a payroll register for Butler Co. for the week ended December 7, 1994.
2. Journalize the entry to record the payroll for the week.

PROBLEM 10-5B
PAYROLL ACCOUNTS AND
YEAR-END ENTRIES
Objectives 1, 2

The following accounts, with the balances indicated, appear in the ledger of Sims and Coen Co. on December 1 of the current year:

212	Salaries Payable	—
213	FICA Tax Payable	$ 7,550
214	Employees Federal Income Tax Payable	9,070
215	Employees State Income Tax Payable	14,586
216	State Unemployment Tax Payable	1,881
217	Federal Unemployment Tax Payable	396
218	Bond Deductions Payable	800
219	Medical Insurance Payable	3,200
611	Sales Salaries Expense	694,430
711	Officers Salaries Expense	342,980
712	Office Salaries Expense	94,050
719	Payroll Taxes Expense	101,673

The following transactions relating to payroll, payroll deductions, and payroll taxes occurred during December:

Dec. 2. Prepared Voucher No. 745 for $800, payable to First National Bank, to purchase U.S. savings bonds for employees.

2. Issued Check No. 728 in payment of Voucher No. 745.

3. Prepared Voucher No. 746 for $16,620, payable to First National Bank for $7,550 of FICA tax and $9,070 of employees' federal income tax due.

3. Issued Check No. 729 in payment of Voucher No. 746.

14. Journalized the entry to record the biweekly payroll. A summary of the payroll record follows:

Salary distribution:		
Sales	$33,660	
Officers	16,720	
Office	4,180	$54,560
Deductions:		
FICA tax	$ 3,575	
Federal income tax withheld	8,569	
State income tax withheld	2,112	
Savings bond deductions	375	
Medical insurance deductions	528	15,159
Net amount		$39,401

Dec. 14. Prepared Voucher No. 757, payable to Payroll Bank Account, for the net amount of the biweekly payroll.

14. Issued Check No. 738 in payment of Voucher No. 757.

14. Journalized the entry to record payroll taxes on employees' earnings of December 14: FICA, $3,575; state unemployment tax, $162; federal unemployment tax, $35.

17. Prepared Voucher No. 758 for $15,719, payable to First National Bank for $7,150 of FICA tax and $8,569 of employees' federal income tax due.

17. Issued Check No. 744 in payment of Voucher No. 758.

18. Prepared Voucher No. 760 for $3,200, payable to Pico Insurance Company, for the semiannual premium on the group medical insurance policy.

19. Issued Check No. 750 in payment of Voucher No. 760.

28. Journalized the entry to record the biweekly payroll. A summary of the payroll record follows:

Salary distribution:		
Sales	$31,350	
Officers	16,720	
Office	4,180	$52,250
Deductions:		
FICA tax	$ 3,311	
Federal income tax withheld	8,322	
State income tax withheld	2,029	
Savings bond deductions	375	14,037
Net amount		$38,213

Dec. 28. Prepared Voucher No. 795, payable to Payroll Bank Account, for the net amount of the biweekly payroll.

28. Issued Check No. 782 in payment of Voucher No. 795.

28. Journalized the entry to record payroll taxes on employees' earnings of December 28: FICA, $3,311; state unemployment tax, $161; federal unemployment tax, $33.

30. Prepared Voucher No. 801 for $750, payable to First National Bank, to purchase U.S. savings bonds for employees.

30. Issued Check No. 791 in payment of Voucher No. 801.

30. Prepared Voucher No. 802 for $14,586, payable to First National Bank, for employees' state income tax due on December 31.

30. Issued Check No. 792 in payment of Voucher No. 802.

Instructions

1. Journalize the transactions.
2. Journalize the adjusting entry on December 31 to record salaries for the incomplete payroll period. Salaries accrued are as follows: sales salaries, $3,245; officers salaries, $1,800; office salaries, $450. The payroll taxes are immaterial and are not accrued. Post to the accounts.

SOLUTIONS SOFTWARE

Instructions for Solving Problem 10-5B Using Solutions Software

1. Load opening balances.
2. Enter your name in the Student Name field in the General Information data entry window. Set the run date to December 31 of the current year.
3. Save the opening balances file to your drive and directory.
4. Select the General Journal entries option and key the journal entries. Leave the reference field blank.
5. Display a journal entries report.
6. Display a trial balance.
7. Key the adjusting entries for payroll only. All other adjustments have been made. Key ADJ.ENT. in the reference field.
8. Display the financial statements.
9. Save a backup copy of your data file.
10. Perform period-end closing.
11. Display a post-closing trial balance.
12. Save your data file to disk.
13. End the session.

PROBLEM 10-6B
INCOME-SHARING
BONUSES
Objective 3

The Chief Operating Officer (COO) of General Products Co. is entitled to an annual income-sharing bonus of 4%. For the current year, income before bonus and income taxes is $720,000, and income taxes are estimated at 40% of income before income taxes.

Instructions

1. Calculate the amount of the bonus, assuming that:
   a. The bonus is based on income before deductions for bonus and income taxes.
   b. The bonus is based on income after deduction for bonus but before deduction for income taxes.
   c. The bonus is based on income after deduction for income taxes but before deduction for bonus.
   d. The bonus is based on income after deductions for bonus and income taxes.
2. a. Which bonus plan would the COO prefer? Discuss.
   b. Would this plan always be the COO's choice, regardless of General Products Co.'s income level? Discuss.

SHARPEN YOUR COMMUNICATION SKILLS ►

PROBLEM 10-7B
PURCHASES AND NOTES
PAYABLE TRANSACTIONS
Objectives 3, 4, 5

The following items were selected from among the transactions completed by Otis Co. during the current year:

Mar. 2. Purchased merchandise on account from Clark Co., $5,000.
       8. Purchased merchandise on account from Malone Co., $10,000.
     12. Paid Clark Co. for the invoice of March 2, less 2% discount.
Apr. 1. Issued a 60-day, 12% note for $10,000 to Malone Co., on account.
May 10. Issued a 120-day, non-interest-bearing note for $45,000 to Garden City Bank. The bank discounted the note at the rate of 14%.
     31. Paid Malone Co. the amount owed on the note of April 1.
Aug. 5. Borrowed $7,500 from First Financial Corporation, issuing a 60-day, 14% note for that amount.
Sep. 7. Paid Garden City Bank the amount due on the note of May 10.
Oct. 4. Paid First Financial Corporation the interest due on the note of August 5 and renewed the loan by issuing a new 30-day, 16% note for $7,500. (Record both the debit and credit to the notes payable account.)
Nov. 3. Paid First Financial Corporation the amount due on the note of October 4.
     15. Purchased store equipment from Sims Equipment Co. for $50,000, paying $8,000 and issuing a series of seven 12% notes for $6,000 each, coming due at 30-day intervals.
Dec. 15. Paid the amount due Sims Equipment Co. on the first note in the series issued on November 15.
     31. Paid $32,400 of the annual pension cost of $45,000. (Record both the payment and the unfunded pension liability.)

Instructions

1. Journalize the transactions.
2. Journalize the adjusting entries for each of the following accrued expenses for the current year:

    a. Vacation pay $17,900
    b. Product warranty cost   15,000

3. Journalize the adjusting entry for the accrued interest at December 31 on the six notes owed to Sims Equipment Co.
4. Assume that a single note for $42,000 had been issued on November 15 instead of the series of seven notes and that its terms required principal payments of $6,000 each 30 days, with interest at 12% on the principal balance before applying the $6,000 payment. Calculate the amount that would have been due and payable on December 15.

**SOLUTIONS
SOFTWARE**

Instructions for Solving Problem 10-7B Using Solutions Software

1. Load opening balances.
2. Enter your name in the Student Name field in the General Information data entry window. Set the run date to December 31 of the current year .
3. Save the opening balances file to your drive and directory.
4. Select the General Journal Entries option and key the journal entries. Leave the reference field blank. Note: To review the chart of accounts, select F-1.
5. Display a journal entries report.
6. Display a trial balance.
7. Key the adjusting entries. Key ADJ.ENT. in the reference field.
8. Display the financial statements.
9. Save a backup copy of your data file.
10. Perform period-end closing.
11. Display a post-closing trial balance.
12. Save your data file to disk.
13. End the session.

MINI-CASE E. ROBB AND CO.

In 1993, your mother retired as president of the family-owned business, E. Robb and Co., and a new president was recruited by an executive search firm. The new president's contract called for an annual base salary of $80,000 plus a bonus of 12% of income after deducting the bonus but before deducting income taxes.

In 1994, the first full year under the new president, E. Robb and Co. reported income of $910,000 before deducting the bonus and income taxes. After being fired on January 3, 1995, the new president demanded immediate payment of a $109,200 bonus for 1994.

Your mother was concerned about the accounting practices used during 1994, and she has asked you to help her in reviewing the accounting records before the bonus is paid. Upon investigation, you have discovered the following facts:

a. The payroll for December 27-31, 1994, was not accrued at the end of the year. The salaries for the five-day period and the applicable payroll taxes are as follows:

Sales salaries	$9,000
Office salaries	3,000
FICA tax	7.5%
State unemployment tax (employer only)	3.2%
Federal unemployment tax	.8%

The payroll was paid on January 9, 1995, for the period December 27, 1994, through January 7, 1995.

b. The semiannual pension cost of $22,500 was not accrued for the last half of 1994. The pension cost was paid to Reliance Insurance Company on January 12, 1995, and was journalized by a debit to Pension Expense and a credit to Cash for $22,500.

c. The estimated product warranty liability of $12,000 for products sold during the year ended December 31, 1994, was not journalized.

d. On July 1, 1994, a one-year insurance policy was purchased for $10,640, debiting the cost to Prepaid Insurance. No adjusting entry was made for insurance expired at December 31, 1994.

e. The vacation pay liability of $12,000 for the year ended December 1994, was not journalized.

Instructions

1. Based on reported 1994 income of $910,000 before deducting the bonus and income taxes, was the president's calculation of the $109,200 bonus correct? Explain.
2. What accounting errors were made in 1994 that would affect the amount of the president's bonus?
3. Based on the employment contract and your answer to (2), what is the correct amount of the president's bonus for 1994?
4. How much did the president's demand for a $109,200 bonus exceed the correct amount of the bonus under the employment contract?
5. ▬▬▬ ► Describe the major advantage and disadvantage of using income-sharing bonuses in employment contracts.

COMPREHENSIVE PROBLEM 3

Selected transactions completed by Key Inc. during its first fiscal year ending December 31 were as follows:

a. Prepared a voucher to establish a petty cash fund of $300 and issued a check in payment of the voucher. (Journalize two entries.)
b. Prepared a voucher to replenish the petty cash fund, based on the following summary of petty cash receipts: office supplies, $95; miscellaneous selling expense, $97; miscellaneous administrative expense, $90.
c. Prepared a voucher for the purchase of $5,000 of merchandise, 1/10, n/30. Purchase invoices are recorded at the net amount using a perpetual inventory system.
d. Paid the invoice in (c) after the discount period had passed.
e. Received cash from daily cash sales for $9,050. The amount indicated by the cash register was $9,060.
f. Received a 60-day, 10% note for $30,000 on account.
g. Discounted note received in (f) at the bank, 30 days prior to maturity, at 12%.
h. Received notice from the bank that the note discounted in (g) had been dishonored. Paid the bank the maturity value of the note.
i. Received amount owed on dishonored note in (h) plus interest for 36 days at 10% computed on the maturity value of the note.
j. Received $800 on account and wrote off the remainder owed on a $1,500 accounts receivable balance. (The allowance method is used in accounting for uncollectible receivables.)

k. Reinstated the account written off in (j) and received $700 cash in full payment.
l. Traded office equipment on May 31 for new equipment with a list price of $125,000. A trade-in allowance of $30,000 was received on the old equipment that had cost $90,000 and had accumulated depreciation of $65,000 as of May 31. A voucher was prepared for the amount owed of $95,000.
m. Journalized the monthly payroll for November, based on the following data:

Salaries:		Deductions:	
Sales salaries	$ 9,500	Income tax withheld	$2,950
Office salaries	4,500	FICA tax withheld	900
	$14,000		

Unemployment tax rates assumed:
State unemployment, 3.8%
Federal unemployment, .8%
Amount subject to unemployment taxes:
State unemployment $2,000
Federal unemployment 2,000

n. Journalized the employer's payroll taxes on the payroll in (m).
o. Issued a 90-day, non-interest-bearing note for $25,000 to the bank, which discounted it at 12%.
p. Journalized voucher for payment of the note in (o) at maturity.
q. The pension cost for the year was $34,000, and a voucher was prepared for $25,000, payable to the trustee for the funded portion.

Instructions

1. Journalize the selected transactions.
2. Based on the following data, prepare a bank reconciliation for November of the current year:

   a. Balance according to the bank statement at November 30, $89,030.
   b. Balance according to the ledger at November 30, $60,130.
   c. Checks outstanding at November 30, $56,630.
   d. Deposit in transit, not recorded by bank, $27,600.
   e. Bank debit memorandum for service charges, $40.
   f. A check for $100 in payment of a voucher was erroneously recorded in the accounts as $10.
3. Based on the bank reconciliation prepared in (2), journalize the entry or entries to be made by Key Inc.
4. Based on the following selected data, journalize the adjusting entries as of December 31 of the current year:

   a. Estimated uncollectible accounts at December 31, $5,950. The balance of Allowance for Doubtful Accounts at December 31 was $900 (debit).
   b. Key Inc. uses a perpetual inventory system. The physical inventory on December 31 indicated an inventory shrinkage of $2,000.
   c. Prepaid insurance expired during the year, $18,400.
   d. Office supplies used during the year, $5,100.
   e. Depreciation is computed as follows:

Asset	Cost	Residual Value	Acquisition Date	Useful Life in Years	Depreciation Method Used
Buildings	$225,000	0	January 2	50	Straight-line
Office Equip.	120,000	$12,000	July 1	5	Sum-of-the-years-digits
Store Equip.	60,000	10,000	January 3	8	Declining-balance (at twice the straight-line rate)

f. A patent costing $18,000 when acquired on January 2 has a remaining legal life of 9 years, and was expected to have value for 6 years.

g. The cost of mineral rights was $50,000. Of the estimated deposit of 25,000 tons of ore, 6,000 tons were mined during the year.

h. Total vacation pay expense for the year, $7,000.

i. A product warranty was granted beginning December 1 and covering a one-year period. The estimated cost is 3% of sales, which totaled $150,000 in December.

5. Based on the following post-closing trial balance and other data, prepare a balance sheet in report form at December 31 of the current year:

Key Inc.
Post-Closing Trial Balance
December 31, 19—

Petty Cash	300	
Cash	59,250	
Marketable Equity Securities	40,000	
Allowance for Decline to Market		4,510
Notes Receivable	50,000	
Accounts Receivable	152,300	
Allowance for Doubtful Accounts		5,950
Merchandise Inventory	220,250	
Prepaid Insurance	12,950	
Office Supplies	2,300	
Land	50,000	
Buildings	225,000	
Accumulated Depreciation—Buildings		4,500
Office Equipment	120,000	
Accumulated Depreciation—Office Equipment		18,000
Store Equipment	60,000	
Accumulated Depreciation—Store Equipment		15,000
Mineral Rights	50,000	
Accumulated Depletion		12,000
Patents	15,000	
FICA Tax Payable		2,100
Employees Federal Income Tax Payable		2,950
State Unemployment Tax Payable		1,520
Federal Unemployment Tax Payable		320
Salaries Payable		14,000
Accounts Payable		88,000
Product Warranty Payable		4,500
Vacation Pay Payable		7,000
Unfunded Pension Liability		2,000
Notes Payable		450,000
Stock Capital		100,000
Retained Earings		325,000
	1,057,350	1,057,350

The following information relating to the balance sheet accounts at December 31 is obtained from supplementary records:

Notes receivable is a current asset.

The merchandise inventory is stated at cost by the lifo method.

The product warranty payable is a current liability.

Vacation pay payable:

Current liability	$ 5,000
Long-term liability	2,000

The unfunded pension liability is a long-term liability.

Notes payable:

Current liability	$ 50,000
Long-term liability	400,000

(continued)

6. Assuming that the general manager had been granted a 4% income-sharing bonus (based on income after deduction for the bonus) and income before the bonus was $325,000, what would have been the amount of the bonus?

7. On February 7 of the following year, the merchandise inventory was destroyed by fire. Based on the following data obtained from the accounting records, estimate the cost of the merchandise destroyed:

Jan. 1 Merchandise inventory	$220,250
Jan. 1–Feb. 7 Purchases (net)	189,750
Sales (net)	350,000
Estimated gross profit rate	35%

SOLUTIONS SOFTWARE

Instructions for Solving Comprehensive Problem 3 Using Solutions Software

1. Load opening balances.
2. Enter your name in the Student Name field in the General Information data entry window. Set the run date to December 31 of the current year.
3. Save the opening balances file to your drive and directory.
4. Select the General Journal Entries option and key the journal entries. Use December 31 of the current year as the date for each entry. Key (a), (b), etc., in the reference field to identify each transaction.
5. Display a journal entries report.
6. Display a trial balance.
7. Key the adjusting entries. Key ADJ.ENT. in the reference field.
8. Display the financial statements.
9. Save a backup copy of your data file.
10. Perform period-end closing.
11. Display a post-closing trial balance.
12. Save your data file to disk.
13. End the session.

ANSWERS TO SELF-EXAMINATION QUESTIONS

1. **D** The amount of net pay of $687.75 (answer D) is determined as follows:

Gross pay:		
40 hours at $20	$800.00	
5 hours at $30	150.00	$950.00
Deductions:		
Federal income tax withheld	$212.00	
FICA:		
$600 × .075	$45.00	
$350 × .015	5.25	50.25	262.25
Net pay		$687.75

2. **B** Employers are usually required to withhold a portion of the earnings of their employees for payment of federal income taxes (answer A), FICA tax (answer C), and state and local income taxes (answer D). Generally, federal unemployment compensation taxes (answer B) are levied against the employer only and thus are not deducted from employee earnings.

3. **D** The employer incurs operating costs for FICA tax (answer A), federal unemployment compensation tax (answer B), and state unemployment compensation tax (answer C). The employees' federal income tax (answer D) is not an operating cost of the employer. It is withheld from the employees' earnings.

4. **C** The maturity value is $5,100, determined as follows:

Face amount of note	$5,000
Plus interest ($5,000 × 12/100 × 60/360)	100
Maturity value	$5,100

5. **B** The net amount available to a borrower from discounting a note payable is called the proceeds. The proceeds of $4,900 (answer B) is determined as follows:

Face amount of note	$5,000
Less discount ($5,000 × 12/100 × 60/360)	100
Proceeds	$4,900

You and Accounting

On August 4, 1993, *The Wall Street Journal* reported that **American Telephone & Telegraph Inc. (AT&T)** bonds due in 2002, paying 7⅛% interest, were selling for 106¼. Does this mean that you could buy these bonds on this date for $106.25 each?

The Wall Street Journal also reported that **Whirlpool Corporation** zero-coupon bonds due in 2011 were selling for 46. Why are these bonds selling at such a low price?

You will learn the answers to these and other questions related to bonds in this chapter.

Chapter 11
Long-Term Liabilities: Bonds Payable

LEARNING OBJECTIVES
After studying this chapter, you should be able to:

Objective 1
List the characteristics of bonds.

Objective 2
Explain the present-value concept and the present value of bonds payable.

Objective 3
Journalize entries for bonds payable.

Objective 4
Journalize entries for bond sinking funds, using future-value concepts.

Objective 5
Journalize entries for bond redemptions.

Objective 6
Prepare a balance sheet that includes bonds payable.

A corporation may finance its operations by borrowing money on a long-term basis. In this chapter, we will discuss the accounting principles and concepts related to issuing long-term debt, including bonds payable.

CHARACTERISTICS OF BONDS PAYABLE

A corporation normally borrows money on a long-term basis by issuing either notes or bonds. A **bond** is a form of interest-bearing note. Long-term notes may be issued to a few lending agencies or to a single investor, such as an insurance company. Bonds are usually sold to underwriters who are dealers and brokers in securities. Underwriters, in turn, sell them to investors. In this chapter, we will focus on the accounting principles and concepts for bonds payable. However, much of this discussion also applies to long-term notes.

When funds are borrowed through issuing bonds, there is a definite commitment to pay interest and to repay the principal at a stated future date. Bondholders are creditors of the issuing corporation, and their claims for interest and for repayment of principal rank ahead of the claims of stockholders.

A corporation that issues bonds enters into a contract, called a **bond indenture** or **trust indenture** with the bondholders. A bond issue is normally divided into a number of individual bonds, which may be of varying denominations. Usually the principal of each bond, called the **face value**, is $1,000 or a multiple of $1,000. The interest on bonds may be payable annually, semiannually, or quarterly. Most bonds pay interest semiannually.

The prices of bonds are quoted on bond exchanges as a percentage of the bonds' face value. Thus, Whirlpool bonds quoted at 106¼ could be purchased for $1,060.25. Likewise, bonds quoted at 109 could be purchased for $1,090.

Registered bonds may be transferred from one owner to another by endorsement on the bond certificate. The issuing corporation records or registers the name and the address of each bondholder. Interest payments are then made to each registered bondholder. Title to **coupon bonds**, also called **bearer bonds**, is transferred merely by delivery. Thus, the issuing corporation does not know the identity of the bondholders. Interest coupons, in the form of checks or drafts payable to bearer, are attached to the bond certificate. At each interest date, the holder detaches the appropriate coupon and presents it to a bank for payment. Although coupon bonds were issued often in the past, they are rarely issued today.

When all bonds of an issue mature at the same time, they are called **term bonds**. If the maturities are spread over several dates, they are called **serial bonds**. For example, one-tenth of an issue of $1,000,000 bonds, or $100,000, may mature 16 years from the issuance date, another $100,000 in the 17th year, and so on until the final $100,000 matures in the 25th year.

Bonds that may be exchanged for other securities under certain conditions are called **convertible bonds**. Bonds issued by a corporation that reserves the right to redeem bonds before maturity are called **callable bonds**.

A **secured bond** is one that gives the bondholder a claim on specific assets in case the issuing corporation fails to meet its liabilities on the bonds. The properties mortgaged or pledged may be specific buildings and equipment, the entire plant, or stocks and bonds of other companies owned by the corporation. Unsecured bonds issued on the basis of the general credit of the corporation are called **debenture bonds**.

THE PRESENT-VALUE CONCEPT AND BONDS PAYABLE

The concept of present value plays an important role in many accounting analyses and business decisions. For example, accounting analyses based on the present-value concept are useful for evaluating proposals for long-term investments in plant and equipment. In this chapter, we discuss the concept of present value as it relates to bonds.

The concept of **present value** is based on the time value of money. What is the time value of money? An amount of cash to be received at some date in the future is not the equivalent of the same amount of cash held at an earlier date. In other words, a sum of cash to be received in the future is not as valuable as the same sum on hand today. This is because cash on hand today can be invested to earn income.

How Refinancing Works

Some of the same factors that influence a corporation's decision on financing are also considered when a company refinances, or changes the structure of its debt and stockholders' equity. These concerns are described in the following excerpt from an article in USA TODAY.

When a major company like Allegis Corp. announces that it is "recapitalizing" [refinancing], many shareholders may be baffled. . . . Recapitalization plans aren't as complicated as they seem, however. Here are some basic questions and answers:

What is capital?

Simply put, it's a company's money. It can come from two sources: stockholders and lenders.

The stockholders' share is called equity. It represents cash the company has raised by selling stock, and profits the company has built up.

The other part of capital is money borrowed from banks or raised by selling bonds.

How companies balance equity and debt is up to them. At IBM Corp., only 11% of total capital is debt. Sears, Roebuck and Co. has 46% debt. The level of debt a company keeps depends on the risk its managers are willing to assume.

What does risk have to do with it?

It's no different for a company than for an individual. The more debt you have, the greater the risk. Reason: Any profit you earn first must go to meet interest payments. If earnings aren't sufficient to cover the interest owed, you'll have to deplete your savings—or sell something—to raise the needed cash.

What happens in a recapitalization?

A company decides to borrow heavily to raise cash for a large, one-time cash . . . payment to shareholders. . . . [In addition,] . . . shareholders also receive new shares to replace their old shares in the company. . . . [In] the process, the company generally [reduces its equity]. It's replaced with debt.

How can the company afford the debt load?

The company is forced to operate more efficiently than ever. It will have to slash expenses to keep earnings up in the face of higher interest expenses. Owens-Corning Fiberglas Corp., for example, pared its research costs significantly after its recapitalization last year. . . .

Is there any advantage in being so heavily in debt?

Debt does have a good side. By borrowing, you gain "leverage"—the ability to control more assets by using someone else's money. That can magnify the return to shareholders, if business is good and the firm operates efficiently. . . .

Source: Neil Budde, "How Company Recapitalization Plans Work," USA TODAY (June 8, 1987).

For example, $100 on hand today would be more valuable than $100 received a year from today. In this case, if the $100 cash on hand today can be invested to earn 10% per year, the $100 will accumulate to $110 ($100 plus $10 earnings) in one year. The $100 on hand today is the present-value amount that is equivalent to $110 to be received a year from today.

When a corporation issues bonds, the price that a buyer is willing to pay for the bonds is the sum of the present values of the following amounts:

1. The face amount of the bonds at a maturity date.
2. Periodic interest at a specified percentage of the face amount.

Present Value of the Face Amount of Bonds

The present value of the face amount of bonds is the value today of the amount to be received at the maturity date. For example, assume you are to receive $1,000 in one year and that the rate of interest is 12%. The present value of the $1,000 is $892.86 ($1,000 ÷ 1.12). If you are to receive the $1,000 one year later (two years in all), with the interest compounded at the end of the first year, the present value is $797.20 ($892.86 ÷ 1.12).

You can determine the present value of a cash sum to be received in the future by a series of divisions as illustrated above. In practice, however, it is normal to use a table of present values for this purpose. The **present value of $1 table** can be used to find the present-value factor for $1 to be received for the appropriate number of periods in the future. The amount of the future cash sum is then multiplied by this factor to determine its present value. Exhibit 1 is a partial table of the present value of $1.[1]

---

[1] To simplify the illustrations and homework assignments, the tables presented in this chapter are limited to 20 periods for a small number of interest rates, and the amounts are carried to only four decimal places. Computer programs are available for determining present value factors for any number of interest rates, decimal places, or periods. More complete interest tables are presented in Appendix A.

Exhibit 1
Present Value of $ 1 at Compound Interest

Periods	5%	5½%	6%	6½%	7%	10%	11%	12%	13%	14%
1	0.9524	0.9479	0.9434	0.9390	0.9346	0.9091	0.9009	0.8929	0.8850	0.8772
2	0.9070	0.8985	0.8900	0.8817	0.8734	0.8264	0.8116	0.7972	0.7832	0.7695
3	0.8638	0.8516	0.8396	0.8278	0.8163	0.7513	0.7312	0.7118	0.6931	0.6750
4	0.8227	0.8072	0.7921	0.7773	0.7629	0.6830	0.6587	0.6355	0.6133	0.5921
5	0.7835	0.7651	0.7473	0.7299	0.7130	0.6209	0.5935	0.5674	0.5428	0.5194
6	0.7462	0.7252	0.7050	0.6853	0.6663	0.5645	0.5346	0.5066	0.4803	0.4556
7	0.7107	0.6874	0.6651	0.6435	0.6228	0.5132	0.4817	0.4523	0.4251	0.3996
8	0.6768	0.6516	0.6274	0.6042	0.5820	0.4665	0.4339	0.4039	0.3762	0.3506
9	0.6446	0.6176	0.5919	0.5674	0.5439	0.4241	0.3909	0.3606	0.3329	0.3075
10	0.6139	0.5854	0.5584	0.5327	0.5083	0.3855	0.3522	0.3220	0.2946	0.2697
11	0.5847	0.5549	0.5268	0.5002	0.4751	0.3505	0.3173	0.2875	0.2607	0.2366
12	0.5568	0.5260	0.4970	0.4697	0.4440	0.3186	0.2858	0.2567	0.2307	0.2076
13	0.5303	0.4986	0.4688	0.4410	0.4150	0.2897	0.2575	0.2292	0.2042	0.1821
14	0.5051	0.4726	0.4423	0.4141	0.3878	0.2633	0.2320	0.2046	0.1807	0.1597
15	0.4810	0.4479	0.4173	0.3888	0.3624	0.2394	0.2090	0.1827	0.1599	0.1401
16	0.4581	0.4246	0.3936	0.3651	0.3387	0.2176	0.1883	0.1631	0.1415	0.1229
17	0.4363	0.4024	0.3714	0.3428	0.3166	0.1978	0.1696	0.1456	0.1252	0.1078
18	0.4155	0.3815	0.3503	0.3219	0.2959	0.1799	0.1528	0.1300	0.1108	0.0946
19	0.3957	0.3616	0.3305	0.3022	0.2765	0.1635	0.1377	0.1161	0.0981	0.0829
20	0.3769	0.3427	0.3118	0.2838	0.2584	0.1486	0.1240	0.1037	0.0868	0.0728

For the preceding example, Exhibit 1 indicates that the present value of $1 to be received in two years with interest of 12% a year is 0.7972. Multiplying $1,000 by 0.7972 yields $797.20. This is the same amount that we determined previously by two consecutive divisions. In Exhibit 1, the Periods column represents the number of compounding periods and the Percentage columns represent the compound interest rate per period. For example, 12% for two years compounded annually, as in the preceding example, is 12% for two periods. Likewise, 12% for two years compounded semiannually would be 6% (12% per year ÷ 2 semiannual periods) for four periods (2 years × 2 semiannual periods). Similarly, 12% for three years compounded semiannually would be 6% (12% ÷ 2) for six periods (3 years × 2 semiannual periods).

Present Value of the Periodic Bond Interest Payments

The present value of the periodic bond interest payments is the value today of the amount of interest to be received at the end of each interest period. Such a series of fixed payments at fixed intervals is called an **annuity**

Exhibit 2 is a partial table of the **present value of an annuity** of $1 at compound interest. Exhibit 2 indicates the present value of $1 to be received at the end of each period for various compound rates of interest. For example, the present value of $1,000 to be received at the end of each of the next five periods at 10% compound interest per period is $3,790.80 ($1,000 × 3.7908).

ACCOUNTING FOR BONDS PAYABLE

Objective 3
Journalize entries for bonds payable.

The interest rate specified in the bond indenture is called the **contract** or **coupon rate**. This rate may differ from the market rate of interest at the time the bonds are issued. If the **market** or **effective rate** is higher than the contract rate, the bonds will sell at a **discount**, or less than their face amount. Why is this the case? Buyers are not willing to pay the face amount for bonds whose contract rate is lower than the market rate. The discount, in effect, represents the amount necessary to make up

Exhibit 2
Present Value of Annuity of $1 at
Compound Interest

Periods	5%	5 ½%	6%	6 ½%	7%	10%	11%	12%	13%	14%
1	0.9524	0.9479	0.9434	0.9390	0.9346	0.9091	0.9009	0.8929	0.8850	0.8772
2	1.8594	1.8463	1.8334	1.8206	1.8080	1.7355	1.7125	1.6901	1.6681	1.6467
3	2.7232	2.6979	2.6730	2.6485	2.6243	2.4869	2.4437	2.4018	2.3612	2.3216
4	3.5460	3.5052	3.4651	3.4258	3.3872	3.1699	3.1024	3.0373	2.9745	2.9137
5	4.3295	4.2703	4.2124	4.1557	4.1002	3.7908	3.6959	3.6048	3.5172	3.4331
6	5.0757	4.9955	4.9173	4.8410	4.7665	4.3553	4.2305	4.1114	3.9976	3.8887
7	5.7864	5.6830	5.5824	5.4845	5.3893	4.8684	4.7122	4.5638	4.4226	4.2883
8	6.4632	6.3346	6.2098	6.0888	5.9713	5.3349	5.1461	4.9676	4.7988	4.6389
9	7.1078	6.9522	6.8017	6.6561	6.5152	5.7590	5.5370	5.3283	5.1317	4.9464
10	7.7217	7.5376	7.3601	7.1888	7.0236	6.1446	5.8892	5.6502	5.4262	5.2161
11	8.3064	8.0925	7.8869	7.6890	7.4987	6.4951	6.2065	5.9377	5.6869	5.4527
12	8.8632	8.6185	8.3838	8.1587	7.9427	6.8137	6.4924	6.1944	5.9176	5.6603
13	9.3936	9.1171	8.8527	8.5997	8.3577	7.1034	6.7499	6.4235	6.1218	5.8424
14	9.8986	9.5896	9.2950	9.0138	8.7455	7.3667	6.9819	6.6282	6.3025	6.0021
15	10.3797	10.0376	9.7123	9.4027	9.1079	7.6061	7.1909	6.8109	6.4624	6.1422
16	10.8378	10.4622	10.1059	9.7678	9.4467	7.8237	7.3792	6.9740	6.6039	6.2651
17	11.2741	10.8646	10.4773	10.1106	9.7632	8.0216	7.5488	7.1196	6.7291	6.3729
18	11.6896	11.2461	10.8276	10.4325	10.0591	8.2014	7.7016	7.2497	6.8399	6.4674
19	12.0853	11.6077	11.1581	10.7347	10.3356	8.3649	7.8393	7.3658	6.9380	6.5504
20	12.4622	11.9504	11.4699	11.0185	10.5940	8.5136	7.9633	7.4694	7.0248	6.6231

for the difference in the market and the contract interest rates. In contrast, if the market rate is lower than the contract rate, the bonds will sell at a **premium**, or more than their face amount. In this case, buyers are willing to pay more than the face amount for bonds whose contract rate is higher than the market rate.

Bonds Issued at Face Amount

To illustrate the journal entries for issuing bonds, assume that on January 1 a corporation issues for cash $100,000 of 12%, five-year bonds, with interest of $6,000 payable semiannually. The market rate of interest at the time the bonds are issued is 12%. Since the contract rate and the market rate of interest are the same, the bonds will sell at their face amount. This amount is the sum of (1) the present value of the face amount of $100,000 to be repaid in five years and (2) the present value of ten semiannual interest payments of $6,000 each. This computation is shown below.[2]

Present value of face amount of $100,000 due in 5 years,
   at 12% compounded semiannually: $100,000 × 0.5584
   (present value of $1 for 10 periods at 6%)...................................... $ 55,840
Present value of 10 semiannual interest payments of $6,000,
   at 12% compounded semiannually: $6,000 × 7.3601 (present
   value of annuity of $1 for 10 periods at 6%).................................. 44,160
Total present value of bonds... $100,000

    The basic data for computing the above amounts were obtained from the present-value tables in Exhibits 1 and 2. The first of the two amounts, **$55,840**, is the present value of the $100,000 that is to be repaid in five years. The $55,840 is determined as follows:

1. The present value of $1 for ten periods (five years of semiannual payments) at 6% semiannually (12% annual rate) is located in Exhibit 1.

[2] Because the present-value tables are rounded to four decimal places, minor rounding differences may appear in the illustrations.

2. The present-value factor in (1) is multiplied by $100,000.

If the bond indenture provided that no interest would be paid during the entire five-year period, the bonds would be worth only $55,840 at the time of their issuance. To express the concept of present value from a different viewpoint, if $55,840 were invested today, with interest at 12% compounded semiannually, the sum accumulated at the end of ten semiannual periods would be $100,000.

The second of the two amounts, **$44,160**, is the present value of the series of ten $6,000 interest payments. The $44,160 is determined as follows:

1. The present value of an annuity of $1 for ten periods (five years of semiannual payments) at 6% semiannually (12% annual rate) is located in Exhibit 2.
2. The present-value factor in (1) is multiplied by $6,000.

You can also view the present value of $44,160 as the amount that must be deposited today at an interest rate of 12% compounded semiannually to provide ten semiannual withdrawals of $6,000 each. At the end of the tenth withdrawal, the original deposit will be reduced to zero.

The entry to record the issuance of the $100,000 bonds at their face amount is shown below.

| Jan. 1 | Cash | 100,000 | |
| | Bonds Payable | | 100,000 |

At six-month intervals following the issuance of the 12% bonds, interest payments of $6,000 are made. The interest payment is recorded in the usual manner by a debit to Interest Expense and a credit to Cash. At the maturity date, the payment of the principal sum of $100,000 is recorded by a debit to Bonds Payable and a credit to Cash.

Bonds Issued at a Discount

What if the market rate of interest is greater than the contract rate of interest? Will the bonds still sell at their face value? If the market rate of interest is 13% and the contract rate is 12%, the bonds will sell at a discount. The present value of the five-year, $100,000 bonds is computed as follows:

Present value of face amount of $100,000 due in
  5 years, at 13% compounded semiannually: $100,000
  × 0.5327 (present value of $1 for 10 periods at 6½%) $53,270
Present value of 10 semiannual interest payments of $6,000,
  at 13% compounded semiannually: $6,000 × 7.1888 (present
  value of an annuity of $1 for 10 periods at 6½%)   43,133
Total present value of bonds $96,403

The two present values that make up the total are both less than the comparable amounts in the preceding example. This is because the market rate of interest was 12% in the first example, while the market rate of interest was 13% in the above example. The present value of a future amount becomes less and less as the interest rate used to compute the present value increases. Stated in another way, the amount that has to be invested today to equal a future amount becomes less and less as the interest rate that is assumed to be earned on the investment increases.

The entry to record the issuance of the preceding 12% bonds is shown below.

Jan. 1	Cash	96,403	
	Discount on Bonds Payable	3,597	
	Bonds Payable		100,000

When bonds payable are issued at a discount, the amount of the discount is recorded in a separate contra account. The $3,597 discount may be viewed as the amount that is needed to entice investors to accept a contract rate of interest that is below the market rate. In other words, the discount is the market's way of adjusting a bond's contract rate of interest to the higher market rate of interest. In this sense, the discount represents an additional interest expense beyond the amounts paid as periodic interest based on the contract rate of interest. The discount is paid to the bondholders at the maturity date. That is, in the above example the issuer must pay the bondholders $100,000 at maturity, even though only $96,403 was initially received when the bonds were issued.

As we discussed above, a discount represents additional interest expense above the amounts paid as periodic interest. Because of this, generally accepted accounting principles require the amortization of discounts to increase the interest expense over the life of a bond issue.

Amortization of a Bond Discount

There are two methods of amortizing discount to interest expense over the life of a bond issue: (1) the **straight-line method** and (2) the **effective interest rate method**, often called the **interest method**. The interest method is required by generally accepted accounting principles.[3] However, both methods amortize the same total amount of discount over the life of the bonds. The straight-line method is acceptable if the results obtained do not materially differ from the results that would be obtained by the use of the interest method.[4] Because it illustrates the basic concept of amortizing discounts and is simpler, we will illustrate the straight-line method in this chapter. We illustrate the interest method in an appendix to this chapter.

The straight-line method of amortizing bond discount provides for amortization in equal periodic amounts. Applying this method to the preceding example yields amortization of 1/10 of $3,597, or $359.70, each half year. The amount of the interest expense on the bonds remains constant for each half year at $6,000 plus $359.70, or $6,359.70. The entry to record the first interest payment and the amortization of the related amount of discount is shown below.

June 30	Interest Expense	6,359.70	
	Discount on Bonds Payable		359.70
	Cash		6,000.00

Instead of recording the amortization each time the interest is paid, it may be recorded only at the end of the year. When this procedure is used, each interest payment is recorded on the periodic payment date as shown below.

| Interest Expense | 6,000.00 | |
| Cash | | 6,000.00 |

The entry to amortize the discount at the end of the first year is shown below. The amount of the discount amortized, $719.40, is made up of the two semiannual amortization amounts of $359.70.

| Dec. 31 | Interest Expense | 719.40 | |
| | Discount on Bonds Payable | | 719.40 |

Bonds Issued at a Premium

If the market rate of interest is 11% and the contract rate is 12%, the bonds will sell at a premium. The present value of the five-year, $100,000 bonds is computed as follows:

Present value of face amount of $100,000 due in 5 years,
  at 11% compounded semiannually: $100,000 × 0.5854
  (present value of $1 for 10 periods at 5½%) .... $ 58,540
Present value of 10 semiannual interest payments of $6,000,
  at 11% compounded semiannually: $6,000 × 7.5376 (present
  value of an annuity of $1 for 10 periods at 5½%) 45,226
Total present value of bonds $103,766

[3] *Opinions of the Accounting Principles Board, No. 21,* "Interest on Receivables and Payables" (New York: American Institute of Certified Public Accountants, 1971), par. 14.
[4] *Ibid.*

The entry to record the issuance of the bonds is as follows:

Jan. 1	Cash	103,766	
	Bonds Payable		100,000
	Premium on Bonds Payable		3,766

Amortization of a Bond Premium

The amortization of bond premiums is basically the same as that for bond discounts, except that interest expense is decreased. In the above example, the straight-line method yields amortization of 1/10 of $3,766, or $376.60, each half year. The entry to record the first interest payment and the amortization of the related premium is as follows:

June 30	Interest Expense	5,623.40	
	Premium on Bonds Payable	376.60	
	Cash		6,000.00

If the amortization of the premium is recorded only at the end of the year, each interest payment is recorded by debiting Interest Expense and crediting Cash. The amortization of the premium at the end of the first year is then recorded as shown below. The amount of the premium amortized, $753.20, is the sum of the two semiannual amounts of $376.60.

| Dec. 31 | Premium on Bonds Payable | 753.20 | |
| | Interest Expense | | 753.20 |

Zero-Coupon Bonds

Some enterprises issue bonds that do not provide for interest payments. Such bonds are called **zero-coupon bonds**.

Zero-coupon bonds provide for only the payment of the face amount of the bonds at the maturity date. Because the bonds do not provide for interest payments, they sell at a large discount. For example, Whirlpool Corporation's zero-coupon bonds maturing in 2011 were selling for 46 on June 25, 1993.

To further illustrate, if the market rate of interest for five-year bonds that pay interest semiannually is 13%, the present value of $100,000 zero-coupon, five-year bonds is as follows:

Present value of $100,000 due in 5 years, at 13% compounded
semiannually: $100,000 × 0.5327 (present value of $1 for
10 periods at 6½%) $53,270

The accounting for zero-coupon bonds is similar to that for interest-bearing bonds that have been sold at a discount. The entry to record the issuance of the bonds is as follows:

Cash	53,270	
Discount on Bonds Payable	46,730	
Bonds Payable		100,000

The discount of $46,730 is amortized as interest expense over the life of the bonds.

Using Accounting

The bonds issued by companies are rated as to their riskiness as investments by such independent financial reporting services as *Moody's* and *Standard and Poor's*. These services rely heavily upon financial statements and the terms of the bond indenture (for example, whether the bonds are secured) in setting the credit rating. These credit ratings, in turn, influence how much the bonds will sell for in the marketplace.

BOND SINKING FUNDS

Objective 4
Journalize entries for bond sinking funds, using future-value concepts.

A bond indenture may restrict dividends payments by a corporation as a means of increasing the assurance that the bonds will be paid at maturity. In addition to or instead of this restriction, the bond indenture may require that funds for the payment of the face value of the bonds at maturity be set aside over the life of the bond issue. The amounts set aside are kept separate from other assets in a special fund called a **sinking fund**.

Cash deposited in a sinking fund is usually invested in income-producing securities. The periodic deposits plus the earnings on the investments should accumulate to the face value of the bonds at maturity. To compute the amount of these periodic deposits, the concept of future value can be used.

Future-Value Concepts

Future value is the amount that will accumulate at some future date as a result of an investment or a series of investments. For example, if you invest $1,000 at 10% per year, the future value at the end of one year will be $1,100 ($1,000 plus $100 earnings). If you leave the $1,100 to accumulate additional earnings for three years, the future value at the end of the second year will be $1,210 ($1,100 plus $110 earnings), and at the end of the third year, $1,331 ($1,210 plus $121 earnings).

The future value of an investment can also be determined by using a table of future values. Exhibit 3 is a partial table of the future value of $1.

Exhibit 3
Future Value of $1 at Compound Interest

Periods	5%	5½%	6%	6½%	7%	10%	11%	12%	13%	14%
1	1.0500	1.0550	1.0600	1.0650	1.0700	1.1000	1.1100	1.1200	1.1300	1.1400
2	1.1025	1.1130	1.1236	1.1342	1.1449	1.2100	1.2321	1.2544	1.2769	1.2996
3	1.1576	1.1742	1.1910	1.2080	1.2250	1.3310	1.3676	1.4049	1.4429	1.4815
4	1.2155	1.2388	1.2625	1.2865	1.3108	1.4641	1.5181	1.5735	1.6305	1.6890
5	1.2763	1.3070	1.3382	1.3701	1.4026	1.6105	1.6851	1.7623	1.8424	1.9254
6	1.3401	1.3788	1.4185	1.4591	1.5007	1.7716	1.8704	1.9738	2.0820	2.1950
7	1.4071	1.4547	1.5036	1.5540	1.6058	1.9487	2.0762	2.2107	2.3526	2.5023
8	1.4775	1.5347	1.5939	1.6550	1.7182	2.1436	2.3045	2.4760	2.6584	2.8526
9	1.5513	1.6191	1.6895	1.7626	1.8385	2.3580	2.5580	2.7731	3.0040	3.2520
10	1.6289	1.7081	1.7909	1.8771	1.9672	2.5937	2.8394	3.1059	3.3946	3.7072
11	1.7103	1.8021	1.8983	1.9992	2.1049	2.8531	3.1518	3.4786	3.8359	4.2262
12	1.7959	1.9012	2.0122	2.1291	2.2522	3.1384	3.4985	3.8960	4.3345	4.8179
13	1.8857	2.0058	2.1329	2.2675	2.4099	3.4523	3.8833	4.3635	4.8980	5.4924
14	1.9799	2.1161	2.2609	2.4149	2.5785	3.7975	4.3104	4.8871	5.5348	6.2614
15	2.0789	2.2325	2.3966	2.5718	2.7590	4.1773	4.7846	5.4736	6.2543	7.1379
16	2.1829	2.3553	2.5404	2.7390	2.9522	4.5950	5.3109	6.1304	7.0673	8.1373
17	2.2920	2.4848	2.6928	2.9171	3.1588	5.0545	5.8951	6.8660	7.9861	9.2765
18	2.4066	2.6215	2.8543	3.1067	3.3799	5.5599	6.5436	7.6900	9.0243	10.5752
19	2.5270	2.7657	3.0256	3.3086	3.6165	6.1159	7.2633	8.6128	10.1974	12.0557
20	2.6533	2.9178	3.2071	3.5237	3.8697	6.7275	8.0623	9.6463	11.5231	13.7435

For the above example, the table indicates that the future value of $1 in three years (periods), with earnings at the rate of 10% a year, is 1.331. The future value of the investment of $1,000 is computed by multiplying $1,000 by 1.331, which yields $1,331. This is the same amount as determined above.

Future value may also arise from an annuity—a series of equal investments made at fixed intervals. For example, assume that you invest $1,000 at the end of each year at 10% interest per year, compounded annually. The future value of your investment (the annuity) at the end of the third year is $3,310, as shown below.

Year	Beginning Balance	Earnings During Year (10% × Beginning Balance)	Annual Deposit (End of Year)	Accumulation at End of Year
	—	—	$1,000	$1,000
2	$1,000	$100	1,000	2,100
3	2,100	210	1,000	3,310

You can also determine the future value of a series of investments by using a table of future values. Exhibit 4 is a partial table of the future value of an annuity of $1.

Exhibit 4
Future Value of Annuity of $1 at Compound Interest (Investments at End of Period)

Periods	5%	5½%	6%	6½%	7%	10%	11%	12%	13%	14%
1	1.0000	1.0000	1.0000	1.0000	1.0000	1.0000	1.0000	1.0000	1.0000	1.0000
2	2.0500	2.0550	2.0600	2.0650	2.0700	2.1000	2.1100	2.1200	2.1300	2.1400
3	3.1525	3.1680	3.1836	3.1992	3.2149	3.3100	3.3421	3.3744	3.4069	3.4396
4	4.3101	4.3423	4.3746	4.4072	4.4399	4.6410	4.7097	4.7793	4.8498	4.9211
5	5.5256	5.5811	5.6371	5.6936	5.7507	6.1051	6.2278	6.3529	6.4803	6.6101
6	6.8019	6.8881	6.9753	7.0637	7.1533	7.7156	7.9129	8.1152	8.3227	8.5355
7	8.1420	8.2669	8.3938	8.5229	8.6540	9.4872	9.7833	10.0890	10.4047	10.7305
8	9.5491	9.7216	9.8975	10.0769	10.2598	11.4359	11.8594	12.2997	12.7573	13.2328
9	11.0266	11.2563	11.4913	11.7319	11.9780	13.5795	14.1640	14.7757	15.4157	16.0854
10	12.5779	12.8744	13.1808	13.4944	13.8165	15.9374	16.7220	17.5487	18.4198	19.3373
11	14.2068	14.5835	14.9716	15.3716	15.7836	18.5312	19.5614	20.6546	21.8143	23.0445
12	15.9171	16.3856	16.8699	17.3707	17.8885	21.3843	22.7132	24.1331	25.6502	27.2708
13	17.7130	18.2868	18.8821	19.4998	20.1406	24.5227	26.2116	28.0291	29.9847	32.0887
14	19.5986	20.2926	21.0151	21.7673	22.5505	27.9750	30.0949	32.3926	34.8827	37.5811
15	21.5786	22.4087	23.2760	24.1822	25.1290	31.7725	34.4054	37.2797	40.4175	43.8424
16	23.6575	24.6411	25.6725	26.7540	27.8881	35.9497	39.1900	42.7533	46.6717	50.9804
17	25.8404	26.9964	28.2129	29.4930	30.8402	40.5447	44.5008	48.8837	53.7391	59.1176
18	28.1324	29.4812	30.9057	32.4101	33.9990	45.5992	50.3959	55.7497	61.7251	68.3941
19	30.5390	32.1027	33.7600	35.5167	37.3790	51.1591	56.9395	63.4397	70.7494	78.9692
20	33.0660	34.8683	36.7856	38.8253	40.9955	57.2750	64.2028	72.0524	80.9468	91.0249

For the above example, the table indicates that the future value of an annuity of $1 in three years (periods), with earnings at the rate of 10% a year, is 3.310. The future value of the series of investments of $1,000 is computed by multiplying $1,000 by 3.310, which yields $3,310. This is the same amount as determined above.

To illustrate the use of the future-value concept to determine the periodic deposits in a bond sinking fund, assume that a corporation issues $100,000 of ten-year bonds, dated January 1. A bond sinking fund for the payment of the bonds at maturity is to be established, with deposits to be made at the end of each year. If the deposits are expected to earn 14% per year, the annual deposit would be $5,171, determined as follows:

$$\text{Annual Deposit} = \frac{\text{Maturity Value of Bonds}}{\text{Future Value of Annuity of \$1 for 10 Periods at 14\%}}$$

$$\text{Annual Deposit} = \frac{\$100,000}{19.3373}$$

Annual Deposit = $5,171 (rounded)

Accounting for Bond Sinking Funds

When cash is transferred to the sinking fund, an account called Sinking Fund Cash is debited and Cash is credited. The purchase of investments is recorded by a debit to Sinking Fund Investments and a credit to Sinking Fund Cash. As income (interest or dividends) is received, the cash is debited to Sinking Fund Cash and Sinking Fund Income is credited.

We will use the preceding example to illustrate the accounting for a bond sinking fund. In this example, annual sinking fund deposits are $5,171. When invested in securities yielding 14% per year, these deposits will accumulate to $100,000 at the end of ten years. Some selected transactions and related entries for this sinking fund during the ten-year period are illustrated below.

Deposit of cash in the fund

Sinking Fund Cash	5,171
Cash	5,171

The first deposit in the sinking fund is recorded. A similar entry would be recorded as deposits are made at the end of each of the nine remaining years.

Purchase of investments

Sinking Fund Investments	5,000
Sinking Fund Cash	5,000

The purchases of securities after the first deposit was made are recorded in a summary entry. The time of purchase and the amount invested at any one time may vary, depending upon market conditions and the unit price of securities purchased.

Receipt of income from investments

Sinking Fund Cash	700
Sinking Fund Income	700

The receipt of income for the year on the securities purchased is recorded in a summary entry. Interest and dividends are received at different times during the year, and the amount earned per year normally increases as the fund increases.

Sale of investments

Sinking Fund Cash	85,100
Sinking Fund Investments	82,480
Gain on Sale of Investments	2,620

The sale of all securities at the end of the tenth year is recorded. Investments may be sold from time to time and the proceeds reinvested. Prior to maturity, all investments are converted into cash.

Payment of bonds

Bonds Payable	100,000
Cash	1,791
Sinking Fund Cash	101,791

The payment of the bonds and the transfer of the remaining sinking fund cash to the cash account are recorded. The cash available in the fund at the end of the tenth year is assumed to be composed of the following:

Proceeds from sale of investments	$ 85,100
Income earned during tenth year	11,520
Last annual deposit	5,171
Total	$101,791

In the above example, the amount of the fund exceeded the amount of the liability by $1,791. This excess is transferred to the regular cash account. But what if the amount of the fund is less than the amount of the liability? For example, assume that the fund totaled only $99,500 at the end of the tenth year. In this case, the $500 deficiency is made up by writing a check on the regular cash account.

Sinking fund income represents earnings of the corporation and is reported in the income statement as *Other income*. The cash and the securities making up the sinking fund are reported in the balance sheet as *Investments*, immediately below the Current Assets section.

BOND REDEMPTION

Objective 5
Journalize entries for bond redemptions.

Callable bonds can be redeemed by the issuing corporation within the period of time and at the price stated in the bond indenture. The call price is normally above the face value. If the market rate of interest declines after issuing the bonds, the corporation may sell new bonds at a lower interest rate and use the funds to redeem the original bond issue. In this way, the corporation can save on future interest expenses. A corporation may also redeem its bonds by purchasing them on the open market.

A corporation usually redeems its bonds at a price different from that of the **carrying value** (or **book value**) of the bonds. The carrying value of bonds payable is the balance of the bonds payable account (face amount of the bonds), less any unamortized discount or plus any unamortized premium. If the price paid for redemption is below the bond carrying value, the difference in these two amounts is recorded as a gain. If the price paid for the redemption is above the carrying amount, a loss is recorded.[5]

To illustrate, assume that on June 30 a corporation has a bond issue of $100,000 outstanding, on which there is an unamortized premium of $4,000. The corporation has the option of calling the bonds for $105,000, which it exercises on this date. The entry to record the redemption is as follows:

June 30	Bonds Payable	100,000	
	Premium on Bonds Payable	4,000	
	Loss on Redemption of Bonds	1,000	
	Cash		105,000

Even when a bond issue is not callable, the corporation may still purchase its bonds on the open market. Assuming that the preceding corporation purchases one-fourth ($25,000) of the bonds for $24,000 on June 30, the entry to record the redemption is as follows:

June 30	Bonds Payable	25,000	
	Premium on Bonds Payable	1,000	
	Cash		24,000
	Gain on Redemption of Bonds		2,000

In the preceding entry, only a portion of the premium relating to the redeemed bonds is written off. The difference between the carrying value of the bonds purchased, $26,000 ($25,000 + $1,000), and the price paid for the redemption, $24,000, is recorded as a gain.

---

[5] Gains and losses on the redemption of bonds are reported in a separate section of the income statement under the heading *Extraordinary items*. This section of the income statement will be discussed in a later chapter.

BALANCE SHEET PRESENTATION OF BONDS PAYABLE

Objective 6
Prepare a balance sheet that
includes bonds payable.

Bonds payable are usually reported on the balance sheet as long-term liabilities. If there are two or more bond issues, the details of each should be reported on the balance sheet or in a supporting schedule or note. Separate accounts are normally maintained for each bond issue.

When the balance sheet date is within one year of the maturity date of the bonds, the bonds may require classification as a current liability. This would be the case if the bonds are to be paid out of current assets. If the bonds are to be paid from a sinking fund or if they are to be refinanced with another bond issue, they should remain in the noncurrent category. In this case, the details of the retirement of the bonds are normally disclosed in a note to the financial statements.

The balance in a discount on bonds payable account is reported in the balance sheet as a deduction from the related bonds payable. Conversely, the balance in a bond premium account is reported as an addition to the related bonds payable. Either on the face of the financial statements or in accompanying notes, a description of the bonds (terms, security, due date, and coupon and effective interest rates) should also be disclosed. In addition, the maturities and sinking fund requirements should be disclosed for each of the next five years.[6] Finally, the market (fair) value of the bonds payable should also be disclosed.[7]

APPENDIX A

EFFECTIVE INTEREST RATE METHOD OF AMORTIZATION

The effective interest rate method of amortization of discounts and premiums provides for a constant *rate of interest* on the carrying amount of the bonds at the beginning of each period. This is in contrast to the straight-line method, which provides for a constant *amount* of interest expense.

The interest rate used in the interest method of amortization is the market rate on the date the bonds are issued. The carrying amount of the bonds to which the interest rate is applied is the face amount of the bonds minus any unamortized discount or plus any unamortized premium. Under the interest method, the interest expense to be reported on the income statement is computed by multiplying the effective interest rate by the carrying amount of the bonds. The difference between the interest expense computed in this way and the periodic interest payment is the amount of discount or premium to be amortized for the period.

AMORTIZATION OF DISCOUNT BY THE INTEREST METHOD

To illustrate the interest method for amortizing bond discounts, we assume the following data from the chapter illustration of the issuance of $100,000 bonds at a discount:

Face value of 12%, 5-year bonds, interest compounded semiannually	$100,000
Present value of bonds at effective (market) rate of interest of 13%	96,403
Discount on bonds payable	$ 3,597

Applying the interest method to these data yields the amortization table in Exhibit 5. You should note the following items in this table:

1. The interest paid (Column A) remains constant at 6% of $100,000, the face amount of the bonds.

[6] *Statement of Financial Accounting Standards, No. 47,* "Disclosure of Long-Term Obligations" (Stamford: Financial Accounting Standards Board, 1981), par. 10.

[7] *Statement of Financial Accounting Standards, No. 107,* "Disclosures about Fair Value of Financial Instruments" (Norwalk: Financial Accounting Standards Board, 1991), par. 10.

2. The interest expense (Column B) is computed at 6½% of the bond carrying value at the beginning of each period. This results in an increasing interest expense each period.

3. The excess of the interest expense over the interest payment of $6,000 is the amount of discount to be amortized (Column C).

4. The unamortized discount (Column D) decreases from the initial balance, $3,597, to a zero balance at the maturity date of the bonds.

5. The carrying value (Column E) increases from $96,403, the amount received for the bonds, to $100,000 at maturity.

Exhibit 5
Amortization of Discount on Bonds Payable

Interest Payment	A Interest Paid (6% of Face Amount)	B Interest Expense (6½% of Bond Carrying Value)	C Discount Amortization (B – A)	D Unamortized Discount (D – C)	E Bond Carrying Value ($100,000 – D)
				$3,597	$ 96,403
1	$6,000	$6,266 (6½% of $96,403)	$266	3,331	96,669
2	6,000	6,284 (6½% of $96,669)	284	3,047	96,953
3	6,000	6,302 (6½% of $96,953)	302	2,745	97,255
4	6,000	6,322 (6½% of $97,255)	322	2,423	97,577
5	6,000	6,343 (6½% of $97,577)	343	2,080	97,920
6	6,000	6,365 (6½% of $97,920)	365	1,715	98,285
7	6,000	6,389 (6½% of $98,285)	389	1,326	98,674
8	6,000	6,415 (6½% of $98,674)	415	911	99,089
9	6,000	6,441 (6½% of $99,089)	441	470	99,530
10	6,000	6,470 (6½% of $99,530)	470	—	100,000

The entry to record the first interest payment on June 30 and the related discount amortization is as follows:

June 30	Interest Expense	6,266	
	Discount on Bonds Payable		266
	Cash		6,000

If the amortization is recorded only at the end of the year, the amount of the discount amortized on December 31 would be $550. This is the sum of the first two semiannual amortization amounts ($266 and $284) from Exhibit 5.

AMORTIZATION OF PREMIUM BY THE INTEREST METHOD

To illustrate the interest method for amortizing bond premiums, we assume the following data from the chapter illustration of the issuance of $100,000 bonds at a premium:

Present value of bonds at effective (market) rate of interest of 11%	$103,766
Face value of 12%, 5-year bonds, interest compounded semiannually	100,000
Premium on bonds payable...	$ 3,766

Using the interest method to amortize the above premium yields the amortization table in Exhibit 6. You should note the following items in this table:

1. The interest paid (Column A) remains constant at 6% of $100,000, the face amount of the bonds.

2. The interest expense (Column B) is computed at 5½% of the bond carrying value at the beginning of each period. This results in a decreasing interest expense each period.
3. The excess of the periodic interest payment of $6,000 over the interest expense is the amount of premium to be amortized (Column C).
4. The unamortized premium (Column D) decreases from the initial balance, $3,766, to a zero balance at the maturity date of the bonds.
5. The carrying value (Column E) decreases from $103,766, the amount received for the bonds, to $100,000 at maturity.

Exhibit 6
Amortization of Premium on Bonds Payable

Interest Payment	A Interest Paid (6% of Face Amount)	B Interest Expense (5½% of Bond Carrying Value)	C Premium Amortization (A – B)	D Unamortized Premium (D – C)	E Bond Carrying Value ($100,000 + D)
				$3,766	$103,766
1	$6,000	$5,707 (5½% of $103,766)	$293	3,473	103,473
2	6,000	5,691 (5½% of $103,473)	309	3,164	103,164
3	6,000	5,674 (5½% of $103,164)	326	2,838	102,838
4	6,000	5,657 (5½% of $102,838)	343	2,495	102,495
5	6,000	5,638 (5½% of $102,495)	362	2,133	102,133
6	6,000	5,618 (5½% of $102,133)	382	1,751	101,751
7	6,000	5,597 (5½% of $101,751)	403	1,348	101,348
8	6,000	5,575 (5½% of $101,348)	425	923	100,923
9	6,000	5,551 (5½% of $100,923)	449	474	100,474
10	6,000	5,526 (5½% of $100,474)	474	—	100,000

The entry to record the first interest payment on June 30 and the related premium amortization is as follows:

June 30	Interest Expense	5,707	
	Premium on Bonds Payable	293	
	Cash		6,000

If the amortization is recorded only at the end of the year, the amount of the premium amortized on December 31 would be $602. This is the sum of the first two semiannual amortization amounts ($293 and $309) from Exhibit 6.

APPENDIX B

INVESTMENTS IN BONDS

Throughout this chapter, we have discussed bonds and related transactions from the standpoint of the issuing corporation (the debtor). However, these transactions also affect investors. In this appendix, we will discuss the accounting for bonds from the point of view of investors.

Investments in bonds or other debt securities that are not intended as a ready source of cash for normal operations are classified as **long-term investments**. The carrying value of a bond investment is normally reported in the balance sheet under the caption *Investments,* following current assets. In addition, the market (fair) value of the bond investment should be disclosed, either on the face of the balance sheet or in an accompanying note.[8]

[8] *Ibid.,* par. 10.

A business may make long-term investments because it has cash that is not needed in its normal operations. A corporation may also purchase bonds in order to establish or maintain business relations with the issuing company. Cash and securities in bond sinking funds are considered long-term investments, because they will be used for paying a bond liability.

Investments in bonds may be purchased directly from the issuing corporation or from other investors. The services of a broker are usually employed in buying and selling bonds listed on the organized bond exchanges. The record of transactions on bond exchanges is reported daily in the financial pages of newspapers. This record usually includes data on the bond interest rate, maturity date, volume of sales, and the high, low, and closing prices for each corporation's bonds traded during the day. Prices for bonds are quoted as a percentage of the face amount. Thus, the price of a $1,000 bond quoted at 104½ would be $1,045.

ACCOUNTING FOR BOND INVESTMENTS—PURCHASE, INTEREST, AND AMORTIZATION

A long-term investment in debt securities is usually carried at cost. The cost of bonds purchased includes the amount paid to the seller plus other costs related to the purchase. For example, such costs would include a broker's commission.

When bonds are purchased between interest dates, the buyer normally pays the seller the interest accrued from the last interest payment date to the date of purchase. The amount of the interest paid is normally debited to Interest Income, since it is an offset against the amount that will be received at the next interest date.

To illustrate, assume that a $1,000 bond is purchased at 102 plus a brokerage fee of $5.30 and accrued interest of $10.20. The transaction is recorded by the following entry:

Apr. 2	Investment in Lewis Co. Bonds	1,025.30	
	Interest Income	10.20	
	Cash		1,035.50

The cost of the bond is recorded in a single investment account. The face amount of the bond and the premium (or discount) are normally not recorded in separate accounts. This is different from the accounting for bonds payable. Separate premium and discount accounts are usually not maintained by investors, since bond investments are often not held by business enterprises until their maturity dates.

When bonds held as long-term investments are purchased at a price other than the face amount, such as above, the premium or discount should be amortized over the remaining life of the bonds. The amortization of premium decreases the amount of the investment in bonds account and interest income. The amortization of discount increases the amount of the investment in bonds account and interest income. The amortization of the premium or discount can be determined using either the straight-line or interest methods. Unlike bonds payable, the amortization of premiums and discounts on bond investments are usually recorded at the end of the period, rather than when interest is received.

Interest received on bond investments is recorded by a debit to Cash and a credit to Interest Income. At the end of a period, the interest accrued should be recorded by a debit to Interest Receivable and a credit to Interest Income.

To illustrate, assume that $50,000 of 8% bonds of Deitz Corporation, due in 8¾ years, are purchased by Crenshaw Inc. on July 1. Crenshaw Inc. purchases the bonds directly from Deitz Corporation to yield an effective interest rate of 11%. The purchase price is $41,706 plus interest of $1,000 ($50,000 × 8% × 3/12) accrued from April 1, the date of the last semiannual interest payment. Entries in the accounts of Crenshaw Inc. at the time of purchase and for the remainder of the fiscal period ending December 31 are as follows:

Payment for investment in bonds and accrued interest	July 1	Investment in Deitz Corp. Bonds Interest Income Cash	41,706 1,000	 42,706

Cost of $50,000 of Deitz Corp. bonds	$41,706
Interest accrued ($50,000 × 8% × 3/12)	1,000
Total	$42,706

Receipt of semiannual interest for April 1–October 1 ($50,000 × 8% × 6/12)	Oct. 1	Cash Interest Income	2,000	 2,000

Adjusting entry for accrued interest from October 1–December 31 ($50,000 × 8% × 3/12)	Dec. 31	Interest Receivable Interest Income	1,000	 1,000

Adjusting entry for amortization of discount by straight-line method for July 1–December 31	Dec. 31	Investment in Deitz Corp. Bonds Interest Income	474	 474

Face value of bonds	$50,000
Cost of bond investment	41,706
Discount on bond investment	$ 8,294
Number of months to maturity (8¾ years × 12)	105 months
Monthly amortization (rounded to nearest dollar)	
($8,294 ÷ 105 months)	$79 per month
Amortization for 6 months ($79 × 6)	$474

The entries in the interest income account in the above illustration are summarized below.

July 1	Paid accrued interest—3 months	$(1,000)
Oct. 1	Received interest payment—6 months	2,000
Dec. 31	Recorded accrued interest—3 months	1,000
31	Recorded amortization of discount—6 months	474
	Interest earned—6 months	$ 2,474

ACCOUNTING FOR BOND INVESTMENTS—SALE

Many long-term investments in bonds are sold before their maturity date. When this occurs, the seller receives the sales price (less commissions and other selling costs) plus any accrued interest since the last interest payment date. Before recording the cash proceeds, the seller should amortize any discount or premium for the current period up to the date of sale. Any gain or loss on the sale can then be recorded when the cash proceeds are recorded. Such gains and losses are normally reported in the Other Income section of the income statement.

To illustrate, assume that the Deitz Corporation bonds in the above example are sold for $47,350 plus accrued interest on June 30, seven years after their purchase. The carrying *amount* of the bonds (cost plus amortized discount) as of *January 1* of the year of sale (78 months after their purchase) is $47,868 [$41,706 + ($79 per mo. × 78 months)]. The entries to amortize the discount for the current year and to record the sale of the bonds are as follows:

Amortization of $474 of discount for current year ($79 × 6 months)	June 30	Investment in Deitz Corp. Bonds Interest Income	474	 474

Receipt of interest and proceeds from sale of bonds and recognition of loss on sale of bonds	June 30	Cash	48,350	
		Loss on Sale of Investments	992	
		Interest Income		1,000
		Investment in Deitz Corp. Bonds		48,342

Interest for April 1–June 30 ($50,000 × 8% × 3/12)	$ 1,000
Carrying value of bonds on January 1	$47,868
Discount amortized, Jan. 1–June 30	474
Carrying value of bonds on June 30	$48,342
Proceeds of sale	47,350
Loss on sale	$ 992

CHAPTER REVIEW

Key Points

Objective 1. List the characteristics of bonds.

The characteristics of bonds depend upon the type of bonds issued by a corporation. Bonds that may be issued include registered bonds, bearer bonds, coupon bonds, term bonds, serial bonds, convertible bonds, callable bonds, secured bonds, and debenture bonds.

Objective 2. Explain the present-value concept and the present value of bonds payable.

The concept of present value is based on the time value of money. That is, an amount of cash to be received at some date in the future is not the equivalent of the same amount of cash held at an earlier date. For example, if $100 cash today can be invested to earn 10% per year, the $100 today is referred to as the present value amount that is equivalent to $110 to be received a year from today.

A price that a buyer is willing to pay for a bond is the sum of (1) the present value of the face amount of the bonds at the maturity date and (2) the present value of the periodic interest payments.

Objective 3. Journalize entries for bonds payable.

The journal entry for issuing bonds payable debits Cash for the proceeds received and credits Bonds Payable for the face value of the bonds. Any difference between the face value of the bonds and the proceeds is debited to Discount on Bonds Payable or credited to Premium on Bonds Payable.

A discount or premium on bonds payable is amortized to interest expense over the life of the bonds. The entry to amortize a discount debits Interest Expense and credits Discount on Bonds Payable. The entry to amortize a premium debits Premium on Bonds Payable and credits Interest Expense.

Objective 4. Journalize entries for bond sinking funds, using future-value concepts.

The amounts set aside to pay a bond at its maturity date are accumulated in a sinking fund. The concept of future value may be used to determine the amount of the periodic deposits in a sinking fund. The journal entry to record deposits in a sinking fund debits Sinking Fund Cash and credits Cash. Investments are recorded by debiting Sinking Fund Investments and crediting Sinking Fund Cash. Income from sinking fund investments is recorded in a sinking fund income account.

At maturity, Bonds Payable is debited for the face value of the bonds and Sinking Fund Cash is credited. Any surplus of sinking fund cash is returned to the regular cash account. Any shortage of sinking fund cash is transferred to the sinking fund from the regular cash account.

Objective 5. Journalize entries for bond redemptions.

When a corporation redeems bonds, Bonds Payable is debited for the face value of the bonds, the premium (discount) on bonds account is debited (credited) for its balance, Cash is credited, and any gain or loss on the redemption is recorded.

Objective 6. Prepare a balance sheet that includes bonds payable.

Bonds payable are usually reported on the balance sheet as long-term liabilities. When the balance sheet date is within one year of the bond maturity date, the bonds should be classified as a current liability if they are to be paid out of current assets. If the bonds are to be paid from a sinking fund or refinanced, they should remain in the noncurrent category. A discount on bonds should be reported in the balance sheet as a deduction from the related bonds payable. A premium on bonds should be reported as an addition to the related bonds payable.

Glossary of Key Terms

Annuity. A series of equal cash flows at fixed intervals. **Objective 2**

Bond. A form of interest-bearing note employed by corporations to borrow on a long-term basis. **Objective 1**

Bond indenture. The contract between a corporation issuing

bonds and the bondholders. **Objective 1**

Carrying value. The amount at which a temporary or a long-term investment or a long-term liability is reported on the balance sheet; also called basis or book value. **Objective 5**

Contract rate. The interest rate specified on a bond; sometimes called the coupon rate of interest. **Objective 3**

Discount. The excess of the face amount of bonds over their issue price. **Objective 3**

Effective rate. The market rate of interest at the time bonds are issued. **Objective 3**

Future value. The amount that will accumulate at some future date as a result of an investment or a series of investments. **Objective 4**

Premium. The excess of the issue price of bonds over the face

amount. **Objective 3**

Present value. The estimated present worth of an amount of cash to be received (or paid) in the future. **Objective 2**

Present value of an annuity. The sum of the present values of a series of equal cash flows to be received at fixed intervals. **Objective 2**

Sinking fund. Assets set aside in a special fund to be used for a specific purpose. **Objective 4**

Self-Examination Questions
Answers at end of chapter.

1. If a corporation plans to issue $1,000,000 of 12% bonds at a time when the market rate for similar bonds is 10%, the bonds can be expected to sell at:
   A. their face amount
   B. a premium
   C. a discount
   D. a price below their face amount

2. The entry to journalize the amortization of a premium on bonds payable is:
   A. debit Interest Expense, credit Bonds Payable
   B. debit Premium on Bonds Payable, credit Interest Expense
   C. debit Interest Expense, credit Premium on Bonds Payable
   D. debit Premium on Bonds Payable, credit Bonds Payable

3. If the bonds payable account has a balance of $500,000 and

the discount on bonds payable account has a balance of $40,000, what is the carrying value of the bonds?
   A. $460,000   C. $540,000
   B. $500,000   D. $580,000

4. The cash and the securities that make up the sinking fund established for the payment of bonds at maturity are classified on the balance sheet as:
   A. current assets   C. long-term liabilities
   B. investments   D. current liabilities

5. The balance in the discount on bonds payable account would usually be reported in the balance sheet in the:
   A. Current Assets section   C. Long-Term Liabilities section
   B. Current Liabilities section   D. Investments section

ILLUSTRATIVE PROBLEM

Dent Inc.'s fiscal year ends December 31. Selected transactions for the period 1993 through 2000, involving bonds payable issued by Dent Inc., are as follows:

1993

June 30. Issued $4,000,000 of 25-year, 9% callable bonds dated June 30, 1993, for cash of $3,840,000. Interest is payable semiannually on June 30 and December 31.

Dec. 31. Paid the semiannual interest on the bonds.
    31. Recorded straight-line amortization of $3,200 discount on the bonds.
    31. Closed the interest expense account.

1994

June 30. Paid the semiannual interest on the bonds.

Dec. 31. Paid the semiannual interest on the bonds.
    31. Recorded straight-line amortization of $6,400 discount on the bonds.
    31. Closed the interest expense account.

2000

June 30. Recorded the redemption of the bonds, which were called at 102. The balance in the bond discount account is $115,200 after the payment of interest and amortization of discount have been recorded. (Record the redemption only.)

Instructions

1. Journalize entries to record the preceding transactions.
2. Determine the amount of interest expense for 1993 and 1994.

3. Estimate the effective annual interest rate by dividing the interest expense for 1993 by the bond carrying amount at the time of issuance and multiplying by 2.
4. Determine the carrying amount of the bonds as of December 31, 1994.

Solution

1.
1993

June 30	Cash	3,840,000	
	Discount on Bonds Payable	160,000	
	Bonds Payable		4,000,000
Dec. 31	Interest Expense	180,000	
	Cash		180,000
31	Interest Expense	3,200	
	Discount on Bonds Payable		3,200
31	Income Summary	183,200	
	Interest Expense		183,200

1994

June 30	Interest Expense	180,000	
	Cash		180,000
Dec. 31	Interest Expense	180,000	
	Cash		180,000
31	Interest Expense	6,400	
	Discount on Bonds Payable		6,400
31	Income Summary	366,400	
	Interest Expense		366,400

2000

June 30	Bonds Payable	4,000,000	
	Loss on Redemption of Bonds Payable	195,200	
	Discount on Bonds Payable		115,200
	Cash		4,080,000

2. a. 1993—$183,200
    b. 1994—$366,400
3. $183,200 ÷ $3,840,000 = 4.77% rate for six months of a year
    4.77% × 2 = 9.54% annual rate
4. Initial carrying value of bonds $3,840,000
    Discount amortized on December 31, 1993   3,200
    Discount amortized on December 31, 1994   6,400
    Carrying value of bonds, December 31, 1994 $3,849,600

DISCUSSION QUESTIONS

1. When underwriters are used by corporations issuing bonds, what function do the underwriters perform?
2. Explain the meaning of each of the following terms as they relate to a bond issue: (a) secured, (b) convertible, (c) callable, and (d) debenture.
3. Describe the two distinct obligations incurred by a corporation when issuing bonds.
4. If you asked your broker to purchase for you a 9% bond when the market interest rate for such bonds was 10%, would you expect to pay more or less than the face value for the bond? Explain.
5. A corporation issues $5,000,000 of 10% coupon bonds to yield interest at the rate of 9%. (a) Was the amount of cash received from the sale of the bonds greater or less than $5,000,000? (b) Identify the following terms related to the bond issue: (1) face amount, (2) market or effective rate of interest, (3) contract or coupon rate of interest, and (4) maturity amount.
6. If bonds issued by a corporation are sold at a premium, is the market rate of interest greater or less than the coupon rate?

7. What is the present value of $1,000 due in two years, if the market rate of interest is 11%?

8. What is the present value of $1,000 to be received in each of the next two years, if the market rate of interest is 11%?

9. If the bonds payable account has a balance of $2,000,000 and the premium on bonds payable account has a balance of $25,500, what is the carrying value of the bonds?

10. The following data are related to a $750,000, 12% bond issue for a selected semiannual interest period:

Bond carrying value at beginning of period	$796,500
Interest paid at end of period	45,000
Interest expense allocable to the period	42,675

(a) Were the bonds issued at a discount or at a premium? (b) What is the balance of the discount or premium account at the beginning of the period? (c) How much amortization of discount or premium is allocable to the period?

11. A corporation issues 10%, 20-year debenture bonds, with a face amount of $5,000,000, for 102½ at the beginning of the current year. Assuming that the premium is to be amortized on a straight-line basis, what is the total amount of interest expense for the current year?

12. In the entry made at year end, indicate the title of (a) the account to be debited and (b) the account to be credited for amortization of (1) discount on bonds payable and (2) premium on bonds payable.

13. What is the purpose of a bond sinking fund?

14. If the earnings rate is 9% compounded annually, what would be the value at the end of the second year for a $1,000 investment?

15. If the earnings rate is 12% compounded annually, what would be the value at the end of the sixth year for a $5,000 investment? Use the table of the future value of $1 presented in this chapter to determine the value.

16. What would be the value at the end of the second year from a series of investments of $5,000 each to be made at the end of each of the first two years, with earnings of 12% compounded annually?

17. If Power Company invests $5,000 at the end of each of the next five years in a sinking fund and the fund investments yield 10% per year compounded annually, what is the value of the fund at the end of five years? Use the table of the future value of an annuity of $1 presented in this chapter to determine the value.

18. What amount must be invested at the end of each of the next five years, in a sinking fund that earns 12% compounded annually, to accumulate to $25,000 at the end of the fifth year? Use the table of the future value of an annuity of $1 presented in this chapter to determine the amount.

19. If the amount accumulated in a sinking fund account exceeds the amount of liability at the redemption date, to what account is the excess transferred?

20. How are cash and securities comprising a sinking fund classified on the balance sheet?

21. Bonds Payable has a balance of $500,000 and Discount on Bonds Payable has a balance of $7,500. If the issuing corporation redeems the bonds at 98, what is the amount of gain or loss on redemption?

22. Indicate how the following accounts should be reported in the balance sheet: (a) Premium on Bonds Payable, and (b) Discount on Bonds Payable.

23. A company purchased a $1,000, 20-year zero-coupon bond for $189 to yield 8.5% to maturity. How is the interest income computed?

Source: "Technical Hotline," *Journal of Accountancy* (January 1989), p. 100.

ETHICS DISCUSSION CASE

Restono Inc. has outstanding a $50,000,000, 25-year, 11% debenture bond issue dated July 1, 1978. The bond issue is due June 30, 2003. The bond indenture requires a sinking fund, which has a balance of $30,000,000 as of July 1, 1995. Restono Inc. is currently experiencing a shortage of funds due to a recent plant expansion. Grace Barker, treasurer of Restono, has suggested using the sinking fund cash to temporarily relieve the shortage of funds. Barker's brother-in-law, who is trustee of the sinking fund, is willing to loan Restono Inc. the necessary funds from the sinking fund.

Discuss whether Grace Barker is behaving in an ethical manner.

WHAT DO YOU
THINK

?

Should all liabilities presented in the balance sheet be valued at present values?

FINANCIAL ANALYSIS AND INTERPRETATION

A financial measure that focuses on the relative risk of the debtholders is the number of times the interest charges are earned during the year. The higher the ratio, the lower the risk that interest payments to the debtholders will not be made if earnings decrease. In other words, the higher the ratio the greater the assurance that interest payments will be made on a continuing basis. This measure also indicates the general financial strength of the enterprise, which is of interest to stockholders and employees as well as creditors.

The amount available to meet interest charges is not affected by taxes on income. This is because interest is deductible in determining taxable income. Thus, the number of times interest charges are earned is computed as shown below:

$$\frac{\text{Number of Times}}{\text{Interest Charges Earned}} = \frac{\text{Income Before Income Tax} + \text{Interest Expense}}{\text{Interest Expense}}$$

a. For Hershey Foods Corporation, determine the number of times interest charges were earned for the years ended December 31, 1992 and 1991. (The makeup of "interest expense, net" as reported on the income statement is described in Note 4 to the statements. Do not include interest income in your computation.)
b. What conclusions can be drawn from the data concerning the risk of the debtholders for the interest payments and the general financial strength of Hershey?

EXERCISES

EXERCISE 11-1
REAL WORLD FOCUS
Objective 3

K Mart Corporation 8⅜% bonds due in 2017 were reported in *The Wall Street Journal* as selling for 106 on August 11, 1993.

**SHARPEN YOUR ►
COMMUNICATION SKILLS**

Were the bonds selling at a premium or at a discount on June 4, 1992? Explain.

EXERCISE 11-2
ENTRIES FOR ISSUANCE OF
BONDS
Objective 3

C. C. Cox Co. issued $10,000,000 of 20-year, 11% bonds on April 1 of the current year, with interest payable on April 1 and October 1. The fiscal year of the company is the calendar year. Journalize the entries to record the following selected transactions for the current year:

Apr. 1. Issued the bonds for cash at their face amount.
Oct. 1. Paid the interest on the bonds.
Dec. 31. Recorded accrued interest for three months.

EXERCISE 11-3
ENTRIES FOR BOND
ISSUANCE; AMORTIZATION
OF DISCOUNT BY
STRAIGHT-LINE METHOD
Objective 3

On the first day of its fiscal year, Mitchell Company issued $10,000,000 of ten-year, 10% bonds, interest payable semiannually, at an effective interest rate of 12%, receiving cash of $8,852,950.
a. Journalize the entries to record the following:
    1. Sale of the bonds.
    2. First semiannual interest payment. (Amortization of discount is to be recorded annually.)
    3. Second semiannual interest payment.
    4. Amortization of discount at the end of the first year, using the straight-line method.
b. Determine the amount of the bond interest expense for the first year.

EXERCISE 11-4
COMPUTATION OF BOND
PROCEEDS, ENTRIES FOR
BOND ISSUANCE, AND
AMORTIZATION OF
PREMIUM BY STRAIGHT-
LINE METHOD
Objectives 2, 3

On March 1, 1994, Brown Corporation issued $1,000,000 of ten-year, 12% bonds at an effective interest rate of 11%. Interest is payable semiannually on March 1 and September 1. Journalize the entries to record the following:
a. Sale of bonds on March 1, 1994. (Use the tables of present values in the chapter to determine the bond proceeds.)
b. First interest payment on September 1, 1994, and amortization of bond premium for six months, using the straight-line method. (Round to the nearest dollar.)

EXERCISE 11-5
DETERMINATION OF
SINKING FUND DEPOSIT
AND ENTRY
Objective 4

L. D. Riley Inc. issued $5,000,000 of 20-year bonds on January 1 of the current year. The bond indenture requires that equal deposits be made in a bond sinking fund at the end of each of the 20 years. The fund is expected to be invested in securities that will yield 12% per year, compounded annually.

a. Determine the amount of each of the 20 deposits to be made in the bond sinking fund.
b. Journalize the entry to record the first deposit made in the sinking fund.

EXERCISE 11-6
ENTRIES FOR BOND
SINKING FUND
Objective 4

Hood Corporation issued $20,000,000 of ten-year bonds on the first day of the fiscal year. The bond indenture provides that a sinking fund be accumulated, assuming 10% interest, by ten annual deposits of $1,254,910, beginning at the end of the first year.

Journalize the entries to record the following selected transactions related to the bond issue:

a. The required amount is deposited in the sinking fund.
b. Investments in securities made from the first sinking fund deposit total $1,250,000.
c. The sinking fund earned $123,600 during the year following the first deposit (summarizing entry).
d. The bonds are paid at maturity, and excess cash of $55,800 in the fund is transferred to the cash account.

EXERCISE 11-7
ENTRIES FOR BOND
SINKING FUND; FUND
DEFICIENCY
Objective 4

Higgins Corporation issued $10,000,000 of 20-year bonds on the first day of the fiscal year. The bond indenture provides that a sinking fund be accumulated by 20 annual deposits of $275,000, beginning at the end of the first year.

Journalize the entries to record the following selected transactions related to the bond issue:

a. The required amount is deposited in the sinking fund.
b. Investments in securities from the first sinking fund deposit total $270,500.
c. The sinking fund earns $18,500 during the year following the first deposit (summarizing entry).
d. The bonds are paid at maturity, and a fund deficiency of $47,750 is transferred from the regular cash account.

EXERCISE 11-8
ENTRIES FOR ISSUANCE
AND CALLING OF BONDS
Objectives 3, 5

Kline Corp. issued $5,000,000 of 20-year, 12% callable bonds on March 1, 1994, with interest payable on March 1 and September 1. The fiscal year of the company is the calendar year. Journalize the entries to record the following selected transactions:

1994
Mar. 1. Issued the bonds for cash at their face amount.
Sep. 1. Paid the interest on the bonds.

1999
Sep. 1. Called the bond issue at 102, the rate provided in the bond indenture. (Omit entry for payment of interest.)

APPENDIX A
EXERCISE 11-9
AMORTIZATION OF
DISCOUNT BY INTEREST
METHOD

On the first day of its fiscal year, Mitchell Company issued $10,000,000 of ten-year, 10% bonds, interest payable semiannually, at an effective interest rate of 12%, receiving cash of $8,852,950.

a. Journalize the entries to record the following:
   1. Sale of the bonds.
   2. First semiannual interest payment. (Amortization of discount is to be recorded annually.)
   3. Second semiannual interest payment.
   4. Amortization of discount at the end of the first year, using the interest method. (Round to the nearest dollar.)
b. Compute the amount of the bond interest expense for the first year.

APPENDIX A
EXERCISE 11-10
COMPUTATION OF BOND
PROCEEDS, AMORTIZATION
OF PREMIUM BY INTEREST
METHOD, AND INTEREST
EXPENSE

On the first day of its fiscal year, Kane Inc. issued $10,000,000 of ten-year, 12% bonds at an effective interest rate of 10%, with interest payable semiannually. Compute the following, presenting figures used in your computations and rounding to the nearest dollar:

a. The amount of cash proceeds from the sale of the bonds. (Use the tables of present values in the chapter.)
b. The annual premium to be amortized for the first semiannual interest payment period, using the interest method.

c. The amount of premium to be amortized for the second semiannual interest payment period, using the interest method.

d. The amount of the bond interest expense for the first year.

APPENDIX B
EXERCISE 11-11
ENTRIES FOR PURCHASE
AND SALE OF INVESTMENT
IN BONDS

Journalize he entries to record the following selected transactions of Fitch Company:

a. Purchased for cash $200,000 of Gray Co. 11% bonds at 102 plus accrued interest of $5,500.

b. Received first semiannual interest.

c. Amortized $360 on the bond investment at the end of the first year.

d. Sold the bonds at 100 plus accrued interest of $2,775. The bonds were carried at $201,750 at the time of the sale.

WhAT'S WRONG
WITH THi2?

At the beginning of the current year, two bond issues (A and B) were outstanding. During the year, bond issue A was redeemed and a significant loss on the redemption of bonds was reported as Other Expense on the income statement. At the end of the year, bond issue B was reported as a current liability because its maturity date was early in the following year. A sinking fund of cash and securities sufficient to pay the series B bonds was reported in the balance sheet as *Investments*. Can you find any flaws in the reporting practices related to the two bond issues?

PROBLEMS

Series A

PROBLEM 11-1A
PRESENT VALUE; BOND
PREMIUM; ENTRIES FOR
BONDS PAYABLE
TRANSACTIONS
Objectives 2, 3

On July 1, 1994, Curry Corporation issued $10,000,000 of ten-year, 12% bonds at an effective interest rate of 11%. Interest on the bonds is payable semiannually on December 31 and June 30. The fiscal year of the company is the calendar year.

Instructions

1. Journalize the entry to record the amount of the cash proceeds from the sale of the bonds. Use the tables of present values in this chapter to compute the cash proceeds, rounding to the nearest dollar.

2. Journalize the entries to record the following:
   a. The first semiannual interest payment on December 31, 1994, and the amortization of the bond premium, using the straight-line method.
   b. The interest payment on June 30, 1995, and the amortization of the bond premium, using the straight-line method.

3. Determine the total interest expense for 1994.

SHARPEN YOUR
COMMUNICATION SKILLS

4. Will the bond proceeds always be greater than the face value of the bonds when the coupon rate is greater than the market rate of interest? Explain.

PROBLEM 11-2A
PRESENT VALUE; BOND
DISCOUNT; ENTRIES FOR
BONDS PAYABLE
TRANSACTIONS
Objectives 2, 3

On July 1, 1994, Allen Corporation issued $12,000,000 of ten-year, 10% bonds at an effective interest rate of 11%. Interest on the bonds is payable semiannually on December 31 and June 30. The fiscal year of the company is the calendar year.

Instructions

1. Journalize the entry to record the amount of the cash proceeds from the sale of the bonds. Use the tables of present values in this chapter to compute the cash proceeds, rounding to the nearest dollar.

2. Journalize the entries to record the following:
   a. The first semiannual interest payment on December 31, 1994, and the amortization of the bond discount, using the straight-line method.
   b. The interest payment on June 30, 1995, and the amortization of the bond discount, using the straight-line method.

3. Determine the total interest expense for 1994.

SHARPEN YOUR
COMMUNICATION SKILLS

4. Will the bond proceeds always be less than the face value of the bonds when the coupon rate is less than the market rate of interest? Explain.

PROBLEM 11-3A
ENTRIES FOR BOND AND
SINKING FUND
TRANSACTIONS; FUND
DEFICIENCY
Objectives 3, 4

The following transactions relate to the issuance of $1,000,000 of ten-year, 10% bonds dated January 1, 1985, and the accumulations in a sinking fund to redeem the bonds at maturity. Interest on the bonds is payable on June 30 and December 31.

1985
Jan.   2. Sold the bond issue at 100.
June 30. Paid semiannual interest on bonds.
Dec. 31. Paid semiannual interest on bonds and deposited $58,000 in a bond sinking fund.

1986
Jan. 13. Purchased $56,100 of investments with bond sinking fund cash.
June 30. Paid semiannual interest on bonds.
Oct. 22. Received $4,125 income on investments.
Dec. 31. Paid semiannual interest on bonds.

(Assume that all intervening transactions have been properly recorded.)

1995
Jan.   2. Sold all investments in the bond sinking fund for $980,500. The sinking fund investments had a carrying value of $999,200.
       11. Paid the bonds at maturity from the sinking fund cash and the regular cash account. The cash available in the sinking fund at this date was $991,900.

Instructions
Journalize the entries to record the foregoing transactions.

PROBLEM 11-4A
ENTRIES FOR BOND AND
SINKING FUND
TRANSACTIONS
Objectives 3, 4

During 1994 and 1995, Norris Company completed the following transactions relating to its $5,000,000 issue of 20-year, 12% bonds dated July 1, 1994. Interest is payable on June 30 and December 31. The corporation's fiscal year is the calendar year.

1994
July   1. Sold the bond issue for $5,402,000 cash.
Dec. 31. Paid the semiannual interest on the bonds.
       31. Recorded bond premium amortization of $10,050, which was determined by using the straight-line method.
       31. Deposited $144,000 cash in a bond sinking fund.
       31. Closed the interest expense account.

1995
Jan.   9. Purchased various securities with sinking fund cash, cost $136,500.
June 30. Paid the semiannual interest on the bonds.
Dec. 20. Recorded the receipt of $10,150 of income on sinking fund securities, depositing the cash in the sinking fund.
       31. Paid the semiannual interest on the bonds.
       31. Recorded bond premium amortization of $20,100, which was determined by using the straight-line method.
       31. Deposited $288,000 cash in the sinking fund.
       31. Closed the interest expense account.

Instructions
1. Journalize the entries to record the foregoing transactions.
2. Prepare a columnar table, using the following headings, and list the information for each of the two years.

Account Balances at End of Year

Year	Bond Interest Expense for Year	Sinking Fund Income for Year	Bonds Payable	Premium on Bonds	Sinking Fund	
					Cash	Investments

SOLUTIONS
SOFTWARE

Instructions for Solving Problem 11-4A Using Solutions Software
1. Load opening balances.
2. Enter your name in the Student Name field on the General Information data entry window. Set the run date to December 31, 1994.
3. Save the opening balances file to your drive and directory.

4. Select the General Journal Entries option and key the journal entries for 1994. Leave the reference field blank. Note: To review the chart of accounts, select F-1.
5. Display a journal entries report.
6. Display a trial balance.
7. Set the run date to December 31, 1995.
8. Select the General Journal Entries option and key the journal entries for 1995. Leave the reference field blank. Note: Be certain to change the year to 1995 when entering the General Journal entries.
9. Display a journal entries report for 1995.
10. Display a trial balance.
11. Save your data file to disk.
12. End the session.

PROBLEM 11-5A
ENTRIES FOR BONDS
PAYABLE TRANSACTIONS
Objectives 3, 5

The following transactions were completed by L. L. Lang Inc., whose fiscal year is the calendar year:

1994
July   1.   Issued $5,000,000 of 10-year, 8% callable bonds dated July 1, 1994, at an effective rate of 10%, receiving cash of $4,376,940. Interest is payable semiannually on December 31 and June 30.
Dec. 31.   Paid the semiannual interest on the bonds.
      31.   Recorded bond discount amortization of $31,153, which was determined by using the straight-line method.
      31.   Closed the interest expense account.

1995
June 30.   Paid the semiannual interest on the bonds.
Dec. 31.   Paid the semiannual interest on the bonds.
      31.   Recorded bond discount amortization of $62,306, which was determined by using the straight-line method.
      31.   Closed the interest expense account.

2002
June 30.   Recorded the redemption of the bonds, which were called at 101. The balance in the bond discount account is $124,612 after payment of interest and amortization of discount have been recorded. (Record the redemption only.)

Instructions
1. Journalize the entries to record the foregoing transactions.
2. Indicate the amount of the interest expense in (a) 1994 and (b) 1995.
3. Determine the carrying value of the bonds as of December 31, 1995.

APPENDIX A
PROBLEM 11-6A
ENTRIES FOR BONDS
PAYABLE TRANSACTIONS;
INTEREST METHOD OF
AMORTIZATION OF BOND
PREMIUM

On July 1, 1994, Curry Corporation issued $10,000,000 of ten-year, 12% bonds at an effective interest rate of 11%, receiving proceeds of $10,597,240. Interest on the bonds is payable semiannually on December 31 and June 30. The fiscal year of the company is the calendar year.

Instructions
1. Journalize the entries to record the following:
   a. The first semiannual interest payment on December 31, 1994, and the amortization of the bond premium, using the interest method. (Round to nearest dollar.)
   b. The interest payment on June 30, 1995, and the amortization of the bond premium, using the interest method. (Round to nearest dollar.)
2. Determine the total interest expense for 1994.

APPENDIX A
PROBLEM 11-7A
ENTRIES FOR BONDS
PAYABLE TRANSACTIONS;
INTEREST METHOD OF
AMORTIZATION OF BOND
DISCOUNT

On July 1, 1994, Allen Corporation issued $12,000,000 of ten-year, 10% bonds at an effective interest rate of 11%, receiving proceeds of $11,282,640. Interest on the bonds is payable semiannually on December 31 and June 30. The fiscal year of the company is the calendar year.

Instructions
1. Journalize the entries to record the following:
   a. The first semiannual interest payment on December 31, 1994, and the amortization of the bond discount, using the interest method. (Round to nearest dollar.)

b. The interest payment on June 30, 1995, and the amortization of the bond discount, using the interest method. (Round to nearest dollar.)

2. Determine the total interest expense for 1994.

APPENDIX B
PROBLEM 11-8A
ENTRIES FOR BOND
INVESTMENTS

The following selected transactions relate to certain securities acquired as a long-term investment by J. Matson Inc., whose fiscal year ends on December 31:

1994
Sep. 1. Purchased $300,000 of Payne Company 10-year, 14% bonds dated July 1, 1994, directly from the issuing company, for $305,900 plus accrued interest of $7,000.
Dec. 31. Received the semiannual interest on the Payne Company bonds.
     31. Recorded bond premium amortization of $200 on the Payne Company bonds. The amortization amount was determined by using the straight-line method.

(Assume that all intervening transactions and adjustments have been properly recorded, and that the number of bonds owned has not changed from December 31, 1994, to December 31, 1999.)

2000
June 30. Received the semiannual interest on the Payne Company bonds.
July 31. Sold one-half of the Payne Company bonds at 102 plus accrued interest. The broker deducted $700 for commission, etc., remitting the balance. Prior to the sale, $175 of premium on one-half of the bonds is to be amortized, reducing the carrying amount of those bonds to $151,175.
Dec. 31. Received the semiannual interest on the Payne Company bonds.
     31. Recorded bond premium amortization of $300 on the Payne Company bonds.

Instructions
Journalize the entries to record the foregoing transactions.

Series B

PROBLEM 11-1B
PRESENT VALUE; BOND
PREMIUM; ENTRIES FOR
BONDS PAYABLE
TRANSACTIONS
Objectives 2, 3

On July 1, 1994, Shute Inc. issued $10,000,000 of ten-year, 11% bonds at an effective interest rate of 10%. Interest on the bonds is payable semiannually on December 31 and June 30. The fiscal year of the company is the calendar year.

Instructions
1. Journalize the entry to record the amount of the cash proceeds from the sale of the bonds. Use the tables of present values in this chapter to compute the cash proceeds, rounding to the nearest dollar.
2. Journalize the entries to record the following:
   a. The first semiannual interest payment on December 31, 1994, including the amortization of the bond premium, using the straight-line method.
   b. The interest payment on June 30, 1995, and the amortization of the bond premium, using the straight-line method.
3. Determine the total interest expense for 1994.

▶ SHARPEN YOUR
COMMUNICATION SKILLS
4. Will the bond proceeds always be greater than the face value of the bonds when the coupon rate is greater than the market rate of interest? Explain.

PROBLEM 11-2B
PRESENT VALUE; BOND
DISCOUNT; ENTRIES FOR
BONDS PAYABLE
TRANSACTIONS
Objectives 2, 3

On July 1, 1994, Cline Inc. issued $15,000,000 of ten-year, 10% bonds at an effective interest rate of 12%. Interest on the bonds is payable semiannually on December 31 and June 30. The fiscal year of the company is the calendar year.

Instructions
1. Journalize the entry to record the amount of the cash proceeds from the sale of the bonds. Use the tables of present values in this chapter to compute the cash proceeds, rounding to the nearest dollar.
2. Journalize the entries to record the following:
   a. The first semiannual interest payment on December 31, 1994, and the amortization of the bond discount, using the straight-line method.
   b. The interest payment on June 30, 1995, and the amortization of the bond discount, using the straight-line method.

3. Determine the total interest expense for 1994.

SHARPEN YOUR COMMUNICATION SKILLS ▶ 4. Will the bond proceeds always be less than the face value of the bonds when the coupon rate is less than the market rate of interest? Explain.

PROBLEM 11-3B
ENTRIES FOR BOND AND
SINKING FUND
TRANSACTIONS; FUND
DEFICIENCY
Objectives 3, 4

The following transactions relate to the issuance of $900,000 of ten-year, 8% bonds dated January 1, 1985, and the accumulations in the sinking fund to redeem the bonds at maturity. Interest on the bonds is payable on June 30 and December 31.

1985
Jan. 2. Sold the bond issue at 100.
June 30. Paid semiannual interest on bonds.
Dec. 31. Paid semiannual interest on bonds and deposited $50,000 in a bond sinking fund.

1986
Jan. 6. Purchased $49,200 of investments with bond sinking fund cash.
June 30. Paid semiannual interest on bonds.
Nov. 11 Received $4,050 income on investments.
Dec. 31. Paid semiannual interest on bonds.

(Assume that all intervening transactions have been properly recorded.)

1995
Jan. 2. Sold all investments in the bond sinking fund for $885,750. The sinking fund investments had a carrying value of $899,200.
       3. Paid the bonds at maturity from the sinking fund cash and the regular cash account. The cash available in the sinking fund at this date was $893,500.

Instructions
Journalize the entries to record the foregoing transactions.

PROBLEM 11-4B
ENTRIES FOR BOND AND
SINKING FUND
TRANSACTIONS
Objectives 3, 4

During 1994 and 1995, Pryor Company completed the following transactions relating to its $4,500,000 issue of 30-year, 11% bonds dated July 1, 1994. Interest is payable on June 30 and December 31. The corporation's fiscal year is the calendar year.

1994
July 1. Sold the bond issue for $4,197,600 cash.
Dec. 31. Paid semiannual interest on the bonds.
       31. Recorded bond discount amortization of $5,040, which was determined by using the straight-line method.
       31. Deposited $30,000 cash in a bond sinking fund.
       31. Closed the interest expense account.

1995
Jan. 15. Purchased various securities with sinking fund cash, cost $27,400.
June 30. Paid the semiannual interest on the bonds.
Dec. 15. Recorded the receipt of $2,900 of income on sinking fund securities, depositing the cash in the sinking fund.
       31. Paid the semiannual interest on the bonds.
       31. Recorded bond discount amortization of $10,080, which was determined by using the straight-line method.
       31. Deposited $60,000 cash in the sinking fund.
       31. Closed the interest expense account.

Instructions
1. Journalize the entries to record the foregoing transactions.
2. Prepare a columnar table, using the following headings, and list the information for each of the two years.

Account Balances at End of Year

Year	Bond Interest Expense for Year	Sinking Fund Income for Year	Bonds Payable	Discount on Bonds	Sinking Fund Cash	Investments

SOLUTIONS SOFTWARE

Instructions for Solving Problem 11-4B Using Solutions Software

1. Load opening balances.
2. Enter your name in the Student Name field in the General Information data entry window. Set the run date to December 31, 1994.
3. Save the opening balances file to your drive and directory.
4. Select the General Journal Entries option and key the journal entries. Leave the reference field blank. Note: To review the chart of accounts, select F-1.
5. Display a journal entries report.
6. Display a trial balance.
7. Set the run date to December 31, 1995.
8. Select the General Journal Entries option and key the journal entries for 1995. Leave the reference field blank. Note: Be certain to change the year to 1995 when entering the General Journal entries.
9. Display a journal entries report for 1995.
10. Display a trial balance.
11. Save your data file to disk.
12. End the session.

PROBLEM 11-5B
ENTRIES FOR BONDS
PAYABLE TRANSACTIONS
Objectives 3, 5

The following transactions were completed by Logan Co., whose fiscal year is the calendar year:

1994
July 1.   Issued $20,000,000 of 10-year, 14% callable bonds dated July 1, 1994, at an effective rate of 12%, receiving cash of $22,293,860. Interest is payable semiannually on December 31 and June 30.
Dec. 31.   Paid the semiannual interest on the bonds.
      31.   Recorded bond premium amortization of $114,693, which was determined by using the straight-line method.
      31.   Closed the interest expense account.

1995
June 30.   Paid the semiannual interest on the bonds.
Dec. 31.   Paid the semiannual interest on the bonds.
      31.   Recorded bond premium amortization of $229,386, which was determined by using the straight-line method.
      31.   Closed the interest expense account.

2000
July 1.   Recorded the redemption of the bonds, which were called at 104. The balance in the bond premium account is $917,544 after the payment of interest and amortization of premium have been recorded. (Record the redemption only.)

Instructions
1. Journalize the entries to record the foregoing transactions.
2. Indicate the amount of the interest expense in (a) 1994 and (b) 1995.
3. Determine the carrying value of the bonds as of December 31, 1995.

APPENDIX A
PROBLEM 11-6B
ENTRIES FOR BONDS
PAYABLE TRANSACTIONS;
INTEREST METHOD OF
AMORTIZATION OF BOND
PREMIUM

On July 1, 1994, Shute Inc. issued $10,000,000 of ten-year, 11% bonds at an effective interest rate of 10%, receiving proceeds of $10,623,210. Interest on the bonds is payable semiannually on December 31 and June 30. The fiscal year of the company is the calendar year.

Instructions
1. Journalize the entries to record the following:
   a. The first semiannual interest payment on December 31, 1994, and the amortization of the bond premium, using the interest method. (Round to nearest dollar.)
   b. The interest payment on June 30, 1995, and the amortization of the bond premium, using the interest method. (Round to nearest dollar.)
2. Determine the total interest expense for 1994.

APPENDIX A
PROBLEM 11-7B
ENTRIES FOR BONDS
PAYABLE TRANSACTIONS;
INTEREST METHOD OF
AMORTIZATION OF BOND
DISCOUNT

On July 1, 1994, Cline Inc. issued $15,000,000 of ten-year, 10% bonds at an effective interest rate of 12%, receiving proceeds of $13,279,425. Interest on the bonds is payable semiannually on December 31 and June 30. The fiscal year of the company is the calendar year.

Instructions
1. Journalize the entries to record the following:
   a. The first semiannual interest payment on December 31, 1994, and the amortization of the bond discount, using the interest method.

b. The interest payment on June 30, 1995, and the amortization of the bond discount, using the interest method.

2. Determine the total interest expense for 1994.

APPENDIX B
PROBLEM 11-8B
ENTRIES FOR BOND
INVESTMENTS

The following selected transactions relate to certain securities acquired by Marsh Company, whose fiscal year ends on December 31:

1994

Sep. 1. Purchased $500,000 of Ellis Company 20-year, 9% bonds dated July 1, 1994, directly from the issuing company, for $476,200 plus accrued interest of $7,500.

Dec. 31. Received the semiannual interest on the Ellis Company bonds.

31. Recorded bond discount amortization of $400 on the Ellis Company bonds. The amortization amount was determined by using the straight-line method.

(Assume that all intervening transactions and adjustments have been properly recorded, and that the number of bonds owned has not changed from December 31, 1994, to December 31, 1998.)

1999

June 30. Received the semiannual interest on the Ellis Company bonds.

July 31. Sold one-half of the Ellis Company bonds at 95 plus accrued interest. The broker deducted $750 for commission, etc., remitting the balance. Prior to the sale, $350 of discount on one-half of the bonds was amortized, reducing the carrying value of those bonds to $241,050.

Dec. 31. Received the semiannual interest on the Ellis Company bonds.

31. Recorded bond discount amortization of $600 on the Ellis Company bonds.

Instructions

Journalize the entries to record the foregoing transactions.

MINI-CASE ST BOTTLING CORPORATION

You hold a 25% interest in the family-owned business, a soft drink bottling distributorship organized as a corporation. Your sister, who is the manager, has proposed an expansion of plant facilities at an expected cost of $1,500,000. Two alternative plans have been suggested as methods of financing the expansion. Each plan is briefly described as follows:

Plan 1. Issue $1,500,000 of 20-year, 12% bonds at face amount.

Plan 2. Issue an additional $500,000 of capital stock and $1,000,000 of 20-year, 12% bonds at face amount.

The balance sheet as of the end of the previous fiscal year is as follows:

ST Bottling Co.
Balance Sheet
December 31, 19—

Assets

Current assets	$2,350,000
Plant assets	5,150,000
Total assets	$7,500,000

Liabilities and Stockholders' Equity

Current liabilities	$2,000,000
Capital stock	600,000
Retained earnings	4,900,000
Total liabilities and stockholders' equity	$7,500,000

Net income has remained relatively constant over the past several years. The expansion program is expected to increase yearly income before bond interest and income tax from $300,000 to $500,000.

Your sister has asked you, as the company treasurer, to prepare an analysis of each financing plan.

Instructions

1. Prepare a tabulation indicating the expected net income under each plan. Interest expense on bonds payable is deducted in determining "income before income taxes." Income taxes should be deducted in determining net income. Apply an income tax rate of 40% to income before income taxes to determine the expected income tax expense for the year.

2. Discuss the factors that should be considered in evaluating the two plans.

ANSWERS TO SELF-EXAMINATION QUESTIONS

1. B Since the contract rate on the bonds is higher than the prevailing market rate, a rational investor would be willing to pay more than the face amount, or a premium (answer B), for the bonds. If the contract rate and the market rate were equal, the bonds could be expected to sell at their face amount (answer A). Likewise, if the market rate is higher than the contract rate, the bonds would sell at a price below their face amount (answer D) or at a discount (answer C).

2. B The entry to amortize a premium on bonds payable decreases interest expense. Therefore, the entry to amortize a premium on bonds payable is to debit Premium on Bonds Payable and credit Interest Expense (answer B).

3. A The bond carrying value, sometimes called the book value, is the face amount plus unamortized premium or less unamortized discount. For this question, the carrying value is $500,000 less $40,000, or $460,000 (answer A).

4. B Although the sinking fund may consist of cash as well as securities, the fund is listed on the balance sheet as an investment (answer B) because it is to be used to pay the long-term liability at maturity.

5. C The balance of Discount on Bonds Payable is usually reported as a deduction from Bonds Payable in the Long-Term Liabilities section (answer C) of the balance sheet. Likewise, a balance in a premium on bonds payable account would usually be reported as an addition to Bonds Payable in the Long-Term Liabilities section of the balance sheet.

You and Accounting

The following stock quotations for Grumman Corporation, an aerospace/defense contractor, were taken from the August 12, 1993, issue of *The Wall Street Journal*. The first stock is a common stock, and the second stock is a preferred stock.

NEW YORK STOCK EXCHANGE COMPOSITE TRANSACTIONS

52 Weeks					Yld		Vol				Net
Hi	Lo	Stock	Sym	Div	%	PE	100s	Hi	Lo	Close	Chg
47⅞	19⅝	Grumman	GQ	1.20	3.1	18	244	39⅛	38⅞	39	+⅛

The preceding quotations are interpreted as follows:

Hi	Highest price during the past 52 weeks
Lo	Lowest price during the past 52 weeks
Stock	Name of the company
Sym	Stock exchange symbol (GQ for Grumman)
Div	Dividends paid per share during the past year
Yld %	Annual dividend yield per share based on the closing price (Grumman's 3.1% yield on common stock is computed as $1.2 ÷ $39)
PE	Price-earnings ratio on common stock
Vol	The volume of stock traded in 100s
Hi	Highest price the previous day
Lo	Lowest price the previous day
Close	Closing price the previous day
Net Chg	The net change in price from the previous day

In this chapter, you will read about accounting for corporate stocks, such as the one listed, and other topics related to the corporate form of organization. This will enable you to better understand corporations and corporate stocks as a potential investment.

Chapter 12
Corporate Equity

In the Dartmouth College case in 1819, Chief Justice Marshall of the United States Supreme Court stated:

A corporation is an artificial being, invisible, intangible, and existing only in contemplation of the law.

The concept underlying the preceding definition has become the basis for the legal doctrine that a corporation is an artificial person, created by law and having a distinct existence separate and apart from the natural persons who are responsible for its creation and operation. Almost all large business enterprises in the United States are organized as corporations.

Throughout the earlier chapters of this text, we have used the corporate form of entity as a basis for illustrations. In this chapter, we further discuss the characteristics of corporate entities. In doing so, we discuss the main sources of equity, various types of paid-in capital, the payment of dividends, and treasury stock transactions. Finally, we describe and illustrate the preparation of a retained earnings statement and the statement of stockholders' equity.

CHARACTERISTICS OF A CORPORATION

Objective 1
Describe the characteristics of the corporate form of organization.

A corporation has a **separate legal existence**. It may acquire, own, and dispose of property in its corporate name. It may also incur liabilities and enter into other types of contracts according to the rights granted by its charter or articles of incorporation. As a separate legal entity, a corporation has certain characteristics that make it different from other forms of business organization. We briefly describe the most important of these characteristics below.

The ownership of a corporation is represented by shares of stock, called **capital stock**. In practice, corporations may have several different classes of stock outstanding. Each share of stock has the same rights as every other share of stock in its class. As we illustrate later in this chapter, each class of stock is accounted for separately.

Shares of stock may be bought and sold without affecting the operations or continued existence of the corporation. Corporations whose shares of stock are traded in public markets are called **public corporations**. Corporations whose shares are not traded publicly are usually owned by a small group of investors and are called **nonpublic** or **private corporations**.

The stockholders of a corporation have **limited liability**. A corporation is responsible for its own acts and obligations under law. Therefore, a corporation's creditors usually may not go beyond the assets of the corporation to satisfy their claims. Thus, the financial loss that a stockholder may suffer is limited to the amount invested. This limited liability feature contributed to the rapid growth of the corporate form of organization.

Stockholders exercise control over the management of a corporation's operations and activities by electing a **board of directors**. Under the authority of the corporate charter, the board of directors meets periodically to establish corporate policies. The board also selects the chief executive officer (CEO) and other major officers to manage the day-to-day affairs of the corporation. Exhibit 1 shows the organizational structure of a corporation.

Exhibit 1
Organizational Structure of a Corporate Enterprise

As a separate legal entity, a corporation is subject to additional **taxes**. For example, corporations must pay federal income taxes. Some states also require corporations to pay income taxes. In addition, when an enterprise is initially organized (incorporated), it usually pays a fee to the state. **Government regulations** may also restrict corporations in such matters as ownership of real estate, retention of earnings, and purchase of their own stock.

A corporation distributes its earnings (income) to stockholders in the form of **dividends**. Although corporations must pay federal and, in some cases, state income taxes, income distributed in the form of dividends is taxed again as income to those receiving the dividends. This **double taxation** of corporate earnings is viewed as a major disadvantage of the corporate form of organization.

Corporations may be organized for nonprofit reasons, such as recreational, educational, charitable, or humanitarian purposes. However, most corporations are organized to earn a profit and a fair rate of return for their stockholders. In the remainder of this chapter, we discuss corporations organized for profit.

SOURCES OF PAID-IN CAPITAL

Objective 2
List the major sources of paid-in capital, including the various classes of capital stock.

As we discussed and illustrated in earlier chapters, the Stockholders' Equity section of the corporate balance sheet has two major subdivisions: **paid-in capital** (or contributed capital) and retained earnings. The main source of paid-in capital is from the issuance of stock. In the following paragraphs, we discuss the characteristics of the various classes of capital stock. We conclude this section with a brief discussion of other sources of paid-in capital.

Capital Stock

The number of shares of capital stock that a corporation is authorized to issue is set forth in its charter. The term *issued* refers to the shares issued to the stockholders. A corporation may, under circumstances we discuss later in this chapter, reacquire some of the stock that it has issued. The stock remaining in the hands of stockholders is then called **outstanding stock**.

The shares of capital stock are often assigned a monetary amount, known as **par**. As a written representation of ownership, corporations may issue **stock certificates** to stockholders.[1] On a stock certificate is printed the par value of the stock, the name of the stockholder, and the number of shares owned. Stock may also be issued without par, in which case it is called **no-par stock**. Some states require the board of directors to assign a **stated value** to no-par stock.

Because of the limited liability feature of corporations, creditors have no claim against the personal assets of stockholders. However, some state laws require that corporations maintain a minimum contribution by the stockholders as protection for creditors. This minimum amount is called **legal capital**. The amount of required legal capital varies among the states, but it usually includes the amount of par or stated value of the shares of capital stock issued.

The major rights that accompany ownership of a share of stock are as follows:

1. The right to vote in matters concerning the corporation.
2. The right to share in distributions of earnings.
3. The **preemptive right**, which is the right to maintain the same fractional interest in the corporation by purchasing shares of any additional issuances of stock.[2]
4. The right to share in assets on liquidation.

When only one class of capital stock is issued, it is called **common stock**. In this case, each share of common stock has equal rights. To appeal to a broader investment market, a corporation may issue one or more classes of stock with various preference rights. A normal preference right is the right to share in distributions of earnings. Such stock is generally called **preferred stock**.

The board of directors has the sole authority to distribute dividends to the stockholders. When such action is taken, the directors are said to *declare* a dividend. Since dividends are normally based on earnings, a corporation cannot guarantee dividends to its stockholders. Rather than distribute dividends, the board of directors may decide to retain earnings in the corporation to provide for expansion, to offset possible future losses, or to provide for other contingencies.

A corporation with both preferred stock and common stock is permitted to declare dividends on the common only after it meets the dividend preference of the preferred stock. The dividend preference of the preferred stock may be stated in monetary terms or as a percent of par. For example, $4 preferred stock has a prior claim to an annual $4 per share dividend. If the par value of the preferred stock were $50, the same claim on dividends could be stated as 8% preferred stock.

---

[1] Some corporations have stopped issuing stock certificates except on special request. In these cases, the corporation maintains records of ownership by using electronic media.
[2] In recent years, stockholders of a number of corporations have, by formal action, given up their preemptive rights.

NONPARTICIPATING AND PARTICIPATING PREFERRED STOCK. The preferred stockholders' dividend preference is usually limited to a certain amount. Such stock is said to be **nonparticipating preferred stock**. To continue the preceding example, assume that a corporation has 1,000 shares of $4 nonparticipating preferred stock and 4,000 shares of common stock outstanding. Also assume that the net income, amount of earnings retained, and the amount of earnings distributed by the board of directors for the first three years of operations are as follows:

	First Year	Second Year	Third Year
Net income	$20,000	$55,000	$100,000
Amount retained	10,000	20,000	40,000
Amount distributed	$10,000	$35,000	$ 60,000

Exhibit 2 shows the distribution of the earnings between the preferred stock and the common stock for each year.

Exhibit 2
Dividends to Nonparticipating Preferred Stock

	First Year	Second Year	Third Year
Amount distributed	$10,000	$35,000	$60,000
Preferred dividend (1,000 shares)	4,000	4,000	4,000
Common dividend (4,000 shares)	$ 6,000	$31,000	$56,000
Dividends per share:			
Preferred	$4.00	$4.00	$ 4.00
Common	$1.50	$7.75	$14.00

In this example, the preferred stockholders received an annual dividend of $4 per share, compared to the common stockholders' dividends of $1.50, $7.75, and $14.00 per share. The preferred stockholders have a greater chance of receiving regular dividends than do the common stockholders. On the other hand, common stockholders have a greater chance of receiving larger dividends than do the preferred stockholders.

Preferred stock may provide for the possibility of receiving additional dividends if certain conditions are met. These conditions often include reaching a certain level of earnings and distributing a certain amount of dividends to common stockholders. Such stock is called **participating preferred stock**. It is rarely used in today's financial markets.

CUMULATIVE AND NONCUMULATIVE PREFERRED STOCK. The preferred stock contract may contain special provisions if regular preferred dividends are passed (not declared) by the board of directors. These provisions normally prohibit the payment of any common stock dividends if any preferred dividends have been passed in prior years. Such preferred stock is said to be **cumulative preferred stock**, and any preferred dividends that have been passed are said to be *in arrears*. Preferred stock not having this cumulative right is called **noncumulative preferred stock**.

To illustrate, we use the corporation in the previous example. This corporation has outstanding 1,000 shares of $4 cumulative preferred stock and 4,000 shares of common stock. We assume that no dividends have been paid in the preceding two years. In the third (current) year, dividends of $22,000 are declared. Exhibit 3 shows the distribution of these dividends between the preferred and common stock.

Exhibit 3
Dividends to Cumulative Preferred Stock

Amount distributed		$22,000
Preferred dividend (1,000 shares):		
First-year dividend in arrears	$4,000	
Second-year dividend in arrears	4,000	
Third-year current dividend	4,000	12,000
Common dividend (4,000 shares)		$10,000
Dividends per share:		
Preferred		$12.00
Common		$ 2.50

OTHER PREFERENTIAL RIGHTS. In the preceding discussion of the preference rights of preferred stock, we emphasized dividend distributions. Preferred stock may also be given preference rights on assets in liquidation of the corporation. However, claims of creditors must be satisfied first before any assets are distributed to stockholders. Any assets remaining after the creditors have been paid are first distributed to preferred stockholders. Any remaining assets are then distributed to common stockholders.

A corporation may have more than one class of preferred stock, with differences as to the amount of dividends, preferences in liquidation, and voting rights. The rights of a class of stock may be determined by reference to the corporate charter, stock certificate, or stock contract.

Preferred Stock—Risks vs. Rewards

Preferred stocks shield shareholders somewhat from the lows of corporate fortunes. If dividend payments must be reduced, preferred stockholders receive dividends before common shareholders. However, preferred stockholders often miss out on the highs of corporate fortunes. If dividend payments are large, because most preferred stock is nonparticipating, preferred shareholders receive a fixed dividend, and the bulk of the large dividends goes to common shareholders. These "safe-but-stodgy" equities can offer dramatic profits, however, as described in the following excerpt from an article in *Business Week*:

. . . In times of grave financial trouble, dividends on preferreds are often suspended and placed in arrears. . . . If and when the company reinstates dividends, current shareholders are entitled to all the back payments, whether or not they owned stock during the arrearage period—if the preferred is cumulative. . . .

The gains [from purchasing preferred stock with dividends in arrears] can be impressive. Bethlehem Steel announced in April that it would pay $22.5 million in arrears and resume the regular quarterly dividend on its two classes of preferred stock. Because Bethlehem had missed four payments, investors receive an extra year's worth of dividends: One class that usually pays $1.25 quarterly will return $6.25—not bad on a stock that traded in the low 30s just a few months ago.

Playing preferreds in arrears requires patience. Long Island Lighting, for instance, recently announced that it would try to resume paying dividends next year after a four-year hiatus. But the larger concern lies in the fact that you're betting on a turnaround. And all bets are off if the company goes bankrupt: You not only lose arrearages but you're also sure to see the share price plummet. On the repayment totem pole, preferreds occupy the second-lowest notch—before the common shareholders but after the creditors and bondholders. . . .

Source: Troy Segal, "Preferred Stock: The Risky Hunt for Hidden Rewards," *Business Week* (June 13, 1988), p. 114.

Other Sources of Paid-In Capital

In addition to the issuance of stock, paid-in capital may arise from donations of real estate or other properties to a corporation. Civic groups and municipalities sometimes give land or buildings to a corporation as an incentive to locate or remain in a community. In such cases, the corporation debits the assets for their fair market value and credits *Donated Capital*.

Paid-in capital may also arise from the redemption of capital stock by a corporation. Preferred stock contracts sometimes provide that the issuing corporation may redeem (retire) the stock at a specific redemption price. When the stock is redeemed, the redemption price may be less than the original issuance price of the stock. In this case, the excess of the original issuance price over the redemption price is credited to *Paid-In Capital from Preferred Stock Redemption*. On the other hand, the redemption price may be greater than the original issuance price of the stock. In this case, the excess of the redemption price over the original issuance price is debited to Retained Earnings.

Paid-in capital may result when a corporation buys and sells its own stock in the market place. Such stock is called **treasury stock**. Later in this chapter, we discuss the recording of treasury stock transactions, including the recording of paid-in capital from such transactions.

Objective 3
Journalize the entries for issuing capital stock.

ISSUING CAPITAL STOCK

A separate account is used for recording the amount of each class of stock issued to investors in a corporation. For example, assume that a corporation is authorized to issue 10,000 shares of preferred stock, $100 par, and 100,000 shares of common stock, $20 par. One-half of each class of authorized shares is issued at par for cash. The entry to record the stockholders' investment and the receipt of the cash is as follows:[3]

Cash	1,500,000	
Preferred Stock		500,000
Common Stock		1,000,000

The capital stock accounts (Preferred Stock, Common Stock) are controlling accounts. A record of each stockholder's name, address, and number of shares held is normally kept in a subsidiary ledger. This subsidiary ledger is called the **stockholders ledger**. It provides the information for issuing dividend checks, annual meeting notices, and financial reports to individual stockholders.[4]

Par stock is often issued by a corporation at a price other than par. This is because the par value of a stock is simply a way of dividing owners' equity into units of ownership. The price at which stock can be sold by a corporation depends on a variety of factors, such as the following:

1. The financial condition, earnings record, and dividend record of the corporation.
2. Investor expectations of the corporation's potential earning power.
3. General business and economic conditions and prospects.

When par stock is issued for a price that is more than its par, the stock has sold at a **premium**. When par stock is issued for a price that is less than its par, the stock has sold at a **discount**. Thus, if stock with a par of $50 is issued for a price of $60, the stock has sold at a premium of $10. If the same stock is issued for a price of $45, the stock has sold at a discount of $5.

Many states do not permit the issuance of stock at a discount. In others, it may be done only under unusual conditions. Since issuing capital stock at a discount is rare, we will not illustrate it.

Premium on Capital Stock

When capital stock is issued at a premium, Cash or other asset accounts are debited for the amount received. The stock account is then credited for the par amount. The excess of the amount paid over par is a part of the total investment of the stockholders in the corporation. Therefore, such an amount in excess of par should be classified as a part of the paid-in capital. An account entitled Paid-In Capital in Excess of Par is usually credited for this amount.

To illustrate, if Caldwell Company issues 2,000 shares of $50 par preferred stock for cash at $55, the entry to record the transaction is as follows:

Cash	110,000	
Preferred Stock		100,000
Paid-In Capital in Excess of Par—Preferred Stock		10,000

Although the $10,000 in excess of par is a part of the paid-in capital, it is recorded in an account separate from the stock account to which it relates. This is be-

---

[3] The accounting for investments in stocks from the point of view of the investor is discussed in a later chapter.
[4] Large public corporations often use a financial institution, such as a bank, as transfer agent or registrar for maintaining stockholder records.

cause, in some states, the amount received in excess of par may not be considered a part of legal capital. If so, this amount may be used for dividends to stockholders. However, if this amount is used for dividends, stockholders should be clearly notified that the dividend is a return of paid-in capital rather than a distribution of earnings.

No-Par Stock

In most states, both preferred and common stock may be issued without a par value. Preferred stock, however, is normally assigned a par value. When no-par stock is issued, the entire proceeds are credited to the capital stock account. This is true even though the issuance price varies from time to time. For example, assume that at the time of organization a corporation issues 10,000 shares of no-par common stock at $40 a share and at a later date issues 1,000 additional shares at $36. The entries to record the issuances of the no-par stock are as follows:

Original issuance of 10,000 shares of no-par common at $40.

Cash	400,000	
Common Stock		400,000

Subsequent issuance of 1,000 shares of no-par common at $36.

Cash	36,000	
Common Stock		36,000

The laws of some states require that the entire proceeds from the issuance of no-par stock be regarded as legal capital. The preceding entries follow this principle. In other states, no-par stock may be assigned a stated value per share. The stated value is treated similarly to par value, and the excess of the proceeds over the stated value is credited to Paid-In Capital in Excess of Stated Value. If we assume that in the preceding example the stated value is $25, the issuance of the no-par stock is recorded as follows:

Original issuance of 10,000 shares of no-par common at $40, stated value $25.

Cash	400,000	
Common Stock		250,000
Paid-In Capital in Excess of Stated Value		150,000

Subsequent issuance of 1,000 shares of no-par common at $36, stated value $25.

Cash	36,000	
Common Stock		25,000
Paid-In Capital in Excess of Stated Value		11,000

Issuing Stock for Assets Other Than Cash

When capital stock is issued in exchange for assets other than cash, such as land, buildings, and equipment, the assets acquired should be recorded at their fair market value. If the fair market value of the assets cannot be objectively determined, the fair market price of the stock issued may be used.

To illustrate, assume that a corporation acquired land for which the fair market value cannot be determined. In exchange, the corporation issued 10,000 shares of its $10 par common. Assuming the stock has a current market price of $12 per share, the transaction is recorded as follows:

Land	120,000	
Common Stock		100,000
Paid-In Capital in Excess of Stated Value		20,000

Objective 4
Journalize the entries for
treasury stock transactions.

TREASURY STOCK TRANSACTIONS

Although some state laws restrict the practice, a corporation may purchase shares of its own outstanding stock from stockholders. A corporation may buy its own stock in order to provide shares for resale to employees, for reissuance as a bonus to employees, or to support the market price of the stock. For example, General Motors bought back its common stock and stated that two primary uses of the treasury stock would be for incentive compensation plans and employee savings plans.

Treasury stock is stock that:

1. Has been issued as fully paid
2. Has been reacquired by the corporation
3. Has not been canceled or reissued

A commonly used method of accounting for the purchase and the resale of treasury stock is the **cost method**.[5] When the stock is purchased by the corporation, the account *Treasury Stock* is debited for its cost (the price paid for it). The par value and the price at which the stock was originally issued are ignored. When the stock is resold, Treasury Stock is credited for its cost, and any difference between the cost and the selling price is normally debited or credited to a paid-in capital account. This latter account is entitled *Paid-In Capital from Sale of Treasury Stock*.

To illustrate the cost method, assume that the paid-in capital of a corporation is as follows:

Common stock, $25 par (20,000 shares authorized and issued)	$500,000	
Excess of issue price over par	150,000	$650,000

The transactions involving treasury stock and the related entries are as follows:

Purchased 1,000 shares of treasury stock at $45.

Treasury Stock	45,000	
Cash		45,000

Sold 200 shares of treasury stock at $60.

Cash	12,000	
Treasury Stock		9,000
Paid-In Capital from Sale of Treasury Stock		3,000

Sold 200 shares of treasury stock at $40.

Cash	8,000	
Paid-In Capital from Sale of Treasury Stock	1,000	
Treasury Stock		9,000

As we illustrated, a sale of treasury stock may result in a decrease in paid-in capital. To the extent that Paid-In Capital from Sale of Treasury Stock has a credit balance, it should be debited for any decrease. Any remaining decrease should then be debited to the retained earnings account.

REPORTING PAID-IN CAPITAL

Objective 5
Prepare the Paid-In Capital
section of a corporate balance
sheet.

As with other sections of the balance sheet, alternative terms and formats may be used in reporting paid-in capital. Exhibit 4 illustrates some examples of these alternatives.

---

[5] Another method, called the *par value method*, is infrequently used and is discussed in advanced accounting texts.

Exhibit 4
Paid-In Capital Section of Stock-holders' Equity

Stockholders' Equity			
Paid-in capital:			
Preferred $5 stock, cumulative, $50 par (2,000 shares authorized and issued)	*450,000*	$100,000	
Excess of issue price over par	*50,000*	10,000	$ 110,000 *500,000*
Common stock, $20 par (50,000 shares authorized, 45,000 shares issued)	*300,000*	$900,000	
Excess of issue price over par	*150,000*	132,000	1,032,000 *450,000*
From stock redemption			60,000
Total paid-in capital			$1,202,000
			950,000

Shareholders' Equity	
Contributed capital:	
Preferred 10% stock, cumulative, $50 par (2,000 shares authorized and issued)	$100,000
Common stock, $20 par (50,000 shares authorized, 45,000 shares issued)	900,000
Additional paid-in capital	202,000
Total contributed capital	$1,202,000

In the first example, each class of stock is listed first, followed by related paid-in capital accounts. In the second example, the capital stock accounts are listed first. The other paid-in capital accounts are listed as a single item described as *Additional paid-in capital*. These combined accounts could also be described as *Capital in excess of par (or stated value) of shares* or other similar title.

How is treasury stock and paid-in capital from the sale of treasury stock reported in the balance sheet? Paid-In Capital from Sale of Treasury Stock is reported in the Paid-In Capital section. Treasury Stock is deducted from the total of the paid-in capital and retained earnings.

To illustrate, Exhibit 5 shows a Stockholders' Equity section with treasury stock.

Exhibit 5
Stockholders' Equity Section with Treasury Stock

Stockholders' Equity			
Paid-in capital:			
Common stock, $25 par (20,000 shares authorized and issued)	*300,000*	$500,000	
Excess of issue price over par	*150,000*	150,000	$650,000 *450,000*
From donated land			2,000
Total paid-in capital			$652,000
Retained earnings			130,000
Total			$782,000
Deduct treasury stock (600 shares at cost)			27,000
Total stockholders' equity			$755,000

The Stockholders' Equity section of the balance sheet indicates that 20,000 shares of stock were issued, of which 600 are held as treasury stock. The number of shares outstanding is therefore 19,400. Owners of 19,400 shares would have the right to vote at a stockholders' meeting.

Significant changes in paid-in capital during a period should also be disclosed.

Such disclosures may be presented either in a *statement of stockholders' equity* or in notes to the financial statements. We describe and illustrate the statement of stockholders' equity later in this chapter.

DIVIDENDS

Objective 6
Journalize the entries for cash dividends and stock dividends.

A dividend usually represents a distribution of retained earnings. Dividends may be paid in cash, in stock of the company, or in other property. A dividend may also represent a distribution of paid-in capital. We discuss cash dividends, stock dividends, and liquidating dividends in the following paragraphs.

Cash Dividends

A cash distribution of earnings by a corporation to its shareholders is called a **cash dividend**. Cash dividends are the most common form of dividend. We have illustrated the payment of cash dividends in the earlier chapters of this text.

Can a corporation pay a cash dividend at any time? There are usually three conditions that a corporation must meet to pay a cash dividend:

1. Sufficient retained earnings
2. Sufficient cash
3. Formal action by the board of directors

A large amount of retained earnings does not always mean that a corporation is able to pay dividends. There must also be enough cash in excess of normal operating needs. The board of directors of a corporation is not required by law to declare dividends. This is true even if both retained earnings and cash are large enough to justify a dividend. When a dividend has been *declared*, however, it becomes a liability of the corporation.

Most corporations try to maintain a stable dividend record in order to make their stock attractive to investors. Dividends may be paid once a year or semiannually or quarterly. The general tendency is to pay quarterly dividends on both common and preferred stock. In periods of high profitability, the board of directors may declare an *extra* dividend on common stock. It may be paid at one of the usual dividend dates or at some other date. The use of the term *extra* dividend indicates that the board of directors does not anticipate an increase in the amount of the *regular* dividend.

You may have seen corporate announcements of dividend declarations in newspapers. Dividend declarations are usually announced and reported in financial newspapers and investor services. Three dates are important in a dividend announcement:

1. The date of declaration
2. The date of record
3. The date of payment

The date of declaration is the date the board of directors takes formal action to declare the dividend. The date of record is the date on which ownership of shares is to be determined. The date of payment is the date on which the dividend is to be paid. For example, a dividend announcement might read:

On June 26, the board of directors of Campbell Soup Co. declared a quarterly cash dividend of $.33 per common share to stockholders of record as of the close of business on July 8, payable on July 31.

The liability for a dividend is recorded on the declaration date. No entry is required on the date of record. This date merely sets the date for determining the identity of the stockholders who will receive the dividend. The period of time between the record date and the payment date allows for the preparation of the dividend checks. During this period, a stock's price is usually quoted as selling *ex-dividends*. This means that since the date of record has passed, a new investor will not receive the unpaid dividends. On the date of payment, the corporation's dividend liability is paid by mailing the dividend checks.

We simplified previous illustrations of dividend entries by assuming that the declaration date and the payment date were the same. In the next illustration, we journalize the dividend entries when this is not the case. Assume that on December 1 the board of directors of Hiber Corporation declares both a preferred stock and common stock dividend. The preferred stock dividend is a regular quarterly dividend of $2.50 on the 5,000 shares of $100 par, 10% preferred stock outstanding (total dividend of $12,500). The common stock dividend is a quarterly dividend of $0.30 on the 100,000 shares of $10 par common stock outstanding (total dividend of $30,000). The record date is December 10, and checks are to be issued to stockholders on January 2. The entry to record the declaration of the dividends is as follows:

Dec. 1	Cash Dividends		42,500	
	Cash Dividends Payable			42,500

The balance in Cash Dividends will be transferred to Retained Earnings as a part of the closing process. Cash Dividends Payable will be listed on the December 31 balance sheet as a current liability. The entry to record the payment of the dividends on January 2 is as follows:

Jan. 2	Cash Dividends Payable		42,500	
	Cash			42,500

If a corporation that holds treasury stock declares a cash dividend, the dividends are not paid on the treasury shares. To do so would place the corporation in the position of earning income through dealing with itself. For example, if Hiber Corporation in the preceding illustration had held 5,000 shares of its own common stock, the cash dividends on the common stock would have been $28,500 [(100,000 − 5,000) x $.30] instead of $30,000.

Dividends on cumulative preferred stock do not become a liability of the corporation until formal action is taken by the board of directors. However, dividends in arrears at a balance sheet date should be disclosed. This disclosure may be made by a footnote or a parenthetical note.

Using Accounting

Potential investors in a corporation often rely on accounting information in assessing the attractiveness of stocks. For example, the existence of dividends in arrears on cumulative preferred stock can serve as a warning that the corporation does not pay dividends every year. Such dividends in arrears must be paid before any dividends are available to common stockholders. Likewise, any liquidation preference of preferred stock ranks ahead of the common stock if the corporation goes out of business. If the ability to earn dividends from investing in the stock is a primary concern, then the size of retained earnings, the dividend history of the corporation, and the amount of cash and cash equivalents as well as cash flows are important pieces of information.

Stock Dividends

What is a **stock dividend**? It is a pro rata distribution of shares of stock to stockholders through a transfer of retained earnings to paid-in capital. Such distributions are usually in common stock and are issued to holders of common stock. It is possible to issue common stock to preferred stockholders or vice versa, but such stock dividends are rare.

Stock dividends are different from cash dividends in that there is no distribution of cash or other assets to stockholders. Stock dividends are often issued by corporations that are experiencing rapid growth. Such corporations use most of the cash generated from operations to acquire new facilities or to expand their operations and thus do not wish to use cash to pay dividends.

When a corporation holding treasury stock declares a stock dividend, the number of shares to be issued may be based on either (1) the number of shares outstanding or (2) the number of shares issued. In practice, the number of shares held as treasury stock usually is a small percent of the number of shares issued. Further, the rate of dividend is normally small, so the difference between the methods is usually not significant.

The effect of a stock dividend on the stockholders' equity of the issuing corporation is to transfer retained earnings to paid-in capital. The amount of this transfer, however, has been subject to some debate in the accounting profession. The laws of most states require that a minimum amount equal to the par or stated value of a stock dividend be transferred from retained earnings to paid-in capital.

For nonpublic (private) corporations, the minimum is usually transferred from retained earnings to paid-in capital. This minimum transfer is often justified on the basis that stockholders of nonpublic corporations have direct knowledge of the affairs of the corporation. Because of this knowledge, the stockholders are able to assess the impact of the stock dividend on the corporation. In addition, since stock of nonpublic corporations is not actively traded, the fair value of the shares of stock issued in a stock dividend usually cannot be objectively determined.

For large public corporations, the *fair value* of the shares issued in a stock dividend is the amount transferred from retained earnings to paid-in capital. The justification for the transfer of *fair value* for public corporations is expressed as follows:

. . . Many recipients of stock dividends look upon them as distributions of corporate earnings and usually in an amount equivalent to the fair value of the additional shares received. . . . [Such] views . . . are . . . strengthened in those instances, which by far are the most numerous where the [stock dividends] are so small in comparison with the shares previously outstanding that they do not have any apparent effect upon the share market price and, consequently, the market value of the shares previously held remains substantially unchanged. . . . [where] these circumstances exist the corporation should in the public interest ... [transfer] from [retained earnings] to . . . [paid-in capital] . . . an amount equal to the fair value of the additional shares issued. . . .[6]

Using the preceding method, Stock Dividends is debited for the fair value of the stock issued as a dividend. Stock Dividends Distributable is credited for the par or stated value of the common stock to be issued. The difference between the fair value of the stock and its par or stated value is credited to Paid-In Capital in Excess of Par—Common Stock. When the stock is issued on the date of payment, Stock Dividends Distributable is debited and Common Stock is credited for the par or stated value of the stock issued. At the end of the period, the stock dividends account is closed to Retained Earnings.

To illustrate a stock dividend for a public corporation, assume that the stockholders' equity accounts of Hendrix Corporation as of December 15 are as follows:

Common Stock, $20 par (2,000,000 shares issued)	$40,000,000
Paid-In Capital in Excess of Par—Common Stock	9,000,000
Retained Earnings	26,600,000

On December 15, the board of directors declares a stock dividend of 5% or 100,000 shares (2,000,000 shares x 5%), to be issued on January 10. The market price of the stock on the declaration date is $31 a share. The entry to record the declaration is as follows:

---

[6] *Accounting Research and Terminology Bulletins—Final Edition,* "No. 43, Restatement and Revision of Accountsing Research Bulletins" (New York: American Institute of Certified Public Accountants, 1961), Ch. 7, Sec. B, par. 10.

Dec. 15	Stock Dividends (100,000 × $31)	3,100,000	
	Stock Dividends Distributable		
	(100,000 × $20)		2,000,000
	Paid-In Capital in Excess of Par—		
	Common Stock		1,100,000

The $3,100,000 debit to Stock Dividends is transferred to Retained Earnings as a part of the closing process at the end of the period. The following entry records the issuance of the stock on January 10:

| Jan. 10 | Stock Dividends Distributable | 2,000,000 | |
| | Common Stock | | 2,000,000 |

The effect of the stock dividend is to transfer $3,100,000 from retained earnings to paid-in capital and to increase by 100,000 the number of shares outstanding. There is no change in the assets, liabilities, or total stockholders' equity of the corporation. If financial statements are prepared between the date of declaration and the date of issuance, the stock dividends distributable account should be listed in the Paid-In Capital section of the balance sheet.

The issuance of the additional stock dividend shares does not affect the total amount of a stockholder's equity. A stock dividend also does not affect a stockholder's proportionate interest (equity) in the corporation. We illustrate this for a stockholder who is assumed to own 1,000 shares.

The Corporation	Before Stock Dividend	After Stock Dividend
Common stock	$40,000,000	$42,000,000
Excess of issue price over par	9,000,000	10,100,000
Retained earnings	26,600,000	23,500,000
Total stockholders' equity	$75,600,000	$75,600,000
Number of shares outstanding	2,000,000	2,100,000
Equity per share	$37.80	$36.00
A Stockholder		
Number of shares owned	1,000	1,050
Total equity	$37,800	$37,800
Portion of corporation owned	.05%	.05%

Liquidating Dividends

A liquidating dividend is a distribution to stockholders from paid-in capital. Such dividends are rare and are usually paid when a corporation is permanently reducing its operations or winding up its affairs completely. Since dividends are normally paid from retained earnings, dividends that reduce paid-in capital should be identified as liquidating dividends when paid.

APPROPRIATIONS OF RETAINED EARNINGS

Objective 7
Journalize appropriations of retained earnings, and prepare the related retained earnings statement.

As we illustrated in prior chapters, retained earnings is reported in the balance sheet, and changes in retained earnings are reported in a separate retained earnings statement. In the following paragraphs, we discuss the recording and reporting of appropriations of retained earnings.

Recording Appropriations of Retained Earnings

A corporation's retained earnings available for use as dividends may be limited (restricted) by action of its board of directors. The amount restricted is called an **appropriation** or a **reserve**. This amount remains a part of retained earnings and is reported as such in the financial statements.

An appropriation is usually reflected in the accounts by transferring the amount from the retained earnings account to a special account. This special account is identified as an appropriation, with a description of its purpose. An example of such an account would be *Appropriation for Plant Expansion*.

Appropriations may be required by contract or law. For example, appropriations may be required by contract for bank loans or cumulative preferred stock dividends in arrears. Appropriations may also be required by state law for the amounts paid for treasury stock.

To illustrate, assume that a corporation with retained earnings of $200,000 purchases treasury stock for $50,000. An appropriation of $50,000 would be transferred to the account Appropriation for Treasury Stock. This appropriation would restrict the payment of dividends to not more than $150,000. In this way, the corporation's legal capital will not be used for dividends. The entry to record the appropriation is as follows:

Apr. 24	Retained Earnings	50,000	
	Appropriation for Treasury Stock		50,000

When a part or all of an appropriation is no longer needed, it is transferred back to the retained earnings account. In the preceding example, when the corporation sells the treasury stock, the following entry is made:

Nov. 10	Appropriation for Treasury Stock	50,000	
	Retained Earnings		50,000

When a corporation borrows a large amount of money, it may issue notes or bonds. The lender or the bond agreement may require restrictions on dividends until the debt is paid. The amount restricted is usually equal to the amount of the debt outstanding. The appropriation of retained earnings may be made in total, or an annual buildup of appropriations may be required. For example, assume that a corporation borrows $700,000 by issuing ten-year bonds. If equal annual appropriations are required over the life of the bonds, there would be a series of ten entries, each in the amount of $70,000. The entry below records the annual appropriation.

Aug. 1	Retained Earnings	70,000	
	Appropriation for Bonded Indebtedness		70,000

Even if the bond agreement does not require the appropriation of retained earnings, the corporation's board of directors might make such an appropriation. In this case, the appropriation is said to be **discretionary** rather than **contractual**. The entries are the same in either case.

An appropriation of retained earnings is not related to any specific assets. Thus, an appropriation does not mean that there is an equivalent amount of cash or other assets set aside in a special fund. *The only purpose of an appropriation is to restrict dividend distributions to stockholders.* The cash that otherwise might be distributed as dividends could be invested in other assets, such as plant and equipment, or used to reduce liabilities.

The board of directors of a corporation may as a separate action set aside assets such as cash or marketable securities for a specific purpose. This setting aside of assets may also be accompanied by an appropriation of retained earnings. In this case, the appropriation is said to be **funded**. As we discussed in a prior chapter, such funds accumulated for the retiring of bonds payable are called **sinking funds**.

The board of directors may establish appropriations for purposes other than those discussed in the preceding paragraphs. For example, a board of directors may appropriate retained earnings for contingencies, such as inventory price declines, a possible settlement of a pending lawsuit, or possible losses from self-insurance.

Reporting Appropriations of Retained Earnings

The retained earnings statement is normally divided into two major sections: (1) appropriated and (2) unappropriated. The first section presents for each appropriation account its beginning balance, any additions or deductions during the period, and its ending balance. The second section presents for the unappropriated retained earnings account its beginning balance, net income or net loss for the period, dividends, transfers to and from the appropriation accounts, and the ending balance. The final figure on the statement is the total retained earnings as of the end of the period. Exhibit 6 shows an example of this form of retained earnings statement for Lester Corporation.

Exhibit 6
Retained Earnings Statement with Appropriations

Lester Corporation
Retained Earnings Statement
For Year Ended December 31, 1995

Appropriated:			
Appropriation for plant expansion, January 1, 1995		$ 180,000	
Additional appropriation (see below)		100,000	
Retained earnings appropriated, December 31, 1995			$ 280,000
Unappropriated:			
Balance, January 1, 1995		$1,414,500	
Net income for the year		580,000	$1,994,500
Cash dividends declared		$ 125,000	
Transfer to appropriation for plant expansion (see above)		100,000	225,000
Retained earnings unappropriated, December 31, 1995			$1,769,500
Total retained earnings, December 31, 1995			$2,049,500

In the balance sheet, the *appropriated* and *unappropriated* portions of retained earnings should be clearly distinguished. An example of such a presentation is shown here.

Retained earnings:		
Appropriated:		
For plant expansion	$ 280,000	
Unappropriated	1,769,500	
Total retained earnings		$2,049,500

Presentations, other than this one, could also be used to report retained earnings in the balance sheet. For example, the preceding data could be presented in a note accompanying the balance sheet. Such a presentation, including the note, might appear as follows:

Retained earnings (see note)   *$2,049,500*

Note:

Retained earnings in the amount of $280,000 are appropriated for expansion of plant facilities; the remaining $1,749,500 is unappropriated.

STATEMENT OF STOCKHOLDERS' EQUITY

Objective 8
Prepare a statement of stockholders' equity.

In preceding chapters, we described and illustrated the financial statements for corporate enterprises. These basic corporate financial statements include the income statement, the retained earnings statement, and the balance sheet. In addition to these basic statements, significant changes in stockholders' equity should be reported for the period in which they occur. These changes are often reported in a statement of stockholders' equity.

The statement of stockholders' equity may be prepared in a columnar format, where each column represents a major stockholders' equity classification. Changes in each classification are then described in the left-hand column. Exhibit 7 is a statement of stockholders' equity for Telex Inc.

Exhibit 7
Statement of Stockholders' Equity

	Telex Inc. Statement of Stockholders' Equity For Year Ended December 31, 1995						
	Preferred Stock	*Common Stock*	*Paid-In Capital in Excess of Par— Common Stock*	*Unappropriated Retained Earnings*	*Retained Earnings Appropriated for Treasury Stock*	*Treasury (Common) Stock*	*Total*
Balance, Jan. 1, 1995	$5,000,000	$10,000,000	$3,000,000	$1,500,000	$500,000	$(500,000)	$19,500,000
Net income				850,000			850,000
Dividends on preferred stock				(250,000)			(250,000)
Dividends on common stock				(400,000)			(400,000)
Issuance of additional common stock		500,000	50,000				550,000
Purchase of treasury stock						(30,000)	(30,000)
Increase in appropriation for treasury stock				(30,000)	30,000		
Balance, Dec. 31, 1995	$5,000,000	$10,500,000	$3,050,000	$1,670,000	$530,000	$(530,000)	$20,220,000

CHAPTER REVIEW

Key Points

Objective 1. Describe the characteristics of the corporate form of organization.
The primary characteristics of the corporate form of organization are separate legal existence, transferable units of stock, and limited liability. Corporations are also subject to federal income taxes.

Objective 2. List the major sources of paid-in capital, including the various classes of capital stock.
The main source of paid-in capital is from the issuance of stock. The two primary classes of capital stock are common stock and preferred stock. Preferred stock is normally non-

participating and may be cumulative or noncumulative. In addition to the issuance of stock, paid-in capital may arise from donations of assets, redemption of capital stock, and from treasury stock transactions.

Objective 3. Journalize the entries for issuing capital stock.
When a corporation issues stock at par for cash, the cash account is debited, and the class of stock issued is credited for its par amount. When a corporation issues stock at more than par, Paid-In Capital in Excess of Par is credited for the difference between the cash received and the par value of the stock.

When capital stock is issued and exchanged for assets other than cash, the assets acquired should be recorded at their fair market price.

When no-par stock is issued, the entire proceeds are credited to the capital stock account. No-par stock may be assigned a stated value per share, and the excess of the proceeds over the stated value may be credited to Paid-In Capital in Excess of Stated Value.

Objective 4. Journalize the entries for treasury stock transactions.

When a corporation purchases its own stock, the cost method of accounting is normally used. Treasury stock is debited for its cost, and Cash is credited. If the stock is resold, Treasury Stock is credited for its cost and any difference between the cost and the selling price is normally debited or credited to Paid-In Capital from Sale of Treasury Stock.

Objective 5. Prepare the Paid-In Capital section of a corporate balance sheet.

Alternative terms and formats may be used in reporting paid-in capital. Using one format, each class of stock is listed first, followed by related paid-in capital accounts, including Paid-In Capital from Sale of Treasury Stock. Treasury Stock is deducted from the total of the paid-in capital and retained earnings.

Objective 6. Journalize the entries for cash dividends and stock dividends.

The entry to record a declaration of cash dividends is to debit Dividends and credit Dividends Payable for each class of stock. The payment of dividends is recorded in the normal manner. When a stock dividend is declared, Stock Dividends is debited for the fair value of the stock to be issued. Stock Dividends Distributable is credited for the par or stated value of

the common stock to be issued. The difference between the fair value of the stock and its par or stated value is credited to Paid-In Capital in Excess of Par—Common Stock. When the stock is issued on the date of payment, Stock Dividends Distributable is debited and Common Stock is credited for the par or stated value of the stock issued.

Objective 7. Journalize appropriations of retained earnings, and prepare the related retained earnings statement.

An appropriation is recorded by debiting the retained earnings account and crediting a special appropriation of retained earnings account. The appropriation account is normally identified according to its purpose. When a part or all of an appropriation is no longer needed, it is transferred back to the retained earnings account by reversing the entry.

A retained earnings statement is normally divided into two major sections: (1) appropriated and (2) unappropriated. The first section presents the beginning balances of any appropriations, any additions or deductions during the period, and an ending balance. The second section presents for the unappropriated retained earnings account its beginning balance, net income or net loss for the period, dividends, transfers to and from the appropriation accounts, and the ending balance. The statement concludes with the total retained earnings as of the end of the period.

Objective 8. Prepare a statement of stockholders' equity.

Significant changes in stockholders' equity should be reported for the period in which they occur. These changes may be reported in a statement of stockholders' equity in a columnar format, where each column represents a major stockholders' equity classification.

Glossary of Key Terms

Appropriation. The amount of a corporation's retained earnings that has been restricted and therefore is not available for distribution to shareholders as dividends. **Objective 7**

Capital stock. Shares of ownership of a corporation. **Objective 1**

Cash dividend. A cash distribution of earnings by a corporation to its shareholders. **Objective 6**

Common stock. The basic ownership class of corporate capital stock. **Objective 2**

Cumulative preferred stock. Preferred stock that is entitled to current and past dividends before dividends may be paid on common stock. **Objective 2**

Discount. The excess of par value of stock over its sales price. **Objective 3**

Funded. An appropriation of retained earnings accompanied by a segregation of cash or marketable securities. **Objective 7**

Liquidating dividend. A distribution out of paid-in capital when a corporation permanently reduces its operations or winds up its affairs completely. **Objective 6**

Nonparticipating preferred stock. Preferred stock where dividend preference is limited to a certain amount. **Objective 2**

Outstanding stock. The stock that has been issued to stock-

holders. **Objective 2**

Paid-in capital. The capital acquired from stockholders. **Objective 2**

Par. The monetary amount printed on a stock certificate. **Objective 2**

Preemptive right. The right of each shareholder to maintain the same fractional interest in the corporation by purchasing shares of any additional issuances of stock. **Objective 2**

Preferred stock. A class of stock with preferential rights over common stock. **Objective 2**

Premium. The excess of the sales price of stock over its par amount. **Objective 3**

Stated value. A value approved by the board of directors of a corporation for no-par stock. Similar to par value. **Objective 2**

Statement of stockholders' equity. A summary of the changes in the stockholders' equity of a corporation that have occurred during a specific period of time. **Objective 8**

Stock dividend. Distribution of a company's own stock to its shareholders. **Objective 6**

Treasury stock. A corporation's own outstanding stock that has been reacquired. **Objective 2**

Self-Examination Questions
Answers at end of chapter.

1. If a corporation has outstanding 1,000 shares of $9 cumulative preferred stock of $100 par and dividends have been passed for the preceding three years, what is the amount of preferred dividends that must be declared in the current year before a dividend can be declared on common stock?
   A. $9,000
   B. $27,000
   C. $36,000
   D. $45,000

   $9 \times 1000 \times 3 = 27,000$
   $27,000 + 9,000 = 36,000$

2. Paid-in capital for a corporation may originate from which of the following sources?
   A. Issuance of cumulative preferred stock
   B. Redemption of the corporation's own stock
   C. Sale of the corporation's treasury stock
   D. All of the above

3. The Stockholders' Equity section of the balance sheet may include:
   A. Common Stock   C. Preferred Stock
   B. Donated Capital   D. All of the above

4. If a corporation reacquires its own stock, the stock is listed on the balance sheet in the:
   A. Current Assets section
   B. Long-Term Liabilities section
   C. Stockholders' Equity section
   D. Investments section

5. An appropriation for plant expansion would be reported on the balance sheet in the:
   A. Plant Assets section
   B. Long-Term Liabilities section
   C. Stockholders' Equity section
   D. Current Liabilities section

ILLUSTRATIVE PROBLEM

During its current fiscal year ended December 31, 1995, Block Inc. completed the following selected transactions:

Jan. 9. Purchased 1,500 shares of its own common stock at $16, recording the stock at cost. (Prior to the purchase, there were 70,000 shares of $10 par common stock outstanding.)

Mar. 16. Discovered that a receipt of $500 cash on account from I. Jonson had been posted in error to the account of I. Johnson. The transaction was journalized correctly.

May 18. Declared a semiannual dividend of $1 on the 10,000 shares of preferred stock and a 20¢ dividend on the common stock to stockholders of record on May 28, payable on June 10.

June 10. Paid the cash dividends.

Aug. 23. Sold 1,000 shares of treasury stock at $18, receiving cash.

Nov. 12. Declared semiannual dividends of $1 on the preferred stock and 20¢ on the common stock. In addition, a 5% common stock dividend was declared on the common stock outstanding, to be capitalized the fair market value of the common stock, which is estimated at $16.

Dec. 4. Paid the cash dividends and issued the certificates for the common stock dividend.

31. The board of directors authorized the appropriation necessitated by the holding of treasury stock.

Instructions
Journalize the entries to record the transactions for Block Inc.

Solution

1995

Jan. 9	Treasury Stock	24,000	
	Cash		24,000
Mar. 16	No entry. Error can be corrected by revising the postings in the subsidiary accounts receivable ledger.		
May 18	Cash Dividends	23,700	
	Cash Dividends Payable		23,700*
	*(10,000 × $1) + [(70,000 - 1,500) × $.20]		
June 10	Cash Dividends Payable	23,700	
	Cash		23,700
Aug. 23	Cash	18,000	
	Treasury Stock		16,000
	Paid-In Capital from Sale of Treasury Stock		2,000

ILLUSTRATIVE PROBLEM

Nov. 12	Cash Dividends	23,900*	
	Cash Dividends Payable		23,900
	*(10,000 × $1) + [(70,000 - 500) × $.20]		
12	Stock Dividends	55,600*	
	Stock Dividends Distributable		34,750
	Paid-In Capital in Excess of Par—Common Stock		20,850
	*(70,000 - 500) × 5% × $16		
Dec. 4	Cash Dividends Payable	23,900	
	Stock Dividends Distributable	34,750	
	Cash		23,900
	Common Stock		34,750
31	Retained Earnings	8,000	
	Appropriation for Treasury Stock		8,000*
	*(500 × $16)		

DISCUSSION QUESTIONS

1. Why are most large business enterprises organized as corporations?
2. What are the titles of the two principal subdivisions of the Stockholders' Equity section of a corporate balance sheet?
3. The charter of a corporation provides for the issuance of a maximum of 50,000 shares of $100 par common stock. The corporation issued 30,000 shares of common stock, and two years later it reacquired 5,000 shares. After the reacquisition, what is the number of shares of stock (a) authorized, (b) issued, and (c) outstanding?
4. Of two corporations organized at approximately the same time and engaged in competing businesses, one issued $25 par common stock, and the other issued $10 par common stock. Do the par designations provide any indication as to which stock is preferable as an investment? Explain.
5. What are the four basic rights that accompany ownership of a share of common stock?
6. a. Differentiate between common stock and preferred stock.
   b. Describe briefly (1) nonparticipating preferred stock and (2) cumulative preferred stock.
7. Assume that a corporation has had outstanding 50,000 shares of $7 cumulative preferred stock of $100 par and dividends were passed for the preceding three years. What amount of total dividends must be paid to the preferred stockholders before the common stockholders are entitled to any dividends in the current year?
8. What are some sources of paid-in capital other than the issuance of capital stock?
9. If a corporation is given land as an inducement to locate in a particular community, (a) how should the amount of the debit to the land account be determined, and (b) what is the title of the account that should be credited for the same amount?
10. If common stock of $20 par is sold for $30, what is the $10 difference between the issue price and par called?
11. What are some of the factors that influence the market price of a corporation's stock?
12. When a corporation issues stock at a premium, is the premium income? Explain.
13. Land is acquired by a corporation for 5,000 shares of its $25 par common stock, which is currently selling for $35 per share on a national stock exchange. (a) At what value should the land be recorded? (b) What accounts and amounts should be credited to record the transaction?
14. a. In what respect does treasury stock differ from unissued stock?
    b. How should treasury stock be presented on the balance sheet?
15. A corporation reacquires 2,000 shares of its own $40 par common stock for $95,000, recording it at cost. (a) What effect does this transaction have on revenue or expense of the period? (b) What effect does it have on stockholders' equity?
16. The treasury stock in Question 15 is resold for $125,000. (a) What is the effect on the corporation's revenue of the period? (b) What is the effect on stockholders' equity?
17. In which section of the corporation balance sheet would Paid-In Capital in Excess of Par—Preferred Stock appear?
18. Indicate which of the following accounts would be reported as part of paid-in capital on

the balance sheet:
   a. Retained Earnings
   b. Common Stock
   c. Donated Capital
   d. Preferred Stock

19. The Stockholders' Equity section of a corporation balance sheet contains the following items:

Preferred $4 stock, $50 par	$300,000	
Excess of issue price over par—preferred stock	30,000	$330,000
Common stock, $10 par	$500,000	
Excess of issue price over par—common stock	70,000 570,000	$900,000
Retained earnings		275,000 $1,175,000

What is the amount of each of the following: (a) paid-in capital attributable to preferred stock, (b) paid-in capital attributable to common stock, (c) earnings retained for use in the business, and (d) total stockholders' equity?

20. The Stockholders' Equity section of a corporation balance sheet contains total paid-in capital of $560,000, retained earnings of $240,000, and treasury stock of $50,000. What is the total stockholders' equity?

21. What are the three conditions for the declaration and the payment of a cash dividend?

22. The dates in connection with the declaration of a cash dividend are April 1, May 15, and May 30. Identify each date.

23. A corporation with both cumulative preferred stock and common stock outstanding has a substantial credit balance in its retained earnings account at the beginning of the current fiscal year. Although net income for the current year is sufficient to pay the preferred dividend of $50,000 each quarter and a common dividend of $200,000 each quarter, the board of directors declares dividends only on the preferred stock. Suggest possible reasons for passing the dividends on the common stock.

24. The board of directors declared a 5% stock dividend of 1,000 shares on $50 par common stock. If the market price is $65 per share on the date of declaration, for what amount should the stock dividends account be debited to record the declaration?

25. State the effect of the following actions on a corporation's total assets, liabilities, and stockholders' equity: (a) declaration of a cash dividend; (b) payment of the cash dividend declared in (a); (c) declaration of a stock dividend; (d) issuance of stock certificates for the stock dividend declared in (c).

26. An owner of 200 shares of Dunston Company common stock receives a stock dividend of 4 shares. (a) What is the effect of the stock dividend on the equity per share of the stock? (b) How does the total equity of 204 shares compare with the total equity of 200 shares before the stock dividend?

27. a. Where should a declared but unpaid cash dividend be reported on the balance sheet?
    b. Where should a declared but unissued stock dividend be reported on the balance sheet?

28. A corporation that had issued 25,000 shares of $10 par common stock subsequently reacquired 1,000 shares, which it now holds as treasury stock. If the board of directors declares a cash dividend of $1 per share, what will be the total amount of the dividend?

29. What term is used to identify a distribution to stockholders from paid-in capital?

30. Appropriations of retained earnings may be (a) required by law, (b) required by contract, or (c) made at the discretion of the board of directors. Give an illustration of each type of appropriation.

31. A credit balance in Retained Earnings does not represent cash. Explain.

32. The board of directors votes to appropriate $250,000 of retained earnings for bonded indebtedness. What is the effect of this action on (a) cash, (b) total retained earnings, and (c) retained earnings available for dividends?

33. Why do some corporations report a statement of stockholders' equity? Describe the normal format of the statement of stockholders' equity.

REAL WORLD FOCUS   34. A stockbroker advises a client to "buy cumulative preferred stock. . . . With that type of stock, . . . [you] will never have to worry about losing the dividends." Is the broker right?

Source: "Investors Guide," *Naples Daily News* (July 21, 1991), p. 13E.

ETHICS DISCUSSION CASE

Ignacio Maglie and Don Tomlin are organizing Mines Unlimited Inc. to undertake a high-risk gold mining venture in Mexico. Maglie and Tomlin tentatively plan to request authorization for 100,000,000 shares of common stock to be sold to the general public. Maglie and Tomlin have decided to establish par of $.10 per share in order to appeal to a wide variety of potential investors. Maglie and Tomlin feel that investors would be more willing to invest in the company if they received a large quantity of shares for what might appear to be a "bargain" price.

SHARPEN YOUR
COMMUNICATION SKILLS ►

Discuss whether Maglie and Tomlin are behaving in an ethical manner.

WHAT DO YOU THINK

Assume that Gravey Inc. recently was authorized to issue 3%, $100 par, redeemable preferred stock. The preferred stock *must* be redeemed by Gravey Inc. at $105 in five years. The preferred stockholders have no voting rights unless dividends are in arrears for more than six quarters. Should you account for the issuance of the preferred stock as debt or equity?

FINANCIAL ANALYSIS AND INTERPRETATION

Two profitability measures included in the stock quotations that appear daily in *The Wall Street Journal* and similar publications are the price-earnings ratio and the dividend yield per share of common stock. The price-earnings (P/E) ratio is an indication of a firm's future earnings prospects and is computed as follows:

$$\text{Price-Earnings Ratio} = \frac{\text{Market Price per Share of Common Stock}}{\text{Earnings per Share of Common Stock}}$$

The market price per common share is the price at a specific date, and the earnings are the annual earnings per common share. A high P/E ratio indicates that investors expect the company's earnings to be above average for comparable companies.

The dividend yield is a profitability measure that shows the rate of return to common stockholders in terms of cash dividends. It is computed as follows:

$$\text{Dividend Yield} = \frac{\text{Dividends per Share of Common Stock}}{\text{Market Price per Share of Common Stock}}$$

The dividends per common share are the annual dividends per share, and the market price per common share is the price at a specific date. Dividend yield is of special interest to investors who look for a current return (dividend) from their investment.

a. Determine Hershey Food Corporation's price-earnings ratio on December 31, 1992 and 1991.
b. Determine Hershey's dividend yield as of December 31, 1992 and 1991 on common stock (exclude Class B Common Stock).

Note: Hershey's common stock price was $47 and $44⅜ on December 31, 1992 and 1991.

SHARPEN YOUR
COMMUNICATION SKILLS ►

c. What conclusions can you reach from an analysis of these data?

EXERCISES

EXERCISE 12-1
DIVIDENDS PER SHARE
Objective 2

Lance Company has stock outstanding as follows: 10,000 shares of $8 (8%) cumulative, nonparticipating preferred stock of $100 par, and 100,000 shares of $20 par common. During its first five years of operations, the following amounts were distributed as dividends: first year, none; second year, $120,000; third year, $180,000; fourth year, $230,000; fifth year, $200,000. Calculate the dividends per share on each class of stock for each of the five years.

EXERCISE 12-2
ENTRIES FOR ISSUANCE OF
PAR STOCK
Objective 3

On April 25, Bonn Company issued for cash 5,000 shares of $10 par common stock at $14, and on August 7, it issued for cash 1,000 shares of $50 par preferred stock at $54.
a. Journalize the entries for April 25 and August 7.
b. What is the total amount invested (total paid-in capital) by all stockholders as of August 7?

EXERCISE 12-3
ENTRIES FOR ISSUANCE OF
NO-PAR STOCK
Objective 3

On January 25, Campbell Company issued for cash 5,000 shares of no-par common stock (with a stated value of $20) at $22, and on August 15, it issued for cash 2,000 shares of $50 par preferred stock at $52.

a. Journalize the entries for January 25 and August 15, assuming that the common stock is to be credited with the stated value.

b. What is the total amount invested (total paid-in capital) by all stockholders as of August 15?

EXERCISE 12-4
ISSUANCE OF STOCK FOR
ASSETS OTHER THAN CASH
Objective 3

On February 9, Morris Corporation acquired land in exchange for 5,000 shares of $25 par common stock with a current market price of $40. Journalize the entry to record the transaction.

EXERCISE 12-5
TREASURY STOCK
TRANSACTIONS
Objective 4

On March 1 of the current year, Curtis Company reacquired 1,000 shares of its common stock at $22 per share. On August 10, 500 of the reacquired shares were sold at $25 per share. The remaining 500 shares were sold at $20 per share on December 19.

a. Journalize the transactions of March 1, August 10, and December 19.

b. What is the balance in Paid-In Capital from Sale of Treasury Stock on December 31 of the current year?

c. Where will the balance in Paid-In Capital from Sale of Treasury Stock be reported on the balance sheet?

SHARPEN YOUR
COMMUNICATION SKILLS ► d. For what reasons might Curtis Company have purchased the treasury stock?

EXERCISE 12-6
ISSUANCE OF STOCK;
REPORTING PAID-IN
CAPITAL
Objectives 3, 5

Slezak Company, with an authorization of 5,000 shares of preferred stock and 50,000 shares of common stock, completed several transactions involving its capital stock on April 1, the first day of operations. The trial balance at the close of the day follows:

Cash	450,000	
Land	90,000	
Buildings	410,000	
Preferred $12 Stock, $100 par		450,000
Paid-In Capital in Excess of Par—Preferred Stock		50,000
Common Stock, $20 par		300,000
Paid-In Capital in Excess of Par—Common Stock		150,000
	950,000	950,000

All shares within each class of stock were sold at the same price. The preferred stock was issued in exchange for the land and buildings.

a. Journalize the two entries to record the transactions summarized in the trial balance.

b. Prepare the Stockholders' Equity section of the balance sheet as of April 1.

EXERCISE 12-7
ISSUANCE OF STOCK;
REPORTING PAID-IN
CAPITAL
Objectives 3, 5

Shaw Products Inc. was organized on January 17 of the current year, with an authorization of 10,000 shares of $9 noncumulative preferred stock, $100 par, and 100,000 shares of $10 par common stock.

The following selected transactions were completed during the first year of operations:

Jan. 17. Issued 20,950 shares of common stock at par for cash.
Feb. 4. Issued 20,000 shares of common stock in exchange for land, buildings, and equipment with fair market prices of $40,000, $120,000, and $45,000 respectively.
Oct. 15. Issued 2,000 shares of preferred stock at $104 for cash.

a. Journalize the transactions.

b. Prepare the Stockholders' Equity section of the balance sheet as of December 31, the end of the current year. The net income for the year amounted to $37,500.

EXERCISE 12-8
REPORTING PAID-IN
CAPITAL
Objective 5

The following accounts and their balances appear in the ledger of ITC Inc. on June 30 of the current year:

Common Stock, $20 par	$300,000
Paid-In Capital in Excess of Par	90,000
Paid-In Capital from Sale of Treasury Stock	5,000

| Retained Earnings | 115,500 |
| Treasury Stock | 15,000 |

Prepare the Stockholders' Equity section of the balance sheet as of June 30. Twenty-five thousand shares of common stock are authorized, and 1,000 shares have been reacquired.

EXERCISE 12-9
REPORTING PAID-IN
CAPITAL
Objective 5

The following accounts and their balances were selected from the unadjusted trial balance of Spielman Company at December 31, the end of the current fiscal year:

Preferred $3 Stock, $25 par	$500,000
Paid-In Capital in Excess of Par—Preferred Stock	75,000
Common Stock, no par, $20 stated value	750,000
Paid-In Capital in Excess of Par—Common Stock	200,000
Paid-In Capital from Redemption of Common Stock	10,000
Paid-In Capital from Sale of Treasury Stock	7,500
Donated Capital	100,000
Retained Earnings	350,000

Prepare the Paid-In Capital portion of the Stockholders' Equity section of the balance sheet. There are 50,000 shares of common stock authorized and 20,000 shares of preferred stock authorized.

EXERCISE 12-10
ENTRIES FOR CASH
DIVIDENDS
Objective 6

The dates of importance in connection with a cash dividend of $25,000 on a corporation's common stock are January 9, January 25, and February 7. Journalize the entries required on each date.

EXERCISE 12-11
ENTRIES FOR STOCK
DIVIDENDS
Objective 6

The following account balances appear on the balance sheet of Long Company: Common stock (10,000 shares authorized), $50 par, $400,000; Paid-in capital in excess of par—common stock, $72,500; and Retained earnings, $199,500. The board of directors declared a 5% stock dividend when the market price of the stock was $65 a share. Long reported no income or loss for the current year.
a. Journalize the entries to record (1) the declaration of the dividend, capitalizing an amount equal to market value, and (2) the issuance of the stock certificates.
b. Determine the following amounts before the stock dividend was declared: (1) total paid-in capital, (2) total retained earnings, and (3) total stockholders' equity.
c. Determine the following amounts after the stock dividend was declared and closing entries were recorded at the end of the year: (1) total paid-in capital, (2) total retained earnings, and (3) total stockholders' equity.

EXERCISE 12-12
ENTRIES FOR TREASURY
STOCK AND
APPROPRIATION
Objectives 4, 7

A corporation purchased for cash 2,500 shares of its own $20 par common stock at $30 a share. In the following year, it sold 1,000 of the treasury shares at $36 a share for cash.
a. Journalize the entries (1) to record the purchase (treasury stock is recorded at cost) and (2) to provide for the appropriation of retained earnings.
b. Journalize the entries (1) to record the sale of the stock and (2) to reduce the appropriation.

EXERCISE 12-13
RETAINED EARNINGS
STATEMENT WITH
APPROPRIATIONS
Objective 7

Jenkins Corporation reports the following results of transactions affecting net income and retained earnings for its first fiscal year of operations ended on December 31:

Appropriation for plant expansion	$ 25,000
Cash dividends declared	60,000
Net income	108,000

Prepare a retained earnings statement for the fiscal year ended December 31.

12-8A

**WhAT'S WROnG
WITH THi2?**

How many errors can you find in the following Stockholders' Equity section of the balance sheet prepared as of the end of the current year?

Stockholders' Equity		
Paid-in capital:		
Preferred $4 stock, cumulative, $50 par		
(5,000 shares authorized and issued)	$250,000	
Excess of issue price over par	60,000	$ 310,000
Retained earnings		140,000
Total paid-in capital		$ 450,000
Common stock, $20 par (50,000 shares		
authorized, 30,000 shares issued)	$600,000	
Excess of issue price over par	210,000	810,000
Total stockholders' equity		$1,260,000

PROBLEMS

Series A

PROBLEM 12-1A
DIVIDENDS ON PREFERRED
AND COMMON STOCK
Objective 2

SPREADSHEET
PROBLEM

Sanford Company has declared the following annual dividends over a six-year period: 1992, $6,000; 1993, $9,000; 1994, $30,000; 1995, $84,000; 1996, $72,000; and 1997, $21,000. During the entire period, the outstanding stock of the company included 1,000 shares of cumulative, nonparticipating, $10 preferred stock, $100 par, and 10,000 shares of common stock, $50 par.

Instructions
1. Calculate the total dividends and the per share dividends declared on each class of stock for each of the six years. There were no dividends in arrears on January 1, 1992. Summarize the data in tabular form, using the following column headings:

		Preferred Dividends		Common Dividends	
Year	Dividends	Total	Per Share	Total	Per Share
1992	$ 6,000				
1993	9,000				
1994	30,000				
1995	84,000				
1996	72,000				
1997	21,000				

2. Calculate the average annual dividend per share for each class of stock for the six-year period.
3. Assuming that the preferred stock was sold at par and common stock was sold at $40 at the beginning of the six-year period, calculate the percentage return on initial shareholders' investment, based on the average annual dividend per share (a) for preferred stock and (b) for common stock.

PROBLEM 12-2A
ISSUANCE OF STOCK;
REPORTING PAID-IN
CAPITAL
Objectives 3, 5

The following accounts and their balances appear in the ledger of Janet Combs Corp. on March 31 of the current year:

Preferred $9 Stock, $100 par (10,000 shares	
authorized, 5,000 shares issued)	$ 500,000
Paid-In Capital in Excess of Par—Preferred Stock	20,000
Common Stock, $20 par (100,000 shares	
authorized, 75,000 shares issued)	1,500,000
Paid-In Capital in Excess of Par—Common Stock	225,000
Retained Earnings	305,000

At the annual stockholders' meeting on April 11, the board of directors presented a plan for modernizing and expanding plant operations at a cost of approximately $500,000. The plan provided (a) that the corporation borrow $175,000, (b) that 1,000 shares of the unissued preferred stock be issued through an underwriter, and (c) that a building, valued at $180,000, and the land on which it is located, valued at $40,000, be acquired in accordance with preliminary negotiations by the issuance of 10,000 shares of common stock. The plan was approved by the stockholders and accomplished by the following transactions:

May 7. Issued 10,000 shares of common stock in exchange for land and building in accordance with the plan.
     20. Issued 1,000 shares of preferred stock, receiving $105 per share in cash from the underwriter.
     31. Borrowed $175,000 from Highland National Bank, giving a 12% mortgage note.

No other transactions occurred during May.

Instructions
1. Journalize the entries to record the preceding transactions.
2. Prepare the Stockholders' Equity section of the balance sheet as of May 31.

PROBLEM 12-3A
STOCK TRANSACTIONS;
REPORTING PAID-IN
CAPITAL
Objectives 3, 4, 5

The following selected accounts appear in the ledger of Helms Corporation on July 1, the beginning of the current fiscal year:

Preferred 10% Stock, $50 par (10,000 shares authorized, 7,000 shares issued)	$350,000
Paid-In Capital in Excess of Par—Preferred Stock	28,000
Common Stock, $20 par (50,000 shares authorized, 25,000 shares issued)	500,000
Paid-In Capital in Excess of Par—Common Stock	90,000
Retained Earnings	337,000

During the year, the corporation completed a number of transactions affecting the stockholders' equity. They are summarized as follows:

a. Purchased 1,000 shares of treasury common for $27,500.
b. Sold 500 shares of treasury common for $15,000.
c. Issued 2,500 shares of common stock at $30, receiving cash.
d. Sold 1,000 shares of preferred 10% stock at $52.50.
e. Sold 250 shares of treasury common for $6,500.

Instructions
1. Journalize the entries to record the transactions. Identify each entry by letter. (The use of T accounts for stockholders' equity accounts will facilitate the determination of the amounts needed in recording some of the transactions and in completing Instruction (2).)
2. Prepare the Stockholders' Equity section of the balance sheet as of June 30, the end of the current fiscal year. The net income for the year was $185,000, and cash dividends declared and paid during the year were $105,000.

SOLUTIONS
SOFTWARE

Instructions for Solving Problem 12-3A Using Solutions Software
1. Load opening balances.
2. Enter your name in the Student Name field in the General Information data entry window. Set the run date to June 30 of the current year.
3. Save the opening balances file to your drive and directory.
4. Select the General Journal Entries option, and key the journal entries. Leave the reference field blank. Note: To review the chart of accounts, select F-1.
5. Display a journal entries report.
6. Display a balance sheet.
7. Save your data file to disk.
8. End the session.

PROBLEM 12-4A
STOCK TRANSACTIONS;
REPORTING PAID-IN
CAPITAL
Objectives 3, 5

Payne Company was organized by Bows, Howe, and Radner. The charter authorized 10,000 shares of common stock with a par of $50. The following transactions affecting stockholders' equity were completed during the first year of operations:

a. Issued 2,000 shares of stock at par to Bows and Howe for cash.
b. Purchased land and a building from Radner. The building is mortgaged for $125,000 for 22 years at 12%, and there is accrued interest of $4,000 on the mortgage note at the time of the purchase. It is agreed that the land is to be priced at $49,000 and the building at $130,000, and that Radner's equity will be exchanged for stock at par. The corporation

agreed to assume responsibility for paying the mortgage note and the accrued interest.

c. Issued 2,000 shares of stock at $60 to various investors for cash.
d. Purchased equipment for $75,000. The seller accepted a 6-month, 11% note for $25,000 and 1,000 shares of stock in exchange for the equipment.

Instructions

1. Journalize the entries to record the transactions.
2. Prepare the Stockholders' Equity section of the balance sheet as of the end of the first year of operations. The Retained Earnings balance is the net income for the year, $67,200, less dividends declared and paid during the year, $5 per share on each share of stock issued.

PROBLEM 12-5A
TREASURY STOCK
TRANSACTIONS;
DIVIDENDS
Objectives 4, 6

As of January 1, the beginning of the current fiscal year, Snyder Corporation had issued 40,000 common, $100 par shares of the 50,000 shares authorized. The retained earnings balance was $947,500. The only transactions affecting common stock during the fiscal year are as follows:

Mar. 1. The board of directors declared a $2 per share dividend on the common stock, payable on April 10 to stockholders of record on March 22.
Apr. 10. Paid the dividends declared on March 1.
May 5. Purchased 1,000 shares of treasury stock for $210,000.
June 1. The board of directors declared a $2 per share dividend on the common stock outstanding, payable on July 12 to stockholders of record on May 25.
July 12. Paid the dividends declared on June 1.
Aug. 21. Sold the treasury stock purchased on May 5 for $216,500.
Sep. 1. The board of directors declared a 5% common stock dividend to be distributed on October 16 to stockholders of record on September 20. The market price of the stock is $220 per share.
Oct. 16. Distributed the stock dividend declared on September 1.

Instructions

Journalize the transactions.

PROBLEM 12-6A
STOCK TRANSACTIONS
AND CORRECTIONS;
BALANCE SHEET
Objectives 3, 4, 5

Grady Company was organized on March 1 of the current year. The accounting clerk prepared the first balance sheet the following December 31, the date that had been adopted as the end of the fiscal year. This balance sheet is as follows:

Grady Company
Balance Sheet
March 1 to December 31, 19—

Assets		Liabilities	
Cash	$ 51,700	Accounts payable	$ 93,000
Accounts receivable	208,900	Preferred stock	200,000
Merchandise inventory	122,500	Common stock	300,000
Prepaid insurance	9,100	Paid-in capital in excess	
Treasury common stock	20,000	of par—common stock	30,000
Equipment	130,000		
Retained earnings (deficit)	80,800		
Total assets	$623,000	Total liabilities	$623,000

You are retained by the board of directors to audit the accounts and to prepare a revised balance sheet. The relevant facts developed during the course of your engagement are:

a. Stock authorized: 5,000 shares of $100 par, $8 preferred, and 50,000 shares of $20 par common.
b. Stock issued: 2,000 shares of preferred at $102.50 and 15,000 shares of common at $22. The premium on preferred stock was credited to Retained Earnings.
c. The company reacquired 1,000 shares of the issued common stock at $25. The difference between par and the price paid was debited to Retained Earnings. (The treasury stock is to be recorded at cost.)
d. Included in merchandise inventory is $4,000 of office supplies.
e. Land to be used as a future building site cost $30,000 and was debited to Equipment.
f. No depreciation has been recognized. The equipment is to be depreciated for 9 months

by the straight-line method, using an estimated life of 10 years and assuming no residual value.

g. No dividends have been declared or paid.

Instructions

1. Journalize the entries to record the corrections. Corrections of net income should be recorded as adjustments to Retained Earnings.
2. Prepare a six-column work sheet, with columns for (a) balances per balance sheet, (b) corrections, and (c) corrected balances. In listing the accounts, leave an extra line blank following the retained earnings account. Complete the work sheet.
3. Prepare a corrected balance sheet in report form as of the end of the fiscal year.
4. Explain why a premium on the sale of capital stock is not considered to be a part of retained earnings.

Instructions for Solving Problem 12-6A Using Solutions Software

1. Load opening balances.
2. Enter your name in the Student Name field in the General Information data entry window. Set the run date to December 31 of the current year.
3. Save the opening balances file to your drive and directory.
4. Select the General Journal Entries option, and key the journal entries. Leave the reference field blank. Note: To review the chart of accounts, select F-1.
5. Display a journal entries report.
6. Display a balance sheet.
7. Save your data file to disk.
8. End the session.

PROBLEM 12-7A
ENTRIES FOR TREASURY
STOCK; DIVIDENDS;
APPROPRIATIONS
Objectives 4, 6, 7

At the beginning of the current fiscal year, Neuman Corporation had 40,000 common shares outstanding. Selected transactions completed by Neuman Corporation during the current year are as follows:

Mar. 10. Purchased 1,000 shares of the corporation's own common stock at $62, recording the stock at cost.

Apr. 11. Discovered that a receipt of $450 cash on account from A. Allen had been posted in error to the account of N. Alden. The transaction was recorded correctly in the journal.

May 1. Declared semiannual dividends of $5 on 5,000 shares of preferred stock and $1 on the common stock to stockholders of record on May 20, payable on July 15.

July 15. Paid the cash dividends.

Aug. 22. Sold 500 shares of treasury stock at $70, receiving cash.

Nov. 30. Declared semiannual dividends of $5 on the preferred stock and $1.25 on the common stock. In addition, a 5% common stock dividend was declared on the common stock outstanding. The fair market value of the common stock is estimated at $72.

Dec. 30. Paid the cash dividends and issued the certificates for the common stock dividend.

30. The board of directors authorized the appropriation necessitated by the holding of treasury stock.

Instructions
Journalize the transactions.

Instructions for Solving Problem 12-7A Using Solutions Software

1. Load opening balances.
2. Enter your name in the Student Name field in the General Information data entry window. Set the run date to December 31 of the current year.
3. Save the opening balances file to your drive and directory.
4. Select the General Journal Entries option, and key the journal entries. Leave the reference field blank. Note: To review the chart of accounts, select F-1.
5. Display a journal entries report.
6. Save a backup copy of your data file.
7. Perform period-end closing.
8. Display a balance sheet.
9. Save your data file to disk.
10. End the session.

PROBLEM 12-8A
APPROPRIATIONS OF
RETAINED EARNINGS;
RETAINED EARNINGS
STATEMENT
Objective 7

The retained earnings accounts of Yoder Corporation for the current fiscal year ended December 31 are as follows:

ACCOUNT APPROPRIATION FOR PLANT EXPANSION   ACCOUNT NO. 3201

Date		Item	Debit	Credit	Balance Debit	Balance Credit
19—						
Jan.	1	Balance				150,000
Dec.	31	Retained earnings		50,000		200,000

ACCOUNT APPROPRIATION FOR TREASURY STOCK   ACCOUNT NO. 3202

Date		Item	Debit	Credit	Balance Debit	Balance Credit
19—						
Jan.	1	Balance				375,000
Dec.	31	Retained earnings	125,000			250,000

ACCOUNT RETAINED EARNINGS   ACCOUNT NO. 3301

Date		Item	Debit	Credit	Balance Debit	Balance Credit
19—						
Jan.	1	Balance				515,000
Dec.	31	Income summary		175,000		690,000
	31	Appropriation for plant expansion	50,000			640,000
	31	Appropriation for treasury stock		125,000		765,000
	31	Cash dividends	90,000			675,000
	31	Stock dividends	185,000			490,000

ACCOUNT CASH DIVIDENDS   ACCOUNT NO. 3302

Date		Item	Debit	Credit	Balance Debit	Balance Credit
19—						
July	27		90,000		90,000	
Dec.	31	Retained earnings		90,000	—	—

ACCOUNT STOCK DIVIDENDS   ACCOUNT NO. 3303

Date		Item	Debit	Credit	Balance Debit	Balance Credit
19—						
July	27		185,000		185,000	
Dec.	31	Retained earnings		185,000	—	—

Instructions
Prepare a retained earnings statement for the fiscal year ended December 31.

PROBLEM 12-9A
STOCK TRANSACTIONS;
APPROPRIATIONS;
STOCKHOLDERS' EQUITY
SECTION OF BALANCE
SHEET
Objectives 3, 4, 5, 6, 7

The stockholders' equity accounts of Zellner Enterprises Inc., with balances on January 1 of the current fiscal year, are as follows:

Common Stock, $25 stated value (100,000 shares authorized, 50,000 shares issued)	$1,250,000
Paid-In Capital in Excess of Stated Value	300,000
Appropriation for Plant Expansion	150,000
Appropriation for Treasury Stock	120,000
Retained Earnings	425,000
Treasury Stock (4,000 shares, at cost)	120,000

The following selected transactions occurred during the year:

Jan. 15. Received land from the city as a donation. The land had an estimated fair market value of $65,000.

30. Paid cash dividends of $1 per share on the common stock. The dividend had been properly recorded when declared on December 20 of the preceding fiscal year for $46,000.

Feb. 25. Sold all the treasury stock for $150,000.

Apr. 1. Issued 5,000 shares of common stock for $190,000.

July 1. Declared a 4% stock dividend on common stock, to be capitalized at the market price of the stock, which is $40 a share.

Aug. 11. Issued the certificates for the dividend declared on July 1.

Nov. 20. Purchased 2,000 shares of treasury stock for $72,000.

Dec. 21. The board of directors authorized an increase of the appropriation for plant expansion by $50,000.

21. Declared a $1.10 per share dividend on common stock.

21. Decreased the appropriation for treasury stock to $72,000.

31. Closed the credit balance of the income summary account, $196,700.

31. Closed the two dividends accounts to Retained Earnings.

Instructions

1. Enter the January 1 balances in T accounts for the stockholders' equity accounts listed. Also prepare T accounts for the following: Paid-In Capital from Sale of Treasury Stock; Donated Capital; Stock Dividends Distributable; Stock Dividends; Cash Dividends.

2. Journalize the entries to record the transactions and post to the eleven selected accounts.

3. Prepare the Stockholders' Equity section of the balance sheet as of December 31 of the current fiscal year.

Instructions for Solving Problem 12-9A Using Solutions Software

1. Load opening balances.

2. Enter your name in the Student Name field in the General Information data entry window. Set the run date to December 31 of the current year.

3. Save the opening balances file to your drive and directory.

4. Select the General Journal Entries option, and key the journal entries, including the two closing entries. Leave the reference field blank. Note: To review the chart of accounts, select F-1.

5. Display a journal entries report.

6. Display a balance sheet.

7. Save your data file to disk.

8. End the session.

SOLUTIONS
SOFTWARE

PROBLEM 12-10A
STATEMENT OF
STOCKHOLDERS' EQUITY
Objective 8

The stockholders' equity accounts of Reese Corporation for the current fiscal year ended December 31 are as follows.

ACCOUNT COMMON STOCK, $10 PAR   ACCOUNT NO.

Date		Item	Debit	Credit	Balance Debit	Balance Credit
19—						
Jan.	1	Balance				800,000
	20	Issued 10,000 shares		100,000		900,000

ACCOUNT PAID-IN CAPITAL IN EXCESS OF PAR   ACCOUNT NO.

Date		Item	Debit	Credit	Balance Debit	Balance Credit
19—						
Jan.	1	Balance				180,000
	20	Issued 10,000 shares		25,000		205,000

ACCOUNT TREASURY STOCK   ACCOUNT NO.

Date		Item	Debit	Credit	Balance Debit	Balance Credit
19—						
Nov.	30	Purchased 1,000 shares	11,000		11,000	

ACCOUNT APPROPRIATION FOR TREASURY STOCK   ACCOUNT NO.

Date		Item	Debit	Credit	Balance Debit	Balance Credit
19—						
Dec.	31	Retained earnings		11,000		11,000

ACCOUNT RETAINED EARNINGS   ACCOUNT NO.

Date		Item	Debit	Credit	Balance Debit	Balance Credit
19—						
Jan.	1	Balance				575,000
Dec.	31	Income summary		215,000		790,000
	31	Appropriation for treasury stock	11,000			779,000
	31	Cash dividends	100,000			679,000

ACCOUNT CASH DIVIDENDS   ACCOUNT NO.

Date		Item	Debit	Credit	Balance Debit	Balance Credit
19—						
Apr.	12		50,000		50,000	
Oct.	17		50,000		100,000	
Dec.	31	Closing		100,000	—	—

Instructions

Prepare a statement of stockholders' equity for the fiscal year ended December 31.

Series B

PROBLEM 12-1B
DIVIDENDS ON PREFERRED
AND COMMON STOCK
Objective 2

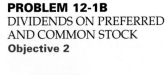

Peabody Company has declared the following annual dividends over a six-year period: 1992, $62,000; 1993, $128,000; 1994, $12,000; 1995, $5,000; 1996, $6,000; and 1997, $45,000. During the entire period, the outstanding stock of the company included 2,000 shares of cumulative, non-participating, $5 preferred stock, $50 par, and 20,000 shares of common stock, $10 par.

Instructions

1. Calculate the total dividends and the per share dividends declared on each class of stock for each of the six years. There were no dividends in arrears on January 1, 1992. Summarize the data in tabular form, using the following column headings:

		Preferred Dividends		Common Dividends	
Year	Dividends	Total	Per Share	Total	Per Share
1992	$ 62,000				
1993	128,000				
1994	12,000				
1995	5,000				
1996	6,000				
1997	45,000				

2. Calculate the average annual dividend per share for each class of stock for the six-year period.
3. Assuming that the preferred stock was sold at par and common stock was sold at $27.50 at the beginning of the six-year period, calculate the percentage return on initial shareholders' investment, based on the average annual dividend per share (a) for preferred stock and (b) for common stock.

PROBLEM 12-2B
ISSUANCE OF STOCK;
REPORTING OF PAID-IN
CAPITAL
Objectives 3, 5

The following accounts and their balances appear in the ledger of Fred Putman Corp. on June 30 of the current year:

Preferred $9 Stock, $100 par (10,000 shares authorized, 8,000 shares issued)	$ 800,000
Paid-In Capital in Excess of Par—Preferred Stock	16,000
Common Stock, $20 par (100,000 shares authorized, 75,000 shares issued)	1,500,000
Paid-In Capital in Excess of Par—Common Stock	210,000
Retained Earnings	305,000

At the annual stockholders' meeting on July 9, the board of directors presented a plan for modernizing and expanding plant operations at a cost of approximately $500,000. The plan provided (a) that the corporation borrow $200,000, (b) that 1,000 shares of the unissued preferred stock be issued through an underwriter, and (c) that a building, valued at $155,000, and the land on which it is located, valued at $40,000, be acquired in accordance with preliminary negotiations by the issuance of 8,000 shares of common stock. The plan was approved by the stockholders and accomplished by the following transactions:

July 29. Issued 8,000 shares of common stock in exchange for land and building in accordance with the plan.
   30. Issued 1,000 shares of preferred stock, receiving $105 per share in cash from the underwriter.
   31. Borrowed $200,000 from Palmer National Bank, giving a 14% mortgage note.

No other transactions occurred during July.

Instructions
1. Journalize the entries to record the preceding transactions.
2. Prepare the Stockholders' Equity section of the balance sheet as of July 31.

PROBLEM 12-3B
STOCK TRANSACTIONS;
PAID-IN CAPITAL
Objectives 3, 4, 5

The following selected accounts appear in the ledger of Hirchfield Corporation on July 1, the beginning of the current fiscal year:

Preferred 12% Stock, $100 par (20,000 shares authorized, 12,500 shares issued)	$1,250,000
Paid-In Capital in Excess of Par—Preferred Stock	62,500
Common Stock, $10 par (500,000 shares authorized, 300,000 shares issued)	3,000,000
Paid-In Capital in Excess of Par—Common Stock	600,000
Retained Earnings	1,450,000

During the year, the corporation completed a number of transactions affecting the stockholders' equity. They are summarized as follows:

a. Purchased 10,000 shares of treasury common for $120,000.
b. Sold 3,000 shares of treasury common for $45,000.
c. Sold 2,000 shares of preferred 12% stock at $105.
d. Issued 50,000 shares of common stock at $15, receiving cash.
e. Sold 2,000 shares of treasury common for $22,000.

Instructions
1. Journalize the entries to record the transactions. Identify each entry by letter. (The use of T accounts for stockholders' equity accounts will facilitate the determination of the amounts needed in recording some of the transactions and in completing Instruction (2).)
2. Prepare the Stockholders' Equity section of the balance sheet as of June 30, the end of the current fiscal year. The net income for the year was $550,000, and cash dividends declared and paid during the year were $420,000.

Instructions for Solving Problem 12-3B Using Solutions Software
1. Load opening balances.
2. Enter your name in the Student Name field in the General Information data entry window. Set the run date to June 30 of the current year.
3. Save the opening balances file to your drive and directory.
4. Select the General Journal Entries option, and key the journal entries. Leave the reference field blank. Note: To review the chart of accounts, select F-1.

5. Display a journal entries report.
6. Display a balance sheet.
7. Save your data file to disk.
8. End the session.

PROBLEM 12-4B
STOCK TRANSACTIONS;
REPORTING PAID-IN
CAPITAL
Objectives 3, 5

Bonita East Corp. was organized by Dunn, Edwards, and Gardner. The charter authorized 50,000 shares of common stock with a par of $10. The following transactions affecting stockholders' equity were completed during the first year of operations:

a. Issued 10,000 shares of stock at par to Dunn for cash.
b. Purchased land and a building from Gardner. The building is mortgaged for $95,500 for 16 years at 13%, and there is accrued interest of $4,000 on the mortgage note at the time of the purchase. It is agreed that the land is to be priced at $40,000 and the building at $125,000, and that Gardner's equity will be exchanged for stock at par. The corporation agreed to assume responsibility for paying the mortgage note and the accrued interest.
c. Issued 10,000 shares of stock at $12 to various investors for cash.
d. Purchased equipment for $75,000. The seller accepted a 6-month, 11% note for $25,000 and 5,000 shares of stock in exchange for the equipment.

Instructions
1. Journalize the entries to record the transactions.
2. Prepare the Stockholders' Equity section of the balance sheet as of the end of the first year of operations. The Retained Earnings balance is the net income for the year, $77,500, less dividends declared and paid during the year, $1 per share on each share of stock issued.

PROBLEM 12-5B
TREASURY STOCK
TRANSACTIONS;
DIVIDENDS
Objectives 4, 6

As of January 1, the beginning of the current fiscal year, Doyle Company had issued 70,000 common, $50 par shares of the 100,000 shares authorized. The retained earnings balance was $995,000. The only transactions affecting common stock during the fiscal year are as follows:

Mar. 8.   The board of directors declared a $2 per share dividend on the common stock, payable on April 10 to stockholders of record on March 22.
Apr. 10.   Paid the dividends declared on March 8.
May   5.   Purchased 1,000 shares of treasury stock for $107,000.
June 7.   The board of directors declared a $2 per share dividend on the common stock outstanding, payable on July 12 to stockholders of record on May 25.
July 12.   Paid the dividends declared on June 7.
Aug. 21.   Sold the treasury stock purchased on May 5 for $116,500.
Sep. 6.   The board of directors declared a 5% common stock dividend to be distributed on October 16 to stockholders of record on September 20. The market price of the stock is $110 per share.
Oct. 16.   Distributed the stock dividend declared on September 6.

Instructions
Journalize the transactions.

PROBLEM 12-6B
STOCK TRANSACTIONS
AND CORRECTIONS;
BALANCE SHEET
Objectives 3, 4, 5

Abrams Company was organized on April 1 of the current year. The accounting clerk prepared the first balance sheet the following December 31, the date that had been adopted as the end of the fiscal year. This balance sheet is as follows:

Abrams Company
Balance Sheet
April 1 to December 31, 19—

Assets		Liabilities	
Cash	$ 65,750	Accounts payable	$ 85,000
Accounts receivable	215,000	Preferred stock	200,000
Merchandise inventory	145,250	Common stock	300,000
Prepaid insurance	6,500	Paid-in capital in	
Treasury common stock	20,000	excess of par—	
Equipment	130,000	common stock	30,000
Retained earnings (deficit)	32,500		
Total assets	$615,000	Total liabilities	$615,000

You are retained by the board of directors to audit the accounts and to prepare a revised balance sheet. The relevant facts developed during the course of your engagement are:

a. Stock authorized: 5,000 shares of $100 par, $11 preferred, and 50,000 shares of $20 par common.

b. Stock issued: 1,000 shares of preferred at $105 and 15,000 shares of common at $22. The premium on preferred stock was credited to Retained Earnings.

c. The company reacquired 1,000 shares of the issued common stock at $30. The difference between par and the price paid was debited to Retained Earnings. (The treasury stock is to be recorded at cost.)

d. Included in merchandise inventory is $1,500 of office supplies.

e. Land to be used as a future building site cost $30,000 and was debited to Equipment.

f. No depreciation has been recognized. The equipment is to be depreciated for 9 months by the straight-line method, using an estimated life of 10 years and assuming no residual value.

g. No dividends have been declared or paid.

Instructions

1. Journalize the entries to record the corrections. Corrections of net income should be recorded as adjustments to Retained Earnings.

2. Prepare a six-column work sheet, with columns for (a) balances per balance sheet, (b) corrections, and (c) corrected balances. In listing the accounts, leave an extra line blank following the retained earnings account. Complete the work sheet.

3. Prepare a corrected balance sheet in report form as of the end of the fiscal year.

SHARPEN YOUR COMMUNICATION SKILLS ► 4. Explain why a premium on the sale of capital stock is not considered to be a part of retained earnings.

SOLUTIONS SOFTWARE

Instructions for Solving Problem 12-6B Using Solutions Software

1. Load opening balances.

2. Enter your name in the Student Name field in the General Information data entry window. Set the run date to December 31 of the current year.

3. Save the opening balances file to your drive and directory.

4. Select the General Journal Entries option, and key the journal entries. Leave the reference field blank. Note: To review the chart of accounts, select F-1.

5. Display a journal entries report.

6. Display a balance sheet.

7. Save your data file to disk.

8. End the session.

PROBLEM 12-7B
ENTRIES FOR TREASURY STOCK; DIVIDENDS; APPROPRIATIONS
Objectives 4, 6, 7

At the beginning of the current fiscal year, Penrod Corporation had 80,000 common shares outstanding. Selected transactions completed by Penrod Corporation during the current year are as follows:

Feb. 3. Declared semiannual dividends of $5 on 10,000 shares of preferred stock and $0.50 on the 80,000 shares of $10 par common stock to stockholders of record on February 28, payable on March 15.

Mar. 15. Paid the cash dividends.

     30. Purchased 5,000 shares of the corporation's own common stock at $16, recording the stock at cost.

Apr. 29. Discovered that a receipt of $750 cash on account from A. C. Green Co. had been posted in error to the account of Greenberg Co. The transaction was recorded correctly in the journal.

July 10. Sold 1,000 shares of treasury stock at $22, receiving cash.

     23. Declared semiannual dividends of $5 on the preferred stock and $0.50 on the common stock. In addition, a 2% common stock dividend was declared on the common stock outstanding, to be capitalized at the fair market value of the common stock, which is estimated at $20.

Aug. 25. Paid the cash dividends and issued the certificates for the common stock dividend.

Nov. 8. Discovered that an invoice of $825 for utilities expense for the month of October was debited to Office Supplies.

Dec. 31. The board of directors authorized the appropriation necessitated by the holding of treasury stock.

Instructions

Journalize the transactions.

SOLUTIONS
SOFTWARE

Instructions for Solving Problem 12-7B Using Solutions Software
1. Load opening balances.
2. Enter your name in the Student Name field in the General Information data entry window. Set the run date to December 31 of the current year.
3. Save the opening balances file to your drive and directory.
4. Select the General Journal Entries option, and key the journal entries. Leave the reference field blank. Note: To review the chart of accounts, select F-1.
5. Display a journal entries report.
6. Save a backup copy of your data file.
7. Perform period-end closing.
8. Display a balance sheet.
9. Save your data file to disk.
10. End the session.

PROBLEM 12-8B
APPROPRIATIONS OF
RETAINED EARNINGS;
RETAINED EARNINGS
STATEMENT
Objective 7

The retained earnings accounts of Elder Corporation for the current fiscal year ended December 31 are as follows:

ACCOUNT **APPROPRIATION FOR PLANT EXPANSION**   ACCOUNT NO. 3201

Date		Item	Debit	Credit	Balance Debit	Balance Credit
19—						
Jan.	1	Balance				300,000
Dec.	31	Retained earnings		50,000		350,000

ACCOUNT **APPROPRIATION FOR TREASURY STOCK**   ACCOUNT NO. 3202

Date		Item	Debit	Credit	Balance Debit	Balance Credit
19—						
Jan.	1	Balance				250,000
Dec.	31	Retained earnings	30,000			220,000

ACCOUNT **RETAINED EARNINGS**   ACCOUNT NO. 3301

Date		Item	Debit	Credit	Balance Debit	Balance Credit
19—						
Jan.	1	Balance				515,000
Dec.	31	Income summary		190,000		705,000
	31	Appropriation for plant expansion	50,000			655,000
	31	Appropriation for treasury stock		30,000		685,000
	31	Cash dividends	50,000			635,000
	31	Stock dividends	100,000			535,000

ACCOUNT **CASH DIVIDENDS**   ACCOUNT NO. 3302

Date		Item	Debit	Credit	Balance Debit	Balance Credit
19—						
Apr.	10		25,000		25,000	
Oct.	13		25,000		50,000	
Dec.	31	Retained earnings		50,000	—	—

ACCOUNT **STOCK DIVIDENDS**   ACCOUNT NO. 3303

Date		Item	Debit	Credit	Balance Debit	Balance Credit
19—						
Oct.	13		100,000		100,000	
Dec.	31	Retained earnings		100,000	—	—

Instructions

Prepare a retained earnings statement for the fiscal year ended December 31.

PROBLEM 12-9B
STOCK TRANSACTIONS;
APPROPRIATIONS;
STOCKHOLDERS' EQUITY
SECTION OF BALANCE
SHEET
Objectives 3, 4, 5, 6, 7

The stockholders' equity accounts of Collins Enterprises Inc., with balances on January 1 of the current fiscal year, are as follows:

Common Stock, $10 stated value (100,000 shares authorized, 80,000 shares issued)	$800,000
Paid-In Capital in Excess of Stated Value	120,000
Appropriation for Plant Expansion	75,000
Appropriation for Treasury Stock	37,500
Retained Earnings	397,750
Treasury Stock (3,000 shares, at cost)	37,500

The following selected transactions occurred during the year:

Feb. 1. Paid cash dividends of $1 per share on the common stock. The dividend had been properly recorded when declared on December 28 of the preceding fiscal year.

Apr. 7. Sold all the treasury stock for $45,000.

May 5. Issued 10,000 shares of common stock for $130,000.

June 11. Received land from the Naples City Council as a donation. The land had an estimated fair market value of $50,000.

July 30. Declared a 5% stock dividend on common stock, to be capitalized at the market price of the stock, which is $15 a share.

Aug. 27. Issued the certificates for the dividend declared on July 30.

Oct. 8. Purchased 2,500 shares of treasury stock for $25,000.

Dec. 20. Declared a $1 per share dividend on common stock.

20. The board of directors authorized an increase of the appropriation for plant expansion by $25,000.

20. Decreased the appropriation for treasury stock to $25,000.

31. Closed the credit balance of the income summary account, $132,500.

31. Closed the two dividends accounts to Retained Earnings.

Instructions

1. Enter the January 1 balances in T accounts for the stockholders' equity accounts listed. Also prepare T accounts for the following: Paid-In Capital from Sale of Treasury Stock; Donated Capital; Stock Dividends Distributable; Stock Dividends; Cash Dividends.

2. Journalize the entries to record the transactions and post to the eleven selected accounts.

3. Prepare the Stockholders' Equity section of the balance sheet as of December 31 of the current fiscal year.

Instructions for Solving Problem 12-9B Using Solutions Software

1. Load opening balances.

2. Enter your name in the Student Name field in the General Information data entry window. Set the run date to December 31 of the current year.

3. Save the opening balances file to your drive and directory.

4. Select the General Journal Entries option, and key the journal entries, including the two closing entries. Leave the reference field blank. Note: To review the chart of accounts, select F-1.

5. Display a journal entries report.

6. Display a balance sheet.

7. Save your data file to disk.

8. End the session.

PROBLEM 12-10B
STATEMENT OF
STOCKHOLDERS' EQUITY
Objective 8

The stockholders' equity accounts of Reese Corporation for the current fiscal year ended December 31 are as follows.

ACCOUNT COMMON STOCK, $1 PAR   ACCOUNT NO.

Date		Item	Debit	Credit	Balance Debit	Balance Credit
19—						
Jan.	1	Balance				100,000
May	20	Issued 50,000 shares		50,000		150,000

ACCOUNT **PAID-IN CAPITAL IN EXCESS OF PAR**   ACCOUNT NO.

Date		Item	Debit	Credit	Balance Debit	Balance Credit
19—						
Jan.	1	Balance				400,000
May	20	Issued 5,000 shares		25,000		425,000

ACCOUNT **TREASURY STOCK**   ACCOUNT NO.

Date		Item	Debit	Credit	Balance Debit	Balance Credit
19—						
Nov.	30	Purchased 1,000 shares	8,000		8,000	

ACCOUNT **APPROPRIATION FOR TREASURY STOCK**   ACCOUNT NO.

Date		Item	Debit	Credit	Balance Debit	Balance Credit
19—						
Dec.	31	Retained earnings		8,000		8,000

ACCOUNT **RETAINED EARNINGS**   ACCOUNT NO.

Date		Item	Debit	Credit	Balance Debit	Balance Credit
19—						
Jan.	1	Balance				925,000
Dec.	31	Income summary		320,000		1,245,000
	31	Appropriation for treasury stock	8,000			1,237,000
	31	Cash dividends	15,000			1,222,000

ACCOUNT **CASH DIVIDENDS**   ACCOUNT NO.

Date		Item	Debit	Credit	Balance Debit	Balance Credit
19—						
Mar.	12		10,000		10,000	
June	17		5,000		15,000	
Dec.	31	Closing		15,000	—	—

Instructions

Prepare a statement of stockholders' equity for the fiscal year ended December 31.

MINI-CASE KOLBY CO.

Kolby Co. has paid quarterly cash dividends since 1987. These dividends have steadily increased from $.20 per share to the latest dividend declaration of $.50 per share. The board of directors would like to continue this trend and are hesitant to suspend or decrease the amount of quarterly dividends. Unfortunately, sales dropped sharply in the fourth quarter of 1995 because of worsening economic conditions and increased competition. As a result, the board is uncertain as to whether it should declare a dividend for the last quarter of 1995.

On November 1, 1995, Kolby Co. borrowed $500,000 from Second National Bank to use in modernizing its retail stores and to expand its product line in reaction to its competition. The terms of the 10-year, 12% loan require Kolby Co. to:

a. Pay monthly the total interest due.
b. Pay $50,000 of the principal each November 1, beginning in 1996.
c. Maintain a current ratio (current assets ÷ current liabilities) of 2:1.
d. Appropriate $500,000 of retained earnings until the loan is fully paid.
e. Maintain a minimum balance (a compensating balance) of $25,000 in its Second National Bank account.

On December 31, 1995, 25% of the $500,000 loan had been disbursed in modernization of the retail stores and in expansion of the product line, and the remainder is temporarily invested in U.S. Treasury Notes. Kolby Co.'s balance sheet as of December 31, 1995, is as follows:

Kolby Co.
Balance Sheet
December 31, 1995

Assets

Current assets:

Cash		$ 40,000	
Marketable securities, at cost (market price, $379,500)		375,000	
Accounts receivable	$ 91,500		
Less allowance for doubtful accounts	6,500	85,000	
Merchandise inventory		120,500	
Prepaid expenses		4,500	
Total current assets			$ 625,000

Plant assets:

Land		$150,000	
Buildings	$950,000		
Less accumulated depreciation	215,000	735,000	
Equipment	$460,000		
Less accumulated depreciation	110,000	350,000	
Total plant assets			1,235,000
Total assets			$1,860,000

Liabilities

Current liabilities:

Accounts payable	$ 71,800	
Notes payable (Second National Bank)	50,000	
Salaries payable	3,200	
Total current liabilities	$125,000	

Long-term liabilities:

Notes payable (Second National Bank)	450,000	
Total liabilities		$ 575,000

Stockholders' Equity

Paid-in capital:

Common stock, $20 par (50,000 shares authorized, 25,000 shares issued)	$500,000		
Excess of issue price over par	40,000		
Total paid-in capital		$540,000	

Retained earnings:

Appropriated for provision of Second National Bank loan	$500,000		
Unappropriated	245,000		
Total retained earnings		745,000	
Total stockholders' equity			1,285,000
Total liabilities and stockholders' equity			$1,860,000

The board of directors is scheduled to meet January 10, 1996, to discuss the results of operations for 1995 and to consider the declaration of dividends for the fourth quarter of 1995. The chairman of the board has asked for your advice on the declaration of dividends.

Instructions

1. What factors should the board consider in deciding whether to declare a cash dividend?
2. The board is considering the declaration of a stock dividend instead of a cash dividend. Discuss the issuance of a stock dividend from the point of view of (a) a stockholder and (b) the board of directors.

ANSWERS TO SELF-EXAMINATION QUESTIONS

1. **C** If a corporation has cumulative preferred stock outstanding, dividends that have been passed for prior years plus the dividend for the current year must be paid before dividends may be declared on common stock. In this case, dividends of $27,000 ($9,000 x 3) have been passed for the preceding three years and the current year's dividends are $9,000, making a total of $36,000 (answer C) that must be paid to preferred stockholders before dividends can be declared on common stock.

2. **D** Paid-in capital is one of the two major subdivisions of the stockholders' equity of a corporation. It may result from many sources, including the issuance of cumulative preferred stock (answer A), the redemption of a corporation's own stock (answer B), and the sale of a corporation's treasury stock (answer C).

3. **D** The Stockholders' Equity section of corporate balance sheets is divided into two principal subsections: (1) investments contributed by the stockholders and (2) net income retained in the business. Included as part of the investments by stockholders is the par of common stock (answer A), donated capital (answer B), and the par of preferred stock (answer C).

4. **C** Reacquired stock, known as treasury stock, should be listed in the Stockholders' Equity section (answer C) of the balance sheet. The price paid for the treasury stock is deducted from the total of all the stockholders' equity accounts.

5. **C** An appropriation for plant expansion is a portion of total retained earnings and would be reported in the Stockholders' Equity section of the balance sheet (answer C).

Part 4

Financial Accounting Reporting Issues

You and Accounting

If you converted 100 U.S. dollars to German deutsche marks, how much foreign currency would you receive? The answer to this question is essential for anyone traveling to Germany. The amount you would receive for $100 of U.S. currency is 165.79 marks.

The amount of German marks received for 100 U.S. dollars was determined by multiplying $100 by the proper exchange rate (1.6579) from a foreign exchange table such as the following:

	Dollar
Canada	1.3073
France	6.0255
Germany	1.7220
Italy	1617.8
Japan	103.64
Switzerland	1.5330
United Kingdom	.68013

Source: *The Wall Street Journal*, August 12, 1993.

If you ordered merchandise priced in a foreign currency, you would also need to be able to determine the equivalent price in U.S. dollars. For example, assume that you ordered a place setting of china from a British firm for an advertised price of 89 pounds. How much is this in U.S. dollars? The answer is $130.86, which is calculated by dividing the amount of foreign currency (89 pounds) by the exchange rate (.68013).

Many business enterprises enter into transactions with foreign companies. Computations such as these are required to determine the amounts to be received and paid. In this chapter, one of the topics that you will read about is the accounting for international transactions.

Chapter 13
Income Statement Issues; Investments in Stocks; International Transactions

LEARNING OBJECTIVES
After studying this chapter, you should be able to:

Objective 1
Journalize the entries for corporate income taxes, including deferred income taxes.

Objective 2
Prepare an income statement reporting the following unusual items:
  Discontinued operations
  Extraordinary items
  Changes in accounting principles

Objective 3
Prepare an income statement reporting earnings per share data.

Objective 4
Prepare a retained earnings statement reporting a prior-period adjustment.

Objective 5
Journalize the entries for long-term investments in stocks, using the cost method and the equity method.

Objective 6
Compute the equity per share of stock.

Objective 7
Describe alternative methods of combining businesses and the preparation of consolidated financial statements.

Objective 8
Journalize the entries for international transactions.

We have discussed a variety of financial accounting topics in the earlier chapters of this text. In this chapter, we discuss some special topics in financial accounting, including the reporting of corporate income taxes, unusual items in the income statement, earnings per share, and prior-period adjustments. In addition, we briefly discuss investments in stocks, business combinations, and the accounting for international transactions.

CORPORATE INCOME TAXES

Objective 1
Journalize the entries for corporate income taxes, including deferred income taxes.

As we mentioned in an earlier chapter, corporations are taxable entities that must pay income taxes. Some corporations pay not only federal income taxes, but also state and local income taxes. Although the following discussion is limited to federal income taxes, the basic concepts also apply to state and local income taxes.

Payment of Income Taxes

Most corporations are required to pay estimated federal income taxes in four installments throughout the year. For example, assume that a corporation with a calendar-year accounting period estimates its income tax expense for the year as $84,000. The entry to record each of the four estimated tax payments of $21,000 (¼ of $84,000) is as follows:

Income Tax	21,000	
Cash		21,000

At year end, the actual taxable income and the actual tax are determined.[1] If additional taxes are owed, the additional liability is recorded. If the total estimated tax payments are greater than the tax liability based on actual income, the overpayment should be debited to a receivable account and credited to Income Tax.

Because income tax is often a significant amount, it is normally reported on the income statement as a special deduction, as shown.

Palmer Corporation Income Statement For the Year ended December 31, 19—	
Sales	$980,000
～～～～～～～～～～～～～～～～～～～～	
Income before income tax	$200,000
Income tax	82,500
Net income	$117,500

Allocation of Income Taxes

The **taxable income** of a corporation must be determined according to the tax laws. It is often different from the *income before income tax* determined and reported according to generally accepted accounting principles. As a result, the income tax based on *taxable income* usually differs from the income tax based on *income before taxes* in the income statement. This difference may need to be allocated between various financial statement periods, depending on the nature of the items causing the differences.

Some differences between *taxable income* and *income before income tax* are created because items are recognized in one period for tax purposes and in another period for income statement purposes. Such differences, called **temporary differences**, reverse or turn around in later years. Some examples of items that create temporary differences are listed here.[2]

1. Revenues or gains are taxed after they are reported in the income statement. Example: The point-of-sale method of realizing revenue is used for financial state-

---

[1] A corporation's income tax returns and supporting records are subject to audits by taxing authorities, who may assess additional taxes. Because of this possibility, the liability for income taxes is sometimes described in the balance sheet as *Estimated income tax payable.*
[2] *Statement of Financial Accounting Standards, No. 109,* "Accounting for Income Taxes" (Norwalk: Financial Accounting Standards Board, 1992), par. 11.

ment reporting, and the installment method of realizing revenue is used for tax reporting.

2. Expenses or losses are deducted in determining taxable income after they are reported in the income statement. Example: Product warranty expense estimated and reported in the year of the sale for financial statement reporting is deducted for tax reporting when paid.

3. Revenues or gains are taxed before they are reported in the income statement. Example: Cash received in advance for magazine subscriptions is included in taxable income when received but included in the income statement only when earned in a future period.

4. Expenses or losses are deducted in determining taxable income before they are reported in the income statement. Example: An accelerated depreciation method is used for tax purposes, and the straight-line method is used for financial reporting purposes.

Over the life of an enterprise, temporary differences do not change or reduce the total amount of tax paid. Temporary differences affect only the *timing* of when the taxes are paid. In most cases, managers use tax-planning techniques so that temporary differences will defer the payment of taxes to later years. As a result, at the end of each year, the amount of the current tax liability and the postponed (deferred) liability must be recorded.

To illustrate, assume that at the end of the first year of operations a corporation reports $300,000 income before income taxes on its income statement. If we assume an income tax rate of 40%, the income tax reported on the income statement is $120,000 ($300,000 × 40%).[3] However, to reduce current income taxes, the corporation uses tax planning to reduce the taxable income to $100,000. Thus, the income tax actually due for the year is only $40,000 ($100,000 × 40%). The $80,000 ($120,000 − $40,000) difference between the two tax amounts is created by timing differences in realizing revenue. It represents a deferment of $80,000 of income tax to future years.

The income tax reported on the income statement is the total tax, $120,000, expected to be paid on the income for the year. This income tax includes the $80,000 that relates to this year's income but that will be paid in future years. In this way, the current year's expenses (including income tax) are matched against the current year's revenue. To achieve this matching on the income statement, income tax is allocated between periods, using the following journal entry:

Income Tax	120,000	
Income Tax Payable		40,000
Deferred Income Tax Payable		80,000

In future years, the $80,000 in Deferred Income Tax Payable will be transferred to Income Tax Payable as the timing differences reverse and the taxes become due. For example, if $48,000 of the deferred tax reverses and becomes due in the second year, the following journal entry would be made in the second year:

Deferred Income Tax Payable	48,000	
Income Tax Payable		48,000

The balance of Deferred Income Tax Payable at the end of a year is reported as a liability. The amount due within one year is classified as a current liability. The remainder is classified as a long-term liability or reported in a Deferred Credits section following the Long-Term Liabilities section.[4]

Differences between taxable income and income (before tax) reported on the income statement may also arise because certain revenues are exempt from tax and cer-

---

[3] For purposes of illustration, the 40% tax rate is assumed to include all federal, state, and local income taxes.
[4] In some cases, a deferred tax asset may arise for tax benefits to be received in the future. Such deferred tax assets are reported as either a current or long-term asset, depending on when the expected benefits are expected to be realized.

tain expenses are not deductible in determining taxable income.[5] For example, interest income on municipal bonds may be exempt from taxation. Such differences create no special financial reporting problems since the amount of income tax determined in accordance with the tax laws is the same amount reported on the income statement.

Are Deferred Taxes Really a Liability?

For those companies that show a significant amount of deferred taxes on their balance sheets, the question that may arise is whether such amounts really are liabilities. For example, the reporting of a liability for "deferred income taxes, $267.7 million," on an Anheuser-Busch balance sheet was discussed in *Forbes*. In this article, excerpts from which follow, it was noted that Anheuser-Busch's deferred tax liability was equal to 19% of the total liabilities and 26% of the stockholders' equity.

. . . *Says Harvey D. Moskowitz, national director of accounting and auditing for Seidman & Seidman, "The deferred taxes on the balance sheet bear no relationship to what is actually going to be owed". . . .*

Here's the explanation for this curious state of affairs: Anheuser-Busch had pretax income of $271.5 million, so, using standard corporate tax rates (less credits), it owed $99.7 mil- *lion to Uncle Sam. That's what it set aside as "provision for income taxes" on its income statement. But it's not what the company actually paid. Like most businesses Anheuser keeps two sets of books, one for tax purposes, one for stock owners. It uses accelerated depreciation for taxes but straight line for reporting to investors. . . . So, out-of-pocket, it really had to pay only $31.9 million in taxes . . . the line marked "current" on the income statement. The other $67.8 million is called "deferred," under the assumption that the company will pay those taxes eventually—when accelerated depreciation runs out, for example.*

That assumption is probably wrong, though. As long as the company keeps growing—in real terms or because of inflation— it will keep adding new assets and new interest costs to replace the ones that are running out. That means those deferred taxes, instead of getting paid, will simply roll over. And over and over and over. It could almost make you dizzy.

Source: Jane Carmichael, "Rollover," *Forbes* (January 18, 1982), pp. 75, 78.

UNUSUAL ITEMS THAT AFFECT THE INCOME STATEMENT

Objective 2
Prepare an income statement reporting the following unusual items:
    Discontinued operations
    Extraordinary items
    Changes in accounting
    principles

Three types of unusual items may affect the current year's net income and are reported separately in the income statement. These three types of items are:

1. The results of discontinued operations
2. Extraordinary items of gain or loss
3. A change from one generally accepted accounting principle to another

We briefly discuss each of the these items in the following paragraphs. We assume that the items illustrated are material to the financial statements. Immaterial items would not affect the normal financial statement presentation.

Discontinued Operations

A gain or loss resulting from disposing of a business segment is reported on the income statement as a gain or loss from **discontinued operations**. The term *discontinued* refers to "the operations of a segment of a business . . . that has been sold, abandoned, spun off, or otherwise disposed of or . . . is the subject of a formal plan for disposal."[6]

The term *business segment* refers to a part of an enterprise whose activities represent a major line of business, such as a division or department or a certain class of customer.[7] For example, assume that an enterprise owns newspapers, television stations, and radio stations. If the enterprise were to sell its radio stations, the results of the sale would be reported as a gain or loss on discontinued operations.

---

[5] Such differences, which will not reverse with the passage of time, are sometimes called *permanent differences*.
[6] *Opinions of the Accounting Principles Board, No. 30*, "Reporting the Results of Operations" (New York: American Institute of Certified Public Accountants, 1973), par. 8.
[7] *Ibid.*, par. 13.

When an enterprise discontinues a segment of its operations, both the *gain or loss from discontinued operations* and the results from *continuing operations* should be reported. The results from continuing operations are presented first, followed by the gain or loss from discontinued operations. Additional data concerning the disposal should also be presented. Such data include the identity of the segment, the disposal date, a description of the segment's assets and liabilities, and the manner of disposal. These data are often disclosed in a note to the financial statements.[8]

Extraordinary Items

Extraordinary gains and losses result from "events and transactions that are unusual in nature and infrequent in occurrence."[9] Such gains and losses, other than those from disposing of a business segment, should be reported in the income statement as **extraordinary items**. To be classified as an extraordinary item, an event must meet both of the following requirements:[10]

1. Unusual nature—the event should be significantly different from the typical or the normal operating activities of the entity.
2. Infrequent occurrence—the event should not be expected to recur often.

Events that meet both of the preceding requirements are uncommon. For example, the 1992 edition of *Accounting Trends & Techniques* indicated that only 55 of the 600 industrial and merchandising companies surveyed reported extraordinary items on their income statements. Usually, extraordinary items result from natural disasters, such as floods, earthquakes, and fires that are not expected to recur. Gains or losses from condemning land or buildings for public use are also considered extraordinary.

Sometimes extraordinary events result in unusual financial results. For example, in its 1989 income statement, Delta Air Lines reported an extraordinary gain of over $5.5 million as the result of the crash of one of its 727 airplanes earlier in the fiscal year. The plane that crashed was insured for $6.5 million, but its book value in Delta's accounting records was $962,000.

Gains and losses on the disposal of plant assets are not extraordinary items. This is because (1) they are not unusual and (2) they recur from time to time in the normal operations of an enterprise. Likewise, gains and losses from the sale of investments are usual and recurring for most enterprises. However, if a company has owned only one type of investment during its entire existence, a gain or loss on its sale might qualify as an extraordinary item, provided there was no intention of acquiring other similar investments in the future.

Changes in Accounting Principles

A change in accounting principle "results from adoption of a generally accepted accounting principle different from the one used previously for reporting purposes."[11] We discussed the consistency concept as it relates to changes in accounting methods in a prior chapter.

A change in generally accepted accounting principles or methods should be disclosed in the financial statements (or in notes to the statements) of the period in which the change is made. This disclosure should include the nature of the change and its justification. In addition, the effects of the change should be disclosed as follows:

1. The effect on the current year's net income should be disclosed.
2. The cumulative effect of the change on the net income of prior periods should be reported in a special section of the income statement.

[8] *Ibid.,* par. 18.
[9] *Ibid.,* par. 20.
[10] *Ibid.*
[11] *Opinions of the Accounting Principles Board, No. 20,* "Accounting Changes" (New York: American Institute of Certified Public Accountants, 1971), par. 7.

The special section in which the cumulative effect is reported should follow any extraordinary items and immediately precede the net income.[12] If financial statements of prior periods are presented on a comparative basis with the current period's statements, the following additional disclosures should be made:

1. The financial statements of the prior periods should be restated as if the change had been made in the prior periods.
2. The effect of the restatement of the prior periods' statements should be reported either on the face of the statements or in a note to the statements.

Using Accounting

An important use of accounting for potential investors is the prediction of future income and cash flows. The identification of unusual items on the income statement allows investors to isolate the effects of such items on income and cash flows. For example, businesses rarely discontinue the opera-tion of a segment of their business or experience a natural disaster such as a hurricane, fire, or flood. By identifying such items on the income statement, investors and other users of the financial statements consider such factors in predicting future income and cash flows for the business enterprise.

Illustration of Reporting Unusual Items

Many different terms and formats may be used in reporting unusual items in the income statement. Exhibit 1 is a partial income statement for Jones Corporation, showing unusual items. You should note that the related tax effects of unusual items are reported with the item to which they are associated. Thus, the loss from discontinued operations, the extraordinary item, and the cumulative effect of the change in depreciation method are reported net of income tax. The amount of income tax related to each of these items may be disclosed on the face of the financial statements or in a note to the statements.

Exhibit 1
Unusual Items in Income Statement

Jones Corporation Income Statement For the Year Ended December 31, 1995	
Net sales	$9,600,000
Income from continuing operations before income tax	$1,310,000
Income tax	620,000
Income from continuing operations	$ 690,000
Loss on discontinued operations (Note A)	100,000
Income before extraordinary items and cumulative effect of a change in accounting principle	$ 590,000
Extraordinary item:	
Gain on condemnation of land, net of applicable income tax of $65,000	150,000
Cumulative effect on prior years of changing to a different depreciation method (Note B)	92,000
Net income	$ 832,000

Note A.

On July 1 of the current year, the electrical products division of the corporation was sold at a loss of $100,000, net of applicable income tax of $50,000. The net sales of the division for the current year were $2,900,000. The assets sold were composed of inventories, equipment and plant totaling $2,100,000. The purchaser assumed liabilities of $600,000.

---

[12] Two exceptions to these disclosures are made for a change from the last-in, first-out inventory method or for a change in the method of accounting for long-term construction contracts. The disclosures for these changes are discussed in advanced accounting texts.

Note B.

Depreciation of all property, plant, and equipment has been computed by the straight-line method in 1995. Prior to 1995, depreciation of equipment for one of the divisions had been computed on the double-declining-balance method. In 1995, the straight-line method was adopted for this division in order to achieve uniformity and to better match depreciation charges with the estimated economic utility of such assets. Consistent with APB Opinion No. 20, *this change in depreciation has been applied to prior years. The effect of the change was to increase income before extraordinary items for 1995 by $30,000. The adjustment of $92,000 (after reduction for income tax of $88,000) to apply the new method to prior years is also included in income for 1995.*

EARNINGS PER COMMON SHARE

Objective 3
Prepare an income statement reporting earnings per share data.

The amount of net income is often used by investors and creditors in evaluating a company's profitability. However, net income by itself is difficult to use in comparing companies of different sizes. For example, a net income of $750,000 may be acceptable for a small computer software company, but it would be unacceptable for Apple Computer Inc. Moreover, trends in net income may be difficult to evaluate, using only net income, when there have been significant changes in a company's stockholders' equity.

In addressing these concerns, the profitability of companies is often expressed as earnings per share. **Earnings per share**, often called **EPS**, is the net income per share of common stock outstanding during a period. Corporations whose stock is traded on stock exchanges, referred to as public companies, must report earnings per share on the income statement.[13]

Using Accounting

Because of its importance, earnings per share is reported in the financial press and by various investor services, such as *Moodys* and *Standard & Poors*. Changes in earnings per share can lead to significant changes in the price of a corporation's stock in the market place.

If a company has only common stock outstanding, the earnings per share of common stock is determined by dividing net income by the number of common shares outstanding. If preferred stock is outstanding, the net income must be reduced by the amount of any preferred dividend requirements before dividing by the number of common shares outstanding.

The effect of unusual items should be considered in computing earnings per share. Otherwise, a single earnings per share amount based on net income could be misleading. For example, assume that Jones Corporation, whose partial income statement for 1995 was presented in Exhibit 1, reported net income of $700,000 for 1994. Also assume that no extraordinary or other special items were reported in 1993. The corporation's capital stock included 200,000 common shares outstanding during 1994 and 1995. The earnings per share is $3.50 ($700,000 ÷ 200,000) for 1994 and $4.16 ($832,000 ÷ 200,000) for 1995. Comparing the two earnings per share amounts for 1994 and 1995 would suggest that operations had significantly improved. However, the current year's per share amount that is comparable to $3.50 is $3.45, which is the income from continuing operations of $690,000 divided by 200,000 shares of common stock outstanding. This latter amount indicates a slight downward trend in normal operations.

---

[13] Nonpublic corporations are exempt from reporting earnings per share under *Statement of Financial Accounting Standards, No. 21*, "Suspension of the Reporting of Earnings per Share and Segment Information by Nonpublic Enterprises" (Stamford: Financial Accounting Standards Board, 1978).

When unusual items exist, earnings per share should be reported for the following items:

1. Income from continuing operations
2. Income before extraordinary items and the cumulative effect of a change in accounting principle
3. The cumulative effect of a change in accounting principle
4. Net income[14]

The reporting of earnings per share for the gain or loss on discontinued operations and for extraordinary items is optional. Earnings per share data may be shown in parentheses or added at the bottom of the statement, as shown in Exhibit 2 for Jones Corporation.

Exhibit 2
Income Statement with Earnings per Share

Jones Corporation Income Statement For the Year Ended December 31, 1995	
Income from continuing operations	$690,000
Net income	832,000
Earnings per common share:	
Income from continuing operations	$3.45
Loss on discontinued operations	.50
Income before extraordinary item and cumulative	
effect of a change in accounting principle	$2.95
Extraordinary item	.75
Cumulative effect on prior years of changing to a	
different depreciation method	.46
Net income	$4.16

In computing the earnings per share of common stock, all factors that could affect the number of common shares outstanding should be considered. For example, an issue of preferred stock or bonds (debt) with the right to convert to common stock may be outstanding. Such securities that are convertible to common stock are often classified as **common stock equivalents.**[15]

When common stock equivalents exist, two amounts for earnings per share are normally reported. One amount is computed without regard to the conversion privilege. This amount is called *Earnings per common share—assuming no dilution* or *Primary earnings per share.* The second amount is based on the assumption that the preferred stock or bonds are converted to common stock. This amount is called *Earnings per common share—assuming full dilution* or *Fully diluted earnings per share.*[16]

A note accompanying the financial statements normally explains how the earnings per share were computed. An example of such a note, taken from the financial statements of The Pillsbury Company, follows:

Net earnings per share are computed using the weighted average number of common shares, including common share equivalents of stock options, outstanding during each year. Net earnings per share assuming full dilution would be substantially the same.

---

[14] *Opinions of the Accounting Principles Board, No. 15,* "Earnings per Share" (New York: American Institute of Certified Public Accountants, 1969) as amended by *Opinions of the Accounting Principles Board, No. 20,* and *Opinions of the Accounting Principles Board, No. 30.*

[15] To be classified as a common stock equivalent, a security must satisfy certain requirements set forth in *Opinions of the Accounting Principles Board, No. 15,* "Earnings per Share" (New York: American Institute of Certified Public Accountants, 1969).

[16] Additional issues related to computing earnings per share are discussed in advanced accounting texts.

PRIOR-PERIOD ADJUSTMENTS

Objective 4
Prepare a retained earnings statement reporting a prior-period adjustment.

Material errors in a prior period's net income may arise from mathematical mistakes and from mistakes in applying accounting principles. The effect of material errors that are not discovered within the same fiscal period in which they occurred should not be included in determining net income for the current period.[17] Corrections of such errors are called **prior-period adjustments**. These errors are reported as an adjustment of the retained earnings balance at the beginning of the period in which the error is discovered and corrected.[18] For example, correcting a material error in computing a prior period's depreciation expense is a prior-period adjustment. In addition, a change from an unacceptable accounting principle to an acceptable accounting principle is considered to be a correction of a material error and is reported as a prior-period adjustment. For example, a change from reporting plant assets at market values to historical costs would be a prior-period adjustment.

Differences arising from using estimates are not prior-period adjustments. Estimates must be used throughout the accounting process. For example, uncollectible accounts receivable must be estimated in preparing the financial statements. As a result, differences between estimated and actual amounts will arise. These differences are not considered errors or prior-period adjustments, but they are included in determining the current period's net income.

Exhibit 3 illustrates the reporting of a prior-period adjustment in the retained earnings statement.

Exhibit 3
Retained Earnings Statement with Prior-Period Adjustment

Casper Inc. Retained Earnings Statement For Year Ended December 31, 1995		
Retained earnings, January 1, 1995	*212,500*	$~~310,500~~
Less prior-period adjustment:		
Correction of error in depreciation expense in 1994, net of applicable income tax of $13,000	*11,000*	29,200
Corrected retained earnings, January 1, 1995	*201,500*	$281,300
Net income for year	*102,500*	$77,350
Less dividends	*60,000*	40,000
Increase in retained earnings		~~37,350~~ *42,500*
Retained earnings, December 31, 1995		$318,650

Prior-period adjustments are reported net of any related income tax. If only the current period's financial statements are presented, the effect of the adjustment on the net income of the preceding period should also be disclosed. If financial statements for prior periods are presented on a comparative basis, the prior periods' statements should be restated and the amount of the adjustment disclosed.

Prior-period adjustments are rare in financial reporting. Annual audits by independent public accountants, combined with good internal control policies and procedures, reduce the chance of such errors.

INVESTMENTS IN STOCKS

Objective 5
Journalize the entries for long-term investments in stocks, using the cost method and the equity method.

A business may purchase long-term investments in **equity securities** (preferred stock and common stock) for a variety of reasons. One reason may be that the enterprise has excess cash that it does not need for normal operations. A corporation may also purchase stocks as a means of developing or maintaining business relationships with the issuing company. In other cases, a corporation may purchase voting stock of another corporation in order to gain control of its activities.

[17] Corrections of errors that are discovered in the same period in which they occur were discussed in a previous chapter.
[18] *Statement of Financial Accounting Standards, No. 16*, "Prior Period Adjustments" (Stamford: Financial Accounting Standards Board, 1977), par. 11.

In this section, we discuss the principles underlying the accounting for investments in stocks that are not intended as a ready source of cash in the normal operations of a business. Such investments are identified as long-term investments and are reported in the balance sheet under the caption *Investments*.[19]

There are two methods of accounting for long-term investments in stock: (1) the **cost method** and (2) the **equity method**. The method used depends on whether the investor (buyer of the stock) has a significant influence over the operating and financing activities of the company (the investee) whose stock is owned. If the investor does not have a significant influence, the cost method is used. If the investor has a significant influence, the equity method is used. Evidence of such influence includes the percentage of ownership, the existence of intercompany transactions, and the interchange of managerial personnel. Generally, if the investor owns 20% or more of the voting stock of the investee, it is assumed that the investor has significant influence over the investee.[20]

Cost Method

As with the purchase of other assets, the cost of stocks purchased includes all expenditures necessary to acquire the stocks. For example, the cost of stocks includes not only the amount paid to the seller but also such costs as a broker's commission. The total cost of a stock purchased is debited to an investment account.

Cash dividends may be received on capital stock held as an investment. When the cost method is used, such dividends are recorded as an increase (debit) to an asset account and an increase (credit) to a dividend income account.

To illustrate, assume that on March 1, Makowski Corporation purchases 100 shares of Compton Corporation common stock at 59 plus a brokerage fee of $40. On April 30, Compton Corporation declares a $2 per share cash dividend payable on June 15 to stockholders of record on May 15. The entries in the accounts of Makowski Corporation to record the purchase of the stock and the receipt of the dividends are as follows:

Purchase of Compton Corp. common stock	Mar. 1	Investment in Compton Corp. Stock	5,940	
		Cash		5,940

Receipt of cash dividends on Compton Corp. common stock	June 15	Cash	200	
		Dividend Income		200

Under the cost method, investments in stocks are reported in the financial statements using a lower-of-cost-or-market rule. This rule is applied on the balance sheet date to all stock investments taken as a whole. If the total cost of the investments is lower than the total market value, no special reporting is necessary. If the total market value is lower, the investments are reported at the market value. The decrease in value is not, however, reported on the income statement as a loss. Instead, the decrease in value is reported as a separate item in the Stockholders' Equity section of the balance sheet.[21]

An exception to the preceding lower-of-cost-or-market rule is made if the decrease in the market value for an individual stock is considered a permanent decrease. This might be the case, for example, if a corporation has filed for bankruptcy. In this case, the carrying amount (cost) of the individual stock is written down (decreased), and the amount of the write-down is reported as a loss on the income statement. After the write-down, the revised carrying value of the individual stock is treated as its cost and is not increased for later recoveries in market value.[22]

[19] Temporary investments in marketable securities were discussed in an earlier chapter.

[20] *Opinions of the Accounting Principles Board, No. 18*, "The Equity Method of Accounting for Investments in Common Stock" (New York: American Institute of Certified Public Accountants, 1971), par. 17.

[21] *Statement of Financial Accounting Standards, No. 12*, "Accounting for Certain Marketable Securities" (Stamford: Financial Accounting Standards Board, 1975), par. 11.

[22] *Ibid.*, par. 21.

Equity Method

Under the equity method, a stock purchase is recorded at its cost in the same manner as if the cost method were used. The equity method, however, is different from the cost method in the way in which net income and cash dividends of the investee are recorded. The equity method of recording these items is summarized as follows:

1. The investor's share of the periodic net income of the investee is recorded as an increase in the investment account on the balance sheet. This increase is also recorded on the income statement as revenue for the period. Likewise, the investor's share of an investee's net loss is recorded as a decrease in the investment and as a loss for the period.
2. The investor's share of cash dividends is recorded as an increase in the cash account and a decrease in the investment account.

To illustrate, assume that on January 2, Hally Inc. pays cash of $350,000 for 40% of the common (voting) stock of Brock Corporation. Assume also that, for the year ending December 31, Brock Corporation reports net income of $105,000 and declares and pays $45,000 in dividends. Using the equity method, Hally Inc. (the investor) records these transactions as follows:

Purchase of 40% of Brock Corp. common stock	Jan. 2	Investment in Brock Corp. Stock	350,000	
		Cash		350,000
Share (40%) of Brock Corp. net income of $105,000	Dec. 31	Investment in Brock Corp. Stock	42,000	
		Income of Brock Corp.		42,000
Share (40%) of cash dividends of $45,000 paid by Brock Corp.	Dec. 31	Cash	18,000	
		Investment in Brock Corp. Stock		18,000

The combined effect of recording 40% of Brock Corporation's net income and dividends is to increase Cash by $18,000, Investment in Brock Corp. Stock by $24,000, and Income of Brock Corp. by $42,000.

Sale of Long-Term Investments in Stocks

When shares of stock are sold, the investment account is credited for the carrying value of the shares sold. The cash or receivable account is debited for the proceeds (sales price less commission and other selling costs). Any difference between the proceeds and the carrying value is recorded as a gain or loss on the sale.

To illustrate, assume that an investment in Drey Inc. stock has a carrying value of $15,700. If the proceeds from the sale of the stock are $17,500, the entry to record the transaction is as follows:

	Cash	17,500	
	Investment in Drey Inc. Stock		15,700
	Gain on Sale of Investments		1,800

EQUITY PER SHARE

Objective 6
Compute the equity per share of stock.

The stockholders' equity reported on the balance sheet is often reported in the financial press in terms of **equity per share** or **book value per share**. Equity per share is one of many factors that influences the market value of a corporation's stock.

Earnings potential, dividend rates, and future expectations also affect the market price of stocks. For example, so-called hot stocks may sell at multiples of more than ten times their equity per share. On the other hand, stock of corporations that have reported losses or unfavorable earnings trends may sell at less than the equity per share.

If there is only one class of stock, equity per share is determined by dividing the total stockholders' equity by the number of shares outstanding. For a corporation with both preferred and common stock, total stockholders' equity must be allocated between the two classes of stock. This allocation must consider any liquidation rights and any cumulative dividend features of the preferred stock. After the total equity is allocated, the equity per share for preferred stock and common stock is determined.

To illustrate, assume that as of the end of the current fiscal year, a corporation has preferred and common shares outstanding, no preferred dividends are in arrears, and preferred stock is entitled to $105 per share on liquidation. The stockholders' equity and the computation of the equity per share is shown.

Stockholders' Equity

Preferred $9 stock, cumulative, $100 par	
(1,000 shares outstanding)	$100,000
Excess of issue price over par—preferred stock	2,000
Common stock, $10 par (50,000 shares outstanding)	500,000
Excess of issue price over par—common stock	50,000
Retained earnings	253,000
Total stockholders' equity	$905,000

Allocation of Total Equity to Preferred and Common Stock

Total stockholders' equity	$905,000
Allocated to preferred stock:	
Liquidation price	105,000
Allocated to common stock	$800,000

Equity per Share

$$\text{Equity per share of preferred stock} = \frac{\text{Total dollar equity of preferred stock}}{\text{Number of shares of preferred stock outstanding}}$$

$$\text{Equity per share of preferred stock} = \frac{\$105,000}{1,000 \text{ shares}} = \$105 \text{ per share}$$

$$\text{Equity per share of common stock} = \frac{\text{Total dollar equity of common stock}}{\text{Number of shares of common stock outstanding}}$$

$$\text{Equity per share of common stock} = \frac{\$800,000}{50,000 \text{ shares}} = \$16 \text{ per share}$$

Assume that the preferred stock is entitled to dividends in arrears on liquidation and dividends are in arrears for two years. The equity per share in the preceding example would then be determined as follows:

Total stockholders' equity		$905,000
Allocated to preferred stock:		
Liquidation price	$105,000	
Dividends in arrears	18,000	123,000
Allocated to common stock		$782,000

$$\text{Equity per share of preferred stock} = \frac{\$123,000}{1,000 \text{ shares}} = \$123 \text{ per share}$$

$$\text{Equity per share of common stock} = \frac{\$782,000}{50,000 \text{ shares}} = \$15.64 \text{ per share}$$

BUSINESS COMBINATIONS

Objective 7
Describe alternative methods of combining businesses and the preparation of consolidated financial statements.

Each year, many business enterprises combine to achieve such objectives as efficiencies of large-scale production and diversification of product lines. Business combinations often involve complex accounting principles and terminology. Our objective in the following paragraphs is to introduce you to some of the unique terminology and concepts related to business combinations. We also briefly describe the use, reporting, and preparation of consolidated statements.

Mergers and Consolidations

A **merger** is the joining of two enterprises in which one corporation acquires the properties of another corporation that is then dissolved. Usually, all the assets and liabilities of the acquired company are taken over by the acquiring company. The acquiring enterprise may use cash, debt obligations, or its own capital stock as the form of payment. Whatever the form of payment, the amount received by the dissolving corporation is distributed to its stockholders in final liquidation.

A **consolidation** is the creation of a new corporation, to which is transferred the assets and liabilities of two or more existing corporations. The new corporation usually issues its own stock in exchange for the net assets acquired. The original corporations are then dissolved.

Parent and Subsidiary Corporations

Business combinations may also occur when one corporation buys a controlling share of the outstanding voting stock of one or more other corporations. In this case, none of the participating corporations dissolve. The corporations continue as separate legal entities in a parent–subsidiary relationship. The corporation owning all or a majority of the voting stock of the other corporation is called the **parent company**. The corporation that is controlled is called the **subsidiary company**. Two or more corporations closely related through stock ownership are sometimes called **affiliated** or **associated companies**.

In accounting terms, parent and subsidiary relationships are created by either a *purchase* or a *pooling of interests*. A corporation may acquire the controlling share of the voting common stock of another corporation by paying cash, exchanging other assets, issuing debt, or some combination of these methods. The stockholders of the acquired company, in turn, transfer their stock to the parent corporation. In such cases, the transaction is recorded like a normal purchase of assets, and the combination is accounted for by the **purchase method**.

A parent–subsidiary relationship may be created by exchanging the voting common stock of the acquiring corporation (the parent) for the common stock of the acquired corporation (the subsidiary). If at least 90% of the stock of the subsidiary is acquired in this way, the transaction is a pooling of interests, and the combination is accounted for by the **pooling-of-interests method**. In a pooling of interests, the stockholders of the acquired company (the subsidiary) become stockholders of the acquiring company (the parent).

The accounting for a purchase and a pooling of interests are significantly different. A purchase is accounted for as a *sale–purchase* transaction, whereas a pooling of interests is accounted for as a *joining of ownership interests*.

Generally accepted accounting principles set forth very strict criteria that must be met before the pooling-of-interests method can be used.[23] As a result, only a few business combinations are accounted for by the pooling-of-interests method. The 1992 edition of *Accounting Trends & Techniques* reported that 91% of the business combinations surveyed were accounted for by the purchase method.

Consolidated Financial Statements

Although the corporations that make up a parent–subsidiary affiliation may operate as a single economic unit, they continue to maintain separate accounting records and prepare their own periodic financial statements. At the end of the year, the financial statements of the parent and subsidiary are combined and reported as a single company. These combined financial statements of the parent and subsidiary are called **consolidated statements**. Such statements are usually identified by adding "and subsidiary(ies)" to the name of the parent corporation or by adding "consolidated" to the statement title.

Consolidated financial statements are considered more meaningful to stockholders of the parent company than separate statements for each corporation. This is because the parent company, *in substance*, controls the subsidiaries even though the parent and its subsidiaries are separate entities.

When the data on the financial statements of the parent corporation and its subsidiaries are combined to form the consolidated statements, special attention should be given to intercompany transactions. For example, intercompany transactions may involve the purchase or sale of goods between the parent and subsidiary or the lending of money by the parent to the subsidiary.

Intercompany transactions by their very nature affect the individual accounts of the parent and subsidiary and thus the financial statements of both companies. For example, assume that a subsidiary company issued a $200,000 note to its parent for cash. In this case, the subsidiary's ledger would include a note payable account with a balance of $200,000, which is reported on the subsidiary's balance sheet. Likewise, the parent's ledger would include a note receivable account with a balance of $200,000, which is reported on the parent's balance sheet.[24]

The effects of intercompany transactions must be eliminated when the financial statements of the parent and subsidiary are consolidated. For example, in the preceding illustration, the parent's $200,000 note receivable and the subsidiary's $200,000 note payable must be eliminated when consolidated financial statements are prepared. This is because consolidated financial statements are prepared as if the parent and subsidiary are one operating unit. In other words, in the preceding example, the consolidated entity cannot owe itself $200,000.

In addition to intercompany transactions, the ownership interest of the parent in the subsidiary's stock, which is represented by the balance in the parent's investment in subsidiary account, must also be eliminated. This is done by eliminating the parent's investment in subsidiary account against the balances of the subsidiary's stockholders' equity accounts.

If the parent owns less than 100% of the subsidiary stock, the subsidiary stock owned by outsiders is called **minority interest**. The minority interest is not eliminated but is normally reported on the consolidated balance sheet immediately preceding consolidated stockholders' equity. The 1992 edition of *Accounting Trends & Techniques* indicates that most of the companies surveyed reported minority interest in the long-term liabilities (noncurrent) section of the consolidated balance sheet.

When a business combination is accounted for as a purchase, the subsidiary's net assets are reported in the consolidated balance sheet at their fair market value

---

[23] *Opinions of the Accounting Principles Board, No. 16*, "Business Combinations" (New York: American Institute of Certified Public Accountants, 1970).

[24] Examples of other accounts often affected by intercompany transactions include accounts receivable and accounts payable, interest receivable and interest payable, sales and purchases (or cost of merchandise sold), and interest expense and interest income.

at the time of the purchase. In some cases, a parent may pay more than the fair market value of a subsidiary's net assets because the subsidiary has prospects for high future earnings. The difference between the amount paid by the parent and the fair market value of the subsidiary's net assets is reported on the consolidated balance sheet as an intangible asset. This asset is identified as **Goodwill** or **Excess of cost of business acquired over related net assets**.

Many U.S. corporations own subsidiaries in foreign countries. Such corporations are often called **multinational corporations**. The financial statements of the foreign subsidiary are usually prepared in foreign currency. Before the financial statements of foreign subsidiaries are consolidated with their domestic parent's financial statements, the amounts shown on the statements for the foreign companies must be converted to U.S. dollars.[25]

ACCOUNTING FOR INTERNATIONAL TRANSACTIONS

Objective 8
Journalize the entries for international transactions.

Many U.S. companies enter into transactions with foreign business enterprises, either as sellers or buyers of products or services. These transactions may require the payment or receipt of currencies other than the U.S. dollar. In the following paragraphs, we discuss the basic principles used in accounting for such international transactions.

If transactions with foreign companies require payment or receipt in U.S. dollars, no special accounting problems arise.[26] Such transactions are recorded as we described and illustrated earlier in this text. For example, the sale of merchandise to a Japanese company that is billed in and paid for in dollars would be recorded by the U.S. company in the normal manner. However, if the transaction is billed and payment is to be received in Japanese yen, the U.S. company may incur an exchange gain or loss.

Realized Currency Exchange Gains and Losses

A U.S. company may enter into a transaction with a foreign company requiring either the receipt of a foreign currency or payment in a foreign currency. When funds are received in a foreign currency, the amount of foreign currency received must be converted to its equivalent in U.S. dollars for recording in the accounts. When payment is to be made in a foreign currency, U.S. dollars must be exchanged for the foreign currency for payment.

To illustrate, assume that a U.S. company purchases merchandise from a British company that requires payment in British pounds. In this case, U.S. dollars ($) must be exchanged for British pounds (£) to pay for the merchandise. This exchange of one currency into another involves the use of an exchange rate. The **exchange rate** is the rate at which one unit of currency (the dollar, for example) can be converted into another currency (the British pound, for example).

To continue the example, assume that the U.S. company had purchased merchandise for £1,000 from a British company on June 1, when the exchange rate was $1.40 per British pound. Thus, $1,400 must be exchanged for £1,000 to make the purchase.[27] The U.S. company records the transaction in dollars, as follows:

June 1	Merchandise Inventory	1,400	
	Cash		1,400
	Payment of Invoice No. 1725 from		
	W. A. Sterling Co., £1,000; exchange		
	rate, $1.40 per British pound.		

[25] Additional discussion of business combinations and multinational corporations can be found in advanced accounting courses and texts.

[26] This discussion is from the point of view of a U.S. company. Unless otherwise indicated, the reference to the dollar refers to the U.S. dollar rather than a dollar of another country, such as Canada.

[27] Foreign exchange rates are quoted in major financial reporting services. Because the exchange rates are quite volatile, those used in this chapter are assumed rates.

Instead of a cash purchase, the purchase may be made on account. In this case, the exchange rate may change between the date of purchase and the payment of the account payable in the foreign currency. In practice, exchange rates vary daily.

To illustrate, assume that the preceding purchase was made on account. The entry to record it is as follows:

June 1	Merchandise Inventory		1,400	
	Accounts Payable—W. A. Sterling Co.			1,400
	Purchase on account; Invoice No. 1725			
	from W. A. Sterling Co., £1,000;			
	exchange rate, $1.40 per British pound.			

Assume that on the date of payment, June 15, the exchange rate was $1.45 per pound. The £1,000 account payable must be settled by exchanging $1,450 (£1,000 × $1.45) for £1,000. In this case, the U.S. company incurs an exchange loss of $50 because $1,450 was needed to settle a $1,400 account payable. The cash payment is recorded as follows:

June 15	Accounts Payable—W. A. Sterling Co.		1,400	
	Exchange Loss		50	
	Cash			1,450
	Cash paid on Invoice No. 1725, for			
	£1,000, or $1,400, when exchange rate			
	was $1.45 per pound.			

We can analyze all transactions with foreign companies in the manner described. For example, assume that a sale on account for $1,000 to a Swiss company on May 1 was billed in Swiss francs. The cost of the merchandise sold was $600, and the selling company uses a perpetual inventory system. If the exchange rate was $.25 per Swiss franc (F) on May 1, the transaction is recorded as follows:

May 1	Accounts Receivable—D. W. Robinson Co.		1,000	
	Sales			1,000
	Invoice No. 9772, F4,000; exchange			
	rate, $.25 per Swiss franc.			

1	Cost of Merchandise Sold		600	
	Merchandise Inventory			600

Assume that the exchange rate increases to $.30 per Swiss franc on May 31 when cash is received. In this case, the U.S. company realizes an exchange gain of $200. This gain is realized because the F4,000, which had a value of $1,000 on the date of sale, has increased in value to $1,200 (F4,000 × $.30) on May 31 when the payment is received. The receipt of the cash is recorded as follows:

May 31	Cash		1,200	
	Accounts Receivable—D. W. Robinson Co.			1,000
	Exchange Gain			200
	Cash received on Invoice No. 9772, for			
	F4,000, or $1,000, when exchange rate was			
	$.30 per Swiss franc.			

Unrealized Currency Exchange Gains and Losses

In the previous examples, the transactions were completed by either the receipt or the payment of cash. On the date the cash was received or paid, any related exchange gain or loss was realized and was recorded in the accounts. However, financial statements may be prepared between the date of the sale or purchase on account and the date the cash is received or paid. In this case, any exchange gain or loss created by a change in exchange rates between the date of the original transaction and the balance sheet date must be recorded. Such an exchange gain or loss is reported in the financial statements as an unrealized exchange gain or loss.

To illustrate, assume that a sale on account for $1,000 had been made to a German company on December 20 and had been billed in deutsche marks (DM). The cost of merchandise sold was $700. On this date, the exchange rate was $.50 per deutsche mark. The transaction is recorded as follows:

Dec. 20	Accounts Receivable—T. A. Mueller Inc.	1,000	
	Sales		1,000
	Invoice No. 1793, DM2,000; exchange rate,		
	$.50 per deutsche mark.		
20	Cost of Merchandise Sold	700	
	Merchandise Inventory		700

Assume that the exchange rate decreases to $.45 per deutsche mark on December 31, the date of the balance sheet. Thus, the $1,000 account receivable on December 31 has a value of only $900 (DM2,000 x $.45). This *unrealized* loss of $100 ($1,000 - $900) is recorded as follows:

Dec. 31	Exchange Loss	100	
	Accounts Receivable—T. A. Mueller Inc.		100
	Invoice No. 1793, DM2,000 $\times$ $.05		
	decrease in exchange rate.		

Any additional change in the exchange rate during the following period is recorded when the cash is received. To continue the illustration, assume that the exchange rate declines from $.45 to $.42 per deutsche mark by January 19, when the DM2,000 is received. The receipt of the cash on January 19 is recorded as follows:

Jan. 19	Cash (DM2,000 $\times$ $.42)	840	
	Exchange Loss ($.03DM $\times$ 2,000)	60	
	Accounts Receivable—T. A. Mueller Inc.		900
	Cash received on Invoice No. 1793, for		
	DM2,000, or $900, when exchange rate was		
	$.42 per deutsche mark.		

In contrast, assume that in the preceding example the exchange rate increases between December 31 and January 19. In this case, an exchange gain would be recorded on January 19. For example, if the exchange rate increases from $.45 to $.47 per deutsche mark during this period, Exchange Gain would be credited for $40 ($.02 $\times$ DM2,000).

A balance in the exchange loss account at the end of the fiscal period is reported in the Other Expense section of the income statement. A balance in the exchange gain account is reported in the Other Income section.

CHAPTER REVIEW

Key Points

Objective 1. Journalize the entries for corporate income taxes, including deferred income taxes.

Corporations are subject to federal income tax and are required to make estimated payments throughout the year. To record the payment of estimated tax, Income Tax is debited and Cash is credited. If additional taxes are owed at the end of the year, Income Tax is debited and Income Tax Payable is credited for the amount owed. If the estimated tax payments

are greater than the actual tax liability, a receivable account is debited and Income Tax is credited.

The tax effects of temporary differences must be allocated between periods. The journal entry for such allocations normally debits Income Tax and credits Income Tax Payable and Deferred Income Tax Payable.

Objective 2. Prepare an income statement reporting the following unusual items: Discontinued operations, Extraordinary items, and Changes in accounting principles.

Discontinued operations: A gain or loss resulting from the disposal of a segment of a business should be identified on the income statement, net of related income tax, as a gain or loss from discontinued operations. The results of continuing operations should also be identified on the income statement.

Extraordinary items: Gains and losses may result from events and transactions that are unusual in nature and infrequent in occurrence. Such items, net of related income tax, should be identified on the income statement as extraordinary items.

Changes in accounting principles: A change in an accounting principle results from the adoption of a generally accepted accounting principle different from the one used previously for reporting purposes. The effect of the change in principle on net income in the current period, as well as the cumulative effect on income of prior periods, should be disclosed in the financial statements. The effects of a change in an accounting principle should be reported net of related income tax.

Objective 3. Prepare an income statement reporting earnings per share data.

Earnings per share data are reported on the income statements of public corporations. If there are nonrecurring items on the income statement, the per share amount should be presented for (1) income from continuing operations, (2) income before extraordinary items and the cumulative effect of a change in accounting principle, (3) the cumulative effect of a change in accounting principle, and (4) net income.

Objective 4. Prepare a retained earnings statement reporting a prior-period adjustment.

Material errors related to a prior period are called prior-period adjustments. Prior-period adjustments are reported as an adjustment to the retained earnings balance at the beginning of the period in which the correction is made.

Objective 5. Journalize the entries for long-term investments in stocks, using the cost method and the equity method.

The cost of purchasing a long-term investment in a stock includes all expenditures necessary to acquire the stock. The total cost of a stock purchased is debited to an investment account.

When the cost method is used, cash dividends are recorded as an increase in the cash account (debit) and an increase in the dividend income account (credit). The lower-of-cost-or-market rule is applied to the total cost or total market price of the stock as of the date of the balance sheet. If total market is lower, the difference is reported as a separate item in the Stockholders' Equity section of the balance sheet. If the decline in market value for an individual security is permanent, the individual security is written down and the write-down is reported as a realized loss on the income statement.

Under the equity method, the investor records its share of periodic net income of the investee as an increase in the investment account (debit) and as an increase in an income account (credit). The investor's share of the investee's periodic net loss is recorded in a loss account (debit) and as a decrease in the investment account (credit). The investor records its share of cash dividends as an increase in the cash account (debit) and as a decrease in the investment account (credit).

When shares of stock held as a long-term investment are sold, cash or a receivable account is debited for the proceeds and the investment account is credited for the carrying amount of the shares sold. Any difference between the proceeds, and the carrying amount is recorded as a gain or loss on the sale.

Objective 6. Compute the equity per share of stock.

If there is only one class of stock, equity per share is determined by dividing the total stockholders' equity by the number of shares outstanding. For a corporation with both preferred and common stock, the total stockholders' equity must be allocated between the two classes of stock. This allocation must consider any liquidation rights and any cumulative dividend features of the preferred stock. After the total equity is allocated, the equity per share for preferred stock and common stock is determined as follows:

$$\text{Equity per share of preferred stock} = \frac{\text{Total dollar equity of preferred stock}}{\text{Number of shares of preferred stock outstanding}}$$

$$\text{Equity per share of common stock} = \frac{\text{Total dollar equity of common stock}}{\text{Number of shares of common stock outstanding}}$$

Objective 7. Describe alternative methods of combining businesses and the preparation of consolidated financial statements.

Businesses may combine in a merger or a consolidation. Business combinations may also occur when one corporation acquires a controlling share of the outstanding voting stock of another corporation. In this case, a parent–subsidiary relationship exists, and the companies are called affiliated or associated companies.

Although the corporations that make up a parent–subsidiary affiliation may operate as a single economic unit, they usually continue to maintain separate accounting records and prepare their own periodic financial statements. The financial statements prepared by combining the parent and subsidiary statements are called consolidated statements.

Under the purchase method, the parent's investment account at the date of acquisition is reciprocal to the parent's share of the subsidiary's stockholders' equity accounts. If the parent pays more than the book value for the subsidiary's stock, the excess is allocated to the subsidiary's net assets or identified as goodwill on the consolidated balance sheet. When a parent corporation purchases less than 100% of the subsidiary's stock, the remaining stockholders' equity is identified as minority interest. The minority interest is reported on the consolidated balance sheet, usually preceding stockholders' equity.

In preparing consolidated income statements for a parent and its subsidiary, all amounts from intercompany transactions, such as management fees, are eliminated. Any intercompany sales of merchandise and any profit included in inventories are also eliminated.

Objective 8. Journalize the entries for international transactions.

When a U.S. company enters into a transaction with a company in a foreign country using a currency other than the dollar, an exchange rate is used to convert the foreign currency into dollars. The transaction is then recorded in dollars, similar to other transactions.

When foreign currency is received in payment of a receivable or when foreign currency is paid in payment of a payable, a foreign exchange gain or loss may be realized. Such a gain or loss will be realized if the foreign exchange rate changes between the initial recording of the transaction and the receipt or payment of the foreign currency. If a foreign transaction has not been completed by the end of the year, an adjusting entry to record any unrealized currency exchange gains or losses may need to be recorded.

Glossary of Key Terms

Consolidated statements. Financial statements resulting from combining parent and subsidiary company statements. **Objective 7**

Consolidation. The creation of a new corporation by the transfer of assets and liabilities from two or more existing corporations. **Objective 7**

Cost method. A method of accounting for an investment in common stock, by which the investor recognizes as income its share of cash dividends of the investee. **Objective 5**

Discontinued operations. The operations of a business segment that have been disposed of. **Objective 2**

Earnings per share (EPS). The profitability ratio of net income available to common shareholders to the number of common shares outstanding. **Objective 3**

Equity method. A method of accounting for investments in common stock, by which the investment account is adjusted for the investor's share of periodic net income and property dividends of the investee. **Objective 5**

Equity per share. The ratio of stockholders' equity to the related number of shares of stock outstanding. **Objective 6**

Equity securities. Preferred or common stock. **Objective 5**

Exchange rate. The rate at which one currency can be converted into another currency. **Objective 8**

Extraordinary items. Events or transactions that are unusual and infrequent. **Objective 2**

Merger. The combining of two corporations by the acquisition of the properties of one corporation by another, with the

dissolution of one of the corporations. **Objective 7**

Minority interest. The portion of a subsidiary corporation's capital stock that is not owned by the parent corporation. **Objective 7**

Parent company. The company owning a majority of the voting stock of another corporation. **Objective 7**

Pooling-of-interests method. A method of accounting for an affiliation of two corporations resulting from an exchange of voting stock of one corporation for substantially all the voting stock of the other corporation. **Objective 7**

Prior-period adjustments. Corrections of material errors related to a prior period or periods, excluded from the determination of net income. **Objective 4**

Purchase method. The accounting method employed when a parent company acquires a controlling share of the voting stock of a subsidiary other than by the exchange of voting common stock. **Objective 7**

Subsidiary company. The corporation that is controlled by a parent company. **Objective 7**

Taxable income. The base on which the amount of income tax is determined. **Objective 1**

Temporary differences. Differences between income before income tax and taxable income created by items that are recognized in one period for income statement purposes and in another period for tax purposes. Such differences reverse or turn around in later years. **Objective 1**

Self-Examination Questions
Answers at end of chapter.

1. During its first year of operations, a corporation elected to use the straight-line method of depreciation for financial reporting purposes and the sum-of-the-years-digits method in determining taxable income. If the income tax is 40% and the amount of depreciation expense is $60,000 under the straight-line method and $100,000 under the sum-of-the-years-digits method, what is the amount of income tax deferred to future years?
   A. $16,000   C. $40,000
   B. $24,000   D. $60,000

2. A material gain resulting from the condemnation of land for public use would be reported on the income statement as:
   A. an extraordinary item   C. revenue from sales
   B. an other income item   D. a change in estimate

3. An item treated as a prior-period adjustment should be reported in the financial statements as:
   A. an extraordinary item
   B. an other expense item
   C. an adjustment of the beginning balance of Retained Earnings
   D. a change in estimate

4. A corporation's balance sheet includes 10,000 outstanding shares of $8 cumulative preferred stock of $100 par; 100,000 outstanding shares of $20 par common stock; paid-in capital in excess of par—common stock of $100,000; and retained earnings of $540,000. If preferred dividends are three years in arrears and the preferred stock is entitled to dividends in arrears plus $110 per share in the event of liquidation, what is the equity per common share?
   A. $20.00   C. $23.00
   B. $22.20   D. $25.40

5. On July 9, 1995, a sale on account for $10,000 to a Mexican company was billed for 25,000,000 pesos. The exchange rate was $.0004 per peso on July 9 and $.0005 per peso on August 8, 1995, when the cash was received on account. Which of the following statements identifies the exchange gain or loss for the fiscal year ended December 31, 1995?
   A. Realized exchange loss, $2,500
   B. Realized exchange gain, $2,500
   C. Unrealized exchange loss, $2,500
   D. Unrealized exchange gain, $2,500

ILLUSTRATIVE PROBLEM

Selected data from the balance sheets of five corporations, identified by letter, are as follows:

A. Common stock, $10 par $ 1,500,000
   Paid-in capital in excess of par—common stock   200,000
   Retained earnings   100,000

B. Preferred $8 stock, $100 par $ 1,000,000
   Paid-in capital in excess of par—preferred stock   50,000
   Common stock, no par, 50,000 shares outstanding   1,250,000
   Deficit   300,000
   Preferred stock has prior claim to assets on liquidation to the extent of par.

C. Preferred 8% stock, $10 par $ 2,000,000
   Paid-in capital in excess of par—preferred stock   280,000
   Common stock, $15 par   3,750,000
   Retained earnings   450,000
   Preferred stock has prior claim to assets on liquidation to the extent of 110% of par.

D. Preferred 6% stock, $1,000 par $25,000,000
   Common stock, $50 par   4,000,000
   Paid-in capital in excess of par—common stock   260,000
   Retained earnings   1,800,000
   Dividends on preferred stock are in arrears for 2 years, including the dividend passed during the current year. Preferred stock is entitled to par plus unpaid cumulative dividends on liquidation to the extent of retained earnings.

E. Preferred $1 stock, $25 par $ 500,000
   Common stock, $8 par   2,000,000
   Deficit   170,000
   Dividends on preferred stock are in arrears for 4 years, including the dividend passed during the current year. Preferred stock is entitled to par plus unpaid cumulative dividends on liquidation, regardless of the availability of retained earnings.

Instructions

Calculate for each corporation the equity per share of each class of stock, presenting the total shareholders' equity allocated to each class and the number of shares outstanding.

Solution

Class of Stock	Total Equity Allocated	÷	Number of Shares	=	Equity per Share
A. Common	$1,800,000		150,000		$ 12.00
B. Preferred	1,000,000		10,000		100.00
Common	1,000,000*		50,000		20.00
*(50,000 + 1,250,000 − 300,000)					
C. Preferred	2,200,000**		200,000		11.00
Common	4,280,000		250,000		17.12
**(2,000,000 × 1.10)					
D. Preferred	26,800,000***		25,000		1,072.00
Common	4,260,000		80,000		53.25
***[25,000,000 + 2(1,500,000) − (3,000,000 − 1,800,000)]					
E. Preferred	580,000		20,000		29.00
Common	1,750,000****		250,000		7.00
****[2,000,000 − 170,000 − 4(20,000)]					

DISCUSSION QUESTIONS

1. A corporation has paid $250,000 of federal income tax during the year on the basis of its estimated income. What entry should be recorded as of the end of the year if it determines that (a) it owes an additional $20,000; (b) it overpaid its tax by $10,000?

2. The income before income tax reported on the income statement for the year is $790,000. Because of temporary differences between accounting and tax methods, the taxable income for the same year is $650,000. Assuming an income tax rate of 40%, determine (a) the amount of income tax to be deducted from the $790,000 on the income statement, (b) the amount of the actual income tax that should be paid for the year, and (c) the amount of the deferred income tax liability.

3. How would the amount of deferred income tax payable be reported in the balance sheet if (a) it is payable within one year and (b) it is payable beyond one year?

4. What two criteria must be met to classify an item as an extraordinary item on the income statement?

5. Indicate where the following should be reported in the financial statements, assuming that financial statements are presented only for the current year:
   a. Loss by a Florida citrus firm from crop damage caused by frost. Frost damage occurs one or two times on the average each decade.
   b. Loss on disposal of equipment considered to be obsolete.
   c. Uninsured loss on building due to hurricane damage. The firm was organized in 1920 and had not previously incurred hurricane damage.

6. Classify each of the following revenue and expense items as either (a) normally recurring or (b) extraordinary. Assume that the amount of each item is material.
   (1) Loss on sale of plant assets.
   (2) Interest income on notes receivable.
   (3) Uninsured flood loss. (Flood insurance is unavailable because of periodic flooding in the area.)
   (4) Salaries of corporate officers.
   (5) Gain on sale of land condemned for public use.
   (6) Uncollectible accounts expense.

7. During the current year, 20 acres of land that cost $100,000 were condemned for construction of an interstate highway. Assuming that an award of $140,000 in cash was received and that the applicable income tax on this transaction is 30%, how would this information be presented in the income statement?

8. If significant changes are made in the accounting principles applied from one period to the next, why should the effect of these changes be disclosed in the financial statements?

9. A corporation reports earnings per share of $9.50 for the most recent year and $7.00 for the preceding year. The $9.50 includes a $3.00 per share gain from a sale of the only investment owned since the business was organized in 1940. (a) Should the composition of the $9.50 be disclosed in the financial reports? (b) What is the earnings per share amount for the most recent year that is comparable to the $7.00 earnings per share of the preceding year? (c) On the basis of the limited information presented, would you conclude that operations had improved or declined?

10. Indicate how prior-period adjustments would be reported on the financial statements presented only for the current period.

11. a. What are two methods of accounting for long-term investments in stock?
    b. Under what caption are long-term investments in stock reported on the balance sheet?

12. Jones Inc. received a $.30 per share cash dividend on 5,000 shares of TCI Corporation common stock, which Jones Inc. carries as a long-term investment. (a) Assuming that Jones Inc. uses the cost method of accounting for its investment in TCI Corporation, what account would be credited for the receipt of the $1,500 dividend? (b) Assuming that Jones Inc. uses the equity method of accounting for its investment in TCI Corporation, what account would be credited for the receipt of the $1,500 dividend?

13. At the end of the current period, a corporation has 5,000 shares of preferred stock and 50,000 shares of common stock outstanding. Assuming that there are no preferred dividends in arrears, that the preferred stock is entitled to receive $56 per share on liquidation, and that total stockholders' equity is $1,750,000, determine the following amounts: (a) equity per share of preferred stock and (b) equity per share of common stock.

14. Differentiate between equity per share and market price per share of stock.

15. Common stock has a par of $10 per share, the current equity per share is $22.50, and the market price per share is $55. Suggest reasons for the comparatively high market price in relation to par and to equity per share.

16. What terms are applied to the following: (a) a corporation that is controlled by another corporation through ownership of a controlling interest in its stock; (b) a corporation that owns a controlling interest in the voting stock of another corporation; (c) a group of corporations related through stock ownership?

17. Which method of accounting for long-term investments in stock (cost or equity) should be used by the parent company in accounting for its investments in stock of subsidiaries?

18. What are the two methods by which a parent–subsidiary relationship may be established?

19. What are consolidated (financial) statements?

20. At the end of the fiscal year, the amount of notes receivable and notes payable reported on the respective balance sheets of a parent and its wholly owned subsidiary are as follows:

	Parent	Subsidiary
Notes receivable	$500,000	$75,000
Notes payable	175,000	70,000

If $50,000 of Subsidiary's notes receivable are owed by Parent, determine the amount of notes receivable and notes payable to be reported on the consolidated balance sheet.

21. Sales and purchases of merchandise by a parent corporation and its wholly owned subsidiary during the year were as follows:

	Parent	Subsidiary
Sales	$5,000,000	$975,000
Purchases	3,200,000	605,000

If $500,000 of the sales of Parent were made to Subsidiary, determine the amount of sales and purchases to be reported on the consolidated income statement.

22. P Company purchases for $10,000,000 the entire common stock of S Corporation. What accounts on S's balance sheet are reciprocal to the investment account on P's balance sheet?

23. Are the eliminations of the reciprocal accounts in consolidating the balance sheets of P and S in Question 22 recorded in the respective ledgers of the two companies? Explain.

24. Parent Corporation owns 90% of the outstanding common stock of Subsidiary Corporation, which has no preferred stock. (a) What is the term applied to the remaining 10% interest? (b) If the total stockholders' equity of Subsidiary Corporation is $750,000, what is the amount of Subsidiary's book equity allocable to outsiders? (c) Where is the amount determined in (b) reported on the consolidated balance sheet?

25. Can a U.S. company incur an exchange gain or loss because of fluctuations in the exchange rate if its transactions with foreign countries, involving receivables or payables, are executed in (a) dollars, (b) the foreign currency?

26. A U.S. company purchased merchandise for 20,000 francs on account from a French company. If the exchange rate was $.19 per franc on the date of purchase and $.18 per franc on the date of payment of the account, what was the amount of exchange gain or loss realized by the U.S. company?

27. What two conditions give rise to unrealized currency exchange gains and losses from sales and purchases on account that are to be settled in the foreign currency?

 28. An annual report of The Campbell Soup Company reported on its income statement $2.4 million as "equity in earnings of affiliates." Journalize the entry that Campbell would have made to record this equity in earnings of affiliates.

 29. The 1991 annual report of The Quaker Oats Company disclosed the discontinuance of its Fisher-Price operations. The estimated loss on disposal of the operations was $30 million, net of $20 million of tax benefits. Indicate how the loss from discontinued operations should be reported by The Quaker Oats Company on its income statement for the year ended June 30, 1991.

 30. Corporation X realized a material gain when its facilities at a designated floodway were acquired by the urban renewal agency. How should the gain be reported in the income statement?

Source: "Technical Hotline," *Journal of Accountancy* (June 1989), p. 32.

ETHICS DISCUSSION CASE

Marchant Company has recently begun selling merchandise to foreign customers. Roberta Douglas, the controller, has implemented a policy that requires all foreign transactions to be executed in U.S. dollars. In this way, Douglas transfers to the customers all risks of foreign transactions on sales to foreign markets.

Discuss whether Roberta Douglas's policy is ethical.

SHARPEN YOUR ►
COMMUNICATION SKILLS

WHAT DO YOU THINK

Federal income taxes are currently reported as an expense on the income statement, according to generally accepted accounting principles. Some accountants argue, however, that income taxes should be considered a distribution of income, similar to dividends, rather than an expense. Likewise, one could argue that interest should be considered a distribution of income to creditors rather than an expense. What do you think are some arguments for accounting for federal income taxes and interest as distributions of income rather than as expenses?

FINANCIAL ANALYSIS AND INTERPRETATION

Hershey Foods Corporation prepares consolidated financial statements that include foreign affiliates. Translation gains or losses related to the consolidation of net assets of foreign affiliates are reported in the Stockholders' Equity section of the balance sheet.

a. Determine Hershey Foods Corporation's basis for carrying investments in affiliate companies.

b. Determine the amount of intangibles (goodwill) resulting from business acquisitions as of December 31, 1992.

c. Determine the amount of the foreign currency translation adjustments for the year ended December 31, 1992. (Note: See the consolidated statements of Stockholders' Equity.)

EXERCISES

EXERCISE 13-1
INCOME TAX ENTRIES
Objective 1

Journalize the entries to record the following selected transactions of Anson Inc.:

Apr. 15. Paid the first installment of the estimated income tax for the current fiscal year ending December 31, $175,000. No entry had been made to record the liability.

June 15. Paid the second installment of $175,000.

Sep. 15. Paid the third installment of $175,000.

Dec. 31. Recorded the estimated income tax liability for the year just ended and the deferred income tax liability, based on the transactions above and the following data:

Income tax rate	40%
Income before income tax	$1,900,000
Taxable income according to tax return	1,775,000

Jan. 15. Paid the fourth installment of $185,000.

EXERCISE 13-2
EXTRAORDINARY ITEM
Objective 2

SHARPEN YOUR
COMMUNICATION SKILLS

A company received life insurance proceeds on the death of its president before the end of its fiscal year. It intends to report the amount in its income statement as an extraordinary item.

Would this be in conformity with generally accepted accounting principles? Discuss.

Source: "Technical Hotline," *Journal of Accountancy* (June 1989), p. 31.

EXERCISE 13-3
INCOME STATEMENT
Objective 2

On the basis of the following data for the current fiscal year ended September 30, prepare an income statement for Root Company, including an analysis of earnings per share in the form illustrated in this chapter. There were 50,000 shares of $20 par common stock outstanding throughout the year.

Administrative expenses	$ 46,250
Cost of merchandise sold	622,500
Cumulative effect on prior years of changing to a different depreciation method (increase in income)	70,000
Gain on condemnation of land (extraordinary item)	57,750
Income tax applicable to change in depreciation method	22,000
Income tax applicable to gain on condemnation of land	16,750
Income tax reduction applicable to loss from discontinued operations	22,500
Income tax applicable to ordinary income	108,000
Loss on discontinued operations	74,500
Sales	992,500
Selling expenses	74,750

EXERCISE 13-4
PRIOR-PERIOD ADJUSTMENT
Objective 4

C. C. Littler and Company reported the following results of transactions affecting retained earnings for the current year ended December 31, 1995:

Net income	$102,500
Dividends	60,000
Prior-period adjustment for understatement of merchandise inventory on December 31, 1994, net of applicable income tax of $9,000	11,000

Assuming that the retained earnings balance reported on the retained earnings statement as of December 31, 1994, was $212,500, prepare a retained earnings statement for the year ended December 31, 1995.

EXERCISE 13-5
EQUITY METHOD
Objective 5

REAL W●RLD FOCUS

The following note to the consolidated financial statements for The Goodyear Tire and Rubber Co. related to the principles of consolidation used in preparing the financial statements:

The Company's investments in 20% to 50% owned companies in which it has the ability to exercise significant influence over operating and financial policies are accounted for by the equity method. Accordingly, the Company's share of the earnings of these companies is included in consolidated net income.

▶ SHARPEN YOUR
COMMUNICATION SKILLS

Is it a requirement that Goodyear use the equity method in this situation? Explain.

EXERCISE 13-6
ENTRIES FOR INVESTMENT IN STOCK, RECEIPT OF DIVIDENDS, AND SALE OF SHARES
Objective 5

On February 10, Gregory Corporation acquired 500 shares of the 50,000 outstanding shares of Dawson Co. common stock at 52¾ plus commission and postage charges of $400. On August 3, a cash dividend of $3 per share and a 5% stock dividend were received. On October 15, 100 shares were sold at 55½, less commission and postage charges of $175. Journalize the entries to record (a) the purchase of the stock, (b) the receipt of dividends, and (c) the sale of the 100 shares.

EXERCISE 13-7
ENTRIES USING EQUITY METHOD FOR STOCK INVESTMENT
Objective 5

At a total cost of $1,500,000, Tower Corporation acquired 100,000 shares of Enviro-Systems Co. common stock as a long-term investment. Tower Corporation uses the equity method of accounting for this investment. Enviro-Systems Co. has 250,000 shares of common stock outstanding, including the shares acquired by Tower Corporation. Journalize the entries by Tower Corporation to record the following information:
a. Enviro-Systems Co. reports net income of $500,000 for the current period.
b. A cash dividend of $1 per common share is paid by Enviro-Systems Co. during the current period.

EXERCISE 13-8
EQUITY PER SHARE
Objective 6

The stockholders' equity accounts of DeViro Company at the end of the current fiscal year are as follows: Preferred $5 Stock, $50 par, $1,000,000; Common Stock, $25 par, $5,000,000; Paid-In Capital in Excess of Par—Common Stock, $200,000; Paid-In Capital in Excess of Par—Preferred Stock, $40,000; Retained Earnings, $860,000.
a. Calculate the equity per share of each class of stock, assuming that the preferred stock is entitled to receive $60 on liquidation.
b. Calculate the equity per share of each class of stock, assuming that the preferred stock is to receive $60 per share plus the dividends in arrears in the event of liquidation and that only the dividends for the current year are in arrears.

EXERCISE 13-9
EQUITY PER SHARE; LIQUIDATION AMOUNTS
Objective 6

The following items were listed in the Stockholders' Equity section of the balance sheet on June 30: Preferred stock, $50 par, $500,000; Common stock, $20 par, $1,500,000; Paid-in capital in excess of par—common stock, $150,000; Deficit, $250,000. On July 1, the board of directors voted to dissolve the corporation immediately. A short time later, after all noncash assets were sold and liabilities were paid, cash of $1,525,000 remained for distribution to stockholders.
a. Assuming that preferred stock is entitled to preference in liquidation of $55 per share, calculate the equity per share on June 30 of (1) preferred stock and (2) common stock.
b. Calculate the amount of the $1,525,000 that will be distributed for each share of (1) preferred stock and (2) common stock.

▶ SHARPEN YOUR
COMMUNICATION SKILLS

c. Explain the reason for the difference between the common stock equity per share on June 30 and the amount of the cash distribution per common share.

EXERCISE 13-10
ELIMINATIONS FOR CONSOLIDATED INCOME STATEMENT
Objective 7

For the current year ended June 30, the results of operations of Paley Corporation and its wholly owned subsidiary, Sims Enterprises, are as follows:

	Paley Corporation		Sims Enterprises	
Sales		$950,000		$400,000
Cost of merchandise sold	$625,000		$240,000	
Selling expenses	155,000		55,000	
Administrative expenses	85,000		35,000	
Interest expense (income)	(12,000)	853,000	12,000	342,000
Net income		$ 97,000		$ 58,000

During the year, Paley sold merchandise to Sims for $75,000. The merchandise was sold by Sims to nonaffiliated companies for $100,000. Paley's interest income was realized from a long-term loan to Sims.

Determine: (1) the amounts to be eliminated from the following items in preparing a consolidated income statement for the current year: (a) sales and (b) cost of merchandise sold and (2) the consolidated net income.

EXERCISE 13-11
ENTRIES FOR SALES MADE
IN FOREIGN CURRENCY
Objective 8

Robb Company makes sales on account to several Swedish companies that it bills in kronas. Journalize the entries for the following selected transactions completed during the current year assuming that Robb uses the perpetual inventory system:

Feb. 2. Sold merchandise on account, 10,000 kronas; exchange rate, $.16 per krona. The cost of merchandise sold was $1,200.
Mar. 4. Received cash from sale of February 2, 10,000 kronas; exchange rate, $.17 per krona.
May 30. Sold merchandise on account, 12,000 kronas; exchange rate, $.17 per krona. The cost of merchandise sold was $1,500..
June 30. Received cash from sale of May 30, 12,000 kronas; exchange rate, $.16 per krona.

EXERCISE 13-12
ENTRIES FOR PURCHASES
MADE IN FOREIGN
CURRENCY
Objective 8

Holzer Company purchases merchandise from a German company that requires payment in deutsche marks. Journalize the entries for the following selected transactions completed during the current year assuming Holzer uses the perpetual inventory system:

June 10. Purchased merchandise on account, net 30, 5,000 deutsche marks; exchange rate, $.58 per deutsche mark.
July 10. Paid invoice of June 10; exchange rate, $.59 per deutsche mark.
Sep. 1. Purchased merchandise on account, net 30, 4,000 deutsche marks; exchange rate, $.59 per deutsche mark.
Oct. 1. Paid invoice of September 1; exchange rate, $.57 per deutsche mark.

WhAT'S WRONG WITH THi2?

How many errors can you find in the following balance sheet?

Simpson Inc. and Subsidiaries
Consolidated Balance Sheet
January 31, 19—

Assets

Current assets:		
Cash		$ 127,500
Investment in bonds of Fox Company		100,000
Accounts and notes receivable	$ 360,000	
Less allowance for doubtful receivables	18,500	341,500
Inventories, at lower of cost (first-in, first-out) or market		460,750
Prepaid expenses		20,000
Unamortized discount on bonds payable		15,000
Total current assets		$1,064,750
Investments:		
Bond sinking fund		$ 210,500
Marketable securities, at lower of cost or market (cost, $80,000)		76,250
Total investments		286,750

	Cost	Accumulated Depreciation	Book Value	
Plant assets:				
Goodwill	$ 400,000		$ 400,000	
Buildings	500,000	$ 190,600	309,400	
Machinery and equipment	1,382,200	583,100	799,100	
Total plant assets	$2,282,200	$ 773,700		1,508,500
Intangible assets:				
Land			$ 150,000	
Goodwill			100,000	
Total intangible assets				250,000
Total assets				$3,110,000

Liabilities

Current liabilities:		
Accounts payable	$ 250,000	
Income tax payable	60,250	
Accrued liabilities	40,750	
Deferred income tax payable	5,000	
Total current liabilities		$ 356,000
Long-term liabilities:		
Debenture 10% bonds payable, due January 31, 2001	$ 500,000	
Minority interest in subsidiaries	57,500	
Total long-term liabilities		557,500
Deferred credits:		
Deferred income tax payable		40,000
Total liabilities		$ 953,500

Stockholders' Equity

Paid-in capital:			
Common stock, $10 par (500,000 shares authorized, 100,000 shares issued)		$1,000,000	
Excess of issue price over par—common stock		160,000	
Total paid-in capital			$1,160,000
Retained earnings:			
Appropriated:			
For bonded indebtedness	$500,000		
For plant expansion	250,000	$ 750,000	
Unappropriated		234,000	
Total retained earnings		984,000	
Cash dividends payable		12,500	
Total stockholders' equity			2,156,500
Total liabilities and stockholders' equity			$3,110,000

PROBLEMS

Series A

PROBLEM 13-1A
INCOME TAX ALLOCATION
Objective 1

Differences between the accounting methods applied to accounts and financial reports and those used in determining taxable income yielded the following amounts for the first four years of a corporation's operations:

	First Year	Second Year	Third Year	Fourth Year
Income before income tax	$236,250	$337,500	$506,250	$549,000
Taxable income	168,750	292,500	483,750	582,750

The income tax rate for each of the four years was 40% of taxable income, and each year's taxes were promptly paid.

SPREADSHEET
PROBLEM

Instructions

1. Determine for each year the amounts described in the following columnar captions, presenting the information in the form indicated:

Year	Income Tax Deducted on Income Statement	Income Tax Payments for the Year	Deferred Income Tax Payable	
			Year's Addition (Deduction)	Year-End Balance

2. Total the first three amount columns.

PROBLEM 13-2A
INCOME TAX; INCOME
STATEMENT
Objectives 1, 2

The following data were selected from the records of A. P. Ryan Inc. for the current fiscal year ended December 31:

Advertising expense	$ 27,250
Cost of merchandise sold	600
Delivery expense	19,750
Depreciation expense—office equipment	5,200
Depreciation expense—store equipment	9,000
Gain on condemnation of land	20,000
Income tax:	
Applicable to continuing operations	35,000
Applicable to loss from disposal of a segment of the business (reduction)	8,200
Applicable to gain on condemnation of land	4,000
Insurance expense	9,000
Interest expense	25,200
Loss from disposal of a segment of the business	40,200
Miscellaneous administrative expense	4,550
Miscellaneous selling expense	8,600
Office salaries expense	42,750
Office supplies expense	1,700
Rent expense	21,000
Sales	997,500
Sales commissions expense	53,500
Sales salaries expense	42,500
Store supplies expense	7,500

SPREADSHEET
PROBLEM

Instructions

Prepare a multiple-step income statement, concluding with a section for earnings per share in the form illustrated in this chapter. There were 25,000 shares of common stock (no preferred) outstanding throughout the year. Assume that the gain on condemnation of land is an extraordinary item.

PROBLEM 13-3A
ENTRIES FOR INVESTMENTS
IN STOCK
Objective 5

The following transactions relate to certain securities acquired by Hidy Company, whose fiscal year ends on December 31:

1993

Feb. 11. Purchased 1,000 shares of the 25,000 outstanding common shares of Huston Corporation at 35 plus commission and other costs of $175.

June 5. Received the regular cash dividend of $1 a share on Huston Corporation stock.

Dec. 5. Received the regular cash dividend of $1 a share plus an extra dividend of $.25 a share on Huston Corporation stock.

(Assume that all intervening transactions have been recorded properly and that the number of shares of stock owned have not changed from December 31, 1993, to December 31, 1997.)

1998

June 7. Received the regular cash dividend of $1 a share and a 5% stock dividend on the Huston Corporation stock.

July 20. Sold 500 shares of Huston Corporation stock at 40. The broker deducted commission and other costs of $125, remitting the balance.

Dec. 9. Received a cash dividend at the new rate of $1.10 a share on the Huston Corporation stock.

Instructions

Journalize the entries for the preceding transactions.

PROBLEM 13-4A
EQUITY PER SHARE
Objective 6

Selected data from the balance sheets of six corporations, identified by letter, are as follows:

A. Common stock, $10 par $ 500,000
    Paid-in capital in excess of par—common stock   100,000
    Deficit   75,000

B. Preferred $2 stock, $25 par $ 500,000
    Common stock, $20 par   1,500,000
    Paid-in capital in excess of par—common stock   130,000
    Retained earnings   410,000
    Preferred stock has prior claim to assets on liquidation to the extent of par.

C. Preferred $9 stock, $100 par $1,000,000
    Paid-in capital in excess of par—preferred stock   50,000
    Common stock, no par,
       25,000 shares outstanding   1,250,000
    Deficit   200,000
    Preferred stock has prior claim to assets on liquidation to the extent of par.

D. Preferred 11% stock, $50 par $2,000,000
    Paid-in capital in excess of par—preferred stock   275,000
    Common stock, $25 par   3,750,000
    Retained earnings   450,000
    Preferred stock has prior claim to assets on liquidation to the extent of 110% of par.

E. Preferred 9% stock, $100 par $1,200,000
    Common stock, $50 par   4,000,000
    Paid-in capital in excess of par—common stock   340,000
    Retained earnings   108,000
    Dividends on preferred stock are in arrears for 2 years, including the dividend passed during the current year. Preferred stock is entitled to par plus unpaid cumulative dividends on liquidation to the extent of retained earnings.

F. Preferred $2 stock, $25 par $ 500,000
    Common stock, $10 par   2,000,000
    Deficit   170,000
    Dividends on preferred stock are in arrears for 3 years, including the dividend passed during the current year. Preferred stock is entitled to par plus unpaid cumulative dividends on liquidation, regardless of the availability of retained earnings.

Instructions

Calculate for each corporation the equity per share of each class of stock, presenting the total shareholders' equity allocated to each class and the number of shares outstanding.

PROBLEM 13-5A
ELIMINATIONS FOR
CONSOLIDATED BALANCE
SHEET AND INCOME
STATEMENT
Objective 7

On January 4 of the current year, Porter Corporation exchanged 30,000 shares of its $10 par common stock for 12,000 shares (the entire issue) of Strong Company's $25 par common stock. Strong purchased from Porter Corporation $125,000 of its $250,000 issue of bonds payable, at face amount. All the items for interest appearing on the balance sheets and income statements of both corporations are related to the bonds.

During the year, Porter Corporation sold merchandise with a cost of $138,000 to Strong Company for $230,000, all of which was sold by Strong Company before the end of the year.

Porter Corporation has correctly recorded the income and dividends reported for the year by Strong Company. Data for the income statements for both companies for the current year are as follows:

	Porter Corporation	Strong Company
Revenues:		
Sales	$1,600,000	$500,000
Income of subsidiary	110,000	—
Interest income	—	12,500
	$1,710,000	$512,500
Expenses:		
Cost of merchandise sold	$ 950,000	$280,000
Selling expenses	165,000	52,000
Administrative expenses	125,000	37,000
Interest expense	25,000	—
Income tax	195,000	33,500
	$1,460,000	$402,500
Net income	$ 250,000	$110,000

Data for the balance sheets of both companies as of the end of the current year are as follows:

	Porter Corporation	Strong Company
Assets		
Cash	$ 62,500	$ 27,050
Accounts receivable (net)	165,000	51,800
Dividends receivable	50,000	—
Interest receivable	—	6,250
Inventories	275,000	126,300
Investment in Strong Company (12,000 shares)	641,550	—
Investment in Porter Corp. bonds (at face amount)	—	125,000
Plant and equipment	1,150,000	496,950
Accumulated depreciation	(650,000)	(108,350)
	$1,694,050	$725,000
Liabilities and Stockholders' Equity		
Accounts payable	$ 75,200	$ 27,750
Income tax payable	20,510	5,700
Dividends payable	30,000	50,000
Interest payable	12,500	—
Bonds payable, 10% (due in 2006)	250,000	—
Common stock, $10 par	1,000,000	—
Common stock, $25 par	—	300,000
Paid-in capital in excess of par	100,000	50,000
Retained earnings	205,840	291,550
	$1,694,050	$725,000

Instructions

1. Determine the amounts to be eliminated from the following items in preparing the consolidated balance sheet as of December 31 of the current year: (a) dividends receivable and dividends payable; (b) interest receivable and interest payable; (c) investment in Strong Company and stockholders' equity; (d) investment in Porter Corporation bonds and bonds payable.
2. Determine the amounts to be eliminated from the following items in preparing the consolidated income statement for the current year ended December 31: (a) sales and cost of merchandise sold; (b) interest income and interest expense; (c) income of subsidiary and net income.
3. Determine the amount of the reduction in consolidated inventories, net income, and retained earnings if Strong Company's inventory had included $50,000 of the merchandise purchased from Porter Corporation.

PROBLEM 13-6A
FOREIGN CURRENCY
TRANSACTIONS
Objective 8

Benton Company sells merchandise to and purchases merchandise from various companies in Canada and the Philippines. These transactions are settled in the foreign currency. The following selected transactions were completed during the current fiscal year:

May 10.   Sold merchandise on account to Salas Company, net 30, 300,000 pesos; exchange rate, $.048 per Philippines peso. The cost of merchandise sold was $7,500.

June 9.   Received cash from Salas Company; exchange rate, $.047 per Philippines peso.

July 5.   Purchased merchandise on account from Mason Company, net 30, $5,000 Canadian; exchange rate, $.82 per Canadian dollar.

Aug. 4.   Issued check for amount owed to Mason Company; exchange rate, $.81 per Canadian dollar.

     31.   Sold merchandise on account to Marcos Company, net 30, 300,000 pesos; exchange rate, $.044 per Philippines peso. The cost of merchandise sold was $6,800.

Sep. 30.   Received cash from Marcos Company; exchange rate, $.046 per Philippines peso.

Oct. 10.   Purchased merchandise on account from Chevalier Company, net 30, $20,000 Canadian; exchange rate, $.83 per Canadian dollar.

Nov. 9.   Issued check for amount owed to Chevalier Company; exchange rate, $.84 per Canadian dollar.

Dec. 15.   Sold merchandise on account to Adams Company, net 30, $50,000 Canadian; exchange rate, $.85 per Canadian dollar. The cost of merchandise sold was $22,500.

     16.   Purchased merchandise on account from Santos Company, net 30, 250,000 pesos; exchange rate, $.047 per Philippines peso.

     31.   Recorded unrealized currency exchange gain and/or loss on transactions of December 15 and 16. Exchange rates on December 31: $.86 per Canadian dollar; $.048 per Philippines peso.

Instructions

1. Journalize the entries to record the transactions and adjusting entries for the year assuming Benton uses the perpetual inventory system.
2. Journalize the entries to record the payment of the December 16 purchase, on January 15, when the exchange rate was $.046 per Philippines peso, and the receipt of cash from the December 15 sale, on January 17, when the exchange rate was $.87 per Canadian dollar.

Instructions for Solving Problem 13-6A Using Solutions Software

1. Load opening balances.
2. Enter your name in the Student Name field in the General Information data entry window. Set the run date to December 31 of the current year.
3. Save the opening balances file to your drive and directory.
4. Select the General Journal Entries option, and key the journal entries. Leave the reference field blank. Note: To review the chart of accounts, select F-1.
5. Display a journal entries report.
6. Display a trial balance.
7. Key the adjusting entries, including the entries to record the exchange gains and losses. Key ADJ.ENT. in the reference field.
8. Display the adjusting entries. Key ADJ.ENT. in the Reference Restriction area of the Selection Options screen.
9. Display an income statement and a balance sheet.
10. Save a backup copy of your data file.
11. Perform period-end closing.
12. Display a post-closing trial balance.
13. Set the run date to January 31 of the following year.
14. Key the journal entries of January 15 and January 17.
15. Display a journal entries report.
16. Display a trial balance.
17. Save your data file to disk.
18. End the session.

Series B

PROBLEM 13-1B
INCOME TAX ALLOCATION
Objective 1

Differences between the accounting methods applied to accounts and financial reports and those used in determining taxable income yielded the following amounts for the first four years of a corporation's operations:

	First Year	Second Year	Third Year	Fourth Year
Income before income tax	$326,250	$416,250	$517,500	$495,000
Taxable income	270,000	382,500	528,750	540,000

The income tax rate for each of the four years was 40% of taxable income, and each year's taxes were promptly paid.

Instructions

1. Determine for each year the amounts described in the following columnar captions, presenting the information in the form indicated:

	Income Tax		Deferred Income Tax Payable	
Year	Deducted on Income Statement	Income Tax Payments for the Year	Year's Addition (Deduction)	Year-End Balance

2. Total the first three amount columns.

PROBLEM 13-2B
INCOME TAX; INCOME
STATEMENT
Objectives 1, 2

The following data were selected from the records of Cullen Inc. for the current fiscal year ended December 31:

Advertising expense	$ 22,500
Cost of merchandise sold	595,000
Delivery expense	10,400
Depreciation expense—office equipment	4,250
Depreciation expense—store equipment	11,500
Gain on condemnation of land	50,000
Income tax:	
Applicable to continuing operations	55,000
Applicable to loss from disposal of a segment of the business (reduction)	5,000
Applicable to gain on condemnation of land	15,000
Insurance expense	9,100
Interest income	13,700
Loss from disposal of a segment of the business	25,000
Miscellaneous administrative expense	2,800
Miscellaneous selling expense	3,500
Office salaries expense	46,000
Office supplies expense	1,750
Rent expense	30,000
Sales	987,500
Sales commissions expense	44,900
Sales salaries expense	56,900
Store supplies expense	2,600

Instructions

Prepare a multiple-step income statement, concluding with a section for earnings per share in the form illustrated in this chapter. There were 50,000 shares of common stock (no preferred) outstanding throughout the year. Assume that the gain on condemnation of land is an extraordinary item.

PROBLEM 13-3B
ENTRIES FOR INVESTMENTS
IN STOCK
Objective 5

The following transactions relate to certain securities acquired by Barnett Company, whose fiscal year ends on December 31:

1993
Feb. 20.   Purchased 1,000 shares of the 20,000 outstanding common shares of Stevens Corporation at 35 plus commission and other costs of $175.
May 15.   Received the regular cash dividend of $1 a share on Stevens Corporation stock.
Nov. 15.   Received the regular cash dividend of $1 a share plus an extra dividend of $.20 a share on Stevens Corporation stock.

(Assume that all intervening transactions have been recorded properly and that the number of shares of stock owned have not changed from December 31, 1993, to December 31, 1997.)

1998

May 20.   Received the regular cash dividend of $1 a share and a 5% stock dividend on the Stevens Corporation stock.

July 20.   Sold 500 shares of Stevens Corporation stock at 30. The broker deducted commission and other costs of $125, remitting the balance.

Nov. 18.   Received a cash dividend at the new rate of $1.10 a share on the Stevens Corporation stock.

Instructions

Journalize the entries for the preceding transactions.

PROBLEM 13-4B
EQUITY PER SHARE
Objective 6

Selected data from the balance sheets of six corporations, identified by letter, are as follows:

A. Common stock, no par, 50,000 shares outstanding $ 750,000
   Deficit   90,000

B. Preferred $2 stock, $25 par $ 750,000
   Common stock, $10 par   2,000,000
   Paid-in capital in excess of par—common stock   50,000
   Retained earnings   450,000
   Preferred stock has prior claim to assets on liquidation to the extent of par.

C. Preferred $12 stock, $100 par $ 500,000
   Paid-in capital in excess of par—preferred stock   30,000
   Common stock, $5 par   1,000,000
   Paid-in capital in excess of par—common stock   55,000
   Deficit   205,000
   Preferred stock has prior claim to assets on liquidation to the extent of par.

D. Preferred 10% stock, $100 par $ 750,000
   Paid-in capital in excess of par—preferred stock   100,000
   Common stock, $20 par   2,500,000
   Deficit   75,000
   Preferred stock has prior claim to assets on liquidation to the extent of 110% of par.

E. Preferred 11% stock, $100 par $ 800,000
   Common stock, $5 par   2,000,000
   Paid-in capital in excess of par—common stock   300,000
   Retained earnings   104,000
   Dividends on preferred stock are in arrears for 2 years, including the dividend passed during the current year. Preferred stock is entitled to par plus unpaid cumulative dividends on liquidation to the extent of retained earnings.

F. Preferred $2 stock, $25 par $ 500,000
   Paid-in capital in excess of par—preferred stock   10,000
   Common stock, $10 par   1,500,000
   Deficit   55,000
   Dividends on preferred stock are in arrears for 3 years, including the dividend passed during the current year. Preferred stock is entitled to par plus unpaid cumulative dividends on liquidation, regardless of the availability of retained earnings.

Instructions

Calculate for each corporation the equity per share of each class of stock, presenting the total shareholders' equity allocated to each class and the number of shares outstanding.

PROBLEM 13-5B
ELIMINATIONS FOR
CONSOLIDATED BALANCE
SHEET AND INCOME
STATEMENT
Objective 7

On January 1 of the current year, Parks Corporation exchanged 25,000 shares of its $10 par common stock for 50,000 shares (the entire issue) of Sota Company's $5 par common stock. Later in the year, Sota purchased from Parks Corporation $100,000 of its $200,000 issue of bonds payable, at face amount. All the items for interest appearing on the balance sheets and income statements of both corporations are related to the bonds.

During the year, Parks Corporation sold merchandise with a cost of $175,000 to Sota Company for $250,000, all of which was sold by Sota Company before the end of the year.

Parks Corporation has correctly recorded the income and dividends reported for the year by Sota Company. Data for the income statements for both companies for the current year are as follows:

	Parks Corporation	Sota Company
Revenues:		
Sales	$1,950,000	$575,000
Income of subsidiary	125,000	—
Interest income	—	3,125
	$2,075,000	$578,125
Expenses:		
Cost of merchandise sold	$1,219,600	$315,750
Selling expenses	185,000	62,275
Administrative expenses	135,000	37,000
Interest expense	12,500	—
Income tax	155,100	38,100
	$1,707,200	$453,125
Net income	$ 367,800	$125,000

Data for the balance sheets of both companies as of the end of the current year are as follows:

	Parks Corporation	Sota Company
Assets		
Cash	$ 66,200	$ 29,150
Accounts receivable (net)	108,400	70,800
Dividends receivable	12,500	—
Interest receivable	—	3,125
Inventories	549,550	199,000
Investment in Sota Company (50,000 shares)	505,800	—
Investment in Parks Corp. bonds (at face amount)	—	100,000
Plant and equipment	837,850	312,000
Accumulated depreciation	(230,300)	(164,075)
	$1,850,000	$550,000
Liabilities and Stockholders' Equity		
Accounts payable	$ 104,400	$ 26,100
Income tax payable	20,000	5,600
Dividends payable	20,000	12,500
Interest payable	6,250	—
Bonds payable, 12½% (due in 2009)	200,000	—
Common stock, $10 par	1,000,000	—
Common stock, $5 par	—	250,000
Paid-in capital in excess of par	40,000	80,000
Retained earnings	459,350	175,800
	$1,850,000	$550,000

Instructions

1. Determine the amounts to be eliminated from the following items in preparing the consolidated balance sheet as of December 31 of the current year: (a) dividends receivable and dividends payable; (b) interest receivable and interest payable; (c) investment in Sota Company and stockholders' equity; (d) investment in Parks Corporation bonds and bonds payable.
2. Determine the amounts to be eliminated from the following items in preparing the con-

solidated income statement for the current year ended December 31: (a) sales and cost of merchandise sold; (b) interest income and interest expense; (c) income of subsidiary and net income.

3. Determine the amount of the reduction in consolidated inventories, net income, and retained earnings if Sota Company's inventory had included $100,000 of the merchandise purchased from Parks Corporation.

PROBLEM 13-6B
FOREIGN CURRENCY
TRANSACTIONS
Objective 8

Lynn Company sells merchandise to and purchases merchandise from various Canadian and Japanese companies. These transactions are settled in the foreign currency. The following selected transactions were completed during the current fiscal year:

Jan. 20. Purchased merchandise on account from Ridge Company, net 30, $50,000 Canadian; exchange rate, $.84 per Canadian dollar.

Feb. 16. Issued check for amount owed to Ridge Company; exchange rate, $.86 per Canadian dollar.

Mar. 3. Sold merchandise on account to Niko Company, net 30, 500,000 yen; exchange rate, $.008 per Japanese yen. The cost of merchandise sold was $1,800.

Apr. 2. Received cash from Niko Company; exchange rate, $.009 per Japanese yen.

May 30. Purchased merchandise on account from Andrews Company, net 30, $30,000 Canadian; exchange rate, $.87 per Canadian dollar.

June 29. Issued check for amount owed to Andrews Company; exchange rate, $.86 per Canadian dollar.

July 3. Sold merchandise on account to Oh Company, net 30, 1,000,000 yen; exchange rate, $.0085 per Japanese yen. The cost of merchandise sold was $5,500.

Aug. 2. Received cash from Oh Company; exchange rate, $.007 per Japanese yen.

Dec. 6. Sold merchandise on account to Claude Company, net 45, $8,000 Canadian; exchange rate, $.85 per Canadian dollar. The cost of merchandise sold was $4,100.

    20. Purchased merchandise on account from Toko Company, net 30, 3,000,000 yen; exchange rate, $.006 per Japanese yen.

    31. Recorded unrealized currency exchange gain and/or loss on transactions of December 6 and 20. Exchange rates on December 31: $.83 per Canadian dollar; $.005 per Japanese yen.

Instructions

1. Journalize the entries to record the transactions and adjusting entries for the year assuming Lynn uses the perpetual inventory system.
2. Journalize the entries to record the payment of the December 20 purchase, on January 19, when the exchange rate was $.0055 per Japanese yen, and the receipt of cash from the December 6 sale, on January 20, when the exchange rate was $.82 per Canadian dollar.

**SOLUTIONS
SOFTWARE**

Instructions for Solving Problem 13-6B Using Solutions Software

1. Load opening balances.
2. Enter your name in the Student Name field in the General Information data entry window. Set the run date to December 31 of the current year.
3. Save the opening balances file to your drive and directory.
4. Select the General Journal Entries option, and key the journal entries. Leave the reference field blank. Note: To review the chart of accounts, select F-1.
5. Display a journal entries report.
6. Display a trial balance.
7. Key the adjusting entries, including the entries to record the exchange gains and losses. Key ADJ.ENT. in the reference field.
8. Display the adjusting entries. Key ADJ.ENT. in the Reference Restriction area of the Selection Options screen.
9. Display an income statement and a balance sheet.
10. Save a backup copy of your data file.
11. Perform period-end closing.
12. Display a post-closing trial balance.

13. Set the run date to January 31 of the following year.
14. Key the journal entries of January 19 and January 20.
15. Display a journal entries report.
16. Display a trial balance.
17. Save your data file to disk.
18. End the session.

MINI-CASE MAXINE MCNEAL

Your grandmother recently retired, sold her home in Chicago, and moved to a retirement community in Sarasota. With some of the proceeds from the sale of her home, she is considering investing $250,000 in the stock market.

In the process of selecting among alternative stock investments, your grandmother collected annual reports from twenty different companies. In reviewing these reports, however, she has become confused and has questions concerning several items that appear in the financial reports. She has asked for your help and has written down the following questions for you to answer:

a. *In reviewing the annual reports, I noticed many references to "consolidated financial statements." What are consolidated financial statements?*
b. *"Excess of cost of business acquired over related net assets" appears on the consolidated balance sheets in several annual reports. What does this mean? Is it an asset (it appears with other assets)?*

c. *What is minority interest?*
d. *A footnote to one of the consolidated statements indicated interest and the amount of a loan from one company to another had been eliminated. Is this good accounting? A loan is a loan. How can a company just eliminate a loan that hasn't been paid off?*
e. *How can financial statements for an American company (in dollars) be combined with a British subsidiary (in pounds)?"*

Instructions

1. ▪▪▪▪ ► Briefly respond to each of your grandmother's questions.
2. While discussing the items in (1) with your grandmother, she asked for your advice on whether she should limit her investment to one stock. What would you advise?

COMPREHENSIVE PROBLEM 4

Selected transactions completed by Walton Inc. during the fiscal year ending March 31, 1995, were as follows:

a. Issued 5,000 shares of $25 par common stock at $35, receiving cash.
b. Issued 5,000 shares of $100 par preferred 8% stock at $110, receiving cash.
c. Declared a dividend of $0.25 per share on common stock and $2 per share on preferred stock. On the date of record, 100,000 shares of common stock were outstanding, no treasury shares were held, and 15,000 shares of preferred stock were outstanding.
d. Paid the cash dividends declared in (c).
e. Redeemed $500,000 of 8-year, 13% bonds at 98. The balance in the bond discount account is $3,900 after the payment of interest and amortization of discount have been recorded. (Record only the redemption of the bonds payable.)
f. Transferred $500,000 of the appropriation for bonded indebtedness back to retained earnings for the bonds redeemed in (e).
g. Purchased 2,000 shares of treasury common stock at $40 per share.
h. Issued $1,000,000 of 10-year, 12% bonds at an effective interest rate of 10%, with interest payable semiannually.
i. Declared a 5% stock dividend on common stock and a $2 cash dividend per share on preferred stock. On the date of declaration, the market value of the common stock was $41 per share. On the date of record, 100,000 shares of common stock were outstanding, 2,000

shares of treasury common stock were held, and 15,000 shares of preferred stock were outstanding.

j. Issued the stock certificates for the stock dividends declared in (i) and paid the cash dividends to the preferred stockholders.

k. Sold, at $45 per share, 1,000 shares of treasury common stock purchased in (g).

l. Purchased 1,000 shares of Hanson Inc. common stock, which represented 5% of the outstanding shares, as a long-term investment. Paid 48 plus commission and other costs of $550.

m. Recorded the payment of semiannual interest on the bonds issued in (h) and the amortization of the premium for six months. The amortization was determined using the straight-line method. (Round the amortization to the nearest dollar.)

n. Deposited $20,000 in a bond sinking fund.

o. Appropriated $50,000 of retained earnings for bonded indebtedness.

p. Received dividends of $675 on the Hanson Inc. stock purchased in (l).

Instructions

1. Journalize the selected transactions.
2. After all the transactions for the year ended March 31, 1995, had been posted (including the transactions recorded in (1) and all adjusting entries), the following data were selected from the records of Walton Inc.:

Income statement data:

Advertising expense	$ 85,000
Cost of merchandise sold	4,000,000
Delivery expense	17,000
Depreciation expense—office equipment	13,100
Depreciation expense—store equipment	45,000
Dividend income	675
Gain on redemption of bonds	6,100
Income tax:	
Applicable to continuing operations	308,975
Applicable to loss from disposal of a	
segment of the business	21,100
Applicable to gain from redemption of bonds	1,150
Interest expense	68,500
Loss from disposal of a segment of the business	80,500
Miscellaneous administrative expenses	1,600
Miscellaneous selling expenses	6,300
Office rent expense	25,000
Office salaries expense	85,000
Office supplies expense	5,300
Sales	5,500,000
Sales commissions	95,000
Sales salaries expense	280,000
Store supplies expense	9,500

Retained earnings and balance sheet data:	
Accounts payable	$ 149,500
Accounts receivable	280,500
Accumulated depreciation—office equipment	835,250
Accumulated depreciation—store equipment	2,214,750
Allowance for doubtful accounts	11,500
Bond sinking fund cash	20,000
Bonds payable, 12%, due 2003	1,000,000
Cash	183,000

Common stock, $25 par (400,000 shares authorized; 104,900 shares outstanding)	2,622,500
Deferred income tax payable (current portion, $4,700)	25,700
Dividends:	
Cash dividends for common stock	$ 100,000
Cash dividends for preferred stock	110,000
Stock dividends for common stock	200,900
Dividends payable	25,000
Income tax payable	55,900
Investment in Hanson Inc. stock (long term)	48,550
Marketable securities at cost, held as a short-term investment (market value, $80,500)	77,500
Merchandise inventory (March 31, 1995), at lower of cost (fifo) or market	425,000
Office equipment	2,410,100
Paid-in capital from sale of treasury stock	5,000
Paid-in capital in excess of par—common stock	325,000
Paid-in capital in excess of par—preferred stock	240,000
Preferred 8% stock, $100 par (30,000 shares authorized; 15,000 shares issued)	1,500,000
Premium on bonds payable	118,400
Prepaid expenses	15,900
Retained earnings:	
Appropriated for bonded indebtedness (April 1, 1994)	500,000
Appropriated for bonded indebtedness (March 31, 1995)	50,000
Appropriated for treasury stock (April 1, 1994)	—
Appropriated for treasury stock (March 31, 1995)	40,000
Unappropriated, April 1, 1994	2,485,950
Store equipment	8,603,950
Treasury stock (1,000 shares of common stock at cost of $40 per share)	40,000

a. Prepare a multiple-step income statement for the year ended March 31, 1995, concluding with earnings per share. In computing earnings per share, assume that the average number of common shares outstanding was 100,000 and preferred dividends were $110,000. Round to nearest cent.

b. Prepare a retained earnings statement for the year ended March 31, 1995.

c. Prepare a balance sheet in report form as of March 31, 1995.

SOLUTIONS SOFTWARE

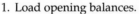

Instructions for Solving Comprehensive Problem 4 Using Solutions Software

1. Load opening balances.
2. Enter your name in the Student Name field in the General Information data entry window. Set the run date to March 31, 1995.
3. Save the opening balances file to your drive and directory.
4. Select the General Journal Entries option, and key the journal entries, including the adjusting entries for the amortization of premium on the bonds payable.
5. Display a journal entries report.
6. Display a trial balance.
7. Display the financial statements.
8. Save a backup copy of your data file.
9. Perform period-end closing.
10. Display a post-closing trial balance.
11. Save your data file to disk.
12. End the session.

ANSWERS TO SELF-EXAMINATION QUESTIONS

1. **A** The amount of income tax deferred to future years is $16,000 (answer A), determined as follows:

Depreciation expense, sum-of-the-years-digits method	$100,000
Depreciation expense, straight-line method	60,000
Excess expense in determination of taxable income	$ 40,000
Income tax rate	× 40%
Income tax deferred to future years	$ 16,000

2. **A** Events and transactions that are distinguished by their unusual nature and by the infrequency of their occurrence, such as a gain on condemnation of land for public use, are reported in the income statement as extraordinary items (answer A).

3. **C** The correction of a material error related to a prior period should be excluded from the determination of net income of the current period and reported as an adjustment of the balance of retained earnings at the beginning of the current period (answer C).

4. **C** The total stockholders' equity is determined as follows:

Preferred stock	$1,000,000
Common stock	2,000,000
Excess of issue price over par—common stock	100,000
Retained earnings	540,000
Total equity	$3,640,000

The amount allocated to common stock is determined as follows:

Total equity		$3,640,000
Allocated to preferred stock:		
Liquidation price	$1,100,000	
Dividends in arrears	240,000	1,340,000
Allocated to common stock		$2,300,000

The equity per common share is determined as follows:

$2,300,000 ÷ 100,000 shares = $23 per share

5. **B** The 25,000,000 pesos billed, which had a value of $10,000 (25,000,000 pesos × $.0004) on July 9, 1995, had increased in value to $12,500 (25,000,000 pesos × $.0005) on August 8, 1995, when payment was received. The gain, which was realized because the transaction was completed by the receipt of cash, was $2,500 (answer B).

You and Accounting

How much cash do you now have in the bank or in your wallet or purse? How much cash did you have at the beginning of this month? The difference between these two amounts is the net change in your cash during the month. Knowing the reasons for the change in cash may be useful in evaluating whether your financial position has improved and whether you will be able to pay your bills in the future.

For example, assume that you had $200 at the beginning of the month and $550 at the end of the month. The net change in cash is $350. Based on this net change, it appears that your financial position has improved. However, this conclusion may or may not be valid, depending upon how the change of $350 was created. If you *borrowed* $1,000 during the month and spent $650 on living expenses, your cash would have increased by $350. On the other hand, if you *earned* $1,000 and spent $650 on living expenses, your cash would have also increased by $350, but your financial position is improved compared to the first scenario.

To assess whether your financial position during a period has improved, it is useful to analyze individual cash transactions. These transactions can then be classified according to basic cash activities. In this chapter, you will be introduced to the statement of cash flows, which reports the results of such analyses for a business.

Chapter 14
Statement of
Cash Flows

LEARNING OBJECTIVES
After studying this chapter, you should be able to:

Objective 1
Explain why the statement of cash flows is one of the basic financial statements.

Objective 2
Summarize the types of cash flow activities reported in the statement of cash flows.

Objective 3
Prepare a statement of cash flows, using the indirect method.

Objective 4
Prepare a statement of cash flows, using the direct method.

The basic financial statements are the (1) income statement, (2) retained earnings statement, (3) balance sheet, and (4) statement of cash flows. In previous chapters, we used the first three statements and other information to analyze the effects of management decisions on an organization's revenues and costs. In this chapter, we will describe and illustrate the statement of cash flows. We will explain how to prepare it and how to interpret and use it.

PURPOSE OF THE STATEMENT OF CASH FLOWS

Objective 1
Explain why the statement of cash flows is one of the basic financial statements.

The **statement of cash flows** reports a firm's major cash inflows and outflows for a period.[1] It provides useful information about a firm's ability to generate cash from operations, maintain and expand its operating capacity, meet its financial obligations, and pay dividends.

The statement of cash flows is one of the basic financial statements.[2] It is useful to managers in evaluating past operations and in planning future investing and financing activities. It is useful to investors, creditors, and others in assessing the firm's profit potential. In addition, it provides a basis for assessing the ability of the firm to pay its maturing debt.

Focus on Cash Flow

In the past, investors have relied heavily on a company's earnings information in judging the company's performance. But this information may be misleading. As a result, more and more investors are focusing on cash flows, as described below.

Follow the money.

That's a guiding principle for . . . stock analysts and investors who study corporate cash flows. While none of them advocate using cash-flow analysis by itself, they say it can be an important tool in piercing the camouflage that sometimes makes reported earnings misleading.

As the term suggests, cash flow is basically a measure of the money flowing into—or out of—a business. If large companies were run, like lemonade stands, on a cash basis, earnings and cash flow would be identical.

Every major corporation, however, keeps its books on an accrual basis. . . . [This] can give a truer picture of corporate profitability, but sometimes it obscures important developments.

Take a company that spent $140 million on new machinery last year. If it depreciates the equipment over a seven-year period, it will be subtracting $20 million from reported profits each year.

But if the machines will stay up to date and useful for 25 years, the company's reported earnings may understate its true strength. . . .

Sometimes the reverse is true. If a company has been neglecting

capital spending, its earnings may look good. But on a cash-flow basis, it will look no better, perhaps worse, than its competitors.

In another article, analysts raised questions about the ability of McDonald's Corp. to continue its growth, given the rate at which McDonald's is consuming cash. Some of these concerns, which illustrate the importance of cash-flow analysis, are presented in the following excerpts:

[To raise cash] McDonald's started selling off more company-owned restaurants as domestic sales went softer. . . .

McDonald's received $131 million cash from sales of [300] restaurants. . . . That works out to an average of $436,000 per store—30% of the previous year's revenues of an average store. A longtime rule of thumb in the fast-food industry is that stores are sold for between 50% and 90% of revenues. . . .

One real surprise . . . is "the magnitude of cash McDonald's needs to consume every year to continue its earnings."

Through last year, the company plowed all of its operating cash flow into capital spending—meaning the business was consuming cash at least as fast as it was generating it. Faster, in fact. . . .

Last year, . . . cash flow from operations was $1.3 billion, while $1.1 billion was spent to build 641 new stores and another $500 million went for other capital expenditures. Add to that figure $133 million in dividends and $160 million to repurchase stock. . . .

[McDonald's] plans include a cut in capital spending to the level of increased operating cash flow this year. . . .

Sources: John R. Dorfman, "Stock Analysts Increase Focus on Cash Flow," *The Wall Street Journal* (February 17, 1987), Section 2, page 1; Dana Wechsler Linden, "R. McDonald, CPA," *Forbes* (September 16, 1991), p. 44.

REPORTING CASH FLOWS

Objective 2
Summarize the types of cash flow activities reported in the statement of cash flows.

The statement of cash flows reports cash flows by three types of activities:[3]

1. **Cash flows from operating activities** are cash flows from transactions that affect net income. Examples of such transactions include the purchase and sale of merchandise by a retailer.

2. **Cash flows from investing activities** are cash flows from transactions that affect the investments in noncurrent assets. Examples of such transactions include the sale and purchase of plant assets, such as equipment and buildings.

---

[1] As used in this chapter, cash refers to cash and cash equivalents. Examples of cash equivalents include marketable securities, certificates of deposit, U.S. Treasury bills, and money market funds.
[2] *Statement of Accounting Standards, No. 95*, "Statement of Cash Flows" (Stamford: Financial Accounting Standards Board, 1987).
[3] *Ibid.*

3. **Cash flows from financing activities** are cash flows from transactions that affect the equity and debt of the entity. Examples of such transactions include the issuance or retirement of equity and debt securities.

The cash flows from operating activities is normally presented first, followed by the cash flows from investing activities and financing activities. The total of the net cash flow from these activities is the net increase or decrease in cash for the period. The cash balance at the beginning of the period is added to the net increase or decrease in cash, and the cash balance at the end of the period is reported. The ending cash balance on the statement of cash flows equals the cash reported on the balance sheet.

Exhibit 1 shows common cash flow transactions reported in each of the three sections of the statement of cash flows. We can use the cash flows reported by operating, investing, and financing activities to identify significant relationships within and among the activities. For example, we can relate the cash receipts from issuing bonds to repayments of borrowings when both are reported as financing activities. Also, we can identify the impact of each of the three activities (operating, investing, and financing) on cash flows. This allows investors and creditors to evaluate the effects of cash flows on a firm's profits and ability to pay debt.

Exhibit 1
Cash Flows

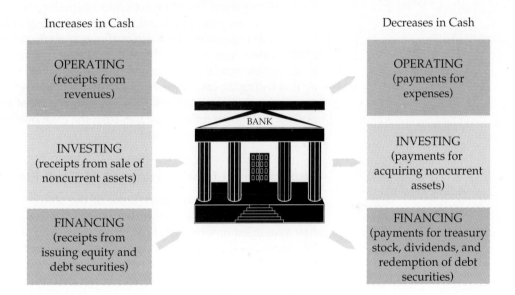

Cash Flows from Operating Activities

The most frequent and often the most important cash flows of an enterprise relate to operating activities. There are two alternative methods for reporting cash flows from operating activities in the statement of cash flows. These methods are (1) the direct method and (2) the indirect method.

The **direct method** reports the sources of operating cash and the uses of operating cash. The major source of operating cash is cash received from customers. The major uses of operating cash include cash paid to suppliers for merchandise and services and cash paid to employees for wages. The difference between these operating cash receipts and cash payments is the **net cash flow from operating activities.**

The primary advantage of the direct method is that it reports the sources and uses of cash in the statement of cash flows. Its primary disadvantage is that the necessary data may not be readily available and may be costly to gather.

The **indirect method** reports the operating cash flows by beginning with net income and adjusting it for revenues and expenses that do not involve the receipt or payment of cash. In other words, accrual net income is adjusted to determine the net amount of cash flows from operating activities.

A major advantage of the indirect method is that it focuses on the differences between net income and cash flows from operations. In this sense, it shows the relationship between the income statement, the balance sheet, and the statement of cash flows. Because the data are readily available, the indirect method is normally less costly to use than the direct method.

Cash Flows from Investing Activities

Cash inflows from investing activities normally arise from selling plant assets, investments, and intangible assets. Cash outflows normally include payments to acquire plant assets, investments, and intangible assets.

Cash flows from investing activities are reported on the statement of cash flows by first listing the cash inflows. The cash outflows are then presented. If the inflows are greater than the outflows, **net cash flow *provided* by investing activities** is reported. If the cash inflows are less than the cash outflows, **net cash flow *used* for investing activities** is reported.

Cash Flows from Financing Activities

Cash inflows from financing activities normally arise from issuing debt or equity securities. Examples of such inflows include issuing bonds, notes payable, and preferred and common stocks. Cash outflows from financing activities include paying cash dividends, repaying debt, and acquiring treasury stock.

Cash flows from financing activities are reported on the statement of cash flows by first listing the cash inflows. The cash outflows are then presented. If the inflows are greater than the outflows, **net cash flow *provided* by financing activities** is reported. If the cash inflows are less than the cash outflows, **net cash flow *used* for financing activities** is reported.

Illustrations of the Statement of Cash Flows

Exhibit 2 presents two illustrations of the statement of cash flows. Both statements are for the same accounting period for Computer King Corporation. The first statement reports cash flows from operating activities by the direct method. The second statement reports cash flows from operating activities by the indirect method. The same amount of net cash flow from operating activities is reported, regardless of the method. We will illustrate both methods in detail later in this chapter.

Exhibit 2
Statements of Cash Flows

Computer King Corporation Statement of Cash Flows—Direct Method For Month Ended November 30, 1994		
Cash flows from operating activities:		
Cash recieved from customers	$7,500	
Deduct cash payments for expenses and payment		
to creditors	4,600	
Net cash flow from operating activities		$ 2,900
Cash flows from investing activities:		
Cash payments for acquisition of land		(10,000)
Cash flows from financing activities:		
Cash received from sale of capital stock	$15,000	
Deduct cash dividends	2,000	
Net cash flow from financing activities		13,000
Net cash flow and November 30, 1994 cash balance		$ 5,900

Computer King Corporation
Statement of Cash Flows—Indirect Method
For Month Ended November 30, 1994

Cash flows from operating activities:		
Net income, per income statement	$ 3,050	
Add increase in accounts payable	400	
	$ 3,450	
Deduct increase in supplies	550	
Net cash flow from operating activities		$ 2,900
Cash flows from investing activities:		
Cash payments for acquisition of land		(10,000)
Cash flows from financing activities:		
Cash received from sale of capital stock	$15,000	
Deduct cash dividends	2,000	
Net cash flow from financing activities		13,000
Net cash flow and November 30, 1994 cash balance		$ 5,900

Noncash Investing and Financing Activities

An enterprise may enter into investing and financing activities that do not directly involve cash. For example, an enterprise may issue common stock to retire long-term debt. Such a transaction does not have a direct effect on cash. However, the transaction does eliminate the need for future cash payments to pay interest and retire the bonds. Thus, such transactions should be reported to readers of the financial statements because of their future effect on cash flows.

When noncash investing and financing transactions occur during a period, their effect is reported in a separate schedule. This schedule accompanies the statement of cash flows. Other examples of noncash investing and financing transactions include acquiring plant assets by issuing bonds or capital stock and issuing common stock in exchange for convertible preferred stock.

Cash Flow per Share

The term *cash flow per share* is sometimes reported in the financial press. Often, the term is used to mean "cash flow from operations per share." Such reporting may be misleading to users of the financial statements. For example, users might interpret cash flow per share as the amount available for dividends. This would not be the case if most of the cash generated by operations is required for repaying loans or for reinvesting in the business. Users might also think that cash flow per share is equivalent or perhaps superior to earnings per share. For these reasons, the financial statements, including the statement of cash flows, should not report cash flow per share.

STATEMENT OF CASH FLOWS—THE INDIRECT METHOD

Objective 3
Prepare a statement of cash flows, using the indirect method.

The indirect method of reporting cash flows from operating activities is normally less costly and more efficient than the direct method. In addition, when the direct method is used, the indirect method must also be used in preparing a supplemental reconciliation of net income with cash flows from operations. The 46th Edition (1992) of *Accounting Trends & Techniques* reported that 97% of the companies surveyed used the indirect method. For these reasons, the indirect method of preparing the statement of cash flows is discussed first.

To collect the data for the statement of cash flows, all the cash receipts and cash payments for a period could be analyzed and then reported by purpose (operating, investing, or financing). However, this procedure is expensive and time-consuming. A more efficient approach is to analyze the changes in the noncash balance sheet accounts. The logic of this approach is that a change in any balance sheet account (including cash) can be analyzed in terms of changes in the other balance sheet accounts. To illustrate, the accounting equation is rewritten below to focus on the cash account:

$$\text{Assets} = \text{Liabilities} + \text{Stockholders' Equity}$$
$$\text{Cash} + \text{Noncash Assets} = \text{Liabilities} + \text{Stockholders' Equity}$$
$$\text{Cash} = \text{Liabilities} + \text{Stockholders' Equity} - \text{Noncash Assets}$$

Any change in the cash account results in a change in one or more noncash balance sheet accounts. That is, if the cash account changes, then a liability, stockholders' equity, or noncash asset account must also change.

Additional explanatory data are also obtained by analyzing the income statement accounts and supporting records. For example, since the net income or net loss for the period is closed to Retained Earnings, a change in the retained earnings account can be partially explained by the net income or net loss reported on the income statement.

There is no order in which the noncash balance sheet accounts must be analyzed. However, it is usually more efficient to analyze the accounts in the reverse order in which they appear on the balance sheet. Thus, the analysis of retained earnings provides the starting point for determining the cash flows from operating activities, which is the first section of the statement of cash flows.

The comparative balance sheet for Rundell Inc. on December 31, 1995 and 1994, is used to illustrate the indirect method. This balance sheet is shown in Exhibit 3. Selected ledger accounts and other data are presented as needed.[4]

Exhibit 3
Comparative Balance Sheet

Rundell Inc.
Comparative Balance Sheet
December 31, 1995 and 1994

	1995	1994	Increase Decrease*
Assets			
Cash	$ 49,000	$ 26,000	$ 23,000
Trade receivables (net)	74,000	65,000	9,000
Inventories	172,000	180,000	8,000*
Prepaid expenses	4,000	3,000	1,000
Investments (long-term)	—	45,000	45,000*
Land	90,000	40,000	50,000
Building	200,000	200,000	—
Accumulated depreciation— building	(36,000)	(30,000)	(6,000)
Equipment	290,000	142,000	148,000
Accumulated depreciation—equipment	(43,000)	(40,000)	(3,000)
Total assets	$800,000	$631,000	$169,000
Liabilities			
Accounts payable (merchandise creditors)	$ 45,000	$ 28,200	$ 16,800
Accrued expenses (operating expenses)	5,000	3,800	1,200
Income tax payable	2,500	4,000	1,500*
Dividends payable	15,000	8,000	7,000
Bonds payable	120,000	245,000	125,000*
Total liabilities	$187,500	$289,000	$101,500*
Stockholders' Equity			
Preferred stock	$150,000	—	$150,000
Paid-in capital in excess of par—preferred stock	10,000	—	10,000
Common stock	280,000	$230,000	50,000
Retained earnings	172,500	112,000	60,500
Total stockholders' equity	$612,500	$342,000	$270,500
Total liabilities and stockholders' equity	$800,000	$631,000	$169,000

[4] An appendix that discusses using a work sheet as an aid in assembling data for the statement of cash flows is presented at the end of this chapter. This appendix illustrates a work sheet that can be used with the indirect method and a work sheet that can be used with the direct method of reporting cash flows from operating activities.

Retained Earnings

The comparative balance sheet for Rundell Inc. shows that retained earnings increased $60,500 during the year. Analyzing the entries posted to the retained earnings account indicates how this change occurred. The retained earnings account for Rundell Inc. is shown below.

ACCOUNT RETAINED EARNINGS   ACCOUNT NO.

Date		Item	Debit	Credit	Balance Debit	Balance Credit
1995						
Jan.	1	Balance				112,000
Dec.	31	Net income		90,500		
	31	Cash dividends	30,000			172,500

The retained earnings account must be carefully analyzed because some of the entries to retained earnings may not affect cash. For example, a decrease in retained earnings resulting from issuing a stock dividend does not affect cash. Likewise, an appropriation of retained earnings does not affect cash. Such transactions are not reported on the statement of cash flows.

For Rundell Inc., the retained earnings account indicates that the $60,500 change resulted from net income of $90,500 and cash dividends declared of $30,000. The effect of each of these items on cash flows is discussed below.

CASH FLOWS FROM OPERATING ACTIVITIES. The net income of $90,500 reported by Rundell Inc. normally is not equal to the amount of cash generated from operations during the period. This is because net income is determined using the accrual method of accounting.

Under the accrual method of accounting, there is often a difference between when revenues and expenses are recorded and when cash is received or paid. For example, merchandise may be sold on account and the cash received at a later date.

Likewise, insurance expense represents the amount of insurance expired during the period. The premiums for the insurance may have been paid in a prior period. Thus, the net income reported on the income statement must be adjusted in determining cash flows from operating activities. The typical adjustments to net income are summarized in Exhibit 4.

Exhibit 4
Adustments to Net Income—
Indirect Method

Net income, per income statement		$XX
Add: Depreciation of plant assets	$XX	
Amortization of bond payable discount and intangible assets	XX	
Decreases in current assets (receivables, inventories, prepaid expenses)	XX	
Increases in current liabilities (accounts and notes payable, accrued liabilities)	XX	
Losses on disposal of assets and retirement of debt	XX	XX
Deduct: Amortization of bond payable premium	$XX	
Increases in current assets (receivables, inventories, prepaid expenses)	XX	
Decreases in current liabilities (accounts and notes payable, accrued liabilities)	XX	
Gains on disposal of assets and retirement of debt	XX	XX
Net cash flow from operating activities		$XX

Some of the adjustment items in Exhibit 4 are for expenses that affect noncurrent accounts but not cash. For example, depreciation of plant assets and amortization of intangible asses are deducted from revenue but do not affect cash. Likewise, the amortization of premium on bonds payable decreases interest expense but does not affect cash.

Some of the adjustment items in Exhibit 4 are for revenues and expenses that affect current assets and current liabilities but not cash flows. For example, a sale of $10,000 on account increases accounts receivable by $10,000. However, cash is not affected. Thus, the increase in accounts receivable of $10,000 between two balance sheet dates is deducted from net income in arriving at cash flows from operating activities.

Cash flows from operating activities should not include investing or financing transactions. For example, assume that land costing $50,000 was sold for $90,000 (a gain of $40,000). The sale should be reported as an investing activity: "Cash receipts from the sale of land, $90,000." However, the $40,000 gain on the sale of the land is included in net income on the income statement. Thus, the $40,000 gain is *deducted from* net income in determining cash flows from operations in order to avoid "double counting" the cash flow from the gain. Losses from the sale of plant assets are *added to* net income in determining cash flows from operations. Likewise, losses on the retirement of debt are added to net income and gains are deducted from net income in determining cash flows from operating activities.

The effect of dividends payable on cash flows from operating activities is omitted from Exhibit 4. Dividends payable is omitted because dividends do not affect net income. Later in the chapter, we will discuss the reporting of dividends in the statement of cash flows.

In the following paragraphs, we will discuss the adjustment of Rundell Inc.'s net income to "Cash flows from operating activities."

DEPRECIATION. The comparative balance sheet in Exhibit 3 indicates that Accumulated Depreciation—Equipment increased by $3,000 and Accumulated Depreciation—Building by $6,000. As shown below, these two accounts indicate that depreciation for the year was $12,000 for the equipment and $6,000 for the building, or a total of $18,000.

ACCOUNT ACCUMULATED DEPRECIATION—EQUIPMENT ACCOUNT NO.

Date		Item	Debit	Credit	Balance Debit	Balance Credit
1995						
Jan.	1	Balance				40,000
May	9	Discarded, no salvage	9,000			
Dec.	31	Depreciation for year		12,000		43,000

ACCOUNT ACCUMULATED DEPRECIATION—BUILDING   ACCOUNT NO.

Date		Item	Debit	Credit	Balance Debit	Balance Credit
1995						
Jan.	1	Balance				30,000
Dec.	31	Depreciation for year		6,000		36,000

The $18,000 of depreciation expense reduced net income but did not require an outflow of cash. Thus, the $18,000 is added to net income in determining cash flows from operating activities, as follows:

Cash flows from operating activities:
Net income $90,500
Add: Depreciation   18,000 $108,500

CURRENT ASSETS AND CURRENT LIABILITIES. As shown in Exhibit 4, decreases in noncash current assets and increases in current liabilities are added to net income. In contrast, increases in noncash current assets and decreases in current liabilities are deducted from net income. The current asset and current liability accounts of Rundell Inc. are as follows:

	December 31		
			Increase
Accounts	*1995*	*1994*	*Decrease**
Trade receivables (net)	$ 74,000	$ 65,000	$ 9,000
Inventories	172,000	180,000	8,000*
Prepaid expenses	4,000	3,000	1,000
Accounts payable			
(merchandise creditors)	45,000	28,200	16,800
Accrued expenses			
(operating expenses)	5,000	3,800	1,200
Income taxes payable	2,500	4,000	1,500*

The $9,000 increase in **trade receivables** indicates that the sales on account during the year are $9,000 more than collections from customers on account. The amount reported as sales on the income statement therefore includes $9,000 that did not result in a cash inflow during the year. Thus, $9,000 is deducted from net income.

The $8,000 decrease in **inventories** indicates that the merchandise sold exceeds the cost of the merchandise purchased by $8,000. The amount deducted as cost of merchandise sold on the income statement therefore includes $8,000 that did not require a cash outflow during the year. Thus, $8,000 is added to net income. The $1,000 increase in prepaid expenses indicates that the cash payments for prepaid expenses exceed the amount deducted as an expense during the year by $1,000. Thus, $1,000 is deducted from net income.

The $16,800 increase in **accounts payable** indicates that the amount incurred during the year for merchandise purchased on account exceeds the cash payments made on account by $16,800. The amount reported on the income statement for cost of merchandise sold therefore includes $16,800 that did not require a cash outflow during the year. Thus, $16,800 is added to net income.

The $1,200 increase in **accrued expenses** indicates that the amount incurred during the year for operating expenses exceeds the cash payments by $1,200. The amount reported on the income statement for operating expenses therefore includes $1,200 that did not require a cash outflow during the year. Thus, $1,200 is added to net income.

The $1,500 decrease in **income taxes payable** indicates that the amount paid for taxes exceeds the amount owed during the year by $1,500. The amount reported on the income statement for income tax therefore is less than the amount paid by $1,500. Thus, $1,500 is deducted from net income.

The preceding adjustments to net income are summarized below.

Cash flows from operating activities:			
Net income		$ 90,500	
Add: Depreciation	$18,000		
Decrease in inventories	8,000		
Increase in accounts payable	16,800		
Increase in accrued expenses	1,200	44,000	
		$134,500	
Deduct: Increase in trade receivables	$ 9,000		
Increase in prepaid expenses	1,000		
Decrease in income taxes payable	1,500	11,500	$123,000

GAIN ON SALE OF INVESTMENTS. The ledger or income statement of Rundell Inc. indicates that the sale of investments resulted in a gain of $30,000. As we discussed previously, the sale proceeds, which include the gain and the carrying value of the investments, are included in cash flows from investing activities. The gain is also included in net income. Thus, to avoid double reporting, the gain of $30,000 is deducted from net income in determining cash flows from operating activities, as shown below.

Cash flows from operating activities:
Net income	$90,500
Deduct: Gain on sale of investments	30,000

REPORTING CASH FLOWS FROM OPERATING ACTIVITIES. All the necessary adjustments to convert the net income to cash flows from operating activities for Rundell Inc. have now been presented. These adjustments are summarized in Exhibit 5 in a format suitable for the statement of cash flows.

Exhbit 5
Cash Flows from Operating Activities—Indirect Method

Cash flows from operating activities:			
Net income, per income statement			$ 90,500
Add: Depreciation	$18,000		
Decrease in inventories	8,000		
Increase in accounts payable	16,800		
Increase in accrued expenses	1,200	44,000	
		$134,500	
Deduct: Increase in trade receivables	$ 9,000		
Increase in prepaid expenses	1,000		
Decrease in income taxes payable	1,500		
Gain on sale of investments	30,000	41,500	
Net cash flow from operating activities			$93,000

Using Accounting

The Chief Financial Officer (CFO) of Honeywell Corporation put all managers through a financial training course in order to help them think about the cash implications of their decisions. The CEO wanted his managers to understand how cash can be tied up in such things as receivables and inventory, and that growth can be achieved with significant working capital requirements on the front end. As a result, Honeywell generated cash by reducing its working capital needs from $2.2 billion to $1.6 billion.

CASH FLOWS USED FOR PAYMENT OF DIVIDENDS. According to the retained earnings account of Rundell Inc., shown earlier in the chapter, cash dividends of $30,000 were declared during the year. However, the dividends payable account, shown below, indicates that dividends of only $23,000 were paid during the year.

ACCOUNT DIVIDENDS PAYABLE   ACCOUNT NO.

Date		Item	Debit	Credit	Balance Debit	Balance Credit
1995						
Jan.	1	Balance				8,000
Jan.	10	Cash paid	8,000		—	—
June	20	Dividend declared		15,000		15,000
July	10	Cash paid	15,000		—	—
Dec.	20	Dividend declared		15,000		15,000

The $23,000 of dividend payments represent a cash outflow that is reported in the financing activities section as follows:

Cash flows from financing activities:
Cash paid for dividends	$23,000

Common Stock

The common stock account increased by $50,000 as shown below. This increase results from issuing stock in exchange for land valued at $50,000.

ACCOUNT COMMON STOCK   ACCOUNT NO.

Date		Item	Debit	Credit	Balance Debit	Balance Credit
1995						
Jan.	1	Balance				230,000
Dec.	28	Issued at par in exchange for land		50,000		280,000

Although no inflow or outflow of cash occurred, the transaction represents a significant investing and financing activity. Such transactions, as discussed previously, are reported in a separate schedule accompanying the statement of cash flows. In this schedule, the transaction is reported as follows:

Noncash investing and financing activities:
    Acquisition of land by issuance of common stock $50,000

Preferred Stock

The preferred stock account increased by $150,000, and the paid-in capital in excess of par—preferred stock account increased by $10,000, as shown below. These increases result from issuing preferred stock for $160,000.

ACCOUNT PREFERRED STOCK   ACCOUNT NO.

Date		Item	Debit	Credit	Balance Debit	Balance Credit
1995						
Nov.	1	30,000 shares issued for cash		150,000		150,000

PAID-IN CAPITAL IN EXCESS OF PAR—
ACCOUNT PREFERRED STOCK   ACCOUNT NO.

Date		Item	Debit	Credit	Balance Debit	Balance Credit
1995						
Nov.	1	30,000 shares issued for cash		10,000		10,000

This cash inflow is reported in the financing activities section as follows:

Cash flows from financing activities:
    Cash received from sale of preferred stock $160,000

Bonds Payable

The bonds payable account decreased by $125,000, as shown below. This decrease results from retiring the bonds by a cash payment for their face value.

ACCOUNT BONDS PAYABLE   ACCOUNT NO.

Date		Item	Debit	Credit	Balance Debit	Balance Credit
1995						
Jan.	1	Balance				245,000
June	30	Retired by payment of cash at face amount		125,000		120,000

This cash outflow is reported in the financing activities section as follows:

Cash flows from financing activities:
    Cash paid to retire bonds payable $125,000

Equipment

The equipment account increased by $148,000, and the accumulated depreciation—equipment account increased by $3,000, as shown below.

ACCOUNT EQUIPMENT   ACCOUNT NO.

Date		Item	Debit	Credit	Balance Debit	Balance Credit
1995						
Jan.	1	Balance			142,000	
May	9	Discarded, no salvage		9,000	—	—
Dec.	7	Purchased for cash	157,000		290,000	

ACCOUNT ACCUMULATED DEPRECIATION—EQUIPMENT ACCOUNT NO.

Date		Item	Debit	Credit	Balance Debit	Balance Credit
1995						
Jan.	1	Balance				40,000
May	9	Discarded, no salvage	9,000		—	—
Dec.	7	Depreciation for the year		12,000		43,000

The $148,000 increase in the equipment account resulted from two separate transactions. The first transaction is the discarding of equipment with a cost of $9,000. The credit of $9,000 in the equipment account and the debit of $9,000 in the accumulated depreciation—equipment account indicate that the discarded equipment was fully depreciated. In addition, the memorandum entry in the accounts indicates that no salvage was realized from the disposal of the equipment. Thus, the first transaction of discarding the equipment did not affect cash and is not reported on the statement of cash flows.

The second transaction is the purchase of equipment for cash of $157,000. This transaction is reported as an outflow of cash in the investing activities section, as follows:

Cash flows from investing activities:
   Cash paid for purchase of equipment $157,000

The credit of $12,000 in the accumulated depreciation account represents depreciation expense for the year. This depreciation expense of $12,000 on the equipment has already been considered as an addition to net income in determining cash flows from operating activities, as reported in Exhibit 5.

Building

The comparative balance sheet in Exhibit 3 indicates no change in buildings during the year. Also, the ledger indicates that no entries were made to the building account during the year. For this reason, the account is not shown.

The credit in the accumulated depreciation—building account, shown earlier, represents depreciation expense for the year. This depreciation expense of $6,000 on the building has already been considered as an addition to net income in determining cash flows from operating activities, as reported in Exhibit 5.

Land

The land account increased by $50,000 as shown below. This increase results from acquiring the land by issuing common stock at par.

ACCOUNT LAND   ACCOUNT NO.

Date		Item	Debit	Credit	Balance Debit	Balance Credit
1995						
Jan.	1	Balance			40,000	
Dec.	28	Acquired by issuing common stock at par	50,000		90,000	

Although no inflow or outflow of cash occurred, the transaction represents a significant investing and financing activity. Such transactions, as discussed previously, are reported in a separate schedule accompanying the statement of cash flows. In this schedule, the transaction is reported as follows:

Noncash investing and financing activities:
    Acquisition of land by issuing common stock $50,000

Investments

The investments account decreased by $45,000 as shown below. This decrease results from selling the investments for $75,000 in cash.

ACCOUNT INVESTMENTS   ACCOUNT NO.

Date		Item	Debit	Credit	Balance Debit	Balance Credit
1995						
Jan.	1	Balance			45,000	
June	8	Sold for $75,000 cash		45,000	—	—

The $75,000 proceeds received from the sale of the investments is reported as a cash flow from investing activities, as follows:

Cash flows from investing activities:
    Cash received from sale of investments (includes $30,000 gain
        reported in net income) $75,000

The proceeds of $75,000 include the $30,000 gain on the sale of investments and the $45,000 carrying value of the investments. As shown in Exhibit 5, the $30,000 gain is also deducted from net income in the cash flows from operating activities section. This is necessary so that the $30,000 cash inflow related to the gain is not included twice as a cash inflow.

Preparing the Statement of Cash Flows

The statement of cash flows for Rundell Inc. is prepared from the data assembled and analyzed above, using the indirect method. Exhibit 6 shows the statement of cash flows prepared by Rundell Inc. The statement indicates that the cash position increased by $23,000 during the year. The most significant increase in net cash flows, $93,000, was from operating activities. The most significant use of cash, $82,000, was for investing activities.

Exhibit 6
Statement of Cash Flows—
Indirect Method

Rundell Inc.
Statement of Cash Flows
For Year Ended December 31, 1995

Cash flows from operating activities:			
Net income, per income statement		$ 90,500	
Add: Depreciation	$ 18,000		
Decrease in inventories	8,000		
Increase in accounts payable	16,800		
Increase in accrued expenses	1,200	44,000	
		$134,500	
Deduct: Increase in trade receivables	$ 9,000		
Increase in prepaid expenses	1,000		
Decrease in income taxes payable	1,500		
Gain on sale of investments	30,000	41,500	
Net cash flow from operating activities			$ 93,000
Cash flows from investing activities:			
Cash received from sale of investments		$ 75,000	
Less: Cash paid for purchase of equipment		157,000	
Net cash flow used for investing activities			(82,000)
Cash flows from financing activities:			
Cash received from sale of preferred stock		$160,000	
Less: Cash paid for dividends	$ 23,000		
Cash paid to retire bonds payable	125,000	148,000	
Net cash flow provided by financing activities			12,000
Increase in cash			$ 23,000
Cash at the beginning of the year			26,000
Cash at the end of the year			$ 49,000
Schedule of Noncash Investing and Financing Activities:			
Acquired land by issuing common stock			$50,000

STATEMENT OF CASH FLOWS—THE DIRECT METHOD

Objective 4
Prepare the statement of cash
flows, using the direct method.

As we discussed previously, the direct method and the indirect method will report the same amount of cash flows from operating activities. In addition, the manner of reporting cash flows from investing and financing activities is the same under both methods. The methods differ in how the cash flow from operating activities data are obtained, analyzed, and reported.

To illustrate how the data for cash flows from operating activities are obtained and analyzed under the direct method, we will use the comparative balance sheet and the income statement for Rundell Inc. In this way, we can compare the statement of cash flows under the direct method and the indirect method.

Exhibit 7 shows the changes in the current asset and liability account balances for Rundell Inc. The income statement in Exhibit 7 shows additional data for Rundell Inc.

Exhibit 7
Balance Sheet and Income
Statement Data for Direct Method

Accounts	December 31		
	1995	*1994*	*Increase Decrease**
Cash	$ 49,000	$ 26,000	$23,000
Trade receivables (net)	74,000	65,000	9,000
Inventories	172,000	180,000	8,000*
Prepaid expenses	4,000	3,000	1,000
Accounts payable (merchandise creditors)	45,000	28,200	16,800
Accrued expenses (operating expenses)	5,000	3,800	1,200
Income taxes payable	2,500	4,000	1,500*

Rundell Inc.
Income Statement
For Year Ended December 31, 1995

Sales		$960,000
Cost of merchandise sold		580,000
Gross profit		$380,000
Operating expenses:		
Depreciation expense	$ 18,000	
Other operating expenses	260,000	
Total operating expenses		278,000
Income from operations		$102,000
Other income:		
Gain on sale of investments	$ 30,000	
Other expense:		
Interest expense	14,000	16,000
Income before income tax		$118,000
Income tax		27,500
Net income		$90,500

The direct method reports cash flows from operating activities by major classes of operating cash receipts and operating cash payments. In the following paragraphs, we will describe and illustrate these classes. The difference between the major classes of total operating cash receipts and total operating cash payments is the net cash flow from operating activities.

Cash Received from Customers

The $960,000 of sales for Rundell Inc. is reported by using the accrual method. To determine the cash received from sales made to customers, the $960,000 must be adjusted. The adjustments necessary to convert the sales reported on the income statement to the cash received from customers is summarized below.

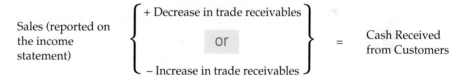

For Rundell Inc., the cash received from customers is $951,000, as shown below.

Sales	$960,000
Less increase in trade receivables	9,000
Cash received from customers	$951,000

The additions to **trade receivables** for sales on account during the year were $9,000 more than the amounts collected from customers on account. Sales reported on the income statement therefore included $9,000 that did not result in a cash inflow during the year. In other words, the increase of $9,000 in trade receivables during 1995 indicates that sales on account exceeded cash received from customers by $9,000. Thus, $9,000 is deducted from sales to determine the cash received from customers. The $951,000 of cash received from customers is reported in the cash flows from operating activities section of the cash flow statement.

Cash Payments for Merchandise

The $580,000 of cost of merchandise sold is reported on the income statement for Rundell Inc., using the accrual method. The adjustments necessary to convert the cost of merchandise sold to cash payments for merchandise made during 1995 are summarized below.

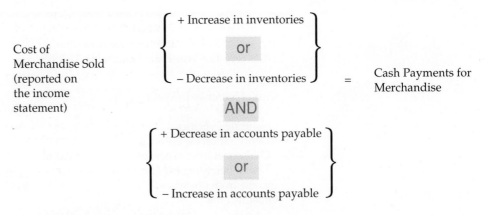

For Rundell Inc., the amount of cash payments for merchandise is $555,200, as determined below.

Cost of merchandise sold		$580,000
Deduct: Decrease in inventories	$ 8,000	
Increase in accounts payable	16,800	24,800
Cash payments for merchandise		$555,200

The $8,000 decrease in **inventories** indicates that the merchandise sold exceeded the cost of the merchandise purchased by $8,000. The amount reported on the income statement for cost of merchandise sold therefore includes $8,000 that did not require a cash outflow during the year. Thus, $8,000 is deducted from the cost of merchandise sold in determining the cash payments for merchandise.

The $16,800 increase in **accounts payable** (merchandise creditors) indicates that merchandise purchases include $16,800 for which there was no cash outflow (payment) during the year. In other words, the increase in accounts payable indicates that cash payments for merchandise were $16,800 less than the purchases on account during 1996. Thus, $16,800 is deducted from the cost of merchandise sold in determining the cash payments for merchandise.

Cash Payments for Operating Expenses

The $18,000 of depreciation expense reported on the income statement did not require a cash outflow. Thus, under the direct method, it is not reported on the statement of cash flows. The $260,000 reported for other operating expenses is adjusted to reflect the cash payments for operating expenses as summarized below.

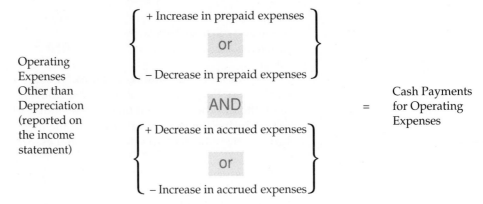

For Rundell Inc., the amount of cash payments for operating expenses is $259,800, determined as follows:

Operating expenses other than depreciation	$260,000
Add increase in prepaid expenses	1,000
	$261,000
Deduct increase in accrued expenses	1,200
Cash payments for operating expenses	$259,800

The cash outflow for **prepaid expenses** exceeded the amount deducted as an expense by $1,000 during the year. Hence, $1,000 is added to the amount of operating expenses (other than depreciation) reported on the income statement in determining the cash payments for operating expenses.

The increase in **accrued expenses** (operating expenses) indicates that operating expenses include $1,200 for which there was no cash outflow (payment) during the year. In other words, the increase in accrued expenses indicates that the cash payments for operating expenses were $1,200 less than the amount reported as an expense during the year. Thus, $1,200 is deducted from the operating expenses on the income statement in determining the cash payments for operating expenses.

Gain on Sale of Investments

The income statement for Rundell Inc. in Exhibit 7 reports a gain of $30,000 on the sale of investments. As we discussed previously, the gain is included in the proceeds from the sale of investments, which is reported as part of the cash flows from investing activities.

Interest Expense

The income statement for Rundell Inc. in Exhibit 7 reports interest expense of $14,000. The interest expense is related to the bonds payable that were outstanding during the year. We assume that interest on the bonds is paid on June 30 and December 31. Thus, $14,000 cash outflow for interest expense is reported on the statement of cash flows as an operating activity.

If interest payable had existed at the end of the year, the interest expense would be adjusted for any increase or decrease in interest payable from the beginning to the end of the year. That is, a decrease in interest payable would be added to and an increase in interest payable would be subtracted from interest expense. This is similar to the adjustment for changes in income taxes payable, which we will illustrate in the following paragraph.

Cash Payments for Income Taxes

The adjustment to convert the income tax reported on the income statement to the cash basis is summarized below.

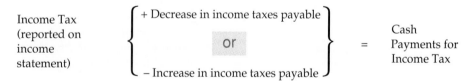

For Rundell Inc., cash payments for income tax are $29,000, determined as follows:

Income tax	$27,500
Add decrease in income taxes payable	1,500
Cash payments for income tax	$29,000

The cash outflow for **income taxes** exceeded the income tax deducted as an expense during the period by $1,500. Thus, $1,500 is added to the amount of income tax reported on the income statement in determining the cash payments for income tax.

Reporting Cash Flows from Operating Activities—Direct Method

Exhibit 8 is a complete statement of cash flows for Rundell Inc., using the direct method for reporting cash flow from operating activities. The portions of this statement that differ from the indirect method are highlighted in color. Exhibit 8 also includes the separate schedule reconciling net income and net cash flow from operating activities. As we mentioned earlier, this schedule must accompany the statement of cash flows when the direct method is used. This schedule is similar to the cash flows from operating activities section of the statement of cash flows prepared by using the indirect method.

Exhibit 8
Statement of Cash Flows—
Direct Method

Rundell Inc.
Statement of Cash Flows
For Year Ended December 31, 1995

Cash flows from operating activities:			
Cash received from customers		$951,000	
Deduct: Cash payments for merchandise	$555,200		
Cash payments for operating expenses	259,800		
Cash payments for interest	14,000		
Cash payments for income tax	29,000	858,000	
Net cash flow from operating activities			$ 93,000
Cash flows from investing activities:			
Cash received from sale of investments		$ 75,000	
Less: Cash paid for purchase of equipment		157,000	
Net cash flow used for investing activities			(82,000)
Cash flows from financing activities:			
Cash received from sale of preferred stock		$160,000	
Less: Cash paid for dividends	$ 23,000		
Cash paid to retire bonds payable	125,000	148,000	
Net cash flow provided by financing activities			12,000
Increase in cash			$ 23,000
Cash at the beginning of the year			26,000
Cash at the end of the year			$ 49,000
Schedule of Noncash Investing and Financing Activities:			
Acquired land by issuing common stock			$ 50,000
Schedule Reconciling Net Income with Cash Flows from Operating Activities:			
Net income, per income statement			$ 90,500
Add: Depreciation	$ 18,000		
Decrease in inventories	8,000		
Increase in accounts payable	16,800		
Increase in accrued expenses	1,200	44,000	
		$134,500	
Deduct: Increase in trade receivables	$ 9,000		
Increase in prepaid expenses	1,000		
Decrease in income taxes payable	1,500		
Gain on sale of investments	30,000	41,500	
Net cash flow from operating activities		$ 93,000	

APPENDIX

WORK SHEET FOR STATEMENT OF CASH FLOWS

Some accountants prefer to use a work sheet to assist them in assembling data for the statement of cash flows. Although a work sheet is not essential, it may be useful when a large number of transactions are to be analyzed. Whether or not a work sheet is used, the concepts of cash flow and the statements of cash flows presented in this chapter are not affected.

In this appendix, we will describe and illustrate the use of work sheets in preparing the statement of cash flows. We will discuss work sheets for both the indirect method and the direct method.

WORK SHEET—INDIRECT METHOD

The data for Rundell Inc., presented in Exhibit 3, are used as a basis for illustrating the work sheet for the indirect method. The procedures used in preparing this work sheet, shown in Exhibit 9, are outlined as follows:

1. List the title of each balance sheet account in the Accounts column. For each account, enter its balance as of December 31, 1994, in the first column, and its balance as of December 31, 1995, in the last column. Place the credit balances in parentheses. The column totals should equal zero, since the total of the debits in a column should equal the total of the credits in a column.

2. Analyze the change during the year in each account to determine the net increase (decrease) in cash and the cash flows from operating activities, investing activities, financing activities, and the noncash investing and financing activities. Show the effect of the change on cash flows by making entries in the Transactions columns.

Analyzing Accounts

As we discussed in this chapter, an efficient method of analyzing cash flows is to determine the type of cash flow activity that led to changes in balance sheet accounts during the period. As we analyze each noncash account, we will make entries on the work sheet for specific types of cash flow activities related to the noncash accounts. After we have analyzed all the noncash accounts, we will make an entry for the increase (decrease) in cash during the period. *These entries, however, are not posted to the ledger.* They only aid in assembling the data on the work sheet for use in preparing the statement of cash flows.

The order in which the accounts are analyzed is unimportant. However, it is more efficient to begin with the retained earnings account and proceed upward in the accounts listing.

RETAINED EARNINGS. The work sheet shows a Retained Earnings balance of $112,000 at December 31, 1994, and $172,500 at December 31, 1995. Thus, retained earnings increased $60,500 during the year. This increase resulted from two factors: (1) net income of $90,500 and (2) declaring cash dividends of $30,000. To identify the cash flows by activity, we will make two entries on the work sheet. These entries also serve to account for or explain, in terms of cash flows, the increase of $60,500.

In closing the accounts at the end of the year, the retained earnings account was credited for the net income of $90,500. The $90,500 is reported on the statement of cash flows as "cash flows from operating activities." The following entry is made in the Transactions columns on the work sheet. This entry (1) accounts for the credit portion of the closing entry (to Retained Earnings) and (2) identifies the cash flow in the bottom portion of the work sheet.

(a) Operating Activities—Net Income	90,500	
Retained Earnings		90,500

Exhibit 9
*Work Sheet for Statement of Cash
Flows—Indirect Method*

Rundell Inc.
Work Sheet for Statement of Cash Flows
For Year Ended December 31, 1995

Accounts	Balance, Dec. 31, 1994	Transactions Debit		Transactions Credit		Balance, Dec. 31, 1995
Cash	26,000	(s)	23,000			49,000
Trade Receivables	65,000	(r)	9,000			74,000
Inventories	180,000			(q)	8,000	172,000
Prepaid Expenses	3,000	(p)	1,000			4,000
Investments	45,000			(o)	45,000	—
Land	40,000	(n)	50,000			90,000
Building	200,000					200,000
Accumulated Depreciation—Building	(30,000)			(m)	6,000	(36,000)
Equipment	142,000	(l)	157,000	(k)	9,000	290,000
Accumulated Depreciation—Equipment	(40,000)	(k)	9,000	(j)	12,000	(43,000)
Accounts Payable	(28,200)			(h)	16,800	(45,000)
Accrued Expenses	(3,800)			(i)	1,200	(5,000)
Income Taxes Payable	(4,000)	(g)	1,500			(2,500)
Dividends Payable	(8,000)			(f)	7,000	(15,000)
Bonds Payable	(245,000)	(e)	125,000			(120,000)
Preferred Stock	—			(d)	150,000	(150,000)
Paid-In Capital in Excess of Par—Preferred Stock	—			(d)	10,000	(10,000)
Common Stock	(230,000)			(c)	50,000	(280,000)
Retained Earnings	(112,000)	(b)	30,000	(a)	90,500	(172,500)
Totals	0		405,500		405,500	0
Operating activities:						
Net Income		(a)	90,500			
Decrease in income taxes payable				(g)	1,500	
Increase in accounts payable		(h)	16,800			
Increase in accrued expenses		(i)	1,200			
Depreciation of equipment		(j)	12,000			
Depreciation of building		(m)	6,000			
Gain on sale of investments				(o)	30,000	
Increase in prepaid expenses				(p)	1,000	
Decrease in inventories		(q)	8,000			
Increase in trade receivables				(r)	9,000	
Investing activities:						
Purchased equipment				(l)	157,000	
Sold investments		(o)	75,000			
Financing activities:						
Declared cash dividends				(b)	30,000	
Issued preferred stock		(d)	160,000			
Retired bonds payable				(e)	125,000	
Increase in dividends payable		(f)	7,000			
Schedule of noncash investing and financing activities:						
Acquired land by issuing common stock		(c)	50,000	(n)	50,000	
Net increase in cash				(s)	23,000	
Totals			426,500		426,500	

In closing the accounts at the end of the year, the retained earnings account was debited for dividends declared of $30,000. The $30,000 is reported as a financing activity on the statement of cash flows. The following entry on the work sheet (1) accounts for the debit portion of the closing entry (to Retained Earnings) and (2) identifies the cash flow in the bottom portion of the work sheet.

| (b) Retained Earnings | 30,000 | |
| Financing Activities—Declared Cash Dividends | | 30,000 |

The $30,000 of declared dividends will be adjusted later for the actual amount of cash dividends paid during the year.

OTHER ACCOUNTS. We discussed in the chapter the analysis of the changes in the other accounts and their effect on cash flows and therefore will not repeat that discussion in this appendix. The related entries are made in the work sheet in a manner similar to entries (a) and (b). A summary of these entries is as follows:

(c)	Schedule of Noncash Investing and		
	Financing Activities—Acquired Land by Issuing Common Stock	50,000	
	Common Stock		50,000
(d)	Financing Activities—Issued Preferred Stock	160,000	
	Preferred Stock		150,000
	Paid-In Capital in Excess of Par—Preferred Stock		10,000
(e)	Bonds Payable	125,000	
	Financing Activities—Retired Bonds Payable		125,000
(f)	Financing Activities—Increase in Dividends Payable	7,000	
	Dividends Payable		7,000
(g)	Income Taxes Payable	1,500	
	Operating Activities—Decrease in Income Taxes Payable		1,500
(h)	Operating Activities—Increase in Accounts Payable	16,800	
	Accounts Payable		16,800
(i)	Operating Activities—Increase in Accrued Expenses	1,200	
	Accrued Expenses		1,200
(j)	Operating Activities—Depreciation of Equipment	12,000	
	Accumulated Depreciation—Equipment		12,000
(k)	Accumulated Depreciation—Equipment	9,000	
	Equipment		9,000
(l)	Equipment	157,000	
	Investing Activities—Purchase of Equipment		157,000
(m)	Operating Activities—Depreciation of Building	6,000	
	Accumulated Depreciation—Building		6,000
(n)	Land	50,000	
	Schedule of Noncash Investing and Financing Activities—Acquired Land by Issuing Common Stock		50,000
(o)	Investing Activities—Sale of Investments	75,000	
	Operating Activities—Gain on Sale of Investments		30,000
	Investments		45,000
(p)	Prepaid Expenses	1,000	
	Operating Activities—Increase in Prepaid Expenses		1,000
(q)	Operating Activities—Decrease in Inventories	8,000	
	Inventories		8,000
(r)	Trade Receivables	9,000	
	Operating Activities—Increase in Trade Receivables		9,000
(s)	Cash	23,000	
	Net Increase in Cash		23,000

Completing the Work Sheet

After we have analyzed all the balance sheet accounts and made the entries on the work sheet, all the operating, investing, and financing activities are identified in the bottom portion of the work sheet. The accuracy of the work sheet entries is verified by the equality of the totals of the debit and credit Transactions columns.

Preparing the Statement of Cash Flows

The statement of cash flows prepared from the work sheet is identical to the statement in Exhibit 6. The data for the three sections of the statement are obtained from the bottom portion of the work sheet. Some of these data may not be reported exactly as they appear in the work sheet. For example, in reporting the cash flows from operating activities, the total depreciation expense ($18,000) is reported instead of the two separate amounts ($12,000 and $6,000).

In the cash flows from operating activities section, the effect of depreciation is normally presented first. The effects of increases and decreases in current assets and current liabilities are then presented. The effects of any gains and losses on operating activities are normally reported last. The cash paid for dividends is reported as $23,000 instead of the amount of dividends declared ($30,000) less the increase in dividends payable ($7,000). The issuing of the common stock for land ($50,000) is reported in a separate schedule.

WORK SHEET—DIRECT METHOD

A work sheet can also be used as an aid in assembling data for preparing a statement of cash flows under the direct method. As a basis for illustration, we will use the balance sheet data for Rundell Inc. in Exhibit 3 and the income statement data in Exhibit 7. The procedures used in preparing the work sheet shown in Exhibit 10 are outlined as follows:

1. List the title of each asset account in the Accounts column. For each account, enter its balance as of December 31, 1994, in the first column, and its balance as of December 31, 1995, in the last column. Place the contra asset account balances (credit balances) in parentheses. Enter the amount of the total assets for December 31, 1994 and 1995, on the work sheet.
2. List the title of each liability and stockholders' equity account in the Accounts column. For each account, enter its balance as of December 31, 1994, in the first column, and its balance as of December 31, 1995, in the last column. Enter the total liabilities and stockholders' equity for December 31, 1994 and 1995, on the work sheet. The total assets and the total liabilities and stockholders' equity should be equal for each year.
3. List the title of each income statement account and "Net Income" on the work sheet.
4. Analyze the effect of each income statement item on cash flows from operating activities. Beginning with sales, enter the balance of each item in the proper Transactions column. Complete the entry in the Transactions columns to show the effect on cash flows.
5. Analyze the change during the year in each balance sheet account to determine the net increase (decrease) in cash and the cash flows from operating activities, investing activities, financing activities, and the noncash investing and financing activities. Show the effect of the change on cash flows by making entries in the Transactions columns.

Analyzing Accounts

Under the direct method of reporting cash flows from operating activities, analyzing accounts begins with the income statement. As we analyze each income statement account, we will make entries on the work sheet that show the effect on cash flows from operating activities. After we have analyzed the income statement accounts, we will analyze changes in the balance sheet accounts.

The order in which the balance sheet accounts are analyzed is unimportant. However, it is more efficient to begin with the retained earnings account and proceed upward in the account listing. As each noncash balance sheet account is analyzed, we will make entries on the work sheet for the related cash flow activities. After we have analyzed all the noncash accounts, we will make an entry for the increase (decrease) in cash during the period.

Exhibit 10   *Work Sheet for Statement of Cash Flows—Direct Method*

Rundell Inc.
Work Sheet for Statement of Cash Flows
For Year Ended December 31, 1995

Accounts	Balance, Dec. 31, 1994	Transactions Debit		Transactions Credit		Balance, Dec. 31, 1995
Balance Sheet						
Cash	26,000	(w)	23,000			49,000
Trade Receivables	65,000	(v)	9,000			74,000
Inventories	180,000			(u)	8,000	172,000
Prepaid Expenses	3,000	(t)	1,000			4,000
Investments	45,000			(e)	45,000	—
Land	40,000	(s)	50,000			90,000
Building	200,000					200,000
Accumulated Depreciation—Building	(30,000)			(c)	6,000	(36,000)
Equipment	142,000	(r)	157,000	(q)	9,000	290,000
Accumulated Depreciation—Equipment	(40,000)	(q)	9,000	(c)	12,000	(43,000)
Total Assets	631,000					800,000
Accounts Payable	28,200			(p)	16,800	45,000
Accrued Expenses	3,800			(o)	1,200	5,000
Income Taxes Payable	4,000	(n)	1,500			2,500
Dividends Payable	8,000			(m)	7,000	15,000
Bonds Payable	245,000	(l)	125,000			120,000
Preferred Stock	—			(k)	150,000	150,000
Paid-In Capital in Excess of Par—Preferred Stock	—			(k)	10,000	10,000
Common Stock	230,000			(j)	50,000	280,000
Retained Earnings	112,000	(i)	30,000	(h)	90,500	172,500
Total Liabilities and Stockholders' Equity	631,000					800,000
Income Statement						
Sales				(a)	960,000	
Cost of Merchandise Sold		(b)	580,000			
Depreciation Expense		(c)	18,000			
Other Operating Expenses		(d)	260,000			
Gain on Sales of Investments				(e)	30,000	
Interest Expense		(f)	14,000			
Income Taxes		(g)	27,500			
Net Income		(h)	90,500			
Cash Flows						
Operating activities:						
Cash received from customers		(a)	960,000	(v)	9,000	
Cash payments:						
Merchandise		(p)	16,800	(b)	580,000	
		(u)	8,000			
Operating expenses		(o)	1,200	(d)	260,000	
				(t)	1,000	
Interest expense				(f)	14,000	
Income taxes				(g)	27,500	
				(n)	1,500	
Investing activities:						
Sold investments		(e)	75,000			
Purchased equipment				(r)	157,000	
Financing activities:						
Declared cash dividends				(i)	30,000	
Issued preferred stock		(k)	160,000			
Retired bonds payable				(l)	125,000	
Increase in dividends payable		(m)	7,000			
Schedule of noncash investing & financing activities:						
Acquired land by issuing common stock		(j)	50,000	(s)	50,000	
Net increase in cash				(w)	23,000	
Totals			2,673,500		2,673,500	

SALES. The income statement for Rundell Inc. shows sales of $960,000 for the year. Sales for cash provide cash when the sale is made. Sales on account provide cash when customers pay their bills. The entry on the work sheet is as follows:

(a) Operating Activities—Receipts from Customers	960,000	
Sales		960,000

COST OF MERCHANDISE SOLD. The income statement for Rundell Inc. shows cost of merchandise sold of $580,000 for the year. The cost of merchandise sold requires cash payments for cash purchases of merchandise. For purchases on account, cash payments are made when the invoices are due. The entry on the work sheet is as follows:

(b) Cost of Merchandise Sold	580,000	
Operating Activities—Payments for Merchandise		580,000

DEPRECIATION EXPENSE. The income statement for Rundell Inc. shows depreciation expense of $18,000. Depreciation expense does not require a cash outflow and thus is not reported on the statement of cash flows. The entry on the work sheet to fully account for the depreciation expense is as follows:

(c) Depreciation Expense	18,000	
Accumulated Depreciation—Building		6,000
Accumulated Depreciation—Equipment		12,000

OTHER ACCOUNTS. We discussed in the chapter the analysis of the changes in the other accounts and their effect on cash flows and therefore will not repeat that discussion in this appendix. The related entries are made on the work sheet in a manner similar to entries (a), (b), and (c). A summary of these entries is as follows:

(d) Other Operating Expenses	260,000	
Operating Activities—Paid Operating Expenses		260,000
(e) Investing Activities—Sold Investments	75,000	
Investments		45,000
Gain on Sales of Investments		30,000
(f) Interest Expense	14,000	
Operating Activities—Paid Interest		14,000
(g) Income Taxes	27,500	
Operating Activities—Paid Income Taxes		27,500
(h) Net Income	90,500	
Retained Earnings		90,500
(i) Retained Earnings	30,000	
Financing Activities—Declared Cash Dividends		30,000
(j) Schedule of Noncash Investing and Financing Activities—Acquired Land by Issuing Common Stock	50,000	
Common Stock		50,000
(k) Financing Activities—Issued Preferred Stock	160,000	
Preferred Stock		150,000
Paid-In Capital in Excess of Par—Preferred Stock		10,000
(l) Bonds Payable	125,000	
Financing Activities—Retired Bonds Payable		125,000
(m) Financing Activities—Increase in Dividends Payable	7,000	
Dividends Payable		7,000
(n) Income Taxes Payable	1,500	
Operating Activities—Decrease in Income Taxes Payable		1,500
(o) Operating Activities—Cash Paid for Operating Expenses	1,200	
Accrued Expenses		1,200

(p)	Operating Activities—Cash Paid for Merchandise	16,800	
	Accounts Payable		16,800
(q)	Accumulated Depreciation—Equipment	9,000	
	Equipment		9,000
(r)	Equipment	157,000	
	Investing Activities—Purchased Equipment		157,000
(s)	Land	50,000	
	Schedule of Noncash Investing and Financing Activities—Acquired Land by Issuing Common Stock		50,000
(t)	Prepaid Expenses	1,000	
	Operating Activities—Cash Paid for Operating Expenses		1,000
(u)	Operating Activities—Cash Paid for Merchandise	8,000	
	Inventories		8,000
(v)	Trade Receivables	9,000	
	Operating Activities—Cash Received from Customers		9,000
(w)	Cash	23,000	
	Net Increase in Cash		23,000

Completing the Work Sheet

After we have analyzed all the income statement and balance sheet accounts and have made the entries on the work sheet, all the operating, investing, and financing activities are identified in the bottom portion of the work sheet. The mathematical accuracy of the work sheet entries is verified by the equality of the totals of the debit and credit Transactions columns.

Preparing the Statement of Cash Flows

The statement of cash flows prepared from the work sheet is identical to the statement in Exhibit 8. The data for the three sections of the statement are obtained from the bottom portion of the work sheet. Some of these data may not be reported exactly as they appear on the work sheet.

CHAPTER REVIEW

Key Points

Objective 1. Explain why the statement of cash flows is one of the basic financial statements.
The statement of cash flows is one of the basic financial statements because it reports useful information about a firm's ability to generate cash from operations, maintain and expand its operating capacity, meet its financial obligations, and pay dividends. This information assists investors, creditors, and others in assessing the firm's profit potential and its ability to pay its maturing debt. The statement of cash flows is also useful to managers in evaluating past operations and in planning future operating, investing, and financing activities.

Objective 2. Summarize the types of cash flow activities reported in the statement of cash flows.
The statement of cash flows reports cash receipts and cash payments by three types of activities: operating activities, investing activities, and financing activities.

Cash flows from operating activities are cash flows from transactions that affect net income. There are two methods of

reporting cash flows from operating activities: (1) the direct method and (2) the indirect method.

Cash inflows from investing activities are cash flows from the sale of investments, plant assets, and intangible assets. Cash outflows generally include payments to acquire investments, plant assets, and intangible assets.

Cash inflows from financing activities include proceeds from issuing equity securities, such as preferred and common stock. Cash inflows also arise from issuing bonds, mortgage notes payable, and other long-term debt. Cash outflows from financing activities arise from paying cash dividends, purchasing treasury stock, and repaying amounts borrowed.

Investing and financing for an enterprise may be affected by transactions that do not involve cash. The effect of such transactions should be reported in a separate schedule accompanying the statement of cash flows.

Because it may be misleading, cash flow per share is not reported in the statement of cash flows.

Objective 3. Prepare a statement of cash flows, using the indirect method.

To prepare the statement of cash flows, changes in the noncash balance sheet accounts are analyzed. This logic relies on the fact that a change in any balance sheet account can by ana-lyzed in terms of changes in the other balance sheet accounts. Thus, by analyzing the noncash balance sheet accounts, those activities that resulted in cash flows can be identified. Al-though the noncash balance sheet accounts may be analyzed in any order, it is usually more efficient to begin with retained earnings. Additional data are obtained by analyzing the in-come statement accounts and supporting records.

Preparing the statement of cash flows using the indirect method of reporting cash flows from operating activities is il-lustrated in this chapter.

Objective 4. Prepare a statement of cash flows, using the direct method.

The direct method and the indirect method will report the same amount of cash flows from operating activities. Also, the manner of reporting cash flows from investing and financing activities is the same under both methods. The methods differ in how the cash flow from operating activities data are ob-tained, analyzed, and reported. The direct method reports cash flows from operating activities by major classes of oper-ating cash receipts and cash payments. The difference be-tween the major classes of total operating cash receipts and to-tal operating cash payments is the net cash flow from operating activities.

The data for reporting cash flows from operating activities by the direct method can be obtained by analyzing the cash flows related to the revenues and expenses reported on the in-come statement. The revenues and expenses are adjusted from the accrual basis of accounting to the cash basis for purposes of preparing the statement of cash flows.

When the direct method is used, a reconciliation of net in-come and net cash flow from operating activities is reported in a separate schedule. This schedule is similar to the cash flows from operating activities section of the statement of cash flows prepared using the indirect method.

Preparing the statement of cash flows using the direct method is illustrated in this chapter.

Glossary of Key Terms

Cash flows from financing activities. The section of the state-ment of cash flows which reports cash flows from transac-tions that affect the equity and debt of the entity. **Objective 2**

Cash flows from investing activities. The section of the state-ment of cash flows which reports cash flows from transac-tions that affect investments in noncurrent assets. **Objec-tive 2**

Cash flows from operating activities. The section of the state-ment of cash flows which reports the cash transactions that affect the determination of net income. **Objective 2**

Direct method. A method of reporting the cash flows from op-erating activities as the difference between the operating cash receipts and the operating cash payments. **Objective 2**

Indirect method. A method of reporting the cash flows from operating activities as the net income from operations ad-justed for all deferrals of past cash receipts and payments and all accruals of expected future cash receipts and pay-ments. **Objective 2**

Statement of cash flows. A summary of the major cash re-ceipts and cash payments for a period. **Objective 1**

Self-Examination Questions

Answers at end of chapter.

1. An example of a cash flow from an operating activity is:
   A. receipt of cash from the sale of capital stock
   B. receipt of cash from the sale of bonds
   C. payment of cash for dividends
   D. receipt of cash from customers on account

2. An example of a cash flow from an investing activity is:
   A. receipt of cash from the sale of equipment
   B. receipt of cash from the sale of capital stock
   C. payment of cash for dividends
   D. payment of cash to acquire treasury stock

3. An example of a cash flow from a financing activity is:
   A. receipt of cash from customers on account
   B. receipt of cash from the sale of equipment
   C. payment of cash for dividends
   D. payment of cash to acquire marketable securities

4. Which of the following methods of reporting cash flows from operating activities adjusts net income for revenues and expenses not involving the receipt or payment of cash?
   A. Direct method   C. Reciprocal method
   B. Purchase method   D. Indirect method

5. The net income reported on the income statement for the year was $55,000, and depreciation of plant assets for the year was $22,000. The balances of the current asset and cur-rent liability accounts at the beginning and end of the year are as follows:

	End	Beginning
Cash	$ 65,000	$ 70,000
Trade receivables	100,000	90,000
Inventories	145,000	150,000
Prepaid expenses	7,500	8,000
Accounts payable (merchandise creditors)	51,000	58,000

The total amount reported for cash flows from operating activities in the statement of cash flows, using the indirect method, is:

   A. $33,000   C. $65,500
   B. $55,000   D. $77,000

ILLUSTRATIVE PROBLEM

The comparative balance sheet of Nesbitt Inc. for December 31, 1995 and 1994, is as follows:

Nesbitt Inc.
Comparative Balance Sheet
December 31, 1995 and 1994

	1995	1994
Assets		
Cash	$ 65,100	$ 42,500
Trade receivables (net)	91,350	61,150
Inventories	104,500	109,500
Prepaid expenses	3,600	2,700
Investments (long-term)	—	35,000
Land	30,000	50,000
Buildings	345,000	210,000
Accumulated depreciation—buildings	(120,600)	(110,400)
Machinery and equipment	255,000	255,000
Accumulated depreciation—machinery and equipment	(92,000)	(65,000)
Patents	35,000	40,000
	$716,950	$630,450
Liabilities and Stockholders' Equity		
Accounts payable (merchandise creditors)	$ 42,800	$ 65,950
Accrued expenses (operating expenses)	18,000	12,600
Income taxes payable	7,000	4,000
Dividends payable	15,000	10,000
Mortgage note payable, due 2001	60,000	—
Bonds payable	—	75,000
Common stock, $20 par	300,000	250,000
Excess of issue price over par—common stock	100,000	75,000
Retained earnings	174,150	137,900
	$716,950	$630,450

The income statement for Nesbitt Inc. is shown below.

Nesbitt Inc.
Income Statement
For Year Ended December 31, 1995

Sales		$800,000
Cost of merchandise sold		480,000
Gross profit		$320,000
Operating expenses:		
Depreciation expense	$ 37,200	
Patent amortization	5,000	
Other operating expenses	140,500	
Total operating expenses		182,700
Income from operations		$137,300
Other income:		
Gain on sale of investments	$ 15,000	
Other expense:		
Interest expense	6,500	8,500
Income before income tax		$145,800
Income tax		49,550
Net income		$ 96,250

An examination of the accounting records revealed the following additional information applicable to 1995:

a. Land costing $20,000 was sold for $20,000.
b. A mortgage note was issued for $60,000.
c. A building costing $135,000 was constructed.
d. 2,500 shares of common stock were issued at 30 in exchange for the bonds payable.
e. Cash dividends declared were $60,000.

Instructions

1. Prepare a statement of cash flows, using the indirect method of reporting cash flows from operating activities.
2. Prepare a statement of cash flows, using the direct method of reporting cash flows from operating activities.

Solution

1.

Nesbitt Inc.
Statement of Cash Flows—Indirect Method
For Year Ended December 31, 1995

Cash flows from operating activities:			
Net income, per income statement		$ 96,250	
Add: Depreciation	$ 37,200		
Amortization of patents	5,000		
Decrease in inventories	5,000		
Increase in accrued expenses	5,400		
Increase in income taxes payable	3,000	55,600	
		$151,850	
Deduct: Increase in trade receivables (net)	$ 30,200		
Increase in prepaid expenses	900		
Decrease in accounts payable	23,150		
Gain on sales of investments	15,000	69,250	
Net cash flow from operating activities			$ 82,600
Cash flows from investing activities:			
Cash received from sale of:			
Investments	$ 50,000		
Land	20,000	$ 70,000	
Less: Cash paid for construction of building		135,000	
Net cash flow used for investing activities			(65,000)
Cash flows from financing activities:			
Cash received from issuing mortgage note payable		$ 60,000	
Less: Cash paid for dividends		55,000	
Net cash flow provided by financing activities			5,000
Increase in cash			$ 22,600
Cash at the beginning of the year			42,500
Cash at the end of the year			$ 65,100

Schedule of Noncash Investing and Financing Activities:

Issued common stock to retire bonds payable	$ 75,000

2.

Nesbitt Inc.
Statement of Cash Flows—Direct Method
For Year Ended December 31, 1995

Cash flows from operating activities:			
Cash received from customers[1]		$769,800	
Deduct: Cash paid for merchandise[2]	$498,150		
Cash paid for operating expenses[3]	136,000		
Cash paid for interest expense	6,500		
Cash paid for income tax[4]	46,550	687,200	
Net cash flow from operating activities			$ 82,600
Cash flows from investing activities:			
Cash received from sale of:			
Investments	$ 50,000		
Land	20,000	$ 70,000	
Less: Cash paid for construction of building		135,000	
Net cash flow used for investing activities			(65,000)
Cash flows from financing activities:			
Cash received from issuing mortgage note payable		$ 60,000	
Less: Cash paid for dividends[5]		55,000	
Net cash flow provided by financing activities			5,000
Increase in cash			$ 22,600
Cash at the beginning of the year			42,500
Cash at the end of the year			$ 65,100

ILLUSTRATIVE

Schedule of Noncash Investing and Financing Activities:
Issued common stock to retire bonds payable $75,000

Computations: ^{1}$800,000 − $30,200 = $769,800
^{2}$480,000 − $5,000 + $23,150 = $498,150
^{3}$140,500 + $900 − $5,400 = $136,000
^{4}$49,550 − $3,000 = $46,550
^{5}$60,000 + $10,000 − $15,000 = $55,000

DISCUSSION QUESTIONS

1. Which financial statement is most useful in evaluating past operations and in planning future investing and financing activities?
2. What are the three types of activities reported on the statement of cash flows?
3. State the effect (cash receipt or payment, and amount) of each of the following transactions, considered individually, on cash flows:
   a. Sold a new issue of $100,000 of bonds at 101.
   b. Sold equipment with a book value of $37,500 for $40,000.
   c. Sold 5,000 shares of $20 par common stock at $35 per share.
   d. Retired $500,000 of bonds on which there was $2,500 of unamortized bond discount for $501,000.
4. Identify the type of cash flow activity for each of the following (operating, investing, or financing):
   a. purchased buildings
   b. issued common stock
   c. sold investments
   d. net income
   e. issued bonds
   f. redeemed bonds
   g. purchased treasury stock
   h. paid cash dividends
   i. purchased patents
   j. issued preferred stock
   k. sold equipment
5. Name the two alternative methods of reporting cash flows from operating activities in the statement of cash flows.
6. What is the principal disadvantage of the direct method of reporting cash flows from operating activities?
7. What are the major advantages of the indirect method of reporting cash flows from operating activities?
8. On the statement of cash flows, if the cash inflows from investing activities exceed the cash outflows, how is the difference described?
9. On the statement of cash flows, if the cash outflows from investing activities exceed the cash inflows, how is the difference described?
10. On the statement of cash flows, if the cash inflows from financing activities exceed the cash outflows, how is the difference described?
11. On the statement of cash flows, if the cash outflows from financing activities exceed the cash inflows, how is the difference described?
12. A corporation issued $200,000 of common stock in exchange for $200,000 of plant assets. Where would this transaction be reported on the statement of cash flows?
13. A corporation acquired as a long-term investment all of the capital stock of XL Co., valued at $5,000,000, by issuing $5,000,000 of its own common stock. Where should the transaction be reported on the statement of cash flows?
14. a. What is the effect on cash flows of declaring and issuing a stock dividend?
    b. Is the stock dividend reported on the statement of cash flows?
15. What is the effect on cash flows of appropriating retained earnings for bonded indebtedness?
16. Indicate whether each of the following would be added to or deducted from net income in determining net cash flow from operating activities by the indirect method:
    a. increase in notes payable due in 90 days
    b. decrease in accounts payable
    c. gain on retirement of long-term debt

    d. depreciation of plant assets

    e. increase in merchandise inventory

    f. amortization of discount on bonds payable

    g. increase in notes receivable due in 90 days

    h. decrease in accounts receivable

    i. loss on disposal of plant assets

    j. amortization of premium on bonds payable

    k. decrease in accrued salaries payable

    l. amortization of patents

    m. decrease in prepaid expenses

17. A retail enterprise, using the accrual method of accounting, owed merchandise creditors (accounts payable) $290,000 at the beginning of the year and $315,000 at the end of the year. How would the $25,000 increase be used to adjust net income in determining the amount of cash flows from operating activities by the indirect method? Explain.

18. If revenue from sales amounted to $900,000 for the year and trade receivables totaled $120,000 at the beginning of the year and $95,000 at the end of the year, what was the amount of cash received from customers during the year?

19. If salaries payable was $75,000 at the beginning of the year and $65,000 at the end of the year, should $10,000 be added to or deducted from income to determine the amount of cash flows from operating activities by the indirect method? Explain.

20. The board of directors declared cash dividends totaling $120,000 during the current year. The comparative balance sheet indicates dividends payable of $25,000 at the beginning of the year and $30,000 at the end of the year. What was the amount of cash payments to stockholders during the year?

21. A long-term investment in bonds with a cost of $75,000 was sold for $80,000 cash. (a) What was the gain or loss on the sale? (b) What was the effect of the transaction on cash flows? (c) How should the transaction be reported in the statement of cash flows if cash flows from operating activities are reported by the indirect method?

22. A corporation issued $5,000,000 of 20-year bonds for cash at 105. How would the transaction be reported on the statement of cash flows?

23. Fully depreciated equipment costing $55,000 was discarded. What was the effect of the transaction on cash flows if (a) $5,000 cash is received, (b) there is no salvage value?

24. For the current year, Accord Company decided to switch from the indirect method to the direct method for reporting cash flows from operating activities on the statement of cash flows. Will the change cause the amount of net cash flow from operating activities to be (a) larger, (b) smaller, or (c) the same as if the indirect method had been used? Explain.

25. Name five common major classes of operating cash receipts or operating cash payments presented on the statement of cash flows when the cash flows from operating activities are reported by the direct method.

26. The cash flows from operating activities are reported by the direct method on the statement of cash flows. If sales for the current year were $750,000 and trade receivables decreased by $25,000 during the year, what was the amount of cash received from customers?

27. The cash flows from operating activities are reported by the direct method on the statement of cash flows. If income tax for the current year was $100,000 and income tax payable decreased by $25,000 during the year, what was the amount of cash payments for income tax?

 28. In a recent annual report, PepsiCo, Inc., reported that during the year it issued treasury stock and debt of $162.7 million for acquisitions. How would this be reported on the statement of cash flows?

ETHICS DISCUSSION CASE

Alice Bowers, controller of Ortiz Inc., has decided to add cash flow per share to the financial statements. She feels that such reporting, although different from past reporting, would be useful to the readers. The cash flow per share would be reported on the statement of cash flows. On a comparative basis with the preceding year, the cash flow per share figure for the current year increased by 20% (as contrasted with a slight decline in net income and earnings per share).

Discuss whether Alice Bowers is behaving in an ethical manner.

 SHARPEN YOUR COMMUNICATION SKILLS

WHAT DO YOU THINK

Assume that you are considering an investment in a new start-up software company. A review of the company's financial statements reveals a negative retained earnings. In addition, it appears as though the company has been running a negative cash flow from operations since the company's inception.

How is the company staying in business under these circumstances? Could this be a good investment?

FINANCIAL ANALYSIS AND INTERPRETATION

The Retailing Division of Walker Company provided the following information on the cash flow from operations:

Net income	$450,000
Increase in accounts receivable	(340,000)
Increase in inventory	(300,000)
Decrease in accounts payable	(90,000)
Depreciation	100,000
Cash flow from operations	$(180,000)

The manager of the Retailing Division provided the accompanying memo with this report:

From: Senior Vice-President, Retailing Division

I am pleased to report that we had earnings of $450,000 over the last period. This resulted in a return on invested capital of 10%, which is near our targets for this division. I have been aggressive in building the revenue volume in the division. As a result, I am happy to report that we have increased the number of new credit card customers as a result of an aggressive marketing campaign. In addition, we have found some excellent merchandise opportunities. Some of our suppliers have made some of their apparel merchandise available at a deep discount. We have purchased as much of these goods as possible in order to improve profitability. I'm also happy to report that our vendor payment problems have improved. We are nearly caught up on our overdue payables balances.

SHARPEN YOUR COMMUNICATION SKILLS ►

Comment on the Senior Vice-President's memo in light of the cash flow information.

EXERCISES

EXERCISE 14-1
CASH FLOWS FROM OPERATING ACTIVITIES—NET LOSS
Objective 2

On its income statement for the current year, Carson Company reported a net loss of $60,000 from operations. On its statement of cash flows, it reported $15,000 of cash flows from operating activities.

SHARPEN YOUR COMMUNICATION SKILLS ►

Explain this apparent contradiction between the loss and the positive cash flows.

EXERCISE 14-2
CASH FLOWS FROM OPERATING ACTIVITIES—INDIRECT METHOD
Objectives 2, 3

The net income reported on the income statement for the current year was $87,100. Depreciation recorded on equipment and a building amounted to $31,750 for the year. Balances of the current asset and current liability accounts at the beginning and end of the year are as follows:

	End of Year	Beginning of Year
Cash	$ 64,250	$ 60,500
Trade receivables (net)	98,750	91,250
Inventories	110,000	95,000
Prepaid expenses	6,400	7,650
Accounts payable (merchandise creditors)	77,200	72,700
Salaries payable	3,250	5,750

a. Prepare the cash flows from operating activities section of the statement of cash flows, using the indirect method.

SHARPEN YOUR COMMUNICATION SKILLS

b. If the direct method had been used, would the net cash flow from operating activities have been the same? Explain.

EXERCISE 14-3
CASH FLOWS FROM
OPERATING ACTIVITIES—
INDIRECT METHOD
Objectives 2, 3

The net income reported on an income statement for the current year was $92,125. Depreciation recorded on store equipment for the year amounted to $43,500. Balances of the current asset and current liability accounts at the beginning and end of the year are as follows:

	End of Year	Beginning of Year	
Cash	$ 70,150	$66,500	3650
Trade receivables (net)	79,250	83,750	⟨4500⟩
Merchandise inventory	110,000	97,000	13,000
Prepaid expenses	8,000	7,500	500
Accounts payable (merchandise creditors)	70,200	73,200	⟨3,000⟩
Wages payable	6,900	5,650	1250

SPREADSHEET
PROBLEM

Prepare the cash flows from operating activities section of a statement of cash flows, using the indirect method.

103,025

EXERCISE 14-4
REPORTING CHANGES IN
EQUIPMENT ON STATEMENT
OF CASH FLOWS
Objectives 2, 3

An analysis of the general ledger accounts indicates that office equipment, which had cost $75,000 and on which accumulated depreciation totaled $67,500 on the date of sale, was sold for $7,000 during the year. Using this information, indicate the items to be reported on the statement of cash flows.

EXERCISE 14-5
REPORTING CHANGES IN
EQUIPMENT ON STATEMENT
OF CASH FLOWS
Objectives 2, 3

An analysis of the general ledger accounts indicates that delivery equipment, which had cost $45,000 and on which accumulated depreciation totaled $39,000 on the date of sale, was sold for $7,750 during the year. Using this information, indicate the items to be reported on the statement of cash flows.

EXERCISE 14-6
REPORTING LAND
TRANSACTIONS ON
STATEMENT OF CASH
FLOWS
Objectives 2, 3

On the basis of the details of the following plant asset account, indicate the items to be reported on the statement of cash flows:

ACCOUNT **LAND**   ACCOUNT NO.

					Balance	
Date		Item	Debit	Credit	Debit	Credit
19--						
Jan.	1	Balance			500,000	
Feb.	5	Purchased for cash	150,000		—	—
Oct.	30	Sold for $75,000		40,000	610,000	

EXERCISE 14-7
REPORTING
STOCKHOLDERS' EQUITY
ITEMS ON STATEMENT OF
CASH FLOWS
Objectives 2, 3

On the basis of the following stockholders' equity accounts, indicate the items, exclusive of net income, to be reported on the statement of cash flows. There were no unpaid dividends at either the beginning or the end of the year.

ACCOUNT **COMMON STOCK, $10 PAR**   ACCOUNT NO.

					Balance	
Date		Item	Debit	Credit	Debit	Credit
19--						
Jan.	1	Balance, 50,000 shares				500,000
Feb.	11	5,000 shares issued for cash		50,000	—	—
June	30	2,750-share stock dividend		27,500		577,500

PAID-IN CAPITAL IN EXCESS
ACCOUNT OF PAR—COMMON STOCK   ACCOUNT NO.

Date		Item	Debit	Credit	Balance Debit	Balance Credit
19--						
Jan.	1	Balance				90,000
Feb.	11	5,000 shares issued for cash		20,000	—	—
June	30	Stock dividend		10,000		120,000

ACCOUNT RETAINED EARNINGS   ACCOUNT NO.

Date		Item	Debit	Credit	Balance Debit	Balance Credit
19--						
Jan.	1	Balance				275,000
June	30	Stock dividend	37,500		—	—
Dec.	30	Cash dividend	55,000			
Dec.	31	Net income		97,500		280,000

EXERCISE 14-8
REPORTING LAND
ACQUISITION FOR CASH
AND MORTGAGE NOTE ON
STATEMENT OF CASH
FLOWS
Objectives 2, 3

On the basis of the details of the following asset account, indicate the items to be reported on the statement of cash flows:

ACCOUNT LAND   ACCOUNT NO.

Date		Item	Debit	Credit	Balance Debit	Balance Credit
19--						
Jan.	1	Balance			450,000	
Feb.	10	Purchased for cash	50,000		—	—
Nov.	20	Purchased with long-term mortgage note	150,000		650,000	

EXERCISE 14-9
DETERMINING NET
INCOME FROM NET CASH
FLOW FROM OPERATING
ACTIVITIES
Objectives 2, 3

Austin Inc. reported a net cash flow from operating activities of $46,500 on its statement of cash flows for the year ended December 31, 1995. The following information was reported in the cash flows from operating activities section of the statement of cash flows, using the indirect method:

Decrease in income tax payable	$ 1,250
Decrease in inventories	5,500
Depreciation	9,400
Gain on sale of investments	14,250
Increase in accounts payable	7,300
Increase in prepaid expenses	500
Increase in trade receivables	4,700

Determine the net income reported by Austin Inc. for the year ended December 31, 1995.

EXERCISE 14-10
DETERMINING SELECTED
AMOUNTS FOR CASH
FLOWS FROM OPERATING
ACTIVITIES—DIRECT
METHOD
Objectives 2, 4

Selected data taken from the accounting records of Brown Company for the current year ended December 31 are as follows:

	Balance January 1	Balance December 31
Accrued expenses (operating expenses)	$12,000	$ 5,500
Accounts payable (merchandise creditors)	85,000	70,000
Inventories	62,500	53,500
Prepaid expenses	17,500	12,500

During the current year, the cost of merchandise sold was $790,000 and the operating expenses other than depreciation were $275,000. The direct method is used for presenting the cash flows from operating activities on the statement of cash flows.

Determine the amount reported on the statement of cash flows for (a) cash payments for merchandise and (b) cash payments for operating expenses.

EXERCISE 14-11
CASH FLOWS FROM
OPERATING ACTIVITIES—
DIRECT METHOD
Objectives 2, 4

The income statement of Jackson Company for the current year ended June 30 is as follows:

Sales	$995,000
Cost of merchandise sold	600,000
Gross profit	$395,000
Operating expenses:	
Depreciation expense	$ 31,500
Other operating expenses	248,500
Total operating expenses	280,000
Income before income tax	$115,000
Income tax	35,000
Net income	$ 80,000

Changes in the balances of selected accounts from the beginning to the end of the current year are as follows:

	Increase (Decrease)
Trade receivables (net)	$(26,000)
Inventories	11,200
Prepaid expenses	(1,250)
Accounts payable (merchandise creditors)	(17,500)
Accrued expenses (operating expenses)	6,800
Income tax payable	(7,100)

Prepare the cash flows from operating activities section of the statement of cash flows, using the direct method.

EXERCISE 14-12
CASH FLOWS FROM
OPERATING ACTIVITIES—
DIRECT METHOD
Objectives 2, 4

The income statement for Regal Company for the current year ended June 30 and balances of selected accounts at the beginning and the end of the year are as follows:

Sales	$872,500
Cost of merchandise sold	500,000
Gross profit	$372,500
Operating expenses:	
Depreciation expense	$ 32,250
Other operating expenses	213,750
Total operating expenses	246,000
Income before income tax	$126,500
Income tax	30,900
Net income	$ 95,600

	End of Year	*Beginning of Year*
Trade receivables (net)	$ 90,000	$80,000
Inventories	102,500	87,500
Prepaid expenses	6,900	7,650
Accounts payable (merchandise creditors)	74,200	69,700
Accrued expenses (operating expenses)	3,750	6,250
Income tax payable	2,225	2,225

Prepare the cash flows from operating activities section of the statement of cash flows, using the direct method.

EXERCISE 14-13
CASH FLOWS FROM
OPERATING ACTIVITIES—
DIRECT METHOD
Objectives 2, 4

The income statement for the current year and balances of selected accounts at the beginning and end of the current year are as follows:

Sales		$1,250,000
Cost of merchandise sold		750,000
Gross profit		$ 500,000
Operating expenses:		
Depreciation expense	$ 43,500	
Other operating expenses	327,875	
Total operating expenses		371,375
Operating income		$ 128,625
Other expense:		
Interest expense		9,000
Income before income tax		$ 119,625
Income tax		27,500
Net income		$ 92,125

	End of Year	Beginning of Year
Trade receivables	$79,750	$84,250
Inventories	99,500	86,500
Prepaid expenses	8,100	7,600
Accounts payable (merchandise creditors)	69,700	72,700
Accrued expenses (operating expenses)	6,900	5,650
Interest payable	1,750	1,750
Income tax payable	3,000	4,500

Prepare the cash flows from operating activities section of the statement of cash flows, using the direct method.

EXERCISE 14-14
CASH FLOWS FROM
OPERATING ACTIVITIES
Objectives 2, 4

REAL WORLD FOCUS

Selected data from the income statement and statement of cash flows of Toys "R" Us, Inc., for the year ending February 1, 1992, are as follows:

Income Statement Data (dollars in thousands)

Net earnings	$339,529
Depreciation and amortization	100,701
Deferred taxes (expense)	23,604

Statement of Cash Flows Data (dollars in thousands)

Decrease in accounts receivable	$ 9,092
Increase in merchandise inventories	115,436
Increase in prepaid expenses and other operating assets	16,176
Increase in accounts payable, accrued expenses, and taxes	461,436

Prepare the cash flows from operating activities section of the statement of cash flows (using the indirect method) for Toys "R" Us, Inc., for the year ending February 1, 1992.

EXERCISE 14-15
ANALYSIS OF STATEMENT
OF CASH FLOWS—DELTA
AIRLINES
Objectives 1, 2

REAL WORLD FOCUS

The following is a condensed version of Delta Airline's Statement of Cash Flows for the years ended June 3, 1990-1992.

Delta Airlines

Statement of Cash Flows (Condensed, 000s)

For the Years Ended June 30, 1992, 1991, 1990

	1992	1991	1990
Cash Flows from Operations:			
Net Income	$ (506,318)	$ (324,380)	$ 302,783
Add: Depreciation	634,528	521,457	459,162
Increase in current liabilities	527,916	327,737	(21,772)
Other items	248,791	166,941	157,896
Deduct: Decrease (increase) in accounts receivable	(420,886)	(106,699)	26,049
Increase in prepaid expenses and			
other current assets	(69,108)	(72,350)	(30,510)
Gain on sale of flight equipment	(34,563)	(16,843)	(17,906)
Other items	(230,846)	(172,073)	(71,936)
Net cash provided by operations	$ 149,514	$ 323,790	$ 803,766
Cash Flows from Investing Activities:			
Property and equipment additions	$(2,481,008)	$(2,144,583)	(1,689,534)
Proceeds from sale of flight equipment	42,693	24,764	29,980
Investments in equity securities	(17)	0	(314,515)
Purchase of Pan Am	(531,000)	0	0
Purchase of leasehold and operating rights	(69,786)	(51,885)	0
Net cash provided by investing activities	$(3,039,118)	$(2,171,704)	$(1,974,069)
Cash Flows from Financing Activities:			
Issuance of long-term obligations	$ 1,500,000	$ 1,050,000	$ 781,400
Sale of treasury stock	0	476,005	0
Issuance of common stock	1,740	1,288	376,157
Net short-term borrowings	744,672	(9,331)	65,351
Repurchase of common stock	0	(220,796)	(591,154)
Payments on noncurrent obligations	(793,619)	(322,169)	(145,004)
Cash dividends	(89,372)	(83,838)	(113,647)
Proceeds from sale and leaseback transactions	812,894	1,652,000	336,000
Net cash provided by financial activities	$ 2,176,315	$ 2,543,159	$ 709,103
Net Increase (Decrease) in Cash	$ (713,289)	$ 695,245	$ (461,200)

SHARPEN YOUR
COMMUNICATION SKILLS ►

a. (1) Is Delta Airline's performance improving or deteriorating over the 1990-1992 time period?

    (2) Cash increased nearly $700 million in 1991, then fell around the same amount in 1992. What caused this reversal?

    (3) Explain how Delta is able to have over a $500 million loss for 1992, but still have positive cash flow from operations.

    (4) Why is "gain on sale of flight equipment" subtracted in determining the cash flow from operations?

    (5) Does Delta appear to be reducing its fleet purchases? Where is the money coming from to purchase aircraft?

b. What do you think a sale and leaseback transaction is?

WhAT'S WRONG
WITH THi2?

How many errors can you find in the following statement of cash flows? The cash balance at the beginning of the year was $70,700. All other figures are correct.

Environmental Products Inc.
Statement of Cash Flows
For Year Ended December 31, 19—

Cash flows from operating activities:			
Net income, per income statement		$ 90,300	
Add: Depreciation	$ 49,000		
Increase in trade receivables	11,200	60,200	
		$150,500	
Deduct: Increase in accounts payable	$ 4,400		
Increase in inventories	22,200		
Gain on sale of investments	5,000		
Decrease in accrued expenses	1,600	33,200	
Net cash flow from operating activities			$117,300
Cash flows from investing activities:			
Cash received from sale of investments		$ 85,000	
Less: Cash paid for purchase of land	$ 70,000		
Cash paid for purchase of equipment	150,100	220,100	
Net cash flow used for investing activities			(135,100)
Cash flows from financing activities:			
Cash received from sale of common stock		$107,000	
Plus cash paid for dividends		45,500	
Net cash flow provided by financing activities			152,500
Increase in cash			$134,700
Cash at the end of the year			100,800
Cash at the beginning of the year			$235,500

PROBLEMS

Series A

PROBLEM 14-1A
STATEMENT OF CASH
FLOWS—INDIRECT
METHOD
Objective 3

The comparative balance sheet of C. T. Green Inc. for June 30, 1995 and 1994, is as follows:

	June 30, 1995	June 30, 1994
Assets		
Cash	$ 82,000	$ 64,800
Trade receivables (net)	104,800	91,000
Inventories	127,400	108,900
Investments	—	90,000
Land	102,000	—
Equipment	425,700	329,700
Accumulated depreciation	(171,800)	(135,800)
	$670,100	$548,600
Liabilities and Stockholders' Equity		
Accounts payable (merchandise creditors)	$ 70,900	$ 63,000
Accrued expenses (operating expenses)	6,100	5,000
Dividends payable	14,400	12,000
Common stock, $10 par	360,000	300,000
Paid-in capital in excess of par—common stock	31,400	19,400
Retained earnings	187,300	149,200
	$670,100	$548,600

The following additional information was taken from the records of C. T. Green Inc.:

a. Equipment and land were acquired for cash.
b. There were no disposals of equipment during the year.
c. The investments were sold for $98,000 cash.

d. The common stock was issued for cash.
e. There was a $88,500 credit to Retained Earnings for net income.
f. There was a $50,400 debit to Retained Earnings for cash dividends declared.

Instructions

Prepare a statement of cash flows, using the indirect method of presenting cash flows from operating activities.

PROBLEM 14-2A
STATEMENT OF CASH
FLOWS—INDIRECT
METHOD
Objective 3

The comparative balance sheet of Kane Inc. at June 30, 1995 and 1994, is as follows:

	June 30, 1995	June 30, 1994
Assets		
Cash	$ 45,100	$ 64,600
Trade receivables (net)	116,300	129,300
Merchandise inventory	354,700	346,400
Prepaid expenses	5,200	3,600
Plant assets	440,000	396,800
Accumulated depreciation—plant assets	(232,300)	(266,600)
	$729,000	$674,100
Liabilities and Stockholders' Equity		
Accounts payable (merchandise creditors)	$ 71,300	$ 65,400
Mortgage note payable	—	101,300
Common stock, $30 par	300,000	270,000
Paid-in capital in excess of par—common stock	39,800	34,800
Retained earnings	317,900	202,600
	$729,000	$674,100

Additional data obtained from the income statement and from an examination of the accounts in the ledger are as follows:

a. Net income, $155,300.
b. Depreciation reported on the income statement, $38,600.
c. An addition to the building was constructed at a cost of $116,100, and fully depreciated equipment costing $72,900 was discarded, with no salvage realized.
d. The mortgage note payable was not due until 2000, but the terms permitted earlier payment without penalty.
e. 1,000 shares of common stock were issued at 35 for cash.
f. Cash dividends declared and paid, $40,000.

Instructions

Prepare a statement of cash flows, using the indirect method of presenting cash flows from operating activities.

PROBLEM 14-3A
STATEMENT OF CASH
FLOWS—INDIRECT
METHOD
Objective 3

The comparative balance sheet of Paton Corporation at December 31, 1995 and 1994, is as follows:

	Dec. 31, 1995	Dec. 31, 1994
Assets		
Cash	$ 72,400	$ 66,800
Trade receivables (net)	87,900	100,500
Inventories	192,100	178,600
Prepaid expenses	6,400	2,900
Land	75,000	75,000
Buildings	480,600	316,800
Accumulated depreciation—buildings	(157,500)	(144,000)
Machinery and equipment	206,300	206,300
Accumulated depreciation—machinery and equipment	(93,000)	(81,300)
Patents	30,000	37,500
	$900,200	$759,100

Liabilities and Stockholders' Equity

Accounts payable (merchandise creditors)	$ 27,200	$ 38,900
Dividends payable	18,800	15,000
Salaries payable	7,900	14,600
Mortgage note payable, due 2001	120,000	—
Bonds payable	—	70,000
Common stock, $10 par	410,000	360,000
Paid-in capital in excess of par—common stock	65,000	45,000
Retained earnings	251,300	215,600
	$900,200	$759,100

An examination of the income statement and the accounting records revealed the following additional information applicable to 1995:

a. Net income, $63,200.
b. Depreciation expense reported on the income statement: buildings, $13,500; machinery and equipment, $11,700.
c. Patent amortization reported on the income statement, $7,500.
d. A building was constructed for $163,800.
e. A mortgage note for $120,000 was issued for cash.
f. 5,000 shares of common stock were issued at 14 in exchange for the bonds payable.
g. Cash dividends declared, $27,500.

Instructions

Prepare a statement of cash flows, using the indirect method of presenting cash flows from operating activities.

SPREADSHEET
PROBLEM

PROBLEM 14-4A
STATEMENT OF CASH
FLOWS—INDIRECT
METHOD
Objective 3

The comparative balance sheet of B. L. Nelson Inc. at December 31, 1995 and 1994, is as follows:

	Dec. 31, 1995	Dec. 31, 1994
Assets		
Cash	$ 97,100	$ 81,400
Trade receivables (net)	170,000	151,700
Income tax refund receivable	9,000	—
Inventories	255,600	269,400
Prepaid expenses	9,300	11,100
Investments	50,000	250,000
Land	180,000	230,000
Buildings	820,000	450,000
Accumulated depreciation—buildings	(207,700)	(193,800)
Equipment	608,400	470,400
Accumulated depreciation—equipment	(218,000)	(205,700)
	$1,773,700	$1,514,500
Liabilities and Stockholders' Equity		
Accounts payable (merchandise creditors)	$ 96,000	$ 108,720
Income tax payable	—	10,880
Bonds payable	350,000	—
Discount on bonds payable	(29,000)	—
Common stock, $10 par	630,000	600,000
Paid-in capital in excess of par—common stock	81,000	72,000
Appropriation for plant expansion	280,000	230,000
Retained earnings	365,700	492,900
	$1,773,700	$1,514,500

The noncurrent asset, the noncurrent liability, and the stockholders' equity accounts for 1995 are as follows:

ACCOUNT INVESTMENTS   ACCOUNT NO.

Date		Item	Debit	Credit	Balance Debit	Balance Credit
1995						
Jan.	1	Balance			250,000	
Mar.	22	Realized $220,000 cash from sale		200,000	50,000	—

ACCOUNT LAND   ACCOUNT NO.

Date		Item	Debit	Credit	Balance Debit	Balance Credit
1995						
Jan.	1	Balance			230,000	
April	20	Realized $62,500 cash from sale		50,000	180,000	

ACCOUNT BUILDINGS   ACCOUNT NO.

Date		Item	Debit	Credit	Balance Debit	Balance Credit
1995						
Jan.	1	Balance			450,000	
April	20	Acquired for cash	370,000		820,000	

ACCOUNT ACCUMULATED DEPRECIATION—BUILDINGS   ACCOUNT NO.

Date		Item	Debit	Credit	Balance Debit	Balance Credit
1995						
Jan.	1	Balance				193,800
Dec.	31	Depreciation for year		13,900		207,700

ACCOUNT EQUIPMENT   ACCOUNT NO.

Date		Item	Debit	Credit	Balance Debit	Balance Credit
1995						
Jan.	1	Balance			470,400	
	26	Discarded, no salvage		48,000		
May	27	Purchased for cash	96,000			
Aug.	11	Purchased for cash	90,000		608,400	

ACCOUNT ACCUMULATED DEPRECIATION—EQUIPMENT   ACCOUNT NO.

Date		Item	Debit	Credit	Balance Debit	Balance Credit
1995						
Jan.	1	Balance				205,700
	26	Equipment discarded	48,000			
Dec.	31	Depreciation for year		60,300		218,000

ACCOUNT BONDS PAYABLE   ACCOUNT NO.

Date		Item	Debit	Credit	Balance Debit	Balance Credit
1995 May	1	Issued 20-year bonds		350,000		350,000

ACCOUNT DISCOUNT ON BONDS PAYABLE   ACCOUNT NO.

Date		Item	Debit	Credit	Balance Debit	Balance Credit
1995 May	1	Bonds issued	30,000		30,000	
Dec.	31	Amortization		1,000	29,000	

ACCOUNT COMMON STOCK, $10 PAR   ACCOUNT NO.

Date		Item	Debit	Credit	Balance Debit	Balance Credit
1995 Jan.	1	Balance				600,000
Dec.	7	Stock dividend		30,000		630,000

ACCOUNT PAID-IN CAPITAL IN EXCESS OF PAR—COMMON STOCK   ACCOUNT NO.

Date		Item	Debit	Credit	Balance Debit	Balance Credit
1995 Jan.	1	Balance				72,000
Dec.	7	Stock dividend		9,000		81,000

ACCOUNT APPROPRIATION FOR PLANT EXPANSION   ACCOUNT NO.

Date		Item	Debit	Credit	Balance Debit	Balance Credit
1995 Jan.	1	Balance				230,000
Dec.	31	Appropriation		50,000		280,000

ACCOUNT RETAINED EARNINGS   ACCOUNT NO.

Date		Item	Debit	Credit	Balance Debit	Balance Credit
1995 Jan.	1	Balance				492,900
Dec.	7	Stock dividend	39,000			
	31	Net loss	6,700			
	31	Cash dividends	31,500			
	31	Appropriated	50,000			365,700

Instructions

Prepare a statement of cash flows, using the indirect method of presenting cash flows from operating activities.

PROBLEM 14-5A
STATEMENT OF CASH
FLOWS—DIRECT METHOD
Objective 4

The comparative balance sheet of C. C. Conley Inc. for December 31, 1994 and 1995, is as follows:

	Dec. 31, 1995	Dec. 31, 1994
Assets		
Cash	$ 72,000	$ 50,500
Trade receivables (net)	88,000	80,000
Inventories	105,900	91,400
Investments	—	50,000
Land	50,000	—
Equipment	375,000	275,000
Accumulated depreciation	(149,000)	(114,000)
	$541,900	$432,900

Liabilities and Stockholders' Equity		
Accounts payable (merchandise creditors)	$ 59,000	$ 57,000
Accrued expenses (operating expenses)	5,000	7,000
Dividends payable	15,000	10,000
Common stock, $40 par	320,000	250,000
Paid-in capital in excess of par—common stock	17,000	12,000
Retained earnings	125,900	96,900
	$541,900	$432,900

The income statement for the year ended December 31, 1995, is as follows:

Sales		$919,500
Cost of merchandise sold		550,000
Gross profit		$369,500
Operating expenses:		
Depreciation expense	$ 35,000	
Other operating expenses	260,000	
Total operating expenses		295,000
Operating income		$ 74,500
Other income:		
Gain on sale of investments		10,000
Income before income tax		$ 84,500
Income tax		20,000
Net income		$ 64,500

Instructions

Prepare a statement of cash flows, using the direct method of presenting cash flows from operating activities.

SPREADSHEET
PROBLEM

SOLUTIONS
SOFTWARE

Instructions for Solving Problem 14-5A Using Solutions Software
1. Load opening balances.
2. Enter your name in the Student Name field in the General Information data entry window. Set the run date to December 31, 1995.
3. Save the opening balances file to your drive and directory.
4. Display a statement of cash flows.
5. Save your data file to disk.
6. End the session.

PROBLEM 14-6A
STATEMENT OF CASH
FLOWS—DIRECT METHOD
APPLIED TO PROBLEM 14-1A
Objective 4

The comparative balance sheet of C. T. Green Inc. for June 30, 1995 and 1994, is as follows:

	June 30, 1995	June 30, 1994
Assets		
Cash	$ 82,000	$ 64,800
Trade receivables (net)	104,800	91,000
Inventories	127,400	108,900
Investments	—	90,000
Land	102,000	—
Equipment	425,700	329,700
Accumulated depreciation	(171,800)	(135,800)
	$670,100	$548,600

	June 30, 1995	June 30, 1994
Liabilities and Stockholders' Equity		
Accounts payable (merchandise creditors)	$ 70,900	$ 63,000
Accrued expenses (operating expenses)	6,100	5,000
Dividends payable	14,400	12,000
Common stock, $10 par	360,000	300,000
Paid-in capital in excess of par—common stock	31,400	19,400
Retained earnings	187,300	149,200
	$670,100	$548,600

The income statement for the year ended June 30, 1995, is as follows:

Sales		$1,194,000
Cost of merchandise sold		708,900
Gross profit		$ 485,100
Operating expenses:		
Depreciation expense	$ 36,000	
Other operating expenses	336,000	
Total operating expenses		372,000
Operating income		$ 113,100
Other income:		
Gain on sale of investments		8,000
Income before income tax		$ 121,100
Income tax		32,600
Net income		$ 88,500

The following additional information was taken from the records of C. T. Green Inc.:

a. Equipment and land were acquired for cash.
b. There were no disposals of equipment during the year.
c. The investments were sold for $98,000.
d. The common stock was issued for cash.
e. There was a $50,400 debit to Retained Earnings for cash dividends declared.

Instructions

Prepare a statement of cash flows, using the direct method of presenting cash flows from operating activities.

PROBLEM 14-7A
STATEMENT OF CASH
FLOWS—DIRECT AND
INDIRECT METHODS
Objectives 3, 4

An income statement and a comparative balance sheet for DABCO Company are as follows:

DABCO Company
Income Statement
For Year Ended December 31, 1995

Sales		$1,520,700
Cost of merchandise sold		1,110,200
Gross profit		$ 410,500
Operating expenses		
Depreciation expense	$ 39,990	
Other operating expenses	227,110	
Total operating expenses		267,100
		$ 143,400
Other income:		
Gain on sale of land	$ 20,500	
Gain on sale of investments	11,000	
	$ 31,500	
Other expense:		
Interest expense	25,000	6,500
Income before income tax		$ 149,900
Income tax		38,500
Net income		$ 111,400

DABCO Company
Comparative Balance Sheet
December 31, 1995 and 1994

	1995	1994
Assets		
Cash	$ 57,870	$ 66,200
Trade receivables (net)	137,180	117,800
Inventories	211,500	190,150
Prepaid expenses	5,160	6,120
Investments	44,500	93,500
Land	77,250	75,000
Buildings	412,500	225,000
Accumulated depreciation—buildings	(91,260)	(81,220)
Equipment	493,700	437,500
Accumulated depreciation—equipment	(179,700)	(149,750)
Total assets	$1,168,700	$980,300
Liabilities and Stockholders' Equity		
Accounts payable (merchandise creditors)	$ 58,715	$ 51,875
Accrued expenses (operating expenses)	11,000	10,500
Interest payable	1,875	1,875
Income tax payable	5,000	8,500
Dividends payable	15,660	12,500
Mortgage note payable	175,000	—
Bonds payable	100,000	250,000
Common stock, $25 par	450,000	375,000
Paid-in capital in excess of par—common stock	47,250	41,250
Retained earnings	304,200	228,800
Total liabilities and stockholders' equity	$1,168,700	$980,300

The following additional information on cash flows during the year was obtained from an examination of the ledger:

a. Investments (long-term) were purchased for $40,500.
b. Investments (long-term) costing $89,500 were sold for $100,500.
c. Equipment was purchased for $56,200. There were no disposals.
d. A building valued at $187,500 and land valued at $62,500 were acquired by a cash payment of $250,000.
e. Land which cost $60,250 was sold for $80,750 cash.

f. A mortgage note payable for $175,000 was issued for cash.
g. Bonds payable of $150,000 were retired by the payment of their face amount.
h. 3,000 shares of common stock were issued for cash at 27.
i. Cash dividends of $36,000 were declared.

Instructions

1. Prepare a statement of cash flows, using the direct method of presenting cash flows from operating activities.

2. Prepare a statement of cash flows, using the indirect method of presenting cash flows from operating activities.

3. Which method of reporting cash flows from operating activities is more widely used? Explain.

SPREADSHEET
PROBLEM

SHARPEN YOUR
COMMUNICATION SKILLS

Series B

PROBLEM 14-1B
STATEMENT OF CASH
FLOWS—INDIRECT
METHOD
Objective 3

The comparative balance sheet of T. A. Kolby Inc. for December 31, 1995 and 1994, is as follows:

	Dec. 31, 1995	Dec. 31, 1994
Assets		
Cash	$ 90,500	$ 60,400
Trade receivables (net)	123,200	112,000
Inventories	150,300	128,100
Investments	—	80,000
Land	70,000	—
Equipment	874,600	724,500
Accumulated depreciation	(208,600)	(159,600)
	$1,100,000	$945,400
Liabilities and Stockholders' Equity		
Accounts payable (merchandise creditors)	$ 75,000	$ 70,600
Accrued expenses (operating expenses)	4,800	6,400
Dividends payable	21,000	14,000
Common stock, $10 par	450,000	350,000
Paid-in capital in excess of par—common stock	23,800	16,800
Retained earnings	525,400	487,600
	$1,100,000	$945,400

The following additional information was taken from the records:

a. The investments were sold for $85,000 cash.
b. Equipment and land were acquired for cash.
c. There were no disposals of equipment during the year.
d. The common stock was issued for cash.
e. There was an $87,800 credit to Retained Earnings for net income.
f. There was a $50,000 debit to Retained Earnings for cash dividends declared.

Instructions

Prepare a statement of cash flows, using the indirect method of presenting cash flows from operating activities.

PROBLEM 14-2B
STATEMENT OF CASH
FLOWS—INDIRECT METHOD
Objective 3

The comparative balance sheet of Roth Corporation at December 31, 1995 and 1994, is as follows:

	Dec. 31, 1995	Dec. 31, 1994
Assets		
Cash	$ 78,300	$ 64,000
Trade receivables (net)	69,300	73,700
Merchandise inventory	121,900	97,400
Prepaid expenses	7,660	5,860
Plant assets	472,440	425,240
Accumulated depreciation—plant assets	(138,500)	(157,500)
	$611,100	$508,700
Liabilities and Stockholders' Equity		
Accounts payable (merchandise creditors)	$ 69,100	$ 53,500
Mortgage note payable	—	60,000
Common stock, $25 par	300,000	250,000
Paid-in capital in excess of par—common stock	34,500	31,500
Retained earnings	207,500	113,700
	$611,100	$508,700

Additional data obtained from the income statement and from an examination of the accounts in the ledger are as follows:

a. Net income, $108,800.
b. Depreciation reported on the income statement, $34,600.
c. An addition to the building was constructed at a cost of $100,800, and fully depreciated equipment costing $53,600 was discarded, with no salvage realized.
d. The mortgage note payable was not due until 2003, but the terms permitted earlier payment without penalty.
e. 2,000 shares of common stock were issued at $26.50 for cash.
f. Cash dividends declared and paid, $15,000.

Instructions

Prepare a statement of cash flows, using the indirect method of presenting cash flows from operating activities.

PROBLEM 14-3B
STATEMENT OF CASH
FLOWS—INDIRECT METHOD
Objective 3

The comparative balance sheet of Courier Corporation at December 31, 1995 and 1994, is as follows:

	Dec. 31, 1995	Dec. 31, 1994
Assets		
Cash	$ 60,900	$ 52,800
Trade receivables (net)	86,100	70,000
Inventories	126,600	136,700
Prepaid expenses	4,400	3,100
Land	65,000	65,000
Buildings	381,500	291,500
Accumulated depreciation—buildings	(154,600)	(143,400)
Machinery and equipment	300,500	300,500
Accumulated depreciation—machinery and equipment	(101,200)	(71,500)
Patents	30,800	38,500
	$800,000	$743,200
Liabilities and Stockholders' Equity		
Accounts payable (merchandise creditors)	$ 58,800	$ 88,800
Dividends payable	9,400	8,250
Salaries payable	5,000	5,450
Mortgage note payable, due 2005	55,000	—
Bonds payable	—	110,000
Common stock, $10 par	450,000	350,000
Paid-in capital in excess of par—common stock	80,000	70,000
Retained earnings	141,800	110,700
	$800,000	$743,200

An examination of the income statement and the accounting records revealed the following additional information applicable to 1995:

a. Net income, $66,100.
b. Depreciation expense reported on the income statement: buildings, $11,200; machinery and equipment, $29,700.
c. A building was constructed for $90,000.
d. Patent amortization reported on the income statement, $7,700.
e. A mortgage note for $55,000 was issued for cash.
f. 10,000 shares of common stock were issued at 11 in exchange for the bonds payable.
g. Cash dividends declared, $35,000.

Instructions

Prepare a statement of cash flows, using the indirect method of presenting cash flows from operating activities.

SPREADSHEET
PROBLEM

PROBLEM 14-4B
STATEMENT OF CASH
FLOWS—INDIRECT METHOD
Objective 3

The comparative balance sheet of Brodell Inc. at December 31, 1995 and 1994, is as follows:

	Dec. 31, 1995	Dec. 31, 1994
Assets		
Cash	$ 36,200	$ 38,800
Trade receivables (net)	60,800	54,100
Inventories	136,750	121,000
Prepaid expenses	3,850	4,100
Investments	—	45,000
Land	28,500	28,500
Buildings	190,000	126,000
Accumulated depreciation—buildings	(46,200)	(41,400)
Equipment	286,200	239,500
Accumulated depreciation—equipment	(86,100)	(77,400)
	$610,000	$538,200
Liabilities and Stockholders' Equity		
Accounts payable (merchandise creditors)	$ 38,700	$ 48,300
Income tax payable	3,600	2,800
Bonds payable	50,000	—
Discount on bonds payable	(2,900)	—
Common stock, $20 par	315,000	300,000
Paid-in capital in excess of par—common stock	40,200	33,000
Appropriation for plant expansion	50,000	30,000
Retained earnings	115,400	124,100
	$610,000	$538,200

The noncurrent asset, the noncurrent liability, and the stockholders' equity accounts for 1995 are as follows:

ACCOUNT INVESTMENTS   ACCOUNT NO.

Date		Item	Debit	Credit	Balance Debit	Balance Credit
1995						
Jan.	1	Balance			45,000	
Mar.	5	Realized $40,500 cash from sale		45,000	—	—

ACCOUNT LAND   ACCOUNT NO.

Date		Item	Debit	Credit	Balance Debit	Balance Credit
1995						
Jan.	1	Balance			28,500	

ACCOUNT BUILDINGS   ACCOUNT NO.

Date		Item	Debit	Credit	Balance Debit	Balance Credit
1995						
Jan.	1	Balance			126,000	
July	1	Acquired for cash	64,000		190,000	

ACCUMULATED
ACCOUNT DEPRECIATION—BUILDINGS   ACCOUNT NO.

Date		Item	Debit	Credit	Balance Debit	Balance Credit
1995						
Jan.	1	Balance				41,400
Dec.	31	Depreciation for year		4,800		46,200

ACCOUNT EQUIPMENT   ACCOUNT NO.

Date		Item	Debit	Credit	Balance Debit	Balance Credit
1995						
Jan.	1	Balance			239,500	
Mar.	1	Discarded, no salvage		21,000		
	5	Purchased for cash	40,000			
Dec.	1	Purchased for cash	27,700		286,200	

ACCUMULATED
ACCOUNT DEPRECIATION—EQUIPMENT   ACCOUNT NO.

Date		Item	Debit	Credit	Balance Debit	Balance Credit
1995						
Jan.	1	Balance				77,400
Mar.	1	Equipment discarded	21,000			
Dec.	31	Depreciation for year		29,700		86,100

ACCOUNT BONDS PAYABLE   ACCOUNT NO.

Date		Item	Debit	Credit	Balance Debit	Balance Credit
1995						
May	1	Issued 20-year bonds		50,000		50,000

ACCOUNT DISCOUNT ON BONDS PAYABLE   ACCOUNT NO.

Date		Item	Debit	Credit	Balance Debit	Balance Credit
1995						
May	1	Bonds issued	3,000		3,000	
Dec.	31	Amortization		100	2,900	

ACCOUNT COMMON STOCK, $10 PAR   ACCOUNT NO.

Date		Item	Debit	Credit	Balance Debit	Balance Credit
1995						
Jan.	1	Balance				300,000
June	29	Stock dividend		15,000		315,000

PAID-IN CAPITAL IN

ACCOUNT   EXCESS OF PAR—COMMON STOCK   ACCOUNT NO.

Date		Item	Debit	Credit	Balance Debit	Balance Credit
1995						
Jan.	1	Balance				33,000
June	29	Stock dividend		7,200		40,200

ACCOUNT   APPROPRIATION FOR PLANT EXPANSION   ACCOUNT NO.

Date		Item	Debit	Credit	Balance Debit	Balance Credit
1995						
Jan.	1	Balance				30,000
Dec.	31	Appropriation		20,000		50,000

ACCOUNT   RETAINED EARNINGS   ACCOUNT NO.

Date		Item	Debit	Credit	Balance Debit	Balance Credit
1995						
Jan.	1	Balance				124,100
June	29	Stock dividend	22,200			
Dec.	31	Net income		53,500		
	31	Cash dividends	20,000			
	31	Appropriated	20,000			115,400

Instructions

Prepare a statement of cash flows, using the indirect method of presenting cash flows from operating activities.

PROBLEM 14-5B
STATEMENT OF CASH
FLOWS—DIRECT METHOD
Objective 4

The comparative balance sheet of A. C. North Co. for December 31, 1995 and 1994, is as follows:

	Dec. 31, 1995	Dec. 31, 1994
Assets		
Cash	$ 59,200	$ 44,900
Trade receivables (net)	91,500	80,000
Inventories	105,900	90,500
Investments	—	75,000
Land	85,000	—
Equipment	362,400	282,400
Accumulated depreciation	(149,000)	(119,000)
	$555,000	$453,800
Liabilities and Stockholders' Equity		
Accounts payable (merchandise creditors)	$ 62,450	$ 55,000
Accrued expenses (operating expenses)	6,000	4,000
Dividends payable	12,000	10,000
Common stock, $20 par	300,000	250,000
Paid-in capital in excess of par—common stock	22,000	12,000
Retained earnings	152,550	122,800
	$555,000	$453,800

The income statement for the year ended December 31, 1995, is as follows:

Sales		$995,000
Cost of merchandise sold		590,750
Gross profit		$404,250
Operating expenses:		
Depreciation expense	$ 30,000	
Other operating expenses	280,000	
Total operating expenses		310,000
Operating income		$ 94,250
Other income:		
Gain on sale of investments		5,000
Income before income tax		$ 99,250
Income tax		22,500
Net income		$ 76,750

The following additional information was taken from the records:

a. Equipment and land were acquired for cash.
b. There were no disposals of equipment during the year.
c. The investments were sold for $80,000 cash.
d. The common stock was issued for cash.
e. There was a $47,000 debit to Retained Earnings for cash dividends declared.

Instructions

Prepare a statement of cash flows, using the direct method of presenting cash flows from operating activities.

Instructions for Solving Problem 14-5B Using Solutions Software

1. Load opening balances.
2. Enter your name in the Student Name field in the General Information data entry window. Set the run date to December 31, 1995.
3. Save the opening balances file to your drive and directory.
4. Display a statement of cash flows.
5. Save your data file to disk.
6. End the session.

SPREADSHEET
PROBLEM

SOLUTIONS
SOFTWARE

PROBLEM 14-6B
STATEMENT OF CASH
FLOWS—DIRECT METHOD
APPLIED TO PROBLEM 14-1B
Objective 4

The comparative balance sheet of T. A. Kolby Inc. for December 31, 1995 and 1994, is as follows:

	Dec. 31, 1995	Dec. 31, 1994
Assets		
Cash	$ 90,500	$ 60,400
Trade receivables (net)	123,200	112,000
Inventories	150,300	128,100
Investments	—	80,000
Land	70,000	—
Equipment	874,600	724,500
Accumulated depreciation	(208,600)	(159,600)
	$1,100,000	$945,400
Liabilities and Stockholders' Equity		
Accounts payable (merchandise creditors)	$ 75,000	$ 70,600
Accrued expenses (operating expenses)	4,800	6,400
Dividends payable	21,000	14,000
Common stock, $10 par	450,000	350,000
Paid-in capital in excess of par—common stock	23,800	16,800
Retained earnings	525,400	487,600
	$1,100,000	$945,400

The income statement for the year ended December 31, 1995, is as follows:

Sales		$1,287,300
Cost of merchandise sold		770,000
Gross profit		$ 517,300
Operating expenses:		
Depreciation expense	$ 49,000	
Other operating expenses	364,000	
Total operating expenses		413,000
Operating income		$ 104,300
Other income:		
Gain on sale of investments		5,000
Income before income tax		$ 109,300
Income tax		21,500
Net income		$ 87,800

The following additional information was taken from the records:

a. The investments were sold for $85,000 cash at the beginning of the year.
b. Equipment and land were acquired for cash.
c. There were no disposals of equipment during the year.
d. The common stock was issued for cash.
e. There was a $50,000 debit to Retained Earnings for cash dividends declared.

Instructions

Prepare a statement of cash flows, using the direct method of presenting cash flows from operating activities.

PROBLEM 14-7B
STATEMENT OF CASH
FLOWS—DIRECT AND
INDIRECT METHODS
Objectives 3, 4

An income statement and a comparative balance sheet for Yoder Company are as follows:

Yoder Company
Income Statement
For Year Ended December 31, 1995

Sales		$1,255,000
Cost of merchandise sold		830,000
Gross profit		$ 425,000
Operating expenses		
Depreciation expense	$ 39,990	
Other operating expenses	220,010	
Total operating expenses		260,000
		$ 165,000
Other income:		
Gain on sale of land	$ 18,750	
Gain on sale of investments	14,250	
	$ 33,000	
Other expense:		
Interest expense	27,500	5,500
Income before income tax		$ 170,500
Income tax		59,100
Net income		$ 111,400

Yoder Company
Comparative Balance Sheet
December 31, 1995 and 1994

	1995	1994
Assets		
Cash	$ 52,370	$ 60,700
Trade receivables (net)	130,080	116,700
Inventories	215,400	188,050
Prepaid expenses	5,160	6,120
Investments	34,250	93,500
Land	65,000	75,000
Buildings	435,000	225,000
Accumulated depreciation—buildings	(91,260)	(81,220)
Equipment	493,700	437,500
Accumulated depreciation—equipment	(179,700)	(149,750)
Total assets	$1,160,000	$971,600
Liabilities and Stockholders' Equity		
Accounts payable (merchandise creditors)	$ 54,640	$ 48,300
Accrued expenses (operating expenses)	12,000	11,000
Interest payable	3,000	3,000
Income tax payable	6,250	9,750
Dividends payable	15,660	12,500
Mortgage note payable	175,000	—
Bonds payable	100,000	250,000
Common stock, $25 par	450,000	375,000
Paid-in capital in excess of par—common stock	47,250	41,250
Retained earnings	296,200	220,800
Total liabilities and stockholders' equity	$1,160,000	$971,600

The following additional information on cash flows during the year was obtained from an examination of the ledger:

a. Investments (long-term) were purchased for $34,500.

b. Investments (long-term) costing $93,750 were sold for $108,000.

c. Equipment was purchased for $56,200. There were no disposals.

d. A building valued at $210,000 and land valued at $40,000 were acquired by a cash payment of $250,000.

e. Land which cost $50,000 was sold for $68,750 cash.

f. A mortgage note payable for $175,000 was issued for cash.
g. Bonds payable of $150,000 were retired by the payment of their face amount.
h. 3,000 shares of common stock were issued for cash at 27.
i. Cash dividends of $36,000 were declared.

Instructions

SPREADSHEET PROBLEM

1. Prepare a statement of cash flows, using the direct method of presenting cash flows from operating activities.

2. Prepare a statement of cash flows, using the indirect method of presenting cash flows from operating activities.

SHARPEN YOUR COMMUNICATION SKILLS ▶

3. Which method of reporting cash flows from operating activities is more widely used? Explain.

MINI-CASE A. J. JOHNS INC.

Alan Johns is the president and majority shareholder of A. J. Johns Inc., a small retail store chain. Recently, Johns submitted a loan application for A. J. Johns Inc. to Bonita National Bank. It called for a $200,000, 11%, ten-year loan to help finance the construction of a building and the purchase of store equipment, costing a total of $250,000 to enable A. J. Johns Inc. to open a store in Bonita. Land for this pur-

pose was acquired last year. The bank's loan officer request-ed a statement of cash flows in addition to the most recent in-come statement, balance sheet, and retained earnings state-ment that Johns had submitted with the loan application.

As a close family friend, Johns asked you to prepare a statement of cash flows. From the records provided, you prepared the following statement:

A. J. Johns Inc.
Statement of Cash Flows
For Year Ended December 31, 19—

Cash flows from operating activities:			
Net income, per income statement		$ 82,500	
Add: Depreciation	$28,000		
Decrease in trade receivables	11,500	39,500	
		$122,000	
Deduct: Increase in inventory	$10,000		
Increase in prepaid expenses	1,500		
Decrease in accounts payable	3,000		
Gain on sale of investments	7,500	22,000	
Net cash flow from operating activities			$100,000
Cash flows from investing activities:			
Cash received from investments sold		$ 42,500	
Less: Cash paid for purchase of store equipment		35,000	
Net cash flow from investing activities			7,500
Cash flows from financing activities:			
Cash paid for dividends		$ 50,000	
Net cash flow used for financing activities			(50,000)
Increase in cash			$ 57,500
Cash at the beginning of the year			27,500
Cash at the end of the year			$ 85,000
Schedule of Noncash Financing and Investing Activities:			
Issued common stock at par for land			$ 40,000

After reviewing the statement, Johns telephoned you and commented, "Are you sure this statement is right?" Johns then raised the following questions:

a. "How can depreciation be a cash flow?"
b. "The issuing of common stock for the land is listed in a separate schedule. This transaction has nothing to do with cash! Shouldn't this transaction be eliminated from the statement?"
c. "How can the gain on sale of investments be a deduc-tion from net income in determining the cash flow from operating activities?"

d. "Why does the bank need this statement anyway? They can compute the increase in cash from the balance sheets for the last two years."

After jotting down Johns's questions, you assured him that this statement was "right." However, to alleviate Johns's concern, you arranged a meeting for the following day.

Instructions

1. How would you respond to each of Johns's questions?
2. ▬▬ ▶ Do you think that the statement of cash flows enhances the chances of A. J. Johns Inc. receiving the loan? Discuss.

ANSWERS TO SELF-EXAMINATION QUESTIONS

1. **D** Cash flows from operating activities affect transactions that enter into the determination of net income such as the receipt of cash from customers on account (answer D). Receipts of cash from the sale of capital stock (answer A) and the sale of bonds (answer B) and payments of cash for dividends (answer C) are cash flows from financing activities.

2. **A** Cash flows from investing activities include receipts from the sale of noncurrent assets, such as equipment (answer A), and payments to acquire noncurrent assets. Receipts of cash from the sale of capital stock (answer B) and payments of cash for dividends (answer C) and to acquire treasury stock (answer D) are cash flows from financing activities.

3. **C** Payment of cash dividends (answer C) is an example of a financing activity. The receipt of cash from customers on account (answer A) is an operating activity. The receipt of cash from the sale of equipment (answer B) is an investing activity. The payment of cash to acquire marketable securities (answer D) is an example of an investing activity.

4. **D** The indirect method (answer D) reports cash flows from operating activities by beginning with net income and adjusting it for revenues and expenses not involving the receipt or payment of cash.

5. **C** The cash flows from operating activities section of the statement of cash flows would report net cash flow from operating activities of $65,500, determined as follows:

Net income		$55,000
Add: Depreciation	$22,000	
Decrease in inventories	5,000	
Decrease in prepaid expenses	500	27,500
		$82,500
Deduct: Increase in trade receivables	$10,000	
Decrease in accounts payable	7,000	17,000
Net cash flow from operating activities		$65,500

Annual Reports and Financial Statement Analysis

Corporate
Annual Reports

Financial
Statement Analysis

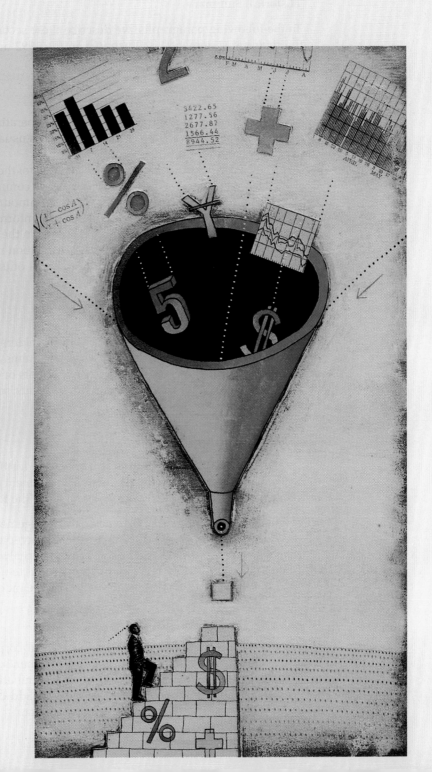

CORPORATE ANNUAL REPORTS

Corporations normally issue annual reports to their stockholders and other interested parties. Such reports summarize the corporation's operating activities for the past year and plans for the future. There are many variations in the form and order of presentation of the major sections of annual reports. However, one section of the annual report is devoted to the financial statements, including the accompanying notes. In addition, annual reports usually include the following sections:

1. Financial Highlights
2. President's Letter to the Stockholders
3. Management Report
4. Independent Auditors' Report
5. Historical Summary

In the following paragraphs, we describe these sections. Each section, as well as the financial statements, is illustrated in the 1992 annual report for Hershey Foods Corporation.

Financial Highlights

The Financial Highlights section summarizes the operating results for the last year or two. It is sometimes called Results in Brief. It is usually presented on the first one or two pages of the annual report.

There are many variations in format and content of the Financial Highlights section. Such items as sales, net income, net income per common share, cash dividends paid, cash dividends per common share, and the amount of capital expenditures are typically presented. In addition to these data, information about the financial position at year end may be presented. As shown in the Financial Highlights section for Hershey Foods Corporation, such information may include the year-end amounts of stockholders' equity, common shares outstanding, book value per share, and the price per share.

President's Letter to the Stockholders

A letter from the company president to the stockholders is also presented in most annual reports. These letters usually discuss such items as reasons for an increase or decrease in net income, changes in existing plants or purchase or construction of new plants, significant new financing commitments, social responsibility issues, and future plans.

Management Report

The management of the corporation is responsible for the corporation's accounting system and financial statements. In the Management Report, the chief financial officer or other corporate officer normally includes the following:

1. A statement that the financial statements are management's responsibility and that they have been prepared according to generally accepted accounting principles.
2. Management's assessment of the company's internal accounting control system.
3. Comments on any other relevant matters related to the accounting system, the financial statements, and the examination by the independent auditor.

Independent Auditors' Report

Before issuing annual statements, all publicly held corporations are required to have an independent audit of their financial statements. Certified public accountants (CPAs) are engaged to conduct an audit (examination) of the financial statements. The purpose of an independent audit is to add credibility to the financial statements that have been prepared by management.

On completion of the audit, which for large corporations may take several weeks or longer, an Independent Auditors' Report is issued. This report accompanies the financial statements. The normal audit report includes the following three paragraphs:

1. An introductory paragraph identifying the financial statements audited.
2. A scope paragraph describing the nature of the audit.
3. An opinion paragraph presenting the auditor's opinion on the fairness of the statements.

For the financial statements of most companies, the auditors render an opinion such as the one for Hershey Foods Corporation. Such an opinion is called an *unqualified* or *clean opinion*. However, it is possible that accounting methods used by the corporation do not conform with generally accepted accounting principles. In such cases, a *qualified opinion* is rendered, and the exception is briefly described. If the departure from accepted principles is severe, an *adverse* or *negative opinion* is issued and the exception described. In rare cases, the auditors may be unable to reach an opinion on the financial statements. The auditor then issues a *disclaimer* and briefly describes why an opinion could not be reached.

Historical Summary

The Historical Summary section reports selected financial and operating data of past periods, usually for five or ten years. It is usually presented in close proximity to the financial statements for the current year. There are wide variations in the types of data reported and the title of this section. In the annual report for Hershey Foods Corporation, this section is called the "Six-Year Consolidated Financial Summary."

Other Information

In the preceding paragraphs, we described the most commonly presented sections of annual reports related to the financial statements. Some annual reports may include other financial information, such as forecasts that indicate financial plans and expectations for the year ahead and other supplemental data.

Hershey Foods Corporation

Management's Discussion and Analysis – Financial Review

Summary of Consolidated Operating Results

The Corporation achieved increased sales and net income in 1992 and 1991. Net sales during this two-year period increased at a compound annual rate of 9%, primarily reflecting volume growth from international acquisitions, new product introductions, and existing confectionery products, and confectionery price increases. The Corporation's pasta business also contributed to growth in sales and earnings during the period.

In March 1992, Hershey Chocolate U.S.A. increased by approximately 5% the wholesale price of its line of packaged candy products, the first increase since 1984. Hershey Chocolate U.S.A. had previously increased the wholesale price of its line of standard bars and certain other pack-types by approximately 12½% in February 1991. These product lines represented over 45% of the Corporation's annual sales in 1992. The price increases were intended to cover the rising costs of certain raw materials, petroleum-based packaging materials, fuel and employee benefits.

Net income, excluding the effect of a net gain on business restructuring in 1990, increased at a compound annual rate of 11% during the two-year period. This increase was a result of the growth in sales, an improved gross profit margin and a lower effective income tax rate, partially offset by higher levels of selling, marketing and administrative expenses.

Summary of Financial Position and Liquidity

The Corporation's financial position remained strong during 1992. The capitalization ratio (total short-term and long-term debt as a percent of stockholders' equity, short-term and long-term debt) was 27% as of December 31, 1992 and 22% as of December 31, 1991. The ratio of current assets to current liabilities was 1.3:1 as of December 31, 1992 and 1.6:1 as of December 31, 1991. The increase in the capitalization ratio was primarily due to higher short-term borrowings associated with the May 1992 purchase of an 18.6% interest in Freia Marabou a.s (Freia), the leading Scandinavian chocolate, confectionery and snack food company, for $179.1 million. The decrease in the current ratio reflects the borrowings for Freia and the current classification of certain long-term debt as discussed below.

In October 1992, the Corporation announced that it was withdrawing its prior bid to acquire the remaining shares of Freia and had tendered its 18.6% interest to Kraft General Foods Holdings Norway, Inc. (KGF). Proceeds from the sale of the Corporation's interest in Freia are expected to be received in the spring of 1993 upon approval by the Norwegian government of KGF's ownership of Freia. A portion of the proceeds will be used for early repayment of $95.2 million of long-term debt. Accordingly, the investment and the debt have been classified as current assets and liabilities, respectively, as of December 31, 1992.

Historically, the Corporation's major source of financing has been cash generated from operations. Generally, seasonal working capital needs peak during the summer months and have been met by issuing commercial paper.

During 1992, the Corporation's cash and cash equivalents decreased by $47.0 million. Cash provided from operating activities, short-term borrowings, and cash and cash equivalents on hand at the beginning of the period were sufficient to finance capital additions, purchase the investment interest in Freia, and pay cash dividends.

During the three-year period ended December 31, 1992, the Corporation's cash and cash equivalents decreased by $28.4 million. Total debt increased by $302.9 million during this same period, reflecting the investment in Freia and several business acquisitions.

Capital Additions
(dollars in millions)

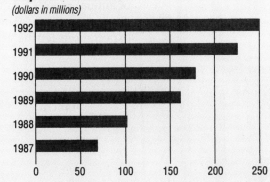

The Corporation anticipates that capital expenditures will be in excess of $200 million per annum during the next several years as a result of the expansion of facilities to support new products and continued modernization of existing facilities. As of December 31, 1992, the Corporation's principal capital commitments included construction of a finished goods production facility adjacent to its new chocolate-processing plant, a pasta plant, manufacturing capacity expansion and modernization.

In February 1991, the Corporation issued $100 million of 8.8% Debentures due 2021 (Debentures), under a Form S-3 Registration Statement (Registration Statement) which was declared effective in June 1990. As of December 31, 1992,

$100 million of additional debt securities remained available for issuance under the Registration Statement.

In the fourth quarter of 1991, the Corporation established an employee stock ownership trust (ESOP) to serve as the primary vehicle for the Corporation's contributions to its existing employee savings and stock investment plan for participating domestic salaried and hourly employees. The ESOP was funded by a 7.75% loan of $47.9 million from the Corporation. The proceeds from this loan were used by the ESOP to purchase from the Corporation 1,193,816 shares of its Common Stock at a market price of $40⅛ per share. This stock had been acquired by the Corporation through open market purchases. The Corporation began making contributions to the ESOP in 1992. Further discussion of the ESOP can be found in Note 9 to the consolidated financial statements.

Acquisitions and Divestiture

Operating results during the period were impacted by the following:

- May 1992 — Completed the acquisition of the 18.6% interest in Freia from Orkla a.s, a diversified Norwegian company. The investment was accounted for under the cost method in 1992. The Corporation expects to sell this interest to KGF during 1993.

- April 1992 — Completed the sale of Hershey do Brasil Participacoes Ltda., a holding company which owned a 41.7% equity interest in Petybon S.A., to the Bunge & Born Group for approximately $7.0 million. Petybon S.A., located in Brazil, is a producer of pasta, biscuits and margarine products.

- October 1991 — Purchased the shares of Nacional de Dulces, S.A. de C.V. (subsequently renamed Hershey Mexico, S.A. de C.V.) owned by its joint venture partner, Grupo Carso, S.A. de C.V. Prior to this transaction, the Corporation owned 50% of the stock. Hershey Mexico has its main offices and manufacturing plant in Guadalajara, Mexico. It produces, imports and markets chocolate products for the Mexican market under the *Hershey's* brand name.

- May 1991 — Acquired from Dairymen, Inc. certain assets of its ultra-high temperature fluid milk-processing

business (aseptically-packaged drink business), including a Savannah, Georgia manufacturing facility.

- May 1991 — Completed the acquisition of the Gubor Schokoladen GmbH and Gubor Schokoladenfabrik GmbH (Gubor) chocolate business from H. Bahlsens Keksfabrik KG. Gubor, which operates two manufacturing plants in Germany, produces and markets high-quality assorted pralines and seasonal chocolates under the *Gubor* brand name. The transaction was effective as of January 1, 1991.

- February 1990 — Acquired from Kraft General Foods, Inc. all of the outstanding voting securities of Ronzoni Foods Corporation.

A further discussion of these acquisitions and the divestiture can be found in Note 3 to the consolidated financial statements.

Contribution to Net Sales of Businesses Acquired 1990 - 1992

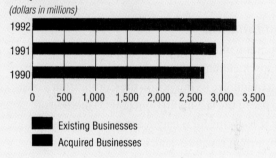

(dollars in millions)

■ Existing Businesses
■ Acquired Businesses

Other Items

The most significant raw material used in the production of the Corporation's chocolate and confectionery products is cocoa beans. Generally, the Corporation has been able to offset the effects of increases in the cost of this raw material through selling price increases or reductions in product weights. Conversely, declines in the cost of cocoa beans have served as a source of funds to maintain selling price stability, enhance consumer value through increases in product weights, respond to competitive activity, develop new products and markets, and offset rising costs of other raw materials and expenses.

The cost of cocoa beans and the prices for the related commodity futures contracts historically have been subject to wide fluctuations attributable to a variety of factors, including the effect of weather on crop yield, other imbalances between supply and demand, currency exchange rates and speculative influences. Over the last few years, the market prices of cocoa beans and cocoa futures have declined as a result of worldwide increases in stocks, as the annual cocoa bean crop exceeded demand for seven consecutive years. The 1991/1992 crop, however, resulted in a small deficit and another deficit is expected for the current crop. Prices in 1992 were relatively stable because of the remaining excess stocks and similar market conditions are expected to continue during the first part of 1993. The Corporation's costs will not necessarily reflect market price fluctuations because of its forward purchasing practices, premiums and discounts reflective of relative values, varying delivery times, and supply and demand for specific varieties and grades of cocoa beans.

Market prices for peanuts began the year at lower levels as compared to the prior year due to an excellent 1991 crop. Prices remained stable during 1992 on reports of favorable growing conditions and a good harvest of the 1992 crop in the fourth quarter. Prices are expected to remain relatively stable through most of 1993.

Effects of Inflation

The Corporation monitors the effects of inflation and takes various steps, including selling price and product weight changes, to minimize its impact on the Corporation's business. The use of the last-in, first-out (LIFO) method of inventory accounting for most inventories matches current costs with current revenues and, in periods of inflation, reduces income taxes and improves cash flow. The capital additions program, through investment in modern plant and equipment, provides for future sales growth and manufacturing efficiencies. These management practices have resulted in inflation having a minimal effect on comparative results of operations and financial condition for the most recent three years.

Capital Structure

The Corporation has two classes of stock outstanding, Common Stock and Class B Common Stock (Class B Stock). The Common Stock and the Class B Stock generally vote together without regard to class on matters submitted to stockholders, including the election of directors, with the Common Stock having one vote per share and the Class B Stock having ten votes per share. However, the Common Stock, voting separately as a class, is entitled to elect

one-sixth of the Board of Directors. With respect to dividend rights, the Common Stock is entitled to cash dividends 10% higher than those declared and paid on the Class B Stock.

The Corporation's Common Stock is listed on the New York Stock Exchange (NYSE), which has a rule generally prohibiting dual classes of common stock. The Corporation's dual class structure has been grandfathered under this rule. In May 1992, the NYSE released for public comment a concept proposal under which dual class capital structures would be permitted, provided certain requirements were met, including approval of the structure by a majority of independent directors and disinterested stockholders. These approval requirements were met when the Corporation adopted its dual class structure in 1984. Additionally, the concept proposal would also grandfather the Corporation's and other listed companies' existing dual class structures.

Market Prices and Dividends

Cash dividends paid on the Corporation's Common Stock and Class B Stock were $91.4 million in 1992 and $83.4 million in 1991. The annual dividend rate on the Common Stock is $1.08 per share, an increase of 10% over the 1991 rate of $.98 per share. The 1992 dividend represents the 18th consecutive year of Common Stock dividend increases. In 1990, the Corporation paid a special dividend of $13.3 million as a result of the sale of its equity interest in AB Marabou (Marabou).

Dividends Paid Per Share of Common Stock
(dollars)

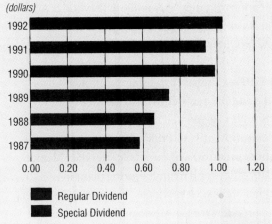

Regular Dividend
Special Dividend

On February 2, 1993, the Corporation's Board of Directors declared a quarterly dividend of $.27 per share of Common Stock payable on March 15, 1993, to stockholders of record as of February 26, 1993. It is the Corporation's 253rd consecutive Common Stock dividend. A quarterly dividend of $.245 per share of Class B Stock was also declared.

Hershey Foods Corporation's Common Stock is listed and traded principally on the NYSE under the ticker symbol "HSY." Approximately 24.1 million shares of the Corporation's Common Stock were traded during 1992. The closing price of the Common Stock on December 31, 1992 was $47. The Class B Stock is not publicly traded. There were 31,642 stockholders of record of the Common Stock and the Class B Stock as of December 31, 1992.

The following table shows the dividends paid per share of Common Stock and Class B Stock and the price range of the Common Stock for each quarter of the past two years:

	Dividends Paid Per Share		Common Stock Price Range*	
	Common Stock	Class B Stock	High	Low
1992				
1st Quarter	$ .245	$.2225	45^{1}/_{4}$	39^{7}/_{8}$
2nd Quarter	.245	.2225	42$^{1}/_{8}$	38$^{1}/_{4}$
3rd Quarter	.270	.2450	45$^{1}/_{2}$	41$^{5}/_{8}$
4th Quarter	.270	.2450	48$^{3}/_{8}$	43$^{1}/_{2}$
	$1.030	$.9350		
1991				
1st Quarter	$ .225	$.2025	42^{3}/_{8}$	35^{1}/_{8}$
2nd Quarter	.225	.2025	43$^{7}/_{8}$	39$^{5}/_{8}$
3rd Quarter	.245	.2225	42$^{5}/_{8}$	38$^{1}/_{2}$
4th Quarter	.245	.2225	44$^{1}/_{2}$	36$^{1}/_{2}$
	$ .940	$.8500		

* NYSE – Composite Quotations for Common Stock by calendar quarter.

Operating Return on Average Stockholders' Equity

The Corporation's operating return on average stockholders' equity was 17.3% in 1992. Over the most recent six-year period, the return has ranged from 16.1% in 1989 to 19.0% in 1987. For the purpose of calculating operating return on average stockholders' equity, earnings is defined as net income, excluding the net gain on the sale of Friendly Ice Cream Corporation (Friendly) in 1988 and the net gain on business restructuring in 1990.

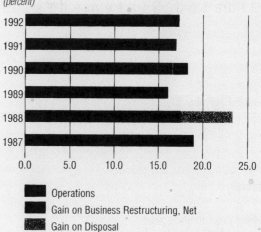

Return on Average Stockholders' Equity
(percent)

Operations
Gain on Business Restructuring, Net
Gain on Disposal

Operating Return on Average Invested Capital

The Corporation's operating return on average invested capital was 14.4% in 1992. Over the most recent six-year period, the return has ranged from 13.2% in 1989 to 14.4% in 1992. Average invested capital consists of the annual average of beginning and ending balances of long-term debt, deferred income taxes and stockholders' equity. For the purpose of calculating operating return on average invested capital, earnings is defined as the sum of net income, excluding the net gains on the sale of Friendly and business restructuring, and the after-tax effect of interest on long-term debt.

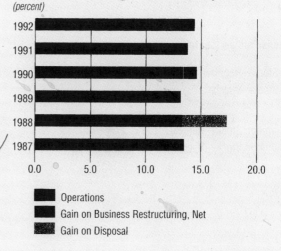

Return on Average Invested Capital
(percent)

Operations
Gain on Business Restructuring, Net
Gain on Disposal

Hershey Foods Corporation

Consolidated Statements of Income

(in thousands of dollars except per share amounts)

For the years ended December 31,	1992	1991	1990
Net Sales	**$3,219,805**	$2,899,165	$2,715,609
Costs and Expenses:			
Cost of sales	**1,833,388**	1,694,404	1,588,360
Selling, marketing and administrative	**958,189**	814,459	776,668
Total costs and expenses	**2,791,577**	2,508,863	2,365,028
Gain on Business Restructuring, Net	**—**	—	35,540
Income before Interest and Income Taxes	**428,228**	390,302	386,121
Interest expense, net	**27,240**	26,845	24,603
Income before Income Taxes	**400,988**	363,457	361,518
Provision for income taxes	**158,390**	143,929	145,636
Net Income	**$ 242,598**	$ 219,528	$ 215,882
Net Income per Share	**$ 2.69**	$ 2.43	$ 2.39

Cash Dividends Paid per Share:			
Common Stock—Regular	**$ 1.030**	$ .940	$ .840
Common Stock—Special	**—**	—	.150
Class B Common Stock—Regular	**.935**	.850	.755
Class B Common Stock—Special	**—**	—	.135

The notes to consolidated financial statements are an integral part of these statements.

Hershey Foods Corporation

Management's Discussion and Analysis – Results of Operations

Net Sales

Net sales rose $320.6 million or 11% in 1992 and $183.6 million or 7% in 1991. The increase in 1992 was due to volume growth from existing brands, sales of new products, confectionery price increases, and the consolidation of Hershey Mexico, the remaining shares of which were acquired in late 1991. The increase in 1991 reflected growth from business acquisitions, confectionery selling price increases, and volume growth from the Corporation's pasta, international and refrigerated puddings businesses.

Costs and Expenses

Cost of sales as a percent of net sales decreased to 56.9% in 1992 from 58.4% in 1991 and 58.5% in 1990. The resulting increase in gross margin in 1992 was primarily due to lower costs for certain major raw materials, confectionery price increases, and manufacturing efficiencies. The increase in gross margin in 1991 reflected confectionery price increases almost entirely offset by a higher average cost per pound of peanuts and cocoa beans, as well as increases in overhead and employee benefits costs.

Selling, marketing and administrative costs increased in 1992, primarily reflecting higher promotion and advertising expenses related to the sales volume growth and the introduction of new products. The increase in selling, marketing and administrative costs in 1991 was a result of business acquisitions and increased promotion expenses offset somewhat by lower advertising expenses.

Gain on Business Restructuring, Net

The Corporation's financial results for 1990 included a net pre-tax gain from business restructuring activities totaling $35.5 million. This gain, which increased net income by $20.3 million is discussed further in Note 2 to the consolidated financial statements.

Interest Expense, Net

Net interest expense was $.4 million higher in 1992 than 1991, due to higher levels of short-term borrowings, offset partially by lower short-term interest rates, lower long-term interest expense, and an increase in capitalized interest. The increase in short-term debt was a result of the Corporation's May 1992 purchase of an 18.6% interest in Freia and interim borrowings to finance capital additions. Long-term interest expense was below 1991 reflecting repayments of long-term debt. A cumulative increase in capital expenditures resulted in significantly higher capitalized interest in 1992 versus 1991.

Net interest expense increased by $2.2 million in 1991 as a result of additional debt required on an interim basis to finance capital additions, working capital requirements and business acquisitions, offset partially by higher capitalized interest.

Provision for Income Taxes

The Corporation's effective income tax rate was 39.5%, 39.6% and 40.3% in 1992, 1991 and 1990, respectively. The principal factors causing differences in the effective income tax rates among the years were a tax benefit in 1992 associated with the sale of the Corporation's equity interest in its Brazilian joint venture, changes in the mix of the Corporation's income among various tax jurisdictions and increases in non-taxable income. These changes more than offset an increase in the Pennsylvania corporate income tax rate in 1991.

Net Income

Net income increased $23.1 million or 11% in 1992. Excluding the effect of the 1990 net gain on business restructuring, net income increased $23.9 million or 12% in 1991. Net income as a percent of net sales was 7.5% in 1992, 7.6% in 1991, and 7.2% in 1990 after excluding the net gain on business restructuring.

Hershey Foods Corporation

Consolidated Statements of Cash Flows

(in thousands of dollars)

For the years ended December 31,	1992	1991	1990
Cash Flows Provided from (Used by) Operating Activities			
Net income	$ 242,598	$ 219,528	$ 215,882
Adjustments to reconcile net income to net cash provided from operations:			
Depreciation and amortization	97,087	85,413	73,889
Deferred income taxes	21,404	20,654	(8,257)
Gain on business restructuring, net	—	—	(35,540)
Changes in assets and liabilities, net of effects from business acquisitions:			
Accounts receivable—trade	(13,841)	(6,404)	(21,028)
Inventories	(20,262)	(43,949)	(61,447)
Accounts payable	(10,715)	4,070	23,300
Other assets and liabilities	(20,707)	94,270	(5,398)
Other, net	649	(26,242)	5,105
Net Cash Provided from Operating Activities	296,213	347,340	186,506
Cash Flows Provided from (Used by) Investing Activities			
Capital additions	(249,795)	(226,071)	(179,408)
Business acquisitions	—	(44,108)	(78,153)
Sale of equity interest	—	—	78,041
Purchase of investment interest	(179,076)	—	—
Other, net	6,581	(1,510)	(4,501)
Net Cash (Used by) Investing Activities	(422,290)	(271,689)	(184,021)
Cash Flows Provided from (Used by) Financing Activities			
Net increase in short-term debt	201,425	56,489	1,131
Long-term borrowings	1,259	23,620	77,117
Repayment of long-term debt	(32,173)	(27,861)	(18,567)
Repayment of assumed debt	—	—	(250)
Loan to ESOP	—	(47,902)	—
Proceeds from sale of Common Stock to ESOP	—	47,902	—
Cash dividends paid	(91,444)	(83,401)	(87,757)
Net Cash Provided from (Used by) Financing Activities	79,067	(31,153)	(28,326)
Increase (Decrease) in Cash and Cash Equivalents	(47,010)	44,498	(25,841)
Cash and Cash Equivalents as of January 1	71,124	26,626	52,467
Cash and Cash Equivalents as of December 31	$ 24,114	$ 71,124	$ 26,626
Interest Paid	$ 29,515	$ 24,468	$ 26,085
Income Taxes Paid	$ 151,490	$ 119,038	$ 147,099

The notes to consolidated financial statements are an integral part of these statements.

Hershey Foods Corporation

Management's Discussion and Analysis – Cash Flows

Summary

Over the past three years, cash requirements for capital additions, dividend payments, purchase of an investment interest in Freia, and several business acquisitions exceeded cash provided from operating activities and the sale of the Corporation's equity interest in Marabou in 1990 by $311.1 million. Total debt, including debt assumed in business acquisitions, increased during the period by $302.9 million. Cash and cash equivalents decreased by $28.4 million during the period.

The Corporation's cash provided from operations during the year is affected by seasonal sales patterns. Chocolate and confectionery seasonal and holiday related sales have typically been highest during the third and fourth quarters of the year, representing the principal seasonal effect. Generally, the Corporation's seasonal working capital needs peak during the summer months and have been met by issuing commercial paper.

Operating Activities

Depreciation and amortization have increased significantly as a result of continuous investment in capital additions and business acquisitions. Cash requirements for accounts receivable and inventories have tended to fluctuate during the three-year period based on sales during December and inventory management practices. The 1992 increase in cash used for other assets and liabilities was primarily related to commodities transactions and payment of income taxes. The 1991 increase in cash flow provided from other assets and liabilities was primarily related to commodities transactions and a corporate owned life insurance program.

Investing Activities

Investing activities included capital additions, the purchase of the 18.6% investment interest in Freia in May 1992, several business acquisitions and, in 1990, the gross proceeds from the sale of the Corporation's equity interest in Marabou. The income taxes paid in 1990 on the Marabou gain were included in operating activities. Capital additions during the past three years included manufacturing

equipment, construction of new facilities and expansion of existing facilities. Cash used for business acquisitions reflected current assets, property, plant and equipment, and intangibles acquired, net of liabilities assumed. Businesses acquired during the past three years included Gubor, the aseptically-packaged drink business and Hershey Mexico in 1991, and Ronzoni in 1990.

Financing Activities

Financing activities included debt borrowings and repayments, payment of dividends and, in 1991, ESOP transactions. In each of the past three years, short-term borrowings in the form of commercial paper or bank borrowings were necessary to fund seasonal working capital requirements. Commercial paper borrowings increased significantly in 1992 due to the purchase of the investment interest in Freia. In February 1991, the Corporation issued $100 million of Debentures under its Form S-3 Registration Statement which was declared effective in June 1990. A portion of the proceeds from issuance of the Debentures was used to repay $76.7 million of domestic commercial paper borrowings which were classified as long-term debt as of December 31, 1990.

During 1991, the Corporation established an ESOP to serve as the primary vehicle for the Corporation's contributions to its existing employee savings and stock investment plan for participating domestic salaried and hourly employees. The ESOP was funded by a 7.75% loan of $47.9 million from the Corporation. The proceeds from this loan were used by the ESOP to purchase from the Corporation 1,193,816 shares of its Common Stock at a market price of $40⅛ per share. This stock had been acquired by the Corporation through open market purchases. The Corporation began making contributions to the ESOP in 1992. ESOP loan payments are due quarterly through 2006.

In 1990, the Corporation paid a one-time special dividend of $13.3 million from the $52.8 million of after-tax proceeds realized upon the sale of the Corporation's equity interest in Marabou. Regular cash dividends paid increased 10% in 1992 over 1991 and 12% in 1991 over 1990.

Hershey Foods Corporation

Consolidated Balance Sheets

(in thousands of dollars)

December 31,	1992	1991
ASSETS		
Current Assets:		
Cash and cash equivalents...	$ 24,114	$ 71,124
Accounts receivable—trade..	173,646	159,805
Inventories...	457,179	436,917
Prepaid expenses and other...	105,966	76,633
Investment interest	179,076	—
Total current assets	939,981	744,479
Property, Plant and Equipment, Net..................................	1,295,989	1,145,666
Intangibles Resulting from Business Acquisitions...................	399,768	421,694
Other Assets..	37,171	29,983
	$2,672,909	$2,341,822
LIABILITIES AND STOCKHOLDERS' EQUITY		
Current Liabilities:		
Accounts payable..	$ 127,175	$ 137,890
Accrued liabilities...	240,816	226,267
Accrued income taxes	5,682	22,000
Short-term debt..	259,045	57,620
Current portion of long-term debt	104,224	26,955
Total current liabilities	736,942	470,732
Long-term Debt...	174,273	282,933
Other Long-term Liabilities	92,950	80,907
Deferred Income Taxes..	203,465	171,999
Total liabilities	1,207,630	1,006,571
Stockholders' Equity:		
Preferred Stock, outstanding shares: none in 1992 and 1991	—	—
Common Stock, outstanding shares:		
74,929,057 in 1992 and 74,921,282 in 1991........................	74,929	74,921
Class B Common Stock, outstanding shares:		
15,257,279 in 1992 and 15,265,054 in 1991........................	15,257	15,265
Additional paid-in capital	52,129	52,509
Cumulative foreign currency translation adjustments	2,484	26,424
Unearned ESOP compensation	(44,708)	(47,902)
Retained earnings	1,365,188	1,214,034
Total stockholders' equity	1,465,279	1,335,251
	$2,672,909	$2,341,822

The notes to consolidated financial statements are an integral part of these balance sheets.

Hershey Foods Corporation

Management's Discussion and Analysis – Financial Condition

Assets

Total assets increased $331.1 million or 14% as of December 31, 1992, primarily as a result of increases in current assets and capital additions.

Current assets increased $195.5 million as of December 31, 1992, primarily due to the 1992 purchase of a $179.1 million investment interest in Freia, which has been classified as a current asset, and an increase in other current assets. The increase in other current assets was primarily related to commodity transactions.

The $150.3 million net increase in property, plant and equipment was primarily the result of capital additions of $249.8 million in 1992 and depreciation expense of $84.4 million.

Liabilities

Total liabilities increased $201.1 million or 20% as of December 31, 1992, primarily due to higher current liabilities.

Current liabilities increased $266.2 million as a result of higher short-term debt and current portion of long-term debt balances. The $201.4 million increase in short-term debt was principally a result of domestic commercial paper borrowings to purchase the investment interest in Freia and interim borrowings to finance capital additions. The increase of $77.3 million in the current portion and the $108.7 million decline in the long-term portion of debt principally reflects the current classification of $95.2 million of long-term debt which will be repaid early using the proceeds from the sale of the Freia investment interest.

The deferred income tax liability as of December 31, 1992 and 1991 has been provided based upon statutory corporate income tax rates in effect at the time of the underlying transactions. The Financial Accounting Standards Board (FASB) has issued Statement of Financial Accounting Standards No. 109, "Accounting for Income Taxes" (FAS No. 109), which must be adopted in 1993 and will modify the way the Corporation accounts for income taxes. Among other provisions, FAS No. 109 requires that tax liabilities be stated at income tax rates currently in effect and allows for either the recording of the entire catch-up effect in the year of adoption or retroactive restatement of prior financial statements. Upon adopting the new accounting rules, the Corporation will record the entire catch-up effect. Management believes that based on the current Federal statutory corporate income tax rate, the adoption will have a favorable impact of approximately $8.0 million on net income in 1993.

The FASB has also issued Statement of Financial Accounting Standards No. 106, "Employers' Accounting for Post-retirement Benefits Other Than Pensions" (FAS No. 106). FAS No. 106 must be adopted in 1993 and requires that the expected cost of post-retirement benefits be accrued during the years that employees render the necessary service. Presently, the Corporation expenses these benefits as paid.

As further discussed in Note 8, the Corporation intends to adopt FAS No. 106 effective January 1, 1993 by means of a cumulative catch-up adjustment. Management expects the accumulated post-retirement benefit obligation as of the implementation date to be approximately $190.0 million, resulting in a one-time charge of approximately $110.0 million after income taxes. In 1993, the incremental expense under FAS No. 106 is expected to be approximately $8.0 million after income taxes. The adoption of this standard will have no effect on the Corporation's cash flows.

Stockholders' Equity

Total stockholders' equity rose 10% in 1992 and has increased at a compound annual rate of 12% over the past five years.

Hershey Foods Corporation

Consolidated Statements of Stockholders' Equity

(in thousands of dollars)	Preferred Stock	Common Stock	Class B Common Stock	Additional Paid-in Capital	Cumulative Foreign Currency Translation Adjustments	Unearned ESOP Compensation	Retained Earnings	Total Stockholders' Equity
Balance as of January 1, 1990	$ —	$74,907	$15,279	$50,212	$ 26,870	$ —	$ 949,782	$1,117,050
Net income							215,882	215,882
Dividends:								
Common Stock, $.990 per share....							(74,161)	(74,161)
Class B Common Stock,								
$.890 per share							(13,596)	(13,596)
Foreign currency translation								
adjustments					(675)			(675)
Conversion of Class B Common Stock								
into Common Stock..............		3	(3)					—
Incentive plan transactions				(963)				(963)
Balance as of December 31, 1990	—	74,910	15,276	49,249	26,195	—	1,077,907	1,243,537
Net income							219,528	219,528
Dividends:								
Common Stock, $.940 per share....							(70,426)	(70,426)
Class B Common Stock,								
$.850 per share							(12,975)	(12,975)
Foreign currency translation								
adjustments...................					229			229
Conversion of Class B Common Stock								
into Common Stock..............		11	(11)					—
Incentive plan transactions				(446)				(446)
Employee stock ownership trust								
transactions...................				3,706		(47,902)		(44,196)
Balance as of December 31, 1991	—	74,921	15,265	52,509	26,424	(47,902)	1,214,034	1,335,251
Net income							242,598	242,598
Dividends:								
Common Stock, $1.030 per share...							(77,174)	(77,174)
Class B Common Stock,								
$.935 per share							(14,270)	(14,270)
Foreign currency translation								
adjustments...................					(23,940)			(23,940)
Conversion of Class B Common Stock								
into Common Stock..............		8	(8)					—
Incentive plan transactions				(741)				(741)
Employee stock ownership trust								
transactions...................				361		3,194		3,555
Balance as of December 31, 1992	$ —	$74,929	$15,257	$52,129	$ 2,484	$(44,708)	$1,365,188	$1,465,279

The notes to consolidated financial statements are an integral part of these statements.

Notes to Consolidated Financial Statements

1. Summary of Significant Accounting Policies

Significant accounting policies employed by the Corporation are discussed below and in other notes to the consolidated financial statements. Certain reclassifications have been made to prior year amounts to conform to the 1992 presentation.

Principles of Consolidation

The consolidated financial statements include the accounts of the Corporation and its subsidiaries after elimination of intercompany accounts and transactions. Investments in affiliated companies are accounted for using the equity method.

Cash Equivalents

All highly liquid debt instruments purchased with a maturity of three months or less are classified as cash equivalents.

Commodities Futures and Options Contracts

In connection with the purchasing of major commodities (principally cocoa and sugar) for anticipated manufacturing requirements, the Corporation enters into commodities futures and options contracts as deemed appropriate to reduce the risk of future price increases. These futures and options contracts are accounted for as hedges and, accordingly, gains and losses are deferred and recognized in cost of sales as part of the product cost.

Property, Plant and Equipment

Property, plant and equipment are stated at cost. Depreciation of buildings, machinery and equipment is computed using the straight-line method over the estimated useful lives.

Intangibles Resulting from Business Acquisitions

Intangible assets resulting from business acquisitions principally consist of the excess of the acquisition cost over the fair value of the net assets of businesses acquired (goodwill). Goodwill is amortized on a straight-line basis over 40 years. Other intangible assets are amortized on a straight-line basis over their estimated useful lives.

Accumulated amortization of intangible assets resulting from business acquisitions was $61.2 million and $50.1 million as of December 31, 1992 and 1991, respectively.

Foreign Currency Translation

Results of operations for international entities are translated using the average exchange rates during the period. For international entities operating in non-highly inflationary economies, assets and liabilities are translated to U.S. dollars using the exchange rates in effect at the balance sheet date. Resulting translation adjustments are recorded in a separate component of stockholders' equity, "Cumulative Foreign Currency Translation Adjustments."

Foreign Exchange Contracts

The Corporation enters into foreign exchange contracts to hedge transactions denominated in international currencies and to hedge payment of intercompany transactions with its non-domestic subsidiaries. Gains and losses are recognized as part of the underlying transactions. In entering into these contracts the Corporation has assumed the risk which might arise from the possible inability of counterparties to meet the terms of their contracts. The Corporation does not expect any losses as a result of counterparty defaults.

As of December 31, 1992, the Corporation had contracts maturing in 1993 and 1994 to purchase at contracted forward rates $57.2 million in foreign currency, primarily Canadian dollars and British sterling, and to sell at contracted forward rates $238.9 million in foreign currency, related to Norwegian kroner expected to be received from the sale of the Corporation's investment interest in Freia Marabou a.s (Freia) as discussed below.

License Agreements

The Corporation has entered into license agreements under which it has access to proprietary technology and manufactures and/or markets and distributes certain products. The Corporation's rights under these agreements are extendable on a long-term basis at the Corporation's option subject to certain conditions, including minimum sales levels. License fees and royalties, payable under the terms of the agreements, are expensed as incurred.

2. Gain on Business Restructuring, Net

The Corporation's financial results for 1990 included a net pre-tax gain from business restructuring activities totaling $35.5 million. This gain, which increased net income by $20.3 million, resulted from two events. In May 1990, the Corporation sold its equity interest in AB Marabou for $78.0 million. The sale resulted in a gain of $60.5 million and had the effect of increasing net income by $35.3 million. In the fourth quarter of 1990, the Corporation recorded a manufacturing restructuring charge of $25.0 million associated with the modernization and relocation of certain manufacturing operations. This charge reduced net income by $15.0 million.

3. Acquisitions and Divestiture

In May 1992, the Corporation acquired an 18.6% interest in Freia from Orkla a.s, a diversified Norwegian company, for $179.1 million. The investment was accounted for under the cost method in 1992.

In October 1992, the Corporation announced that it was withdrawing its prior bid to acquire the remaining shares of Freia and had tendered its 18.6% interest to Kraft General Foods Holdings Norway, Inc. (KGF). The KGF offer is subject to certain conditions, including approval by the Norwegian government of KGF's ownership of Freia which is expected in the spring of 1993. The price will be adjusted for interest to be earned from the date of tender until the payment date. The sale of the Corporation's Freia shares will result in a one-time, pre-tax gain of approximately $80.0 million.

In April 1992, the Corporation completed the sale of Hershey do Brasil Participacoes Ltda., a holding company which owned a 41.7% equity interest in Petybon S.A., to the Bunge & Born Group for approximately $7.0 million. Petybon S.A., located in Brazil, is a producer of pasta, biscuits and margarine products. The sale resulted in a modest pre-tax gain and a reduction in the effective income tax rate of .8% for 1992.

In accordance with the purchase method of accounting, the purchase prices of the acquisitions summarized below were allocated to the underlying assets and liabilities at the date of acquisition based on their estimated respective fair values. Results subsequent to the dates of acquisition are included in the consolidated financial statements. Had the results of these acquisitions been included in consolidated results for the entire length of each period presented, the effect would not have been material.

In October 1991, the Corporation purchased the shares of Nacional de Dulces, S.A. de C.V. (NDD) owned by its joint venture partner, Grupo Carso, S.A. de C.V., for $10.0 million. Prior to the acquisition, the Corporation owned 50% of the outstanding stock of NDD. Subsequent to the acquisition, NDD was renamed Hershey Mexico, S.A. de C.V. (Hershey Mexico). Hershey Mexico has its main offices and manufacturing plant in Guadalajara, Mexico. It produces, imports and markets chocolate products for the Mexican market under the *Hershey's* brand name.

In May 1991, the Corporation purchased certain assets of Dairymen, Inc.'s ultra-high temperature fluid milk-processing business, including a Savannah, Georgia manufacturing facility for $2.2 million, plus the assumption of $8.5 million in debt.

Also in May 1991, the Corporation completed the acquisition of the Gubor Schokoladen GmbH and Gubor Schokoladenfabrik GmbH (Gubor) chocolate business from H. Bahlsens Keksfabrik KG for $31.9 million, plus the assumption of $9.0 million in debt. Gubor manufactures and markets high-quality assorted pralines and seasonal chocolates in Germany. The acquisition was effective as of January 1, 1991.

In February 1990, the Corporation purchased all of the outstanding voting securities of Ronzoni Foods Corporation from Kraft General Foods, Inc. for $78.2 million, plus the assumption of $3.7 million in debt.

4. Interest Expense

Interest expense, net consisted of the following:

For the years ended December 31,	1992	1991	1990
(in thousands of dollars)			
Long-term debt and lease obligations	$ 30,435	$ 32,252	$ 24,258
Short-term debt	11,328	7,403	7,936
Capitalized interest	(12,055)	(10,386)	(5,875)
	29,708	29,269	26,319
Interest income	(2,468)	(2,424)	(1,716)
Interest expense, net	$ 27,240	$ 26,845	$ 24,603

5. Short-term Debt

Generally the Corporation's short-term borrowings are in the form of commercial paper or bank loans with an original maturity of three months or less. The Corporation maintained lines of credit arrangements with commercial banks, under which it could borrow up to $377 million as of December 31, 1992 and up to $168 million as of December 31, 1991 at the lending banks' prime commercial interest rates or lower. These lines of credit, which may be used to support commercial paper borrowings, may be terminated at the option of the Corporation. The Corporation had outstanding domestic commercial paper borrowings and short-term international bank loans against these lines of credit of $259.0 million and $57.6 million as of December 31, 1992 and 1991, respectively.

Lines of credit were supported by commitment fee arrangements. The fees were generally 1/8 % per annum of the commitment. There were no significant compensating balance agreements which legally restricted these funds.

As a result of maintaining a consolidated cash management system, the Corporation maintains overdraft positions at certain banks. Such overdrafts, which were included in accounts payable, were $22.0 million and $23.5 million as of December 31, 1992 and 1991, respectively.

6. Long-term Debt

Long-term debt consisted of the following:

December 31,	1992	1991
(in thousands of dollars)		
Medium-term Notes, 8.45% to 9.92%, due 1992-1998	$ 55,400	$ 73,800
9.5% Sinking Fund Debentures due 2009	42,000	49,500
9.125% Sinking Fund Debentures due 2016	50,000	50,000
8.8% Debentures due 2021	100,000	100,000
Other obligations, net of unamortized debt discount	31,097	36,588
	278,497	309,888
Less — current portion	104,224	26,955
Total long-term debt	$174,273	$282,933

The Corporation intends to use a portion of the proceeds from the sale of its investment interest in Freia for early repayment of $95.2 million of long-term debt during 1993. Accordingly, these borrowings were classified as current as of December 31, 1992.

Aggregate annual maturities and sinking fund requirements during the next five years, including the long-term debt expected to be repaid in 1993 with the proceeds from the sale of the Freia investment interest, are: 1993, $104.2 million; 1994, $14.2 million; 1995, $7.5 million; 1996, $2.1 million; and 1997, $15.9 million. The Corporation's debt is principally unsecured and of equal priority. None of the debt is convertible into stock of the Corporation. The Corporation is in compliance with all covenants included in the related debt agreements.

7. Income Taxes

The provision for income taxes is based on income before income taxes as reported in the consolidated statements of income. Tax credits are recognized as a reduction in the provision using the flow-through method.

Deferred income taxes are provided to reflect timing differences between reported results of operations for financial statement and income tax purposes. Timing differences related primarily to accelerated depreciation and, in 1990, the manufacturing restructuring charge. The provision for income taxes was as follows:

For the years ended December 31,	1992	1991	1990
(in thousands of dollars)			
Current:			
Federal	$104,223	$ 96,074	$121,924
State	30,968	25,128	17,580
International	1,795	2,073	14,389
Current provision for income taxes	136,986	123,275	153,893
Deferred:			
Federal	11,770	12,618	(3,185)
State	4,579	6,111	6,726
International	5,055	1,925	(11,798)
Deferred provision (benefit) for income taxes	21,404	20,654	(8,257)
Total provision for income taxes	$158,390	$143,929	$145,636

The following table reconciles the Federal statutory income tax rate with the Corporation's effective income tax rate:

For the years ended December 31,	1992	1991	1990
Federal statutory tax rate	34.0%	34.0%	34.0%
Increase (reduction) resulting from:			
State income taxes, net of Federal income tax benefits	6.0	5.5	4.4
Non-deductible acquisition costs	0.9	1.0	1.0
Sale of equity interest	(0.8)	—	—
Corporate owned life insurance	(1.0)	(1.1)	(0.5)
Other, net	0.4	0.2	1.4
Effective income tax rate	39.5%	39.6%	40.3%

The Financial Accounting Standards Board (FASB) has issued Statement of Financial Accounting Standards No. 109, "Accounting for Income Taxes" (FAS No. 109). FAS No. 109 accounting and disclosure rules must be adopted in 1993. Among other provisions, FAS No. 109 requires that tax liabilities be stated at income tax rates currently in effect and allows for either the recording of the entire catch-up effect in the year of adoption or retroactive restatement of prior financial statements. Upon adopting the new accounting rules, the Corporation will record the entire catch-up effect. Management believes that based on the current Federal statutory corporate income tax rate, the adoption will have a favorable impact of approximately $8.0 million on net income in 1993.

8. Retirement Plans and Other Benefits

The Corporation and its subsidiaries sponsor a number of defined benefit retirement plans covering substantially all employees. Plans covering most domestic salaried and hourly employees provide retirement benefits based on individual account balances which are increased annually by pay-related and interest credits. Plans covering certain non-domestic employees provide retirement benefits based on career average pay, final pay, or final average pay as defined within the provisions of the individual plans. The Corporation also participates in several multi-employer retirement plans which provide defined benefits to employees covered under certain collective bargaining agreements.

The Corporation's policy is to fund domestic pension liabilities in accordance with the minimum and maximum limits imposed by the Employee Retirement Income Security Act of 1974 and Federal income tax laws. Non-domestic pension liabilities are funded in accordance with applicable local laws and regulations. Plan assets are invested in a broadly diversified portfolio consisting primarily of domestic and international common stocks and fixed income securities.

Pension expense included the following components:

For the years ended December 31,	1992	1991	1990
(in thousands of dollars)			
Service cost	$ 22,858	$ 20,056	$ 19,369
Interest cost on projected benefit obligation	24,098	22,148	18,392
Investment loss (return) on plan assets	(12,331)	(53,627)	2,427
Net amortization and deferral	(15,245)	30,161	(27,420)
Corporate sponsored plans	19,380	18,738	12,768
Multi-employer plans	580	1,231	1,603
Other	630	645	801
Total pension expense	$ 20,590	$ 20,614	$ 15,172

The funded status and amounts recognized in the consolidated balance sheets for the retirement plans were as follows:

	December 31, 1992		December 31, 1991	
	Assets Exceed Accumulated Benefits	Accumulated Benefits Exceed Assets	Assets Exceed Accumulated Benefits	Accumulated Benefits Exceed Assets
(in thousands of dollars)				
Actuarial present value of:				
Vested benefit obligation	$1,643	$319,635	$238,780	$ 32,524
Accumulated benefit obligation	$1,987	$344,091	$254,468	$ 39,406
Actuarial present value of projected benefit obligation	$3,255	$375,715	$280,647	$ 48,020
Plan assets at fair value	2,566	305,255	295,743	9,554
Plan assets greater than (less than) projected benefit obligation	(689)	(70,460)	15,096	(38,466)
Net (gain) loss unrecognized at date of transition	(79)	1,306	(1,809)	3,255
Prior service cost not yet recognized in earnings	6	12,815	6,864	959
Unrecognized net (gain) loss from past experience different than that assumed	708	29,664	(11,118)	5,835
Minimum liability adjustment	—	(18,999)	—	(5,300)
Prepaid pension expense (pension liability)	$ (54)	$(45,674)	$ 9,033	$(33,717)

The projected benefit obligation for the plans was determined principally using a discount rate of 7.0% and 7.5% as of December 31, 1992 and 1991, respectively. For both 1992 and 1991 the assumed long-term compensation increase rate and the assumed long-term rate of return on plan assets were primarily 6.0% and 9.5%, respectively.

The Corporation and its subsidiaries provide certain health care and life insurance benefits for retired employees. Substantially all of the Corporation's domestic employees become eligible for these benefits at early retirement age. Retiree health care benefits and life insurance premiums of $5.4 million, $4.3 million and $3.6 million, were expensed as paid during 1992, 1991 and 1990, respectively.

The FASB has issued Statement of Financial Accounting Standards No. 106, "Employers' Accounting for Post-retirement Benefits Other Than Pensions" (FAS No. 106). FAS No. 106 must be adopted in 1993 and requires that the expected cost of post-retirement benefits be accrued during the years that employees render the necessary service.

The Corporation intends to adopt FAS No. 106 effective January 1, 1993 by means of a cumulative catch-up adjustment. Management expects the accumulated post-retirement benefit obligation as of the implementation date to be approximately $190.0 million, resulting in a one-time charge of approximately $110.0 million after income taxes. In 1993, the incremental expense under FAS No. 106 is expected to be approximately $8.0 million after income taxes. The adoption of this standard will have no effect on the Corporation's cash flows.

As part of its long-range financing plans, the Corporation, in 1989, implemented a corporate owned life insurance program covering most of its domestic employees. After paying employee death benefits, proceeds from this program will be available for general Corporate purposes and may be used to offset future employee benefits costs, including retiree medical benefits. The Corporation's investment in corporate owned life insurance policies was recorded net of policy loans in other assets, and interest accrued on the policy loan was included in accrued liabilities as of December 31, 1992. Net life insurance expense, including interest expense, was included in selling, marketing and administrative expenses.

9. Employee Stock Ownership Trust

In 1991, the Corporation established an employee stock ownership trust (ESOP) to serve as the primary vehicle for the Corporation's contributions to its existing employee savings and stock investment plan for participating domestic salaried and hourly employees. The ESOP was funded by a 15-year 7.75% loan of $47.9 million from the Corporation. The proceeds from this loan were used by the ESOP to purchase, at a market price of $40 1/8 per share, 1,193,816 shares of the Corporation's Common Stock which it had previously acquired through open market purchases.

During 1992, the ESOP received a combination of dividends on unallocated shares and contributions from the Corporation equal to the amount required to meet its principal and interest payments under the loan. Simultaneously, the ESOP allocated to participants 79,588 shares of Common Stock. The Corporation recognized net compensation expense equal to the shares allocated multiplied by the original cost of $40 1/8 per share less dividends received by the ESOP on unallocated shares. Dividends paid on ESOP shares were $.9 million in 1992. The unearned ESOP compensation balance as of December 31, 1992 represented deferred compensation expense to be recognized by the Corporation in future years as additional shares are allocated to participants.

10. Capital Stock and Net Income Per Share

As of December 31, 1992, the Corporation had 530,000,000 authorized shares of capital stock. Of this total, 450,000,000 shares were designated as Common Stock, 75,000,000 shares as Class B Common Stock (Class B Stock), and 5,000,000 shares as Preferred Stock, each class having a par value of one dollar per share. As of December 31, 1992, there was a combined total of 90,186,336 shares of both classes of common stock outstanding. No shares of the Preferred Stock were issued or outstanding during the three-year period ended December 31, 1992.

The Common Stock and the Class B Stock generally vote together without regard to class on matters submitted to stockholders, including the election of directors, with the Common Stock having one vote per share and the Class B Stock having ten votes per share. However, the Common Stock, voting separately as a class, is entitled to elect one-sixth of the Board of Directors. With respect to dividend rights, the Common Stock is entitled to cash dividends 10% higher than those declared and paid on the Class B Stock.

Class B Stock can be converted into Common Stock on a share-for-share basis at any time. During 1992, 1991 and 1990, a total of 7,775, 11,350 and 2,900 shares, respectively, of Class B Stock were converted into Common Stock.

Hershey Trust Company, as Trustee for Milton Hershey School, as institutional fiduciary for estates and trusts unrelated to Milton Hershey School, and as direct owner of investment shares, held a total of 23,428,494 shares of the Common Stock, and as Trustee for Milton Hershey School, held 15,153,003 shares of the Class B Stock as of December 31, 1992, and is entitled to cast approximately

77% of the total votes of both classes of the Corporation's common stock. Hershey Trust Company, as Trustee for Milton Hershey School, must approve the issuance of shares of Common Stock or any other action which would result in the Hershey Trust Company, as Trustee for Milton Hershey School, not continuing to have voting control of the Corporation.

Net income per share has been computed based on the 90,186,336 weighted average number of shares of the Common Stock and the Class B Stock outstanding during the year, for all years presented.

11. Incentive Plan

The long-term portion of the 1987 Key Employee Incentive Plan (Plan) provides for grants or awards to senior executives and key employees of one or more of the following: performance stock units, non-qualified stock options (stock options), stock appreciation rights and restricted stock units. The Plan also provides for the deferral of performance stock unit awards by participants.

As of December 31, 1992, a total of 198,932 contingent performance stock units and restricted stock units had been granted for potential future distribution, primarily related to three-year cycles ending December 31, 1992, 1993 and 1994. Deferred performance stock units and accumulated dividend amounts totaled 244,190 shares as of December 31, 1992.

Stock options are granted at exercise prices of not less than 100% of the fair market value of a share of Common Stock at the time the option is granted and are exercisable for periods no longer than ten years from the date of grant. Each option may be used to purchase one share of Common Stock. No compensation expense is recognized under the stock options portion of the Plan.

Stock option activity was as follows:

	Shares under Options	
	Number of Shares	Option Price per Share
Outstanding — January 1, 1990	415,700	$23¾ to 28
Granted	502,700	$35⅜
Exercised	(77,840)	$25⅜ to 28
Cancelled	(5,600)	$35⅜
Outstanding — December 31, 1990 . . .	834,960	$23¾ to 35⅜
Granted	59,800	$36¼
Exercised	(30,135)	$23¾ to 28
Cancelled	(7,500)	$35⅜
Outstanding — December 31, 1991 . . .	857,125	$23¾ to 36¼
Granted	939,000	$41⅛ to 44¾
Exercised	(69,650)	$23¾ to 35⅜
Cancelled	(9,500)	$44¾
Outstanding — December 31, 1992 . . .	1,716,975	$25⅜ to 44¾

No stock appreciation rights had been granted or awarded as of December 31, 1992.

12. Supplemental Income Statement Information

Supplemental income statement information is provided in the table below. These costs were expensed in the year incurred.

For the years ended December 31,	1992	1991	1990
(in thousands of dollars)			
Promotion.	$398,577	$325,465	$315,242
Advertising	137,631	117,049	146,297
Maintenance and repairs	79,563	72,192	66,203
Depreciation expense.	84,434	72,735	61,725
Rent expense.	23,960	23,288	20,758
Research and development	24,203	22,770	19,152

Rent expense pertains to all operating leases which were principally related to certain administrative buildings, distribution facilities and transportation equipment. Future minimum rental payments under non-cancellable operating leases with a remaining term in excess of one year as of December 31, 1992, were: 1993, $9.7 million; 1994, $12.1 million; 1995, $11.1 million; 1996, $10.8 million; 1997, $10.7 million; 1998 and beyond, $113.4 million.

Amounts for taxes other than payroll and income taxes, amortization of intangibles resulting from business acquisitions, and royalties were less than 1% of net sales.

13. Supplemental Balance Sheet Information

Accounts Receivable — Trade

In the normal course of business, the Corporation extends credit to customers which satisfy pre-defined credit criteria. The Corporation believes that it has little concentration of credit risk due to the diversity of its customer base. Receivables, as shown on the consolidated balance sheets, were net of allowances of $10.4 million and $9.5 million as of December 31, 1992 and 1991, respectively.

Inventories

The Corporation values the majority of its inventories under the last-in, first-out (LIFO) method and the remaining inventories at the lower of first-in, first-out (FIFO) cost or market. LIFO cost of inventories valued using the LIFO method was $350.4 million as of December 31, 1992 and $334.5 million as of December 31, 1991 and all inventories were stated at amounts that did not exceed realizable values. Total inventories were as follows:

December 31, (in thousands of dollars)	1992	1991
Raw materials	$243,243	$236,846
Goods in process	30,965	30,039
Finished goods	231,313	227,405
Inventories at FIFO	505,521	494,290
Adjustment to LIFO	(48,342)	(57,373)
Total inventories	$457,179	$436,917

Property, Plant and Equipment

Property, plant and equipment balances included construction in progress of $196.9 million and $170.5 million as of December 31, 1992 and 1991, respectively.

Major classes of property, plant and equipment were as follows:

December 31, (in thousands of dollars)	1992	1991
Land	$ 40,163	$ 37,911
Buildings	385,545	384,117
Machinery and equipment	1,371,729	1,159,268
	1,797,437	1,581,296
Accumulated depreciation	501,448	435,630
Property, plant and equipment, net	$1,295,989	$1,145,666

Accrued Liabilities

Accrued liabilities were as follows:

December 31, (in thousands of dollars)	1992	1991
Payroll and other compensation	$ 63,088	$ 55,346
Advertising and promotion	72,735	63,344
Interest	22,744	24,366
Other	82,249	83,211
Total accrued liabilities	$240,816	$226,267

14. Segment Information

The Corporation operates in a single consumer foods line of business, encompassing the domestic and international manufacture, distribution and sale of chocolate, confectionery, pasta and other food products.

Operations in Canada represent the majority of the Corporation's international business. Historically, transfers of product between geographic areas have not been significant. Net sales, income before interest and income taxes, and identifiable assets by geographic segment were as follows:

For the years ended December 31,	1992	1991	1990
(in thousands of dollars)			
Net sales:			
Domestic	$2,871,438	$2,566,448	$2,508,542
International	348,367	332,717	207,067
Total	$3,219,805	$2,899,165	$2,715,609
Income before interest and income taxes:			
Domestic	$ 419,317	$ 381,549	$ 344,303
International	8,911	8,753	6,278
Gain on Business Restructuring, Net	—	—	35,540
Total	$ 428,228	$ 390,302	$ 386,121
Identifiable assets as of December 31:			
Domestic	$2,353,230	$2,003,425	$1,820,434
International	319,679	338,397	258,394
Total	$2,672,909	$2,341,822	$2,078,828

15. Quarterly Data (Unaudited)

Summary quarterly results were as follows:

(in thousands of dollars except per share amounts)

Year 1992	First	Second	Third	Fourth	Year
Net sales	$800,967	$621,840	$827,475	$969,523	$3,219,805
Gross profit	337,529	266,791	352,792	429,305	1,386,417
Net income	58,924	34,475	66,880	82,319	242,598
Net income per share[a]	.65	.39	.74	.91	2.69

Year 1991	First	Second	Third	Fourth	Year
Net sales	$684,565	$585,166	$765,502	$863,932	$2,899,165
Gross profit	272,733	245,703	319,754	366,571	1,204,761
Net income	48,636	31,903	64,085	74,904	219,528
Net income per share[a]	.54	.35	.71	.83	2.43

[a] The weighted average number of shares outstanding was 90,186,336 for all periods presented.

Responsibility for Financial Statements

Hershey Foods Corporation is responsible for the financial statements and other financial information contained in this report. The Corporation believes that the financial statements have been prepared in conformity with generally accepted accounting principles appropriate under the circumstances to reflect in all material respects the substance of applicable events and transactions. In preparing the financial statements, it is necessary that management make informed estimates and judgments. The other financial information in this annual report is consistent with the financial statements.

The Corporation maintains a system of internal accounting controls designed to provide reasonable assurance that financial records are reliable for purposes of preparing financial statements and that assets are properly accounted for and safeguarded. The concept of reasonable assurance is based on the recognition that the cost of the system must be related to the benefits to be derived. The Corporation believes its system provides an appropriate balance in this regard. The Corporation maintains an Internal Audit Department which reviews the adequacy and tests the application of internal accounting controls.

The financial statements have been audited by Arthur Andersen & Co., independent public accountants, whose appointment was ratified by stockholder vote at the stockholders' meeting held on April 27, 1992. Their report expresses an opinion that the Corporation's financial statements are fairly stated in conformity with generally accepted accounting principles, and they have indicated to us that their examination was performed in accordance with generally accepted auditing standards which are designed to obtain reasonable assurance about whether the financial statements are free of material misstatement.

The Audit Committee of the Board of Directors of the Corporation, consisting solely of outside directors, meets regularly with the independent public accountants, internal auditors and management to discuss, among other things, the audit scopes and results. Arthur Andersen & Co. and the internal auditors both have full and free access to the Audit Committee, with and without the presence of management.

Report of Independent Public Accountants

To the Stockholders and Board of Directors
of Hershey Foods Corporation:

We have audited the accompanying consolidated balance sheets of Hershey Foods Corporation (a Delaware Corporation) and subsidiaries as of December 31, 1992 and 1991, and the related consolidated statements of income, stockholders' equity and cash flows for each of the three years in the period ended December 31, 1992, appearing on pages 22, 24, 26, 28 and 29 through 37. These financial statements are the responsibility of the Corporation's management. Our responsibility is to express an opinion on these financial statements based on our audits.

We conducted our audits in accordance with generally accepted auditing standards. Those standards require that we plan and perform the audit to obtain reasonable assurance about whether the financial statements are free of material misstatement. An audit includes examining, on a test basis, evidence supporting the amounts and disclosures in the financial statements. An audit also includes assessing the accounting principles used and significant estimates made by management, as well as evaluating the overall financial statement presentation. We believe that our audits provide a reasonable basis for our opinion.

In our opinion, the financial statements referred to above present fairly, in all material respects, the financial position of Hershey Foods Corporation and subsidiaries as of December 31, 1992 and 1991, and the results of their operations and cash flows for each of the three years in the period ended December 31, 1992 in conformity with generally accepted accounting principles.

New York, N.Y.
January 29, 1993

Hershey Foods Corporation

Six-Year Consolidated Financial Summary

make a money on appreciation, not on dividend.

(all dollar and share amounts in thousands except market price and per share statistics)

	1992	1991	1990	1989	1988	1987
Summary of Operations[a]						
Net Sales	$3,219,805	2,899,165	2,715,609	2,420,988	2,168,048	1,863,816
Cost of Sales	$1,833,388	1,694,404	1,588,360	1,455,612	1,326,458	1,149,663
Selling, Marketing and Administrative	$ 958,189	814,459	776,668	655,040	575,515	468,062
Gain on Business Restructuring, Net	$ —	—	35,540	—	—	—
Interest Expense, Net	$ 27,240	26,845	24,603	20,414	29,954	22,413
Income Taxes	$ 158,390	143,929	145,636	118,868	91,615	99,604
Income from Continuing Operations	$ 242,598	219,528	215,882	171,054	144,506	124,074
Discontinued Operations	$ —	—	—	—	69,443	24,097
Net Income	$ 242,598	219,528	215,882	171,054	213,949	148,171
Income Per Share from Continuing Operations	$ 2.69	2.43	2.39[e]	1.90	1.60	1.38
Net Income Per Share	$ 2.69	2.43	2.39[e]	1.90	2.37	1.64
Weighted Average Shares Outstanding	90,186	90,186	90,186	90,186	90,186	90,186
Dividends Paid on Common Stock	$ 77,174	70,426	74,161[b]	55,431	49,433	43,436
Per Share	$ 1.030	.940	.990[b]	.740	.660	.580
Dividends Paid on Class B Common Stock	$ 14,270	12,975	13,596[b]	10,161	9,097	8,031
Per Share	$ .935	.850	.890[b]	.665	.595	.525
Income from Continuing Operations before Interest and Income Taxes as a Percent of Net Sales	13.3%	13.5%	12.9%[c]	12.8%	12.3%	13.2%
Income from Continuing Operations as a Percent of Net Sales	7.5%	7.6%	7.2%[c]	7.1%	6.7%	6.7%
Depreciation	$ 84,434	72,735	61,725	54,543	43,721	35,397
Advertising	$ 137,631	117,049	146,297	121,182	99,082	97,033
Promotion	$ 398,577	325,465	315,242	256,237	230,187	171,162
Payroll	$ 433,162	398,661	372,780	340,129	298,483	263,529
Year-end Position and Statistics[a]						
Working Capital	$ 203,039	273,747	320,552	281,821	273,716	190,069[d]
Capital Additions	$ 249,795	226,071	179,408	162,032	101,682	68,504
Total Assets	$2,672,909	2,341,822	2,078,828	1,814,101	1,764,665	1,544,354
Long-term Debt	$ 174,273	282,933	273,442	216,108	233,025	280,900
Stockholders' Equity	$1,465,279	1,335,251	1,243,537	1,117,050	1,005,866	832,410
Current Ratio	1.3:1	1.6:1	1.9:1	2.0:1	1.8:1	1.7:1[d]
Capitalization Ratio	27%	22%	19%	17%	22%	27%
Net Book Value Per Share	$ 16.25	14.81	13.79	12.39	11.15	9.23
Operating Return on Average Stockholders' Equity	17.3%	17.0%	16.6%	16.1%	17.5%	19.0%
Operating Return on Average Invested Capital	14.4%	13.8%	13.4%	13.2%	13.3%	13.5%
Full-time Employees at Year-end	13,700	14,000	12,700	11,800	12,100	10,540
Stockholders' Data						
Outstanding Shares of Common Stock and Class B Common Stock at Year-end	90,186	90,186	90,186	90,186	90,186	90,186
Market Price of Common Stock at Year-end	$ 47	44³⁄₈	37½	35⅞	26	24½
Range During Year	$48³⁄₈-38¼	44½-35⅛	39⅝-28¼	36⅞-24¾	28⅝-21⅞	37³⁄₄-20³⁄₄
Year-end Common Stock and Class B Common Stock Holders	31,642	31,029	30,052	29,998	30,430	29,151
Approximate Annual Composite Trading Volume	24,146	27,975	31,024	41,220	46,693	48,145

[handwritten: pays per share has some extend of money]

Notes:

(a) Amounts for 1987 have been restated for discontinued operations, where applicable. Operating Return on Average Stockholders' Equity and Operating Return on Average Invested Capital have been computed using Net Income, excluding the gain on the sale of Friendly Ice Cream Corporation and the Gain on Business Restructuring, Net.

(b) Amounts included a special dividend for 1990 of $11.2 million or $.15 per share of Common Stock and $2.1 million or $.135 per share of Class B Common Stock.

(c) Calculated percent excludes the Gain on Business Restructuring, Net. Including the gain, Income from Continuing Operations before Interest and Income Taxes as a Percent of Net Sales was 14.2% and Income from Continuing Operations as a Percent of Net Sales was 7.9%.

(d) Amounts exclude net assets of discontinued operations.

(e) Income Per Share from Continuing Operations and Net Income Per Share for 1990 included a $.22 per share Gain on Business Restructuring, Net. Excluding the impact of this gain, Income Per Share from Continuing Operations and Net Income Per Share would have been $2.17.

FINANCIAL STATEMENT ANALYSIS

The basic financial statements provide much of the information users need to make economic decisions about business enterprises. In the following paragraphs, we discuss various ways in which financial statement data are analyzed.

BASIC ANALYTICAL PROCEDURES

The analytical measures obtained from financial statements are often expressed as ratios or percentages. For example, the relationship of $300,000 to $200,000 ($300,000/$200,000, or $300,000:$200,000) may be expressed as 1.5, 1.5:1, or 150%.

Analytical procedures may be used to compare items on a current statement with related items on earlier statements. For example, cash of $150,000 on the current balance sheet may be compared with cash of $100,000 on the balance sheet of a year earlier. The current year's cash may be expressed as 1.5 or 150% of the earlier amount or as an increase of 50% or $50,000.[1]

Analytical procedures are also widely used to examine relationships within a financial statement. To illustrate, assume that cash of $50,000 and inventories of $250,000 are included in the total assets of $1,000,000 on a balance sheet. In relative terms, the cash balance is 5% of the total assets, and the inventories are 25% of the total assets.

In the following discussion, we emphasize the importance of each of the various analytical measures illustrated. The measures are not ends in themselves; they are only guides in evaluating financial and operating data. Many other factors, such as trends in the industry and general economic conditions, should also be considered.

Horizontal Analysis

The percentage analysis of increases and decreases in related items in comparative financial statements is called **horizontal analysis**. The amount of each item on the most recent statement is compared with the related item on one or more earlier statements. The amount of increase or decrease in the item is listed, along with the percent of increase or decrease.

Horizontal analysis may include a comparison between two statements. In this case, the earlier statement is used as the base. Horizontal analysis may also include three or more comparative statements. In this case, the earliest date or period may be used as the base for comparing all later dates or periods. Alternatively, each statement may be compared to the immediately preceding statement. Exhibit 1 is a condensed comparative balance sheet for two years for Marlea Company, with horizontal analysis.

We cannot fully evaluate the significance of the various increases and decreases in the items shown in Exhibit 1 without additional information. Although total assets at the end of 1995 were $91,000 (7.4%) less than at the beginning of the year, liabilities were reduced by $133,000 (30%), and stockholders' equity increased $42,000 (5.3%). It appears that the reduction of $100,000 in long-term liabilities was achieved mostly through the sale of long-term investments.

The balance sheet in Exhibit 1 may be expanded to include the details of the various categories of assets and liabilities. An alternative is to present the details in separate schedules. Exhibit 2 is a supporting schedule with horizontal analysis.

The decrease in accounts receivable may be due to changes in credit terms or improved collection policies. Likewise, a decrease in inventories during a period of increased sales may indicate an improvement in the management of inventories.

The changes in the current assets in Exhibit 2 appear favorable. This assessment is supported by the 24.8% increase in net sales shown in Exhibit 3.

---

[1] Increases or decreases in items may be expressed in percentage terms only when the initial or base amount is positive. If the base amount is zero or a negative value, the amount of change cannot be expressed as a percentage.

Exhibit 1
Comparative Balance Sheet—
Horizontal Analysis

Marlea Company Comparative Balance Sheet December 31, 1995 and 1994				
	1995	1994	Increase Amount	(Decrease) Percent
Assets				
Current assets	$ 550,000	$ 533,000	$ 17,000	3.2%
Long-term investments	95,000	177,500	(82,500)	(46.5%)
Plant assets (net)	444,500	470,000	(25,500)	(5.4%)
Intangible assets	50,000	50,000	—-	
Total assets	$1,139,500	$1,230,500	($ 91,000)	(7.4%)
Liabilities				
Current liabilities	$ 210,000	$ 243,000	($ 33,000)	(13.6%)
Long-term liabilities	100,000	200,000	(100,000)	(50.0%)
Total liabilities	$ 310,000	$ 443,000	($133,000)	(30.0%)
Stockholders' Equity				
Preferred 6% stock, $100 par	$ 150,000	$ 150,000	—-	—-
Common stock, $10 par	500,000	500,000	—-	—-
Retained earnings	179,500	137,500	$ 42,000	30.5%
Total stockholders' equity	$ 829,500	$ 787,500	$ 42,000	5.3%
Total liabilities and stockholders' equity	$1,139,500	$1,230,500	($ 91,000)	(7.4%)

Exhibit 2
Comparative Schedule of Current Assets—
Horizontal Analysis

Marlea Company Comparative Schedule of Current Assets December 31, 1995 and 1994				
	1995	1994	Increase Amount	(Decrease) Percent
Cash	$ 90,500	$ 64,700	$25,800	39.9%
Marketable securities	75,000	60,000	15,000	25.0%
Accounts receivable (net)	115,000	120,000	(5,000)	(4.2%)
Inventories	264,000	283,000	(19,000)	(6.7%)
Prepaid expenses	5,500	5,300	200	3.8%
Total current assets	$550,000	$533,000	$17,000	3.2%

An increase in net sales may not have a favorable effect on operating performance. The percentage increase in Marlea Company's net sales is accompanied by a greater percentage increase in the cost of goods (merchandise) sold. This has the effect of reducing gross profit. Selling expenses increased significantly, and administrative expenses increased slightly. Overall operating expenses increased by 20.7%, whereas gross profit increased by only 19.7%.

The increase in operating income and in net income is favorable. However, a study of the expenses and additional analyses and comparisons should be made before reaching a conclusion.

Exhibit 4 illustrates a comparative retained earnings statement with horizontal analysis. It reveals an increase of 30.5% in retained earnings for the year. The increase is due to net income of $91,000 for the year less dividends of $49,000.

Vertical Analysis

A percentage analysis may also be used to show the relationship of each component to the total within a single statement. This type of analysis is called **vertical analysis**. Like horizontal analysis, the statements may be prepared in either de-

Exhibit 3
Comparative Income Statement—
Horizontal Analysis

Marlea Company
Comparative Income Statement
December 31, 1995 and 1994

	1995	1994	Increase Amount	(Decrease) Percent
Sales	$1,530,500	$1,234,000	$296,500	24.0%
Sales returns and allowances	32,500	34,000	(1,500)	(4.4%)
Net sales	$1,498,000	$1,200,000	$298,000	24.8%
Cost of goods sold	1,043,000	820,000	223,000	27.2%
Gross profit	$ 455,000	$ 380,000	$ 75,000	19.7%
Selling expenses	$ 191,000	$ 147,000	$ 44,000	29.9%
Administrative expenses	104,000	97,400	6,600	6.8%
Total operating expenses	$ 295,000	$ 244,400	$ 50,600	20.7%
Operating income	$ 160,000	$ 135,600	$ 24,400	18.0%
Other income	8,500	11,000	(2,500)	(22.7%)
	$ 168,500	$ 146,600	$ 21,900	14.9%
Other expense	6,000	12,000	(6,000)	(50.0%)
Income before income tax	$ 162,500	$ 134,600	$ 27,900	20.7%
Income tax	71,500	58,100	13,400	23.1%
Net income	$ 91,000	$ 76,500	$ 14,500	19.0%

Exhibit 4
Comparative Retained Earnings
Statement—
Horizontal Analysis

Marlea Company
Comparative Retained Earnings Statement
December 31, 1995 and 1994

	1995	1994	Increase Amount	(Decrease) Percent
Retained earnings, January 1	$137,500	$100,000	$37,500	37.5%
Net income for the year	91,000	76,500	14,500	19.0%
Total	$228,500	$176,500	$52,000	29.5%
Dividends:				
On preferred stock	$ 9,000	$ 9,000	—	—
On common stock	40,000	30,000	$10,000	33.3%
Total	$ 49,000	$ 39,000	$10,000	25.6%
Retained earnings, December 31	$179,500	$137,500	$42,000	30.5%

tailed or condensed form. In the latter case, additional details of the changes in individual items may be presented in supporting schedules. In such schedules, the percentage analysis may be based on either the total of the schedule or the statement total. Although vertical analysis is limited to an individual statement, its significance may be improved by preparing comparative statements.

In vertical analysis of the balance sheet, each asset item is stated as a percent of the total assets. Each liability and stockholders' equity item is stated as a percent of the total liabilities and stockholders' equity. Exhibit 5 is a condensed comparative balance sheet with vertical analysis for Marlea Company.

The major percentage changes in Marlea Company's assets are in the current asset and long-term investment categories. In the Liabilities and Stockholders' Equity sections of the balance sheet, the greatest percentage changes are in long-term liabilities and retained earnings. Stockholders' equity increased from 64% to 72.8% of total liabilities and stockholders' equity in 1995. There is a comparable decrease in liabilities.

In a vertical analysis of the income statement, each item is stated as a percent of net sales. Exhibit 6 is a condensed comparative income statement with vertical analysis for Marlea Company.

Exhibit 5
Comparative Balance Sheet—
Vertical Analysis

Marlea Company
Comparative Balance Sheet
December 31, 1995 and 1994

	1995 Amount	1995 Percent	1994 Amount	1994 Percent
Assets				
Current assets	$ 550,000	48.3%	$ 533,000	43.3%
Long-term investments	95,000	8.3	177,500	14.4
Plant assets (net)	444,500	39.0	470,000	38.2
Intangible assets	50,000	4.4	50,000	4.1
Total assets	$1,139,500	100.0%	$1,230,500	100.0%
Liabilities				
Current liabilities	$ 210,000	18.4%	$ 243,000	19.7%
Long-term liabilities	100,000	8.8	200,000	16.3
Total liabilities	$ 310,000	27.2%	$ 443,000	36.0%
Stockholders' Equity				
Preferred 6% stock, $100 par	$ 150,000	13.2%	$ 150,000	12.2%
Common stock, $10 par	500,000	43.9	500,000	40.6
Retained earnings	179,500	15.7	137,500	11.2
Total stockholders' equity	$ 829,500	72.8%	$ 787,500	64.0%
Total liabilities and stockholders' equity	$1,139,500	100.0%	$1,230,500	100.0%

Exhibit 6
Comparative Income Statement—
Vertical Analysis

Marlea Company
Comparative Income Statement
For Years Ended December 31, 1995 and 1994

	1995 Amount	1995 Percent	1994 Amount	1994 Percent
Sales	$1,530,500	102.2%	$1,234,000	102.8%
Sales returns and allowances	32,500	2.2	34,000	2.8
Net sales	$1,498,000	100.0%	$1,200,000	100.0%
Cost of goods sold	1,043,000	69.6	820,000	68.3
Gross profit	$ 455,000	30.4%	$ 380,000	31.7%
Selling expenses	$ 191,000	12.8%	$ 147,000	12.3%
Administrative expenses	104,000	6.9	97,400	8.1
Total operating expenses	$ 295,000	19.7%	$ 244,400	20.4%
Operating income	$ 160,000	10.7%	$ 135,600	11.3%
Other income	8,500	.6	11,000	.9
	$ 168,500	11.3%	$ 146,600	12.2%
Other expense	6,000	.4	12,000	1.0
Income before income tax	$ 162,500	10.9%	$ 134,600	11.2%
Income tax	71,500	4.8%	58,100	4.8
Net income	$ 91,000	6.1%	$ 76,500	6.4%

We must use care in judging the significance of differences between percentages for the two years. For example, the decline of the gross profit rate from 31.7% in 1994 to 30.4% in 1995 is only 1.3 percentage points. In terms of dollars of potential gross profit, however, it represents a decline of approximately $19,500 (1.3% × $1,498,000).

Common-Size Statements

Horizontal and vertical analyses with both dollar and percentage amounts are useful in assessing relationships and trends in financial condition and operations of an enterprise. Vertical analysis with both dollar and percentage amounts is also useful in comparing one company with another or with industry averages. Such comparisons are easier to make with the use of common-size statements. In a **common-size statement**, all items are expressed in percentages.

Common-size statements are useful in comparing the current period with prior periods, individual businesses, or one business with industry percentages. Industry data are often available from trade associations and financial information services. Exhibit 7 is a comparative common-size income statement for two enterprises.

Exhibit 7
Common-Size Income Statement

Marlea Company and Gram Corporation Condensed Common-Size Income Statement For Year Ended December 31, 1995		
	Marlea Company	Gram Corporation
Sales	102.2%	102.3%
Sales returns and allowances	2.2	2.3
Net sales	100.0%	100.0%
Cost of goods sold	69.6	70.0
Gross profit	30.4%	30.0%
Selling expenses	12.8%	11.5%
Administrative expenses	6.9	4.1
Total operating expenses	19.7%	15.6%
Operating income	10.7%	14.4%
Other income	.6	.6
	11.3%	15.0%
Other expense	.4	.5
Income before income tax	10.9%	14.5%
Income tax	4.8	5.5
Net income	6.1%	9.0%

Exhibit 7 indicates that Marlea Company has a slightly higher rate of gross profit than Gram Corporation. However, this advantage is more than offset by Marlea Company's higher percentage of selling and administrative expenses. As a result, the operating income of Marlea Company is 10.7% of net sales, compared with 14.4% for Gram Corporation—an unfavorable difference of 3.7 percentage points.

Other Analytical Measures

In addition to the preceding analyses, other relationships may be expressed in ratios and percentages. Often, these items are taken from the financial statements and thus are a type of vertical analysis. Comparison of these items with items from earlier periods is a type of horizontal analysis.

FOCUS OF FINANCIAL STATEMENT ANALYSES

Some aspects of an enterprise's financial condition and operations are of greater importance to some users than others. However, all users are interested in the ability of an enterprise to pay its debts as they are due and to earn income. These two aspects of an enterprise are called factors of **solvency** and **profitability**

An enterprise that cannot pay its debts on a timely basis may experience difficulty in obtaining credit. A lack of available credit may, in turn, lead to a decline in the enterprise's profitability. Eventually, the enterprise may be forced into bankruptcy. Likewise, an enterprise that is less profitable than its competitors is likely to be at a disadvantage in obtaining credit or new capital from stockholders. Thus, the factors of solvency and profitability are interrelated.

Analyses of historical data are useful in assessing the past performance of an enterprise and in forecasting its future performance. The results of financial analyses may be even more useful when they are compared with those of competing enterprises and with industry averages.

In the following paragraphs, we discuss various types of financial analyses useful in evaluating the solvency and profitability of an enterprise. The examples are based on Marlea Company's financial statements presented earlier. In some cases, data from Marlea Company's financial statements of the preceding year and from other sources are also used.

SOLVENCY ANALYSIS

Solvency is the ability of a business to meet its financial obligations (debts) as they are due. Solvency analysis, therefore, focuses on the ability of an enterprise to pay or otherwise satisfy its current and noncurrent liabilities. This ability is normally assessed by examining balance sheet relationships. Major analyses used in assessing solvency include the following:

1. Current position analysis
2. Accounts receivable analysis
3. Inventory analysis
4. The ratio of plant assets to long-term liabilities
5. The ratio of liabilities to stockholders' equity
6. The number of times interest charges are earned

Current Position Analysis

To be useful in assessing solvency, a ratio or other financial measure must relate to an enterprise's ability to pay or otherwise satisfy its liabilities. The use of such measures to assess the ability of an enterprise to pay its current liabilities is called **current position analysis**. Such analysis is of special interest to short-term creditors.

An analysis of a firm's current position normally includes determining the working capital, the current ratio, and the acid-test ratio. The current and acid-test ratios are most useful when analyzed together and compared to previous periods and other firms in the industry.

WORKING CAPITAL. The excess of the current assets of an enterprise over its current liabilities is called **working capital**. *The working capital is often used in evaluating a company's ability to meet currently maturing debts.* It is especially useful in making monthly or other period-to-period comparisons for a company. However, amounts of working capital are difficult to assess when comparing companies of different sizes or in comparing such amounts with industry figures. For example, working capital of $250,000 may be adequate for a small residential contractor, but it may be inadequate for a large commercial contractor.

CURRENT RATIO. Another means of expressing the relationship between current assets and current liabilities is the **current ratio**. This ratio is sometimes called the **working capital ratio** or **bankers' ratio**. The ratio is computed by dividing the total current assets by the total current liabilities. For Marlea Company, working capital and the current ratio for 1995 and 1994 are as follows:

	1995	1994
Current assets	$550,000	$533,000
Current liabilities	210,000	243,000
Working capital	$340,000	$290,000
Current ratio	2.6:1	2.2:1

The current ratio is a more reliable indicator of solvency than is working capital. To illustrate, assume that as of December 31, 1995, the working capital of a competitor is much greater than $340,000, but its current ratio is only 1.3:1. Considering these facts alone, Marlea Company, with its current ratio of 2.6:1, is in a more favorable position to obtain short-term credit than the competitor, which has the greater amount of working capital.

ACID-TEST RATIO. The working capital and the current ratio do not consider the makeup of the current assets. To illustrate the importance of this consideration, the current position data for Marlea Company and Wilson Corporation as of December 31, 1995, are as follows:

	Marlea Company	Wilson Corporation
Current assets:		
Cash	$ 90,500	$ 45,500
Marketable securities	75,000	25,000
Accounts receivable (net)	115,000	90,000
Inventories	264,000	380,000
Prepaid expenses	5,500	9,500
Total current assets	$550,000	$550,000
Current liabilities	210,000	210,000
Working capital	$340,000	$340,000
Current ratio	2.6:1	2.6:1

Both companies have working capital of $340,000 and a current ratio of 2.6:1. But the ability of each company to pay its current debts is significantly different. Wilson Corporation has more of its current assets in inventories. Some of these inventories must be sold and the receivables collected before the current liabilities can be paid in full. Thus, a large amount of time may be necessary to convert these inventories into cash. Declines in market prices and a reduction in demand could also impair the ability to pay current liabilities. In contrast, Marlea Company has cash and current assets (marketable securities and accounts receivable) that can generally be converted to cash rather quickly to meet its current liabilities.

A ratio that measures the "instant" debt-paying ability of a company is called the **acid-test ratio** *or* **quick ratio.** It is the ratio of the total quick assets to the total current liabilities. **Quick assets** are cash and other current assets that can be quickly converted to cash. Quick assets normally include cash, marketable securities, and receivables. The acid-test ratio data for Marlea Company are as follows:

	1995	1994
Quick assets:		
Cash	$ 90,500	$ 64,700
Marketable securities	75,000	60,000
Accounts receivable (net)	115,000	120,000
Total	$280,500	$244,700
Current liabilities	$210,000	$243,000
Acid-test ratio	1.3:1	1.0:1

Accounts Receivable Analysis

The size and makeup of accounts receivable change constantly during business operations. Sales on account increase accounts receivable, whereas collections from customers decrease accounts receivable. Firms that grant long credit terms usually have larger accounts receivable balances than those granting short credit terms. Increases or decreases in the volume of sales also affect the balance of accounts receivable.

It is desirable to collect receivables as promptly as possible. The cash collected from receivables improves solvency. In addition, the cash generated by prompt collections from customers may be used in operations for such purposes as purchasing merchandise in large quantities at lower prices. The cash may also be used for payment of dividends to stockholders or for other investing or financing purposes. Prompt collection also lessens the risk of loss from uncollectible accounts.

ACCOUNTS RECEIVABLE TURNOVER. The relationship between credit sales and accounts receivable may be stated as the **accounts receivable turnover**. This ratio is computed by dividing net sales on account by the average net accounts receivable. It is desirable to base the average on monthly balances, which allows for seasonal changes in sales. When such data are not available, it may be necessary to use the average of the accounts receivable balance at the beginning and the end of the year. If there are trade notes receivable as well as accounts, the two may be combined. The accounts receivable turnover data for Marlea Company are as follows. All sales were made on account.

	1995	1994
Net sales on account	$1,498,000	$1,200,000
Accounts receivable (net):		
Beginning of year	$ 120,000	$ 140,000
End of year	115,000	120,000
Total	$ 235,000	$ 260,000
Average	$ 117,500	$ 130,000
Accounts receivable turnover	12.7	9.2

The increase in the accounts receivable turnover for 1995 indicates that there has been an improvement in the collection of receivables. This may be due to a change in the granting of credit or the collection practices or both.

NUMBER OF DAYS' SALES IN RECEIVABLES. Another measure of the relationship between credit sales and accounts receivable is the **number of days' sales in receivables**. This ratio is computed by dividing the net accounts receivable at the end of the year by the average daily sales on account. Average daily sales on account is determined by dividing net sales on account by 365 days. The number of days' sales in receivables is computed for Marlea Company as follows:

	1995	1994
Accounts receivable (net), end of year	$ 115,000	$ 120,000
Net sales on account	$1,498,000	$1,200,000
Average daily sales on account	$ 4,104	$ 3,288
Number of days' sales in receivables	28.0	36.5

(Accounts receivable ÷ avg. daily sales on account)

The number of days' sales in receivables is an estimate of the length of time the accounts receivable have been outstanding. Comparing this measure with the credit terms provides information on the efficiency in collecting receivables. For example, assume that the number of days' sales in receivables for Empire Inc. is 40. If Empire Inc.'s credit terms are n/45, then its collection process appears to be efficient. On the other hand, if Empire Inc.'s credit terms are n/30, its collection process does not appear to be efficient. A comparison with other firms in the same industry and with prior years also provides useful information. Such comparisons may indicate efficiency of collection procedures and trends in credit management.

Inventory Analysis

An enterprise should keep enough inventory on hand to meet the needs of its customers and its operations. At the same time, however, an excessive amount of inventory reduces solvency by tying up funds. Excess inventories also increase insurance expense, property taxes, storage costs, and other related expenses. These expenses further reduce funds that could be used elsewhere to improve operations.

Finally, excess inventory also increases the risk of losses because of price declines or obsolescence of the inventory. Two measures that are useful for evaluating the management of inventory are the inventory turnover and the number of days' sales in inventory.

INVENTORY TURNOVER. The relationship between the volume of goods (merchandise) sold and inventory may be stated as the **inventory turnover**. It is computed by dividing the cost of goods sold by the average inventory. If monthly data are not available, the average of the inventories at the beginning and the end of the year may be used. The inventory turnover for Marlea Company is computed as follows:

	1995	1994
Cost of goods sold	$1,043,000	$820,000
Inventories:		
Beginning of year	$ 283,000	$311,000
End of year	264,000	283,000
Total	$ 547,000	$594,000
Average	$ 273,500	$297,000
Inventory turnover	3.8	2.8

The inventory turnover improved for Marlea Company because of an increase in the cost of goods sold and a decrease in the average inventories. Differences across inventories, companies, and industries are too great to allow a general statement on what is a good inventory turnover. For example, a firm selling food should have a higher turnover than a firm selling furniture or jewelry. Likewise, the perishable foods department of a supermarket should have a higher turnover than the soaps and cleansers department. However, for each business or each department within a business, there is a reasonable turnover rate. A turnover lower than this rate could mean that inventory is not being managed properly.

NUMBER OF DAYS' SALES IN INVENTORY. Another measure of the relationship between the cost of goods sold and inventory is the **number of days' sales in inventory**. This measure is computed by dividing the inventory at the end of the year by the average daily cost of goods sold (cost of goods sold divided by 365). The number of days' sales in inventory for Marlea Company is computed as follows:

	1995	1994
Inventories, end of year	$ 264,000	$283,000
Cost of goods sold	$1,043,000	$820,000
Average daily cost of goods sold	$ 2,858	$ 2,247
Number of days' sales in inventory	92.4	125.9

(Inventories ÷ avg. daily cost of goods sold)

The number of days' sales in inventory is a rough measure of the length of time it takes to acquire, sell, and replace the inventory. For Marlea Company, there is a major improvement in the number of days' sales in inventory during 1995. However, a comparison with earlier years and similar firms would be useful in assessing Marlea Company's overall inventory management.

Ratio of Plant Assets to Long-Term Liabilities

Long-term notes and bonds are often secured by mortgages on plant assets. The **ratio of total plant assets to long-term liabilities** *is a solvency measure that indicates the margin of safety of the noteholders or bondholders. It also indicates the ability of the enterprise to borrow additional funds on a long-term basis.* The ratio of plant assets to long-term liabilities for Marlea Company is as follows:

	1995	1994
Plant assets (net)	$444,500	$470,000
Long-term liabilities	$100,000	$200,000
Ratio of plant assets to long-term liabilities	4.4:1	2.4:1

The major increase in this ratio at the end of 1995 is mainly due to liquidating one-half of Marlea Company's long-term liabilities. If the company needs to borrow additional funds on a long-term basis in the future, it is in a strong position to do so.

Ratio of Liabilities to Stockholders' Equity

Claims against the total assets of an enterprise are divided into two groups: (1) claims of creditors and (2) claims of owners. *The relationship between the total claims of the creditors and owners is a solvency measure that indicates the margin of safety for creditors. It also indicates the ability of the enterprise to withstand adverse business conditions.* When the claims of creditors are large in relation to the equity of the stockholders, there are usually significant interest payments. If earnings decline to the point where the company is unable to meet its interest payments, the business may be taken over by the creditors.

The relationship between creditor and stockholder equity is shown in the vertical analysis of the balance sheet. For example, the balance sheet of Marlea Company in Exhibit 5 indicates that on December 31, 1995, liabilities represented 27.2% and stockholders' equity represented 72.8% of the total liabilities and stockholders' equity (100.0%). Instead of expressing each item as a percent of the total, this relationship may be expressed as a ratio of one to the other, as follows:

	1995	1994
Total liabilities	$310,000	$443,000
Total stockholders' equity	$829,500	$787,500
Ratio of liabilities to stockholders' equity	.37:1	.56:1

The balance sheet of Marlea Company shows that the major factor affecting the change in the ratio was the $100,000 decrease in long-term liabilities during 1995. The ratio at the end of both years shows a large margin of safety for the creditors.

Number of Times Interest Charges Earned

Corporations in some industries, such as public utilities, normally have high ratios of debt to stockholders' equity. For such corporations, *the relative risk of the debtholders is normally measured as the* **number of times the interest charges are earned** during the year. The higher the ratio, the lower the risk that interest payments will not be made if earnings decrease. In other words, the higher the ratio, the greater the assurance that interest payments will be made on a continuing basis. *This measure also indicates the general financial strength of the enterprise, which is of interest to stockholders and employees as well as creditors.*

The amount available to meet interest charges is not affected by taxes on income. This is because interest is deductible in determining taxable income. Thus, the number of times interest charges are earned is computed as shown.

	1995	1994
Income before income tax	$ 900,000	$ 800,000
Add interest expense	300,000	250,000
Amount available to meet interest charges	$1,200,000	$1,050,000
Number of times interest charges earned	4	4.2

Analysis such as this can also be applied to dividends on preferred stock. In such a case, net income is divided by the amount of preferred dividends to yield the number of times preferred dividends are earned. This measure indicates the risk that dividends to preferred stockholders may not be paid.

PROFITABILITY ANALYSIS

Profitability is the ability of an entity to earn profits. This ability to earn profits depends on the effectiveness and efficiency of operations as well as resources available to the enterprise. Profitability analysis, therefore, focuses primarily on the relationship between operating results as reported in the income statement and resources available to the enterprise as reported in the balance sheet. Major analyses used in assessing profitability include the following:

1. Ratio of net sales to assets
2. Rate earned on total assets
3. Rate earned on stockholders' equity
4. Rate earned on common stockholders' equity
5. Earnings per share on common stock
6. Price-earnings ratio
7. Dividend yield

Ratio of Net Sales to Assets

The **ratio of net sales to assets** *is a profitability measure that shows how effectively a firm utilizes its assets.* For example, two competing enterprises have equal amounts of assets. If the sales of one are double the sales of the other, the enterprise with the higher sales is making better use of its assets.

In computing the ratio of net sales to assets, any long-term investments are excluded from total assets. This is because such investments are unrelated to normal operations involving the sale of goods or services. Assets may be measured as the total at the end of the year, the average at the beginning and the end of the year, or the average of monthly totals. The basic data and the computation of this ratio for Marlea Company are as follows:

	1995	1994
Net sales	$1,498,000	$1,200,000
Total assets (excluding long-term investments):		
Beginning of year	$1,053,000	$1,010,000
End of year	1,044,500	1,053,000
Total	$2,097,500	$2,063,000
Average	$1,048,750	$1,031,500
Ratio of net sales to assets	1.4:1	1.2:1

There was an improvement in this ratio during 1995. This was primarily due to an increase in sales volume. A comparison with similar companies or industry averages would be helpful in assessing the effectiveness of Marlea Company's use of its assets.

Rate Earned on Total Assets

The **rate earned on total assets** *measures the profitability of total assets, without considering how the assets are financed.* This rate is therefore not affected by whether the assets are financed primarily by creditors or stockholders.

The rate earned on total assets is computed by adding interest expense to net income and dividing this sum by the average total assets. The addition of interest expense to net income eliminates the effect of whether the assets are financed by debt or equity. The rate earned by Marlea Company on total assets is computed as follows:

	1995	1994
Net income	$ 91,000	$ 76,500
Plus interest expense	6,000	12,000
Total	$ 97,000	$ 88,500
Total assets:		
Beginning of year	$1,230,500	$1,187,500
End of year	1,139,500	1,230,500
Total	$2,370,000	$2,418,000
Average	$1,185,000	$1,209,000
Rate earned on total assets	8.2%	7.3%

The rate earned on total assets of Marlea Company during 1995 improved over that of 1994. A comparison with similar companies and industry averages would be useful in evaluating Marlea Company's profitability on total assets.

Sometimes it may be desirable to compute the rate of operating income to total assets. This is especially true if significant amounts of nonoperating income and expense are reported on the income statement. In this case, any assets related to the nonoperating income and expense items should be excluded from total assets in computing the rate. In addition, using operating income (which is before tax) has the advantage of eliminating the effects of any changes in the tax structure on the rate of earnings. When evaluating published data on rates earned on assets, you should be careful to determine the exact nature of the measure that is reported.

Rate Earned on Stockholders' Equity

Another measure of profitability is the **rate earned on stockholders' equity**. It is computed by dividing net income by average total stockholders' equity. In contrast to the rate earned on total assets, *this measure emphasizes the rate of income earned on the amount invested by the stockholders.*

The total stockholders' equity may vary throughout a period. For example, an enterprise may issue or retire stock, pay dividends, and earn net income. If monthly amounts are not available, the average of the stockholders' equity at the beginning and the end of the year is normally used to compute this rate. For Marlea Company, the rate earned on stockholders' equity is computed as follows:

	1995	1994
Net income	$ 91,000	$ 76,500
Stockholders' equity:		
Beginning of year	$ 787,500	$ 750,000
End of year	829,500	787,500
Total	$1,617,000	$1,537,500
Average	$ 808,500	$ 768,750
Rate earned on stockholders' equity	11.3%	10.0%

The rate earned by an enterprise on the equity of its stockholders is usually higher than the rate earned on total assets. This occurs when the amount earned on assets acquired with creditors' funds is more than the interest paid to creditors. This difference in the rate on stockholders' equity and the rate on total assets is called **leverage**.

Marlea Company's rate earned on stockholders' equity for 1995, 11.3%, is greater than the rate of 8.2% earned on total assets. The leverage of 3.1% (11.3% – 8.2%) for 1995 compares favorably with the 2.7% (10.0% – 7.3%) leverage for 1994. Exhibit 8 shows the 1995 and 1994 leverage for Marlea Company.

Exhibit 8
Leverage

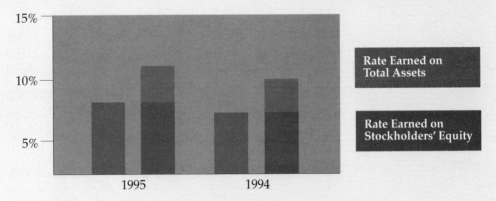

Rate Earned on Common Stockholders' Equity

A corporation may have both preferred and common stock outstanding. In this case, the common stockholders have the residual claim on earnings. The **rate earned on common stockholders' equity** focuses only on the rate of profits earned on the amount invested by the common stockholders. It is computed by subtracting preferred dividend requirements from the net income and dividing by the average common stockholders' equity.

Marlea Company has $150,000 of 6% nonparticipating preferred stock outstanding on December 31, 1995 and 1994. Thus, the annual preferred dividend requirement is $9,000 ($150,000 x 6%). The common stockholders' equity equals the total stockholders' equity, including retained earnings, less the par of the preferred stock ($150,000). The basic data and the rate earned on common stockholders' equity for Marlea Company are as follows:

	1995	1994
Net income	$ 91,000	$ 76,500
Preferred dividends	9,000	9,000
Remainder—identified with common stock	$ 82,000	$ 67,500
Common stockholders' equity:		
Beginning of year	$ 637,500	$ 600,000
End of year	679,500	637,500
Total	$1,317,000	$1,237,500
Average	$ 658,500	$ 618,750
Rate earned on common stockholders' equity	12.5%	10.9%

The rate earned on common stockholders' equity differs from the rates earned by Marlea Company on total assets and total stockholders' equity. This occurs if there are borrowed funds and also preferred stock outstanding, which rank ahead of the common shares in their claim on earnings. Thus, the concept of leverage, as we discussed in the preceding section, can also be applied to the use of funds from the sale of preferred stock as well as borrowing. Funds from both sources can be used in an attempt to increase the return on common stockholders' equity.

Earnings per Share on Common Stock

One of the profitability measures most commonly quoted by the financial press is **earnings per share (EPS)** on common stock. It is also normally reported in the income statement in corporate annual reports. If a company has issued only one class of stock, the earnings per share is computed by dividing net income by the number of shares of stock outstanding. If preferred and common stock are outstanding, the net income is first reduced by the amount of preferred dividend requirements.

The data on the earnings per share of common stock for Marlea Company are as follows:

	1995	1994
Net income	$91,000	$76,500
Preferred dividends	9,000	9,000
Remainder—identified with common stock	$82,000	$67,500
Shares of common stock outstanding	50,000	50,000
Earnings per share on common stock	$1.64	$1.35

Since earnings are the primary basis for dividends, earnings per share and dividends per share on common stock are commonly used by investors in assessing alternative stock investments. Earnings per share can be reported with dividends per share to indicate the relationship between earnings and dividends. A comparison of these two per share amounts indicates the extent to which the corporation is retaining its earnings for use in operations. Exhibit 9 shows these relationships for Marlea Company:

Exhibit 9
Earnings and Dividends per Share of Common Stock

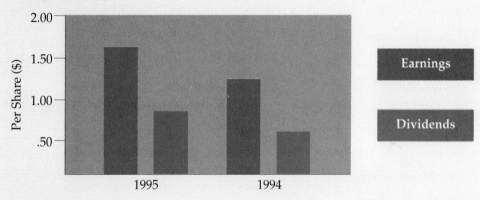

Price-Earnings Ratio

Another profitability measure commonly quoted by the financial press is the price-earnings (P/E) ratio on common stock. *The price-earnings ratio is an indicator of a firm's future earnings prospects.* It is computed by dividing the market price per share of common stock at a specific date by the annual earnings per share. To illustrate, assume that the market prices per common share are 20½ at the end of 1995 and 13½ at the end of 1994. The price-earnings ratio on common stock of Marlea Company is computed as follows:

	1995	1994
Market price per share of common stock	$20.50	$13.50
Earnings per share on common stock	$ 1.64	$ 1.35
Price-earnings ratio on common stock	12.5	10.0

The price-earnings ratio indicates that a share of common stock of Marlea Company was selling for 10 times the amount of earnings per share at the end of 1994. At the end of 1995, the common stock was selling for 12.5 times the amount of earnings per share.

Dividend Yield

The dividend yield on common stock is a profitability measure that shows the rate of return to common stockholders in terms of cash dividends. It is of special interest to investors whose main investment objective is to receive current returns (dividends) on an investment rather than an increase in the market price of the investment. The dividend yield is computed by dividing the annual dividends paid per share of common stock by the market price per share on a specific date. To illustrate, assume that dividends were $0.80 per common share and the market price was 20½ at the end of 1995. Dividends were $0.60 per share, and the market price was 13½ at the end of 1994. The dividend yield on common stock of Marlea Company is as follows:

	1995	1994
Dividends per share of common stock	$ .80	$ .60
Market price per share of common stock	$20.50	$13.50
Dividend yield on common stock	3.9%	4.4%

SUMMARY OF ANALYTICAL MEASURES

Exhibit 10 presents a summary of the analytical measures that we have discussed. These measures can be computed for most medium-size enterprises. Depending on the specific enterprise being analyzed, some measures might be omitted or additional measures could be developed. The type of industry, the capital structure, and the diversity of the enterprise's operations usually affect the measures used. For example, analysis for an airline might include revenue per passenger mile and cost per available seat as measures. Likewise, analysis for a hotel might focus on occupancy rates.

Percentage analyses, ratios, turnovers, and other measures of financial position and operating results are useful analytical measures. They are helpful in assessing an enterprise's past performance and predicting its future. They are not, however, a substitute for sound judgment. In selecting and interpreting analytical measures, conditions peculiar to an enterprise or its industry should be considered. In addition, the influence of the general economic and business environment should be considered.

In determining trends, the interrelationship of the measures used in assessing an enterprise should be carefully studied. Comparable indexes of earlier periods should also be studied. Data from competing enterprises may be useful in assessing the efficiency of operations for the firm under analysis. In making such comparisons, however, the effects of differences in the accounting methods used by the enterprises should be considered.

Exhibit 10
Summary of Analytical Measures

	Method of Computation	Use
Solvency measures:		
Working capital	Current assets − Current liabilities	To indicate the ability to meet currently maturing obligations
Current ratio	$\dfrac{\text{Current assets}}{\text{Current liabilities}}$	
Acid-test ratio	$\dfrac{\text{Quick assets}}{\text{Current liabilities}}$	To indicate instant debt-paying ability
Accounts receivable turnover	$\dfrac{\text{Net sales on account}}{\text{Average accounts receivable}}$	To assess the efficiency in collecting receivables and in the management of credit
Number of days' sales in receivables	$\dfrac{\text{Accounts receivable, end of year}}{\text{Average daily sales on account}}$	
Inventory turnover	$\dfrac{\text{Cost of goods sold}}{\text{Average inventory}}$	To assess the efficiency in the management of inventory
Number of days' sales in inventory	$\dfrac{\text{Inventory, end of year}}{\text{Average daily cost of goods sold}}$	
Ratio of plant assets to long-term liabilities	$\dfrac{\text{Plant assets (net)}}{\text{Long-term liabilities}}$	To indicate the margin of safety to long-term creditors
Ratio of liabilities to stockholders' equity	$\dfrac{\text{Total liabilities}}{\text{Total stockholders' equity}}$	To indicate the margin of safety to creditors
Number of times interest charges earned	$\dfrac{\text{Income before income tax + Interest expense}}{\text{Interest expense}}$	To assess the risk to debtholders in terms of number of times interest charges were earned

Exhibit 10 continued

Profitability measures:

Ratio of net sales to assets	$$\frac{\text{Net sales}}{\text{Average total assets (excluding long-term investments)}}$$	To assess the effectiveness in the use of assets
Rate earned on total assets	$$\frac{\text{Net income + Interest expense}}{\text{Average total assets}}$$	To assess the profitability of the assets
Rate earned on stockholders' equity	$$\frac{\text{Net income}}{\text{Average total stockholders' equity}}$$	To assess the profitability of the investment by stockholders
Rate earned on common stockholders' equity	$$\frac{\text{Net income – Preferred dividends}}{\text{Average common stockholders' equity}}$$	To assess the profitability of the investment by common stockholders
Earnings per share on common stock	$$\frac{\text{Net income – Preferred dividends}}{\text{Shares of common stock outstanding}}$$	
Dividends per share of common stock	$$\frac{\text{Dividends}}{\text{Shares of common stock outstanding}}$$	To indicate the extent to which earnings are being distributed to common stockholders
Price-earnings ratio	$$\frac{\text{Market price per share of common stock}}{\text{Earnings per share of common stock}}$$	To indicate future earnings prospects, based on the relationship between market value of common stock and earnings
Dividend yield	$$\frac{\text{Dividends per share of common stock}}{\text{Market price per share of common stock}}$$	To indicate the rate of return to common stockholders in terms of dividends

PROBLEMS

PROBLEM FSA-1
HORIZONTAL ANALYSIS
FOR INCOME STATEMENT

For 1995, Getz Company reported its most significant increase in net income in years. At the end of the year, Jane Getz, the president, is presented with the following condensed comparative income statement:

Getz Company
Comparative Income Statement
For Years Ended December 31, 1995 and 1994

	1995	1994
Sales	$907,200	$803,200
Sales returns and allowances	7,200	3,200
Net sales	$900,000	$800,000
Cost of goods sold	557,000	488,000
Gross profit	$343,000	$312,000
Selling expenses	$108,000	$136,000
Administrative expenses	81,000	65,000
Total operating expenses	$189,000	$201,000
Operating income	$154,000	$111,000
Other income	2,000	1,000
Income before income tax	$156,000	$112,000
Income tax	48,000	32,000
Net income	$108,000	$ 80,000

Instructions

1. Prepare a comparative income statement with horizontal analysis for the two-year period, using 1994 as the base year.

2. To the extent the data permit, comment on the significant relationships revealed by the horizontal analysis prepared in (1).

SHARPEN YOUR COMMUNICATION SKILLS

PROBLEM FSA-2
VERTICAL ANALYSIS FOR
INCOME STATEMENT

For 1995, Hartley Company initiated an extensive sales promotion campaign that included the expenditure of an additional $50,000 for advertising. At the end of the year, Ann Hartley, the president, is presented with the following condensed comparative income statement:

Hartley Company
Comparative Income Statement
For Years Ended December 31, 1995 and 1994

	1995	1994
Sales	$612,000	$363,600
Sales returns and allowances	12,000	3,600
Net sales	$600,000	$360,000
Cost of goods sold	372,000	216,000
Gross profit	$228,000	$144,000
Selling expenses	$108,000	$ 57,600
Administrative expenses	24,000	16,200
Total operating expenses	$132,000	$ 73,800
Operating income	$ 96,000	$ 70,200
Other income	1,800	1,440
Income before income tax	$ 97,800	$ 71,640
Income tax	22,800	16,200
Net income	$ 75,000	$ 55,440

SPREADSHEET
PROBLEM

Instructions

1. Prepare a comparative income statement for the two-year period, presenting an analysis of each item in relationship to net sales for each of the years.
2. To the extent the data permit, comment on the significant relationships revealed by the vertical analysis prepared in (1).

SHARPEN YOUR
COMMUNICATION SKILLS

PROBLEM FSA-3
COMMON-SIZE INCOME
STATEMENT

Revenue and expense data for the current calendar year for Harpo Publishing Company and for the publishing industry are as follows. The Harpo Publishing Company data are expressed in dollars; the publishing industry averages are expressed in percentages.

	Harpo Publishing Company	Publishing Industry Average
Sales	$8,072,000	100.5%
Sales returns and allowances	72,000	.5
Cost of goods sold	5,760,000	69.0
Selling expenses	656,000	9.0
Administrative expenses	496,000	8.2
Other income	48,000	.6
Other expense	104,000	1.4
Income tax	384,000	5.0

Instructions

1. Prepare a common-size income statement comparing the results of operations for Harpo Publishing Company with the industry average.
2. As far as the data permit, comment on significant relationships revealed by the comparisons.

SHARPEN YOUR
COMMUNICATION SKILLS

PROBLEM FSA-4
EFFECT OF TRANSACTIONS
ON CURRENT POSITION
ANALYSIS

Data pertaining to the current position of Osborn Inc. are as follows:

Cash	$137,000
Marketable securities	40,000
Accounts and notes receivable (net)	303,000
Inventories	490,500
Prepaid expenses	29,500
Accounts payable	297,500
Notes payable (short-term)	75,000
Accrued expenses	27,500

Instructions

1. Compute (a) the working capital, (b) the current ratio, and (c) the acid-test ratio.
2. List the following captions on a sheet of paper:

Transaction	Working Capital	Current Ratio	Acid-Test Ratio

Compute the working capital, the current ratio, and the acid-test ratio after each of the following transactions, and record the results in the appropriate columns. Consider each transaction separately, and assume that only that transaction affects the data given.

a. Sold marketable securities, $40,000.
b. Paid accounts payable, $100,000.
c. Purchased goods on account, $80,000.
d. Paid notes payable, $75,000.
e. Declared a cash dividend, $50,000.
f. Declared a common stock dividend on common stock, $72,500.
g. Borrowed cash from bank on a long-term note, $200,000.
h. Received cash on account, $150,000.
i. Issued additional shares of stock for cash, $150,000.
j. Paid cash for prepaid expenses, $40,000.

PROBLEM FSA-5
EFFECT OF ERRORS ON
CURRENT POSITION
ANALYSIS

Prior to approving an application for a short-term loan, Citizens National Bank required that Fite Company provide evidence of working capital of at least $300,000, a current ratio of at least 1.5:1, and an acid-test ratio of at least 1.0:1. The chief accountant of Fite Company compiled the following data pertaining to the current position:

Fite Company
Schedule of Current Assets and Current Liabilities
December 31, 1995

Current assets:		Current liabilities:	
Cash	$115,250	Accounts payable	$325,000
Marketable securities	101,250	Notes payable	75,000
Accounts receivable	330,500	Total current liabilities	$400,000
Notes receivable	50,000		
Interest receivable	3,000		
Inventories	179,250		
Supplies	20,750		
Total current assets	$800,000		

Instructions

1. Compute (a) the working capital, (b) the current ratio, and (c) the acid-test ratio.
2. At the request of the bank, a firm of independent auditors was retained to examine data submitted with the loan application. This examination disclosed several errors. Prepare correcting entries for each of the following errors:
   a. A canceled check indicates that a bill for $25,000 for repairs on factory equipment had not been recorded in the accounts.
   b. Accounts receivable of $30,500 are uncollectible and should be immediately written off. In addition, it was estimated that of the remaining receivables, 5% would eventually become uncollectible. An allowance should be made for these future uncollectible accounts.
   c. Six months' interest had been accrued on the $50,000, 12%, six-month note receivable dated October 1, 1995.
   d. Supplies on hand at December 31, 1995, total $9,750.
   e. The marketable securities portfolio includes $50,000 of Porter Company stock that is held as a long-term investment.
   f. The notes payable account consists of a 12%, 90-day note dated November 1, 1995. No interest had been accrued on the note.
   g. Accrued wages as of December 31, 1995, totaled $30,000.

h. Rental Income had been credited on receipt of $72,000, which was the full amount of a year's rent for warehouse space leased to C. Pena and Son, effective July 1, 1995.

3. Giving effect to each of the preceding errors separately and assuming that only that error affects the current position of Fite Company, compute (a) the working capital, (b) the current ratio, and (c) the acid-test ratio. Use the following column headings for recording your answers:

| Error | Working Capital | Current Ratio | Acid-Test Ratio |

4. Prepare a revised schedule of working capital as of December 31, 1995, and recompute the current ratio and the acid-test ratio, giving effect to the corrections of all the preceding errors.

SHARPEN YOUR COMMUNICATION SKILLS ► 5. Discuss the action you would recommend that the bank take regarding the pending loan application.

PROBLEM FSA-6
EIGHTEEN MEASURES OF SOLVENCY AND PROFITABILITY

The comparative financial statements of C. C. Shelton and Co. are as follows. The market price of C. C. Shelton and Co. common stock was $30.25 on December 31, 1994, and $27 on December 31, 1995.

C. C. Shelton and Co.
Comparative Income Statement
For Years Ended December 31, 1995 and 1994

	1995	1994
Sales (all on account)	$7,779,200	$6,528,000
Sales returns and allowances	299,200	128,000
Net sales	$7,480,000	$6,400,000
Cost of goods sold	4,874,800	3,840,000
Gross profit	$2,605,200	$2,560,000
Selling expenses	$1,205,200	$ 985,600
Administrative expenses	540,000	526,400
Total operating expenses	$1,745,200	$1,512,000
Operating income	$ 860,000	$1,048,000
Other income	140,000	112,000
	$1,000,000	$1,160,000
Other expense (interest)	200,000	180,000
Income before income tax	$ 800,000	$ 980,000
Income tax	320,000	400,000
Net income	$ 480,000	$ 580,000

C. C. Shelton and Co.
Comparative Retained Earnings Statement
For Years Ended December 31, 1995 and 1994

	1995	1994
Retained earnings, January 1	$2,416,000	$1,936,000
Add net income for year	480,000	580,000
Total	$2,896,000	$2,516,000
Deduct dividends:		
On preferred stock	$ 30,000	$ 30,000
On common stock	50,000	70,000
Total	$ 80,000	$ 100,000
Retained earnings, December 31	$2,816,000	$2,416,000

C. C. Shelton and Co.
Comparative Balance Sheet
December 31, 1995 and 1994

	1995	1994
Assets		
Current assets:		
Cash	$ 105,000	$ 95,000
Marketable securities	225,000	175,000
Accounts receivable (net)	440,000	400,000
Inventories	769,600	674,800
Prepaid expenses	70,400	35,200
Total current assets	$1,610,000	$1,380,000
Long-term investments	300,000	250,000
Plant assets	4,506,000	4,086,000
Total assets	$6,416,000	$5,716,000
Liabilities		
Current liabilities	$ 700,000	$ 600,000
Long-term liabilities		
Mortgage note payable, 10%, due 2001	$ 200,000	—
Bonds payable, 15%, due 2009	1,200,000	$1,200,000
Total long-term liabilities	$1,400,000	$1,200,000
Total liabilities	$2,100,000	$1,800,000
Stockholders' Equity		
Preferred $6 stock, $100 par	$ 500,000	$ 500,000
Common stock, $10 par	1,000,000	1,000,000
Retained earnings	2,816,000	2,416,000
Total stockholders' equity	$4,316,000	$3,916,000
Total liabilities and stockholders' equity	$6,416,000	$5,716,000

SPREADSHEET
PROBLEM

Instructions

Determine the following measures for 1995:

1. Working capital.
2. Current ratio.
3. Acid-test ratio.
4. Accounts receivable turnover.
5. Number of days' sales in receivables.
6. Inventory turnover.
7. Number of days' sales in inventory.
8. Ratio of plant assets to long-term liabilities.
9. Ratio of liabilities to stockholders' equity.
10. Number of times interest charges earned.
11. Number of times preferred dividends earned.
12. Ratio of net sales to assets.
13. Rate earned on total assets.
14. Rate earned on stockholders' equity.
15. Rate earned on common stockholders' equity.
16. Earnings per share on common stock.
17. Price-earnings ratio.
18. Dividend yield.

PROBLEM FSA-7
REPORT ON DETAILED
FINANCIAL ANALYSIS

Ann Raines is considering making a substantial investment in C. C. Shelton and Co. The company's comparative financial statements for 1995 and 1994 are given in Problem FSA-6. To assist in the evaluation of the company, Raines secured the following additional data taken from the balance sheet at December 31, 1993:

Accounts receivable (net)	$ 350,000
Inventories	654,800
Long-term investments	250,000
Total assets	5,284,000
Total stockholders' equity (preferred and common stock outstanding same as in 1994)	3,684,000

SHARPEN YOUR COMMUNICATION SKILLS ▶ **Instructions**

Prepare a report for Raines, based on an analysis of the financial data presented. In preparing your report, include all ratios and other data that will be useful in arriving at a decision regarding the investment. (Note: If you are using the Solutions Software, you may want to complete the following instructions before you prepare this report.)

SOLUTIONS SOFTWARE

Instructions for Solving Problem FSA-7 Using Solutions Software

1. Load opening balances.
2. Save the opening balances file to your drive and directory.
3. Set the run date to December 31, 1994, and enter your name.
4. Display a horizontal analysis of the income statement.
5. Display a vertical analysis of the income statement.
6. Display a horizontal analysis of the balance sheet.
7. Display a vertical analysis of the balance sheet.
8. Save your data file to disk.
9. End the session.

INTEREST TABLES

The following present value and future value tables contain factors carried to six decimal places for interest rates of 5% to 14% for 50 periods.

Present Value of 1 at Compound Interest Due in n Periods: $p_{\overline{n}|i} = \dfrac{1}{(1+i)^n}$

n	5%	5.5%	6%	6.5%	7%	8%	9%	10%	11%	12%	13%	14%
1	0.952381	0.94787	0.943396	0.93897	0.934580	0.925926	0.917431	0.909091	0.90090	0.892857	0.88496	0.87719
2	0.907029	0.89845	0.889996	0.88166	0.873439	0.857339	0.841680	0.826446	0.81162	0.797194	0.78315	0.76947
3	0.863838	0.85161	0.839619	0.82785	0.816298	0.793832	0.772183	0.751315	0.73119	0.711780	0.69305	0.67497
4	0.822702	0.80722	0.792094	0.77732	0.762895	0.735030	0.708425	0.683013	0.65873	0.635518	0.61332	0.59208
5	0.783526	0.76513	0.747258	0.72998	0.712986	0.680583	0.649931	0.620921	0.59345	0.567427	0.54276	0.51937
6	0.746215	0.72525	0.704961	0.68533	0.666342	0.630170	0.596267	0.564474	0.53464	0.506631	0.48032	0.45559
7	0.710681	0.68744	0.665057	0.64351	0.622750	0.583490	0.547034	0.513158	0.48166	0.452349	0.42506	0.39964
8	0.676839	0.65160	0.627412	0.60423	0.582009	0.540269	0.501866	0.466507	0.43393	0.403883	0.37616	0.35056
9	0.644609	0.61763	0.591898	0.56735	0.543934	0.500249	0.460428	0.424098	0.39092	0.360610	0.33288	0.30751
10	0.613913	0.58543	0.558395	0.53273	0.508349	0.463193	0.422411	0.385543	0.35218	0.321973	0.29459	0.26974
11	0.584679	0.55491	0.526788	0.50021	0.475093	0.428883	0.387533	0.350494	0.31728	0.287476	0.26070	0.23662
12	0.556837	0.52598	0.496969	0.46968	0.444012	0.397114	0.355535	0.318631	0.28584	0.256675	0.23071	0.20756
13	0.530321	0.49856	0.468839	0.44102	0.414964	0.367698	0.326179	0.289664	0.25751	0.229174	0.20416	0.18207
14	0.505068	0.47257	0.442301	0.41410	0.387817	0.340461	0.299246	0.263331	0.23199	0.204620	0.18068	0.15971
15	0.481017	0.44793	0.417265	0.38883	0.362446	0.315242	0.274538	0.239392	0.20900	0.182696	0.15989	0.14010
16	0.458112	0.42458	0.393646	0.36510	0.338735	0.291890	0.251870	0.217629	0.18829	0.163122	0.14150	0.12289
17	0.436297	0.40245	0.371364	0.34281	0.316574	0.270269	0.231073	0.197845	0.16963	0.145644	0.12522	0.10780
18	0.415521	0.38147	0.350344	0.32189	0.295864	0.250249	0.211994	0.179859	0.15282	0.130040	0.11081	0.09456
19	0.395734	0.36158	0.330513	0.30224	0.276508	0.231712	0.194490	0.163508	0.13768	0.116107	0.09806	0.08295
20	0.376889	0.34273	0.311805	0.28380	0.258419	0.214548	0.178431	0.148644	0.12403	0.103667	0.08678	0.07276
21	0.358942	0.32486	0.294155	0.26648	0.241513	0.198656	0.163698	0.135131	0.11174	0.092560	0.07680	0.06383
22	0.341850	0.30793	0.277505	0.25021	0.225713	0.183941	0.150182	0.122846	0.10067	0.082643	0.06796	0.05599
23	0.325571	0.29187	0.261797	0.23494	0.210947	0.170315	0.137781	0.111678	0.09069	0.073788	0.06014	0.04911
24	0.310068	0.27666	0.246979	0.22060	0.197147	0.157699	0.126405	0.101526	0.08170	0.065882	0.05323	0.04308
25	0.295303	0.26223	0.232999	0.20714	0.184249	0.146018	0.115968	0.092296	0.07361	0.058823	0.04710	0.03779
26	0.281241	0.24856	0.219810	0.19450	0.172195	0.135202	0.106393	0.083905	0.06631	0.052521	0.04168	0.03315
27	0.267848	0.23560	0.207368	0.18263	0.160930	0.125187	0.097608	0.076278	0.05974	0.046894	0.03689	0.02908
28	0.255094	0.22332	0.195630	0.17148	0.150402	0.115914	0.089548	0.069343	0.05382	0.041869	0.03264	0.02551
29	0.242946	0.21168	0.184557	0.16101	0.140563	0.107328	0.082155	0.063039	0.04849	0.037383	0.02889	0.02237
30	0.231377	0.20064	0.174110	0.15119	0.131367	0.099377	0.075371	0.057309	0.04368	0.033378	0.02557	0.01963
31	0.220359	0.19018	0.164255	0.14196	0.122773	0.092016	0.069148	0.052099	0.03935	0.029802	0.02262	0.01722
32	0.209866	0.18027	0.154957	0.13329	0.114741	0.085200	0.063438	0.047362	0.03545	0.026609	0.02002	0.01510
33	0.199873	0.17087	0.146186	0.12516	0.107235	0.078889	0.058200	0.043057	0.03194	0.023758	0.01772	0.01325
34	0.190355	0.16196	0.137912	0.11752	0.100219	0.073045	0.053395	0.039143	0.02878	0.021212	0.01568	0.01162
35	0.181290	0.15352	0.130105	0.11035	0.093663	0.067635	0.048986	0.035584	0.02592	0.018940	0.01388	0.01019
40	0.142046	0.11746	0.097222	0.08054	0.066780	0.046031	0.031838	0.022095	0.01538	0.010747	0.00753	0.00529
45	0.111297	0.08988	0.072650	0.05879	0.047613	0.031328	0.020692	0.013719	0.00913	0.006098	0.00409	0.00275
50	0.087204	0.06877	0.054288	0.04291	0.033948	0.021321	0.013449	0.008519	0.00542	0.003460	0.00222	0.00143

Present Value of Ordinary Annuity of 1 per Period: $P_{\overline{n}|i} = \dfrac{1 - \dfrac{1}{(1+i)^n}}{i}$

n	5%	5.5%	6%	6.5%	7%	8%	9%	10%	11%	12%	13%	14%
1	0.952381	0.94787	0.943396	0.93897	0.934579	0.925926	0.917431	0.909091	0.90090	0.892857	0.88496	0.87719
2	1.859410	1.84632	1.833393	1.82063	1.808018	1.783265	1.759111	1.735537	1.71252	1.690051	1.66810	1.64666
3	2.723248	2.69793	2.673012	2.64848	2.624316	2.577097	2.531295	2.486852	2.44371	2.401831	2.36115	2.32163
4	3.545951	3.50515	3.465106	3.42580	3.387211	3.312127	3.239720	3.169865	3.10245	3.037349	2.97447	2.91371
5	4.329477	4.27028	4.212364	4.15568	4.100197	3.992710	3.889651	3.790787	3.69590	3.604776	3.51723	3.43308
6	5.075692	4.99553	4.917324	4.84101	4.766540	4.622880	4.485919	4.355261	4.23054	4.111407	3.99755	3.88867
7	5.786373	5.68297	5.582381	5.48452	5.389289	5.206370	5.032953	4.868419	4.71220	4.563757	4.42261	4.28830
8	6.463213	6.33457	6.209794	6.08875	5.971299	5.746639	5.534819	5.334926	5.14612	4.967640	4.79677	4.63886
9	7.107822	6.95220	6.801692	6.65610	6.515232	6.246888	5.995247	5.759024	5.53705	5.328250	5.13166	4.94637
10	(7.721735)	7.53763	7.360087	7.18883	7.023582	6.710081	6.417658	6.144567	5.88923	5.650223	5.42624	5.21612
11	8.306414	8.09254	7.886875	7.68904	7.498674	7.138964	6.805191	6.495061	6.20652	5.937699	5.68694	5.45273
12	8.863252	8.61852	8.383844	8.15873	7.942686	7.536078	7.160725	6.813692	6.49236	6.194374	5.91765	5.66029
13	9.393573	9.11708	8.852683	8.59974	8.357651	7.903776	7.486904	7.103356	6.74987	6.423548	6.12181	5.84236
14	9.898641	9.58965	9.294984	9.01384	8.745468	8.224237	7.786150	7.366687	6.96187	6.628168	6.30249	6.00207
15	10.379658	10.03758	9.712249	9.40267	9.107914	8.559479	8.060688	7.606080	7.19087	6.810864	6.46238	6.14217
16	10.837770	10.46216	10.105895	9.76776	9.446649	8.851369	8.312558	7.823709	7.37916	6.973986	6.60388	6.26506
17	11.274066	10.86461	10.477260	10.11058	9.763223	9.121638	8.543631	8.021553	7.54879	7.119630	6.72909	6.37286
18	11.689587	11.24607	10.827603	10.43247	10.059087	9.371887	8.755625	8.201412	7.70162	7.249670	6.83991	6.46742
19	12.085321	11.60765	11.158116	10.73471	10.335595	9.603599	8.950115	8.364920	7.83929	7.365777	6.93797	6.55037
20	12.462210	11.95038	11.469921	11.01851	10.594014	9.818147	9.128546	8.513564	7.96333	7.469444	7.02475	6.62313
21	12.821153	12.27524	11.764077	11.28498	10.835527	10.016803	9.292244	8.648694	8.07507	7.562003	7.10155	6.68696
22	13.163003	12.58317	12.041582	11.53520	11.061241	10.200744	9.442425	8.771540	8.17574	7.644646	7.16951	6.74294
23	13.488574	12.87504	12.303379	11.77014	11.272187	10.371059	9.580207	8.883218	8.26643	7.718434	7.22966	6.79206
24	13.798642	13.15170	12.550358	11.99074	11.469334	10.528758	9.706612	8.984744	8.34814	7.784316	7.28288	6.83514
25	14.093945	13.41393	12.783356	12.19788	11.653583	10.674776	9.822580	9.077040	8.42174	7.843139	7.32998	6.87293
26	14.375185	13.66250	13.003166	12.39237	11.825779	10.809978	9.928972	9.160945	8.48806	7.895660	7.37167	6.90608
27	14.643034	13.89810	13.210534	12.57500	11.986709	10.935165	10.026580	9.237223	8.54780	7.942554	7.40856	6.93515
28	14.898127	14.12142	13.406164	12.74648	12.137111	11.051078	10.116128	9.306567	8.60162	7.984423	7.44120	6.96066
29	15.141074	14.33310	13.590721	12.90749	12.277674	11.158406	10.198283	9.369606	8.65011	8.021806	7.47009	6.98304
30	15.372451	14.53375	13.764831	13.05868	12.409041	11.257783	10.273654	9.426914	8.69379	8.055184	7.49565	7.00266
31	15.592811	14.72393	13.929086	13.20063	12.531814	11.349799	10.342802	9.479013	8.73315	8.084986	7.51828	7.01988
32	15.802677	14.90420	14.084043	13.33393	12.646555	11.434999	10.406240	9.526376	8.76860	8.111594	7.53830	7.03498
33	16.002549	15.07507	14.230230	13.45909	12.753790	11.513888	10.464441	9.569432	8.80054	8.135352	7.55602	7.04823
34	16.192904	15.23703	14.368141	13.57661	12.854009	11.586934	10.517835	9.608553	8.82932	8.156564	7.57170	7.05985
35	16.374194	15.39055	14.498246	13.68696	12.947672	11.654568	10.566821	9.644159	8.85524	8.175504	7.58557	7.07005
40	17.159086	16.04612	(15.046297)	14.14553	13.331709	11.924613	10.757360	9.779051	8.95105	8.243777	7.63438	7.10504
45	17.774070	16.54773	15.455832	14.48023	13.605522	12.108402	10.881197	9.862808	9.00791	8.282516	7.66086	7.12322
50	18.255925	16.93152	15.761861	14.72452	13.800746	12.233485	10.961683	9.914814	9.04165	8.304498	7.67524	7.13266

Future Amount of 1 at Compound Interest Due in n Periods: $a_{\overline{n}|i} = (1+i)^n$

n \ i	5%	5.5%	6%	6.5%	7%	8%	9%	10%	11%	12%	13%	14%
1	1.050000	1.05500	1.060000	1.06500	1.070000	1.080000	1.090000	1.100000	1.11000	1.120000	1.13000	1.14000
2	1.102500	1.11303	1.123600	1.13423	1.144900	1.166400	1.188100	1.210000	1.23210	1.254400	1.27690	1.29960
3	1.157625	1.17424	1.191016	1.20795	1.225043	1.259712	1.295029	1.331000	1.36763	1.404928	1.44290	1.48154
4	1.215506	1.23882	1.262477	1.28647	1.310796	1.360489	1.411582	1.464100	1.51807	1.573519	1.63047	1.68896
5	1.276282	1.30696	1.338226	1.37009	1.402552	1.469328	1.538624	1.610510	1.68506	1.762342	1.84244	1.92541
6	1.340096	1.37884	1.418519	1.45914	1.500730	1.586874	1.677100	1.771561	1.87041	1.973823	2.08195	2.19497
7	1.407100	1.45468	1.503630	1.55399	1.605781	1.713824	1.828039	1.948717	2.07616	2.210681	2.35261	2.50227
8	1.477455	1.53469	1.593848	1.65500	1.718186	1.850930	1.992563	2.143589	2.30454	2.475963	2.65844	2.85259
9	1.551328	1.61909	1.689479	1.76257	1.838459	1.999005	2.171893	2.357948	2.55804	2.773079	3.00404	3.25195
10	1.628895	1.70814	1.790848	1.87714	1.967151	2.158925	2.367364	2.593742	2.83942	3.105848	3.39457	3.70722
11	1.710339	1.80209	1.898299	1.99915	2.104852	2.331639	2.580426	2.853117	3.15176	3.478550	3.83586	4.22623
12	1.795856	1.90121	2.012196	2.12910	2.252192	2.518170	2.812665	3.138428	3.49845	3.895976	4.33452	4.81790
13	1.885649	2.00577	2.132928	2.26749	2.409845	2.719624	3.065805	3.452271	3.88328	4.363493	4.89041	5.49241
14	1.979932	2.11609	2.260904	2.41487	2.578534	2.937194	3.341727	3.797498	4.31044	4.887112	5.53475	6.26135
15	2.078928	2.23248	2.396558	2.57184	2.759032	3.172169	3.642482	4.177248	4.78459	5.473566	6.25427	7.13794
16	2.182875	2.35526	2.540352	2.73901	2.952164	3.425943	3.970306	4.594973	5.31089	6.130394	7.06733	8.13725
17	2.292018	2.48480	2.692773	2.91705	3.158815	3.700018	4.327633	5.054470	5.89509	6.866041	7.98608	9.27646
18	2.406619	2.62147	2.854339	3.10665	3.379932	3.996019	4.717120	5.559917	6.54355	7.689966	9.02427	10.57517
19	2.526950	2.76565	3.025600	3.30859	3.616528	4.315701	5.141661	6.115909	7.26334	8.612762	10.19742	12.05569
20	2.653298	2.91776	3.207135	3.52365	3.869684	4.660957	5.604411	6.727500	8.06231	9.646293	11.52309	13.74349
21	2.785963	3.07823	3.399564	3.75268	4.140562	5.033834	6.108808	7.400250	8.94917	10.803848	13.02109	15.66758
22	2.925261	3.24754	3.603537	3.99661	4.430402	5.436540	6.658600	8.140275	9.93357	12.100310	14.71383	17.86104
23	3.071524	3.42615	3.819750	4.25639	4.740530	5.871464	7.257874	8.954302	11.02627	13.552347	16.62663	20.36158
24	3.225100	3.61459	4.048935	4.53305	5.072367	6.341181	7.911083	9.849733	12.23916	15.178629	18.78809	23.21221
25	3.386355	3.81339	4.291871	4.82770	5.427433	6.848475	8.623081	10.834706	13.55546	17.000064	21.23054	26.46192
26	3.555673	4.02313	4.549383	5.14150	5.807353	7.396353	9.399158	11.918177	15.07986	19.040072	23.99051	30.16658
27	3.733456	4.24440	4.822346	5.47570	6.213868	7.988061	10.245082	13.109944	16.73865	21.324881	27.10928	34.38991
28	3.920129	4.47784	5.111687	5.83162	6.648838	8.627106	11.167140	14.420994	18.57990	23.883866	30.63349	39.20449
29	4.116136	4.72412	5.418388	6.21067	7.114257	9.317275	12.172182	15.863093	20.62369	26.749930	34.61584	44.69312
30	4.321942	4.98395	5.743491	6.61437	7.612255	10.062657	13.267678	17.449402	22.89230	29.959922	39.11590	50.95016
31	4.538039	5.25807	6.088101	7.04430	8.145113	10.867669	14.461770	19.194342	25.41045	33.555113	44.20096	58.08318
32	4.764941	5.54726	6.453387	7.50218	8.715271	11.737083	15.763329	21.113777	28.20560	37.581726	49.94709	66.21483
33	5.003189	5.85236	6.840590	7.98982	9.325340	12.676050	17.182028	23.225154	31.30821	42.091533	56.44021	75.48490
34	5.253348	6.17424	7.251025	8.50916	9.978114	13.690134	18.728411	25.547670	34.75212	47.142517	63.77744	86.05279
35	5.516015	6.51383	7.686087	9.06225	10.676581	14.785344	20.413968	28.102437	38.57485	52.799620	72.06851	98.10018
40	7.039989	8.51331	10.285718	12.41607	14.974458	21.724521	31.409420	45.259256	65.00087	93.050970	132.78155	188.88351
45	8.985008	11.12655	13.764611	17.01110	21.002452	31.920449	48.327286	72.890484	109.53024	163.987604	244.64140	363.67907
50	11.467400	14.54196	18.420154	23.30668	29.457025	46.901613	74.357520	117.390853	184.56483	289.002190	450.73593	700.23299

Future Amount of Ordinary Annuity of 1 per Period: $A_{\overline{n}|i} = \dfrac{(1 + i)^n - 1}{i}$

n	5%	5.5%	6%	6.5%	7%	8%	9%	10%	11%	12%	13%	14%
1	1.000000	1.00000	1.000000	1.00000	1.000000	1.000000	1.000000	1.000000	1.00000	1.000000	1.00000	1.00000
2	2.050000	2.05500	2.060000	2.06500	2.070000	2.080000	2.090000	2.100000	2.11000	2.120000	2.13000	2.14000
3	3.152500	3.16802	3.183600	3.19922	3.214900	3.246400	3.278100	3.310000	3.34210	3.374400	3.40690	3.43960
4	4.310125	4.34227	4.374616	4.40717	4.439943	4.506112	4.573129	4.641000	4.70973	4.779328	4.84980	4.92114
5	5.525631	5.58109	5.637093	5.69364	5.750740	5.866601	5.984711	6.105100	6.22780	6.352847	6.48027	6.61010
6	6.801913	6.88805	6.975319	7.06373	7.153291	7.335929	7.523335	7.715610	7.91286	8.115189	8.32271	8.53552
7	8.142008	8.26689	8.393838	8.52287	8.654021	8.922803	9.200435	9.487171	9.78327	10.089012	10.40466	10.73049
8	9.549109	9.72157	9.897468	10.07686	10.259803	10.636628	11.028474	11.435888	11.85943	12.299693	12.75726	13.23276
9	11.026564	11.25626	11.491316	11.73185	11.977989	12.487558	13.021036	13.579477	14.16397	14.775656	15.41571	16.08535
10	12.577893	12.87535	13.180795	13.49442	13.816448	14.486562	15.192930	15.937425	16.72201	17.548735	18.41975	19.33730
11	14.206787	14.58350	14.971643	15.37156	15.783599	16.645487	17.560293	18.531167	19.56143	20.654583	21.81432	23.04452
12	15.917127	16.38559	16.869941	17.37071	17.888451	18.977126	20.140720	21.384284	22.71319	24.133133	25.65018	27.27075
13	17.712983	18.28680	18.882138	19.49981	20.140643	21.495297	22.953385	24.522712	26.21164	28.029109	29.98470	32.08865
14	19.598632	20.29257	21.015066	21.76730	22.550488	24.214920	26.019189	27.974983	30.09492	32.392602	34.88271	37.58107
15	21.578564	22.40866	23.275970	24.18217	25.129022	27.152114	29.360916	31.772482	34.40536	37.279715	40.41746	43.84241
16	23.657492	24.64114	25.672528	26.75401	27.888054	30.324283	33.003399	35.949730	39.18995	42.753280	46.67173	50.98035
17	25.840366	26.99640	28.212880	29.49302	30.840217	33.750226	36.973705	40.544703	44.50084	48.883674	53.73906	59.11760
18	28.132385	29.48120	30.905653	32.41007	33.999033	37.450244	41.301338	45.599173	50.39594	55.749715	61.72514	68.39407
19	30.539004	32.10267	33.759992	35.51672	37.378965	41.446263	46.018458	51.159090	56.93949	63.439681	70.74941	78.96923
20	33.065954	34.86832	36.785591	38.82531	40.995492	45.761964	51.160120	57.274999	64.20283	72.052442	80.94683	91.02493
21	35.719252	37.78608	39.992727	42.34895	44.865177	50.422921	56.764530	64.002499	72.26514	81.698736	92.46992	104.76842
22	38.505214	40.86431	43.392290	46.10164	49.005739	55.456755	62.873338	71.402749	81.21431	92.502584	105.49101	120.43600
23	41.430475	44.11185	46.995828	50.09824	53.436141	60.893296	69.531939	79.543024	91.14788	104.602894	120.20484	138.29704
24	44.501999	47.53800	50.815577	54.35463	58.176671	66.764759	76.789813	88.497327	102.17415	118.155241	136.83147	158.65862
25	47.727099	51.15259	54.864512	58.88768	63.249038	73.105940	84.700896	98.347059	114.41331	133.333870	155.61956	181.87083
26	51.113454	54.96598	59.156383	63.71538	68.676470	79.954415	93.323977	109.181765	127.99877	150.333934	176.85010	208.33274
27	54.669126	58.98911	63.705766	68.85688	74.483823	87.350768	102.723135	121.099942	143.07864	169.374007	200.84061	238.49933
28	58.402583	63.23351	68.528112	74.33257	80.697691	95.338830	112.968217	134.209936	159.81729	190.698887	227.94989	272.88923
29	62.322712	67.71135	73.629798	80.16419	87.346529	103.965936	124.135356	148.630930	178.39719	214.582754	258.58338	312.09373
30	66.438848	72.43548	79.058186	86.37486	94.460786	113.283211	136.307539	164.494023	199.02088	241.332684	293.19922	356.78685
31	70.760790	77.41943	84.801677	92.98923	102.073041	123.345868	149.575217	181.943425	221.91317	271.292606	332.31511	407.73701
32	75.298829	82.67750	90.889778	100.03353	110.218154	134.213537	164.036987	201.137767	247.32362	304.847719	376.51608	465.82019
33	80.063771	88.22476	97.343165	107.53571	118.933425	145.950620	179.800315	222.251544	275.52922	342.429446	426.46317	532.03501
34	85.066959	94.07712	104.183755	115.52553	128.258765	158.626670	196.982344	245.476699	306.83744	384.520979	482.90338	607.51991
35	90.320307	100.25136	111.434780	124.03469	138.236878	172.316804	215.710755	271.024368	341.58955	431.663496	546.68082	693.57270
40	120.799774	136.60561	154.761966	175.63192	199.635112	259.056519	337.882445	442.592556	581.82607	767.091420	1013.70424	1342.02510
45	159.700156	184.11917	212.743514	246.32459	285.749311	386.505617	525.858734	718.904837	986.63856	1358.230032	1874.16463	2590.56480
50	209.347996	246.21748	290.335905	343.17967	406.528929	573.770156	815.083556	1163.908529	1668.77115	2400.018249	3459.50712	4994.52135

CODES OF PROFESSIONAL ETHICS FOR ACCOUNTANTS

In recent years, governments, businesses, and the public have given increased attention to ethical conduct. They have insisted upon a level of human behavior that goes beyond that required by laws and regulations. Thus many businesses, as well as professional groups (such as accountants) and governmental organizations, have established standards of ethical conduct. This text emphasizes the ethical conduct of accountants, who serve various business interests as well as the public.

This appendix sets forth the standards of professional conduct expected of accountants in public accounting and private accounting. For accountants employed in public accounting, the American Institute of Certified Public Accountants' *Code of Professional Conduct* is presented.[1] For accountants employed in private accounting, the Institute of Management Accountants' *Standards of Ethical Conduct for Management Accountants* is presented as a guide to professional conduct.[2]

Supplementing the codes of professional ethics are ethics discussion cases that appear after the discussion questions in each chapter. These cases represent "real world" examples of ethical issues facing accountants. It should be noted that codes of professional ethics are general guides to good behavior and their application to specific situations often requires the exercise of professional judgment. In some cases, the line between right and wrong may be quite fine, and reasonable people may disagree. In addition, business is dynamic and everchanging, and what society considers to be acceptable behavior changes from time to time.

Code of Professional Conduct
as amended May 20, 1991

Composition, Applicability, and Compliance

The Code of Professional Conduct of the American Institute of Certified Public Accountants consists of two sections—(1) the Principles and (2) the Rules. The Principles provide the framework for the Rules, which govern the performance of professional services by members. The Council of the American Institute of Certified Public Accountants is authorized to designate bodies to promulgate technical standards under the Rules, and the bylaws require adherence to those Rules and standards.

The Code of Professional Conduct was adopted by the membership to provide guidance and rules to all members—those in public practice, in industry, in government, and in education—in the performance of their professional responsibilities.

Compliance with the Code of Professional Conduct, as with all standards in an open society, depends primarily on members' understanding and voluntary actions, secondarily on reinforcement by peers and public opinion, and ultimately on disciplinary proceedings, when necessary, against members who fail to comply with the Rules.

Other Guidance

The Principles and Rules as set forth herein are further amplified by interpretations and rulings contained in *AICPA Professional Standards.*

Interpretations of Rules of Conduct consist of interpretations which have been adopted, after exposure to state societies, state boards, practice units and other interested parties, by the professional ethics division's executive committee to pro-

---

[1] *Code of Professional Conduct* (New York: American Institute of Certified Public Accountants, 1992), pp. 3–8.
[2] *Standards of Ethical Conduct for Management Accountants* (Montvale, New Jersey: Institute of Management Accountants, 1992), pp. 1–2.

vide guidelines as to the scope and application of the Rules but are not intended to limit such scope or application. A member who departs from such guidelines shall have the burden of justifying such departure in any disciplinary hearing.

Ethics Rulings consist of formal rulings made by the professional ethics division's executive committee after exposure to state societies, state boards, practice units and other interested parties. These rulings summarize the application of Rules of Conduct and interpretations to a particular set of factual circumstances. Members who depart from such rulings in similar circumstances will be requested to justify such departures.

Publication of an interpretation or ethics ruling in the *Journal of Accountancy* constitutes notice to members. Hence, the effective date of the pronouncement is the last day of the month in which the pronouncement is published in the *Journal of Accountancy.* The professional ethics division will take into consideration the time that would have been reasonable for the member to comply with the pronouncement.

Members should also consult, if applicable, the ethical standards of their state CPA society, state board of accountancy, the Securities and Exchange Commission, and any other governmental agency which may regulate their client's business or use their reports to evaluate the client's compliance with applicable laws and related regulations.

Section I—Principles

Preamble

Membership in the American Institute of Certified Public Accountants is voluntary. By accepting membership, a certified public accountant assumes an obligation of self-discipline above and beyond the requirements of laws and regulations.

These Principles of the Code of Professional Conduct of the American Institute of Certified Public Accountants express the profession's recognition of its responsibilities to the public, to clients, and to colleagues. They guide members in the performance of their professional responsibilities and express the basic tenets of ethical and professional conduct. The Principles call for an unswerving commitment to honorable behavior, even at the sacrifice of personal advantage.

Article I
Responsibilities
In carrying out their responsibilities as professionals, members should exercise sensitive professional and moral judgments in all their activities.
As professionals, certified public accountants perform an essential role in society. Consistent with that role, members of the American Institute of Certified Public Accountants have responsibilities to all those who use their professional services. Members also have a continuing responsibility to cooperate with each other to improve the art of accounting, maintain the public's confidence, and carry out the profession's special responsibilities for self-governance. The collective efforts of all members are required to maintain and enhance the traditions of the profession.

Article II
The Public Interest
Members should accept the obligation to act in a way that will serve the public interest, honor the public trust, and demonstrate commitment to professionalism.
A distinguishing mark of a profession is acceptance of its responsibility to the public. The accounting profession's public consists of clients, credit grantors, governments, employers, investors, the business and financial community, and others who rely on the objectivity and integrity of certified public accountants to maintain the orderly functioning of commerce. This reliance imposes a public interest responsibility on certified public accountants. The public interest is defined as the collective well-being of the community of people and institutions the profession serves.

In discharging their professional responsibilities, members may encounter conflicting pressures from among each of those groups. In resolving those conflicts, members should act with integrity, guided by the precept that when members fulfill their responsibility to the public, clients' and employers' interests are best served.

Those who rely on certified public accountants expect them to discharge their responsibilities with integrity, objectivity, due professional care, and a genuine interest in serving the public. They are expected to provide quality services, enter into fee arrangements, and offer a range of services—all in a manner that demonstrates a level of professionalism consistent with these Principles of the Code of Professional Conduct.

All who accept membership in the American Institute of Certified Public Accountants commit themselves to honor the public trust. In return for the faith that the public reposes in them, members should seek continually to demonstrate their dedication to professional excellence.

Article III
Integrity
To maintain and broaden public confidence, members should perform all professional responsibilities with the highest sense of integrity.

Integrity is an element of character fundamental to professional recognition. It is the quality from which the public trust derives and the benchmark against which a member must ultimately test all decisions.

Integrity requires a member to be, among other things, honest and candid within the constraints of client confidentiality. Service and the public trust should not be subordinated to personal gain and advantage. Integrity can accommodate the inadvertent error and the honest difference of opinion; it cannot accommodate deceit or subordination of principle.

Integrity is measured in terms of what is right and just. In the absence of specific rules, standards, or guidance, or in the face of conflicting opinions, a member should test decisions and deeds by asking: "Am I doing what a person of integrity would do? Have I retained my integrity?" Integrity requires a member to observe both the form and the spirit of technical and ethical standards; circumvention of those standards constitutes subordination of judgment.

Integrity also requires a member to observe the principles of objectivity and independence and of due care.

Article IV
Objectivity and Independence
A member should maintain objectivity and be free of conflicts of interest in discharging professional responsibilities. A member in public practice should be independent in fact and appearance when providing auditing and other attestation services.

Objectivity is a state of mind, a quality that lends value to a member's services. It is a distinguishing feature of the profession. The principle of objectivity imposes the obligation to be impartial, intellectually honest, and free of conflicts of interest. Independence precludes relationships that may appear to impair a member's objectivity in rendering attestation services.

Members often serve multiple interests in many different capacities and must demonstrate their objectivity in varying circumstances. Members in public practice render attest, tax, and management advisory services. Other members prepare financial statements in the employment of others, perform internal auditing services, and serve in financial and management capacities in industry, education, and government. They also educate and train those who aspire to admission into the profession. Regardless of service or capacity, members should protect the integrity of their work, maintain objectivity, and avoid any subordination of their judgment.

For a member in public practice, the maintenance of objectivity and independence requires a continuing assessment of client relationships and public responsibility. Such a member who provides auditing and other attestation services should be independent in fact and appearance. In providing all other services, a member should maintain objectivity and avoid conflicts of interest.

Although members not in public practice cannot maintain the appearance of independence, they nevertheless have the responsibility to maintain objectivity in rendering professional services. Members employed by others to prepare financial statements or to perform auditing, tax, or consulting services are charged with the same responsibility for objectivity as members in public practice and must be scrupulous in their application of generally accepted accounting principles and candid in all their dealings with members in public practice.

Activity V
Due Care

A member should observe the profession's technical and ethical standards, strive continually to improve competence and the quality of services, and discharge professional responsibility to the best of the member's ability.

The quest for excellence is the essence of due care. Due care requires a member to discharge professional responsibilities with competence and diligence. It imposes the obligation to perform professional services to the best of a member's ability with concern for the best interest of those for whom the services are performed and consistent with the profession's responsibility to the public.

Competence is derived from a synthesis of education and experience. It begins with a mastery of the common body of knowledge required for designation as a certified public accountant. The maintenance of competence requires a commitment to learning and professional improvement that must continue throughout a member's professional life. It is a member's individual responsibility. In all engagements and in all responsibilities, each member should undertake to achieve a level of competence that will assure that the quality of the member's services meets the high level of professionalism required by these Principles.

Competence represents the attainment and maintenance of a level of understanding and knowledge that enables a member to render services with facility and acumen. It also establishes the limitations of a member's capabilities by dictating that consultation or referral may be required when a professional engagement exceeds the personal competence of a member or a member's firm. Each member is responsible for assessing his or her own competence—of evaluating whether education, experience, and judgment are adequate for the responsibility to be assumed.

Members should be diligent in discharging responsibilities to clients, employers, and the public. Diligence imposes the responsibility to render services promptly and carefully, to be thorough, and to observe applicable technical and ethical standards.

Due care requires a member to plan and supervise adequately any professional activity for which he or she is responsible.

Article VI
Scope and Nature of Services

A member in public practice should observe the Principles of the Code of Professional Conduct in determining the scope and nature of services to be provided.

The public interest aspect of certified public accountants' services requires that such services be consistent with acceptable professional behavior for certified public accountants. Integrity requires that service and the public trust not be subordinated to personal gain and advantage. Objectivity and independence require that members be free from conflicts of interest in discharging professional responsibilities. Due care requires that services be provided with competence and diligence.

Each of these Principles should be considered by members in determining whether or not to provide specific services in individual circumstances. In some instances, they may represent an overall constraint on the nonaudit services that might be offered to a specific client. No hard-and-fast rules can be developed to help members reach these judgments, but they must be satisfied that they are meeting the spirit of the Principles in this regard.

In order to accomplish this, members should

- Practice in firms that have in place internal quality-control procedures to ensure that services are competently delivered and adequately supervised.
- Determine, in their individual judgments, whether the scope and nature of other services provided to an audit client would create a conflict of interest in the performance of the audit function for that client.
- Assess, in their individual judgments, whether an activity is consistent with their role as professionals (for example, Is such activity a reasonable extension or variation of existing services offered by the member or others in the profession?).

STANDARDS OF ETHICAL CONDUCT FOR MANAGEMENT ACCOUNTANTS

Management accountants have an obligation to the organizations they serve, their profession, the public, and themselves to maintain the highest standards of ethical conduct. In recognition of this obligation, the Institute of Management Accountants has promulgated the following standards of ethical conduct for management accountants. Adherence to these standards is integral to achieving the *Objectives of Management Accounting.*[3] Management accountants shall not commit acts contrary to these standards nor shall they condone the commission of such acts by others within their organizations.

Competence

Management accountants have a responsibility to:
- Maintain an appropriate level of professional competence by ongoing development of their knowledge and skills.
- Perform their professional duties in accordance with relevant laws, regulations, and technical standards.
- Prepare complete and clear reports and recommendations after appropriate analyses of relevant and reliable information.

Confidentiality

Management accountants have a responsibility to:
- Refrain from disclosing confidential information acquired in the course of their work except when authorized, unless legally obligated to do so.
- Inform subordinates as appropriate regarding the confidentiality of information acquired in the course of their work and monitor their activities to assure the maintenance of that confidentiality.
- Refrain from using or appearing to use confidential information acquired in the course of their work for unethical or illegal advantage either personally or through third parties.

Integrity

Management accountants have a responsibility to:
- Avoid actual or apparent conflicts of interest and advise all appropriate parties of any potential conflict.
- Refrain from engaging in any activity that would prejudice their ability to carry out their duties ethically.
- Refuse any gift, favor, or hospitality that would influence or would appear to influence their actions.

---

[3] National Association of Accountants, *Statements on Management Accounting: Objectives of Management Accounting,* Statement No. 1B, New York, N.Y., June 17, 1982.

- Refrain from either actively or passively subverting the attainment of the organization's legitimate and ethical objectives.
- Recognize and communicate professional limitations or other constraints that would preclude responsible judgment or successful performance of an activity.
- Communicate unfavorable as well as favorable information and professional judgments or opinions.
- Refrain from engaging in or supporting any activity that would discredit the profession.

Objectivity

Management accountants have a responsibility to:
- Communicate information fairly and objectively.
- Disclose fully all relevant information that could reasonably be expected to influence an intended user's understanding of the reports, comments, and recommendations presented.

ALTERNATIVE METHODS OF RECORDING DEFERRALS

As we discussed in Chapter 3, deferrals are created by recording a transaction in a way that delays or defers the recognition of an expense or a revenue. Deferrals may be either deferred expenses (prepaid expenses) or deferred revenues (unearned revenues).

In Chapter 2, deferred expenses (prepaid expenses) were debited to an *asset* account at the time of payment. As an alternative, deferred expenses may be debited to an *expense* account at the time of payment. In Chapter 2, deferred revenues (unearned revenues) were credited to a *liability* account at the time of receipt. As an alternative, deferred revenues may be credited to a *revenue* account at the time of receipt. In this appendix, we describe and illustrate these alternative methods of recording deferred expenses and deferred revenues.

DEFERRED EXPENSES (PREPAID EXPENSES)

As a basis for illustrating the alternative methods of recording deferred expenses, we will use the insurance premium paid by Computer King Corporation in Chapter 2. The amounts related to this insurance are as follows:

Prepayment of insurance for 24 months, starting December 1	$2,400
Insurance premium expired during December	100
Unexpired insurance premium at the end of December	$2,300

Based on the above data, the entries to account for the deferred expense (prepaid insurance) recorded initially as an *asset* are shown in the journal and T accounts in Exhibit 1. The adjusting entry in Exhibit 1 was shown in Chapter 3. The entries to account for the prepaid insurance recorded initially as an *expense* are shown in the journal and T accounts in Exhibit 2.

Exhibit 1				*Exhibit 2*			
Prepaid Expense **Recorded Initially as Asset**				*Prepaid Expense* **Recorded Initially as Expense**			
Initial entry (to record initial payment):				Initial entry (to record initial payment):			
Dec. 1	Prepaid Insurance	2,400		Dec. 1	Insurance Expense	2,400	
	Cash		2,400		Cash		2,400
Adjusting entry (to transfer amount **used** to proper expense account):				Adjusting entry (to transfer amount **unused** to the proper asset account):			
Dec. 31	Insurance Expense	100		Dec. 31	Prepaid Insurance	2,300	
	Prepaid Insurance		100		Insurance Expense		2,300
Closing entry (to close income statement accounts with debit balances):				Closing entry (to close income statement accounts with debit balances):			
Income Summary		XXXX		Income Summary		XXXX	
Purchases			XXXX	Purchases			XXXX
Insurance Expense			100	Insurance Expense			100

Prepaid Insurance				Prepaid Insurance			
Dec. 1	2,400	Dec. 31 Adjusting	100	Dec. 31 Adjusting	2,300		

Insurance Expense				Insurance Expense			
Dec. 31 Adjusting	100	Dec. 31 Closing	100	Dec. 1	2,400	Dec. 31 Adjusting	2,300
						31 Closing	100

Either of the two methods of recording deferred expenses (prepaid expenses) may be used. As illustrated in Exhibits 1 and 2, both methods result in the same account balances after the adjusting entries have been recorded. Therefore, the amounts reported as expenses in the income statement and as assets on the balance sheet will not be affected by the method used. To avoid confusion, the method used by an enterprise for each kind of prepaid expense should be followed consistently from year to year.

Some enterprises record all deferred expenses using one method. Other enterprises use one method to record the prepayment of some expenses and the other method for other expenses. Initial debits to the asset account are logical for prepayments of insurance, which are usually for periods of one to three years. On the other hand, rent on a building may be prepaid on the first of each month. The prepaid rent will expire by the end of the month. In this case, it is logical to record the payment of rent by initially debiting an expense account rather than an asset account.

DEFERRED REVENUES (UNEARNED REVENUES)

As a basis for illustrating the alternative methods of recording deferred revenues, we will use the rent received by Computer King Corporation in Chapter 2. Computer King rented land on December 1 to a local retailer for use as a parking lot for three months, receiving $360 for the entire three months. On December 31, $120 (1/3 × $360) of the rent has been earned, and $240 (2/3 × $360) of the rent is still unearned.

Based on the above data, the entries to account for the deferred revenue (unearned rent) recorded initially as a liability are shown in the journal and ledger in Exhibit 3. The adjusting entry in Exhibit 3 was shown in Chapter 3. The entries to account for the unearned rent recorded initially as revenue are shown in the journal and ledger in Exhibit 4.

Exhibit 3	*Exhibit 4*
*Unearned Revenue **Recorded Initially as Liability***	*Unearned Revenue **Recorded Initially as Revenue***

Exhibit 3			Exhibit 4		
Initial entry (to record initial receipt):			Initial entries (to record initial receipt):		
Dec. 1 Cash	360		Dec. 1 Cash	360	
Unearned Rent		360	Rent Income		360
Adjusting entry (to transfer amount **earned** to proper **revenue** account):			Adjusting entry (to transfer amount **unearned** to proper **liability** account):		
Dec. 31 Unearned Rent	120		Dec. 31 Rent Income	240	
Rent Income		120	Unearned Rent		240
Closing entry (to close income statement accounts with credit balances):			Closing entry (to close income statement accounts with credit balances):		
Dec. 31 Sales	XXXX		Dec. 31 Sales	XXXX	
Rent Income	120		Rent Income	120	
Income Summary		XXXX	Income Summary		XXXX

Unearned Rent						Unearned Rent				
Dec. 31	Adjusting	120	Dec. 1	360					Dec. 31	Adjusting	240

Rent Income						Rent Income				
Dec. 31	Closing	120	Dec. 31	Adjusting	120	Dec. 31	Adjusting	240	Dec. 1	360
						Dec. 31	Closing	120		

As illustrated in Exhibits 3 and 4, both methods result in the same account balances after the adjusting entries have been recorded. Therefore, the amounts reported as revenues in the income statement and as liabilities on the balance sheet will not be affected by the method used. Either of the methods may be used for all revenues received in advance. Alternatively, the first method may be used for advance receipts of some kinds of revenue and the second method for other kinds. To avoid confusion, the method used by an enterprise for each kind of unearned revenue should be followed consistently from year to year.

REVERSING ENTRIES FOR DEFERRALS

As we discussed in the appendix at the end of Chapter 4, the use of reversing entries is optional. However, the use of reversing entries generally simplifies the analysis of transactions and reduces the likelihood of errors in the subsequent recording of transactions. Normally, reversing entries are prepared for deferrals in the following two cases:

1. When a deferred expense (prepaid expense) is initially recorded as an expense.
2. When a deferred revenue (unearned revenue) is initially recorded as a revenue.

The entry to reverse the adjustment to record the prepaid insurance in Exhibit 2 is as follows:

Jan. 1	Insurance Expense	2,300	
	Prepaid Insurance		2,300

The entry to reverse the adjustment to record the unearned rent in Exhibit 4 is as follows:

Jan. 1	Unearned Rent	240	
	Rent Income		240

EXERCISES

EXERCISE C-1
ADJUSTING ENTRIES FOR
OFFICE SUPPLIES

The office supplies purchased during the year total $5,450, and the amount of office supplies on hand at the end of the year is $1,530.

a. Record the following transactions directly in T accounts for Office Supplies and Office Supplies Expense, using the system of initially recording supplies as an asset: (1) purchases for the period; (2) adjusting entry at the end of the period. Identify each entry by number.
b. Record the following transactions directly in T accounts for Office Supplies and Office Supplies Expense, using the system of initially recording supplies as an expense: (1) purchases for the period; (2) adjusting entry at the end of the period. Identify each entry by number.

EXERCISE C-2
ADJUSTING ENTRIES FOR
PREPAID INSURANCE

During the first year of operations, insurance premiums of $4,500 were paid. At the end of the year, unexpired premiums totaled $2,000. Journalize the adjusting entry at the end of the year, assuming that (a) prepaid expenses were initially recorded as assets and (b) prepaid expenses were initially recorded as expenses.

EXERCISE C-3
ADJUSTING ENTRIES FOR
ADVERTISING REVENUE

The advertising revenues received during the year totaled $280,000, and the unearned advertising revenue at the end of the year is $40,000.

a. Record the following transactions directly in T accounts for Unearned Advertising Revenue and Advertising Revenue, using the system of initially recording advertising fees as a liability: (1) revenues received during the period; (2) adjusting entry at the end of the period. Identify each entry by number.
b. Record the following transactions directly in T accounts for Unearned Advertising Revenue and Advertising Revenue, using the system of initially recording advertising fees as revenue: (1) revenues received during the period; (2) adjusting entry at the end of the period. Identify each entry by number.

EXERCISE C-4
YEAR-END ENTRIES FOR
DEFERRED REVENUES

In their first year of operations, Snyder Publishing Co. received $400,000 from advertising contracts and $675,000 from magazine subscriptions, crediting the two amounts to Unearned Advertising Revenue and Circulation Revenue, respectively. At the end of the year, the unearned advertising revenue amounts to $60,000, and the unearned circulation revenue amounts to $150,000. Journalize the adjusting entries that should be made at the end of the year.

PERIODIC INVENTORY SYSTEMS

In this text, we emphasize the perpetual inventory system of accounting for purchases and sales of merchandise. Not all merchandise enterprises, however, use perpetual inventory systems. Some managers/owners of small merchandise enterprises, such as locally owned hardware stores, may feel more comfortable using manually kept records. Because a manual perpetual inventory system is time-consuming and costly to maintain, the periodic inventory system is often used in these cases.

MERCHANDISE TRANSACTIONS IN A PERIODIC INVENTORY SYSTEM

In a periodic inventory system, the revenues from sales are recorded when sales are made in the same manner as in a perpetual inventory system. However, no attempt is made on the sale date to record the cost of the merchandise sold. Instead, the merchandise inventory on hand at the end of the period is counted. This physical inventory is then used to determine (1) the cost of merchandise sold during the period and (2) the cost of merchandise on hand at the end of the period.

In a periodic inventory system, purchases of inventory are recorded in a purchases account rather than in a merchandise inventory account. No attempt is made to keep a detailed record of the amount of inventory on hand at any given time.

The purchases account is normally debited for the amount of the invoice before considering any purchases discounts. Purchases discounts are normally recorded in a separate purchases discounts account.[1] The balance of this account is reported as a deduction from the amount initially recorded in Purchases for the period. Thus, the purchases discounts account is viewed as a contra (or offsetting) account to Purchases.

Purchases returns and allowances are recorded in a similar manner as purchases discounts. A separate account is used to keep a record of the amount of purchases returns and allowances during a period. Purchases returns and allowances are reported as a deduction from the amount initially recorded as Purchases. Like Purchases Discounts, the purchases returns and allowances account is a contra (or offsetting) account to Purchases.

When merchandise is purchased FOB shipping point, the buyer is responsible for paying the freight charges. In a periodic inventory system, freight charges paid when purchasing merchandise FOB shipping point are debited to Transportation In, Freight In, or a similarly titled account.

To illustrate the recording of merchandise transactions in a periodic system, we will use the following selected transactions for Taylor Co. We will also explain how the transaction would have been recorded under a perpetual system.

June 5. Purchased $30,000 of merchandise on account from Owen Clothing, terms 2/10, n/30.

Purchases	30,000	
Accounts Payable		30,000

Under the perpetual inventory system, such purchases would be recorded in the merchandise inventory account.

June 8. Returned merchandise purchased on account from Owen Clothing on June 5, $500.

Accounts Payable	500	
Purchases Returns and Allowances		500

Under the perpetual inventory system, returns would be recorded as a credit to the merchandise inventory account.

---

[1] Some businesses prefer to credit the purchases account. If this alternative is used, the balance of the purchases account will be a net amount—the total purchases less the total purchases discounts for the period.

June 15. Paid Owen Clothing for purchase of June 5, less return of $500 and discount of $590 [($30,000 – $500) × 2%].

Accounts Payable	29,500	
Cash		28,910
Purchases Discounts		590

Under a perpetual inventory system, purchases discounts would be recorded directly as a reduction in the cost of the merchandise inventory.

June 18. Sold merchandise on account to Jones Co., $12,500, 1/10, n/30. The cost of the merchandise sold was $9,000.

Accounts Receivable	12,500	
Sales		12,500

The entry to record the sale is the same under both systems. Under the perpetual inventory system, the cost of merchandise sold and the reduction in merchandise inventory would also be recorded on the date of sale.

June 21. Received merchandise returned on account from Jones Co., $4,000. The cost of the merchandise returned was $2,800.

Sales Returns and Allowances	4,000	
Accounts Receivable		4,000

The entry to record the sales return is the same under both systems. In addition, the cost of the merchandise returned would be debited to the merchandise inventory account and credited to the cost of merchandise sold account under the perpetual inventory system.

June 22. Purchased merchandise from Norcross Clothiers, $15,000, terms FOB shipping point, 2/15, n/30, with prepaid transportation charges of $750 added to the invoice.

Purchases	15,000	
Transportation In	750	
Accounts Payable		15,750

This entry is similar to the June 5 entry for the purchase of merchandise. Since the transportation terms were FOB shipping point, the prepaid freight charges of $750 must be added to the invoice cost of $15,000. Under the perpetual inventory system, the total cost of the purchase of $15,750 would be debited to the merchandise inventory account.

June 28. Received $8,415 as payment on account from Jones Co., less return of June 21 and less discount of $85 [($12,500 – $4,000) × 1%].

Cash	8,415	
Sales Discounts	85	
Accounts Receivable		8,500

This entry is the same under the perpetual inventory system.

June 29. Received $19,600 from cash sales. The cost of the merchandise sold was $13,800.

Cash	19,600	
Sales		19,600

The entry to record the sale is the same under both systems. Under the perpetual inventory system, the cost of merchandise sold and the reduction in merchandise inventory would also be recorded on the date of sale.

COST OF MERCHANDISE SOLD

Under the periodic inventory system, the cost of merchandise sold during a period is reported in a separate section in the income statement. To illustrate, assume that on January 3, 1995, Computer King Corporation opened a merchandising outlet selling microcomputers and software. During 1995, Computer King Corporation purchased $340,000 of merchandise. The inventory at December 31, 1995, the end of the year, is $59,700. The cost of merchandise sold during 1995 is reported as follows:

Cost of merchandise sold:		
Purchases		$340,000
Less merchandise inventory, December 31, 1995		59,700
Cost of merchandise sold		$280,300

To continue the example, assume that during 1996 Computer King Corporation purchased additional merchandise of $521,980. Computer King Corporation also received credit for purchases returns and allowances of $9,100, took purchases discounts of $2,525, and paid transportation costs of $17,400. The purchases returns and allowances and the purchases discounts are deducted from the total purchases to yield the net purchases. The transportation costs are then added to the net purchases to yield the cost of merchandise purchased. These amounts are reported in the cost of merchandise sold section of Computer King Corporation's income statement for 1996 as follows:

Purchases		$521,980
Less: Purchases returns and allowances	$9,100	
Purchases discounts	2,525	11,625
Net purchases		$510,355
Add transportation in		17,400
Cost of merchandise purchased		$527,755

The ending inventory of Computer King Corporation on December 31, 1995, $59,700, becomes the beginning inventory for 1996. In the cost of merchandise sold section of the income statement for 1996, this beginning inventory is added to the cost of merchandise purchased to yield the merchandise available for sale. The ending inventory on December 31, 1996, $62,150, is then subtracted from the merchandise available for sale to yield the cost of merchandise sold. Exhibit 1 shows the cost of merchandise sold during 1996.

Exhibit 1
Cost of Merchandise Sold—
Periodic Inventory System

Cost of merchandise sold:			
Merchandise inventory, January 1, 1996			$ 59,700
Purchases		$521,980	
Less: Purchases returns and allowances	$9,100		
Purchases discounts	2,525	11,625	
Net purchases		$510,355	
Add transportation in		17,400	
Cost of merchandise purchased			527,755
Merchandise available for sale			$587,455
Less merchandise inventory, December 31, 1996			62,150
Cost of merchandise sold			$525,305

The multiple-step income statement under the periodic inventory system is illustrated in Exhibit 2. The multiple-step income statement under a perpetual inventory system is similar, except that the cost of merchandise sold section has been expanded in Exhibit 2.[2]

[2] Small differences in the amount reported as cost of merchandise sold may arise under the periodic and perpetual inventory methods. These differences result from how purchases discounts are recorded. To simplify, we have ignored such differences for the purposes of this discussion.

Exhibit 2
Multiple-Step Income
Statement—Periodic
Inventory System

Computer King, Corporation
Income Statement
For Year Ended December 31, 1996

Revenue from sales:				
Sales			$720,185	
Less: Sales returns and allowances		$ 6,140		
Sales discounts		5,790	11,930	
Net Sales				$708,255
Cost of merchandise sold:				
Merchandise inventory				
January 1, 1996			$ 59,700	
Purchases		$521,980		
Less: Purchases returns and allowances	$9,100			
Purchases discounts	2,525	11,625		
Net purchases		$510,355		
Add transportation in		17,400		
Cost of merchandise purchased			527,755	
Merchandise available for sale			587,455	
Less merchandise inventory,				
December 31, 1996			62,150	
Cost of merchandise sold				525,305
Gross profit				$182,950
Operating expenses:				
Selling expenses:				
Sales salaries expense		$ 60,030		
Advertising expense		10,860		
Depreciation expense—store equipment		3,100		
Miscellaneous selling expense		630		
Total selling expenses			$ 74,620	
Administrative expenses:				
Office salaries expense		$ 21,020		
Rent expense		8,100		
Depreciation expense—office equipment		2,490		
Insurance expense		1,910		
Office supplies expense		610		
Miscellaneous administrative expense		760		
Total administrative expenses			34,890	
Total operating expenses				109,510
Income from operations				$ 73,440
Other income:				
Interest income		$ 3,800		
Rent income		600		
Total other income			$ 4,400	
Other expense:				
Interest expense			2,440	1,960
Net income				$ 75,400

CHART OF ACCOUNTS FOR A PERIODIC INVENTORY SYSTEM

Exhibit 3 is the chart of accounts for Computer King Corporation when a periodic inventory system is used. The periodic inventory accounts related to merchandising transactions are shown in color.

END-OF-PERIOD PROCEDURES IN A PERIODIC INVENTORY SYSTEM

The end-of-period procedures are generally the same for the periodic and perpetual inventory systems. In the remainder of this appendix, we will discuss the dif-

Exhibit 3
Chart of Accounts—Periodic Inventory System

Balance Sheet Accounts	Income Statement Accounts

Balance Sheet Accounts

100 Assets
110 Cash
111 Notes Receivable
112 Accounts Receivable
113 Interest Receivable
115 Merchandise Inventory
116 Office Supplies
117 Prepaid Insurance
120 Land
123 Store Equipment
124 Accumulated Depreciation— Store Equipment
125 Office Equipment
126 Accumulated Depreciation— Office Equipment
200 Liabilities
210 Accounts Payable
211 Salaries Payable
212 Unearned Rent
215 Notes Payable
300 Stockholders' Equity
310 Capital Stock
311 Retained Earnings
312 Dividends
313 Income Summary

Income Statement Accounts

400 Revenues
410 Sales
411 Sales Returns and Allowances
412 Sales Discounts
500 Costs and Expenses
510 Purchases
511 Purchases Returns and Allowances
512 Purchases Discounts
513 Transportation In
520 Sales Salaries Expense
521 Advertising Expense
522 Depreciation Expense—Store Equipment
529 Miscellaneous Selling Expense
530 Office Salaries Expense
531 Rent Expense
532 Depreciation Expense—Office Equipment
533 Insurance Expense
534 Office Supplies Expense
539 Misc. Administrative Expense
600 Other Income
610 Rent Income
611 Interest Income
700 Other Expense
710 Interest Expense

ferences in procedures for the two systems, which affect the work sheet, the adjusting entries, and the closing entries. As the basis for illustration, we will use the data for Computer King Corporation, presented in Chapter 4.

Work Sheet

The differences in the work sheet for a merchandising enterprise that uses the periodic inventory system are highlighted in the work sheet for Computer King in Exhibit 4. As we illustrated earlier, accounts for purchases, purchases returns and allowances, purchases discounts, and transportation in are used in a periodic inventory system.

Under the periodic inventory system, a separate merchandise inventory account is maintained in the ledger. Throughout the accounting period, this account shows the inventory at the beginning of the period. As shown in Exhibit 1, the merchandise inventory on January 1, 1996, $59,700, is a part of the merchandise available for sale. At the end of the period, the beginning inventory amount in the ledger is replaced with the ending inventory amount. To record this updating of the inventory account, two adjusting entries are used.[3] The first adjusting entry transfers the beginning inventory balance to Income Summary. This entry, shown below, has the effect of increasing the cost of merchandise sold and decreasing net income.

| Dec. 31 | Income Summary | 59,700 | |
| | Merchandise Inventory | | 59,700 |

After the first adjusting entry has been recorded and posted, the balance of the merchandise inventory account is zero. The second adjusting entry records the cost

---

[3] Another method of updating the merchandise inventory account at the end of the period is called the *closing method*. This method adjusts the merchandise inventory through the use of closing entries. This method is not appropriate for use in computerized accounting systems. Since the financial statements are the same under both methods and since computerized accounting systems are used by most businesses, the closing method is not illustrated.

Exhibit 4
Work Sheet—Periodic
Inventory System

Computer King Corporation
Work Sheet
For Year Ended December 31, 1996

Account Title	Trial Balance Dr.	Trial Balance Cr.	Adjustments Dr.	Adjustments Cr.	Adjusted Trial Balance Dr.	Adjusted Trial Balance Cr.	Income Statement Dr.	Income Statement Cr.	Balance Sheet Dr.	Balance Sheet Cr.
Cash	52,950				52,950				52,950	
Notes Receivable	40,000				40,000				40,000	
Accounts Receivable	60,880				60,880				60,880	
Interest Receivable			(a) 200		200				200	
Merchandise Inventory	59,700		(c) 62,150	(b) 59,700	62,150				62,150	
Office Supplies	1,090			(d) 610	480				480	
Prepaid Insurance	4,560			(e) 1,910	2,650				2,650	
Land	10,000				10,000				10,000	
Store Equipment	27,100				27,100				27,100	
Accum. Depr.—Store Equip.		2,600		(f) 3,100		5,700				5,700
Office Equipment	15,570				15,570				15,570	
Accum. Depr.—Office Equipment		2,230		(g) 2,490		4,720				4,720
Accounts Payable		22,420				22,420				22,420
Salaries Payable				(h) 1,140		1,140				1,140
Unearned Rent		2,400	(i) 600			1,800				1,800
Notes Payable (final payment, 2000)		25,000				25,000				25,000
Capital Stock		15,000				15,000				15,000
Retained Earnings		138,800				138,800				138,800
Dividends	18,000				18,000				18,000	
Income Summary			(b) 59,700	(c) 62,150	59,700	62,150	59,700	62,150		
Sales		720,185				720,185		720,185		
Sales Returns and Allowances	6,140				6,140		6,140			
Sales Discounts	5,790				5,790		5,790			
Purchases	521,980				521,980		521,980			
Purchases Returns & Allowances		9,100				9,100		9,100		
Purchases Discounts		2,525				2,525		2,525		
Transportation In	17,400				17,400		17,400			
Sales Salaries Expense	59,250		(h) 780		60,030		60,030			
Advertising Expense	10,860				10,860		10,860			
Depr. Exp.—Store Equip.			(f) 3,100		3,100		3,100			
Miscellaneous Selling Expense	630				630		630			
Office Salaries Expense	20,660		(h) 360		21,020		21,020			
Rent Expense	8,100				8,100		8,100			
Depr. Ex.—Office Equip.			(g) 2,490		2,490		2,490			
Insurance Expense			(e) 1,910		1,910		1,910			
Office Supplies Expense			(d) 610		610		610			
Misc. Administrative Expense	760				760		760			
Rent Income				(i) 600		600		600		
Interest Income		3,600		(a) 200		3,800		3,800		
Interest Expense	2,440				2,440		2,440			
	943,860	943,860	131,900	131,900	1,012,940	1,012,940	722,960	798,360	289,980	214,580
Net Income							75,400			75,400
							798,360	798,360	289,980	289,980

(a) Interest earned but not received on notes receivable, $200.

(b) Beginning merchandise inventory, $59,700.

(c) Ending merchandise inventory, $62,150.

(d) Office supplies used, $610 ($1,090–$480).

(e) Insurance expired, $1,910.

(f) Depreciation of store equipment, $3,100.

(g) Depreciation of office equipment, $2,490.

(h) Salaries accrued but not paid (sales salaries, $780; office salaries, $360), $1,140.

(i) Rent earned from amount received in advance, $600.

of the merchandise on hand at the end of the period by debiting Merchandise Inventory. Since the merchandise inventory at December 31, 1996, $62,150, is subtracted from the cost of merchandise available for sale in determining the cost of merchandise sold, Income Summary is credited. This credit has the effect of decreasing the cost of merchandise available for sale during the period, $587,455, by the cost of the unsold merchandise. The second adjusting entry is shown below.

Dec.31   Merchandise Inventory   62,150
                Income Summary   62,150

After the second adjusting entry has been recorded and posted, the balance of the merchandise inventory account is the amount of the ending inventory. The accounts for Merchandise Inventory and Income Summary after both entries have been posted would appear as follows, in T account form:

Merchandise Inventory

1996					
Jan. 1	Beginning inventory	59,700	Dec. 31	Beginning inventory	59,700
Dec. 31	Ending inventory	62,150			

Income Summary

Dec. 31 Beginning inventory	59,700	Dec. 31 Ending inventory	62,150

No separate adjusting entry can be made for merchandise inventory shrinkage in a periodic inventory system. This is because no perpetual inventory records are available to show what inventory should be on hand at the end of the period. One disadvantage of the periodic inventory system is that inventory shrinkage cannot be measured.[4]

Completing the Work Sheet

After all of the necessary adjustments have been entered on the work sheet, the work sheet is completed in the normal manner. An exception to the usual practice of extending only account balances is Income Summary. Both the debit and credit amounts for Income Summary are extended to the Adjusted Trial Balance columns. Extending both amounts aids in the preparation of the income statement because the debit adjustment (the beginning inventory of $59,700) and the credit adjustment (the ending inventory of $62,150) are reported as part of the cost of merchandise sold.

The purchases, purchases discounts, purchases returns and allowances, and transportation in accounts are extended to the Income Statement Columns of the work sheet, since they are used in computing the cost of merchandise sold. You should note that the two merchandise inventory amounts in Income Summary are extended to the Income Statement columns. After all of the items have been extended to the statement columns, the four columns are totaled and the net income or net loss is determined.

Financial Statements

The financial statements for Computer King Corporation are essentially the same under both the perpetual and periodic inventory systems.[5] As illustrated in Exhibit 1, the major difference is in the manner in which cost of merchandise sold is reported in a multiple-step income statement when the periodic inventory system is used.[6]

[4] Any inventory shrinkage that does exist is part of the cost of merchandise sold, reported on the income statement, since a smaller ending inventory is deducted from the merchandise available for sale.
[5] To simplify the discussion, we assume that the accounts payable for Computer King Corporation on December 31, 1996, were not subject to any cash discounts.
[6] The single-step income statement would be the same for both the perpetual and the periodic inventory systems.

Adjusting and Closing Entries

The adjusting entries are the same under both the perpetual and periodic inventory systems, except for merchandise inventory. As indicated previously, two adjusting entries for beginning and ending merchandise inventory are necessary in a periodic inventory system.

The closing entries differ in the periodic inventory system in that their is no cost of merchandise sold account to be closed to Income Summary. Instead, the purchases, purchases discounts, purchases returns and allowances, and transportation in accounts are closed to Income Summary.[7] To illustrate, the adjusting and closing entries under a periodic inventory system for Computer King Corporation are shown below.

	DATE		DESCRIPTION	POST. REF.	DEBIT	CREDIT	
1			Adjusting Entries				1
2	Dec. 1996	31	Interest Receivable	113	2 0 0 00		2
3			Interest Income	611		2 0 0 00	3
4							4
5		31	Income Summary	312	59 7 0 0 00		5
6			Merchandise Inventory	115		59 7 0 0 00	6
7							7
8		31	Merchandise Inventory	115	62 1 5 0 00		8
9			Income Summary	312		62 1 5 0 00	9
10							10
11		31	Office Supplies Expense	534	6 1 0 00		11
12			Office Supplies	116		6 1 0 00	12
13							13
14		31	Insurance Expense	533	1 9 1 0 00		14
15			Prepaid Insurance	117		1 9 1 0 00	15
16							16
17		31	Depreciation Expense—Store Equip.	522	3 1 0 0 00		17
18			Accumulated Depr.—Store Equip.	124		3 1 0 0 00	18
19							19
20		31	Depreciation Expense—Office Equip.	532	2 4 9 0 00		20
21			Accumulated Depr.—Office Equip.	126		2 4 9 0 00	21
22							22
23		31	Sales Salaries Expense	520	7 8 0 00		23
24			Office Salaries Expense	530	3 6 0 00		24
25			Salaries Payable	211		1 1 4 0 00	25
26							26
27		31	Unearned Rent	212	6 0 0 00		27
28			Rent Income	610		6 0 0 00	28

[7] The balance of Income Summary, after the merchandise inventory adjustments and the first two closing entries have been posted, is the net income or net loss for the period.

	DATE		DESCRIPTION	POST. REF.	DEBIT	CREDIT	
			JOURNAL			PAGE 29	
1			Closing Entries				1
2	1996 Dec.	31	Sales	410	720 1 8 5 00		2
3			Purchases Returns and Allowances	511	9 1 0 0 00		3
4			Purchases Discounts	512	2 5 2 5 00		4
5			Rent Income	610	6 0 0 00		5
6			Interest Income	611	3 8 0 0 00		6
7			Income Summary	313		736 2 1 0 00	7
8							8
9		31	Income Summary	313	663 2 6 0 00		9
10			Sales Returns and Allowances	411		6 1 4 0 00	10
11			Sales Discounts	412		5 7 9 0 00	11
12			Purchases	510		521 9 8 0 00	12
13			Transportation In	513		17 4 0 0 00	13
14			Sales Salaries Expense	520		60 0 3 0 00	14
15			Advertising Expense	521		10 8 6 0 00	15
16			Depreciation Exp.—Store Equip.	522		3 1 0 0 00	16
17			Miscellaneous Selling Expense	529		6 3 0 00	17
18			Office Salaries Expense	530		21 0 2 0 00	18
19			Rent Expense	531		8 1 0 0 00	19
20			Depreciation Exp.—Office Equip.	532		2 4 9 0 00	20
21			Insurance Expense	533		1 9 1 0 00	21
22			Office Supplies Expense	534		6 1 0 00	22
23			Miscellaneous Administrative Exp.	539		7 6 0 00	23
24			Interest Expense	710		2 4 4 0 00	24
25							25
26		31	Income Summary	313	75 4 0 0 00		26
27			Retained Earnings	311		75 4 0 0 00	27
28							28
29		31	Retained Earnings	311	18 0 0 0 00		29
30			Dividends	312		18 0 0 0 00	30
31							31

EXERCISES

EXERCISE D-1
PURCHASES RELATED TRANSACTIONS— PERIODIC INVENTORY SYSTEM

Journalize entries for the following related transactions, assuming that Glavine Company uses the periodic inventory system.

a. Purchased $5,000 of merchandise from Smoltz Co. on account, terms 1/10, n/30.
b. Discovered that some of the merchandise was defective and returned items with an invoice price of $1,000, receiving credit.
c. Paid the amount owed on the invoice within the discount period.
d. Purchased $2,000 of merchandise from Statton Co. on account, terms 1/10, n/30.
e. Paid the amount owed on the invoice within the discount period.

EXERCISE D-2
SALES RELATED TRANSACTIONS— PERIODIC INVENTORY SYSTEM

Journalize entries for the following related transactions, assuming that Courier Company uses the periodic inventory system.

May 5. Sold merchandise to a customer for $10,000, terms FOB shipping point, 2/10, n/30.

5. Paid the transportation charges of $120, debiting the amounts to Accounts Receivable.

10. Issued a credit memorandum for $1,000 to a customer for merchandise returned.

15. Received a check for the amount due from the sale.

EXERCISE D-3
ADJUSTING ENTRIES FOR MERCHANDISE INVENTORY—PERIODIC INVENTORY SYSTEM

Data assembled for preparing the work sheet for T. C. Randall Co. for the fiscal year ended December 31, 1993, included the following:

Merchandise inventory as of January 1, 1993	$145,000
Merchandise inventory as of December 31, 1993	137,500

Journalize the two adjusting entries for merchandise inventory that would appear on the work sheet, assuming that the periodic inventory system is used.

EXERCISE D-4
IDENTIFICATION OF MISSING ITEMS FROM INCOME STATEMENT—PERIODIC INVENTORY SYSTEM

For (a) through (i), identify the items designated by "X."

a. Sales – (X + X) = Net sales
b. Purchases – (X + X) = Net purchases
c. Net purchases + X = Cost of merchandise purchased
d. Merchandise inventory (beginning) + cost of merchandise purchased = X
e. Merchandise available for sale – X = Cost of merchandise sold
f. Net sales – cost of merchandise sold = X
g. X + X = Operating expenses
h. Gross profit – operating expenses = X
i. Income from operations + X – X = Net income

EXERCISE D-5
MULTIPLE-STEP INCOME STATEMENT—PERIODIC INVENTORY SYSTEM

Selected data for Simone Company for the current year ended December 31 are as follows:

Merchandise inventory, January 1	$ 55,000
Merchandise inventory, December 31	57,500
Purchases	562,000
Purchases discounts	8,000
Purchases returns and allowances	15,500
Sales	705,000
Sales discounts	6,500
Sales returns and allowances	8,700
Transportation in	12,500

Prepare a multiple-step income statement through gross profit for Simone Company for the current year ended December 31.

EXERCISE D-6
ADJUSTING AND CLOSING ENTRIES—PERIODIC INVENTORY SYSTEM

Selected account titles and related amounts appearing in the Income Statement and Balance Sheet columns of the work sheet of Jones Company for the year ended December 31 are listed in alphabetical order as follows:

Administrative Expenses	$ 79,500
Building	312,500
Capital Stock	100,000
Cash	58,500
Dividends	60,000
Interest Expense	2,500
Merchandise Inventory (1/1)	225,000
Merchandise Inventory (12/31)	230,000
Notes Payable	25,000
Office Supplies	10,600
Purchases	850,000
Purchases Discounts	8,000
Purchases Returns and Allowances	12,000
Retained Earnings	200,000
Salaries Payable	4,220
Sales	1,275,000
Sales Discounts	10,200
Sales Returns and Allowances	34,300
Selling Expenses	132,700
Store Supplies	7,700
Transportation In	11,300

All selling expenses have been recorded in the account entitled Selling Expenses, and all administrative expenses have been recorded in the account entitled Administrative Expenses.

Assuming that Jones Company uses the periodic inventory system, journalize (a) the adjusting entries for merchandise inventory and (b) the closing entries.

PROBLEMS

PROBLEM D-1
SALES-RELATED AND
PURCHASE-RELATED
TRANSACTIONS—
PERIODIC INVENTORY
SYSTEM

The following were selected from among the transactions completed by Freeman Company during November of the current year:

Nov. 3. Purchased office supplies for cash, $720.
5. Purchased merchandise on account from Butler Co., list price $20,000, trade discount 37.5%, terms FOB destination, 1/10, n/30.
6. Sold merchandise for cash, $2,950.
7. Purchased merchandise on account from Mattox Co., $6,400, terms FOB shipping point, 2/10, n/30, with prepaid transportation costs of $190 added to the invoice.
7. Returned merchandise purchased on November 5 from Butler Co., $2,500.
11. Sold merchandise on account to Bowles Co., list price $2,250, trade discount 20%, terms 1/10, n/30.
15. Paid Butler Co. on account for purchase of November 5, less return of November 7 and discount.
16. Sold merchandise on nonbank credit cards and reported accounts to the card company, $3,850.
17. Paid Mattox Co. on account for purchase of November 7, less discount.
19. Purchased merchandise for cash, $3,500.
21. Received cash on account from sale of November 11 to Bowles Co., less discount.
24. Sold merchandise on account to Clemons Co., $4,200, terms 1/10, n/30.
28. Received cash from card company for nonbank credit card sales of November 16, less $190 service fee.
30. Received merchandise returned by Clemons Co. from sale on November 24, $2,700.

Instructions
Journalize the transactions for Freeman Co.

PROBLEM D-2
SALES-RELATED AND
PURCHASE-RELATED
TRANSACTIONS—
PERIODIC INVENTORY
SYSTEM

The following were selected from among the transactions completed by Montrose Company during May of the current year:

May 3. Purchased merchandise on account from Floyd Co., list price $5,000, trade discount 20%, terms FOB shipping point, 2/10, n/30, with prepaid transportation costs of $120 added to the invoice.
5. Purchased merchandise on account from Kramer Co., $8,500, terms FOB destination, 1/10, n/30.
6. Sold merchandise on account to C. F. Howell Co., list price $4,000, trade discount 30%, terms 2/10, n/30.
8. Purchased office supplies for cash, $650.
10. Returned merchandise purchased on May 5 from Kramer Co., $1,300.
13. Paid Floyd Co. on account for purchase of May 3, less discount.
14. Purchased merchandise for cash, $10,500.
15. Paid Kramer Co. on account for purchase of May 5, less return of May 10 and discount.
16. Received cash on account from sale of May 6 to C. F. Howell Co., less discount.
19. Sold merchandise on nonbank credit cards and reported accounts to the card company, $2,450.
22. Sold merchandise on account to Comer Co., $3,480, terms 2/10, n/30.
24. Sold merchandise for cash, $4,350.
30. Received merchandise returned by Comer Co. from sale on May 22, $1,480.
28. Received cash from card company for nonbank credit card sales of May 19, less $140 service fee.

Instructions
Journalize the transactions for Montrose Co.

PROBLEM D-3
SALES-RELATED AND

The following selected transactions were completed during October between Sims Company and J. C. Power Co.:

PURCHASE-RELATED
TRANSACTIONS FOR
SELLER AND BUYER—
PERIODIC INVENTORY
SYSTEM

Oct. 4. Sims Company sold merchandise on account to J. C. Power Co., $10,000, terms FOB destination, 1/15, n/eom.

4. Sims Company paid transportation costs of $600 for delivery of merchandise sold to J. C. Power Co. on October 4.

10. Sims Company sold merchandise on account to J. C. Power Co., $15,000, terms FOB shipping point, n/eom.

12. J. C. Power Co. returned merchandise purchased on account on October 4 from Sims Company, $2,000.

14. J. C. Power Co. paid transportation charges of $1,200 on October 10 purchase from Sims Company.

18. Sims Company sold merchandise on account to J. C. Power Co., $18,000, terms FOB shipping point, 2/10, n/30. Sims Company prepaid transportation costs of $1,500, which were added to the invoice.

19. J. C. Power Co. paid Sims Company for purchase of October 4, less discount and less return of October 11.

28. J. C. Power Co. paid Sims Company on account for purchase of October 18, less discount.

31. J. C. Power Co. paid Sims Company on account for purchase of October 10.

Instructions

Journalize the October transactions for (1) Sims Company and (2) J. C. Power Co.

PROBLEM D-4
PREPARATION OF WORK
SHEET, FINANCIAL
STATEMENTS, AND
ADJUSTING AND CLOSING
ENTRIES—PERIODIC
INVENTORY SYSTEM

The accounts and their balances in the ledger of Gant Inc. on December 31 of the current year are as follows:

Cash	$ 68,175
Accounts Receivable	112,500
Merchandise Inventory	180,000
Prepaid Insurance	9,700
Store Supplies	4,250
Office Supplies	2,100
Store Equipment	112,000
Accumulated Depreciation—Store Equipment	40,300
Office Equipment	50,000
Accumulated Depreciation—Office Equipment	17,200
Accounts Payable	66,700
Salaries Payable	—
Unearned Rent	1,200
Note Payable (final payment, 2000)	105,000
Capital Stock	100,000
Retained Earnings	120,510
Dividends	40,000
Income Summary	—
Sales	995,000
Sales Returns and Allowances	11,900
Sales Discounts	7,100
Purchases	635,000
Purchases Returns and Allowances	10,100
Purchases Discounts	4,900
Transportation In	6,200
Sales Salaries Expense	86,400
Advertising Expense	30,000
Depreciation Expense—Store Equipment	—
Store Supplies Expense	—
Miscellaneous Selling Expense	1,335
Office Salaries Expense	54,000
Rent Expense	36,000
Insurance Expense	—
Depreciation Expense—Office Equipment	—
Office Supplies Expense	—
Miscellaneous Administrative Expense	1,650
Rent Income	—
Interest Expense	12,600

The data needed for year-end adjustments on December 31 are as follows:

Merchandise inventory on December 31		$220,000
Insurance expired during the year		7,260
Supplies on hand on December 31:		
Store supplies		1,700
Office supplies		400
Depreciation for the year:		
Store equipment		9,500
Office equipment		4,800
Salaries payable on December 31:		
Sales salaries	$2,750	
Office salaries	1,150	3,900
Unearned rent on December 31		400

Instructions

1. Prepare a work sheet for the fiscal year ended December 31, listing all accounts in the order given.
2. Prepare a multiple-step income statement.
3. Prepare a statement of owner's equity.
4. Prepare a report form of balance sheet, assuming that the current portion of the note payable is $15,000.
5. Journalize the adjusting entries.
6. Journalize the closing entries.

SPECIAL JOURNALS AND SUBSIDIARY LEDGERS

A manual accounting system is used in the text because such a system enables you to focus on the basic principles of accounting. In practice, a manual system is often modified in order to process accounting data more efficiently. In this appendix, we will describe and illustrate two such modifications.

In the text, we recorded all transactions manually in a two-column journal. We then posted the journal entries individually to the accounts in the ledger. Such manual accounting systems are simple to use and easy to understand. Manually kept records may serve a business reasonably well when the amount of data collected, stored, and used by an enterprise, called its **database,** is relatively small. For a large retailer with a large database, however, manual processing is too costly and too time-consuming. For example, a large retailer such as J.C. Penney Co. has thousands of credit sale transactions with thousands of customers daily. Each credit sale requires an entry debiting Accounts Receivable and crediting Sales. In addition, a record of each customer's receivable must be kept.

When an enterprise has a large number of similar transactions, the use of a two-column journal is inefficient and impractical. In such cases, special journals and subsidiary ledgers are useful. In addition, the manual system can be supplemented or replaced by a computerized system. Although in the following paragraphs we illustrate the manual use of special journals and subsidiary ledgers, the basic principles apply in a computerized accounting system.

SPECIAL JOURNALS

One method of processing data more efficiently in a manual accounting system is to expand the two-column journal to a multicolumn journal. Each column in a multicolumn journal is used only for recording transactions that affect a certain account. For example, a special column could be used only for recording debits to the cash account and another special column could be used only for recording credits to the cash account. The addition of the two special columns would eliminate the writing of *Cash* in the journal for every receipt and payment of cash. Also, there would be no need to post each individual debit and credit to the cash account. Instead, the *Cash Dr.* and *Cash Cr.* columns could be totaled periodically and only the totals posted. In a similar way, special columns could be added for recording credits to Sales, debits and credits to Accounts Receivable and Accounts Payable, and for other entries that are often repeated.

An all-purpose multicolumn journal may be adequate for a small business enterprise that has many transactions of a similar nature. However, a journal that has many columns for recording many different types of transactions is impractical for larger enterprises.

The next logical extension of the accounting system is to replace the single multicolumn journal with a number of **special journals.** Each special journal is designed to be used for recording a single kind of transaction that occurs frequently. For example, since most enterprises have many transactions in which cash is paid out, it is common practice to use a special journal for recording cash payments. Likewise, another special journal normally is used to record cash receipts.

The format and number of special journals that an enterprise uses depends upon the nature of the business. An enterprise that sells merchandise to customers on account might use a special journal designed for recording only credit sales. On the other hand, a business that does not give credit would have no need for such a journal. In other cases, record-keeping costs may be reduced by using sales and purchases documents as special journals.

The transactions that occur most often in a medium-size merchandising enterprise and the special journals in which they are recorded are as follows:

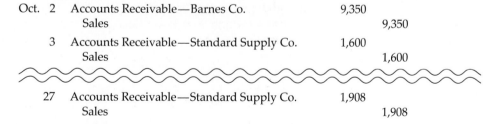

Sale of merchandise on account	recorded in	Sales journal
Receipt of cash from any source	recorded in	Cash receipts journal
Purchase of merchandise or other items on account	recorded in	Purchases journal
Payment of cash for any purpose	recorded in	Cash payments journal

The standard two-column journal, called the **general journal** or simply the **journal,** can be used for entries that do not fit into any of the special journals. For example, adjusting and closing entries are recorded in the general journal.

SUBSIDIARY LEDGERS

As we discussed in the text, when there are a large number of individual accounts with a common characteristic, they can be grouped together in a separate ledger called a **subsidiary ledger.** The primary ledger, which contains all of the balance sheet and income statement accounts, is then called the **general ledger.** Each subsidiary ledger is represented in the general ledger by a summarizing account, called a **controlling account.** The sum of the balances of the accounts in a subsidiary ledger must equal the balance of the related controlling account. Thus, a subsidiary ledger can be thought of as a secondary ledger that supports a controlling account in the general ledger.

The individual accounts with customers are arranged in alphabetical order in a subsidiary ledger called the **accounts receivable ledger** or **customers ledger.** The controlling account in the general ledger that summarizes the debits and credits to the individual customer's accounts is Accounts Receivable. The individual accounts with creditors are arranged in alphabetical order in a subsidiary ledger called the **accounts payable ledger** or **creditors ledger.** The related controlling account in the general ledger is Accounts Payable. Exhibit 1 illustrates the relationship between the general ledger and these subsidiary ledgers.

SALES JOURNAL

The **sales journal** is only used for recording **sales of merchandise on account.** *Cash sales are recorded in the cash receipts journal.* To illustrate the efficiency of using a sales journal, consider the following sales transactions of Kannon Co., recorded in a general journal:[1]

Oct.	2	Accounts Receivable—Barnes Co.	9,350	
		Sales		9,350
	3	Accounts Receivable—Standard Supply Co.	1,600	
		Sales		1,600

~~~~~~

| | 27 | Accounts Receivable—Standard Supply Co. | 1,908 | |
| | | Sales | | 1,908 |

If Kannon Co. had a total of 9 credit sales transactions during October, 18 account titles and amounts would be recorded. In addition, 27 postings must be made—9 postings to Accounts Receivable, 9 to the accounts receivable subsidiary ledger, and 9 to Sales. In contrast, these transactions could be recorded more efficiently in a sales journal, as shown in Exhibit 2.

The first sale recorded by Kannon Co. in October is to Barnes Co. for $9,350 (Invoice No. 615). Since the amount of the debit to Accounts Receivable is the same as the credit to Sales, only a single amount column is necessary. The date, invoice number, customer name, and amount are entered for each sale.

[1] The periodic inventory system is used throughout this appendix.

Exhibit 1
General Ledger and Subsidiary Ledgers

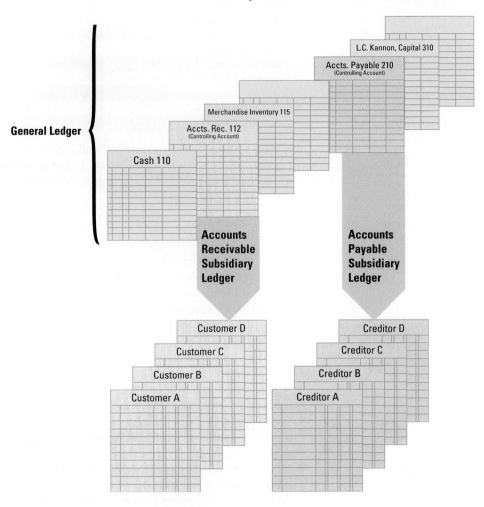

Exhibit 2
Sales Journal After Posting

SALES JOURNAL

	DATE	INVOICE NO.	AMOUNT DEBITED	POST. REF.	ACCTS. REC. DR. SALES CR.	
1	1995 Oct. 2	615	Barnes Co.	✓	9 3 5 0 00	1
2	3	616	Standard Supply Co.	✓	1 6 0 0 00	2
3	5	617	David T. Mattox	✓	15 3 0 5 00	3
4	9	618	Barnes Co.	✓	1 3 9 6 00	4
5	10	619	Adler Company	✓	6 7 5 0 00	5
6	17	620	Hamilton Co.	✓	7 8 5 0 00	6
7	23	621	Cooper & Co.	✓	1 5 0 2 00	7
8	26	622	Tracy & Lee Co.	✓	3 2 7 9 00	8
9	27	623	Standard Supply Co.	✓	1 9 0 8 00	9
10	31				48 9 4 0 00	10
11					(113) (411)	11

Posting the Sales Journal

When sales on account are recorded in a sales journal, individual transactions are posted to customer accounts in the accounts receivable ledger. A single monthly total is posted to Accounts Receivable and Sales. Exhibit 3 shows the basic procedure of posting from a sales journal to an accounts receivable ledger and the general ledger.

The individual amounts in Exhibit 3, such as the $9,350 debit to Barnes Co., are posted to the accounts receivable ledger. Since the balances in the customer ac-

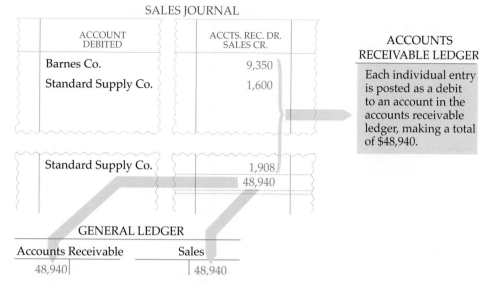

Exhibit 3
Flow of Data from Sales Journal to Ledgers

counts are usually debit balances, a three-column account form shown below is often used.

NAME	Barnes Co.							
ADDRESS	9350 Ridge Ave., Los Angeles, CA 90048-3694							

DATE		ITEM	POST. REF.	DEBIT	CREDIT	BALANCE
Sep.^{1995}	25		S34	5 8 0 0 00		5 8 0 0 00
Oct.	2		S35	9 3 5 0 00		15 1 5 0 00

The source of the entries posted to the subsidiary ledger is indicated in the Posting Reference column of each account by inserting the letter *S* and the page number of the sales journal. A check mark (✓) instead of a number is then inserted in the Posting Reference column of the sales journal, as shown in Exhibit 2.

The customer accounts in the subsidiary ledger are maintained in alphabetical order. They are usually not numbered because the order changes each time a new account is inserted or an old account is removed. If a customer's account has a credit balance, that fact should be indicated by an asterisk or parentheses in the Balance column. When an account's balance is zero, a line may be drawn in the balance column. At the end of each month, the amount column of the sales journal is totaled and ruled. This total is equal to the sum of the month's debits to the individual accounts in the subsidiary ledger. It is posted in the general ledger as a debit to Accounts Receivable and a credit to Sales, as shown below. The respective account numbers are then inserted below the total in the sales journal to indicate that the posting is completed, as shown in Exhibit 2.

ACCOUNT	*Accounts Receivable*				ACCOUNT NO.	113	
DATE		ITEM	POST. REF.	DEBIT	CREDIT	BALANCE	
						DEBIT	CREDIT
Oct.^{1995}	1	Balance	✓	16 1 1 9 00		16 1 1 9 00	
	31		S35	48 9 4 0 00		64 8 0 9 00	

ACCOUNT	*Sales*				ACCOUNT NO.	411	
DATE		ITEM	POST. REF.	DEBIT	CREDIT	BALANCE	
						DEBIT	CREDIT
Oct.^{1995}	31		S35		48 9 4 0 00		48 9 4 0 00

Sales Returns and Allowances

When merchandise sold is returned or a price adjustment is granted, an entry is made in the general journal. Sales returns are recorded in the general journal because they do not fit in any of the special journals. During October, Kannon Co. issued a credit memorandum and recorded the transaction in a two-column general journal, as shown below.

	DATE	DESCRIPTION	POST. REF.	DEBIT	CREDIT	
1	1995 Oct. 13	Sales Returns and Allowances	412	2 5 0 00		1
2		Accounts Receivable—				2
3		Adler Company	113 ✓		2 5 0 00	3
4		Credit Memo No. 32.				4

JOURNAL   PAGE 18

The debit portion of the entry is posted to Sales Returns and Allowances (No. 412) in the general ledger. The credit portion of the entry is posted to Accounts Receivable (No. 113) in the general ledger and also to the customer's account in the subsidiary ledger (✓). At the time these entries are journalized, a diagonal line is drawn in the Posting Reference column to indicate the need for posting the credits to two different accounts. The account number and check mark are inserted at the time the entry is posted.

If a cash refund is made because of merchandise returned or for an allowance, Sales Returns and Allowances is debited and Cash is credited. Since this Transaction involves the payment of cash, the entry would be recorded in the cash payments journal.

CASH RECEIPTS JOURNAL

All transactions that involve the receipt of cash are recorded in a **cash receipts journal.** Thus, the cash receipts journal has a special column entitled *Cash Dr.,* as shown in the cash receipts journal of Kannon Co. in Exhibit 4.

The kinds of transactions in which cash is received and how often they occur determine the titles of the other columns. In a typical merchandising business, the most frequent sources of cash receipts are likely to be cash sales and collections from customers on account. Thus, the cash receipts journal in Exhibit 4 also has special columns for Sales Cr., Accounts Receivable Cr., and Sales Discounts Dr.

Entries in the Cash Receipts Journal

All transactions recorded in the cash receipts journal will involve an entry in the Cash Dr. column. For example, on October 2, Kannon Co. received cash of $2,544 and entered that amount in the Cash Dr. column.

The Sales Cr. column is used for recording sales of merchandise for cash. Each sale is normally recorded on a cash register. The cash register totals are accumulated and are recorded in the cash receipts journal daily, weekly, or at other regular intervals. For example, the entry of October 7 records weekly sales and cash receipts of $3,700. The total of the Sales Cr. column will be posted at the end of the month. Thus, a check mark is inserted in the Posting Reference column to indicate that the $3,700 item needs no further attention.

The Accounts Receivable Cr. column is used for recording credits to customer accounts for payments of invoices on account. If a cash discount is granted, it is recorded in the Sales Discounts Dr. column. To illustrate, cash was received on October 5 from Barnes Co. in payment of its account less a cash discount. Entries are made in the Cash Dr. column for $5,684, in the Sales Discounts Dr. column for $116, and in the Accounts Receivable Cr. column for $5,800.

Exhibit 4
Cash Receipts Journal after Posting

CASH RECEIPTS JOURNAL — PAGE 14

	DATE		ACCOUNT CREDITED	POST. REF.	OTHER ACCOUNTS CR.	SALES CR.	ACCOUNTS REC. CR.	SALES DISCOUNTS DR.	CASH DR.	
1	1995 Oct.	2	Notes Receivable	112	2 4 0 0 00				2 5 4 4 00	1
2			Interest Income	812	1 4 4 00					2
3		5	Barnes Co.	✓			5 8 0 0 00	1 1 6 00	5 6 8 4 00	3
4		6	Fogarty & Jacobs	✓			2 6 2 5 00		2 6 2 5 00	4
5		7	Sales	✓		3 7 0 0 00			3 7 0 0 00	5
6		10	David T. Mattox	✓			6 0 0 00	1 2 00	5 8 8 00	6
7		13	Standard Supply Co.	✓			1 6 0 0 00	3 2 00	1 5 6 8 00	7
8		14	Sales	✓		1 6 3 2 00			1 6 3 2 00	8
9		17	Adler Company	✓			6 5 0 0 00	1 3 0 00	6 3 7 0 00	9
10		19	Hamilton Co.	✓			4 8 6 5 00		4 8 6 5 00	10
11		21	Sales	✓		1 9 2 0 00			1 9 2 0 00	11
12		23	Purchases Returns and Allowances	512	8 6 00				8 6 00	12
13		24	Wallace Co.	✓			2 2 2 9 00		2 2 2 9 00	13
14		27	Hamilton Co.	✓			7 8 5 0 00	1 5 7 00	7 6 9 3 00	14
15		28	Sales	✓		2 0 8 6 00			2 0 8 6 00	15
16		31	Sales	✓		2 4 2 3 00			2 4 2 3 00	16
17		31			2 6 3 0 00	11 7 6 1 00	32 0 6 9 00	4 4 7 00	46 0 1 3 00	17
18					(√)	(4 1 1)	(1 1 3)	(4 1 3)	(1 1 1)	18

The Other Accounts Cr. column is used for recording credits to any account for which there is no special credit column. For example, Kannon Co. received cash on October 2 in payment of an interest-bearing note. Since no special columns exist for Notes Receivable or Interest Income, Notes Receivable of $2,400 and Interest Income of $144 are entered in the Other Accounts Cr. column.

Posting the Cash Receipts Journal

Exhibit 5 shows the flow of data from the cash receipts journal to the ledgers of Kannon Co. At regular intervals, each amount in the Other Accounts Cr. column of the cash receipts journal is posted to the proper account in the general ledger. The posting is indicated by inserting the account number in the Posting Reference column of the cash receipts journal. The posting reference CR and the proper page number are inserted in the Posting Reference columns of the accounts.

The amounts in the Accounts Receivable Cr. column are posted at regular intervals to the customer accounts in the accounts receivable ledger. These customers are identified in the Account Credited column of the cash receipts journal. The initials *CR* and the proper page number are inserted in the Posting Reference column of each customer's account. A check mark is placed in the Posting Reference column of the cash receipts journal to show that each amount has been posted. None of the individual amounts in the Sales Cr., Sales Discounts Dr., and Cash Dr. columns are posted separately.

At the end of the month, all of the amount columns are totaled and ruled. The equality of the debits and credits should then be verified. Because each amount in the Other Accounts Cr. column has been posted individually to a general ledger account, a check mark is inserted below the column total to indicate that no further action is needed. The totals of the other four columns are posted to the proper accounts in the general ledger, and their account numbers are inserted below the totals to show that the posting has been completed.

Exhibit 5
Flow of Data from Cash Receipts
Journal to Ledgers

CASH RECEIPTS JOURNAL

ACCOUNT CREDITED	P. R.	OTHER ACCOUNTS CR.	SALES CR.	ACCOUNTS RECEIVABLE CR.	SALES DISCOUNTS DR.	CASH DR.
Notes Receivable	112	2,400				2,544
Interest Income	811	144				
Barnes Co.	✓			5,800	116	5,684
Fogarty & Jacobs	✓			2,625		2,625
Sales	✓		3,700			3,700
David T. Mattox	✓			600	12	588
Sales	✓		2,423			2,423
		2,630	11,761	32,069	447	46,013

ACCOUNTS RECEIVABLE LEDGER

Each individual entry is posted as a credit to an account in the accounts receivable ledger, making a total of $32,069.

GENERAL LEDGER

Notes Receivable		Sales		Sales Discounts	
2,400			11,761	447	

Interest Income		Accounts Receivable		Cash	
	144		32,069	46,013	

ACCOUNTS RECEIVABLE CONTROL AND SUBSIDIARY LEDGER

During October, the following postings were made to Accounts Receivable in the general ledger of Kannon Co.:

	Debits	
Oct. 31	Total sales on account (sales journal)	$48,940
	Credits	
Oct. 13	A sales return (general journal)	250
Oct. 31	Total cash received on account (cash receipts journal)	32,069

Exhibit 6 is the accounts receivable controlling account, and Exhibit 7 is the subsidiary accounts receivable ledger of Kannon Co.

Exhibit 6
Accounts Receivable Account in the General Ledger at the End of the Month

ACCOUNT *Accounts Receivable*　　　　ACCOUNT NO.113

DATE		ITEM	POST. REF.	DEBIT	CREDIT	BALANCE DEBIT	BALANCE CREDIT
Oct. 1995	1	Balance	✓	16 1 1 9 00		16 1 1 9 00	
	13		J18		2 5 0 00	15 8 6 9 00	
	31		S35	48 9 4 0 00		64 8 0 9 00	
	31		CR14		32 0 6 9 00	32 7 4 0 00	

ACCOUNTS RECEIVABLE LEDGER

Exhibit 7
Accounts Receivable Ledger at the End of the Month

NAME　Adler Company
ADDRESS　7608 Melton Ave., Los Angeles, CA 90025-3942

DATE		ITEM	POST. REF.	DEBIT	CREDIT	BALANCE
Oct. 1995	10	Balance	S35	6 7 5 0 00		6 7 5 0 00
	13		J18		2 5 0 00	6 5 0 0 00
	17		CR14		6 5 0 0 00	

Exhibit 7 (continued)
Accounts Receivable Ledger at
the End of the Month

NAME   Barnes Co.

ADDRESS   9350 Ridge Ave., Los Angeles, CA 90048-3694

DATE		ITEM	POST. REF.	DEBIT	CREDIT	BALANCE
Sep. 1995	25		S34	5 8 0 0 00		5 8 0 0 00
Oct.	2		S35	9 3 5 0 00		15 1 5 0 00
	5		CR14		5 8 0 0 00	9 3 5 0 00
	9		S35	1 3 9 6 00		10 7 4 6 00

NAME   Cooper & Co.

ADDRESS   650 Wilson, Portland, OR 97209-1406

DATE		ITEM	POST. REF.	DEBIT	CREDIT	BALANCE
Oct. 1995	23		S35	1 5 0 2 00		1 5 0 2 00

NAME   Fogarty & Jacobs

ADDRESS   142 West 8th, Los Angeles, CA 90014-1225

DATE		ITEM	POST. REF.	DEBIT	CREDIT	BALANCE
Sep. 1995	17		S34	2 6 2 5 00		2 6 2 5 00
Oct.	6		CR14		2 6 2 5 00	——

NAME   Hamilton Co.

ADDRESS   5200 Charter Ave., San Francisco, CA 94110-1732

DATE		ITEM	POST. REF.	DEBIT	CREDIT	BALANCE
Sep. 1995	10		S33	4 8 6 5 00		4 8 6 5 00
Oct.	17		S35	7 8 5 0 00		12 7 1 5 00
	19		CR14		4 8 6 5 00	7 8 5 0 00
	27		CR14		7 8 5 0 00	——

NAME   David T. Mattox

ADDRESS   1200 Capital Ave., Sacramento, CA 95814-1048

DATE		ITEM	POST. REF.	DEBIT	CREDIT	BALANCE
Sep. 1995	30		S34	6 0 0 00		6 0 0 00
Oct.	5		S35	15 3 0 5 00		15 9 0 5 00
	10		CR14		6 0 0 00	15 3 0 5 00

NAME   Standard Supply Co.

ADDRESS   9554 W. Colorado Blvd., Pasadena, CA 91107-1318

DATE		ITEM	POST. REF.	DEBIT	CREDIT	BALANCE
Oct. 1995	3		S35	1 6 0 0 00		1 6 0 0 00
	13		CR14		1 6 0 0 00	——
	27		S35	1 9 0 8 00		1 9 0 8 00

Exhibit 7 (concluded)
Accounts Receivable Ledger at the End of the Month

NAME   Tracy & Lee Co.
ADDRESS   521 Scottsdale Blvd., Phoenix, AZ 85004-1100

DATE	ITEM	POST. REF.	DEBIT	CREDIT	BALANCE
1995 Oct. 26		S35	3 2 7 9 00		3 2 7 9 00

NAME   Wallace Co.
ADDRESS   1004 Market St., Sacramento, CA 95814-1048

DATE	ITEM	POST. REF.	DEBIT	CREDIT	BALANCE
1995 Sep. 12		S34	2 2 2 9 00		2 2 2 9 00
Oct. 24		CR14		2 2 2 9 00	—

After all posting has been completed for the month, the sum of the balances in the accounts receivable ledger should be compared with the balance of the accounts receivable account in the general ledger. If the controlling account and the subsidiary ledger do not agree, the error or errors must be located and corrected. The balances of the individual customer accounts may be summarized on a computer printout, or a schedule may be prepared, as shown below. The total of the schedule, $32,740, agrees with the balance of the accounts receivable account shown in Exhibit 6.

Kannon Co.
Schedule of Accounts Receivable
October 31, 1995

Barnes Co.	$10,746
Cooper & Co.	1,502
David T. Mattox	15,305
Standard Supply Co.	1,908
Tracy & Lee Co.	3,279
Total accounts receivable	$32,740

PURCHASES JOURNAL

The types of items purchased most often on account by a merchandising enterprise are:

1. Merchandise for resale to customers.
2. Supplies for use in the business.
3. Equipment and other plant assets.

The **purchases journal** should be designed to allow for the recording of **all items purchased on account.** *Cash purchases of items are recorded in the cash payments journal.* Exhibit 8 shows the form of a purchases journal used by Kannon Co.

For each transaction recorded in the purchases journal, the credit is entered in the Accounts Payable Cr. column. The next three amount columns are used for recording debits to the accounts most often affected. Invoice amounts for merchandise purchased for sale to customers are recorded in the Purchases Dr. column. Likewise, purchases of store supplies and office supplies are entered in the Store Supplies Dr. and Office Supplies Dr. columns. If supplies are purchased only once in a while, the two columns could be omitted from the journal.

The Other Accounts Dr. column is used to record purchases, on account, of any item for which there is not a special debit column. The title of the account to be debited is entered in the Account column and the amount is entered in the Amount column. A separate Posting Reference column is provided for this section of the purchases journal.

Exhibit 8
Purchases Journal after Posting

	DATE		ACCOUNT CREDITED	POST. REF.	ACCOUNTS PAYABLE CR.	PURCHASES DR.	STORE SUPPLIES DR.	OFFICE SUPPLIES DR.	OTHER ACCOUNTS DR.			
									ACCOUNT	POST. REF.	AMOUNT	
1	Oct. 1995	2	Video Co.	✓	5 7 2 4 00	5 7 2 4 00						1
2		3	Marsh Co.	✓	7 4 0 0 00	7 4 0 0 00						2
3		9	Parker Supply Co.	✓	2 5 7 00		1 3 1 00	1 2 6 00				3
4		10	Beale Office									4
5			Equipment	✓	5 0 0 0 00				Office Equipment	111	5 0 0 0 00	5
6		11	Marsh Co.	✓	3 2 0 0 00	3 2 0 0 00						6
7		16	Dunlap Co.	✓	3 5 9 3 00	3 5 9 3 00						7
8		17	Robinson Supply	✓	1 5 0 0 00	1 5 0 0 00						8
9		20	Walton Co.	✓	15 1 2 5 00				Store Equipment		15 1 2 5 00	9
10		23	Parker Supply Co.	✓	1 3 2 00		7 5 00	5 7 00				10
11		27	Dunlap Co.	✓	6 3 8 9 00	6 3 8 9 00						11
12		31			48 3 2 0 00	27 8 0 6 00	2 0 6 00	1 8 3 00			20 1 2 5 00	12
13					(2 1 1)	(5 1 1)	(1 1 5)	(1 1 6)			(√)	13

Posting the Purchases Journal

The principles used in posting the purchases journal are similar to those used in posting the sales and cash receipts journals. The source of the entries posted to the subsidiary and general ledgers is indicated in the Posting Reference column of each account by inserting the letter *P* and the page number of the purchases journal, as shown below. A check mark (✓) is inserted in the Posting Reference column of the purchases journal after each credit is posted to a creditor's account in the subsidiary accounts payable ledger.

NAME	Robinson Supply					
ADDRESS	3800 Mission Street, San Francisco, CA 94110-1732					
DATE		ITEM	POST. REF.	DEBIT	CREDIT	BALANCE
Oct. 1995 17			P19		1 5 0 0 00	1 5 0 0 00

Exhibit 9 shows the flow of data from the purchases journal of Kannon Co. to the ledgers. At regular intervals, the amounts in the Other Accounts Dr. column of the purchases journal are posted to the accounts in the general ledger. As each amount is posted, the related general ledger account number is inserted in the Posting Reference column of the Other Accounts section.

At the end of each month, the purchases journal is totaled and ruled, as shown in Exhibit 8. Before the totals are posted to the general ledger, the sum of the totals of the four debit columns should be compared with the total of the credit column to prove their equality.

The totals of the four special columns are posted to the appropriate general ledger accounts in the usual manner, with the related account numbers inserted below the columnar totals. Because each amount in the Other Accounts Dr. column was posted individually, a check mark is placed below the $20,125 total to show that no further action is needed.

Exhibit 9
*Flow of Data from Purchases
Journal to Ledgers*

PURCHASES JOURNAL

ACCOUNT CREDITED	P. R.	ACCTS. PAYABLE CR.	PURCHASES DR.	STORE SUP. DR.	OFFICE SUP. DR.	OTHER ACCOUNTS DEBIT		
						ACCOUNT	P.R.	AMOUNT
Video Co.	✓	5,724	5,724					
Marsh Co.	✓	7,400	7,400					
Parker Supply Co.	✓	257		131	126			
Robinson Supply	✓	1,500	1,500					
Walton Co.	✓	15,125				Store Equip.	121	15,125
Parker Supply Co.	✓	132		75	57			
Dunlap Co.	✓	6,389	6,389					
		48,320	27,806	206	183			20,125

GENERAL LEDGER

Accounts Payable	Store Supplies	Office Supplies
48,320	206	183

Purchases	Store Equipment
27,806	15,125

ACCOUNTS PAYABLE LEDGER

Each individual entry is posted as a credit to an account in the accounts payable ledger, making a total of $48,320.

Purchases Returns and Allowances

When merchandise purchased is returned or a price adjustment is granted, an entry is made in the general journal. Purchases returns are recorded in the general journal because they do not fit in any of the special journals. To illustrate, assume that Kannon Co. issued a debit memorandum for a return of merchandise during October. The transaction may be recorded in a two-column general journal, as shown below.

JOURNAL   PAGE 18

	DATE		DESCRIPTION	POST. REF.	DEBIT	CREDIT	
17	Oct.	20	Accounts Payable—Dunlap Co.	211 ✓	1 0 0 00		17
18			Purchases Returns and Allowances	512		1 0 0 00	18
19			Debit Memo No. 20.				19

The debit portion of the entry is posted to Accounts Payable (No. 211) in the general ledger and to the creditor's account in the subsidiary ledger (✓). At the time these entries are journalized, the need for posting the debits to two different accounts is indicated by drawing a diagonal line in the Posting Reference column. The account number and check mark are inserted at the time the entry is posted.

After the entry has been recorded, the memorandum is attached to the related unpaid invoice. If the invoice had been paid before the return or allowance was granted, a cash refund might be received.

If goods other than merchandise are returned or a price adjustment is granted, the account to which the goods were first debited should be credited. For example, if a purchase of office equipment is returned, the credit would be to Office Equipment rather than Purchases Returns and Allowances.

D – Pure
e – each

CASH PAYMENTS JOURNAL

The special columns for the **cash payments journal** are determined in the same manner as for the sales, cash receipts, and purchases journals. The determining factors are the kinds of transactions to be recorded and how often they occur. It is necessary to have a Cash Cr. column. Payments to creditors on account happen often enough to require columns for Accounts Payable Dr. and Purchases Discounts Cr. The cash payments journal in Exhibit 10 has these three columns and an additional column for Other Accounts Dr.

Exhibit 10
Cash Payments Journal after Posting

	DATE		CK. NO.	ACCOUNT DEBITED	POST. REF.	OTHER ACCOUNTS DR.	ACCOUNTS PAYABLE DR.	PURCHASES DISCOUNTS CR.	CASH CR.	
1	1995 Oct.	2	312	Purchases	511	1 2 7 5 00			1 2 7 5 00	1
2		4	313	Store Equipment	121	3 5 0 00			3 5 0 00	2
3		12	314	Marsh Co.	✓		7 4 0 0 00	7 4 00	7 3 2 6 00	3
4		12	315	Sales Salaries Exp.	611	2 5 6 0 00			2 5 6 0 00	4
5		12	316	Office Salaries Exp.	711	8 8 0 00			8 8 0 00	5
6		14	317	Misc. Admin. Exp.	719	5 6 00			5 6 00	6
7		16	318	Prepaid Insurance	117	9 8 4 00			9 8 4 00	7
8		20	319	Marsh Co.	✓		3 2 0 0 00	3 2 00	3 1 6 8 00	8
9		20	320	Heath Co.	✓		4 8 5 0 00		4 8 5 0 00	9
10		21	321	Sales Ret. & Allow.	412	4 6 2 00			4 6 2 00	10
11		23	322	Robinson Supply	✓		1 5 0 0 00	3 0 00	1 4 7 0 00	11
12		23	323	Video Co.	✓		7 6 0 0 00		7 6 0 0 00	12
13		23	324	Rent Expense	712	7 9 0 00			7 9 0 00	13
14		24	325	Walton Co.	✓		9 5 2 5 00		9 5 2 5 00	14
15		26	326	Sales Salaries Exp.	611	2 5 6 0 00			2 5 6 0 00	15
16		26	327	Office Salaries Exp.	711	8 8 0 00			8 8 0 00	16
17		26	328	Advertising Exp.	612	7 8 6 00			7 8 6 00	17
18		27	329	Misc. Selling Exp.	619	4 2 00			4 2 00	18
19		28	330	Office Equipment	123	9 0 0 00			9 0 0 00	19
20		31				12 5 2 5 00	34 0 7 5 00	1 3 6 00	46 4 6 4 00	20
21						(✓)	(2 1 1)	(5 1 3)	(1 1 1)	21
22										22
23										23
24										24
25										25

All payments by Kannon Co. are made by check. As each transaction is recorded in the cash payments journal, the related check number is entered in the column at the right of the Date column. The check numbers are helpful in controlling cash payments, and they provide a useful cross-reference.

The Other Accounts Dr. column is used for recording debits to any account for which there is no special column. For example, Kannon Co. paid $1,275 on October 2 for a purchase of merchandise. The transaction was recorded by writing *Purchases* in the space provided and $1,275 in the Other Accounts Dr. and the Cash Cr. columns. The Posting Reference (511) was inserted at the time the debit was posted.

Debits to creditor accounts for invoices paid are recorded in the Accounts Payable Dr. column and credits for the amounts paid are recorded in the Cash Cr. column. If a discount is taken, the debit to the account payable will differ from the amount of the payment. Cash discounts taken on merchandise purchased for re-sale are recorded in the Purchases Discounts Cr. column.

Exhibit 11 shows the flow of data from the cash payments journal to the ledgers of Kannon Co. At frequent intervals during the month, the amounts entered in the Accounts Payable Dr. column are posted to the creditor accounts in the accounts payable ledger. After each posting, *CP* and the page number of the journal are in-serted in the Posting Reference column of the account. A check mark is placed in the Posting Reference column of the cash payments journal to indicate that each amount has been posted.

Exhibit 11
Flow of Data from Cash
Payments Journal to Ledgers

CASH PAYMENTS JOURNAL

ACCOUNT DEBITED	P. R.	OTHER ACCOUNTS DR.	ACCOUNTS PAYABLE DR.	PURCHASES DISCOUNTS CR.	CASH CR.
Purchases	511	1,275			1,275
Store Equipment	121	350			350
Marsh Co.	✓		7,400	74	7,326
Sales Salaries Expense	611	2,560			2,560
Misc. Selling Expense	619	42			42
Office Equipment	123	900			900
		12,525	34,075	136	46,464

GENERAL LEDGER

	Accounts Payable	Purchases Discounts	Cash
Other Accounts	34,075	136	46,464

Each entry is posted separately to the appropriate account.

ACCOUNTS PAYABLE LEDGER

Each individual entry is posted as a debit to an account in the accounts payable ledger, making a total of $34,075.

The items in the Other Accounts Dr. column are also posted to the accounts in the general ledger at regular intervals. The posting is indicated by writing the ac-count numbers in the Posting Reference column of the cash payments journal. At the end of the month, each of the amount columns in the cash payments journal is totaled. The sum of the two debit totals is compared with the sum of the two credit totals to determine their equality, and the journal is ruled.

A check mark is placed below the total of the Other Accounts Dr. column to in-dicate that it is not posted. When each of the totals of the other three columns is posted to a general ledger account, the account numbers are inserted below the col-umn totals.

ACCOUNTS PAYABLE CONTROL AND SUBSIDIARY LEDGER

During October, the following postings were made to Accounts Payable in the gen-eral ledger of Kannon Co.:

Credits to Accounts Payable	
Oct. 31 Total purchases on account (purchases journal)	$48,320
Debits to Accounts Payable	
Oct. 20 A return of merchandise (general journal)	100
Oct. 31 Total cash payments on account	
(cash payments journal)	34,075

Exhibit 12 shows the accounts payable controlling account of Kannon Co. as of October 31. The procedures for posting and balancing the accounts payable subsidiary ledger are similar to those for accounts receivable. Therefore, the accounts payable subsidiary ledger is not illustrated.

Exhibit 12
Accounts Payable Account in the General Ledger at the End of the Month

ACCOUNT Accounts Payable					ACCOUNT NO. 211	
DATE	ITEM	POST. REF.	DEBIT	CREDIT	BALANCE	
					DEBIT	CREDIT
1995 Oct. 1	Balance	✓				21 9 7 5 00
20		J18	1 0 0 00			21 8 7 5 00
31		P19		48 3 2 0 00		70 1 9 5 00
31		CP16	34 0 7 5 00			36 1 2 0 00

After all posting has been completed for the month, the sum of the balances in the accounts payable ledger should be compared with the balance of the accounts payable account in the general ledger. If the controlling account and the subsidiary ledger do not agree, the error or errors must be located and corrected. The balances of the individual creditor accounts may be summarized on a schedule, as shown below. The total of the schedule, $36,120, agrees with the balance of the accounts payable account shown in Exhibit 12.

Kannon Co.
Schedule of Accounts Payable
October 31, 1995

Beale Office Equipment	$ 5,000
Dunlap Co.	9,882
Parker Supply Co.	389
Video Co.	5,724
Walton Co.	15,125
Total accounts payable	$36,120

PROBLEMS

PROBLEM E-1
DETERMINING PROPER
SPECIAL JOURNALS TO
USE

For the past few years, your aunt has operated a small jewelry store, Creative Jewelers. Its current annual revenues are approximately $450,000. Because the company's accountant has been taking more and more time each month to record all transactions in a two-column journal and to prepare the financial statements, your aunt is considering improving the company's accounting system by adding special journals and subsidiary ledgers. Your aunt has asked you to help her with this project. She has compiled the following information:

1.

Type of Transaction	Estimated Frequency per Month
Purchases of merchandise on account	200
Sales on account	175
Cash receipts from customers on account	150
Daily cash register summaries of cash sales	25
Purchases of merchandise for cash	20
Purchases of office supplies on account	5
Purchases of store supplies on account	5
Cash payments for utilities expenses	4
Cash purchases of office supplies	4
Cash purchases of store supplies	4

2. For merchandise purchases of high dollar-value items, Creative Jewelers issues notes payable at current interest rates to vendors. These notes are issued because many of the high-value items may not sell immediately and the issuance of the notes reduces the need to maintain large balances of cash or assets that can be readily converted to cash. Notes are issued for approximately 10% of the purchases on account.

3. All purchases discounts are taken when available.

4. A sales discount of 1/10, n/30 is offered to all credit customers.

5. A local sales tax of 6% is collected on all intrastate sales of merchandise.

6. Monthly financial statements are prepared.

Instructions

1. Briefly discuss the circumstances under which special journals would be used in place of a two-column journal. Include in your answer your recommendations for Creative Jewelers' accounting system.

2. Assume that your aunt has decided to use a sales journal and a purchases journal. Design the format for each journal, giving special consideration to the needs of Creative Jewelers.

3. Which subsidiary ledgers would you recommend for Creative Jewelers?

PROBLEM E-2
SALES JOURNAL;
ACCOUNTS RECEIVABLE
AND GENERAL LEDGERS

C. L. Wolfe Co. was established on May 20 of the current year. Its sales of merchandise on account and related returns and allowances during the remainder of the month are as follows. Terms of all sales were 1/10, n/30, FOB destination.

May 21. Sold merchandise on account to Boritz Co., Invoice No. 1, $1,200.
   22. Sold merchandise on account to Stark Co., Invoice No. 2, $2,750.
   24. Sold merchandise on account to Morris Co., Invoice No. 3, $3,175.
   25. Issued Credit Memorandum No. 1 for $100 to Boritz Co. for merchandise returned.
   27. Sold merchandise on account to C. D. Walters Co., Invoice No. 4, $2,500.
   28. Sold merchandise on account to A. Udall Co., Invoice No. 5, $1,500.
   28. Issued Credit Memorandum No. 2 for $150 to Stark Co. for merchandise returned.
   30. Sold merchandise on account to Stark Co., Invoice No. 6, $2,925.
   30. Issued Credit Memorandum No. 3 for $75 to C. D. Walters Co. for damages to merchandise caused by faulty packing.
   31. Sold merchandise on account to Morris Co., Invoice No. 7, $995.

Instructions

1. Journalize the transactions for May, using a single-column sales journal and a two-column general journal. Post to the following customer accounts in the accounts receivable ledger and insert the balance immediately after recording each entry: Boritz Co.; Morris Co.; Stark Co.; A. Udall Co.; C. D. Walters Co.

2. Post the general journal and the sales journal to the following accounts in the general ledger, inserting the account balances only after the last postings:

   113   Accounts Receivable
   411   Sales
   412   Sales Returns and Allowances

3. a. What is the sum of the balances of the accounts in the subsidiary ledger at May 31?
   b. What is the balance of the controlling account at May 31?

4. Assume that on June 1, C. L. Wolfe Co. decides to sell to retail as well as wholesale customers. Briefly explain how the sales journal may be modified to accommodate sales on account that require the collection of a state sales tax.

SHARPEN YOUR ► COMMUNICATION SKILLS

PROBLEM E-3
SALES AND CASH
RECEIPTS JOURNALS;
ACCOUNTS RECEIVABLE
AND GENERAL LEDGERS

If the working papers correlating with the textbook are not used, omit Problem E-3.

Three journals, the accounts receivable ledger, and portions of the general ledger of Unisac Co. are presented in the working papers. Sales invoices and credit memorandums were entered in the journals by an assistant. Terms of sales on account are 2/10, n/30, FOB shipping point. Transactions in which cash and notes receivable were received during July are as follows:

July 1. Received $5,880 from C. D. Martin Co. in payment of June 21 invoice less discount.
   3. Received $10,300 in payment of $10,000 note receivable and interest of $300.
      Post transactions of July 1, 2, and 6 to accounts receivable ledger.
   7. Received $6,370 from Janet Rowe Co. in payment of June 28 invoice less discount.
   8. Received $2,200 from R. C. Fellows Co. in payment of June 10 invoice, no discount.

Post transactions of July 7, 8, 10, 12, and 15 to accounts receivable ledger.

July 16. Cash sales for first half of July totaled $4,610.

    19. Received $1,000 refund for return of defective equipment purchased for cash in June.

    20. Received $2,842 from C. D. Martin Co. in payment of balance due on July 10 invoice less discount.

    22. Received $5,684 from R. C. Fellows Co. in payment of July 12 invoice less discount.

    Post transactions of July 17, 20, 22, and 23 to accounts receivable ledger.

    27. Received $40 for sale of office supplies at cost.

    31. Received $1,750 cash and a $2,500 note receivable from Ignacio and Co. in settlement of the balance due on the invoice of July 2, no discount. (Journalize the receipt of the note in the general journal.)

    31. Cash sales for the second half of July totaled $4,150.

    Post transactions of July 27, 28, 30, and 31 to accounts receivable ledger.

Instructions

1. Journalize the cash receipts in the cash receipts journal and the note in the general journal. Before journalizing a receipt of cash on account, determine the balance of the customer's account. Post the entries from the three journals, in date sequence, to the accounts receivable ledger in accordance with the instructions in the narrative of transactions. Insert the new balance after each posting to an account.

2. Post the appropriate individual entries from the cash receipts journal and the general journal to the general ledger.

3. Total each of the columns of the sales journal and the cash receipts journal and post the appropriate totals to the general ledger. Insert the balance of each account after the last posting.

4. Prepare a schedule of accounts receivable as of July 31 and compare the total with the balance of the controlling account.

PROBLEM E-4
SALES AND CASH
RECEIPTS JOURNALS;
ACCOUNTS RECEIVABLE
AND GENERAL LEDGERS

Transactions related to sales and cash receipts completed by Environmental Products of Collier County during the period June 15–30 of the current year are as follows. The terms of all sales on account are 2/10, n/30, FOB shipping point.

June 15. Issued Invoice No. 793 to Towers Co., $4,425.

    16. Received cash from F. G. Black Co. for the balance owed on its account less discount.

    19. Issued Invoice No. 794 to Halloway Co., $7,500.

    20. Issued Invoice No. 795 to Ross and Son, $2,975.

    Post all journals to the accounts receivable ledger.

    23. Received cash from Halloway Co. for the balance owed on June 15, no discount.

    24. Issued Credit Memorandum No. 35 to Towers Co., $275.

    24. Issued Invoice No. 796 to Halloway Co., $4,950.

    24. Received $1,560 in payment of a $1,500 note receivable and interest of $60.

    Post all journals to the accounts receivable ledger.

    25. Received cash from Towers Co. for the balance due on invoice of June 15 less discount.

    28. Received cash from Halloway Co. for invoice of June 19 less discount.

    28. Issued Invoice No. 797 to F. G. Black Co., $2,100.

    30. Issued Credit Memorandum No. 36 to F. G. Black Co., $250.

    30. Recorded cash sales for the second half of the month, $8,155.

    Post all journals to the accounts receivable ledger.

Instructions

1. Insert the following balances in the general ledger as of June 1:

111	Cash	$13,705
112	Notes Receivable	7,500
113	Accounts Receivable	15,975
411	Sales	—
412	Sales Returns and Allowances	—
413	Sales Discounts	—
811	Interest Income	—

2. Insert the following balances in the accounts receivable ledger as of June 15:

F. G. Black Co. $8,900
Halloway Co.   9,825
Ross and Son   —
Towers Co.   —

3. In a single-column sales journal and a cash receipts journal similar to the ones illustrated in this appendix, insert *June 15 Total(s) Forwarded* on the left side of the first line of the journal. Insert a check mark (✓) in the Post. Ref. column, and the following dollar figures in the respective amount columns:

Sales journal: 25,350
Cash receipts journal: 3,467; 13,470; 22,600; 366; 39,171.

4. Using the two special journals and a two-column general journal, journalize the transactions for the remainder of June. Post to the accounts receivable ledger and insert the balances at the points indicated in the narrative of transactions. *Determine the balance in the customer's account before recording a cash receipt.*

5. Total each of the columns of the special journals and post the individual entries and totals to the general ledger. Insert account balances after the last posting.

6. Determine that the subsidiary ledger agrees with the controlling account in the general ledger.

Instructions for Solving Problem E-4 Using Solutions Software

1. Load opening balances.
2. Save the opening balances file to your drive and directory.
3. Set the run date to June 30 of the current year and enter your name.
4. Key the journal entries.
5. Display the journal entries.
6. Display a trial balance.
7. Save your data file to disk.
8. End the session.

PROBLEM E-5
PURCHASES AND
PURCHASES RETURNS,
ACCOUNTS PAYABLE
ACCOUNT, AND
ACCOUNTS PAYABLE
LEDGER

Purchases on account and related returns and allowances completed by Chan and Son Sales during May of the current year are as follows:

May 1. Purchased merchandise on account from Yu Co., $6,150.50.
      4. Purchased merchandise on account from O'Grady Co., $9,250.
      5. Received a credit memorandum from Yu Co. for merchandise returned, $200.
      9. Purchased office supplies on account from Tyler Supply, $175.30.
     13. Purchased merchandise on account from Yu Co., $4,370.50.
     14. Purchased office equipment on account from Diamond Equipment Co., $5,500.
     17. Purchased merchandise on account from James Co., $3,100.
     19. Received a credit memorandum from Tyler Supply for office supplies returned, $22.50.
     20. Purchased merchandise on account from Craig Co., $1,130.30.
     24. Purchased store supplies on account from Tyler Supply, $325.
     27. Received a credit memorandum from O'Grady Co. as an allowance for damaged merchandise, $500.
     29. Purchased merchandise on account from James Co., $475.15.
     31. Purchased office supplies on account from Tyler Supply, $210.50.

Instructions
1. Insert the following balances in the general ledger as of May 1:

114	Store Supplies	$ 460.00
115	Office Supplies	327.40
122	Office Equipment	32,500.00
211	Accounts Payable	12,212.30
511	Purchases	89,917.40
512	Purchases Returns and Allowances	2,170.10

2. Insert the following balances in the accounts payable ledger as of May 1:

Craig Co.	$2,177.70
Diamond Equipment Co.	—
James Co.	4,550.25
O'Grady Co.	5,484.35
Tyler Supply	—
Yu Co.	—

3. Journalize the transactions for May, using a purchases journal similar to the one illustrated in this appendix and a two-column general journal. Post to the creditor accounts in the accounts payable ledger immediately after each entry.
4. Post the general journal and the purchases journal to the accounts in the general ledger.
5. a. What is the sum of the balances in the subsidiary ledger at May 31?
   b. What is the balance of the controlling account at May 31?

PROBLEM E-6
PURCHASES AND CASH
PAYMENTS JOURNALS;
ACCOUNTS PAYABLE AND
GENERAL LEDGERS

Fashion Clothiers Co. was established on June 16 of the current year. Transactions related to purchases, returns and allowances, and cash payments during the remainder of June are as follows:

June 16. Issued Check No. 1 in payment of rent for the remainder of June, $900.
   16. Purchased office equipment on account from Harper Equipment Co., $7,250.
   16. Purchased merchandise on account from Hernandez Clothing Co., $15,500.
   17. Issued Check No. 2 in payment of store supplies, $410, and office supplies, $290.
   18. Purchased merchandise on account from Carter Clothing, $9,720.
   19. Purchased merchandise on account from Adams Co., $2,150.
   20. Received a credit memorandum from Carter Clothing for returned merchandise, $720.
   Post the journals to the accounts payable ledger.
   23. Issued Check No. 3 to Harper Equipment Co. in payment of invoice, $7,250.
   23. Received a credit memorandum from Adams Co. for defective merchandise, $465.
   24. Issued Check No. 4 to Hernandez Clothing Co. in payment of invoice of $15,500 less 1% discount.
   25. Issued Check No. 5 to a cash customer for merchandise returned, $215.
   26. Issued Check No. 6 to Carter Clothing in payment of the balance owed less 2% discount.
   27. Purchased merchandise on account from Adams Co., $1,610.
   Post the journals to the accounts payable ledger.
   30. Purchased the following from Harper Equipment Co. on account: store supplies, $150; office supplies, $75; store equipment, $1,500.
   30. Issued Check No. 7 to Adams Co. in payment of invoice of $2,150 less the credit of $465.
   30. Purchased merchandise on account from Hernandez Clothing Co., $6,200.
   30. Issued Check No. 8 in payment of sales salaries, $1,775.
   30. Received a credit memorandum from Harper Equipment Co. for defect in office equipment, $75.
   Post the journals to the accounts payable ledger.

SPREADSHEET
PROBLEM

Instructions
1. Journalize the transactions for June. Use a purchases journal and a cash payments journal, similar to those illustrated in this appendix, and a two-column general journal. Refer to the following partial chart of accounts:

111	Cash	412	Sales Returns and Allowances
116	Store Supplies	511	Purchases
117	Office Supplies	512	Purchases Returns and Allowances
121	Store Equipment	513	Purchases Discounts
123	Office Equipment	611	Sales Salaries Expense
211	Accounts Payable	712	Rent Expense

At the points indicated in the narrative of transactions, post to the following accounts in the accounts payable ledger:

Adams Co.	Harper Equipment Co.
Carter Clothing	Hernandez Clothing Co.

2. Post the individual entries (Other Accounts columns of the purchases journal and the cash payments journal; both columns of the general journal) to the appropriate general ledger accounts.

3. Total each of the columns of the purchases journal and the cash payments journal and post the appropriate totals to the general ledger. (Because the problem does not include transactions related to cash receipts, the cash account in the ledger will have a credit balance.)

4. Prepare a schedule of accounts payable.

PROBLEM E-7
ALL JOURNALS AND
GENERAL LEDGER; TRIAL
BALANCE

The transactions completed by Miles Company during July, the first month of the current fiscal year, were as follows:

July 1. Issued Check No. 610 for July rent, $1,400.   *CPJ*
     2. Purchased merchandise on account from Bidwell Co., $2,590.   *PJ*
   PJ 3. Purchased equipment on account from Glass Equipment Co., $9,600.
   SJ 5. Issued Invoice No. 940 to W. Cox Co., $1,700.
   CRJ 6. Received check for $2,772 from Powell Co. in payment of $2,800 invoice less 1% discount.
   CPJ 6. Issued Check No. 611 for miscellaneous selling expense, $310.
   GJ 9. Received credit memorandum from Bidwell Co. for returned merchandise, $290.
   SS 9. Issued Invoice No. 941 to Collins Co., $8,500.
   CP 10. Issued Check No. 612 for $9,405 to Howell Co. in payment of $9,500 invoice less 1% discount.
   CR 10. Received check for $7,375 from Sax Manufacturing Co. in payment of $7,375 invoice, no discount.
   CP 10. Issued Check No. 613 to Bone Enterprises in payment of $2,120 invoice, no discount.
   SJ 11. Issued Invoice No. 942 to Joy Co., $3,120.
   CP 11. Issued Check No. 614 for $705 to Porter Co. in payment of account, no discount.
   CR 12. Received check for $1,683 from W. Cox Co. in payment of $1,700 invoice less 1% discount.
   GJ 13. Issued credit memorandum to Joy Co. for damaged merchandise, $320.
   CP 13. Issued Check No. 615 for $2,254 to Bidwell Co. in payment of $2,300 balance less 2% discount.
   CP 16. Issued Check No. 616 for $2,725 for cash purchase of merchandise.
   CR 16. Cash sales for July 1–16, $21,520.
   PJ 17. Purchased merchandise on account from Bone Enterprises, $7,920.
   CR 18. Received check for return of merchandise that had been purchased for cash, $790.
   CP 18. Issued Check No. 617 for miscellaneous administrative expense, $238.
   PJ 19. Purchased the following on account from Moore Supply Co.: store supplies, $248; office supplies, $197.
   CP 20. Issued Check No. 618 in payment of advertising expense, $1,850.
   SS 23. Issued Invoice No. 943 to Sax Manufacturing Co., $8,172.
   PS 24. Purchased the following on account from Howell Co.: merchandise, $5,127; store supplies, $292.
   SS 25. Issued Invoice No. 944 to Collins Co., $4,650.
   CR 25. Received check for $2,800 from Powell Co. in payment of $2,800 balance, no discount.
   CP 26. Issued Check No. 619 to Glass Equipment Co. in payment of $9,600 invoice of July 3, no discount.
   CP 30. Issued Check No. 620 for monthly salaries as follows: sales salaries; $9,100; office salaries, $3,800.
   CR 31. Cash sales for July 17–31, $18,150.
   CP 31. Issued Check No. 621 in payment of transportation charges for merchandise purchased during the month, $930.

Instructions

1. Enter the following account balances in the general ledger as of July 1:

111	Cash	$ 9,850
113	Accounts Receivable	12,975
114	Merchandise Inventory	35,500
115	Store Supplies	545

116	Office Supplies	360
117	Prepaid Insurance	2,100
121	Equipment	47,250
122	Accumulated Depreciation	22,250
211	Accounts Payable	13,530
311	Capital Stock	10,000
312	Retained Earnings	62,800
313	Dividends	—
411	Sales	—
412	Sales Returns and Allowances	—
413	Sales Discounts	—
511	Purchases	—
512	Purchases Returns and Allowances	—
513	Purchases Discounts	—
514	Transportation In	—
611	Sales Salaries Expense	—
612	Advertising Expense	—
619	Miscellaneous Selling Expense	—
711	Office Salaries Expense	—
712	Rent Expense	—
719	Miscellaneous Administrative Expense	—

2. Journalize the transactions for July, using the following journals similar to those illustrated in this appendix: single-column sales journal, cash receipts journal, purchases journal, cash payments journal, and two-column general journal. The terms of all sales on account are FOB shipping point, 1/10, n/30. Assume that an assistant makes daily postings to the individual accounts in the accounts payable ledger and the accounts receivable ledger.
3. Post the appropriate individual entries to the general ledger.
4. Total each of the columns of the special journals and post the appropriate totals to the general ledger; insert the account balances.
5. Prepare a trial balance.
6. Verify the agreement of each subsidiary ledger with its controlling account. Balances of the accounts in the subsidiary ledgers as of July 31 are as follows:

Accounts receivable: 13,150; 8,172; 2,800
Accounts payable: 5,419; 7,920; 1,650

SOLUTIONS SOFTWARE

Instructions for Solving Problem E-7 Using Solutions Software

1. Load opening balances.
2. Save the opening balances file to your drive and directory.
3. Set the run date to July 31 of the current year and enter your name.
4. Key the journal entries.
5. Display the journal entries.
6. Display a trial balance.
7. Save your data file to disk.
8. End the session.

PROBLEM E-8
SALES JOURNAL WITH
SALES TAX PAYABLE
COLUMN; ACCOUNTS
RECEIVABLE AND
GENERAL LEDGERS

Rivera Company was established on May 15 of the current year. Its sales of merchandise on account and related returns and allowances during the remainder of the month are as follows. Terms of all sales were 1/15, n/30, FOB shipping point. The sales tax was 5%.

May 18. Sold merchandise on account to JCM Co., Invoice No. 1, $1,500 plus sales tax of $75.

20. Sold merchandise on account to Reese Co., Invoice No. 2, $3,300 plus sales tax of $165.

22. Sold merchandise on account to Innis Co., Invoice No. 3, $3,600 plus sales tax of $180.

23. Issued Credit Memorandum No. 1 for $300 plus sales tax of $15 to JCM Co. for merchandise returned.

27. Sold merchandise on account to D. L. Victor Co., Invoice No. 4, $2,800 plus sales tax of $140.

28. Sold merchandise on account to Tyson Co., Invoice No. 5, $500 plus sales tax of $25.

May 28. Issued Credit Memorandum No. 2 for $100 plus sales tax of $5 to Reese Co. for merchandise returned.

   30. Sold merchandise on account to Reese Co., Invoice No. 6, $1,800 plus sales tax of $90.

   30. Issued Credit Memorandum No. 3 for $200 plus sales tax of $10 to D. L. Victor Co. for damages to merchandise caused by faulty packing.

   31. Sold merchandise on account to Innis Co., Invoice No. 7, $2,500 plus sales tax of $125.

SPREADSHEET PROBLEM

Instructions

1. Journalize the transactions for May, using a three-column sales journal and a two-column general journal. Post to the following customer accounts in the accounts receivable ledger and insert the balance immediately after recording each entry: JCM Co.; Innis Co.; Reese Co.; Tyson Co.; D. L. Victor Co.

2. Post the general journal and the sales journal to the following accounts in the general ledger, inserting the account balances only after the last postings:

    113   Accounts Receivable
    215   Sales Tax Payable
    411   Sales
    412   Sales Returns and Allowances

3. a. What is the sum of the balances of the accounts in the subsidiary ledger at May 31?
   b. What is the balance of the controlling account at May 31?

GLOSSARY

A

Accelerated depreciation methods. Depreciation methods that provide for a high depreciation expense in the first year of use of an asset and a gradually declining expense thereafter. (329)

Account. The form used to record additions and deductions for each individual asset, liability, owner's equity, revenue, and expense. (42)

Account form of balance sheet. A form of balance sheet with assets on the left-hand side and liabilities and stockholders' equity on the right-hand side. (21, 182)

Account payable. A liability created by a purchase made on credit. (15)

Account receivable. A claim against a customer for services rendered or goods sold on credit. (16)

Accounting. The process of identifying, measuring, and communicating economic information to permit informed judgments and decisions by users of the information. (8)

Accounting cycle. The sequence of basic accounting procedures during a fiscal period. (138)

Accounting equation. The expression of the relationship between assets, liabilities, and owner's equity; it is most commonly stated as Assets = Liabilities + Owner's Equity. (14)

Accounting system. The methods and procedures used by an enterprise to record and report financial data for use by management and external users. (218)

Accrual basis. Revenues are recognized in the period earned and expenses are recognized in the period incurred in the process of generating revenues. (90)

Accruals. Expenses that have been incurred or revenues that have been earned, but have not been recorded. (91)

Accrued expenses. Expenses that have been incurred but not recorded in the accounts. Sometimes called accrued liabilities. (91)

Accrued revenues. Revenues that have been earned but not recorded in the accounts. Sometimes called accrued assets. (91)

Accumulated depreciation account. The contra asset account used to accumulate the depreciation recognized to date on plant assets. (98)

Adjusting entries. Entries required at the end of an accounting period to bring the ledger up to date. (91)

Adjusting process. The process of updating the accounts at the end of a period. (90)

Administrative expenses. Expenses incurred in the administration or general operations of a business. (181)

Aging the receivables. The process of analyzing the account receivable and classifying them according to various age groupings, with the due date being the base point for determining age. (265)

Allowance method. A method of accounting for uncollectible receivables, whereby advance provision for the uncollectibles is made. (262)

Amortization. The periodic expense attributed to the decline in usefulness of an intangible asset. (341)

Appropriation. The amount of a corporation's retained earnings that has been restricted and therefore is not available for distribution to shareholders as dividends. (455)

Assets. Physical items (tangible) or rights (intangible) that have value and that are owned by the business entity. (14)

Average cost method. The method of inventory costing that is based on the assumption that costs should be charged against revenue in accordance with the weighted average unit costs of the items sold. (295)

B

Balance of the account. The amount of difference between the debits and the credits that have been entered into an account. (44)

Balance sheet. A financial statement listing the assets, liabilities, and owner's equity of a business entity as of a specific date. (19)

Bank reconciliation. The method of analysis that details the items that are responsible for the difference between the cash balance reported in the bank statement and the balance of the cash account in the ledger. (226)

Betterment. An expenditure that increases operating efficiency or capacity for the remaining useful life of a plant asset. (334)

Bond. A form of interest-bearing note employed by corporations to borrow on a long-term basis. (412)

Bond indenture. The contract between a corporation issuing bonds and the bondholders. (412)

Book value of the asset. The difference between the balance of a plant asset account and its related accumulated depreciation account. (98)

Boot. The balance owed the supplier when an old asset is traded for a new asset. (337)

Business entity concept. The concept that accounting applies to individual economic units and that each unit is separate from the persons who supply its assets. (13)

Business transaction. The occurrence of an economic event or a condition that must be recorded in the accounting records. (14)

C

Capital expenditures. Costs that add to the utility of assets for more than one accounting period. (334)

Capital leases. Leases that include one or more of four provisions that result in treating the leased assets as purchased assets in the accounts. (340)

Capital stock. Shares of ownership of a corporation. (444)

Carrying amount. The amount at which a temporary investment is reported on the balance sheet; also called basis or book value. (269, 422)

Cash basis. Revenue is recognized in the period cash is received, and expenses are recognized in the period cash is paid. (90)

Cash dividend. A cash distribution of earnings by a corporation to its shareholders. (452)

Cash equivalents. Highly liquid investments that are usually reported on the balance sheet with cash. (235)

Cash flows from financing activities. The section of the statement of cash flows which reports cash flows from transactions that affect the equity and debt of the entity. (525)

Cash flows from investing activities. The section of the statement of cash flows which reports cash flows from transactions that affect investments in noncurrent assets. (524)

Cash flows from operating activities. The section of the statement of cash flows which reports the cash transactions that affect the determination of net income. (524)

Chart of accounts. The system of accounts that make up the ledger for a business enterprise. (42)

Closing entries. Entries necessary to eliminate the balances of temporary accounts in preparation for the following accounting period. (129)

Common stock. The basic ownership class of corporate capital stock. (445)

Completed-contract method. The method that recognizes revenue from long-term construction contracts when the project is completed. (304)

Composite-rate depreciation method. A method of depreciation based on the use of a single rate that applies to entire groups of assets. (333)

Consolidated statements. Financial statements resulting from combining parent and subsidiary company statements. (495)

Consolidation. The creation of a new corporation by the transfer of assets and liabilities from two or more existing corporations. (495)

Contingent liabilities. Potential obligations that will become liabilities only if certain events occur in the future. (261, 386)

Contra accounts. Accounts that are offset against other accounts. (98)

Contract rate. The interest rate specified on a bond; sometimes called the coupon rate of interest. (414)

Controlling account. The account in the general ledger that summarizes the balances of the accounts in a subsidiary ledger. (219)

Corporation. A separate legal entity that is organized in accordance with state or federal statutes and in which ownership is divided into shares of stock. (13)

Cost accounting. A branch of managerial accounting concerned with accumulating costs for financial reporting purposes. (374)

Cost method. A method of accounting for an investment in common stock, by which the investor recognizes as income its share of cash dividends of the investee. (492)

Cost principle. The principle that the monetary record for properties and services purchased by a business should be maintained in terms of actual cost. (13)

Credit. (1) The right side of an account; (2) the amount entered on the right side of an account; (3) to enter an amount on the right side of an account. (43)

Credit memorandum. The form issued by a seller to inform a buyer that a credit has been posted to the buyer's account receivable. (172)

Cumulative preferred stock. Preferred stock that is entitled to current and past dividends before dividends may be paid on common stock. (446)

Current assets. Cash or other assets that are expected to be converted to cash or sold or used up, usually within a year or less, through the normal operations of a business. (128)

Current liabilities. Liabilities that will be due within a short time (usually one year or less) and that are to be paid out of current assets. (128)

D

Debit. (1) The left side of an account; (2) the amount entered on the left side of an account; (3) to enter an amount on the left side of an account. (43)

Debit memorandum. The form issued by a buyer to inform a seller that a debit has been posted to the seller's account payable. (169)

Declining-balance depreciation method. A method of depreciation that provides declining periodic depreciation expense over the estimated life of an asset. (328)

Deferrals. Delays in the recognition of expenses that have been incurred or revenues that have been received. (91)

Deferred expenses. Items that are initially recorded as assets but are expected to become expenses over time or through the normal operations of the enterprise. Sometimes called prepaid expenses. (91)

Deferred revenues. Items that are initially recorded as liabilities but are expected to become revenues over time or through the normal operations of the enterprise. Sometimes called unearned revenues. (91)

Depletion. The cost of metal ores and other minerals removed from the earth. (341)

Depreciation. In a general sense, the decrease in usefulness of plant assets other than land. In accounting, refers to the systematic allocation of a plant asset's cost to expense. The periodic cost expiration for the use of all plant assets except land. (98, 325)

Direct labor. The cost of wages of employees who are directly involved in converting materials into the manufactured project. (304)

Direct materials. The cost of materials that are an integral part of the manufactured product. (304)

Direct method. A method of reporting the cash flows from operating activities as the difference between the operating cash receipts and the operating cash payments. (525)

Direct write-off method. A method of accounting for uncollectible receivables, whereby an expense is recognized only when specific accounts are judged to be uncollectible. (262)

Discontinued operations. The operations of a business segment that have been disposed of. (486)

Discount. The interest deducted from the maturity value of a note receivable. The excess of the face amount of bonds over their issue price. The excess of par value of stock over its sales price. (260, 414, 448)

Discount rate. The rate used in computing the interest to be deducted from the maturity value of a note. (385)

Dishonored note receivable. A note that the maker fails to pay on its due date. (261)

Dividends. A distribution of earnings of a corporation to its owners (stockholders). (17, 42)

Double-entry accounting. A system for recording transactions, based on recording increases and decreases in accounts so that debits always equal credits. (46)

E

Earnings per share (EPS). The profitability ratio of net income available to common shareholders to the number of common shares outstanding. (489)

Effective rate. The market rate of interest at the time bonds are issued. (414)

Electronic funds transfer (EFT). A payment system that uses computerized electronic impulses rather than paper (money, checks. etc.) to effect a cash transaction. (236)

Employee's earnings record. A detailed record of each employee's earnings. (376)

Equity method. A method of accounting for investments in common stock, by which the investment account is adjusted for the investor's share of periodic net income and property dividends of the investee. (492)

Equity per share. The ratio of stockholders' equity to the related number of shares of stock outstanding. (492)

Equity securities. Preferred or common stock. (491)

Exchange rate. The rate at which one currency can be converted into another currency. (497)

Expenses. Assets used up or services consumed in the process of generating revenues. (16, 42)

Extraordinary items. Events or transactions that are unusual and infrequent. (487)

Extraordinary repair. An expenditure that increases the useful life of an asset beyond the original estimate. (334)

F

Factory overhead. All the remaining costs of manufacturing the product that are not included in direct materials or direct labor. (304)

FICA tax. Federal Insurance Contributions Act tax used to finance federal programs for old-age and disability benefits (social security) and health insurance for the aged (Medicare). (368)

Financial Accounting. Standards Board (FASB). An authoritative body for the development of accounting principles. (12)

Finished goods. Manufactured goods in the state in which they are to be sold. (304)

First-in, first-out (fifo) method. A method inventory costing based on the assumption that the costs of merchandise sold should be charged against revenue in the order in which the costs were incurred. (293)

Fiscal year. The annual accounting period adopted by an enterprise. (132)

FOB destination. Terms of agreement between buyer and seller whereby ownership passes when merchandise is received by the buyer, and the seller pays the transportation costs. (174)

FOB shipping point. Terms of agreement between buyer and seller whereby ownership passes when merchandise is delivered to the freight carrier, and the buyer pays the transportation costs. (174)

Funded. An appropriation of retained earnings accompanied by a segregation of cash or marketable securities. (456)

Future value. The amount that will accumulate at some future date as a result of an investment or a series of investments. (419)

G

General ledger. The primary ledger, when used in conjunction with subsidiary ledgers, that contains all of the balance sheet and income statement accounts. (219)

Generally accepted accounting principles (GAAP). Generally accepted guidelines for the preparation of financial statements. (11)

Goodwill. An intangible asset that attaches to a business as a result of such favorable factors as location, product superiority, reputation, and managerial skill. (342)

Gross pay. The total earnings of an employee for a payroll period. (368)

Gross profit. The excess of net sales over the cost of merchandise sold. (180)

Gross profit method. A means of estimating inventory on hand based on the relationship of gross profit to sales. (303)

I

Income from operations. The excess of gross profit over total operating expenses. (181)

Income statement. A summary of the revenues and expenses of a business entity for a specific period of time. (19)

Income Summary. The account used in the closing process for transferring the revenue and expense account balances to Retained Earnings at the end of the period. (130)

Indirect method. A method of reporting the cash flows from operating activities as the net income from operations adjusted for all deferrals of past cash receipts and payments and all accruals of expected future cash receipts and payments. (525)

Installment method. The method of recognizing revenue, whereby each receipt of cash from installment sales is considered to be part cost of merchandise sold and part gross profit. (268)

Intangible assets. Long-lived assets that are useful in the operations of an enterprise, are not held for sale, and are without physical qualities. (324)

Internal controls. The detailed policies and procedures used by an enterprise to direct operations and provide reasonable assurance that the enterprise objectives are achieved. (218)

Internal control structure. Consists of the following three elements: (1) the accounting system, (2) the control environment, and (3) the control procedures. (220)

Invoice. The bill provided by the seller (who refers to it as a *sales invoice*) to a buyer (who refers to it as a *purchase invoice*) for items purchased. (167)

J

Journal. The initial record in which the effects of a transaction on accounts are recorded. (44)

Journalizing. The process of recording a transaction in a journal. (45)

L

Last-in, first-out (lifo) method. A method of inventory costing based on the assumption that the most recent merchandise costs incurred should be charged against revenue. (294)

Ledger. The group of accounts used by an enterprise. (42)

Liabilities. Debts of a business enterprise owed to outsiders (creditors). (14, 42)

Liquidating dividend. A distribution out of paid-in capital when a corporation permanently reduces its operations or winds up its affairs completely. (455)

Long-term liabilities. Liabilities that are not due for a long time (usually more than one year). (128)

Lower-of-cost-or-market method. A method of valuing inventory that reports the inventory at the lower of its cost or current market value (replacement cost). (300)

M

Marketable securities. Investments insecurities that can be readily sold when cash is needed. (268)

Matching concept. The concept that all expenses incurred should be matched with the revenue they generate during a period of time. (19, 90)

Materiality. The concept that recognizes the practicality of ignoring small or insignificant deviations from generally accepted accounting principles. (61)

Materials. Goods in the state in which they were acquired for use in a manufacturing process. (304)

Maturity value. The amount due at the maturity or due date of a note. (259)

Merchandise inventory. Merchandise on hand and available for sale to customers. (166)

Merger. The combining of two corporations by the acquisition of the properties of one corporation by another, with the dissolution of one of the corporations. (495)

Minority interest. The portion of a subsidiary corporation's capital stock that is not owned by the parent corporation. (496)

Multiple-step income statement. An income statement with several sections, subsections, and subtotals. (180)

N

Natural business year. A year that ends when a business's activities have reached the lowest point in its annual operating cycle. (132)

Net income. The final figure in the income statement when revenues exceed expenses. (19)

Net loss. The final figure in the income statement when expenses exceed revenues. (19)

Net pay. Gross pay less payroll deductions; the amount the employer is obligated to pay the employee. (368)

Net realizable value. The amount at which merchandise that can be sold only at prices below cost should be valued; it is determined as the estimated selling price less any direct costs of disposal. (301)

Nominal accounts. Revenue or expense accounts that are periodically closed to the income summary account; temporary owner's equity accounts. (130)

Nonparticipating preferred stock. Preferred stock where dividend preference is limited to a certain amount. (446)

Note receivable. A written promise to pay, representing an amount to be received by a business. (256)

O

Operating leases. Leases that do no meet the criteria for capital leases and thus are accounted for as operating expenses. (340)

Other expense. An expense that cannot be traced directly to operations. (181)

Other income. Revenue from sources other than the primary operating activity of a business. (181)

Outstanding stock. The stock that has been issued to stockholders. (445)

Owner's equity. The rights of the owners in a business enterprise. The claim of owners against the assets of the business after the total liabilities are deducted. (14, 42)

P

Paid-in capital. The capital acquired from stockholders. (445)

Par. The monetary amount printed on a stock certificate. (445)

Parent company. The company owning a majority of the voting stock of another corporation. (495)

Partnership. An unincorporated business owned by two or more individuals. (13)

Payroll. The total amount paid to employees for a certain period. (368)

Payroll register. A multicolumn form used to assemble and summarize payroll data at the end of each payroll period. (372)

Percentage-of-completion method. A method of recognizing revenue, whereby the revenue is determined to be realized at the time that title passes to the buyer. (304)

Periodic inventory system. A system of inventory accounting in which only the revenue from sales is recorded each time a sale is made. The cost of merchandise on hand at the end of a period is determined by a detailed listing (physical inventory) of the merchandise on hand. (166)

Perpetual inventory system. A system of inventory accounting in which both the revenue from sales and the cost of merchandise sold are recorded each time a sale is made so that the records continually disclose the amount of the inventory on hand. (166)

Petty cash fund. A special cash fund used to pay relatively small amount. (234)

Physical inventory. The detailed listing of merchandise on hand. (166, 290)

Plant assets. Tangible assets that are owned by a business enterprise, are permanent or have a long life, and are used in the business. (97, 324)

Point-of-sale method. The method of recognizing revenue, whereby the revenue is determined to be realized at the time that title passes to the buyer. (268)

Pooling-of-interests method. A method of accounting for an affiliation of two corporations resulting from an exchange of voting stock of one corporation for substantially all the voting stock of the other corporation. (495)

Post-closing trial balance. A trial balance prepared after all the temporary accounts have been closed. (131)

Posting. The process of transferring debits and credits from a journal to the accounts. (48)

Postretirement benefits. Rights to benefits that employees earn during their term of employment for themselves and their dependents after they retire. (382)

Preemptive right. The right of each shareholder to maintain the same fractional interest in the corporation by purchasing shares of any additional issuances of stock. (445)

Preferred stock. A class of stock with preferential rights over common stock. (445)

Premium. The excess of the issue price of bonds over the face amount. The excess of the sales price of stock over its par amount. (415, 448)

Prepaid expenses. Purchased commodities or services that have not been used up at the end of an accounting period. (15)

Present value. The estimated present worth of an amount of cash to be received (or paid) in the future. (412)

Present value of an annuity. The sum of the present values of a series of equal cash flows to be received at fixed intervals. (414)

Private accounting. The profession whose members are accountants employed by a business firm or not-for-profit organization. (9)

Proceeds. The net amount available from discounting a note or issuing a bond. (260, 385)

Prior-period adjustments. Corrections of material errors related to a prior period or periods, excluded from the determination of net income. (491)

Promissory note. A written promise to pay a sum in money on demand or at a definite time. (256)

Public accounting. The profession whose members render accounting services on a fee basis. (9)

Purchase method. The accounting method employed when a parent company acquires a controlling share of the voting stock of a subsidiary other than by the exchange of voting common stock. (495)

Purchases discounts. An available discount taken by a buyer for early payment of an invoice. (168)

Purchases returns and allowances. Reductions in purchases, resulting from merchandise being returned to the seller or from the seller's reduction in the original purchase price. (169)

R

Real accounts. Balance sheet accounts. (130)

Report form of balance sheet. A form of balance sheet with the liabilities and owner's equity sections below the asset section. (21, 182)

Residual value. The estimated recoverable cost of a depreciable asset as of the time of its removal from service. (326)

Retail inventory method. A method of inventory costing based on the relationship of the cost and the retail price of merchandise. (302)

Retained earnings. Net income retained in a corporation. (16)

Revenue expenditures. Expenditures that benefit only the current period. (334)

Revenues. Increases in owner's equity as a result of providing services or selling products to customers. (16, 42)

S

Sales discounts. An available discount granted by a seller for early payment of an invoice; a contra account to Sales. (171)

Sales returns and allowances. Reductions in sales, resulting from merchandise being returned by customers or from the seller's reduction in the original sales price; a contra account to Sales. (172)

Selling expenses. Expenses incurred directly in the sale of merchandise. (181)

Single-step income statement. An income statement in which the total of all expenses is deducted in one step from the total of all revenues. (182)

Sinking fund. Assets set aside in a special fund to be used for a specific purpose. (419)

Slide. The erroneous movement of all digits in a number, one or more spaces to the right or the left, such as writing $542 as $5,420. (59)

Sole proprietorship. An unincorporated business owned by one individual. (13)

Stated value. A value approved by the board of directors of a corporation for no-par stock. Similar to par value. (445)

Statement of cash flows. A summary of the major cash receipts and cash payments for a period. (524)

Statement of retained earnings. A summary of the changes in the earnings retained in the business entity *for a specific period of time,* such as a month or a year. (19)

Statement of stockholders' equity. A summary of the changes in the stockholders' equity of a corporation that have occurred during a specific period of time. (458)

Stockholders' equity. The equity of the stockholders of a corporation. (22)

Stock options. Rights given by a corporation to its employees to purchase shares of the corporation's stock at a stated price. (382)

Straight-line depreciation method. A method of depreciation that provides for equal periodic depreciation expense over the estimated life of an asset. (327)

Subsidiary company. The corporation that is controlled by a parent company. (495)

Subsidiary ledger. A ledger containing individual accounts with a common characteristic. (219)

Sum-of-the-years-digits depreciation method. A method of depreciation that provides for declining periodic depreciation expense over the estimated life of an asset. (328)

T

T account. A form of account resembling the letter T. (43)

Taxable income. The base on which the amount of income tax is determined. (484)

Temporary accounts. Revenue or expense accounts that are periodically closed to the income summary account; nominal accounts. (130)

Temporary differences. Differences between income before income tax and taxable income created by items that are recognized in one period for income statement purposes and in another period for tax purposes. Such differences reverse or turn around in later years. (484)

Temporary investments. Investments in securities that can be readily sold when cash is needed. (268)

Trade discounts. Special discounts from published list prices offered by sellers to certain classes of buyers. (174)

Transposition. The erroneous arrangement of digits in a number, such as writing $542 as $524. (59)

Treasury stock. A corporation's own outstanding stock that has been reacquired. (447)

Trial balance. A summary listing of the titles and balances of the accounts in the ledger. (58)

U

Units-of-production depreciation method. A method of depreciation that provides for depreciation expense based on the expected productive capacity of an asset. (327)

V

Voucher. A document that serves as evidence of authority to pay cash. (231)

Voucher system. Records, methods, and procedures employed in verifying and recording liabilities and paying and recording cash payments. (231)

W

Work in process. Goods in the process of manufacture. (304)

Work sheet. A working paper used to summarize adjusting entries and assist in the preparation of financial statements. (99)

INDEX

CHECK FIGURES FOR SELECTED PROBLEMS

Prob.	Check Figure	Prob.	Check Figure
1-1A	1. Apr. 30, Cash, $1,070	8-7A	Income from contracts, 1995, $465,000
1-2A	1. Net income, $27,655	8-1B	3. $196,250
1-3A	1. Net income, $2,350	8-2B	2. Gross profit, $198,750
1-4A	2. Net income, $3,050	8-3B	1. $8,807
1-5A	3. Net income, $1,430	8-4B	LCM, $54,605
1-6A	1. Net income, $35,900	8-5B	2. a. Net income, $77,000
1-1B	1. Oct. 31, Cash, $4,595	8-6B	1. $207,200
1-2B	1. Net income, $18,300	8-7B	Income from contracts, 1995, $275,000
1-3B	1. Net income, $2,470	9-2A	Declining bal. dep., 1995, $4,000
1-4B	2. Net income, $2,675	9-3A	d. Sum-of-years-digits dep., 1994, $28,750
1-5B	3. Net income, $2,105	9-4A	4. $195,000
1-6B	1. Net income, $93,375	9-6A	Accum. depr., June 30, 1996, $1,875
2-1A	3. Total credits, $24,960	9-7A	Acc. Dep.-Printing Equip., Sep. 30, 1994, $257,850
2-2A	3. Total debits, $36,350	9-8A	1. Net income, $103,000
2-3A	3. Total debits, $29,950	9-9A	1. c. $1,550
2-4A	4. Total credits, $100,040	9-2B	Declining bal. dep., 1995, $2,000
2-5A	4. Total credits, $248,065	9-3B	d. Sum-of-years-digits dep., 1994, $35,000
2-6A	7. Total debits, $33,338.10	9-4B	4. $166,200
2-7A	1. Total credits, $98,190	9-6B	Accum. depr., Dec. 31, 1995, $1,525
2-1B	3. Total debits, $27,100	9-7B	Acc. Dep.-Printing Equip., Mar. 31, 1994, $262,350
2-2B	3. Total credits, $58,400	9-8B	1. Net income, $96,344
2-3B	3. Total debits, $20,125	9-9B	1. c. $1,250
2-4B	4. Total credits, $103,015	10-3A	2. d. Total payroll tax exp., $20,204.50
2-5B	4. Total credits, $304,950	10-4A	1. Total employee earnings, $6,293.00
2-6B	7. Total debits, $33,338.10	10-6A	1. d. $9,000
2-7B	1. Total debits, $123,090	10-7A	4. $5,500
3-3A	1. Adjusted trial balance totals, $66,980	10-3B	2. d. Total payroll tax exp. $20,427.15
3-6A	3. Adjusted trial balance totals, $468,720	10-4B	1. Total employee earnings, $6,323.00
3-7A	2. Corrected total stockholders' equity, $58,850	10-6B	1. d. $16,875
3-3B	1. Adjusted trial balance totals, $66,980	10-7B	4. $6,420
3-6B	3. Adjusted trial balance totals, $470,500	Comp. Pb. 3	5. Total assets, $997,390
3-7B	2. Corrected total stockholders' equity, $79,000	11-1A	1. Proceeds, $10,597,240
4-1A	2. Net income, $9,710	11-2A	3. $635,868
4-2A	3. Retained earnings, April 30, 1995, $48,955	11-4A	2. 1995 Premium on Bonds, $371,850
4-3A	2. Net income, $3,561.11	11-5A	3. Carrying amt. of bonds, Dec. 31, 1995, $4,470,399
4-4A	2. Net income, $42,870	11-1B	1. Proceeds, $10,623,210
4-5A	3. Net income, $22,424	11-2B	3. $836,029
4-1B	2. Net income, $25,490	11-4B	2. 1995 Discount on Bonds, $287,280
4-2B	3. Retained earnings, Dec. 31, $103,450	11-5B	3. Carrying amt. of bonds, Dec. 31, 1995, $21,949,781
4-3B	2. Net income, $3,692.71	12-1A	1. Total common dividends per share, $16.20
4-4B	2. Net income, $44,830	12-2A	2. Total stockholders' equity, $2,875,000
4-5B	3. Net income, $22,590	12-3A	2. Total stockholders' equity, $1,506,500
Comp. Pb. 1	4. Net income, $5,235	12-4A	2. Total stockholders' equity, $357,200
5-5A	Net income, $11,960	12-6A	3. Total assets, $514,700
5-6A	2. Net income, $111,800	12-8A	Total retained earnings, Dec. 31, $940,000
5-7A	3. Total assets, $550,000	12-9A	3. Total stockholders' equity, $2,593,980
5-8A	1. Net income, $70,000	12-10A	Total stockholders' equity, $1,784,000
5-9A	2. Net income, $138,905	12-1B	1. Total common dividends per share, $9.90
5-5B	Net income, $50,420	12-2B	2. Total stockholders' equity, $3,131,000
5-6B	2. Net income, $106,050	12-3B	2. Total stockholders' equity, $7,399,500
5-7B	3. Total assets, $390,200	12-4B	2. Total stockholders' equity, $381,450
5-8B	1. Net income, $52,490	12-6B	3. Total assets, $555,000
5-9B	2. Net income, $139,805	12-8B	Retained earnings, Dec. 31, $1,105,000
Comp. Pb. 2	4. Net income, $55,340	12-9B	3. Total stockholders' equity, $1,633,250
6-1A	Adj. bal., $23,037.55	12-10B	Total stockholders' equity, $1,797,000
6-2A	1. Adj. bal., $20,879.87	13-1A	1. Year-end balances, 4th year, $40,500
6-3A	1. Adj. bal., $9,898.02	13-2A	Net income, $69,000
6-1B	Adj. bal., $17,629.90	13-4A	D. Common stock, $28.50
6-2B	1. Adj. bal., $17,091.88	13-5A	3. Reduction in consolidated net income, $20,000
6-3B	1. Adj. bal., $12,026.09	13-1B	1. Year-end balance, 4th year, $13,500
7-2A	2. Note 3, (d) $6,352.83	13-2B	Net income, $120,000
7-4A	3. $662,300	13-4B	D. Common stock, $19.60
7-5A	1. Bal. of Allow., Year 4, $11,850	13-5B	3. Reduction in consolidated net income, $30,000
7-6A	2. Net income, third year, $58,650	Comp. Pb. 4	2. a. Net income, $400,950
7-7A	3. Loss on repossession, $30	14-1A	Net cash flow from operating activities, $93,200
7-8A	1. Net income, $99,500	14-2A	Net cash flow from operating activities, $202,900
7-2B	2. Note 1, (d) $15,130	14-3A	Net cash flow from operating activities, $73,100
7-4B	3. $320,300	14-4A	Net cash flow from operating activities, $700
7-5B	1. Bal. of Allow., Year 4, $8,750	14-5A	Net cash flow from operating activities, $67,000
7-6B	2. Net income, third year, $39,200	14-6A	Net cash flow from operating activities, $93,200
7-7B	3. Gain on repossession, $38	14-7A	Net cash flow from operating activities, $83,960
7-8B	1. Net income, $99,700	14-1B	Net cash flow from operating activities, $101,200
8-1A	3. $4,650	14-2B	Net cash flow from operating activities, $137,100
8-2A	2. Gross profit, $4,455	14-3B	Net cash flow from operating activities, $76,950
8-3A	1. $11,256	14-4B	Net cash flow from operating activities, $61,600
8-4A	LCM, $54,745	14-5B	Net cash flow from operating activities, $84,300
8-5A	2. a. Net income, $72,000	14-6B	Net cash flow from operating activities, $101,200
8-6A	1. $347,200	14-7B	Net cash flow from operating activities, $82,460

Classification of Accounts

Account Title	Account Classification	Normal Balance	Financial Statement
Accounts Payable	Current liability	Credit	Balance sheet
Accounts Receivable	Current asset	Debit	Balance sheet
Accumulated Depreciation	Plant asset	Credit	Balance sheet
Accumulated Depletion	Plant asset	Credit	Balance sheet
Advertising Expense	Operating expense	Debit	Income statement
Allowance for Doubtful Accounts	Current asset	Credit	Balance sheet
Amortization Expense	Operating expense	Debit	Income statement
Appropriation for _____	Stockholder's equity	Credit	Retained earnings statement/ Balance sheet
Bonds Payable	Long-term liability	Credit	Balance sheet
Building	Plant asset	Debit	Balance sheet
Capital Stock	Stockholders' equity	Credit	Balance sheet
Cash	Current asset	Debit	Balance sheet
Cash Dividends	Stockholders' equity	Debit	Retained earnings statement
Cash Dividends Payable	Current liability	Credit	Balance sheet
Common Stock	Stockholders' equity	Credit	Balance sheet
Cost of Merchandise (Goods) Sold	Cost of merchandise (goods sold)	Debit	Income statement
Deferred Income Tax	Current liability/Long-term liability	Credit	Balance sheet
Depletion Expense	Operating expense	Debit	Income statement
Discount on Bonds Payable	Long-term liability	Debit	Balance sheet
Discounts Lost	Other expense	Debit	Income statement
Dividend Income	Other income	Credit	Income statement
Dividends	Stockholders' equity	Debit	Retained earnings statement
Donated Capital	Stockholders' equity	Credit	Balance sheet
Employees Federal Income Tax Payable	Current liability	Credit	Balance sheet
Equipment	Plant asset	Debit	Balance sheet
Exchange Gain	Other income	Credit	Income statement
Exchange Loss	Other expense	Debit	Income statement
Factory Overhead (Overapplied)	Deferred credit	Credit	Balance sheet (interim)
Factory Overhead (Underapplied)	Deferred debit	Debit	Balance sheet (interim)
Federal Income Tax Payable	Current liability	Credit	Balance sheet
Federal Unemployment Tax Payable	Current liability	Credit	Balance sheet
FICA Tax Payable	Current liability	Credit	Balance sheet
Finished Goods	Current asset	Debit	Balance sheet
Gain on Disposal of Plant Assets	Other income	Credit	Income statement
Gain on Redemption of Bonds	Extraordinary item	Credit	Income statement
Gain on Sale of Investments	Other income	Credit	Income statement
Goodwill	Intangible asset	Debit	Balance sheet
Income Tax	Income tax	Debit	Income statement
Income Tax Payable	Current liability	Credit	Balance sheet
Insurance Expense	Operating expense	Debit	Income statement
Interest Expense	Other expense	Debit	Income statement
Interest Income	Other income	Credit	Income statement
Interest Receivable	Current asset	Debit	Balance sheet
Investment in Bonds	Investment	Debit	Balance sheet
Investment in Stocks	Investment	Debit	Balance sheet
Investment in Subsidiary	Investment	Debit	Balance sheet

Abbreviations and Acronyms Commonly Used in Business and Accounting

AAA	American Accounting Association
ABC	Activity-based costing
ACRS	Accelerated Cost Recovery System
AICPA	American Institute of Certified Public Accountants
CEO	Chief Executive Officer
CFO	Chief Financial Officer
CIA	Certified Internal Auditor
CIM	Computer-integrated manufacturing
CMA	Certified Management Accountant
CPA	Certified Public Accountant
Cr.	Credit
Dr.	Debit
EDI	Electronic data interchange
EPS	Earnings per share
FAF	Financial Accounting Foundation
FASB	Financial Accounting Standards Board
FEI	Financial Executives Institute
FICA tax	Federal Insurance Contributions Act tax
FIFO	First-in, first-out
FOB	Free on board
GAAP	Generally accepted accounting principles
GASB	Governmental Accounting Standards Board
GNP	Gross National Product
IMA	Institute of Management Accountants
IRC	Internal Revenue Code
IRS	Internal Revenue Service
JIT	Just-in-time
LIFO	Last-in, first-out
MACRS	Modified Accelerated Cost Recovery System
n/30	Net 30
n/eom	Net, end-of-month
P/E Ratio	Price-earnings ratio
ROI	Return on investment
SEC	Securities and Exchange Commission
TQM	Total quality management